Adult Psychopathology
and Diagnosis

Adult Psychopathology and Diagnosis

Eighth Edition

Edited by

Deborah C. Beidel and B. Christopher Frueh

WILEY

This eighth edition first published 2018
© 2018 John Wiley & Sons, Inc.

Edition History
John Wiley & Sons, Inc. (7e, 2014), John Wiley & Sons, Inc. (6e, 2012), John Wiley & Sons, Inc. (5e, 2007).

Registered Office
John Wiley & Sons, Inc., 111 River Street, Hoboken, NJ 07030, USA

Editorial Office
111 River Street, Hoboken, NJ 07030, USA

For details of our global editorial offices, customer services, and more information about Wiley products visit us at www.wiley.com.

Wiley also publishes its books in a variety of electronic formats and by print-on-demand. Some content that appears in standard print versions of this book may not be available in other formats.

Library of Congress Cataloging-in-Publication Data

Names: Beidel, Deborah C., editor. | Frueh, B. Christopher, editor.
Title: Adult psychopathology and diagnosis / edited by Deborah C. Beidel,
    University of Central Florida, Florida, USA, B. Christopher Frueh,
    University of Hawaii, Hilo, USA.
Description: Eighth edition. | Hoboken, NJ : Wiley, 2018. | Revised edition
    of: Adult psychopathology and diagnosis / edited by Deborah C. Beidel, B.
    Christopher Frueh, and Michel Hersen. Seventh edition. 2014. | Includes
    bibliographical references and indexes. |
Identifiers: LCCN 2017053901 (print) | LCCN 2017054485 (ebook) | ISBN
    9781119383499 (pdf) | ISBN 9781119384175 (epub) | ISBN 9781119383604
    (hardback)
Subjects: LCSH: Psychology, Pathological. | BISAC: PSYCHOLOGY /
    Psychopathology / General.
Classification: LCC RC454 (ebook) | LCC RC454 .A324 2018 (print) | DDC
    616.89–dc23
LC record available at https://lccn.loc.gov/2017053901

Cover image: © Ekely/iStockphoto
Cover design by Wiley

Set in 10/12 pt PalatinoLTStd-Roman by Thomson Digital, Noida, India

Printed in the United States of America

SKY10037610_102822

Contents

Contributors

Michelle Accardi-Ravid
School of Medicine
University of Washington
Seattle, WA

Candice Alfano, PhD
Department of Psychology
University of Houston
Houston, TX

Gordon Asmundson, PhD
Department of Psychology
University of Regina
Regina, Saskatchewan, Canada

Jeffrey Bedwell, PhD
Department of Psychology
University of Central Florida
Orlando, FL

Deborah C. Beidel, PhD
Department of Psychology
University of Central Florida
Orlando, FL

Melanie Bennett, PhD
Department of Psychiatry
University of Maryland Medical School
Baltimore, MD

Joanna M. Berg
Center of Excellence in Substance Abuse
    and Treatment Education
VA Puget Sound Healthcare System
Seattle, WA

Jo Bower, PhD
Department of Psychology
University of Houston
Houston, TX

Laurent Breithhaupt
George Mason University
Fairfax, VA

Lori Brotto, PhD
Department of Psychology
University of British Columbia
Vancouver, BC, Canada

Cynthia Bulik, PhD
Department of Psychiatry
University of North Carolina-Chapel Hill
Neurosciences Hospital
Chapel Hill, NC

L. Kevin Chapman, PhD
Park Plaza Avenue,
Louisville, KY

Dennis Combs, PhD
Department of Psychology
University of Texas at Tyler
Tyler, TX

Cristina Crego, MS
Department of Psychology
University of Kentucky
Lexington, KY

Stacey B. Daughters, PhD
Psychology Department
University of North Carolina at Chapel
    Hill
Chapel Hill, NC

Ryan C. T. DeLapp
Department of Psychology
University of Louisville
Louisville, KY

Leilani Feliciano, PhD
Psychology Department
University of Colorado
Colorado Springs, CO

J. Christopher Fowler, PhD
Menninger Department of Psychiatry &
    Behavioral Sciences at Baylor College
of Medicine
Houston, TX

Gerald Goldstein, PhD
Psychology Service
VA Pittsburgh Healthcare System
Pittsburgh, PA

Timo Giesbrecht
Faculty of Psychology and Neuroscience
Maastrict University
Maastricht, the Netherlands

Rachel W. Gow, PhD
Departments of Psychology and Pediatrics
Virginia Commonwealth University
Richmond, VA

Michael A. Gramlich
Department of Psychology
University of Central Florida
Orlando, FL

Colette Gramszlo
Department of Psychological and Brain
    Sciences
University of Louisville
Louisville, KY

Anouk Grubaugh, PhD
Department of Psychiatry and Behavioral
    Sciences
Medical University of South Carolina
Charleston, SC

Christopher J. Hopwood, PhD
Department of Psychology
Michigan State University
East Lansing, MI

Michelle M. Hospital, PhD
School of Integrated Science and
    Humanity
Florida International University
Miami, FL

Vicie Hurst, PhD
Department of Psychology
University of Central Florida
Orlando, FL

Sheri Johnson
Downey St
San Francisco, CA

Susan C. Kleiman, PhD
Center for Clinical and Translational
    Science and Training
Cincinnati Children's Hospital Medical
    Center
Cincinnati, OH

Anne A. Lawrence, MD, PhD
28th Ave NE
Seattle, WA

Daniel LeBouthiller
Department of Psychology
University of Regina
Regina, Saskatchewan, Canada

Angela Lee
Department of Psychological and Brain
    Sciences
University of Louisville
Louisville, KY

Scott O. Lilienfeld
Department of Psychology
Emory University
Atlanta, GA

Steven Jay Lynn
Department of Psychology
Binghamton University (SUNY)
Binghamton, New York

Suzanne E. Mazzeo
Departments of Psychology and Pediatrics
Virginia Commonwealth University
Richmond, VA

Harald Merckelbach
Faculty of Psychology and Neuroscience
Maastricht University
Maastricht, the Netherlands

David J. Miklowitz, PhD
Department of Psychiatry
University of California at Los Angeles
Los Angeles, CA

Colleen Mundo
Colorado Center for Assessment and
  Counseling
Ft Collins, CO

Sandra Morales
Department of Psychology
University of Texas at Tyler
Tyler, TX

Kim T. Mueser
Center for Psychiatric Rehabilitation
Boston, MA

Anjana Muralidharan, PhD
Baltimore VA Medical Center Annex
Baltimore, MD

Sandra Neer, PhD
Department of Psychology
University of Central Florida
Orlando, FL

John P. O'Donnell
Department of Psychology
University of Central Florida
Orlando, FL

John Oldham, PhD
Menninger Department of Psychiatry &
  Behavioral Sciences at Baylor
  College of Medicine
Houston, TX

Jason Peer, PhD
Baltimore VA Medical Center – VA
  Maryland Health Care System
Baltimore, MD

Craig P. Polizzi
Department of Psychology
Binghamton University
Binghamton, NY

Katie A. Ragsdale
Department of Psychiatry and Behavioral
  Sciences
Emory University School of Medicine
Atlanta, GA

Brenna N. Renn, PhD
University of Washington School of
  Medicine
Seattle, WA

Natalie Rosen, PhD
Department of Psychology and
  Neuroscience
Department of Obstetrics and
  Gynaecology
Dalhousie University Life Sciences Centre
Halifax, Canada

Daniel L. Segal
Psychology Department
University of Colorado
Colorado Springs, CO

Cortni Smith
Department of Psychology
University of Texas at Tyler
Tyler, TX

Linda C. Sobell, PhD
Department of Clinical and School
  Psychology
Fort Lauderdale, FL

Mark B. Sobell, PhD
Department of Clinical and School
  Psychology
Fort Lauderdale, FL

Christophe C. Spencer
Department of Psychology
University of Central Florida
Orlando, FL

Katherine M. Thomas
Department of Psychological Sciences
Purdue University
West Lafayette, IN

Sara Trace, PhD
South Estes Drive
Chapel Hill, NC

Dalena Van-Heugten-Van Der Kloet
Department of Psychology
Oxford Brookes University
Oxford, UK

Eric F. Wagner, PhD
Department of Public Health and Social
  Work
Florida International University
Miami, FL

Thomas A. Widiger, PhD
Department of Psychology
University of Kentucky
Lexington, KY

Monnica T. Williams, PhD
Department of Psychology
University of Connecticut
Storrs, CT

Janet Woodruff-Borden
Department of Psychological and Brain
  Sciences
University of Louisville
Louisville, KY

Jennifer Y. Yi
Psychology Department
University of North Carolina at Chapel
  Hill
Chapel Hill, NC

Zeynep Yilmaz
University of North Carolina at Chapel
  Hill
Neurosciences Hospital
Chapel Hill, NC

Kenneth Zucker, PhD
Child, Youth and Family Program
Centre for Addiction and Mental Health
Toronto, Ontario

Preface

This is the eighth edition of *Adult Psychopathology and Diagnosis*, a series that Samuel M. Turner and Michel Hersen began in 1984, and it is the first edition without Michel's co-editorship.

Since publication of the previous edition, much research into the *DSM-5* has been conducted and new data continue to emerge that force us to continuously reconsider how we approach and conceptualize psychological disorders. Psychopathology is a vibrant field, and ongoing discoveries regarding the roles of genetics, neurobiology, and behavior require that we continue to update this volume for students and professionals alike. We believe that our eminent authors (some of whom are contributing to this volume for the first time) have captured both major changes and more nuanced findings in their respective chapters.

As much as possible, we have asked our contributors to follow a standard format. Exceptions, of course, were granted as dictated by the data inherent in each chapter. Generally, however, each chapter has a description of the disorder, a case study, and material documenting epidemiology, clinical picture, course and prognosis, diagnostic considerations, psychological and biological assessment, and etiological considerations. Each chapter also contains a summary.

Many individuals have contributed to the eighth edition of this book. First, we thank our experts, who agreed to share their vast knowledge about their areas of study. And, as always, we thank Patricia Rossi and her exceptionally professional staff at John Wiley & Sons for understanding the importance of this area to clinical psychology and psychiatry.

Deborah C. Beidel, Orlando, Florida
B. Christopher Frueh, Hilo, Hawaii

About the Companion Website

This book is accompanied by a companion website:

www.wiley.com/go/beidel/psychopathology8e

The website hosts supplementary resources for students and instructors.

For Instructors:

- A testbank of multiple choice questions to accompany each chapter in the book

For Students:

- PowerPoint slides to accompany each chapter in the book

PART I

OVERVIEW

CHAPTER 1

Mental Disorders as Discrete Clinical Conditions: Dimensional Versus Categorical Classification

THOMAS A. WIDIGER and CRISTINA CREGO

IN *DSM-IV*, THERE [was] "no assumption that each category of mental disorder is a completely discrete entity with absolute boundaries dividing it from other mental disorders or from no mental disorder" (American Psychiatric Association [APA], APA, 2000, p. xxxi). This carefully worded disclaimer, however, was somewhat hollow, as it was the case that "*DSM-IV* [was] a categorical classification that divides mental disorders into types based on criterion sets with defining features" (APA, 2000, p. xxxi). The categorical model of classification is consistent with a medical tradition in which it is believed (and often confirmed in other areas of medicine) that disorders have specific etiologies, pathologies, and treatments (Guze, 1978; Guze & Helzer, 1987; Zachar & Kendler, 2007).

Clinicians, following this lead, diagnosed and conceptualized the conditions presented in *DSM-IV-TR* as disorders that are qualitatively distinct from normal functioning and from one another. *DSM-IV-TR* provided diagnostic criterion sets to help guide clinicians toward a purportedly correct diagnosis and an additional supplementary section devoted to differential diagnosis that indicated "how to differentiate [the] disorder from other disorders that have similar presenting characteristics" (APA, 2000, p. 10). The intention of the manual was to help the clinician determine which particular mental disorder provides the best explanation for the symptoms and problems facing the patient. Clinicians devote initial time with a new patient to identify, through differential diagnosis, which specific disorder best explains a patient's presenting complaints. The assumption is that the person is suffering from a single, distinct clinical condition, caused by a specific pathology for which there will be a specific treatment (Frances, First, & Pincus, 1995).

Authors of the diagnostic manual devote a considerable amount of time writing, revising, and researching diagnostic criteria to improve differential diagnosis. They buttress each disorder's criterion set, trying to shore up discriminant validity and distinctiveness, following the rubric of Robins and Guze (1970) that the validity of a

Adult Psychopathology and Diagnosis, Eighth Edition. Edited by Deborah C. Beidel and B. Christopher Frueh.
© 2018 John Wiley & Sons, Inc. Published 2018 by John Wiley & Sons, Inc.
Companion website: www.wiley.com/go/beidel/psychopathology8e

diagnosis rests in large part on its "delimitation from other disorders" (p. 108). "These criteria should . . . permit exclusion of borderline cases and doubtful cases (an undiagnosed group) so that the index group may be as homogeneous as possible" (Robins & Guze, 1970, p. 108).

Scientists may devote their careers to attempting to identify the specific etiology, pathology, or treatment for a respective diagnostic category. Under the assumption that the diagnoses do in fact refer to qualitatively distinct conditions, it follows that there should be a specific etiology, pathology, and perhaps even a specific treatment for each respective disorder. The theories, hypotheses, findings, and disputes regarding the specific etiology, pathology, and/or treatment of a respective mental disorder largely inform the respective chapters of professional, graduate, and undergraduate texts on psychopathology, such as this current edition of *Adult Psychopathology and Diagnosis*.

However, the question of whether mental disorders are, in fact, discrete clinical conditions or arbitrary distinctions along continuous dimensions of functioning has been a long-standing issue (Kendell, 1975) and its significance is escalating with the growing recognition of the limitations of the categorical model (Goldberg, 2015; Hyman, 2010; Stephan et al., 2016; Widiger & Clark, 2000; Widiger & Samuel, 2005). The principal model for the validation of mental disorder diagnostic categories was provided by Robins and Guze (1970), who articulated five fundamental phases: clinical description, laboratory study, delimitation from other disorders, follow-up, and family studies. However, the research that has accumulated to date has not supported the validity of the delimitation of the disorders from one another. "Indeed, in the last 20 years, the categorical approach has been increasingly questioned as evidence has accumulated that the so-called categorical disorders like major depressive disorder and anxiety disorders, and schizophrenia and bipolar disorder seem to merge imperceptibly both into one another and into normality . . . with no demonstrable natural boundaries" (First, 2003, p. 661). As expressed by the vice chair of *DSM-5*, "the failure of DSM-III criteria to specifically define individuals with only one disorder served as an alert that the strict neo-Kraepelinian categorical approach to mental disorder diagnoses advocated by Robins and Guze (1970), Spitzer, Endicott, and Robins (1978), and others could have some serious problems" (Regier, 2008, p. xxi). As acknowledged by Kendell and Jablensky (2003), "it is likely that, sooner or later, our existing typology will be abandoned and replaced by a dimensional classification" (p. 8).

In 1999, a DSM-5 Research Planning Conference was held under joint sponsorship of the APA and the National Institute of Mental Health (NIMH), the purpose of which was to set research priorities that would optimally inform future classifications. One impetus for this effort was the frustration with the existing nomenclature.

In the more than 30 years since the introduction of the Feighner criteria by Robins and Guze, which eventually led to *DSM-III*, the goal of validating these syndromes and discovering common etiologies has remained elusive. Despite many proposed candidates, not one laboratory marker has been found to be specific in identifying any of the *DSM*-defined syndromes. Epidemiologic and clinical studies have shown extremely high rates of comorbidities among the disorders, undermining the hypothesis that the syndromes represent distinct etiologies. Furthermore, epidemiologic studies have shown a high degree of short-term diagnostic instability for many disorders. With regard to treatment, lack of treatment specificity is the rule rather than the exception (Kupfer, First, & Regier, 2002, p. xviii).

DSM-5 Research Planning Work Groups were formed to develop white papers that would set an effective research agenda for the next edition of the diagnostic manual. The Nomenclature Work Group, charged with addressing fundamental assumptions of the diagnostic system, concluded that it will be "important that consideration be given to advantages and disadvantages of basing part or all of DSM-V on dimensions rather than categories" (Rounsaville et al., 2002, p. 12).

The white papers developed by the DSM-5 Research Planning Work Groups were followed by a series of international conferences whose purpose was to further enrich the empirical database in preparation for the eventual development of *DSM-5* (a description of this conference series can be found at www.dsm5.org). The first conference was devoted to shifting personality disorders to a dimensional model of classification (Widiger, Simonsen, Krueger, Livesley, & Verheul, 2005). The final conference was devoted to dimensional approaches across the diagnostic manual, including substance use disorders, major depressive disorder, psychoses, anxiety disorders, and developmental psychopathology, as well as the personality disorders (Helzer et al., 2008a).

Nevertheless, despite all this preparatory work toward a shift to a dimensional classification, *DSM-5* retained the categorical model for all its diagnoses. The apparent failure of the categorical model of classification was at least duly noted within the introduction to *DSM-5*. "The historical aspiration of achieving diagnostic homogeneity by progressively subtyping within disorder categories is no longer sensible; like most common human ills, mental disorders are heterogeneous at many levels, ranging from genetic risk factors to symptoms" (APA, 2013, p. 12). The authors of *DSM-5* further suggested that "dimensional approaches to diagnosis . . . will likely supplement or supersede current categorical approaches in the coming years" (APA, 2013, 13).

The purpose of this chapter is to review the *DSM-IV-TR* and *DSM-5* categorical diagnostic approach. The chapter begins with a discussion of the problematic boundaries among the *DSM-IV-TR* and *DSM-5* categorical diagnoses. We then focus in particular on depression, alcohol abuse and dependence, personality disorders, and intellectual disability. We conclude with a discussion of the shifts within *DSM-5* toward a dimensional classification.

DIAGNOSTIC BOUNDARIES

In an effort to force differential diagnosis, a majority of diagnoses in *DSM-III* (APA, 1980) contained exclusionary criteria specifying that a respective disorder could not be diagnosed if it occurred in the presence of another disorder. These exclusions by fiat did not prove to be effective (Boyd et al., 1984) and many were deleted in *DSM-III-R* (APA, 1987). As expressed at the time by Maser and Cloninger (1990), "it is clear that the classic Kraepelinian model in which all psychopathology is comprised of discrete and mutually exclusive diseases must be modified or rejected" (p. 12).

Many *DSM-5* diagnostic criterion sets, however, continue to include exclusionary criteria that attempt to force clinicians to make largely arbitrary choices among alternative diagnoses (APA, 2013), and it is also evident that there will likely continue to be a highly problematic rate of diagnostic co-occurrence (Krueger & Markon, 2006; Maser & Patterson, 2002; Widiger & Clark, 2000). The term *comorbidity* refers to the co-occurrence of distinct disorders, apparently interacting with one another, each presumably with its own independent etiology, pathology, and treatment implications (Feinstein, 1970). If one considers the entire diagnostic manual (which has not yet been done by any epidemiological study), it would likely be exceedingly rare for any patient to meet the criteria for just one disorder, and the comorbidity rises even further if one considers lifetime co-occurrence. Brown, Campbell, Lehman, Grisham, and Mancill (2001), for instance, reported that 95% of individuals in a clinical setting who meet criteria for lifetime major depression or dysthymia also meet criteria for a current or past anxiety disorder. Comorbidity is the norm rather than the exception (Brown & Barlow, 2009; Friborg, Martinussen, Kaiser, Øvergård, & Rosenvinge, 2013; Friborg et al., 2014; Kessler, Chiu, Demler, & Walters, 2005; Kotov, Perlman, Gámez, & Watson, 2015). The excessive comorbidity across the APA diagnostic manual may be saying more about the invalidity of existing diagnostic distinctions than the presence of multiple coexisting conditions (Krueger, 2002; Widiger & Edmundson, 2011).

Diagnostic comorbidity has become so prevalent that some researchers have argued for an abandonment of the term *comorbidity* in favor of a term (e.g., *co-occurrence*) that does not imply the presence of distinct clinical entities (Lilienfeld, Waldman, & Israel, 1994). There are instances in which the presence of multiple diagnoses suggests the presence of distinct yet comorbid psychopathologies, but in most instances the presence of co-occurring diagnoses does appear to suggest a common, shared pathology and, therefore, a failing of the current diagnostic system (Krueger & Markon, 2006; Widiger & Clark, 2000). "Comorbidity may be trying to show us that many current treatments are not so much treatments for transient 'state' mental disorders of affect and anxiety as they are treatments for core processes, such as negative affectivity, that span normal and abnormal variation as well as undergird multiple mental disorders" (Krueger, 2002, p. 44).

Diagnostic criteria have traditionally been developed and subsequently modified in order to construct a disorder that is as homogeneous as possible, thereby facilitating the likelihood of identifying a specific etiology, pathology, and treatment (Robins & Guze, 1970). However, the typical result of this effort is to leave a large number of cases unaccounted for, given that many, if not most patients, have a complex, hetergenous array of symptoms. (Smith & Combs, 2010). New diagnostic categories are added to the nomenclature in large part to decrease clinicians' reliance on the nonspecific, wastebasket label of "not otherwise specified" (NOS). NOS has been among the most frequent diagnoses within clinical populations (Widiger & Edmundson, 2011). The function of many of the new disorders that have been added to recent editions of the manual have not involved the identification of uniquely new forms of psychopathology. Their purpose was generally instead to fill problematic gaps. Notable examples for *DSM-IV* included bipolar II (filling a gap between *DSM-III-R* bipolar and cyclothymic mood disorders), mixed anxiety-depressive disorder (a gap between anxiety and mood disorders), depressive personality disorder (personality and mood disorders), and postpsychotic depressive disorder of schizophrenia (schizophrenia and major depression) (Frances et al., 1995).

When new diagnoses are added to fill gaps, they have the ironic effect of creating additional boundary problems (i.e., more gaps), thereby making differential diagnosis even more problematic (Phillips, Price, Greenburg, & Rasmussen, 2003; Pincus, Frances, Davis, First, & Widiger, 1992; Pincus, McQueen, & Elinson, 2003). One must ask, for instance, whether it is really meaningful or useful to determine whether mixed anxiety-depressive disorder is a mood or an anxiety disorder, whether schizoaffective disorder is a mood disorder or a form of schizophrenia (Craddock & Owen, 2010), whether postpsychotic depressive disorder of schizophrenia is a form of depression or schizophrenia, whether early-onset dysthymia is a mood or a personality disorder (Widiger, 2003), whether acute stress disorder is an anxiety or a dissociative disorder (Cardena, Butler, & Spiegel, 2003), whether hypochondriasis is an anxiety disorder or a somatoform disorder, whether body dysmorphic disorder is an anxiety, eating, or somatoform disorder, and whether generalized social phobia is an anxiety or a personality disorder (Widiger, 2001a). In all these cases the most accurate answer is likely to be that each respective disorder includes features of different sections of the diagnostic manual. Yet the arbitrary and procrustean decision of which single section of the manual in which to place each diagnosis must be made by the authors of a categorical diagnostic manual, and a considerable amount of effort and research are conducted to guide this decision, followed by further discussion and research to refute and debate whatever particular categorical decision was made.

There are comparable examples of what might be arbitrary splitting of categories in *DSM-5* (APA, 2013). *DSM-5* split out from reactive attachment disorder a new diagnosis of disinhibited social engagement disorder. Binge eating disorder (which was originally included within the diagnosis of bulimia nervosa) obtained official recognition. However, for the most part, changes that occurred in *DSM-5* were consistent with the intention to shift the manual more closely toward a dimensional model. For example, there are cases in which previously "distinct" diagnoses were lumped together rather than split apart. For example, *DSM-5* autism spectrum disorder subsumes within one diagnosis *DSM-IV-TR* autistic disorder, Asperger's disorder, childhood disintegrative disorder, and pervasive developmental disorder not otherwise specified (Lord & Bishop, 2015). The archaic subtypes of schizophrenia were deleted. "Instead a dimensional approach to rating severity of core symptoms of schizophrenia is included in *DSM-5* Section III" (APA, 2013, p. 810). The problematic categorical distinction of substance abuse versus dependence was replaced by a level of severity, from mild, moderate, to severe, based simply on the number of diagnostic criteria. Included in Section III of *DSM-5* is a proposed dimensional trait model that would subsume all of the existing personality disorder categories.

DEPRESSION

Mood disorders is a section of the APA diagnostic manual for which the presence of qualitatively distinct conditions is particularly difficult to defend, especially for the primary diagnoses of dysthymia and major depressive disorder (Brown & Barlow, 2009). Discussed here will be early-onset dysthymia, the continuum of depression, and subthreshold major depression, along with more general points concerning the boundary between mood and personality disorder.

There is no meaningful distinction between early-onset dysthymia, an officially recognized mood disorder diagnosis, and depressive personality disorder, a diagnosis proposed for *DSM-IV* but included within its appendix (APA, 2000). In fact, much of the empirical and conceptual basis for adding dysthymia to the *DSM-III* (i.e., Keller, 1989) came from research and clinical literature concerning depressive personality. As acknowledged by the principal architects of *DSM-III*, dysthymia is "roughly equivalent to the concept of depressive personality" (Spitzer, Williams, & Skodol, 1980, p. 159). Depressive personality disorder was included within the mood disorders section of *DSM-III* despite the recommendations to recognize its existence as a disorder of personality (Klerman, Endicott, Spitzer, & Hirschfeld, 1979), because it resembled the symptomatology of other mood disorders (i.e., depressed mood) more than it resembled the symptoms of other personality disorders (e.g., schizoid). However, whereas mood disorders are defined largely by similarity in content (i.e., mood being the predominant feature; APA, 2013), the personality disorders are defined largely by form (i.e., early onset, pervasive, and chronic) often with quite different content (e.g., schizoid personality disorder has little resemblance to histrionic personality disorder).

After *DSM-III* was published, it became evident that many of the persons who were consistently and characteristically pessimistic, gloomy, cheerless, glum, and sullen (i.e., dysthymic) had been that way since childhood and that in many cases no apparent or distinct age of onset could be established. In other words, its conceptualization as a personality disorder became apparent. *DSM-III-R*, therefore, added an early-onset subtype (APA, 1987) and acknowledged that "this disorder usually begins in childhood, adolescence, or early adult life, and for this reason has often been referred to as a Depressive Personality" (APA, 1987, p. 231).

Personality disorder researchers proposed again for *DSM-IV* to include a depressive personality disorder diagnosis. They were told that in order for it to be included, it would need to be distinguished from the already established diagnosis of early-onset dysthymia, a task that might be considered rather difficult, if not unfair, given that the construction of dysthymia had been based in large part on the research and literature concerning depressive personality (Keller, 1989). Nevertheless, the DSM-IV Personality Disorders Work Group developed a proposed diagnostic criterion set that placed relatively more emphasis on cognitive features not currently included within the criterion set for dysthymia (including early-onset), as well as excluding somatic features (Task Force on DSM-IV, 1991). This criterion set was provided to the DSM-IV Mood Disorders Work Group to include within their *DSM-IV* field trial to determine empirically whether it was indeed possible to demarcate an area of functioning not yet covered by early-onset dysthymia, or at least identify persons not yet meeting diagnostic criteria for early-onset dysthymia.

The proposed criterion set was successful in reaching this goal (Phillips et al., 1998), which, perhaps, should not be surprising because no criterion set for a categorical diagnosis appears to be entirely successful in covering all cases. However, the Mood Disorders Work Group was equally impressed with the potential utility of the depressive personality diagnostic criteria for further describing and expanding the coverage of dysthymia (Keller et al., 1995) and, therefore, incorporated much of the proposed criteria for depressive personality into their proposed revisions for dysthymia, including early-onset dysthymia (Task Force on DSM-IV, 1993). The DSM-IV Task Force recognized that it might be problematic to now require the personality disorder researchers to further redefine depressive personality to distinguish it from this new version of dysthymia. Therefore, the DSM-IV Task Force decided instead to include both criterion sets in the appendix to *DSM-IV* (along with the original criterion set for dysthymia within the mood disorders section), with the acknowledgment that there may not be any meaningful distinction between them (APA, 1994; Frances et al., 1995). However, depressive personality disorder was not even included within the appendix for *DSM-5*, in large part because the DSM-5 Personality and Personality Disorders Work Group was not interested in adding any new categorical diagnoses to the manual (Skodol, 2012). Nevertheless, included within DSM-5 Section III, for emerging measures and models, is a five-domain, 25-trait, dimensional model of personality disorder, which includes the personality trait of "depressivity" that would likely be very difficult to distinguish from an early onset dysthymia.

The Continuum of Depression   The common view is that many instances of sadness (or even depression) do not constitute a mental disorder. Persons can be very sad without having a mental disorder (Horwitz & Wakefield, 2007). However, a simple inspection of the diagnostic criteria for major depressive disorder would not lend confidence to a conceptualization of this condition as being qualitatively distinct from "normal" depression or sadness (Andrews et al., 2008). Persons who are just very sad will have the same symptoms of a major depressive disorder but just at a lesser degree of severity. Persons who are very sad will have a depressed mood, decreased interest in pleasurable activities, appetite change, decreased energy, and lower self-esteem. Each of the diagnostic criteria for a major depressive disorder is readily placed along a continuum of severity that would shade imperceptibly into what would be considered a "normal" sadness. *DSM-5,* therefore, includes specific thresholds for each of them, but they are clearly arbitrary thresholds that simply demarcate a relatively higher level of severity from a lower level of severity (e.g., "nearly every day" or "markedly diminished," and at least a "2-week" period; APA, 2013, p. 188). The diagnosis requires five of these nine criteria, with no apparent rationale for this threshold other than it would appear to be severe enough to be defensible to be titled as a "major" depressive episode, as distinguished from a "minor" depressive episode, which is then distinguished from "normal" sadness (APA, 2013).

Depression does appear to shade imperceptibly into "normal" sadness (Andrews et al., 2008). Üstün and Sartorius (1995) conducted a study of 5,000 primary-care patients in 14 countries and reported a linear relationship between disability and number of depressive symptoms. Kessler, Zhao, Blazer, and Swartz (1997) examined the distribution of minor and major symptoms of depression using data from the National Comorbidity Survey. They considered the relationship of these symptoms with parental history of mental disorder, number and duration of depressive episodes, and comorbidity with other forms of psychopathology. Respective relationships increased with increasing number of symptoms, with no clear, distinct break. Sakashita, Slade, and Andrews (2007) examined the relationship between the number of symptoms of depression and four measures of impairment using data from the Australian National Survey of Mental Health and Well-Being, and found that the relationship was again simply linear, with no clear or natural discontinuity to support the selection of any particular cutoff point.

Taxometrics refers to a series of related statistical techniques to detect whether a set of items is optimally understood as describing (assessing) a dimensional or a categorical construct (Beauchaine, 2007; Ruscio & Ruscio, 2004). Other statistical techniques, such as cluster or factor analyses, presume that the construct is either categorical or dimensional (respectively) and then determines how best to characterize the variables or items in either a categorical or dimensional format, respectively. Taxometric analyses are uniquely intriguing in providing a direct test of which structural model is most valid in characterizing the set of items or variables.

A number of taxometric studies have been conducted on various symptoms and measures of depression. The first was provided by Ruscio and Ruscio (2000) in their taxometric analyses of items from the Beck Depression Inventory and, independently, items from the Zung Self-Rating Depression Scale in a sample of 996 male veterans who had received a diagnosis of post-traumatic stress disorder but who also had a high prevalence rate of major depressive disorder, as well as a sample of 8,045 individuals from the general population (60% female) who completed the items from the Depression scale of the Minnesota Multiphasic Personality Inventory. They indicated that "results of both studies, drawing on three widely used measures of depression, corroborated the dimensionality of depression" (Ruscio & Ruscio, 2000, p. 473).

The taxometric findings of Ruscio and Ruscio (2000) have been subsequently replicated, including taxometric analyses of: (a) structured interview assessments of *DSM-IV-TR* major depressive disorder symptoms and, independently, items from the Beck Depression Inventory in a sample of 960 psychiatric outpatients (Slade, 2007); (b) major depressive disorder diagnostic criteria assessed in the 1,933 persons who endorsed at least one criterion in the Australian National Survey of Mental Health and Well-Being (Slade & Andrews, 2005); (c) self- and parent-reported depressive symptoms in 845 children and adolescents drawn from the population-based Georgia Health and Behavior Study (Hankin, Fraley, Lahey, & Waldman, 2005); (d) responses to MMPI-2 depression scales completed by 2,000 psychiatric inpatients and outpatients (Franklin, Strong, & Greene, 2002); (e) epidemiologic survey of depressive symptoms within 392 college students (Baldwin & Shean, 2006); (f) Beck Depression Inventory items reported by 2,260 college students (Ruscio & Ruscio, 2002); and (g) depression items in the Composite International Diagnostic Interview as administered in the National Comorbidity Survey to 4,577 participants who endorsed the item concerning a lifetime occurrence of sad mood or loss of interest (Prisciandoro & Roberts, 2005). However, in contrast to the findings from these eight taxometric studies, three taxometric studies have supported a latent class taxon, including semistructured interview assessments of *DSM-IV-TR* major depressive disorder symptoms in 1,800 psychiatric outpatients (Ruscio, Zimmerman, McGlinchey, Chelminski, & Young, 2007), interview and self-report assessments of depression in 1,400 high school students (Solomon, Ruscio, Seeley, & Lewinsohn, 2006), and self-report and interview data on depression in 378 adolescents receiving treatment for depression (Ambrosini, Bennett, Cleland, & Haslam, 2002). In sum, the bulk of the evidence does appear to support a dimensional understanding of depression, but there is some ambiguity and inconsistency in the taxometric findings (Beach & Amir, 2003; Beauchaine, 2007; Widiger, 2001b).

Subthreshold Major Depression   Depression is a section of the diagnostic manual that does have considerable difficulty identifying or defining a clear boundary with "normal" sadness. Subthreshold cases of depression (i.e., persons with depressive symptoms below the threshold for a *DSM-5* mental disorder diagnosis) are clearly responsive to pharmacologic interventions, do seek treatment for their sadness, and are often being treated within primary care settings (Judd, Schettler, & Akiskal, 2002; Pincus et al., 2003). These facts contributed to the proposal to include within an appendix to *DSM-IV* a diagnosis of "minor depressive disorder," which it is acknowledged "can be difficult to distinguish from periods of sadness that are an inherent part of everyday life" (APA, 2000, p. 776).

Wakefield (2016) has been critical of the criteria for major depressive disorder for including an inconsistently applied exclusion criterion. The *DSM-IV-TR* excluded most instances of depressive reactions to the loss of a loved one (i.e., uncomplicated bereavement). Depression after the loss of a loved one could be considered a mental disorder if "the symptoms persist for longer than 2 months" (APA, 2000, p. 356). Allowing persons just 2 months to grieve before one is diagnosed with a mental disorder does appear to be rather arbitrary. More importantly, it is also unclear if depression in response to other losses should not also then be comparably excluded, such as depression secondary to the loss of a job or physical health (Wakefield, Schimtz, First, & Horwitz, 2007). Why the loss of a person is treated so differently from the loss of health or a job is not clear.

On the other hand, one could argue alternatively that all exclusion criteria should be removed. Perhaps the problem is not that depression in response to a loss of a job or physical disorder should not be a disorder, analogous to bereavement (Wakefield, 2007), but that bereavement should be a mental disorder (Bonanno et al., 2007; Forstmeier & Maercker, 2007; Widiger & Miller, 2008). What is currently considered to be a normal depression in response to the loss of a loved one does often, if not always, include pain and suffering, meaningful impairment to functioning, and is outside of the ability of the bereaved person to fully control, the essential hallmarks of a mental disorder (Widiger & Sankis, 2000). The depression is a reasonable response to the loss of a loved one, a psychological trauma, but many physical disorders and injuries are reasonable and understandable responses to a physical trauma. The loss is perhaps best understood as part of the etiology for the disorder, not a reason for which a disorder is not considered to be present (Widiger, 2012a).

One of the major revisions for *DSM-5* was indeed to weaken the distinction between normal bereavement and a mental disorder of depression. *DSM-5* no longer excludes the diagnosis of a major depressive disorder if the depression is secondary to the loss of a loved one. "Responses to a significant loss (e.g., bereavement, financial ruin, losses from a natural disaster, a serious medical illness or disability)" (APA, 2013, p. 161) can now all be diagnosed as a mental disorder.

ALCOHOL ABUSE AND DEPENDENCE

One of the sections of the diagnostic manual for which a categorical model of classification and conceptualization has had a firmly entrenched tradition has been the substance use disorders. Alcoholism, in particular, has long been conceptualized as a qualitatively distinct disease (Garbutt, 2008; Goodwin & Guze, 1996; Nathan, Conrad, & Skinstad, 2016). A significant change to its diagnosis and conceptualization occurred with *DSM-III-R* (APA, 1987) when it shifted from being understood as a purely physiological dependence to a broader and less specific behavioral dependence (Carroll, Rounsaville, & Bryant, 1994; Edwards & Gross, 1976). "Dependence is seen as a complex process that reflects the central importance of substances in an individual's life, along with a feeling of compulsion to continue taking the substance and subsequent problems controlling use" (Schuckit et al., 1999, p. 41). To many, though, the diagnosis does still refer to a disease, but one that is developed through a normal social-learning history (Kandel, 1998).

However, the diagnosis has been broadened considerably in *DSM-5* wherein it is referred to as a behavioral addiction, and would, therefore, be listed along with pathological gambling (Martin, 2005; Petry, 2006; Potenza, 2006). Pathological gambling has been considered by many substance use and pathological gambling researchers and clinicians to be an addiction, but it could not be included within the substance-related disorders section because it does not involve the ingestion of a substance (Bradford, Geller, Lesieur, Rosenthal, & Wise, 1996). This requirement has been deleted in *DSM-5*, with the section renamed "substance-related and addictive disorders" (APA, 2013).

This new class of disorders could eventually contain a wide variety of possible behavioral addictions, including an excessive participation in shopping, sex, or the Internet. As stated at one point on the *DSM-5* website, along with pathological gambling, "other addiction-like behavioral disorders such as 'Internet addiction' . . . will be considered as potential additions to this category as research data accumulate" (APA, 2010, "Substance Related Disorders," para. 1). The preface to this section of the diagnostic manual explicitly states that Internet, sex, and shopping addictions are not included because there is currently insufficient evidence to support their validity. However, it is apparent that the broadening of the concept of substance dependence to include behavioral forms of addiction will encourage clinicians to diagnose these additional variants. "This 'slippery slope' makes it difficult to know where to draw the line demarcating any excessive behavior as an addiction" (Petry, 2005a, p. 7). Provided within an appendix to *DSM-5* for conditions needing further study is Internet gaming disorder (i.e., behavioral addiction to Internet games), including its diagnostic criteria, risk factors, prevalence, and differential diagnosis. Proposed for inclusion in the sex disorders section of *DSM-5* was hypersexual disorder, which can indeed be identified as a sex addiction (Kafka, 2010; Ragan & Martin, 2000; Winters, 2010).

The distinction between harmful substance use and a substance use disorder is itself unclear and indistinct. Presumably, persons can choose to consume alcohol without being compelled to do so by the presence of a mental disorder. The *DSM-5* diagnostic criteria for a substance use disorder are fallible indicators for harmful and dyscontrolled usage (e.g., use more than originally intended, continue to use despite social consequences, and reduction of other activities in preference for the substance; APA, 2013). The more of these indicators of dyscontrol that are present, the more likely it is that there is, in fact, dyscontrol, but none can be considered infallible in the identification of dyscontrol and no particular number of them clearly demarcates a boundary between the presence and absence of dyscontrolled usage. It is not even clear how much purportedly volitional or regulatory control a normal, healthy person has over adaptive, healthy behaviors (Bargh & Ferguson, 2000; Howard & Conway, 1986; Kirsch & Lynn, 2000; Wegner & Wheatley, 2000), let alone the boundary between controlled and dyscontrolled harmful behaviors. Both normal and abnormal human functioning are, at best, the result of a complex interaction of apparent volitional choice with an array of biogenetic and environmental determinants.

The distinction between *DSM-IV-TR* alcohol abuse and dependence was equally fuzzy. Abuse has generally been considered to be simply a residual category and/or a less severe form of dependence (Saunders, 2006). Some of the diagnostic criteria for abuse were contained with the criterion set for dependence (e.g., interference with social, occupational, or recreational activities), which is always a problem for disorders that would be considered to be qualitatively distinct. It is largely for this reason that the formal distinction between abuse and dependence was abandoned in *DSM-5* (APA, 2013).

The diagnostic criteria for alcohol dependence were written largely in an effort to describe a prototypic case of the disorder, a practice that is still followed for all but a few of the disorders throughout *DSM-5*. However, prototypic cases are typically understood to be the most severe cases and/or the cases that involve all possible features or symptoms of the disorder (First & Westen, 2007). The construction of diagnostic criterion sets in terms of prototypic cases does work to an extent, but it also fails to adequately describe many of the actual cases, including the subthreshold cases, and perhaps even the typical cases, depending upon the distribution of features and symptomatology within the population. Constructing criterion sets in terms of prototypic cases can be comparable to confining the description and diagnosis of (for instance) intellectual disability to the most severe variant, and then attempting to apply this description to mild and moderate variants; a method of diagnosis that would obviously be sorely limited in the description, assessment, and diagnosis of intellectual disability. The limitations of the prototypic case approach are now becoming more closely appreciated in the diagnosis of dyscontrolled substance use and, more specifically, alcohol use disorders, where the existing criterion sets are failing to adequately describe (for instance) dyscontrolled and impairing alcohol usage in adolescents (Crowley, 2006) and other "diagnostic orphans" (Saunders, 2006).

The limitation is perhaps most clearly demonstrated in studies using item response theory (IRT) methodology. IRT allows the researcher to investigate the fidelity with which items are measuring a latent trait along the length of its continuum, contrasting, for instance, the amount of information that different diagnostic criteria provide at different levels of the latent trait (Muthen, 2006). Some diagnostic criteria, for instance, might be most useful in distinguishing among mild cases of the disorder, whereas other diagnostic criteria are most useful in distinguishing among the more severe cases of the disorder. A number of IRT analyses have now been conducted for the diagnosis of substance dependence (and other disorders) and the findings are remarkably consistent (Reise & Waller, 2009). The existing diagnostic criterion sets (and/or symptoms currently assessed in existing instruments) cluster around the high end of the disorder, as opposed to being spread out across the entire range of the continuum (e.g., Kahler & Strong, 2006; Langenbucher et al., 2004; Muthen, 2006; Proudfoot, Baillie, & Teesson, 2006; Saha, Chou, & Grant, 2006). This consistent pattern of results is in stark contrast to what is traditionally found in cognitive ability testing, where IRT analyses have been largely developed and previously applied (Reise & Waller, 2009).

It is evident from the IRT analyses that the existing diagnostic criterion sets are sorely inadequate in characterizing the lower and even middle range of substance use dysfunction, consistent with the *DSM-IV-TR* and *DSM-5* descriptions being confined to a prototypic (most severe) case. If alcohol usage was conceptualized along a continuum, the job of the authors of the diagnostic manual would be to construct a description and measurement of the disorder that adequately represent each of the levels or degrees to which the disorder appears along this continuum, rather than attempting to describe the prototypic case. The *DSM-IV-TR* criterion set was confined to the most severe cases and was not describing well a large proportion of persons with clinically significant alcohol use dysfunction. As a result, clinicians had to rely on the nondescriptive, wastebasket diagnosis of NOS to describe the lower range of the continuum (Saunders, 2006).

A step in the direction of recognizing the continuous nature of substance use disorder was incorporated in *DSM-5*. Along with the abandonment of the distinction between abuse and dependence, *DSM-5* also includes a rating of severity for a substance use disorder, depending upon the number of diagnostic criteria that are met. For example, a "mild" substance use disorder is suggested by the presence of just two to three features (APA, 2013). However, the features for the mildest and the most severe cases are still the same. What would be more informative would be to have the different levels defined by the features that are relatively specific to that level, analogous to how the comparable distinctions are made between the levels of severity for an intellectual disability.

Personality Disorders

There are three major problematic boundaries for the personality disorders: the boundaries between personality disorders and other mental disorders; the boundaries between personality disorders and normal personality; and the boundaries among the personality disorders. The boundaries with other mental disorders will be discussed first, followed by the other two boundaries.

Boundaries with Other Mental Disorders   Among the proposals considered for the personality disorders at the DSM-5 Research Planning Conference (Kupfer et al., 2002) was the suggestion to replace the diagnosis of personality disorder with early-onset and chronic variants of existing Axis I mental disorders (First et al., 2002). This might appear at first blush to be a radical proposal, and perhaps it is. However, it does have support from a variety of sources.

There is no clear or consistent boundary between the personality disorders and many other mental disorders, particularly the mood, anxiety, impulse dyscontrol, and psychotic disorders (Krueger, 2005). In fact, *DSM-5* schizotypal personality disorder has long been classified as a form of schizophrenia rather than as a personality disorder in the World Health Organization's *International Classification of Diseases* (ICD-10; WHO, 1992), the parent classification for the APA's *DSM-5*. Schizotypal personality disorder is genetically related to schizophrenia, most of its neurobiological risk factors and psychophysiological correlates are shared with schizophrenia (e.g., eye tracking, orienting, startle blink, and neurodevelopmental abnormalities), and the treatments that are effective in ameliorating schizotypal symptoms overlap with treatments used for persons with Axis I schizophrenia (Kwapil & Barrantes-Vidal, 2012).

On the other hand, there are also compelling reasons for continuing to consider schizotypal as a personality disorder (Kwapil & Barrantes-Vidal, 2012; Raine, 2006). Simply because a personality disorder shares a genetic foundation with another disorder does not then indicate that it is a form of that other disorder. Running counter to viewing schizotypal personality disorder as a variant of schizophrenia are the following: the disorder is far more comorbid with other personality disorders than it is with any other schizophrenia-related disorder; persons with schizotypal personality disorder rarely go on to develop schizophrenia; and schizotypal symptomatology is seen in quite a number of persons within the general population who lack any genetic association with schizophrenia and who would not be appropriately described as having some form of schizophrenia (Raine, 2006).

However, a fate similar to that of schizotypal personality disorder in *ICD-10* (WHO, 1992) and depressive personality disorder in *DSM-IV* (APA, 1994) could await the other personality disorder diagnostic categories in a future edition of the diagnostic manual (First et al., 2002). For example, social phobia was a new addition to *DSM-III* (Spitzer et al., 1980; Turner & Beidel, 1989). It was considered then to be a distinct, circumscribed condition, consistent with the definition of a phobia as a "persistent, irrational fear of a *specific* object, activity, or situation" (APA, 1994, p. 336, our emphasis). However, it became apparent to anxiety disorder researchers and clinicians that the fears of many of their patients were rarely so discrete and circumscribed (Spitzer & Williams, 1985). Therefore, the authors of *DSM-III-R* developed a generalized subtype for when "the phobic situation includes most social situations" (APA, 1987, p. 243). *DSM-III-R* generalized social phobia, however, overlapped substantially with the *DSM-III* diagnosis of avoidant personality disorder. Both were concerned with a pervasive, generalized social insecurity, discomfort, and timidity. Efforts to distinguish them have indicated only that avoidant personality disorder tends to be, on average, relatively more dysfunctional than generalized social phobia (Sanislow, da Cruz, Gianoli, & Reagan, 2012; Turner, Beidel, & Townsley, 1992).

DSM-IV provided no solution. In fact, it was acknowledged that generalized social phobia emerged "out of a childhood history of social inhibition or shyness" (APA, 1994, p. 414), consistent with the fundamental definition of a personality disorder. An argument raised for classifying this condition as an anxiety disorder rather than a personality disorder was that many persons with the disorder benefit from pharmacologic interventions (Liebowitz, 1992). "One may have to rethink what the personality disorder concept means in an instance where 6 weeks of phenelzine therapy begins to reverse long-standing interpersonal hypersensitivity as well as discomfort in socializing" (Liebowitz, 1992, p. 251). Of course, one might also have to rethink what the anxiety disorder concept means when an antidepressant is an effective form of treating an anxiety disorder. In addition, it is unclear why a maladaptive personality trait should not be responsive to a pharmacologic intervention (Knorr & Kessing, 2010; Knutson et al., 1998; Tang et al., 2009). In any case, the authors of *DSM-IV-TR* concluded that these two conditions "may be alternative conceptualizations of the same or similar conditions" (APA, 2000, p. 720).

There does not currently appear to be a meaningful distinction between avoidant personality disorder and generalized social phobia (APA, 2000; Sanislow et al., 2012; Tyrer, 2005; Widiger, 2003). Some suggest that the best solution is to simply abandon the personality disorder diagnosis in favor of the generalized anxiety disorder (First et al., 2002; Schneider, Blanco, Anita, & Liebowitz, 2002). "We believe that the more extensive evidence for syndromal validity of social phobia, including pharmacological and cognitive-behavioral treatment efficacy, make it the more useful designation in cases of overlap with avoidant personality" (Liebowitz et al., 1998, p. 1060). The reference to treatment efficacy by Liebowitz et al. (1998) falls on receptive ears for many clinicians who struggle to obtain insurance coverage for the treatment of maladaptive personality functioning. It is often reported that a personality disorder diagnosis is stigmatizing, due in large part to its placement on a distinct axis that carries the implication of being an untreatable, lifetime disorder (Frances et al., 1991; Kendell, 1983). For reasons such as these, the Assembly of the APA (which has authoritative governance over the approval of revisions to the diagnostic manual) has repeatedly passed resolutions to explore proposals to move one or more personality disorders to Axis I, in large part to address the stigma and lack of reimbursement for their treatment. This proposal is now moot, given the abandonment of the multiaxial system in *DSM-5* (APA, 2013).

Future proposals of the Assembly, though, might now take the form of shifting individual personality disorders into a respective mood, anxiety, or impulse dyscontrol disorder as an early-onset, chronic variant. Just as the depressive, schizotypal, and avoidant personality disorders could be subsumed within an existing section of Axis I, borderline personality disorder could be reclassified as a mood dysregulation and/or impulse dyscontrol disorder; obsessive-compulsive personality disorder could be reclassified as a generalized and chronic variant of obsessive-compulsive anxiety disorder (although there is, in fact, only weak evidence to support a close relationship between the obsessive-compulsive anxiety and personality disorders; Samuels & Costa, 2012); and antisocial personality disorder could be reclassified as an adult variant of conduct (disruptive behavior) disorder. In *DSM-5*, schizotypal personality disorder is cross-listed within the schizophrenia spectrum section, and antisocial is cross-listed within the disruptive behavior disorders section (APA, 2013).

In sum, the future for many of the personality disorder diagnostic categories might be reformulations as early-onset chronic variants of existing Axis I disorders, as explicitly proposed at the initial DSM-5 Research Planning Conference (First et al., 2002). A difficulty for any such proposal, beyond the fundamental concern that the diagnostic manual would no longer recognize the existence of maladaptive personality functioning, is that it might just create more problems than it solves (Widiger, 2003). It is well established that persons have constellations of maladaptive personality traits that have significant consequential life outcomes (Ozer & Benet-Martinez, 2006; Roberts & DelVecchio, 2000). These personality traits are not currently well described by just one or even multiple personality disorder diagnoses (Clark, 2007; Trull & Durrett, 2005; Widiger, 2012b) and will be described even less well by multiple diagnoses across the broad classes of mood, anxiety, impulse dyscontrol, psychotic, and disruptive behavior disorders.

Boundaries with Other Personality Disorders and Normal Personality   Rounsaville et al. (2002) suggested that the first section of the diagnostic manual to shift to a dimensional classification should be the personality disorders. The personality disorders have been among the most problematic of disorders to be diagnosed categorically (First et al., 2002; Kendell, 1989). It is the norm for patients to meet diagnostic criteria for more than one personality disorder (Clark, 2007; Lilienfeld et al., 1994; Livesley, 2003; Trull & Durrett, 2005). Excessive diagnostic co-occurrence was, in fact, the primary reason that five of the 10 personality disorder diagnoses were proposed for deletion in *DSM-5* (Skodol, 2012). The excessive co-occurrence may be the result of the nature of the construct of personality. For instance, it is perhaps self-evident that persons are not well described by just one trait term (e.g., introverted). Each person has instead a constellation of personality traits, many of which are adaptive, and some of which may also be maladaptive. There is little reason to think that it would be different when a person is said to have a personality disorder (Widiger & Trull, 2007).

There also appears to be no clear or distinct boundary between normal and abnormal personality functioning. The *DSM-IV-TR* diagnostic thresholds were not set at a point that has any theoretical or clinical significance. They were arbitrarily set at half or one more than half of the diagnostic criteria (APA, 2000). In fact, all the personality disorders are readily understood as extreme and/or maladaptive variants of normal personality traits distributed within the general population; more specifically, the domains and facets of the five-factor dimensional model (FFM) of general personality structure (Widiger, Samuel, Mullins-Sweatt, Gore, & Crego, 2012; Widiger & Trull, 2007).

The FFM consists of five broad domains of general personality functioning: neuroticism (or emotional instability), extraversion versus introversion, openness versus closedness, agreeableness versus antagonism, and conscientiousness versus undependability. Studies have now well documented that all of the *DSM-IV-TR* personality disorder symptomatology is readily understood as maladaptive variants of the domains and facets of the FFM (O'Connor, 2002, 2005; Samuel & Widiger, 2008; Saulsman & Page, 2004; Widiger & Costa, 2002; Widiger et al., 2012). Saulsman and Page (2004) concluded on the basis of their meta-analytic review of the FFM-personality disorder research that "each of the personality disorders shows associations with the five-factor model that are meaningful and predictable given their diagnostic criteria" (p. 1075). As acknowledged by Livesley (2001b), "all categorical diagnoses of *DSM* can be accommodated within the five-factor framework" (p. 24). As expressed by Clark (2007), "the five-factor model of personality is widely accepted as representing the higher-order structure of both normal and abnormal personality traits" (p. 246). The problematic diagnostic co-occurrence among the *DSM-IV-TR* personality disorders is well explained by the extent to which each of the personality disorders shares traits of the FFM (Lynam & Widiger, 2001; O'Connor, 2005).

A team of researchers are now working together to develop a Hiearchical Taxonomy of Psychopathology (HiTOP) as an alternative to the existing categorical nomenclature (Kotov et al., 2017). The HiTOP model includes two broad domains of externalizing dysfunction and emotional dysregulation that cut across the mood, anxiety, substance use, psychotic, and personality disorders. At the five-domain level are maladaptive personality traits (i.e., internalizing, thought disorder, misconduct, antagonism, and detachment) which are said to align with the FFM of general personality structure (Kotov et al., 2017).

Proposed for *DSM-5* was another five-domain, 25-trait dimensional model that represented "maladaptive variants of the five domains of the extensively validated and replicated personality model known as the 'Big Five,' or the Five Factor Model of personality" (APA, 2013, p. 773). These five domains are negative affectivity (FFM neuroticism), detachment (FFM introversion), psychoticism (FFM openness), antagonism (FFM antagonism), and disinhibition (low FFM conscientiousness) (Krueger, Derringer, Markon, Watson, & Skodol, 2012). The *DSM-5* dimensional trait model does differ in important ways from the FFM; more specifically, it is confined to maladaptive personality functioning and it is unipolar in structure (e.g., it does not recognize any maladaptive variants of extraversion that is opposite to detachment, or agreeableness that is opposite to antagonism). Nevertheless, there is strong conceptual and empirical support for its alignment with the five domains of the FFM (APA, 2013; De Fruyt, De Clerq, De Bolle, Markon, & Krueger, 2013; Gore & Widiger, 2013; Krueger & Markon, 2014; Thomas et al., 2013).

The FFM of personality disorder has a number of advantages over the existing categorical approach (Widiger et al., 2012). It would help with the stigmatization of a personality disorder diagnosis because no longer would a personality disorder be conceptualized as something that is qualitatively distinct from general personality traits. All persons vary in the extent of their neuroticism, the extent to which they are agreeable versus antagonistic, and the extent to which they are conscientious, impulsive, and/or undependable (McCrae & Costa, 2003). The FFM of personality disorder provides not only a more precise description of each person's individual personality structure but also a more complete picture through the inclusion of normal, adaptive traits, recognizing thereby that a person is more than just the personality disorder and that there are aspects to the self that can be adaptive, even commendable, despite the presence of the maladaptive personality traits. Some of the personality strengths may also be quite relevant to treatment, such as openness to experience, indicating an interest in exploratory psychotherapy; agreeableness, indicating an engagement in group therapy; and conscientiousness, indicating a willingness and ability to adhere to the demands and rigor of dialectical behavior therapy (Sanderson & Clarkin, 2002). The FFM of personality disorder would also bring to the psychiatric nomenclature a wealth of knowledge concerning the origins, childhood antecedents, stability, and universality of the dispositions that are known with respect to the FFM (Widiger et al., 2012; Widiger & Trull, 2007).

The Nomenclature Work Group at the initial DSM-5 Research Planning Conference called for the replacement of the *DSM-IV-TR* diagnostic categories by a dimensional model (Rounsaville et al., 2002). "If a dimensional system of personality performs well and is acceptable to clinicians, it might then be appropriate to explore dimensional approaches in other domains" (Rounsaville et al., 2002, p. 13). A subsequent APA *DSM-5* preparatory conference was devoted to making this shift, providing its extensive empirical support (Widiger et al., 2005). The proposal of the DSM-5 Personality and Personality Disorders Work Group, however, was more conservative. The initial proposal was not to replace the diagnostic categories with a dimensional trait model. It was only to provide a dimensional trait model as a supplement for the existing diagnostic categories to be used when the patient failed to meet the diagnostic criteria for a respective personality disorder category (Skodol, 2012). In the final version of the proposal, six diagnostic categories remained. The only time in which a clinician would describe a patient in terms of the five trait domains would be when the patient failed to meet the criteria for one of the six traditional syndromes. Traits from the dimensional model were now included with the diagnostic criterion sets of these categories, but they were not even considered to be sufficient for the diagnosis. Also included were deficits in the sense of self and interpersonal relatedness obtained from psychodynamic literature that were considered to be independent of maladaptive personality traits (Skodol, 2012).

The proposal was ultimately rejected, largely because of inadequate empirical support (Skodol, Morey, Bender, & Oldham, 2013). The initial dimensional trait proposal had been created *de novo* by work group members, thereby lacking a strong empirical foundation. In addition, rather than closely tying the proposal to the well-validated FFM, the authors explicitly distanced the proposal from the FFM (i.e., Clark & Krueger, 2010). In the last year of the proposal it was more closely tied to the FFM (APA, 2012) but the DSM-5 Scientific Review Committee was not provided with the FFM-personality disorder research (Widiger, 2013). By then strong opposition to the proposal had also accumulated (e.g., Clarkin & Huprich, 2011; Gunderson, 2010; Shedler et al., 2010). Further, the dimensional trait model was structurally embedded within a much more extensive and complex proposal that included the additional features of self pathology derived from psychodynamic theory and research (Skodol, 2012). Nevertheless, the proposal was at least included in Section III of *DSM-5* for emerging measures and models as an alternative to the *DSM-5* diagnostic categories that were equivalent to the *DSM-IV-TR* syndromes, carried over without any revision.

A more radical proposal has been made for the 11th edition of the WHO *International Classification of Diseases*, in which all of the current *ICD-10* personality syndromes (comparable to the *DSM-IV* and *DSM-5* syndromes) would be replaced with five broad domains of maladaptive personality traits: negative affective, detachment, dissocial, disinhibition, and anankastic. These traits are also said to be aligned with the FFM: "Negative Affective with neuroticism, Detachment with low extraversion, Dissocial with low agreeableness, Disinhibited with low conscientiousness and Anankastic with high conscientiousness" (Mulder, Horwood, Tyrer, Carter, & Joyce, 2016, p. 85). Most importantly, "the proposed *ICD-11* classification abolishes all type-specific categories of personality disorder" (Tyrer et al., 2015, p. 721). In this regard, the *ICD-11* proposal may indeed represent a paradigm shift in how personality disorders are conceptualized and diagnosed within the next edition of the ICD (Tyrer, 2014). This *ICD-11* proposal may, of course, meet the same fate as the *DSM-5* proposal.

INTELLECTUAL DISABILITY

Rounsaville et al. (2002) and others suggested that the personality disorders section should be the first to shift toward a dimensional classification, apparently not fully appreciating that one section has long been dimensional: intellectual disability (previously called mental retardation). Many persons write as if a shift to a dimensional classification represents a new, fundamental change to the diagnostic manual (e.g., Regier, 2008). For much of the manual such a shift would certainly represent a fundamental change in how mental disorders are conceptualized and classified (Guze, 1978; Guze & Helzer, 1987; Robins & Guze, 1970). Nevertheless, there is a clear precedent for a dimensional classification of psychopathology already included within *DSM-5*: the diagnosis of intellectual disability (APA, 2013).

Intellectual disability in *DSM-5* is diagnosed along a continuum of cognitive and social functioning—more precisely, deficits in adaptive functioning and intellectual functions confirmed by standardized intelligence testing. This typically translates to an intelligence quotient (IQ) score of 70 ± 5 (APA, 2013). An IQ of 70 does not carve nature at a discrete joint or identify the presence of a qualitatively distinct condition, disease, or disorder. On the contrary, it is a quantitative cutoff point along the dimension of intelligence. An IQ of 70 is simply two standard deviations below the mean (American Association of Mental Retardation [AAMR], AAMR, 2002).

Intelligence involves the ability to reason, plan, solve problems, think abstractly, comprehend complex ideas, learn quickly, and learn from experience (AAMR, 2002). Intelligence, like personality, is distributed as a hierarchical, multifactorial continuous variable. Most persons' levels of intelligence, including most of those with an intellectual disability, are the result of a complex interaction of multiple genetic, fetal, and infant development, and environmental influences (Deary, Spinath, & Bates, 2006). There are no discrete breaks in its distribution that would provide an absolute distinction between normal and abnormal intelligence. The point of demarcation for the diagnosis of an intellectual disability is an arbitrary, quantitative distinction along the normally distributed levels of hierarchically and multifactorially defined intelligence. This point of demarcation is arbitrary in the sense that it does not carve nature at a discrete joint, but it was not, of course, randomly or mindlessly chosen. It is a defensible selection that was informed by the impairments in adaptive functioning commonly associated with an IQ of 70 or below (AAMR, 2002). For example, a previous cutoff point of an IQ of 79 identified too many persons who were in fact able to function independently.

In addition, the disorder of intellectual disability is not diagnosed simply on the basis of an IQ of 70 or below (an IQ score is not even necessarily required in *DSM-5*; APA, 2013). It must be accompanied by a documented impairment to functioning. "Mental retardation is a disability characterized by significant limitation in both intellectual functioning and in adaptive behavior as expressed in conceptual, social and practical adaptive skills" (AAMR, 2002, p. 23). Persons with IQ scores lower than 70 who can function effectively would not be diagnosed with the disorder (APA, 2013). The diagnosis is understood in the context of the social and practical requirements of everyday functioning that must be met by the person (Luckasson & Reeve, 2001). The purpose of the diagnosis is not to suggest that a specific pathology is present, but to identify persons who, on the basis of their intellectual disability, would be eligible for public health care services and benefits to help them overcome or compensate for their relatively lower levels of intelligence.

Many instances of intellectual disability are due in large part to specific etiologies, such as tuberous sclerosis, microcephaly, von Recklinghausen's disease, trisomy 21, mosaicism, Prader–Willi syndrome, and many, many more (Kendell & Jablensky, 2003). Nevertheless, the disorders that result from these specific etiologies are generally understood as medical conditions, an associated feature of which is also the intellectual disability that would be diagnosed concurrently and independently. The intellectual disability that is diagnosed as a mental disorder within *DSM-5* is itself a multifactorially determined and heterogeneous dimensional construct falling along the broad continuum of intellectual functioning. "The causes of intellectual disabilities are typically complex interactions of biological, behavioral/psychological, and socio-cultural factors" (Naglieri, Salter, & Rojahn, 2008, p. 409). An important postnatal cause for intellectual disability is "simply" psychosocial deprivation, resulting from poverty, chaotic living environment, and/or child abuse or neglect. No clear etiology will be evident in up to 40% of cases. In sum, intellectual disability may serve as an effective model for the classification of the rest of the diagnostic manual, including mood, psychotic, personality, anxiety, and other mental disorders.

DSM-5 AND DIMENSIONAL CLASSIFICATION

The modern effort to demarcate a taxonomy of distinct clinical conditions is often traced to Kraepelin (1917). Kraepelin (1917), however, had himself acknowledged that "wherever we try to mark out the frontier between mental health and disease, we find a neutral territory, in which the imperceptible change from the realm of normal life to that of obvious derangement takes place" (p. 295). The Robins and Guze (1970) paradigm for the validation of categorical diagnosis has also been widely influential within psychiatry (Klerman, 1983; Kupfer et al., 2002). In 1989, L. Robins and Barrett (1989) edited a text in honor of this classic paper. Kendell (1989) provided the final word in his closing chapter. His conclusions, however, were curiously negative. "Ninety years have now elapsed since Kraepelin first provided the framework of a plausible classification of mental disorders. Why then, with so many potential validators available, have we made so little progress since that time?" (Kendell, 1989, p. 313). He answered his rhetorical question in the next paragraph: "One important possibility is that the discrete clusters of psychiatric symptoms we are trying to delineate do not actually exist but are as much a mirage as discrete personality types" (Kendell, 1989, p. 313).

It is stated in the preface to *DSM-5* that "this edition of *DSM* was designed first and foremost to be a useful guide to clinical practice" (APA, 2013, p. xii). First (2005) argued, in his rejoinder to a proposal to shift the diagnostic manual into a dimension model, that "the most important obstacle standing in the way of its implementation in *DSM-5* (and beyond) is questions about clinical utility" (p. 561). However, one should question whether the existing diagnostic manual in fact has appreciable clinical utility

(Mullins-Sweatt & Widiger, 2009). "Apologists for categorical diagnoses argue that the system has clinical utility being easy to use and valuable in formulating cases and planning treatment [but] there is little evidence for these assertions" (Livesley, 2001a, p. 278). First (2005) suggested that "the current categorical system of *DSM* has clinical utility with regard to the treatment of individuals" (p. 562), yet elsewhere has stated that "with regard to treatment, lack of treatment specificity is the rule rather than the exception" (Kupfer et al., 2002, p. xviii). The heterogeneity of diagnostic membership, the lack of precision in description, the excessive diagnostic co-occurrence, the failure to lead to a specific diagnosis, the reliance on the "not otherwise specified" wastebasket diagnosis, and the unstable and arbitrary diagnostic boundaries of the *DSM-IV-TR* and *DSM-5* categories, are matters of clinical utility that are a source of considerable frustration for clinicians and public health care agencies (Mullins-Sweatt & Widiger, 2009).

The primary goal of the authors of the *DSM-5* was to shift the manual toward a dimensional classification (Helzer, Wittchen, Krueger, & Kraemer, 2008b; Regier, Narrow, Kuhl, & Kupfer, 2010). This intention represented an explicit recognition of the failure of the categorical system (Goldberg, 2010, 2015). And the *DSM-5* does indeed include a number of clear and potentially significant shifts toward a dimensional classification. The introduction to the manual explicitly acknowledges the failure of the categorical model: "The once plausible goal of identifying homogeneous populations for treatment and research resulted in narrow diagnostic categories that did not capture clinical reality, symptom heterogeneity within disorders, and significant sharing of symptoms across multiple disorders" (APA, 2013, p. 12). Many of the changes that were made to the nomenclature reflected a preference for a more dimensional conceptualization (e.g., the autism spectrum disorder, the conceptualization of a schizophrenia spectrum, the level of severity for substance use disorder, and the reference within the introduction of the manual to the broad dimensions of internalizing and externalizing dysfunction that cut across existing categories). Included in Section III of *DSM-5* for emerging models and measures is a five-domain, 25-trait dimensional model of maladaptive personality functioning (Krueger et al., 2011) that is aligned conceptually and empirically with the FFM dimensional model of general personality structure (APA, 2013; De Fruyt et al., 2013; Gore & Widiger, 2013; Thomas et al., 2013). This model is presented as an alternative to the traditional diagnostic categories "to address numerous shortcomings of the current approach" (APA, 2013, p. 761) and its presence within the diagnostic manual will help to stimulate further research as well as increase the familiarity and interest of clinicians with respect to this alternative approach (Widiger, 2013).

Nevertheless, it is also acknowledged that "DSM-5 remains a categorical classification of separate disorders" (APA, 2013, p. xii). The shifts that did occur were frankly tentative, if not timid. "What is being proposed for DSM-V is not to substitute dimensional scales for categorical diagnoses, but to add a dimensional option to the usual categorical diagnoses for DSM-V" (Kraemer, 2008, p. 9). None of the mental disorders, including even the personality disorders, converted to a dimensional classification. There was a shift toward the conceptualization of some disorders as existing along a spectrum (e.g., autism and schizophrenia), and substance use disorder collapsed the problematic distinction between abuse and dependence into one disorder that includes four levels of severity. However, with respect to the latter, there remains no acknowledgement of the continuum into normal substance usage. There will continue to be a reliance on the NOS category to identify subthreshold conditions (the threshold for a substance use diagnosis was, in fact, raised from one criterion to two).

DSM-III is often said to have provided a significant paradigm shift in how psychopathology is diagnosed (Kendell & Jablensky, 2003; Klerman, 1983; Regier, 2008). Much of the credit for the innovative nature and success of *DSM-III* is due to the foresight, resolve, and perhaps even courage of its Chair, Dr. Robert Spitzer. The primary authors of *DSM-5* fully recognized the failure of the categorical model of classification (Kupfer et al., 2002; Regier, 2008; Regier et al., 2010). They had the empirical support and the opportunity to lead the field of psychiatry to a comparably bold new future in diagnosis and classification, but no true paradigm shift in the classification of psychopathology has occurred.

There was never an intention to actually shift the diagnostic manual into a dimensional system. As acknowledged by Helzer, Kraemer, and Krueger (2006), "our proposal [for *DSM-5*] not only preserves categorical definitions but also does not alter the process by which these definitions would be developed. Those charged with developing criteria for specific mental disorders would operate just as their predecessors have" (p. 1675). In other words, work groups, for the most part, continued to develop diagnostic criteria to describe prototypic cases in a manner that would maximize homogeneity and differential diagnosis (Robins & Guze, 1970; Spitzer et al., 1980), thereby continuing to fail to adequately describe typical cases and again leaving many patients to receive the diagnosis of NOS. Dimensional proposals for *DSM-5* were only to develop "supplementary dimensional approaches to the categorical definitions that would also relate back to the categorical definitions" (Helzer et al., 2008b, p. 116). It was the intention for these dimensions to serve only as ancillary descriptions that lacked any official representation within a patient's medical record. They have no official alphanumerical code and may then not even be communicated to any public health care agency.

Kraemer, Noda, and O'Hara (2004) argued that in psychiatry "a categorical diagnosis is necessary" (p. 21). "Clinicians who must decide whether to treat or not treat a patient, to hospitalize or not, to treat a patient with a drug or with psychotherapy, or what type, must inevitably use a categorical approach to diagnosis" (Kraemer et al., 2004, p. 12). This is a not uncommon perception, but it is not an accurate characterization of actual clinical practice (Mullins-Sweatt & Widiger, 2009). In many common clinical situations, the decision is not, in fact, black and white. Clinicians and social agencies make decisions with respect to a frequency of therapy sessions, an extent of insurance coverage, a degree of medication dosage, and even degrees of hospitalization (e.g., day hospital, partial hospitalization, residential program, or traditional hospitalization).

It is evident that these different clinical decisions are not well informed by a single, uniform diagnostic threshold. The current diagnostic thresholds are not set at a point that is optimal for any one particular social or clinical decision, and the single diagnostic threshold is used to inform a wide variety of different decisions. A dimensional system has the flexibility to provide different thresholds for different social and clinical decisions and would then be considerably more useful for clinicians and more credible for social agencies than the current system. A flexible (dimensional) classification would be preferable to governmental, social, and professional agencies because it would provide a more reliable, valid, explicitly defined, and tailored means for making each respective social and clinical concern. It is for this reason that the authors of *DSM-5* included the supplementary dimensional scales to facilitate particular clinical decisions (e.g., Shear, Bjelland, Beesdo, Gloster, & Wittchen, 2008).

The NIMH has largely rejected *DSM-5*, indicating that they are no longer interested in funding studies that rely upon this nomenclature. As expressed by the director of the NIMH, "it is critical to realize that we cannot succeed if we use DSM categories" (Insel, 2013). NIMH has developed its own nomenclature, referred to as the Research Domain Criteria (RdoC; Insel, 2009; Sanislow et al., 2010), consisting of five broad areas of research (i.e., negative valence systems, positive valence systems, cognitive systems,

systems for social processes, and arousal/modulatory systems) that cut across the existing *DSM-5* diagnoses. The RDoC nomenclature is described as dimensional, because it is concerned with underlying mechanisms that are best described in terms of levels or degrees of functioning rather than distinct categories (Cuthbert, 2014). "Each level of analysis needs to be understood across a dimension of function" (Insel, 2013). However, the primary distinction with *DSM-5* is that the RDoC system emphasizes a neurobiological model of psychopathology. "Mental disorders are biological disorders involving brain circuits that implicate specific domains of cognition, emotion, or behavior" (Insel, 2013). NIMH is primarily critical of the *DSM-5* for deriving its diagnoses on the basis of overt symptoms (Craddock & Owen, 2010; Kapur, Phillips, & Insel, 2012). "Unlike our definitions of ischemic heart disease, lymphoma, or AIDS, the *DSM* diagnoses are based on a consensus about clusters of clinical symptoms, not any objective laboratory measure" (Insel, 2013). However, it is also unclear if a biological reductionism will be any more successful (Kendler, 2005).

Most (if not all) mental disorders appear to be the result of a complex interaction of an array of interacting biological vulnerabilities and dispositions with a number of significant environmental, psychosocial events that often exert their effects over a progressively developing period of time (Rutter, 2003). The most complete and compelling explanation will not likely be achieved through a biological reductionism because much will be lost by a failure to appreciate that explanation and understanding at the level of behavior and cognition remains fundamentally valid, and necessary (Kendler, 2005). The symptoms and pathologies of mental disorders appear to be highly responsive to a wide variety of neurobiological, interpersonal, cognitive, and other mediating and moderating variables that help to develop, shape, and form a particular individual's psychopathology profile. This complex etiological history and individual psychopathology profile are unlikely to be well described by single diagnostic categories that attempt to make distinctions at nonexistent discrete joints along the continuous distributions (Widiger & Samuel, 2005). The publication of *DSM-III* was said to have provided a significant, major advance in the diagnosis and classification of psychopathology (Klerman, 1983). The APA diagnostic nomenclature, however, is now beset by substantial criticism (Frances, 2013; Greenberg, 2013; Widiger & Crego, 2015), with NIMH openly rejecting it (Insel, 2013). Perhaps it is time for a paradigm shift.

REFERENCES

Ambrosini, P. J., Bennett, D. S., Cleland, C. M., & Haslam, N. (2002). *Journal of Psychiatric Research, 36*, 247–256.

American Association on Mental Retardation. (2002). *Mental retardation: Definition, classification, and systems of support* (10th ed.). Washington, DC: Author.

American Psychiatric Association. (1980). *Diagnostic and statistical manual of mental disorders* (3rd ed.). Washington, DC: Author.

American Psychiatric Association. (1987). *Diagnostic and statistical manual of mental disorders* (3rd ed., rev. ed.) Washington, DC: Author.

American Psychiatric Association. (1994). *Diagnostic and statistical manual of mental disorders* (4th ed.). Washington, DC: Author.

American Psychiatric Association. (2000). *Diagnostic and statistical manual of mental disorders* (4th ed., text rev.) Washington, DC: Author.

American Psychiatric Association (February, 2010). *Include pathological (disordered) gambling within addiction and related disorders.* Retrieved from http://www.dsm5.org/ProposedRevisions/Pages/proposedrevision.aspx?rid=210

American Psychiatric Association (May 1, 2012). *Rationale for the proposed changes disorders classification in DSM-5*. Retrieved from http://www.dsm5.o Personality%20Disorders/Rationale%20for%20the%20Proposed%20change: 20Personality%20Disorders%20in%20DSM-5%205-1-12.pdf

American Psychiatric Association. (2013). *Diagnostic and statistical manual of mental disorders* (5th ed.). Arlington, VA: American Psychiatric Publishing.

Andrews, G., Brugha, T., Thase, M., Duffy, F. F., Rucci, P., & Slade, T. (2008). Dimensionality and the category of major depressive episode. In J. E. Helzer, H. C. Kraemer, R. F. Krueger, H-U. Wittchen, P. J. Sirovatka, & D. A. Regier (Eds.), *Dimensional approaches to diagnostic classification. Refining the research agenda for DSM-V* (pp. 35–51). Washington, DC: American Psychiatric Association.

Baldwin, G., & Shean, G. D. (2006). A taxometric study of the Center for Epidemiological Studies depression scale. *Genetic, Social, and General Psychology Monographs, 132*, 101–128.

Bargh, J. A., & Ferguson, M. J. (2000). Beyond behaviorism: On the automaticity of higher mental processes. *Psychological Bulletin, 126*, 925–945.

Beach, S. R. H., & Amir, N. (2003). Is depression taxonic, dimensional, or both? *Journal of Abnormal Psychology, 112*, 2228–2236.

Beauchaine, T. P. (2007). A brief taxometrics primer. *Journal of Clinical Child and Adolescent Psychology, 36*, 654–676.

Bonanno, G. A., Neria, Y., Mancini, A., Coifman, K. G., Litz, B., & Insel, B. (2007). Is there more to complicated grief than depression and posttraumatic stress disorder? A test of incremental validity. *Journal of Abnormal Psychology, 116*, 342–351.

Boyd, J. H., Burke, J. D. Jr. Gruenberg, E., Holzer, C. E. III Rae, D. S., George, L. K., . . . Nestadt, G. (1984). Exclusion criteria of DSM-III: A study of co-occurrence of hierarchy-free syndromes. *Archives of General Psychiatry, 41*, 983–989.

Bradford, J., Geller, J., Lesieur, H. R., Rosenthal, R., & Wise, M. (1996). Impulse control disorders. In T. A. Widiger, A. J. Frances, H. A. Pincus, R. Ross, M. B. First, & W. W. Davis (Eds.), *DSM-IV sourcebook* (Vol. 2, pp. 1007–1031). Washington, DC: American Psychiatric Association.

Brown, T. A., & Barlow, D. H. (2009). A proposal for a dimensional classification system based on the shared features of the DSM-IV anxiety and mood disorders: implications for assessment and treatment. *Psychological Assessment, 21*(3), 256.

Brown, T. A., Campbell, L. A., Lehman, C. L., Grisham, J. R., & Mancill, R. B. (2001). Current and lifetime comorbidity of the DSM-IV anxiety and mood disorders in a large clinical sample. *Journal of Abnormal Psychology, 110*, 585–599.

Cardena, E., Butler, L. D., & Spiegel, D. (2003). Stress disorders. In I. Weiner (Series Ed.) & G. Stricker & T. A. Widiger (Vol. Eds.), *Handbook of psychology: Volume 8*. Clinical psychology (pp. 229–249). Hoboken, NJ: Wiley.

Carroll, K. M., Rounsaville, B. J., & Bryant, K. J. (1994). Should tolerance and withdrawal be required for substance dependence disorder? *Drug and Alcohol Dependence, 36*, 15–20.

Clark, L. A. (2007). Assessment and diagnosis of personality disorder. Perennial issues and an emerging reconceptualization. *Annual Review of Psychology, 58*, 227–257.

Clark, L. A., & Krueger, R. F. (2010, February 10). Rationale for a six-domain trait dimensional diagnostic system for personality disorder. Retrieved from http://www.dsm5.org/Proposed Revisions/Pages/RationaleforaSixDomainTraitDimensionalDiagnosticSystemforPersonality Disorder.aspx

Clarkin, J. F., & Huprich, S. K. (2011). Do DSM-5 personality disorder proposals meet criteria for clinical utility? *Journal of Personality Disorders, 25*, 192–205.

Craddock, N., & Owen, M. J. (2010). The Kraepelinian dichotomy—going, going, but still not gone. *British Journal of Psychiatry, 196*, 92–95.

Crowley, T. J. (2006). Adolescents and substance-related disorders: Research agenda to guide decisions on Diagnostic and Statistical Manual Disorders, fifth edition (DSM-V). *Addiction, 101*(Suppl. 1), 115–124.

Cuthbert, B. N. (2014). The RDoC framework: facilitating transition from ICD/DSM to dimensional approaches that integrate neuroscience and psychopathology. *World Psychiatry, 13*(1), 28–35.

Deary, I. J., Spinath, F. M., & Bates, T. C. (2006). Genetics of intelligence. *European Journal of Human Genetics, 14*, 690–700.

De Fruyt, F., De Clerq, B., De Bolle, M., Willie, B., Markon, K. E., & Krueger, R. F. (2013). General and maladaptive traits in a five-factor framework for DSM-5 in a university student sample. *Assessment, 20*, 295–307.

Edwards, G., & Gross, M. (1976). Alcohol dependence: Provisional description of a clinical syndrome. *British Medical Journal, 1*, 1058–1061.

Feinstein, A. R. (1970). The pre-therapeutic classification of co-morbidity in chronic disease. *Chronic Disease, 23*, 455–468.

First, M. B. (2003). Psychiatric classification. In A. Tasman, J. Kay, & J. Lieberman (Eds.), *Psychiatry* (2nd ed., Vol. 1, pp. 659–676). Hoboken, NJ: Wiley.

First, M. B. (2005). Clinical utility: A prerequisite for the adoption of a dimensional approach in DSM. *Journal of Abnormal Psychology, 114*, 560–564.

First, M. B., Bell, C. B., Cuthbert, B., Krystal, J. H., Malison, R., Offord, D. R., . . . Wisner, K. L. (2002). Personality disorders and relational disorders: A research agenda for addressing crucial gaps in DSM. In D. J. Kupfer, M. B. First, & D. A. Regier (Eds.), *A research agenda for DSM-V* (pp. 123–199). Washington, DC: American Psychiatric Association.

First, M. B., & Westen, D. (2007). Classification for clinical practice: How to make ICD and DSM better able to serve clinicians. *International Review of Psychiatry, 19*, 473–481.

Forstmeier S., & Maercker, A. (2007). Comparison of two diagnostic systems for complicated grief. *Journal of Affective Disorders, 99*, 203–211.

Frances, A. J. (2013). *Saving normal.* New York, NY: HarperCollins.

Frances, A. J., First, M. B., & Pincus, H. A. (1995). *DSM-IV guidebook.* Washington, DC: American Psychiatric Press.

Frances, A. J., First, M. B., Widiger, T. A., Miele, G., Tilly, S. M., Davis, W. W., & Pincus, H. A. (1991). An A to Z guide to DSM-IV conundrums. *Journal of Abnormal Psychology, 100*, 407–412.

Franklin, C. L., Strong, D. R., & Greene, R. L. (2002). A taxometric analysis of the MMPI-2 depression scales. *Journal of Personality Assessment, 79*, 110–121.

Friborg, O., Martinussen, M., Kaiser, S., Øvergård, K. T., & Rosenvinge, J. H. (2013). Comorbidity of personality disorders in anxiety disorders: a meta-analysis of 30 years of research. *Journal of Affective Disorders, 145*, 143–155.

Friborg, O., Martinsen, E. W., Martinussen, M., Kaiser, S., Overgard, K. T., & Rosenvinge, J. H. (2014). Comorbidity of personality disorders in mood disorders: A meta-analytic review of 122 studies from 1988 to 2010. *Journal of Affective Disorders, 152*, 1–11

Garbutt, J. C. (2008). Alcoholism. In S. H. Fatemi & P. J. Clayton (Eds.), *The medical basis of psychiatry* (3rd ed., pp. 227–249). Totowa, NJ: Humana Press.

Goldberg, D. (2010). Should our major classifications of mental disorders be revised? *British Journal of Psychiatry, 196*, 255–256.

Goldberg, D. (2015). Psychopathology and classification in psychiatry. *Social Psychiatry and Psychiatric Epidemiology, 50*, 1–5.

Goodwin, D. W., & Guze, S. B. (1996). *Psychiatric diagnosis* (5th ed) New York, NY: Oxford University Press.

Gore, W. L., & Widiger, T. A. (2013). The DSM-5 dimensional trait model and five factor models of general personality. *Journal of Abnormal Psychology, 122*, 816–821.

Greenberg, G. (2013). *The book of woe: The DSM and the unmaking of psychiatry.* New York, NY: Blue Rider Press.

Gunderson, J. G. (2010). Commentary on "Personality traits and the classification of mental disorders: Toward a more complete integration in DSM-5 and an empirical model of psychopathology." *Personality Disorders: Theory, Research, and Treatment 1,* 119–122.

Guze, S. B. (1978). Nature of psychiatric illness: Why psychiatry is a branch of medicine. *Comprehensive Psychiatry, 19,* 295–307.

Guze, S. B., & Helzer, J. E. (1987). The medical model and psychiatric disorders. In R. Michels & J. Cavenar (Eds.), *Psychiatry* (Vol. 1, chap. 51, pp. 1–8). Philadelphia, PA: Lippincott.

Hankin, B. L., Fraley, R. C., Lahey, B. B., & Waldman, I. D. (2005). Is depression best viewed as a continuum or discrete category? A taxometric analysis of childhood and adolescent depression in a population-based sample. *Journal of Abnormal Psychology, 114,* 96–110.

Helzer, J. E., Kraemer, H. C., & Krueger, R. F. (2006). The feasibility and need for dimensional psychiatric diagnoses. *Psychological Medicine, 36,* 1671–1680.

Helzer, J. E., Kraemer, H. C., Krueger, R. F., Wittchen, H.-U., Sirovatka, P. J., & Regier, D. A. (Eds.). (2008a). *Dimensional approaches in diagnostic classification.* Washington, DC: American Psychiatric Association.

Helzer, J. E., Wittchen, H-U., Krueger, R. F., & Kraemer, H. C. (2008b). Dimensional options for DSM-V: The way forward. In J. E. Helzer, H. C. Kraemer, R. F. Krueger, H-U. Wittchen, P. J. Sirovatka, & D. A. Regier (Eds.), *Dimensional approaches to diagnostic classification. Refining the research agenda for DSM-V* (pp. 115–127). Washington, DC: American Psychiatric Association.

Horwitz, A. V., & Wakefield, J. C. (2007). *The loss of sadness: How psychiatry transformed normal sorrow into depressive disorder.* New York, NY: Oxford University Press.

Howard, G. S., & Conway, C. G. (1986). Can there be an empirical science of volitional action? *American Psychologist, 41,* 1241–1251.

Hyman, S. (2010). The diagnosis of mental disorders: The problem of reification. *Annual Review of Clinical Psychology, 6,* 155–179.

Insel, T. R. (2009). Translating scientific opportunity into public health impact. A strategic plan for research on mental illness. *Archives of General Psychiatry, 66,* 128–133.

Insel, T. R. (2013). *Director's blog: Transforming diagnosis.* Retrieved from http://www.nimh.nih.gov/about/director/2013/transforming-diagnosis.shtml

Judd, L. L., Schettler, P. J., & Akiskal, H. S. (2002). The prevalence, clinical relevance, and public health significance of subthreshold depressions. *Psychiatric Clinics of North America, 25,* 685–698.

Kafka, M. P. (2010). Hypersexual disorder: A proposed diagnosis for DSM-V. *Archives of Sexual Behavior, 39,* 377–400.

Kahler, C. W., & Strong, D. R. (2006). A Rasch model analysis of DSM-IV alcohol abuse and dependence items in the National Epidemiological Survey on Alcohol and Related Conditions. *Alcoholism: Clinical and Experimental Research, 30,* 1165–1175.

Kandel, E. R. (1998). A new intellectual framework for psychiatry. *American Journal of Psychiatry, 155,* 457–469.

Kapur, S., Phillips, A. G., & Insel, T. R. (2012). Why has it taken so long for biological psychiatry to develop clinical tests and what to do about it? *Molecular Psychiatry, 17,* 1174–1179.

Keller, M. B. (1989). Current concepts in affective disorders. *Journal of Clinical Psychiatry, 50,* 157–162.

Keller, M. B., Klein, D. N., Hirschfeld, R. M. A., Kocsis, J. H., McCullough, J. P., Miller, I., . . . Shea, M. T. (1995). Results of the DSM-IV mood disorders field trial. *American Journal of Psychiatry, 152,* 843–849.

Kendell, R. E. (1975). *The role of diagnosis in psychiatry.* Oxford, England: Blackwell Scientific Publications.

Kendell, R. E. (1983). DSM-III: A major advance in psychiatric nosology. In R. L. Spitzer, J. B. W. Williams, & A. E. Skodol (Eds.), *International perspectives on DSM-III* (pp. 55–68). Washington, DC: American Psychiatric Press.

Kendell, R. E. (1989). Clinical validity. In L. N. Robins J. E. Barrett (Eds.), *The validity of psychiatric diagnosis* (pp. 305–321). New York, NY: Raven Press.

Kendell, R. E., & Jablensky, A. (2003). Distinguishing between the validity and utility of psychiatric diagnosis. *American Journal of Psychiatry, 160,* 4–12.

Kendler, K. S. (2005). Toward a philosophical structure for psychiatry, *American Journal of Psychiatry, 162,* 433–440.

Kessler, R. C., Chiu, W. T., Demler, O., & Walters, E. E. (2005). Prevalence, severity, and comorbidity of 12-month DSM-IV disorders in the National Comorbidity Survey replication. *Archives of General Psychiatry, 62,* 617–627.

Kessler, R. C., Zhao, S., Blazer, D. G., & Swartz, M. (1997). Prevalence, correlates, and course of minor depression and major depression in the National Comorbidity Survey. *Journal of Affective Disorders, 45,* 19–30.

Kirsch, I., & Lynn, S. J. (2000). Automaticity in clinical psychology. *American Psychologist, 54,* 504–515.

Klerman, G. L. (1983). The significance of DSM-III in American psychiatry. In R. L. Spitzer, J. B. W. Williams, & A. E. Skodol (Eds.), *International perspectives on DSM-III* (pp. 3–26). Washington, DC: American Psychiatric Press.

Klerman, G. L., Endicott, J., Spitzer, R. L., & Hirschfeld, R. M. (1979). Neurotic depressions: A systematic analysis of multiple criteria and meanings. *American Journal of Psychiatry, 136,* 57–61.

Knorr, U., & Kessing, L. V. (2010). The effect of selective serotonin reuptake in healthy subjects. A systematic review. *Nordic Journal of Psychiatry, 64,* 153–163.

Knutson, B., Wolkowitz, O. M., Cole, S. W., Chan, T., Moore, E. A., Johnson, R. C., . . . Reus, V. H. (1998). Selective alteration of personality and social behavior by serotonergic intervention. *American Journal of Psychiatry, 155,* 373–379.

Kotov, R., Krueger, R. F., Watson, D., Achenbach, T. M., Althoff, R. R., Bagby, M., . . . Zimmerman, M. (2017). The Hierarchical Taxonomy of Psychopathology (HiTOP): A dimensional alternative to traditional nosologies. *Journal of Abnormal Psychology, 126,* 454–477.

Kotov, R., Perlman, G., Gámez, W., & Watson, D. (2015). The structure and short-term stability of the emotional disorders: a dimensional approach. *Psychological Medicine, 45,* 1687–1698.

Kraemer, H. C. (2008). DSM categories and dimensions in clinical and research contexts. In J. E. Helzer, H. C. Kraemer, R. F. Krueger, H-U. Wittchen, P. J. Sirovatka, & D. A. Regier (Eds.), *Dimensional approaches to diagnostic classification. Refining the research agenda for DSM-V* (pp. 5–17). Washington, DC: American Psychiatric Association.

Kraemer, H. C., Noda, A., & O'Hara, R. (2004). Categorical versus dimensional approaches to diagnosis: Methodological challenges. *Journal of Psychiatric Research, 38,* 17–25.

Kraepelin, E. (1917). *Lectures on clinical psychiatry* (3rd ed.). New York, NY: William Wood.

Krueger, R. F. (2002). Psychometric perspectives on comorbidity. In J. E. Helzer & J. J. Hudziak (Eds.), *Defining psychopathology in the 21st century: DSM-V and beyond* (pp. 41–54). Washington, DC: American Psychiatric Publishing.

Krueger, R. F. (2005). Continuity of axes I and II: Toward a unified model of personality, personality disorders, and clinical disorders. *Journal of Personality Disorders, 19,* 233–261.

Krueger, R. F., Clark, L. A., Watson, D., Markon, K. E., Derringer, J., Skodol, A., & Livesley, W. J. (2011). Deriving an empirical structure of personality pathology for *DSM-5. Journal of Personality Disorders, 24,* 170–191.

Krueger, R. F., Derringer, J., Markon, K. F., Watson, D., & Skodol, A. E. (2012). Initial construction of a maladaptive personality trait model and inventory for DSM-5. *Psychological Medicine, 42,* 1879–1890.

Krueger, R. F., & Markon, K. E. (2006). Reinterpreting comorbidity: A model-based approach to understanding and classifying psychopathology. *Annual Review of Clinical Psychology, 2,* 111–133.

Krueger, R. F., & Markon, K. E. (2014). The role of the DSM-5 personality trait model in moving toward a quantitative and empirically based approach to classifying personality and psychopathology. *Annual Review of Clinical Psychology, 10,* 477–501.

Kupfer, D. J., First, M. B., & Regier, D. A. (Eds.). (2002). Introduction. In D. J. Kupfer, M. B. First, & D. A. Regier (Eds.), *A research agenda for DSM-V* (pp. xv–xxiii) Washington, DC: American Psychiatric Association.

Kwapil, T. R., & Barrantes-Vidal, N. (2012) Schizotypal personality disorder: An integrative review. In T. A. Widiger (Ed.), *The Oxford handbook of personality disorders* (pp. 437–476). New York, NY: Oxford University Press.

Langenbucher, J. W., Labouvie, E., Martin, C. S., Sanjuan, P. M., Bavly, L., Kirisci, L., & Chung, T. (2004). Application of item response theory analysis to alcohol, cannabis, and cocaine criteria in DSM-IV. *Journal of Abnormal Psychology, 113,* 72–80.

Liebowitz, M. R. (1992). Diagnostic issues in anxiety disorders. In A. Tasman &M. B. Riba (Eds.), *Review of psychiatry* (Vol. 11, pp. 247–259). Washington, DC: American Psychiatric Press.

Liebowitz, M. R., Barlow, D. H., Ballenger, J. C., Davidson, J., Foa, E. B., Fyer, A. J., . . . Spiegel, D. (1998). DSM-IV anxiety disorders: Final overview. In T. A. Widiger, A. J. Frances, H. A. Pincus, R. Ross, M. B. First, W. Davis, & M. Kline (Eds.), *DSM-IV sourcebook* (Vol. 4, pp. 1047–1076). Washington, DC: American Psychiatric Association.

Lilienfeld, S. O., Waldman, I. D., & Israel, A. C. (1994). A critical examination of the use of the term "comorbidity" in psychopathology research. *Clinical Psychology: Science and Practice, 1,* 71–83.

Livesley, W. J. (2001a). Commentary on reconceptualizing personality disorder categories using trait dimensions. *Journal of Personality, 69,* 277–286.

Livesley, W. J. (2001b). Conceptual and taxonomic issues. In W. J. Livesley (Ed.), *Handbook of personality disorders. Theory, research, and treatment* (pp. 3–38). New York, NY: Guilford Press.

Livesley, W. J. (2003). Diagnostic dilemmas in classifying personality disorder. In K. A. Phillips, M. B. First, & H. A. Pincus (Eds.), *Advancing DSM. Dilemmas in psychiatric diagnosis* (pp. 153–190). Washington, DC: American Psychiatric Association.

Lord, C., & Bishop, S. L. (2015). Recent advances in autism research as reflected in DSM-5 criteria for autism spectrum disorder. *Annual Review of Clinical Psychology, 11,* 53–70.

Luckasson, R., & Reeve, A. (2001). Naming, defining, and classifying in mental retardation. *Mental Retardation, 39,* 47–52.

Lynam, D. R., & Widiger, T. A. (2001). Using the five factor model to represent the DSM-IV personality disorders: An expert consensus approach. *Journal of Abnormal Psychology, 110,* 401–412.

Martin, P. R. (2005). Affirmative viewpoint. *American Journal on Addictions, 14,* 1–3.

Maser, J. D., & Cloninger, C. R. (1990). Comorbidity of anxiety and mood disorders: Introduction and overview. In J. D. Maser & C. R. Cloninger (Eds.), *Comorbidity of mood and anxiety disorders* (pp. 3–12). Washington, DC: American Psychiatric Press.

Maser, J. D., & Patterson, T. (2002). Spectrum and nosology: Implications for DSM-V. *Psychiatric Clinics of North America, 25,* 855–885.

McCrae, R. R., & Costa, P. T. (2003). *Personality in adulthood. A five-factor theory perspective* (2nd ed.). New York, NY: Guilford Press.

Mulder, R. T., Horwood, J., Tyrer, P., Carter, J., & Joyce, P. R. (2016). Validating the proposed ICD-11 domains. *Personality and Mental Health, 10*(2), 84–95.

Mullins-Sweatt, S. N., & Widiger, T. A. (2009). Clinical utility and DSM-V. *Psychological Assessment, 21,* 302–312.

Muthen, B. (2006). Should substance use disorders be considered as categorical or dimensional? *Addiction, 101*(Suppl 1), 6–16.

Naglieri, J., Salter, C., & Rojahn, J. (2008). Cognitive disorders of childhood. Specific learning and intellectual disabilities. In J. E. Maddux & B. A. Winstead (Eds.), *Psychopathology: Foundations for a contemporary understanding* (2nd ed., pp. 401–416). Mahwah, NJ: Erlbaum.

Nathan, P. E., Conrad, M., & Skinstad, A. H. (2016). History of the concept of addiction. *Annual Review of Clinical Psychology, 12*, 29–51.

O'Connor, B. P. (2002). A quantitative review of the comprehensiveness of the five-factor model in relation to popular personality inventories. *Assessment, 9*, 188–203.

O'Connor, B. P. (2005). A search for consensus on the dimensional structure of personality disorders. *Journal of Clinical Psychology, 61*, 323–345.

Ozer, D. J., & Benet-Martinez, V. (2006). Personality and the prediction of consequential outcomes. *Annual Review of Psychology, 57*, 401–421.

Petry, N. M. (2005a). Negative rebuttal. *American Journal on Addictions, 14*, 6–7.

Petry, N. M. (2005b). Negative viewpoint. *American Journal on Addictions, 14*, 4–5.

Petry, N. M. (2006). Should the scope of addictive behaviors be broadened to include pathological gambling? *Addiction, 101*(Suppl. 1), 152–160.

Phillips, K. A., Gunderson, J. G., Triebwasser, J., Kimble, C. R., Faedda, G., Lyoo, I. K., & Renn, J. (1998). Reliability and validity of depressive personality disorder. *American Journal of Psychiatry, 155*, 1044–1048.

Phillips, K. A., Price, L. H., Greenburg, B. D., & Rasmussen, S. A. (2003). Should the DSM diagnostic groupings be changed? In K. A. Phillips, M. B. First, & H. A. Pincus (Eds.), *Advancing DSM. Dilemmas in psychiatric diagnosis* (pp. 57–84). Washington, DC: American Psychiatric Association.

Pincus, H. A., Frances, A., Davis, W., First, M., & Widiger, T. (1992). DSM-IV and new diagnostic categories: Holding the line on proliferation. *American Journal of Psychiatry, 149*, 112–117.

Pincus, H. A., McQueen, L. E., & Elinson, L. (2003). Subthreshold mental disorders: Nosological and research recommendations. In K. A. Phillips, M. B. First, & H. A. Pincus (Eds.), *Advancing DSM: Dilemmas in psychiatric diagnosis* (pp. 129–144). Washington, DC: American Psychiatric Association.

Potenza, M. N. (2006). Should addictive disorders include non-substance-related conditions? *Addiction, 101*(Suppl. 1), 142–151.

Prisciandaro, J. J., & Roberts, J. E. (2005). A taxometric investigation of unipolar depression in the National Comorbidity Survey. *Journal of Abnormal Psychology, 114*, 718–728.

Proudfoot, H., Baillie, A. J., & Teesson, M. (2006). The structure of alcohol dependence in the community. *Drug and Alcohol Dependence, 81*, 21–26.

Ragan, P. W., & Martin, P. R. (2000). The psychobiology of sexual addiction. *Sexual Addiction & Compulsivity, 7*, 161–175.

Raine, A. (2006). Schizotypal personality: Neurodevelopmental and psychosocial trajectories. *Annual Review of Clinical Psychology, 2*, 291–326.

Regier, D. A. (2008). Forward: Dimensional approaches to psychiatric classification. In J. E. Helzer, H. C. Kraemer, R. F. Krueger, H.-U. Wittchen, P. J. Sirovatka, & D. A. Regier (Eds.), *Dimensional approaches to diagnostic classification. Refining the research agenda for DSM-V* (pp. xvii–xxiii) Washington, DC: American Psychiatric Association.

Regier, D. A., Narrow, W. E., Kuhl, E. A., & Kupfer, D. J. (2010). The conceptual development of DSM-V. *American Journal of Psychiatry, 166*, 645–655.

Reise, S. P., & Waller, N. G. (2009). Item response theory and clinical measurement. *Annual Review of Clinical Psychology, 5*, 27–48.

Roberts, B. W., & DelVecchio, W. F. (2000). The rank-order consistency of personality traits from childhood to old age: A quantitative review of longitudinal studies. *Psychological Bulletin, 126*, 3–25.

Robins, E., & Guze, S. B. (1970). Establishment of diagnostic validity in psychiatric illness: Its application to schizophrenia. *American Journal of Psychiatry, 126,* 107–111.

Robins, L. N. & Barrett, J. E. (Eds.). (1989). *The validity of psychiatric diagnosis.* New York, NY: Raven Press.

Rounsaville, B. J., Alarcon, R. D., Andrews, G., Jackson, J. S., Kendell, R. E., & Kendler, K. (2002). Basic nomenclature issues for DSM-V. In D. J. Kupfer, M. B. First, & D. E. Regier (Eds.), *A research agenda for DSM-V* (pp. 1–29). Washington, DC: American Psychiatric Association.

Ruscio, A. M., & Ruscio, J. (2002). The latent structure of analogue depression: Should the Beck Depression Inventory be used to classify groups? *Psychological Assessment, 14,* 135–145.

Ruscio, J., & Ruscio, A. M. (2000). Informing the continuity controversy: A taxometric analysis of depression. *Journal of Abnormal Psychology, 109,* 473–487.

Ruscio, J., & Ruscio, A. M. (2004). Clarifying boundary issues in psychopathology: The role of taxometrics in a comprehensive program of structural research. *Journal of Abnormal Psychology, 113,* 24–38.

Ruscio, J., Zimmerman, M., McGlinchey, J. B., Chelminski, I., & Young, D. (2007). Diagnosing major depressive disorder XI. A taxometric investigation of the structure underlying DSM-IV symptoms. *Journal of Nervous and Mental Disease, 195,* 10–19.

Rutter, M., (2003, October). *Pathways of genetic influences on psychopathology.* Zubin Award Address at the 18th Annual Meeting of the Society for Research in Psychopathology, Toronto, Ontario.

Saha, T. D., Chou, S. P., & Grant, B. F. (2006). Toward an alcohol use disorder continuum using item response theory: Results from the National Epidemiologic Survey on Alcohol and Related Conditions. *Psychological Medicine, 36,* 931–941.

Sakashita, C., Slade, T., & Andrews, G. (2007). An empirical analysis of two assumptions in the diagnosis of DSM-IV major depressive episode. *Australian and New Zealand Journal of Psychiatry, 41,* 17–23.

Samuel, D. B., & Widiger, T. A. (2008). A meta-analytic review of the relationships between the five-factor model and DSM-IV-TR personality disorders: A facet level analysis. *Clinical Psychology Review, 28,* 1326–1342.

Samuels, J., & Costa, P. T. (2012). Obsessive-compulsive personality disorder. In T. A. Widiger (Ed.), *The Oxford handbook of personality disorders* (pp. 566–581). New York, NY: Oxford University Press.

Sanderson, C. J., & Clarkin, J. F. (2002). Further use of the NEO PI-R personality dimensions in differential treatment planning. In P. T. Costa & T. A. Widiger (Eds.), *Personality disorders and the five factor model of personality* (2nd ed., pp. 351–75). Washington, DC: American Psychological Association.

Sanislow, C. A., da Cruz, K. L., Gianoli, M. O., & Reagan, E. (2012). Avoidant personality disorder, traits, and types. In T. A. Widiger (Ed.), *The Oxford handbook of personality disorders* (pp. 549–565). New York, NY: Oxford University Press.

Sanislow, C. A., Pine, D. S., Quinn, K. J., Kozak, M. J., Garvey, M. A., Heinssen, R. K., . . . Cuthbert, B. N. (2010). Developing constructs for psychopathology research: Research domain criteria. *Journal of Abnormal Psychology, 119,* 631–638.

Saulsman, L. M., & Page, A. C. (2004). The five-factor model and personality disorder empirical literature: A meta-analytic review. *Clinical Psychology Review, 23,* 1055–1085.

Saunders, J. B. (2006). Substance dependence and non-dependence in the Diagnostic and Statistical Manual of Mental Disorders (DSM) and the International Classification of Diseases (ICD): Can an identical conceptualization be achieved? *Addiction, 101*(Suppl. 1), 48–58.

Schneider, F. R., Blanco, C., Anita, S., & Liebowitz, M. R. (2002). The social anxiety spectrum. *Psychiatric Clinics of North America, 25,* 757–774.

Schuckit, M. A., Daeppen, J-B., Danko, G. P., Tripp, M. L., Smith, T. L., Li, T-K., . . . Bucholz, K. K. (1999). Clinical implications for four drugs of the DSM-IV distinction between substance dependence with and without a physiological component. *American Journal of Psychiatry, 156,* 41–49.

Shear, M. K., Bjelland, I., Beesdo, K., Gloster, A. T., & Wittchen, H.-U. (2008). Supplementary dimensional assessment in anxiety disorders. In J. E. Helzer, H. C. Kraemer, R. F. Krueger, H.-U. Wittchen, P. J. Sirovatka, & D. A. Regier (Eds.), *Dimensional approaches to diagnostic classification. Refining the research agenda for DSM-V* (pp. 65–84). Washington, DC: American Psychiatric Association.

Shedler, J., Beck, A., Fonagy, P., Gabbard, G. O., Gunderson, J. G., Kernberg, O., . . . Westen, D. (2010). Personality disorders in DSM-5. *American Journal of Psychiatry, 167,* 1027–1028.

Skodol, A. E. (2012) Personality disorders in DSM-5. *Annual Review of Clinical Psychology, 8,* 317–344.

Skodol, A. E., Morey, L. C., Bender, D. S., & Oldham, J. M. (2013). The ironic fate of the personality disorders in DSM-5. *Personality Disorders: Theory, Research, & Treatment, 4,* 342–349.

Slade, T. (2007). Taxometric investigation of depression: Evidence of consistent latent structure across clinical and community samples. *Australian and New Zealand Journal of Psychiatry, 41,* 403–410.

Slade, T., & Andrews, G. (2005). Latent structure of depression in a community sample: A taxometric analysis. *Psychological Medicine, 35,* 489–497.

Smith, G. T., & Combs, J. (2010). Issues of construct validity in psychological diagnoses. In T. Millon, R. F. Krueger, and E. Simonsen (Eds.), *Contemporary directions in psychopathology: Toward the DSM-V and ICD-11* (pp. 205–222). New York, NY: Guilford Press.

Solomon, A., Ruscio, J., Seeley, J. R., & Lewinsohn, P. M. (2006). A taxometric investigation of unipolar depression in a large community sample. *Psychological Medicine, 36,* 973–985.

Spitzer, R. L., Endicott, J., & Robins, E. (1978). Research diagnostic criteria: Rationale and reliability. *Archives of General Psychiatry, 35,* 773–782.

Spitzer, R. L., & Williams, J. B. W. (1985). Proposed revisions in the DSM-III classification of anxiety disorders based on research and clinical experience. In A. H. Tuma & J. Maser (Eds.), *Anxiety and the anxiety disorders* (pp. 759–773). Hillsdale, NJ: Erlbaum.

Spitzer, R. L., Williams, J. B. W., & Skodol, A. E. (1980). DSM-III: The major achievements and an overview. *American Journal of Psychiatry, 137,* 151–164.

Stephan, K. E., Bach, D. R., Fletcher, P. C., Flint, J., Frank, M. J., Friston, K. J., . . . Dayan, P. (2016). Charting the landscape of priority problems in psychiatry, part 1: classification and diagnosis. *Lancet Psychiatry, 3,* 77–83.

Tang, T. Z., DeRubeis, R. J., Hollon, S. D., Amsterdam, J., Shelton, R., & Schalet, B. (2009). Personality change during depression treatment. A placebo-controlled trial. *Archives of General Psychiatry, 66,* 1322–1330.

Task Force on DSM-IV. (1991, September). *DSM-IV options book: Work in progress.* Washington, DC: American Psychiatric Association.

Task Force on DSM-IV. (1993, March). *DSM-IV draft criteria.* Washington, DC: American Psychiatric Association.

Thomas, K. M., Yalch, M. M., Krueger, R. F., Wright, A. G. C., Markon, K. E., & Hopwood, C. J. (2013). The convergent structure of DSM-5 personality trait facets and Five-Factor Model trait domains. *Assessment, 20,* 308–311.

Trull, T. J., & Durrett, C. A. (2005). Categorical and dimensional models of personality disorder. *Annual Review of Clinical Psychology, 1,* 355–380.

Turner, S. M., & Beidel, D. C. (1989). Social phobia: Clinical syndrome, diagnosis, and comorbidity. *Clinical Psychology Review, 9,* 3–18.

Turner, S. M., Beidel, D. C., & Townsley, R. M. (1992). Social phobia: A comparison of specific and generalized subtypes and avoidant personality disorder. *Journal of Abnormal Psychology, 101,* 326–331.

Tyrer, P. (2005). The anxious cluster of personality disorders: A review. In M. Maj, H. S. Akiskal, J. E. Mezzich, & A. Okasha (Eds.), *Personality disorders* (pp. 349–375). Hoboken, NJ: Wiley.

Tyrer, P. (2014). Time to choose DSM-5, ICD-11, or both? *Archives of Psychiatry and Psychotherapy, 3*, 5–8.

Tyrer, P., Reed, G. M., & Crawford, M. J. (2015). Classification, assessment, prevalence, and effect of personality disorder. *Lancet, 385*, 717–726.

Üstün, T. B., & Sartorius, N. (Eds.). (1995). *Mental illness in general health care: An international study.* London, England: Wiley.

Wakefield, J. C. (2016). Diagnostic issues and controversies in DSM-5: Return of the false positives problem. *Annual Review of Clinical Psychology, 12*, 105–132.

Wakefield, J. C., Schmitz, M. F., First, M. B., & Horwitz, A. V. (2007). Extending the bereavement exclusion for major depression to other losses—Evidence from the National Comorbidity Survey. *Archives of General Psychiatry, 64*, 433–440.

Wegner, D. M., & Wheatley, T. (2000). Apparent mental causation: Sources of the experience of will. *American Psychologist, 54*, 480–492.

Widiger, T. A. (2001a). Social anxiety, social phobia, and avoidant personality disorder. In W. R. Corzier & L. Alden (Eds.), *International handbook of social anxiety* (pp. 335–356). New York, NY: Wiley.

Widiger, T. A. (2001b). What can we learn from taxometric analyses? *Clinical Psychology: Science and Practice, 8*, 528–533.

Widiger, T. A. (2003). Personality disorder and Axis I psychopathology: The problematic boundary of Axis I and Axis II. *Journal of Personality Disorders, 17*, 90–108.

Widiger, T. A. (2012a). Classification and diagnosis: Historical development and contemporary issues. In J. Maddux and B. Winstead (Eds.), *Psychopathology: Foundations for a contemporary understanding* (3rd ed., pp. 63–83). Erlbaum.

Widiger, T. A. (2012b). Historical developments and current issues. In T. A. Widiger (Ed.), *The Oxford handbook of personality disorders* (pp. 13–34). New York: Oxford University Press.

Widiger, T. A. (2013). DSM-5 personality disorders. A postmortem and future look. *Personality Disorders: Theory, Research, and Treatment, 4*, 382–387.

Widiger, T. A., & Clark, L. A. (2000). Toward DSM-V and the classification of psychopathology. *Psychological Bulletin, 126*, 946–963.

Widiger, T. A., & Costa, P. T. (2002). Five-factor model personality disorder research. In T. A. Widiger & P. T. Costa (Eds.) *Personality disorders and the five-factor model of personality* (2nd ed., pp. 59–87). Washington, DC: American Psychological Association.

Widiger, T. A., & Crego, C. (2015). Process and content of DSM-5. *Psychopathology Review, 2*, 162–176.

Widiger, T. A., & Edmundson, M. (2011). Diagnoses, dimensions, and DSM-V. In D. Barlow (Ed.), *Oxford handbook of clinical psychology* (pp. 254–278). New York, NY: Oxford University Press.

Widiger, T. A., & Miller, J. D. (2008). Psychological diagnosis. In D. Richard & S. Huprich (Eds.), *Clinical psychology, assessment, treatment, and research* (pp. 69–88). Oxford, England: Elsevier.

Widiger, T. A., & Samuel, D. B. (2005). Diagnostic categories or dimensions: A question for DSM-V. *Journal of Abnormal Psychology, 114*, 494–504.

Widiger, T. A., Samuel, D. B., Mullins-Sweat, S., Gore, W. L., & Crego, C. (2012). Integrating normal and abnormal personality structure: The five-factor model. In T. A. Widiger (Ed.), *The Oxford handbook of personality disorders* (pp. 82–107). New York, NY: Oxford University Press.

Widiger, T. A., & Sankis, L. (2000). Adult psychopathology: Issues and controversies. *Annual Review of Psychology, 51*, 377–404.

Widiger, T. A., Simonsen, E., Krueger, R. F., Livesley, W. J., & Verheul, R. (2005). Personality disorder research agenda for the DSM-V. *Journal of Personality Disorders, 19*, 317–340.

Widiger, T. A., & Trull, T. J. (2007). Plate tectonics in the classification of personality disorder: Shifting to a dimensional model. *American Psychologist, 62,* 71–83.

Winters, J. (2010). Hypersexual disorder: A more cautious approach. *Archives of Sexual Behavior, 39,* 594–596.

World Health Organization. (1992). *The ICD-10 classification of mental and behavioural disorders. Clinical descriptions and diagnostic guidelines.* Geneva, Switzerland: Author.

Zachar, P., & Kendler, K. S. (2007). Psychiatric disorders: A conceptual taxonomy. *American Journal of Psychiatry, 164,* 557–565.

CHAPTER 2

Promise and Challenges with the Research Domain Criteria Framework

JEFFREY S. BEDWELL, CHRISTOPHER C. SPENCER, and JOHN P. O'DONNELL

RESEARCH DOMAIN CRITERIA: DESCRIPTION AND REASONS FOR DEVELOPMENT

Compared with other areas of clinical practice, there has been relatively little progress in the development of more effective treatments and prevention strategies for mental illness over the past several decades, despite rapid advances in neuroscience (Kozak & Cuthbert, 2016). One likely obstacle has been problems with the validity of the current mental illness classification systems (Cuthbert & Kozak, 2013)—the *Diagnostic and Statistical Manual of Mental Disorders* (*DSM*), currently in its fifth edition (American Psychiatric Association, 2013), and the mental and behavioral disorders section of the *International Classification of Diseases* (ICD), now in its 10th edition (World Health Organization, 1990).

The *DSM-I* was published in 1952 and contained approximately 100 disorders that were modeled from the Veterans Administration classification and an eclectic mixture of Kraepelinian and psychoanalytic concepts (Cooper & Blashfield, 2016). These initial disorders were given names and very short descriptions to assist in communication between medical professionals. The *DSM-II* was published in 1968 and expanded the classification of disorders from two to 10 divisions while eliminating the notion that all disorders were a reaction to idiosyncratic life events (Fischer, 2012). The *DSM-II* was widely criticized as the diagnoses were shown to be unreliable, which led to the publication of the *DSM-III* in 1980. This represented a larger paradigm shift by introducing checklists of mostly behavioral features, which improved diagnostic reliability, but potentially at the expense of validity (Fischer, 2012). The checklist of symptoms was polythetic, in that many listed symptoms were not required or essential to the diagnosis. This polythetic checklist approach was maintained in the remaining *DSM* versions— *DSM-III-R* (1987), *DSM-IV* (1994), *DSM-IV-TR* (2000), and *DSM-5* (2013).

Although an improvement upon previous classification systems, there have been many criticisms of the current polythetic criteria approach. For example, using the polythetic method of diagnosis with the *DSM-5*, there are 636,120 symptom combinations that meet diagnostic criteria for post-traumatic stress disorder, 23,442 ways to meet criteria for panic disorder, and 227 ways to meet criteria for a major depressive episode,

Adult Psychopathology and Diagnosis, Eighth Edition. Edited by Deborah C. Beidel and B. Christopher Frueh.
© 2018 John Wiley & Sons, Inc. Published 2018 by John Wiley & Sons, Inc.
Companion website: www.wiley.com/go/beidel/psychopathology8e

which highlights the significant within-disorder heterogeneity problem (DiMauro, Carter, Folk, & Kashdan, 2014; Galatzer-Levy & Bryant, 2013). Further, changes to the *DSM* based on empirical literature are slow to become adopted (e.g., the trait-based personality system was placed in an alternative section of *DSM-5*), and decisions are subject to financial and political pressures (Pilecki, Clegg, & McKay, 2011). Individual disorders appearing in the *DSM* and *ICD* were developed based on observed symptom clusters, associated features, and course of illness, as interpreted using informal clinical intuition (Kozak & Cuthbert, 2016). Unfortunately, symptoms in these classification systems are often heterogeneous within diagnoses and overlapping across diagnoses, which impede efforts to establish convergent and discriminant validity (Kozak & Cuthbert, 2016). While updated editions of these systems have refined the symptoms based on observation, the disorders themselves became reified as actual disease entities without sufficient support for validity (Cuthbert & Kozak, 2013). This led to continued reliance on these potentially invalid diagnoses in mental health research, which may explain the inability of researchers to identify reliable, sensitive, and specific markers of an underlying disease process for any of the disorders (Pearlson, 2015).

In reaction to the prolonged lack of progress in identifying more effective treatments for mental illness, the National Institute of Mental Health (NIMH) introduced a new Strategic Plan in 2008 for the development of new ways to classify mental illnesses based on "observable behavioral and neurobiological measures" (National Institute of Mental Health, 2016). In response to this plan, NIMH introduced the Research Domain Criteria (RDoC) framework in 2009 to guide future research in a manner that addresses the aims of this plan and does not rely on a presumably flawed diagnostic system (Insel et al., 2010; Sanislow et al., 2010). RDoC was modeled after a separate NIMH-funded project called Cognitive Neuroscience for Translational Research in Cognition on Schizophrenia (CNTRICS), which aimed to identify circuit-based measures of cognitive constructs to serve as treatment targets for schizophrenia (Barch et al., 2009). The NIMH eventually developed a designated "RDoC Unit" within its organization to facilitate communication with researchers and the public about RDoC intent, methodology, and funding opportunities (see https://www.nimh.nih.gov/research-priorities/rdoc/index.shtml).

While the current *DSM* and *ICD* systems primarily reflect a top-down model in which theoretical syndromes direct and constrain subsequent research, the RDoC approach uses a bottom-up model that begins with empirical findings from studies that are agnostic to existing theoretical diagnoses, with intentions to use that knowledge to create a future classification system. RDoC also represents a new dimensional approach to psychopathology that encourages examination of the entire range from normal to abnormal functioning on the constructs (Cuthbert & Insel, 2013). Importantly, RDoC does not attempt to represent an alternative diagnostic system—it is a framework for psychopathology research, which may eventually lead to a more valid diagnostic system. In addition, some investigators believe that RDoC has strong potential to identify currently unknown early developmental markers of psychopathology that may lead to directed early intervention and prevention techniques (Sonuga-Barke, 2014). Specifically RDoC advocates "(a) the development and validation of dimensional constructs that (b) integrate elements of psychology and biology that (c) are theoretically linked to narrowly defined impairments of psychiatric clinical importance" (Kozak & Cuthbert, 2016).

THE RDoC MATRIX

The RDoC template consists of a matrix of units of analysis in relation to particular dimensional domains, constructs, and subconstructs (see Figure 2.1 for an example

Negative Valence Systems

Construct/Subconstruct	Genes Notice	Molecules	Cells	Circuits	Physiology	Behavior	Self-Report	Paradigms
Acute Threat ("Fear")		Elements	Elements	Elements	Elements	Elements	Elements	Elements
Potential Threat ("Anxiety")		Elements	Elements	Elements	Elements		Elements	Elements
Sustained Threat		Elements	Elements	Elements	Elements	Elements	Elements	
Loss		Elements		Elements	Elements	Elements	Elements	Elements
Frustrative Nonreward		Elements		Elements		Elements	Elements	Elements

Positive Valence Systems

Construct/Subconstruct		Genes Notice	Molecules	Cells	Circuits	Physiology	Behavior	Self-Report	Paradigms
Approach Motivation	Reward Valuation		Elements		Elements			Elements	Elements
	Effort Valuation / Willingness to Work		Elements		Elements			Elements	Elements
	Expectancy / Reward Prediction Error		Elements		Elements	Elements	Elements	Elements	Elements
	Action Selection / Preference-Based Decision Making				Elements				
Initial Responsiveness to Reward Attainment			Elements		Elements		Elements	Elements	Elements
Sustained/Longer-Term Responsiveness to Reward Attainment			Elements		Elements	Elements	Elements	Elements	
Reward Learning			Elements	Elements	Elements	Elements	Elements	Elements	Elements
Habit			Elements	Elements	Elements		Elements	Elements	Elements

Figure 2.1   Depiction of the Research Domain Criteria Matrix's negative and positive valence system domains. Note that this figure is a portion of the larger matrix that contains additional domains. *Source*: National Institute of Mental Health (2017). RDoC Matrix. Retrieved February 28, 2017, from https://www.nimh.nih.gov/research-priorities/rdoc/constructs/rdoc-matrix.shtml.

portion of the matrix). The units of analysis span a micro-to-macro level, starting with genes, molecules, and cells—then expanding to circuits (e.g., as measured by functional neuroimaging and event-related potentials) and physiology (i.e., biological indices that do not directly map on to circuits)—followed by the more downstream units of behavior (e.g., performance on tasks or systematic behavioral observations) and self-reports (e.g., interview-based scales and psychometric self-report scales). These units of analyses are intended to be independent, with no unit viewed as more important or causally linked to another unit. There is a separate column for paradigms, which are well-validated means of measuring the respective construct, which may include more than one unit of analysis. As depicted in Figure 2.1, the units of analysis and paradigms are presented in the vertical columns of the grid, while the constructs comprise the rows. The matrix is not a fixed framework, as the NIMH encourages scientists to suggest additions and changes, which has resulted in updates to the matrix on the NIMH website since the initial release.

Currently there are five domains: negative valence systems (e.g., acute threat, loss), positive valence systems (e.g., approach motivation, reward learning), cognitive systems (e.g., attention, working memory), social processes (e.g., affiliation and attachment, social communication), and arousal and regulatory systems (e.g., arousal, circadian rhythms). Under each of these domains are rows for each construct, examples of which are as outlined. Some constructs also have subconstructs. The constructs and subconstructs were chosen in workshops by experts in the field to have a level of granularity that facilitates research, as higher-level psychological constructs (e.g., executive functioning) contain excessive heterogeneity (Kozak & Cuthbert, 2016). In addition, the initial workshops required that constructs must meet two criteria to be considered for inclusion in the matrix—"There must be strong evidence for the validity of the suggested construct itself [as a behavioral function]"; and "There must be strong evidence that the suggested construct maps onto a specific biological system, such as a brain circuit" (Cuthbert & Insel, 2013). Within the cells of the matrix are "elements," which are empirically supported components or instruments related to the respective construct and unit of analysis. The elements are continually updated based on new scientific findings, and the goal of the RDoC paradigm is to fill in all of the cells with elements that have strong and consistent empirical support and psychometric properties. Readers are encouraged to view the most recent version at the official NIMH RDoC website: https://www.nimh .nih.gov/research-priorities/rdoc/index.shtml.[1]

Two additional important aspects of the RDoC framework are not explicitly included in the matrix itself, as they represent additional dimensions that could not be represented on the two-dimensional matrix. These are neurodevelopmental trajectories and interactions with the environment. The RDoC explicitly seeks to better understand developmental trajectories across all phases of the lifespan. In particular it seeks to better understand the trajectories that mark the transition from normal to abnormal behavior, with a goal of identifying pre-symptomatic dysfunction that could be targeted by prevention strategies (Cuthbert, 2014). The NIMH also recognizes that it is widely accepted that most mental illnesses result from the interaction of neuropathology with environmental influences. The RDoC encourages investigators to measure and consider the bidirectional influence of environmental effects on a construct of interest (Cuthbert, 2014). Environmental factors also interact with the developmental factors as there may be critical windows of development in which particular environmental factors (e.g., sexual abuse, viral infection) have a larger influence on changing a construct from the normal to abnormal range of functioning. The NIMH does not offer formal guidance or strategies on how to incorporate the role of development or environment in a particular RDoC project, and instead encourages investigators to be creative and follow the most promising methodological ideas as applied to the construct of interest (Cuthbert, 2014).

ILLUSTRATIVE EXAMPLE FOR THE RDoC MATRIX

As an example, we will examine the current state of knowledge (i.e., elements) inside of the cells of the subconstruct "acute threat (fear)," which is found under the construct "negative valence systems." For the sake of brevity, only two elements will be listed for

---

[1] Details in this paragraph were based on the latest information available from this NIMH website as of February 2017.

each cell, although many cells contain more. Starting from left to right across columns, genes includes "BDNF" and "5HT/5HTRs," molecules includes "dopamine" and "GABA," cells includes "GABAergic cells" and "glia," circuits includes "autonomic nervous system" and "basal amygdala," physiology includes "blood pressure" and "context startle," behavior includes "analgesia" and "avoidance," and self-report includes "fear survey schedule" and "subjective units of distress scale (SUDS)." The separate "paradigms" column on the far right includes "behavior approach test" and "CO_2 challenge test." While the role of development and environment are not listed in the matrix, investigators are strongly encouraged to measure and describe the influence of these factors on acute threat/fear.

For this example of acute threat/fear, one RDoC methodology approach might consist of recruiting participants in a manner that would represent a relatively continuous dimension of severity of fear response. This may involve multiple targeted advertisements/recruitment strategies to include individuals with no history of psychopathology, individuals with disorders that are likely to include exaggerated acute fear responses (e.g., post-traumatic stress disorder or panic disorder), individuals who may have abnormally reduced fear response (e.g., psychopathy or amygdala lesion), and individuals with other psychiatric disorders. The researcher may then choose to use a behavior approach test to elicit temporary acute fear and examine dependent variables across multiple units of analysis such as blood pressure and SUDS ratings, as well as pre-existing units such as polymorphisms on BDNF-related genes. This hypothetical study could then contribute to the elements under "genes" by identifying a single nucleotide polymorphism of a particular BDNF-related gene that related to an abnormal fear response to the behavior approach test (as indexed by blood pressure and SUDS). The researcher could add examination of the potential moderating role of environment by collecting information on current/recent life stressors, social support, and history of traumatic events, as well as the potential moderating role of development by including a wide range of ages.

RDoC CRITIQUES AND RESPONSES

As the RDoC framework is a radical departure from the long tradition of diagnoses based on the medical model (e.g., *DSM*), there have been many criticisms and concerns since its release. A central concern raised by different investigators is that RDoC is reductionistic and places more emphasis on biology while under-emphasizing the role of the environment (Kirmayer & Crafa, 2014; Lilienfeld, 2014; Miller, 2010; Paris & Kirmayer, 2016; Zoellner & Foa, 2016). This concern may stem from the observation that five of the seven units of analyses are at a biological level, with behavior and self-reports being the two exceptions, which also appear at the far right of the list. However, the NIMH has clarified that the units of analyses are not intended to be "levels" of analysis, as each is fully independent and not dependent on other units (Kozak & Cuthbert, 2016). In addition, although the environment (e.g., social or cultural context) is not explicitly present in the units of analysis, likely due to difficulty in standardizing definitions and measurement, the RDoC website strongly encourages researchers to examine the influence of environment on the constructs, as well as the interaction of environment with the other units of analysis. Thus, while examination of the RDoC matrix table may give a superficial impression that it places more emphasis on biology, the NIMH has clarified on both the website and in publications that RDoC is agnostic regarding the relative influence of biology and environment on the constructs.

Others have criticized the lack of emphasis on self-report which captures the embodied experience, and in some cases may have more established psychometric support than behavioral or physiological methods (Paris & Kirmayer, 2016; Zoellner & Foa, 2016). However, the RDoC matrix includes a "units of analysis" column for self-report with the intent of capturing this important element (Cuthbert, 2014). Similar to the previous criticism, there appears to be some misunderstanding in the field about how the units of analysis are not assuming causal direction or level of importance. Given its agnostic stance, the framework can incorporate growing knowledge regarding phenomenology. For example, it is possible that individual differences in the functioning of a particular circuit may have several different dimensional ways in which individuals experience and self-report that disturbance. An existing example can be found under the domain of negative valence systems and the construct of potential threat ("anxiety"). In that self-report cell there are several scales listed that assess various manners in which an individual may experience dimensional differences in the functioning of the related construct, including social anxiety (Fear of Negative Evaluation Scale), anxiety regarding physical sensations related to anxiety (Anxiety Sensitivity Index), and anxiety of the unknown (Intolerance of Uncertainty Scale). As there are no causal inferences between the units of analysis, the matrix allows for the possibility that an environmental insult (e.g., chronic bullying) during a critical developmental window (e.g., late childhood) may cause an enduring self-experience of social anxiety which may then have a cascading effect of changing the layers of related biological units, including epigenetic changes as the most micro level. However, the self-report unit of analysis is currently limited to existing self-report measures and clinical interviews, and thus may not be sensitive to unique phenomenological experiences that do not have a corresponding instrument with strong psychometric properties. The NIMH acknowledges that RDoC is not intended to capture all aspects of psychopathology and therefore continues to fund projects that fall outside of the RDoC framework (Cuthbert, 2014).

Some investigators have highlighted problems with disparate and largely unknown levels of measurement error present in particular instruments/paradigms identified in the matrix (Lilienfeld, 2014; Peterson, 2015). This is a general problem in the field of cognitive/behavioral testing and neuroimaging, which will present an obstacle to RDoC research until investigators clarify the measurement error of existing measures and create new measures with less error (Cuthbert & Kozak, 2013). This effort has already begun— one example is a study examining the psychometric properties of the startle and corrugator response in the no shock, predictable shock, unpredictable shock task (Kaye, Bradford, & Curtin, 2016).

Another issue is that RDoC does not explicitly address how individuals vary in their characteristic developmental adaptations (i.e., behavioral expressions) of underlying basic tendencies/traits (Franklin, Jamieson, Glenn, & Nock, 2015; Lilienfeld, 2014). Therefore, the relationship between the units of analysis for a particular construct interacts with individualized behavioral expression of that construct. Until varying behavioral expressions of a particular construct are operationally defined and measured, this will present a confound to understanding the relationships across the units of analysis for that construct.

Some have argued that, given these difficulties with RDoC, a more fruitful approach would involve iterative study of potential biomarkers for diagnoses, establishing convergent validity through variables such as course of illness, family history, and response to treatment (Carroll, 2015). However, this has been the general approach attempted by many investigators over the last several decades and little progress has been made in terms of treatment or prevention targets. This lack of progress is what prompted the NIMH to design a radically different research paradigm with the hope of fostering the development of more effective and individually targeted treatments and prevention techniques (Cuthbert, 2014).

EXAMPLES OF INDIVIDUAL RESEARCH PROJECTS
USING RDoC-COMPATIBLE METHODOLOGIES

Since the public release of RDoC, a number of research studies have been published using methodologies consistent with the RDoC. These studies have generally used one of five strategies for participant sampling:

- recruitment of a nonpsychiatric community sample to identify, using exploratory analyses, one or more psychiatric symptom severity scales that relate to an RDoC construct;
- recruitment of participants to include two or more specified *DSM* disorders and explore symptoms that relate to an RDoC construct across the combined sample;
- recruitment of a group with a lifetime history of a specific psychiatric symptom or behavior of interest, regardless of diagnosis, to compare with a control group on a RDoC construct;
- recruitment of participants using techniques that result in a full range of severity for a single psychiatric symptom of interest, regardless of disorder, and examining how the symptom relates to a RDoC construct;
- recruitment of multiple *DSM* diagnoses and use of a clustering method to examine groups that emerge based on individual differences on an RDoC construct—often referred to as "biotypes"—and then examining the relation of the biotypes/groups to *DSM* diagnoses and clinical outcome variables.

Many studies across these categories have used the word "transdiagnostic" or "cross-diagnostic" to refer to relationships that are found across two or more diagnoses when analyzed as a single sample. We provide examples of published empirical studies within each of these respective categories in the following.

Some studies recruit nonpsychiatric community participants and explore how severity of one or more psychiatric symptoms relates to an RDoC construct. This is relevant as RDoC attempts to understand the full range of severity, including subclinical levels in a community-based sample. One such study found that the error-related negativity (ERN) amplitude from electroencephalogram (EEG) was reduced in nonpsychiatric adults reporting more depressive symptoms (Weinberg et al., 2016). Another similar design using nonpsychiatric adults found relationships between specific psychiatric symptoms with threat sensitivity and inhibitory control (Nelson, Strickland, Krueger, Arbisi, & Patrick, 2016). A study assessing nonpsychiatric children used structural equation modeling and found that increased externalizing symptoms were related to reduced working memory performance (Huang-Pollock, Shapiro, Galloway-Long, & Weigard, 2017). Another project recruited a community sample of children using a longitudinal design and found that temperamental positive and negative affect measured at the age of 6 was related to differences in the late positive potential amplitude from EEG in reaction to emotional images at the age of 9 (Kessel et al., 2017).

Other studies examine the relationship of specific psychiatric symptom severity and RDoC constructs using analyses that combine two or more psychiatric disorders. An example comes from one of the first RDoC studies to be published, which examined speech characteristics in a study that combined individuals diagnosed with depression, bipolar I disorder, and schizophrenia (Cohen, Najolia, Kim, & Dinzeo, 2012). Results revealed relationships between speech characteristics and symptom measures that were found across the disorders and did not significantly vary between the disorders. Other research combined all treatment-seeking patients with any of the *DSM-IV* anxiety disorders and created five ranked severity bins based on a dimensional defensive reactivity index derived from physiological measures (Lang, McTeague, & Bradley, 2016). They found that all primary anxiety diagnoses were represented in each bin, providing evidence for the transdiagnostic nature of the range of severity for defensive reactivity across anxiety disorders. Another example is a study that recruited participants with three different anxiety disorders and found that the trait of anxiety sensitivity mediated most relationships between diagnosis and sleep dysfunction, suggesting that anxiety sensitivity is a transdiagnostic trait that is more directly related to sleep dysfunction than to the related diagnoses (Baker et al., 2016). Finally, two studies from our laboratory conducted analyses that combined participants with a wide range of schizophrenia-spectrum and mood disorders, along with individuals with no history of a psychiatric disorder (Bedwell, Butler, Chan, & Trachik, 2015; Bedwell et al., 2016). Exploratory stepwise regressions across the entire sample revealed that specific clinician-rated and self-reported psychiatric symptoms were related to event-related potential amplitudes from EEG during visual processing and reward tasks. When a significant relationship was found across the entire sample, we then examined whether that relationship interacted with diagnostic class to determine whether the relationship was relatively transdiagnostic or a result of a strong relationship within a particular diagnostic class.

Some designs compare a group with a lifetime history of a particular psychiatric symptom or behavior of interest with a group that did not experience this symptom. One of these studies reported a relationship between a history of psychosis, regardless of disorder, and a reduced ERN amplitude during a metacognition task (Chan, Trachik, & Bedwell, 2015). Another examined individuals with a history of violence or criminal offending, regardless of diagnosis, and found that increased self-reported aggressive tendencies were related to reduced inhibitory control processing during presentation of threatening words (Verona & Bresin, 2015). A neuroimaging study included participants with and without a history of psychosis and used hierarchical regression to show differences in functional magnetic resonance imaging (fMRI) activation that were related to a history of a psychosis after first entering diagnosis in the model, and no differences in fMRI activation related to diagnosis when psychotic symptoms were entered first in the model (Sabharwal et al., 2016). This clever use of contrasting hierarchical modeling indicates that the results are not notably influenced by the inclusion of a particular diagnostic group in the sample, and that the relationship was relatively transdiagnostic in nature.

Some RDoC studies recruit participants in a manner that represents a full range of severity on a psychiatric symptom of interest, regardless of the disorder. One example is a study that recruited both psychiatric and nonpsychiatric adolescents representing a full range of anhedonia severity, which found that severity of anhedonia was related to a specific fMRI activation pattern during a reward sensitivity task (Bradley, Case, Freed, Stern, & Gabbay, 2017).

Finally, another group of studies include recruitment of multiple *DSM* diagnoses and use of a clustering method to examine groups that emerge based on individual differences on an RDoC construct. One such study used cluster analysis across adolescents with attention deficit-hyperactivity disorder, bipolar disorder, and both comorbid disorders to examine sustained attention performance, and found that two new groups emerged that did not map onto the *DSM* diagnoses (Kleinman et al., 2015). A large seminal study using this technique examined individuals with schizophrenia, schizoaffective disorder, and bipolar disorder with psychosis, along with their first-degree relatives and nonpsychiatric controls, and used multivariate taxometric analyses on a large set of biomarkers (Clementz et al., 2016; Ivleva et al., 2017). Results revealed three psychosis biotypes that did not map onto diagnoses, and external measures suggested that the biotypes may be more clinically informative than the diagnoses. Finally, a different research group identified four distinct biotypes in individuals with depression based on patterns of dysfunctional connectivity from neuroimaging, and these biotypes predicted response to transcranial magnetic stimulation therapy (Drysdale et al., 2017).

Overall, investigators have used a variety of methodologies to add knowledge to the RDoC matrix. RDoC does not constrain the possible methodological approaches, and there are likely other creative approaches that are not reviewed here. One of the goals of RDoC is to allow researchers the flexibility to use methodologies that seem most appropriate for a given research question.

SUMMARY

The RDoC appears to be a promising framework to direct research which may lead to a new and more valid classification of mental illness, with hopes that this will improve treatment effectiveness and lead to prevention and early detection strategies. The NIMH released RDoC in response to continued frustration regarding the relative lack of progress in mental illness treatment and prevention. The goal is to initiate a new way of conducting research in the field that has greater potential to lead to effective clinical applications than do the existing techniques, which have largely relied on the *DSM* and *ICD* systems. RDoC is still relatively new and requires further refinement as knowledge evolves and a wider range of investigators provide input into the organization of the matrix. Many investigators have been critical of the framework, which has created useful debate that will likely serve to refine and optimize RDoC. One aspect that all investigators can agree on is that any research framework that actually leads to rapid clinical progress in effective treatment and prevention of mental illness is invaluable. Only the future can determine whether the RDoC is that framework.

REFERENCES

American Psychiatric Association (2013). *Diagnostic and statistical manual of mental disorders: DSM-V*. Washington, DC: American Psychiatric Assocation.

Baker, A. W., Keshaviah, A., Goetter, E. M., Bui, E., Swee, M., Rosencrans, P. L., & Simon, N. M. (2016). Examining the role of anxiety sensitivity in sleep dysfunction across anxiety disorders. *Behavioral Sleep Medicine, 15*(3), 216–227.

Barch, D. M., Carter, C. S., Arnsten, A., Buchanan, R. W., Cohen, J. D., Geyer, M., . . . Heinssen, R. (2009). Selecting paradigms from cognitive neuroscience for translation into use in clinical trials: proceedings of the third CNTRICS meeting. *Schizophrenia Bulletin, 35*(1), 109–114.

Bedwell, J. S., Butler, P. D., Chan, C. C., & Trachik, B. J. (2015). Transdiagnostic psychiatric symptoms related to visual evoked potential abnormalities. *Psychiatry Research, 230*(2), 262–270.

Bedwell, J. S., Potts, G. F., Gooding, D. C., Trachik, B. J., Chan, C. C., & Spencer, C. C. (2016). Transdiagnostic psychiatric symptoms and event-related potentials following rewarding and aversive outcomes. *PLoS One, 11*(6), e0157084.

Bradley, K. A., Case, J. A., Freed, R. D., Stern, E. R., & Gabbay, V. (2017). Neural correlates of RDoC reward constructs in adolescents with diverse psychiatric symptoms: A Reward Flanker Task pilot study. *Journal of Affective Disorders, 216*, 36–45.

Carroll, B. J. (2015). Clinical science and biomarkers: against RDoC. *Acta Psychiatriatica Scandinavica, 132*(6), 423–424.

Chan, C. C., Trachik, B. J., & Bedwell, J. S. (2015). An event-related potential investigation of error monitoring in adults with a history of psychosis. *Clinical Neurophysiology, 126*(9), 1717–1726.

Clementz, B. A., Sweeney, J. A., Hamm, J. P., Ivleva, E. I., Ethridge, L. E., Pearlson, G. D., . . . Tamminga, C. A. (2016). Identification of distinct psychosis biotypes using brain-based biomarkers. *American Journal of Psychiatry, 173*(4), 373–384.

Cohen, A. S., Najolia, G. M., Kim, Y., & Dinzeo, T. J. (2012). On the boundaries of blunt affect/alogia across severe mental illness: implications for Research Domain Criteria. *Schizophrenia Research, 140*(1–3), 41–45.

Cooper, R., & Blashfield, R. K. (2016). Re-evaluating DSM-I. *Psychological Medicine, 46*(3), 449–456.

Cuthbert, B. N. (2014). Response to Lilienfield. *Behaviour Research and Therapy, 62*, 140–142.

Cuthbert, B. N., & Insel, T. R. (2013). Toward the future of psychiatric diagnosis: the seven pillars of RDoC. *BMC Medicine, 11*, 126.

Cuthbert, B. N., & Kozak, M. J. (2013). Constructing constructs for psychopathology: the NIMH research domain criteria. *Journal of Abnormal Psychology, 122*(3), 928–937.

DiMauro, J., Carter, S., Folk, J. B., & Kashdan, T. B. (2014). A historical review of trauma-related diagnoses to reconsider the heterogeneity of PTSD. *Journal of Anxiety Disorders, 28*(8), 774–786.

Drysdale, A. T., Grosenick, L., Downar, J., Dunlop, K., Mansouri, F., Meng, Y., . . . Liston, C. (2017). Resting-state connectivity biomarkers define neurophysiological subtypes of depression. *Nat Med, 23*(1), 28–38.

Fischer, B. A. (2012). A review of American psychiatry through its diagnoses: the history and development of the Diagnostic and Statistical Manual of Mental Disorders. *Journal of Nervous and Mental Disease, 200*(12), 1022–1030.

Franklin, J. C., Jamieson, J. P., Glenn, C. R., & Nock, M. K. (2015). How developmental psychopathology theory and research can inform the research domain criteria (RDoC) project. *Journal of Clinical Child and Adolescent Psychology, 44*(2), 280–290.

Galatzer-Levy, I. R., & Bryant, R. A. (2013). 636,120 ways to have posttraumatic stress disorder. *Perspectives on Psychological Science, 8*(6), 651–662.

Huang-Pollock, C., Shapiro, Z., Galloway-Long, H., & Weigard, A. (2017). Is poor working memory a transdiagnostic risk factor for psychopathology? *Journal of Abnormal Child Psychology, 45*(8): 1477–1490.

Insel, T., Cuthbert, B., Garvey, M., Heinssen, R., Pine, D. S., Quinn, K., . . . Wang, P. (2010). Research domain criteria (RDoC): toward a new classification framework for research on mental disorders. *American Journal of Psychiatry, 167*(7), 748–751.

Ivleva, E. I., Clementz, B. A., Dutcher, A. M., Arnold, S. J., Jeon-Slaughter, H., Aslan, S., . . . Tamminga, C. A. (2017). Brain structure biomarkers in the psychosis biotypes: Findings from the bipolar-schizophrenia network for intermediate phenotypes. *Biological Psychiatry, 82*(1), 26–39.

Kaye, J. T., Bradford, D. E., & Curtin, J. J. (2016). Psychometric properties of startle and corrugator response in NPU, affective picture viewing, and resting state tasks. *Psychophysiology, 53*(8), 1241–1255.

Kessel, E. M., Kujawa, A., Goldstein, B., Hajcak, G., Bufferd, S. J., Dyson, M., & Klein, D. N. (2017). Behavioral observations of positive and negative valence systems in early childhood predict physiological measures of emotional processing three years later. *Journal of Affective Disorders, 216*, 70–77.

Kirmayer, L. J., & Crafa, D. (2014). What kind of science for psychiatry? *Frontiers in Human Neuroscience, 8*, 435.

Kleinman, A., Caetano, S. C., Brentani, H., Rocca, C. C., dos Santos, B., Andrade, E. R., . . . Lafer, B. (2015). Attention-based classification pattern, a research domain criteria framework, in youths with bipolar disorder and attention-deficit/hyperactivity disorder. *Australian and New Zealand Journal of Psychiatry, 49*(3), 255–265.

Kozak, M. J., & Cuthbert, B. N. (2016). The NIMH Research Domain Criteria initiative: Background, issues, and pragmatics. *Psychophysiology, 53*(3), 286–297.

Lang, P. J., McTeague, L. M., & Bradley, M. M. (2016). RDoC, DSM, and the reflex physiology of fear: A biodimensional analysis of the anxiety disorders spectrum. *Psychophysiology, 53*(3), 336–347.

Lilienfeld, S. O. (2014). The Research Domain Criteria (RDoC): an analysis of methodological and conceptual challenges. *Behaviour Research and Therapy, 62*, 129–139.

Miller, G. A. (2010). Mistreating psychology in the decades of the brain. *Perspectives on Psychological Science, 5*(6), 716–743.

National Institute of Mental Health (2016). *Behavioral assessment methods for RDoC contructs.* Retrieved from https://www.nimh.nih.gov/about/advisory-boards-and-groups/namhc/reports/rdoc_council_workgroup_report_153440.pdf.

Nelson, L. D., Strickland, C., Krueger, R. F., Arbisi, P. A., & Patrick, C. J. (2016). Neurobehavioral Traits as Transdiagnostic Predictors of Clinical Problems. *Assessment, 23*(1), 75–85.

Paris, J., & Kirmayer, L. J. (2016). The National Institute of Mental Health Research Domain Criteria: A bridge too far. *Journal of Nervous and Mental Disease, 204*(1), 26–32.

Pearlson, G. D. (2015). Etiologic, phenomenologic, and endophenotypic overlap of schizophrenia and bipolar disorder. *Annual Review of Clinical Psychology, 11*, 251–281.

Peterson, B. S. (2015). Editorial: Research Domain Criteria (RDoC): a new psychiatric nosology whose time has not yet come. *Journal of Child Psychol Psychiatry, 56*(7), 719–722.

Pilecki, B. C., Clegg, J. W., & McKay, D. (2011). The influence of corporate and political interests on models of illness in the evolution of the DSM. *European Psychiatry, 26*(3), 194–200.

Sabharwal, A., Szekely, A., Kotov, R., Mukherjee, P., Leung, H. C., Barch, D. M., & Mohanty, A. (2016). Transdiagnostic neural markers of emotion-cognition interaction in psychotic disorders. *Journal of Abnormal Psychology, 125*(7), 907–922.

Sanislow, C. A., Pine, D. S., Quinn, K. J., Kozak, M. J., Garvey, M. A., Heinssen, R. K., . . . Cuthbert, B. N. (2010). Developing constructs for psychopathology research: research domain criteria. *Journal of Abnormal Psychology, 119*(4), 631–639.

Sonuga-Barke, E. J. (2014). 'What's up, (R)DoC?'—can identifying core dimensions of early functioning help us understand, and then reduce, developmental risk for mental disorders? *Journal of Child Psychol Psychiatry, 55*(8), 849–851.

Verona, E., & Bresin, K. (2015). Aggression proneness: Transdiagnostic processes involving negative valence and cognitive systems. *International Journal of Psychophysiology, 98*(2 Pt 2) 321–329.

Weinberg, A., Meyer, A., Hale-Rude, E., Perlman, G., Kotov, R., Klein, D. N., & Hajcak, G. (2016). Error-related negativity (ERN) and sustained threat: Conceptual framework and empirical evaluation in an adolescent sample. *Psychophysiology, 53*(3), 372–385.

World Health Organization. (2016). *International statistical classification of diseases and related health problems* (10th revision) Geneva: Author.

Zoellner, L. A., & Foa, E. B. (2016). Applying Research Domain Criteria (RDoC) to the study of fear and anxiety: A critical comment. *Psychophysiology, 53*(3), 332–335.

CHAPTER 3

The Problem of Dual Diagnosis

MELANIE E. BENNETT, JASON PEER, and ANJANA MURALIDHARAN

RESEARCH INDICATES THAT a substantial percentage of the general population with a lifetime psychiatric disorder has a history of some other disorder (Kessler, 1997; Kessler et al., 1994), and more than half of patients in psychiatric treatment meet criteria for more than one diagnosis (Wolf, Schubert, Patterson, Marion, & Grande, 1988). The issue of comorbidity broadly refers to combinations of any type of psychiatric disorder that co-occur in the same individual. A diagnostic pair that has received significant attention over the last two decades is that of mental illness and substance abuse. The term *dual diagnosis* describes individuals who meet diagnostic criteria for a mental disorder (or disorders) along with one or more substance use disorders (SUDs). Although dual diagnosis has likely been a prevalent and persistent condition for a long time, it began to receive attention as both a clinical problem and research domain some 25 years ago. Today, there have been many years of research and thinking about the frequent association between mental disorders and SUDs, how this association complicates the provision of mental health and substance abuse treatment services, and the impact of this association on all aspects of psychopathology research and clinical practice. In this chapter, we will review rates of dual diagnosis, both generally and for specific disorder domains, as well as discussing how dual diagnosis impacts the course, prognosis, assessment, and treatment of adult psychopathology. Finally, we will review current research and thinking on the etiology of dual diagnosis and highlight clinical and research directions.

METHODOLOGICAL ISSUES IN THE ASSESSMENT DIAGNOSIS

There are several methodological issues to consider when reviewing the literature on dual diagnosis. These include how the sample under study shapes the findings, the methods used to assess psychiatric disorders and SUDs, how different methods and measures shape study findings, and the critical impact of one's definition of dual diagnosis on study findings.

Adult Psychopathology and Diagnosis, Eighth Edition. Edited by Deborah C. Beidel and B. Christopher Frueh.
© 2018 John Wiley & Sons, Inc. Published 2018 by John Wiley & Sons, Inc.
Companion website: www.wiley.com/go/beidel/psychopathology8e

SAMPLE SELECTION INFLUENCES FINDINGS

There have been several large-scale epidemiological studies examining rates of dual diagnosis in general population samples since the mid-1980s. These studies provide rates of mental illness and SUDs, use structured diagnostic interviews, and generate results that are reliable and relevant to the population. Most information on rates of dual diagnosis comes from studies of clinical populations. Although not representative of the general population, they illustrate the types of problems faced by individuals in treatment, as well as links between dual diagnosis, service utilization, the impact on illness, and treatment outcome. Importantly, individuals with multiple disorders are more likely to seek treatment, a condition known as Berkson's fallacy (Berkson, 1949), so that estimates of the prevalence of comorbid disorders will be higher in clinical samples. Relatedly, factors such as inpatient or outpatient status and chronicity of illness may affect rates of dual diagnosis found in clinical samples. For example, research on patients with schizophrenia has found that more severely impaired inpatients are less likely to abuse substances than patients who are less ill (Mueser et al., 1990). Dual diagnosis rates also differ by setting, with hospital emergency rooms reflecting higher estimates than other settings (Barbee, Clark, Crapanzano, Heintz, & Kehoe, 1989; Galanter, Castaneda, & Ferman, 1988). In addition, demographic variables correlate with substance abuse, and differences in these variables in clinical samples can influence prevalence rates. For example, gender and age both correlate with substance abuse: males and those of younger age are more likely to abuse substances. Because studies of comorbidity in schizophrenia often use samples of inpatients, who are more likely to be male, the comorbidity rate in schizophrenia found in research with clinical samples may be inflated, because males are both more likely to have SUDs and more likely to be inpatients in psychiatric hospitals.

Another sample-related methodological issue involves the split between the mental health treatment system and the substance abuse treatment system. The literature on dual diagnosis really includes two largely separate areas of investigation: research on substance abuse in individuals with mental illness, and research on mental illness in primary substance abusers. To get an accurate picture of dual diagnosis and its full impact on clinical functioning and research in psychopathology, both aspects of this literature must be examined.

STUDY METHODS AND ASSESSMENT MEASURES INFLUENCE FINDINGS

Diagnostic measures include structured research interviews, nonstructured clinical interviews, self-report ratings, and reviews of medical records. Although structured interviews are the most reliable method of diagnosis (Mueser, Bellack, & Blanchard, 1992a), research with clinical samples will often use less well-standardized assessments. Relatedly, studies measure different substances in their assessments of dual diagnosis, typically including alcohol, cocaine, heroin, hallucinogens, stimulants, and marijuana. Importantly, some substances are not typically considered in assessments of dual diagnosis. For example, nicotine is not usually considered a substance of abuse in dual diagnosis research, despite the high rates of use among individuals with both mental illness (Lasser et al., 2000) and substance abuse (Bien & Burge, 1990), as well as a growing literature that suggests that nicotine dependence has links, perhaps biological in nature, to both major depression (Quattrocki, Baird, & Yurgelun-Todd, 2000) and schizophrenia (Dalack & Meador-Woodruff, 1996; Ziedonis & George, 1997). Others have found elevated rates of psychiatric and SUDs in smokers (Keuthen et al., 2000).

Taken together, factors such as the type of problematic substance use assessed, the measures that are used, and the specific substances that are included in an assessment all contribute to varying meanings of the term *dual diagnosis*.

THERE IS NO SINGLE DEFINITION OF DUAL DIAGNOSIS

Definitions of what constitutes dual diagnosis are far from uniform. Studies often use differing definitions and measures of SUDs, making prevalence rates diverse and difficult to compare. For example, definitions used to determine rates of dual diagnosis vary, ranging from problem use of a substance based on the frequency of use or the number of negative consequences experienced as a result of use, to abuse or dependence based on formal diagnostic criteria. This is a particularly important issue when formal diagnostic criteria for SUDs are used to assess dual diagnosis.

The latest version of the *Diagnostic and Statistical Manual* (*DSM-5*) (American Psychiatric Association, 2013) contains many changes that have important implications for defining dual diagnosis. The category title was revised from substance use disorders (*DSM-IV*) to substance-related and addictive disorders (*DSM-5*); this revision reflects several changes that will have a substantial impact both on how disorders related to alcohol and drug use are diagnosed, and on the inclusion of other conditions as addictions. To begin, whereas *DSM-IV* had separate diagnostic groups for substance abuse and dependence, *DSM-5* combines abuse and dependence into one diagnostic category (SUD) that is rated on a continuum from mild to severe, with the severity rating based on the number of criteria met (mild = two to three criteria met; moderate = four to five criteria met; severe = six or more criteria met).

DSM-5 lists 11 criteria for SUDs, with a minimum of two criteria necessary for the disorder. Finally, nicotine abuse and dependence have been organized into a single tobacco use disorder diagnosis, which is diagnosed using the same criteria as are used for other SUDs. As noted earlier, tobacco use has historically been viewed as less important or less serious an issue than problem drinking or illicit drug use. Bringing tobacco use disorders in line with the way we diagnose other SUDs highlights the great harm that tobacco use confers and may yield more attention to providing smoking cessation interventions within mental health and substance use treatment programs. Combining abuse and dependence into one diagnostic category can have the effect of identifying what might have previously been thought of as a less problematic or separate state (abuse) as a more serious condition that is potentially related to something more serious (dependence), with rates of dual diagnosis increasing as a result. Importantly, the longer list of diagnostic criteria and the severity rating symptom are a visible indication of the thinking that mild substance-related problems are fundamentally related to more severe ones. That is, these are not separate diagnostic categories but ones that are related, different not in the make-up of the conditions but by degree. This pathway from mild to moderate to severe SUD has the potential to impact dual diagnosis by including less severe substance use problems within the dual diagnosis framework. Whereas problem or heavy substance use that did not meet the threshold for a dependence diagnosis previously may not have been considered as part of a definition of dual diagnosis, now less severe expressions of substance use are considered a disorder that would be captured within the definition of dual diagnosis.

Another important change in *DSM-5* is expansion of the chapter on SUDs to include gambling disorder, based on a body of research that now indicates that many of the same underlying neurobiological processes that are activated and make substance use biologically reinforcing are found in problem gamblers, and that symptoms of problematic gambling are similar in many ways to those of SUDs (Petry, 2006). The inclusion of a non-substance-related addiction alongside substance-related ones provides an interesting set of questions. Should gambling disorders now be included in the thinking about dual diagnosis? What does this mean for (the likely increase in) prevalence rates of dual diagnosis that might accompany such a change, our understanding of the causes of dual diagnosis, and implications for assessment and treatment?

The inclusion of gambling disorder in *DSM-5* and the questions this change raises for definitions of dual diagnosis illustrate a broader issue: what one identifies as a diagnosis is key to any definition of dual diagnosis. Gambling provides but one example. Another example can be seen with tobacco dependence. Although there is a large literature documenting higher rates of smoking among individuals with psychiatric disorders (Farrell et al., 2003), tobacco dependence has not traditionally been included as part of the definition of dual diagnosis. This is generally because, with such high rates of smoking among those with psychiatric disorders, including it would yield extremely high rates of dual diagnosis, potentially sapping the concept of its meaning—if everyone has dual diagnosis, does it become less important? However, with growing evidence that smoking may be related to the neurophysiology of some psychiatric disorders (Wing, Wass, Soh, & George, 2012), it may be that tobacco dependence represents an especially important SUD to include as part of a definition of dual diagnosis. The greater attention to gambling disorder and tobacco dependence illustrates the ways in which changing ideas about mental health problems and addictions can impact rates of dual diagnosis.

FINDINGS FROM MAJOR EPIDEMIOLOGICAL STUDIES

Over the past 25 years, several large-scale epidemiological studies of mental illness have examined rates of dual diagnosis, including the Epidemiologic Catchment Area Study (ECA; Regier et al., 1990), the National Comorbidity Survey (NCS; Kessler et al., 1994), the National Comorbidity Survey Replication (NCS-R; Kessler & Merikangas, 2004), and the National Longitudinal Alcohol Epidemiology Study (NLAES; Grant et al., 1994). Although each study differs somewhat from the others in methodology, inclusion/exclusion criteria, and diagnostic categories assessed (see Table 3.1 for a brief description of methods for these studies), we can take several points from this literature that can contribute to our thinking about and understanding of dual diagnosis.

DUAL DIAGNOSIS IS HIGHLY PREVALENT IN COMMUNITY SAMPLES

First, dual diagnosis is highly prevalent in community samples. People with mental illness are at greatly increased risk of having a co-occurring SUD, and people with a SUD are likewise much more likely to meet criteria for an Axis I mental disorder. For example, the ECA (Regier et al., 1990), the first large-scale study of comorbidity of psychiatric and SUDs in the general population, documented high rates of dual diagnosis among both individuals with primary mental disorders and those with primary SUDs. Overall, individuals with a lifetime history of a mental illness had an odds ratio (OR) of 2.3 for a lifetime history of alcohol use disorder and 4.5 for drug use disorder. Antisocial personality disorder (ASP) showed the highest comorbidity rate (83.6%), followed by bipolar disorder (60.7%), schizophrenia (47.0%), panic disorder (35.8%), obsessive-compulsive disorder (32.8%), and major depression (27.2%). Substantial rates of dual diagnosis were also found in primary substance abusers (Regier et al., 1990). Overall, 37%

Table 3.1

Methods of Several Major Epidemiological Studies on Dual Diagnosis

Study	Years	Methods
Epidemiologic Catchment Area Study (Regier et al., 1990)	1980–1984	Surveyed more than 20,000 adults in five cities across the United States both in the community and in institutions. Trained interviewers used the Diagnostic Interview Schedule to determine *DSM-III* diagnoses. Included affective, anxiety, and schizophrenia-spectrum disorders.
National Comorbidity Survey (Kessler et al., 1994)	1990–1992	Assessed 12-month and lifetime prevalence rates for a range of psychiatric disorders in more than 8,000 noninstitutionalized individuals aged 15–54 across 48 states using the Composite International Diagnostic Interview (CIDI) and based on *DSM-III-R* criteria.
National Longitudinal Alcohol Epidemiology Study (Grant et al., 1994)	1991–1992	Examined rates of co-occurrence of alcohol and drug use disorders and affective disorders in a general population sample. The NLAES is a household survey of over 42,000 adults in the United States that utilized diagnostic interviews to assess *DSM-IV* diagnostic criteria for alcohol use disorders.
National Comorbidity Survey Replication (Kessler et al., 2004)	2001–2002	Nationally representative face-to-face household survey of over 9,000 noninstitutionalized people aged 18 years or older. Diagnoses based on *DSM-IV* criteria assessed via CIDI interviews.
National Epidemiologic Survey on Alcohol and Related Conditions (Grant et al., 2004)	2001–2002	Nationally representative face-to-face survey of 43,093 noninstitutionalized respondents, 18 years of age or older, conducted by NIAAA. *DSM-IV* criteria for substance use disorders and nine independent mood and anxiety disorders were assessed with the Alcohol Use Disorders and Associated Disabilities Interview Schedule-*DSM-IV* Version (AUDADIS-IV), a structured diagnostic interview administered by lay interviewers.

of individuals with an alcohol disorder and 53% of those with a drug use disorder had comorbid mental illness.

Further analyses (Helzer & Pryzbeck, 1988) found that among those with alcohol use disorders, the strongest association was with ASP (OR = 21.0), followed by mania (OR = 6.2) and schizophrenia (OR = 4.0). Like the ECA study, the NCS and the NLAES found markedly high rates of dual diagnosis. NCS findings (Kessler et al., 1994) showed that respondents with mental illness had at least twice the risk of lifetime alcohol or drug use disorder, with an even greater risk for individuals with certain types of mental illness. Findings were similar for primary substance abusers: most respondents with an alcohol or drug use disorder had a history of some non-substance use psychiatric disorder (Kendler, Davis, & Kessler, 1997; Kessler, 1997). Overall, 56.8% of men and 72.4% of women with alcohol abuse met diagnostic criteria for at least one psychiatric disorder, as did 78.3% of men and 86.0% of women with alcohol dependence (Kendler et al., 1997). Moreover, 59% of those with a lifetime drug use disorder also met criteria for a lifetime psychiatric disorder (Kessler, 1997). Likewise, the NLAES (Grant et al., 1994; Grant &

Harford, 1995) found that, among respondents with major depression, 32.5% met criteria for alcohol dependence during their lifetime, as compared with 11.2% of those without major depression. Those with primary alcohol use disorders were almost four times more likely to be diagnosed with lifetime depression, and the associations were even stronger for drug use disorders: individuals with drug dependence were nearly seven times more likely than those without to report lifetime major depression (see Bucholz, 1999, for a review). Overall, these studies find that a psychiatric diagnosis yields at least double the risk of a lifetime alcohol or drug use disorder.

HIGH PREVALENCE RATES OF DUAL DIAGNOSIS PERSIST OVER TIME

A second important feature of rates of dual diagnosis is that they appear to be persistent. Examining how rates persist or change over time is important for several reasons. When the ECA and NCS findings were first published, the findings of high rates of both single and dual disorders were significant because they illustrated the many ways in which the understanding, assessment, and treatment of mental illness and SUDs were incomplete. The NCS, in particular, came under increased scrutiny, given that the rates it found for mental illness were even higher than those found by the ECA. Findings from several replications of large epidemiologic studies indicate that even with changes in diagnostic criteria and attitudes about psychological distress, rates of dual disorders remain high. For example, the NCS was recently replicated in the NCS-R. The NCS-R (Kessler & Merikangas, 2004) shared much of the same methodology as the original NCS, repeated many questions from the original survey, and included additional questions to tap *DSM-IV* diagnostic criteria. Comparisons of data from both studies illustrate the persistent nature of dual diagnosis. For example, for major depressive disorder (MDD; Kessler et al., 1996) 38.6% of respondents who met criteria for lifetime MDD also had a diagnosis of SUD, whereas 18.5% of respondents who met criteria for 12-month MDD also had a diagnosis of SUD. Results from the NCS-R confirmed the high prevalence rates of dual diagnosis in people with MDD: 24.0% of those with lifetime MDD also met criteria for a SUD, and 27.1% of those who met criteria for 12-month MDD also met criteria for a SUD (Kessler et al., 2005a).

Similar comparisons can be made between the NLAES and a more recent National Institute on Alcohol Abuse and Alcoholism survey called the National Epidemiologic Survey on Alcohol and Related Conditions (NESARC; Grant et al., 2004). The NESARC stressed the need to ensure that diagnoses of mood and anxiety disorders were independent of SUDs. A comparison of the two studies shows that dual mood/anxiety and SUDs continue to be highly prevalent in community samples. For example, in the NLAES (Grant & Harford, 1995), respondents with a past-year diagnosis of major depression had a 21.36% rate of a co-occurring alcohol use disorder, compared with 6.92% of those without 12-month major depression (OR = 3.65). Similarly, high ORs were found for 12-month major depression and drug use disorders (Grant, 1995).

DUAL DIAGNOSIS IS ONLY ONE PART OF THE COMORBIDITY PUZZLE

The term and typical understanding of dual diagnosis may not accurately reflect the complexity of the problem of co-occurring mental health disorders and SUDs. That is, co-occurring disorders can take many forms, and limiting attention to a particular number or combination of problems may restrict what we can learn about the links and interactions between mental illness and SUDs. As discussed previously, the term dual diagnosis has most often been used to refer to a combination of one mental illness and one SUD. However, epidemiologic studies find high prevalence rates of three or more co-occurring disorders that include but are not limited to dual mental–SUD combinations. For example, Kessler et al. (1994) found that 14% of the NCS sample met criteria for three or more comorbid *DSM* disorders, and that these respondents accounted for well over half of the lifetime and 12-month diagnoses found in the sample.

Other data from the NCS (Kessler et al., 1996) showed that 31.9% of respondents with lifetime MDD and 18.5% of those with 12-month MDD met criteria for three or more comorbid conditions. In the NCS-R, Kessler et al. (2005a) found that 17.3% of respondents met criteria for three or more lifetime disorders. In examining 12-month disorders in the NCS-R sample, Kessler et al. (2005b) found that 23% of the sample met criteria for three or more diagnoses. Taken together, these findings illustrate the importance of thinking about dual diagnosis in the context of the broader picture of comorbid conditions. This includes the newly-introduced diagnostic categories of gambling disorder and tobacco dependence to which we now turn attention.

Gambling Disorder   Although gambling disorder was introduced in *DSM-5*, previous investigations have documented the comorbidity of other psychiatric disorders and SUDs among those who report problem gambling. Lorains, Cowlishaw, and Thomas (2011) reported that tobacco and other SUDs were found in the majority of gamblers (60.1% met criteria for tobacco dependence and 57.5% for some other SUD); mood and anxiety disorders were also common (37.9% and 37.4%, respectively). These rates are mirrored in clinical samples of problem gamblers, where research shows a high rate of current (74.8%) and lifetime (75.5%) psychiatric disorders (Dowling et al., 2015). Epidemiological studies have also looked at rates of problem gambling among individuals identified as having a psychiatric disorder. Using the NESARC data, Cowlishaw, Hakes, and Dowling (2016) examined rates of at-risk gambling (one to two *DSM-IV* symptoms) or problem gambling (three or more symptoms) among 3,007 respondents who were seeking treatment for mood and anxiety problems and reported gambling at least five times in a 1-year period. Overall, lifetime rates were 5.8% for at-risk gambling and 3.1% for problem gambling; past year rates were lower but still meaningful (at-risk gambling = 3.5%; problem gambling = 1.4%).

Tobacco Dependence   Tobacco is the most widely used substance of abuse among individuals with mental health diagnoses (Farrell et al., 2003) and rates of smoking for individuals with mental health disorders are two to three times higher than the general population (Lawrence, Mitrou, & Zubrick, 2009). Smokers with mental health disorders have longer smoking histories and, importantly, are less likely to quit: whereas tobacco use and dependence have been on the decline in the general population, rates have generally remained stable among smokers with mental health disorders (Dickerson et al., 2012; Secades-Villa et al., 2013; Williams, Steinberg, Griffiths, & Cooperman, 2013).

Despite these high prevalence rates, tobacco dependence has not often been considered in research on dual diagnosis. There are several reasons for this. First, including tobacco dependence would serve to define a great number of people with a mental health disorder as having a dual diagnosis. Second, there is a complicated history of tolerance and even encouragement of smoking among those with mental health disorders, as many treatment providers believed that individuals would experience symptom relapse or display increased disruptive behavior if not able to smoke, ideas that have since been found to be untrue (El-Guebaly, Cathcart, Currie, Brown, & Gloster, 2002). Third, in the past, tobacco dependence was not fully considered an addiction in the same way as chronic and harmful use of alcohol or illicit drugs, because rates of smoking in the general population were similarly high and the negative consequences of smoking, unlike other substances, were often far removed from the time of the actual behavior (i.e., the health effects were more likely to manifest after many years of smoking).

There are several reasons to consider tobacco dependence when conceptualizing dual diagnosis. The addictive nature of tobacco/nicotine, its negative health effects and other negative consequences—cost, stigma, second-hand smoke—have been identified (see Bennett, Wilson, Genderson, & Saperstein, 2013, and Graham, Frost-Pineda, & Gold, 2007 for reviews). As information about tobacco dependence has increased, rates of smoking in the general population have decreased dramatically, although it is still a significant problem for individuals with mental health disorders. Estimates suggest that individuals with mental health disorders smoke 50% of all cigarettes consumed in this country (Lasser et al., 2000) and that individuals with mental health disorders have a disproportionately difficult time quitting smoking (see Mackowick, Lynch, Weinberger, & George, 2012, for a review). Moreover, nicotine may have a unique connection with genetics and brain functioning in some psychiatric disorders, including depression and schizophrenia (de Leon & Diaz, 2012; Wing, Wass, Soh, & George, 2012), and quitting might be more difficult for individuals with mental health disorders due to biological factors that may make smoking more reinforcing (Berg et al., 2014) or withdrawal symptoms more problematic (Leventhal, Ameringer, Osborn, Zvolensky, & Langdon, 2013; Weinberger, Desai, & McKee, 2010) than what is experienced by other smokers. For these reasons, we believe a comprehensive review of dual diagnosis should include information on tobacco dependence, and have provided this in the following sections.

The epidemiological studies just listed provide information on rates of tobacco dependence among those with mental health disorders. Lawrence et al. (2009) used data from the NCS-R to examine rates of comorbid tobacco dependence and mental health disorders (affective, anxiety, and SUDs) as measured by the WHO Composite International Diagnostic Interview (CIDI). Among respondents with a mental health disorder in the past 12 months, 40.1% were current smokers (almost double the 21.3% smoking prevalence in adults without a mental health disorder in the last 12 months). Rates were highest among those with SUDs (63.6%), followed by individuals with affective disorders (45.1%) and anxiety disorders (37.6%). Goodwin, Zvolensky, Keyes, and Hasin (2012) examined rates of tobacco dependence among those with mental health disorders in the NESARC sample. Diagnoses of specific phobia, personality disorder, MDD, and bipolar disorder were associated with increased odds of nicotine dependence, as well as with increased risk of persistent nicotine dependence over a 3-year follow-up (Goodwin, Pagura, Spiwak, Lemeshow, & Sareen, 2011). In an examination of associations between smoking and personality disorders using the NESARC sample, Pulay et al. (2010) found that the nicotine dependence had the strongest associations with schizotypal, borderline, narcissistic, and obsessive-compulsive personality disorder diagnoses.

Cross-National Epidemiological Studies   The preceding review of epidemiological studies focuses on findings from studies conducted in the United States. An interesting and important complement to findings from the United States comes from findings from the WHO World Mental Health Surveys (WMHS; Kessler et al., 2006), an assessment of diagnosis of mental health disorders using the WHO CIDI carried out in 28 countries around the world with a sample of over 150,000 respondents. Findings from this international survey confirm results from the United States: mental health disorders are prevalent in all regions of the world, and rates of comorbid SUDs are substantially higher among those with mental health disorders. For example, in an examination of prevalence rates and correlates of bipolar spectrum disorder in a subset of the WHO WMHS sample ($n = 61,392$), Merikangas et al. (2011) found that 36.6% of those with a bipolar spectrum disorder met criteria for a co-occurring SUD. Other findings from the WHO WMHS replicate findings reviewed earlier: comorbidity of multiple mental health disorders, including diagnostic combinations that include psychiatric and substance use disorders, is associated with greater impairments such as higher risk for suicide (Nock et al., 2009). As more cross-national data are collected and analyzed, it will be important to expand on this work to examine if and how different processes and cultural factors influence the development and persistence of dual diagnosis.

Prevalence of Dual Diagnosis in Age-Related Subgroups Dual diagnosis among young adults has become of greater interest to clinicians, researchers, and policymakers over recent years as more attention has been given to early intervention to provide treatment that could alter the illness trajectory and prevent long-term disability. In one investigation (Lipari & Hedden, 2014), 6.4% of young adults have a dual mental health and SUD diagnosis, which translates to 2.2 million young adults. An additional 1.6% (555,000) met criteria for a serious mental illness and comorbid SUD. Other studies confirm that among young adults, SUDs are commonly found comorbid with mood (Lubman et al., 2007) and schizophrenia spectrum disorders, including first-episode psychosis (Archie et al., 2007; Bennett & Dixon, 2011). Compton and colleagues (2009) surveyed a sample of 109 hospitalized young adults experiencing a first episode of psychosis and found that 46% reported weekly drinking and 11% drank daily. In addition, 61% reported weekly use of cannabis, 45% used daily, and 57% met criteria for cannabis use disorder. Research shows that dual diagnosis confers significant cost and burden for young adults worldwide (Patel et al., 2007).

Among young adults, continued substance use after mental illness diagnosis, especially continued regular use of cannabis, is associated with poor longitudinal outcomes. González-Pinto et al. (2011) followed a sample of 112 young adults for 8 years following a first admission for psychosis (82 were re-interviewed at the 8-year follow-up assessment). Participants were classified according to cannabis use: 25 had cannabis use before their first psychotic episode and continuous use during follow-up, 27 had cannabis use before their first episode but stopped its use during follow-up, and 40 never used cannabis. The three groups did not differ significantly in symptoms or functional outcome at the baseline, 1-year, or 3-year assessments. However, those who continued cannabis use showed significantly poorer symptom ratings and Global Assessment of Functioning scores at the 5- and 8-year assessments. Interestingly, those who had used and stopped showed the strongest positive symptom and functional outcomes over time. Clausen et al. (2014) followed 314 young people for 5 years after their involvement in a treatment study for individuals with first-episode psychosis. Findings show that nonusers and those who had stopped during follow-up had better outcomes (lower symptom levels, better social functioning) than did starters and continuers.

Another special population comprises older adults. In the general population, rates of psychiatric and SUDs appear to decline in older adults with lower rates of diagnosis of mood, anxiety, and SUDs for those aged 65 years and older compared with those aged 18–64 (Gum, King-Kallimanis, & Kohn, 2009). When stratified by older age groups—young-old (55–64), middle-old (65–74), old-old (75–84), and oldest-old (85 and up)—rates of psychiatric and SUDs decreased with increasing age, as did the mean number of psychiatric disorders, with the young-old group having the highest number of comorbidities (Reynolds, Pietrzak, El-Gabalawy, Mackenzie, & Sareen, 2015). As with young and middle-aged adults, men in the sample had higher rates of SUDs than women; however, gender differences in SUD rates decreased with increasing age (Reynolds et al., 2015). With samples of individuals with psychiatric illnesses, rates of SUDs also appear to decline with age (Kerfoot, Petrakis, & Rosenheck, 2011). Importantly, however, older adults with psychiatric disorders remain at elevated risk for SUDs compared with their same-age peers without mental illness. In a nationally representative sample of non-institutionalized US residents, presence of a mental health disorder significantly pre-dicted current smoking status across age groups (Cook et al., 2014). Results from the NESARC (Chou & Cheung, 2013) found that although the overall prevalence of MDD is low in older adults (2.95% for the past year and 8.82% lifetime), among those with lifetime MDD, 20% met criteria for an alcohol use disorder. Findings from a study of a large cohort of individuals with severe psychotic disorders indicate substantially ele-vated rates of smoking, heavy alcohol use, and recreational drug use across age groups in this sample, relative to the general population (Hartz et al., 2014).

Dual diagnosis may play an important role in a subset of older adults who experience chronic mental health disorders. Mackenzie, El-Gabalawy, Chou, & Sareen (2013) examined factors that may contribute to persistence of three mental health diag-noses—mood, anxiety, and SUDs—over time in older adults surveyed in the NESARC study. Their findings showed that although most disorders were not persistent from one assessment to a second one that was conducted 3 years later, comorbidity of another mental health disorder (including SUDs) was a significant predictor of persistence of any disorder over time.

In line with the idea of including gambling disorder within the definition of dual diagnosis, several studies using NESARC data have found high rates of dual mental and gambling disorders among older adults (Chou & Cheung, 2013; Pilver, Libby, Hoff, & Potenza, 2013), highlighting the way in which older age may impact the traditional definition of dual diagnosis. For example, Pietrzak, Morasco, Blanco, Grant, and Petry (2006) examined over 10,000 older adults in the NESARC survey and found significantly elevated rates of SUDs (alcohol, tobacco, and drugs), as well as mood, anxiety, and personality disorders among those with disordered gambling.

Interplay of Psychiatric Disorders and Comorbid Medical Conditions Over the past two decades, mounting evidence has confirmed that medical conditions are highly comorbid with mental health disorders (Druss & Walker, 2011), with several identified complex and bidirectional pathways. First, the presence of a chronic medical condition increases risk for mental health disorders (Chou, Huang, Goldstein, & Grant, 2013). Secondly, the presence of a mental health disorder increases risk for medical conditions (Goff et al., 2005). Finally, medical and mental health disorders share a number of common risk factors, such as low socioeconomic status and chronic stress (Druss & Walker, 2011). Further complicating matters, the presence of a SUD can increase risk of psychiatric/medical comorbidity (Dickey, Normand, Weiss, Drake, & Azeni, 2002; Lin, Zhang, Leung, & Clark, 2011). Conversely, individuals with chronic medical conditions who abuse substances are at increased risk for adverse psychiatric outcomes; current smoking status is a predictor of incident major depression among individuals with coronary artery disease, in the 3 months following discharge from the hospital for a cardiac event (Stafford, Berk, & Jackson, 2013). Among individuals infected with HIV, those who are drug users are at increased risk for mental illness compared with those who are not (Altice, Kamarulzaman, Soriano, Schechter, & Friedland, 2010). Finally, the intersection of dual diagnosis with medical comorbidity is associated with significantly increased burden of illness, complexity of medical condition, and poorer treatment outcomes (Altice et al., 2010; Lin et al., 2011; Stafford et al., 2013).

FINDINGS FROM STUDIES OF CLINICAL SAMPLES

The fact that dual diagnosis is fairly common in the general population serves to highlight the even higher rates found in treatment settings. Clinical studies of dual diagnosis have assessed general psychiatric patients, patients with specific psychiatric disorders, and primary substance abusing patients.

DUAL DIAGNOSIS IN GENERAL PSYCHIATRIC PATIENTS

One-third to three-quarters of general psychiatric patients may meet criteria for comorbid psychiatric and SUDs, depending on the diagnostic make-up and chronicity of the sample (Ananth et al., 1989; Galanter et al., 1988; McLellan, Druley, & Carson, 1978; Mezzich, Ahn, Fabrega, & Pilkonis, 1990; Safer, 1987). Rates seem to fall in the higher end of this range for samples comprising more impaired patient populations. For example, Ananth et al. (1989) found that 72.0% of a sample of patients with schizophrenia, bipolar disorder, and atypical psychosis received a comorbid substance use diagnosis. Mezzich et al. (1990) conducted a large-scale assessment of dual diagnosis in more than 4,000 patients presenting for evaluation and referral for mental health problems over an 18-month period and found substantial rates of dual diagnosis among several diagnostic subsamples. The highest rates were seen among patients with severe mental illnesses such as bipolar disorder (45% diagnosed with an alcohol use disorder and 39% diagnosed with a drug use disorder) and schizophrenia or paranoid disorders (42% and 38% were diagnosed with alcohol use disorder and other SUDs, respectively). However, dual diagnosis was also pronounced in other patient groups. Specifically, 33% of patients with major depression were diagnosed with an alcohol use disorder, and 18% were diagnosed with a drug use disorder. Among patients with anxiety disorders, 19% and 11% were diagnosed with alcohol use disorder and other SUDs, respectively.

DUAL DIAGNOSIS IN SAMPLES OF PATIENTS WITH SPECIFIC DISORDERS

Rates of dual diagnosis have been extensively studied among patients with severe mental illness, including schizophrenia (Dixon, Haas, Weiden, Sweeney, & Frances, 1991; Mueser et al., 1990), bipolar disorder (Bauer et al., 2005; McElroy et al., 2001; Salloum & Thase, 2000; Vieta et al., 2000), and major depression (Goodwin & Jamison, 1990; Lynskey, 1998; Merikangas, Leckman, Prusoff, Pauls, & Weissman, 1985; Swendsen & Merikangas, 2000). Findings show that dual diagnosis is common in such samples. Mueser et al. (1990) reported that 47% had a lifetime history of alcohol abuse, whereas many had abused stimulants (25%), cannabis (42%), and hallucinogens (18%). Dixon et al. (1991) found that 48% of a sample of schizophrenia patients met criteria for an alcohol or drug use disorder. Chengappa, Levine, Gershon, and Kupfer (2000) evaluated the prevalence of substance abuse and dependence in patients with bipolar disorder.

Among patients with bipolar I, 58% met abuse or dependence criteria for at least one substance, and 11% abused or were dependent on three or more substances. In the bipolar II group, the rate of dual diagnosis was approximately 39%. Baethge et al. (2005) followed a group of first-episode bipolar I patients and found that about one-third of the sample had a SUD at the baseline assessment, and that patients using two or more substances showed poorer outcomes over the 2 years of the study. Bauer et al. (2005) conducted structured interviews with a large sample of inpatient veterans with bipolar disorder across 11 sites ($n = 328$) to examine rates of comorbid anxiety and SUDs. Results showed high rates of current (33.8%) and lifetime (72.3%) SUDs in the sample, along with a rate of 29.8% meeting criteria for multiple current disorders.

Hasin, Endicott, and Lewis (1985) examined rates of comorbidity in a sample of patients with affective disorder presenting for treatment as part of the National Institute of Mental Health (NIMH) Collaborative Study of Depression and found that 24% of these patients reported serious problems with alcohol and 18% met diagnostic criteria for an alcohol use disorder. In an examination of patients with major depression, bipolar disorder, and controls participating in the NIMH Collaborative Program on the Psycho-biology of Depression, Winokur et al. (1998) found that affective disorder patients had substantially higher rates of dual SUDs than did controls.

Dual diagnosis is also common among patients with anxiety disorders. In their review of studies of dual anxiety disorders and SUDs, Kushner, Sher, and Beitman (1990) found that rates differ by type of anxiety disorder, with social phobia (ranging from 20% to 36% rate of dual diagnosis) and agoraphobia (ranging from 7.0% to 27.0% rate of dual diagnosis) showing the highest rates of substance abuse comorbidity. Others have found a 22% rate of lifetime alcohol use disorder among patients with social phobia (Himle & Hill, 1991), a 10–20% rate for patients with agoraphobia (Bibb & Chambless, 1986), and up to a 12% rate of lifetime alcohol dependence among patients with obsessive-compulsive disorder (Eisen & Rasmussen, 1989). In addition, more attention is being given recently to dual substance abuse and post-traumatic stress disorder (PTSD) in clinical samples. A growing literature examining this diagnostic combination finds high rates of dual diagnosis among patients with PTSD, with some findings as high as 80% (Keane, Gerardi, Lyons, & Wolfe, 1988). Research with both samples of veterans with PTSD and samples of women with assault- or trauma-related PTSD show strikingly high rates of comorbid substance abuse and dependence (see Stewart, Pihl, Conrod, & Dongier, 1998, for a review), as well as other disorders. Moreover, Breslau, Davis, Peterson, and Schultz (1997) interviewed a sample of 801 women and found that PTSD significantly increased the likelihood for later alcohol use disorder. Research with community mental health patients with several mental illnesses shows extremely high rates of co-occurring PTSD (14–53%, usually undiagnosed; Grubaugh, Zinzow, Paul, Egede, & Frueh, 2011).

Research documents high rates of dual diagnosis among those with eating disorders. Higher rates of drug use have been found in samples of individuals with eating disorders than in controls (Krug et al., 2008), and studies of clinical samples show high overall rates of alcohol and drug use disorders. For example, Grillo, White, and Masheb (2009) assessed *DSM-IV* lifetime and current psychiatric disorder comorbidity in patients with binge-eating disorder and found that more than 73% of respondents had at least one lifetime diagnosis and 43% had at least one current psychiatric diagnosis, with almost 25% of the sample meeting criteria for a lifetime SUD. Several studies have shown variation in rates of SUDs across the different types of eating disorders—anorexia nervosa, bulimia nervosa, binge-eating disorder—and subsets of disorders within these (Root et al., 2010). In addition, rates of comorbidity, including that with SUDs, may be associated with eating disorder severity, with those with more severe symptoms of eating disorder showing the highest rates of comorbid SUDs (Spindler & Milos, 2007).

Some of the highest rates of comorbidity are found for patients with personality disorders, especially ASP. Studies show that comorbid ASP accelerates the development of alcoholism (Hesselbrock, Hesselbrock, & Workman-Daniels, 1986), and that 80% of patients with ASP have a history of problem use of alcohol (Schuckit, 1983). In a recent review of studies on dual SUDs and borderline personality disorder (BPD), Trull, Sher, Minks-Brown, Durbin, and Burr (2000) found that, across studies, more than 48% of patients with BPD met criteria for alcohol use disorders, and 38% of those with BPD met criteria for a drug use disorder. In a recent re-analysis of the NESARC data, Trull et al. (2010) found high rates of dual personality disorders and SUDs. More than one-quarter of those with ASP (26.65%) met criteria for drug dependence, although even higher rates of drug dependence were found for those with histrionic (29.72%) and dependent (27.34%) personality disorders. Goldstein, Compton, and Grant (2010) examined rates of ASP in individuals with PTSD and how this combination of disorders affected risk of further comorbid psychiatric disorders. Compared with those with PTSD only, those with PTSD + ASP showed much higher rates of additional comorbid diagnoses. Specifically, those with PTSD + ASP met criteria for, on average, 5.7 additional lifetime Axis I diagnoses, whereas those with PTSD only met criteria for only 2.3 additional lifetime Axis I diagnoses. Rates of additional Axis II diagnosis were similar (2.5 additional Axis II diagnoses for those with PTSD + ASP vs. 0.7 for those with PTSD only).

Wildes, Marcus, and Fagiolini (2008) examined rates of eating disorders in individuals with bipolar disorder and found that a subset of individuals with bipolar disorder and loss of control over eating showed elevated rates of SUDs. In another study of individuals with bipolar disorder, Bauer et al. (2005) interviewed inpatients using the Structured Clinical Interview for *DSM-IV* and found that rates of comorbidity with SUDs were high (33.8% current, 72.3% lifetime), but that almost 30% of respondents had comorbid bipolar, SUD, and anxiety disorders. Such findings illustrate the importance of expanding our thinking regarding dual diagnosis into multiple comorbidities.

As noted earlier, rates of tobacco dependence are high among individuals with mental health disorders. Studies indicate that more than 60% of adults with schizophrenia, 40% with bipolar disorder, and 30% with major depression in the United States smoke, compared with fewer than 20% in the overall adult population (Dickerson et al., 2012; Heffner et al., 2011). Similarly, research has found higher rates of smoking among those with a range of anxiety disorders, although directionality is unclear—there is evidence to suggest that smoking is a risk factor for panic disorder and generalized anxiety disorder (Moylan, Jacka, Pasco, & Berk, 2012).

Some speculate that those with mental health disorders who smoke may experience a more severe subtype of disorder than those who do not smoke. For example, Strong et al. (2010) examined differences in smoking behavior among those with no history of MDD, those with a single episode, or those with recurrent major episodes in 1,560 participants in the NCS-R. Those with comorbid recurrent major depression reported more smoking, greater nicotine dependence, more comorbid mental health disorders, and greater impairment in functioning than those with no or a single episode of major depression. Saiyad and El-Mallakh (2012) studied the impact of smoking on symptoms of bipolar disorders ($n = 134$) and found that those with bipolar disorder who smoked reported more severe symptoms of anxiety, depression, and mania. Others have suggested that smoking may be a marker for a more chronic form of schizophrenia (Dalack & Meador-Woodruff, 1996) or a subtype of bulimia nervosa characterized by more depression and alcohol abuse (Sandager et al., 2008).

DUAL DIAGNOSIS IN PATIENTS WITH PRIMARY SUDs

Substance-abusing patients in treatment are a heterogeneous group, encompassing a range of substances and levels of severity. Nonetheless, researchers have found high rates of dual disorders across diverse samples of patients seeking substance abuse treatment (Arendt & Munk-Jorgensen, 2004; Falck, Wang, Siegal, & Carlson, 2004; Herz, Volicer, D'Angelo, & Gadish, 1990; Mirin, Weiss, Griffin, & Michael, 1991; Mirin, Weiss, & Michael, 1988; Penick et al., 1984; Powell, Penick, Othmer, Bingham, & Rice, 1982; Ross, Glaser, & Stiasny, 1988a; Rounsaville, Weissman, Kleber, & Wilber, 1982a; Watkins et al., 2004; Weissman & Meyers, 1980). Findings of lifetime rates of psychiatric disorder range from 73.5% of a sample of cocaine abusers (Rounsaville et al., 1991), to 77% of a sample of hospitalized alcoholics (Hesselbrock, Meyer, & Keener, 1985), to 78% of a sample of patients in an alcohol and drug treatment facility (Ross, Glaser, & Germanson, 1988b). Findings of current psychiatric disorder are similarly high, ranging from 55.7% of a group of cocaine abusers (Rounsaville et al., 1991) to 65% in a general substance-abusing sample (Ross et al., 1988).

Further reflecting their diagnostic heterogeneity, substance abusers in treatment experience a range of comorbid psychiatric disorders. Among the most widely studied have been affective disorders, and treatment-seeking substance abusers show high rates of both major depression (Hasin, Grant, & Endicott, 1988; Hesselbrock et al., 1985; Merikangas & Gelernter, 1990; Mezzich et al., 1990; Miller, Klamen, Hoffmann, & Flaherty, 1996; Rounsaville, Weissman, Wilber, Crits-Christoph, & Kleber, 1982b; Weissman & Meyers, 1980) and bipolar disorder (Strakowski & DelBello, 2000). Miller et al. (1996) surveyed a sample of more than 6,000 substance abuse treatment patients from 41 sites and found that 44% had a lifetime history of major depression. In a review of comorbidity of affective and SUDs, Lynskey (1998) found that the prevalence of unipolar depression among patients receiving treatment for SUDs ranged from a low of 25.8% for lifetime depression in a sample of 93 alcohol-dependent men (Sellman & Joyce, 1996) to a high of 67% meeting a lifetime diagnosis of major depression among a sample of 120 inpatients (Grant, Hasin, & Harford, 1989). Busto, Romach, and Sellers (1996) evaluated rates of dual diagnosis in a sample of 30 patients admitted to a medical facility for benzodiazepine detoxification and found that 33% met *DSM-II-R* criteria for lifetime major depression.

Results from large studies of treatment-seeking substance abusers find that these patients show five to eight times the risk of having a comorbid bipolar diagnosis (see Strakowski & DelBello, 2000, for a review). The importance of dual mental illness in substance-abusing samples lies in its link to functioning and treatment outcome. Burns, Teesson, and O'Neill (2005) studied the impact of dual anxiety disorders and/or depression on outcome of 71 patients seeking outpatient alcohol treatment. Comorbid patients showed greater problems at baseline (more disabled, drank more heavily) than did substance abuse-only patients, a difference that persisted at a follow-up assessment 3 months later.

An extensive literature documents high rates of comorbid personality disorders in primary substance abusers (Khantzian & Treece, 1985; Nace, 1990; Nace, Davis, & Gaspari, 1991), especially ASP (Herz et al., 1990; Hesselbrock et al., 1985; Liskow, Powell, Nickel, & Penick, 1991; Morgenstern, Langenbucher, Labouvie, & Miller, 1997; Penick et al., 1984; Powell et al., 1982). In their evaluation of a large sample of treatment-seeking substance abusers, Mezzich et al. (1990) found that 18% of those with alcohol use disorders and almost 25% of those with drug use disorders met criteria for an Axis II disorder. Busto et al. (1996) found that 42% of their sample of patients undergoing benzodiazepine detoxification met *DSM-III-R* criteria for ASP. Morgenstern et al. (1997) assessed prevalence rates of personality disorders in a multisite sample of 366 substance abusers in treatment. Results showed that more than 57% of the sample met criteria for at least one personality disorder. ASP was the most prevalent (22.7% of the sample), followed by borderline (22.4%), paranoid (20.7%), and avoidant (18%) personality disorders. Moreover, the presence of a personality disorder doubled the likelihood of meeting criteria for a comorbid Axis I disorder. Brooner, King, Kidorf, Schmidt, and Bigelow (1997) assessed psychiatric disorders in 716 opioid abusers on methadone maintenance therapy and found that 47% of the sample met criteria for at least one disorder, with ASP and major depression being the most common co-occurring diagnoses. In addition, psychiatric comorbidity was associated with more severe SUD. Kokkevi, Stephanis, Anastasopoulou, & Kostogianni (1998) surveyed 226 treatment-seeking individuals with drug dependence in Greece and found a 59.5% prevalence rate of personality disorder, with more than 60% of these patients meeting criteria for more than one personality disorder. Furthermore, those with personality disorders were at twice the risk for meeting an additional Axis I diagnosis.

Findings are similar with anxiety disorders, with high rates of comorbid phobias (Bowen, Cipywnyk, D'Arcy, & Keegan, 1984; Hasin et al., 1988; Ross et al., 1988), panic disorder (Hasin et al., 1988; Penick et al., 1984), and obsessive-compulsive disorder (Eisen & Rasmussen, 1989) documented in substance-abusing populations. Thomas, Thevos, and Randall (1999) reported a 23% prevalence rate of social phobias in a large study of both inpatients and outpatients with alcohol dependence. Substance abusers also appear to be especially affected by PTSD (Cottler, Compton, Mager, Spitznagel, & Janca, 1992; Davis & Wood, 1999; Triffleman, Marmar, Delucchi, & Ronfeldt, 1995).

In an analysis of cocaine-dependent patients in the National Institute on Drug Abuse Collaborative Cocaine Treatment Study, Najavitis et al. (1998) found that 30.2% of women and 15.2% of men met *DSM-II-R* criteria for PTSD. Recently, Back et al. (2000) found that 42.9% of a sample of cocaine-dependent individuals met criteria for PTSD, and Bonin, Norton, Asmundson, Dicurzio, and Pidlubney (2000) found a 37.4% rate of PTSD in a sample of patients attending a community substance abuse treatment program. In sum, the literature clearly documents high rates of dual substance abuse and psychiatric disorders for a variety of psychopathological conditions and in a range of patient populations. Findings from epidemiological studies show that dual diagnosis is relatively common in the general population, and results of clinical studies illustrate the frequency of dual diagnosis among individuals in treatment. That rates of dual diagnosis are similarly high in both mentally ill and primary substance-abusing populations serves to highlight the serious difficulties in having two separate and independent systems of care for mental illness and substance abuse (Grella, 1996; Ridgely, Lambert, Goodman, Chichester, & Ralph, 1998), because both populations of patients are quite likely to be suffering from both types of disorders.

CLINICAL IMPACT OF DUAL DISORDERS

The importance of dual diagnosis lies in its negative impact on the course and prognosis of both psychiatric and SUDs, as well as its influence on assessment, diagnosis, and treatment outcome. In the next section, we review the ways that dual diagnosis impacts three general areas: patient functioning, clinical care, and research.

IMPACT OF DUAL DIAGNOSIS ON FUNCTIONING

Dual diagnosis has a profound impact on many domains of functioning. This section reviews the many ways that dual diagnosis affects symptoms of mental illness, course of mental illness over time, cognitive functioning, and compliance with treatment.

Symptoms, Course of Illness, and Life Functioning   Dual diagnosis severely impacts the severity and course of many disorders, especially among patients with serious mental illnesses such as schizophrenia, bipolar disorder, and recurrent major depression. Often these dually diagnosed individuals show a poorer and more chaotic course of disorder, with more severe symptoms (Alterman, Erdlen, Laporte, & Erdlen, 1982; Barbee et al., 1989; Hays & Aidroos, 1986; Negrete and Knapp, 1986), more frequent hospitalizations (Carpenter, Heinrichs, & Alphs, 1985; Drake & Wallach, 1989; Sonne, Brady, & Morton, 1994), and more frequent relapses than patients without co-occurring substance abuse (Linszen, Dingemans, & Lenior, 1994; O'Connell, Mayo, Flatow, Cuthbertson, & O'Brien, 1991; Sokolski et al., 1994). Haywood et al. (1995) found that substance abuse, along with medication noncompliance, was the most important predictor of more frequent rehospitalization among schizophrenia patients.

Recently, Margolese, Malchy, Negrete, Tempier, and Gill (2004) compared three groups of schizophrenia patients: those with current SUD, those with lifetime but not current SUD, and those with no current or history of SUD. Patients with current SUD showed more positive symptoms than did the other patient groups, had higher scores on measures of depression as compared with the single diagnosis group, and were more likely than the single diagnosis group to be noncompliant with their medications. Winokur et al. (1998) found that patients with drug abuse and bipolar disorder had an earlier age of onset of bipolar disorder than did those with bipolar disorder alone, as well as a stronger family history of mania.

Nolan et al. (2004) rated patients with bipolar or schizoaffective disorder on severity of manic symptoms, severity of depressive symptoms, and number of illness episodes over a 1-year period ($n = 258$). Results showed that ratings for mania severity were associated with comorbid substance abuse. Lehman, Myers, Thompson, and Corty (1993) compared individuals with dual mental illness and substance use diagnoses against those with just a primary mental illness and found that the dual diagnosis group had a higher rate of personality disorder and more legal problems. Hasin, Endicott, and Keller (1991) followed 135 individuals with dual mood and alcohol use disorders who were originally studied as part of the NIMH Collaborative Study on the Psychobiology of Depression. Although most had experienced at least one 6-month period of remission of the alcohol disorder at some point during the follow-up period, most had relapsed after 5 years. Mueller et al. (1994) examined the impact of alcohol dependence on the course of major depression over 10 years among individuals with depression who participated in the NIMH Collaborative Depression Study. Those who were alcohol-dependent at baseline had a much lower rate of recovery from major depression than those with major depression alone, illustrating the negative impact of alcohol use disorders on the course of MDD.

Dual diagnosis is also a serious issue for patients with PTSD (Najavitis, Weiss, & Shaw, 1997; Ouimette, Brown, & Najavitis, 1998). Overall, the combination of substance abuse and PTSD appears to be linked to higher rates of victimization, more severe PTSD symptoms in general, more severe subgroups of PTSD symptoms, and higher rates of Axis II comorbidity (Ouimette, Wolfe, & Chrestman, 1996). Saladin, Brady, Dansky, and Kilpatrick (1995) compared 28 women with both substance abuse and PTSD with 28 women with PTSD only and found that the dual diagnosis group reported more symptoms of avoidance and arousal, more sleep disturbance, and greater traumatic event exposure than the PTSD-only group. Back et al. (2000) similarly found higher rates of exposure to traumatic events, more severe symptomatology, and higher rates of other psychiatric disorders among cocaine-dependent individuals with PTSD as compared with those without lifetime PTSD. Moreover, evidence suggests that the combination of

PTSD and cocaine dependence remains harmful over several years, with patients showing a greater likelihood of continued PTSD as well as revictimization several years after an initial substance abuse treatment episode (Dansky, Brady, & Saladin, 1998).

Dual diagnosis also exerts a profound impact on overall life functioning. Patients with severe mental illnesses, such as schizophrenia, who abuse substances appear to be particularly hard hit in this regard (see Bradizza & Stasiewicz, 1997, for a review; Kozaric-Kovacic, Folnegovic-Smalc, Folnegovic, & Marusic, 1995). Drake and colleagues have consistently found that individuals with schizophrenia and comorbid substance abuse show substantially poorer life adjustment than do individuals with schizophrenia without substance abuse, and eat fewer regular meals (Drake, Osher, & Wallach, 1989; Drake & Wallach, 1989). Havassy and Arns (1998) surveyed 160 frequently hospitalized adult psychiatric patients and found not only high rates of dual disorders (48% of patients had at least one current SUD; of these, 55.1% met criteria for polysubstance dependence) but also that dual diagnosis was related to increased depressive symptoms, poor life functioning, lower life satisfaction, and a greater likelihood of being arrested or in jail. Research similarly shows that patients with dual affective and alcohol use disorders show greater difficulties in overall functioning and social functioning than do patients with depression (Hirschfeld, Hasin, Keller, Endicott, & Wunder, 1990) or bipolar disorder (Singh, Mattoo, Sharan, & Basu, 2005).

Newman, Moffitt, Caspi, and Silva (1998) examined the impact of different types of comorbidity (including but not limited to substance abuse–psychiatric disorder combinations) on life functioning in a large sample of young adults. Multiple-disordered cases showed poorer functioning than single-disordered cases in almost every area measured, including health status, suicide attempts, disruption in performance of daily activities, the number of months disabled because of psychiatric illness, greater life dissatisfaction, less social stability (more residence changes, greater use of welfare for support, greater rates of adult criminal conviction records), greater employment problems, lower levels of educational attainment, and greater reports of physical health problems. Weiss et al. (2005) examined the interplay between bipolar disorder and recovery from SUDs on a range of quality-of-life factors in a sample of 1,000 patients with current or lifetime bipolar disorder. Specifically, three groups were compared: those with no history of SUDs, those with past SUDs, and those with current SUDs. Results showed that the current SUD group had the poorest functioning, and both SUD groups reported lower quality of life and higher lifetime rates of suicide attempts than did the non-SUD group. Moreover, the toxic effects of psychoactive substances in individuals with schizophrenia and bipolar disorder can be present even at use levels that may not be problematic in the general population (Lehman, Myers, Dixon, & Johnson, 1994; Mueser et al., 1990).

Cognitive Functioning   There is a range of cognitive impairments associated with psychiatric disorders, particularly serious mental illness (e.g., schizophrenia, bipolar disorder). Individuals with schizophrenia spectrum disorders demonstrate cognitive impairments across a range of cognitive domains when compared with normative comparison samples (Heinrichs & Zakzanis, 1998). Although not as severe, individuals with affective disorders demonstrate similar impairments across a range of cognitive domains (Depp et al., 2007; Goldberg et al., 1993; Schretlen et al., 2007). These impairments are linked by modest to strong correlations to functional outcomes in schizophrenia (Green 1996) and bipolar disorder (Dickerson et al., 2004; Dickerson, Sommerville, Origoni, Ringel, & Parente, 2001).

There is also evidence that, in samples of individuals with primary SUDs, chronic or sustained substance use can contribute to cognitive impairment and resulting brain dysfunction (Bowden, Crews, Bates, Fals-Stewart, & Ambrose, 2001; Rogers & Robbins, 2001). Moreover, cognitive impairment has been implicated in substance abuse treatment outcomes in this population (Aharonovich, Nunes, & Hasin, 2003; Fals-Stewart & Schafer, 1992). Such findings suggest that substance use might exacerbate existing cognitive impairment, which could, in part, contribute to the poorer outcomes, experienced by persons with co-occurring serious mental illness and SUD.

Although this recognition has prompted clinical research efforts to adapt and develop new substance abuse interventions designed to accommodate some of the cognitive and motivational impairments associated with serious mental illness (e.g., Addington et al., 1998; Bellack, Bennett, Gearon, Brown, & Yang, 2006; Ziedonis & George, 1997), other research efforts have been directed toward further description and explication of the role of cognitive impairment in individuals with dual diagnosis. The majority of this work has focused on serious mental illness samples. On the one hand, there is concern about the possible exacerbation of existing cognitive impairment resulting from substance use among individuals with dual disorders, suggesting that these individuals would demonstrate poorer cognitive functioning compared with those without SUD. On the other hand, some data suggest that engaging in behaviors necessary to obtain access to substances requires a higher level of functioning (Dixon, 1999; Mueser et al., 1990), and, thus, these individuals with dual disorders would have better cognitive functioning than individuals without SUD.

With regard to cognitive functioning, the data are in fact mixed, and overall suggest that there are few differences between those with serious mental illness who have a current or history of SUD and those who do not. In a meta-analysis of 22 studies investigating neurocognitive functioning among individuals with schizophrenia, Potvin, Joyal, Pelletier, and Stip (2008) found that there was no difference on a composite score of cognitive functioning between those with SUD and those without. Furthermore, they found few differences between groups on specific cognitive domains or specific cognitive measures. Depp et al. (2007) also found no differences in cognitive functioning among a sample of individuals with bipolar disorder with and without SUDs. In contrast, Carey, Carey, and Simons (2003), in a sample of individuals with schizophrenia spectrum and bipolar disorders, found that those with a current SUD or former SUD both demonstrated better cognitive functioning than did those who had never used substances.

The interpretation of these data is complicated by several substantive and methodological issues. First, there is some indication that impairment may vary depending on primary substance of abuse. Across the meta-analytic data, alcohol use was associated with poorer working memory performance, whereas cannabis use was associated with better problem-solving and visual memory performance (Potvin et al., 2008). This finding is consistent with neuropsychological data from SUD samples without psychiatric diagnoses, where alcohol is associated with greater impairments than are other drugs such as cocaine (Goldstein et al., 2004). However, types of substances are not always accounted for in dual disorder studies (e.g., Carey et al., 2003). Second, consistent with methodological limitations across the dual diagnosis research literature, the rigor with which samples have been characterized has been quite variable. Some studies have relied on chart diagnoses as opposed to diagnostic interview to identify SUD, few have verified drug status with urinalysis, and others have failed to characterize the severity, recency, or chronicity of substance use. With regard to the latter, analyses included in the Potvin et al. (2008) study indicated that as age increased, so did the cognitive impairment among those with SUD, suggesting that chronicity of use may be a moderating factor in cognitive functioning among dual disorders. Similarly, Carpenter and Hittner (1997) found that lifetime use of alcohol or cocaine (i.e., number of years of regular use) was the strongest predictor of cognitive impairment among a sample of individuals with mixed psychiatric diagnoses (affective and anxiety disorders) and SUDs.

These latter findings raise the related question of how cognitive impairment changes over time as a result of substance use in individuals with dual disorders. Few investigations have addressed this question. Using a group comparison design with carefully characterized samples, Carey et al. (2003) found no difference in cognitive functioning between individuals with serious mental illness and current SUD versus those with past history of SUD (defined as not meeting full criteria for the past 6 months). Peer, Bennett, and Bellack (2009) compared individuals with schizophrenia who met *DSM-IV* criteria for current cocaine dependence and those who met criteria for remission on a brief neuropsychological battery and found few differences. This study also included a parallel analysis of samples of individuals with affective disorders and cocaine dependence versus remission, which yielded similar results. Although these studies used rigorous diagnostic criteria to characterize the samples, they are limited by their cross-sectional nature. That is, they did not evaluate change within subjects in cognitive functioning as a result of discontinuation of substance use.

At least two longitudinal studies have been conducted that address this question. A brief longitudinal study of inpatients with schizophrenia with or without current cocaine dependence at admission found few changes in cognition as a result of abstinence from cocaine over an 18-day study period (Cooper et al., 1999). Furthermore, there were few differences in cognition between groups at baseline or at follow-up. McCleery, Addington, and Addington (2006) followed 183 individuals with a first episode of psychosis over a 2-year study period and assessed cognition and substance use. Results indicated that cognition largely remained stable over time, while substance use declined over the study period. Together these findings suggest that cognitive functioning may be relatively static among individuals with dual disorders. Indeed, in the general SUD literature, longitudinal data suggest there are only slight and/or inconsistent improvements in neurocognitive functioning after a period of abstinence from substances (Bates, Voelbel, Buckman, Labouvie, & Barry, 2005; Di Sclafani, Tolou-Shams, Price, & Fein, 2002; Horner, 1999).

There are at least two possible interpretations of these data: (1) given the significant cognitive impairment associated with serious mental illness, substance use causes only minimal additional impairment; and (2) the toxic effects of substance use on cognition are not easily resolved following abstinence. In part, this research may be limited by the lack of sensitivity of the neuropsychological measures used for these particular research questions. With further advances in cognitive neuroscience, more refined measures that are more tightly linked to brain structures and functions impacted by chronic substance use will likely be developed (Rogers & Robbins, 2001). Although candidate brain structures and neurotransmitter pathways are increasingly being identified in the general SUD literature (e.g., Goldstein et al., 2004; Goldstein & Volkow, 2002), significantly more work is needed to understand the specifics of cognitive functioning in dual disorders, with regard both to pre-existing impairment and sequelae of chronic substance use.

Treatment Noncompliance and Violence Substance abuse often interferes with compliance with both behavioral and psychopharmacological treatments. Lambert, Griffith, and Hendrickse (1996) surveyed patients on a general psychiatry unit in a Veterans Administration medical center and found that discharges against medical advice were more likely to occur among patients with alcohol and/or SUDs. Pages et al. (1998) similarly assessed predictors of discharge against medical advice in psychiatric patients. The presence of SUD and a greater quantity and frequency of substance use were among the most important predictors. Owen, Fischer, Booth, and Cuffel (1996) followed a sample of 135 inpatients after discharge and found that medication noncompliance was related to substance abuse, and that this combination was significantly associated with lack of outpatient contact in the follow-up period. Specifically, those with dual diagnoses were more than eight times more likely to be noncompliant with their medication. In a large-scale study of factors related to medication adherence in schizophrenia patients, Gilmer et al. (2004) found that substance abusers were less likely to be adherent to antipsychotic medication regimens than were schizophrenia patients who did not abuse substances.

Similar results were found in a review of factors that impede use of medication in individuals with bipolar disorder (Velligan et al., 2009). Many studies have found that substance use is a critical barrier to medication adherence. Such findings are especially important when linked to functioning and service use. For example, schizophrenia patients who were nonadherent with their medications were more than 2.5 times more likely to be hospitalized than those who were adherent (Gilmer et al., 2004). Verduin, Carter, Brady, Myrick, and Timmerman (2005) compared bipolar only, alcohol-dependent only, and comorbid bipolar and alcohol-dependent patients on several treatment variables, including number of outpatient psychiatric visits and length of psychiatric hospitalizations, in the year leading up to and including an index hospitalization at a veterans' hospital from 1999 through 2003. The comorbid group had fewer outpatient psychiatric visits and shorter inpatient hospitalizations than did either of the single disorder groups.

For many disorders, substance abuse and its associated noncompliance with treatment is linked not only to poorer outcomes but also to greater risk for violence (Marzuk, 1996; Poldrugo, 1998; Sandberg, McNiel, & Binder, 1998; Scott et al., 1998; Soyka, 2000; Steadman et al., 1998; Swanson, Borum, Swartz, & Hiday, 1999; Swartz et al., 1998) and suicide (Cohen, Test, & Brown, 1990; Goodwin & Jamison, 1990; Karmali et al., 2000; Landmark, Cernovsky, & Merskey, 1987; Pages, Russo, Roy-Byrne, Ries, & Cowley, 1997; Verduin et al., 2005). In terms of violence, Fulwiler, Grossman, Forbes, and Ruthazer (1997) compared differences between two groups of outpatients with chronic mental illness: those with and without a history of violence. The only significant differences between the two groups involved alcohol or drug use. McFall, Fontana, Raskind, and Rosenheck (1999) examined 228 male Vietnam veterans seeking inpatient treatment for PTSD and found that levels of substance abuse were positively correlated with violence and aggression. The combination of schizophrenia and ASP appears to put people at high risk for violence, especially when they are drinking (Joyal, Putkonen, Paavola, & Tiihonen, 2004).

In their recent examination of population-based registers of hospital discharge diagnoses and violent crime in a Swedish sample over 30 years, Fazel, Lichtenstein, Grann, Goodwin, and Langstrom (2010) found that risk for violent crime among individuals with bipolar disorders was almost entirely due to substance abuse comorbidity, with those with bipolar-only diagnoses showing extremely low risk for violence crime. Such findings illustrate the problematic impact of substance use on violence in individuals with psychiatric disorders.

Research also shows links between dual disorders and rate of suicide. In an analysis of epidemiological data from the NESARC, Oquendo et al. (2010) found that lifetime rates of suicide attempts were higher for those with dual bipolar disorder and alcohol use disorders (25.29%) than for respondents with bipolar disorder alone (14.78%). Pages et al. (1997) surveyed 891 psychiatric inpatients with MDD and found that both substance use and substance dependence were associated with higher levels of suicidal ideation. Potash et al. (2000) examined the relationship between alcohol use disorders and suicidality in bipolar patients and found that 38% of subjects with dual bipolar and alcohol use disorders had attempted suicide, as compared with 22% of those with bipolar disorder only. Recently, McCloud, Barnaby, Omu, Drummond, and Aboud (2004) examined alcohol disorders and suicidality (defined as any record of self-harm or thoughts or plans of self-harm or suicide written in the medical record) in consecutive admissions to a psychiatric hospital. Problem drinking (as measured by the Alcohol Use Disorders Identification Test [AUDIT]) was strongly related to suicidality, with higher AUDIT scores (representing greater severity of problems with alcohol) showing higher rates of suicidality.

Importantly, those with multiple comorbidities—patients who have more than two comorbid diagnoses—are at even higher risk for suicide. In such cases, the added impact on suicidality of trauma in general or comorbid PTSD in particular is great. Tarrier and Picken (2011) examined rates of suicide in individuals with dual schizophrenia and SUDs and found that rates of suicidality (based on scores on the Beck Suicidality Scale) were higher among those with comorbid PTSD. Cacciola, Koppenhaver, Alterman, and McKay (2009) identified four groups among a sample of 466 male veterans: SUD only; SUD + PTSD; SUD + PTSD + another Axis I disorder; and SUD + another Axis I disorder. Lifetime rates of both suicidal ideation and suicide attempts were highest in the SUD + PTSD + another Axis I disorder group. Such findings illustrate the ways that multiple comorbidities can further increase risk for suicidality.

IMPACT OF DUAL DIAGNOSIS ON CLINICAL CARE AND RELATED FACTORS

Dual diagnosis impacts clinical care on many levels. This section reviews the many ways that dual diagnosis impacts service use and health care costs, as well as related factors such a medical illness, legal problems, and homelessness.

Service Utilization and Health Care Costs   Increased service utilization among the dually diagnosed has been borne out in both large-scale household surveys and clinical studies. For example, Helzer and Pryzbeck (1988) examined data from the ECA study and found that, for respondents of both sexes with alcohol use disorders, the number of additional non-substance-use-disorder diagnoses had a significant impact on seeking treatment: those with more diagnoses reported greater utilization of treatment services. Grant (1997) examined the influence of comorbid major depression and substance abuse on rates of seeking alcohol and drug treatment in data collected from the NLAES (Grant et al., 1994). The percentage of individuals with alcohol use disorders seeking treatment practically doubled, from 7.8% to 16.9%, when a comorbid MDD was also present. Interestingly, the greatest rate of seeking treatment (35.3%) was found among respondents who met criteria for all three disorders—alcohol, drug, and depression—illustrating how the term *dual diagnosis* is somewhat misleading, because some individuals have two or more substance use and psychiatric disorders, and each might have an additive effect on negative outcomes.

Similarly, Wu, Kouzis, and Leaf (1999), analyzing data from the NCS, found that although 14.5% of patients with a pure alcohol disorder reported using mental health and substance abuse intervention services, more than 32% of patients with comorbid alcohol and mental disorders used such services. Menezes et al. (1996) studied the impact of substance use problems on service utilization over 1 year in a sample of 171 individuals with serious mental illness. Although the number of inpatient admissions was equivalent for those with dual disorders and those with mental illness only, the dual diagnosis group used psychiatric emergency services 1.3 times more frequently and spent 1.8 times as many days in the hospital than did the single disorder group.

Given their increased rates of service utilization, it is not surprising that dual diagnosis patients generally accrue greater health care costs than do patients with a single diagnosis (Maynard & Cox, 1998; McCrone et al., 2000). Dickey and Azeni (1996) examined the costs of psychiatric treatment for more than 16,000 seriously mentally ill individuals with and without comorbid SUDs. Patients with dual diagnoses had psychiatric treatment costs that were nearly 60% higher than the costs of psychiatrically impaired individuals without substance abuse. Interestingly, most of the increased cost was a result of greater rates of inpatient psychiatric treatment, suggesting that the impact of substance abuse on psychiatric symptoms and illness relapse is realized when patients require costly psychiatric hospitalization. Garnick, Hendricks, Comstock, and Horgan (1997) examined health insurance data files over 3 years from almost 40,000 employees and found that those with dual diagnoses routinely accrued substantially higher health care costs than those with substance abuse only. Such findings suggest that individuals with dual disorders access the most expensive treatment options (inpatient hospitalization, visits to emergency rooms), which are short-term in order to manage acute distress, and fail to get the comprehensive and ongoing care they require.

These findings on rates of services use can be perplexing. For example, if dual diagnosis patients are accessing more and more expensive services, why do they consistently have more severe psychiatric symptoms, more substance-related problems, and poorer outcomes than do those with single disorders? As noted earlier, dual diagnosis patients appear to access expensive but short-term or acute treatment options more often while being noncompliant or not adhering to longer-term medication and outpatient treatment regiments. Other factors include lack of integrated care, as well as increased numbers of problems to treat associated with treating more than one disorder (Watkins, Burnam, Kung, & Paddock, 2001). In addition, researchers have recently begun to examine more closely the quality of services accessed by dual diagnosis patients. For example, in their study of patients with bipolar disorder with and without comorbid SUDs, Verduin et al. (2005) found that patients with bipolar disorder and comorbid substance abuse were less likely than patients with substance abuse alone to be referred to intensive substance abuse treatment.

Watkins et al. (2001) looked at the delivery of appropriate care to probable dual diagnosis patients assessed as part of the Healthcare for Communities Survey (a study of a subset of respondents from the Community Tracking Study, a nationally representative study of the civilian, noninstitutionalized people in the United States—see Kemper et al., 1996, for details). Appropriate care included medications for severe mental illness (a mood stabilizer for bipolar disorder, antipsychotic medication for a psychiatric disorder), medications and/or psychosocial interventions for anxiety disorders or major depression, and at least four sessions of any sort of treatment in the past year. In addition, variables addressed included whether patients are receiving integrated care for dual disorders (receiving both mental health and substance abuse treatment from one provider) or comprehensive substance abuse treatment (defined as including inpatient or outpatient substance use treatment that included a physical examination, a mental health evaluation, or job or relationship counseling). Results showed that 72% of dual diagnosis patients did not receive any specialty mental health or substance abuse services (i.e., services provided by a mental health or substance abuse professional rather than a primary care physician), 8% received both mental health and substance abuse treatment (either integrated or by different providers), 23% received appropriate mental health care, and 9% received comprehensive substance abuse treatment.

Other studies have found a disconnect between services accessed and services needed in dual diagnosis samples (Najavits, Sullivan, Schmitz, Weiss, & Lee, 2004). Such findings suggest that the complicated clinical picture presented by dual diagnosis patients makes it difficult for patients and providers to determine and administer appropriate care.

Physical Illness   The negative health effects of smoking are well known, and those with mental health disorders who smoke similarly share these risks. However, some populations fare even worse when it comes to the negative effects of smoking. For example, people with serious mental illness represent a special population that is even more markedly affected by the negative effects of smoking. People with serious mental illness suffer from a range of life-threatening medical conditions at rates that are significantly higher than the general population (Jeste, Gladsjo, Lindamer, & Lacro, 1996; Muir-Cochrane, 2006) and are also more likely to have multiple chronic illnesses (Carney & Jones, 2006; Carney, Jones, & Woolson, 2006; Dickerson et al., 2006). This high rate of medical comorbidity results in worsened psychosis and psychiatric symptoms, lowered quality of life, and higher rates of mortality in people with serious mental illness (Auquier, Lancon, Rouillon, Lader, & Holmes, 2006; Dixon, Postrado, Delahanty, Fischer, & Lehman, 1999; Dixon et al., 2007).

Smoking and tobacco dependence significantly impact, complicate, or are known to be a primary cause of the medical diseases that lead to significantly elevated rates of mortality for people with serious mental illness (Compton, Daumit, & Druss, 2006). Smoking increases the metabolism of some antipsychotic medications, producing reduced antipsychotic blood levels and requiring substantial increases in medication dosages in some cases (Goff, Henderson, & Amico, 1992; Ziedonis, Kosten, Glazer, & Frances, 1994). Serious mental illness smokers have a poorer course of illness, with earlier onset and more psychiatric hospitalizations (Goff et al., 1992; Sandyk & Kay, 1991; Ziedonis et al., 1994). Finally, other important consequences of smoking for people with serious mental illness include the high financial cost of smoking in people with limited income (Steinberg, Williams, & Ziedonis, 2004), as well as additional negative social perceptions in a population that is already subject to significant social stigma.

One of the most significant health problems among those with dual diagnosis is risk for HIV and AIDS. People with schizophrenia and other severe mental illness are one of the highest-risk groups for HIV (Gottesman & Groome, 1997; Krakow, Galanter, Dermatis, & Westreich, 1998), and substance use substantially increases unsafe sex practices (Carey, Carey, & Kalichman, 1997) and other high-risk behaviors. McKinnon, Cournos, Sugden, Guido, and Herman (1996) found that 17.5% of a sample of psychiatric patients had a history of injection drug use, 35% reported using drugs during sex, and 30% traded sex for drugs—all substance use behaviors that are highly risky in terms of the transmission of HIV and AIDS. In their sample of 145 psychiatric inpatients and outpatients in Australia, Thompson et al. (1997) found that 15.9% of dual diagnosis patients reported injection drug use, a figure that is 10 times higher than that found in the general population. Hoff, Beam-Goulet, and Rosenheck (1997) examined data from the 1992 National Survey of Veterans and found that the combination of PTSD and substance abuse increased the risk of HIV infection almost 12-fold over individuals with either disorder alone.

There is increasing evidence that other physical illnesses and high-risk health habits are also found more often in people with dual disorders. Stuyt (2004) found that 29.7% of a dual diagnosis sample had hepatitis C, a rate that is 16 times higher than that found in the general population. Salloum, Douaihy, Ndimbie, and Kirisci (2004) examined physical health and disorders in three groups of psychiatric patients hospitalized on a dual diagnosis treatment unit: a group with both alcohol and cocaine dependence, a group with alcohol dependence only, and a group with cocaine dependence only. Results showed that the group with both alcohol and cocaine dependence showed higher rates of a range of medical problems, including multiple hepatitis infections, than both single diagnosis groups.

Jones et al. (2004) examined physical health problems among people with severe mental illness and found that 74% of the sample were treated for one chronic health condition, and 50% were treated for two or more. The two most highly prevalent chronic health conditions—pulmonary disease and infectious disease—were both associated with SUDs in this sample. Moreover, results of regression analysis showed that substance abuse, along with age and obesity, was a significant predictor of health problem severity. Ouimette, Goodwin, and Brown (2007) identified medical problems in SUD patients with and without PTSD. Those with dual SUD + PTSD had more cardiovascular, neurological, and total physical symptoms than those with SUDs alone. Others have found high rates of mortality and other dangerous health conditions among those with dual diagnosis (Batki et al., 2009; Dickey, Dembling, Azeni & Normand, 2004; Lambert, LePage, & Schmitt, 2003). Importantly, these higher rates of physical health problems can serve as additional barriers to achieving important recovery goals (Conover, Arno, Weaver, Ang, & Ettner, 2006).

Legal Problems Individuals with dual diagnoses have more frequent contacts with the legal system. Clark, Ricketts, and McHugo (1999) followed a sample of individuals with mental illness and SUDs over 3 years to longitudinally examine legal involvement and its correlates in this population. While rates of arrest were high, patients were four times more likely to have encounters with the legal system that did not result in arrest. This suggests that frequency of arrest, although significant, is an under-representation of the frequency of contact that dual diagnosis patients have with the legal system. Continued substance abuse over the follow-up period was significantly associated with a greater likelihood of arrest. Among samples of incarcerated prisoners, rates of severe mental illnesses and co-occurring psychiatric disorders are far higher than in the general US population (Wolff et al., 2011).

Homelessness The combination of mental illness and substance abuse also increases risk for homelessness. Among patients with schizophrenia (Dixon, 1999), those who used substances had greater psychotic symptoms and relapses, a higher incidence of violent behavior and suicide, elevated rates of HIV infection, increased mortality, and higher rates of treatment and medication noncompliance. They were also more likely to live in an unstable housing situation or be homeless. Caton et al. (1994) compared a sample of mentally ill homeless men with a sample of mentally ill men who were not homeless and found higher rates of drug use disorders among the homeless group. Leal, Galanter, Dermatis, and Westreich (1999) assessed 147 patients with dual diagnosis and found that protracted homelessness (no residence for 1 year or more) were significantly more likely among patients with a history of injection drug use. Recently, Folsom et al. (2005) examined risk factors for homelessness and patterns of service use among a large sample of patients ($n = 10,340$). Patients with mental illness and substance abuse were more than four times as likely to be homeless as patients who did not abuse substances.

Issues for Women with Serious Mental Illness and Substance Abuse Importantly, dual diagnosis is often particularly problematic for individuals who are also otherwise underserved. As noted, individuals with schizophrenia appear to be particularly hard hit by the additional difficulties of SUD. Another such population is women with severe mental illness and substance abuse. Women with comorbid severe mental illness and substance abuse show poorer retention in treatment (Brown, Melchior, & Huba, 1999) and elevated levels of anxiety, depression, and medical illness (Brunette & Drake, 1998), as well as being more difficult to engage in treatment and more under-represented in treatment overall (Comtois & Ries, 1995). In addition, women with dual diagnoses have higher rates of sexual and physical victimization compared with women in the general population (Gearon & Bellack, 1999; Goodman, Rosenburg, Mueser, & Drake, 1997). Prevalence of physical victimization for women with serious mental illness ranges between 42% and 64% (Jacobson, 1989), and other research finds that 21–38% of women with serious mental illness report adult sexual abuse (Goodman, Dutton & Harris, 1995). Among women in a residential therapeutic community, 49% reported physical abuse and 40% reported sexual abuse (Palacios, Urmann, Newel, & Hamilton, 1999). Data from 28 women and 24 men with serious mental illness and SUDs indicated that, when compared with men, women were more likely to report being physically (60% of women vs. 29% of men) and sexually (47% of women vs. 17% of men) victimized (Gearon, Bellack, Nidecker, & Bennett, 2003).

Issues related to pregnancy and parenting often affect women with dual diagnosis. Grella (1997) summarized some of the many difficulties in terms of providing services for pregnant women with dual disorders, including receiving adequate prenatal care, use of substances and psychiatric medications while pregnant, and lack of coordinated treatment planning and provision among medical, psychiatric, and addictions professionals. Kelly et al. (1999) found that women with both psychiatric and substance use diagnoses were at greatly elevated risk of receiving inadequate prenatal care. There are also substantial barriers to treatment and medical care, including fears of losing custody of the unborn child or of their other children, lack of medical insurance, and the often disjointed nature of available services for the medical and psychiatric care of these patients (Grella, 1997). Finally, when compared with men, women with dual diagnosis may have different treatment needs. Grella (2003) reported greater needs for family and trauma-related services, and women with psychotic disorders had the greatest level of need of all the groups for basic services.

PROVISION OF TREATMENT AND TREATMENT OUTCOME

Co-occurring SUDs raise problems for interventions that have been designed to impact specific psychiatric symptoms, or ones that have been validated on samples that have excluded dual diagnosis patients. In addition, clinicians often experience difficulties in making referrals for dual diagnosis patients in the current system of single disorder treatment, which effectively separates the treatment systems for mental illness and substance abuse. The fact that patients must often be forced into single diagnostic categories no doubt results in SUDs being overlooked or ignored by treatment professionals who have expertise in treating only single conditions, or in dual diagnosis patients not receiving both the psychiatric and the substance abuse treatment they require (Blanchard, 2000). Patients with dual diagnosis are more difficult to treat and show poorer retention in treatment as well as poorer treatment outcomes as compared with single disorder patients. Such findings tend to be true both for patients with primary mental illness and co-occurring substance abuse (see Drake et al., 1998, and Polcin, 1992 for reviews; Goldberg, Garno, Leon, Kocsis, & Portera, 1999) and for patients identified through substance abuse treatment programs with comorbid mental illness (Glenn &

Parsons, 1991; Ouimette, Ahrens, Moos, & Finney, 1998; Rounsaville, Kosten, Weissman, & Kleber, 1986). An early study by McLellan, Luborsky, Woody, O'Brien, & Cruley (1983) found that higher psychiatric severity was associated with poorer treatment outcome among alcohol and drug abuse treatment patients. Tomasson and Vaglum (1997) examined the impact of psychiatric comorbidity on 351 treatment-seeking substance abusers over a 28-month period and found that patients with comorbid psychiatric disorders at admission showed worse outcome in terms of mental health functioning at follow-up.

Ouimette, Gima, Moos, and Finney (1999) reported findings of a 1-year follow-up of three groups of patients with dual substance use and psychiatric disorders (psychotic disorders, affective/anxiety disorders, and personality disorders) as compared with a group of substance abuse-only patients. Although all the groups showed comparable decreases in substance use at follow-up, patients with dual diagnoses showed greater levels of psychological distress and psychiatric symptoms and lower rates of employment than did patients with only SUDs. In a 3-year follow-up of a sample of patients with alcohol use disorders, Kranzler, Del Boca, and Rounsaville (1996) found that the presence of comorbid psychiatric disorders, including depression and ASP, is generally associated with worse 3-year outcomes.

Thomas, Melchert, and Banken (1999) examined treatment outcome in 252 patients in substance abuse treatment and found that the likelihood of relapse within the year following treatment was significantly increased in patients with dual personality disorders. Specifically, 6% of patients with personality disorders were abstinent at 1 year post-treatment, as compared with 44% of those with no diagnosed personality disorders. A study by Havassy, Shopshire, and Quigley (2000) examined the effects of substance dependence on treatment outcome in 268 psychiatric patients following two different case management programs. Regardless of program, dual diagnosis patients showed more negative outcomes than did patients with only a psychiatric disorder.

IMPACT OF DUAL DISORDERS ON ASSESSMENT AND DIAGNOSIS

There are numerous ways that dual diagnosis affects assessment and diagnosis, including symptom overlap, multiple impairments owing to different disorders, and substance-induced disorders resembling psychiatric disorders.

SYMPTOM OVERLAP

The symptoms of many psychiatric disorders overlap with those of SUDs, making diagnosis of either class of disorders difficult. For example, *DSM* lists problems in social functioning as symptoms of both schizophrenia and SUDs. That some criteria can count toward multiple diagnoses can potentially increase comorbidity rates and make diagnosis of substance abuse difficult. This overlap can work against identification of the psychiatric disorder in some cases. For example, high rates of dual substance use and bipolar disorders lead to an underdiagnosis of bipolar disorder, because of the often incorrect assumption that the behavioral manifestations of bipolar disorder are secondary to substance use (Evans, 2000). Others suggest that underdiagnosis can also be an issue with dual PTSD and SUDs (Brady, Killeen, Brewerton, & Lucerini, 2000; Brunello et al., 2001).

MULTIPLE IMPAIRMENTS OWING TO DIFFERENT DISORDERS

Substance use disorders are often overlooked in mental health settings. It is exceedingly difficult to determine the impact of substance abuse when serious mental illness profoundly affects all areas of functioning. *DSM-IV* diagnoses of substance abuse and dependence were largely based on diagnostic criteria that reflected substance use becoming more pervasive in a person's life and interfering with normal functioning. Criteria involving substance use impair one's ability to work, engage in relationships, complete responsibilities, and participate in activities. However, such factors often do not apply to many patients with mental illness whose substantial level of impairment associated with the psychiatric disorder often precludes them from having a job, being in relationships, or engaging in other activities. It becomes unclear how to measure the negative impact of substance use when there are few competing demands, activities, or responsibilities to be disrupted.

SUBSTANCE-INDUCED DISORDERS RESEMBLE PSYCHIATRIC DISORDERS

Diagnosis of psychopathology in the presence of substance abuse and dependence is especially difficult because symptoms of substance use and withdrawal can resemble psychiatric disorders (Schuckit, 1983; Schuckit & Monteiro, 1988). Long-term alcohol use and withdrawal can lead to psychotic symptoms, and abuse of amphetamines often results in psychotic symptoms that are identical to schizophrenia. Alcohol abuse and withdrawal also resemble symptoms of anxiety disorders (Kushner et al., 1990). Panic and obsessive behavior are often found with stimulant use and withdrawal from depressant drugs (Schuckit, 1983). Rates of dual diagnosis might be inflated, with individuals experiencing psychiatric disorders concurrent with alcohol or drug dependence being counted among those with dual disorder, although many of these symptoms will likely fade following a period of abstinence.

Incorrect treatment decisions may occur if interventions are aimed at what appear to be acute symptoms of psychiatric disorder but are, in fact, substance-induced symptoms. For example, Rosenthal and Miner (1997) review the issue of differential diagnosis of substance-induced psychosis and schizophrenia, and stress that medicating what appears to be acute psychosis due to schizophrenia but is actually substance-induced psychosis is not only incorrect but also ineffective treatment. Schuckit et al. (1997) suggest that too little attention has been paid to the "independent versus concurrent distinction" as it applies to dual diagnosis. Some alcoholics suffer from long-term psychiatric disorders that are present before, during, and after alcohol dependence and require treatment independent of that for their alcohol abuse or dependence.

Others have also found that a majority of dual diagnosis patients have concurrent psychiatric diagnoses that are likely a result of the effects of heavy substance use. Rosenblum et al. (1999) used an algorithm to determine whether individuals with co-occurring mood and cocaine use disorders have either an "autonomous" mood disorder—that is, one that either existed prior to the cocaine use disorder or persists during times of abstinence (similar to Schuckit's independent distinction)—or a "non-autonomous" mood disorder that followed from the cocaine use disorder and would remit during cocaine abstinence. Results showed that 27% of subjects were rated as having an autonomous mood disorder, whereas 73% were rated as having a non-autonomous mood disorder.

At this point, differentiating independent from concurrent dual disorders requires significant investment in training interviewers and in interviewing patients. Such requirements often cannot be met in the day-to-day operations of mental health treatment programs. Moreover, multiple assessments may be necessary. For example, Ramsey, Kahler, Read, Stuart, and Brown (2004) examined changes in classifying depressive episodes in alcohol-dependent patients as either substance-induced depression or independent MDD. Patients in a partial hospital program for alcohol treatment were assessed five times over a year for symptoms of MDD. Results showed that many (more than 25%) of the cases first categorized as substance-induced MDD were reclassified as independent MDD at some point during the year, owing to depressive symptoms that persisted once the patients had achieved a long period of abstinence.

IMPLICATIONS FOR NOSOLOGY

The fact that two disorders co-occur with great regularity raises the question of whether both categories actually represent two distinct disorders at all (Sher & Trull, 1996). For example, the literature regarding SUDS and ASP finds a high rate of comorbidity between the two disorders, one that is likely enhanced by the symptom overlap inherent in the ASP diagnosis. However, some suggest (Widiger & Shea, 1991) that such a high degree of co-occurrence between these two disorders could mean that these are not, in fact, unique diagnoses, but rather that such a pattern of comorbidity indicates the presence of a single disorder.

IMPACT OF DUAL DIAGNOSIS ON PSYCHOPATHOLOGY RESEARCH

Dual diagnosis affects several areas that are critical to psychopathology research, including diagnosis, sample selection, and interpretation of research findings.

DIAGNOSTIC AND SAMPLE SELECTION ISSUES IN PSYCHOPATHOLOGY RESEARCH

An accurate diagnosis is a necessary starting point for any psychopathology study, and dual diagnosis presents an abundance of diagnostic challenges. Individuals with dual diagnoses may provide unreliable diagnostic information, or their data may be inaccurate because of greater severity of impairments. Alternatively, they might minimize their substance use and associated consequences, especially if they have much to lose by admitting to or honestly discussing their substance use, such as services, benefits (Ridgely, Goldman, & Willenbring, 1990), or child custody. The timing of a research diagnostic interview can also impact results, as answers and resulting diagnostic decisions may vary depending on type of use, stage of treatment, and psychiatric stabilization. The method of assessment can also impact diagnostic findings (Regier et al., 1998), and diagnoses given in a clinical setting may vary with those obtained through more structured methods (Fennig, Craig, Tanenberg-Karant, & Bromet, 1994). As presented previously, establishing an accurate diagnosis in individuals with active substance use or withdrawal can be problematic, as the effects of substance use can imitate the symptoms of various psychiatric disorders. Most diagnostic systems used in psychopathology research contend with this difficulty by asking if psychiatric symptoms have been experienced solely during the course of substance use, and may recommend assessment only after a sustained period of abstinence. However, patient reports may be inaccurate, and histories may be too extensive and complicated to allow for this level of precise understanding.

Finally, the issue of overlapping diagnostic criteria can pose a significant difficulty for psychopathology research, as common diagnostic criteria may contribute to the diagnosis of multiple disorders when in fact the psychopathology is better understood as a single pathological process rather than two distinct disorders (Blashfield, 1990; Sher & Trull, 1996). The overlap of SUDs with ASP is notably problematic, and this frequent comorbidity has long been recognized (Widiger & Shea, 1991). Krueger (1999) examined 10 common mental disorders using structural equation modeling and found that ASP loads onto a common "externalizing" factor along with alcohol and drug dependence, suggesting that substance dependence and ASP may share certain underlying features. Whether this overlap is indeed because of common conceptual characteristics or is an artifact of similar diagnostic criteria is unknown. These diagnostic issues impact research findings, in that poor diagnoses will necessarily lead to poor-quality data. Researchers can improve diagnostic reliability by conducting structured interviews, using collateral information and behavioral observation to inform diagnostic decisions, and assessing the patient at multiple time points (Carey & Correia, 1998).

In terms of sample selection, psychopathology and treatment outcome research tends to focus on single or pure disorders and routinely excludes dual diagnosis cases, a practice that has several implications for research. First, screening out dual diagnosis patients yields samples that are atypical. Most patients with one psychiatric disorder meet criteria for some other disorder. Eliminating patients with dual disorders means that the resulting sample is less impaired and less representative of patients who present for treatment, resulting in limited generalizability of research findings (Krueger, 1999). In addition, dual diagnosis patients often have other characteristics that are not adequately represented in the resultant study sample. For example, Partonen, Sihvo, and Lonnqvist (1996) report descriptive data on patients excluded from an antidepressant efficacy that screened out individuals with "chronic alcohol or drug misuse." As a result, younger male patients were likely to be excluded, with current substance abuse as the strongest excluding influence.

Second, dual diagnosis impacts required sample sizes. In their examination of the impact of comorbid disorders on sample selection, Newman et al. (1998) discuss findings related to effect sizes of examining only single disorder cases versus the inclusion of dual disorder cases when analyzing group differences. Results showed that when dual disorder cases are excluded, larger sample sizes are required in order to detect small effect sizes. In contrast, retaining dual disorder cases yielded greater variance on study measures, resulting in larger effect sizes requiring smaller sample sizes.

Third, psychopathology and treatment outcome research most often combines those with dual diagnoses without classification by the specific type of drug use disorder. Whereas some might limit the scope of the study to alcohol only, most cast a wide net and include patients with alcohol, drug, and polysubstance use disorders. For example, research on substance abuse among patients with severe mental illness typically includes disorders of any number or combination of substances, including alcohol, marijuana, cocaine, and heroin. The impact of grouping all SUDs together is unclear, but it certainly raises the possibility that research may miss important issues that are potentially particular to one substance. For example, it would not be surprising if interventions for patients with a greater number of drug use disorders or with both alcohol and drug use disorders required adaptations that are not necessary for patients with single-drug or alcohol use disorders. Similarly, there are likely meaningful differences between patients who inject drugs and those who do not, patients who have long histories of substance dependence and those who do not, or patients who are dependent on cocaine or heroin and those who are abusing marijuana.

INTERPRETATION OF PSYCHOPATHOLOGY AND TREATMENT OUTCOME RESEARCH

The overall result of screening out those with SUDs from psychopathology and treatment outcome research is that there are very few data to inform treatment. For example, following completion of an antidepressant efficacy trial, Partonen et al. (1996) point out that they were left without information regarding the efficacy of antidepressants among patients with dual disorders. In their discussion of the many complex issues surrounding comorbidity and psychopathology research, Sher and Trull (1996) question the advantage of studying pure cases when certain disorders occur together with such great frequency that there really may be no ultimate benefit of studying either one alone. It is also unclear how well findings from psychopathology and treatment outcome research will generalize to the larger population of individuals with a particular disorder if patients with dual diagnoses are not included. The relevance of single disorder research to this substantial population of dually impaired individuals is highly suspect, and excluding dual diagnosis cases yields samples that are not representative of those presenting for treatment.

However, routinely including dual diagnosis cases in psychopathology and treatment outcome research has its drawbacks. Sher and Trull (1996) and Krueger (1999) discuss the fact that if dual diagnosis cases are included in psychopathology research, understanding of both mental and SUDs is compromised, in that samples would be less well defined. As a result, it would be unclear whether results could be attributed to the disorder under study or to comorbid disorders represented in the sample. In addition, comorbidity complicates longitudinal data because different patterns of comorbidity may emerge over time within individuals (Sher and Trull, 1996). One possible strategy for dealing with dual disorders in psychopathology and treatment outcome research is the use of samples that include comorbid cases in percentages found in the general population in order to increase the generalizability of findings (Newman et al., 1998; Sher and Trull, 1996). Widiger and Shea (1991) offer additional options, including having one diagnosis take precedence over another, adding criteria in order to make a differential diagnosis, or removing criteria shared by disorders. Sher and Trull (1996) additionally suggest statistically controlling for comorbidity via regression techniques but acknowledge that this practice can mask important common features of disorders.

THEORIES OF DUAL DIAGNOSIS

This review makes two points clear: dual diagnosis is highly prevalent, and it has a pervasive impact on both clinical and research domains. Models to explain dual diagnoses tend to fall into one of four general categories (see Mueser, Drake, & Wallach, 1998, for a review). Third variable or common factors models suggest that some shared influence is responsible for the development of both psychiatric and SUDs. The two types of causal models—secondary SUD models and secondary psychiatric disorder models—posit that either type of disorder causes the other. Bidirectional models suggest that either psychiatric or SUDs can increase risk for and exacerbate the impact of the other. These models have been described depending on the particular area of psychopathology. Examination of this literature finds that models of dual diagnosis are typically organized by disorder, with research focused on specific combinations of dual disorders rather than on the issue of dual diagnosis across disorders. Extensive reviews of models in each of these categories can be found (Blanchard, 2000; Mueser et al., 1998).

COMMON FACTORS MODELS

Common factors models suggest a shared etiological basis for psychiatric disorders and SUDs. Most research has focused on genetics as the likely common factor. Results of numerous twin, adoption, and family studies clearly show that both mental illness and substance abuse run in families, and that familial aggregation of single disorders is substantial (Kendler et al., 1997; Kushner, Sher, & Beitman, 1990; Merikangas et al., 1985; Merikangas & Gelernter, 1990). Such findings have led to the hypothesis that commonly co-occurring disorders might be linked via common genetic factors. However, for genetics to serve as a viable common factor, family studies must show high rates of transmission of pure forms of both substance use and psychiatric disorders. For example, a proband with depression only should have an increased rate of alcoholism only in the individual's relatives in order to provide evidence of shared genetic etiology.

Studies of familial transmission of a range of comorbid psychiatric and SUDs find that the evidence for a common genetic factor is lacking. Merikangas and Gelernter (1990) reviewed family, twin, and adoption studies of alcoholism and depression and concluded that familial transmission of pure forms of the disorders was not supported: "Depressed only" probands did not have increased rates of "alcoholism only" in their relatives, and "alcoholism only" probands did not have increased rates of "depression only" in their relatives. These authors stress that although familial aggregation of disorders is evident, the notion of a common genetic factor underlying the two is not supported, and the disorders appear to be transmitted separately.

In subsequent analyses of familial transmission of comorbid depression and SUDs using data from the Yale Family Study of Comorbidity of Substance Disorders, Swendsen and Merikangas (2000) similarly found that there was no support for a common factors model: mood disorders in the proband were not associated with an increased risk of alcohol dependence in relatives. Similar results have been reported with schizophrenia (Kendler, 1985), ASP (Hesselbrock, 1986), and patients with schizoaffective and bipolar disorders (Gershon et al., 1982).

Importantly, common factors other than genetics may exist. Several possible common factors might link SUDs and severe mental illness, including comorbid ASP, low socioeconomic status, and poor cognitive functioning (Mueser et al., 1998). For example, ASP is associated with both SUDs and severe mental illness. Mueser et al. (1999) examined the links among conduct disorder, ASP, and SUDs in patients with severe mental illness and found that both childhood conduct disorder and adult ASP were significant risk factors for SUDs. However, the status of ASP as a risk factor is unclear, given that problem substance use is part of the diagnosis of ASP, raising the possibility that ASP may be a byproduct of SUD. Also, ASP is based in large part on criminality and socioeconomic status, both of which are difficulties that often go along with both SUD and severe mental illness (Mueser et al., 1998).

Other researchers are proposing multivariate approaches to identifying common factors of dual disorders. One such model is described by Trull et al. (2000) to explain the high prevalence of dual SUDs and BPD. These authors suggest that a family history of psychopathology inspires both dysfunctional family interactions and the inheritance of maladaptive personality traits that are associated with the development of both BPD and SUDs. Specifically, the personality traits of affective instability and impulsivity are central to both disorders and are conceptualized as stemming from a combination of "constitutional and environmental factors" (Trull et al., 2000) that include inherited deficiencies in serotonergic functioning, in combination with a stressful family environment that may include associated childhood trauma. These factors in turn impact the development of BPD and SUD, both alone and in combination. These authors stress that although this model is currently speculative, more prospective longitudinal studies with a developmental and multivariate focus will enable the pieces of the models to be evaluated simultaneously. This model provides an example of combining strategies from family studies and psychopathology research into a multivariate framework that provides rich details as to how two disorders could be developmentally related.

In fact, the description and measurement of multivariate influences in the development and maintenance of dual disorders are becoming increasingly sophisticated, spanning from neurophysiology to postnatal development factors such as family stress (Fishbein & Tarter, 2009). Several studies have focused on the identification of neuro-cognitive and neurophysiological vulnerability indicators for substance use and psychiatric disorders. The P3 event-related potential (ERP) is a neurophysiological measure of brain activity that occurs between 300 and 600 milliseconds after stimulus presentation and is implicated in cognitive information processing, response inhibition, and self-regulation (Begleiter & Porjesz, 1995; Fishbein & Tarter, 2009). Reduced P3 amplitude has been fairly consistently identified among individuals with an alcohol SUD who are abstinent, as well as in populations at high risk for SUD (e.g., sons of fathers with alcohol dependence), suggesting that it is a heritable pre-existing vulnerability marker, or endophenotype, for alcohol use disorders (Begleiter & Porjesz, 1995).

As discussed previously, conduct disorder or, more generally, externalizing disorders often co-occur with SUDs. Reduced P3 has also been associated with externalizing disorders (e.g., attention deficit disorder; Klorman, 1991), which suggests it may represent a common factor to both of these disorders (Iacono, Carlson, Malone, & McGue, 2002). In a large longitudinal community-based sample, Iacono et al. (2002) measured P3 amplitude and assessed for a series of disorders including attention deficit hyperactivity disorder, conduct disorder, ASP, and SUD in a sample of 502 male adolescents and their parents. Participants were assessed at age 17 and then reassessed 3 years later. Results indicated that reduced P3 amplitude was associated with a paternal history not only of SUD but also of ASP. It was also associated with childhood disorders of disinhibition, including SUDs, and P3 amplitude at age 17 predicted the development of several disorders of disinhibition including SUD. The authors conclude that reduced P3 amplitude may be a common, genetically transmitted risk factor for a broad range of psychiatric disorders including SUD that share the common feature of behavioral disinhibition. It is anticipated that with continued advancements in cognitive neuroscience, similar endophenotypes will be identified that will facilitate the identification of common genetic risk factors for dual disorders.

SECONDARY SUBSTANCE ABUSE MODELS

Secondary substance abuse models contend that mental illness increases vulnerability to SUDs. Probably the most widely discussed model of this type is the self-medication model, which asserts that individuals with psychiatric disorders use substances as a way to self-medicate psychopathological symptoms and relieve discomfort associated with the primary psychiatric disorder.

There are several types of studies used to examine applicability of a self-medication model to different forms of psychopathology. Some determine the ages of onset of dual disorders, with the idea being that SUDs developing after other Axis I psychopathology support the self-medication hypothesis. Some examine subjective reasons for use among patients with different disorders, while others correlate levels of symptoms with levels of substance abuse (from a self-medication perspective, greater symptoms should correlate with greater substance abuse). Another line of self-medication research involves investigating the types of substances used by different patient groups. According to a self-medication hypothesis, patients with certain psychopathological conditions should preferentially seek out and use substances that will directly impact symptoms associated with their specific psychopathology.

Support for a self-medication model varies depending on the type of mental illness under investigation. For example, although the model is popular among treatment providers working with patients with severe mental illness, empirical support for a self-medication model has not been compelling (see Mueser et al., 1998, for a review). Although it has been suggested that schizophrenia patients preferentially abuse stimulants to self-medicate negative symptoms (Schneier & Siris, 1987), this finding has not been replicated in other studies (Mueser, Yarnold, & Bellack, 1992b). Most importantly, studies fail to find evidence that specific substances are used in response to specific symptoms. Rather, patterns of drug use appear to be strongly associated with demographic factors and drug availability (Mueser et al., 1992b). In addition, a self-medication model of SUDs in severe mental illness would predict that the more symptomatic patients would be at higher risk for SUDs (Mueser et al., 1992a). Several studies, however, have found the opposite to be true: more severely ill patients are less likely to abuse substances (Chen et al., 1992; Cohen & Klein, 1970; Mueser et al., 1992b), and patients with SUDs have better premorbid social functioning (Dixon et al., 1991).

Although individuals with schizophrenia and other severe mental illnesses report a range of reasons for substance use—to alleviate social problems, insomnia, or depression; to get high; to relieve boredom; and to increase energy—few endorse using specific substances to combat particular psychiatric symptoms (see Brunette, Mueser, Xie, & Drake, 1997, for a review). Moreover, many studies have found that patients with schizophrenia report worsening of symptoms with substance abuse, including increased hallucinations, delusions, and paranoia (Barbee et al., 1989; Cleghorn et al., 1991; Dixon et al., 1991; Drake et al., 1989), and others have found that more severe symptoms of schizophrenia are not linked to more severe substance abuse (Brunette et al., 1997). Similarly, findings of increased rates of cocaine use among patients with bipolar disorder, interpreted by some to indicate self-medication of depressive symptoms, have been found upon review to more likely reflect attempts to prolong euphoric feelings associated with mania (Goodwin & Jamison, 1990).

Other secondary substance abuse models may be more relevant to patients with severe mental illness. A social facilitation model suggests that patients with severe mental illness may have fewer available opportunities for social interaction, and that substance abuse helps smooth the process of social engagement in patients who lack appropriate social and interpersonal skills. Finding that a large portion of substance use/abuse by individuals with schizophrenia occurs in a public setting, Dixon, Haas, Weiden, Sweeney, and Frances (1990) suggest that drug use may provide "isolated, socially handicapped individuals with an identity and a social group" (p. 74) or fulfill needs for contact and acceptance (Mueser et al., 1992a).

Others offer an alleviation of dysphoria model; substance abuse represents an attempt to alleviate these negative mood states. Evidence for self-medication may be more relevant to dual diagnosis within other psychopathological disorders. For example, several reviews have found that self-medication may apply to dual PTSD and SUDs, especially among women with trauma-related PTSD. Three main theories (Chilcoat &

Breslau, 1998) are the *self-medication hypothesis*, which suggests that drugs are used to medicate PTSD symptoms; the *high-risk hypothesis*, which suggests that drug use puts individuals at heightened risk for trauma that can lead to PTSD; and the *susceptibility hypothesis*, which suggests that drug users are more likely to develop PTSD following exposure to a traumatic event. They then use data from a sample of more than 1,000 young adults who were randomly selected from enrollees in a large health maintenance organization and were followed longitudinally over 5 years in order to examine the timing of the development of both PTSD and SUDs. Those with a history of PTSD at baseline were four times more likely than those without PTSD to develop drug abuse or dependence at some point during the 5 years of the study. In contrast, baseline drug abuse/dependence did not confer any increased risk of subsequent exposure to trauma or to developing PTSD in those who did experience some traumatic event during the follow-up period.

Other data on dual SUD and PTSD (Stewart et al., 1998) that also lend support to a self-medication model include: (a) development of substance abuse most often follows development of PTSD; (b) patients often report that they perceive substance use to be effective in controlling PTSD symptoms; (c) patients with both PTSD and SUD report more severe trauma and a greater severity of PTSD symptoms, suggesting that substances are used in an effort to control greater psychiatric symptomatology; and (d) drugs of abuse may be related to different clusters of PTSD symptoms, suggesting that substance abuse may be linked to attempts to control intrusion or arousal symptoms of PTSD. These authors stress that although a self-medication model is likely too simplistic to explain all forms of PTSD–SUD comorbidity, at this point it provides a good fit for the current literature.

Recently there has been increased interest in neurobiological mechanisms that underlie dual diagnosis, particularly with respect to the ways in which mental illness and addiction share common neurological pathways. The foundation for this research is that neurobiological deficits and abnormalities that provide the basis for different forms of mental illness may predispose those with mental illness to substance abuse.

This literature includes animal studies of dual diagnosis, where brain lesions are produced to simulate different forms of psychopathology. Factors such as the ability to experience reinforcement from drug use and differential patterns of use and/or cravings are examined. A good summary of this approach to dual diagnosis in schizophrenia is presented by Chambers, Krystal, and Self (2001). Briefly, increased vulnerability to SUDs in schizophrenia results from impairment in brain systems that are central to schizophrenia—the most important of which may be the mesolimbic dopamine system. According to this model, the mesolimbic dopamine system is implicated in the reinforcing effects of drug use (drug use increases dopamine levels), as well as in the development of schizophrenia (high dopamine levels are implicated as a major factor in the development of schizophrenia). In other words, these authors suggest that the neuropathology of schizophrenia may contribute to the vulnerability to addiction by facilitating neural substrates that mediate positive reinforcement. The putative neuropathology underlying schizophrenia involves alterations in neuroanatomic circuitry that regulate positive reinforcement, incentive motivation, behavioral inhibition, and addictive behavior (Chambers et al., 2001, p. 71).

Thus, the neurobiological problems that give rise to schizophrenia also put the individual at heightened risk for developing SUDs. Several studies have found support for this sort of neurological linkage in schizophrenia. Chambers and Self (2002) studied rats with neonatal ventral hippocampal lesions (NVHL rats), a procedure that produces behavioral disturbances in rats that resemble the psychopathological behaviors seen in schizophrenia, including positive and negative symptoms and abnormal cognitive functioning (see Chambers & Self, 2002, and Chambers & Taylor, 2004, for details of the procedure and its effects). In comparison to controls (rats with sham lesions), NVHL rats showed faster rates of cocaine self-administration, a higher degree of binge cocaine use, and faster relapse to cocaine use following a period of nonuse. Other studies using this and similar methodologies have generated similar findings (Chambers & Taylor, 2004).

Similar animal models are available for depression and substance use. In one model for depression, rats undergo bilateral olfactory bulbectomy (OBX), creating behavior that is biologically and behaviorally similar to depression in humans, including decreased pleasure-seeking, disruptions in sleep, agitation, and other cognitive problems that respond only to chronic (and not acute) antidepressant treatment (see Holmes et al., 2002, for a thorough review). Importantly, this procedure also causes dopamine dysregulation in areas of the brain implicated in the reinforcing effects of drugs of abuse, again similar to those found in humans. In comparison to rats with sham lesions (Holmes et al., 2002), those with OBX lesions were more sensitive to the reinforcing effects of amphetamine. Specifically, they learned to self-administer amphetamine more quickly and had higher levels of stable amphetamine administration.

Other studies have used rats genetically bred for signs of learned helplessness as an operational definition of depression in rats. For example, Vengeliene, Vollmayr, Henn, and Spanagel (2005) examined differences in alcohol intake between congenital learned helplessness rats (cLH) and congenital nonlearned helplessness rats (cNLH)—two lines of rats selectively bred for different escape reactions following inescapable shock (cLH rats do not try to escape the shock, even though they have not been exposed to it before, whereas cNLH rats will try to escape the shock). In this study, these two groups of rats were given access to alcohol and tap water for self-administration for 6 weeks and then underwent 2 weeks of no alcohol access followed by renewed access to alcohol for 4 days. Although results showed no differences in males, female cLH rats consumed greater amounts of alcohol than did cNLH rats during the self-administration portion of the study and showed a more pronounced alcohol deprivation effect (greater consumption of alcohol following a period with no alcohol consumption). The authors suggest that inborn "depressive-like" behavior in female rats is associated with increase alcohol intake. These and other animal models of depression (Fagergren, Overstreet, Goiny, & Hurd, 2005) appear to be a useful avenue for the study of dual diagnosis involving depression and substance abuse. Such studies are finding that "depressed" animals respond differently than other animals to drugs and alcohol, providing interesting new leads in the search for biological mechanisms that lead to dual diagnosis.

The high rate of smoking among individuals with schizophrenia is another possible instance in which a neurophysiological deficit predisposes individuals to engage in substance use. Rates of smoking among individuals with schizophrenia are exceedingly high when compared with the general population (de Leon et al., 1995; Hughes, Hatsukami, Mitchell, & Dahlgren, 1986). Individuals with schizophrenia tend to smoke more cigarettes (de Leon et al., 1995), smoke higher nicotine content cigarettes, and smoke harder in an attempt to extract higher doses of nicotine from cigarettes (Olincy, Young, & Freedman, 1997).

Somewhat different than the self-medication of symptoms of schizophrenia discussed previously, intriguing data suggest that, for some individuals with schizophrenia, smoking may be an attempt to adapt to a neurophysiological deficit related to sensory gating. Specifically, Adler, Hoffer, Wiser, and Freedman (1993) investigated the impact of cigarette smoking on the P50 ERP. This ERP is involved in habituation to stimuli and functions to screen out irrelevant information. It is typically elicited with a sensory gating paradigm where two auditory clicks are presented in close temporal sequence. In intact sensory gating there is a diminished neurophysiological response to the second click. Functionally, this represents a screening out of less relevant information, thus allowing for the availability of more cognitive resources for the processing of new salient stimuli.

Consistent with other research, Adler et al. (1993) found that in the case of individuals with schizophrenia, there is a failure to inhibit the response to the second click. However, when allowed to smoke freely, there was a normalization (i.e., greater inhibition in response to the second click), albeit lasting only briefly. In a second experiment, Adler, Hoffer, Griffith, Waldo, & Freedman (1992) investigated the impact of nicotine gum in first-degree relatives of individuals with schizophrenia who were nonsmokers and had a demonstrated sensory gating deficit (as measured by P50). Results were similar to the patient sample: relatives demonstrated a transient improvement in P50 ERP. Interestingly, these effects were only found with a higher dose of nicotine gum (6 mg); pilot testing with lower doses failed to yield an effect (Adler et al., 1992).

Another well-documented psychophysiological deficit in individuals with schizophrenia that has also been identified in first-degree relatives is that of eye tracking dysfunction, namely smooth pursuit eye movement (SPEM; e.g., Holzman, 1987). Briefly, when required to visually track a moving object, impaired individuals demonstrate an increase in "catch-up" (due to tracking too slowly) and "leading" eye saccades (due to tracking too quickly or visually "jumping" ahead of the stimuli; Olincy, Ross, Young, Roath, & Freedman, 1998). Essentially, these saccades decrease the accuracy and efficiency with which individuals visually track a moving object. Olincy et al. (1998) found that in individuals with schizophrenia, performance on a SPEM task significantly improved when patients were allowed to smoke freely (compared with task performance after a 10-hour period of abstinence from smoking).

Notably, after smoking, there was a significant decrease in leading saccades, which the authors postulated was an indication of enhanced inhibition and similar to nicotine's normalizing effect in the P50 ERP. These neurophysiological findings have been linked to the alpha-7 nicotinic receptor, a low-affinity receptor that requires high doses of nicotine for activation, which may partially explain heavy smoking (i.e., extracting higher doses of nicotine) among individuals with schizophrenia (Adler et al., 1998). In addition to furthering our understanding of the impact of nicotine on the pathophysiology of schizophrenia, these findings have also helped contribute to the development of new cognitive-enhancing medications for individuals with the disorder (e.g., Olincy et al., 2006).

SECONDARY PSYCHIATRIC DISORDER MODELS

With some specific differences, these models suggest that substance abuse causes psychopathology. Schuckit and Monteiro (1988; Schuckit, 1983) stress that the use of or withdrawal from many psychoactive substances causes reactions that appear indistinguishable from psychiatric disorders. The case for substance-induced psychiatric disorder appears particularly relevant to dual SUDs and major depression. Raimo and Schuckit (1998) review the evidence in support of the idea that most cases of comorbid depression and alcohol dependence are substance-induced, including findings that drinking can cause severe depressive symptoms; treatment-seeking substance abusers show increased rates of depression that often remit following abstinence and in the absence of specific treatments for depression; individuals with substance-induced depression do not show elevated rates of depression in family members; and children of alcoholics show higher rates of alcohol use disorders but do not show elevated rates of major depression. These authors stress that, although having independent depression in addition to alcohol abuse or dependence is certainly possible, most of the depression that is comorbid with alcohol use disorders is substance-induced and not independent in nature.

Following this example, Swendson and Merikangas (2000) reviewed findings that are relevant to an etiological model of dual substance abuse and depression: the onset of alcohol dependence typically precedes the onset of unipolar depression; symptoms of depression often remit following several weeks of abstinence from alcohol; and genetic studies do not support a shared genetic basis for comorbidity of depression and alcohol dependence. They suggest that the association between unipolar depression and alcohol dependence may best be described via a secondary psychiatric disorder model, in which chronic alcohol use causes unipolar depression, either through the considerable life stress that alcohol dependence promotes for the drinker in many important domains of functioning, or through the pharmacological properties of alcohol as a depressant substance.

Epidemiological data and laboratory studies suggest a potential role of cannabis in the etiology of psychosis (Andrade, 2016; Ranganathan, Skosnik, & D'Souza, 2016). Several large longitudinal epidemiologic studies have found that cannabis use is associated with an earlier age of onset of psychotic illness (Helle et al., 2016; van Os, Bak, Hanssen, Bijl, de Graaf, & Verdoux, 2002) and increases the risk of conversion to psychosis among individuals at high risk for psychotic disorders (Kraan et al., 2016). A large meta-analysis of 83 studies that investigated age of onset and substance use identified that individuals who used cannabis experience onset of psychosis 2.7 years younger than those who did not use substances (Large, Sharma, Compton, Slade & Nielssen, 2011). While other substance use was also associated with a 2-year earlier age of onset, only cannabis made a unique contribution to risk of psychosis above and beyond all substance use. Alcohol use had no significant impact on age of onset.

Data also suggest a dose and strength (potency) relationship between cannabis use and psychosis. A meta-analysis evaluating amount of cannabis use (e.g., frequency) and psychosis identified that the heaviest users had an almost four-fold increased risk of schizophrenia and other psychotic-related conditions (Marconi, Di Forti, Lewis, Murray, & Vassos, 2016). It should be noted that this study did not include other risk factors as covariates, such as other substance use. With regard to potency, a case-controlled study conducted in south London compared type and amount of cannabis use among individuals receiving mental health treatment for psychosis and sociodemo-graphically similar controls recruited from the local community (Di Forti et al., 2009). While there was no difference in ever use or age of first use, members of the patient group showed a pattern of heavier use for a longer period and were more likely to have used high-potency cannabis. The authors suggest that higher-potency cannabis increases the risk of psychosis, although other risk factor variables were not investigated.

These epidemiological data converge with human laboratory studies evaluating the neurophysiological effects of cannabis and related cannabinoids such as tetrahydro-cannabinol (THC). As reviewed by Sherif, Radhakrishan, D'Souza, & Ranganathan (2016), in double-blind controlled studies, THC and other synthetic cannabinoids, when administered at a range of doses to healthy adults, can result in psychotic experiences, cognitive impairments and psychophysiological decrements similar to schizophrenia. Further, they point out that laboratory studies show these effects can be reversed in healthy adults with single-dose administration of dopamine antagonists such as haloperidol—suggesting that cannabinoid's interaction with the dopamine system may be one mechanism of action that results in psychotic symptoms. Finally, there are some mixed data that suggest the effects of THC may be modulated by genes implicated in schizophrenia such as catechol-O-methyltransferase (COMT), such that individuals who possess a certain COMT genotype may be more sensitive to the cognitive impairing effects (Sherif et al., 2016).

Collectively, these data have led researchers to suggest a contributing role of marijuana in the onset of psychosis. This relationship may not likely to be a direct single causal role but could instead be a component cause that interacts with other risk factors in the manifestation of psychosis (Large et al., 2011; Ranganathan et al., 2016). An alternative hypothesis suggest that common factors confer risk of both using marijuana and developing psychosis (Ksir & Hart, 2016). A critique of some of the epidemiological data is that it fails to account for general substance use, does not always include other risk factors and cannot account for the incidence of schizophrenia among individuals who have not been exposed to cannabis (Ksir & Hart, 2016; Sherif et al., 2016). Further research is needed to fully elucidate the complex relationship between cannabinoids and psychosis. In the meantime, the available evidence has led to public health education efforts to inform individuals at risk for psychosis about the potential health risks of using marijuana as well as substance use intervention and harm reduction efforts (Andrade, 2016).

BIDIRECTIONAL MODELS

Bidirectional models propose that ongoing, interactional effects account for increased rates of comorbidity. Support for a bidirectional model for anxiety and alcohol dependence (Kushner, Abrams, & Borchardt, 2000) includes the following: (a) most patients with anxiety and alcohol use disorders report drinking to control fears and reduce tension; (b) drinking can cause anxiety (i.e., anxiety can result from long-term alcohol use, patients report increased anxiety after drinking, and withdrawal from alcohol can cause physiological symptoms of anxiety); (c) alcohol dependence can lead to anxiety disorders (i.e., alcohol dependence puts one at increased risk for later development of an anxiety disorder, and chronic drinking can cause neurochemical changes that cause anxiety and panic); and (d) anxiety disorders can lead to alcohol dependence (i.e., having an anxiety disorder puts one at increased risk for later development of alcohol dependence, alcohol provides stress-response dampening and reduces the clinical symptoms of anxiety, and many people use alcohol to self-medicate anxiety symptoms). The authors conclude that alcohol and anxiety interact to produce an exacerbation of both anxiety symptoms and drinking. Whereas initial use of alcohol provides short-term relief of anxiety symptoms, it negatively reinforces further drinking, leading to increased physiological symptoms of anxiety. They then propose a so-called feed-forward cycle wherein drinking is promoted by the short-term anxiety-reducing effects of alcohol, whereas anxiety symptoms are worsened by heavy drinking, leading to continued drinking in response to these worsened anxiety symptoms.

SUMMARY AND FUTURE DIRECTIONS

We are at a critical juncture in the field of dual diagnosis and its impact both clinically and in research. Over the past three decades, efforts have focused primarily on identifying the problem of dual diagnosis—including its rates and consequences—and getting clinicians and researchers to think about dual disorders when pursuing their clinical or research work. We have learned much about the prevalence and impact of dual disorders from general population and clinical studies over the last several decades.

Currently we can say with certainty that dual diagnosis is common, both in the general population and among clients in mental health and substance abuse treatment. Comorbid psychiatric disorder and SUDs impact a large percentage of people, and dual disorders persist over time. These patterns are likely to shift as a broadened definition of SUD that routinely includes tobacco dependence makes its way into the mainstream of thinking around dual diagnosis. It will be interesting to see how the new definitions and conceptualizations that are part of *DSM-5* impact dual diagnosis. As noted previously, changes in the diagnosis of SUDs that include merging abuse and dependence into one disorder, the addition of gambling disorder, and changes to the diagnostic requirements for other disorder could lead to higher rates of dual diagnosis. Individuals with less severe problems (abuse) who may have been overlooked or not included previously may now be counted.

Importantly, we are now beginning to see that patients who present with multiple diagnoses are the most difficult and complex patients to understand and treat. The notion of dual disorders may require reconceptualization as the frequency of individuals with two, three, or more comorbid psychiatric and SUDs continues to climb. Such findings highlight the potential need to adjust our thinking about *dual* diagnosis and whether the term should updated from *dual* to *multiple* as a way to more accurately capture the reality that many cases of dual diagnosis really reflect multiple comorbid conditions.

The issue of multiple comorbidities—multiple substance use, psychiatric, and even medical disorders within individuals—is probably the most critical issue facing assessment and diagnosis of dual disorders. Research is starting to examine the interrelationships among mental health, somatic disease, and addiction. The inclusion of tobacco dependence within the framework of dual diagnosis plays an important role in this shift. For example, work on the relationships among mood disorders, smoking and tobacco dependence, and the presence of and recovery from physical illnesses such as heart disease is finding complex associations that impact treatment, recovery, and relapse (Stafford, Berk, & Jackson, 2013). Findings that individuals with mental health disorders have more health risk factors such as diabetes, obesity, and smoking but receive less medical treatment for them (Briskman, Bar, Boaz, & Shargorodsky, 2012) highlight the need for more attention to the public health impacts of multiple comorbidities.

Second, it is clear that research on psychopathology and its treatments is complicated by questions of dual diagnosis. Dual diagnosis impacts basic questions of research methodology and impact: who is included and excluded in dual diagnosis research; how are dual disorders handled in data collection and analysis; and how are research findings to be understood when individuals have multiple disorders? Although acknowledging and adapting to the reality of multiple comorbidites within individuals will further complicate treatment research, it is essential that research explore ways to include and be applicable to individuals with multiple conditions. That is, it is increasingly less useful to explore the relationships between only two disorders, or to limit the development of treatments to individuals with two disorders, when many of those with comorbid conditions have more than two problems. Practically speaking, issues of mood, anxiety, and substance use are intertwined for many people, and research will need to address the understanding and treatment of these syndromes together rather than separately.

Finally, several models that explain dual diagnosis take into account the different types of psychopathology and substances of abuse, as well as the differences in disorder severity. Research linking neurobiological development of psychiatric disorders to substance abuse vulnerability highlights the need to incorporate biological and psychological constructs as we proceed in trying to understand dual diagnosis. The next step is to further examine causal mechanisms and determine how these models work, given the significant heterogeneity seen in the dual diagnosis population. Although a range of theories has been proposed, more specific work is required to fully examine the links between mental illness and SUDs. Here again, research will have to adapt to the current reality of multiple comorbidities. At present it is unclear how prevailing models of dual disorders that are organized around a pair of problems are going to be relevant to individuals with three or more diagnoses. Overall, moving forward in our understanding of dual disorders will require that we focus on comorbidity and the connections among multiple problems as a way to best learn about and treat individuals.

REFERENCES

Addington, J., el-Guebaly, N., Campbell, W., Hodgins, D. C., & Addington, D. (1998). Smoking cessation treatment for patients with schizophrenia. *American Journal of Psychiatry, 155,* 974–976.

Adler, L. E., Hoffer, L. J., Griffith, J., Waldo, M. C., & Freedman, R. (1992). Normalization by nicotine of deficient auditory sensory gating in the relatives of schizophrenics. *Biological Psychiatry, 32,* 607–616.

Adler, L. E., Hoffer, L. D., Wiser, A., & Freedman, R. (1993). Normalization of auditory physiology by cigarette smoking in schizophrenic patients. *American Journal of Psychiatry, 150,* 1865–1861.

Adler, L. E., Olincy, A., Waldo, M., Harris, J. G., Griffith, J., Stevens, K., . . . Freedman, R. (1998). Schizophrenia, sensory gating, and nicotinic receptors. *Schizophrenia Bulletin, 24,* 189–202.

Aharonovich, E., Nunes, E., & Hasin, D. (2003). Cognitive impairment, retention, and abstinence among cocaine abusers in cognitive-behavioral treatment. *Drug and Alcohol Dependence, 71,* 207–211.

Alterman, A. I., Erdlen, D. L., Laporte, D. L., & Erdlen, F. R. (1982). Effects of illicit drug use in an inpatient psychiatric setting. *Addictive Behaviors, 7*(3), 231–242.

Altice, F. L., Kamarulzaman, A., Soriano, V. V., Schechter, M., & Friedland, G. H. (2010). Treatment of medical, psychiatric, and substance-use comorbidities in people infected with HIV who use drugs. *The Lancet, 376*(9738), 367–387.

American Psychiatric Association. (1994). *Diagnostic and statistical manual of mental disorders* (4th ed.). Washington, DC: Author.

American Psychiatric Association. (2013). *Diagnostic and statistical manual of mental disorders* (5th ed.). Arlington, VA: American Psychiatric Publishing.

Ananth, J., Vandewater, S., Kamal, M., Brodsky, A., Gamal, R., & Miller, M. (1989). Mixed diagnosis of substance abuse in psychiatric patients. *Hospital and Community Psychiatry, 40,* 297–299.

Andrade, C. (2016). Cannabis and neuropsychiatry: the longitudinal risk of psychosis as an adverse outcome. *Journal of Clinical Psychiatry, 77,* 739–742.

Archie, S., Rush, B.R., Akhtar-Danesh, N., Norman, R., Malla, A., Roy, P., Zipursky, R.B. (2007). Substance use and abuse in first-episode psychosis: prevalence before and after early intervention. *Schizophrenia Bulletin, 33*(6), 1354–1363.

Arendt, M., & Munk-Jorgensen, P. (2004). Heavy cannabis users seeking treatment: Prevalence of psychiatric disorders. *Social Psychiatry and Psychiatric Epidemiology, 39*(2), 97–105.

Auquier, P., Lancon, C., Rouillon, F., Lader, M., & Holmes, C. (2006). Mortality in schizophrenia. *Pharmacoepidemiology & Drug Safety, 15*(12), 873–879.

Back, S., Dansky, B. S., Coffey, S. F., Saladin, M. E., Sonne, S., & Brady, K. T. (2000). Cocaine dependence with and without post-traumatic stress disorder: A comparison of substance use, trauma history, and psychiatric comorbidity. *American Journal on Addictions, 9*(1), 51–62.

Baethge, C., Baldessarini, R. J., Khalsa, H. M., Hennen, J., Salvatore, P., & Tohen, M. (2005). Substance abuse in first-episode bipolar I disorder: Indications for early intervention. *American Journal of Psychiatry, 162*(5), 1008–1010.

Barbee, J. G., Clark, P. D., Crapanzano, M. S., Heintz, G. C., & Kehoe, C. E. (1989). Alcohol and substance abuse among schizophrenic patients presenting to an emergency psychiatric service. *Journal of Nervous and Mental Disease, 177,* 400–407.

Bates, M. E., Voelbel, G. T., Buckman, J. F., Labouvie, E. W., & Barry, D. (2005). Short-term neuropsychological recovery in clients with substance use disorders. *Alcoholism: Clinical and Experimental Research, 29*(3), 367–377.

Batki, S. L., Meszaros, Z. S., Strutynski, K., Dimmock, J. A., Leontieva, L., Ploutz-Snyder, R., . . . Drayer, R. A. (2009). Medical comorbidity in patients with schizophrenia and alcohol dependence. *Schizophrenia Research, 107*(2–3), 139–146.

Bauer, M. S., Altshuler, L., Evans, D. R., Beresford, T., Williford, W. O., & Hauger, R. (2005). Prevalence and distinct correlates of anxiety, substance, and combined comorbidity in a multi-site public sector sample with bipolar disorder. *Journal of Affective Disorders, 85,* 301–315.

Begleiter, H., & Porjesz, B. (1995). Neurophysiological phenotypic factors in the development of alcoholism. In H. Begleiter& B. Kissin (Eds.), *The genetics of alcoholism* (pp. 269–293). New York, NY: Oxford University Press.

Bellack, A. S., Bennett, M. E., Gearon, J. S., Brown, C. H., & Yang, Y. (2006). A randomized clinical trail of a new behavioral treatment for drug abuse in people with severe and persistent mental illness. *Archives of General Psychiatry, 63,* 426–432.

Bennett, M. E., & Dixon, L. (2011). Taking issue: substance use and first-episode psychosis. *Psychiatric Services, 62*(9), 997.

Bennett, M. E., Wilson, A. L., Genderson, M., & Saperstein, A. M. (2013). Smoking cessation in people with schizophrenia. *Current Drug Abuse Reviews, 6*(3), 180–190.

Berg, S. A., Sentir, A. M., Cooley, B. S., Engleman, E. A., & Chambers, R. A. (2014). Nicotine is more addictive, not more cognitively therapeutic in a neurodevelopmental model of schizophrenia produced by neonatal ventral hippocampal lesions. *Addiction Biology, 19*(6), 1020–1031.

Berkson, J. (1949). Limitations of the application of four-fold tables to hospital data. *Biometric Bulletin, 2,* 47–53.

Bibb, J. L., & Chambless, D. L. (1986). Alcohol use and abuse among diagnosed agoraphobics. *Behavior Research and Therapy, 24*(1), 49–58.

Bien, T. H., & Burge, J. (1990). Smoking and drinking: A review of the literature. *International Journal of the Addictions, 25,* 1429–1454.

Blanchard, J. J. (2000). The co-occurrence of substance use in other mental disorders: Editor's introduction. *Clinical Psychology Review, 20*(2), 145–148.

Blashfield, R. K. (1990). Comorbidity and classification. In J. D. Master & C. R. Cloninger (Eds.), *Comorbidity of mood and anxiety disorders* (pp. 61–82). Washington, DC: American Psychiatric Publishing.

Bonin, M. F., Norton, G. R., Asmundson, G. J., Dicurzio, S., & Pidlubney, S. (2000). Drinking away the hurt: The nature and prevalence of posttraumatic stress disorder in substance abuse patient attending a community-based treatment program. *Journal of Behavior Therapy and Experimental Psychiatry, 31*(1), 55–66.

Bowden, S. C., Crews, F. T., Bates, M. E., Fals-Stewart, W., & Ambrose, M. L. (2001). Neurotoxicity and neurocognitive impairments with alcohol and drug-use disorders: Potential roles in addiction and recovery. *Alcoholism: Clinical and Experimental Research, 25,* 317–321.

Bowen, R. C., Cipywnyk, D., D'Arcy, C., & Keegan, D. (1984). Alcoholism, anxiety disorders, and agoraphobia. *Alcoholism Clinical and Experimental Research, 8*(1), 48–50.

Bradizza, C. M., & Stasiewicz, P. R. (1997). Integrating substance abuse treatment for the seriously mentally ill into inpatient psychiatric treatment. *Journal of Substance Abuse Treatment, 14*(2), 103–111.

Brady, K. T., Killeen, T. K., Brewerton, T., & Lucerini, S. (2000). Comorbidity of psychiatric disorders and posttraumatic stress disorder. *Journal of Clinical Psychiatry, 61*(Suppl. 7), 22–32.

Breslau, N., Davis, G. C., Peterson, E. L., & Schultz, L. (1997). Psychiatric sequelae of posttraumatic stress disorder in women. *Archives of General Psychiatry, 54*(1), 81–87.

Briskman, I., Bar, G., Boaz, M., & Shargorodsky, M. (2012). Impact of co-morbid mental illness on the diagnosis and management of patients hospitalized for medical conditions in a general hospital. *International Journal of Psychiatry in Medicine, 43*(4), 339–348.

Brooner, R. K., King, V. L., Kidorf, M., Schmidt, C. W., & Bigelow, G. E. (1997). Psychiatric and substance use comorbidity among treatment-seeking opioid abusers. *Archives of General Psychiatry, 54*(1), 71–80.

Brown, V. B., Melchior, L. A., & Huba, G. J. (1999). Level of burden among women diagnosed with severe mental illness and substance abuse. *Journal of Psychoactive Drugs, 31*(1), 31–40.

Brunello, N., Davidson, J. R., Deahl, M., Kessler, R. C., Mendlewicz, J., Racagni, G., . . . Zohar, J. (2001). Posttraumatic stress disorder: Diagnosis and epidemiology, comorbidity and social consequences, biology and treatment. *Neuropsychobiology, 43*(3), 150–162.

Brunette, M. F., & Drake, R. E. (1998). Gender differences in homeless persons with schizophrenia and substance abuse. *Community Mental Health Journal, 34*, 627–642.

Brunette, M. F., Mueser, K. T., Xie, H., & Drake, R. E. (1997). Relationships between symptoms of schizophrenia and substance abuse. *Journal of Nervous and Mental Disease, 185*, 13–20.

Bucholz, K. K. (1999). Nosology and epidemiology of addictive disorders and their comorbidity. *Psychiatric Clinics of North America, 22*(2), 221–239.

Burns, L., Teesson, M., & O'Neill, K. (2005). The impact of comorbid anxiety and depression on alcohol treatment outcomes. *Addiction, 100*(6), 787–796.

Busto, U. E., Romach, M. K., & Sellers, E. M. (1996). Multiple drug use and psychiatric comorbidity in patients admitted to the hospital with severe benzodiazepine dependence. *Journal of Clinical Psychopharmacology, 16*(1), 51–57.

Cacciola, J. S., Koppenhaver, J. M., Alterman, A. I., & McKay, J. R. (2009). Posttraumatic stress disorder and other psychopathology in substance abusing patients. *Drug and Alcohol Dependence, 101*(1–2), 27–33.

Carey, K. B., & Correia, C. J. (1998). Severe mental illness and addictions: Assessment considerations. *Addictive Behaviors, 23*(6), 735–748.

Carey, K. B., Carey, M. P., & Simons, J. S. (2003). Correlates of substance use disorder among psychiatric outpatients: Focus on cognition, social role functioning, and psychiatric status. *Journal of Nervous and Mental Disease, 191*, 300–308.

Carey, M. P., Carey, K. B., & Kalichman, S. C. (1997). Risk for human immunodeficiency virus (HIV) infection among persons with severe mental illnesses. *Clinical Psychology Review, 17*, 271–291.

Carney, C. P., & Jones, L. E. (2006). Medical comorbidity in women and men with bipolar disorders: A population-based controlled study. *Psychosomatic Medicine, 68*(5), 684–691.

Carney, C. P., Jones, L., & Woolson, R. F. (2006). Medical comorbidity in women and men with schizophrenia. *Journal of General Internal Medicine, 21*, 1133–1137.

Carpenter, K. M., & Hittner, J. B. (1997). Cognitive impairment among the dually diagnosed: Substance use history and depressive symptom correlates. *Addiction, 92*, 747–759.

Carpenter, W. T. J., Heinrichs, D. W., & Alphs, L. D. (1985). Treatment of negative symptoms. *Schizophrenia Bulletin, 11*, 440–452.

Caton, C. L., Shrout, P. E., Eagle, P. F., Opler, L. A., Felix, A., & Dominguez, B. (1994). Risk factors for homelessness among schizophrenic men: A case-control study. *American Journal of Public Health, 84*, 265–270.

Chambers, R. A., Krystal, J. H., & Self, D. W. (2001). A neurobiological basis for substance abuse comorbidity in schizophrenia. *Biological Psychiatry, 50,* 71–83.

Chambers, R. A., & Self, D. W. (2002). Motivational responses to natural and drug rewards in rats with neonatal ventral hippocampal lesions: An animal model of dual diagnosis schizophrenia. *Neuropsychopharmacology, 27,* 889–905.

Chambers, R. A., & Taylor, J. R. (2004). Animal modeling dual diagnosis schizophrenia: Sensitization to cocaine in rats with neonatal ventral hippocampal lesions. *Biological Psychiatry, 56,* 308–316.

Chen, C., Balogh, R., Bathija, J., Howanitz, E., Plutchik, R., & Conte, H. R. (1992). Substance abuse among psychiatric inpatients. *Comprehensive Psychiatry, 33,* 60–64.

Chengappa, K. N., Levine, J., Gershon, S., & Kupfer, D. J. (2000). Lifetime prevalence of substance or alcohol abuse and dependence among subjects with bipolar I and II disorders in a voluntary registry. *Bipolar Disorder, 2*(3, Pt. 1), 191–195.

Chilcoat, H. D., & Breslau, N. (1998). Investigations of causal pathways between posttraumatic stress disorder and drug use disorders. *Addictive Behaviors, 23*(6), 827–840.

Chou, K., & Cheung, K. (2013). Major depressive disorder in vulnerable groups of older adults, their course and treatment, and psychiatric comorbidity. *Depression and Anxiety, 30,* 528–537.

Chou, S. P., Huang, B., Goldstein, R., & Grant, B. F. (2013). Temporal associations between physical illnesses and mental disorders – Results from the Wave 2 National Epidemiologic Survey on Alcohol and Related Conditions (NESARC). *Comprehensive Psychiatry, 54*(6), 627–638.

Clark, R. E., Ricketts, S. K., & McHugo, G. J. (1999). Legal system involvement and costs for persons in treatment for severe mental illness and substance use disorders. *Psychiatric Services, 50*(5), 641–647.

Clausen L., Hjorthøj C.R., Thorup A., Jeppesen P., Petersen L., Bertelsen M., Nordentoft M. (2014). Change in cannabis use, clinical symptoms and social functioning among patients with first-episode psychosis: a 5-year follow-up study of patients in the OPUS trial. *Psychological Medicine,* 44(1), 117–126.

Cleghorn, J. M., Kaplan, R. D., Szechtman, B., Szechtman, H., Brown, G. M., & Franco, S. (1991). Substance abuse and schizophrenia: Effect on symptoms but not on neurocognitive function. *Journal of Clinical Psychiatry, 52,* 26–30.

Cohen, L. J., Test, M. A., & Brown, R. J. (1990). Suicide and schizophrenia: Data from a prospective community treatment study. *American Journal of Psychiatry, 147,* 602–607.

Cohen, M., & Klein, D. F. (1970). Drug abuse in a young psychiatric population. *American Journal of Orthopsychiatry, 40,* 448–455.

Compton, M. T., Daumit, G. L., & Druss, B. G. (2006). Cigarette smoking and overweight/obesity among individuals with serious mental illness: A preventative perspective. *Harvard Review of Psychiatry, 14*(4), 212–222.

Compton M. T., Kelley M. E., Ramsay C. E., Pringle M., Goulding S. M., Esterberg M. L., . . . Walker E. F. (2009). Association of pre-onset cannabis, alcohol, and tobacco use with age at onset of prodrome and age at onset of psychosis in first-episode patients. *American Journal of Psychiatry, 166*(11), 1251–1257.

Comtois, K. A., & Ries, R. (1995). Sex differences in dually diagnosed severely mentally ill clients in dual diagnosis outpatient treatment. *American Journal on Addictions, 4,* 245–253.

Conover, C. J., Arno, P., Weaver, M., Ang, A., & Ettner, S. L. (2006). Income and employment of people living with combined HIV/AIDS, chronic mental illness, and substance abuse disorders. *Journal of Mental Health Policy and Economics, 9*(2), 71–86.

Cook, B. L., Wayne, G. F., Kafali, E. N., Liu, Z., Shu, C., Flores, M. (2014). Trends in smoking among adults with mental illness and association between mental health treatment and smoking cessation. *Journal of the American Medical Association, 311*(2), 172–182.

Cooper, L., Liberman, D., Tucker, D., Nuechterlein, K. H., Tsuang, J., & Barnett, H. L. (1999). Neurocognitive deficits in the dually diagnosed with schizophrenia and cocaine abuse. *Psychiatric Rehabilitation Skills, 3,* 231–245.

Cottler, L. B., Compton, W. M., III Mager, D., Spitznagel, E. L., & Janca, A. (1992). Posttraumatic stress disorder among substance users from the general population. *American Journal of Psychiatry, 149*(5), 664–670.

Cowlishaw, S., Hakes, J. K., & Dowling, N. A. (2016). Gambling problems in treatment for affective disorders: Results from the National Epidemiologic Survey on Alcohol and Related Conditions (NESARC). *Journal of Affective Disorders, 15,* 110–114.

Dalack, G. W., & Meador-Woodruff, J. H. (1996). Smoking, smoking withdrawal and schizophrenia: Case reports and a review of the literature. *Schizophrenia Research, 22,* 133–141.

Dansky, B. S., Brady, K. T., & Saladin, M. E. (1998). Untreated symptoms of posttraumatic stress disorder among cocaine-dependent individuals: Changes over time. *Journal of Substance Abuse Treatment, 15*(6), 499–504.

Davis, T. M., & Wood, P. S. (1999). Substance abuse and sexual trauma in a female veteran population. *Journal of Substance Abuse Treatment, 16*(2), 123–127.

De Leon, J., Dadvand, M., Canuso, C., White, A. O., Stanilla, J. K., & Simpson, G. M. (1995). Schizophrenia and smoking: An epidemiological survey in a state hospital. *American Journal of Psychiatry, 152*(3), 453–455.

de Leon, J., & Diaz, F. J. (2012). Genetics of schizophrenia and smoking: An approach to studying their comorbidity based on epidemiological findings. *Human Genetics, 131*(6), 877–901.

Depp, C. A., Moore, D. J., Sitzer, D., Palmer, B. W., Eyler, L. T., Roesch, S., . . . Jeste, D. V. (2007). Neurocognitive impairment in middle-aged and older adults with bipolar disorder: Comparison to schizophrenia and normal comparison subjects. *Journal of Affective Disorders, 101,* 201–209.

Dickerson, F. B., Boronow, J. J., Stallings, C. R., Origoni, A. E., Cole, S., & Yolken, R. H. (2004). Association between cognitive functioning and employment status of persons with bipolar disorder. *Psychiatric Services, 55*(1), 54–58.

Dickerson, F., Stallings, C. R., Origoni, A. E., Vaughan, C., Khushalani, S., Schroeder, J., & Yolken, R. H. (2012). Cigarette smoking among persons with schizophrenia or bipolar disorder in routine clinical settings, 1999–2011. *Psychiatric Services, 64*(1), 44–50.

Dickerson, F. B., Brown, C. H., Daumit, G. L., Fang, L., Goldberg, R. W., Wohlheiter, K., & Dixon, L. B. (2006). Health status of individuals with serious mental illness. *Schizophrenia Bulletin, 32*(3), 584–589.

Dickerson, F. B., Sommerville, J., Origoni, A. E., Ringel, N. B., & Parente, F. (2001). Outpatients with schizophrenia and bipolar I disorder: Do they differ in their cognitive and social functioning? *Psychiatry Research, 102*(1), 21–27.

Dickey, B., & Azeni, H. (1996). Persons with dual diagnoses of substance abuse and major mental illness: Their excess costs of psychiatric care. *American Journal of Public Health, 86*(7), 973–977.

Dickey, B., Dembling, B., Azeni, H., & Normand, S. T. (2004). Externally caused deaths for adults with substance use and mental disorders. *Journal of Behavioral Health Services & Research, 31*(1), 75–85.

Dickey, B., Normand, S. L. T., Weiss, R. D., Drake, R. E., & Azeni, H. (2002). Medical morbidity, mental illness, and substance use disorders. *Psychiatric Services, 53*(7), 861–867.

Di Forti, M., Morgan, C., Dazzan, P., Pariante, C., Mondelli, V., Marques, T. R. . . . Murray, R. M. (2009). High-potency cannabis and the risk of psychosis. *British Journal of Psychiatry, 195,* 488–491.

Di Sclafani, V., Tolou-Shams, M., Price, L. J., & Fein, G. (2002). Neuropsychological performance of individuals dependent on crack-cocaine, or crack-cocaine and alcohol, at 6 weeks and 6 months of abstinence. *Drug and Alcohol Dependence, 66,* 161–171.

Dixon, L. (1999). Dual diagnosis of substance abuse in schizophrenia: Prevalence and impact on outcomes. *Schizophrenia Research, 35*, S93–S100.

Dixon, L., Haas, G., Weiden, P., Sweeney, J., & Frances, A. J. (1990). Acute effects of drug abuse in schizophrenic patients: Clinical observations and patients' self-reports. *Schizophrenia Bulletin, 16*(1), 69–79.

Dixon, L., Haas, G., Weiden, P., Sweeney, J., & Frances, A. J. (1991). Drug abuse in schizophrenic patients: Clinical correlates and reasons for use. *American Journal of Psychiatry, 149*, 231–234.

Dixon, L. D., Medoff, D. R., Wohlheiter, K., DiClemente, C., Golderberg, R., Kreyenbuhl, J., . . . Davin, C. (2007). Correlates of severity of smoking among persons with severe mental illness. *The American Journal on Addictions, 16*, 101–110.

Dixon, L. D., Postrado, L., Delahanty, J., Fischer, P. J., & Lehman, A. (1999). The association of medical comorbidity in schizophrenia with pool physical and mental health. *Journal of Nervous and Mental Disease, 187*(8), 496–502.

Dowling, N. A., Cowlishaw, S., Jackson, A. C., Merkouris, S. S., Francis, K. L., & Christensen, D. R. (2015). Prevalence of psychiatric co-morbidity in treatment-seeking problem gamblers: A systematic review and meta-analysis. *Australian & New Zealand Journal of Psychiatry, 49*(6), 519–539.

Drake, R. E., Mercer-McFadden, C., Mueser, K. T., McHugo, G. J., & Bond, G. R. (1998). Review of integrated mental health and substance abuse treatment for patients with dual disorders. *Schizophrenia Bulletin, 24*(4), 589–608.

Drake, R. E., Osher, F. C., & Wallach, M. A. (1989). Alcohol use and abuse in schizophrenia: A prospective community study. *Journal of Nervous and Mental Disease, 177*, 408–414.

Drake, R. E., & Wallach, M. A. (1989). Substance abuse among the chronically mentally ill. *Hospital and Community Psychiatry, 40*, 1041–1046.

Druss, B. G. & Walker, E. R. (2011). Mental disorders and medical comorbidity. *Robert Wood Johnson Foundation, The Synthesis Project, Research Synthesis Report No. 21*.

Eisen, J. L., & Rasmussen, S. A. (1989). Coexisting obsessive compulsive disorder and alcoholism. *Journal of Clinical Psychiatry, 50*(3), 96–98.

El-Guebaly, N., Cathcart, J., Currie, S., Brown, D., & Gloster, S. (2002). Public health and therapeutic aspects of smoking bans in mental health and addiction settings. *Psychiatric Services, 53*(12), 1617–1622.

Evans, D. L. (2000). Bipolar disorder: Diagnostic challenges and treatment consideration. *Journal of Clinical Psychiatry, 61*(Suppl. 13), 26–31.

Fagergren, P., Overstreet, D. H., Goiny, M., & Hurd, Y. L. (2005). Blunted response to cocaine in the Flinders hypercholinergic animal model of depression. *Neuroscience, 132*, 1159–1171.

Falck, R. S., Wang, J., Siegal, H. A., & Carlson, R. G. (2004). The prevalence of psychiatric disorder among a community sample of crack cocaine users: An exploratory study with practical implications. *Journal of Nervous and Mental Disease, 192*(7), 503–507.

Fals-Stewart, W., & Schafer, J. (1992). The relationship between length of stay in drug-free therapeutic communities and neurocognitive functioning. *Journal of Clinical Psychology, 48*(4), 539–543.

Farrell, M., Howes, S., Bebbington, P., Brugha, T., Jenkins, R., Lewis, G., Marsden, J., . . . Meltzer, H. (2003). Nicotine, alcohol, and drug dependence, and psychiatric comorbidity—Results of a national household survey. *Review of Psychiatry, 15*(1–2), 50–56.

Fazel, S., Lichtenstein, P., Grann, M., Goodwin, G. M., & Langstrom, N. (2010). Bipolar disorder and violent crime: New evidence from population-based longitudinal studies and systematic review. *Archives of General Psychiatry, 67*(9), 931–938.

Fennig, S., Craig, T. J., Tanenberg-Karant, M., & Bromet, E. J. (1994). Comparison of facility and research diagnoses in first-admission psychotic patients. *American Journal of Psychiatry, 151*(10), 1423–1429.

Fishbein, D., & Tarter, R. (2009). Infusing neuroscience into the study and prevention of drug misuse and co-occurring aggressive behavior. *Substance Use and Misuse, 44*, 1204–1235.

Folsom, D. P., Hawthorne, W., Lindamer, L., Gilmer, T., Bailey, A., Golshan, S., . . . Jeste, D. V. (2005). Prevalence and risk factors for homelessness and utilization of mental health services among 10,340 patients with serious mental illness in a large public mental health system. *American Journal of Psychiatry*, 162(2), 370–376.

Fulwiler, C., Grossman, H., Forbes, C., & Ruthazer, R. (1997). Early-onset substance abuse and community violence by outpatient with chronic mental illness. *Psychiatric Services*, 48(9), 1181–1185.

Galanter, M., Castaneda, R., & Ferman, J. (1988). Substance abuse among general psychiatric patients: Place of presentation, diagnosis, and treatment. *American Journal of Drug and Alcohol Abuse*, 14(2), 211–235.

Garnick, D. W., Hendricks, A. M., Comstock, C., & Horgan, C. (1997). Do individuals with substance abuse diagnoses incur higher charges than individuals with other chronic conditions? *Journal of Substance Abuse Treatment*, 14(5), 457–465.

Gearon, J. S., & Bellack, A. S. (1999). Women with schizophrenia and co-occurring substance use disorders: An increased risk for violent victimization and HIV. *Journal of Community Mental Health*, 35, 401–419.

Gearon, J. S., Bellack, A. S., Nidecker, M., & Bennett, M. E. (2003). Gender differences in drug use behavior in people with serious mental illness. *American Journal on Addictions*, 12(3), 229–241.

Gershon, E. S., Hamovit, J., Guroff, J. J., Dibble, E., Leckman, J. F., Sceery, W., . . . Bunney, W. E. (1982). A family study of schizoaffective, bipolar I, bipolar II, and normal probands. *Archives of General Psychiatry*, 39(10), 1157–1167.

Gilmer, T. P., Dolder, C. R., Lacro, J. P., Folsom, D. P., Lindamer, L., Garcia, P., & Jeste, D. V. (2004). Adherence to treatment with antipsychotic medication and health care costs among Medicaid beneficiaries with schizophrenia. *American Journal of Psychiatry*, 161, 692–699.

Glenn, S. W., & Parsons, O. A. (1991). Prediction of resumption of drinking in posttreatment alcoholics. *International Journal of the Addictions*, 26(2), 237–254.

Goff, D. C., Henderson, D. C., & Amico, E. (1992). Cigarette smoking in schizophrenia: Relationship to psychopathology and medication side effects. *American Journal of Psychiatry*, 149, 1189–1194.

Goff, D. C., Sullivan, L. M., McEvoy, J. P., Meyer, J. M., Nasrallah, H. A., Daumit, G. L., & Lieberman, J. A. (2005). A comparison of ten-year cardiac risk estimates in schizophrenia patients from the CATIE study and matched controls. *Schizophrenia Research*, 80(1), 45–53.

Goldberg, J. F., Garno, J. L., Leon, A. C., Kocsis, J. H., & Portera, L. (1999). A history of substance abuse complicates remission from acute mania in bipolar disorder. *Journal of Clinical Psychiatry*, 60(11), 733–740.

Goldberg, T. E., Gold, J. M., Greenberg, M. D., Griffin, S., Schulz, C., Pickar, D., . . . Weinberger, D. R. (1993). Contrasts between patients with affective disorders and patients with schizophrenia on a neuropsychological test battery. *American Journal of Psychiatry*, 150, 1355–1362.

Goldstein, R. B., Compton, W. M., & Grant, B. F. (2010). Antisocial behavioral syndromes and additional psychiatric comorbidity in posttraumatic stress disorder among U.S. adults: Results from Wave 2 of the National Epidemiologic Survey on Alcohol and Related Conditions. *Journal of the American Psychiatric Nurses Association*, 16, 145–165.

Goldstein, R. Z., Leskovjan, A. C., Hoff, A. L., Hitzemann, R., Bashan, F., Khalsa, S. S., . . . Volkow, N. D. (2004). Severity of neuropsychological impairment in cocaine and alcohol addiction: association with metabolism in the prefrontal cortex. *Neuropsychologia*, 42(11), 1447–58.

Goldstein, R. Z., & Volkow, N. D. (2002). Drug addiction and its underlying neurobiological basis: Neuroimaging evidence for the involvement of the frontal cortex. *American Journal of Psychiatry*, 159, 1642–1652.

González-Pinto A., Alberich S., Barbeito S., Gutierrez M., Vega P., Ibáñez B., . . . Arango C. (2011). Cannabis and first-episode psychosis: different long-term outcomes depending on continued or discontinued use. *Schizophrenia Bulletin*, 37(3), 631–639.

Goodman, L. A., Dutton, M. A., & Harris, M. (1995). The relationship between violence dimensions and symptom severity among homeless, mentally ill women. *Journal of Traumatic Stress, 10*(1), 51–70.

Goodman, L., Rosenburg, S., Mueser, K. T., & Drake, R. (1997). Physical and sexual assault history in women with SMI: Prevalence, correlates, treatment, and future research directions. *Schizophrenia Bulletin, 23,* 685–696.

Goodwin, F. K., & Jamison, K. R. (1990). *Manic-depressive illness.* New York, NY: Oxford University Press.

Goodwin, R. D., Pagura, J., Spiwak, R., Lemesho, A. R., & Sareen, J. (2011). Predictors of persistent nicotine dependence among adults with United States. *Drug and Alcohol Dependence, 188*(2–3), 127–133.

Goodwin R. D., Zvolensky, M. J., Keyes, K. M., & Hasin, D. S. (2012). Mental disorders and cigarette use among adults in the United States. *American Journal on Addiction, 21*(5), 416–423.

Gottesman, I. I., & Groome, C. S. (1997). HIV/AIDS risks as a consequence of schizophrenia. *Schizophrenia Bulletin, 23,* 675–684.

Graham, N. A., Frost-Pineda, K., & Gold, M. S. (2007). Tobacco and psychiatric dual disorders. *Journal of Addictive Diseases, 26*(Suppl. 1), 5–12.

Grant, B. F. (1995). Comorbidity between *DSM-IV* drug use disorders and major depression: Results of a national survey of adults. *Journal of Substance Abuse, 7*(4), 481–497.

Grant, B. F. (1997). The influence of comorbid major depression and substance use disorders on alcohol and drug treatment: Results of a national survey. *National Institute on Drug Abuse Research Monograph, 172,* 4–15.

Grant, B. F., & Harford, T. C. (1995). Comorbidity between *DSM-IV* alcohol use disorders and major depression: Results of a national survey. *Drug and Alcohol Dependence, 39,* 197–206.

Grant, B. F., Harford, T. C., Dawson, D. A., Chou, P., Dufour, M., & Pickering, R. (1994). Prevalence of *DSM-IV* alcohol abuse and dependence: United States, 1992. *Alcohol Health and Research World, 18*(3), 243–248.

Grant, B. F., Hasin, D. S., & Harford, T. C. (1989). Screening for major depression among alcoholics: An application of receiver operating characteristic analysis. *Drug and Alcohol Dependence, 23,* 123–131.

Grant, B. F., Stinson, F. S., Dawson, D. A., Chou, S. P., Dufour, M. C., Compton, W., . . . Kaplan, K. (2004). Prevalence and co-occurrence of substance use disorders and independent mood and anxiety disorders: Results from the National Epidemiologic Survey on Alcohol and Related Conditions. *General Psychiatry, 61*(8), 807–816.

Green, M. F. (1996). What are the functional consequences of neurocognitive deficits in schizophrenia? *American Journal of Psychiatry, 153,* 321–330.

Grella, C. E. (1996). Background and overview of mental health and substance abuse treatment systems: Meeting the needs of women who are pregnant or parenting. *Journal of Psychoactive Drugs, 28*(4), 319–343.

Grella, C. E. (1997). Services for perinatal women with substance abuse and mental health disorders: The unmet need. *Journal of Psychoactive Drugs, 29*(1), 67–78.

Grella, C. E. (2003). Effects of gender and diagnosis on addiction history, treatment utilization, and psychosocial functioning among a dually-diagnosed sample in drug treatment. *Journal of Psychoactive Drugs, 35*(1), 169–179.

Grillo, C. M., White, M. A., & Masheb, R. M. (2009). *DSM-IV* psychiatric disorder comorbidity and its correlates in binge eating disorder. *International Journal of Eating Disorders, 42*(3), 228–234.

Grubaugh, A. L., Zinzow, H. M., Paul, L., Egede, L. E., & Frueh, B. C. (2011). Trauma exposure and posttraumatic stress disorder in adults with severe mental illness: A critical review. *Clinical Psychology Review, 31,* 883–899.

Gum, A. M., King-Kallimanis, B. & Kohn, R. (2009). Prevalence of mood, anxiety, and substance-abuse disorders for older Americans in the National Comorbidity Survey-Replication. *American Journal of Geriatric Psychiatry*, 17(9), 769–781.

Hartz, S. M., Pato, C. N., Medeiros, H., Cavazos-Rehg, P., Sobell, J. L., Knowles, J. A., Bierut, L. J., Pato, M. T., for the Genomic Psychiatry Cohort Consortium. (2014). Comorbidity of severe psychotic disorders with measures of substance use. *JAMA Psychiatry*, 71(3), 248–254.

Hasin, D. (2003). Classification of alcohol use disorders. *Alcohol Research and Health*, 27(1), 5–17.

Hasin, D. S., Endicott, J., & Keller, M. B. (1991). Alcohol problems in psychiatric patients: 5-year course. *Comprehensive Psychiatry*, 32(4), 303–316.

Hasin, D. S., Endicott, J., & Lewis, C. (1985). Alcohol and drug abuse in patients with affective syndromes. *Comprehensive Psychiatry*, 26(3), 283–295.

Hasin, D. S., Grant, B. F., & Endicott, J. (1988). Lifetime psychiatric comorbidity in hospitalized alcoholics: Subject and familial correlates. *International Journal of the Addictions*, 23(8), 827–850.

Havassy, B. E., & Arns, P. G. (1998). Relationship of cocaine and other substance dependence to well-being of high-risk psychiatric patients. *Psychiatric Services*, 49(7), 935–940.

Havassy, B. E., Shopshire, M. S., & Quigley, L. A. (2000). Effects of substance dependence on outcomes of patients in a randomized trial of two case management models. *Psychiatric Services*, 51(5), 639–644.

Hays, P., & Aidroos, N. (1986). Alcoholism followed by schizophrenia. *Acta Psychiatrica Scandinavica*, 74(2), 187–189.

Haywood, T. W., Kravitz, H. M., Grossman, L. S., Cavanaugh, J. L., Jr. Davis, J. M., & Lewis, D. A. (1995). Predicting the "revolving door" phenomenon among patients with schizophrenic, schizoaffective, and affective disorders. *American Journal of Psychiatry*, 152, 856–861.

Heffner, J. L., Strawn, J. R., DelBello, M. P., Strakowski, S. M., & Anthenelli, R. M. (2011). The co-occurrence of cigarette smoking and bipolar disorder: Phenomenology and treatment considerations. *Bipolar Disorder*, 13(5–6), 439–453.

Heinrichs, R. W., & Zakzanis, K. K. (1998). Neurocognitive deficit in schizophrenia: A quantitative review of the evidence. *Neuropsychology*, 12, 426–445.

Helle, S., Ringen, P. A., Melle, I., Larsen, T., Gjestad, R., Johnsen, E. . . . Loberg, E. (2016). Cannabis use is associated with 3 years earlier onset of schizophrenia spectrum disorder in a naturalistic, multi-site sample (N = 1119). *Schizophrenia Research*, 170, 217–221.

Helzer, J. E., & Pryzbeck, T. R. (1988). The co-occurrence of alcoholism with other psychiatric disorders in the general population and its impact on treatment. *Journal of Studies on Alcohol*, 49(3), 219–224.

Herz, L. R., Volicer, L., D'Angelo, N., & Gadish, D. (1990). Additional psychiatric illness by Diagnostic Interview Schedule in male alcoholics. *Comprehensive Psychiatry*, 30(1), 72–79.

Hesselbrock, M. N., Meyer, R. E., & Keener, J. J. (1985). Psychopathology in hospitalized alcoholics. *Archives of General Psychiatry*, 42, 1050–1055.

Hesselbrock, V. M. (1986). Family history of psychopathology in alcoholics: A review and issues. In R. E. Meyer (Ed.), *Psychopathology and addictive disorders* (pp. 41–56). New York, NY: Guilford Press.

Hesselbrock, V. M., Hesselbrock, M. N., & Workman-Daniels, K. L. (1986). Effect of major depression and antisocial personality on alcoholism: Course and motivational patterns. *Journal of Studies on Alcohol*, 47(3), 207–212.

Himle, J. A., & Hill, E. M. (1991). Alcohol abuse and anxiety disorders: Evidence from the Epidemiologic Catchment Area Survey. *Journal of Anxiety Disorders*, 5, 237–245.

Hirschfeld, R. M. A., Hasin, D., Keller, M. D., Endicott, J., & Wunder, J. (1990). Depression and alcoholism: Comorbidity in a longitudinal study. In J. D. Maser and C. R. Cloninger (Eds.),

Comorbidity of mood and anxiety disorders (pp. 293–304). Washington, DC: American Psychiatric Publishing.

Hoff, R. A., Beam-Goulet, J., & Rosenheck, R. A. (1997). Mental disorder as a risk factor for human immunodeficiency virus infection in a sample of veterans. *Journal of Nervous and Mental Disease, 185*(9), 556–560.

Holmes, P. V., Masini, C. V., Primuaux, S. D., Garrett, J. L., Zellner, A., Stogner, K. S., . . . Crystal, J. D. (2002). Intravenous self-administration of amphetamine is increased in a rat model of depression. *Synapse, 46*(4), 4–10.

Holzman, P. S. (1987). Recent studies of psychophysiology in schizophrenia. *Schizophrenia Bulletin, 13,* 49–75.

Horner, D. (1999). Attentional functioning in abstinent cocaine abusers. *Drug and Alcohol Dependence, 54,* 19–33.

Hughes, J. R., Hatsukami, D. K., Mitchell, J. E., & Dahlgren, L. A. (1986). Prevalence of smoking among psychiatric outpatients. *American Journal of Psychiatry, 143*(8), 993–997.

Iacono, W. G., Carlson, S. R., Malone, S. M., & McGue, M. (2002). P3 event-related potential amplitude and the risk for disinhibitory disorders in adolescent boys. *Archives of General Psychiatry, 59,* 750–757.

Jacobson, A. (1989). Physical and sexual assault histories among psychiatric outpatients. *American Journal of Psychiatry, 146*(6), 755–758.

Jeste, D. V., Gladsjo, J. A., Lindamer, L. A., & Lacro, J. P. (1996). Medical comorbidity in schizophrenia. *Schizophrenia Bulletin, 22*(3), 413–430.

Jones, D. R., Macias, C., Barreira, P. J., Fisher, W. H., Hargreaves, W. A., & Harding, C. M. (2004). Prevalence, severity, and co-occurrence of chronic physical health problems of persons with severe mental illness. *Psychiatric Services, 55*(11), 1250–1257.

Joyal, C. C., Putkonen, A., Paavola, P., & Tiihonen, J. (2004). Characteristics and circumstances of homicidal acts committed by offenders with schizophrenia. *Psychological Medicine, 34*(3), 433–442.

Karmali, M., Kelly, L., Gervin, M., Browne, S., Larkin, C., & O'Calleghan, E. (2000). The prevalence of comorbid substance misuse and its influence on suicidal ideation among inpatients with schizophrenia. *Acta Psychiatrica Scandinavica, 101*(6), 452–456.

Keane, T. M., Gerardi, R. J., Lyons, J. A., & Wolfe, J. (1988). The interrelationship of substance abuse and posttraumatic stress disorder: Epidemiological and clinical considerations. In M. Galanter (Ed.), *Recent developments in alcoholism.* New York, NY: Plenum Press.

Kelly, R. H., Danielsen, B. H., Golding, J. M., Anders, T. F., Gilbert, W. M., & Zatzick, D. F. (1999). Adequacy of prenatal care among women with psychiatric diagnoses giving birth in California in 1994 and 1995. *Psychiatric Services, 50*(12), 1584–1590.

Kemper, P., Blumenthal, D., Corrigan, J. M., Cunningham, P. J., Felt, S. M., Grossman, J. M., . . . Ginsburg, P. B. (1996). The design of the community tracking study: A longitudinal study of health system change and its effects on people. *Inquiry, 33*(2), 195–206.

Kendler, K. S. (1985). A twin study of individuals with both schizophrenia and alcoholism. *British Journal of Psychiatry, 147,* 48–53.

Kendler, K. S., Davis, C. G., & Kessler, R. C. (1997). The familial aggregation of common psychiatric and substance use disorders in the National Comorbidity Survey: A family history study. *British Journal of Psychiatry, 170,* 541–548.

Kerfoot, K. E., Petrakis, I. L., & Rosenheck, R. A. (2011). Dual diagnosis in an aging population: Prevalence of psychiatric disorders, comorbid substance abuse, and mental health service utilization in the Department of Veterans Affairs. *Journal of dual diagnosis, 7*(1–2), 4–13.

Kessler, R. C. (1997). The prevalence of psychiatric comorbidity. In S. Wetzler & W. C. Sanderson (Eds.), *Treatment strategies for patients with psychiatric comorbidity* (pp. 23–48). New York, NY: Wiley.

Kessler, R. C., Berglund, P., Demler, O., Jin, R., Koretz, D., Merikangas, K. R., . . . Wang, P. S. (2003). The epidemiology of major depressive disorder: Results from the National Comorbidity Survey Replication (NCS-R). *Journal of the American Medical Association, 289*(23), 3095–3105.

Kessler, R. C., Berglund, P., Demler, O., Jin, R., Merikangas, K. R., & Walters, E. E. (2005a). Lifetime prevalence and age-of-onset distributions of *DSM-IV* disorders in the National Comorbidity Survey Replication. *Archives of General Psychiatry, 62*, 593–602.

Kessler, R. C., Chiu, W. T., Demler, O., Merikangas, A. R., & Walters, E. E. (2005b). Prevalence, severity, and comorbidity of 12-month *DSM-IV* disorders in the National Comorbidity Survey Replication. *Archives of General Psychiatry, 62*, 617–627.

Kessler, R. C., Haro, J. M., Heeringa, S. G., Pennell, B. E., & Ustun, T. B. (2006). The World Health Organization World Mental Health Survey Initiative. *Epidemiologia e Psichiatria Sociale, 15*(3), 161–166.

Kessler, R. C., McGonagle, K. A., Zhao, S., Nelson, C. B., Hughes, M., Eshleman, S., . . . Kendler, K. S. (1994). Lifetime and 12-month prevalence of *DSM-II-R* psychiatric disorders in the United States. *Archives of General Psychiatry, 51*, 8–19.

Kessler, R. C., & Merikangas, K. R. (2004). The National Comorbidity Survey Replication (NCS-R): Background and aims. *International Journal of Methods in Psychiatric Research, 13*(2), 60–68.

Kessler, R. C., Nelson, C. B., McGonagle, K. A., Liu, J., Swartz, M., & Blazer, D. G. (1996). Comorbidity of *DSM-III-R* major depressive disorder in the general population: Results from the US National Comorbidity Survey. *British Journal of Psychiatry, 168*(30), 17–30.

Keuthen, N. J., Niaura, R. S., Borrelli, B., Goldstein, M., DePue, J., Murphy, C., . . . Abrams, D. (2000). Comorbidity, smoking behavior, and treatment outcome. *Psychotherapy and Psychosomatics, 69*, 244–250.

Khantzian, E. J., & Treece, C. (1985). *DSM-III* psychiatric diagnoses of narcotic addicts. *Archives of General Psychiatry, 42*, 1067–1071.

Klorman, R. (1991). Cognitive event-related potentials and attention deficit disorder. *Journal of Learning Disability, 64*, 179–192.

Kokkevi, A., Stephanis, N., Anastasopoulou, E., & Kostogianni, C. (1998). Personality disorders in drug abusers: Prevalence and their association with Axis I disorders as predictors of treatment retention. *Addictive Behaviors, 23*(6), 841–853.

Kozaric-Kovacic, D., Folnegovic-Smalc, V., Folnegovic, Z., & Marusic, A. (1995). Influence of alcoholism on the prognosis of schizophrenia patients. *Journal of Studies on Alcohol, 56*, 622–627.

Kraan, T., Velthourst, E., Koenders, L., Zwaart, K., Ising, H. K., van den Berg, D., . . . van der Gaag, M. (2015). Cannabis use and transition to psychosis in individuals at ultra-high risk: review and meta-analysis. *Psychological Medicine, 46*, 673–681.

Krakow, D. S., Galanter, M., Dermatis, H., & Westreich, L. M. (1998). HIV risk factors in dually diagnosed patients. *American Journal of Addictions, 7*(1), 74–80.

Kranzler, H. R., DelBoca, F. K., & Rounsaville, B. J. (1996). Comorbid psychiatric diagnosis predicts three-year outcomes in alcoholics: A posttreatment natural history study. *Journal of Studies on Alcohol, 57*, 619–626.

Krueger, R. F. (1999). The structure of common mental disorders. *Archives of General Psychiatry, 56*, 921–926.

Krug, I., Treasure, J., Anderluh, M., Bellodi, L., Cellini, E., diBernardo, . . . Fernández-Aranda, F. (2008). Present and lifetime comorbidity of tobacco, alcohol and drug use in eating disorders: A European multicenter study. *Drug and Alcohol Dependence, 97*(1–2), 169–179.

Ksir, C. & Hart, C. L. (2016). Cannabis and psychosis: a critical overview of the relationship. *Current Psychiatry Reports, 18*, 1–11.

Kushner, M. G., Abrams, K., & Borchardt, C. (2000). The relationship between anxiety disorders and alcohol use disorders: A review of major perspectives and findings. *Clinical Psychology Review, 20*(2), 149–171.

Kushner, M. G., Sher, K. J., & Beitman, B. D. (1990). The relation between alcohol problems and the anxiety disorders. *American Journal of Psychiatry, 147*(6), 685–695.

Lambert, M. T., Griffith, J. M., & Hendrickse, W. (1996). Characteristics of patients with substance abuse diagnoses on a general psychiatry unit in a VA medical center. *Psychiatric Services, 47*(10), 1104–1107.

Lambert, M. T., LePage, J. P., & Schmitt, A. L. (2003). Five-year outcomes following psychiatric consultation to a tertiary care emergency room. *American Journal of Psychiatry, 160*(7), 1350–1353.

Landmark, J., Cernovsky, Z. Z., & Merskey, H. (1987). Correlates of suicide attempts and ideation in schizophrenia. *British Journal of Psychiatry, 151*, 18–20.

Large, M., Sharma, S., Compton, M. T., Slade, T., & Nielssen, O. (2011). Cannabis use and earlier onset of psychosis: a systematic meta-analysis. *Archives of General Psychiatry, 68*, 555–561.

Lasser, K., Boyd, J. W., Woolhandler, S., Himmelstein, D. U., McCormick, D., & Bor, D. H. (2000). Smoking and mental illness: A population-based study. *Journal of the American Medical Association, 284*(2), 2606–2610.

Lawrence, D., Mitrou, F., & Zubrick, S. R. (2009). Smoking and mental illness: Results from population surveys in Australia and the United States. *BMC Public Health, 9*, 285.

Leal, D., Galanter, M., Dermatis, H., & Westreich, L. (1999). Correlates of protracted homelessness in a sample of dually diagnosed psychiatric inpatients. *Journal of Substance Abuse Treatment, 16*(2), 143–147.

Lehman, A. F., Myers, C. P., Dixon, L. B., & Johnson, J. L. (1994). Defining subgroups of dual diagnosis patients for service planning. *Hospital and Community Psychiatry, 45*(6), 556–561.

Lehman, A. F., Myers, C. P., Thompson, J. W., & Corty, E. (1993). Implications of mental and substance use disorders: A comparison of single and dual diagnosis patients. *Journal of Nervous and Mental Disease, 181*(6), 365–370.

Leventhal, A. M., Ameringer, K. J., Osborn, E., Zvolensky, M. J., & Langdon, K. J. (2013). Anxiety and depressive symptoms and affective patterns of tobacco withdrawal. *Drug and Alcohol Dependence 133*(2), 324–329.

Lin, W., Zhang, J., Leung, G. Y., & Clark, R. E. (2011). Chronic physical conditions in older adults with mental illness and/or substance use disorders. *Journal Of The American Geriatrics Society, 59*(10), 1913–1921.

Linszen, D. H., Dingemans, P. M., & Lenior, M. E. (1994). Cannabis abuse and the course of recent-onset schizophrenic disorders. *Archives of General Psychiatry, 51*, 273–279.

Lipari, R. N., & Hedden, S. L. (2014). *Serious mental health challenges among older adolescents and young adults.* The CBHSQ Report: May 6, 2014. Center for Behavioral Health Statistics and Quality. Substance Abuse and Mental Health Services Administration, Rockville, MD.

Liskow, B., Powell, B. J., Nickel, E. J., & Penick, E. (1991). Antisocial alcoholics: Are there clinically significant diagnostic subtypes? *Journal of Studies on Alcohol, 52*(1), 62–69.

Lorains, F. K., Cowlishaw, S., & Thomas, S. A. (2011). Prevalence of comorbid disorders in problem and pathological gambling: Systematic review and meta-analysis of population surveys. *Addiction, 106*(3), 490–498.

Lubman, D. I., Allen, N. B., Rigers, N., Cementon, E., & Bonomo, T. (2007). The impact of co-occurring mood and anxiety disorder among substance-abusing youth. *Journal of Affective Disorders, 103*, 105–112.

Lynskey, M. T. (1998). The comorbidity of alcohol dependence and affective disorders: Treatment implications. *Drug and Alcohol Dependence, 52*, 201–209.

Mackenzie, C. S., El-Gabalawy, R., Chou, K. L., & Sareen, J. (2013). Prevalence and predictors and persistent versus remitting mood, anxiety, and substance disorders in a national sample of older adults. *American Journal of Geriatric Psychiatry, 22*(9), 854–865.

Mackowick, K. M., Lynch, M. J., Weinberger, A. H., & George, T. P. (2012). Treatment of tobacco dependence in people with mental health and addictive disorders. *Current Psychiatry Reports, 14,* 478–485.

Marconi, A., Di Forti, M., Lewis, C., Murray, R. M., & Vassos, E. (2016). Meta-analysis of the association between the level of cannabis use and risk of psychosis. *Schizophrenia Bulletin, 42,* 1262–1269.

Margolese, H. C., Malchy, L., Negrete, J. C., Tempier, R., & Gill, K. (2004). Drug and alcohol use among patients with schizophrenia and related psychosis: Levels and consequences. *Schizophrenia Research, 67*(2–3), 157–166.

Marzuk, P. M. (1996). Violence, crime, and mental illness: How strong a link? *Archives of General Psychiatry, 53,* 481–486.

Maynard, C., & Cox, G. B. (1988). Psychiatric hospitalization of persons with dual diagnoses: estimates from two national surveys. *Psychiatric Services, 49*(12), 1615–1617.

McCleery, A., Addington, J., & Addington, D. (2006). Substance misuse and cognitive functioning in early psychosis: A 2-year follow-up. *Schizophrenia Research, 88,* 187–191.

McCloud, A., Barnaby, B., Omu, N., Drummond, C., & Aboud, A. (2004). Relationship between alcohol use disorders and suicidality in a psychiatric population: In-patient prevalence study. *British Journal of Psychiatry, 184,* 439–445.

McCrone, P., Menezes, P. R., Johnson, S., Scott, H., Thornicroft, G., Marshall, J., . . . Kuipers, E. (2000). Service use and costs of people with dual diagnosis in South London. *Acta Psychiatrica Scandinavica, 101*(6), 464–472.

McElroy, S. L., Altshuler, L. L., Suppes, T., Keck, P. E., Jr. Frye, M. A., Denicoff, K. D., . . . Post, R. M. (2001). Axis I psychiatric comorbidity and its relationship to historical illness variables in 288 patients with bipolar disorder. *American Journal of Psychiatry, 158*(3), 420–426.

McFall, M., Fontana, A., Raskind, M., & Rosenheck, R. (1999). Analysis of violent behavior in Vietnam combat veteran psychiatric inpatients with posttraumatic stress disorder. *Journal of Traumatic Stress, 12*(3), 501–517.

McKinnon, K., Cournos, F., Sugden, R., Guido, J. R., & Herman, R. (1996). The relative contributions of psychiatric symptoms and AIDS knowledge to HIV risk behaviors among people with severe mental illness. *Journal of Clinical Psychiatry, 57*(11), 506–513.

McLellan, A. T., Druley, K. A., & Carson, J. E. (1978). Evaluation of substance abuse in a psychiatric hospital. *Journal of Clinical Psychiatry, 39*(5), 425–430.

McLellan, A. T., Luborsky, L., Woody, G. E., O'Brien, C. P., & Cruley, K. A. (1983). Predicting response to alcohol and drug abuse treatments: Role of psychiatric severity. *Archives of General Psychiatry, 40,* 620–625.

Menezes, P. R., Johnson, S., Thornicroft, G., Marshall, J., Prosser, D., Bebbington, P., & Kuipers, E. (1996). Drug and alcohol problems among individuals with severe mental illnesses in South London. *British Journal of Psychiatry, 168,* 612–619.

Merikangas K. R., Jin, R., He, J., Kessler, R. C., Lee, S., Sampson, N. A., . . . Zarkov, A. (2011). Prevalence and correlates of bipolar spectrum disorder in the World Mental Health Survey Initiative. *Archives of General Psychiatry, 68*(3), 241–251.

Merikangas, K. R., & Gelernter, C. S. (1990). Comorbidity for alcoholism and depression. *Psychiatric Clinics of North America, 13*(4), 613–633.

Merikangas, K. R., Leckman, J. F., Prusoff, B. A., Pauls, D. L., & Weissman, M. M. (1985). Familial transmission of depression and alcoholism. *Archives of General Psychiatry, 42,* 367–372.

Mezzich, J. E., Ahn, C. W., Fabrega, H., & Pilkonis, P. (1990). Patterns of psychiatric comorbidity in a large population presenting for care. In J. D. Maser & C. R. Cloninger (Eds.), *Comorbidity of mood and anxiety disorders* (pp. 189–204). Washington, DC: American Psychiatric Publishing.

Miller, N. S., Klamen, D., Hoffmann, N. G., & Flaherty, J. A. (1996). Prevalence of depression and alcohol and other drug dependence in addictions treatment populations. *Journal of Psychoactive Drugs, 28*, 111–124.

Mirin, S. M., Weiss, R. D., Griffin, M. L., & Michael, J. L. (1991). Psychopathology in drug abusers and their families. *Comprehensive Psychiatry, 32*(1), 36–51.

Mirin, S. M., Weiss, R. D., & Michael, J. L. (1988). Psychopathology in substance abusers: Diagnosis and treatment. *American Journal of Drug and Alcohol Abuse, 14*, 139–157.

Morgenstern, J., Langenbucher, J., Labouvie, E., & Miller, K. J. (1997). The comorbidity of alcoholism and personality disorders in a clinical population: Prevalence rates and relation to alcohol typology variables. *Journal of Abnormal Psychology, 106*(1), 74–84.

Moylan, S., Jacka, F. N., Pasco, J. A., & Berk, M. (2012). Cigarette smoking, nicotine dependence, and anxiety disorder: A systematic review of population-based, epidemiological studies. *BMC Medicine, 10*(123).

Mueller, T. I., Lavori, P. W., Keller, M. B., Swartz, A., Warshaw, M., Hasin, D., . . . Akiskal, H. (1994). Prognostic effect of the variable course of alcoholism on the 10-year course of depression. *American Journal of Psychiatry, 151*(5), 701–706.

Mueser, K. T., Bellack, A. S., & Blanchard, J. J. (1992a). Comorbidity of schizophrenia and substance abuse: Implications for treatment. *Journal of Consulting and Clinical Psychology, 60*(6), 845–856.

Mueser, K. T., Drake, R. E., & Wallach, M. A. (1998). Dual diagnosis: A review of etiological theories. *Addictive Behaviors, 23*(6), 717–734.

Mueser, K. T., Rosenberg, S. D., Drake, R. E., Miles, K. M., Wolford, G., Vidaver, R., & Carrieri, K. (1999). Conduct disorder, antisocial personality disorder, and substance use disorders in schizophrenia and major affective disorders. *Journal of Studies on Alcohol, 60*(2), 278–284.

Mueser, K. T., Yarnold, P. R., & Bellack, A. S. (1992b). Diagnostic and demographic correlates of substance abuse in schizophrenia and major affective disorder. *Acta Psychiatrica Scandinavica, 85*, 48–55.

Mueser, K. T., Yarnold, P. R., Levinson, D. F., Singh, H., Bellack, A. S., Kee, K., . . . Yadalam, K. G. (1990). Prevalence of substance abuse in schizophrenia: Demographic and clinical correlates. *Schizophrenia Bulletin, 16*(1), 31–56.

Muir-Cochrane, E. (2006). Medical cormorbidty risk factors and barriers to care for people with schizophrenia. *Journal of Psychiatric and Mental Health Nursing, 13*, 447–452.

Nace, E. P. (1990). Personality disorder in the alcoholic patient. *Psychiatric Annals, 19*, 256–260.

Nace, E. P., Davis, C. W., & Gaspari, J. P. (1991). Axis II comorbidity in substance abusers. *American Journal of Psychiatry, 148*(1), 118–120.

Najavitis, L. M., Gastfriend, D. R., Barber, J. P., Reif, S., Muenz, L. R., Blaine, J., . . . Weiss, R. D. (1998). Cocaine dependence with and without posttraumatic stress disorder among subjects in the National Institute on Drug Abuse Collaborative Cocaine Treatment Study. *American Journal of Psychiatry, 155*(2), 214–219.

Najavitis, L. M., Sullivan, T. P., Schmitz, M., Weiss, R. D., & Lee, C. S. (2004). Treatment utilization by women with PTSD and substance dependence. *American Journal of Addictions, 13*(3), 215–224.

Najavitis, L. M., Weiss, R. D., & Shaw, S. R. (1997). The link between substance abuse and posttraumatic stress disorder in women: A review. *American Journal of Addiction, 6*(4), 273–283.

Negrete, J. C., & Knapp, W. P. (1986). The effects of cannabis use on the clinical condition of schizophrenics. *National Institute on Drug Abuse Research Monograph, 67*, 321–327.

Newman, D. L., Moffitt, T. E., Caspi, A., & Silva, P. (1998). Comorbid mental disorders: Implications for treatment and sample selection. *Journal of Abnormal Psychology, 107*(2), 305–311.

Nock, M. K., Hwang, I., Sampson, N., Kessler, R. C., Angermeyer, M., Beautrais, A., . . . Williams, D. R. (2009). Cross-national analysis of the associations among mental disorders and suicidal behavior: Findings from the WHO World Mental Health Surveys. *PLoS Medicine* (www .plosmedicine.org), *6*(8), 1–17.

Nolan, W. A., Luckenbaugh, D. A., Altshuler, L. L., Suppes, T., McElroy, S. L., Frye, M. A., . . . Post, R. M. (2004). Correlates to 1-year prospective outcome in bipolar disorder: Results from the Stanley Foundation Bipolar Network. *American Journal of Psychiatry, 161*(8), 1447–1454.

O'Connell, R. A., Mayo, J. A., Flatow, L., Cuthbertson, B., & O'Brien, B. E. (1991). Outcome of bipolar disorder on long-term treatment with lithium. *British Journal of Psychiatry, 159*, 123–129.

Olincy, A., Harris, J. G., Johnson, L. L., Pender, V., Kongs, S., Allensworth, D., . . . Freedman, R. (2006). Proof-of-concept trial of an alpha7 nicotinic agonist in schizophrenia. *Archives of General Psychiatry, 63*(6), 630–638.

Olincy, A., Ross, R. G., Young, D. A., Roath, M., & Freedman, R. (1998). Improvement in smooth pursuit eye movements after cigarette smoking in schizophrenic patients. *Neuropsychopharmacology, 18*(3), 175–185.

Olincy, A., Young, D. A., & Freedman, R. (1997). Increased levels of the nicotine metabolite cotinine in schizophrenic smokers compared to other smokers. *Biological Psychiatry, 42*, 1–5.

Oquendo, M. A., Currier, D., Liu, S. M., Hasin, D. S., Grant, B. F., & Blanco, C. (2010). Increased risk for suicidal behavior in comorbid bipolar disorder and alcohol use disorders: Results from the National Epidemiologic Survey on Alcohol and Related Conditions. *Journal of Clinical Psychiatry, 71*(7), 902–909.

Ouimette, P. C., Ahrens, C., Moos, R. H., & Finney, J. W. (1998). During treatment changes in substance abuse patients with posttraumatic stress disorder: The influence of specific interventions and program environments. *Journal of Substance Abuse Treatment, 15*(6), 555–564.

Ouimette, P. C., Brown, P. J., & Najavitis, L. M. (1998). Course and treatment of patients with both substance use and posttraumatic stress disorders. *Addictive Behaviors, 23*(6), 785–795.

Ouimette, P. C., Gima, K., Moos, R. H., & Finney, J. W. (1999). A comparative evaluation of substance abuse treatment IV: The effect of comorbid psychiatric diagnoses on amount of treatment, continuing care, and 1-year outcomes. *Alcoholism: Clinical and Experimental Research, 23*(3), 552–557.

Ouimette, P., Goodwin, E., & Brown, P. J. (2007). Health and well being of substance use disorder patients with and without posttraumatic stress disorder. *Addictive Behaviors, 31*(8), 1415–1423.

Ouimette, P. C., Wolfe, J., & Chrestman, K. R. (1996). Characteristics of posttraumatic stress disorder-alcohol abuse comorbidity in women. *Journal of Substance Abuse, 8*(3), 335–346.

Owen, R. R., Fischer, E. P., Booth, B. M., & Cuffel, B. J. (1996). Medication noncompliance and substance abuse among persons with schizophrenia. *Psychiatric Services, 47*(8), 853–858.

Pages, K. P., Russo, J. E., Roy-Byrne, P. P., Ries, R. K., & Cowley, D. S. (1997). Determinants of suicidal ideation: The role of substance use disorders. *Journal of Clinical Psychiatry, 58*(11), 510–515.

Pages, K. P., Russo, J. E., Wingerson, D. K., Ries, R. K., Roy-Byrne, P. P., & Cowley, D. S. (1998). Predictors and outcome of discharge against medical advice from the psychiatric units of a general hospital. *Psychiatric Services, 49*(9), 1187–1192.

Palacios, S., Urmann, C. F., Newel, R., & Hamilton, N. (1999). Developing a sociological framework for dually diagnosed women. *Journal of Substance Abuse Treatment, 17*(1–2), 91–102.

Partonen, T., Sihvo, S., & Lonnqvist, J. K. (1996). Patients excluded from an antidepressant efficacy trial. *Journal of Clinical Psychiatry, 57*(12), 572–575.

Patel, V., Flisher, A. J., Hetrick, S., & McGorry, P. (2007). Mental health of young people: a global public-health Challenge. *Lancet, 369*, 1302–1313.

Peer, J., Bennett, M. E., & Bellack, A. S. (2009). Neurocognitive characteristics of individuals with schizophrenia and cocaine dependence: Comparison of currently dependent and remitted groups. *Journal of Nervous and Mental Disease, 197*, 631–634.

Penick, E. C., Powell, B. J., Othmer, E., Bingham, S. F., Rice, A. S., & Liese, B. S. (1984). Subtyping alcoholics by coexisting psychiatric syndromes: Course, family history, outcome. In D. W. Goodwin, K. T. VanDusen, & S. A. Mednick (Eds.), *Longitudinal research in alcoholism* (pp. 167–196). Boston, MA: Kluwer-Nijhoff.

Petry, N. (2006). Should the scope of addictive behaviors be broadened to include pathological gambling? *Addiction, 101*(Suppl 1), 152–160.

Pietrzak, R. H., Morasco, B. J., Blanco, C., Grant, B. F., & Petry, N. M. (2006). Gambling level and psychiatric and medical disorders in older adults: results from the National Epidemiologic Survey on Alcohol and Related Conditions. *American Journal of Geriatric Psychiatry, 15*(4), 301–313.

Pilver, C. E., Libby, D. J., Hoff, R. A., & Potenza, M. N. (2013). Problem gambling severity and the incidence of Axis I psychopathology among older adults in the general population. *Journal of Psychiatric Research, 47*, 534–541.

Polcin, D. L. (1992). Issues in the treatment of dual diagnosis clients who have chronic mental illness. *Professional Psychology: Research and Practice, 23*(1), 30–37.

Poldrugo, F. (1998). Alcohol and criminal behavior. *Alcohol and Alcoholism, 33*(1), 12–15.

Potash, J. B., Kane, H. S., Chiu, Y. F., Simpson, S. G., MacKinnon, D. F., McInnis, M. G., . . . DePaulo, J. R. Jr. (2000). Attempted suicide and alcoholism in bipolar disorder: Clinical and familial relationships. *American Journal of Psychiatry, 157*(12), 2048–2050.

Potvin, S., Joyal, C. C., Pelletier, J., & Stip, E. (2008). Contradictory cognitive capacities among substance-abusing patients with schizophrenia: A meta-analysis. *Schizophrenia Research, 100*, 242–251.

Powell, B. J., Penick, E. C., Othmer, E., Bingham, S. F., & Rice, A. S. (1982). Prevalence of additional psychiatric syndromes among male alcoholics. *Journal of Clinical Psychiatry, 43*(10), 404–407.

Pulay, A. J., Stinson, F. S., Ruan, W. J., Smith, S. M., Pickering, R. P., Dawson, D. A., & Grant, B. F. (2010). The relationship of DSM-IV personality disorders to nicotine dependence—Results from a national survey. *Drug and Alcohol Dependence, 108*(1–2), 141–145.

Quattrocki, E., Baird, A., & Yurgelun-Todd, D. (2000). Biological aspects of the link between smoking and depression. *Harvard Review of Psychiatry, 8*(3), 99–110.

Raimo, E. B., & Schuckit, M. A. (1998). Alcohol dependence and mood disorders. *Addictive Behaviors, 23*(6), 933–946.

Ramsey, S. E., Kahler, C. W., Read, J. P., Stuart, G. L., & Brown, R. A. (2004). Discriminating between substance-induced and independent depressive episodes in alcohol dependent patients. *Journal of Studies on Alcohol, 65*(5), 672–676.

Ranganathan, M., Skosnik, P. D., & D'Souza, C. P. (2016). Marijuana and madness: associations between cannibinoids and psychosis. *Biological Psychiatry, 79* 511–513.

Regier, D. A., Farmer, M. E., Rae, D. S., Locke, B. Z., Keither, S. J., Judd, L. L., & Goodwin, F. K. (1990). Comorbidity of mental disorders with alcohol and other drug abuse. *Journal of the American Medical Association, 264*, 2511–2518.

Regier, D. A., Kaelber, C. T., Rae, D. S., Farmer, M. E., Knauper, B., Kessler, R. C., & Norquist, G. S. (1998). Limitations of diagnostic criteria and assessment instruments for mental disorders: Implications for research and policy. *Archives of General Psychiatry, 55*, 109–115.

Reynolds, K., Pietrzak, R. H., El-Gabalawy, R., Mackenzie, C. S., & Sareen, J. (2015). Prevalence of psychiatric disorders in U.S. older adults: findings from a nationally representative survey. *World Psychiatry, 14*: 74–81.

Ridgely, M. S., Goldman, H. H., & Willenbring, M. (1990). Barriers to the case of persons with dual diagnoses: Organizational and financing issues. *Schizophrenia Bulletin, 16*(1), 123–132.

Ridgely, M. S., Lambert, D., Goodman, A., Chichester, C. S., & Ralph, R. (1998). Interagency collaboration in services for people with co-occurring mental illness and substance use disorder. *Psychiatric Services, 49*, 236–238.

Rogers, R. D., & Robbins, T. W. (2001). Investigating the neurocognitive deficits associated with chronic drug misuse. *Current Opinion in Neurobiology, 11,* 250–257.

Root, T. L., Pinheiro, A. P., Thornton, L., Strober, M., Fernandez-Aranda, F., Brandt, H., . . . Bulik, C. M. (2010). Substance use disorders in women with anorexia nervosa. *International Journal of Eating Disorders, 43*(1), 14–21.

Rosenblum, A., Fallon, B., Magura, S., Handelsman, L., Foote, J., & Bernstein, D. (1999). The autonomy of mood disorders among cocaine-using methadone patients. *American Journal of Drug and Alcohol Abuse, 25*(1), 67–80.

Rosenthal, R. N., & Miner, C. H. (1997). Differential diagnosis of substance-induced psychosis and schizophrenia in patients with substance use disorders. *Schizophrenia Bulletin, 23*(2), 187–193.

Ross, H. E., Glaser, F. B., & Germanson, T. (1988b). The prevalence of psychiatric disorders in patients with alcohol and other drug problems. *Archives of General Psychiatry, 45,* 1023–1031.

Ross, H. E., Glaser, F. B., & Stiasny, S. (1988a). Differences in the prevalence of psychiatric disorders in patients with alcohol and drug problems. *British Journal of Addiction, 83,* 1179–1192.

Rounsaville, B. J., Anton, S. F., Carroll, K., Budde, D., Prusoff, B. A., & Gawin, F. (1991). Psychiatric diagnoses of treatment seeking cocaine abusers. *Archives of General Psychiatry, 48,* 43–51.

Rounsaville, B. J., Kosten, T. R., Weissman, M. M., & Kleber, H. D. (1986). Prognostic significance of psychopathology in treated opiate addicts. *Archives of General Psychiatry, 43,* 739–745.

Rounsaville, B. J., Weissman, M. M., Kleber, H., & Wilber, C. (1982a). Heterogeneity of psychiatric diagnosis in treated opiate addicts. *Archives of General Psychiatry, 39,* 161–166.

Rounsaville, B. J., Weissman, M. M., Wilber, C. H., Crits-Christoph, K., & Kleber, H. D. (1982b). Diagnosis and symptoms of depression in opiate addicts: Course and relationship to treatment outcome. *Archives of General Psychiatry, 39,* 151–156.

Safer, D. J. (1987). Substance abuse by young adult chronic patients. *Hospital and Community Psychiatry, 38*(5), 511–514.

Saiyad, M., & El-Mallakh, R. S. (2012). Smoking is associated with greater symptom load in bipolar disorder patients. *Annals of Clinical Psychiatry, 24*(4), 305–309.

Saladin, M. E., Brady, K. T., Dansky, B. S., & Kilpatrick, D. G. (1995). Understanding comorbidity between posttraumatic stress disorder and substance use disorders: Two preliminary investigations. *Addictive Behaviors, 20*(5), 643–655.

Salloum, I. M., Douaihy, A., Ndimbie, O. K., & Kirisci, L. (2004). Concurrent alcohol and cocaine dependence impact on physical health among psychiatric patients. *Journal of Addictive Disorders, 23*(2), 71–81.

Salloum, I. M., & Thase, M. E. (2000). Impact of substance abuse on the course and treatment of bipolar disorder. *Bipolar Disorder, 2*(3, Pt. 2), 269–280.

Sandager, N., Peterson, C. B., Allen, S., Henderson, K. E., Crow, S., & Thuras, P. (2008). Tobacco use and comorbidity in bulimia nervosa. *International Journal of Eating Disorders, 41*(8), 734–738.

Sandberg, D. A., McNiel, D. E., & Binder, R. L. (1998). Characteristics of psychiatric inpatients who stalk, threaten, or harass hospital staff after discharge. *American Journal of Psychiatry, 155*(8), 1102–1105.

Sandyk, R., & Kay, S. R. (1991). Tobacco addiction as a marker of age at onset of schizophrenia. *International Journal of Neuroscience, 57*(3–4), 259–262.

Schneier, F. R., & Siris, S. G. (1987). A review of psychoactive substance use and abuse in schizophrenia: Patterns of drug choice. *Journal of Nervous and Mental Disease, 175,* 641–650.

Schretlen, D. J., Cascella, N. G., Meyer, S. M., Kingery, L. R., Testa, S. M., Munro, C. A., . . . Pearlson, G. D. (2007). Neuropsychological functioning in bipolar disorder and schizophrenia. *Biological Psychiatry, 62,* 179–186.

Schuckit, M. A. (1983). Alcoholism and other psychiatric disorders. *Hospital and Community Psychiatry, 34*(11), 1022–1027.

Schuckit, M. A., & Monteiro, M. G. (1988). Alcoholism, anxiety, and depression. *British Journal of Addiction, 83*, 1373–1380.

Schuckit, M. A., Tipp, J. E., Bucholz, K. K., Nurnberger, J. I., Hesselbrock, V. M., Crowe, R. R., & Kramer, J. (1997). The life-time rates of three major mood disorder and four major anxiety disorders in alcoholics and controls. *Addiction, 92*(10), 1289–1304.

Scott, H., Johnson, S., Menezes, P., Thornicroft, G., Marshall, J., Bindman, J., . . . Kuipers, E. (1998). Substance misuse and risk of aggression and offending among the severely mentally ill. *British Journal of Psychiatry, 172*, 345–350.

Secades-Villa, R., Olfson, M., Okuda, M., Velasquez, N., Perez-Fuentes, S., Liu, S. S., & Blanco, C. (2013). Trends in the prevalence of tobacco use in the United States, 1991–1992 to 2004–2005. *Psychiatric Services, 64*(5), 458–465.

Sellman, J. D., & Joyce, P. R. (1996). Does depression predict relapse in the 6 months following treatment for men with alcohol dependence? *Australian New Zealand Journal of Psychiatry, 30*, 573–578.

Sher, K. J., & Trull, T. J. (1996). Methodological issues in psychopathology research. *Annual Review of Psychology, 47*, 371–400.

Sherif, M., Radhakrishan, R., D'Souza, D. C., & Ranganathan (2016). Human laboratory studies on cannabinoids and psychosis. *Biological Psychiatry, 79*, 526–538.

Singh, J., Mattoo, S. K., Sharan, P., & Basu, D. (2005). Quality of life and its correlates in patients with dual diagnosis of bipolar affective disorder and substance dependence. *Bipolar Disorder, 7*(2), 187–191.

Sokolski, K. N., Cummings, J. L., Abrams, B. I., DeMet, E. M., Katz, L. S., & Costa, J. F. (1994). Effects of substance abuse on hallucination rates and treatment responses in chronic psychiatric patients. *Journal of Clinical Psychiatry, 55*, 380–387.

Sonne, S. C., Brady, K. T., & Morton, W. A. (1994). Substance abuse and bipolar affective disorder. *Journal of Nervous and Mental Disease, 182*(6), 349–352.

Soyka, M. (2000). Substance misuse, psychiatric disorder and violent and disturbed behaviour. *British Journal of Psychiatry, 176*, 345–350.

Spindler, A., & Milos, G. (2007). Links between eating disorder symptom severity and psychiatric comorbidity. *Eating Behavior, 8*(3), 364–367.

Stafford, L., Berk, M., & Jackson, H. J. (2013). Tobacco smoking predicts depression nd poorer quality of life in heart disease. *BMC Cardiovasular Disorders, 13*(35).

Steadman, H. J., Mulvey, E. P., Monahan, J., Robbins, P. C., Appelbaum, P. S., Grisson, T., . . . Silver, E. (1998). Violence by people discharged from acute psychiatric inpatient facilities and by others in the same neighborhoods. *Archives of General Psychiatry, 55*(5), 393–401.

Steinberg, M. L., Williams, J. M., & Ziedonis, D. M. (2004). Financial implications of cigarette smoking among individuals with schizophrenia. *Tobacco Control, 13*, 206.

Stewart, S. H., Pihl, R. O., Conrod, P. J., & Dongier, M. (1998). Functional associations among trauma, posttraumatic stress disorder and substance-related disorders. *Addictive Behaviors, 23*(6), 797–812.

Strakowski, S. M., & DelBello, M. P. (2000). The co-occurrence of bipolar and substance use disorders. *Clinical Psychology Review, 20*(2), 191–206.

Strong, D. R., Cameron, A., Feuer, S., Cohn, A., Abrantes, A. M., & Brown, R. A. (2010). Single versus recurrent depression history: Differentiating risk factors among current US smokers. *Drug and Alcohol Dependence, 109*(1–3), 90–95.

Stuyt, E. B. (2004). Hepatitis C in patients with co-occurring mental disorders and substance use disorders: Is tobacco use a possible risk factor? *American Journal of Addictions, 13*(1), 46–52.

Swanson, J., Borum, R., Swartz, M., & Hiday, V. (1999). Violent behavior preceding hospitalization among persons with severe mental illness. *Law and Human Behavior, 23*(2), 185–204.

Swartz, M. S., Swanson, J. W., Hiday, V. A., Borum, R., Wagner, H. R., & Burns, B. J. (1998). Violence and severe mental illness: The effects of substance abuse and nonadherence to medication. *American Journal of Psychiatry, 155*(2), 226–231.

Swendsen, J. D., & Merikangas, K. R. (2000). The comorbidity of depression and substance use disorders. *Clinical Psychology Review, 20*(2), 173–189.

Tarrier, N., & Picken, A. (2011). Co-morbid PTSD and suicidality in individuals with schizophrenia and substance and alcohol abuse. *Social Psychiatry and Psychiatric Epidemiology, 46*(11), 1079–1086.

Thomas, S. E., Thevos, A. K., & Randall, C. L. (1999). Alcoholics with and without social phobia: A comparison of substance use and psychiatric variables. *Journal of Studies on Alcohol, 60*, 472–479.

Thomas, V. H., Melchert, T. P., & Banken, J. A. (1999). Substance dependence and personality disorders: Comorbidity and treatment outcome in an inpatient treatment population. *Journal of Studies on Alcohol, 60*(2), 271–277.

Thompson, S. C., Checkley, G. E., Hocking, J. S., Crofts, N., Mijch, A. M., & Judd, F. K. (1997). HIV risk behavior and HIV testing of psychiatric patients in Melbourne. *Australia and New Zealand Journal of Psychiatry, 31*(4), 566–576.

Tomasson, K., & Vaglum, P. (1997). The 2-year course following detoxification treatment of substance abuse: The possible influence of psychiatric comorbidity. *European Archives of Psychiatry and Clinical Neuroscience, 247*(6), 320–327.

Triffleman, E. G., Marmar, C. R., Delucchi, K. L., & Ronfeldt, H. (1995). Childhood trauma and posttraumatic stress disorder in substance abuse inpatients. *Journal of Nervous and Mental Disease, 183*(3), 172–176.

Trull, T. J., Jahng, S., Tomko, R. L., Wood, P. K., & Sher, K. J. (2010). Revised NESARC personality disorder diagnoses: Gender, prevalence, and comorbidity with substance dependence disorders. *Journal of Personality Disorders, 24*(4), 412–426.

Trull, T. J., Sher, K. J., Minks-Brown, C., Durbin, J., & Burr, R. (2000). Borderline personality disorder and substance use disorders: A review and integration. *Clinical Psychology Review, 20*(2), 235–253.

van Os J., Bak M., Hanssen M., Bijl R. V., de Graaf R., Verdoux H. (2002). Cannabis use and psychosis: A longitudinal population-based study. *American Journal of Epidemiology, 156*, 319–327.

Velligan, D. I., Weiden, P. J., Sajatovic, M., Scott, J., Carpenter, D., Ross, R., & Docherty, J. P. Expert Consensus Panel on Adherence Problems in Serious and Persistent Mental Illness. (2009). The Expert Consensus Guideline Series: Adherence problems in patients with serious and persistent mental illness. *Journal of Clinical Psychiatry, 70*(Suppl 4), 1–46.

Vengeliene, V., Vollmayr, B., Henn, F. A., & Spanagel, R. (2005). Voluntary alcohol intake in two rat lines selectively bred for learned helpless and non-helpless behavior. *Psychopharmacology, 178*, 125–132.

Verduin, M. L., Carter, R. E., Brady, K. T., Myrick, H., & Timmerman, M. A. (2005). Health service use among persons with comorbid bipolar and substance use disorders. *Psychiatric Services, 56*(4), 475–480.

Vieta, E., Colom, F., Martinez-Aran, A., Benabarre, A., Reinares, M., & Gasto, C. (2000). Bipolar II disorder and comorbidity. *Comprehensive Psychiatry, 41*(5), 339–343.

Watkins, K. E., Burnam, A., Kung, F. Y., & Paddock, S. (2001). A national survey of care for persons with co-occurring mental and substance use disorders. *Psychiatric Services, 52*(8), 1062–1068.

Watkins, K. E., Hunter, S. B., Wenzel, S. L., Tu, W., Paddock, S. M., Griffin, A., & Ebener, P. (2004). Prevalence and characteristics of clients with co-occurring disorders in outpatient substance abuse treatment. *American Journal of Drug and Alcohol Abuse, 30*(4), 749–764.

Weinberger, A. H., Desai, R. A., & McKee, S. A. (2010). Nicotine withdrawal in U.S. smokers with current mood, anxiety, alcohol use, and substance use disorders. *Drug and Alcohol Dependence*, *108*, 7–12.

Weiss, R. D., Ostacher, M. J., Otto, M. W., Calabrese, J. R. Fossey, M., Wisiewski, S. R., . . . STEP-BD Investigators. (2005). Does recovery from substance use disorder matter in patients with bipolar disorder? *Journal of Clinical Psychiatry*, *66*(6), 730–750.

Weissman, M. M., & Myers, J. K. (1980). Clinical depression in alcoholism. *American Journal of Psychiatry*, *137*, 372–373.

Widiger, T. A., & Shea, T. (1991). Differentiation of Axis I and Axis II disorders. *Journal of Abnormal Psychology*, *100*(3), 399–406.

Wildes, J. E., Marcus, M. D., & Fagiolini, A. (2008). Prevalence and correlates of eating disorder co-morbidity in patients with bipolar disorder. *Psychiatry Research*, *161*(1), 51–58.

Williams, J. M., Steinberg, M. L., Griffiths, K. G., & Cooperman, N. (2013). Smokers with behavioral health comorbidity should be designated a tobacco use disparity group. *American Journal of Public Health*, *103*(9), 1549–1555.

Wing, V. C., Wass, C. E., Soh, D. W., & George, T. P. (2012). A review of neurobiological vulnerability factors and treatment implications for comorbid tobacco dependence in schizophrenia. *Annals of the New York Academy of Sciences*, *1248*, 89–106.

Winokur, G., Turvey, C., Akiskal, H., Coryell, W., Solomon, D., Leon, A., . . . Keller, M. (1998). Alcoholism and drug abuse in three groups—bipolar I, unipolars, and their acquaintances. *Journal of Affective Disorders*, *50*(2–3), 81–89.

Wolf, A. W., Schubert, D. S. P., Patterson, M. B., Marion, B., & Grande, T. P. (1988). Associations among major psychiatric disorders. *Journal of Consulting and Clinical Psychology*, *56*, 292–294.

Wolff, N., Frueh, B. C., Shi, J., Gerardi, D., Fabrikant, N., & Schumann, B. E. (2011). Trauma exposure and mental health characteristics of incarcerated females self-referred to specialty PTSD treatment. *Psychiatric Services*, *62*, 954–958.

Wu, L., Kouzis, A. C., & Leaf, P. J. (1999). Influence of comorbid alcohol and psychiatric disorders on utilization of mental health services in the National Comorbidity Survey. *American Journal of Psychiatry*, *156*, 1230–1236.

Ziedonis, D. M., & George, T. P. (1997). Schizophrenia and nicotine use: Report of a pilot smoking cessation program and review of neurobiological and clinical issues. *Schizophrenia Bulletin*, *23*, 247–254.

Ziedonis, D. M., Kosten, T. R., Glazer, W. M., & Frances, R. J. (1994). Nicotine dependence and schizophrenia. *Hospital and Community Psychiatry*, *45*, 204–206.

CHAPTER 4

Structured and Semistructured Interviews for Differential Diagnosis: Fundamental Issues, Applications, and Features

VICIE HURST and DEBORAH C. BEIDEL

STRUCTURED AND SEMISTRUCTURED interviews were developed to address the difficulties that clinicians and researchers historically have had in making accurate diagnoses of mental disorders with traditional unstructured clinical interviews. A major contributing factor to diagnostic imprecision was the lack of uniformity or standardization of questions asked of respondents in evaluating the nature and extent of their psychiatric symptoms and arriving at a formal diagnosis. Structured and semistructured interviews solve this problem by their very nature, leading to vastly improved diagnostic clarity and precision. This chapter provides a basic introduction to the structured and semistructured interviews used to diagnose psychopathology among adults. We begin by discussing the basic types of structured and semistructured interviews, and this is followed by an exploration of their major features, advantages, and drawbacks. We conclude with a discussion of the most popular multidisorder structured and semistructured interviews that are used to diagnose clinical disorders and personality disorders.

The publication of the fifth edition of *Diagnostic and Statistical Manual of Mental Disorders* (*DSM-5*; American Psychiatric Association [APA], 2013) introduced many changes, especially regarding the classification and organization of many clinical disorders. One major change was the removal of the multiaxial system, which previously denoted an important distinction between clinical disorders and personality disorders on separate diagnostic axes. Notably, no changes were made to the classification and diagnostic criteria for the personality disorders. In this chapter, we describe the changes made to some of the major structured and semistructured interviews, as these measures have been updated to reflect the changes in *DSM-5* (APA, 2013).

BASIC ISSUES REGARDING STRUCTURED AND SEMISTRUCTURED INTERVIEWS

The most common method used by mental health professionals to evaluate and diagnose their clients is the direct clinical interview (Segal & Hersen, 2010). Such interviews, however, can vary tremendously, especially with regard to the amount of *structure* that is imposed. Indeed, there are some important differences between less structured interviews and more structured ones. Unstructured clinical interviews are dependent on the clinician's unique background, knowledge base, theoretical model, and interpersonal style, and thus are highly flexible. Within this unstructured approach, clinicians are entirely responsible for asking whatever questions they decide are necessary to reach a diagnostic conclusion. In fact, any type of question or topic (relevant or not) can be pursued in any way that fits the mood, preferences, training, specific interests, or philosophy of the clinician. One can easily imagine the resulting variability across interviews from one clinician to another. On the other hand, structured interviews conform to a standardized list of questions (including follow-up questions), a uniform sequence of questioning, and systematized ratings of the client's responses. These questions are designed to measure the specific criteria for many mental disorders as presented in the *DSM*. These essential elements of structured interviews serve several important purposes, most notably that their use:

- increases coverage of many mental disorders that otherwise might be overlooked;
- enhances the diagnostician's ability to accurately determine whether particular symptoms are present or absent;
- reduces variability among interviewers, which improves reliability.

These features of structured interviews add much in terms of developing clinical psychology into a true science. For example, structured interviews are subject to evaluation and statistical analysis, and they can be modified and improved, based on the published literature regarding their psychometric properties.

Not all structured interviews are the same. In fact, the term *structured interview* is broad, and the actual extent of structure provided by an interview varies considerably. Structured interviews can be divided into one of two types: *fully structured* or *semistructured*. In a fully structured interview, questions are asked of the respondent verbatim, the wording of probes used to follow up on initial questions is specified, and interviewers are trained not to deviate from this rigid format. In a semistructured interview, although initial questions regarding each symptom are specified and are typically asked verbatim, the interviewer has substantial latitude to follow up on responses. The interviewer can modify or augment the standard inquiries with individualized and contextualized probes to more accurately rate specific symptoms. The extent of structure provided in an interview clearly impacts the amount of clinical experience and judgment that are required to administer the interview appropriately: semistructured interviews require clinically experienced examiners to administer the interview and to make diagnoses, whereas fully structured interviews can be administered by nonclinicians who receive training on the specific instrument. This latter difference makes fully structured interviews popular and economical, especially in large-scale research studies in which accurate diagnoses are essential.

Structured and semistructured interviews assist with the differential diagnosis of all major clinical disorders and personality disorders. Interviews used for psychiatric diagnosis are typically aligned with the *DSM* system and, therefore, assess the formal diagnostic criteria specified in the manual. However, structured interviews exist beyond those designed for *DSM* differential diagnosis. Other structured interviews are narrower in focus; for example, to assess a specific problem or form of psychopathology in great depth (e.g., eating disorders, substance abuse, borderline personality disorder features). An excellent resource for information on a host of specialized interviews is provided by Rogers (2001). Our focus now turns to a discussion of some common functions of structured and semistructured interviews.

APPLICATIONS OF STRUCTURED AND SEMISTRUCTURED INTERVIEWS

Whereas structured and semistructured interviews are used in many different venues and for many different purposes, their application falls into three broad areas: research, clinical practice, and clinical training.

Research   The research domain is the most common application, whereby structured or semistructured interviews are used to formally diagnose participants for inclusion into a study so that etiology, comorbidity, and treatment approaches (among other topics) can be explored for a diagnosis or group of diagnoses. Sound empirical research on mental disorders certainly requires that individuals assigned a diagnosis truly meet full criteria for that diagnosis. Another research application for structured interviews is to provide a standardized method for assessing change in one's clinical status over time. As noted by Rogers (2003), these types of longitudinal comparison are essential for establishing outcome criteria, which is vital to diagnostic validity.

Clinical Practice   In clinical settings, administration of a structured or semistructured interview may be used as part of a comprehensive and standardized intake evaluation. Routine and complete administration of a structured interview is increasingly common in psychology training clinics, but doing so requires considerable training for clinicians and time for full administration. A variation on this theme is that sections of a structured interview may be administered subsequent to a traditional unstructured interview to clarify and confirm the diagnostic impressions. Widiger and Samuel (2005) provide another thoughtful alternative, especially regarding the assessment of personality disorders in clinical practice. They recommend the strategy of administering an objective self-report inventory, which is followed by a semistructured interview that focuses on the personality disorders that received elevated scores from the testing. This strategy is responsive to time constraints in clinical practice but also allows for collection of standardized, systematic, and objective data from the structured interview. Finally, we wish to emphasize that in clinical settings, structured interviews should not take the place of traditional clinical interviews. Both can be performed, although at various times and for different purposes. The combination of the two approaches, integrated flexibly to meet the needs of individual clinicians and their clients, reflects the best of the scientist–practitioner model, in which the science and art of assessment are both valued and valuable (Rogers, 2003).

Clinical Training   Use of structured or semistructured interviews for training mental health professionals is an increasingly popular and ideal application, because interviewers can learn (through repeated administrations) specific questions and follow-up probes used to elicit information and evaluate specific diagnostic criteria provided by the *DSM*. Modeling the questions, sequence, and flow from a structured interview can be an invaluable source of training for beginning clinicians.

Table 4.1

Advantages and Disadvantages of Structured and Semistructured Interviews

Advantages	Disadvantages
Increased reliability	**May hinder rapport**
Because questions are standardized, structured interviews decrease variability among interviewers, which enhances interrater reliability. Structured interviews also increase the reliability of assessment for a client's symptoms across time, as well as the reliability between client report and collateral information.	Use of structured interviews may damage rapport because they are problem-centered, not person-centered, and poorly trained interviewers may neglect to use their basic clinical skills during the assessment.
Increased validity	**Limited by the validity of the classification system itself**
Structured interviews assure that diagnostic criteria are covered systematically and completely. This is important because it serves to increase the validity of diagnosis.	Structured interviews used for diagnosis are inherently tied to diagnostic systems. Thus, they are only as valid as the systems upon which they are based. Furthermore, it is difficult to establish the validity of particular structured interviews because there is no gold standard in psychiatric diagnosis.
Utility as training tools	**The trade-off of breadth versus depth**
Structured interviews are excellent training tools for clinicians in training because they promote the learning of specific diagnostic questions and probes used by experienced clinical interviewers. In addition, nonclinicians can easily be trained to administer fully structured interviews, which can be cost-effective in both research and clinical settings.	Structured interviews are limited because they cannot cover all disorders or topic areas. When choosing a structured interview, one must evaluate carefully the trade-offs of breadth versus depth of assessment.

ADVANTAGES AND DISADVANTAGES OF STRUCTURED AND SEMISTRUCTURED INTERVIEWS

No assessment device in the mental health field is perfect, and structured and semi-structured interviews are no exception. In this section, the strengths and weaknesses of structured interviews are discussed. Our intention is to give readers an appreciation of the key issues to be considered when deciding whether to use the structured interview approach to assessment. A summary of the advantages and disadvantages is presented in Table 4.1.

Advantage: Increased Reliability Perhaps the most important advantage of structured interviews centers on their ability to increase diagnostic reliability (reliability defined in this context refers to consistency or agreement about diagnoses assigned by different raters; Coolidge & Segal, 2010a). By systemizing and standardizing the questions interviewers ask, and the way answers to those questions are recorded and interpreted, structured interviews decrease the amount of information variance in diagnostic evaluations (e.g., Rogers, 2001). That is, structured interviews decrease the chances that two different interviewers will elicit different information from the same client, which may result in different diagnoses. Thus, interrater reliability, or the likelihood that two different interviewers examining the same individual will arrive at the same diagnosis, is greatly increased.

Increased interrater reliability has broad implications in clinical and research settings. Because many psychological and psychopharmacological treatments are intimately tied to specific diagnoses, it is imperative that those diagnoses are accurate (Segal & Coolidge, 2001). Thus, if different clinicians interviewing the same client arrive at different diagnostic conclusions, it would be challenging to make a definitive decision about treatment. Similarly, accurate diagnosis is also essential for many types of clinical research, for example, studies that address causes and treatments of specific forms of psychopathology (Segal & Coolidge). Imagine a study examining different treatments for bipolar disorder. In such a study, it would be imperative to be certain that those individuals in the treatment groups have accurate diagnoses of bipolar disorder. Researchers must be able to accurately and definitively diagnose participants with the disorder being studied before researchers can even begin to examine theories of etiology or the effectiveness of treatment for that mental disorder.

In addition to increasing interrater reliability, structured interviews increase the likelihood that the diagnosis is reliable across time and across various sources of information (Rogers, 2001). In many clinical and research settings, individuals are, in fact, assessed on different occasions. Making multiple assessments could be dangerous if an interviewer evaluates a client in a different manner with different questions on different occasions. The client's presentation may be substantially altered because the way he or she is asked about those symptoms has changed, rather than the client's symptoms or diagnosis being different. Using a standardized interview for multiple assessments helps to ensure that if a client's presentation has changed, it is because his or her symptoms are actually different, not because of variance in interviews (Rogers, 2001). This type of reliability is particularly important for pre- and post-assessments for both clinical and research outcomes. Likewise, in many settings, clinicians conduct collateral interviews with significant people in the client's life to glean a broader picture of the client's symptoms, problems, and experiences. Using a structured interview for both a client and a collateral source will likely increase the chances that discrepancies between the client and collateral informant are real, rather than a consequence of different interviewing styles (Rogers, 2001).

Advantage: Increased Validity   Validity of psychiatric diagnosis refers to the meaningfulness or usefulness of the diagnosis (Coolidge & Segal, 2010b). A required prerequisite for validity is reliability. Thus, because structured interviews greatly increase the reliability of diagnosis, they also increase the likelihood that the diagnosis is valid. Structured interviews also improve the validity of diagnoses in other ways. The systematic construction of structured interviews lends a methodological validity to these types of assessment compared with unstructured approaches. Because structured interviews are designed to thoroughly and accurately assess well-defined diagnostic criteria, they are often better assessments of those criteria than are unstructured interviews (Rogers, 2001). According to Rogers, clinicians who use unstructured interviews sometimes diagnose too quickly, narrow their diagnostic options too early, and miss comorbid diagnoses. Because structured interviews essentially force clinicians to assess all specified criteria for a broad range of diagnoses, they offer a more thorough and valid assessment of many disorders than do unstructured interviews.

In our experience, it is common for beginning clinicians who are conducting an unstructured clinical interview to gather information about the presence or absence of only a few common mental disorders. Coverage of other disorders may be neglected during an unstructured interview if the interviewer is unfamiliar with the specific criteria of some disorders. Some unstructured interviews may also provide limited information about whether comorbid psychopathology exists or about the severity of the psychopathology. Because they incorporate systematic ratings, structured and semistructured interviews easily provide information that allows for the determination of the level of severity and the level of impairment associated with a diagnosis. Structured interviews provide the same information about comorbid disorders as well.

Advantage: Utility as Training Tools Structured interviews can be invaluable training tools for beginning mental health professionals as well as experienced clinicians who want to enhance their diagnostic skills. Use of structured interviews in the training context can help clinicians to develop or enhance their understanding of the flow, format, and questions inherent in a comprehensive diagnostic interview. With repeated administrations, much of a structured interview can be internalized by the clinician. In addition, use of structured interviews for training can reduce anxiety, especially among inexperienced clinicians, because the format and flow are clearly outlined for the interviewer. This type of structure can be helpful and calming for beginning clinicians, who may be initially overwhelmed by the diagnostic process and its inherent complexity.

Structured interviews can also be useful in training those who make preliminary mental health assessments, for example, intake staff at hospitals, so that clients are thoroughly and accurately evaluated in preparation for treatment planning. In the case of nonclinician interviewers, fully structured interviews are advisable, because they minimize the amount of clinical judgment needed for accurate administration. Use of these trained paraprofessionals can make large-scale research studies cost-effective.

Disadvantage: May Hinder Rapport Despite the advantages of structured interviews, their application is not without controversy. The most common criticism of structured interviews is that their use may damage rapport or the therapeutic alliance (Segal, Maxfield, & Coolidge, 2008), which is widely viewed as an essential component of effective psychotherapy. Attaining a reliable and accurate diagnosis for a client is a hollow victory if the process prevents the therapeutic alliance from forming, or, in a more dramatic example of clinical failure, the client does not return to continue treatment. The well-known joke poking fun at medicine, "the operation was a success but the patient died," might be recast in terms of structured interviews as "the diagnosis was impeccable but the client never came back for another session."

How exactly might structured interviews damage rapport? Perhaps most importantly, structured interviews may impede the connection between client and clinician because interviews are problem-centered rather than person-centered. There is a danger that interviewers become so concerned with the protocol of their interview that they fail to demonstrate the warmth, empathy, and genuine regard necessary to form a therapeutic alliance. Indeed, the standardization of the interview may play out as "routinization" (Rogers, 2003). In addition, interviewers who are overly focused on the questions that they must "get through" in an interview may, consequently, miss important behavioral cues or other information that could prove essential to the case.

Proponents of structured interviews note that the problem of rapport-building during a structured interview can be overcome with training, experience, and flexibility (Rogers, 2003). We concur, and emphasize the observation that "rapid inquiries or monotonous questioning represents clear misuses of structured interviews" (Rogers, 2003, p. 22). If interviewers use their basic clinical skills, structured interviews can and should be conducted in such a way that establishes rapport and enhances understanding of the client. To ensure that this is the case, however, interviewers must be aware of the potential negative effects of structured interviews on rapport-building and make the nurturance of the therapeutic alliance a prominent goal during an interview, even while they are focused on following the protocol. It behooves those who use structured interviews to engage their respondents in a meaningful way during the interview and to avoid a rote-like interviewing style that may alienate. On the other hand, not all clients have a negative perception of a structured interview that must be intentionally overcome. Some clients like the structured approach to assessment because it is perceived as thorough and detailed, and in these cases rapport is easily attained.

Disadvantage: Limited by the Validity of the Classification System Itself Earlier, we noted that proponents of structured interviews claim that they render more valid diagnoses in general. The assumption inherent in this argument is that the *DSM* diagnostic criteria are inherently valid, which is a debatable point. One should recognize that *DSM* diagnostic criteria were developed to *operationalize* theoretical constructs (e.g., depression, panic disorder, schizophrenia) so there is no absolute basis on which criteria were created. Furthermore, mental disorders are social constructions, which implies that they evolve over time as societies evolve.

Although successive editions of the *DSM* have been better grounded in empirical research, and the criteria for some disorders (e.g., major depression) have solid research support, other disorders (e.g., most of the personality disorders) and their criteria have not been examined as consistently or as completely, therefore leaving questions about their validity (Widiger & Trull, 2007). This point is also bolstered by the fact that the criteria for some disorders have changed significantly from one edition to another in the evolution of the *DSM* (Coolidge & Segal, 1998; Segal, 2010).

Furthermore, criteria for many disorders in the *DSM* are impacted by cultural and subcultural variations in the respondent, as well as by the age of the respondent. Indeed, the diagnostic criteria for many mental disorders do not fit the context of later life and, therefore, some criteria do not adequately capture the presentation of the disorders among many older adults (e.g., Segal, Coolidge, & Rosowsky, 2006; Segal, Qualls, & Smyer, 2011). Thus, certain criteria may be valid only for certain individuals, at a particular point in time, at a particular age. The primary method clinicians currently use to conceptualize diagnoses (the *DSM*), while improving, is far from perfect. Because the *DSM* generally does poorly in attending to these issues of age and diversity, interviews based on poorly fitting diagnostic criteria are similarly limited.

In addition to potential problems with *DSM* diagnostic criteria, another issue regarding structured interviews is that it is difficult to establish their validity firmly. The quandary is that our best means of establishing the validity of a structured interview is to compare diagnoses obtained from such interviews with diagnoses obtained by expert clinicians or by other structured interviews. This is inherently problematic because we cannot be certain that diagnoses by experts or other structured interviews are in fact valid in the first place (Segal et al., 2008).

Disadvantage: The Trade-Off of Breadth Versus Depth A final criticism of structured interviews centers on the fact that no one structured interview can be all things in all situations, covering all disorders and eventualities. For example, if a structured interview has been designed to cover an entire diagnostic system (like the *DSM*, which identifies several hundred specific mental disorders), then inquiries about each disorder must be limited to a few inclusion criteria. In this case, the fidelity of the official diagnostic criteria has been compromised for the sake of a comprehensive interview. If the fidelity of the criteria is not compromised, then the structured interview becomes unwieldy in terms of time and effort required for its full administration. Most structured interviews attempt some kind of compromise between these two points of tension.

Thus, in terms of breadth versus depth of approach, users of structured interviews are forced to make a choice regarding what is most useful in each situation. Both choices have their limitations. If clinicians or researchers decide to use an interview that provides great breadth of information, they ensure that a wide range of disorders and a great many different areas of a respondent's life are assessed. However, one may not have the depth of information needed to fully conceptualize a case. On the other hand, deciding to use an interview focused on a few specific areas will provide clinicians and researchers with a wealth of information about those specific areas, but it may result in missing information that could lead to additional diagnoses or a different case conceptualization. Thus, it is essential to understand that when choosing a particular structured or semistructured interview, there are often trade-offs regarding breadth and depth of information.

Weighing Advantages and Disadvantages

Our examination of the strengths and limitations of structured interviews highlights the importance of carefully contemplating what is needed for the clinical or research situation before choosing a structured interview. Structured interviews can be invaluable tools in both clinical and research work; however, it is essential that one does not use such tools without accounting for the problems inherent in their use. Rogers (2001) voiced the helpful perspective that it would be unwise to view the interviewing process as an either/or proposition (i.e., unstructured vs. structured interview). In certain situations, unstructured interviews may meet the objectives more efficiently than a structured interview. For example, in a crisis, flexibility on the part of the clinician is required to meet the pressing demands of this fluid and potentially volatile interaction. However, in other cases, greater assurances that the diagnostic conclusions are valid and meaningful would take priority, for example, in clinical research or in the delivery of clearly defined psychotherapeutic intervention protocols. As noted earlier, the integration of a non-standardized or clinical interview with a structured or semistructured interview may also be an excellent option for clinicians and researchers.

Finally, despite some potential limitations of structured and semistructured interviews, their use has clearly revolutionized the diagnostic process, vastly improving diagnostic reliability and validity. Such interviews have greatly improved clinical and research endeavors by providing a more standardized, scientific, and quantitative approach to the evaluation of specific symptoms and mental disorders. As such, it is likely that the use of structured and semistructured interviews will increase in the coming decades.

STRUCTURED AND SEMISTRUCTURED INTERVIEWS FOR DIFFERENTIAL DIAGNOSIS

In this section, we examine several popular structured and semistructured interviews. These interviews can be divided into those that focus on clinical disorders and those that focus on personality disorders. As noted earlier, although the *DSM-5* no longer makes a distinction between clinical disorders and personality disorders (with the replacement of the multiaxial coding system by a nonaxial coding system), the distinction is still relevant to the current crop of structured and semistructured interviews which were developed with this difference in mind. In addition, the names and content of many of the instruments for personality disorders remain unchanged, which reflects the absence of changes from *DSM-IV* to *DSM-5*. Instruments that focus on clinical disorders include the Anxiety Disorders Interview Schedule for *DSM-5*, the Diagnostic Interview Schedule for *DSM-5*, the Schedule for Affective Disorders and Schizophrenia, and the Structured Clinical Interview for *DSM-5*. Instruments that measure personality disorders include the Diagnostic Interview for *DSM* Personality Disorders, the International Personality Disorder Examination, the Structured Clinical Interview for *DSM-5* Personality Disorders, and the Structured Interview for *DSM-IV* Personality.

Where possible, we describe updates made to some of these instruments as they were revised to conform to the current *DSM-5* system. However, not all instruments have been updated to reflect *DSM-5* criteria; this lack of changes, and any instruments that are still awaiting changes, will also be noted in the descriptions of each. A general overview of each instrument is provided in Table 4.2. Each instrument assesses a variety of mental disorders and, therefore, can assist in the important task of differential diagnosis (i.e., a systematic means of discriminating among numerous possible disorders to identify specific ones for which the client meets the diagnostic threshold). Each interview also allows for an assessment of many comorbid mental disorders. The instruments presented in this chapter do not represent an exhaustive list of structured and semistructured interviews, but they are among the most common and well-validated ones. Interested readers are referred to Rogers (2001), Segal and Hersen (2010), and Summerfeldt, Kloosterman, and Antony (2010) for information on instruments not reviewed in this chapter.

Table 4.2

Comparison of Major Diagnostic Interviews

Name	Time Required	Format	Comment
Anxiety Disorders Interview Schedule for *DSM-5* (Brown & Barlow, 2014a)	45–60 minutes	Semistructured, interviewer administered	Provides in-depth assessment of anxiety disorders and other frequently comorbid conditions (e.g., mood disorders, substance abuse). Designed to be administered by trained mental health professionals with training in administration. Available in separate current and lifetime versions.
Diagnostic Interview Schedule (Robins et al., 2000)	90–150 minutes	Fully structured, computerized, closed-ended questions	Designed for epidemiological research. Includes most diagnoses in *DSM-5*. Can be administered by nonclinicians, although interviewers must receive specialized training.
Schedule for Affective Disorders and Schizophrenia (Endicott & Spitzer, 1978)	90–150 minutes	Semistructured, interviewer administered	Provides in-depth coverage on clinical disorders, namely mood and psychotic disorders. Designed for administration by trained mental health professionals, and additional training in administration is required.
Structured Clinical Interview for *DSM-5* (First, Williams, Karg, & Spitzer, 2016b)	45–90 minutes	Semistructured, interviewer administered	Covers *DSM-5* clinical disorders most commonly seen in clinical settings. Designed for use by professionals with knowledge of psychopathology, *DSM-5* diagnostic criteria, and basic interviewing skills. Research Version, Clinical Version and Clinical Trials Version available.

(continued)

Table 4.2

continued

Name	Time Required	Format	Comment
Diagnostic Interview for *DSM-IV* Personality Disorders (Zanarini, Frankenburg, Sickel, & Yong, 1996)	90 minutes	Semistructured, interviewer administered	Designed to assess the 10 standard *DSM-IV* personality disorders. Requirements for administration include, at a minimum, a bachelor's degree, at least 1 year of clinical experience with personality-disordered clients, and several training interviews.
International Personality Disorder Examination (Loranger, 1999)	15 minutes (self-administered screen), 90 minutes (interview)	Contains self-administered pencil-and-paper questionnaire and semistructured interview	Evaluates personality disorders for both the *DSM-IV* and the *International Classification of Diseases*, 10th ed. (*ICD-10*). Intended for use by experienced clinicians with specialized training in administration.
Structured Clinical Interview for *DSM-5* Personality Disorders (First, Williams, Benjamin, & Spitzer, 2016)	20 minutes (self-administered screen), 60 minutes (interview)	Contains self-report screening questionnaire and semistructured interview	Assesses the 10 standard *DSM-5* personality disorders. Designed for administration by professionals with knowledge of psychopathology, *DSM-5* diagnostic criteria, and basic interviewing skills.
Structured Interview for *DSM-IV* Personality (Pfohl, Blum, & Zimmerman, 1997)	60–90 minutes	Semistructured interview	Comprehensive interview for *DSM-IV* personality disorders. Collateral sources encouraged. Requirements for administration include an undergraduate degree in the social sciences and 6 months' experience with diagnostic interviewing in addition to specialized training.

Anxiety Disorders Interview Schedule for DSM-5   The Anxiety Disorders Interview Schedule for *DSM-5* (ADIS-5; Brown & Barlow, 2014a) is a semistructured clinician-administered interview designed to assess anxiety disorders as defined by the *DSM-5*. It provides differential diagnosis among anxiety disorders and includes sections on mood, somatoform, and substance use disorders, as anxiety disorders are frequently comorbid with such conditions. There are two versions of the adult ADIS-5: the Standard Version, which provides only current diagnostic information, and the Lifetime Version (ADIS-5L; Brown & Barlow, 2014b), which offers both past and current diagnostic information. The ADIS-5L is similar in structure to the ADIS-5, but contains separate sections that assess the prior occurrence of disorders. The ADIS-5 can be used in both clinical and research settings.

At the beginning of the ADIS-5, basic demographic information is collected, as well as a short description of the presenting problem. This information gives the examiner an idea of which topics should be pursued in more detail throughout the interview. Following the presenting problem, the examiner asks the respondent, "What would you say is the main reason that brought you here today?" and the response is recorded verbatim. Next, the respondent is asked to describe any recent struggles in functioning within the past year (e.g., school, work, relationships). Notably, medical/treatment history has been moved to the front of the ADIS-5, before the diagnostic portion of the instrument, for several reasons, one of which is to consider the influence of current medications and medical problems on current symptomatology.

The interview then continues with the assessment of anxiety disorders. This section begins with the more prevalent anxiety disorders (e.g., panic disorder, agoraphobia, social anxiety disorder) and is organized logically to reflect the shared symptoms among many anxiety disorders. Next are sections assessing mood disorders, somatoform disorders, post-traumatic stress disorder, depressive disorders, mood disorders, somatic disorders, alcohol and substance use/dependence, and screening for other disorders (e.g., hoarding). A segment assessing the individual's family history of psychological disorders is also included. Prior to the *DSM-5* revisions to the ADIS, Brown, DiNardo, and Barlow (1994b) recommended administering the Hamilton Rating Scale for Depression and the Hamilton Anxiety Rating scale for additional information regarding anxiety and depression; however, the authors of the ADIS-5 (Brown & Barlow, 2014a) no longer recommend administration of the Hamilton scales following the administration of the ADIS, and the two measures have been separated.

Each section on the ADIS-5 includes items assessing diagnostic criteria for the given disorder. The examiner begins with several dichotomous yes/no initial inquiry questions, and affirmative answers warrant further questioning to gauge the presence or absence of the disorder. In some sections, these dichotomous items are considered skip-out points in which, pending negative ratings, continuation is not necessary. Dimensional ratings are also obtained regarding both current and past experiences of major symptoms of the given disorder. As noted previously, the ADIS-5L contains separate sections for current and past occurrences of disorders, whereas the ADIS-5 assesses only current disorders. However, the ADIS-5 contains screening questions for past episodes in the initial inquiry items. If the respondent denotes a positive response to these screening questions, the clinician's manual recommends that the interviewer adapt other items in that section to obtain information about previous disorders. The manual notes that this information may be useful in differential diagnosis.

After the initial inquiry section, the clinician continues with the current episode segment of the interview, which provides items that collectively assess all diagnostic criteria for a specific disorder. The questions in the current episode section are arranged so that they begin as open-ended and are followed by more specific inquiries. The need for the more specific inquiries is contingent upon the response to the initial open-ended question. For instance, if the respondent provides a specific response to a question regarding the timeline of a given symptom (e.g., "The symptom began around 1 month ago"), then follow-up questions may not be needed. The current episode section also contains questions that assess the onset of the disorder and etiological factors. After the current episode section, the administrator again asks about past episodes of the disorder. The purpose of this repeated item is that the interviewer can reassess the previous occurrence of the disorder given the wealth of diagnostic information collected in that section. In the ADIS-5L, the current episode portion of the interview is followed by the past episode section, which is similar in structure to the current episode segment.

The ADIS-5 contains a score sheet in which the interviewer records diagnoses (including dates of onset) in addition to a diagnostic confidence rating (0–100, with 100 indicating complete certainty). If the diagnostic confidence rating is less than 100, the interviewer must indicate why. Each disorder listed is given a rating of clinical severity ranging from 0 to 8, with higher numbers indicating more distress. Ratings of 0 indicate that there are no features of a given disorder present. These ratings are used to identify clinical versus subclinical disorders, such that ratings of 3 or below indicate subsyndromal symptomatology, and ratings of 4 and above indicate the presence of a disorder (as per the *DSM-5* criteria). The ADIS-5L also contains a "diagnostic timeline" page that synthesizes information regarding the temporal sequence of disorders as well as etiology.

The ADIS-5 is designed for use by experienced clinicians who are familiar with the *DSM-5* as well as the ADIS-5. Examiners are encouraged to use clinical judgment to determine whether an item should be read verbatim or reworded as needed (e.g., shortening length and complexity of questions for those with lower levels of education). Examiners are also encouraged to use their clinical judgment to gather further clarifying information from respondents, and to decide when to skip certain sections of the interview.

Overall, both the ADIS-5 and ADIS-5L are popular and valuable tools in diagnosing anxiety disorders as well as frequently comorbid conditions. Studies of the previous versions of the ADIS (e.g., ADIS-IV; see Grisham, Brown, and Campbell, 2004 for a summary) indicated empirical support regarding the reliability and validity of the instrument); however, due to the recent publication of the ADIS-5, psychometric properties of the newest version are yet to be established and will likely be the focus of future studies. Previous versions of the ADIS have been translated into at least five other languages (the ADIS-5 is likely to follow this trend). There is an adapted version for use with children. The ADIS-5 interview and manual are available from Oxford University Press (global.oup.com).

Diagnostic Interview Schedule for DSM-5 The Diagnostic Interview Schedule (DIS; Robins et al., 2000) is designed to ascertain the presence or absence of major mental disorders of the *DSM-5* (APA, 2013). It is unique among the multidisorder diagnostic interviews in that it is a *fully structured* interview specifically designed for use by nonclinician interviewers, whereas the other interviews are semistructured. By definition, a fully structured interview clearly specifies all questions and probes, and does not permit deviations.

The original DIS was developed in 1978 at the request of the National Institute of Mental Health Division of Biometry and Epidemiology, which was commencing a series of large-scale, multicenter epidemiological investigations of mental disorders in the general adult population in the United States. The development of a structured interview that could be administered by nonclinicians was imperative because of the prohibitive cost of using professional clinicians as interviewers. As a result, the DIS was designed as a fully structured diagnostic interview explicitly crafted so that it could be administered and scored by nonclinician interviewers.

The most recent DIS (DIS-5; "History and Scope", n.d.) has been revised to map onto the *DSM-5* diagnostic criteria and includes revisions prompted by field experience and associated feedback. The DIS-5 comprises changes in the assessment of current syndrome, assessing for whether a disorder has been present in the last 12 months and having interviewees indicate when in the last 12 months the symptoms were present. The DIS-5 also covers substance use disorders as coded by the *DSM-5* and the *International Classification of Diseases*, 10th ed. (*ICD-10*). Separation anxiety and somatization disorders are omitted from the DIS-5; however, the DIS-IV modules for these disorders can still be obtained for use. In addition, the DIS-5 no longer includes screening for cognitive concerns (e.g., dementia).

To assure standardization of the DIS-5, computerized administration is required, which may be either administered by the interviewer or self-administered. In both formats, the exact wording of all questions and probes is presented to the respondent in a fixed order on a computer screen. Rephrasing of questions is discouraged, although DIS-5 interviewers can repeat questions as necessary to ensure that the respondent understands them. All questions are closed-ended, and replies are coded with a forced-choice yes/no response format. The DIS-5 gathers all necessary information about the person from his or her self-report. Collateral sources of information are not used. The DIS-5 is self-contained and covers all necessary symptoms to make most *DSM-5* diagnoses. To this end, the *DSM-5* diagnostic criteria for the disorders have been faithfully turned into specific questions in the DIS-5. The coded responses are directly entered into a database during the interview, and the diagnosis is made according to the explicit rules of the *DSM-5* diagnostic system.

Because the DIS was designed for epidemiological research with normative samples, interviewers do not elicit a presenting problem from the respondent, as would be typical in unstructured clinical interviews. Rather, interviewers begin by asking questions about symptoms in a standardized order. Like most of the other structured interviews examined here, the DIS-5 has sections that cover different disorders. Each diagnostic section is independent, except where one diagnosis pre-empts another. Once a symptom is reported to be present, further closed-ended questions are asked about diagnostically relevant information, such as severity, frequency, time frame, and possibility of organic etiology of the symptom. The DIS-5 includes a set of core questions that are asked of each respondent. Core questions are followed by contingent questions which are administered only if the preceding core question is endorsed. Interviewers use a probe flowchart that indicates which probes to select in which circumstances.

For each symptom, the respondent is asked to state whether it has ever been present and how recently. All data about the presence or absence of symptoms and time frames of occurrence are coded and entered into the computer. Consistent with its use of non-clinician interviewers who may not be overly familiar with the *DSM-5* or psychiatric diagnosis, the diagnostic output of the DIS-5 is generated by a computer program that analyzes data from the completed interview. The output provides estimates of prevalence for two time periods: current and lifetime.

Due to its highly structured format, full administration of the DIS-5 typically requires between 90 and 150 minutes. To shorten administration time, the modular format makes it possible to drop evaluation of disorders that are not of interest in a study. Another option is to drop further questioning for a disorder once it is clear that the threshold number of symptoms needed for diagnosis will not be met. Although designed for use by nonclinician administrators, training for competent administration of the DIS-5 is necessary. Trainees typically attend a 3-day training program at University of Florida (Gainesville, Florida) or at their own location. The training entails review of the DIS-5 manual, didactic presentations about the structure and conventions of the DIS-5, homework exercises, and practice interviews followed by feedback and review. Additional supervised practice is also recommended.

The psychometric properties of the original DIS and its revisions are excellent, and such data have been documented in an impressive array of studies; however, due to the newness of the DIS-5, psychometric properties for the newest version have not yet been established. Interested readers are referred to Compton and Cottler (2004) for an excellent summary of the psychometric characteristics of the DIS-IV. Overall, the DIS has proven to be a popular and useful diagnostic assessment tool, especially for large-scale epidemiological research.

The DIS has been translated into more than a dozen languages, is used in countries across the globe for epidemiological research, and served as the basis for the Composite International Diagnostic Interview used by the World Health Organization. For further information on DIS-5 materials, training, and developments, refer to the DIS website (http://epidemiology.phhp.ufl.edu/assessments/c-dis-5-and-c-sam-5/).

Schedule for Affective Disorders and Schizophrenia   The Schedule for Affective Disorders and Schizophrenia (SADS; Endicott & Spitzer, 1978) is a semistructured diagnostic interview designed to evaluate a range of clinical disorders, with a focus on mood and psychotic disorders. Ancillary coverage is provided for anxiety symptoms, substance abuse, psychosocial treatment history, and antisocial personality features. The SADS provides in-depth but focused coverage of the mood and psychotic disorders and supplies meaningful distinctions of impairment in the clinical range for these disorders. The SADS can be used to make many *DSM-IV* diagnoses, but it is not completely aligned with the *DSM* system, representing a significant point of concern. With substantive changes made in *DSM-5*, the SADS is at risk of becoming more outdated if it is not revised substantially.

The SADS is intended to be administered to adult respondents by trained mental health professionals. It focuses heavily on the differential diagnosis of mood and psychotic disorders, with great depth of assessment in these areas. In the beginning of the interview, a brief overview of the respondent's background and psychiatric problems is elicited via an open-ended inquiry. The SADS is then divided into two parts, each focusing on a different time period. Part I provides for a thorough evaluation of current psychiatric problems and concomitant functional impairment. A unique feature of the SADS is that, for the current episode, symptoms are rated when they were at their worst levels to increase diagnostic sensitivity and validity. In contrast, Part II provides a broad overview of past episodes of psychopathology and treatment. Overall, the SADS covers more than 20 diagnoses in a systematic and comprehensive fashion and provides for diagnosis of both current and lifetime psychiatric disorders. Some examples include schizophrenia (with six subtypes), schizoaffective disorder, manic disorder, hypomanic disorder, major depressive disorder (with 11 subtypes), minor depressive disorder, panic disorder, obsessive- compulsive disorder, phobic disorder, alcoholism, and antisocial personality disorder (Endicott & Spitzer, 1978). In *DSM-5*, the subtypes of schizophrenia have been deleted (due to poor validity and clinical utility), so the distinction made by the SADS in this area may not be of much use in the future.

In the SADS, questions are clustered according to specific diagnoses. For each disorder, standard questions are specified to evaluate specific symptoms of that disorder. Questions are either dichotomous or rated on a Likert-type scale, which allows for uniform documentation of levels of severity, persistence, and functional impairment associated with each symptom. To supplement client self-report and obtain the most accurate symptom picture, the SADS allows for consideration of all available sources of information (i.e., chart records, input from relatives). In addition to the standard questions asked of each respondent, optional probes may be selectively used to clarify responses, and unstructured questions may be generated by the interviewer to augment answers to the optional probes. Thus, considerable clinical experience and judgment are needed to administer the SADS. To reduce length of administration and evaluation of symptoms that are not diagnostically significant, many diagnostic sections begin with screening questions that provide for skip-outs to the next section if the respondent shows no evidence of having the disorder. Administration of the SADS typically takes between 90 and 150 minutes. The interviewer makes formal diagnostic appraisals after the interview is completed. No computer scoring applications have been designed for the SADS because of the complex nature of the diagnostic process and the strong reliance on clinical judgment.

As noted earlier, the SADS was designed for use by trained clinicians. Considerable clinical judgment, interviewing skills, and familiarity with diagnostic criteria and psychiatric symptoms are requisite for competent administration. As such, it is recommended that the SADS only be administered by professionals with graduate degrees and clinical experience, such as clinical psychologists, psychiatrists, and psychiatric social workers (Endicott & Spitzer, 1978). Training in the SADS is intensive and can encompass several weeks. The process includes reviewing the most recent SADS manual and practice in rating written case vignettes and videotaped SADS interviews. Additionally, trainees typically watch and score live interviews as if participating in a reliability study with a simultaneous-rating design. Throughout, discussion and clarification with expert interviewers regarding diagnostic disagreements or difficulties add to the experience. Finally, trainees conduct their own SADS interviews, which are observed and critiqued by the expert trainers.

Numerous additional versions of the SADS have been devised, each with a distinct focus and purpose. Perhaps the most common is the SADS-L (Lifetime version), which can be used to make both current and lifetime diagnoses but has significantly fewer details about current psychopathology than the full SADS and results in a quicker administration time. The SADS-L generally is used with nonpsychiatric samples in which there is no assumption of a significant current psychiatric problem. The SADS-Change Version is also popular and consists of 45 key symptoms from the SADS Part 1. Extensive study of the SADS suggests that it possesses excellent psychometric characteristics. See Rogers, Jackson, and Cashel (2004) for a comprehensive review of these data.

The SADS has been translated into several languages, but its primary use has been in North America. The SADS has been widely used in clinical research over the past three decades, and consequently has a large body of empirical data associated with it. As such, it is often the instrument of choice for clinical researchers desiring in-depth assessment of depression and schizophrenia. The extensive subtyping of disorders provided by the SADS is also highly valued by clinical researchers. However, owing to its length and complexity, the SADS is infrequently chosen for use in many traditional, purely clinical settings (e.g., community mental health centers). Because the SADS is most closely aligned with the Research Diagnostic Criteria (and not the *DSM* criteria), there are no plans to update the measure to fit the *DSM-5* (J. Endicott, personal communication, January 6, 2017). The SADS can be obtained directly from the instrument's developers.

Structured Clinical Interview for DSM-5 Disorders The Structured Clinical Interview for *DSM-5* 5 Disorders (SCID-5) is a flexible, semistructured diagnostic interview designed for use by trained clinicians to diagnose many adult *DSM-5* clinical disorders. The SCID has widespread popularity as an instrument to obtain reliable and valid psychiatric diagnoses for clinical, research, and training purposes, and the previous versions have been used in more than 1,000 studies.

The original SCID was designed for application in both research and clinical settings. Recently, the SCID has been split into three distinct versions: the Research Version, the Clinician Version, and the Clinical Trials Version. The Research Version covers more disorders, subtypes, and course specifiers than the Clinician Version and, therefore, takes longer to complete. The benefit, however, is that it provides for a wealth of diagnostic data that is particularly valued by clinical researchers. The coverage of the Clinical Trials Version is customizable and depends on the inclusion/exclusion criteria for specific clinical trials (First, Williams, Karg, & Spitzer, 2016b).

The most up-to-date version of the SCID has been modified to reflect changes in the *DSM-5*. The updated instrument contains several new disorders (e.g., hoarding, premenstrual dysphoric disorder, trichotillomania, gambling disorder, and attention-deficit/hyperactivity disorder), updated and new questions, and adjustments to the original SCID algorithm (First et al., 2016b).

The Clinician Version of the SCID (SCID-5-CV; First et al. 2016b) is designed for use in clinical settings. It has been trimmed to encompass only those *DSM-5* disorders that are most typically seen in clinical practice and can further be abbreviated on a module-by-module basis. The SCID-5-CV contains 10 self-contained modules of major diagnostic categories (mood episodes, psychotic symptoms, psychotic disorders, mood disorders, substance use disorders, and anxiety disorders, obsessive-compulsive disorder and post-traumatic stress disorder, attention-deficit/hyperactivity disorder, screening for other disorders, and adjustment disorder).

The modular design of the SCID represents a major strength of the instrument, because administration can be customized easily to meet the unique needs of the user. For example, the SCID can be shortened or lengthened to include only those categories of interest, and the order of modules can be altered. The format and sequence of the SCID were designed to approximate the flowcharts and decision trees followed by experienced diagnostic interviewers. The SCID begins with an open-ended overview portion, during which the development and history of the present psychological disturbance are elicited, and tentative diagnostic hypotheses are generated. In addition, screening for substance abuse occurs prior to the diagnostic modules of the SCID so that the effects of the client's substance use can be clarified from the beginning of the interview. Then, the SCID systematically presents modules that allow for assessment of specific disorders and symptoms. Most disorders are evaluated for two time periods: current (meets criteria for the past month) and lifetime (ever-met criteria).

Consistent with its linkage with *DSM*, formal diagnostic criteria are included in the SCID booklet, thus permitting interviewers to see the exact criteria to which the SCID questions pertain. This unique feature makes the SCID an outstanding training tool for clinicians, because it facilitates the learning of diagnostic criteria and presents excellent questions to assess the criteria. The SCID has many open-ended prompts that encourage respondents to elaborate freely about their symptoms. At times, open-ended prompts are followed by closed-ended questions to fully clarify a specific symptom. Although the SCID provides structure to cover criteria for each disorder, its semistructured format provides significant latitude for interviewers to re-state questions, ask for further clarification, probe, and challenge if the initial prompt was misunderstood by the interviewee or clarification is needed to rate a symptom. SCID interviewers are encouraged to use all sources of information about a respondent, and gentle challenging of the respondent is encouraged if discrepant information is suspected.

During administration, each symptom is rated as either absent (or below threshold) or present (and clinically significant). The SCID flowchart instructs interviewers to skip out of a diagnostic section when essential symptoms are judged to be below threshold or absent. These skip-outs result in decreased time of administration as well as the skipping of items with no diagnostic significance. Administration of the SCID is typically completed in one session and takes 45–90 minutes. Once administration is completed, all current and past disorders for which criteria are met are listed on a Diagnostic Summary sheet.

The SCID is optimally administered by trained clinicians. Because of the semistructured format of the SCID, proper administration often requires that interviewers re-state or clarify questions in ways that are sometimes not clearly outlined in the manual to judge accurately if a diagnostic criterion has been met. The task requires that SCID assessors have a working knowledge of psychopathology, *DSM-5* diagnostic criteria, and basic interviewing skills. Standard procedures for training to use the SCID include carefully reading the *Users Guide to the SCID* (First et al., 2016b), reviewing the SCID administration booklet and score sheet, viewing SCID videotape training materials that are available from the SCID authors, and conducting role-played practice administrations with extensive feedback discussions. Next, trainees may administer the SCID to representative participants who are jointly rated so that a discussion about sources of disagreements can ensue. In research settings, a formal reliability study is advantageous. The reliability and validity of the previous versions of the SCID in adult populations with diverse disorders have been evaluated in several investigations, with generally excellent results among widely varied participant samples and experimental designs (see review by First & Gibbon, 2004; Segal, Hersen & Van Hasselt, 1994).

Overall, the SCID is a widely used and respected assessment instrument. Previous versions have been translated into 12 languages and it has been applied successfully in research studies and clinical practice in many countries. As clinicians and researchers shift to using the updated instrument, the SCID-5 is likely to gain similar utilization and support. For more information on the SCID, visit the SCID website (www.scid5.org).

SEMISTRUCTURED INTERVIEWS FOR PERSONALITY DISORDERS

Diagnostic Interview for Personality Disorders   The Diagnostic Interview for *DSM-IV* Personality Disorders (DIPD-IV; Zanarini, Frankenburg, Sickel, & Yong, 1996) is a semistructured interview designed to assess the presence or absence of the 10 standard *DSM-IV* personality disorders as well as depressive personality disorder and passive-aggressive personality disorder in the *DSM-IV* appendix. Prior to personality disorder assessment, a full screening for clinical disorders is recommended. Additionally, an assessment of the respondent's general functioning (e.g., in the domains of work, school, and social life) is advised before administration of the DIPD-IV (Zanarini et al., 1996).

The interview is conducted on a disorder-by-disorder basis. The interview contains 108 sets of questions, each designed to assess a specific *DSM-IV* personality disorder diagnostic criterion. The *DSM-IV* criterion is provided in bold below each set of questions for easy cross-reference. The initial question for each criterion typically has a yes/no format which is followed by open-ended questions to explore clients' experiences more fully. Clients are informed that the interview pertains to the past 2 years of their life and that the interviewer wants to learn about the thoughts, feelings, and behaviors that have been typical for them during the 2-year period. Whereas clients are the sole source of information for rating most of the diagnostic criteria, behavior exhibited during the interview is valued and may override client self-report if there are contradictions. The administrator is encouraged to probe further if responses appear incomplete or fallacious.

Each diagnostic criterion is rated on the following scale: 0, absent or clinically insignificant; 1, present but of uncertain clinical significance; 2, present and clinically significant; and NA, not applicable. After all 108 criteria are evaluated, final categorical diagnosis for each personality disorder is made based on the number of criteria met. The final output is recorded as 2, indicating yes or met full criteria, 1 indicating subthreshold (one less than required number of criteria), or 0 indicating no.

Information about administration and scoring of the DIPD-IV is relatively sparse, at least compared with the other interviews focusing on personality disorders. The training requirements include, at a minimum, a bachelor's degree, at least 1 year of clinical experience with personality-disordered clients, and several training interviews in which the person observes skilled administrators and then administers the interview. Training tapes and workshops are available, as is a Spanish version. Administration time is typically about 90 minutes. Most notably, the DIPD-IV has been chosen as the primary diagnostic measure for personality disorders in the Collaborative Longitudinal Personality Disorders Study, which is a large, multisite, prospective naturalistic longitudinal study of personality disorders and comorbid mental health problems. Because personality disorder criteria have not changed in the DSM-5 there are no anticipated changes to the DIPD-IV at this time (M.C. Zanarini, personal communication, January 25, 2017). For further information on the DIPD-IV, contact Dr. Mary C. Zanarini (zanarini@mclean.harvard.edu).

International Personality Disorder Examination   The International Personality Disorder Examination (IPDE; Loranger, 1999) is an extensive, semistructured diagnostic interview administered by experienced clinicians to evaluate personality disorders for both the *DSM-IV* and *ICD-10* classification systems. The IPDE was developed within the Joint Program for the Diagnosis and Classification of Mental Disorders of the World Health Organization and US National Institutes of Health aimed at producing a standardized assessment instrument to measure personality disorders on a worldwide basis. As such, the IPDE is the only personality disorder interview based on worldwide field trials. The IPDE manual contains the interview questions to assess either the 11 *DSM-IV* or the 10 *ICD-10* personality disorders. The two IPDE modules (*DSM-IV* and *ICD-10*) contain both a self-administered screening questionnaire and a semistructured interview booklet with scoring materials.

The Screening Questionnaire is a self-administered form that contains 77 *DSM-IV* or 59 *ICD-10* items written at a fourth-grade reading level. Items are answered either "true" or "false," and the questionnaire is typically completed in about 15 minutes. The clinician can quickly score the questionnaire and identify those respondents whose scores suggest the presence of a personality disorder. Subsequently, the IPDE clinical interview is administered.

The IPDE Interview modules (for either the *DSM-IV* or *ICD-10* systems) contain questions, each reflecting a personality disorder criterion, which are grouped into six thematic headings: work, self, interpersonal relationships, affects, reality testing, and impulse control (Loranger, 1999). Because disorders are not covered on a one-by-one basis, the intent of the evaluation is less transparent, similar to the SIDP-IV. At the beginning of each section, open-ended inquiries are provided to enable a smooth transition from the previous section and to encourage respondents to elaborate about themselves in a less structured fashion. Then, specific questions are asked to evaluate each personality disorder criterion. For each question, the corresponding personality disorder and the specific diagnostic criterion are identified with specific scoring guidelines.

Respondents are encouraged to report their typical or usual functioning, rather than their personality functioning during times of episodic psychiatric disturbance. The IPDE requires that a trait be prominent during the past 5 years to be considered a part of the respondent's personality. Information about age of onset of particular behaviors is explored to determine if a late-onset diagnosis (after age 25 years) is appropriate. When a respondent acknowledges a particular trait, interviewers follow up by asking for examples and anecdotes to clarify the trait or behavior, gauge the impact of the trait on the person's functioning, and fully substantiate the rating. Such probing requires significant clinical judgment and knowledge on the part of interviewers about each criterion. Items may also be rated based on observation of the respondent's behavior during the session, and this too requires a certain level of clinical expertise. To supplement self-report, an interview of informants is encouraged. Clinical judgment is needed to ascertain which source is more reliable if inconsistencies arise.

Each criterion is rated on a scale with the following definitions: 0 indicates that the behavior or trait is absent or within normal limits, 1 refers to exaggerated or accentuated degree of the trait, 2 signifies criterion level or pathological, and ? indicates the respondent refuses or is unable to answer. Comprehensive item-by-item scoring guidelines are provided in the manual (Loranger, 1999). At the end of the interview, the clinician records the scores for each response on the appropriate IPDE Answer Sheet. Ratings are then collated by hand or computer. The ultimate output is extensive, including presence or absence of each criterion, number of criteria met for each personality disorder, a dimensional score (sum of individual scores for each criterion for each disorder), and a categorical diagnosis (definite, probable, or negative) for each personality disorder (Loranger, 1999). Such comprehensive output is often of value to clinical researchers.

The IPDE is intended to be administered by experienced clinicians who have also received specific training in its use. Such training typically involves a workshop with demonstration videotapes, discussions, and practice. The average administration time for the interview is 90 minutes, which can be reduced by using the screening questionnaire (omitting interview items associated with unlikely personality disorders). Because the IPDE has been selected by the WHO for international application, it has been translated into numerous languages to facilitate cross-cultural research. Ample evidence of reliability and validity of the IPDE has been documented (Loranger, 1999; Loranger et al., 1994). Because of the instrument's ties to the *DSM-IV* and *ICD-10* classification systems, and adoption by the WHO, the IPDE is widely used for international and cross-cultural investigations of personality disorders. No major updates to the IPDE are planned at present (S. Fox, representative of PAR Inc., personal communication, January 23, 2017). The instrument can be purchased through PAR Inc. at http://www4.parinc.com/. The user manual is available through http://www.who.int/en/.

Structured Clinical Interview for DSM-5 Personality Disorders   To complement the clinical disorder version of the SCID, a version focusing on personality disorders was developed: the Structured Clinical Interview for *DSM-5* Personality Disorders (SCID-5-PD; First, Williams, Benjamin, & Spitzer, 2016a). The SCID-5-PD is the *DSM-5*-updated version of the Structured Clinical Interview for DSM-IV Axis II Personality Disorders (First, Gibbon, Spitzer, Williams, & Benjamin, 1997). The SCID-5-PD has a similar semistructured format as the original SCID but it covers the 10 standard *DSM-5* personality disorders, as well as other specified personality disorders. This version also provides cluster categorization (e.g., Cluster A includes paranoid, schizotypal, and schizoid personality disorders) of the personality disorders, as well as a dimensional scoring component.

For comprehensive assessment, the SCID-5-PD may be easily used in conjunction with the original SCID that would be administered prior to personality disorder assessment. This is encouraged so that the respondent's present mental state can be considered when judging accuracy of self-reported personality traits. The basic structure and conventions of the SCID-5-PD closely resemble those of the SCID-5. An additional feature of the SCID-5-PD is that it includes a 106-item self-report screening component called the Screening Personality Questionnaire which may be administered prior to the interview portion and takes about 20 minutes. The purpose of the Screening Personality Questionnaire is to reduce overall administration time, because only those items that are scored in the pathological direction are further evaluated during the structured interview portion.

During the structured interview component, the pathologically endorsed screening responses are further pursued to determine whether the symptoms are experienced at clinically significant levels. Here, the respondent is asked to elaborate on each suspected personality disorder criterion, and specified prompts are provided. Like the original SCID, the *DSM-5* diagnostic criteria are printed on the interview page for easy review, and responses are coded as follows: ?, inadequate information; 0, absent or false; 1, subthreshold; and 2, threshold or true. Each personality disorder is assessed completely, and diagnoses are completed before proceeding to the next disorder. The modular format permits researchers and clinicians to tailor the SCID-5-PD to their specific needs and reduce administration time. Clinicians who administer the SCID-5-PD are expected to use their clinical judgment to clarify responses, gently challenge inconsistencies, and ask for additional information as required to rate each criterion accurately. Collection of diagnostic information from ancillary sources is permitted. Complete administration of the SCID-5-PD typically takes less than 60 minutes.

Training requirements and interviewer qualifications are similar to those of the original SCID. There is no separate clinician version of the SCID-5-PD. The psychometric properties of the SCID-5-PD are expected to be comparable to the SCID-II as minimal changes were instituted and personality disorder diagnostic criteria remain the same; however, establishment of the psychometric properties of the updated instrument is needed. For a comprehensive review of the SCID-II (previous version) psychometric properties, see First and Gibbon (2004). Given the extensive coverage of the personality disorders, the modular approach, and strong operating characteristics, the SCID-5-PD should remain a popular and effective tool for personality disorder assessment. The SCID-5-PD website is the same as for the original SCID (www.scid5.org).

Structured Interview for DSM-IV Personality   The Structured Interview for *DSM-IV* Personality (SIDP-IV; Pfohl, Blum, & Zimmerman, 1997) is a comprehensive semistructured diagnostic interview for *DSM-IV* personality disorders. It covers 14 *DSM-IV* personality disorder diagnoses, including the 10 standard personality disorders, self-defeating personality disorder, depressive personality disorder, negativistic personality disorder, and mixed personality disorder. Prior to the SIDP-IV structured interview, a full evaluation of the respondent's current mental state is required (Pfohl et al., 1997). This is not surprising given that self-report of enduring personality characteristics can be seriously compromised in a respondent who is experiencing acute psychopathology. Indeed, the aim of all personality assessment measures is to rate the respondent's typical, habitual, and lifelong personal functioning rather than acute or temporary states.

Interestingly, the SIDP-IV does not cover *DSM* personality categories on a disorder-by-disorder basis. Rather, *DSM-IV* personality disorder criteria are reflected in items that are grouped according to 10 topical sections that reflect a different dimension of personality functioning. These sections include interests and activities, work style, close relationships, social relationships, emotions, observational criteria, self-perception, perception of others, stress and anger, and social conformity. These categories are not scored; rather, they reflect broad areas of personal functioning under which personality disorder items can logically be subsumed (Pfohl et al., 1997).

Each SIDP-IV question corresponds to a unique *DSM-IV* personality disorder crite-rion, except that one item addresses two criteria. An attractive feature is that the specific *DSM-IV* criterion associated with each question is provided for interviewers to easily view. All questions are administered, and there are no options to skip out. Most questions are conversational in tone and open-ended to encourage respondents to talk about their *usual* behaviors and long-term functioning. In fact, respondents are specifically instructed to focus on their typical or habitual behavior when addressing each item and are prompted to "remember what you are like when you are your usual self." Based on client responses, each criterion is rated on a scale with four anchor points: a rating of 0 indicates that the criterion was not present; 1 corresponds to a subthreshold level where there is some evidence of the trait but it is not sufficiently prominent; 2 refers to the criterion being present for most of the past 5 years; and 3 signifies a strongly present and debilitating level. The SIDP-IV requires that a trait be prominent for most of the past 5 years to be considered a part of the respondent's personality. This 5-year rule helps to ensure that the personality characteristic is stable and of long duration, as required by the General Diagnostic Criteria for Personality Disorders.

A strong point of the organizational format by personality dimensions (rather than by disorders) is that data for specific diagnoses are minimized until final ratings have been collated on the summary sheet. This feature can potentially reduce interviewer biases, such as the halo effect or changing thresholds, if it is obvious that a respondent needs to meet one additional criterion to make the diagnosis. This topical organization also makes the interview's intent less transparent compared with the disorder-by-disorder approach of some other interviews.

Significant clinical judgment is required to properly administer the SIDP-IV, because interviewers are expected to ask additional questions to clarify client responses when necessary. Also, data are not limited to self-report; rather, chart records and significant others such as relatives and friends who know the client well should be consulted when available, and a standard informed consent is included for informant interviews. Such collateral information is particularly prized when evaluating personality-disordered individuals who may lack insight into their own maladaptive personality traits and distort facts about their strengths and limitations. Moreover, informants can also provide diagnostic data that can help resolve the state/trait distinction about specific criterion behaviors.

If discrepancies between sources of information are noted, interviewers must consider all data and use their own judgment to determine the veracity of each source. Making this distinction can be one of the challenges faced by SIDP-IV administrators. Given the multiple sources of diagnostic data, final ratings are made after all sources of information are considered. Such ratings are then transcribed onto a summary sheet that lists each criterion organized by personality disorder, and formal diagnoses are assigned. As required by the *DSM*, diagnoses are made only if the minimum number of criteria (or threshold) has been met for that disorder.

Minimum qualifications for competent administration consist of an interviewer with an undergraduate degree in the social sciences and 6 months' experience with diagnostic interviewing. Moreover, an additional month of specialized training and practice with the SIDP is required to become a competent interviewer (Pfohl et al., 1997). Admin-istrators are required to possess an understanding of manifest psychopathology and the typical presentation and course of clinical and personality disorders. Training tapes and workshop information are available from the instrument authors. The SIDP typically requires 60–90 minutes for the client interview, 20 minutes for interview of significant informants, and approximately 20 minutes to fill out the summary score sheet. Studies documenting the strong psychometric properties of the SIDP are plentiful, and they are summarized in the manual for the instrument (Pfohl et al., 1997). At the time of publication of this chapter, there were no intended changes to the SIDP-IV (N. Blum, personal communication, February 13, 2017). The SIDP-IV is available for purchase through https://www.appi.org/.

THE CULTURAL FORMULATION INTERVIEW (CFI) OF *DSM-5*

New to *DSM-5* is the Cultural Formulation Interview (CFI), which is a 16-question semistructured interview designed to assess the impact of cultural factors on an individual's mental health. The CFI is based on the Outline for Cultural Formulation, a framework for assessing cultural factors as they relate to individuals' mental health that was first introduced in the *DSM-IV*. Although the CFI is not used to diagnose mental disorders *per se*, we have included it in this chapter because the CFI can be used to understand important cultural issues that can impact the expression and diagnosis of mental disorders in diverse populations.

According to the *DSM-5*, cultural concepts are essential to effective diagnostic assessment and clinical management for several reasons, including:

- aiding in avoiding misdiagnosis;
- obtaining useful clinical information;
- improving clinical rapport and engagement as well as therapeutic efficacy;
- clarifying cultural epidemiology;
- guiding clinical research (APA, 2013, p. 759).

The purpose of the CFI is to provide a guide for cultural assessment that improves "cultural validity of diagnostic assessment," aids in treatment planning, and fosters the individual's commitment and satisfaction (APA, 2013). There are two versions of the CFI: the core CFI, which is used to interview the individual, and the CFI-Informant Version, which is used when individuals are unable to answer the question for themselves, as is the case with children, or persons who are cognitively impaired or psychotic. Information for the CFI-Informant version is collected from a person who knows the individual well, and is knowledgeable about the individual's clinical problems and the person's important life circumstances. The information gathered from the CFI-Informant version can be used as a supplement to, or a replacement for, the core CFI.

The CFI is rooted in a person-centered approach focusing on the individual's perspective of their cultural experiences and social contexts. It is suggested that the CFI be used in conjunction with previously obtained demographic information in order to tailor the questions to the individual's current cultural context (APA, 2013). The information collected from the CFI and or the CFI-Informant version along with all other clinical information should be integrated to create a comprehensive evaluation.

The CFI is composed of four main sections, each focusing on a different aspect of cultural factors encountered in diagnostic assessment. The first section (questions 1–3) focuses on the cultural definition of the problem; the second section (questions 4–10) concentrates on cultural perceptions of cause, contacts, and support; the third section (questions 11–13) focuses on cultural factors affecting self-coping and past help-seeking; and the fourth section (questions 14–16) focuses on cultural factors affecting current help-seeking. The CFI is formatted into two columns. The left-hand column provides information to the interviewer on both how to administer the CFI and the goals of the section. The right-hand column offers suggested questions that can be used in the interview. The CFI is a semistructured interview so the questions are flexible and may be rephrased. Clinicians are also encouraged to ask follow-up questions as needed to clarify individuals' answers. The *DSM-5* suggests that the CFI be used flexibly to maintain a natural flow during the interview and therapeutic rapport (APA, 2013). Additional modules have been created to guide clinicians who wish to expand on any of the sections and explore them further during the interview, and for specific populations such as older adults, children, and immigrants. The instrument and supplemental modules can be found online at www.psychiatry.org/dsm5.

SUMMARY AND CONCLUSIONS

This chapter highlights the fact that structured and semistructured interviews have greatly facilitated psychiatric diagnosis, objective measurement of symptoms, and problem clarification in a diverse range of clinical and research settings. Reliability of diagnosis is much improved with the use of structured interviews compared with the nonstandardized approach that is common in clinical practice, and improved reliability provides the foundation for enhanced validity and utility of diagnosis. Given the field's recent emphasis on empirically supported psychotherapeutic interventions and processes (e.g., Barlow, 2014; Castonguay & Beutler, 2006; McHugh & Barlow, 2010; Nathan & Gorman, 2007), we hope that a concomitant focus on clinically relevant, standardized, objective, and validated assessment procedures will be realized as well. Structured and semistructured interviews play a key role in the advancement of the science of clinical psychology.

This chapter provided a broad overview of the basic issues surrounding structured and semistructured interviews, and it described many interviews available to clinicians and researchers. We hope that this information enables clinicians and researchers to choose instruments that will most appropriately suit their needs. Finally, as noted earlier, with the publication of *DSM-5*, many of the structured and semistructured interviews described in this chapter have undergone significant revisions to match the classification changes that occurred for many diagnostic categories. The structured and semistructured interviews that are used to diagnose personality disorders have not required imminent revisions because the classification and criteria of the personality disorders did not change in the move from *DSM-IV-TR* to *DSM-5*. The areas of classification and clinical assessment will undoubtedly continue to evolve and change in the coming years. As such, this is an exciting time for researchers and clinicians who use structured and semistructured interviews and other empirically based assessment tools.

REFERENCES

American Psychiatric Association. (1994). *Diagnostic and statistical manual of mental disorders* (4th ed.). Washington, DC: Author.

American Psychiatric Association. (2000). *Diagnostic and statistical manual of mental disorders* (4th ed., text rev.) Washington, DC: Author.

American Psychiatric Association. (2013). *Diagnostic and statistical manual of mental disorders* (5th ed.). Arlington, VA: American Psychiatric Publishing.

Barlow, D. H. (Ed.). (2014). *Clinical handbook of psychological disorders: A step-by-step treatment manual* (5th ed.). New York, NY: Guilford Press.

Brown, T. A., & Barlow, D. H. (2014a). *Anxiety and Related Disorders Interview Schedule for DSM-5 (ADIS-5): Adult version.* New York, NY: Oxford University Press.

Brown, T. A., & Barlow, D. H. (2014b). *Anxiety and Related Disorders Interview Schedule for DSM-5 (ADIS-5): Lifetime version.* New York, NY: Oxford University Press.

Brown, T. A., DiNardo, P. A., & Barlow, D. H. (1994a). *Anxiety Disorders Interview Schedule for DSM-IV (ADIS-IV)* Albany, NY: Graywind Publications.

Brown, T. A., DiNardo, P. A., & Barlow, D. H. (1994b). *Anxiety Disorders Interview Schedule for DSM-IV: Adult and Lifetime Version, Clinician Manual.* Albany, NY: Graywind Publications.

Castonguay, L. G., & Beutler, L. E. (Eds.). (2006). *Principles of therapeutic change that work.* New York, NY: Oxford University Press.

Compton, W. M., & Cottler, L. B. (2004). The Diagnostic Interview Schedule (DIS) In M. Hilsenroth & D. L. Segal (Eds.), *Personality assessment* (pp. 153–162). Vol. 2 in M. Hersen (Ed.-in-Chief), *Comprehensive handbook of psychological assessment.* Hoboken, NJ: Wiley.

Coolidge, F. L. & Segal, D. L. (1998). Evolution of the personality disorder diagnosis in the *Diagnostic and Statistical Manual of Mental Disorders. Clinical Psychology Review, 18,* 585–599.

Coolidge, F. L., & Segal, D. L. (2010a). Reliability. In I. Weiner & W. E. Craighead (Eds.), *The Corsini encyclopedia of psychology and behavioral science* (4th ed., pp. 1448–1449). Hoboken, NJ: Wiley.

Coolidge, F. L., & Segal, D. L. (2010b). Validity. In I. Weiner & W. E. Craighead (Eds.), *The Corsini encyclopedia of psychology and behavioral science* (4th ed., pp. 1826–1828). Hoboken, NJ: Wiley.

DiNardo, P. A., Brown, T. A., & Barlow, D. H. (1994). *Anxiety Disorders Interview Schedule for DSM-IV: Lifetime version (ADIS-IV-L)* Albany, NY: Graywind Publications.

Endicott, J., & Spitzer, R. L. (1978). A diagnostic interview: The Schedule for Affective Disorders and Schizophrenia. *Archives of General Psychiatry, 35,* 837–844.

First, M. B., & Gibbon, M. (2004). The Structured Clinical Interview for *DSM-IV* Axis I Disorders (SCID-I) and the Structured Clinical Interview for *DSM-IV* Axis II Disorders (SCID-II) In M. Hilsenroth & D. L. Segal (Eds.), *Personality assessment* (pp. 134–143). Vol. 2 in M. Hersen (Ed.-in-Chief), *Comprehensive handbook of psychological assessment.* Hoboken, NJ: Wiley.

First, M. B., Gibbon, M., Spitzer, R. L., Williams, J. B. W., & Benjamin, L. S. (1997). *Structured Clinical Interview for DSM-IV Axis II Personality Disorders (SCID-II)* Washington, DC: American Psychiatric Press.

First, M. B., Williams, J. B. W., Benjamin, L. S., & Spitzer, R. L. (2016a). *The user's guide for the structured clinical interview for DSM-5 personality disorders (SCID-5-PD)* Arlington, VA: American Psychiatric Association.

First, M. B., Williams, J. B. W., Karg, B. S., & Spitzer, R. L. (2016b). *The user's guide for the structured clinical interview for DSM-5 disorders—clinician version (SCID-5-CV)* Arlington, VA: American Psychiatric Association.

Grisham, J. R., Brown, T. A., & Campbell, L. A. (2004). The Anxiety Disorders Interview Schedule for *DSM-IV* (ADIS-IV) In M. J. Hilsenroth & D. L. Segal (Eds.), *Personality assessment* (pp. 163–177). Vol. 2 in M. Hersen (Ed.-in-Chief), *Comprehensive handbook of psychological assessment.* Hoboken, NJ: Wiley, History and Scope. (n.d.) Retrieved from http://epidemiology.phhp.ufl .edu/assessments/c-dis-5/history-and-scope/ on February 16, 2017.

Loranger, A. W. (1999). *International Personality Disorder Examination (IPDE)* Odessa, FL: Psychological Assessment Resources.

Loranger, A. W., Sartorius, N., Andreoli, A., Berger, P., Buchheim, P., Channabasavanna, S. M., . . . Regier, D. A. (1994). The International Personality Disorder Examination: The World Health Organization/Alcohol, Drug Abuse, and Mental Health Administration international pilot study of personality disorders. *Archives of General Psychiatry, 51,* 215–224.

McHugh, R. K., & Barlow, D. H. (2010). The dissemination and implementation of evidence-based psychological treatments. *American Psychologist, 65,* 73–84.

Nathan, P. E., & Gorman, J. M. (Eds.). (2007). *A guide to treatments that work* (3rd ed.) New York, NY: Oxford University Press.

Pfohl, B., Blum, N., & Zimmerman, M. (1997). *Structured Interview for DSM-IV Personality.* Washington, DC: American Psychiatric Press.

Robins, L. N., Cottler, L. B., Bucholz, K. K., Compton, W. M., North, C. S., & Rourke, K. (2000). *Diagnostic Interview Schedule for DSM-IV (DIS-IV).* St. Louis, MO: Washington University School of Medicine.

Rogers, R. (2001). *Handbook of diagnostic and structured interviewing.* New York, NY: Guilford Press.

Rogers, R. (2003). Standardizing DSM-IV diagnoses: The clinical applications of structured interviews. *Journal of Personality Assessment, 81,* 220–225.

Rogers, R., Jackson, R. L., & Cashel, M. (2004). The Schedule for Affective Disorders and Schizophrenia (SADS) In M. Hilsenroth & D. L. Segal (Eds.), *Personality assessment* (pp. 144–152). Vol. 2 in M. Hersen (Ed.-in-Chief), *Comprehensive handbook of psychological assessment.* Hoboken, NJ: Wiley.

Segal, D. L. (2010). Diagnostic and statistical manual of mental disorders (DSM-IV-TR) In Weiner & W. E. Craighead (Eds.), *The Corsini encyclopedia of psychology and behavioral science* (4th ed., pp. 495–497). Hoboken, NJ: Wiley.

Segal, D. L., & Coolidge, F. L. (2001). Diagnosis and classification. In M. Hersen & V. B. Van Hasselt (Eds.), *Advanced abnormal psychology* (2nd ed., pp. 5–22). New York, NY: Kluwer Academic/ Plenum.

Segal, D. L., Coolidge, F. L., & Rosowsky, E. (2006). *Personality disorders and older adults: Diagnosis, assessment, and treatment.* Hoboken, NJ: Wiley.

Segal, D. L., & Hersen, M. (Eds.). (2010). *Diagnostic interviewing* (4th ed.). New York, NY: Springer.

Segal, D. L., Hersen, M., & Van Hasselt, V. B. (1994). Reliability of the Structured Clinical Interview for DSM-III-R: An evaluative review. *Comprehensive Psychiatry, 35,* 316–327.

Segal, D. L., Maxfield, M., & Coolidge, F. L. (2008). Diagnostic interviewing. In M. Hersen & M. Gross (Eds.), *Handbook of clinical psychology: Vol. 1. Adults* (pp. 371–394). Hoboken, NJ: Wiley.

Segal, D. L., Qualls, S. H., & Smyer, M. A. (2011). *Aging and mental health* (2nd ed.). Hoboken, NJ: Wiley.

Summerfeldt, L. J., Kloosterman, P. H., & Antony, M. M. (2010). Structured and semi- structured diagnostic interviews. In M. M. Antony & D. H. Barlow (Eds.), *Handbook of assessment and treatment planning for psychological disorders* (2nd ed., pp. 95–140). New York, NY: Guilford Press.

Widiger, T. A., & Samuel, D. B. (2005). Evidence based assessment of personality disorders. *Psychological Assessment, 17,* 278–287.

Widiger, T. A., & Trull, T. J. (2007). Plate tectonics in the classification of personality disorder: Shifting to a dimensional model. *American Psychologist, 62,* 71–83.

Zanarini, M. C., Frankenburg, F. R., Sickel, A. E., & Yong, L. (1996). *The Diagnostic Interview for DSM-IV Personality Disorders (DIPD-IV)* Belmont, MA: McLean Hospital.

CHAPTER 5

Impact of Race, Ethnicity, and Culture on the Expression and Assessment of Psychopathology

L. KEVIN CHAPMAN, RYAN C. T. DELAPP, and MONNICA T. WILLIAMS

THIS CHAPTER PROVIDES an overview and framework for understanding race, ethnicity, and culture as factors that affect adult psychopathology. Of primary interest are the assessment and treatment of psychopathology that integrates culturally salient values, ideologies, and behaviors into the mental health care of ethnic minorities. Moreover, the chapter is organized into two sections. In the first section, we present a model that highlights relevant multicultural factors that should be considered when working with ethnic minorities. The second section provides a discussion of how to effectively apply the knowledge of these multicultural factors when assessing or treating individuals with diverse ethnic backgrounds. Ultimately, the main objective of this chapter is to encourage mental health professionals to acknowledge the impact of race, ethnicity, and culture on adult psychopathology in order to optimize the efficaciousness of mental health services provided to ethnic minority individuals.

The existing literature has clearly demonstrated the importance of multicultural competency in the assessment and treatment of ethnic minorities. In particular, the relevance of ethnicity (or "a voluntaristic self-identification with a group culture, identified in terms of language, religion, marriage patterns and real or imaginary origins"; Bradby, 2012, p. 955) in adult psychopathology has been substantiated by evidence identifying disparities in prevalence rates, symptom presentation, and severity, as well as mental health service utilization across diverse ethnic groups. For example, Himle et al. (2009) found that most anxiety disorders (with the exception of post-traumatic stress disorder [PTSD]) were more prevalent among non-Hispanic Whites than among African Americans and Caribbean Blacks. However, despite their lower prevalence rates, researchers reported that African Americans and Caribbean Blacks experienced anxiety disorders that were greater in severity and more functionally impairing, which demonstrates how experiences with mental illness can vary by ethnicity. Moreover, ethnicity has been implicated as a differentiating factor in the diagnosis and treatment of schizophrenia (Fabrega et al., 1994; Gara et al., 2012).

Adult Psychopathology and Diagnosis, Eighth Edition. Edited by Deborah C. Beidel and B. Christopher Frueh.
© 2018 John Wiley & Sons, Inc. Published 2018 by John Wiley & Sons, Inc.
Companion website: www.wiley.com/go/beidel/psychopathology8e

These studies highlight the susceptibility of misdiagnosed schizophrenia in African American patients due to the tendency for African Americans to endorse more psychotic symptoms during diagnostic assessments. As a result, Gara et al. (2012) emphasize the importance of culturally sensitive diagnostic assessment tools by explaining how an inability to effectively discriminate schizophrenia and schizoaffective disorders can lead to poor treatment outcomes. Additionally, the relevance of ethnicity in adult psychopathology is bolstered by the findings of Alegria et al. (2007), who used data from the National Latino and Asian Study (NLAAS) to identify factors that influence the treatment-seeking behaviors of Latino individuals. Specifically, researchers found that age of migration, Latino ethnicity (e.g., Mexican, Puerto Rican), birth origin (e.g., U.S.-born, foreign-born), primary language spoken, and years of residency in the United States were all influential factors in the use of mental health services and the satisfaction with care received. Most notably, these findings highlight the impact of varied immigration statuses on the perspectives that ethnic minority individuals bring to the mental health arena. Overall, the aforementioned studies clearly underscore the need for multicultural competency in mental health professionals given that one's self-identification with an ethnic heritage has proven to be a vital differentiating factor in the presentation of symptoms and treatment outcomes across diverse adult samples.

RELEVANCE OF ETHNIC IDENTITY AND ACCULTURATION IN ADULT PSYCHOPATHOLOGY

An understanding of the interaction between multicultural factors (e.g., ethnic identity, acculturation) and sociocultural factors (e.g., socioeconomic status, life stress) in ethnic minority patients has become undeniably germane to providing these individuals with effective mental health care. Prior to learning "how" to integrate the understanding of this interaction within assessment, diagnostic, and treatment practices, mental health professionals must possess the knowledge of "what" multicultural factors exist. Inasmuch, Carter, Sbrocco, and Carter (1996) proposed a theoretical model that acknowledges the role of ethnicity, or a "shared culture and lifestyle," as a pivotal underlying construct in the epidemiology, symptom expression, and treatment of psychopathology in ethnic minority individuals (p. 456). Though initially created to explain variations of anxiety disorders in African Americans, the Carter et al. (1996) model can be utilized to more broadly understand the relationship between ethnicity and adult psychopathology by comprehending the salience of ethnic identity and acculturation in all ethnic minorities.

In particular, ethnic identity is a multifarious construct characterized by how people develop and maintain a sense of belonging to their ethnic heritage (Roberts et al., 1999). Important factors influencing a person's ethnic identity include whether they personally identify as a member of an ethnic group, their sentiments and evaluations of the ethnic group, their self-perception of their group membership, their knowledge and commitment to the group, and their ethnic-related behaviors and practices (Burnett-Zeigler, Bohnert, & Ilgen, 2013). Extant literature has provided several models explaining the developmental stages of ethnic identity (Cross, 1978; Cross & Vandiver, 2001; Marcia et al., 1993; Phinney, 1989). Collectively, each model describes identity shifts between ethnic ambivalence (lack of interest or pride in one's ethnic background), ethnic exploration (curiosity in one's ethnic background potentially accompanied by a devaluing of other ethnic heritages), and multicultural acceptance (integration of commitment to one's ethnic background and an appreciation for other ethnic heritages). Evidence supports the idea that individuals high in ethnic identity (i.e., closer to multicultural acceptance) typically have higher levels of self-esteem, develop more protective coping mechanisms, experience more optimism, and report less psychological symptoms (Chavez-Korvell, Benson-Florez, Rendon, & Farias, 2014; Roberts et al., 1999; Smith, Walker, Fields, Brookins, & Seay, 1999; McMahon & Watts, 2002; Williams, Chapman, Wong, and Turkheimer, 2012). Notably, the protective nature of a strong ethnic identity is not ubiquitous and may vary across ethnic minority groups. For example, Ai, Nicadao, Appel, and Lee (2015) compared the relationships between ethnic identity and diagnosis of major depressive disorder (MDD) among Chinese, Filipino, and Vietnamese American adult samples. Researchers found that higher levels of ethnic identity were related to lower likelihood of MDD among Filipino Americans and higher likelihood of MDD among Chinese Americans. Ethnic identity was unrelated to MDD in the Vietnamese sample. Though the buffering effects of ethnic identity are evident for some, such findings, along with other research (Yip, Gee, & Takeuchi, 2008), suggest that experiencing a strong sense of belonging to a native heritage can amplify the impact of culturally specific stressors (e.g., discrimination, social inequalities), thereby enhancing an individual's focus on their differences from majority culture. Past literature has found that the stage of ethnic identity development, age, and level of perceived stress can attenuate the buffering influence of high ethnic identity (see review by Burnett-Zeigler et al., 2013).

Another relevant construct implicated in the Carter et al. (1996) model is acculturation, traditionally defined as the extent to which ethnic minorities adopt the values and participate in the traditional activities of mainstream culture. Recent re-conceptualizations of the acculturation process utilize a multidimensional perspective where ethnic minorities must reconcile discrepancies in their identity (the salience of one's ethnic versus national identity), value system (individualism versus collectivism), language proficiency, cultural attitudes and knowledge, as well as cultural practices (Park & Rubin, 2012; Schwartz et al., 2013; Yoon et al., 2013).

According to a meta-analysis of 325 studies about the relationship between acculturation and mental health, Yoon et al. (2013) found that mainstream language proficiency was negatively associated with negative mental health, whereas endorsing an ethnic identity was positively related to positive mental health. Most importantly, these findings demonstrate how complex the relationship between acculturation and psychopathology can be, which emphasizes the need for mental health professionals to consider the relevance of each acculturation dimension (e.g., identity, language, value system, behaviors) when working with ethnic minorities. Furthermore, the acculturative stress of integrating disparities in ethnic and mainstream culture across these dimensions can result in difficulties adapting to mainstream culture and/or perceived rejection from one's native heritage (Schwartz et al., 2013), which has been associated with psychopathology in ethnic minority adults (e.g., more eating-disorder symptoms (Van Diest, Tartakovsky, Stachon, Pettit, & Perez, 2013) and greater levels of depression (Ai et al., 2015; Driscoll & Torres, 2013; Jaggers & MacNeil, 2015; Park & Rubin, 2012). When confronted with such cultural disparities, extant literature has identified biculturalism, or the ability for ethnic minorities to effectively integrate elements of two cultural streams, as one of the most protective acculturation statuses against negative health outcomes (Schwartz et al., 2013). For example, Wei et al. (2010) found that high levels of bicultural competence (or the ability to navigate between two groups without undermining one's cultural identity) among ethnic minority college students were protective against depressive symptoms despite experiencing high levels of minority stress.

Alternative acculturative statuses include strongly adhering to the mainstream culture and devaluing native heritage (assimilation), strongly adhering to the native heritage and devaluing the mainstream culture (separation), and exhibiting little interest in adhering to either cultural stream (marginalization; see Matsunga, Hecht, Elek, & Ndiaye, 2010; Yoon et al., 2013). Overall, the existing literature has yielded inconclusive findings clarifying the impact of acculturation on the mental health of ethnic minorities (see Concepcion, Kohatsu, & Yeh, 2013), which has been accredited to the multiple definitions of acculturation (e.g., time since immigration, language fluency, acculturation status) and examining this construct in few ethnic minority groups (Burnett-Zeigler et al., 2013; Yoon et al., 2013).

Aside from having knowledge of ethnic identity and acculturation, mental health professionals must also understand how these constructs interact to influence the psychopathology expressed in many ethnic minority individuals (Yoon et al., 2013). In referencing the Carter et al. (1996) model, African Americans who maintain a strong ethnic identity and are highly assimilated in the dominant culture are believed to endorse traditional beliefs of mainstream society (e.g., individualism) and exhibit symptom presentations consistent with the current diagnostic nomenclature. Notably, it is theorized that these individuals may feel conflicted by being acculturated to believe psychological treatment is effective while embodying a mistrust of societal systems in mainstream culture as a result of historically significant cultural experiences (e.g., perceived discrimination from individuals of the dominant culture). Similarly, Carter et al. (1996) conceptualized that African Americans low in ethnic identity yet highly assimilated will exhibit a traditional symptom presentation, but will be more willing to seek, persist through, and benefit from traditional treatment practices. In contrast, individuals high in ethnic identity who strongly de-identify with mainstream culture (separation acculturation status) represent a subset of ethnic minorities who may display unique symptom presentations and utilize culturally specific explanations for their symptoms, thereby resulting in a greater likelihood of misdiagnosed psychopathology. Further, these individuals are theorized to be less likely to seek treatment due to mistrust in and/or a limited knowledge of mental health care.

Although there is a dearth of literature devoted to examining the additive impact of ethnic identity and acculturation on adult psychopathology (Chae & Foley, 2010), several studies provide evidence supporting the broad application of the Carter et al. (1996) model across diverse ethnic minority groups. Burnett-Zeigler et al. (2013) examined the relationship among ethnic identity, acculturation, and the lifetime prevalence of mental illness and substance use in African American, Latino, and Asian samples. Results indicated that higher levels of ethnic identity, and not higher acculturation, were related to decreased lifetime prevalence of psychiatric illness and substance use for each minority group. Notably, higher acculturation (e.g., use of English language or social preference for individuals not in ethnic group) was associated with increased prevalence of depression in African Americans and Hispanics, increased bipolar diagnoses in Hispanics, and increased anxiety disorder diagnoses for all minority groups. Regarding substance use, higher acculturation was related to increased lifetime prevalence of alcohol and drug use among the Hispanic and Asian sample. These findings suggest that having a strong sense of pride and belonging to an ethnic heritage is protective; however, nondominant individuals who are unable to maintain cultural ties with their native heritage (e.g., first language, relationships with members of ethnic group) may be more susceptible to negative health outcomes.

Nascent literature has provided a more specific understanding of the interaction between these two constructs by utilizing acculturation statuses (e.g., integration, assimilation, separation) instead of a broad definition of acculturation (e.g., English literacy; time of residency). In particular, Matsunaga, Hecht, Elek, & Ndiaye (2010) examined the interaction between ethnic identity and acculturation status in Mexican-heritage adolescents living in the southwest region of the United States and found that an integration acculturation status was more prevalent than assimilation, as well as more predictive of a strong ethnic identification, which suggests that a strong ethnic identity and a successful integration of two cultures are closely associated. Furthermore, Chae and Foley (2010) found that high ethnic identity strongly predicted positive psychological well-being among Chinese, Japanese, and Korean Americans, whereas an assimilation acculturation status predicted poorer psychological well-being among Korean Americans. Also, researchers found that Asian Americans with an integration acculturation status experienced significantly higher psychological well-being compared with other acculturation statuses. Most importantly, these findings suggest that ethnic minorities who maintain a strong sense of belonging to their ethnic heritage (high ethnic identity) and who have successfully integrated the identities, value systems, and cultural practices of their native and mainstream heritages (integration) exhibit fewer clinical symptoms and more life satisfaction.

RELEVANCE OF SOCIOCULTURAL FACTORS IN ADULT PSYCHOPATHOLOGY

Although an understanding of the aforementioned constructs is essential, it is equally important to examine the impact of other sociocultural variables that also exert a considerable degree of influence over the symptom presentation and treatment outcomes of ethnic minorities. Although extant literature has identified myriad variables that impact minority mental health, the current chapter solely focuses on socioeconomic status (SES), stressful life events, and age cohort, which were each identified by the Carter et al. (1996) model as important contributors to the mental health of ethnic minorities.

Researchers propose that SES can provide a more precise understanding of the relationship between ethnicity and adult psychopathology by focusing on the specific environmental elements that characterize each social class. Past literature has shown that high SES is related to better health outcomes. One study by Shen and Takeuchi (2001), examining the relationship between acculturation, SES, and depression in Chinese Americans, found that SES was a better indicator of depressive symptoms than acculturation and that high-SES individuals (i.e., high educational attainment and increased income) had better mental health outcome (i.e., fewer depressive symptoms) compared with low-SES individuals. These findings suggest that it is through the variance in SES and related variables (e.g., perceptions of stress, social support, and physical health) that acculturation may impact the mental health of nondominant individuals (Shen & Takeuchi, 2001). By contrast, nascent literature has begun to propose that the association between social class and mental health is much more complex in that evidence has supported that low-SES and/or foreign-born individuals are not automatically guaranteed poor health outcomes (John, de Castro, Martin, Duran, & Takeuchi, 2012). Rather, it has also been shown that middle class status may be associated with higher rates of affective disorders relative to lower and high classes (Prins, Bates, Keyes, & Muntaner, 2015). Given such findings, it suggests that mental health professionals should acknowledge the detrimental as well as the protective elements of one's social class.

Also, the Carter et al. (1996) model identifies stressful life events as a contributor to the variability in the psychopathology of ethnic minorities. Though a comprehensive understanding of the multiple forms of stress (e.g., violence exposures, neighborhood context, poverty, etc) is beyond the scope of this chapter, extant literature pinpoints race/ethnic-based stress as influential to the mental health of ethnic minority individuals. In particular, Greer (2011) describes racism as "complex systems of privilege and power, which ultimately serve to threaten and/or exclude racial and ethnic minorities from access to societal resources and other civil liberties" (p. 215). As a result of such racial/ethnic injustice, many ethnic minorities are subjected to damaging race/ethnic-focused attitudinal appraisals (i.e., prejudice), race/ethnic-focused assumptions (i.e., stereotypes), and unjust treatment based upon their race/ethnicity (Greer, 2011).

Past studies have indicated that exposure to such race/ethnic-based experiences are strong indicators of mental health outcomes across diverse ethnic minority groups [e.g., discrimination was related to increased lifetime prevalence of generalized anxiety disorder in African Americans (Soto, Dawson-Andoh, & BeLue, 2011) and perceived discrimination was associated with increased anxiety, affective, substance abuse disorders among African Americans, Hispanic Americans, and Asian Americans (Chou, Asnaani, & Hofmann, 2011)]. Notably, empirical evidence suggests that perceived discrimination may be particularly salient to African American clients, given that several studies have found that African Americans endorse greater degrees of perceived discrimination in comparison to other ethnic minority groups in the United States (Cokley, Hall-Clark, & Hicks, 2011; Donovan et al., 2013). Overall, when utilizing ethnic identity and acculturation to gain insight into the culturally specific worldviews of nondominant individuals, it is imperative that mental health professionals also examine the occurrence and impact of race/ethnic-based stressors on the psychopathology of ethnic minorities.

Finally, the Carter et al. (1996) model discusses the relevance of age cohort in the manifestation of psychopathology in ethnic minorities. The evolution of the "social, economic, and political climate" in the United States has yielded diverse experiences across generations of ethnic minorities in this country, thereby impacting the meaning of ethnicity for each generation (Carter et al., 1996, p. 460). In the context of each ethnic group, there are different historical details separating each generation; however, the impact of age cohort on psychopathology remains a relevant consideration. In general, existing literature has implicated intergenerational disparities in perceived racial discrimination (Yip et al., 2008), ethnic identity (Yip et al., 2008), acculturation status (Buscemi, Williams, Tappen, & Blais, 2012), and lifetime prevalence of psychiatric illness (Breslau et al., 2006) across the adult lifespan. One study particularly relevant to this chapter's discussion of the Carter et al. (1996) model examined the protective and/or exacerbating nature of ethnic identity in the relationship between racial discrimination and psychological distress in Asian adults (Yip et al., 2008). Results indicated that ethnic identity appeared to buffer the negative impact of racial discrimination on the psychological distress for adults aged 41–50 years, yet exacerbate the effects of racial discrimination for adults aged 31–40 years and 51 and older. In an attempt to explain these findings, Yip et al. (2008) theorize that the former age cohort is more likely to have a stable lifestyle with more coping mechanisms for stress, whereas the latter age cohorts may characterize adults who are in the exploration phase of their ethnic identity, which, therefore, heightens their sensitivity to being unfairly treated on the basis of their race/ethnicity. Furthermore, the parent–child relationship is another important way that intergenerational differences can impact adult psychopathology, especially for immigrant families (Kim, 2011; Vu & Rook, 2012).

In a study examining intergenerational acculturation conflict and depressive symptoms among Korean American parents, Kim (2011) found that greater discrepancies in cultural values between parent and child (greater intergenerational conflict) were related to increased parental depressive symptoms—an association more pronounced in mothers than in fathers. It was proposed that the cultural expectations of the Korean mother (e.g., to be a "wise and benevolent" primary caregiver) was conflicted by an incongruence with the value system of mainstream culture (Kim, 2011, p. 691). Collectively, such findings provide evidence that the Carter et al. (1996) model elucidates culturally specific considerations for psychological distress among diverse ethnic minorities.

EXPRESSION/ASSESSMENT OF PSYCHOPATHOLOGY

Aside from the administration of culturally sensitive assessment tools to aid in the accurate diagnosis of psychopathology among ethnic minority patients, the current literature has implicated cultural factors endemic to ethnic groups that may influence the expression of their symptomology. The following section presents a general overview of how factors, such as stigma surrounding mental illness and perceived discrimination, impact various forms of symptom expression among non-Western and Western ethnic groups.

EXPRESSION OF PSYCHOPATHOLOGY DIFFERS ACROSS CULTURAL GROUPS

It is often unclear how symptom profiles may differ between ethnic groups when typical research studies use structured instruments, based on an *a priori* set of questions believed to exemplify the disorder under investigation. Measures based on Western notions of prototypical symptoms will fail to capture cultural differences in the expression of all disorders. Thus, variations in symptom patterns are often overlooked or misunderstood. Such misunderstandings affect how we, in turn, conceptualize even seemingly well-defined disorders. The *DSM-5* recognizes several cultural concepts of distress or mental disorders that are generally limited to specific cultural groups for certain dysfunctional and/or distressing behaviors, experiences, and observations (American Psychiatric Association, 2013).

Many culture-bound syndromes are likely unrecognized variations of common Western ailments. For example, susto is a folk illness seen in many Latin American and Native American communities that is attributed to having an extremely frightening experience. Although it is historically translated as "soul loss," a closer meaning to this may actually be loss of "vital force," as the soul is typically not thought to have actually left the body until death (Glazer, Baer, Weller, Garcia de Alba, & Liebowitz, 2004). People afflicted with susto may have symptoms that include nervousness, loss of appetite, insomnia, listlessness, despondency, involuntary muscle tics, and diarrhea. The symptoms of susto are actually quite similar to PTSD, which includes anxiety, avoidance, dissociation, jumpiness, sleep disturbances, and depression. Loss of "vital force" could resemble the fatigue and anhedonia, which may be a part of depressive symptoms within PTSD. Additionally, feeling as if one's soul has been lost may be an idiom of distress for dissociation. Therefore, the concept of susto as a culture-bound syndrome may be better conceptualized as a culture-specific description of PTSD itself.

Interestingly, Latin American folk treatments for the disorder include elements of exposure-based therapies for PTSD (e.g., Williams, Cahill, & Foa, 2010). During the treatment ritual, the individual afflicted with susto must recount their terrifying experience while lying on the axis of a crucifix on the floor. Fresh herbs are swept over the afflicted individual's body while the folk healer says a series of healing prayers (Gillette, 2013). If the first session is not effective, the process is repeated every third day until the patient is recovered. This repeated recounting process is a critical active ingredient in prolonged exposure and cognitive processing therapy, both highly effective treatments for PTSD, which likely accounts for some of the effectiveness of this folk remedy. Sugar, water, and tea may also be used to treat symptoms of chronic susto (Glazer et al., 2004), and in fact herbs used in traditional Mexican medicine have been found to possess anxiolytic effects (Herrera-Ruiz et al., 2011). In terms of conventional treatment for susto, because it is a folk illness, with roots deep in the Hispanic culture, patients may not believe they can be cured by modern methods, and therefore may be less likely to seek mental health care and less likely to believe they can be helped by Western treatments (Gillette, 2013). However, it is worth noting that effective folk remedies for susto have been available for centuries, whereas modern psychological treatments like prolonged exposure were developed relatively recently.

Another example of the connection between *DSM* disorders and culture-bound syndromes can be seen in the enigmatic ailment called koro. Though uncommon in Western cultures, koro is characterized by anxiety over the possibility of one's genitalia receding into the body, resulting in infertility or death (Chowdhury, 1990). To prevent any envisioned shrinkage or retraction of the genitals, a koro sufferer will perform certain behaviors (i.e., pulling of genitals, spiritual rituals, securing genitals to prevent retraction) intended to reduce or eliminate this risk. Obsessive-compulsive disorder (OCD) is characterized by distressing and typically implausible obsessions, with compulsions designed to reduce the anxiety caused by the obsessions. Davis, Steever, Terwilliger, and Williams (2012) note the possibility that koro is simply a form of OCD, as an alternative to the current conceptualization as a culture-bound syndrome or cultural concept of distress. The most salient feature of koro concerns the anxiety surrounding the retraction and shrinkage of genitalia. The degree to which this distress can impair the daily functioning of those with koro has marked similarities to the construct of obsessions in OCD. This, coupled with the improbability of one's genitalia actually receding into one's body for good, makes it possible to categorize this fear as an implausible obsession.

Sexual obsessions are extremely common in OCD worldwide (Williams & Steever, 2015), but these types of thoughts are considered taboo or embarrassing in most cultures. Thus, the stigma and shame attached to the experience of sexual symptoms of OCD are exceptionally distressing (Glazier, Wetterneck, Singh, & Williams, 2015). Furthermore, Bernstein and Gaw (1990) note that sexual identity questions and conflicting feelings about sexuality are common in the experience of koro. Similarly, approximately 10% of treatment-seeking OCD patients report concerns about their sexual identity as a main concern (Williams & Farris, 2011). In OCD, these worries often manifest as fears of experiencing a change in sexual orientation, which is strikingly similar to the worries reported to underlie many cases of koro. Finally, koro has been shown to respond well to behavioral psychotherapy and medications like selective serotonin reuptake inhibitors (SSRIs; Buckle, Chuah, Fones, & Wong, 2007). These same treatments have long been the preferred method of treatment for OCD and its subtypes. Thus, koro is likely simply a cultural variant of OCD.

Although listed in the *DSM-5* as a cultural concept of distress, neurasthenia, or shenjing shuairuo, is currently a recognized mental disorder in the World Health Organization's *International Classification of Diseases* (*ICD-10*) and in the *Chinese Classification of Mental Disorders*. Traditional Chinese medicine describes shenjing shuairuo as a depletion of vital energy and reduced functioning in critical internal organs. The *Chinese Classification of Mental Disorders* considers it a mental disorder that may include weakness, emotional symptoms, excitement symptoms, tension-induced pain, and sleep disturbances. Neurasthenia has been considered a somatic illness, similar to or the same as MDD, but involving culturally sanctioned idioms of distress.

Likewise, there are many conditions that may be considered Western culture-bound syndromes, due to their infrequency or absence in other cultures. These may include anorexia nervosa, substance use disorders, chronic fatigue syndrome, animal hoarding, attention deficit hyperactivity disorder, Munchhausen by proxy, premenstrual dysphoric disorder, dissociative identity disorder, and even type A personality. Many maintain that all psychiatric disorders, regardless of culture, are always culturally influenced constructs. Still others assert that the *DSM* is itself a culture-bound document and question whether it should be used at all outside its country of origin (Nadkarni & Santhouse, 2012).

Expression of Psychopathology Differs Within National Borders

It may be misleading to present cultural differences in psychopathology as an issue only applicable to those in non-Western or developing nations. The expression of psychopathology can and does differ among US ethnic groups that may be considered fairly acculturated (i.e., that share a common language and national borders).

For example, African Americans have been an integral part of American life for centuries, yet notable differences in psychopathology are nonetheless evident. An investigation of OCD in African Americans (Williams, Elstein, Buckner, Abelson, & Himle, 2012) found obsessive-compulsive concerns in five major areas, including contamination and washing, sexual obsessions and reassurance, aggression and mental compulsions, symmetry and perfectionism, and doubt and checking. These dimensions are similar to findings of studies in primarily White samples (i.e., Bloch et al., 2008). However, African Americans with OCD report more contamination symptoms and were twice as likely to report excessive concerns with animals compared with European Americans with OCD.

These notable cultural differences are consistent with findings among nonclinical samples (e.g., Thomas, Turkheimer, & Oltmanns, 2000). Williams and Turkheimer (2007) studied racial differences in OCD symptoms and found that a nonclinical sample of African Americans scored significantly higher on an animal attitude factor than European Americans, meaning they had greater concerns about animals, and it was determined that cultural factors explained this difference. It was hypothesized that the Western perspective of animals as pets is more socially acceptable among European Americans than other cultures which are more likely to regard animals as a source of food or vehicle for labor. Other cultural differences may relate to earlier practices such as the use of dogs as a means to hunt slaves or attack protesters during the Civil Rights era. This is consistent with recent work suggesting that African Americans may experience greater phobias of animals (Chapman et al., 2008). As such, cultural differences are plausible contributing factors for increased animal sensitivity among those with OCD. Fear of being misunderstood was also more frequently endorsed by African Americans with OCD (Williams et al., 2012). An obsessive need to be perfectly understood could be a unique finding for African Americans related to fears of appearing unintelligent, resulting in stereotype compensation—an intentional effort to present oneself in a counterstereotypical manner (Williams, Turkheimer, Magee, & Guterbock, 2008). Finally, one epidemiological study found that that OCD symptom severity was significantly correlated to racial discrimination but not other forms of discrimination, such as discrimination based on gender or sexual orientation.

PREVALENCE RATES MAY DIFFER FOR CULTURAL REASONS

Prevalence rates of various disorders may also differ for cultural reasons. For example, the National Survey of American Life (NSAL) conducted a comprehensive nationwide study of African American and Caribbean Blacks. They interviewed a large number of adults ($n = 5,191$) and adolescents ($n = 1,170$) in their homes, using professionally trained, ethnically matched interviewers. Their study was the first to examine the prevalence, age of onset, and gender differences in a number of mental disorders in a nationally representative Black sample (Taylor, Caldwell, Baser, Faison, & Jackson, 2007). Findings were consistent with previous research indicating that anorexia nervosa is rare among African Americans. In fact, not a single woman in the study met criteria for anorexia in the previous 12 months, and there were no reports at all of anorexia in Caribbean adults. These findings indicate that Black Americans are at lower risk of anorexia than their White counterparts. Likewise, a related study found that Hispanic and Asian American female adults experienced similarly low rates of anorexia nervosa (Franko, 2007). The authors of that study suggested that detection and barriers to treatment may be a factor in the lower rates, but there has been very little research focused on what cultural factors may differentially protect minorities from this disorder and yet promote it in European Americans.

Another way in which culture may impact psychopathology can be found in the frequencies of specific symptoms within a disorder. For example, Chapman and colleagues (Chapman et al., 2008, 2011) found that both African American college students (2008) and African American adults from the community (2011) reported more animal and social fears than did their European American counterparts. These results indicate the need for further exploration of cultural factors and their impact on psychopathology.

STIGMA AND SOMATIZATION OF DISTRESS ACROSS CULTURES

Although there is a general tendency toward somatization across all cultures, ethnic minority individuals in the United States appear more likely to express psychological distress through bodily symptoms for two primary reasons: (1) as compared with European Americans, there is a higher level of stigma associated with mental illness and, therefore, physical symptoms are more socially acceptable; and (2) there is more holistic conceptualization of the person, and, therefore, less of a distinction between mind and body among ethnic minorities (USDHHS, 2001).

For many groups there is considerable stigma attached to being afflicted by mental illness, and thus clients from these groups may be more comfortable reporting physical symptoms over affective and cognitive symptoms. One study of African Americans found that concerns about stigma prompted most mental health care consumers to initially avoid or delay treatment, and once in treatment, they commonly faced stigmatizing reactions from others (Alvidrez, Snowden, & Kaiser, 2008). Hunter and Schmidt (2010) developed a model that incorporates stigma, racism, and somatization into the expression of anxiety in African Americans. The emphasis on physical illnesses over mental illness in African American communities is thought to be related to physical explanations of somatic symptoms of anxiety, including attributing these to conditions like cardiovascular disease, and subsequent help-seeking oriented to these explanations. In particular, anxiety disorders among African Americans are likely to include both fears related to minority status and catastrophic interpretations of somatic symptoms. They propose that these differences, because of their implications for measurement and diagnosis, can explain reduced detection of certain anxiety disorders in African Americans compared with European Americans.

Western models of health and illness often depict a fragmented representation of the person to conceptualize mental and physical processes. For example the mind and body are regarded as separate (called dualism), and then the mind is even further divided in many common models (e.g., psychodynamic personality model of id, ego, and superego; cognitive behavioral therapy's affective, behavioral, and cognitive components). However, many cultures do not make a distinction between the mind and body. Additionally, many cultural traditions recognize the spirit as an integral part of the person, inseparable from the mind and body (e.g., Parham, 2002). Thus, omitting this component will reduce the salience of the treatment in such clients.

SPIRITUALITY AND RELIGION

Spirituality and religious beliefs can be the most important facets of a person's identity, and thus appreciating spiritual and religious diversity is essential to multicultural competency. In the United States, 89% of adults say they believe in God, 77% have a religious affiliation, and 53% say their beliefs are very important to their lives (Pew Research Center, 2015). When help is sought, clients typically look for someone who shares the same values. Thus, therapists will be viewed as more credible in the community if they are competent in religious/spiritual issues.

Devout or orthodox members of most religious traditions tend to have negative perceptions of the mental health professions, distrust therapists, and under-utilize mental health services. This is in part because traditionally the field of psychology has been hostile toward religion. Psychologists are more secular and less religious than the population at large, and therapists have tended to reject organized religious involvement; thus, there is a religiosity gap between mental health providers and the US majority. As a result, building trust may be challenging when working with devout clients, and, in such cases, learning about a client's religious tradition is essential to building rapport. At the very least, it is essential for therapists to avoid interventions that conflict with normative religious beliefs, and at best therapists can incorporate a client's religious practices into treatment. Therapists need to be able to understand individuals and their beliefs within their cultural context (Richards, Keller, & Smith, 2004).

Over the past few years, an uneasy truce has developed between psychology and religion. This is due in part to new research that shows the important role of religion in mental health and well-being. For example, meditation and prayer are correlated with reduced blood pressure and pulse, lower endocrine activity, and lower metabolism. Religious involvement has also been shown to buffer against emotional difficulties, such as depression and anger. Thus a variety of psychological and spiritual interventions may be appropriate with religious clients, depending on the client, the nature of the problem, and the therapist's religious knowledge.

RACISM AND DISCRIMINATION

As previously noted, the experience of being a stigmatized ethnoracial minority is a common phenomenon across cultures, with profound implications for mental health. This includes visible minorities in the United States and Canada, as well as ethnic and cultural groups in other countries, such as Blacks in the United Kingdom, Turks in Germany, and the Dalit in India. Many studies have established a link between discrimination and mental health outcomes. In the United States, African Americans experience the greatest amount of racial discrimination, followed by Asian Americans and Hispanic Americans (Chou et al., 2012). Perceived discrimination has been found to be negatively correlated with mental health, and the effects seem to be strongest (most detrimental) for Asian Americans, followed by Hispanic Americans, followed by African Americans (Cokley et al., 2011).

In addition to overall psychological distress, racism and discrimination have been associated with several specific mental health problems, including stress (Clark, Anderson, Clark, & Williams, 1999), depression (Banks & Kohn-Wood, 2007; Torres, Driscoll, & Burrow, 2010), anxiety (Hunter & Schmidt, 2010), binge drinking (Blume, Lovato, Thyken, & Denny, 2012), PTSD (Pieterse, Todd, Neville, & Carter, 2012), and psychosis (Berger & Sarnyai, 2015). A strong, positive ethnic identity has been shown to be a potential protective factor against psychopathology among minorities (e.g., Williams, Chapman, et al., 2012), except when discriminatory events are severe (Chae, Lincoln, & Jackson, 2011). Failure to understand the role of racism and discrimination limits our understanding of mental health in stigmatized people groups.

Focusing specifically on the link between racism and PTSD can help us to understand how Eurocentric models may sometimes be inadequate for identifying distress in minority populations. The criteria for a PTSD diagnosis implies that a traumatizing event must involve a threat to an individual's physical well-being. Although this description may address many forms of ethnoracially motivated traumatic events, it does not take into account how ongoing lower levels of racism that can lead to a general sense of distress and uncontrollability (Carter, 2007). These experiences, though they may not be physical in nature, attack the individual's identity and force the person to re-experience traumas associated with their culture's history (Helms, Nicholas, & Green, 2010).

Previous editions of the *DSM* recognized racism as trauma only when an individual met criteria for PTSD in relation to a discrete racist event. This is problematic given that many minorities experience cumulative experiences of racism as traumatic, with a discrete event acting as "the last straw," triggering trauma reactions (Carter, 2007). Thus, current conceptualizations of trauma as a discrete horrific event may be limiting for minorities. Recent changes to the *DSM* may open the door for wider recognition of racism-related trauma. It is now within criteria that a person can have PTSD from learning about a traumatic event involving a close friend or family member, or if a person is repeatedly exposed to details about trauma (APA, 2013). This could encompass trauma resulting from ongoing racial stressors (Malcoun, Williams, & Bahojb Nouri, 2014).

Moreover, existing PTSD measures aimed at identifying an index trauma fail to include racism among listed choice response options, leaving such events to be reported as "other" or made to fit into an existing category that may not fully capture the nature of the trauma (e.g., physical assault). This can be problematic since minorities may be reluctant to report experiences of racism to European American therapists (Carter, 2007), who comprise the majority of mental health clinicians in the United States. Minority clients also may not link current PTSD symptoms to a single experience of racism if their symptoms relate to cumulative experiences of discrimination.

Bryant-Davis and Ocampo (2005) noted the similar courses of psychopathology between rape victims and victims of racism. Similar to rape victims, race-related trauma victims may respond with dissociation or shock, which can prevent them from responding to the incident in a functional manner. Victims may then feel shame and self-blame because they were unable to respond or defend themselves, which may lead to self-blame or self-destructive behaviors (Bryant-Davis & Ocampo, 2005). In the same investigation, a parallel was drawn between race-related trauma victims and victims of domestic violence. In both situations, survivors may feel shame over allowing themselves to be victimized.

LANGUAGE AND SYMPTOM EXPRESSION

Another influence on symptom expression is the language used by clinician and client. For example, Diaz et al. (2009) examined the influence of language in the diagnosis of major mental disorders. A total of 259 bilingual Latino, monolingual English-speaking Latino, and European American adults with a history of MDD or psychotic symptoms were compared using structured interviews. Compared with European Americans and mono-lingual English-speaking Latinos, bilingual Latinos had significantly higher rates of diagnosed MDD and significantly lower levels of mania. No significant differences were found between monolingual English-speaking Latinos and European Americans. Between the three study groups, there was no significant difference in level of functioning, psychotic symptoms, or severity of depression. The authors concluded that the diagnostic process is affected by the combination of culture and language, notably being bilingual English/Spanish speaking. Thus, there appears to be an important effect of language on the report and diagnosis of psychopathology (Malgady & Constantino, 1998).

TREATMENT ISSUES

As the US continues to diversify, the understanding of the role of culture, race, and ethnicity in treatment remains paramount and is essential to culturally proficient work with ethnic minority patients. In the following section, a discussion of how such factors can influence various domains of the treatment process (e.g., therapeutic alliance, clinical judgments, and client perspectives) is presented. It is worth noting that the following treatment considerations are not comprehensive, but rather a general overview of how acknowledging the impact of certain cultural factors when working with ethnic minority patients can enhance the efficiency and effectiveness of treatment.

CLINICIAN AND CLIENT INTERPLAY

As noted in the previous edition, ethnic minority clients report feeling more comfortable discussing psychological problems with someone of the same ethnoracial background (for review, see Chapman, DeLapp, & Williams, 2014; Jackson et al., 2004), and they may answer questions about symptoms differently when this match is present (e.g., Williams & Turkheimer, 2008). Ethnic minority clients may perceive their counseling experience to be more effective when they are ethnoracially matched (Lee, Sutton, France, & Uhlemann, 1983), and non-Hispanic White clients may feel more comfortable with someone of the same ethnoracial group (Davis, Williams, & Chapman, 2011). Matching has been shown to strengthen the therapeutic alliance and improve retention (Flicker et al., 2008). However, cultural matching is not always possible due to a lack of availability of a clinician of the same ethnicity as the client, and it may not be desirable from the client's perspective (e.g., could be perceived as "forced segregation"; Pole, Gone, & Kulkarni, 2008). Moreover, cross-cultural understanding of the client–therapist relationship may be enhanced by examining dynamics and issues surrounding race. Thus cross-cultural training is essential for all clinicians (Miller et al., 2015).

Cultural traditions vary in relation to the manner in which clinicians are regarded. Many consider therapists as authority figures and will feel uncomfortable challenging or disagreeing with their clinician. For example, when a Japanese client enters a consulting room, it is common for the client to just sit very tensely in front of the therapist and calmly answer questions. Japanese clients typically want to perform ideally, and this is reflected in therapist–client relationship. Clients tell the therapist their issues, and then just wait for the therapist to analyze them. Clients expect the therapist to tell them what to do. From a Western viewpoint, this can be seen as dependent, but it is actually a way for Japanese people to show respect by giving power to those in authority. Non-Hispanic White therapists can find it difficult to work with Japanese clients if the therapist is not aware of the power dynamics within the Japanese culture. When the Japanese utilize psycho-therapy services, they generally apply Japanese methods of forming relationships, creating a hierarchical relationship between client and therapist. A Japanese client was assessed by a Western therapist without this understanding and the therapist believed the client had no sense of self, describing the client as passive, needy, and repressed. Japanese clients sometimes appear helpless and this might be misinterpreted as playing a victim role. However, from the client's view, it is considered culturally appropriate (Nipoda, 2002). This example also illustrates how cultures differ in terms of what they consider to be the role of the therapist or healer. For example, within the Afrocentric framework, the essence of all things is spiritual. The spirit is energy and life force in each person, which constitutes a self-healing power. Thus, therapy becomes a process or vehicle in which individuals are helped to access their own self-healing power (Parham, 2002).

ROLE OF STEREOTYPES, BIASES, AND THE CLINICIAN'S CULTURE

Although most clinicians are now receiving some multicultural education in their training programs (Green, Callands, Radcliffe, Luebbe, & Klonoff, 2009), practical skills for working with members of specific minority groups are often not included. When clinicians and researchers lack the needed skills and education for effective cross-cultural interactions, they may rely on a *color-blind approach*. Color-blindness is the ideology that different ethnoracial groups should all be treated the same, without regard to cultural differences (Terwilliger, Bach, Bryan, & Williams, 2013). Minorities are often treated as if they lack characteristics that make them different from the dominant majority. Although the intent of color-blindness is to promote fairness, it often causes confusion and can paradoxically increase prejudice (e.g., Richeson & Nussbaum, 2004). When the idea of "treating everyone the same" is proposed, it is typically from the perspective of the dominant majority, implying that clients should be treated as if they were culturally non-Hispanic Whites (Terwilliger et al., 2013).

From a clinical standpoint, color-blindness could result in negative consequences for an ethnic minority client if a therapist were to suggest that the client engage in behaviors that are generally considered adaptive within European American psychological tradi-tion but which may in fact be culturally incongruent outside of that tradition. For example, a therapist may encourage an adult client to move out of the parents' home and find his or her own apartment to assert autonomy. But in more collectivistic cultures, it may be abnormal for unmarried children to move out. Thus such an event could potentially result in a family crisis, conflict, and loss of needed emotional support. The goal, therefore, is not to treat participants as if they were European American, but as they should be treated based on the norms and customs of their particular culture. This approach, called *multiculturalism*, embraces the differences, strengths, and uniqueness of each cultural group (Terwilliger et al., 2013; Williams, Tellawi, Wetterneck, & Chapman, 2013).

Another issue of which clinicians must be aware concerns preconceived notions about clients based solely on ethnic group membership, or pathological stereotypes (Williams, Gooden, & Davis, 2012). These are generalizations about people used as a means of explaining and justifying differences between groups and thereby using these differences to oppress the "out-group." Social status or group position determines the content of stereotypes, and not actual personal characteristics of group members (Jost & Banaji, 1994). Groups that have fewer social and economic advantages will be stereotyped in a way that seemingly explains disparities, such as lower employment or higher illiteracy rates. Although disadvantaged group members may have greater difficulty finding a job due to in-group favoritism, discrimination, and institutional racism, the disadvantaged group member is characterized as unmotivated (could have found a job if he looked hard enough), unintelligent (not smart enough to have that job), lazy (would rather take handouts than work), and criminal (will steal rather than work) (Williams, Gooden, & Davis, 2012).

It is important to understand that pathological stereotypes about cultural groups are unfair and inaccurate. Furthermore, all members of a society are affected by the negative social messages that espouse these stereotypes, casting disadvantaged groups in a negative light (Devine & Elliott, 1995). When we uncritically accept these negative messages, racism follows, even from professionals who mean well. This can lead to harmful, discriminatory behaviors toward clients, which may be conscious or unconscious, and overt or covert.

Perhaps the most common act of discrimination by clinicians is what is termed as a *microaggression* (Sue et al., 2007). A microaggression is a brief, everyday exchange that sends denigrating messages to a target simply because they belong to a racial minority group. Microaggressions are often unconsciously delivered in the form of slights or subtle dismissive behaviors. The target of a microaggression is often forced to ascertain whether another individual did in fact, perpetrate a discriminatory act. This attributional ambiguity is inherently stressful and is different from an overt discriminatory act, which is more easily identified and explained. As such, the influence of racial microaggressions on stress and anxiety may lie in the uncertainty generated from such interactions (Torres, Driscoll, & Burrow, 2010). One study found that racial microaggressions directed against African American clients was predictive of a weaker therapeutic alliance with White therapists. This, in turn, predicted lower ratings of general competence and multicultural counseling competence, and, unsurprisingly, lower counseling satisfaction ratings. Racial microaggressions had a significant indirect effect on client ratings of the counseling competence of White counselors through the therapeutic working alliance (Constantine, 2007).

It is important to understand that microaggressions can be particularly harmful to vulnerable clients, who may already feel stigmatized and exposed even attempting therapy. Minority clients may find it difficult to respond to such remarks in counseling situations due to self-doubt and power dynamics. These problems contribute to feelings of distance from the therapist, unwillingness to disclose sensitive information, and early termination from treatment. Thus, clients may be unable to overcome the condition for which they sought help due to undesirable therapist factors. The degree of harm therapists may cause in this manner is unknown and likely underestimated (Constantine, 2007).

Culture as an Integral Part of Assessment

Americans are socialized not to acknowledge race and ethnicity, due in part to concerns of appearing biased or racist (Gaertner & Dovidio, 2005). However, this avoidance contributes to difficulty in recognizing, discussing, and adapting to cultural differences (Terwilliger et al., 2013). Many European American therapists are uncomfortable discussing race in cross-racial therapeutic dyads (Knox et al., 2003). However, therapists actually have more success working cross-culturally when they address differences directly. Raising the issue of race early in the therapeutic relationship conveys cultural sensitivity and may address clients' concerns about a racially different counselor. When counselors communicate their own cultural background and acknowledge their client's cultural values, clients are more likely to see their counselor as credible and feel more relaxed in therapy (Owen, Tao, Leach, & Rodolfa, 2011). Culturally competent counselors are aware of how their own cultural backgrounds and experiences influence their attitudes and values surrounding psychological processes, and this recognition enables them to better access the client's needs (Delsignore et al., 2010).

Thus, it is important that clinicians understand culture-specific differences, which can range from amount of eye contact to specific idioms of psychological distress. Mental health professionals must make culture an integral part of each assessment, as it influences patterns of communication between clinician and patient and subsequent diagnostic and treatment outcomes (Alarcón et al., 2009). There are too many different groups for any one person to have an in-depth understanding of all, so clinicians should at least receive training specific to the ethnoracial groups most commonly served, and seek additional information and consultation when confronted with clients from completely foreign cultures.

In its ongoing effort to more widely recognize cultural context, the *DSM-5* now includes a cultural formulation interview guide designed to help clinicians assess cultural factors influencing client perspectives on their symptoms and treatment options. It includes questions about client background in terms of culture, race, ethnicity, religion and geographical origin. The interview facilitates the process for individuals to describe distress in their own words and then relate this to how others, who may not share their culture, see their difficulties. This gives the clinician a more comprehensive basis for diagnosis and care, and may be a good starting point for those clinicians working with ethnically different clients.

MISTRUST OF MEDICAL INSTITUTIONS AND ESTABLISHMENT

According to the US Surgeon General, "research documents that many members of minority groups fear, or feel ill at ease, with the mental health system" (NIH, 1999). African Americans have greater distrust of the medical establishment and mental health care, many believing that medical institutions hold racist attitudes (Gamble, 1993; Whaley, 2001). Negative perceptions may be rooted in historical abuses of slaves, who were often used to test and perfect medical procedures before they were attempted on Whites (Gamble, 1997).

The most well-known example of such abuses is The Tuskegee Study of Untreated Syphilis in the African American Male. This is the longest nontherapeutic experiment on human beings in medical history. Begun in 1932 by the United States Public Health Service (USPHS), the study was designed to determine the natural course of untreated syphilis in 400 African American men in Tuskegee, Alabama. The research subjects, who had syphilis when they were enrolled in the study, were matched against 200 uninfected subjects who served as controls (Heintzelman, 2003).

The subjects were recruited with misleading promises of "special free treatment," which were actually spinal taps done without anesthesia to study the neurological effects of syphilis, and they were enrolled without informed consent. The subjects were denied antibiotic therapy when it became clear in the 1940s that peni[treatment for the disease. On several occasions, the USPHS actual subjects from obtaining treatment elsewhere (Heintzelman, 200[

In many cases, the infected subjects passed the disease to their newborn babies. Over 100 people, died directly from advanced syp[an investigatory panel found the study was ethically unjustified and that peni[should have been provided. The National Research Act, passed in 1974, mandated that all federally funded proposed research with human subjects be approved by an institutional review board (IRB). By 1992, settlement payments of approximately $40,000 were made to survivors. President Clinton publicly apologized on behalf of the federal government to the handful of study survivors in April 1997 (Heintzelman, 2003).

Many African Americans see the Tuskegee Study as representative of much current medical research even today (Freimuth et al., 2001). For instance, one study examined attitudes toward biomedical research across four ethnically diverse adults samples and found that African Americans endorsed more fear of participation in research than non-Hispanic White adults, which suggests that a cultural mistrust of research remains salient among African Americans (Katz et al., 2006). Most importantly, in cases where ethnic minorities appear hesitant or distrusting of mental health care, it is important for mental health professionals to remember the historical significance of a cultural mistrust in health care systems. Cultural knowledge of institutional abuses, combined with regular experiences of racism, maintains cultural mistrust surrounding health care.

LACK OF AWARENESS CAN RESULT IN MISDIAGNOSIS

Evidence shows that minorities are often misdiagnosed, due to the factors described previously. These include:

- Misuse of assessment instruments that are considered to be "gold standards."
- Diagnostic criteria based on Eurocentric observations and conceptualizations, resulting in missed or misunderstood symptoms.
- Research findings based on Eurocentric diagnostic criteria, providing less helpful information about psychopathology in non-White populations.
- Lack of adequate multicultural training for clinicians, often resulting in a problematic color-blind approach.
- Pathological stereotypes about members of specific cultural groups that affect clinician judgments.
- Poor therapeutic working alliance due to lack of cultural awareness and micro-aggressions against clients.

These problems are not simply academic, but result in substandard care, inappropriate treatments, and premature termination from treatment. In particular, African Americans are more often given the diagnosis of paranoid schizophrenia than non-Hispanic Whites with similar symptoms (Snowden & Pingitore, 2002). This could be due in part to misinterpretation by clinicians of "healthy cultural paranoia"—a defensive posture taken by African Americans when approaching a new situation that could involve racism or discrimination (Whaley, 2001). This paranoia is not completely unfounded given the reality of discrimination and racial tensions in the United States. Additionally, African Americans are more likely to be admitted as inpatients, even after controlling for severity of illness and demographic variables (Snowden, Hastings, & Alvidrez, 2009).

or Hispanic Americans the research results are mixed. Chui (1996) finds that spanics receive a diagnosis of schizophrenia less often than African Americans and non-Hispanic Whites, but they more often receive diagnoses of other mental illnesses. Solomon (1992) reports that more Puerto Ricans are diagnosed as schizophrenic than any other group, including other Hispanics. This could be due to the intersection of race and ethnicity, as many Puerto Ricans are both Black and Hispanic. Furthermore, when minorities are diagnosed with psychotic or affective disorders the conditions are more likely to be considered chronic rather than acute when compared with European Americans with the same diagnoses.

Likewise, assessments of dangerousness and potential for violence are overestimated for African American inpatients, in accordance with violent and criminal stereotypes (Good, 1996; Wood, Garb, Lilienfeld, & Nezworski, 2002). One result of this bias is the overmedication of Black psychiatric patients (Wood et al., 2002). This is compounded by the fact that African Americans, like many other ethnic minorities, metabolize anti-depressants and antipsychotic medications more slowly than Whites and may be more sensitive to the medications. This higher sensitivity is manifested in a faster and higher rate of response and more severe side-effects, including delirium, when treated with doses commonly used for White patients (Munoz & Hilgenberg, 2006). Thus, African Americans may exhibit poorer medication compliance, which then may be misinterpreted as resistance to treatment.

Interestingly, Hispanic Americans are less likely to be medicated at all (Hodgkin, Volpe-Vartanian, & Alegria, 2007). Aside from limited health care access among Latino populations (Perez-Escamilla, 2010), another potential explanation could be a lack of adherence to medication throughout the course of mental illness (Hodgkin et al., 2007; Colby, Wang, Chhabra, & Pérez-Escamilla, 2012). In particular, Hodgkin et al. (2007) utilized data from the NLAAS and found that 18.9% of Hispanic Americans who discontinued antidepressant medication decided to do so without consulting a health professional. Researchers noted that proficiency in the English language, older age, being married, having insurance, and consistent visits to see a therapist were related to better antidepressant adherence in this sample.

African Americans are diagnosed less accurately than non-Hispanic Whites when they are suffering from depression and seen in primary care (Borowsky et al., 2000), or when they are seen for psychiatric evaluation in an emergency room (Strakowski et al., 1997). One study found that African Americans were less likely than Whites to receive an antidepressant when their depression was first diagnosed (27% vs. 44%), and among those who did receive antidepressant medications, African Americans were less likely to receive the newer SSRI medications than were the White patients (Melfi, Croghan, & Hanna, 2000).

In terms of substance abuse, 15% of the general population will abuse a substance in their lifetime and 4% will abuse a substance within 12 months (Kessler et al., 2005a; Kessler et al., 2005b). Negative social stereotypes dictate that drug users are largely Black and Hispanic. Most people are surprised to learn that African American youth are significantly less likely to use tobacco, alcohol or drugs than non-Hispanic Whites or Hispanic Americans (Centers for Disease Control, 2000). In fact, African Americans spend 25% less than Whites on alcohol (U.S. Department of Labor, 2002). The National Longitudinal Alcohol Epidemiological Survey (1996) indicated that Whites were more likely to use drugs over the lifetime but Blacks were more dependent than Whites, underscoring differential access to effective treatments (Grant, 1996). Blacks and Whites tend to abuse different drugs (e.g. crack vs. cocaine), and the drugs used by African Americans carry harsher penalties and are more likely to be the targets of law enforcement efforts (e.g., Beckett, Nyrop, & Pfingst, 2006). Thus, institutionalized racism may play a role in drug abuse outcomes and access to treatment.

CONCLUSIONS

This chapter represents a charge to mental health professionals to fully consider and subsequently integrate racial, ethnic, and cultural variables into the assessment and treatment of ethnic minority individuals. The importance of such integration undoubtedly has a profound impact on several areas, including but not limited to the following: assessment, expression of psychopathology, diagnostic practices, mental health disparities, treatment outcome studies, continued dearth of ethnic minorities involved in research studies, and a continued paucity of researchers and practitioners of color. Explicit acknowledgment of inherent biases that we all possess and an understanding of the importance of incorporating cultural variables throughout *all* portions of our work with ethnic minority populations are important first steps to decreasing mental health disparities. Additionally, we continue to underscore the importance of reviewing the empirical literature as it pertains to ethnic minority populations since "all measures are *not* created equal." Moreover, there continues to be a disconnect between much of our scientific training with regard to making decisions about assessment measures, how psychopathology is expressed in many ethnic minority individuals, which often deviates from "traditional" expressions, and our subsequent implementation of treatment. Spiritual identity is also essential to many ethnic minority individuals, and incorporating such variables into both the assessment and treatment process is essential. We are additionally emphasizing the importance of respecting (and sometimes incorporating when agreed upon by the client) and seeking assistance from traditional healers or spiritual elders into the treatment process.

Although significant strides have been made in the more recent empirical literature endemic to ethnic minority individuals, we as mental health professionals have to be increasingly cognizant of integrating identified cultural factors throughout all facets of our own work and in training the next generation. Ethnoracial minorities are currently 36.6% of the US population, and 50.4% of all births (U.S. Census Bureau, 2011, 2012), with non-Hispanic Whites projected to be a minority in the United States by 2050 (Nagayama Hall, 2001). Thus, much of the work that we have highlighted is vitally important to our cultural competence in the 21st century.

REFERENCES

Ai, A. L., Nicdao, E. G., Appel, H. B., & Lee, D. H. J. (2015). Ethnic identity and major depression in Asian American subgroups nationwide: Differential findings in relation to subcultural contexts. *Journal of Clinical Psychology, 71*(12), 1225–1244.

Alarcón, R. D., Becker, A. E., Lewis-Fernández, R., Like, R. C., Desai, P., Foulks, E., . . . Cultural Psychiatry Committee of the Group for the Advancement of Psychiatry. (2009). Issues for *DSM-V*: The role of culture in diagnosis. *Journal of Nervous and Mental Disease, 197*(8), 559–560.

Alegria, M., Mulvaney-Day, N., Woo, M., Torres, M., Gao, S., & Oddo, V. (2007). Correlates of past-year mental health service use among Latinos: Results from the National Latino and Asian American study. *American Journal of Public Health, 97*(1), 76–83.

Alvidrez, J., Snowden, L. R., & Kaiser, D. M. (2008). The experience of stigma among Black mental health consumers. *Journal of Health Care for the Poor and Underserved, 19*(3), 874–893.

American Psychiatric Association. (2000). *Diagnostic and statistical manual of mental disorders* (4th ed., text rev.). Washington, DC: Author.

American Psychiatric Association (2013). *Diagnostic and statistical manual of mental disorders*. (5th ed.). Arlington, VA: American Psychiatric Publishing.

Banks, K., & Kohn-Wood, L. P. (2007). The influence of racial identity profiles on the relationship between racial discrimination and depressive symptoms. *Journal of Black Psychology, 33*(3), 331–354.

Beckett, K., Nyrop, K., & Pfingst, L. (2006). Race, drugs, and policing: Understanding disparities in drug delivery arrests. *Criminology, 44*(1), 105–137.

Berger, M., & Sarnyai, Z. (2015). 'More than skin deep': Stress neurobiology and mental health consequences of racial discrimination. *Stress: The International Journal on the Biology of Stress, 18*(1), 1–10.

Bernstein, R. L., & Gaw, A. C. (1990). Koro: Proposed classification for DSM-IV. *American Journal of Psychiatry, 147*(12), 1670–1674.

Bloch, M. H., Landeros-Weisenberger, A., Sen, S., Dombrowski, P., Kelmendi, B., Coric, V., . . . Leckman, J. F. (2008). Association of the serotonin transporter polymorphism and obsessive-compulsive disorder: Systematic review. *American Journal of Medical Genetics Part B: Neuro-psychiatric Genetics, 147*(6), 850–858.

Blume, A. W., Lovato, L. V., Thyken, B. N., & Denny, N. (2012). The relationship of micro-aggressions with alcohol use and anxiety among ethnic minority college students in a histori-cally White institution. *Cultural Diversity and Ethnic Minority Psychology, 18*(1), 45–54.

Borowsky, S. J., Rubenstein, L. V., Meredith, L. S., Camp, P., Jackson-Triche, M., & Wells, K. B. (2000). Who is at risk of nondetection of mental health problems in primary care? *Journal of General Internal Medicine, 15*(6), 381–388.

Bradby, H. (2012). Race, ethnicity and health: The costs and benefits of conceptualizing racism and ethnicity. *Social Science & Medicine, 75*, 955–958.

Breslau, J., Aguilar-Gaxiola, S., Kendler, K. S., Su, M., Williams, D., & Kessler, R. C. (2006). Specifying race-ethnic differences in risk for psychiatric disorder in a U.S. National Sample. *Psychological Medicine, 36*(1), 57–68.

Bryant-Davis, T., & Ocampo, C. (2005). Racist incident–based trauma. *The Counseling Psychologist, 33*(4), 479–500.

Buckle, C., Chuah, Y., Fones, C & Wong, A. (2007). A conceptual history of koro. *Transcultural Psychiatry, 44*(1), 27–43.

Burnett-Zeigler, I., Bohnert, K. M., & Ilgen, M. A. (2013). Ethnic identity, acculturation and the prevalence of lifetime psychiatric disorders among Black, Hispanic, and Asian adults in the U.S. *Journal of Psychiatric Research, 47*, 56–63.

Buscemi, C. P., Williams, C., Tappen, R. M., & Blais, K. (2012). Acculturation and health status among Hispanic American elders. *Journal of Transcultural Nursing, 23*(3), 229–236.

Carter, R. T. (2007). Racism and psychological and emotional injury: recognizing and assessing race-based traumatic stress. *The Counseling Psychologist, 35*(1), 13–105.

Carter, M. M., Sbrocco, T. & Carter, C. (1996). African Americans and anxiety disorders research: Development of a testable theoretical framework. *Psychotherapy, 33*(3), 449–463.

Centers for Disease Control (2000). Youth risk behavior surveillance, United States, 1999. *Mortality and Morbidity Weekly Report: Surveillance Summaries, 49*(SS05), 1–96.

Chae, M. H., & Foley, P. F. (2010). Relationship of ethnic identity, acculturation, and psychological well-being among Chinese, Japanese, and Korean Americans. *Journal of Counseling & Develop-ment, 88*, 466–476.

Chae, D. H., Lincoln, K. D., & Jackson, J. S. (2011). Discrimination, attribution, and racial group identification: Implications for psychological distress among Black Americans in the National Survey of American Life (2001–2003). *American Journal of Orthopsychiatry, 81*(4), 498–506.

Chapman, L. K., Delapp, R. C. T., & Williams, M. T. (2014). Impact of race, ethnicity, and culture on the expression and assessment of psychopathology. In Beidel, D. C., Frueh, B. C., & Hersen, M. (Eds.), *Adult psychopathology and diagnosis* (7th ed., pp. 131–162). Hoboken, NJ: Wiley.

Chapman, L. K., Vines, L., & Petrie, J. (2011). Fear factors: Cross validation of specific phobia domains in a community-based sample of African American adults. *Journal of Anxiety Disorders*, 25(4), 539–544.

Chapman, L. K., Kertz, S. J., Zurlage, M., & Woodruff-Borden, J. (2008). A confirmatory factor analysis of specific phobia domains in African American and Caucasian American young adults. *Journal of Anxiety Disorders*, 22(5), 763–771.

Chavez-Korell, S., Benson-Flórez, G., Rendón, A. D., & Farías, R. (2014). Examining the relationships between physical functioning, ethnic identity, acculturation, familismo, and depressive symptoms for Latino older adults. *The Counseling Psychologist*, 42(2), 255–277.

Chou, T., Asnaani, A., & Hofmann, S. G. (2012). Perception of racial discrimination and psychopathology across three U.S. ethnic minority groups. *Cultural Diversity and Ethnic Minority Psychology*, 18(1), 74–81.

Chowdhury, A. N. (1990). Trait anxiety profile of koro patients. *Indian Journal of Psychiatry*, 32(4), 330.

Chui, T. L. (1996). Problems caused for mental health professionals worldwide by increasing multicultural populations and proposed solutions. *Journal of Multicultural Counseling & Development*, 24, 129–140.

Clark, R., Anderson, N. B., Clark, V. R., & Williams, D. R. (1999). Racism as a stressor for African Americans: A biopsychosocial model. *American Psychologist*, 54(10), 805–816.

Cokley, K., Hall-Clark, B., & Hicks, D. (2011). Ethnic minority-majority status and mental health: The mediating role of perceived discrimination. *Journal of Mental Health Counseling*, 33(3), 243–263.

Colby, J. A., Wang, F., Chhabra, J., & Pérez-Escamilla, R. (2012). Predictors of medication adherence in an urban Latino community with healthcare disparities. *Journal of Immigrant and Minority Health*, 14(4), 589–595.

Concepcion, W. R., Kohatsu, E. L., & Yeh, C. J. (2013). Using racial identity and acculturation to analyze experiences of racism among Asian Americans. *Asian American Journal of Psychology*, 4(2), 136–142.

Constantine, M. G. (2007). Racial microaggressions against African American clients in cross-racial counseling relationships. *Journal of Counseling Psychology*, 54(1), 1–16.

Cross, W. E. (1978). The Thomas and Cross models of psychological nigrescence: A review. *Journal of Black Psychology*, 5(1), 13–31.

Cross, W. J., & Vandiver, B. J. (2001). Nigrescence theory and measurement: Introducing the Cross Racial Identity Scale (CRIS). In J. G. Ponterotto, J. M. Casas, L. A. Suzuki, C. M. Alexander, J. G. Ponterotto, J. M. Casas, . . . C. M. Alexander (Eds.), *Handbook of multicultural counseling* (2nd ed., pp. 371–393). Thousand Oaks, CA, US: Sage Publications, Inc.

Davis, D. M., Williams, M. T., Chapman, L. K. (2011). Anxiety and affect in racially unmatched dyads: Implications for a therapeutic relationship. Poster presented for the *45th Annual Convention of the Association of Behavioral and Cognitive Therapies*, Toronto, ON, November 10–13, 2011.

Davis, D., Steever, A., Terwilliger, J. M., & Williams, M. T. (2012). The relationship between the culture-bound syndrome koro and obsessive-compulsive disorder. In G. R. Hayes & M. H. Bryant (Eds.), *Psychology of culture* (pp. 213–221). Hauppauge, NY: Nova Science Publishers.

Delsignore, A. M., Petrova, E., Harper, A., Stowe, A. M., Mu'Min, A. S., & Middleton, R. A. (2010). Critical incidents and assistance-seeking behaviors of White mental health practitioners: A transtheoretical framework for understanding multicultural counseling competency. *Cultural Diversity and Ethnic Minority Psychology*, 16(3), 352.

Devine, P. G. & Elliot, A. J. (1995). Are racial stereotypes really fading? The Princeton trilogy revisited. *Personality and Social Psychology Bulletin*, 21(11), 1139–1150.

Diaz, E., Miskemen, T., Vega, W. A., Gara, M., Wilson, D. R., Lesser, I., . . . Starkowski, S. (2009). Inconsistencies in diagnosis and symptoms among bilingual and English-speaking Latinos and Euro-Americans. *Psychiatric Services*, 60(10), 1379–1382.

Donovan, R. A., Huynh, Q., Park, I. K., Kim, S. Y., Lee, R. M., & Robertson, E. (2013). Relationships among identity, perceived discrimination, and depressive symptoms in eight ethnic-generational groups. *Journal of Clinical Psychology*, 69(4), 397–414.

Driscoll, M. W., & Torres, L. (2013). Acculturative stress and Latino depression: The mediating role of behavioral and cognitive resources. *Cultural Diversity and Ethnic Minority Psychology*, 1–10.

Fabrega, H., Mulsant, B. M., Rifai, A. H., Sweet, R. A., Pasternak, R., Ulrich, R., & Zubenko, G. S. (1994). Ethnicity and Psychopathology in an Aging Hospital-Based Population: Comparison of African-American and Anglo-European Patients. *Journal of Nervous and Mental Disease*, 182(3), 136–144.

Flicker, S., Waldron, H., Turner, C., Brody, J., & Hops, H. (2008). Ethnic matching and treatment outcome with Hispanic and Anglo substance-abusing adolescents in family therapy. *Journal of Family Psychology*, 22(3), 439–447.

Franko, D. L. (2007). Race, ethnicity, and eating disorders: Considerations for *DSM-V*. *International Journal of Eating Disorders*, 40, S31–S34.

Freimuth, V. S., Quinn, S. C., Thomas, S. B., Cole, G., Zook, E., & Duncan, T. (2001). African Americans' views on research and the Tuskegee Syphilis Study. *Social Science & Medicine*, 52(5), 797–808.

Gaertner, S. L., & Dovidio, J. F. (2005). Understanding and addressing contemporary racism: From aversive racism to the common ingroup identity model. *Journal of Social Issues*, 61(3), 615–639.

Gamble, V. N. (1993). A legacy of distrust: African Americans and medical research. *American Journal of Preventive Medicine*, 9 (6 Suppl.): 35–38.

Gamble, V. N. (1997). Under the shadow of Tuskegee: African Americans and health care. *American Journal of Public Health*, 87(11), 1773–1778.

Gara, M. A., Vega, W. A., Arndt, S., Escamilla, M., Fleck, D. E., Lawson, W. B., . . . Strakowski, S. M. (2012). Influence of patient race and ethnicity on clinical assessment in patients with affective disorders. *Journal of American Medical Association*, 69(6), 593–600.

Gillette, H. The science behind "Susto"—a Latin American folk illness. Saludify. June 6, 2013. Retrieved from https://newstaco.com/2013/06/07/the-science-behind-susto/

Glazer, M., Baer, R. D., Weller, S. C., Garcia, de Alba, J. E. G., & Liebowitz, S. W. (2004). Susto and soul loss in Mexicans and Mexican Americans. *Cross-Cultural Research*, 38(3), 270–288.

Glazier, K., Wetterneck, C. T., Singh, S., & Williams, M. T. (2015). Stigma and shame as barriers to treatment in obsessive-compulsive and related disorders. *Journal of Depression and Anxiety*, 4(3), 191.

Good, B. J. (1996). Culture and *DSM-IV*: Diagnosis, knowledge and power. *Culture, Medicine and Psychiatry*, 20, 127–132.

Grant, B. F. (1996). Prevalence and correlates of drug use and DSM-IV drug dependence in the United States: results of the National Longitudinal Alcohol Epidemiologic Survey. *Journal of Substance Abuse*, 8(2), 195–210.

Green, D., Callands, T. A., Radcliffe, A. M., Luebbe, A. M., & Klonoff, E. A. (2009). Clinical psychology students' perceptions of diversity training: a study of exposure and satisfaction. *Journal of Clinical Psychology*, 65(10), 1056–1070.

Greer, T. M. (2011). Coping strategies as moderators of the relation between individual race-related stress and mental health symptoms for African American women. *Psychology of Women Quarterly*, 35(2), 215–226.

Heintzelman, C. A. (2003). The Tuskegee Syphilis Study and its implications for the 21st century. *The New Social Worker*, 10 (4).

Helms, J. E., Nicholas, G., & Green, C. E. (2012). Racism and ethnoviolence as trauma: Enhancing professional and research training. *Traumatology*, 18, 65–74.

Herrera-Ruiz, M., González-Carranza, A., Zamilpa, A., Jiménez-Ferrer, E., Huerta-Reyes, M., & Navarro-García, V. M. (2011). The standardized extract of Loeselia mexicana possesses anxiolytic activity through the y-amino butyric acid mechanism. *Journal of Ethnopharmacology, 138*(2), 261–267.

Himle, J. A., Baser, R. E., Taylor, R. J., Campbell, R. D., & Jackson, J. S. (2009). Anxiety disorders among African Americans, Blacks of Caribbean descent, and non-Hispanic Whites in the United States. *Journal of Anxiety Disorders, 23*(5), 578–590.

Hodgkin, D., Volpe-Vartanian, J., & Alegría, M. (2007). Discontinuation of antidepressant medication among Latinos in the USA. *Journal of Behavioral Health Services & Research, 34* (3), 329–342.

Hunter, L. R., & Schmidt, N. B. (2010). Anxiety psychopathology in African American adults: Literature review and development of an empirically informed sociocultural model. *Psychological Bulletin, 2010, 136*(2), 211–235.

Jackson, J. S., Torres, M., Caldwell, C. H., Neighbors, H. W., Nesse, R. M., Taylor, R. J., . . . Williams, D. R. (2004). The National Survey of American Life: A study of racial, ethnic and cultural influences on mental disorders and mental health. *International Journal of Methods in Psychiatric Research, 13*(4), 196–207.

Jaggers, J., & MacNeil, G. (2015). Depression in Hispanic Adults Who Immigrated as Youth: Results from the National Latino and Asian American Study. *Best Practices in Mental Health, 11*(2), 1–23.

John, D. A., de Castro, A. B., Martin, D. P., Duran, B., Takeuchi, D. T. (2012). Does an immigrant health paradox exist among Asian Americans? Associations of nativity and occupational class with self-rated health and mental disorders. *Social Science & Medicine, 75*, 2085–2098.

Jost, J. T., & Banaji, M. R. (1994). The role of stereotyping in system-justification and the production of false consciousness. *British Journal of Social Psychology, 33*(1), 1–27.

Katz, R. V., Russell, S. L., Kegeles, S. S., Kressin, N. R., Green, B. L., Wang, M. Q., . . . Claudio, C. (2006). The Tuskegee Legacy Project: Willingness of minorities to participate in biomedical research. *Journal of Health Care for the Poor and Underserved, 17*(4), 698–715.

Kessler, R. C., Berglund, P., Demler, O., Jin, R., Merikangas, K. R., & Walters, E. E. (2005a). Lifetime prevalence and age-of-onset distributions of DSM-IV disorders in the National Comorbidity Survey Replication. *Archives of General Psychiatry, 62*(6), 593–602.

Kessler et al. (2005b). Prevalence, severity, and comorbidity of 12-month DSM-IV disorders in the National Comorbidity Survey Replication. *Archives of General Psychiatry, 62*, 617–627.

Kim, E. (2011). Intergenerational acculturation conflict and Korean American parents' depression symptoms. *Issues in Mental Health Nursing, 32*, 687–695.

Knox, S., Burkard, A. W., Johnson, A. J., Suzuki, L. A., & Ponterotto, J. G. (2003). African American and European American therapists' experiences of addressing race in cross-racial psychotherapy dyads. *Journal of Counseling Psychology, 50*(4), 466–481.

Lee, D., Sutton, R., France, H. & Uhlemann, M. (1983). Effects of counselor race on perceived counselor effectiveness. *Journal of Counseling Psychology, 30*(3), 447–450.

Malcoun, E., Williams, M. T., & Bahojb-Nouri, L. V. (2014). Assessment of posttraumatic stress disorder in African Americans. In L. T. Benuto (Ed.), *Guide to psychological assessment with African Americans.* New York, NY: Springer.

Malgady, R. G., & Constantino, G. (1998). Symptom severity in bilingual Hispanics as a function of clinician ethnicity and language of interview. *Psychological Assessment, 10*(2), 120–127.

Marcia, J.E., Waterman, A. S., Matteson, D. R., Archer, S. L., Orlofsky, J. L. (1993). Ego identity: a handbook for psychosocial research. New York: Springer-Verlag.

Matsunaga, M., Hecht, M. L., Elek, E., & Ndiaye, K. (2010). Ethnic identity development and acculturation: A longitudinal analysis of Mexican-heritage youth in the Southwest United States. *Journal of Cross-Cultural Psychology, 41*(3), 410–427.

McMahon, S. D., & Watts, R. J. (2002). Ethnic identity in urban African American youth: Exploring links with self-worth, aggression, and other psychosocial variables. *Journal of Community Psychology, 30*(4), 411–431.

Melfi, C. A., Croghan, T. W., & Hanna, M. P. (2000). Psychiatric briefs. *Journal of Clinical Psychiatry, 61*, 16–21.

Miller, A., Williams, M. T., Wetterneck, C. T., Kanter, J., & Tsai, M. (2015). Using functional analytic psychotherapy to improve awareness and connection in racially diverse client-therapist dyads. *The Behavior Therapist, 38*(6), 150–156.

Muñoz, C., & Hilgenberg, C. (2006). Ethnopharmacology: understanding how ethnicity can affect drug response is essential to providing culturally competent care. *Holistic Nursing Practice, 20*(5), 227–234.

Nadkarni, A. & Santhouse, A. (2012). Diagnostic and statistical manual of mental disorders (DSM): A culture bound syndrome? Letter to the editor. *Asian Journal of Psychiatry, 5*, 118–119.

Nagayama Hall, G. C. (2001). Psychotherapy research with ethnic minorities: Empirical, ethical, and conceptual issues. *Journal of Consulting and Clinical Psychology, 69*(3), 502–510.

National Institutes of Health. (1999). The fundamentals of mental health and mental illness. In *Mental health: A report of the surgeon general* (chap. 2). Rockville, MD: U.S. Department of Health and Human Services, Substance Abuse and Mental Health Services Administration, Center for Mental Health Services, National Institutes of Health, National Institute of Mental Health.

Nipoda, Y. (2002). Japanese culture and therapeutic relationship. In W. J. Lonner, D. L. Dinnel, S. A. Hayes, & D. N. Sattler (Eds.), *Online readings in psychology and culture* (Unit 10, chap. 3). Bellingham: Center for Cross-Cultural Research, Western Washington University.

Owen, J. J., Tao, K., Leach, M. M., & Rodolfa, E. (2011). Clients' perceptions of their psychotherapists' multicultural orientation. *Psychotherapy, 48*(3), 274–282.

Parham, T. A. (2002). Counseling models for African Americans. In T. A. Parham (Ed.), *Counseling persons of African descent* (pp. 100–118). Thousand Oaks, CA: Sage.

Park, H., & Rubin, A. (2012). The mediating role of acculturative stress in the relationship between acculturation level and depression among Korean immigrants in the U.S. *International Journal of Intercultural Relations, 36*, 611–623.

Perez-Escamilla, R. (2010). Health care access among Latinos: Implications for social and health care reforms. *Journal of Hispanic Higher Education, 9*(1), 43–60.

Pew Research Center. (2015, November 3). *U.S. public becoming less religious: Modest drop in overall rates of belief and practice, but religiously affiliated Americans are as observant as before.* Retrieved from http://www.pewforum.org/2015/11/03/u-s-public-becoming-less-religious/

Phinney, J. S. (1989). Stages of ethnic identity development in minority group adolescents. *The Journal of Early Adolescence, 9*(1–2), 34–49.

Pieterse, A. L., Todd, N. R., Neville, H. A., & Carter, R. T. (2012). Perceived racism and mental health among Black American adults: A meta-analytic review. *Journal of Counseling Psychology, 59*(1), 1–9.

Pole, N., Gone, J. P., & Kulkarni, M. (2008). Posttraumatic stress disorder among ethnoracial minorities in the United States. *Clinical Psychology: Science and Practice, 15*(1), 35–61.

Prins, S. J., Bates, L. M., Keyes, K. M., & Muntaner, C. (2015). Anxious? Depressed? You might be suffering from capitalism: contradictory class locations and the prevalence of depression and anxiety in the USA. *Sociology of health & illness, 37*(8), 1352–1372.

Richeson, J. A., & Nussbaum, R. J. (2004). The impact of multiculturalism versus color-blindness on racial bias. *Journal of Experimental Social Psychology, 40*(3), 417–423.

Richards, P. S., Keller, R. R., & Smith, T. B. (2004). Religious and spiritual diversity in counseling and psychotherapy. In T. B. Smith (Ed.), *Practicing multiculturalism: Affirming diversity in counseling and psychology.* Hoboken, NJ: Wiley.

Roberts, R. E., Phinney, J. S., Masse, L. C., Chen, Y. R., Roberts, C. R., & Romero, A. (1999). The structure of ethnic identity of young adolescents from diverse ethnocultural groups. *Journal of Early Adolescence, 19*, 301–322.

Schwartz, S. J., Waterman, A. S., Umana-Taylor, A. J., Lee, R. M., Kim, S. Y., Vazsonyi, A. T., . . . Williams, M. K. (2013). Acculturation and well-being among college students from immigrant families. *Journal of Clinical Psychology, 69*(4), 298–318.

Shen, B., & Takeuchi, D. T. (2001). A structural model of acculturation and mental health status among Chinese Americans. *American Journal of Community Psychology, 29*(3), 497–415.

Smith, E. P., Walker, K., Fields, L., Brookins, C., & Seay, R. C. (1999). Ethnic identity and its relationship to self-esteem, perceived efficacy, and prosocial attitudes in early adolescence. *Journal of Adolescence, 22*, 867–880.

Snowden, L., Hastings, J., & Alvidrez, J. (2009). Overrepresentation of black Americans in psychiatric inpatient care. *Psychiatric Services, 60*(6), 779–785.

Snowden, L. R., & Pingitore, D. (2002). Frequency and scope of mental health service delivery to African Americans in primary care. *Mental Health Services Research, 4*(3), 123–130.

Solomon, A. (1992). Clinical diagnosis among diverse populations: A multicultural perspective. *Families in Society: The Journal of Contemporary Human Services, 73*, 371–377.

Soto, J. A., Dawson-Andoh, N. A., & BeLue, R. (2011). The relationship between perceived discrimination and generalized anxiety disorders among African Americans, Afro Caribbeans, and non-Hispanic Whites. *Journal of Anxiety Disorder, 25*, 258–265.

Strakowski, S. M., Hawkins, J. M., Keck, J., Paul, E., McElroy, S. L., West, S. A., . . . Tugrul, K. C. (1997). The effects of race and information variance on disagreement between psychiatric emergency room service and research diagnoses in first-episode psychosis. *Journal of Clinical Psychiatry, 58*, 457–463.

Sue, D. W., Capodilupo, C. M., Torino, G. C., Bucceri, J. M., Holder, A., Nadal, K. L., & Esquilin, M. (2007). Racial microaggressions in everyday life: Implications for clinical practice. *American Psychologist, 62*(4), 271.

Taylor, J. Y., Caldwell, C. H., Baser, R. E., Faison, N., & Jackson, J. S. (2007). Prevalence of eating disorders among Blacks in the National Survey of American Life. *International Journal of Eating Disorders, 40*(S3), S10–S14.

Terwilliger, J. M., Bach, N., Bryan, C., & Williams, M. T. (2013). Multicultural versus colorblind ideology: Implications for mental health and counseling. In A. Di Fabio (Ed.), *Psychology of counseling*, Hauppauge, NY: Nova Science Publishers.

Thomas, J., Turkheimer, E., & Oltmanns, T. F. (2000). Psychometric analysis of racial differences on the Maudsley Obsessional Compulsive Inventory. *Assessment, 7*(3), 247–258.

Torres, L., Driscoll, M. W., & Burrow, A. L. (2010). Racial microaggressions and psychological functioning among highly achieving African-Americans: A mixed-methods approach. *Journal of Social & Clinical Psychology, 29*(10), 1074–1099.

U.S. Census Bureau. (2012). *Most children younger than age 1 are minorities*, Census Bureau Reports. Release CB12-90. Retrieved from https://www.census.gov/newsroom/releases/archives/population/cb12-90.html

U.S. Department of Health and Human Services (U.S. DHHS). (2001). *Mental health: Culture, race, and ethnicity—A supplement to mental health: A report of the Surgeon General*. Rockville, MD: Substance Abuse and Mental Health Services Administration, Center for Mental Health Services.

U.S. Department of Labor. (2002). Consumer expenditures in 2000, *Bureau of Labor Statistics, Report 958* (also Table 51). Retrieved from http://www.bls.gov/cex

Van Diest, A. M. K., Tartakovsky, M., Stachon, C., Pettit, J. W., & Perez, M. (2013). The relationship between acculturative stress and eating disorder symptoms: Is it unique from general life stress? *Journal of Behavioral Medicine, 1*–13.

Vu, H. Q., & Rook, K. S. (2012). Acculturation and intergenerational relationships in Vietnamese American families: The role of gender. *Asian American Journal of Psychology*, 1–12.

Wei, M., Liao, K. Y. H., Chao, R. C. L., Mallinckrodt, B., Tsai, P. C., & Botello-Zamarron, R. (2010). Minority stress, perceived bicultural competence, and depressive symptoms among ethnic minority college students. *Journal of Counseling Psychology*, 57(4), 411.

Whaley, A. L. (2001). Cultural mistrust and mental health services for African Americans A review and meta-analysis. *The Counseling Psychologist*, 29(4), 513–531.

Williams, M. T., & Farris, S. G. (2011). Sexual orientation obsessions in obsessive-compulsive disorder: Prevalence and correlates. *Psychiatry Research*, 187(1), 156–159.

Williams, M. T., Chapman, L. K., Wong, J., & Turkheimer, E. (2012). The role of ethnic identity in symptoms of anxiety and depression in African Americans. *Psychiatry Research*, 199, 31–36.

Williams, M. T., Elstein, J., Buckner, E., Abelson, J. M., & Himle, J. A. (2012). Symptom dimensions in two samples of African Americans with obsessive–compulsive disorder. *Journal of Obsessive-Compulsive and Related Disorders*, 1(3), 145–152.

Williams, M. T., & Turkheimer, E. (2007). Identification and explanation of racial differences on contamination measures. *Behaviour Research and Therapy*, 45(12), 3041–3050.

Williams, M. T., Turkheimer, E., Magee, E., & Guterbock, T. (2008). The effects of race and racial priming on self-report of contamination anxiety. *Personality and Individual Differences*, 44(3), 746–757.

Williams, M. T., Gooden, A. M., & Davis, D. (2012). African Americans, European Americans, and pathological stereotypes: An African-centered perspective. In G. R. Hayes & M. H. Bryant (Eds.), *Psychology of culture*. Hauppauge, NY: Nova Science Publishers.

Williams, M., Cahill, S., & Foa, E. (2010). Psychotherapy for post-traumatic stress disorder. In D. Stein, E. Hollander, & B. Rothbaum (Eds.), *Textbook of anxiety disorders* (2nd ed.) Arlington, VA: American Psychiatric Publishing.

Williams, M. T., Tellawi, G., Wetterneck, C. T., & Chapman, L. K. (2013). Recruitment of Ethnoracial Minorities for Mental Health Research. *The Behavior Therapist*, 36(6), 151–156.

Williams, M. T., & Steever, A. (2015). Cultural manifestations of obsessive-compulsive disorder. In C. W. Lack (Ed.), *Obsessive-compulsive disorder: Etiology, phenomenology, and treatment*. Fareham, UK: Onus Books.

Wood, J. M., Garb, H. N., Lilienfeld, S. O., & Nezworski, M. T. (2002). Clinical assessment. *Annual Review of Psychology*, 53, 519–543.

Yip, T., Gee, G. C., & Takeuchi, D. T. (2008). Racial discrimination and psychological distress: The impact of ethnic identity and age among immigrant and United States-born Asian adults. *Developmental Psychology*, 44(3), 787–800.

Yoon, E., Chang, C., Kim, S., Clawson, A., Cleary, S. E., Hansen, M., . . . Gomes, A. M. (2013). A meta-analysis of acculturation/enculturation and mental health. *Journal of Counseling Psychology*, 60(1), 15–30.

PART II

SPECIFIC DISORDERS

CHAPTER 6

Schizophrenia Spectrum and Other Psychotic Disorders

DENNIS R. COMBS, KIM T. MUESER, SANDRA MORALES, and CORTNI SMITH

INTRODUCTION

Schizophrenia is considered the most debilitating and costly of all adult psychiatric illnesses. Despite the recent trend toward community-oriented treatment, about 25% of all psychiatric hospital beds are occupied by persons with schizophrenia. The costs of treating schizophrenia are significant, both financially and personally. It was estimated that the fiscal cost of schizophrenia in the United States was $62.7 billion in 2002 (Wu et al., 2005) and $6.85 billion in Canada in 2004 (Goeree et al., 2005). About one-third (roughly 22.7 billion) of the US dollars spent on schizophrenia is directed to the treatment and medical needs of this population. Despite the economic costs, the impact on the person's social and occupational functioning over a lifetime may be even more devastating (Knapp, Mangalore, & Simon, 2004). In fact, the largest indirect cost associated with schizophrenia is the loss of productivity over the lifetime. The burden of schizophrenia places the disorder as one of the top 10 most disabling conditions in the world in terms of illness-adjusted life years (Mueser & McGurk, 2004; Murray & Lopez, 1996). Even when persons with schizophrenia receive optimal treatments, many continue to experience substantial impairments throughout most of their lives.

Since schizophrenia was first described more than 100 years ago, the nature of the disorder has been hotly debated, and public misconceptions about it have been commonplace. In recent years, there has been a growing consensus among clinicians and researchers to more rigorously define the psychopathology of this disorder. Once referred to as a "wastebasket diagnosis," the term *schizophrenia* is now used to describe a specific clinical syndrome whose features are found in the *DSM-5* (American Psychiatric Association [APA], 2013). Current arguments about the disorder have focused on the validity of the diagnostic category of schizophrenia, and alternative models argue that it is more beneficial to focus on psychotic symptoms (e.g., paranoia, hallucinations, and delusions) (Bentall, Jackson, & Pilgrim, 1988). Nonetheless, an understanding of the core clinical features of schizophrenia is necessary for diagnosis and treatment planning. After many years of struggling to improve the long-term course of schizophrenia, there is

Adult Psychopathology and Diagnosis, Eighth Edition. Edited by Deborah C. Beidel and B. Christopher Frueh.
© 2018 John Wiley & Sons, Inc. Published 2018 by John Wiley & Sons, Inc.
Companion website: www.wiley.com/go/beidel/psychopathology8e

now abundant evidence that combined pharmacological and psychosocial interventions can have a major impact on improving functioning. This chapter provides an up-to-date review of schizophrenia, with a particular focus on the psychopathology of the illness and its impact on other domains of functioning.

DESCRIPTION OF THE DISORDER

Schizophrenia is characterized by impairments in social functioning, including difficulty establishing and maintaining interpersonal relationships, problems working or fulfilling other instrumental roles (e.g., student, homemaker, employee), and difficulties caring for oneself (e.g., poor grooming and hygiene). These problems in daily living, in the absence of significant impairment in intellectual functioning, are the most distinguishing characteristics of schizophrenia and are a necessary criterion for its diagnosis according to most diagnostic systems (e.g., DSM-5). Consequently, many individuals with the illness depend on others to meet their daily living needs. For example, estimates suggest that between 25% and 60% of persons with schizophrenia live with relatives, and an even higher percentage rely on relatives for caregiving (Goldman, 1982; Torrey, 2001). Time spent providing support and care for a person with schizophrenia can be substantial (with reports as high as 6–9 hours per day for some families; Magliano et al., 1998). It appears that the emotional and physical burden on caregivers is found across cultures (Breitborde, Lopez, Chang, Kopelowicz, & Zarate, 2009; Huang, Hung, Sun, Lin, & Chen, 2009; Zahid & Ohaeri, 2010). Individuals without family support typically rely on mental health, residential, and case management services to get their basic needs met. In the worst-case scenario, persons with schizophrenia who have insufficient contact with relatives and who fall between the cracks of the social service delivery system end up in jail (Torrey et al., 1992) or become homeless, with between 10% and 20% of homeless persons having schizophrenia (Susser, Stuening, & Conover, 1989).

In addition to the problems of daily living that characterize schizophrenia, individuals with the illness experience a range of different symptoms. The most common symptoms include positive symptoms (e.g., hallucinations, delusions, disorganization), negative symptoms (e.g., social withdrawal, apathy, anhedonia, poverty of speech), cognitive impairments (e.g., memory difficulties, planning ability, abstract thinking), and problems with mood (e.g., depression, anxiety, anger). The specific nature of these symptoms is described in greater detail in the following section. The symptoms of schizophrenia appear to account for some, but not all, of the problems in social functioning (Glynn, 1998).

The various impairments associated with schizophrenia tend to be long-term, punctuated by fluctuations in severity (i.e., relapse) over time. For this reason, schizophrenia has a broad impact on the family, and individuals are often impeded from pursuing personal life goals. Despite the severity of the disorder, advances in the treatment of schizophrenia provide solid hope for improving the outcome.

CLINICAL PICTURE

Most studies on the dimensions of schizophrenia agree on at least three major groups of symptoms (Liddle, 1987; Mueser, Curran, & McHugo, 1997a; Van Der Does, Dingemans, Linszen, Nugter, & Scholte, 1993), including positive symptoms, negative symptoms, and cognitive impairments. Positive symptoms refer to thoughts, sensory experiences, and behaviors that are present in persons with the disorder but are ordinarily absent in persons without the illness. Common examples of positive symptoms include hallucinations (e.g., hearing voices, seeing visions), delusions (e.g., believing that others are persecuting the person), and bizarre, disorganized behavior (e.g., maintaining a peculiar posture for no apparent reason, wearing multiple layers of clothes). Persecutory delusions (i.e., belief that some entity, group, or person has clear ongoing or future intentions to harm the person) are the most common type of delusion found in schizophrenia (Appelbaum, Robbins, & Roth, 1999; as reviewed in Bentall, Corcoran, Howard, Blackwood, & Kinderman, 2001). About 75% of persons with schizophrenia report hallucinations (Cutting, 1995). Auditory hallucinations are the most common form and are frequently derogatory, negative, or abusive, although some can be benevolent, comforting, and kind (Chadwick & Birchwood, 1995; Copolov, Mackinnon, & Trauer, 2004; Cutting, 1995). Less frequent, but more specific to schizophrenia, are voices that keep a running commentary on the person's actions or consist of two or more voices having a conversation. Auditory hallucinations can range from inaudible sounds (buzzing sounds, noises, muffled speech) or clearly perceived voices of either gender and can occur intermittently or on a continuous basis. It has been assumed that visual hallucinations were infrequent in schizophrenia and were more reflective of a medical condition (prevalence of 10–15% in schizophrenia), but recent evidence suggests that these symptoms are more common than initially believed, especially in more severe forms of the disorder (Bracha, Wolkowitz, Lohr, Karson, & Bigelow, 1989; Mueser, Bellack, & Brady, 1990a).

Negative symptoms, conversely, refer to the absence or diminution of cognitions, feelings, or behaviors that are ordinarily present in persons without the illness. Common negative symptoms include blunted or flattened affect (e.g., diminished facial expressiveness), poverty of speech (i.e., diminished verbal communication), anhedonia (i.e., inability to experience pleasure), apathy, psychomotor retardation (e.g., slow rate of speech), and physical inertia. The positive symptoms of schizophrenia tend to fluctuate over the course of the disorder and are often in remission between episodes of the illness. In addition, positive symptoms tend to be responsive to the effects of antipsychotic medication (Kane & Marder, 1993). In contrast, negative symptoms and cognitive impairments tend to be stable over time and are less responsive to antipsychotic medications (Greden & Tandon, 1991). However, there is some evidence that atypical antipsychotic medications, such as clozapine, risperidone, and olanzapine, have a beneficial impact on negative symptoms and cognitive functioning (Breier, 2005; Green et al., 1997; Tollefson & Sanger, 1997; Wahlbeck, Cheine, Essali, & Adams, 1999).

Aside from the core symptoms of schizophrenia, many persons with schizophrenia experience negative emotions (e.g., depression, anxiety, and anger) as a consequence of their illness (Freeman & Garety, 2003). Depression is quite common (estimated comorbidity rate of 45%; Leff, Tress, & Edwards, 1988) among people with schizophrenia and has been associated with poor outcomes (e.g., increased hospital use, lower employment rates) and suicidal tendencies (Sands & Harrow, 1999). Depressive symptoms can occur during all phases of the illness (prepsychotic, prodrome, acute, and remission), but they tend to attenuate as the active psychotic symptoms remit (Birchwood, Iqbal, Chadwick, & Trower, 2000). In addition, it was generally estimated that approximately 10% of the persons with this illness die from suicide (Bromet, Naz, Fochtmann, Carlson, & Tanenberg-Karant, 2005; Drake, Gates, Whitaker, & Cotton, 1985; Jobe & Harrow, 2005; Roy, 1986), but recent research examining suicide rates has lowered this estimate to around 4.0–5.6% (Inskip, Harris, & Barraclough, 1998; Palmer, Pankratz, & Bostwick, 2005). Risk of suicide is greater in the presence of mood symptoms and substance use, if previous suicide attempts were made during the initial onset of the disorder (Hawton, Sutton, Haw, Sinclair, & Deeks, 2005; first psychotic episode; rates 11–26%, as reviewed in Malla & Payne, 2005), and in time immediately preceding and following inpatient hospitalization (Qin & Nordentoft, 2005). Anxiety is also common in schizophrenia (estimated comorbidity rate of 43%) and is a frequent precursor to psychosis (Argyle, 1990; Braga, Mendlowicz, Marrocos, & Figueria, 2005; Cosoff & Hafner, 1998; Penn, Hope, Spaulding, & Kucera, 1994; Tien & Eaton, 1992). Specifically, there is evidence for the role of anxiety in both the formation and maintenance of persecutory delusions (threat beliefs) as well as hallucinations (Freeman et al., 2002; Freeman & Garety, 2003). Finally, anger, hostility, and social avoidance may also be present, especially when the person is paranoid (Bartels, Drake, Wallach, & Freeman, 1991; Freeman, Garety, & Kuipers, 2001; Gay & Combs, 2005). Interestingly, as paranoia increases, so does the tendency to perceive ambiguous interactions in a negative, threatening manner (Combs & Penn, 2004; Freeman et al., 2005).

In addition to the positive symptoms and negative emotions commonly present in schizophrenia, individuals with this diagnosis often have comorbid substance use disorders. Epidemiological surveys have repeatedly found that persons with psychiatric disorders are at increased risk for alcohol and drug abuse (Mueser et al., 1990a; Mueser, Yarnold, & Bellack, 1992). This risk is highest for persons with the most severe psychiatric disorders, including schizophrenia and bipolar disorder. For example, individuals with schizophrenia are more than four times as likely to have a substance abuse disorder as are individuals in the general population (Regier et al., 1990). In general, approximately 50% of all persons with schizophrenia have a lifetime history of substance use disorder, and 25–35% have a recent history of such a disorder (Mueser, Bennett, & Kushner, 1995). The presence of comorbid substance use disorders in schizophrenia has consistently been found to be associated with a worse course of the illness, including increased vulnerability to relapses and hospitalizations, housing instability and homelessness, violence, economic family burden, and treatment noncompliance (Drake & Brunette, 1998). For these reasons, the recognition and treatment of substance use disorders in persons with schizophrenia are crucial to the overall management of the illness.

Another important clinical feature of schizophrenia is lack of insight and compliance with treatment (Amador & Gorman, 1998; Amador, Strauss, Yale, & Gorman, 1991). Many individuals with schizophrenia have little or no insight into the fact that they have a psychiatric illness or even that they have any problems at all. This denial of illness can lead to noncompliance with recommended treatments, such as psychotropic medications and psychosocial therapies (McEvoy et al., 1989). Furthermore, fostering insight into the illness is a difficult and often impossible task with these persons.

Noncompliance with treatment is a related problem, but it can also occur because of the severe negativity often present in the illness, independent of poor insight. Problems with paranoia and distrust may contribute to noncompliance, in that some persons may believe medications or treatment providers are dangerous to them. Furthermore, the side-effects of some medications (e.g., sedation, dry mouth, motor side-effects), particularly the conventional antipsychotics, are unpleasant and can also lead to noncompliance. Medication noncompliance increases the risk of relapse, and between 50% and 75% of individuals who discontinue their medication will relapse within 1 year. Therefore, treatment compliance is a major concern to clinical treatment providers (Buchanan, 1992). It has been argued that the newer atypical antipsychotics may lead to higher rates of compliance owing to better side-effect profiles (Breier, 2005). However, a recent study of 63,000 individuals with schizophrenia in the Veterans Affairs medical system found widespread noncompliance (compliance measured in terms of filling needed prescriptions) across both conventional and atypical antipsychotics (Valenstein et al., 2004). Strategies for enhancing compliance involve helping the person become a more active participant in his or her treatment, identifying personal goals of treatment that have high relevance for that individual, and helping the person to develop strategies for taking medications into the daily routines (Azrin & Teichner, 1998; Corrigan, Liberman, & Engle, 1990; Kemp, Hayward, Applewhaite, Everitt, & David, 1996; Kemp, Kirov, Everitt, Hayward, & David, 1998).

People with schizophrenia are sometimes assumed to be violent or otherwise dangerous. Indeed, rates of violence have been found to be relatively higher in people with schizophrenia and other severe mental illnesses compared with the general population (Hodgins, Mednick, Brennan, Schulsinger, & Engberg, 1996; Swanson, Holzer, Ganju, & Jono, 1990). However, a more accurate comparison may be to examine the rates of violence between schizophrenia and other psychiatric disorders. Data from the MacArthur Risk Assessment Study found that the actual rates of violence for persons with schizophrenia was 8% for the first 20 weeks following discharge (most violent events occur in the first 20 weeks) and 14% over the course of a 1-year period (Monahan et al., 2001). In comparison, the rates of violence for persons with schizophrenia were actually lower than those for persons with depression and bipolar disorder for the same time period. A prospective study of violent behaviors in females with severe mental illness reported a prevalence rate of 17% over a 2-year period (Dean et al., 2006). Rates vary widely depending upon source of information (e.g., self-report vs. collateral reports), definition of violence, population studied (e.g., inpatients vs. outpatients), and where the research takes place (e.g., country). However, it should be emphasized that the majority of people with schizophrenia and other mental illnesses are not violent (Swanson, 1994). When violence does occur, it is often associated with substance abuse (Steadman et al., 1998), or the combination of substance abuse and medication non-compliance (Swartz et al., 1998). Other factors such as psychopathy (Nolan, Volavka, Mohr, & Czobor, 1999) or antisocial personality disorder (Hodgins & Côté, 1993, 1996) have also been implicated. Finally, targets of violence tend to be family members or friends rather than strangers, which is not unexpected given that most persons with schizophrenia rely heavily on family members for support (Steadman et al., 1998).

Although there is an increased rate of violence in schizophrenia, people with schizophrenia are much more likely to be the victims of violence and violent crime (Hiday, Swartz, Swanson, Borum, & Wagner, 1999). About 34–53% of individuals with severe mental illness report childhood sexual or physical abuse (Greenfield, Strakowski, Tohen, Batson, & Kolbrener, 1994; Jacobson & Herald, 1990; Rose, Peabody, & Stratigeas, 1991; Ross, Anderson, & Clark, 1994), and 43–81% report some type of victimization over their lives (Carmen, Rieker, & Mills, 1984; Hutchings & Dutton, 1993; Jacobson, 1989; Jacobson & Richardson, 1987; Lipschitz et al., 1996). Two recent surveys of a large number of people with severe mental illness found high rates of severe physical or sexual assault in the past year (Goodman et al., 2001; Silver, Arseneault, Langley, Caspi, & Moffitt, 2005). These numbers are striking compared with estimates of the general population, in which 0.3% of women and 3.5% of men reported assault in the past year (Tjaden & Thoennes, 1998). Studies of the prevalence of interpersonal trauma in women with severe mental illness indicate especially high vulnerability to victimization, with rates as high as 77–97% for episodically homeless women (Davies-Netzley, Hurlburt, & Hough, 1996; Goodman, Dutton, & Harris, 1995).

The prevalence of post-traumatic stress disorder (PTSD) among people with schizophrenia and other severe mental illnesses in various samples has ranged from 14% to 43% (Cascardi, Mueser, DeGirolomo, & Murrin, 1996; Craine, Henson, Colliver, & MacLean, 1988; Grubaugh, Zinzow, Paul, Egede, & Frueh, 2011; Mueser, Bond, Drake, & Resnick, 1998a; Mueser et al., 2004; Switzer et al., 1999), but has been as low as 3.8% (Braga et al.,

2005). These current rates of PTSD are far in excess of the lifetime prevalence of PTSD in the general population, with estimates ranging between 8% and 12% (Breslau, Davis, Andreski, & Peterson, 1991; Kessler, Sonnega, Bromet, Hughes, & Nelson, 1995; Resnick, Kilpatrick, Dansky, Saunders, & Best, 1993). Thus, interpersonal violence is so common in the serious mental illness population that it must sadly be considered a normative experience (Goodman, Dutton, & Harris, 1997).

DIAGNOSTIC CONSIDERATIONS

The diagnostic criteria for schizophrenia are fairly similar across a variety of different diagnostic systems. In general, the diagnostic criteria specify some degree of work, social, or self-care impairment, combined with positive and negative symptoms lasting a significant duration (e.g., 6 months or more). The diagnostic criteria for schizophrenia according to *DSM-5* (APA, 2013) must include the presence of two or more of the following five symptoms: delusions, hallucinations, disorganized speech, grossly disorganized or catatonic behavior, or negative symptoms. One of the symptoms must be delusions, hallucinations, or disorganized speech. The symptoms must have been present at least for a month, unless successfully treated. Since the disorder's onset, the symptoms must be accompanied by a decrease in functioning such as work or social interaction, or self-care must be below the level that existed prior to the disorder's onset. Also, for a diagnosis of schizophrenia, there must be continuous signs of the disturbance for at least 6 months.

The diagnosis of schizophrenia requires a clinical interview with the patient, a thorough review of all available records, and standard medical evaluations to rule out the possible role of organic factors (e.g., computed tomography [CT] scan to rule out a brain tumor). In addition, because many persons with schizophrenia are poor historians or may not provide accurate accounts of their behavior, information from significant others, such as family members, is often critical to establish a diagnosis of schizophrenia. The use of family and other informants is especially important in the assessment of prodromal and prepsychotic states. Because of the wide variety of symptoms characteristic of schizophrenia and variations in interviewing style and format across different clinical interviewers, the use of structured clinical interviews, such as the Structured Clinical Interview for DSM (SCID; First, Spitzer, Gibbon, & Williams, 1996), can greatly enhance the reliability and validity of psychiatric diagnosis.

Structured clinical interviews have two main advantages over more open clinical interviews. First, structured interviews provide definitions of the key symptoms, agreed upon by experts, thus making explicit the specific symptoms required for diagnosis. Second, by conducting the interview in a standardized format, including a specific sequence of asking questions, variations in interviewing style are minimized, thus enhancing the comparability of diagnostic assessments across different clinicians. The second point is especially crucial considering that most research studies of schizophrenia employ structured interviews to establish diagnoses. It is important that interviewers are properly trained and interrater reliability with a criterion-trained or expert rater is established before the use of structured interviews are initiated. If the findings of clinical research studies are to be generalized into clinical practice, efforts must be taken to ensure the comparability of the patient populations and the assessment techniques employed.

The symptoms of schizophrenia overlap with many other psychiatric disorders. Establishing a diagnosis of schizophrenia requires particularly close consideration of four other overlapping disorders: substance use disorders, affective disorders, schizoaffective disorder, and delusional disorder. We discuss issues related to each of these disorders and the diagnosis of schizophrenia in the following sections.

SUBSTANCE USE DISORDERS

Substance use disorder, such as alcohol dependence or drug abuse, can be either a differential diagnosis to schizophrenia or a comorbid disorder (i.e., the individual can have both schizophrenia and a substance use disorder). With respect to differential diagnosis, substance use disorders can interfere with a clinician's ability to diagnose schizophrenia and can lead to misdiagnosis if the substance abuse is covert, denied, or not reported accurately (Corty, Lehman, & Myers, 1993; Kranzler et al., 1995). Psychoactive substances, such as alcohol, marijuana, cocaine, and amphetamines, can produce symptoms that mimic those found in schizophrenia, such as hallucinations, delusions, and social withdrawal (Schuckit, 1995). In those cases in which the substance is involved in the etiology of psychosis, a diagnosis of substance-induced psychotic disorder would be appropriate. Further complicating matters, the use of these substances can exacerbate psychotic symptoms and, in many cases, lead to a return of acute psychosis.

Because the diagnosis of schizophrenia requires the presence of specific symptoms in the absence of identifiable organic factors, schizophrenia can only be diagnosed in persons with a history of substance use disorder by examining the individual's functioning during sustained periods of abstinence from drugs or alcohol. When such periods of abstinence can be identified, a reliable diagnosis of schizophrenia can be made. However, persons with schizophrenia who have a long history of substance abuse, with few or no periods of abstinence, are more difficult to assess. For example, in a sample of 461 individuals admitted to a psychiatric hospital, a psychiatric diagnosis could be neither confirmed nor ruled out because of a history of substance abuse in 71 persons (15%; Lehman, Myers, Dixon, & Johnson, 1994).

Substance use disorder is the most common comorbid diagnosis for persons with schizophrenia. Because substance abuse can worsen the course and outcome of schizophrenia, recognition and treatment of substance abuse in schizophrenia are critical goals of treatment. The diagnosis of substance abuse in schizophrenia is complicated by several factors. Substance abuse, as in the general population, is often denied because of social and legal sanctions (Galletly, Field, & Prior, 1993; Stone, Greenstein, Gamble, & McLellan, 1993), a problem that may be worsened in this population because of a fear of losing benefits. Denial of problems associated with substance abuse, a core feature of primary substance use disorders, may be further heightened by psychotic distortions and cognitive impairments present in schizophrenia. Furthermore, the criteria used to establish a substance use disorder in the general population are less useful for diagnosis in schizophrenia (Corse, Hirschinger, & Zanis, 1995). For example, the common consequences of substance abuse in the general population of loss of employment, driving under the influence of alcohol, and relationship problems are less often experienced by people with schizophrenia, who are often unemployed, do not own cars, and have limited interpersonal relationships. Rather, persons with schizophrenia more often experience increased symptoms and rehospitalizations, legal problems, and housing instability because of substance abuse (Drake & Brunette, 1998).

Individuals with schizophrenia tend to use smaller quantities of drugs and alcohol (Cohen & Klein, 1970; Crowley, Chesluk, Dilts, & Hart, 1974; Lehman et al., 1994) and rarely develop the full physical dependence syndrome that is often present in persons with a primary substance use disorder (Corse et al., 1995; Drake et al., 1990; Test, Wallisch, Allness, & Ripp, 1989) or show other physical consequences of alcohol such as stigmata (Mueser et al., 1999). Even very low scores on instruments developed for the primary substance use disorder population, such as the Addiction Severity Inventory, may be indicative of substance use disorder in persons with schizophrenia (Appleby, Dyson, Altman, & Luchins, 1997; Corse et al., 1995; Lehman, Myers, Dixon, & Johnson, 1996). Because of the difficulties in using existing measures of substance abuse for people with schizophrenia and other severe mental illnesses, a screening tool was developed specifically for these populations: the Dartmouth Assessment of Lifestyle Instrument (DALI; Rosenberg et al., 1998). The DALI is an 18-item questionnaire that has high classification accuracy for current substance use disorders of alcohol, cannabis, and cocaine for people with severe mental illness.

Despite the difficulties involved in assessing comorbid substance abuse in persons with schizophrenia, recent developments in this area indicate that if appropriate steps are taken, reliable diagnoses can be made (Drake, Rosenberg, & Mueser, 1996; Maisto, Carey, Carey, Gordon, & Gleason, 2000). The most critical recommendations for diagnosing substance abuse in schizophrenia include: (a) maintain a high index of suspicion of current substance abuse, especially if a person has a past history of substance abuse; (b) use multiple assessment techniques, including self-report instruments, interviews, clinician reports, reports of significant others, and biological assays for the presence of substances, which are routinely collected on admission to inpatient treatment; and (c) be alert to signs that may be subtle indicators of the presence of a substance use disorder, such as unexplained symptom relapses, familial conflict, money management problems, and sudden depression or suicidality. Once a substance use disorder has been diagnosed, integrated treatment that addresses both the schizophrenia and the substance use disorder (co-occurring disorders) is necessary to achieve a favorable clinical outcome (Drake, Mercer-McFadden, Mueser, McHugo, & Bond, 1998).

MOOD DISORDERS

Schizophrenia overlaps more prominently with the major mood disorders than any other psychiatric disorder. The differential diagnosis of schizophrenia from mood disorders is critical, because the disorders respond to different treatments, particularly pharmacological interventions. Two different mood disorders can be especially difficult to distinguish from schizophrenia: bipolar disorder with psychotic features and major depression. The differential diagnosis of these disorders from schizophrenia is complicated by the fact that mood symptoms are frequently present in all phases of schizophrenia (prodrome, acute, and remission), and psychotic symptoms (e.g., hallucinations, delusions) may be present in persons with severe mood disorders (APA, 2013; Pope & Lipinski, 1978).

The crux of making a differential diagnosis between schizophrenia and a major mood disorder is determining whether psychotic symptoms are present in the absence of mood symptoms. If there is strong evidence that psychotic symptoms persist even when the person is not experiencing symptoms of mania or depression, then the diagnosis is either schizophrenia or the closely related disorder of schizoaffective disorder (see the following section). If, on the other hand, symptoms of psychosis are present only during a mood episode, but disappear when the person's mood is stable, then the appropriate diagnosis is either major depression or bipolar disorder. For example, it is common for people with bipolar disorder to have hallucinations and delusions during the height of a manic episode, but for these psychotic symptoms to remit when the person's mood becomes stable again. Similarly, persons with major depression often experience hallucinations or delusions during a severe depressive episode, which subside as their mood improves. If the patient experiences chronic mood problems, meeting criteria for manic, depressive, or mixed episodes, it may be difficult or impossible to establish a diagnosis of schizophrenia, because there are no sustained periods of stable mood.

SCHIZOAFFECTIVE DISORDER

Schizoaffective disorder is a diagnostic entity that overlaps with both the mood disorders and schizophrenia (APA, 2013). Three conditions must be met for a person to be diagnosed with schizoaffective disorder: the person must meet criteria for a major mood episode (depressive or manic mood episodes) along with symptoms from criterion A from schizophrenia; the person has delusions or hallucinations for 2 or more weeks in the absence of a major mood episode; and the mood symptoms have to be present for a majority of the illness's duration (i.e., a person who experiences brief, transient mood states and who is chronically psychotic and has other long-standing impairments would be diagnosed with schizophrenia, rather than schizoaffective disorder).

Schizoaffective disorder and major mood disorder are frequently mistaken for one another because it is incorrectly assumed that schizoaffective disorder simply requires the presence of both psychotic and mood symptoms at the same time. Rather, as described in the preceding section, if psychotic symptoms always coincide with mood symptoms, the person has a mood disorder, whereas if psychotic symptoms are present in the absence of a mood episode, the person meets criteria for either schizoaffective disorder or schizophrenia. Thus, schizoaffective disorder requires longitudinal information about the relationship between mood and psychosis to make a diagnosis. This information is often obtained from the individual but is subject to memory and self-reporting biases (poor insight, or lack of awareness of mood states). The distinction between schizophrenia and schizoaffective disorder can be more difficult to make, because judgment must be made as to whether the affective symptoms have been present for a substantial part of the person's illness. Decision rules for determining the extent to which mood symptoms must be present to diagnose a schizoaffective disorder have not been clearly established.

Although the differential diagnosis between schizophrenia and schizoaffective disorder is difficult to make, the clinical implications of this distinction are less important than between the mood disorders and either schizophrenia or schizoaffective disorder. Research on family history and treatment response suggests that schizophrenia and schizoaffective disorder are similar disorders and respond to the same interventions (Kramer et al., 1989; Levinson & Levitt, 1987; Levinson & Mowry, 1991; Mattes & Nayak, 1984). In fact, many studies of schizophrenia routinely include persons with schizoaffective disorder and find few differences. Therefore, the information provided in this chapter on schizophrenia also pertains to schizoaffective disorder, and the differential diagnosis between the two disorders is not of major importance from a clinical perspective.

Delusions can be found in schizophrenia, schizoaffective disorder, severe mood disorders, organic conditions, and delusional disorder and are a nonspecific symptom in many cases. Persons with delusional disorder develop fixed delusions and do not show the other symptoms of schizophrenia (prominent auditory hallucinations, disorganization, odd or bizarre behaviors, negative symptoms). The delusion may lead to problems with others, but in general the person has good social, educational, and occupational functioning. Tactile and olfactory hallucinations can be present and will usually be incorporated into the delusional belief. Delusional disorder is three times more common in females than in males and has a later age of onset (mean age of 40; Evans,

Paulsen, Harris, Heaton, & Jeste, 1996; Manschreck, 1996; Yamada, Nakajima, & Noguchi, 1998). Delusional disorder accounts for 1–4% of all inpatient admissions and is relatively rare in clinical practice (Kendler, 1982).

In previous editions of the *DSM*, the differential diagnosis between delusional disorder and schizophrenia is based on the presence of nonbizarre delusions and absence of other symptoms of schizophrenia. Nonbizarre delusions are based on events or situations that could occur in real life but are highly improbable and lack supporting evidence (Sedler, 1995). Examples of nonbizarre delusions include being watched, followed, spied upon, harassed, loved, or poisoned. In contrast, bizarre delusions involve mechanisms not believed to exist in an individual's culture, such as beliefs of thought insertion, control, and broadcasting. In reality, the distinction between nonbizarre and bizarre beliefs is highly subjective and difficult (Junginger, Barker, & Coe, 1992; Sammons, 2005). However, in the *DSM-5* the issue of nonbizarre versus bizarre delusions has been removed and it emphasizes the presence of fixed delusions of any type that are present for 1 month. Many persons with delusions will provide convincing arguments that their beliefs are true, and a decision on whether the belief is plausible must often be made with very little corroborating evidence (Flaum, Arndt, & Andreasen, 1991; Jones, 1999). An examination of the person's history, premorbid and current functioning, and symptom profile can be useful in distinguishing delusional disorder from schizophrenia. A structured interview, such as the SCID, can be useful in assessing delusional beliefs along with the other symptoms of schizophrenia.

EPIDEMIOLOGY

It is estimated that approximately 2.2 million persons in the United States have schizophrenia at any given time (Narrow, Rae, Robins, & Regier, 2002; Torrey, 2001). It is believed that 51 million persons have schizophrenia worldwide. The annual incidence of new cases of schizophrenia ranges from 8 to 40 per 100,000 persons (Jablensky, 2000; McGrath et al., 2004, as cited in Tandon, Kesavan, & Nasrallah, 2008a). Point prevalence for any given time period ranges between 3% and 7% per 1,000 persons, with some estimates as high as 10% (Goldner, Hsu, Waraich, & Somers, 2002; Jablensky, 2000; Saha, Chant, Welham, & McGrath, 2005). The lifetime risk for developing schizophrenia appears to be about 0.7% on average (see Saha et al., 2005, as reviewed in Tandon et al., 2008a).

In general, the prevalence of schizophrenia is believed to be remarkably stable across a wide range of different populations and cultures (Crow, 2008; Saha, Welham, Chant, & McGrath, 2006; Tandon et al., 2008a). There has been little difference in the rates of schizophrenia according to gender, race, religion, or level of industrialization (Jablensky, 1999). Similar incidence rates and symptom patterns were found across 10 countries in a study sponsored by the World Health Organization (WHO; Jablensky et al., 1992). However, a more recent review of prevalence studies showed considerable heterogeneity in the rates of schizophrenia among different countries that may be partly owing to variations in diagnostic criteria (Goldner et al., 2002). Furthermore, there is evidence that schizophrenia is more heavily concentrated in urban areas of industrialized countries and, in fact, persons from developing countries may have a better prognosis and course of illness (Jablensky, 2000; Jablensky et al., 2000; Peen & Dekker, 1997; Takei, Sham, O'Callaghan, Glover, & Murray, 1995; Torrey, Bowler, & Clark, 1997). This increased risk appears to be related not only to the likelihood of people with schizophrenia drifting to urban areas, but also to being born in urban areas as well, which suggests that "urbanicity" has an effect on schizophrenia (Torrey et al., 1997).

Because schizophrenia frequently has an onset during early adulthood when important educational, social, and occupational milestones are often achieved, persons with the illness are especially affected in that they are less likely to marry or remain married, particularly males (Eaton, 1975; Munk-Jørgensen, 1987), and they are less likely to complete higher levels of education (Kessler, Foster, Saunders, & Stang, 1995) and they are more likely to have problems in occupational performance (Marwaha & Johnson, 2004). In terms of employment rates, only 14–20% of persons with schizophrenia hold competitive employment despite reporting a desire to work (Mueser, Salyers, & Mueser, 2001; Rosenheck et al., 2006). It has long been known that there is an association between poverty and schizophrenia, with people belonging to lower socioeconomic classes more likely to develop the disorder (Hollingshead & Redlich, 1958; Salokangas, 1978).

Historically, two theories have been advanced to account for this association. The social drift hypothesis postulates that the debilitating effects of schizophrenia on capacity to work result in a lowering of socioeconomic means, and hence poverty (Aro, Aro, & Keskimäki, 1995). The environmental stress hypothesis proposes that the high levels of stress associated with poverty precipitate schizophrenia in some individuals who would not otherwise develop the illness (Bruce, Takeuchi, & Leaf, 1991). Recently, attention has been aimed at different ethnic and migratory groups, such as second-generation Afro-Caribbeans living in the United Kingdom, who show higher incidence rates of schizophrenia (Boydell et al., 2001; Cantor-Graae & Selten, 2005).

It is believed that being a minority in a potentially hostile social environment where racism and discrimination are present may lead to increased stress and potentially higher rates of symptoms (Clark, Anderson, Clark, & Williams, 1999; Combs et al., 2006). Both of these explanations may be partly true, and longitudinal research on changes in socio-economic class status (SES) and schizophrenia provide conflicting results. For example, Fox (1990) reanalyzed data from several longitudinal studies and found that after controlling for initial levels of socioeconomic class, downward drift was not evident. Furthermore, Samele et al. (2001) found that a downward drift in occupational functioning over a 2-year period was not linked to illness course or prognosis. However, Dohrenwend et al. (1992) did find evidence of social drift, even after controlling for socioeconomic class. Also, it is possible that SES level may interact with gender, as males from higher SES homes show poorer clinical outcomes (Parrott & Lewine, 2005). Thus, more work is needed to sort out the relationships between SES and schizophrenia.

PSYCHOLOGICAL AND BIOLOGICAL ASSESSMENT

Diagnostic assessment provides important information about the potential utility of interventions for schizophrenia (e.g., antipsychotic medications). However, assessment does not end with a diagnosis. It must be supplemented with additional psychological and biological assessments.

PSYCHOLOGICAL ASSESSMENT

A wide range of different psychological formulations have been proposed for understanding schizophrenia. For example, there are extensive writings about psychodynamic and psychoanalytic interpretations of schizophrenia. Although this work has made contributions to the further development of these theories, these formulations do not appear to have improved the ability of clinicians to understand persons with this disorder or led to more effective interventions (Mueser & Berenbaum, 1990). Therefore, the use of projective assessment techniques based on psychodynamic concepts of personality, such as the Rorschach and Thematic Apperception Test, is not considered here.

One of the primary areas to assess is severity of psychotic symptoms, because treatment progression is mainly judged by a reduction of symptoms (Andreasen et al., 2005). This includes an assessment of positive and negative symptoms and general psychopathology due to the high comorbidity with anxiety and mood disorders. Measures such as the Positive and Negative Syndrome Scale (PANN S; Kay, Fiszbein, & Opler, 1987), the Brief Psychiatric Rating Scale (BPRS; Overall & Gorham, 1962), and the Psychotic Rating Scale (PSYRATS; Haddock, McCarron, Tarrier, & Faragher, 1999) have been frequently used in schizophrenia research and have good psychometric properties. Scales specific to positive (Scale for the Assessment of Positive Symptoms; Andreasen & Olsen, 1982) and negative symptoms (Scale for the Assessment of Negative Symptoms; Andreasen, 1982) can be used for a more in-depth and detailed assessment of these areas. There are also self-report and interview-based measures of insight available as well (see Amador & David, 2004). Commonly, these symptom measures are used in conjunction with a structured diagnostic interview in the assessment of schizophrenia.

As noted earlier, schizophrenia is often associated with a variety of neuro-psychological impairments. Core areas to assess in terms of cognitive functioning are verbal and visual learning and memory, working memory, attention/vigilance, abstract reasoning/executive functioning, and speed of information processing. These areas are part of the National Institute of Mental Health—Measurement and Treatment Research to Improve Cognition in Schizophrenia cognitive battery (NIMH-MATRICS; Green et al., 2004). Having information on cognitive functioning in these areas will aid in examining the beneficial effects of antipsychotic medication on cognition. It also is important to consider the generalization of these impairments to different situations (i.e., transfer of training problems). Thus, assessment needs to be conducted in the environments in which the skills are to be used in order to provide a more ecologically valid assessment. For example, successful employment interventions incorporate assessment on the job on an ongoing basis rather than extensive prevocational testing batteries that do not generalize to real-world settings (Bond, 1998; Drake & Becker, 1996). Similarly, when assessing independent living skills, it is important that these be measured directly in the living environment of the patient or in simulated tests (Wallace, Liberman, Tauber, & Wallace, 2000).

An emerging area of assessment is social cognition, which is defined as the perception, interpretation, and processing of social stimuli (Penn et al. 1997). Recent research has suggested that emotion perception, attributional style, and theory of mind may be valuable in persons with schizophrenia, as they predict social and community functioning. A review of the psychometric properties of these measures can be found in Pinkham et al. (2014).

A great deal of research has been done on the functional assessment of social skills in people with schizophrenia. Social skills refer to the individual behavioral components, such as eye contact, voice loudness, and the specific choice of words, which in combination are necessary for effective communication with others (Mueser & Bellack, 1998). As previously described, poor social competence is a hallmark of schizophrenia. Although not all problems in social functioning are the consequence of poor social skills, many social impairments appear to be related to skill deficits (Bellack, Morrison, Wixted, & Mueser, 1990c).

These interviews can focus on answering questions such as: Is the patient lonely? Would the patient like more or closer friends? Is the patient able to stand up for his or her rights? Is the patient able to get others to respond positively to him or her? Patient interviews are most informative when combined with interviews with significant others, such as family members and clinicians who are familiar with the nature and quality of the patient's social interactions, as well as naturalistic observations of the patient's social interactions. The combination of these sources of information is useful for identifying specific areas in need of social skills training.

One strategy for assessing social skills that yields the most specific type of information is role-play assessment. Role-plays usually involve brief simulated social interactions between the person and a confederate taking the role of an interactive partner. During role-plays, individuals are instructed to act as though the situation were actually happening in real life. Role-plays can be as brief as 15–30 seconds to assess skill areas such as initiating conversations, or they can be as long as several minutes to assess skills such as problem-solving ability. Role-plays can be audiotaped or videotaped and later rated on specific dimensions of social skill. Alternatively, role-playing can be embedded into the procedures of social skills training, in which persons with schizophrenia practice targeted social skills in role-plays, followed by positive and corrective feedback and additional role-play rehearsal. In the latter instance, the assessment of social skills is integrated into the training of new skills, rather than preceding skills training.

A commonly used assessment measure for social skill is the Maryland Assessment of Social Competence (MASC; Bellack & Thomas-Lohrman, 2003). The MASC is a structured role-play assessment that consists of four 3-minute interactions. Following each role-play, ratings on verbal and nonverbal skill and effectiveness are made, thus allowing the clinician to examine social skill across different situations and contexts.

Recent research on the reliability and validity of social skill assessments, and the benefits of social skills training for persons with schizophrenia, has demonstrated the utility of the social skills construct. Persons with schizophrenia have consistently been found to have worse social skills than those with other psychiatric disorders (Bellack et al., 1990c; Bellack, Mueser, Wade, Sayers, & Morrison, 1992; Mueser, Bellack, Douglas, & Wade, 1991b), and approximately half of the persons with schizophrenia demonstrate stable deficits in basic social skills compared with the nonpsychiatric population (Mueser, Bellack, Douglas, & Morrison, 1991a). In the absence of skills training, social skills tend to be stable over periods of time as long as 6 months to 1 year (Mueser et al., 1991). Social skill in persons with schizophrenia is moderately correlated with the level of premorbid social functioning, current role functioning, and quality of life (Mueser, Bellack, Morrison, & Wixted, 1990c). Social skills tend to be associated with negative symptoms (Appelo et al., 1992; Bellack et al., 1990c; Lysaker, Bell, Zito, & Bioty, 1995; Penn, Mueser, Spaulding, Hope, & Reed, 1995), but not with positive symptoms (Mueser, Douglas, Bellack, & Morrison, 1991; Penn et al., 1995). Furthermore, role-play assessments of social skill are also strongly related to social skill in more natural contexts, such as interactions with significant others (Bellack, Morrison, Mueser, Wade, & Sayers, 1990b).

Persons with schizophrenia show a wide range of impairments in social skills, including areas such as conversational skill, conflict resolution, assertiveness, and problem-solving (Bellack, Sayers, Mueser, & Bennett, 1994; Douglas & Mueser, 1990). Thus, ample research demonstrates that social skills are impaired in persons with schizophrenia, tend to be stable over time in the absence of intervention, and are strongly related to other measures of social functioning. Furthermore, there is growing evidence supporting the efficacy of social skills training for schizophrenia (Bellack, 2004; Heinssen, Liberman, & Kopelowicz, 2000).

The broadest area of psychological assessment is community functioning, and improvement in this area is linked to the concept of recovery (see the section on "Course and prognosis"). Persons with schizophrenia show not only poor social skills but also poor adaptive functioning in the community. Ideally, treatment programs should aim to improve the person's quality of life and satisfaction. Independent living skills, quality of life, and social functioning may need to be assessed in order to examine the person's current functional capacity level. The Social Functioning Scale (Birchwood, Smith, Cochrane, Wetton, & Copstake, 1990) and UCSD Performance-Based Skills Assessment (UPSA; Patterson, Goldman, McKibbin, Hughs, & Jeste, 2001) are widely used measures of adaptive and community functioning.

Family Assessment

The assessment of family functioning has high relevance in schizophrenia for two reasons. First, expressed emotion (EE), which refers to the presence of hostile, critical, or emotionally overinvolved attitudes and behaviors on the part of close relatives of persons with schizophrenia, is an important stressor that can increase the chance of relapse and rehospitalization (Butzlaff & Hooley, 1998). Second, caring for an individual with a psychiatric illness can lead to a significant burden on relatives (Webb et al., 1998), which ultimately can threaten their ability to continue to provide emotional and material support to the individual. Family burden has its own negative consequences and can be related to EE and the ability of the family to care for the person with schizophrenia. Thus, a thorough assessment of these family factors is important in order to identify targets for family intervention.

Several specific methods can be used to assess a negative emotional climate in the family and the burden of the illness. Interviews with individual family members, including the person with schizophrenia, as well as with the entire family, coupled with observation of more naturalistic family interactions, can provide invaluable information about the quality of family functioning. The vast majority of research on family EE has employed a semistructured interview with individual family members, the Camberwell Family Interview (Leff & Vaughn, 1985). This instrument is primarily a research instrument, and it is too time-consuming to be used in clinical practice. Alternatives to the Camberwell Family Interview have been proposed (e.g., Magaña et al., 1986), although none has gained widespread acceptance as yet. Several studies have successfully employed the Family Environment Scale (Moos & Moos, 1981), a self-report instrument completed by family members, which has been found to be related to symptoms and outcome in patients with schizophrenia (Halford, Schweitzer, & Varghese, 1991).

Many instruments have been developed for the assessment of family burden. The most comprehensive instrument, with well-established psychometric properties, is the Family Experiences Interview Schedule (Tessler & Gamache, 1995). This measure provides information regarding both dimensions of subjective burden (e.g., emotional strain) and objective burden (e.g., economic impact), as well as specific areas in which the burden is most severe (e.g., household tasks). The importance of evaluating family functioning is supported by research demonstrating clinical benefits of family intervention for schizophrenia. Numerous controlled studies of family treatment for schizophrenia have shown that family intervention has a significant impact on reducing relapse rates and rehospitalizations (Dixon et al., 2001; Pitschel-Walz, Leucht, Bäuml, Kissling, & Engel, 2001). The critical elements shared across different models of family intervention are education about schizophrenia, the provision of ongoing support, improved communication skills, and a focus on helping all family members improve the quality of their lives (Dixon & Lehman, 1995; Glynn, 1992; Lam, 1991).

BIOLOGICAL ASSESSMENT

Biological assessments are becoming more common in the clinical management of schizophrenia. For diagnosis, biological assessments may be used to rule out possible organic factors such as a tumor, stroke, or covert substance abuse. Urine and blood specimens are sometimes obtained in order to evaluate the presence of substance abuse. Similarly, blood samples may be obtained in order to determine whether the person is compliant with the prescribed antipsychotic medication, although the specific level of medication in the blood has not been conclusively linked to clinical response. Blood levels may also be monitored to ensure appropriate levels of mood stabilizers (e.g., lithium). Some newer medications (e.g., Clozaril) also require ongoing blood tests to detect very rare, but potentially lethal, blood disorders (Alvir, Lieberman, & Safferman, 1995; Young, Bowers, & Mazure, 1998). Client participation in this type of medical monitoring is crucial when using these medications.

Biological measures are sometimes used to characterize impairments in brain functioning associated with schizophrenia, although these assessments do not have clear implications for treatment of the illness at this time and are expensive. In addition, many clinicians do not have access to imaging technology, and its use has been specific to research settings. In terms of brain function and structure, CT scans indicate that between one-half and two-thirds of all persons with schizophrenia display enlarged cerebral ventricles, particularly the lateral and third ventricles, which is indicative of cortical atrophy (Liddle, 1995).

Magnetic resonance imaging (MRI) studies have found structural changes and a reduction in gray matter volumes in the prefrontal, superior temporal, amygdala, hippocampus, and thalamus (Lawrie & Abukmeil, 1998; Wright et al., 2000). These findings have also been found in first-episode and nonill relatives as well, and may be a pathophysiological marker for the disorder (Fannon et al., 2000; McDonald et al., 2002). These gross structural impairments in brain functioning, such as enlarged ventricles, tend to be associated with a wide range of neuropsychological impairments and negative symptoms often present in schizophrenia (Andreasen, Flaum, Swayze, Tyrrell, & Arndt, 1990; Buchanan et al., 1993; Merriam, Kay, Opler, Kushner, & van Praag, 1990). In addition, positron emission tomography (PET) and single photon emission computerized tomography (SPECT) have shown reduced metabolism and blood flow in several of the prefrontal and temporal cortexes, and abnormal activation of the thalamus (Kindermann, Karimi, Symonds, Brown, & Jeste, 1997; Liddle, 1997; McClure, Keshavan, & Pettegrew, 1998; Miyamoto et al., 2003). Functional MRI studies have found less activation in the prefrontal cortex and anterior cingulate cortex during working memory tasks (Carter, MacDonald, Ross, & Stenger, 2001; Perlstein, Carter, Noll, & Cohen, 2001). Finally, diffuse tensor imaging methods, which assess the integrity of white matter pathways in the brain, have found problems in myelinated neurons in the prefrontal lobes specifically and in the connections between the frontal, temporal, and parietal lobes (Burns et al., 2003; Lim, Hedehus, deCrespigny, Menon, & Moseley, 1998).

To date, most of the advances in the treatment of schizophrenia have been in psychopharmacology. Biological assessments are still not useful for diagnosing the illness or for guiding treatment. However, the clinical utility of biological assessment is likely to increase in the years to come as advances continue to be made in the understanding of the biological roots of schizophrenia.

ETIOLOGICAL CONSIDERATIONS

Behavioral Genetics and Molecular Genetics

The etiology of schizophrenia has been a topic of much debate over the past 100 years. Kraepelin (1919/1971) and Bleuler (1911/1950) clearly viewed the illness as having a biological origin. However, from the 1920s to the 1960s, alternative theories gained prominence, speculating that the disease was the result of disturbed family interactions (Bateson, Jackson, Haley, & Weakland, 1956). Psychogenic theories of the etiology of schizophrenia, positing that the illness was psychological in nature rather than biological, played a dominant role in shaping the attitudes and behavior of professionals toward persons with schizophrenia and their relatives (Fromm-Reichmann, 1950; Searles, 1965). These theories have not been supported empirically (Jacob, 1975; Waxler & Mishler, 1971). Moreover, in many cases, psychogenic theories fostered poor relationships between mental health professionals and relatives (Terkelsen, 1983), which have only begun to mend in recent years (Mueser & Glynn, 1999). For more than a century, clinicians have often noted that schizophrenia tends to "run in families." However, the clustering of schizophrenia in family members could reflect learned behavior that is passed on from one generation to the next, rather than predisposing biological factors.

In the 1950s and 1960s, two paradigms were developed for evaluating the genetic contributions to the illness. The first approach, the high-risk paradigm, involves examining the rate of schizophrenia in adopted-away or biological offspring of mothers with schizophrenia. If the rate of schizophrenia in children of biological parents with schizophrenia is higher than in the general population, then even in the absence of contact with those parents, a role for genetic factors in developing the illness is supported. The second approach, the monozygotic/dizygotic twin paradigm, involves comparing the concordance rate of schizophrenia in identical twins (monozygotic) with that in fraternal twins (dizygotic). Because monozygotic twins share the exact same gene pool, whereas dizygotic twins share only approximately half their genes, a higher concordance rate of schizophrenia among monozygotic twins than among dizygotic twins, even reared in the same environment, would support a role for genetic factors in the etiology of schizophrenia.

Over the past 30 years, numerous studies employing either the high-risk or twin paradigm have been conducted examining the role of genetic factors in schizophrenia. There has been almost uniform agreement across studies indicating that the risk of developing schizophrenia in biological relatives of persons with schizophrenia is greater than in the general population, even in the absence of any contact between the relatives (Kendler & Diehl, 1993). Thus, support exists for the role of genetic factors in the etiology of at least some cases of schizophrenia. For example, the odds of developing schizophrenia if one parent has the disorder is 13% and rises to about 50% if both parents have the disorder, compared with only 1% risk in the general population (Gottesman, 1991, 2001; McGuffin, Owen, & Farmer, 1995). Similarly, the concordance rate of one identical twin developing schizophrenia if his or her co-twin also has schizophrenia is between 25% and 50%, compared with about 6% and 15% for fraternal twins (Cardno et al., 1999; Faraone & Tsuang, 1985; Torrey, 1992; Walker, Downey, & Caspi, 1991). It also appears that the risk of developing schizophrenia is greater in more severe types of schizophrenia (average 20% for disorganized and catatonic types; see Gottesman & Shields, 1982).

The fact that identical twins do not have a 100% concordance rate of schizophrenia (heritability rates = 0.80 on average), as might be expected if the disorder were purely genetic, has raised intriguing questions about the etiology of schizophrenia. In a review of 40 studies on genetic risk, it was found that 80% of persons with psychotic symptoms do not have a single parent with the disorder, and 60% have a negative family history (Gottesman, 2001). It is likely that the development of schizophrenia results from an interaction between genetic and environmental factors. The results of a series of longitudinal studies support this case. Tienari and colleauges (Tienari, 1991; Tienari et al., 1987, 2004) compared the likelihood of developing schizophrenia in three groups of children raised by adoptive families. Two groups of children had biological mothers with schizophrenia, and the third group had biological mothers with no psychiatric disorder. The researchers divided the adoptive families of the children into two broad groups based on the level of disturbance present in the family: healthy adoptive families and disturbed adoptive families. Follow-up assessments were conducted to determine the presence of schizophrenia and other severe psychiatric disorders in the adopted children raised in all three groups. The researchers found that biological children of mothers with schizophrenia who were raised by adoptive families with high levels of disturbance were significantly more likely to develop schizophrenia or another psychotic disorder (46%) than were either similarly vulnerable children raised in families with low levels of disturbance (5%) or children with no biological vulnerability raised in either disturbed (24%) or healthy (3%) adoptive families. This study raises the intriguing possibility that some cases of schizophrenia develop as a result of the interaction between biological vulnerability and environmental stress.

Although families do not cause schizophrenia, there are important interactions between the family and person with schizophrenia that deserve consideration. First, as previously mentioned, it has repeatedly been found that critical attitudes and high levels of emotional overinvolvement (EE) on the part of the relatives toward the individual with schizophrenia are strong predictors of the likelihood that persons with schizophrenia will relapse and be rehospitalized (Butzlaff & Hooley, 1998). The importance of family factors is underscored by the fact that the severity of persons' psychiatric illness or their social skill impairments is not related to family EE (Mueser et al., 1993). Rather, family EE seems to act as a stressor, increasing the vulnerability of persons with schizophrenia to relapse.

A second important family consideration is the amount of burden on relatives caring for a mentally ill person. Family members of persons with schizophrenia typically experience a wide range of negative emotions related to coping with the illness, such as anxiety, depression, guilt, and anger (Hatfield & Lefley, 1987, 1993; Oldridge & Hughes, 1992). Burden is even associated with negative health consequences for relatives (Dyck, Short, & Vitaliano, 1999). Family burden may be related to levels of EE, ability to cope with the illness, and ultimately the ability of the family to successfully monitor and manage the schizophrenia in a family member (Mueser & Glynn, 1999). Thus, EE and family burden are important areas for assessment and intervention. Finally, researchers have been interested in discovering genes and chromosomal areas involved in schizophrenia.

Current research has focused on nine chromosomes (the most important appear to be areas 8p and 22q) and seven candidate genes, which may be important in schizophrenia (see Harrison & Owen, 2003). In particular, researchers are particularly interested in identifying genes found across family members with the disorder (linkage studies) or directly related to the underlying pathophysiology of schizophrenia (e.g., genes that affect neurotransmitter functioning such as dopamine, serotonin, or glutamate). This area of research has been hampered by the lack of independent replication of these genetic markers. The exact mechanism for genetic transmission of the disorder is unknown, but it appears that schizophrenia does not follow a Mendelian single gene pattern of inheritance. It is more likely that schizophrenia is a polygenetic condition or that it arises from an interaction of multiple genes, which increase the susceptibility to the disorder (Craddock, O'Donovan, & Owen, 2006; Miyamoto et al., 2003). Regardless, genes and gene–environment interactions are estimated to account for 80% of the risk for schizophrenia, according to a review of the literature (as reviewed in Tandon et al., 2008b).

NEUROANATOMY AND NEUROBIOLOGY

Although there is clear evidence that genetic factors can play a role in the development of schizophrenia, there is also a growing body of evidence pointing to the influence of other biological, nongenetic factors playing a critical role. For example, obstetric complications, maternal exposure to the influenza virus, and other environmental-based insults to the developing fetus (e.g., maternal starvation) are all associated with an increased risk of developing schizophrenia (Geddes & Lawrie, 1995; Kirch, 1993; Rodrigo, Lusiardo, Briggs, & Ulmer, 1991; Susser & Lin, 1992; Susser et al., 1996; Takei et al., 1996; Thomas et al., 2001; Torrey, Bowler, Rawlings, & Terrazas, 1993). Thus, there is a growing consensus that the etiology of schizophrenia may be heterogeneous, with genetic factors playing a role in the development of some cases and early environmental-based factors playing a role in the development of other cases. This heterogeneity may account for the fact that the genetic contribution to schizophrenia has consistently been found to be lower than the genetic contribution to bipolar disorder (Goodwin & Jamison, 1990). Other biological and physiological factors include alterations in brain chemistry and structure.

Pharmacological research has identified many neurochemical changes associated with schizophrenia. By far, the neurotransmitter most commonly implicated in the onset of schizophrenia is dopamine. The dopamine hypothesis proposes that alterations in levels of dopamine are responsible for the symptoms of schizophrenia. Originally, this hypothesis was based on findings that substances that increase dopamine (e.g., levadopa used to treat Parkinson's disease) increase psychotic symptoms, and substances that decrease dopamine reduce psychotic symptoms. Current versions of this hypothesis suggest that an overabundance of dopamine in certain limbic areas of the brain may be responsible for positive symptoms, whereas a lack of dopamine in cortical areas may be responsible for negative symptoms (Davis, Kahn, Ko, & Davidson, 1991; Moore, West, & Grace, 1999). Other neurochemicals also appear to be implicated in schizophrenia. In particular, serotonin may directly or indirectly (e.g., by mediating dopamine) affect symptoms of schizophrenia, because several of the newer antipsychotic medications impact serotonin levels (Lieberman et al., 1998). In addition, glutamate and gamma-aminobutyric acid (GABA) may be altered in schizophrenia (Pearlson, 2000).

As discussed in the section on "Biological assessment," abnormalities in several brain structures have also been identified. In particular, enlarged ventricles and decreased brain volume and blood flow to cortical areas have been associated with a wide range of cognitive impairments and negative symptoms of schizophrenia (Andreasen et al., 1990; Buchanan et al., 1993; Merriam et al., 1990).

LEARNING, MODELING, AND LIFE EVENTS

Although schizophrenia is broadly accepted to be a biologically based disorder and not a learned one, learning and modeling may play a role in the course, outcome, and symptom expression of the disorder. In terms of symptom expression, there is empirical support for the role of operant conditioning in delusions and hallucinations (e.g., hallucinations increase when reinforced). Furthermore, research has shown that psychotic behavior can be modified using differential reinforcement (i.e., attention for any other behavior besides the expression of delusional statements) or punishment principles (Jimenez, Todman, Perez, Godoy, & Landon-Jimenez, 1996; Schock, Clay, & Cipani, 1998). However, these processes are probably more relevant for the maintenance of psychotic symptoms than for etiology. Haynes (1986) proposed a behavioral model of paranoia in which suspiciousness partially stems from the reinforcement of paranoid statements and parental modeling, but this theory has been largely untested.

As described in the following section, the stress-vulnerability model of schizophrenia posits that coping skills mediate the noxious effects of stress on psychobiological vulnerability to symptoms and relapses (Liberman et al., 1986; Nuechterlein & Dawson, 1984). Coping skills, such as social skills for developing and maintaining close relationships with others and strategies for managing negative emotions and distorted thinking processes, can be acquired either naturalistically through access to good role models (e.g., family, friends) or through social learning-based programs, such as social skills training (Bellack, Mueser, Gingerich, & Agresta, 1997) or cognitive-behavior therapy (Chadwick & Birchwood, 1995; Fowler, Garety, & Kuipers, 1995). Thus, improving coping skills, as well as other life skills, through the systematic application of social learning methods is a common treatment goal in schizophrenia.

Although stressful life events alone are not the cause of schizophrenia, some theories hypothesize that life events may contribute to the development of the disorder and can play an important role in the course of schizophrenia. The stress-vulnerability model (Liberman et al., 1986; Zubin & Spring, 1977) assumes that symptom severity and related impairments of psychiatric disorders such as schizophrenia have a biological basis (psychobiological vulnerability) determined by a combination of genetic and early environmental factors. This vulnerability can be decreased by medications and worsened by substance use disorder. Stress, including discrete events (such as traumas) and exposure to ongoing conditions (such as a hostile environment) can impinge on vulnerability, precipitating relapses and worse outcomes. Finally, coping resources, such as coping skills or the ability to obtain social support, can minimize the effects of stress on relapse and the need for acute care.

As described earlier, EE represents a stressful familial environment that may increase relapse and hospitalization in people with schizophrenia. In addition, in the "Clinical picture" section, we discussed that people with schizophrenia are often the targets of violence and have frequently been exposed to physical and/or sexual assault. Exposure to traumatic events may lead to PTSD, a condition characterized by re-living the traumatic experience (e.g., nightmares, intrusive memories), avoidance of people, places, and things that remind the person of the event, and increased arousal symptoms (e.g., irritability, sleep problems). Exposure to trauma and the presence of PTSD are likely to worsen the course of schizophrenia and complicate treatment (Mueser, Rosenberg, Goodman, & Trumbetta, 2002). For example, research shows that both discrete stressors (e.g., life events) and exposure to a stressful environment can worsen psychotic disorders (Butzlaff & Hooley, 1998). PTSD is also associated with substance abuse (Chilcoat & Breslau, 1998), which, as described earlier, can have severe consequences for people with schizophrenia.

Cognitive impairments refer to difficulties in verbal and visual learning and memory, working memory, attention/vigilance, abstract reasoning/executive functioning (i.e., understanding a concept, planning, organizing), and speed of information processing (Green et al., 2004). These cognitive deficits have been observed in unmedicated, medicated, first-episode, remitted, and high-risk children prior to developing the disorder. Thus, cognitive impairments are so commonplace that they are now considered a core feature of schizophrenia (Palmer et al., 1997; Wilk et al., 2005). A recent meta-analysis of cognitive performance found that normal controls without a history of schizophrenia perform consistently better (about 1 standard deviation) than persons with schizophrenia on most cognitive tasks, which suggests that a generalized cognitive deficit is present (Heinrichs, 2005). These deficits also appear to be relatively stable over time and do not appear to reflect a progressive deterioration (Heaton et al., 2001). These cognitive impairments may interfere with the person's ability to focus for sustained periods on work or recreational pursuits, interact effectively with others, perform basic activities of daily living, or participate in conventional psychotherapeutic interventions (Bellack, Gold, & Buchanan, 1999; Brekke, Raine, Ansel, Lencz, & Bird, 1997; Green, Kern, Braff, & Mintz, 2000; Sevy & Davidson, 1995; Velligan et al., 1997). Cognitive impairments also result in difficulties with generalizing training or knowledge to other areas (i.e., transfer of training problems) (Mueser et al., 1991a; Smith, Hull, Romanelli, Fertuck, & Weiss, 1999). Thus, many rehabilitative efforts focus on teaching persons with schizophrenia directly in the environment in which skills will be used, or involve specialized teaching methods, such as errorless learning procedures (Kern, Liberman, Kopelowicz, Mintz, & Green, 2002).

In addition to cognitive deficits, it has become apparent that impairments in social cognition (defined as the way people perceive, interpret, and understand social information) are also found in schizophrenia (Penn, Corrigan, Bentall, Racenstein, & Newman, 1997). Deficits in emotion and social cue perception, problems inferring the intentions and motivations of others (theory of mind), and impairments in social knowledge and schemata have all been found in schizophrenia (Brune, 2005; Corrigan & Penn, 2001; Edwards, Jackson, & Pattison, 2002). More specifically, persons with persecutory delusions exhibit an attributional style in which they tend to blame others rather than situations for negative events (e.g., personalizing attributional style; see Garety & Freeman, 1999). Deficits in social cognition appear to be independent of nonsocial cognition (e.g., memory, attention) in that they predict incremental variance in social functioning and social skill and may arise from distinct brain structures involved in social information processing (Penn, Combs, & Mohamed, 2001; Penn et al., 1997; Pinkham, Penn, Perkins, & Lieberman, 2003). The exact nature of the relationship between social cognition and cognitive functioning is unclear, but social cognition appears to be important in the social functioning of persons with schizophrenia (Green, Oliver, Crawley, Penn, & Silverstein, 2005).

SEX AND RACIAL-ETHNIC CONSIDERATIONS

Several issues related to gender are important for understanding the psychopathology in the course of schizophrenia. As described in the section on course and prognosis, women tend to have a milder overall course and later onset of schizophrenia than do men. The net consequence is that, although similar numbers of men and women have schizophrenia, men are more likely to receive treatment for the disorder. In fact, most research on the treatment of schizophrenia is conducted on samples ranging from 60% to 100% male.

Because treatment studies usually sample persons with schizophrenia who are currently receiving treatment, often inpatient treatment, the efficacy of widely studied psychosocial interventions, such as social skills training and family therapy, has been less adequately demonstrated in women. For example, some research suggests that social skills training may be more helpful to men than to women (Mueser, Levine, Bellack, Douglas, & Brady, 1990d; Schaub, Behrendt, Brenner, Mueser, & Liberman, 1998; Smith et al., 1997). There is a need for more research on the effects of treatments for women with schizophrenia. At the same time, further consideration needs to be given to the different needs of women with this illness. For example, women with schizophrenia are much more likely than men to marry and have children. It is crucial, therefore, that psychosocial interventions be developed to address the relationship, family planning, and parenting needs of women with schizophrenia (Apfel & Handel, 1993; Brunette & Dean, 2002; Coverdale & Grunebaum, 1998).

Another issue related to gender that is in need of further consideration is exposure to trauma. As described earlier, people with schizophrenia are at risk of being the victims of violence. Although both men and women with schizophrenia report histories of abuse and assault, women report more sexual assault (Goodman et al., 2001; Mueser et al., 1998b). Furthermore, in the general population, women are more likely to be abused than men, are more likely to sustain injuries, and are more likely to be economically dependent upon perpetrators of domestic violence. Thus, there is a particular need to recognize and address trauma in the lives of women with schizophrenia. Accurate detection of trauma is further complicated by the fact that most severely mentally ill persons who have been physically or sexually assaulted deny that they have been abused (Cascardi et al., 1996). The development of programs that address both the causes of domestic violence and their sequelae, especially for women with schizophrenia, is a priority in this area (Harris, 1996; Rosenberg et al., 2001).

Research on the relationships between race, ethnicity, and severe psychiatric disorders demonstrates that cultural factors are critical to understanding how persons with schizophrenia are perceived by others in their social milieu, as well as the course of the illness. Although the prevalence of schizophrenia is comparable across different cultures, several studies have shown that the course of the illness is more benign in developing countries than in industrialized nations (Lo & Lo, 1977; Murphy & Raman, 1971; Sartorius et al., 1986). Westermeyer (1989) has raised questions about the comparability of clinical samples in cross-cultural studies, but a consensus remains that the course of schizophrenia tends to be milder in nonindustrialized countries (Jablensky, 1989).

A variety of different interpretations have been offered to account for the better prognosis of schizophrenia in some cultures (Lefley, 1990). It is possible that the strong stigma and social rejection that result from serious mental illness and pose an obstacle to the ability of persons with schizophrenia to cope effectively with their disorder and assimilate into society (Fink & Tasman, 1992) are less prominent in some cultures (Parra, 1985). Greater cultural, familial, and societal acceptance of the social deviations present in schizophrenia may enable these persons to live less stressful and more productive lives. This may be especially true for Hispanic families, who show less EE than do White families (Dorian, Garcia, Lopez, & Hernandez, 2008; Lopez et al., 2009). Hispanic families are typically characterized as more accepting and less blaming of persons with schizophrenia (Kymalainen & Weisman de Mamani, 2008). This is important given the link between EE and relapse, and, in fact, lower rates of relapse have been found in minority families (Aguilera, Lopez, Breitborde, Kopelowicz, & Zarate, 2010).

Cultures with a stronger degree of family ties, in particular, may be less vulnerable to the effects of mental illness (Lin & Kleinman, 1988). For example, Liberman (1994) described how the strong functional ties of seriously mentally ill persons to their families and work foster the reintegration of persons with schizophrenia back into Chinese society following psychiatric hospitalization. In contrast, until recently, families of persons with schizophrenia in many Western societies were viewed by mental health professionals as either irrelevant, or, worse, as causal agents in the development of the illness (Lefley, 1990; Mueser & Glynn, 1999), thus precluding them from a role in psychiatric rehabilitation. Furthermore, the use of other social supports may vary across different ethnic groups or cultures, such as the importance of the church to the African American community and its potential therapeutic benefits (Griffith, Young, & Smith, 1984; Lincoln & Mamiya, 1990).

Some have hypothesized that different cultural interpretations of the individual's role in society and of the causes of mental illness may interact to determine course and outcome. Estroff (1989) has suggested that the emphasis on the self in Western countries, compared with a more family or societally based identification, has an especially disabling effect on persons with schizophrenia, whose sense of self is often fragile or fragmented. Another important consideration is the availability of adaptive concepts for understanding mental illness. For example, *espiritismo* in Puerto Rican culture is a system of beliefs involving the interactions between the invisible spirit world and the visible world, in which spirits can attach themselves to persons (Comas-Díaz, 1981; Morales-Dorta, 1976). Spirits are hierarchically ordered in terms of their moral perfection, and the practice of *espiritismo* is guided by helping individuals who are spiritually ill to achieve higher levels of this perfection. Troubled persons are not identified as sick, nor are they blamed for their difficulties; in some cases, symptoms such as hallucinations may be interpreted favorably as signs that the person is advanced in his or her spiritual development, resulting in some prestige (Comas-Díaz, 1981). Thus, certain cultural interpretations of schizophrenia may promote more acceptance of persons who display the symptoms of schizophrenia, as well as avoiding the common assumption that these phenomenological experiences are the consequence of a chronic, unremitting condition.

Understanding different cultural beliefs, values, and social structures can have important implications for the diagnosis of schizophrenia. Religious practices and beliefs may complicate diagnosis. For example, high levels of religiosity have been found in people with schizophrenia (Brewerton, 1994). Without a clear understanding of the religious and cultural background, patients may be misdiagnosed (May, 1997). Ethnic groups may differ in their willingness to report symptoms, as illustrated by one study that reported that African American persons were less likely than Hispanics or non-Hispanic Whites to report symptoms (Skilbeck, Acosta, Yamamoto, & Evans, 1984). Several studies have shown that ethnic differences in diagnosis vary as a function of both the client's and the interviewer's ethnicity (Baskin, Bluestone, & Nelson, 1981; Loring & Powell, 1988). Misdiagnosis of mood disorders as schizophrenia is the most common problem with the diagnosis of ethnic minorities in the United States (e.g., Jones, Gray, & Parsons, 1981, 1983).

Other studies have found that African Americans are more likely than Whites to be inappropriately diagnosed with paranoid schizophrenia, which has been viewed as a clinician bias in the interpretation of mistrust (Adams, Dworkin, & Rosenberg, 1984; Combs, Penn, & Fenigstein, 2002; Combs et al., 2006; Whaley, 1997, 2001). Alternatively, this finding may also represent the effects of stress and poverty in the development of schizophrenia given the numbers of minorities who live in poverty (Bruce, Takeuchi, & Leaf, 1991; as discussed in the section on "Epidemiology"). Knowledge of cultural norms appears critical to avoid the possible misinterpretation of culturally bound beliefs, experiences, and practices when arriving at a diagnosis.

Cultural differences are also critical in the treatment of schizophrenia, both with respect to service utilization and the nature of treatment provided. There is a growing body of information documenting that ethnic groups differ in their use of psychiatric services. Several studies have indicated that Hispanics and Asian Americans use fewer psychiatric services than do non-Hispanic Whites, whereas Blacks use more emergency and inpatient services (Cheung & Snowden, 1990; Hough et al., 1987; Hu, Snowden,

Jerrell, & Nguyen, 1991; Padgett, Patrick, Burns, & Schlesinger, 1994; Sue, Fujino, Hu, Takeuchi, & Zane, 1991). Aside from cultural-based practices that may cause some individuals to seek assistance outside the mental health system (e.g., practitioners of *santería*; González-Wippler, 1992), access to and retention in mental health services may be influenced by the proximity of mental health services (Dworkin & Adams, 1987) and by the ethnicity of treatment providers. Sue et al. (1991) reported that matching clinician and client ethnicity resulted in higher retention of ethnic minorities in mental health services. Increasing access to needed services for racial/ethnic minorities may require a range of strategies, including ensuring that services are available in the communities where clients live, working with the natural social supports in the community, awareness of relevant cultural norms, and adequate representation of ethnic minorities as treatment providers.

Cultural factors may have an important bearing on psychotherapeutic treatments provided for schizophrenia. Sue and Sue (1990) have described the importance of providing psychotherapy driven by goals that are compatible with clients' cultural norms. This requires both knowledge of subcultural norms and familiarity with the other social support mechanisms typically available to those individuals. Interventions developed for one cultural group may need substantial modification to be effective in other groups. For example, Telles et al. (1995) reported that behavioral family therapy, which has been found to be effective at reducing relapse in schizophrenia for samples of non-Hispanic White and African American individuals (Mueser & Glynn, 1999), was significantly less effective for Hispanic Americans (of Mexican, Guatemalan, and Salvadoran descent) with low levels of acculturation than for more acculturated individuals. In addition, behavioral family therapy has been found to be effective when implemented in Spain and China (Montero et al., 2001; Xiong et al., 1994; Zhang, Wang, Li, & Phillips, 1994). These findings underscore the importance of tailoring psychosocial interventions to meet the unique needs of clients from different cultural backgrounds.

A final cultural factor is stigma—that is, negative attitudes that lead to prejudice and discrimination against people with schizophrenia. Although stigma can be present for a variety of disabilities, attitudes toward people with serious mental illness tend to be more negative (Corrigan & Penn, 1999). Stigma may stem from characteristics of the disorder itself, such as poor social skills, bizarre behavior, and unkempt appearance, and stigma may develop and be maintained through negative media portrayals and myths (e.g., dangerousness, unpredictability) (Farina, 1998). Stigma and discrimination can greatly undermine the person's ability to recover from the effects of schizophrenia and integrate into society. For example, people with serious mental illness identify role functioning, such as employment, developing and maintaining friendships and intimate relationships, and regular activities as critical to their recovery (Uttaro & Mechanic, 1994). However, many studies have shown that these are the very areas most affected by stigma (Farina, 1998). Much is being done to try to reduce stigma associated with schizophrenia and other mental illness. In particular, strategies that involve active education and increased contact with people with mental illness (best if they are of the same status and background) may be most effective for eradicating this serious problem (Corrigan & Penn, 1999).

COURSE AND PROGNOSIS

Schizophrenia usually has an onset in late adolescence or early adulthood, most often between the ages of 16 and 25. However, there is evidence that signs of the disorder are present long before the clinical symptoms of psychosis appear. Children who later develop schizophrenia show impairments in sociability, emotional expressiveness (less positive and more negative facial expressions), and neuromotor functioning (Schiffman et al., 2004; Walker, Grimes, Davis, & Smith, 1993). Data from the New York High Risk Project, which followed a cohort of children at high risk for schizophrenia, found that deficits in verbal memory, attentional vigilance, and gross motor skills in childhood (ages 7–12) predicted the development of schizophrenia later in life (Erlenmeyer-Kimling et al., 2000).

Some individuals display a maladaptive pattern of behaviors, including disruptive behavior, problems in school, poor interpersonal relationships, and impulsivity (Amminger et al., 1999; Baum & Walker, 1995; Fuller et al., 2002; Hans, Marcus, Henson, Auerbach, & Mirsky, 1992). Similarly, symptoms of conduct disorder in childhood, such as repeated fighting, truancy, and lying, have been found to be predictive of the later development of schizophrenia (Asarnow, 1988; Cannon et al., 1993; Neumann, Grimes, Walker, & Baum, 1995; Robins, 1966; Robins & Price, 1991; Rutter, 1984; Watt, 1978). However, other persons with schizophrenia display no unusual characteristics in their premorbid functioning or competence (Zigler & Glick, 1986). The signs of schizophrenia in childhood may be subtle, irregular, and gradual in onset, but they become increasingly more apparent as adolescence approaches (Dworkin et al., 1991).

Prior to the emergence of schizophrenia, many persons enter a prodromal period of the illness, which is characterized by changes in mood and behavior (Yung & McGorry, 1996). The prodrome is an intensification of the core features of the disorder which can last up to 5 years. Prodromal symptoms are subclinical or attenuated symptoms that fail to reach the threshold for a clinical diagnosis but become increasingly apparent to others. Disruptions in sleep, anxiety, depression, aggression/irritability, paranoia, and odd beliefs are common in the prodromal phase (Häfner, Maurer, Trendler, an der Heiden, & Schmidt, 2005; Malla & Payne, 2005; Norman, Scholten, Malla, & Ballageer, 2005; Yung & McGorry, 1996). Social isolation, withdrawal, changes in role functioning, and avolition may be present during this stage as well.

The initial emergence of clinical symptoms (first-episode or first break) is a crucial time for treatment and intervention (Lincoln & McGorry, 1995). Recent research has shown that the average duration of untreated psychosis in this population is 74 weeks (Addington et al., 2015) and it is widely believed that the earlier that antipsychotic medications are initiated, the better the long-term outcome becomes (Penn, Waldheter, Perkins, Mueser, & Lieberman, 2005). In fact, a critical time for treatment appears to be during the first 5 years of the disorder (Malla, Norman, & Joober, 2005). This finding, combined with the efficacy of antipsychotic medications (50% show remission after 3 months and 80% show remission at 1 year; as reviewed in Penn et al., 2005) in first-episode individuals, makes early intervention programs a crucial aspect of treatment. NIMH-funded treatment programs such as the recent RAISE initiative have shown that early intervention does produce better gains in quality of life compared with standard community treatment over a 2-year period (Kane et al., 2015, 2016; Kreyenbuhl et al., 2016). Unfortunately, even after symptom remission is attained, most individuals with schizophrenia still have deficits in social, vocational, and community functioning (Tohen et al., 2000). Negative symptoms in first-episode individuals have been linked to poor cognitive functioning and longer durations of untreated psychosis (Malla & Payne, 2005).

It is extremely rare for the first onset of schizophrenia to occur before adolescence (e.g., before the age of 12), with most diagnostic systems considering childhood-onset schizophrenia to be a different disorder than adolescent or adult-onset. More common than childhood schizophrenia, but nevertheless rare in the total population of persons with schizophrenia, are individuals who develop the illness later in life, such as after the age of 40 (late-onset schizophrenia) or after the age of 60 (very-late-onset schizophrenia) (Cohen, 1990; Howard, Rabins, Seeman, Jeste, & the International Late-Onset Schizophrenia Group, 2000). It is estimated that approximately 23% of individuals with schizophrenia develop symptoms after the age of 40 (Harris & Jeste, 1988). Late-onset schizophrenia is more common in women, and there is evidence of better social, educational, and occupational functioning as compared with early-onset schizophrenia (Howard et al., 2000).

Late-onset schizophrenia is more likely to involve positive symptoms (visual, tactile, and olfactory hallucinations; persecutory delusions) and less likely to involve formal thought disorder or negative symptoms (Bartels, Mueser, & Miles, 1998). Late-onset schizophrenia is further complicated by the lack of clear-cut distinguishing characteristics that discriminate this disorder from a variety of other disorders that develop later in old age such as dementia (Howard, Almeida, & Levy, 1994). Thus, it is important to emphasize that the symptoms of schizophrenia can arise at any point in life and are a developmental phenomenon.

The onset, course, and prognosis of the illness are closely tied to gender (Haas & Garratt, 1998). Women tend to have later age of onset of the illness (average onset is between 25 to 29 years), spend less time in hospitals, have fewer negative symptoms, demonstrate less cognitive impairment, and have better social competence and social functioning than men with the illness (Goldstein, 1988; Häfner et al., 1993; Leung & Chue, 2000; Mueser, Bellack, Morrison, & Wade, 1990; Salem & Kring, 1998). The benefits experienced by women do not appear to be explained by societal differences in tolerance for deviant behavior. A variety of different hypotheses have been advanced to account for the superior outcome of women with schizophrenia (e.g., role of estrogen on dopamine receptors, more adaptive coping with socioenvironmental stressors, improved social networks and competence [Castle & Murray, 1991; Flor-Henry, 1985; Halari et al., 2004]), but no single theory has received strong support.

In general, the onset of schizophrenia can be described as either gradual or acute. The gradual onset of schizophrenia can take place over many months or years, and it may be difficult for family members and others to clearly distinguish onset of the illness (prepsychotic and prodromal signs). In other cases, the symptoms develop rapidly over a period of a few weeks, with dramatic and easily observed changes occurring over this time. People with acute onset of schizophrenia have a somewhat better prognosis than those with a more insidious illness (Fenton & McGlashan, 1991; Kay & Lindenmayer, 1987).

Although schizophrenia is a long-term and severe psychiatric illness, there is considerable interindividual variability in the course and outcome of the illness over time (Marengo, 1994). Generally, though, once schizophrenia has developed, the illness usually continues to be present at varying degrees of severity throughout most of the person's life. Schizophrenia is usually an episodic illness, with periods of acute symptom exacerbation (i.e., relapse) requiring more intensive, often inpatient, treatment interspersed by periods of higher functioning between episodes (i.e., remission). Preventing relapse is a significant clinical concern, because each relapse leads to more persistent symptoms and greater cognitive and psychosocial impairment. Although most persons with schizophrenia live in the community, it is comparatively rare, at least in the short term, for individuals to return to their premorbid levels of functioning between episodes.

Remission is the reduction of active symptoms to nonproblematic, less severe levels (Andreasen et al., 2005). Recovery is much broader and includes both symptom remission and an improvement in social, community, occupational, and adaptive functioning. Recovery is also largely based on consumer perceptions of improvement. A recent review of 10 longitudinal studies on outcome in schizophrenia, some of which followed individuals for more than 20 years, reported that between 21% and 57% of persons with schizophrenia showed periodic episodes of recovery (improved symptoms; greater social, educational, and occupational functioning; Jobe & Harrow, 2005). In fact, some of these individuals showed extended periods of recovery without mental health treatment (Harrow, Grossman, Jobe, & Herbener, 2005; Jobe & Harrow, 2005).

Some general predictors of the course and outcome of schizophrenia have been identified, such as premorbid functioning, but overall, the ability to predict outcome is rather poor (Avison & Speechley, 1987; Tsuang, 1986). The primary reason for this is that symptom severity and functioning are determined by the dynamic interplay among biological vulnerability, environmental factors, and coping skills (Liberman et al., 1986; Nuechterlein & Dawson, 1984). Factors such as compliance with medication (Buchanan, 1992), substance abuse (Drake, Osher, & Wallach, 1989), exposure to a hostile or critical environment (Butzlaff & Hooley, 1998), availability of psychosocial programming (Bellack & Mueser, 1993), and assertive case management and outreach (Mueser et al., 1998a; Mueser, Drake, & Bond, 1997b; Phillips et al., 2001; Quinlivan et al., 1995) are all environmental factors that, in combination, play a large role in determining outcome.

The importance of environmental factors and rehabilitation programs in determining the outcome of schizophrenia is illustrated by two long-term outcome studies conducted by Harding and colleagues (DeSisto, Harding, McCormick, Ashikaga, & Brooks, 1995; Harding, Brooks, Ashikaga, Strauss, & Breier, 1987a,b). The first study was conducted in Vermont, which had a highly developed system of community-based rehabilitation programs for persons with severe mental illness. Persons with schizophrenia in this study demonstrated surprisingly positive outcomes (60% recovery rate) over the 20- to 40-year follow-up period. In contrast, similar individuals in Maine, which had more traditional hospital-based treatment programs, fared substantially worse over the long-term course of their illness. Thus, the outcome of most cases of schizophrenia is not predetermined by specific biological factors, but rather is influenced by the interaction between biological and environmental factors.

In summary, the prognosis of schizophrenia is usually considered poor to fair, and there is general agreement that it is worse than that for other major psychiatric disorders, such as bipolar disorder or major depression (Jobe & Harrow, 2005). Despite the widespread acceptance that schizophrenia is usually a lifelong disability, recent research on the long-term outcome of schizophrenia has challenged this assumption. Many persons with schizophrenia can attain symptom remission and recovery with the appropriate pharmacological and psychosocial treatments (Ciompi, 1980; Harding et al., 1987a,b; Harrow et al., 2005).

CASE STUDY

CASE IDENTIFICATION

Isaac is a 30-year-old, never-married man who lives independently and receives Social Security Supplemental Income because of impaired functioning due to schizophrenia, which developed approximately 10 years ago. Isaac maintains close contact with his parents, who live in the same town, and has occasional contact with his two older brothers and a younger sister. Isaac receives outpatient treatment at his local community mental health center, including antipsychotic medications, involvement in a group program aimed at teaching him how to manage his illness, and participation in a supported employment program that helps him maintain a part-time competitive job at a local grocery store.

PRESENTING COMPLAINTS

Isaac is dissatisfied with several areas of his life that are the focus of treatment. Although medication significantly reduced many of his paranoid symptoms, he continues to have suspicious thoughts in some social situations and feels anxious around other people. He has few friends, none of them women, and he would like to have more friends, including a girlfriend. Although his hygiene is generally good, when his psychotic symptoms increase, he becomes more disheveled, smokes more cigarettes, and becomes agitated. In addition to Isaac's mild paranoia and social anxiety, his social skills are not strong. For example, Isaac maintains poor eye contact and speaks in a low tone of voice when talking with other people, he rarely smiles spontaneously, and he has difficulty coming up with interesting conversational topics. Isaac is also dissatisfied with not completing his college degree because his three siblings have all graduated college, but he doesn't want to return to school until he has proved to himself that he can hold down his part-time job. He has a very low energy level and sometimes has trouble following through regularly on his goals, including his part-time job. Isaac recognizes that he has problems and needs help, but he lacks basic insight into his psychiatric disorder and he does not believe he has schizophrenia. Isaac also does not like having to take medications, partly because of the weight gain he has experienced from his antipsychotic medication. He periodically stops taking his medications when he feels better, which often leads to relapses in his symptoms, a deterioration in functioning, and sometimes rehospitalization.

HISTORY

Isaac first began to experience psychiatric problems 10 years ago. During the summer before his junior year in college, he was working in a busy office. He became increasingly concerned that his officemates were "out to get him" and that there was an intricate plot to discredit him. He also believed that his coworkers were secretly communicating with each other about him through certain facial expressions, choice of clothing, and the configuration of items on their desks. As his paranoia escalated, he became more disorganized in his thinking and behavior, he was less able to take care of his daily activities, and he experienced increased difficulties performing his job because of a combination of difficulties with attention and fear of his co-workers, and he eventually stopped coming to work. Isaac began to believe he was dying and attributed a variety of factors that were playing a role in his demise, including being poisoned by indoor air pollution. Isaac moved back home with his parents and informed them that he would not be returning to school in the fall. As a result of Isaac's symptoms, combined with the deterioration in his ability to take care of himself and meet role expectations at work and school, his parents took him to a mental health professional, who arranged for him to be hospitalized due to the extent of his functional impairment.

During this hospitalization, Isaac was first diagnosed with provisional schizophreniform disorder and treated with antipsychotic medication. Isaac benefited from his treatment, and his most flagrant symptoms improved substantially, including his belief that others were plotting against him. He was discharged after a 4-week period and referred to his local community mental health center for follow-up treatment and rehabilitation. Although Isaac's symptoms were improved, he continued to have impairments in his functioning, including his self-care skills, limited social relationships, and decreased ability to work or attend school in his previous capacity. When these impairments in psychosocial functioning had persisted for 6 months, his diagnosis was changed to schizophrenia.

Although Isaac continued to have symptoms and impairments of schizophrenia after he first developed the disorder 10 years ago, he also made some positive steps toward improving the quality of his life, with the help of his treatment team and his family. After several years of living at home, Isaac moved out 2 years ago to his own apartment. Isaac has been able to live on his own with the support of his family members and his case manager, who coordinates his care with Isaac's treatment team. At first when Isaac moved back home, there was a significant amount of tension in the household, as his parents and younger sister did not understand the nature of his illness and were upset by his occasionally disruptive living habits, such as staying up much of the night. With the help of a clinician who worked with Isaac and his family for 15 months after he returned home, his family was able to learn more about schizophrenia, the principles of its treatment, and strategies for solving problems together.

Last, after attending a local day treatment program, Isaac became interested in working. The mental health center where he receives his treatment had a supported employment program in which an employment specialist was assigned to Isaac to help him find a job in his area of interest and to provide supports to help him keep that job. Isaac said that he was interested in working with animals, so his employment specialist helped him get a part-time job at a local pet store, where he cares for the animals, feeds them, and cleans their cages. Isaac has kept this job for almost 2 years; on two occasions he has had to take some time off when he had a relapse of his symptoms and had to return to the hospital. Isaac's employment specialist arranged with his employer for him to be able to return to his job when he had recovered from his relapse. Isaac's case manager and employment specialist also worked together to motivate Isaac to participate in a program designed to teach him more about his psychiatric disorder and how to manage it in collaboration with others, in order to achieve his recovery goal of returning to school and completing his college degree.

ASSESSMENT

A diagnosis of schizophrenia was confirmed using the SCID. Many of the symptoms described in this vignette are highlighted in *DSM-5* criteria for schizophrenia. Regarding the A criteria, Isaac clearly experienced three "characteristic symptoms," including delusions (e.g., his beliefs about his coworkers and being poisoned by air pollution), disorganized speech and behavior, and negative symptoms (e.g., flattened affect, apathy). In terms of the B criteria, Isaac has experienced clear impairments in his social and occupational functioning—at the time of diagnosis, he was no longer able to care for himself or go to work, and he had dropped out of school. The duration criteria of *DSM-5* were met because these difficulties lasted longer than 6 months. In addition, with respect to the D and E diagnostic criteria for schizophrenia, other diagnoses were ruled out (e.g., mood disorders, substance abuse, developmental disorders). In addition to illustrating some of the symptoms and characteristic impairments of schizophrenia, this vignette illustrates that people with this illness are often able to lead rewarding and productive lives, usually with the help of pharmacological and psychological treatments, as well as social supports, despite continued symptoms and impairment due to the illness.

SUMMARY

Schizophrenia is a severe, long-term psychiatric illness characterized by impairments in social functioning, the ability to work, self-care skills, positive symptoms (hallucinations, delusions), negative symptoms (social withdrawal, apathy), and cognitive impairments. Schizophrenia is a relatively common illness, afflicting approximately 1% of the population, and tends to have an episodic course over the lifetime, with symptoms gradually improving over the long term. Most evidence indicates that schizophrenia is a biological illness that may be caused by a variety of factors, such as genetic contributions and early environmental influences (e.g., insults to the developing fetus).

Despite the biological nature of schizophrenia, environmental stress can either precipitate the onset of the illness or symptom relapses. Schizophrenia can be reliably diagnosed with structured clinical interviews, with particular attention paid to the differential diagnosis of affective disorders. There is a high comorbidity of substance use disorders in persons with schizophrenia, which must be treated if positive outcomes are to accrue. Psychological assessment of schizophrenia is most useful when it focuses on behavioral, rather than dynamic, dimensions of the illness. Thus, assessments and interventions focused on social skill deficits and family functioning have yielded promising treatment results. Biological assessments are useful at this time, primarily for descriptive rather than clinical purposes. Finally, there are a great many issues related to gender and racial or ethnic factors that remain unexplored.

Although schizophrenia remains one of the most challenging psychiatric illnesses to treat, substantial advances have been made in recent years in developing reliable diagnostic systems, understanding the role of various etiological factors, development of effective pharmacological and psychosocial treatments, and the identification of factors that mediate the long-term outcome of the illness, such as stress and substance abuse. These developments bode well for the ability of researchers and clinicians to continue to make headway in treating this serious illness.

REFERENCES

Adams, G. L., Dworkin, R. J., & Rosenberg, S. D. (1984). Diagnosis and pharmacotherapy issues in the care of Hispanics in the public sector. *American Journal of Psychiatry, 141*, 970–974.

Addington, J., Heinssen, R.K., Robinson, D. G., Schooler, N. R., Marcy, P., Brunette, M. F., . . . Kane, J. M. (2015). Duration of untreated psychosis in community treatment settings in the United States. *Psychiatric Services, 66*, 753–756.

Aguilera, A., Lopez, S. R., Breitborde, N. J. K., Kopelowicz, A., & Zarate, R. (2010). Expressed emotion and sociocultural moderation in the course of schizophrenia. *Journal of Abnormal Psychology, 119*, 875–885.

Alvir, J. M. J., Lieberman, J. A., & Safferman, A. Z. (1995). Do white-cell count spikes predict agranulocytosis in clozapine recipients? *Psychopharmacology Bulletin, 31*, 311–314.

Amador, X. F., & David, A. (2004). *Insight and psychosis: Awareness of illness in schizophrenia and related disorders*. New York, NY: Oxford University Press.

Amador, X. F., & Gorman, J. M. (1998). Psychopathologic domains and insight in schizophrenia. *Psychiatric Clinics of North America, 21*, 27–42.

Amador, X. F., Strauss, D., Yale, S., & Gorman, J. M. (1991). Awareness of illness in schizophrenia. *Schizophrenia Bulletin, 17*, 113–132.

American Psychiatric Association. (2013). *Diagnostic and statistical manual of mental disorders* (5th ed.). Arlington, VA: American Psychiatric Publishing.

Amminger, G. P., Pape, S., Rock, D., Roberts, S. A., Ott, S. L., Squires-Wheeler, E. . . . Erlenmeyer-Kimling, L. (1999). Relationship between childhood behavioral disturbance and later schizophrenia in the New York high-risk project. *American Journal of Psychiatry, 156*, 525–530.

Andreasen, N. C. (1982). Negative symptoms in schizophrenia: Definition and reliability. *Archives of General Psychiatry, 39*, 784–788.

Andreasen, N. C., Carpenter, W. T., Kane, J. M., Lasser, R. A., Marder, S. R., & Weinberger, D. R. (2005). Remission in schizophrenia: Proposed criteria and rationale for consensus. *American Journal of Psychiatry, 162*, 441–449.

Andreasen, N. C., Flaum, M., Swayze, II, V. W., Tyrrell, G., & Arndt, S. (1990). Positive and negative symptoms in schizophrenia: A critical reappraisal. *Archives of General Psychiatry, 47*, 615–621.

Andreasen, N. C., & Olsen, S. (1982). Negative versus positive schizophrenia: Definition and validation. *Archives of General Psychiatry, 39*, 784–788.

Apfel, R. J., & Handel, M. H. (1993). *Madness and loss of motherhood: Sexuality, reproduction, and long-term mental illness*. Washington, DC: American Psychiatric Press.

Appelbaum, P. S., Robbins, P. C., & Roth, L. H. (1999). Dimensional approach to delusions: Comparison across types and diagnoses. *American Journal of Psychiatry, 156*, 1938–1943.

Appelo, M. T., Woonings, F. M. J., vanNieuwenhuizen, C. J., Emmelkamp, P. M. G., Sloof, C. J., & Louwerens, J. W. (1992). Specific skills and social competence in schizophrenia. *Acta Psychiatrica Scandinavica, 85*, 419–422.

Appleby, L., Dyson, V., Altman, E., & Luchins, D. (1997). Assessing substance use in multi-problem patients: Reliability and validity of the Addiction Severity Index in a mental hospital population. *Journal of Nervous and Mental Disease, 185*, 159–165.

Argyle, N. (1990). Panic attacks in chronic schizophrenia. *British Journal of Psychiatry, 157*, 430–433.

Aro, S., Aro, H., & Keskimäki, I. (1995). Socio-economic mobility among patients with schizophrenia or major affective disorder: A 17-year retrospective follow-up. *British Journal of Psychiatry, 166*, 759–767.

Asarnow, J. R. (1988). Children at risk for schizophrenia. Converging lines of evidence. *Schizophrenia Bulletin, 14*, 613–631.

Avison, W. R., & Speechley, K. N. (1987). The discharged psychiatric patient: A review of social, social-psychological, and psychiatric correlates of outcome. *American Journal of Psychiatry, 144*, 10–18.

Azrin, N. H., & Teichner, G. (1998). Evaluation of an instructional program for improving medication compliance for chronically mentally ill outpatients. *Behaviour Research and Therapy, 36*, 849–861.

Bartels, S. J., Drake, R. E., Wallach, M. A., & Freeman, D. H. (1991). Characteristic hostility in schizophrenic outpatients. *Schizophrenia Bulletin, 17*, 163–171.

Bartels, S. J., Mueser, K. T., & Miles, K. M. (1998). Schizophrenia. In M. Hersen & V. B. VanHasselt (Eds.), *Handbook of clinical geropsychology* (pp. 173–194). New York, NY: Plenum Press.

Baskin, D., Bluestone, H., & Nelson, M. (1981). Ethnicity and psychiatric diagnosis. *Journal of Clinical Psychology, 37*, 529–537.

Bateson, G., Jackson, D. D., Haley, J., & Weakland, J. (1956). Toward a theory of schizophrenia. *Behavioral Science, 1*, 251–264.

Baum, K. M., & Walker, E. F. (1995). Childhood behavioral precursors of adult symptom dimensions in schizophrenia. *Schizophrenia Research, 16*, 111–120.

Bellack, A. S. (2004). Skills training for people with severe mental illness. *Psychiatric Rehabilitation Journal, 27*, 375–391.

Bellack, A. S., Gold, J. M., & Buchanan, R. W. (1999). Cognitive rehabilitation for schizophrenia: Problems, prospects, and strategies. *Schizophrenia Bulletin, 25*, 257–74.

Bellack, A. S., Morrison, R. L., Mueser, K. T., Wade, J. H., & Sayers, S. L. (1990a). Role play for assessing the social competence of psychiatric patients. *Psychological Assessment, 2*, 248–255.

Bellack, A. S., Morrison, R. L., Wixted, J. T., & Mueser, K. T. (1990b). An analysis of social competence in schizophrenia. *British Journal of Psychiatry, 156*, 809–818.

Bellack, A. S., & Mueser, K. T. (1993). Psychosocial treatment for schizophrenia. *Schizophrenia Bulletin, 19*, 317–336.

Bellack, A. S., Mueser, K. T., Gingerich, S., & Agresta, J. (1997). *Social skills training for schizophrenia: A step-by-step guide.* New York, NY: Guilford Press.

Bellack, A. S., Mueser, K. T., Wade, J. H., Sayers, S. L., & Morrison, R. L. (1992). The ability of schizophrenics to perceive and cope with negative affect. *British Journal of Psychiatry, 160*, 473–480.

Bellack, A. S., Sayers, M., Mueser, K. T., & Bennett, M. (1994). An evaluation of social problem solving in schizophrenia. *Journal of Abnormal Psychology, 103*, 371–378.

Bellack, A. S., & Thomas-Lohrman, S. (2003). *Maryland assessment of social competence.* Unpublished assessment manual, Baltimore, MD.

Bentall, R. P., Corcoran, R., Howard, R., Blackwood, N., & Kinderman, P. (2001). Persecutory delusions: A review and theoretical integration. *Clinical Psychology Review, 21*, 1143–1192.

Bentall, R. P., Jackson, H. F., & Pilgrim, D. (1988). Abandoning the concept of schizophrenia: Some implications of validity arguments for psychological research into psychotic phenomena. *British Journal of Clinical Psychology, 27*, 156–169.

Birchwood, M., Iqbal, Z., Chadwick, P., & Trower, P. (2000). Cognitive approach to depression and suicidal thinking in psychosis I: Ontogeny of post-psychotic depression. *British Journal of Psychiatry, 177*, 516–521.

Birchwood, M., Smith, J., Cochrane, R., Wetton, S., & Copstake, S. (1990). The social functioning scale: The development and validation of a new scale of social adjustment for the use in family intervention programmes with schizophrenic patients. *British Journal of Psychiatry, 157*, 853–859.

Bleuler, E. (1911/1950). *Dementia praecox or the group of schizophrenias.* New York, NY: International Universities Press.

Bond, G. R. (1998). Principles of the individual placement and support model: Empirical support. *Psychiatric Rehabilitation Journal, 22*, 11–23.

Boydell, J., vanOs, J., McKenzie, K., Allardyce, J., Goel, R., McCreadie, R. G., & Murray, R. M. (2001). Incidence of schizophrenia in ethnic minorities in London: Ecological study into interactions with environment. *British Medical Journal, 323*, 1336–1338.

Bracha, H. S., Wolkowitz, O. M., Lohr, J. B., Karson, C. N., & Bigelow, L. B. (1989). High prevalence of visual hallucinations in research subjects with chronic schizophrenia. *American Journal of Psychiatry, 146*, 526–528.

Braga, R. J., Mendlowicz, M. V., Marrocos, R. P., & Figueria, I. L. (2005). Anxiety disorders in outpatients with schizophrenia: Prevalence and impact on the subjective quality of life. *Journal of Psychiatric Research, 39*, 409–414.

Breier, A. (2005). Developing drugs for cognitive impairment in schizophrenia. *Schizophrenia Bulletin, 31*, 816–822.

Breitborde, N. J. K., Lopez, S. R., Chang, C., Kopelowicz, A., & Zarate, R. (2009). Emotional over-involvement can be deleterious for caregivers' health: Mexican Americans caring for a relative with schizophrenia. *Social Psychiatry and Psychiatric Epidemiology, 44*, 716–723.

Brekke, J. S., Raine, A., Ansel, M., Lencz, T., & Bird, L. (1997). Neuropsychological and psychophysiological correlates of psychosocial functioning in schizophrenia. *Schizophrenia Bulletin, 23*, 19–28.

Breslau, N., Davis, G. C., Andreski, P., & Peterson, E. (1991). Traumatic events and posttraumatic stress disorder in an urban population of young adults. *Archives of General Psychiatry, 48*, 216–222.

Brewerton, T. D. (1994). Hyperreligiosity in psychotic disorders. *Journal of Nervous and Mental Disease, 182*, 302–304.

Bromet, E. J., Naz, B., Fochtmann, L. J., Carlson, G. A., & Tanenberg-Karant, M. (2005). Longterm diagnostic stability and outcome in recent first-episode cohort studies of schizophrenia. *Schizophrenia Bulletin, 31,* 639–649.

Bruce, M. L., Takeuchi, D. T., & Leaf, P. J. (1991). Poverty and psychiatric status: Longitudinal evidence from the New Haven Epidemiologic Catchment Area Study. *Archives of General Psychiatry, 48,* 470–474.

Brune, M. (2005). "Theory of mind" in schizophrenia: A review of the literature. *Schizophrenia Bulletin, 31,* 21–42.

Brunette, M. F., & Dean, W. (2002). Community mental health care of women with severe mental illness who are parents. *Community Mental Health Journal, 38,* 153–165.

Buchanan, A. (1992). A two-year prospective study of treatment compliance in patients with schizophrenia. *Psychological Medicine, 22,* 787–797.

Buchanan, R. W., Breier, A., Kirkpatrick, B., Elkashef, A., Munson, R. C., Gellad, F., & Carpenter, W. T. (1993). Structural abnormalities in deficit and nondeficit schizophrenia. *American Journal of Psychiatry, 150,* 59–65.

Burns, H., Job, M., Bastin, M. E., Whalley, H., Macgillivray, T., Johnstone, E. C., & Lawrie, S. M. (2003). Structural disconnectivity in schizophrenia: A diffusion tensor magnetic resonance imaging study. *British Journal of Psychiatry, 182,* 439–443.

Butzlaff, R. L., & Hooley, J. M. (1998). Expressed emotion and psychiatric relapse: A meta-analysis. *Archives of General Psychiatry, 55,* 547–552.

Cannon, T. D., Mednick, S. A., Parnas, J., Schulsinger, F., Praestholm, J., & Vestergaard, A. (1993). Developmental brain abnormalities in the offspring of schizophrenic mothers. *Archives of General Psychiatry, 50,* 551–564.

Cantor-Graae, E., & Selten, J. P. (2005). Schizophrenia and migration: A meta-analysis and review. *American Journal of Psychiatry, 162,* 12–24.

Cardno, A., Marshall, E. J., Coid, B., Macdonald, A. M., Ribchester, T. R., Davies, N. J., . . . Murray, R. M. (1999). Heritability estimates for psychotic disorders: The Maudsley twin psychosis series. *Archives of General Psychiatry, 56,* 162–168.

Carmen, E., Rieker, P. P., & Mills, T. (1984). Victims of violence and psychiatric illness. *American Journal of Psychiatry, 141,* 378–383.

Carter, C. S., MacDonald, A. W., Ross, L. L., & Stenger, V. A. (2001). Anterior cingulate cortex activity and impaired self-monitoring of performance in patients with schizophrenia: An event related fMRI study. *American Journal of Psychiatry, 158,* 1423–1428.

Cascardi, M., Mueser, K. T., DeGirolomo, J., & Murrin, M. (1996). Physical aggression against psychiatric inpatients by family members and partners: A descriptive study. *Psychiatric Services, 47,* 531–533.

Castle, D. J., & Murray, R. M. (1991). The neurodevelopmental basis of sex differences in schizophrenia [Editorial]. *Psychological Medicine, 21,* 565–575.

Chadwick, P., & Birchwood, M. (1995). The omnipotence of voices II: The beliefs about voices questionnaire. *British Journal of Psychiatry, 166,* 773–776.

Cheung, F. K., & Snowden, L. R. (1990). Community mental health and ethnic minority populations. *Community Mental Health Journal, 26,* 277–289.

Chilcoat, H. D., & Breslau, N. (1998). Posttraumatic stress disorder and drug disorders: Testing causal pathways. *Archives of General Psychiatry, 55,* 913–917.

Ciompi, L. (1980). Catamnestic long-term study of life and aging in chronic schizophrenic patients. *Schizophrenia Bulletin, 6,* 606–618.

Clark, R., Anderson, N. B., Clark, V. R., & Williams, D. R. (1999). Racism as a stressor for African Americans. *American Psychologist, 54,* 805–816.

Cohen, C. I. (1990). Outcome of schizophrenia into later life: An overview. *The Gerontologist, 30,* 790–797.

Cohen, M., & Klein, D. F. (1970). Drug abuse in a young psychiatric population. *American Journal of Orthopsychiatry, 40,* 448–455.

Comas-Díaz, L. (1981). Puerto Rican espiritismo and psychotherapy. *American Journal of Orthopsychiatry, 51,* 636–645.

Combs, D. R., & Penn, D. L. (2004). The role of sub-clinical paranoia on social perception and behavior. *Schizophrenia Research, 69,* 93–104.

Combs, D. R., Penn, D. L., Cassisi, J., Michael, C. O., Wood, T. D., Wanner, J., & Adams, S. D. (2006). Perceived racism as a predictor of paranoia among African Americans. *Journal of Black Psychology, 32*(1), 87–104.

Combs, D. R., Penn, D. L., & Fenigstein, A. (2002). Ethnic differences in sub-clinical paranoia: An expansion of norms of the paranoia scale. *Cultural Diversity & Ethnic Minority Psychology, 8,* 248–256.

Copolov, D. L., Mackinnon, A., & Trauer, T. (2004). Correlates of the affective impact of auditory hallucinations in psychotic disorders. *Schizophrenia Bulletin, 30,* 163–171.

Corrigan, P. W., Liberman, R. P., & Engle, J. D. (1990). From noncompliance to collaboration in the treatment of schizophrenia. *Hospital and Community Psychiatry, 41,* 1203–1211.

Corrigan, P. W., & Penn, D. L. (1999). Lessons from social psychology on discrediting psychiatric stigma. *American Psychologist, 54,* 765–776.

Corrigan, P. W., & Penn, D. L. (2001). *Social cognition in schizophrenia.* Washington, DC: American Psychological Association.

Corse, S. J., Hirschinger, N. B., & Zanis, D. (1995). The use of the Addiction Severity Index with people with severe mental illness. *Psychiatric Rehabilitation Journal, 19,* 9–18.

Corty, E., Lehman, A. F., & Myers, C. P. (1993). Influence of psychoactive substance use on the reliability of psychiatric diagnosis. *Journal of Consulting and Clinical Psychology, 61,* 165–170.

Cosoff, S. J., & Hafner, R. J. (1998). The prevalence of comorbid anxiety in schizophrenia, schizoaffective disorder, and bipolar disorder. *Australian and New Zealand Journal of Psychiatry, 32,* 67–72.

Coverdale, J. H., & Grunebaum, H. (1998). Sexuality and family planning. In K. T. Mueser and N. Tarrier (Eds.), *Social functioning in schizophrenia* (pp. 224–237). Boston, MA: Allyn & Bacon.

Craddock, N., O'Donovan, M. C., & Owen, M. J. (2006). Genes for schizophrenia and bipolar disorder? Implications for psychiatric nosology. *Schizophrenia Bulletin, 32,* 9–16.

Craine, L. S., Henson, C. E., Colliver, J. A., & MacLean, D. G. (1988). Prevalence of a history of sexual abuse among female psychiatric patients in a state hospital system. *Hospital and Community Psychiatry, 39,* 300–304.

Crow, T. (2008). The "big bang" theory of the origin of psychosis and the faculty of language. *Schizophrenia Research, 102,* 31–52.

Crowley, T. J., Chesluk, D., Dilts, S., & Hart, R. (1974). Drug and alcohol abuse among psychiatric admissions. *Archives of General Psychiatry, 30,* 13–20.

Cutting, J. (1995). Descriptive psychopathology. In S. R. Hirsch & D. R. Weinberger (Eds.), *Schizophrenia.* New York, NY: Cambridge University Press.

Davies-Netzley, S., Hurlburt, M. S., & Hough, R. (1996). Childhood abuse as a precursor to homelessness for homeless women with severe mental illness. *Violence and Victims, 11,* 129–142.

Davis, K. L., Kahn, R. S., Ko, G., & Davidson, M. (1991). Dopamine in schizophrenia: A review and reconceptualization. *American Journal of Psychiatry, 148,* 1474–1486.

Dean, K., Walsh, E., Moran, P., Tyrer, P., Creed, F., Byford, S., . . . Fahy, T. (2006). Violence in women with psychosis in the community: A prospective study. *British Journal of Psychiatry, 188,* 264–270.

DeSisto, M. J., Harding, C. M., McCormick, R. V., Ashikaga, T., & Brooks, G. W. (1995). The Maine and Vermont three-decade studies of serious mental illness: I. Matched comparison of cross-sectional outcome. *British Journal of Psychiatry, 167,* 331–342.

Dixon, L. B., & Lehman, A. F. (1995). Family interventions for schizophrenia. *Schizophrenia Bulletin*, *21*, 631–643.

Dixon, L. B., McFarlane, W., Lefley, H., Lucksted, A., Cohen, C., Falloon, I., . . . Sondheimer, D., (2001). Evidence-based practices for services to family members of people with psychiatric disabilities. *Psychiatric Services, 52* 903–910.

Dohrenwend, B. R., Levav, I., Shrout, P. E., Schwartz, S., Naveh, G., Link, B. G., . . . Stueve, A. (1992). Socioeconomic status and psychiatric disorders: The causation-selection issue. *Science, 255*, 946–952.

Dorian, M., Garcia, J. I. R., Lopez, S. R., & Hernandez, B. (2008). Acceptance and expressed emotion in Mexican American caregivers of relatives with schizophrenia. *Family Process, 47*, 215–228.

Douglas, M. S., & Mueser, K. T. (1990). Teaching conflict resolution skills to the chronically mentally ill: Social skills training groups for briefly hospitalized patients. *Behavior Modification, 14*, 519–547.

Drake, R. E., & Becker, D. R. (1996). The individual placement and support model of supported employment. *Psychiatric Services, 47*, 473–475.

Drake, R. E., & Brunette, M. F. (1998). Complications of severe mental illness related to alcohol and drug use disorders. In M. Galanter (Ed.), *Recent developments in alcoholism, Vol. 14: The consequences of alcoholism* (pp. 285–299). New York, NY: Plenum Press.

Drake, R. E., Gates, C., Whitaker, A., & Cotton, P. G. (1985). Suicide among schizophrenics: A review. *Comprehensive Psychiatry, 26*, 90–100.

Drake, R. E., Mercer-McFadden, C., Mueser, K. T., McHugo, G. J., & Bond, G. R. (1998). Review of integrated mental health and substance abuse treatment for patients with dual disorders. *Schizophrenia Bulletin, 24*, 589–608.

Drake, R. E., Osher, F. C., Noordsy, D. L., Hurlbut, S. C., Teague, G. B., & Beaudett, M. S. (1990). Diagnosis of alcohol use disorders in schizophrenia. *Schizophrenia Bulletin, 16*, 57–67.

Drake, R. E., Osher, F. C., & Wallach, M. A. (1989). Alcohol use and abuse in schizophrenia: A prospective community study. *Journal of Nervous and Mental Disease, 177*, 408–414.

Drake, R. E., Rosenberg, S. D., & Mueser, K. T. (1996). Assessment of substance use disorder in persons with severe mental illness. In R. E. Drake & K. T. Mueser (Eds.), *Dual diagnosis of major mental illness and substance abuse disorder, II: Recent research and clinical implications*. Vol. 70: New directions in mental health services (pp. 3–17). San Francisco, CA: Jossey-Bass.

Dworkin, R. J., & Adams, G. L. (1987). Retention of Hispanics in public sector mental health services. *Community Mental Health Journal, 23*, 204–216.

Dworkin, R. H., Bernstein, G., Kaplansky, L. M., Lipsitz, J. D., Rinaldi, A., Slater, S. L., . . . Erlenmeyer-Kimling, L. (1991). Social competence and positive and negative symptoms: A longitudinal study of children and adolescents at risk for schizophrenia and affective disorder. *American Journal of Psychiatry, 148*, 1182–1188.

Dyck, D. G., Short, R., & Vitaliano, P. P. (1999). Predictors of burden and infectious illness in schizophrenia caregivers. *Psychosomatic Medicine, 61*, 411–419.

Eaton, W. W. (1975). Marital status and schizophrenia. *Acta Psychiatrica Scandinavica, 52*, 320–329.

Edwards, J., Jackson, H. J., & Pattison, P. E. (2002). Emotion recognition via facial expression and affective prosody in schizophrenia: A methodological review. *Clinical Psychology Review, 22*, 789–832.

Erlenmeyer-Kimling, L., Rock, D., Roberts, S. A., Janal, M., Kestenbaum, C., Cornblatt, B., . . . Gottesman, I. I., (2000). Attention, memory, and motor skills as childhood predictors of schizophrenia-related psychoses: The New York High-Risk project. *American Journal of Psychiatry, 157* 1416–1422.

Estroff, S. E. (1989). Self, identity, and subjective experiences of schizophrenia: In search of the subject. *Schizophrenia Bulletin, 15*, 189–196.

Evans, J. D., Paulsen, J. S., Harris, M. J., Heaton, R. K., & Jeste, D. V. (1996). A clinical and neuropsychological comparison of delusional disorder and schizophrenia. *The Journal of Neuropsychiatry and Clinical Neurosciences, 8,* 281–286.

Fannon, D., Chitnis, X., Doku, V., Tennakoon, L., Ó'Ceallaigh, S., Soni, W., . . . Sharma, T. (2000). Features of structural brain abnormality detected in early first episode psychosis. *American Journal of Psychiatry, 157,* 1829–1834.

Faraone, S. V., & Tsuang, M. T. (1985). Quantitative models of the genetic transmission of schizophrenia. *Psychological Bulletin, 98,* 41–66.

Farina, A. (1998). Stigma. In K. T. Mueser & N. Tarrier (Eds.), *Handbook of social functioning in schizophrenia* (pp. 247–279). Boston, MA: Allyn & Bacon.

Fenton, W. S., & McGlashan, T. H. (1991). Natural history of schizophrenia subtypes, II: Positive and negative symptoms and long term course. *Archives of General Psychiatry, 48,* 978–986.

Fink, P. J., & Tasman, A. (Eds.). (1992). *Stigma and mental illness.* Washington, DC: American Psychiatric Press.

First, M. B., Spitzer, R. L., Gibbon, M., & Williams, J. B. W. (1996). *Structured clinical interview for Axes I and II DSM-IV Disorders—Patient Edition (SCID-I/P).* New York: Biometrics Research Department, New York State Psychiatric Institute.

Flaum, M., Arndt, S., & Andreasen, N. C. (1991). The reliability of "bizarre" delusions. *Comparative Psychiatry, 32,* 59–65.

Flor-Henry, P. (1985). Schizophrenia: Sex differences. *Canadian Journal of Psychiatry, 30,* 319–322.

Fowler, D., Garety, P., & Kuipers, E. (1995). *Cognitive behaviour therapy for psychosis: Theory and practice.* Chichester, England: Wiley.

Fox, J. W. (1990). Social class, mental illness, and social mobility: The social selection-drift hypothesis for serious mental illness. *Journal of Health and Social Behavior, 31,* 344–353.

Freeman, D., & Garety, P. A. (2003). Connecting neurosis and psychosis: The direct influence of emotion on delusions and hallucinations. *Behaviour Research and Therapy, 41,* 923–947.

Freeman, D., Garety, P. A., Bebbington, P. E., Slater, M., Kuipers, E., Fowler, D., . . . Dunn, G., (2005). The psychology of persecutory ideation, II: A virtual reality experimental study. *Journal of Nervous and Mental Disease, 193,* 309–315.

Freeman, D., Garety, P. A., & Kuipers, E. (2001). Persecutory delusions: Developing the understanding of belief maintenance and emotional distress. *Psychological Medicine, 31,* 1293–1306.

Freeman, D., Garety, P. A., Kuipers, E., Fowler, D., & Bebbington, P. E. (2002). A cognitive model of persecutory delusions. *British Journal of Clinical Psychology, 41,* 331–347.

Fromm-Reichmann, F. (1950). *Principles of intensive psychotherapy.* Chicago, IL: University of Chicago Press.

Fuller, R., Nopoulos, P., Arndt, S., O'Leary, D., Ho, B., & Andreasen, N. C. (2002). Longitudinal assessment of premorbid cognitive functioning in patients with schizophrenia through examination of standardized scholastic test performance. *American Journal of Psychiatry, 159,* 1183–1189.

Galletly, C. A., Field, C. D., & Prior, M. (1993). Urine drug screening of patients admitted to a state psychiatric hospital. *Hospital and Community Psychiatry, 44,* 587–589.

Garety, P. A., & Freeman, D., (1999). Cognitive approaches to delusions: A critical review of theories and evidence. *British Journal of Clinical Psychology, 38* 113–154.

Gay, N. W., & Combs, D. R. (2005). Social behaviors in persons with and without persecutory delusions. *Schizophrenia Research, 80,* 2–3.

Geddes, J. R., & Lawrie, S. M. (1995). Obstetric complications and schizophrenia: A meta-analysis. *British Journal of Psychiatry, 167,* 786–793.

Glynn, S. M. (1992). Family-based treatment for major mental illness: A new role for psychologists. *The California Psychologist, 25,* 22–23.

Glynn, S. M. (1998). Psychopathology and social functioning in schizophrenia. In K. T. Mueser & N. Tarrier (Eds.), *Handbook of social functioning in schizophrenia* (pp. 66–78). Boston, MA: Allyn & Bacon.

Goeree, R., Farahati, F., Burke, N., Blackhouse, G., O'Reilly, D., Pyne, J., & Tarride, J. E. (2005). The economic burden of schizophrenia in Canada in 2004. *Current Medical Research & Opinion, 21,* 2017–2028.

Goldman, H. H. (1982). Mental illness and family burden: A public health perspective. *Hospital and Community Psychiatry, 33,* 557–560.

Goldner, E. M., Hsu, L., Waraich, P., & Somers, J. M. (2002). Prevalence and incidence studies of schizophrenic disorders: A systematic review of the literature. *Canadian Journal of Psychiatry, 47,* 833–843.

Goldstein, J. M. (1988). Gender differences in the course of schizophrenia. *American Journal of Psychiatry, 146,* 684–689.

González-Wippler, M. (1992). *Powers of the orishas: Santería and the worship of saints.* New York, NY: Original Publications.

Goodman, L. A., Dutton, M. A., & Harris, M. (1995). Physical and sexual assault prevalence among episodically homeless women with serious mental illness. *American Journal of Orthopsychiatry, 65,* 468–478.

Goodman, L. A., Dutton, M. A., & Harris, M. (1997). The relationship between violence dimensions and symptom severity among homeless, mentally ill women. *Journal of Traumatic Stress, 10,* 51–70.

Goodman, L. A., Salyers, M. P., Mueser, K. T., Rosenberg, S. D., Swartz, M., Essock, S. M., . . . the 5 Site Health and Risk Study Research Committee. (2001). Recent victimization in women and men with severe mental illness: Prevalence and correlates. *Journal of Traumatic Stress, 14,* 615–632.

Goodwin, F. K., & Jamison, K. R. (1990). *Manic-depressive illness.* New York, NY: Oxford University Press.

Gottesman, I. I. (1991). *Schizophrenia genesis: The origins of madness.* New York, NY: Freeman.

Gottesman, I. I. (2001). Psychopathology through a life span-genetic prism. *American Psychologist, 56,* 867–878.

Gottesman, I. I., & Shields, J. (1982). *Schizophrenia: The epigenetic puzzle.* New York, NY: Cambridge University Press.

Greden, J. F., & Tandon, R. (Eds.). (1991). *Negative schizophrenic symptoms: Pathophysiology and clinical implications.* Washington, DC: American Psychiatric Press.

Green, M. F., Kern, R. S., Braff, D. L., & Mintz, J. (2000). Neurocognitive deficits and functional outcome in schizophrenia: Are we measuring the "right stuff"? *Schizophrenia Bulletin, 26,* 119–136.

Green, M. F., Marshall, B. D., Jr., Wirshing, W. C., Ames, D., Marder, S. R., McGurk, S., . . . Mintz, J. (1997). Does risperidone improve verbal working memory in treatment-resistant schizophrenia? *American Journal of Psychiatry, 154,* 799–804.

Green, M. F., Nuechterlein, K. H., Gold, J. M., Barch, D. M., Cohen, J., Essock, S., . . . Marder, S. R. (2004). Approaching a consensus battery for clinical trials in schizophrenia: The NIMH-MATRICS conference to select cognitive domains and test criteria. *Biological Psychiatry, 56,* 301–307.

Green, M. F., Olivier, B., Crawley, J. N., Penn, D. L., & Silverstein, S. (2005). Social cognition in schizophrenia: Recommendations from the measurement and treatment research to improve cognition in schizophrenia new approaches conference. *Schizophrenia Bulletin, 31,* 882–887.

Greenfield, S. F., Strakowski, S. M., Tohen, M., Batson, S. C., & Kolbrener, M. L. (1994). Childhood abuse in first-episode psychosis. *British Journal of Psychiatry, 164,* 831–834.

Griffith, E. E. H., Young, J. L., & Smith, D. L. (1984). An analysis of the therapeutic elements in a black church service. *Hospital and Community Psychiatry, 35,* 464–469.

Grubaugh, A. L., Zinzow, H. M., Paul, L., Egede, L. E., & Frueh, B. C. (2011). Trauma exposure and posttraumatic stress disorder in adults with severe mental illness: A critical review. *Clinical Psychology Review, 31,* 883–899.

Haas, G. L., & Garratt, L. S. (1998). Gender differences in social functioning. In K. T. Mueser & N. Tarrier (Eds.), *Handbook of social functioning in schizophrenia* (pp. 149–180). Boston, MA: Allyn & Bacon.

Haddock, G., McCarron, J., Tarrier, N., & Faragher, E. B. (1999). Scales to measure dimensions of hallucinations and delusions: The psychotic symptom rating scales (PSYRATS). *Psychological Medicine, 29*(4), 879–889.

Häfner, H., Maurer, K., Trendler, G., an der Heiden, W., & Schmidt, M. (2005). The early course of schizophrenia and depression. *European Archives of Psychiatry and Clinical Neuroscience, 255,* 167–173.

Häfner, H., Riecher-Rössler, A., an der Heiden, W., Maurer, K., Fätkenheuer, B., & Löffler, W. (1993). Generating and testing a causal explanation of the gender difference in age at first onset of schizophrenia. *Psychological Medicine, 23,* 925–940.

Halari, R., Kumari, V., Mehorotra, R., Wheeler, M., Hines, M., & Sharma, T. (2004). The relationship of sex hormones and cortisol with cognitive functioning in schizophrenia. *Journal of Pharmacology, 18,* 366–374.

Halford, W. K., Schweitzer, R. D., & Varghese, F. N. (1991). Effects of family environment on negative symptoms and quality of life on psychotic patients. *Hospital and Community Psychiatry, 42,* 1241–1247.

Hans, S. L., Marcus, J., Henson, L., Auerbach, J. G., & Mirsky, A. F. (1992). Interpersonal behavior of children at risk for schizophrenia. *Psychiatry, 55,* 314–335.

Harding, C. M., Brooks, G. W., Ashikaga, T., Strauss, J. S., & Breier, A. (1987a). The Vermont longitudinal study of persons with severe mental illness, I: Methodology, study sample, and overall status 32 years later. *American Journal of Psychiatry, 144,* 718–726.

Harding, C. M., Brooks, G. W., Ashikaga, T., Strauss, J. S., & Breier, A. (1987b). The Vermont longitudinal study of persons with severe mental illness, II: Long-term outcome of subjects who retrospectively met DSM-II criteria for schizophrenia. *American Journal of Psychiatry, 144,* 727–735.

Harris, M. (1996). Treating sexual abuse trauma with dually diagnosed women. *Community Mental Health Journal, 32,* 371–385.

Harris, M. J., & Jeste, D. V. (1988). Late-onset schizophrenia: An overview. *Schizophrenia Bulletin, 14,* 39–45.

Harrison, P. J., & Owen, M. J. (2003). Genes for schizophrenia: Recent findings and their pathophysiological implications. *The Lancet, 361,* 417–419.

Harrow, M., Grossman, L. S., Jobe, T. H., & Herbener, E. S. (2005). Do patients with schizophrenia ever show periods of recovery? A 15-year multi-follow-up study. *Schizophrenia Bulletin, 31,* 723–734.

Hatfield, A. B., & Lefley, H. P. (Eds.) (1987). *Families of the mentally ill: Coping and adaptation.* New York, NY: Guilford Press.

Hatfield, A. B., & Lefley, H. P. (Eds.) (1993). *Surviving mental illness: Stress, coping, and adaptation.* New York, NY: Guilford Press.

Hawton, K., Sutton, L., Haw, C., Sinclair, J., & Deeks, J. J. (2005). Schizophrenia and suicide: Systematic review of risk factors. *British Journal of Psychiatry, 187,* 9–20.

Haynes, S. (1986). Behavioral model of paranoid behaviors. *Behavior Therapy, 17,* 266–287.

Heaton, R. K., Gladsjo, J. A., Palmer, B. W., Kuck, J., Marcotte, T. D., & Jeste, D. V. (2001). Stability and course of neuropsychological deficits in schizophrenia. *Archives of General Psychiatry, 58,* 24–32.

Heinrichs, R. W. (2005). The primacy of cognition in schizophrenia. *American Psychologist, 60,* 229–242.

Heinssen, R. K., Liberman, R. P., & Kopelowicz, A. (2000). Psychosocial skills training for schizophrenia: Lessons from the laboratory. *Schizophrenia Bulletin, 26,* 21–46.

Hiday, V. A., Swartz, M. S., Swanson, J. W., Borum, R., & Wagner, H. R. (1999). Criminal victimization of persons with severe mental illness. *Psychiatric Services, 50,* 62–68.

Hodgins, S., & Côté, G. (1993). Major mental disorder and antisocial personality disorder: A criminal combination. *Bulletin of the American Academy of Psychiatry Law, 21,* 155–160.

Hodgins, S., & Côté, G. (1996). Schizophrenia and antisocial personality disorder: A criminal combination. In L. B. Schlesinger (Ed.), *Explorations in criminal psychopathology: Clinical syndromes with forensic implications* (pp. 217–237). Springfield, IL: Charles C. Thomas.

Hodgins, S., Mednick, S. A., Brennan, P. A., Schulsinger, F., & Engberg, M. (1996). Mental disorder and crime: Evidence from a Danish birth cohort. *Archives of General Psychiatry, 53,* 489–496.

Hollingshead, A. B., & Redlich, F. C. (1958). *Social class and mental illness: A community study.* New York, NY: Wiley.

Hough, R. L., Landsverk, J. A., Karno, M., Burnam, A., Timbers, D. M., Escobar, J. I., & Regier, D. A. (1987). Utilization of health and mental health services by Los Angeles Mexican Americans and non-Hispanic whites. *Archives of General Psychiatry, 44,* 702–709.

Howard, R., Almeida, O., & Levy, R. (1994). Phenomenology, demography and diagnosis in late paraphrenia. *Psychological Medicine, 24,* 397–410.

Howard, R., Rabins, P. V., Seeman, M. V., Jeste, D. V., & the International Late-Onset Schizophrenia Group. (2000). Late-onset schizophrenia and very-late-onset schizophrenia-like psychosis: An international consensus. *American Journal of Psychiatry, 157,* 172–178.

Hu, T., Snowden, L. R., Jerrell, J. M., & Nguyen, T. D. (1991). Ethnic populations in public mental health: Services choices and level of use. *American Journal of Public Health, 81,* 1429–1434.

Huang, X. Y., Hung, B. J., Sun, F. K., Lin, J. D., & Chen, C. C. (2009). The experiences of carers in Taiwanese culture who have long-term schizophrenia in their families: A phenomenological study. *Journal of Psychiatric and Mental Health Nursing, 16,* 874–883.

Hutchings, P. S., & Dutton, M. A. (1993). Sexual assault history in a community mental health center clinical population. *Community Mental Health Journal, 29,* 59–63.

Inskip, H. M., Harris, E. C., & Barraclough, B. (1998). Lifetime risk of suicide for affective disorder, alcoholism, and schizophrenia. *British Journal of Psychiatry, 172,* 35–37.

Jablensky, A. (1989). Epidemiology and cross-cultural aspects of schizophrenia. *Psychiatric Annals, 19,* 516–524.

Jablensky, A. (1999). Schizophrenia: Epidemiology. *Current Opinion in Psychiatry, 12,* 19–28.

Jablensky, A. (2000). Epidemiology of schizophrenia: The global burden of disease and disability. *European Archives of Psychiatry and Clinical Neuroscience, 250,* 274–285.

Jablensky, A., McGrath, J., Herman, H., Castle, D., Gureje, O., Evans, M., . . . Harvey, C. (2000). Psychotic disorders in urban areas: An overview of the study on low prevalence disorders. *Australian and New Zealand Journal of Psychiatry, 34,* 221–236.

Jablensky, A., Sartorius, N., Ernberg, G., Anker, M., Korten, A., & Cooper, J. E. (1992). Schizophrenia: Manifestations, incidence, and course in different cultures—A World Health Organization ten country study. *Psychological Medical Monograph Supplement, 20,* 1–97.

Jacob, T. (1975). Family interaction in disturbed and normal families: A methodological and substantive review. *Psychological Bulletin, 82,* 33–65.

Jacobson, A. (1989). Physical and sexual assault histories among psychiatric outpatients. *American Journal of Psychiatry, 146,* 755–758.

Jacobson, A., & Herald, C. (1990). The relevance of childhood sexual abuse to adult psychiatric inpatient care. *Hospital and Community Psychiatry, 41,* 154–158.

Jacobson, A., & Richardson, B. (1987). Assault experiences of 100 psychiatric inpatients: Evidence of the need for routine inquiry. *American Journal of Psychiatry, 144,* 508–513.

Jimenez, J. M., Todman, M., Perez, M., Godoy, J. F., & Landon-Jimenez, D. V. (1996). The behavioral treatment of auditory hallucinatory responding of a schizophrenic patient. *Journal of Behavioral Therapy and Experimental Psychiatry, 27,* 299–310.

Jobe, T. H., & Harrow, M. (2005). Long-term outcome of patients with schizophrenia: A review. *Canadian Journal of Psychiatry, 50,* 892–900.

Jones, B. E., Gray, B. A., & Parsons, E. B. (1981). Manic-depressive illness among poor urban blacks. *American Journal of Psychiatry, 138,* 654–657.

Jones, B. E., Gray, B. A., & Parsons, E. B. (1983). Manic-depressive illness among poor urban Hispanics. *American Journal of Psychiatry, 140,* 1208–1210.

Jones, E. (1999). The phenomenology of abnormal belief. *Philosophy, Psychiatry, and Psychology, 6,* 1–16.

Junginger, J., Barker, S., & Coe, D. (1992). Mood theme and bizarreness of delusions in schizophrenia and mood psychosis. *Journal of Abnormal Psychology, 101,* 287–292.

Kane, J. M., & Marder, S. R. (1993). Psychopharmacologic treatment of schizophrenia. *Schizophrenia Bulletin, 19,* 287–302.

Kane, J. M., Robinson, D. G., Schooler, N. R., Mueser, K. T., Penn, D. L., Rosenheck, R. A., . . . Heinssen, R. K. (2016). Comprehensive versus usual community care for first-episode psychosis: 2-year outcomes from the NIMH RAISE early treatment program. *American Journal of Psychiatry, 173,* 362–372.

Kane, J. M., Schooler, N. R., Marcy, P., Correll, C. U., Brunette, M. F., Mueser, K. T., . . . Robinson, D. G. (2015). The RAISE early treatment program for first-episode psychosis: Background, rationale, and study design. *Journal of Clinical Psychiatry, 76,* 240–246.

Kay, S. R., Fiszbein, A., & Opler, L. A. (1987). The positive and negative syndrome scale (PANSS) for schizophrenia. *Schizophrenia Bulletin, 13,* 261–276.

Kay, S. R., & Lindenmayer, J. (1987). Outcome predictors in acute schizophrenia: Prospective significance of background and clinical dimensions. *Journal of Nervous and Mental Disease, 175,* 152–160.

Kemp, R., Hayward, P., Applewhaite, G., Everitt, B., & David, A. (1996). Compliance therapy in psychotic patients: Randomised controlled trial. *British Medical Journal, 312,* 345–349.

Kemp, R., Kirov, G., Everitt, B., Hayward, P., & David, A. (1998). Randomised controlled trial of compliance therapy: 18-month follow-up. *British Journal of Psychiatry, 173,* 271–272.

Kendler, K. S. (1982). Demography of paranoid psychosis (delusional disorder): A review and comparison with schizophrenia and affective illness. *Archives of General Psychiatry, 39,* 890–902.

Kendler, K. S., & Diehl, S. R. (1993). The genetics of schizophrenia. *Schizophrenia Bulletin, 19,* 261–285.

Kern, R. S., Liberman, R. P., Kopelowicz, A., Mintz, J., & Green, M. F. (2002). Applications of errorless learning for improving work performance in persons with schizophrenia. *American Journal of Psychiatry, 159,* 1921–1926.

Kessler, R. C., Foster, C. L., Saunders, W. B., & Stang, P. E. (1995). Social consequences of psychiatric disorders, I: Educational attainment. *American Journal of Psychiatry, 152,* 1026–1032.

Kessler, R. C., Sonnega, A., Bromet, E., Hughes, M., & Nelson, C. B. (1995). Posttraumatic stress disorder in the National Comorbidity Survey. *Archives of General Psychiatry, 52,* 1048–1060.

Kindermann, S. S., Karimi, A., Symonds, L., Brown, G. G., & Jeste, D. V. (1997). Review of functional magnetic resonance imaging in schizophrenia. *Schizophrenia Research, 27,* 143–156.

Kirch, D. G. (1993). Infection and autoimmunity as etiologic factors in schizophrenia: A review and reappraisal. *Schizophrenia Bulletin, 19,* 355–370.

Knapp, M., Mangalore, R., & Simon, J. (2004). The global costs of schizophrenia. *Schizophrenia Bulletin, 30,* 279–293.

Kraepelin, E. (1971). *Dementia praecox and paraphrenia* (R. M. Barclay, Trans.). New York, NY: Robert E. Krieger. (Original work published 1919)

Kramer, M. S., Vogel, W. H., DiJohnson, C., Dewey, D. A., Sheves, P., Cavicchia, S., . . . Kimes, I. (1989). Antidepressants in "depressed" schizophrenic inpatients. *Archives of General Psychiatry, 46,* 922–928.

Kranzler, H. R., Kadden, R. M., Burleson, J. A., Babor, T. F., Apter, A., & Rounsaville, B. J. (1995). Validity of psychiatric diagnoses in patients with substance use disorders: Is the interview more important than the interviewer? *Comprehensive Psychiatry, 36,* 278–288.

Kreyenbuhl, J. A., Medoff, D. R., McEvoy, J. P., Smith, T. E., Hackman, A. L., Nossel, I. R., Dixon, L. B., Essok, S. M., & Buchanan, R. W. (2016). The RAISE Connection Program: Psychopharmacological treatment of people with a first episode of schizophrenia. *Psychiatric Services, 1*(67), 1300–1306.

Kymalainen, J. A., & Weisman de Mamani, A. G. (2008). Expressed emotion, communication deviance, and culture in families of patients with schizophrenia: A review of the literature. *Cultural Diversity and Ethnic Minority Psychology, 14,* 85–91.

Lam, D. H. (1991). Psychosocial family intervention in schizophrenia: A review of empirical studies. *Psychological Medicine, 21,* 423–441.

Lawrie, S. M., & Abukmeil, S. S. (1998). Brain abnormality in schizophrenia: A systematic and quantitative review of volumetric magnetic resonance imaging studies. *British Journal of Psychiatry, 172,* 110–120.

Leff, J., Tress, K., & Edwards, B. (1988). The clinical course of depressive symptoms in schizophrenia. *Schizophrenia Research, 1,* 25–30.

Leff, J., & Vaughn, C. (1985). *Expressed emotion in families: Its significance for mental illness.* New York, NY: Guilford Press.

Lefley, H. P. (1990). Culture and chronic mental illness. *Hospital and Community Psychiatry, 41,* 277–286.

Lehman, A. F., Myers, C. P., Dixon, L. B., & Johnson, J. L. (1994). Defining subgroups of dual diagnosis patients for service planning. *Hospital and Community Psychiatry, 45,* 556–561.

Lehman, A. F., Myers, C. P., Dixon, L. B., & Johnson, J. L. (1996). Detection of substance use disorders among psychiatric inpatients. *Journal of Nervous and Mental Disease, 184,* 228–233.

Leung, A., & Chue, P. (2000). Sex differences in schizophrenia: A review of the literature. *Acta Psychiatrica Scandinavica, 401,* 3–38.

Levinson, D. F., & Levitt, M. M. (1987). Schizoaffective mania reconsidered. *American Journal of Psychiatry, 144,* 415–425.

Levinson, D. F., & Mowry, B. J. (1991). Defining the schizophrenia spectrum: Issues for genetic linkage studies. *Schizophrenia Bulletin, 17,* 491–514.

Liberman, R. P. (1994). Treatment and rehabilitation of the seriously mentally ill in China: Impressions of a society in transition. *American Journal of Orthopsychiatry, 64,* 68–77.

Liberman, R. P., Mueser, K. T., Wallace, C. J., Jacobs, H. E., Eckman, T., & Massel, H. K. (1986). Training skills in the psychiatrically disabled: Learning coping and competence. *Schizophrenia Bulletin, 12,* 631–647.

Liddle, P. F. (1987). Schizophrenic syndromes, cognitive performance and neurological dysfunction. *Psychological Medicine, 17,* 49–57.

Liddle, P. F. (1995). Brain imaging. In S. R. Hirsch & D. R. Weinberger (Eds.), *Schizophrenia* (pp. 425–439). Cambridge, MA: Blackwell Science.

Liddle, P. F. (1997). Dynamic neuroimaging with PET, SPET or fMRI. *International Review of Psychiatry, 9,* 331–337.

Lieberman, J. A., Mailman, R. B., Duncan, G., Sikich, L., Chakos, M., Nichols, D. E., & Kraus, J. E. (1998). A decade of serotonin research: Role of serotonin in treatment of psychosis. *Biological Psychiatry, 44,* 1099–1117.

Lim, K. O., Hedehus, M., deCrespigny, A., Menon, V., & Moseley, M. (1998). Diffusion tensor imaging of white matter tracts in schizophrenia. *Biological Psychiatry, 43*(Suppl. 8S) 11S.

Lin, K-M., & Kleinman, A. M. (1988). Psychopathology and clinical course of schizophrenia: A cross-cultural perspective. *Schizophrenia Bulletin, 14*, 555–567.

Lincoln, E. C., & Mamiya, L. H. (1990). *The black church in the African American experience.* Durham, NC: Duke University Press.

Lincoln, C. V., & McGorry, P. (1995). Who cares? Pathways to psychiatric care for young people experiencing a first episode of psychosis. *Psychiatric Services, 46*, 1166–1171.

Lipschitz, D. S., Kaplan, M. L., Sorkenn, J. B., Faedda, G. L., Chorney, P., & Asnis, G. M. (1996). Prevalence and characteristics of physical and sexual abuse among psychiatric outpatients. *Psychiatric Services, 47*, 189–191.

Lo, W. H., & Lo, T. (1977). A ten-year follow-up study of Chinese schizophrenics in Hong Kong. *British Journal of Psychiatry, 131*, 63–66.

Lopez, S. R., Ramirez Garcia, J. I., Ullman, J. B., Kopelowicz, A., Jenkins, J., Breitborde, N. J. K., & Placencia, P. (2009). Cultural variability in the manifestation of expressed emotion. *Family Process, 48*, 179–194.

Loring, M., & Powell, B. (1988). Gender, race, and *DSM-II*: A study of the objectivity of psychiatric diagnostic behavior. *Journal of Health and Social Behavior, 29*, 1–22.

Lysaker, P. H., Bell, M. D., Zito, W. S., & Bioty, S. M. (1995). Social skills at work: Deficits and predictors of improvement in schizophrenia. *Journal of Nervous and Mental Disease, 183*, 688–692.

Magaña, A. B., Goldstein, M. J., Karno, M., Miklowitz, D. J., Jenkins, J., & Falloon, I. R. H. (1986). A brief method for assessing expressed emotion in relatives of psychiatric patients. *Psychiatry Research, 17*, 203–212.

Magliano, L., Fadden, G., Madianos, M., deAlmeida, J. M., Held, T., Guarneri, M., . . . Maj, M. (1998). Burden on the families of patients with schizophrenia: Results of the BIOMED I study. *Social Psychiatry and Psychiatric Epidemiology, 33*, 405–412.

Maisto, S. A., Carey, M. P., Carey, K. B., Gordon, C. M., & Gleason, J. R. (2000). Use of the AUDIT and the DAST-10 to identify alcohol and drug use disorders among adults with a severe and persistent mental illness. *Psychological Assessment, 12*, 186–192.

Malla, A. K., Norman, R. M. G., & Joober, R. (2005). First-episode psychosis, early intervention, and outcome: What haven't we learned? *Canadian Journal of Psychiatry, 50*, 881–891.

Malla, A., & Payne, J. (2005). First-episode psychosis: Psychopathology, quality of life, and functional outcome. *Schizophrenia Bulletin, 31*, 650–671.

Manschreck, T. C. (1996). Delusional disorder: The recognition and management of paranoia. *The Journal of Clinical Psychiatry, 57*, 32–38.

Marengo, J. (1994). Classifying the courses of schizophrenia. *Schizophrenia Bulletin, 20*, 519–536.

Marwaha, S., & Johnson, S. (2004). Schizophrenia and employment: A review. *Social Psychiatry and Psychiatric Epidemiology, 39*, 337–349.

Mattes, J. A., & Nayak, D. (1984). Lithium versus fluphenazine for prophylaxis in mainly schizophrenic schizoaffectives. *Biological Psychiatry, 19*, 445–449.

May, A. (1997). Psychopathology and religion in the era of "enlightened science": A case report. *European Journal of Psychiatry, 11*, 14–20.

McClure, R. J., Keshavan, M. S., & Pettegrew, J. W. (1998). Chemical and physiologic brain imaging in schizophrenia. *Psychiatric Clinics of North America, 21*, 93–122.

McDonald, C., Grech, A., Toulopoulou, T., Schulze, K., Chapple, B., Sham, P., . . . Murray, R. M. (2002). Brain volumes in familial and non-familial schizophrenic probands and their unaffected relatives. *American Journal of Medical Genetics and Neuropsychiatric Genetics, 114*, 616–625.

McEvoy, J. P., Freter, S., Everett, G., Geller, J. L., Appelbaum, P., Apperson, L. J., & Roth, L. (1989). Insight and the clinical outcome of schizophrenic patients. *The Journal of Nervous and Mental Disease, 177*, 48–51.

McGrath, J., Saha, S., Welham, J., El Saadi, O., MacCauley, C., & Chant, D. (2004). A systematic review of the incidence of schizophrenia: The distribution and the influence of sex, urbanicity, migrant status, and methodology. *BMC Medicine, 2,* 13.

McGuffin, P., Owen, M. J., & Farmer, A. E. (1995). Genetic basis of schizophrenia. *The Lancet, 346,* 678–682.

Merriam, A. E., Kay, S. R., Opler, L. A., Kushner, S. F., & van Praag, H. M. (1990). Neurological signs and the positive-negative dimension in schizophrenia. *Biological Psychiatry, 28,* 181–192.

Miyamoto, S., LaMantia, A. S., Duncan, G. E., Sullivan, P., Gilmore, J. H., & Lieberman, A. (2003). Recent advances in the neurobiology of schizophrenia. *Molecular Interventions, 3,* 27–39.

Monahan, J., Steadman, H. J., Silver, E., Appelbaum, P. S., Robbins, P. C., Mulvey, E. P., . . . Banks, S. (2001). *Rethinking risk assessment: The MacArthur study of mental disorder and violence.* New York, NY: Oxford University Press.

Montero, I., Asencio, A., Hernández, I., Masanet, M. J., Lacruz, M., Bellver, F., . . . Ruiz, I. (2001). Two strategies for family intervention in schizophrenia. A randomized trial in a Mediterranean environment. *Schizophrenia Bulletin, 27,* 661–670.

Moore, H., West, A. R., & Grace, A. A. (1999). The regulation of forebrain dopamine transmission: Relevance to the pathophysiology and psychopathology of schizophrenia. *Biological Psychiatry, 46,* 40–55.

Moos, R. H., & Moos, B. S. (1981). *Family environment scale manual.* Palo Alto, CA: Consulting Psychologists Press.

Morales-Dorta, J. (1976). *Puerto Rican espiritismo: Religion and psychotherapy.* New York, NY: Vantage Press.

Mueser, K. T., & Bellack, A. S. (1998). Social skills and social functioning. In K. T. Mueser and N. Tarrier (Eds.), *Handbook of social functioning in schizophrenia* (pp. 79–96). Boston, MA: Allyn & Bacon.

Mueser, K. T., Bellack, A. S., & Brady, E. U. (1990a). Hallucinations in schizophrenia. *Acta Psychiatrica Scandinavica, 82,* 26–29.

Mueser, K. T., Bellack, A. S., Douglas, M. S., & Morrison, R. L. (1991a). Prevalence and stability of social skill deficits in schizophrenia. *Schizophrenia Research, 5,* 167–176.

Mueser, K. T., Bellack, A. S., Douglas, M. S., & Wade, J. H. (1991b). Prediction of social skill acquisition in schizophrenic and major affective disorder patients from memory and symptomatology. *Psychiatry Research, 37,* 281–296.

Mueser, K. T., Bellack, A. S., Morrison, R. L., & Wade, J. H. (1990b). Gender, social competence, and symptomatology in schizophrenia: A longitudinal analysis. *Journal of Abnormal Psychology, 99,* 138–147.

Mueser, K. T., Bellack, A. S., Morrison, R. L., & Wixted, J. T. (1990c). Social competence in schizophrenia: Premorbid adjustment, social skill, and domains of functioning. *Journal of Psychiatric Research, 24,* 51–63.

Mueser, K. T., Bellack, A. S., Wade, J. H., Sayers, S. L., Tierney, A., & Haas, G. (1993). Expressed emotion, social skill, and response to negative affect in schizophrenia. *Journal of Abnormal Psychology, 102,* 339–351.

Mueser, K. T., Bennett, M., & Kushner, M. G. (1995). Epidemiology of substance use disorders among persons with chronic mental illnesses. In A. Lehman & L. Dixon (Eds.), *Double jeopardy: Chronic mental illness and substance abuse* (pp. 9–25). Chur, Switzerland: Harwood Academic.

Mueser, K. T., & Berenbaum, H. (1990). Psychodynamic treatment of schizophrenia: Is there a future? *Psychological Medicine, 20,* 253–262.

Mueser, K. T., Bond, G. R., Drake, R. E., & Resnick, S. G. (1998a). Models of community care for severe mental illness: A review of research on case management. *Schizophrenia Bulletin, 24,* 37–74.

Mueser, K. T., Curran, P. J., & McHugo, G. J. (1997a). Factor structure of the Brief Psychiatric Rating Scale in schizophrenia. *Psychological Assessment, 9*, 196–204.

Mueser, K. T., Douglas, M. S., Bellack, A. S., & Morrison, R. L. (1991c). Assessment of enduring deficit and negative symptom subtypes in schizophrenia. *Schizophrenia Bulletin, 17*, 565–582.

Mueser, K. T., Drake, R. E., & Bond, G. R. (1997b). Recent advances in psychiatric rehabilitation for patients with severe mental illness. *Harvard Review of Psychiatry, 5*, 123–137.

Mueser, K. T., & Glynn, S. M. (1999). *Behavioral family therapy for psychiatric disorders* (2nd ed.). Oakland, CA: New Harbinger.

Mueser, K. T., Goodman, L. B., Trumbetta, S. L., Rosenberg, S. D., Osher, F. C., Vidaver, R., . . . Foy, D. W. (1998b). Trauma and posttraumatic stress disorder in severe mental illness. *Journal of Consulting and Clinical Psychology, 66*, 493–499.

Mueser, K. T., Levine, S., Bellack, A. S., Douglas, M. S., & Brady, E. U. (1990d). Social skills training for acute psychiatric patients. *Hospital and Community Psychiatry, 41*, 1249–1251.

Mueser, K. T., & McGurk, S. R. (2004). Schizophrenia. *The Lancet, 363*, 2063–2072.

Mueser, K. T., Rosenberg, S. D., Drake, R. E., Miles, K. M., Wolford, G., Vidaver, R., & Carrieri, K. (1999). Conduct disorder, antisocial personality disorder, and substance use disorders in schizophrenia and major affective disorders. *Journal of Studies on Alcohol, 60*, 278–284.

Mueser, K. T., Rosenberg, S. D., Goodman, L. A., & Trumbetta, S. L. (2002). Trauma, PTSD, and the course of schizophrenia: An interactive model. *Schizophrenia Research, 53*, 123–143.

Mueser, K. T., Salyers, M. P., & Mueser, P. R. (2001). A prospective analysis of work in schizophrenia. *Schizophrenia Bulletin, 27*, 281–296.

Mueser, K. T., Salyers, M. P., Rosenberg, S. D., Goodman, L. A., Essock, S. M., Osher, F. C., . . . the 5 Site Health & Risk Study Research Committee. (2004). Interpersonal trauma and posttraumatic stress disorder in patients with severe mental illness: Demographic, clinical, and health correlates. *Schizophrenia Bulletin, 30*, 45–57.

Mueser, K. T., Yarnold, P. R., & Bellack, A. S. (1992). Diagnostic and demographic correlates of substance abuse in schizophrenia and major affective disorder. *Acta Psychiatrica Scandinavica, 85*, 48–55.

Munk-Jørgensen, P. (1987). First-admission rates and marital status of schizophrenics. *Acta Psychiatrica Scandinavica, 76*, 210–216.

Murphy, H. B. M., & Raman, A. C. (1971). The chronicity of schizophrenia in indigenous tropical peoples. *British Journal of Psychiatry, 118*, 489–497.

Murray, C. J. L., & Lopez, A. D. (Eds.). (1996). *The global burden of disease and injury series, Vol. I: A comprehensive assessment of mortality and disability from diseases, injuries, and risk factors in 1990 and projected to 2020.* Cambridge, MA: Harvard University Press.

Narrow, W. E., Rae, D. S., Robins, L. N., & Regier, D. A. (2002). Revised prevalence estimates of mental disorders in the United States. *Archives of General Psychiatry, 59*, 115–123.

Neumann, C. S., Grimes, K., Walker, E., & Baum, K. (1995). Developmental pathways to schizophrenia: Behavioral subtypes. *Journal of Abnormal Psychology, 104*, 558–566.

Nolan, K. A., Volavka, J., Mohr, P., & Czobor, P. (1999). Psychopathy and violent behavior among patients with schizophrenia or schizoaffective disorder. *Psychiatric Services, 50*, 787–792.

Norman, R. M., Scholten, D. J., Malla, A. K., & Ballageer, T. (2005). Early signs in schizophrenia spectrum disorders. *The Journal of Nervous and Mental Disease, 193*, 17–23.

Nuechterlein, K. H., & Dawson, M. E. (1984). A heuristic vulnerability/stress model of schizophrenic episodes. *Schizophrenia Bulletin, 10*, 300–312.

Oldridge, M. L., & Hughes, I. C. T. (1992). Psychological well-being in families with a member suffering from schizophrenia. *British Journal of Psychiatry, 161*, 249–251.

Overall, J. E., & Gorham, D. R. (1962). The brief psychiatric rating scale. *Psychological Reports, 10*, 799–812.

Padgett, D. K., Patrick, C., Burns, B. J., & Schlesinger, H. J. (1994). Women and outpatient mental health services: Use by black, Hispanic, and white women in a national insured population. *Journal of Mental Health Administration, 21,* 347–360.

Palmer, B. W., Heaton, R. K., Paulsen, J. S., Kuck, J., Braff, D., Harris, M. J., . . . Jeste, D. V. (1997). Is it possible to be schizophrenic yet neuropsychologically normal? *Neuropsychology, 11,* 437–446.

Palmer, B. A., Pankratz, V. S., & Bostwick, J. M. (2005). The lifetime risk of suicide in schizophrenia: A reexamination. *Archives of General Psychiatry, 62,* 247–253.

Parra, F. (1985). Social tolerance of the mentally ill in the Mexican American community. *International Journal of Social Psychiatry, 31,* 37–47.

Parrott, B., & Lewine, R. (2005). Socioeconomic status of origin and the clinical expression of schizophrenia. *Schizophrenia Research, 75,* 417–424.

Patterson, T. L., Goldman, S., McKibbin, C. L., Hughs, T., & Jeste, D. (2001). UCSD performance-based skills assessment: Development of a new measure of everyday functioning for severely mentally ill adults. *Schizophrenia Bulletin, 27,* 235–245.

Pearlson, G. D. (2000). Neurobiology of schizophrenia. *Annals of Neurology, 48,* 556–566.

Peen, J., & Dekker, J. (1997). Admission rates for schizophrenia in the Netherlands: An urban/rural comparison. *Acta Psychiatrica Scandinavica, 96,* 301–305.

Penn, D. L., Combs, D. R., & Mohamed, S. (2001). Social cognition and social functioning in schizophrenia. In P. W. Corrigan & D. L. Penn (Eds.), *Social cognition and schizophrenia* (pp. 97–122). Washington, DC: American Psychological Association.

Penn, D. L., Corrigan, P. W., Bentall, R. P., Racenstein, J. M., & Newman, L. (1997). Social cognition in schizophrenia. *Psychological Bulletin, 121,* 114–132.

Penn, D., Hope, D. A., Spaulding, W. D., & Kucera, J. (1994). Social anxiety in schizophrenia. *Schizophrenia Research, 11,* 277–284.

Penn, D. L., Mueser, K. T., Spaulding, W. D., Hope, D. A., & Reed, D. (1995). Information processing and social competence in chronic schizophrenia. *Schizophrenia Bulletin, 21,* 269–281.

Penn, D. L., Waldheter, E. J., Perkins, D. O., Mueser, K. T., & Lieberman, J. A. (2005). Psychosocial treatment for first-episode psychosis: A research update. *American Journal of Psychiatry, 162,* 2220–2232.

Perlstein, W. M., Carter, C. S., Noll, D. C., & Cohen, J. D. (2001). Relation of prefrontal cortex dysfunction to working memory and symptoms of schizophrenia. *American Journal of Psychiatry, 158,* 1105–1113.

Phillips, S. D., Burns, B. J., Edgar, E. R., Mueser, K. T., Linkins, K. W., Rosenheck, R. A., . . . Herr, E. C. M. (2001). Moving assertive community treatment into standard practice. *Psychiatric Services, 52,* 771–779.

Pinkham, A. L., Penn, D. L., Green, M. F., Buck, B., Healey, K., & Harvey, P. D. (2014). The social cognition psychometric evaluation study: Results of the expert survey and RAND panel. *Schizophrenia Bulletin, 40,* 813–823.

Pinkham, A., Penn, D., Perkins, D., & Lieberman, J. (2003). Implications for the neural basis of social cognition for the study of schizophrenia. *American Journal of Psychiatry, 160,* 815–824.

Pitschel-Walz, G., Leucht, S., Bäuml, J., Kissling, W., & Engel, R. R. (2001). The effect of family interventions on relapse and rehospitalization in schizophrenia: A meta-analysis. *Schizophrenia Bulletin, 27,* 73–92.

Pope, H. G., & Lipinski, J. F. (1978). Diagnosis in schizophrenia and manic-depressive illness. *Archives of General Psychiatry, 35,* 811–828.

Qin, P., & Nordentoft, M. (2005). Suicide risk in relation to psychiatric hospitalization: Evidence based on longitudinal registers. *Archives of General Psychiatry, 62,* 427–432.

Quinlivan, R., Hough, R., Crowell, A., Beach, C., Hofstetter, R., & Kenworthy, K. (1995). Service utilization and costs of care for severely mentally ill clients in an intensive case management program. *Psychiatric Services, 46,* 365–371.

Regier, D. A., Farmer, M. E., Rae, D. S., Locke, B. Z., Keith, S. J., Judd, L. L., & Goodwin, F. K. (1990). Comorbidity of mental disorders with alcohol and other drug abuse. *Journal of the American Medical Association, 264,* 2511–2518.

Resnick, H. S., Kilpatrick, D. G., Dansky, B. S., Saunders, B. E., & Best, C. L. (1993). Prevalence of civilian trauma and post-traumatic stress disorder in a representative national sample of women. *Journal of Consulting and Clinical Psychology, 61,* 984–991.

Robins, L. N. (1966). *Deviant children grown up.* Huntington, NY: Krieger.

Robins, L. N., & Price, R. K. (1991). Adult disorders predicted by childhood conduct problems: Results from the NIMH Epidemiologic Catchment Area project. *Psychiatry, 54,* 116–132.

Rodrigo, G., Lusiardo, M., Briggs, G., & Ulmer, A. (1991). Differences between schizophrenics born in winter and summer. *Acta Psychiatrica Scandinavica, 84,* 320–322.

Rose, S. M., Peabody, C. G., & Stratigeas, B. (1991). Undetected abuse among intensive case management clients. *Hospital and Community Psychiatry, 42,* 499–503.

Rosenberg, S. D., Drake, R. E., Wolford, G. L., Mueser, K. T., Oxman, T. E., Vidaver, R. M., . . . Luckoor, R. (1998). Dartmouth assessment of lifestyle instrument (DALI): A substance use disorder screen for people with severe mental illness. *American Journal of Psychiatry, 155,* 232–238.

Rosenberg, S. D., Mueser, K. T., Friedman, M. J., Gorman, P. G., Drake, R. E., Vidaver, R. M., . . . Jankowski, M. K. (2001). Developing effective treatments for posttraumatic disorders: A review and proposal. *Psychiatric Services, 52,* 1453–1461.

Rosenheck, R., Leslie, D., Keefe, R., McEvoy, J., Swartz, M., Perkins, D., . . . Lieberman, J. (2006). Barriers to employment for people with schizophrenia. *American Journal of Psychiatry, 163,* 411–417.

Ross, C. A., Anderson, G., & Clark, P. (1994). Childhood abuse and the positive symptoms of schizophrenia. *Hospital and Community Psychiatry, 45,* 489–491.

Roy, A. (Ed.) (1986). *Suicide.* Baltimore, MD: Williams and Wilkins.

Rutter, M. (1984). Psychopathology and development, I: Childhood antecedents of adult psychiatric disorder. *Australian and New Zealand Journal of Psychiatry, 18,* 225–234.

Saha, S., Chant, D., Welham, J., & McGrath, J. (2005). A systematic review of the prevalence of schizophrenia. *Public Library of Science, 2,* e141.

Saha, S., Welham, J., Chant, D., & McGrath, J. (2006). Incidence of schizophrenia does not vary with economic status of the country. *Social Psychiatry and Psychiatric Epidemiology, 41,* 338–340.

Salem, J. E., & Kring, A. M. (1998). The role of gender in the reduction of etiologic heterogeneity in schizophrenia. *Clinical Psychology Review, 18,* 795–819.

Salokangas, R. K. R. (1978). Socioeconomic development and schizophrenia. *Psychiatria Fennica,* 103–112.

Samele, C., vanOs, J., McKenzie, K., Wright, A., Gilvarry, C., Manley, C., . . . Murray, R. (2001). Does socioeconomic status predict course and outcome in patients with psychosis? *Social Psychiatry and Psychiatric Epidemiology, 36,* 573–581.

Sammons, M. T. (2005). Pharmacotherapy for delusional disorder and associated conditions. *Professional Psychology: Research and Practice, 36,* 476–479.

Sands, J. R., & Harrow, M. (1999). Depression during the longitudinal course of schizophrenia. *Schizophrenia Bulletin, 25,* 157–171.

Sartorius, N., Jablensky, A., Korten, A., Ernberg, G., Anker, M., Cooper, J. E., & Day, R. (1986). Early manifestations and first-contact incidence of schizophrenia in different cultures. *Psychological Medicine, 16,* 909–928.

Schaub, A., Behrendt, B., Brenner, H. D., Mueser, K. T., & Liberman, R. P. (1998). Training schizophrenic patients to manage their symptoms: Predictors of treatment response to the German version of the symptom management module. *Schizophrenia Research, 31,* 121–130.

Schiffman, J., Walker, E., Ekstrom, M., Schulsinger, F., Sorensen, H., & Mednick, S. (2004). Childhood videotaped social and neuromotor precursors of schizophrenia: A prospective investigation. *American Journal of Psychiatry, 161,* 2021–2027.

Schock, K., Clay, C., & Cipani, E. (1998). Making sense of schizophrenic symptoms: Delusional statements and behavior may be functional in purpose. *Journal of Behavior Therapy and Experimental Psychiatry, 29,* 131–141.

Schuckit, M. A. (1995). *Drug and alcohol abuse: A clinical guide to diagnosis and treatment (Critical issues in psychiatry)* (4th ed.). New York, NY: Plenum Press.

Searles, H. (1965). *Collected papers on schizophrenia and related subjects.* New York, NY: International Universities Press.

Sedler, M. J. (1995). Understanding delusions. *Psychiatric Clinics of North America, 18,* 251–262.

Sevy, S., & Davidson, M. (1995). The cost of cognitive impairment in schizophrenia. *Schizophrenia Research, 17,* 1–3.

Silver, E., Arseneault, L., Langley, J., Caspi, A., & Moffitt, T. E. (2005). Mental disorder and violent victimization in a total birth cohort. *American Journal of Public Health, 95,* 2015–2021.

Skilbeck, W. M., Acosta, F. X., Yamamoto, J., & Evans, L. A. (1984). Self-reported psychiatric symptoms among black, Hispanic, and white outpatients. *Journal of Clinical Psychology, 40,* 1184–1189.

Smith, T. E., Hull, J. W., Anthony, D. T., Goodman, M., Hedayat-Harris, A., Felger, T., . . . Romanelli, S. (1997). Post-hospitalization treatment adherence of schizophrenic patients: Gender differences in skill acquisition. *Psychiatry Research, 69,* 123–129.

Smith, T. E., Hull, J. W., Romanelli, S., Fertuck, E., & Weiss, K. A. (1999). Symptoms and neurocognition as rate limiters in skills training for psychotic patients. *American Journal of Psychiatry, 156,* 1817–1818.

Steadman, H. J., Mulvey, E. P., Monahan, J., Robbins, P. C., Appelbaum, P. S., Grisso, T., . . . Silver, E. (1998). Violence by people discharged from acute psychiatric inpatient facilities and by others in the same neighborhoods. *Archives of General Psychiatry, 55,* 393–401.

Stone, A., Greenstein, R., Gamble, G., & McLellan, A. T. (1993). Cocaine use in chronic schizophrenic outpatients who receive depot neuroleptic medications. *Hospital and Community Psychiatry, 44,* 176–177.

Sue, D. W., & Sue, D. C. (1990). *Counseling the culturally different: Theory and practice* (2nd ed.). New York, NY: Wiley.

Sue, S., Fujino, D. C., Hu, L.-T., Takeuchi, D. T., & Zane, N. W. S. (1991). Community mental health services for ethnic minority groups: A test of the cultural responsiveness hypothesis. *Journal of Consulting and Clinical Psychology, 59,* 533–540.

Susser, E., & Lin, S. (1992). Schizophrenia after prenatal exposure to the Dutch Hunger Winter of 1944–1945. *Archives of General Psychiatry, 49,* 983–988.

Susser, E., Neugebauer, R., Hoek, H. W., Brown, A. S., Lin, S., Labovitz, D., & Gorman, J. M. (1996). Schizophrenia after prenatal famine: Further evidence. *Archives of General Psychiatry, 53,* 25–31.

Susser, E., Struening, E. L., & Conover, S., (1989). Psychiatric problems in homeless men: Lifetime psychosis, substance use, and current distress in new arrivals at New York City shelters. *Archives of General Psychiatry, 46,* 845–850.

Swanson, J. W. (1994). Mental disorder, substance abuse, and community violence: An epidemiological approach. In J. Monahan & H. Steadman (Eds.), *Violence and mental disorder: Developments in risk assessment* (pp. 101–136). Chicago, IL: University of Chicago Press.

Swanson, J. W., Holzer, C. E., Ganju, V. K., & Jono, R. T. (1990). Violence and psychiatric disorder in the community: Evidence from the Epidemiologic Catchment Area Surveys. *Hospital and Community Psychiatry, 41,* 761–770.

Swartz, M. S., Swanson, J. W., Hiday, V. A., Borum, R., Wagner, H. R., & Burns, B. J. (1998). Violence and severe mental illness: The effects of substance abuse and nonadherence to medication. *American Journal of Psychiatry, 155,* 226–231.

Switzer, G. E., Dew, M. A., Thompson, K., Goycoolea, J. M., Derricott, T., & Mullins, S. D. (1999). Posttraumatic stress disorder and service utilization among urban mental health center clients. *Journal of Traumatic Stress, 12,* 25–39.

Takei, N., Mortensen, P. B., Klaening, U., Murray, R. M., Sham, P. C., O'Callaghan, E., & Munk-Jørgensen, P. (1996). Relationship between in utero exposure to influenza epidemics and risk of schizophrenia in Denmark. *Biological Psychiatry, 40,* 817–824.

Takei, N., Sham, P. C., O'Callaghan, E., Glover, G., & Murray, R. M. (1995). Schizophrenia: Increased risk associated with winter and city birth—A case-control study in 12 regions within England and Wales. *Journal of Epidemiology and Community Health, 49,* 106–109.

Tandon, R., Keshavan, M. S., & Nasrallah, H. A. (2008a). Schizophrenia "just the facts": What we know in 2008, Part 1: Overview. *Schizophrenia Research, 100,* 4–19.

Tandon, R., Keshavan, M. S., & Nasrallah, H. A. (2008b). Schizophrenia "just the facts": What we know in 2008, Part 2: Epidemiology and etiology. *Schizophrenia Research, 102,* 1–18.

Telles, C., Karno, M., Mintz, J., Paz, G., Arias, M., Tucker, D., & Lopez, S. (1995). Immigrant families coping with schizophrenia: Behavioral family intervention v. case management with a low-income Spanish-speaking population. *British Journal of Psychiatry, 167,* 473–479.

Terkelsen, K. G. (1983). Schizophrenia and the family, II: Adverse effects of family therapy. *Family Process, 22,* 191–200.

Tessler, R., & Gamache, G. (1995). *Evaluating family experiences with severe mental illness:* To be used in conjunction with the Family Experiences Interview Schedule (FEI S): The Evaluation Center @ HSRI toolkit. Cambridge, MA: The Evaluation Center.

Test, M. A., Wallisch, L. S., Allness, D. J., & Ripp, K. (1989). Substance use in young adults with schizophrenic disorders. *Schizophrenia Bulletin, 15,* 465–476.

Thomas, H. V., Dalman, C., David, A. S., Gentz, J., Lewis, G., & Allebeck, P. (2001). Obstetric complications and risk of schizophrenia: Effect of gender, age at diagnosis and maternal history of psychosis. *British Journal of Psychiatry, 179,* 409–414.

Tien, A. Y., & Eaton, W. W. (1992). Psychopathologic precursors and sociodemographic risk factors for the schizophrenia syndrome. *Archives of General Psychiatry, 49,* 37–46.

Tienari, P. (1991). Interaction between genetic vulnerability and family environment: The Finnish Adoptive Family Study of schizophrenia. *Acta Psychiatrica Scandinavica, 84,* 460–465.

Tienari, P., Sorri, A., Lahti, I., Naarala, M., Wahlberg, K., Moring, J., . . . Wynne, L. C. (1987). Genetic and psychosocial factors in schizophrenia: The Finnish Adoptive Family Study. *Schizophrenia Bulletin, 13,* 477–484.

Tienari, P., Wynne, L. C., Sorri, A., Lahti, I., Lasky, K., Moring, J., . . . Wahlberg, K. (2004). Genotype-environment interaction in schizophrenia spectrum disorder. *British Journal of Psychiatry, 184,* 216–222.

Tjaden, P., & Thoennes, N. (1998, November). *Prevalence, incidence, and consequences of violence against women: Findings from the National Violence against Women Survey (Research in Brief).* Washington, DC: U.S. Department of Justice, National Institute of Justice.

Tohen, M., Strakowski, S. M., Zarate, C., Hennen, J., Stoll, A. L., Suppes, T., . . . Baldessarinis, R. J. (2000). The McLean-Harvard first episode project: Six month symptomatic and functional outcome in affective and nonaffective psychosis. *Biological Psychiatry, 48,* 467–476.

Tollefson, G. D., & Sanger, T. M. (1997). Negative symptoms: A path analytic approach to a double-blind, placebo- and haloperidol-controlled clinical trial with olanzapine. *American Journal of Psychiatry, 154,* 466–474.

Torrey, E. F. (1992). Are we overestimating the genetic contribution to schizophrenia? *Schizophrenia Bulletin, 18,* 159–170.

Torrey, E. F. (2001). *Surviving schizophrenia* (4th ed.). New York, NY: HarperCollins.

Torrey, E. F., Bowler, A. E., & Clark, K. (1997). Urban birth and residence as risk factors for psychoses: An analysis of 1880 data. *Schizophrenia Research, 25,* 169–176.

Torrey, E. F., Bowler, A. E., Rawlings, R., & Terrazas, A. (1993). Seasonality of schizophrenia and stillbirths. *Schizophrenia Bulletin, 19,* 557–562.

Torrey, E. F., Stieber, J., Ezekiel, J., Wolfe, S. M., Sharfstein, J., Noble, J. H., & Flynn, L. M. (1992). *Criminalizing the seriously mentally ill: The abuse of jails as mental hospitals.* Joint Report of the National Alliance of the Mentally Ill. Washington, DC: Public Citizen's Health Research Group.

Tsuang, M. T. (1986). Predictors of poor and good outcome in schizophrenia. In L. Erlenmeyer-Kimling & N. E. Miller (Eds.), *Life-span research on the prediction of psychopathology.* Hillsdale, NJ: Erlbaum.

Uttaro, T., & Mechanic, D. (1994). The NAMI consumer survey analysis of unmet needs. *Hospital and Community Psychiatry, 45,* 372–374.

Valenstein, M., Blow, F. C., Copeland, L. A., McCarthy, J. F., Zeber, J. E., Gillon, L., . . . Stavenger, T. (2004). Poor antipsychotic adherence among patients with schizophrenia: Medication and patient factors. *Schizophrenia Bulletin, 30,* 255–264.

Van Der Does, A. J. W., Dingemans, P. M. A. J., Linszen, D. H., Nugter, M. A., & Scholte, W. F. (1993). Symptom dimensions and cognitive and social functioning in recent-onset schizophrenia. *Psychological Medicine, 23,* 745–753.

Velligan, D. I., Mahurin, R. K., Diamond, P. L., Hazleton, B. C., Eckert, S. L., & Miller, A. L. (1997). The functional significance of symptomatology and cognitive function in schizophrenia. *Schizophrenia Research, 25,* 21–31.

Wahlbeck, K., Cheine, M., Essali, A., & Adams, C. (1999). Evidence of clozapine's effectiveness in schizophrenia: A systematic review and meta-analysis of randomized trials. *American Journal of Psychiatry, 156,* 990–999.

Walker, E., Downey, G., & Caspi, A. (1991). Twin studies of psychopathology: Why do the concordance rates vary? *Schizophrenia Research, 5,* 211–221.

Walker, E. F., Grimes, K. E., Davis, D. M., & Smith, A. J. (1993). Childhood precursors of schizophrenia: Facial expressions of emotion. *American Journal of Psychiatry, 150,* 1654–1660.

Wallace, C. J., Liberman, R. P., Tauber, R., & Wallace, J. (2000). The Independent Living Skills Survey: A comprehensive measure of the community functioning of severely and persistently mentally ill individuals. *Schizophrenia Bulletin, 26,* 631–658.

Watt, N. F. (1978). Patterns of childhood social development in adult schizophrenics. *Archives of General Psychiatry, 35,* 160–165.

Waxler, N. E., & Mishler, E. G. (1971). Parental interaction with schizophrenic children and well siblings. *Archives of General Psychiatry, 25,* 223–231.

Webb, C., Pfeiffer, M., Mueser, K. T., Mensch, E., DeGirolamo, J., & Levenson, D. F. (1998). Burden and well-being of caregivers for the severely mentally ill: The role of coping style and social support. *Schizophrenia Research, 34,* 169–180.

Westermeyer, J. (1989). Psychiatric epidemiology across cultures: Current issues and trends. *Transcultural Psychiatric Research Review, 26,* 5–25.

Whaley, A. L. (1997). Ethnicity, race, paranoia, and psychiatric diagnoses: Clinician bias versus socio-cultural differences. *Journal of Psychopathology and Behavioral Assessment, 19,* 1–20.

Whaley, A. L. (2001). Cultural mistrust: An important psychological construct for diagnosis and treatment of African-Americans. *Professional Psychology: Research and Practice, 32,* 555–562.

Wilk, C. M., Gold, J. M., McMahon, R. P., Humber, K., Iannone, V. N., & Buchanan, R. W. (2005). No, it is not possible to be schizophrenic yet neuropsychologically normal. *Neuropsychology, 6,* 778–786.

Wright, I. C., Rabe-Hesketh, S., Woodruff, P. W. R., David, A. S., Murrary, R. M., & Bullmore, E. T. (2000). Meta-analysis of regional brain volumes in schizophrenia. *American Journal of Psychiatry, 157,* 16–25.

Wu, E. Q., Birnbaum, H. G., Shi, L., Ball, D. E., Kessler, R. C., Moulis, M., & Aggarwal, J. (2005). The economic burden of schizophrenia in the United States in 2002. *Journal of Clinical Psychiatry, 66,* 1122–1129.

Xiong, W., Phillips, M. R., Hu, X., Ruiwen, W., Dai, Q., Kleinman, J., & Kleinman, A. (1994). Family-based intervention for schizophrenic patients in China: A randomised controlled trial. *British Journal of Psychiatry, 165,* 239–247.

Yamada, N., Nakajima, S., & Noguchi, T. (1998). Age at onset of delusional disorder is dependent on the delusional theme. *Acta Psychiatrica Scandinavica, 97,* 122–124.

Young, C. R., Bowers, M. B., & Mazure, C. M. (1998). Management of the adverse effects of clozapine. *Schizophrenia Bulletin, 24,* 381–390.

Yung, A. R., & McGorry, P. D. (1996). The initial prodrome in psychosis: Descriptive and qualitative aspects. *Australian and New Zealand Journal of Psychiatry, 30,* 587–599.

Zahid, M. A., & Ohaeri, J. U. (2010). Relationship of family caregiver burden with quality of care and psychopathology in a sample of Arab subjects with schizophrenia. *BMC Psychiatry, 10,* 71.

Zhang, M., Wang, M., Li, J., & Phillips, M. R. (1994). Randomised-control trial of family intervention for 78 first-episode male schizophrenic patients: An 18-month study in Suzhou, *Jiangsu. British Journal of Psychiatry, 165,* 96–102.

Zigler, E., & Glick, M. (1986). *A developmental approach to adult psychopathology.* New York, NY: Wiley.

Zubin, J., & Spring, B. (1977). Vulnerability: A new view of schizophrenia. *Journal of Abnormal Psychology, 86,* 103–123.

CHAPTER 7

Bipolar and Related Disorders

SHERI L. JOHNSON and DAVID J. MIKLOWITZ

O VER THE PAST two decades, there has been a considerable resurgence of interest in bipolar disorder (BD; formerly known as manic-depressive illness). This resurgence is attributable in part to the availability of new data on pharmacological agents and psychological treatments for the disorder, as well as a growing body of work on the genetic, neurophysiological and neuroanatomical contributors. It has also been driven by the increasing recognition that the onset of the disorder is often in childhood or adolescence.

In this chapter, we describe diagnostic criteria, epidemiology, and course and prognosis of BD, with particular attention to developmental considerations pertinent to early-onset bipolar illness. Although few studies have examined psychosocial factors relevant to the onset of BD, there is now a considerable literature on psychosocial stressors that affect the course and outcome of the disease and we consider these psychosocial factors as we review the course and prognosis of BD. We then discuss the pharmacological and psychological approaches to treatment of BD. We describe current diagnostic debates and considerations, and we summarize available diagnostic tools. A case study then illustrates diagnosis and treatment. Current etiological models view BD as a primarily genetic illness that creates a biological vulnerability to symptoms. Although the nature of biological vulnerability remains unclear, biological vulnerability is assumed to intensify the individual's vulnerability to environmental stressors. In the final sections, we offer directions for further research.

DESCRIPTION OF THE DISORDER

Several forms of BD have been recognized. All are defined by manic symptoms of varying degrees of severity and duration. The core symptoms believed to constitute mania—elation, grandiosity, and hyperactivation—have been recognized for well over 100 years and remain fairly consistent across editions of the *Diagnostic and Statistical Manual of Mental Disorders* (*DSM*). In this section, we describe the core features of mania, hypomania and depression according to *DSM-5* (American Psychiatric Association [APA], APA, 2013).

According to the *DSM-5* (APA, 2013), manic episodes are defined by elated, expansive, or irritable mood (or any combination of these) and increased activity, plus at least

---

Adult Psychopathology and Diagnosis, Eighth Edition. Edited by Deborah C. Beidel and B. Christopher Frueh.
© 2018 John Wiley & Sons, Inc. Published 2018 by John Wiley & Sons, Inc.
Companion website: www.wiley.com/go/beidel/psychopathology8e

three (four if the mood is only irritable) of the following symptoms: decreased need for sleep; racing thoughts or flight of ideas; rapid speech; inflated self-esteem (also called grandiosity); impulsive, reckless behavior (e.g., spending sprees, hypersexuality); and distractibility. These symptoms must be present for at least 1 week or interrupted by hospitalization or emergency treatment. They must also cause functional impairment. Hypomania is characterized by parallel symptoms, but the criteria specify only that the symptoms last at least 4 days and result in a distinct, observable change in functioning rather than severe impairment.

DSM-5 criteria differ from *DSM-IV-TR* (APA, 2000) in listing increased activity as one of the cardinal symptoms of mania and hypomania. It has been argued that changes in activity are more easily recognized than changes in subjective mood state. As such, it is hoped that the *DSM-5* criteria may lead to improved accuracy in the detection of manic and hypomanic episodes.

Major depressive episodes, when present, are defined by at least five symptoms lasting at least 2 weeks, including sad mood or loss of interest/pleasure in daily activities. Other symptoms include insomnia or hypersomnia, psychomotor agitation or retardation, increases or decreases in weight or appetite, loss of energy, difficulty concentrating or making decisions, feelings of worthlessness, and suicidal ideation or behavior. To meet diagnostic criteria for a major depressive episode, the depressive symptoms must also be associated with functional impairment.

Manic, hypomanic or depressive episodes that are clearly related to an ingested substance or to biological treatments—including antidepressant medications—are classified as substance-induced mood disorders, unless the individual continues to have symptoms and impairment that exceed the expected duration of the substance. In the latter case, the bipolar diagnosis is applied.

The *DSM-5* refers to mixed features as a course specifier that can occur in mania or depression. Mixed features are denoted if a manic episode is accompanied by at least three co-occurring symptoms of depression, or if a major depressive episode is accompanied by at least three co-occurring manic symptoms. For example, a manic or hypomanic patient meets the mixed specifier criteria if he or she has manic symptoms of irritability, increased activity, decreased need for sleep, impulsive behavior, grandiosity, and pressured speech along with depressive symptoms of loss of interest, suicidal thinking, and feelings of worthlessness.

Bipolar I disorder is defined by the presence of at least one lifetime manic episode that is not substance-induced (see the case study toward the end of this chapter). In other words, patients need not have experienced a major depressive episode to meet the diagnostic criteria for bipolar I disorder. Rates of "unipolar mania" (mania without depression) are between 25% and 33% in community samples but only about 10% in clinical samples (Depue & Monroe, 1978; Karkowski & Kendler, 1997; Kessler, Chiu, Demler, & Walters, 2005; Weissman & Myers, 1978). Most patients with unipolar mania eventually develop depressive episodes, however. In a 20-year study of unipolar mania, 20 of 27 patients had episodes of depression during the follow-up period (Solomon et al., 2003).

Bipolar II disorder is characterized by major depressive episodes alternating with hypomanic episodes. Both must be present; one cannot be diagnosed with bipolar II disorder on the basis of hypomanic episodes alone. About 10% of bipolar II patients develop a full manic or mixed episode within a 10-year period, and, thus, convert to bipolar I disorder (Coryell et al., 1995).

Cyclothymic disorder is a variant of BD characterized by 2 years or more (or 1 year among youths) of alternations between hypomanic and depressive symptoms, but none of these alternations meet the full *DSM-5* criteria for a hypomanic, manic, or major depressive episode. Unspecified BD (previously "not otherwise specified" [NOS]) is reserved for patients whose disorder meets the minimum number of required symptoms but not the duration requirements for a full manic, hypomanic, or depressive, episode; or those who meet the duration criteria but fall short by one to two symptoms. Many childhood-onset patients receive this subthreshold diagnosis. Among children with unspecified BD who have one or more relatives with a lifetime history of mania, more than 50% "convert" to bipolar I or II disorder over 5 years (Axelson et al., 2011b).

EPIDEMIOLOGY

Differences in prevalence estimates vary across studies, depending in part on culture and on how broadly the bipolar spectrum is defined. The largest available multinational study, conducted by the World Health Organization, reported lifetime prevalence rates in 61,392 adults in 11 countries: 0.6% for bipolar I disorder, 0.4% for bipolar II disorder, and 1.4% for subthreshold BD defined by at least one symptom of mania. The highest rates were observed in the United States; lifetime prevalence rates were 1.0% for bipolar I disorder, 1.1% for bipolar II, and 2.4% for subthreshold BD (Merikangas et al., 2011). Although there are fewer epidemiological data on cyclothymic disorder, it is believed to affect as much as 4.2% of the general population (Regeer et al., 2004).

AGE AT ONSET

The onset of mood disorders appears to be getting younger in successive birth cohorts (Kessler et al., 2005; Wickramaratne, Weissman, Leaf, & Holford, 1989). Kessler et al. (2005) reported that the lifetime risk of bipolar I or II disorders in 18- to 29-year-olds was 22 times higher than in persons over 60. It is possible, however, that younger persons feel less stigmatized by psychiatric symptoms and are more likely than older persons to report manic symptoms.

In a large ($N = 10,123$) community sample of adolescents in the United States, 2.5% met lifetime *DSM-IV* criteria for bipolar I or II disorder (Merikangas et al., 2012). Many investigators suspect that BD is more likely to be diagnosed by practitioners in the US (e.g., Reichart & Nolen, 2004). In a large US database of outpatient insurance visits, the rate of BD diagnoses in young people increased by 67% and the rate of hospitalizations for BD diagnoses in young people increased by 75% from 1995 to 2000 (Harpaz-Rotem, Leslie, Martin, & Rosenheck, 2005; Harpaz-Rotem & Rosenheck, 2004). In a US nationally representative survey of office visits to outpatient medical practitioners, the number of visits for youths with a diagnosis of BD increased 40-fold between 1994–1995 and 2002–2003 (Moreno et al., 2007). However, this increase reflected a change from 0.01% to 0.4%, suggesting the disorder is still rarely diagnosed in younger patients.

The base rates of bipolar spectrum disorders (types I and II, and BD not elsewhere classified) in youths appear comparable across countries when standardized diagnostic interviews are used. An aggregate analysis of 17 clinical studies of 31,443 children (ages 7 to 21) across the world reported a rate of 1.6% in US sites and 2.2% in non-US sites, a nonsignificant difference. The prevalence of more narrowly defined bipolar I disorder also did not differ significantly across US (0.5%) and non-US sites (0.26%) (Goldstein et al., 2017; Van Meter, Moreira, & Youngstrom, 2011).

The mean age of onset of bipolar I disorder is 18.4 years, and of bipolar II is 20 years (Merikangas et al., 2011), but there is substantial variability. About half of those diagnosed develop the disease by age 25 (Merikangas et al., 2011), with a lower median age of onset of about 18 in treatment samples; about 28% report onset before age 13 (Perlis et al., 2004). Earlier age at onset is associated with rapid cycling and other negative outcomes in adulthood (Coryell et al., 2003; Schneck et al., 2004). Early onset may be a more virulent form of the disorder Children with parents who have an early onset of BD are at higher risk for BD than those whose parents have later onsets (Hafeman et al., 2016).

GENDER AND RACIAL-ETHNIC ISSUES

Women and men are equally likely to develop bipolar I disorder. Women, however, report more depressive episodes than do men and, correspondingly, some (but not all) studies report that women are more likely than men to have bipolar II disorder (e.g., Leibenluft, 1997; Schneck et al., 2004). Women are also more likely to experience rapid-cycling BD (at least four episodes per year), again potentially related to the greater vulnerability to depression (Schneck et al., 2004).

There appear to be important racial and ethnic disparities in the treatment of BD. In the National Comorbidity Survey-Replication (NCS-R) large epidemiological sample, none of the African American persons who were diagnosed with BD were receiving adequate treatment (Johnson & Johnson, 2014). Disparity appears to persist even in specialized treatment centers – in the Systematic Treatment Enhancement Program for BD (STEP-BD), African American and Latino patients received fewer prescriptions for psychiatric medications than European American patients (Gonzalez et al., 2007). Moreover, African American bipolar patients were less likely than Caucasian patients to have an outpatient follow-up visit within 3 months of the initial diagnosis (Kilbourne et al., 2005).

There is a long history of research suggesting that clinicians are likely to over-diagnose psychosis among African American patients (Snowden, 2001). One study found that adult African American patients were less likely than Caucasians to be prescribed mood stabilizers or benzodiazepines and more likely to be given antipsychotic medications (Kupfer, Frank, Grochocinski, Houck, & Brown, 2005). African American adolescents with BD are treated with atypical antipsychotic medications for longer periods than are Caucasian adolescents, even when adjusting for the severity of psychotic symptoms (Patel, DelBello, Keck, & Strakowski, 2005). Not surprisingly given these treatment disparities, the course of BD illness may be worse among African American patients, with greater rates of attempted suicide and hospitalization. The reasons for these racial disparities in treatment are unclear, but are not explained by lack of insurance, lack of treatment-seeking, or lack of acknowledgment of symptoms among African American patients (Johnson & Johnson, 2014). Implicit racial biases have been documented among mental health providers (McMaster, 2016).

CLINICAL PICTURE

Researchers who have examined the factor structure of the manic syndrome typically identify a pure mania cluster of symptoms along with other frequently concomitant symptoms. A principal component analysis of data from 576 diagnosed manic patients identified seven stable underlying factors: depressive mood, irritable aggression, insomnia, depressive inhibition, pure manic symptoms, emotional lability/agitation, and psychosis (Sato, Bottlender, Kleindienst, & Moller, 2002). Through cluster analysis, Sato et al. identified four phenomenological subtypes of acute mania: pure, aggressive, psychotic, and depressive-mixed mania.

The pattern of manic symptoms has been investigated in youths with BD. A meta-analysis of seven studies of youth aged 5–18 years indicated that the most common symptoms during manic episodes were increased energy, distractibility, and pressure of speech (Kowatch, Youngstrom, Danielyan, & Findling, 2005b). Approximately 80% showed irritability and grandiosity, whereas 70% had the "cardinal" manic symptoms of elated mood, decreased need for sleep, or racing thoughts. Less common symptoms included hypersexuality and psychotic symptoms. Thus, most manic children showed symptoms that also characterize adult mania.

SUICIDE

Bipolar disorder is associated with multiple threats to health and livelihood, but the most fundamental concern is the risk of suicide. In two prospective studies, one of 3,291,891 Veterans Administration patients and another of a national cohort of individuals who were followed for 36 years after a first psychiatric contact, BD was found to be the psychiatric condition with the highest rate of suicide (Ilgen, Bohnert, Ignacio et al., 2010; Nordentoft, Mortensen, & Pedersen, 2011). In the national cohort study, 8% of men and 5% of women diagnosed with BD died from suicide (Nordentoft et al, 2011). Large-scale studies such as these are usually based on patient samples, which may over-estimate risk for suicide. In the internationally representative sample of the World Mental Health Survey, one in four persons diagnosed with bipolar I disorder reported a suicide attempt and more than half reported suicidal ideation within the past 12 months (Merikangas et al., 2011). Similar rates of ideation and attempts were reported in a community representative sample of those with bipolar I disorder in the Netherlands (Regeer, Rosso, Ten Have, Vollebergh, & Nolen, 2002). There appear to be neural differences between patients with BD who have attempted and those who have not attempted suicide, such as reductions in gray matter volume in orbitofrontal cortex, hippocampus, and cerebellum (Johnston et al., 2017).

FUNCTIONAL IMPAIRMENT

Many patients with BD experience ongoing impairments in social, occupational, and familial functioning even between episodes, especially if they have unresolved symptoms (Gitlin, Mintz, Sokolski, Hammen, & Altshuler, 2011). In a Stanley Foundation Network study of 253 adult patients with bipolar I or II disorder, only about one in three worked full-time outside of the home (Suppes et al., 2001). More than half (57%) were unable to work or worked only in sheltered settings. Only 42% of bipolar I manic patients who were hospitalized for mania showed steady work performance an average of 1.7 years after hospital discharge (Harrow, Goldberg, Grossman, & Meltzer, 1990). In community samples, people with BD are at four times greater likelihood of work disability compared with the general population (Mitchell, Slade, & Andrews, 2004). Those with difficulties in recovering their premorbid levels of function are at risk for earlier recurrence of symptoms (Weinstock & Miller, 2010).

There is considerable variability in functional impairment, however. For example, there appears to be a link between BD and creativity or productivity: many famous artists, musicians, writers, and politicians probably had manic symptoms (Jamison, 1993). In a Swedish study of over 1 million persons, BD was unique among psychiatric illness in having above average rates of participation in creative occupations (Kyaga et al., 2012). Creativity, whether measured by occupation, lifetime accomplishment, or laboratory tasks, has been found to be particularly high among persons with milder forms of the disorder and among their unaffected family members (Johnson et al., 2015). The presence of creativity in those with no manic episodes suggests that it is *not* the case that creativity is driven by manic symptoms. Highly creative persons and those with BD appear to share temperamental commonalities, such as high levels of drive and ambition (Johnson, Edge, Holmes, & Carver, 2012b). Children diagnosed with BD and children who are the offspring of bipolar parents scored higher than healthy control children on a creativity index (Simeonova, Chang, Strong, & Ketter, 2005). The question of whether medications facilitate or interfere with creativity has not been adequately considered.

MEDICAL COMORBIDITY AND MORTALITY

A growing body of evidence has indicated that those diagnosed with BD are at high risk for premature mortality from medical disorders. Even in countries with accessible medical care for all, BD has been found to relate to dying an average of 8.5–9 years earlier than those in the general population (Crump et al., 2013). Increased risk of death from cardiovascular disease has been particularly well documented, with estimates of a two-fold increase in risk of death by age group for those with BD compared with the general population (Laursen et al., 2013). Risks, though, do not appear to be constrained to cardiovascular disease—several large national cohort studies suggest higher mortality from a range of medical conditions (Roshanaei-Moghaddam & Katon, 2009). There are many potential mechanisms that could explain the premature mortality, ranging from lifestyle complications of the disorder, to infrequent medical care for those with acute psychiatric symptoms, to intrinsic biological (e.g., immune or inflammation) processes inherent in the disorder.

COURSE AND PROGNOSIS

Virtually all patients with BD have illness recurrences. A meta-analysis of eight studies of first-episode patients ($N = 734$) found that rates of recurrence averaged 41% in 1 year and 60% over 4 years, with higher recurrence rates among younger patients (Gignac et al., 2015). The majority of these patients were treated with mood stabilizers. Approximately one in five patients meets criteria for rapid cycling, defined by four or more distinct episodes of mania, hypomania, mixed, or depressive disorder within 1 year (Schneck et al., 2004).

Equally significant are the persistent, mild-to-moderate residual symptoms that most patients experience between episodes, even when undergoing pharmacotherapy (Judd et al., 2002; Keller, Lavori, Coryell, Endicott, & Mueller, 1993; Post et al., 2003). Over a 13-year follow-up of patients with BD, subsyndromal symptoms were present during about half the weeks of follow-up (Judd et al., 2002). These symptoms were predominantly depressive rather than manic. A study of children with bipolar I, II, and unspecified disorders observed similar patterns of residual symptoms over a 15-month follow-up (Birmaher et al., 2009). Indeed, one of the most formidable issues in the treatment of the disorder is the stabilization of depressive symptoms (e.g., Perlis et al., 2006).

PSYCHOSOCIAL PREDICTORS OF THE COURSE OF BIPOLAR DISORDER

By the end of the 1980s, researchers began to acknowledge that biological and genetic models of BD did not explain the enormous heterogeneity in the course of the illness over time (Prien & Potter, 1990). This recognition contributed to a renewed emphasis on psychosocial predictors of the course of the disorder. For example, Ellicott, Hammen, Gitlin, Brown, and Jamison (1990) found that BD patients with severe negative life events were at 4.5 times greater risk for relapse in a 2-year follow-up than were patients with less severe life events. A large body of work has supported the importance of life events in the course of BD (Johnson, 2005a). In addition, Miklowitz, Goldstein, Nuechterlein, Snyder, and Mintz (1988) found that bipolar I manic patients who returned after a hospitalization to families who demonstrated high levels of expressed emotion (EE—criticism, hostility, or emotional over-involvement) or caregiver-to-patient affective negativity (criticism, hostility, or guilt induction) during face-to-face interactions were at high risk for relapse. Those whose families had both high EE and high affective negativity were most likely to relapse within 9 months (94%), whereas those whose families rated low on both attributes were unlikely to relapse within this time frame (17%). These findings have also been well replicated (Johnson, Cuellar, & Gershon, 2016).

Of particular concern, as many as half of those with BD report a history of serious childhood abuse or trauma, although rates are not significantly higher than in other psychiatric disorders (Palmier-Claus, Berry, Bucci, Mansell, & Varese, 2016). Early adversity, defined as physical or sexual maltreatment, predicted the first onset of mania in a large-scale 3-year follow-up of the National Epidemiologic Survey on Alcohol and Related Conditions (Gilman et al., 2015). Among persons who develop the disorder, early childhood trauma exposure correlates with a more severe illness course, including an earlier onset, more hospitalizations, higher likelihood of psychosis, increased suicidality, greater symptom severity, more recurrences, lower quality of life, and higher rates of psychiatric comorbidity (see Daruy-Filho, Brietzke, Lafer, & Grassi-Oliveira, 2011). Further, emotional abuse from parents is approximately four times more likely to be reported by people with BD than by non-clinical controls (Palmier-Claus et al., 2016). Verbal abuse from parents predicts an earlier age of onset and a more severe course of BD (Post et al., 2015).

Although these first-generation studies established the prognostic role of psychosocial factors, they did not distinguish between depression and mania as outcomes. A second generation of research has examined which psychosocial variables influence the course of BD depression versus mania.

PSYCHOSOCIAL PREDICTORS OF DEPRESSION WITHIN BD

The symptomatology and neurobiology of unipolar and BD depression have many strong parallels (Cuellar, Johnson, & Winters, 2005). Given these parallels, one might expect that psychosocial predictors of unipolar depression would influence BD depression. Here, we focus on some of the variables that are well-established predictors of unipolar depression, including negative life events (Monroe, Harkness, Simons, & Thase, 2001), low social support (Brown & Andrews, 1986), EE (Butzlaff & Hooley, 1998), neuroticism (Gunderson, Triebwasser, Phillips, & Sullivan, 1999), and negative cognitive styles (Alloy, Reilly-Harrington, Fresco, Whitehouse, & Zechmeister, 1999).

Negative life events are perhaps the most comprehensively examined predictors of bipolar depression. As reviewed by Johnson (2005a), three cross-sectional studies that used interview-based measures of life events found that negative life events are equally common before episodes of BD depression and unipolar depression (Malkoff-Schwartz et al., 2000; Pardoen et al., 1996; Perris, 1984). Findings of prospective studies with interview-based measures also indicate that stressful life events are correlated with slow recovery from depression (Johnson & Miller, 1997) and predict increases in bipolar depression over several months (Johnson et al., 2008). Thus, the most methodologically rigorous studies suggest that negative life events are precipitants of bipolar depression. There is also evidence that chronic stress can intensify the risk of bipolar depression (Gershon, Johnson, & Miller, 2013).

Other variables involved in unipolar depression also appear to have validity as predictors of bipolar depression. For example, neuroticism (Heerlein, Richter, Gonzalez, & Santander, 1998; Lozano & Johnson, 2001), low social support (Johnson, Winett, Meyer, Greenhouse, & Miller, 1999), family EE (Kim & Miklowitz, 2004; Yan, Hammen, Cohen, Daley, & Henry, 2004), family criticism (Weinstock & Miller, 2010), and rejection sensitivity (Ng & Johnson, 2013) have been found to predict increases in depressive symptoms but not manic symptoms over time. Although negative cognitive styles are often documented in BD (see Cuellar et al., 2005, for review), they are most likely to be found during depression compared with well periods (Cuellar et al., 2005), can be explained by the presence of depressive history rather than manic history (Alloy et al., 1999), and predict increases in depression, but not mania, over time (Johnson & Fingerhut, 2004; Johnson, Meyer, Winett, & Small, 2000a).

In sum, variables that influence the course of unipolar depression also influence bipolar depression. Key predictors of depression include negative life events, poor social support, family EE, negative cognitive styles, and low self-esteem.

PSYCHOSOCIAL PREDICTORS OF MANIA

Available models highlight two sets of predictors for manic symptoms: goal engagement and sleep/schedule disruption.

Goal Dysregulation Drawing on biological models of overly sensitive reward pathways, the goal dysregulation model suggests that people with BD show more extreme responses to rewarding stimuli (Johnson et al., 2012b). People with a history of mania and students who are vulnerable to mania describe themselves as more sensitive to rewards, and this sensitivity predicts the onset and course of manic symptoms (Johnson et al., 2012b). People with BD also place high emphasis on pursuing highly ambitious goals, even when they are not in an episode (Johnson, Eisner, & Carver, 2009). This reward sensitivity would be expected to influence reactions to life events that involve major successes. Consistent with this idea, life events involving goal attainments (such as new relationships, births of children, or career successes) predict increases in manic symptoms but not depressive symptoms (Johnson et al., 2000b, 2008). Such effects are apparent even after controlling for baseline levels of manic symptoms and excluding life events that could have been caused by the patients' symptoms.

Why might attaining an important goal trigger manic symptoms? A set of studies suggest that for people with BD, cognition becomes much more positive during good moods than it does for other people. Available evidence suggests that mood states are associated with distinct positive shifts in confidence (Johnson et al., 2012b; Stern & Berrenberg, 1979), autobiographical recall (Eich, Macaulay, & Lam, 1997), and attention to positively valenced stimuli (Murphy et al., 1999). Impulsivity, or the tendency to pursue rewards without awareness of potential negative consequences, also becomes elevated as people become manic (Swann, Dougherty, Pazzaglia, Pham, & Moeller, 2004) or even more mildly happy (Muhtadie, Johnson, Carver, Gotlib, & Ketter, 2014). Mood state-dependent shifts in confidence may contribute to increased goal setting (Johnson, 2005b). In turn, the increased time and energy spent pursuing goals predict increases in manic symptoms over several months (Lozano & Johnson, 2001). Consistent with these findings, experience sampling data suggest that goal attainments trigger increased goal pursuit for those with BD, which, in turn, may trigger manic symptoms (Fulford, Johnson, Llabre, & Carver, 2010; Johnson, Carver, & Gotlib, 2012a).

It is important to note that those with BD may be overly responsive to indicators of both progress and failure to progress (Eisner, Johnson, & Carver, 2008). In one study (Miklowitz, Alatiq, Geddes, Goodwin, & Williams, 2010), remitted or partially remitted patients with BD, patients with major depressive disorder (MDD), and healthy controls unscrambled six-word strings into five-word sentences, leaving out one word. The extra word allowed the sentences to be completed in a negative, neutral, or "hyperpositive" (goal-oriented) way. Under conditions of positive feedback (a pleasing bell tone for every four sentences completed), all participants completed more sentences than in the non-feedback conditions. However, patients with BD unscrambled more negative sentences under conditions of feedback than did patients with MDD. Thus, simple positive feedback may increase the accessibility of negative thoughts among bipolar patients. This is consistent with other evidence showing that those with BD are highly reactive to signals of their progress or failure (Ruggero & Johnson, 2006; Fulford, Johnson, Llabre, & Carver, 2010).

Sleep and Schedule Disruption   Experimental studies (Barbini et al., 1998) as well as longitudinal studies (Leibenluft, Albert, Rosenthal, & Wehr, 1996) suggest that sleep deprivation is an important trigger of manic symptoms. Wehr, Sack, and Rosenthal (1987) hypothesized that sleep disruption might be one way in which life events trigger episodes of BD, noting that illness episodes are often preceded by life events interfering with the ability to sleep (e.g., transmeridian flights, childbearing). This theory was broadened by Ehlers and colleagues (Ehlers, Frank, & Kupfer, 1988; Ehlers, Kupfer, Frank, & Monk, 1993), who suggested that social disruptions to other aspects of circadian rhythms could trigger symptoms (the "social zeitgebers model").

Consistent with this idea, people with BD, and those at risk for BD, demonstrate more variability in their daily schedules than do healthy controls (Ankers & Jones, 2009; Jones, Hare, and Evershed, 2005). In two studies, Malkoff-Schwartz et al. (1998, 2000) found that bipolar patients reported more life events that disrupted daily routines, sleep or wake times in the weeks preceding manic episodes compared with the weeks preceding depressive episodes. Those with BD also appear to experience a more pronounced shift in mood with daily fluctuations in sleep quality compared with those with no mood disorder (Gershon et al., 2012).

In sum, sleep or schedule disruption is proposed to trigger manic symptoms (Grunze et al., 2010; Leibenluft et al., 1996). As discussed next, some of these risk factors are amenable to modification through psychosocial intervention.

TREATMENT OF BD

Because BD episodes are a product of genetic, biological, and psychosocial agents, optimal treatment regimens should involve combined pharmacological and psychosocial interventions. Unfortunately, in the era of managed care cost containment, drug treatments often are the only treatment provided. Of even more concern, patients with BD often are not diagnosed and provided with initial treatment. Even when the diagnosis and treatment are initiated, patients are prone to discontinuing their medications. Worldwide estimates indicate that about half of those with a lifetime history of treatment received no treatment in the past year (Merikangas et al., 2011). On the other hand, innovative work has considered not just the best treatment, but stronger ways to organize treatment delivery. Bauer and his colleagues have shown that providing psychoeducation through a specialized clinic focused on BD that provides rapid access to nurses for discussion of symptom concerns can reduce relapse and hospitalization (Bauer et al., 2006a,b).

Pharmacological Treatments   Distinctions are usually made between acute pharmacological treatment and maintenance treatment. The goal of acute treatment is to stabilize an existing manic or depressive episode (for review of acute pharmacotherapy studies, see Geddes & Miklowitz, 2013). Adjunctive psychotherapy is usually introduced after the episode stabilization phase and continued throughout maintenance treatment. The goals of adjunctive psychotherapy are to hasten recovery from episodes, minimize residual symptoms and prevent recurrences. Untreated residual symptoms of mania or depression are prospectively associated with illness recurrences (Perlis et al., 2006).

Current pharmacotherapy algorithms for mania for adult- and childhood-onset patients often combine mood stabilizers (e.g., lithium carbonate, divalproex sodium, carbamazepine) with atypical antipsychotic medications (e.g., olanzapine, quetiapine, risperidone, aripiprazole, ziprasidone, lurasidone, asenapine, and less frequently, clozapine) (e.g., Kowatch et al., 2005a; McAllister-Williams, 2006). Adjunctive antidepressant agents are often prescribed for bipolar depression (Baldessarini, Henk, Sklar, Chang, & Leahy, 2008). When given alone, antidepressant medications can cause manic switching and acceleration of cycles in a significant number of patients (Ghaemi, Lenox, & Baldessarini, 2001). When given with mood stabilizers, however, antidepressants do not appear to cause an increase in cycling (Altshuler et al., 2003; Sachs et al., 2007). There has been some debate about the added benefit of antidepressants above and beyond the role of mood stabilizers, with one meta-analysis indicating no significant benefit (Sidor & McQueen, 2012), and recent guidelines suggesting that the evidence is mixed and may vary by drug (Grunze et al., 2010; Sidor & MacQueen, 2012). Findings have been more positive for the antidepressant effects of the anticonvulsant lamotrigine (Malhi et al., 2009), the second-generation antipsychotic lurasidone (Loebel et al., 2014), and the combination of olanzapine with fluoxetine (Tohen et al., 2003).

Patients who discontinue their pharmacotherapy abruptly are at a high risk for recurrence and suicide attempts (Keck, McElroy, Strakowski, Bourne, & West, 1997; Suppes, Baldessarini, Faedda, Tondo, & Tohen, 1993; Tondo & Baldessarini, 2000). For example, in an early study of adolescent BD patients followed for 18 months after a hospitalization, relapse was three times more likely among patients who discontinued lithium than among patients who remained on it (Strober, Morrell, Lampert, & Burroughs, 1990). Patients describe barriers to compliance including missing high periods, objecting to having one's moods controlled by medications, side-effects, lack of information about the disorder, or lack of social or familial supports (for review, see Colom et al., 2000).

Psychotherapy as an Adjunct to Medication Maintenance   Randomized controlled trials indicate positive benefits for several different psychotherapy approaches. The modalities investigated in the trials have included individual, family, and group formats. Treatments supported by multiple randomized controlled trials include group and individual psychoeducation (e.g., Colom et al., 2003; Perry, Tarrier, Morriss, McCarthy, & Limb, 1999; Simon et al., 2005; Torrent et al., 2013), family psychoeducation and skill training (e.g., Fristad, Verducci, Walters, & Young, 2009; Miklowitz, George, Richards, Simoneau, & Suddath, 2003; Rea et al., 2003; West et al., 2014), cognitive-behavioral therapy (CBT; e.g., Lam et al., 2003), and interpersonal and social rhythm therapy (IPSRT; e.g., Frank et al., 2005) (for review, see Geddes & Miklowitz, 2013).

Table 7.1

Common Therapeutic Elements of Psychoeducational Treatment

---

* Teach emotion-regulation skills when challenged by stressors
* Encourage daily monitoring of moods and sleep cycles
* Enhance patient's (or family members') ability to identify and intervene early with relapses
* Track and encourage medication adherence
* Assist patient in stabilizing sleep/wake rhythms and other daily or nightly routines
* Educate family members about the disorder and enhance intrafamilial communication
* Increase access to social and treatment supports
* Help patient acquire balanced attitudes toward the self in relation to the illness
* Encourage acceptance of the disorder

As summarized in Table 7.1, these treatments have several elements in common. First, they typically include an active psychoeducational component, which often involves teaching patients (and, in some cases, family members) to recognize and obtain early treatment for manic episodes before they develop fully. Most treatments emphasize medication adherence, avoiding alcohol and street drugs, and the use of skills to cope more effectively with stressful events. Treatment approaches differ in the emphasis on specific strategies, including involvement of family members in psychoeducation (family-focused treatment, or FFT), stabilizing sleep/wake rhythms (IPSRT and, more recently, CBT for insomnia; Harvey et al., 2015), and cognitive restructuring (CBT).

It is worth highlighting one approach that is fairly distinct compared with other psychotherapy approaches. Functional remediation treatment involves cognitive exercises to address neurocognitive deficits that are often observed in BD, with the aim of improving functional outcomes. In a 10-site study, 268 participants who were euthymic with sustained psychosocial impairments were randomly assigned to functional remediation, group psychoeducation, or treatment as usual. The patients in functional remediation completed a broad array of exercises designed to address memory, attention, problem-solving, reasoning, and organization. The functional remediation group had greater improvements in functioning than did those who received treatment as usual but not compared with those who received group psychoeducation. The mechanism of effect does not appear to have been neurocognitive processes, as neurocognition did not differentially improve in the remediational intervention (Torrent et al., 2013).

Each of the psychological treatments described here has been found in at least one study to delay relapses of BD when combined with pharmacotherapy. The control conditions have varied and have included treatment as usual, individual supportive therapy, unstructured group support, active clinical management, and psychoeducation. There are failed replication studies as well. In a large-scale multicenter study, Scott et al. (2006) found that CBT was no more effective than treatment as usual in delaying recurrences. *Post hoc* analyses, however, revealed that relative to treatment as usual, CBT was associated with longer time to recurrence among patients who had had fewer than 12 lifetime episodes, and less time to recurrence among patients with 12 or more prior episodes. A recent study of 100 patients randomly assigned to IPSRT versus psychoeducation and supportive care did not find an advantage for IPSRT (Inder et al., 2015). This parallels recent trials finding no particular advantage to intensive CBT or functional remediation as compared with psychoeducation for BD (Meyer et al., 2012; Parikh et al., 2012; Torrent et al., 2013). One study found benefits of offering IPSRT acutely, but little gain in offering IPSRT as compared with clinical management after recovery (Frank et al., 2005).

The large-scale STEP-BD examined the effects of psychosocial interventions in a practical clinical trial across 15 US treatment centers (Miklowitz et al., 2007). In this trial, 293 bipolar I and II patients were randomly assigned to one of three intensive psychosocial interventions (30 sessions over 9 months of FFT, IPSRT, or CBT, or a control treatment called collaborative care [CC]). The CC involved three psychotherapy sessions over 6 weeks and focused on developing a relapse prevention plan. All patients were in an acute episode of bipolar depression at the time of randomization. All received "best practice" pharmacotherapy (i.e., mood stabilizers, atypical antipsychotic agents, or antidepressants, in various combinations) in combination with psychotherapy.

Over 1 year, being in any of the intensive psychotherapies was associated with a faster recovery from depression than being in CC. On average, patients in intensive treatment recovered within 169 days, as compared with 279 days in the CC condition. Patients in intensive treatment were also 1.6 times more likely than patients in CC to be clinically well in any given study month. Rates of recovery over 1 year were as follows: FFT, 77%; IPSRT, 65%; CBT, 60%; and CC, 52%. The differences among the three intensive modalities were not significant.

There are still many gaps in research on psychosocial treatment. It remains difficult to know which patient will respond best to which approach. Few studies have identified the mechanisms of action of psychosocial interventions (e.g., whether they enhance medication adherence, improve the patient's ability to recognize prodromal symptoms of recurrence, or increase insight).

The applicability of psychosocial interventions to early-onset BD, or children at risk for developing the illness, has begun to be investigated systematically. Several randomized trials find that family-based treatments are effective in reducing symptom severity in children with bipolar spectrum disorders (Fristad et al., 2009) and adolescents with bipolar I or II disorder (Miklowitz et al., 2008). FFT has also been found to protect against the worsening of depressive and manic symptoms in children at high genetic risk for developing BD (Miklowitz et al., 2013). One study failed to find advantages of FFT over brief psychoeducation in adolescents with BD (Miklowitz et al., 2014).

DIAGNOSTIC CONSIDERATIONS

Although the diagnosis of BD appears straightforward according to *DSM-5*, there is considerable controversy as to its boundaries with other conditions. Here, we address controversies regarding the definition of the bipolar spectrum, diagnosis in pediatric populations, and dual diagnosis (comorbidity) considerations.

The Bipolar Spectrum

There is increasing recognition that many patients have bipolar spectrum disorders, which, depending on the definition, may include subsyndromal manic episodes, manic or hypomanic episodes triggered by antidepressants, subsyndromal mixed episodes, or agitated depression (Akiskal, Benazzi, Perugi, & Rihmer, 2005a; Akiskal et al., 2000). In a sample of young adults treated for recurrent depression at a university health service, 16% met the *DSM-IV* criteria for BD and 83% for recurrent unipolar major depressive illness, but a larger number endorsed having at least brief experiences of hypomanic symptoms on a self-report measure, a hypomanic response to antidepressants, or a family history of hypomania (Smith, Harrison, Muir, & Blackwood, 2005). Indeed, in a study of 229 offspring of persons with BD followed for 16 years, 3.41% met bipolar I disorder criteria, 6.24% met bipolar II disorder, and 7.29% developed BD unspecified per the Schedule for Affective Disorders and Schizophrenia (Duffy et al., 2014). Some caution is warranted in interpreting results in this domain, however, as the interrater reliability of interviews designed to assess milder spectrum forms of BD is low (Kessler et al., 2006).

What is the evidence that spectrum patients are really bipolar in the classic sense? Although they do not necessarily follow the same course of illness patterns as patients with bipolar I or II disorder, patients with subsyndromal forms of BD, such as those with one less symptom than the number required by *DSM-5* criteria, are more likely to have family histories of BD and higher rates of hypomania induced by antidepressants than people without subsyndromal BD symptoms. They also have high rates of suicide, marital disruption, and mental health service utilization compared with those with no history of mental illness (Judd & Akiskal, 2003; Nusslock & Frank, 2011).

Some researchers have examined subsyndromal mood symptoms as a risk factor for the development of fully syndromal BD. Several scales have been developed to assess risk for BD, using items designed to capture different facets of affective disturbance. Although many studies have validated these instruments cross-sectionally, we focus here on the longitudinal evidence.

The Temperament Evaluation of Memphis, Pisa, Paris, and San Diego—autoquestionnaire version (TEMPS-A; Akiskal et al., 2005b) is a self- or parent-rated assessment of positive and negative affectivity tendencies. Scores on the TEMPS-A predicted onset of BD in a 2-year follow-up of 80 children and adolescents with depression (Kochman et al., 2005).

The 79-item General Behavior Inventory (GBI; Depue, Kleinman, Davis, Hutchinson, & Krauss, 1985) covers lifetime frequency of experiences of depressive and manic symptoms, as well as cyclothymia (mood variability). The Cyclothymia scale has been found to be elevated among those with bipolar spectrum disorder diagnoses (Klein, Depue, & Slater, 1985). Reichart et al. (2005) found that higher scores on the GBI depression subscale predicted BD onset at 5-year follow-up among adolescents with depression (Findling et al., 2013).

A childhood version of the GBI rated by parents discriminated pediatric BD from attention deficit hyperactivity disorder (ADHD) in one study (Danielson, Youngstrom, Findling, & Calabrese, 2003). The four-site Longitudinal Assessment of Manic Symptoms study examined a large group of outpatients aged 6–12 ($N = 621$) whose parents had rated them as high on GBI manic symptoms. Most (85%) showed decreasing manic symptoms over 24 months, but 15% showed unstable or rising symptoms. This latter group was more likely than those with decreasing symptoms to develop BD during the follow-up (Findling et al., 2013).

Finally, the Hypomanic Personality Scale was developed to assess subsyndromal manic symptoms and related traits (Eckblad & Chapman, 1986). Kwapil et al. (2000) found that high scores on this scale predicted the onset of bipolar spectrum disorders over a 13-year follow-up of a large sample of college students. These findings have been replicated in another undergraduate sample (Walsh, DeGeorge, Barrantes-Vidal, & Kwapil, 2015).

Thus, self-report measures of spectrum symptoms can be used to predict the onset of bipolar spectrum disorders in longitudinal studies. In virtually all of the studies there have been a substantial number of false positives, suggesting that spectrum symptoms are not uniformly related to BD and may in some cases reflect other disorders, the effects of transient stressors, or, in children or adolescents, developmental phases. Integrating correlates of spectrum symptoms that contribute to risk (e.g., a family history of BD) will be necessary to develop predictive algorithms.

Diagnosis in Children and Adolescents

Perhaps the most controversial diagnostic dilemma is where to draw the boundaries of the bipolar diagnosis in children. Before about 1980, belief was widespread that neither mania nor depression could occur before puberty, although individual case reports of the phenomenon existed (e.g., Anthony & Scott, 1960; Strecker, 1921). This belief has changed significantly in the past two decades (for review, see Luby & Navsaria, 2010). Unfortunately, no separate diagnostic criteria exist for juvenile BD, and, as a result, there has been little cross-national agreement on the operational definition of a manic or mixed episode in childhood. More specifically, debate continues about whether well-demarcated episodes of mania and depression must occur, the minimum duration of these episodes, whether childhood symptoms persist into adult disorders, and whether irritable outbursts deserve their own diagnostic category (e.g., Axelson et al., 2011b; Carlson & Klein, 2014).

Strong interrater reliability of the bipolar diagnosis appears to be more challenging to achieve with younger age groups (Meyer & Carlson, 2010). Unfortunately, DSM-5 has done little to improve the situation. One diagnosis, disruptive mood dysregulation disorder (DMDD), has been added to the mood disorders section to give a "diagnostic home" to children and adolescents who have recurrent irritable outbursts as well as chronic negative affectivity. These youths have often been diagnosed with bipolar spectrum disorders in community settings. Unfortunately, the DMDD diagnosis has significant problems, such as the lack of distinction with oppositional defiant disorder, the lack of a distinctive set of associated symptoms, questions about stability over time, and little data to guide treatment (Axelson et al., 2011a).

Considerable debate exists about using broader definitions of BD among youth. The NIMH Course and Outcome of Bipolar Youth (COBY) study provides strong empirical support for one approach to phenotyping high-risk youth. This long-term prospective study showed that young people with BD unspecified, characterized by one DSM-IV symptom less than full criteria for a manic or hypomanic episode, a clear change in functioning, and a minimum symptom duration of 4 hours within a day and a minimum of four lifetime episodes, were at substantially elevated risk for "converting" to bipolar I or II disorder by 4- to 5-year follow-up (Birmaher et al., 2009). Further, among patients presenting with a BD unspecified phenotype, the risk of conversion to bipolar I or II disorder was 52% over 4 years among those with first- or second-degree family members who had a lifetime manic episode, compared with 36% in BD unspecified patients with a negative family history for mania (Axelson et al., 2011b; Birmaher et al., 2009). Thus, transient manic episodes, when present in a child with a bipolar first- or second-degree relative, are a high-risk phenotype for later bipolar onset.

The Pittsburgh Bipolar Offspring Study (BIOS; Hafemann et al., 2016) found that 8.4% of the offspring (ages 6–18) of bipolar parents had bipolar spectrum disorders at a study baseline, and an additional 15% developed new onset bipolar spectrum disorders by 8-year follow-up. The best predictors of a bipolar spectrum onset were dimensions, such as severity of anxiety/depression, affective lability (i.e., instability of mood states), and manic symptoms before the transition to a bipolar spectrum disorder, as well as having a relative with a comparatively early onset of BD. This combination of risk factors accounted for 49% of new-onset bipolar spectrum disorders over 8 years; the rate among children without these risk factors was 2% (Hafeman et al., 2016).

Another long-term study found developmental continuity for a narrow BD phenotype from late adolescence to early adulthood, but not for a broader BD phenotype marked by irritability and euphoria without associated manic symptoms (Lewinsohn, Seeley,

Buckley, & Klein, 2002). A follow-up of manic children (mean age 11) who met strict *DSM-IV* criteria revealed that 73.3% relapsed into mania over 8 years. Most importantly, youths spent 60% of the weeks in their lives with mood episodes, and 40% in manic states. Between the ages of 18 and 21 years, 44% had a recurrence of mania and 35% had developed substance use disorders (Geller, Tillman, Bolhofner, & Zimerman, 2008).

In a reanalysis of a large-scale longitudinal study of youths in semirural parts of New York (*N* = 776, mean age 13.8), two categories of risk were defined: (1) episodic irritability (based on the parents' and child's answer to questions such as "Are there times when [the child] feels irritable or jumpy?" and "Do these times last for a week or more?"); and (2) chronic irritability (persistent arguing and temper tantrums across the home and school settings). Females exhibited higher levels of episodic and chronic irritability than males. Episodic irritability was stable over time. Moreover, episodic irritability in adolescence predicted the onset of a mania by age 16 (Leibenluft, Cohen, Gorrindo, Brook, & Pine, 2006). Episodic irritability was also a unique predictor of mania by age 22, although this relationship was mediated by the cross-sectional correlation between episodic irritability and depression in early adolescence. In contrast, chronic irritability was associated with ADHD by mid-adolescence and major depressive illness in early adulthood. Clearly, the episodicity of symptoms is an important feature to assess when attempting to distinguish risk for BD from risk for other psychiatric disorders, notably ADHD.

DUAL DIAGNOSIS

BD patients are highly likely to be diagnosed with one or more comorbid disorders. When 12-month prevalence rates in a community epidemiological sample are considered, the highest associations are found of mania/hypomania with ADHD and anxiety disorders (e.g., Kessler et al., 2005). In an international community-based representative sample, 63% of those with bipolar spectrum disorder, and 76.5% of those with bipolar I disorder met lifetime criteria for at least one anxiety disorder (Merikangas et al., 2011).

Community and clinical studies (Brady, Casto, Lydiard, Malcolm, & Arana, 1991; Goldberg, Garno, Leon, Kocsis, & Portera, 1999; Kessler et al., 1997) have documented rates of lifetime substance use disorder ranging from 21% to 45%. Patients with BD have been estimated to have a six-fold increase in substance use disorders compared with those in the general population. One study found that patients were more likely to use alcohol during depressive episodes and more likely to use cocaine and marijuana during manic episodes (Strakowski, DelBello, Fleck, & Arndt, 2000).

Comorbid diagnoses—and even subsyndromal symptoms of comorbid disorders—are associated with a poor prognosis of child and adult BD (Otto et al., 2006; Yen et al., 2016). For example, anxiety comorbidity has been linked with younger onset of BD, lower likelihood of recovery, poorer role functioning and quality of life, a greater likelihood of suicide attempts, and poorer response to medications (Henry et al., 2003; Simon et al., 2004). Studies have also documented slower depression recovery rates among adult or pediatric patients with BD with a comorbid substance use disorder (Yen et al., 2016).

A separate issue is how to distinguish BD from comorbid disorders. A case in point is ADHD. In a sample of children, Geller et al. (1998) compared the frequency of symptoms that are considered classic or pathognomonic of mania with those typically seen in either mania or ADHD. Elated mood, grandiosity, hypersexuality, decreased need for sleep, daredevil acts, and uninhibited people-seeking were far more common in mania than in ADHD. Distractibility, increased activity, and increased energy were observed in both disorders (see also Kim & Miklowitz, 2002). Some studies find that, among children of bipolar parents, the comorbid presence of major depressive episode and ADHD increases risk for developing BD (Chang, Steiner, & Ketter, 2000; Faraone, Biederman, Mennin, Wozniak, & Spencer, 1997a; Faraone et al., 1997b; Leibenluft et al., 2006). This does not seem to generalize to samples without a bipolar parent;, long-term longitudinal studies of girls with ADHD find high rates of depression and suicidal behavior at follow-up, and low rates of BD (Hinshaw et al., 2012; Turgay & Ansari, 2006).

DIAGNOSTIC ASSESSMENT METHODS

There are no biological tests that verify the diagnosis of BD. Structured diagnostic interviews are highly recommended, given the evidence that unstructured clinical interviews can be highly unreliable, particularly for the milder forms of disorder. In the field trials of *DSM-5*, researchers examined whether two clinicians would independently agree on the diagnosis of BD, using their standard clinical interviews. Reliability was poor for bipolar I disorder in adults (0.52 across sites) and for bipolar I and II disorder in youth (also 0.52) (Regier et al., 2013). Overdiagnosis of BD may be particularly common when the patient has other conditions involving mood lability, such as in borderline personality disorder (Ruggero, Zimmerman, Chelminski, & Young, 2010).

The Structured Diagnostic Interview for *DSM* (SCID; First, Spitzer, Gibbon, & Williams, 1995) is the most widely used structured interview for adults, and the Kiddie Schedule for Affective Disorders and Schizophrenia (KSADS) is the most widely used for children. The *DSM-IV* version of the SCID had strong interrater reliability, but estimates are not yet available for diagnoses of BD using the *DSM-5* version.

As with debates about how narrow or broad the criteria for BD should be, there has been some debate about the sensitivity and specificity of diagnoses based on these clinical and structured interviews. The SCID and the KSADS are less sensitive in identifying the milder forms of BD than are clinical interviews (Chambers et al., 1985; Kaufman et al., 1997). For example, the SCID is less likely to identify hypomanic episodes when comparing with diagnoses based on unstructured interviews by experienced clinicians (Dunner & Tay, 1993). This type of discrepancy appears to be the case even in severe samples—in a study of 145 inpatients who had previously received a clinical diagnosis of BD, only 43% met diagnostic criteria for BDs (including BD unspecified) using the SCID (Zimmerman, Ruggero, Chelminski, & Young, 2008). Although one possibility is that the structured diagnostic interviews are insensitive, caution is warranted, in that SCID-based diagnoses of BD were associated with greater risk of a positive family history of BD than an absence of diagnosis, whereas clinical diagnoses were not (Zimmerman, Ruggero, Chelminski, & Young, 2008).

With these important discrepancies across assessment approaches, it is important to conduct a thorough and multi-method clinical assessment. Instruments like the SCID and KSADS should be supplemented by data from self-report questionnaires (especially those that examine subsyndromal forms of mania) as well as a thorough interview to capture the timeline of prior episodes, such as the National Institute of Mental Health (NIMH) Life Charting method (Leverich & Post, 1998). Life charting enables the clinician to investigate the frequency, severity, and timing of prior episodes, so as to consider whether depressive, mixed, or manic episodes have dominated the clinical picture; whether other disorders (e.g., substance dependence) preceded, coincided with, or developed after the onset of the mood disorder; and, to consider potential triggers of episodes.

ETIOLOGICAL CONSIDERATIONS

Current etiological models of BD are multifactorial. Although it is well established that the disorder is highly heritable, current etiological models emphasize that genetic and neurobiological vulnerabilities to BD increase the person's reactivity to socioenvironmental factors.

HERITABILITY

Although heritability estimates have varied, estimates of heritability based on representative community samples are less likely to be biased than those focused on hospitalized or patient samples. In epidemiological twin studies, heritability estimates of 85%-93% have been reported (Kieseppä, Partonen, Haukka, Kaprio, & Lönnqvist, 2004; McGuffin et al., 2003)

The risk of BD among children of bipolar parents is four times greater than among children of healthy parents, and as high as eight times when bipolar spectrum conditions are included. Children of bipolar parents, however, are also at approximately 2.7 times higher risk for developing nonaffective disorders (including ADHD and conduct disorder) compared with the children of well parents. Thus, a proportion of the familial risk is not specific to bipolar illness (Hafeman et al., 2016; Hodgins et al., 2002; LaPalme, Hodgins, & LaRoche, 1997).

At a molecular level, a large number of genes are thought to contribute to the onset of BD. Several genomic regions relevant to BD have been identified. Because the effects of a given genetic region or polymorphism are so small, findings have not been entirely consistent from study to study. Accordingly, researchers have moved toward examining very large samples. In recent genetic studies of over 20,000 individuals, 56 single nucleotide polymorphisms related to BD have been identified, each of which appears to contribute a very small amount to the onset of disorder (Mühleisen et al., 2014). In a recent genome-wide association study (GWAS) of 13,902 cases and 19,279 controls, eight GWAS regions were implicated in BD (Charney, Ruderfer, Moran, Chambert, & Belliveau, 2017). There is likely an overlap between some of the genetic vulnerability to BD and that of schizophrenia, although unique pathways are also suggested (Murray et al., 2004).

Given the very small effect sizes of genetic polymorphisms and genetic regions in predicting symptom outcomes, a growing focus is on identifying neurobiological correlates of the disorder that might be genetically driven. Quantitative trait methods such as these may eventually help to identify genetic loci and pathways related to the disease (Fears et al., 2014). One multinational study examined two genetically isolated populations—the Central Valley of Costa Rica and the Antioquia region of Colombia—and included 738 individuals, 181 of whom had bipolar I disorder. The authors identified more than 40 behavioral and neural phenotypes (e.g., structural changes in the prefrontal cortex) that appeared both highly heritable and genetically linked to BD. They identified a smaller set of phenotypes (e.g., cortical thickness in prefrontal and temporal regions) that appeared to be particularly promising candidate traits for genetic mapping in BD based on degree of heritability and associations with the disorder.

As another example of fruitfully linking genetic profiles to phenotypes, researchers examined genes that had been implicated in BD across multiple datasets, and then examined how these genes were related to biological pathways (Nurnberger, Koller, Jung, Edenberg, & Faroud, 2014). The genes identified to date were related to six different pathways, including genes that were implicated in G proteins and second messenger systems.

NEUROTRANSMITTER DYSREGULATION

Increasingly, BD is being described as an "impairment of synaptic and cellular plasticity" (Manji, 2009, p. 2). This means that people with BD have genetically influenced problems with processing in synapses and circuits (the neuronal connections between different brain structures).

Traditional neurotransmitter models of mood disorders have focused on norepinephrine, dopamine, and serotonin (Charney, Menkes, & Heninger, 1981; Thase, Jindal, & Howland, 2002). It is now widely believed that dysregulations in these systems interact with deficits in other neurotransmitter systems, such as gamma-aminobutyric acid (GABA) and substance P, to produce symptoms of mood disorders (Stockmeier, 2003). Current research focuses on the functioning of neurotransmitter systems rather than on simple models of neurotransmitter levels being either high or low, by measuring sensitivity of the postsynaptic receptors through pharmacological challenges or neuroimaging. Molecular genetic research has also informed researchers about key neurotransmitter systems to investigate. This type of research has progressed more rapidly in understanding dysregulation in serotonin and dopamine systems.

Dopamine Among people without BD, several different dopamine agonists, including stimulants, have been found to trigger manic symptoms, including increases in mood, energy, and talkativeness (Willner, 1995). People with BD show pronounced behavioral effects to stimulants (Anand et al., 2000). Several paradigms have been used to challenge the dopamine system, including behavioral sensitization (the study of how repeated administration of dopamine agonists changes the sensitivity of dopaminergic reward pathways; Kalivas, Duffy, DuMars, & Skinner, 1988; Robinson & Becker, 1986) and sleep deprivation, which appears to interfere with normalizing the sensitivity of dopamine receptors (Ebert, Feistel, Barocks, Kaschka, & Pirner, 1994). Results obtained using these paradigms are consistent with the idea that people with BD have hypersensitive dopamine systems (Strakowski, Sax, Setters, & Keck, 1996; Strakowski, Sax, Setters, Stanton, & Keck, 1997). Those with BD also show a greater sensitivity to dopamine agonists on behavioral tasks, such as willingness to take risks for the possibility of high rewards (Burdick et al., 2014). Imaging studies are consistent with the idea of a dysregulation in glutamate, which has downstream effects on dopaminergic regulation (Whitton, Treadway, & Pizzagalli, 2015). Also relevant to the idea of dopamine dysfunction, a large meta-analysis suggested a link with the A1 polymorphism of the DRD2 gene Taq IA1 (Zou et al., 2012). In animal models, a set of candidate genes for BD have been identified that relate to modulating dopamine signaling within reward pathways (Ogden et al., 2004).

Serotonin Neuroimaging studies indicate that mood disorders, including depressive and bipolar conditions, are generally associated with decreased sensitivity of the serotonin receptors (Stockmeier, 2003). The functioning of the serotonin system can also be tested by manipulating levels of tryptophan, the precursor to serotonin (Staley, Malison, & Innis, 1998). Findings of tryptophan-manipulation studies indicate serotonin receptor dysfunction among persons with a family history of BD (Sobczak, Honig, Schmitt, & Riedel, 2003; Sobczak et al., 2002). Meta-analyses of the more than 20 studies of the serotonin transporter polymorphism in BD have yielded positive but small effects (e.g., Cho et al., 2005; Lasky-Su, Faraone, Glatt, & Tsuang, 2005).

INFLAMMATORY MARKERS

There has been increasing interest in the relevance of the immune system to BD, paralleling research on neuroinflammation in depression. Increases in inflammatory cytokines or cytokine inducers are associated with depressive behaviors, including changes in sleep, anhedonia, and decreased activity. Patients with MDD can be distinguished from healthy controls by higher levels of proinflammatory cytokines (Miller, Maletic, & Raison, 2009). In BD, a meta-analysis of 30 studies concluded that adult patients could be distinguished from healthy controls on concentrations of interleukin-4 (IL-4), IL-10, soluble IL-2 and IL-6 receptors, recombinant tumor necrosis factor (TNF)-α, soluble TNF receptor 1 (sTNFR1), and an IL-1 receptor antagonist (Modabbernia, Taslimi, Brietzke, & Ashrafi, 2013). However, these group differences are greatest when comparing acutely ill patients with controls; they do not necessarily persist when patients are euthymic (e.g., Brietzke et al., 2009).

Two studies have investigated neuroinflammatory activity in pediatric samples. A within-group study of 123 adolescents and young adults with BD found that levels of IL-6, high-sensitivity C-reactive protein, and TNF-α were associated with longer illness duration, more severe depressive symptoms, and more suicidal behavior (Goldstein et al., 2015). A direct comparison of adolescents with bipolar spectrum disorders, adolescents with MDD, and healthy volunteers found that high levels of nuclear factor kappa B in peripheral blood mononuclear cells distinguished the adolescents with BD (Miklowitz et al., 2016).

Less is known about whether increased levels of inflammatory activity normalize with medication treatments. Kim et al. (2004) found that medication-free patients with mania could be distinguished from healthy controls on elevated levels of IFN-y and IL-4, and lower TGF-B1 at the time of a hospital admission. Interestingly, TGF-B1 levels increased significantly from admission to a reassessment after 8 weeks of mood stabilizer treatment. Lithium treatment was associated with normalization of inflammatory markers in one small trial (Boufidou, Nikkolaou, Alevizios, Liappas, & Christodoulou, 2004). Mood state and medications appear to be important covariates in studies that attempt to show that excessive immunoreactivity is a stable feature of BD. There is a need for studies that examine inflammatory activity in those at risk.

BRAIN REGIONS INVOLVED IN BIPOLAR DISORDER

Although findings are not entirely consistent, neuroimaging studies implicate a set of structures in the pathophysiology of BD. Abnormal development and function of the amygdala (involved in detection of the significance of emotionally salient stimuli), nucleus accumbens (involved in motivating responses to reward and incentive cues), and decreased inhibitory control in areas of the prefrontal cortex (involved in effective cognitive regulation of emotions and goal planning), in combination with aberrant connectivity among these structures have been postulated to be at the core of mood dysregulation in BD (Almeida et al., 2009; Townsend & Altshuler, 2012; Versace et al., 2010; Wang et al., 2009). Many of the implicated regions overlap substantially with those involved in emotional reactivity and regulation, and as such, many parallels are present with the brain correlates of unipolar depression (Davidson, Pizzagalli, & Nitschke, 2002; Mayberg, Keightley, Mahurin, & Brannan, 2004). Differences between bipolar and unipolar depression are also found (Delvecchio et al., 2012), in that hyperactivity of regions involved in reward sensitivity, such as the nucleus accumbens, are implicated in BD but not in unipolar depression (Phillips & Swartz, 2014).

In adults, positron emission tomography and functional magnetic resonance imaging (fMRI) studies of neural activity during cognitive or emotional tasks have shown a pattern of amygdala hyperactivity among adults and children with bipolar I disorder (Chen et al., 2011; Lee et al., 2014). Although there has been some debate about how amygdala hyperactivity to emotion stimuli may shift with mood state, findings of a large meta-analysis of fMRI studies indicated that at least some disturbance in this domain can be observed across mood state (Chen et al., 2011).

Research with adults has also consistently indicated atypical neural responses to reward and positive stimuli in BD. Key regions that appear to be dysregulated for those with BD during reward tasks include the nucleus accumbens, left ventrolateral prefrontal cortex, and left orbitofrontal cortex (see Whitton, Treadway, & Pizzagalli, 2015 for review). Heightened activity of the amygdala and medial prefrontal cortex has also been observed in response to positive emotional faces (Keener et al., 2012; Surguladze et al., 2010). Both at rest and during motor tasks, the level of activity in the basal ganglia, a key structure in reward processing, is positively correlated with the concurrent level of manic symptoms (Blumberg et al., 1999; Caligiuri et al., 2003; Delvecchio et al., 2012). Hence, brain regions involved in identifying the importance of negative stimuli appear to become less active during manic episodes, while those involved in processing reward become more active.

Across a broad array of studies, adults and young people with BD demonstrate deficits in the ability to activate the ventrolateral prefrontal cortex and other regions involved in regulatory control. Intriguingly, a growing body of research suggests that the regions involved in effective cognitive control are also activated when people effectively engage in emotion regulation (Ochsner, Silvers, & Buhle, 2012). Blunted responsivity of this network of regions, including the ventrolateral prefrontal cortex and the anterior cingulate, has been shown during emotion regulation tasks and cognitive control tasks across mood states for adults with BD (Lee et al., 2014; Strakowski et al., 2012). Diminished function of the prefrontal cortex and related circuits might interfere with effective planning and goal pursuit in the context of emotion and reward, leading to a low capacity to regulate emotion. Prefrontal cortical deficits have been implicated in schizophrenia as well (Barch, 2005).

Taken together, fMRI studies suggest that BD is characterized by increased activity in regions involved in emotion reactivity and reward sensitivity, combined with diminished activity in regions involved in effective thinking and planning in response to emotional cues (Phillips & Swartz, 2014). These neural patterns do not appear to be merely an effect of the illness progression, in that offspring of bipolar parents who are unaffected by any psychiatric disorder show amygdala hyperactivation when rating emotional faces, and aberrant prefrontal activation and connectivity when processing rewards (Garrett et al., 2012; Olsavsky et al., 2012; Singh et al., 2014).

Multiple structural deficits have been observed that are congruent with the functional profiles observed. In a recent review of structural findings in the medial prefrontal cortex, BD was found to be related to diminished volume, reduced neuronal size or density, lower glial cell density, and changes in gene expression (Savitz, Price, & Drevets, 2014). Diffusion imaging studies indicate abnormal characteristics in the axons in frontal and temporal regions of importance to emotion regulation and reward processing of adults with BD (Phillips & Swartz, 2014). Structural studies have found that BD is associated with a smaller-than-average volume in the amygdala, hippocampus and prefrontal cortex, but findings differ across the life course and with pharmacological treatment history (Lee et al., 2014; Phillips & Swartz, 2014). Findings regarding atypical volume of the hippocampus, amygdala and regions of the prefrontal cortex have been identified in those at risk for BD or in early stages of the disorder (Phillips and Swartz, 2014).

Patterns of neural activation appear to shift with mood episodes. During depression, diminished activity in the anterior cingulate is observed (Mayberg et al., 2004). During mania, persons with BD may show diminished reactivity to negative stimuli compared with healthy or euthymic persons. For example, after viewing faces with negative emotional expressions, patients with mania showed less amygdala and subgenual anterior cingulate cortex activity compared with controls (Lennox, Jacob, Calder, Lupson, & Bullmore, 2004).

In sum, current theory suggests that BD is related to dysregulation in brain regions relevant to emotional reactivity, such as the amygdala, and to reward processing, such as the nucleus accumbens, as well as regions in the prefrontal cortex involved in the regulation of emotion and cognitive control. These regions show atypical patterns of activation in fMRI studies, disturbances in connectivity, and diminished volume. Evidence suggests that neural activation is somewhat mood state-dependent.

CASE STUDY

CASE IDENTIFICATION AND PRESENTING COMPLAINTS

Leonard, a 57-year-old White male, lived with his wife, Helen, and 15-year-old son in a rented house in the suburbs of a major metropolitan area. His wife requested treatment because of his angry outbursts, sleep disturbance, and bizarre preoccupations. He had become preoccupied with kickboxing and was spending hours on the Internet examining relevant websites and writing about it. She discovered that he had written a 500-page manuscript describing the mechanics of kickboxing, containing sections that were rambling, philosophical, and at times incoherent. She explained that he was frequently awake until 4 A.M. and went to bed smelling of alcohol. For nearly 5 years he had been unable to hold down a job.

Leonard presented in his first interview as combative and oppositional. He admitted that he had been feeling "revved" over the past 2 weeks, that he felt full of energy and ideas, and that he needed little sleep, but he denied any negative effects of his symptoms. He described an incident that appeared to be related to his recent manic behavior. He had made contact with a kickboxing champion in another state and had started writing to this man about setting up a new television network devoted to kickboxing. He also claimed he was going to start his own studio. The plans seemed unrealistic given that he had little formal training in this sport and had no money to rent a studio. The kickboxing champion had stopped responding to Leonard's emails, which, Leonard claimed, might be because "he's raising money and wants to surprise me."

Leonard had one manic episode accompanied by hospitalization when he was in college. He had become entranced by a female professor and believed that she was related to him by blood. He began calling her continually and finally followed her to a parking lot where he tried to block her from getting into her car. A passerby called the police, and Leonard was taken to the hospital. He was admitted with the diagnosis of bipolar I, manic episode.

Since this time Leonard had functioned poorly. His work had been intermittent, and he had been fired several times because, as he explained, "My bosses are always idiots and I'm more than happy to tell them so." He had tried to set up a web-based business selling automobile window shields but had made little money. He met Helen during a hiking excursion for singles. They had married approximately 1 year after they met (a period of relative stability for Leonard) and had a child 1 year later.

Leonard had begun medication shortly after his son was born, explaining that he wanted to become a stable father. His psychiatrist recommended lithium carbonate 1,200 mg and divalproex sodium (Depakote) 2,000 mg. Although Leonard did not have further manic episodes, he had several hypomanic periods and complained of an ongoing depression that never fully remitted. He had thought of suicide several times, and these fantasies usually had a dramatic quality. For example, he fantasized about setting himself on fire and then jumping from a tall building. He never made an attempt.

The clinician who evaluated Leonard administered the Structured Clinical Interview for *DSM-IV* (First et al., 1995), which involved an individual interview with him, followed by a separate interview with his wife. The interview confirmed the presence of elated and irritable mood for the past 2 weeks, along with inflated self-esteem, increased activity, decreased need for sleep, flight of ideas and racing thoughts, pressure of speech, and increased spending. His behavior did not require hospitalization but clearly interfered with his functioning. He was given a diagnosis of bipolar I disorder, manic episode and was started on a regimen of lithium, divalproex, and an atypical antipsychotic agent, quetiapine (Seroquel).

SUMMARY

Much progress has been made in clarifying the diagnostic boundaries, genetic pathways, and neurobiological mechanisms relevant to bipolar illness. Research documents the strong influence of psychosocial variables against this background of biological and genetic vulnerability. Psychotherapy is an effective adjunct to pharmacotherapy in the long-term maintenance treatment of the illness, notably interventions that focus on enhancing the patient's understanding of the disorder and effectiveness in coping with symptoms and their potential triggers.

Major focal areas for future studies include clarifying the validity of the bipolar spectrum. It is unclear whether bipolar illness should include only *DSM-5*-defined bipolar I, bipolar II disorder, and cyclothymic disorder, or whether it should also include episodes of mania, hypomania, or depression that do not meet the full severity or duration criteria (unspecified BD). Nowhere are these questions more critical than in defining childhood-onset BD, for which there has been a dramatic increase in rates of treatment in the US over the past 20 years. In the future, it may be that fMRI or other imaging techniques will identify brain changes uniquely associated with bipolar illness, but until that time we must rely on clinical interviews and supplemental questionnaires to diagnose these conditions. Research that improves the reliability, clinical utility, and consumer acceptance of existing diagnostic methods is therefore critical.

The interface between psychosocial and biological risk factors deserves considerable study, especially as these factors relate differentially to the two poles of the disorder. As we have summarized, responses to reward and goal attainment, and factors that disrupt sleep are strongly correlated with the onset of manic episodes. High intrafamilial EE and negative life events are most consistently associated with depressive episodes. Translational research is needed to help clarify the avenues from specific stressors to biological changes to manic versus depressive symptom exacerbations.

The optimal combinations of psychotherapy and pharmacotherapy must be identified in trials that include samples of diverse ethnicity, socioeconomic status, psychiatric and medical comorbidity, and chronicity. Large-scale studies such as STEP-BD are a move in this direction (Deckersbach et al., 2014), but even studies of this size can be under-powered for examining treatment effects within specific subgroups (e.g., patients with comorbid substance dependence or personality disorders). Studies that enhance care and reduce treatment disparities for those from minority groups are essential to moving the field forward.

Last, treatment studies should consider the synergy between biological and psychosocial interventions, and under what conditions combining one with the other will produce the most enduring effects. For example, drugs that stabilize mood symptoms may also energize patients to the extent that they become more amenable to the skill-oriented tasks of CBT. Psychoeducational treatments may increase medication adherence, which in turn may allow patients to remain stable on fewer medications or on lower dosages. Interpersonal or family interventions that increase the patient's ability to benefit from social support and decrease the impact of family or life stressors may also decrease the level of medication required in long-term maintenance. Ideally, the next generation of clinical research in BD will address these questions.

REFERENCES

Akiskal, H. S., Benazzi, F., Perugi, G., & Rihmer, Z. (2005a). Agitated "unipolar" depression reconceptualized as a depressive mixed state: Implications for the antidepressant-suicide controversy. *Journal of Affective Disorders, 85,* 245–258.

Akiskal, H. S., Bourgeois, M. L., Angst, J., Post, R., Moller, H., & Hirschfeld, R. (2000). Reevaluating the prevalence of and diagnostic composition within the broad clinical spectrum of bipolar disorders. *Journal of Affective Disorders, 59,* S5–S30.

Akiskal, H. S., Mendlowicz, M. V., Jean-Louis, G., Rapaport, M. H., Kelsoe, J. R., Gillin, J. C., & Smith, T. L. (2005b). TEMPS-A: Validation of a short version of a self-rated instrument designed to measure variations in temperament. *Journal of Affective Disorders, 85,* 45–52.

Alloy, L. B., Reilly-Harrington, N., Fresco, D. M., Whitehouse, W. G., & Zechmeister, J. S. (1999). Cognitive styles and life events in subsyndromal unipolar and bipolar disorders: Stability and prospective prediction of depressive and hypomanic mood swings. *Journal of Cognitive Psychotherapy, 13,* 21–40.

Almeida, J. R., Versace, A., Mechelli, A., Hassel, S., Quevedo, K., Kupfer, D. J., & Phillips, M. L. (2009). Abnormal amygdala-prefrontal effective connectivity to happy faces differentiates bipolar from major depression. *Biological Psychiatry, 66,* 451–459.

Altshuler, L., Suppes, T., Black, D., Nolen, W. A., Keck, P. E. Jr. Frye, M. A., . . . Post, R. (2003). Impact of antidepressant discontinuation after acute bipolar depression remission on rates of depressive relapse at 1-year follow-up. *American Journal of Psychiatry, 160,* 1252–1262.

American Psychiatric Association. (2000). *Diagnostic and statistical manual of mental disorders* (4th ed., text rev.) Washington, DC: Author.

American Psychiatric Association. (2013). *Diagnostic and statistical manual of mental disorders* (5th ed.). Arlington, VA: American Psychiatric Publishing.

Anand, A., Verhoeff, P., Seneca, N., Zoghbi, S. S., Seibyl, J. P., Charney, D. S., . . . Cohen, M. S. (2000). Brain SPECT imaging of amphetamine-induced dopamine release in euthymic bipolar disorder patients. *American Journal of Psychiatry, 157,* 1109–1114.

Ankers, D., & Jones, S. H. (2009). Objective assessment of circadian activity and sleep patterns in individuals at behavioural risk of hypomania. *Journal of Clinical Psychology, 65,* 1071–1086.

Anthony, E. J., & Scott, P. (1960). Manic-depressive psychosis in childhood. *Child Psychology and Psychiatry, 1,* 53–72.

Axelson, D. A., Birmaher, B., Findling, R. L., Fristad, M. A., Kowatch, R. A., Youngstrom, E. A., . . . Diler, R. S. (2011a). Concerns regarding the inclusion of temper dysregulation disorder with dysphoria in the *Diagnostic and Statistical Manual of Mental Disorders,* Fifth Edition. *Journal of Clinical Psychiatry, 72,* 1257–1262.

Axelson, D. A., Birmaher, B., Strober, M. A., Goldstein, B. I., Ha, W., Gill, M. K., . . . Keller, M. B. (2011b). Course of subthreshold bipolar disorder in youth: Diagnostic progression from bipolar disorder not otherwise specified. *Journal of the American Academy of Child & Adolescent Psychiatry, 50,* 1001–1016.

Barbini, B., Colombo, C., Benedetti, F., Campori, C., Bellodi, L., & Smeraldi, E. (1998). The unipolar-bipolar dichotomy and the response to sleep deprivation. *Psychiatry Research, 79,* 43–50.

Baldessarini, R., Henk, H., Sklar, A., Chang, J., & Leahy, L. Psychotropic medications for patients with bipolar disorder in the United States: polytherapy and adherence. (2008). *Psychiatr Serv, 59* (10), 1175–83.

Barch, D. M. (2005). The cognitive neuroscience of schizophrenia. *Annual Review of Clinical Psychology, 1,* 321–353.

Bauer, M. S., McBride, L., Williford, W. O., Glick, H., Kinosian, B., Altshuler, L., . . . Sajatovic, M. (2006a). Collaborative care for bipolar disorder: Part I. Intervention and implementation in a randomized effectiveness trial. *Psychiatric Services, 57,* 927–936.

Bauer, M. S., McBride, L., Williford, W. O., Glick, H., Kinosian, B., Altshuler, L., . . . Sajatovic, M. (2006b). Collaborative care for bipolar disorder: Part II. Impact on clinical outcome, function, and costs. *Psychiatric Services, 57,* 937–945.

Birmaher, B., Axelson, D., Goldstein, B., Strober, M., Gill, M. K., Hunt, J., . . . Keller, M. (2009). Four-year longitudinal course of children and adolescents with bipolar spectrum disorders: The Course and Outcome of Bipolar Youth (COBY) study. *American Journal of Psychiatry, 166,* 795–804.

Blumberg, H. P., Stern, E., Ricketts, S., Martinez, D., deAsis, J., White, T., . . . Silbersweig, D. A. (1999). Rostral and orbital prefrontal cortex dysfunction in the manic state of bipolar disorder. *American Journal of Psychiatry, 156,* 1986–1988.

Boufidou, F., Nikkolaou, C., Alevizios, B., Liappas, I. A., & Christodoulou, G. N. (2004). Cytokine production in bipolar affective disorder patients under lithium treatment. *Journal of Affective Disorders, 82,* 309–313.

Brady, K. T., Casto, S., Lydiard, R. B., Malcolm, R., & Arana, G. (1991). Substance abuse in an inpatient psychiatric sample. *American Journal of Drug and Alcohol Abuse, 17,* 389–397.

Brietzke, E., Stertz, L., Fernandes, B. S., Kauer-Sant'anna, M., Mascarenhas, M., Escosteguy, V. A., . . . Kapczinski, F. (2009). Comparison of cytokine levels in depressed, manic and euthymic patients with bipolar disorder. *Journal of Affective Disorders, 116,* 214–217.

Brown, G. W., & Andrews, B. (1986). Social support and depression. In R. Trumbull & M. H. Appley (Eds.), *Dynamics of stress: Physiological, psychological, and social perspectives* (pp. 257–282). New York, NY: Plenum Press.

Burdick, K. E., Braga, R. J., Gopin, C. B., & Malhotra, A. K. (2014). Dopaminergic influences on emotional decision making in euthymic bipolar patients. *Neuropsychopharmacology, 39,* 274–282.

Butzlaff, R. L., & Hooley, J. M. (1998). Expressed emotion and psychiatric relapse: A meta- analysis. *Archives of General Psychiatry, 55,* 547–552.

Caligiuri, M. P., Brown, G. G., Meloy, M. J., Eberson, S. C., Kindermann, S. S., Frank, L. R., . . . Lohr, J. B. (2003). An fMRI study of affective state and medication on cortical and subcortical regions during motor performance in bipolar disorder. *Psychiatry Research: Neuroimaging, 123,* 171–182.

Carlson, G. A., & Klein, D. N. (2014). How to understand divergent views on bipolar disorder in youth. *Annual Review of Clinical Psychology, 10,* 529–551.

Chambers, W. J., Puig-Antich, J., Hirsch, M., Paez, P., Ambrosini, P. J., Tabrizi, M. A., & Davies, M. (1985). The assessment of affective disorders in children and adolescents by semi- structured interview: Test-retest reliability. *Archives of General Psychiatry, 42,* 696–702.

Chang, K. D., Steiner, H., & Ketter, T. A. (2000). Psychiatric phenomenology of child and adolescent bipolar offspring. *Journal of the American Academy of Child & Adolescent Psychiatry, 39,* 453–460.

Charney, D. S., Menkes, D. B., & Heninger, G. R. (1981). Receptor sensitivity and the mechanism of action of antidepressants. *Archives of General Psychiatry, 38,* 1160–1180.

Charney, A. W., Ruderfer, D. M., Stahl, E. A., Moran, J. L., Chambert, K., Belliveau, R. A., . . . & Bromet, E. J. (2017). Evidence for genetic heterogeneity between clinical subtypes of bipolar disorder. *Translational Psychiatry, 7,* e993.

Chen, C. H., Suckling, J., Lennox, B. R., Ooi, C., & Bullmore, E. T. (2011). A quantitative meta-analysis of fMRI studies in bipolar disorder. *Bipolar Disorders, 13,* 1–15.

Cho, H. J., Meira-Lima, I., Cordeiro, Q., Michelon, L., Sham, P., Vallada, H., . . . Collier, D. A. (2005). Population-based and family-based studies on the serotonin transporter gene polymorphisms and BD: A systematic review and meta-analysis. *Molecular Psychiatry, 10,* 771–781.

Colom, F., Vieta, E., Martinez-Aran, A., Reinares, M., Benabarre, A., & Gasto, C. (2000). Clinical factors associated with treatment noncompliance in euthymic bipolar patients. *Journal of Clinical Psychiatry, 61,* 549–555.

Colom, F., Vieta, E., Martinez-Aran, A., Reinares, M., Goikolea, J. M., Benabarre, A., . . . Cominas, J. (2003). A randomized trial on the efficacy of group psychoeducation in the prophylaxis of recurrences in bipolar patients whose disease is in remission. *Archives of General Psychiatry, 60,* 402–407.

Coryell, W. D. S., Turvey, C., Keller, M., Leon, A. C., Endicott, J., Schettler, P., . . . Mueller, T. (2003). The long-term course of rapid-cycling bipolar disorder. *Archives of General Psychiatry, 60,* 914–920.

Coryell, W., Endicott, J., Maser, J. D., Keller, M. B., Leon, A. C., & Akiskal, H. S. (1995). Long- term stability of polarity distinctions in the affective disorders. *American Journal of Psychiatry, 152,* 385–390.

Cuellar, A., Johnson, S. L., & Winters, R. (2005). Distinctions between bipolar and unipolar depression. *Clinical Psychology Review, 25,* 307–339.

Crump, C., Ioannidis, J. P., Sundquist, K., Winkleby, M. A., & Sundquist, J. (2013). Mortality in persons with mental disorders is substantially overestimated using inpatient psychiatric diagnoses. *Journal of Psychiatric Research, 47*(10), 1298–130.

Danielson, C. K., Youngstrom, E. A., Findling, R. L., & Calabrese, J. R. (2003). Discriminative validity of the general behavior inventory using youth report. *Journal of Abnormal Child Psychology, 31,* 29–39.

Daruy-Filho, L., Brietzke, E., Lafer, B., & Grassi-Oliveira, R. (2011). Childhood maltreatment and clinical outcomes of bipolar disorder. *Acta Psychiatrica Scandinavica, 124,* 427–434.

Davidson, R. J., Pizzagalli, D., & Nitschke, J. B. (2002). The representation and regulation of emotion in depression: Perspectives from affective neuroscience. In C. L. Hammen & I. H. Gotlib (Eds.), *Handbook of depression* (pp. 219–244). New York, NY: Guilford Press.

Deckersbach, T., Peters, A., Sylvia, L., Urdahl, A., Vieira da Silva Magalhaes, P., Otto, M. W., . . . Nierenberg, A. (2014). Do comorbid anxiety disorders moderate the effects of psychotherapy for bipolar disorder? Results from STEP-BD. *American Journal of Psychiatry, 171,* 178–86.

Delvecchio, G., Fossati, P., Boyer, P., Brambilla, P., Falkai, P., Gruber, O., . . . Frangou, S. (2012). Common and distinct neural correlates of emotional processing in Bipolar Disorder and Major Depressive Disorder: A voxel-based meta-analysis of functional magnetic resonance imaging studies. *European Neuropsychopharmacology, 22,* 100–113.

Depue, R. A., Kleinman, R. M., Davis, P., Hutchinson, M., & Krauss, S. P. (1985). The behavioral high-risk paradigm and bipolar affective disorder, Part VII: Serum free cortisol in nonpatient cyclothymic subjects selected by the General Behavior Inventory. *American Journal of Psychiatry, 142,* 175–181.

Depue, R. A., & Monroe, S. M. (1978). The unipolar-bipolar distinction in the depressive disorders. *Psychological Bulletin, 85,* 1001–1029.

Duffy, A., Horrocks, J., Doucette, S., Keown-Stoneman, C., McCloskey, S., & Grof P. (2014). The developmental trajectory of bipolar disorder. *The British Journal of Psychiatry*, 204(2) 122–128.

Dunner, D. L., & Tay, L. K. (1993). Diagnostic reliability of the history of hypomania in bipolar II patients and patients with major depression. *Comprehensive Psychiatry*, 34, 303–307.

Ebert, D., Feistel, H., Barocks, A., Kaschka, W. P., & Pirner, A. (1994). SPECT assessment of cerebral dopamine D2 receptor blockade in depression before and after sleep deprivation. *Biological Psychiatry*, 35, 880–885.

Eckblad, M., & Chapman, L. J. (1986). Development and validation of a scale for hypomanic personality. *Journal of Abnormal Psychology*, 95, 214–222.

Ehlers, C. L., Frank, E., & Kupfer, D. J. (1988). Social zeitgebers and biological rhythms: A unified approach to understanding the etiology of depression. *Archives of General Psychiatry*, 45, 948–952.

Ehlers, C. L., Kupfer, D. J., Frank, E., & Monk, T. H. (1993). Biological rhythms and depression: The role of zeitgebers and zeitstorers. *Depression*, 1, 285–293.

Eich, E., Macaulay, D., & Lam, R. W. (1997). Mania, depression, and mood dependent memory. *Cognition and Emotion*, 11, 607–618.

Eisner, L., Johnson, S. L., & Carver, C. S. (2008). Cognitive responses to failure and success relate uniquely to bipolar depression versus mania. *Journal ofAbnormal Psychology*, 117, 154–163.

Ellicott, A., Hammen, C., Gitlin, M., Brown, G., & Jamison, K. (1990). Life events and the course of bipolar disorder. *American Journal of Psychiatry*, 147, 1194–1198.

Faraone, S. V., Biederman, J., Mennin, D., Wozniak, J., & Spencer, T. (1997a). Attention-deficit hyperactivity disorder with bipolar disorder: A familial subtype? *Journal of the American Academy of Child & Adolescent Psychiatry*, 36, 1378–1387.

Faraone, S. V., Biederman, J., Wozniak, J., Mundy, E., Mennin, D., & O'Donnell, D. (1997b). Is comorbidity with ADHD a marker for juvenile-onset mania? *Journal of the American Academy of Child & Adolescent Psychiatry*, 36, 1046–1055.

Fears, S. C., Kremeyer, B., Araya, C., Araya, X., Bejarano, J., Ramirez, M., . . . Bearden, C. E. (2014). Multisystem component phenotypes of bipolar disorder for genetic investigations of extended pedigrees. *JAMA Psychiatry*, 71, 375–387.

Findling, R. L., Jo, B., Frazier, T. W., Youngstrom, E. A., Demeter, C. A., Fristad, M. A., . . . Horwitz, S. M. (2013). The 24-month course of manic symptoms in children. *Bipolar Disorders*, 15, 669–679.

First, M. B., Spitzer, R. L., Gibbon, M., & Williams, J. B. W. (1995). *Structured clinical interview for DSM-IV Axis I disorders*. New York, NY: Biometrics Research Department, New York State Psychiatric Institute.

Frank, E., Kupfer, D. J., Thase, M. E., Mallinger, A. G., Swartz, H. A., Fagiolini, A. M., . . . Monk, T. (2005). Two-year outcomes for interpersonal and social rhythm therapy in individuals with bipolar I disorder. *Archives of General Psychiatry*, 62, 996–1004.

Fristad, M. A., Verducci, J. S., Walters, K., & Young, M. E. (2009). Impact of multifamily psycho-educational psychotherapy in treating children aged 8 to 12 years with mood disorders. *Archives of General Psychiatry*, 66, 1013–1021.

Fulford, D., Johnson, S. L., Llabre, M. M., & Carver, C. S. (2010). Pushing and coasting in dynamic goal pursuit: Coasting is attenuated in bipolar disorder. *Psychological Sciences*, 21, 1021–1027.

Garrett, A. S., Reiss, A. L., Howe, M. E., Kelley, R. G., Singh, M. K., Adleman, N. E., . . . Chang, K. D. (2012). Abnormal amygdala and prefrontal cortex activation to facial expressions in pediatric bipolar disorder. *Journal of the American Academy of Child & Adolescent Psychiatry*, 51, 821–831.

Geddes, J. R., & Miklowitz, D. J. (2013). Treatment of bipolar disorder. *Lancet*, 381, 1672–1682.

Geller, B., Tillman, R., Bolhofner, K., & Zimerman, B. (2008). Child bipolar I disorder: Prospective continuity with adult bipolar I disorder; characteristics of second and third episodes; predictors of 8-year outcome. *Archives of General Psychiatry*, 65, 1125–1133.

Geller, B., Williams, M., Zimerman, B., Frazier, J., Beringer, I., & Warner, K. L. (1998). Prepubertal and early adolescent bipolarity differentiated from ADHD by manic symptoms, grandiose delusions, ultra-rapid or ultraradian cycling. *Journal of Affective Disorders, 51*, 81–91.

Gershon, A., Johnson, S. L., & Miller, I. (2013). Chronic stressors and trauma: Prospective influences on the course of bipolar disorder. *Psychological Medicine, 43*, 2583–2592.

Gershon, A., Thompson, W. K., Eidelman, P., McGlinchey, E. L., Kaplan, K. A., & Harvey, A. G. (2012). Restless pillow, ruffled mind: Sleep and affect coupling in interepisode bipolar disorder. *Journal of Abnormal Psychology, 121*, 863.

Ghaemi, S. N., Lenox, M. S., & Baldessarini, R. J. (2001). Effectiveness and safety of long-term antidepressant treatment in bipolar disorder. *Journal of Clinical Psychiatry, 62*, 565–569.

Gignac, A., McGirr, A., Lam, R. W., & Yatham, L. N. (2015). Recovery and recurrence following a first episode of mania: a systematic review and meta-analysis of prospectively characterized cohorts. *J Clinical Psychiatry, 76*, 1241–1248.

Gilman, S. E., Ni, M. Y., Dunn, E. C., Breslau, J., McLaughlin, K. A., Smoller, J. W., & Perlis, R. H. (2015). Contributions of the social environment to first-onset and recurrent mania. *Molecular Psychiatry, 20*, 329–336.

Gitlin, M. J., Mintz, J., Sokolski, K., Hammen, C., & Altshuler, L. L. (2011). Subsyndromal depressive symptoms after symptomatic recovery from mania are associated with delayed functional recovery. *Journal of Clinical Psychiatry, 72*, 692–697.

Goldberg, J., Garno, J., Leon, A., Kocsis, J., & Portera, L. (1999). A history of substance abuse complicates remission from acute mania in bipolar disorder. *Journal of Clinical Psychiatry, 60*, 733–740.

Goldstein, B. I., Birmaher, B., Carlson, G., DelBello, M. P., Findling, R. L., Fristad, M. A., . . . Youngstrom, E. A. (2017). The International Society for Bipolar Disorders Task Force Report on Pediatric Bipolar Disorder: knowledge to date and directions for future research. *Bipolar Disorders*, epub ahead of print. doi: 10.1111/bdi.12556.

Goldstein, B. I., Lotrich, F., Axelson, D., Gill, M. K., Hower, H., Goldstein, T. R., . . . Birmaher, B. (2015). Inflammatory markers among adolescents and young adults with bipolar spectrum disorders. *Journal of Clinical Psychiatry, 76*, 1556–1563.

Gonzalez, J. M., Thompson, P., Escamilla, M., Araga, M., Singh, V., Farrelly, N., . . . Bowden, C. L. (2007). Treatment characteristics and illness burden among European Americans, African Americans, and Latinos in the first 2,000 patients of the systematic treatment enhancement program for bipolar disorder. *Psychopharmacology Bulletin, 40*, 31–46.

Grunze, H., Vieta, E., Goodwin, G. M., Bowden, C., Licht, R. W., Möller, H. J., & Kasper, S. (2010). The World Federation of Societies of Biological Psychiatry (WFSBP) guidelines for the biological treatment of bipolar disorders: Update 2010 on the treatment of acute bipolar depression. *The World Journal of Biological Psychiatry, 11*, 81–109.

Gunderson, J. G., Triebwasser, J., Phillips, K. A., & Sullivan, C. N. (1999). Personality and vulnerability to affective disorders. In R. C. Cloninger (Ed.), *Personality and psychopathology* (pp. 3–32). Washington, DC: American Psychiatric Press.

Hafeman, D. M., Merranko, J., Axelson, D., Goldstein, B. I., Goldstein, T., Monk, K., . . . Brent, D. (2016). Toward the definition of a bipolar prodrome: dimensional predictors of bipolar spectrum disorders in at-risk youths. *American Journal of Psychiatry, 173*, 695–704.

Harpaz-Rotem, I., Leslie, D. L., Martin, A., & Rosenheck, R. A. (2005). Changes in child and adolescent inpatient psychiatric admission diagnoses between 1995 and 2000. *Social Psychiatry and Psychiatric Epidemiology, 40*, 642–647.

Harpaz-Rotem, I., & Rosenheck, R. A. (2004). Changes in outpatient psychiatric diagnosis in privately insured children and adolescents from 1995 to 2000. *Child Psychiatry & Human Development, 34*, 329–340.

Harrow, M., Goldberg, J. F., Grossman, L. S., & Meltzer, H. Y. (1990). Outcome in manic disorders: A naturalistic follow-up study. *Archives of General Psychiatry, 47*, 665–671.

Harvey, A. G., Soehner, A. M., Kaplan, K. A., Hein, K., Lee, J., Kanady, J., . . . Buysse, D. J. (2015). Treating insomnia improves mood state, sleep, and functioning in bipolar disorder: A pilot randomized controlled trial. *Journal of Consulting and Clinical Psychology, 83*, 564.

Heerlein, A., Richter, P., Gonzalez, M., & Santander, J. (1998). Personality patterns and outcome in depressive and bipolar disorders. *Psychopathology, 31*, 15–22.

Henry, C., Van denBulke, D., Bellivier, F., Etain, B., Rouillon, F., & Leboyer, M. (2003). Anxiety disorders in 318 bipolar patients: Prevalence and impact on illness severity and response to mood stabilizer. *Journal of Clinical Psychiatry, 64*, 331–335.

Hinshaw, S. P., Owens, E. B., Zalecki, C., Huggins, S. P., Montenegro-Nevado, A. J., Schrodek, E., & Swanson, E. N. (2012). Prospective follow-up of girls with attention-deficit/hyperactivity disorder into early adulthood: Continuing impairment includes elevated risk for suicide attempts and self-injury. *Journal of Consulting and Clinical Psychology, 80*, 1041–1051.

Hodgins, S., Faucher, B., Zarac, A., & Ellenbogen, M. (2002). Children of parents with bipolar disorder: A population at high risk for major affective disorders. *Child and Adolescent Psychiatric Clinics of North America, 11*, 533–553.

Ilgen, M. A., Bohnert, A. S., Ignacio, R. V., McCarthy, J. F., Valenstein, M. M., Kim, H. M., & Blow, F. C. (2010). Psychiatric diagnoses and risk of suicide in veterans. *Archives of General Psychiatry, 67*, 1152–1158.

Inder, M. L., Crowe, M. T., Luty, S. E., Carter, J. D., Moor, S., Frampton, C. M., & Joyce, P. R. (2015). Randomized, controlled trial of Interpersonal and Social Rhythm Therapy for young people with bipolar disorder. *Bipolar Disorders, 17*, 128–138.

Jamison, K. R. (1993). *Touched with fire: Manic-depressive illness and the artistic temperament.* New York, NY: *Maxwell* Macmillan International.

Johnson, K. R., & Johnson, S. L. (2014). Inadequate treatment of black Americans with bipolar disorder. *Psychiatric Services, 65*, 255–258.

Johnson, S. L. (2005a). Life events in bipolar disorder: Towards more specific models. *Clinical Psychology Review, 25*, 1008–1027.

Johnson, S. L. (2005b). Mania and dysregulation in goal pursuit. *Clinical Psychology Review, 25*, 241–262.

Johnson, S. L., Carver, C. S., & Gotlib, I. H. (2012a). Elevated ambitions for fame among persons diagnosed with bipolar I disorder. *Journal of Abnormal Psychology, 121*, 602–609.

Johnson, S. L., Cuellar, A. K., & Gershon, A. (2016). The influence of trauma, life events, and social relationships on bipolar depression. *Psychiatric Clinics of North America, 39*, 87–94.

Johnson, S. L., Cuellar, A., Ruggero, C., Perlman, C., Goodnick, P., White, R., & Miller, I. (2008). Life events as predictors of mania and depression in bipolar I disorder. *Journal of Abnormal Psychology, 117*, 268–277.

Johnson, S. L., Eisner, L., & Carver, C. S. (2009). Elevated expectancies among persons diagnosed with bipolar disorders. *British Journal of Clinical Psychology, 48*, 217–222.

Johnson, S. L., Edge, M. D., Holmes, M. K., & Carver, C. S. (2012b). The behavioral activation system and mania. *Annual Review of Clinical Psychology, 8*, 143–167.

Johnson, S. L., & Fingerhut, R. (2004). Negative cognitions predict the course of bipolar depression, not mania. *Journal of Cognitive Psychotherapy, 18*, 149–162.

Johnson, S. L., Meyer, B., Winett, C., & Small, J. (2000a). Social support and self-esteem predict changes in bipolar depression but not mania. *Journal of Affective Disorders, 58*, 79–86.

Johnson, S. L., & Miller, I. (1997). Negative life events and time to recovery from episodes of bipolar disorder. *Journal of Abnormal Psychology, 106*, 449–457.

Johnson, S. L., Murray, G., Fredrickson, B., Youngstrom, E. A., Hinshaw, S., Bass, J. M., . . . Salloum, I. (2012c). Creativity and bipolar disorder: Touched by fire or burning with questions? *Clinical Psychology Review, 32*, 1–12.

Johnson, S. L., Murray, G., Hou, S., Staudenmaier, P. J., Freeman, M. A., & Michalak, E. E. (2015). Creativity is linked to ambition across the bipolar spectrum. *Journal of Affective Disorders, 178,* 160–164.

Johnson, S. L., Sandrow, D., Meyer, B., Winters, R., Miller, I., Solomon, D., & Keitner, G. (2000b). Increases in manic symptoms following life events involving goal-attainment. *Journal of Abnormal Psychology, 109,* 721–727.

Johnson, S. L., Winett, C. A., Meyer, B., Greenhouse, W. J., & Miller, I. (1999). Social support and the course of bipolar disorder. *Journal of Abnormal Psychology, 108,* 558–566.

Johnston, J. A., Wang, F., Liu, J., Blond, B. N., Wallace, A., Liu, J., . . . Hermes, E. (2017). Multimodal neuroimaging of frontolimbic structure and function associated with suicide attempts in adolescents and young adults with bipolar disorder. *American Journal of Psychiatry, 174,* 667–675.

Jones, S. H., Hare, D. J., & Evershed, K. (2005). Actigraphic assessment of circadian activity and sleep patterns in bipolar disorder. *Bipolar Disorders, 7,* 176–186.

Judd, L. L., & Akiskal, H. S. (2003). The prevalence and disability of bipolar spectrum disorders in the US population: Re-analysis of the ECA database taking into account subthreshold cases. *Journal of Affective Disorders, 73*(1–2), 123–131.

Judd, L. L., Akiskal, H. S., Schettler, P. J., Endicott, J., Maser, J., Solomon, D. A., . . . Keller, M. B. (2002). The long-term natural history of the weekly symptomatic status of bipolar I disorder. *Archives of General Psychiatry, 59,* 530–537.

Kalivas, P. W., Duffy, P., DuMars, L. A., & Skinner, C. (1988). Behavioral and neurochemical effects of acute and daily cocaine administration in rats. *Journal of Pharmacology and Experimental Therapeutics, 245,* 485–492.

Karkowski, L. M., & Kendler, K. S. (1997). An examination of the genetic relationship between bipolar and unipolar illness in an epidemiological sample. *Psychiatric Genetics, 7,* 159–163.

Kaufman, J., Birmaher, B., Brent, D., Rao, U., Flynn, C., Moreci, P., . . . Ryan, N. (1997). Schedule for Affective Disorders and Schizophrenia for School-Age Children—Present and Lifetime Version (K-SADS-PL): Initial reliability and validity data. *Journal of the American Academy of Child & Adolescent Psychiatry, 36,* 98–988.

Keck, P. E. Jr. McElroy, S. L., Strakowski, S. M., Bourne, M. L., & West, S. A. (1997). Compliance with maintenance treatment in bipolar disorder. *Psychopharmacology Bulletin, 33,* 87–91.

Keener, M. T., Fournier, J. C., Mullin, B. C., Kronhaus, D., Perlman, S. B., LaBarbara, E., . . . Phillips, M. L. (2012). Dissociable patterns of medial prefrontal and amygdala activity to face identity versus emotion in bipolar disorder. *Psychological medicine, 42,* 1913–1924.

Keller, M. B., Lavori, P. W., Coryell, W., Endicott, J., & Mueller, T. I. (1993). Bipolar I: A five-year prospective follow-up. *Journal of Nervous and Mental Disease, 181,* 238–245.

Kessler, R. C., Akiskal, H. S., Angst, J., Guyer, M. H., Hirschfeld, R. M., Merikangas, K. R., & Stang, P. E. (2006). Validity of the assessment of bipolar spectrum disorders in the WHO CIDI 3.0. *Journal of Affective Disorders, 96,* 259–269.

Kessler, R. C., Chiu, W. T., Demler, O., & Walters, E. E. (2005). Prevalence, severity, and comorbidity of 12-month *DSM-IV* disorders in the National Comorbidity Survey Replication. *Archives of General Psychiatry, 62,* 617–627.

Kessler, R. C., Crum, R. C., Warner, L. A., Nelson, C. B., Schulenberg, J., & Anthony, J. C. (1997). Lifetime co-occurrence of *DSM-III-R* alcohol abuse and dependence with other psychiatric disorders in the National Comorbidity Survey. *Archives of General Psychiatry, 54,* 313–321.

Kieseppä, T., Partonen, T., Haukka, J., Kaprio, J., & Lönnqvist, J. (2004). High concordance of Bipolar I Disorder in a nationwide sample of twins. *American Journal of Psychiatry, 161,* 1814–1821.

Kilbourne, A. M., Bauer, M. S., Han, X., Haas, G. L., Elder, P., Good, C. B., . . . Pincus, H. (2005). Racial differences in the treatment of veterans with bipolar disorder. *Psychiatric Services, 56,* 1549–1555.

Kim, E. Y., & Miklowitz, D. J. (2002). Childhood mania, attention deficit hyperactivity disorder, and conduct disorder: A critical review of diagnostic dilemmas. *Bipolar Disorders, 4,* 215–225.

Kim, E. Y., & Miklowitz, D. J. (2004). Expressed emotion as a predictor of outcome among bipolar patients undergoing family therapy. *Journal of Affective Disorders, 82,* 343–352.

Kim, Y. K., Myint, A. M., Lee, B. H., Han, C. S., Lee, S. W., Leonard, B. E., & Steinbusch, H. W. (2004). T-helper types 1, 2, and 3 cytokine interactions in symptomatic manic patients *Psychiatry Research, 129,* 267–272.

Klein, D. N., Depue, R. A., & Slater, J. F. (1985). Cyclothymia in the adolescent offspring of parents with bipolar affective disorder. *Journal of Abnormal Psychology, 94,* 115.

Kochman, F. J., Hantouche, E. G., Ferrari, P., Lancrenon, S., Bayart, D., & Akiskal, H. S. (2005). Cyclothymic temperament as a prospective predictor of bipolarity and suicidality in children and adolescents with major depressive disorder. *Journal of Affective Disorders, 85,* 181–189.

Kowatch, R. A., Fristad, M., Birmaher, B., Wagner, K. D., Findling, R. L., Hellander, M. & The Child Psychiatric Workgroup on Bipolar Disorder. (2005a). Treatment guidelines for children and adolescents with bipolar disorder. *Journal of the American Academy of Child & Adolescent Psychiatry, 44,* 213–235.

Kowatch, R. A., Youngstrom, E. A., Danielyan, A., & Findling, R. L. (2005b). Review and meta-analysis of the phenomenology and clinical characteristics of mania in children and adolescents. *Bipolar Disorders, 7,* 483–496.

Kupfer, D. J., Frank, E., Grochocinski, V. J., Houck, P. R., & Brown, C. (2005). African-American participants in a bipolar disorder registry: Clinical and treatment characteristics. *Bipolar Disorders, 7,* 82–88.

Kwapil, T. R., Miller, M. B., Zinser, M. C., Chapman, L. J., Chapman, J., & Eckblad, M. (2000). A longitudinal study of high scorers on the hypomanic personality scale. *Journal of Abnormal Psychology, 109,* 222–226.

Kyaga, S., Landén, M., Boman, M., Hultman, C. M., Långström, N., & Lichtenstein, P. (2012). Mental illness, suicide and creativity: 40-year prospective total population study. *Journal of Psychiatric Research, 47,* 83–90.

Lam, D. H., Watkins, E. R., Hayward, P., Bright, J., Wright, K., Kerr, N., . . . Sham, P. (2003). A randomized controlled study of cognitive therapy of relapse prevention for bipolar affective disorder: Outcome of the first year. *Archives of General Psychiatry, 60,* 145–152.

LaPalme, M., Hodgins, S., & LaRoche, C. (1997). Children of parents with bipolar disorder: A meta-analysis of risk for mental disorders. *Canadian Journal of Psychiatry, 42,* 623–631.

Laursen T. M., Wahlbeck, K., Hällgren, J., Westman, J., Ösby, U., Alinaghizadeh, H., . . . Nordentoft, M. (2013). Life expectancy and death by diseases of the circulatory system in patients with bipolar disorder or schizophrenia in the Nordic countries. *PLoS One, 8*(6), e67133.

Lasky-Su, J. A., Faraone, S. V., Glatt, S. J., & Tsuang, M. T. (2005). Meta-analysis of the association between two polymorphisms in the serotonin transporter gene and affective disorders. *American Journal of Medical Genetics, 133,* 110–115.

Lee M. S., Anumagalla P., Talluri P., Pavuluri M. N. (2014). Meta-analyses of developing brain function in high-risk and emerged bipolar disorder. *Frontiers in Psychiatry, 5,* 1–10.

Leibenluft, E. (1997). Issues in the treatment of women with bipolar illness. *Journal of Clinical Psychiatry, 58,* 5–11.

Leibenluft, E., Albert, P. S., Rosenthal, N. E., & Wehr, T. A. (1996). Relationship between sleep and mood in patients with rapid-cycling bipolar disorder. *Psychiatry Research, 63,* 161–168.

Leibenluft, E., Cohen, P., Gorrindo, T., Brook, J. S., & Pine, D. S. (2006). Chronic vs. episodic irritability in youth: A community-based, longitudinal study of clinical and diagnostic associations. *Journal of Child and Adolescent Psychopharmacology, 16,* 456–466.

Lennox, R., Jacob, R., Calder, A. J., Lupson, V., & Bullmore, E. T. (2004). Behavioral and neurocognitive responses to sad facial affect are attenuated in patients with mania. *Psychological Medicine, 34,* 795–802.

Leverich, G. S., & Post, R. M. (1998). Life charting of affective disorders. *CNS Spectrums, 3,* 21–37.

Lewinsohn, P. M., Seeley, J. R., Buckley, M. E., & Klein, D. N. (2002). Bipolar disorder in adolescence and young adulthood. *Child and Adolescent Psychiatric Clinics of North America, 11,* 461–475.

Loebel, A., Cucchiaro, J., Silva, R., Kroger, H., Hsu, J., Sarma, K., & Sachs, G. (2014). Lurasidone monotherapy in the treatment of bipolar I depression: A randomized, double-blind, placebo-controlled study. *American Journal of Psychiatry, 171,* 160–168.

Lozano, B. L., & Johnson, S. L. (2001). Can personality traits predict increases in manic and depressive symptoms? *Journal of Affective Disorders, 63,* 103–111.

Luby, J. L., & Navsaria, N. (2010). Pediatric bipolar disorder: Evidence for prodromal states and early markers. *Journal of Child Psychology and Psychiatry, 51,* 459–471.

Malhi, G. S., Adams, D., & Berk, M. (2009). Medicating mood with maintenance in mind: Bipolar depression pharmacotherapy. *Bipolar Disorders, 11,* 55–76.

Malkoff-Schwartz, S., Frank, E., Anderson, B., Sherrill, J. T., Siegel, L., Patterson, D., & Kupfer, D. J. (1998). Stressful life events and social rhythm disruption in the onset of manic and depressive bipolar episodes: A preliminary investigation. *Archives of General Psychiatry, 55,* 702–707.

Malkoff-Schwartz, S., Frank, E., Anderson, B. P., Hlastala, S. A., Luther, J. F., Sherrill, . . . Kupfer, D. J. (2000). Social rhythm disruption and stressful life events in the onset of bipolar and unipolar episodes. *Psychological Medicine, 30,* 1005–1016.

Manji, H. (2009). The role of synaptic and cellular plasticity cascades in the pathophysiology and treatment of mood and psychotic disorders. *Bipolar Disorders, 11,* 2–3.

Mayberg, H. S., Keightley, M., Mahurin, R. K., & Brannan, S. K. (2004). Neuropsychiatric aspects of mood and affective disorders. In R. E. Hales & S. C. Yudofsky (Eds.), *Essentials of neuropsychiatry and clinical neurosciences* (pp. 489–517). Washington, DC: American Psychiatric Publishing.

McAllister-Williams, R. H. (2006). Relapse prevention in bipolar disorder: A critical review of current guidelines. *Journal of Psychopharmacology, 20,* 12–16.

McGuffin, P., Rijsdijk, F., Andrew, M., Sham, P., Katz, R., & Cardno, A. (2003). The heritability of bipolar affective disorder and the genetic relationship to unipolar depression. *Archives of General Psychiatry, 60,* 497–502.

McMaster, K. (2016). *Explaining racial disparity in bipolar disorder treatment: How do providers contribute?* Unpublished doctoral dissertation, University of California, Berkeley.

Merikangas, K. R., Cui, L., Kattan, G., Carlson, G. A., Youngstrom, E. A., & Angst, J. (2012). Mania with and without depression in a community sample of US adolescents. *Archives of General Psychiatry, 69,* 943–951.

Merikangas, K. R., Jin, R., He, J. P., Kessler, R. C., Lee, S., Sampson, N. A., . . . Zarkov, Z. (2011). Prevalence and correlates of bipolar spectrum disorder in the World Mental Health Survey Initiative. *Archives of General Psychiatry, 68,* 241–251.

Meyer, S. E., & Carlson, G. A. (2010). Development, age of onset, and phenomenology in bipolar disorder. In D. J. Miklowitz & D. Cicchetti (Eds.), *Understanding bipolar disorder: A developmental psychopathology perspective* (pp. 35–66). New York, NY: Guilford Press.

Meyer, T. D., & Hautzinger, M. (2012). Cognitive behaviour therapy and supportive therapy for bipolar disorders: relapse rates for treatment period and 2-year follow-up. *Psychological Medicine, 42*(7), 1429–1439.

Miklowitz, D. J., Alatiq, Y., Geddes, J. R., Goodwin, G. M., & Williams, J. M. (2010). Thought suppression in patients with bipolar disorder. *Journal of Abnormal Psychology, 119,* 355–365.

Miklowitz, D. J., Axelson, D. A., Birmaher, B., George, E. L., Taylor, D. O., Schneck, C. D., . . . Brent, D. A. (2008). Family-focused treatment for adolescents with bipolar disorder: Results of a 2-year randomized trial. *Archives of General Psychiatry, 65,* 1053–1061.

Miklowitz, D. J., George, E. L., Richards, J. A., Simoneau, T. L., & Suddath, R. L. (2003). A randomized study of family-focused psychoeducation and pharmacotherapy in the out- patient management of bipolar disorder. *Archives of General Psychiatry, 60,* 904–912.

Miklowitz, D. J., Goldstein, M. J., Nuechterlein, K. H., Snyder, K. S., & Mintz, J. (1988). Family factors and the course of bipolar affective disorder. *Archives of General Psychiatry, 45,* 225–231.

Miklowitz, D. J., Otto, M. W., Frank, E., Reilly-Harrington, N. A., Wisniewski, S. R., Kogan, J. N., & Sachs, G. S. (2007). Psychosocial treatments for bipolar depression: A 1-year randomized trial from the Systematic Treatment Enhancement Program. *Archives of General Psychiatry, 64,* 419–427.

Miklowitz, D. J., Portnoff, L. C., Armstrong, C. C., Keenan-Miller, D., Breen, E. C., Muscatell, K. A., . . . Irwin, M. R. (2016). Inflammatory cytokines and nuclear factor-kappa B activation in adolescents with bipolar and major depressive disorders. *Psychiatry Research, 241,* 315–322.

Miklowitz, D. J., Schneck, C. D., Singh, M. K., Taylor, D. O., George, E. L., Cosgrove, V. E., . . . Chang, K. D. (2013). Early intervention for symptomatic youth at risk for bipolar disorder: A randomized trial of family-focused therapy. *Journal of the American Academy of Child & Adolescent Psychiatry, 52,* 121–131.

Miller, A. H., Maletic, V., & Raison, C. L. (2009). Inflammation and its discontents: the role of cytokines in the pathophysiology of major depression. *Biological Psychiatry, 65,* 732–741.

Mitchell, P. B., Slade, T., & Andrews, G. (2004). Twelve month prevalence and disability of DSM-IV bipolar disorder in an Australian general population survey. *Psychological Medicine, 34,* 777–785.

Modabbernia, A., Taslimi, S., Brietzke, E., & Ashrafi, M. (2013). Cytokine alterations in bipolar disorder: a meta-analysis of 30 studies. *Biological Psychiatry, 74,* 15–25.

Monroe, S. M., Harkness, K., Simons, A., & Thase, M. (2001). Life stress and the symptoms of major depression. *Journal of Nervous and Mental Disease, 189,* 168–175.

Moreno, C., Laje, G., Blanco, C., Jiang, H., Schmidt, A. B., & Olfson, M. (2007). National trends in the outpatient diagnosis and treatment of bipolar disorder in youth. *Archives of General Psychiatry, 64,* 1032–1039.

Muhtadie, L., Johnson, S. L., Carver, C. S., Gotlib, I. H., & Ketter, T. A. (2014). A profile approach to impulsivity in bipolar disorder: The key role of strong emotions. *Acta Psychiatrica Scandinavaca, 129,* 100–108.

Mühleisen, T. W., Leber, M., Schulze, T. G., Strohmaier, J., Degenhardt, F., Treutlein, J., . . . Cichon S. (2014). Genome-wide association study reveals two new risk loci for bipolar disorder. *Nature Communications, 11*(5), 3339.

Murphy, F. C., Sahakian, B. J., Rubinsztein, J. S., Michael, A., Rogers, R. D., Robbins, T. W., & Paykel, E. S. (1999). Emotional bias and inhibitory control processes in mania and depression. *Psychological Medicine, 29,* 1307–1321.

Murray, R. M., Sham, P., VanOs, J., Zanelli, J., Cannon, M., & McDonald, C. (2004). A developmental model for similarities and dissimilarities between schizophrenia and bipolar disorder. *Schizophrenia Research, 71,* 405–416.

Ng, T., & Johnson, S. L. (2013). Rejection sensitivity is associated with quality of life, psychosocial outcome, and the course of depression in euthymic patients with Bipolar I Disorder. *Cognitive Therapy and Research, 37,* 1169–1178.

Nordentoft, M., Mortensen, P. B., & Pedersen, C. B. (2011). Absolute risk of suicide after first hospital contact in mental disorder. *Archives of General Psychiatry, 68*(10), 1058–1064.

Nurnberger, J. I., Koller, D. L., Jung, J., Edenberg, H. J., Foroud, T., Guella, I., . . . Kelsoe, J. R. (2014). Identification of pathways for bipolar disorder: A meta-analysis. *JAMA Psychiatry, 71,* 657–664.

Nusslock, R., & Frank, E. (2011). Subthreshold bipolarity: Diagnostic issues and challenges. *Bipolar Disorders, 13*, 587–603.

Ochsner, K. N., Silvers, J. A., & Buhle, J. T. (2012). Functional imaging studies of emotion regulation: a synthetic review and evolving model of the cognitive control of emotion. *Annals of the New York Academy of Sciences, 1251*, E1–E24.

Ogden, C. A., Rich, M. E., Schork, N. J., Paulus, M. P., Geyer, M. A., Lohr, J. B., . . . Niculescu, A. B. (2004). Candidate genes, pathways, and mechanisms for bipolar (manic-depressive) and related disorders: An expanded convergent functional genomics approach. *Molecular Psychiatry, 9*, 1007–1029.

Olsavsky, A. K., Brotman, M. A., Rutenberg, J. G., Muhrer, E. J., Deveney, C. M., Fromm, S. J., . . . Leibenluft, E. (2012). Amygdala hyperactivation during face emotion processing in unaffected youth at risk for bipolar disorder. *Journal of the American Academy of Child & Adolescent Psychiatry, 51*, 294–303.

Otto, M. W., Simon, N. M., Wisniewski, S. R., Miklowitz, D. J., Kogan, J. N., Reilly-Harrington, N. A., . . . STEP-BD Investigators. (2006). Prospective 12-month course of bipolar disorder in outpatients with and without anxiety comorbidity. *British Journal of Psychiatry, 189*, 20–25.

Palmier-Claus, J. E., Berry, K., Bucci, S., Mansell, W., & Varese, F. (2016). Relationship between childhood adversity and bipolar affective disorder: systematic review and meta-analysis. *British Journal of Psychiatry, 209*, 454–459.

Parikh, S. V., Zaretsky, A., Beaulieu, S., Yatham, L. N., Young, L. T., Patelis-Siotis, I., . . . Streiner, D. L. (2012). A randomized controlled trial of psychoeducation or cognitive-behavioral therapy in bipolar disorder: a Canadian Network for Mood and Anxiety treatments (CANMAT) study [CME]. *Journal of Clinical Psychiatry, 73*(6), 803–810.

Pardoen, D., Bauewens, F., Dramaix, M., Tracy, A., Genevrois, C., Staner, L., & Mendlewicz, J. (1996). Life events and primary affective disorders: A one-year prospective study. *British Journal of Psychiatry, 169*, 160–166.

Patel, N. C., DelBello, M. P., Keck, P. E. Jr., & Strakowski, S. M. (2005). Ethnic differences in maintenance antipsychotic prescription among adolescents with bipolar disorder. *Journal of Child and Adolescent Psychopharmacology, 15*, 938–946.

Perlis, R. H., Miyahara, S., Marangell, L. B., Wisniewski, S. R., Ostacher, M., DelBello, M. P., . . . STEP-BD Investigators. (2004). Long-term implications of early onset in bipolar disorder: Data from the first 1000 participants in the Systematic Treatment Enhancement Program for Bipolar Disorder (STEP-BD). *Biological Psychiatry, 55*, 875–881.

Perlis, R. H., Ostacher, M. J., Patel, J., Marangell, L. B., Zhang, H., Wisniewski, S. R., . . . Thase, M. E. (2006). Predictors of recurrence in bipolar disorder: Primary outcomes from the Systematic Treatment Enhancement Program for Bipolar Disorder (STEP-BD). *American Journal of Psychiatry, 163*, 217–224.

Perris, H. (1984). Life events and depression, Part 2: Results in diagnostic subgroups and in relation to the recurrence of depression. *Journal of Affective Disorders, 7*, 25–36.

Perry, A., Tarrier, N., Morriss, R., McCarthy, E., & Limb, K. (1999). Randomised controlled trial of efficacy of teaching patients with bipolar disorder to identify early symptoms of relapse and obtain treatment. *British Medical Journal, 16*, 149–153.

Phillips, M. L., & Swartz, H. A. (2014). A critical appraisal of neuroimaging studies of bipolar disorder: toward a new conceptualization of underlying neural circuitry and a road map for future research. *American Journal of Psychiatry, 171*, 829–843.

Post, R. M., Denicoff, K. D., Leverich, G. S., Altshuler, L. L., Frye, M. A., Suppes, . . . Nolen, W. A. (2003). Morbidity in 258 bipolar outpatients followed for 1 year with daily prospective ratings on the NIMH life chart method. *Journal of Clinical Psychiatry, 64*, 680–690.

Post, R. M., Altshuler, L. L., Kupka, R., McElroy, S. L., Frye, M. A., Rowe, M., . . . Nolen, W. (2015). Verbal abuse, like physical and sexual abuse, in childhood is associated withan earlier onset and more difficult course of bipolar disorder. *Bipolar Disord* (17), 323–330.

Prien, R. F., & Potter, W. Z. (1990). NIMH Workshop report on treatment of bipolar disorder. *Psychopharmacology Bulletin, 26,* 409–427.

Rea, M. M., Tompson, M., Miklowitz, D. J., Goldstein, M. J., Hwang, S., & Mintz, J. (2003). Family focused treatment vs. individual treatment for bipolar disorder: Results of a randomized clinical trial. *Journal of Consulting and Clinical Psychology, 71,* 482–492.

Regeer, E. J., Ten Have, M., Rosso, M. L., Hakkaart-van Roijen, L., Vollebergh, W., & Nolen, W. A. (2004). Prevalence of bipolar disorder in the general population: A reappraisal study of the Netherlands Mental Health Survey and Incidence Study. *Acta Psychiatrica Scandinavica, 110,* 374–382.

Regeer, E. J., Rosso, M. L., Ten Have, M., Vollebergh, W. and Nolen, W. A. (2002), Prevalence of bipolar disorder: a further study in The Netherlands. *Bipolar Disorders, 4:* 37–38.

Regier, D. A., Narrow, W. E., Clarke, D. E., Kraemer, H. C., Kuramoto, S. J., Kuhl, E. A., & Kupfer, D. J. (2013). DSM-5 field trials in the United States and Canada, Part II: Test-retest reliability of selected categorical diagnoses. *American Journal of Psychiatry, 170,* 59–70.

Reichart, C. G., & Nolen, W. A. (2004). Earlier onset of bipolar disorder in children by anti-depressants or stimulants? An hypothesis. *Journal of Affective Disorders, 78,* 81–84.

Reichart, C. G., van derEnde, J., Wals, M., Hillegers, M. H., Nolen, W. A., Ormel, J., & Verhulst, F. C. (2005). The use of the GBI as predictor of bipolar disorder in a population of adolescent offspring of parents with a bipolar disorder. *Journal of Affective Disorders, 89,* 147–155.

Robinson, T. E., & Becker, J. B. (1986). Enduring changes in brain and behavior produced by chronic amphetamine administration: A review and evaluation of animal models of amphetamine psychosis. *Brain Research Review, 11,* 157–198.

Roshanaei-Moghaddam, B., Katon, W. (2009). Premature mortality from general medical illnesses among persons with bipolar disorder: a review. *Psychiatr Serv, 60*(2), 147–56.

Ruggero, C. J., & Johnson, S. L. (2006). Reactivity to a laboratory stressor among individuals with bipolar I disorder in full or partial remission. *Journal of Abnormal Psychology, 115,* 539.

Ruggero, C. J., Zimmerman, M., Chelminski, I., & Young, D. (2010). Borderline personality disorder and the misdiagnosis of bipolar disorder. *Journal of Psychiatric Research, 44,* 405–408.

Sachs, G. S., Nierenberg, A. A., Calabrese, J. R., Marangell, L. B., Wisniewski, S. R., Gyulai, L., . . . Ketter, T. A. (2007). Effectiveness of adjunctive antidepressant treatment for bipolar depression. *New England Journal of Medicine, 356,* 1711–1722.

Sato, T., Bottlender, R., Kleindienst, N., & Moller, H. J. (2002). Syndromes and phenomenological subtypes underlying acute mania: A factor analytic study of 576 manic patients. *American Journal of Psychiatry, 159,* 968–974.

Savitz, J. B., Price, J. L., & Drevets, W. C. (2014). Neuropathological and neuromorphometric abnormalities in bipolar disorder: View from the medial prefrontal cortical network. *Neuroscience & Biobehavioral Reviews, 42,* 132–147.

Schneck, C. D., Miklowitz, D. J., Calabrese, J. R., Allen, M. H., Thomas, M. R., Wisniewski, S. R., . . . Sachs, G. S. (2004). Phenomenology of rapid cycling bipolar disorder: Data from the first 500 participants in the Systematic Treatment Enhancement Program. *American Journal of Psychiatry, 161,* 1902–1908.

Scott, J., Paykel, E., Morriss, R., Bentall, R., Kinderman, P., Johnson, T., . . . Hayhurst, H. (2006). Cognitive behaviour therapy for severe and recurrent bipolar disorders: A randomised controlled trial. *British Journal of Psychiatry, 188,* 313–320.

Sidor, M. M., & MacQueen, G. M. (2012). An update on antidepressant use in bipolar depression. *Current Psychiatry Reports, 14,* 696–704.

Simeonova, D. I., Chang, K. D., Strong, C., & Ketter, T. A. (2005). Creativity in familial bipolar disorder. *Journal of Psychiatric Research, 39,* 623–631.

Simon, G. E., Ludman, E. J., Unutzer, J., Bauer, M. S., Operskalski, B., & Rutter, C. (2005). Randomized trial of a population-based care program for people with bipolar disorder. *Psychological Medicine, 35,* 13–24.

Simon, N. M., Otto, M. W., Weiss, R., Bauer, M. S., Miyahara, S., Wisniewski, S. R., . . . Calabrese, J. R., (2004). Pharmacotherapy for bipolar disorder and comorbid conditions: Baseline data from STEP-BD. *Journal of Clinical Psychopharmacology, 24,* 512–520.

Singh, M. K., Kelley, R. G., Howe, M. E., Reiss, A. L., Gotlib, I. H., & Chang, K. D. (2014). Reward processing in healthy offspring of parents with bipolar disorder. *JAMA psychiatry, 71,* 1148–1156.

Smith, D.J., Harrison, N., Muir, W. (2005). The high prevalence of bipolar spectrum disorders in young adults with recurrent depression: toward an innovative diagnostic framework. *Journal of Affective Disorders, 84,* 167–178.

Snowden, L. R. (2001). Barriers to effective mental health services for African Americans. *Mental Health Services Research, 3,* 181–187.

Sobczak, S., Honig, A., Schmitt, J. A. Jr., & Riedel, W. J. (2003). Pronounced cognitive deficits following an intravenous L-tryptophan challenge in first-degree relatives of bipolar patients compared to healthy controls. *Neuropsychopharmacology, 28,* 711–719.

Sobczak, S., Riedel, W. J., Booij, L., AanhetRot, M., Deutz, N. E. P., & Honig, A. (2002). Cognition following acute tryptophan depletion: Differences between first-degree relatives of bipolar disorder patients and matched healthy control volunteers. *Psychological Medicine, 32,* 503–515.

Solomon, D. A., Leon, A. C., Endicott, J., Coryell, W. H., Mueller, T. I., Posternak, M. A., & Keller, M. B. (2003). Unipolar mania over the course of a 20-year follow-up study. *American Journal of Psychiatry, 160,* 2049–2051.

Staley, J. K., Malison, R. T., & Innis, R. B. (1998). Imaging of the serotonergic system: Interactions of neuroanatomical and functional abnormalities of depression. *Biological Psychiatry, 44,* 534–549.

Stern, G. S., & Berrenberg, J. L. (1979). Skill-set, success outcome, and mania as determinants of the illusion of control. *Journal of Research in Personality, 13,* 206–220.

Stockmeier, C. A. (2003). Involvement of serotonin in depression: Evidence from postmortem and imaging studies of serotonin receptors and the serotonin transporter. *Journal of Psychiatric Research, 37,* 357–373.

Strakowski, S. M., Adler, C. M., Almeida, J., Altshuler, L. L., Blumberg, H. P., Chang, K. D., . . . Sussman, J. E. (2012). The functional neuroanatomy of bipolar disorder: A consensus model. *Bipolar Disorders, 14,* 313–325.

Strakowski, S. M., DelBello, M. P., Fleck, D. E., & Arndt, S. (2000). The impact of substance abuse on the course of bipolar disorder. *Biological Psychiatry, 48,* 477–485.

Strakowski, S. M., Sax, K. W., Setters, M. J., & Keck, P. E. Jr. (1996). Enhanced response to repeated d-amphetamine challenge: Evidence for behavioral sensitization in humans. *Biological Psychiatry, 40,* 827–880.

Strakowski, S. M., Sax, K. W., Setters, M. J., Stanton, S. P., & Keck, P. E. Jr. (1997). Lack of enhanced behavioral response to repeated d-amphetamine challenge in first-episode psychosis: Implications for a sensitization model of psychosis in humans. *Biological Psychiatry, 42,* 749–755.

Strecker, E. A. (1921). The prognosis in manic-depressive psychosis. *New York Medical Journal, 114,* 209–211.

Strober, M., Morrell, W., Lampert, C., & Burroughs, J. (1990). Relapse following discontinuation of lithium maintenance therapy in adolescents with bipolar I illness: a naturalistic study. *American Journal of Psychiatry, 147,* 457–461.

Suppes, T., Baldessarini, R. J., Faedda, G. L., Tondo, L., & Tohen, M. (1993). Discontinuation of maintenance treatment in bipolar disorder: Risks and implications. *Harvard Review of Psychiatry, 1,* 131–144.

Suppes, T., Leverich, G. S., Keck, P. E., Nolen, W. A., Denicoff, K. D., Altshuler, L. L., . . . Post, R. M. (2001). The Stanley Foundation Bipolar Treatment Outcome Network, Part II: Demographics and illness characteristics of the first 261 patients. *Journal of Affective Disorders, 67,* 45–59.

Surguladze, S. A., Marshall, N., Schulze, K., Hall, M. H., Walshe, M., Bramon, E., . . . McDonald, C. (2010). Exaggerated neural response to emotional faces in patients with bipolar disorder and their first-degree relatives. *Neuroimage, 53,* 58–64.

Swann, A. C., Dougherty, D. M., Pazzaglia, P. J., Pham, M., & Moeller, F. G. (2004). Impulsivity: A link between bipolar disorder and substance abuse. *Bipolar Disorders, 6,* 204–212.

Thase, M. E., Jindal, R., & Howland, R. H. (2002). Biological aspects of depression. In I. H. Gotlib & C. L. Hammen (Eds.), *Handbook of Depression* (pp. 192–218). New York, NY: Guilford Press.

Tohen, M., Vieta, E., Calabrese, J., Ketter, T. A., Sachs, G., Bowden, C., . . . Breier, A. (2003). Efficacy of olanzapine and olanzapine-fluoxetine combination in the treatment of bipolar I depression. *Archives of General Psychiatry, 60,* 1079–1088 (erratum in: *Archives of General Psychiatry* 2004; *61,* 176).

Tondo, L., & Baldessarini, R. J. (2000). Reducing suicide risk during lithium maintenance treatment. *Journal of Clinical Psychiatry, 61,* 97–104.

Torrent, C., Bonnin, C. D. M., Martínez-Arán, A., Valle, J., Amann, B. L., González-Pinto, A., . . . Vieta, E. (2013). Efficacy of functional remediation in bipolar disorder: A multicenter randomized controlled study. *American Journal of Psychiatry, 170,* 852–859.

Townsend, J., & Altshuler, L. L. (2012). Emotion processing and regulation in bipolar disorder: a review. *Bipolar Disorders, 14,* 326–339.

Turgay, A., & Ansari, R. (2006). Major depression with ADHD: In children and adolescents. *Psychiatry 3,* 30–32.

Van Meter, A. R., Moreira, A. L., & Youngstrom, E. A. (2011). Meta-analysis of epidemiologic studies of pediatric bipolar disorder. *Journal of Clinical Psychiatry, 72,* 1250–1256.

Versace, A., Thompson, W. K., Zhou, D., Almeida, J. R., Hassel, S., Klein, C. R., . . . Phillips, M. L. (2010). Abnormal left and right amygdala-orbitofrontal cortical functional connectivity to emotional faces: State versus trait vulnerability markers of depression in bipolar disorder. *Biological Psychiatry, 67,* 422–431.

Walsh, M. A., DeGeorge, D. P., Barrantes-Vidal, N., & Kwapil, T. R. (2015). A 3-year longitudinal study of risk for bipolar spectrum psychopathology. *Journal of Abnormal Psychology, 124,* 486.

Wang, F., Kalmar, J. H., He, Y., Jackowski, M., Chepenik, L. G., Edmiston, E. E., . . . Blumberg, H. P. (2009). Functional and structural connectivity between the perigenual anterior cingulate and amygdala in bipolar disorder. *Biological Psychiatry, 66,* 516–521.

Wehr, T. A., Sack, D. A., & Rosenthal, N. E. (1987). Sleep reduction as a final common pathway in the genesis of mania. *American Journal of Psychiatry, 144,* 210–214.

Weinstock, L. M. & Miller, I. W. (2010). Psychosocial predictors of mood symptoms 1 year after acute phase treatment of bipolar I disorder. *Comprehensive Psychiatry, 51*(5), 497–503.

Weissman, M. M., & Myers, J. K. (1978). Affective disorders in a U.S. urban community: The use of research diagnostic criteria in an epidemiological survey. *Archives of General Psychiatry, 35,* 1304–1311.

West, A. E., Weinstein, S. M., Peters, A. T., Katz, A. C., Henry, D. B., Cruz, R. A., & Pavuluri, M. N. (2014). Child- and family-focused cognitive-behavioral therapy for pediatric bipolar disorder: a randomized clinical trial. *Journal of the American Academy of Child and Adolescent Psychiatry, 53,* 1168–1178.

Whitton, A. E., Treadway, M. T., & Pizzagalli, D. A. (2015). Reward processing dysfunction in major depression, bipolar disorder and schizophrenia. *Current Opinion in Psychiatry, 28,* 7.

Wickramaratne, P. J., Weissman, M. M., Leaf, J. P., & Holford, T. R. (1989). Age, period and cohort effects on the risk of major depression: Results from five United States communities. *Journal of Clinical Epidemiology, 42,* 333–343.

Willner, P. (1995). Sensitization of dopamine D-sub-2- or D-sub-3-type receptors as a final common pathway in antidepressant drug action. *Clinical Neuropharmacology, 18,* S49–S56.

Yan, L. J., Hammen, C., Cohen, A. N., Daley, S. E., & Henry, R. M. (2004). Expressed emotion versus relationship quality variables in the prediction of recurrence in bipolar patients. *Journal of Affective Disorders, 83*, 199–206.

Yen, S., Stout, R., Hower, H., Killam, M. A., Weinstock, L. M., Topor, D. R., . . . Keller, M. B. (2016). The influence of comorbid disorders on the episodicity of bipolar disorder in youth. *Acta Psychiatrica Scandinavica, 133*(4), 324–334.

Zimmerman, M., Ruggero, C. J., Chelminski, I., & Young, D. (2008). Is bipolar disorder over-diagnosed?. *The Journal of Clinical Psychiatry, 69*, 935–940.

Zou, Y.-F., Wang, F., Feng, X.-L., Li, W.-F., Tian, Y. H., Tao, J. H., . . . Huang, F. (2012). Association of DRD2 gene polymorphisms with mood disorders: A meta-analysis. *Journal of Affective Disorders, 136*, 229–237.

CHAPTER 8

Depressive Disorders

LEILANI FELICIANO, BRENNA N. RENN, and DANIEL L. SEGAL

D EPRESSIVE DISORDERS ARE among the most common mental disorders occurring throughout adulthood and later life. These disorders are characterized by a diverse array of symptoms, including feelings of sadness, lack of interest in formerly enjoyable pursuits, sleep and appetite disturbances, lethargy, feelings of worthlessness, and, at times, thoughts of death and dying. Further, they can be extremely debilitating and negatively impact the quality of life of those afflicted.

At the beginning of this millennium, depressive disorders were second only to heart disease as the illness most responsible for poor quality of life and disability (Pincus & Pettit, 2001). By the year 2030, major depressive disorder (MDD) is predicted to be among the leading causes of disability globally, comparable to heart disease and second only to HIV/AIDS (Mathers & Loncar, 2006); however, it is already the leading cause of disability among middle- and high-income countries, including the United States (World Health Organization [WHO], 2017). Depression is also associated with increased suicide risk. In a large cross-national sample of 17 countries, individuals with a depressive disorder had an odds ratio of 3.4–5.9 over that of individuals without depression, even after controlling for such factors as age, education, and relationship status (Nock et al., 2008). In terms of suicide completion, the lifetime risk of completed suicide ranges between 2.2% (Bostwick & Pankratz, 2000) and 4.2% (Coryell & Young, 2005) in individuals with depressive disorders, although the precise mechanisms for these relationships are not firmly established. Comorbid substance use and personality disorders (borderline personality disorder in particular) increase the risk of attempted and completed suicide in people with depressive disorders (Bolton, Pagura, Enns, Grant, & Sareen, 2010). Fortunately, depressive disorders can be treated successfully with psychotherapy, antidepressant medication, or both, suggesting that this significant burden can be reduced (Khan, Faucett, Lichtenberg, Kirsch, & Brown, 2012).

Research on these disorders continues to grow, and substantial knowledge exists about how depressive disorders are presented, including their etiology, course, and prognosis. The purpose of this chapter is to describe the depressive disorders and their criteria, discuss their prevalence and effects on people who have these disorders, examine the best methods for assessing depressive disorders, and present the latest research on

Adult Psychopathology and Diagnosis, Eighth Edition. Edited by Deborah C. Beidel and B. Christopher Frueh.
© 2018 John Wiley & Sons, Inc. Published 2018 by John Wiley & Sons, Inc.
Companion website: www.wiley.com/go/beidel/psychopathology8e

their etiology. The chapter concludes with a brief summary of treatment and case examples to illustrate the complexity of the depressive disorders.

DESCRIPTION OF THE DISORDERS

According to the fifth edition of the *Diagnostic and Statistical Manual of Mental Disorders* (*DSM-5*; American Psychiatric Association [APA], 2013), depressive disorders include several categories of illnesses: disruptive mood dysregulation disorder (applicable to children up to age 18 only), MDD, persistent depressive disorder (formerly dysthymic disorder), premenstrual dysphoric disorder, substance/medication-induced depressive disorder, depressive disorder due to another medical condition, other specified depressive disorder, and unspecified depressive disorder. Using three of the diagnostic categories as an example, Table 8.1 illustrates how depressive disorders in adulthood share common symptoms and clinical features. First, all disorders consist of mood symptoms, which often include feeling sad, empty, irritable, or guilty. Second, these disorders are characterized by vegetative symptoms, which may include fatigue, social withdrawal, or agitation.

Among the depressive disorders, disturbances in sleep and appetite are also common, with lack of sleep and appetite being more typical with depression, although patients with an atypical presentation (discussed later) may complain of hypersomnia (increased sleep) or weight gain caused by frequent eating/overeating. Finally, depressive disorders often include cognitive symptoms, for example, difficulty concentrating; difficulty making decisions; low self-esteem; negative thoughts about oneself, the world, and others; and suicidal ideation. As with all mental disorders, these symptoms must cause significant personal distress or meaningfully disrupt the person's functioning. The

Table 8.1
Sample Diagnostic Criteria

Symptoms	Major Depressive Disorder	Persistent Depressive Disorder (Dysthymia)	Other Specified Depressive Disorder
Depressed mood	At least five of nine symptoms must be present for no less than 2 weeks, all day nearly every day, including either depressed mood or anhedonia.	Depressed mood, plus two or more symptoms must be present for at least 2 years, occurring more days than not.	Either depressed mood or anhedonia, plus other symptoms specific to disorder specified. Duration is variable depending on disorder specified.
Anhedonia			
Change in appetite			
Change in sleep			
Psychomotor agitation or slowing			
Loss of energy			
Decreased concentration/ trouble making decisions			
Thoughts of death/suicide			
Feeling guilty or worthless			

Source: Adapted from the American Psychiatric Association (2013).

degree to which these features occur and the number of symptoms present will determine which type of depressive disorder a person may be experiencing. Next, we discuss each depressive disorder that occurs in adulthood to clarify how it can be distinguished from the others.

MAJOR DEPRESSIVE DISORDER

Major depressive disorder is the most serious and most widely studied depressive disorder, often referred to as the "common cold of psychopathology." It is characterized by at least one *major depressive episode* (MDE), with no history of mania (defined as an acute period of intense energy, euphoria, distorted thinking, and behavioral excesses). To qualify as an MDE, either depressed mood or lack of interest or pleasure in usual activities (anhedonia) must be present, most of the day, nearly every day, and the episode must last at least 2 weeks. In addition, at least five out of nine possible symptoms (listed in Table 8.1) must be present during that same period. The symptoms must cause clinically significant distress or be severe enough to interfere with the individual's social, educational, or occupational functioning. Lastly, the symptom picture should not be better accounted for by another condition (e.g., a medical condition, directly related to use or withdrawal of a substance, a psychotic disorder) (APA, 2013).

Specifiers Major depressive disorder is further qualified as to its severity, chronicity, and remission status. Severity is generally determined by the degree of disability experienced by the affected person. If the person can continue to pursue obligations (work, family, and social activities) and the symptoms are distressing but manageable, then the depression is rated as *mild*. If the person has trouble getting out of bed and can no longer effectively engage in some obligated activities, then the depression is rated as *moderate*. If a person is thinking of death or dying; is so vegetative that he or she has not gotten out of bed, eaten, or engaged in limited self-management activities, then the depression is rated as *severe*. With severe cases, if the person exhibits psychotic symptoms (e.g., delusions and hallucinations, often of the negatively tinged variety), the specifier of *with psychotic features* would be designated as well. Although it is rare, individuals with depression can exhibit symptoms of catatonia, which is characterized by immobility, excessive motor activity, extreme negativism or mutism, and bizarre posturing. In these cases, the qualifier *with catatonia* would be most appropriate. See the "Diagnostic Specifiers" section later for more details.

A person will be diagnosed as having MDD, single episode, if the current episode is the only one the person has ever experienced. In contrast, MDD, recurrent episode, is diagnosed if the person has previously had at least one other discrete and well-defined episode of depression, whether diagnosed or not. In addition to these qualifiers, clinicians should also note features of the disorder related to its presentation (e.g., with anxious distress, mixed features, atypical presentation) (discussed in detail later in the Diagnostic Specifiers section).

PERSISTENT DEPRESSIVE DISORDER

Persistent depressive disorder (previously called *dysthymia*) is typically considered to be less severe than MDD, as it requires fewer symptoms for diagnosis. However, given that the duration required for diagnosis of persistent depressive disorder is longer (2 years vs. 2 weeks), it is, by definition, a chronic state. Therefore, the severity difference in terms of overall distress between the two diagnostic categories may be debatable.

For diagnosis, the symptoms of persistent depressive disorder (listed in Table 8.1) must be present for 2 years, during which time there should be no more than a 2-month period in which the person is symptom-free. The criteria for an MDE may be present during the most recent 2-year period, and such cases are commonly referred to as *double depression*. As in MDD, the person must not ever have met criteria for manic episode, hypomanic episode, or cyclothymic disorder, and the disorder should not be better accounted for by any of the psychotic disorders (e.g., occur only during the course of a psychotic disorder). Finally, symptoms of persistent depressive disorder must not be due exclusively to other disorders (including medical conditions) or to the direct physiological effects of a substance (including medication) (APA, 2013).

Specifiers   If persistent depressive disorder occurs before the age of 21, it is described as having *early onset*; otherwise, it is described as having *late onset*. In addition to onset qualifiers, clinicians should note the specific features of the disorder (e.g., with anxious distress, mixed features, atypical presentation, psychotic features) (discussed in the "Diagnostic Specifiers" section). Clinicians should also note whether the disorder has a *pure dysthymic syndrome*, where the full criteria for an MDE have never been met in at least the preceding 2-year period. However, if the full criteria for an MDE have been met consistently during this 2-year span, then clinicians would specify that a *persistent MDE* was present. If there were 2-month periods within the current episode in which symptoms were subthreshold for an MDE but some depressive symptoms were present, then a specifier of *intermittent MDE, within current episode* would be given. Similarly, if intermittent MDEs have occurred previously, but not within the context of the current episode, a specifier of *intermittent MDE, without current episode* would be noted.

PREMENSTRUAL DYSPHORIC DISORDER

Premenstrual dysphoric disorder is included as part of the depressive disorder section of *DSM-5*, after having been subject to many years of empirical scrutiny in the prior edition of the *DSM*. This disorder is thought to be caused by hormonal fluctuations in the female menstrual cycle (with symptoms more severe than those typically seen with premenstrual syndrome). The distinguishing characteristics of premenstrual dysphoric disorder include the presence of five or more mood symptoms (i.e., significant depressed mood, significant mood swings, irritability, anxiety, decreased interest in activities, difficulty concentrating, lethargy, appetite changes, sleep difficulties, feeling overwhelmed and physical symptoms) that occur in the majority of menstrual cycles (minimally over two cycles) and are tied to the course of the menstrual cycle. Thus, onset of symptoms begins during the premenstrual phase (approximately 1 week before menses), begins to remit during or shortly after menses, and is absent or minimally present in the week post-menses. As with all depressive disorders, the symptoms of premenstrual dysphoric disorder must be associated with significant distress or impairment in meaningful activity (e.g., negatively impacts or interferes with work, school, or social performance). The mood disturbance should not be better accounted for by another disorder (e.g., MDD, panic disorder), although it may be comorbid with other disorders.

SUBSTANCE/MEDICATION-INDUCED DEPRESSIVE DISORDER

Substance/medication-induced depressive disorder is diagnosed when an individual experiences symptoms of a depressive disorder that begin after exposure to a substance or medication capable of producing such effects. As can be seen in Table 8.2, a number of

Table 8.2
Medical Conditions and Medications Associated with Depressive Disorders

Medical Conditions

Neurological disorders
Stroke, Huntington's disease, Parkinson's disease, multiple sclerosis, traumatic brain injury
Coronary artery disease
Hypertension, myocardial infarction, coronary artery bypass surgery, congestive heart failure
Metabolic disturbances
Hypothyroidism or hyperthyroidism, Cushing's disease, diabetes mellitus
Other conditions
Chronic obstructive pulmonary disease, rheumatoid arthritis, deafness, chronic pain, sexual dysfunction, renal
    dialysis

Medications
Antiviral agents
Cardiovascular agents (primarily antihypertensive medications)
Retinoic acid derivatives
Psychotropic medications (including antidepressants and antipsychotics)
Anticonvulsants
Anti-migraine agents
Hormonal agents (including oral contraceptives)
Smoking cessation agents
Immunological agents

Source: Adapted from the American Psychiatric Association (2013).

medications (including some common ones) are associated with depressive symptoms. This diagnosis is based on findings from the individual's history, physical examination, and/or laboratory tests that provide evidence for a temporal link between the depressive symptoms and medication/substance use or intoxication. For example, the depressive disturbance should not precede use of the substance or medication. Like other depressive disorders, symptoms of substance/medication-induced depressive disorder must be severe enough to result in clinically significant distress and/or impairment in important areas of functioning.

Although the symptoms of depression seen in this disorder may be similar to those of MDD and other depressive disorders, the disturbance seen in this diagnosis should not be better explained by another depressive disorder. Like all diagnoses, clinical judgment is essential. The clinician should evaluate whether the medication or substance is truly causative of the depressive mood symptoms, or whether an independent depressive disorder happened to co-occur with the use of medication or substances. The symptoms of this disorder often remit within days to weeks, depending on the half-life of the substance; depressive disturbances that carry this diagnosis should not persist for a substantial length of time (e.g., 1 month) after discontinuation of substance or medication use. The clinician must also rule out delirium as a cause of this mood disturbance (APA, 2013).

Depressive Disorder due to Another Medical Condition

Depressive disorder due to another medical condition refers to a distinct and notable period of depressive symptoms in which there is clear "evidence from the history, physical examination, or laboratory findings that the disturbance is the direct pathophysiological consequence of another medical condition" (APA, 2013, p. 258). That is, the clinician determines that a medical condition is present and that it is causally related to the depressive disorder through a physiological pathway. For example, the clinician should evaluate the temporal relationship between any changes in the medical condition (i.e., onset, worsening, or remission) and the onset of depressive symptoms. As shown in Table 8.2, a wide variety of medical conditions are known to cause depressive symptoms. This disorder must be distinguished from those disorders in which the depressive symptoms are caused by a psychological reaction to having health problems or a medical illness, for example when the person's coping resources are overwhelmed from dealing with the consequences of being ill. As part of the diagnostic process, delirium should also be ruled out as the cause of the symptoms.

OTHER SPECIFIED DEPRESSIVE DISORDER AND UNSPECIFIED DEPRESSIVE DISORDER

In previous editions of the *DSM*, the "depressive disorder not otherwise specified" diagnosis was treated as a catch-all for depressive conditions that were provisional in nature or did not meet the full criteria for any other depressive disorder. In the *DSM-5*, this category has been phased out and replaced by two options: other specified depressive disorder and unspecified depressive disorder.

Other specified depressive disorder is characterized by depressive disorders that are *subclinical* in that they do not meet the full criteria for any of the other depressive disorders mentioned here, yet the symptoms cause significant distress or impairment in functioning. The *DSM-5* describes three examples of disorders that would fit under this category, including recurrent brief depression, short-duration depressive episode, and depressive episode with insufficient symptoms, although this is not an exhaustive list. In a similar vein, *unspecified depressive disorder* is diagnosed in those situations in which the clinician determines that the individual's symptom presentation is characteristic of a depressive disorder (e.g., depressed mood, significant distress, or impairment in functioning), but the symptoms do not meet criteria for any specific depressive disorder listed in the *DSM*. This category allows for clinical judgment and the flexibility of diagnosing the presence of a depressive disorder when there is inadequate information available to make a more specific diagnosis (e.g., in short-term, integrated care settings in which there is more emphasis on current functioning and solutions to problems rather than on conducting a full comprehensive intake; in emergency departments; and in situations where the individual is a poor historian and no collateral informants are available).

DIAGNOSTIC SPECIFIERS

Clinicians may add specifiers as appropriate to provide more information about an individual's unique presentation. Specifiers can be thought of as subtypes of depressive disorders and are classified with the following: (a) anxious distress, (b) mixed features, (c) melancholic features, (d) atypical features, (e) mood-congruent psychotic features, (f) mood-incongruent psychotic features, (g) catatonia, (h) peripartum onset, and (i) seasonal pattern. *Anxious distress* may be used to describe an MDE or persistent depressive disorder characterized by psychomotor agitation such as feeling excessively tense or restless, or having anxious thoughts such as worry, fear, or a sense of losing control. *Mixed features* refer to an MDE that presents with at least three hypomanic/manic symptoms, such as expansive mood or increased psychomotor activity (e.g., decreased need for sleep, flight of ideas, pressured speech).

Major depressive episode and persistent depressive disorder can also present with *melancholic features*, such that the mood disturbance is characterized by a near-absence of the capacity for pleasure and/or an inability to feel better, even briefly, when something good happens (no mood reactivity). This melancholic presentation is further classified by a sense of despondency and despair, psychomotor symptoms, early morning awakening, and depression that is worse in the morning. Researchers have suggested that this subtype is more typically associated with biological etiology and that it may be more responsive to psychopharmacological intervention than to psychotherapies (Andrus et al., 2012).

Conversely, *atypical features* are specified during a depressive disorder in which mood reactivity is notable (i.e., the individual's mood brightens in response to something positive) and occurs in conjunction with psychomotor symptoms of weight gain or increased appetite, hypersomnia, and/or leaden paralysis (i.e., feeling as though one's limbs are heavy, leaden, or weighed down). These individuals may also present with a long-standing pattern of sensitivity to "interpersonal rejection." This depressive subtype is thought to be primarily triggered by stressful life events or a specific psychosocial problem. Although most researchers agree there is likely to be some genetic component to this subtype as well, depression would only be expressed in the face of a major problem that a person could not solve immediately (e.g., loss of employment). This tends to be interpreted as suggesting a depressive disorder that is more likely to respond to psychosocial interventions than to medications (Nutt et al., 2010).

Specifiers related to *psychotic features* provide information about whether the depressive disorder presents with delusions and/or hallucinations, and whether these symptoms are either *congruent* with depressed mood (i.e., having depressive themes, such as disease, death, or guilt) or *incongruent* with depressed mood (i.e., the content does not have notable depressive themes). If catatonic features occur during an MDE, the *catatonia* specifier is used to describe this marked decrease in reactivity to the environment. Although historically associated with schizophrenia, catatonia can occur in other disorders, such as severe MDD.

Finally, two other specifiers provide information about depressive disturbances that are related to context-specific factors. First, *peripartum onset* is specified when onset of symptoms in an MDE occurring during pregnancy (*prepartum*) or within the first 4 weeks following delivery (*postpartum*). These symptoms can occur with or without psychotic features. Second, if an individual experiences recurrent MDEs that are temporally associated with a particular time of year (usually fall or winter), his/her depression is specified *with seasonal pattern* (sometimes called seasonal affective disorder).

In addition to providing more information about a context for a depressive disorder, these specifiers have clinical and prognostic utility. For example, individuals with a mixed feature presentation are at risk of receiving a bipolar disorder diagnosis in the future. Melancholic features are more frequently seen on an inpatient rather than an outpatient basis and may co-occur with psychotic features. Psychotic features are associated with lower recovery rates compared with depressive episodes not complicated by psychotic presentation. Peripartum onset of an MDE with psychotic features is associated with infanticide when the mother experiences command hallucinations to kill the infant or delusions of the infant's possession by a malevolent entity.

WHEN DEPRESSION IS NOT A DEPRESSIVE DISORDER

Sometimes symptoms of depression may be present in an individual who is not diagnosed as having one of the depressive disorders *per se*. For example, people who develop depressive symptoms after a significant life stressor are more likely to be suffering from an *adjustment disorder* rather than a depressive disorder (in the *DSM-5*, adjustment disorders are found under the section called "trauma- and stressor-related disorders"). In addition, a previous manic episode will also exclude a diagnosis of MDD or persistent depressive disorder. If the individual with depression has symptoms that are better accounted for by another diagnostic category, then that diagnostic category should be assigned in lieu of a depressive disorder (e.g., schizoaffective disorder). We revisit this theme later in the chapter.

Finally, we wish to emphasize that everyone experiences feelings of sadness from time to time. This is a normal experience that should not be pathologized, especially if the context for the feelings is reasonable. Depressive symptoms are considered problematic when they cluster together, persist for at least 2 weeks, and are accompanied by meaningful distress or considerable difficulty managing day-to-day activities. In the next section, we provide more examples of some clinical features of the depressive disorders.

CLINICAL PICTURE

Major depressive disorder, persistent depressive disorder, and other specified and unspecified depressive disorders all vary to a degree in their presentation but share several features that distinguish these disorders from other mental disorders. People with depressive disorders can be identified by their pessimistic and negativistic thinking, difficulty solving everyday problems, and lack of initiative. People with depressive disorders may become very disabled by their symptoms and often report having multiple somatic symptoms.

Most people with a depressive disorder exhibit what is called *negativistic thinking*. This term was coined by Aaron Beck (1961) and has since been used extensively to describe the cognitive style of people suffering from depressive disorders. Negativistic thinking is best described as a style of thinking that is overly pessimistic and critical. People with depression tend to expect failure and disappointment at every turn and will focus only on their past failures as a way to confirm these beliefs (Alloy et al., 2000). People with negativistic thinking also have poor self-esteem and are more likely than people without this cognitive bias to experience depressive symptoms (Verplanken, Friborg, Wang, Trafimow, & Woolf, 2007).

Another facet of negativistic thinking, *rumination*, or repeatedly "focusing on the fact that one is depressed; on one's symptoms of depression; and on the causes, meanings, and consequences of depressive symptoms" (Nolen-Hoeksema, 1991, p. 569), is also common in individuals with depressive disorders. Rumination is considered to be a risk factor not only for depression, but also for anxiety disorders and bipolar disorder (Calmes & Roberts, 2007; Gruber, Eidelman, Johnson, Smith & Harvey, 2011; Huffziger, Reinhard, & Kuehner, 2009). Two meta-analyses examining the relationship of ruminative thinking in individuals with mood and/or anxiety disorders found large effect sizes ($r = 0.55$ and $r = 0.42$ in clinical samples, respectively) (Aldao, Nolen-Hoeksema, & Schweizer, 2010), and that adults with depressive disorders engaged in rumination significantly more often than both those with anxiety disorders and healthy controls (Olatunji, Naragon-Gainey, & Wolitzky-Taylor, 2013). Furthermore, Olatunji et al. qualified the type of rumination (e.g., overall, brooding, emotion driven) and examined the extent to which the rumination subtype might impact depressive or anxious symptoms. Results showed moderate correlations with all subtypes except for cognitive coping and depression. Similar results were found for anxiety, suggesting that rumination may be an important contributor to the clinical picture of both depressive disorders and anxiety disorders. These studies indicate that rumination is a useful facet to consider when examining negativistic thinking in individuals with depression.

The presence of negativistic thinking in depression is a bit of a "chicken or egg" problem: Does depression cause negativistic thinking, or does negativistic thinking cause depression? Research suggests that the cause of depression is more likely an imbalanced thinking style and that negativistic thinking may have a clearer association with repeated exposure to failure and disappointment. In a study by Isaacowitz and Seligman (2001), people with pessimistic thinking as well as those with optimistic thinking were at risk for developing depressive symptoms after exposure to stressful life events. In fact, optimists were at higher risk for developing depression than pessimists were, although pessimists tended to have more persistent depression. Therefore, objective perceptions of one's abilities, of one's environment, and of other people are likely to be more protective than overly optimistic or overly pessimistic styles of thinking.

Negativistic thinking is primarily responsible for why individuals with depression find it difficult to engage in and enjoy activities that once gave them pleasure, and thus social isolation is a common feature of depressive disorders (Cacioppo, Hawkley, & Thisted, 2010). Many people with a depressive disorder will report that they have stopped socializing or engaging in pleasant activities, largely because they anticipate no enjoyment from the activity (Chentsova-Dutton & Hanley, 2010). As will be discussed in the section on etiology, it is thought that repeated exposure to stress influences the reward centers of the brain; animal studies have demonstrated that repeated exposure to negative events will result in the adoption of avoidance motivation over appetitive motivation. In other words, people who experience too many negative experiences begin to anticipate that all experiences will be negative and, therefore, they will be motivated by pain reduction (avoidance of aversive stimuli) rather than by need for pleasure (Ho & Wang, 2010).

It is important that people who have depression attempt to re-engage in social activities. Increased social isolation puts the individual with depression at greater risk of severe depression. Several studies show that social support can offset the occurrence or worsening of depression, and thus increasing exposure to socialization is an important process in recovering from depression (Barros-Loscertales et al., 2010; Dichter, Felder, & Smoski, 2010; Jakupcak, Wagner, Paulson, Varra, & McFall, 2010; Mazzucchelli, Kane, & Rees, 2010).

People with depressive disorders also tend to use passive coping skills, or they avoid solving problems (Nolen-Hoeksema, Larson, & Grayson, 1999). This is sometimes due to a pre-existing skills deficit or to *learned helplessness*, a condition caused by repeated attempts and failures to cope with problems (Folkman & Lazarus, 1986). Most often, after people develop depression, they avoid proactive attempts to solve problems because they anticipate that they are not capable of implementing a successful solution (Nezu, 1986). This avoidance often results in more problems; for instance, avoiding marital problems potentially results in increased conflict or divorce.

A relatively recent movement, *positive psychology*, focuses on one's strengths (virtues) as well as any skills deficits in the treatment of depressive disorders (Sin & Lyubomirsky, 2009). Seligman and Csikszentmihalyi (2000) discuss positive psychology as an adjunct to treatment of mental health concerns to provide treatment to the whole person rather than a focus on treating only the depressive symptoms. The main tenets involve putting a person's strengths to work in achieving a balance of three lives: the pleasant life, the good life, and the meaningful life. Seligman and colleagues have designed and researched a series of Internet exercises designed to increase happiness and decrease suffering. For a more detailed review, see Seligman, Steen, Park, and Peterson (2005).

Many people are often surprised to discover how disabling depression can be. People who have depression often complain of somatic problems, such as fatigue, stomach upset, headaches, and joint pain (Viinamaeki et al., 2000). These symptoms, coupled with the pessimism and avoidant style associated with depression, are related to the increased number of disability days reported by people with depressive disorders (Pincus & Pettit, 2001). In the National Comorbidity Survey (NCS; Kessler & Frank, 1997), people with depression reported a five-fold increase in time lost from work compared with those without depression. In fact, individuals treated for depression incurred greater disability costs to employers than did people needing treatment for hypertension and had costs comparable to those with more severe chronic illness like diabetes (Conti & Burton, 1995; Druss, Rosenheck, & Sledge, 2000). Data from the NCS-R (Greenberg et al., 2003) suggested that the economic burden of depression stabilized somewhat between 1990 and 2000, rising from $77.4 billion to $83.1 billion (adjusted for inflation). The majority of this burden was associated with workplace costs (e.g., lost productivity). Interestingly, costs related to treating depression are almost as great as the costs due to disability days from depression (Kessler et al., 1999), and some studies have found the treatment of depression to decrease the number of disability days (Simon et al., 2000). In spite of the availability of efficacious treatments, such as cognitive behavioral therapy and problem-solving therapy (Cuijpers, Karyotaki, Pot, Park, & Reynolds, 2014a; Renn & Areán, 2017), depression remains a significant health care concern for older adults, and depression is associated with disability or decline in functional abilities, reduced quality of life, increased morbidity and mortality, and increased utilization of health care services in late life (Chapman & Perry, 2008; Charney et al., 2003).

DIAGNOSTIC CONSIDERATIONS

Although the *DSM-5* provides guidelines for the diagnosis of depressive disorders, the comorbidity of other medical and psychiatric disorders can complicate a diagnostic decision. To make an accurate diagnosis of depression, the provider must consider physical health and medical history, medications (prescription and over-the-counter), family and personal history, and psychosocial stressors. With regard to the latter, the *DSM-IV-TR* previously required that an individual with *bereavement* be excluded from an MDE diagnosis, regardless of symptom presentation, unless their symptoms lasted more than 2 months or resulted in marked impairment, suicidality, or psychotic features.

As discussed in more detail later (see "Grief and Bereavement"), the *DSM-5* instituted a change in that bereavement is no longer an exclusion criterion for a diagnosis of depression; people who are suffering from the loss of a significant other can be diagnosed concomitantly with a depressive disorder if they meet the clinical characteristics of MDE (Corruble, Falissard, & Gorwood, 2011). This is not to say that bereavement automatically results in a depressive episode; rather, this change reflects the clinical understanding that the loss of a loved one, as well as other stressful life events, can trigger a genuine depressive disorder when out of proportion to a "normal" response (Kendler et al., 2003). Clinicians are urged to consider the culture of the individual in determining what is a normal or expected response to grief/loss, as grief may be expressed differently across cultures.

MEDICAL ILLNESS

The first important step in diagnosing depressive disorders is to have the patient get a complete physical. Depressive disorders commonly co-occur with other mental disorders (e.g., anxiety disorders) and physical disorders (King-Kallimanis, Gum, & Kohn, 2009), which can further exacerbate distress and disability, and can challenge treatment efforts. Because many medical illnesses are related to the onset of a depressive episode, at times treating both the illness and the MDE is a more efficient way to effect symptom change (Gupta, Bahadur, Gupta, & Bhugra, 2006; Katon, 2003; Simon, Von Korff, & Lin, 2005; Stover, Fenton, Rosenfeld, & Insel, 2003; Trivedi, Clayton, & Frank, 2007). For example, in endocrinological disorders like hyperthyroidism and hypothyroidism, individuals experience radical changes in mood and fluctuations in their weight. Sleep disorders, such as obstructive sleep apnea, may also present with symptom overlap with depression, including signs and symptoms of fatigue, weight gain, difficulty with concentration, and mood disturbances (Ejaz, Khawaja, Bhatia, & Hurwitz, 2011); this overlap often complicates accurate diagnosis. Moreover, people with chronic illnesses like diabetes mellitus have high rates of depressive symptoms (de Groot, Jacobson, Samson, & Welch, 1999; Renn, Steers, Jay, & Feliciano, 2013), but not necessarily higher rates of MDD or persistent depressive disorder (Fisher, Glasgow, & Strycker, 2010a; Fisher et al., 2010b). Of note, the construct of *diabetes-related distress* refers to the common negative emotional adjustment to diabetes (e.g., helplessness) that is distinct from a clinical diagnosis of a depressive disorder (Gonzalez et al., 2011). It is important for clinicians to assess disease-specific burden (e.g., emotional distress, poor social support, treatment burden; Martin et al., 2017) to better expand assessment beyond frank depressive disorders and improve psychological and physical interventions for such vulnerable patients.

Other medical illnesses such as stroke (Sagen et al., 2010), Parkinson's disease (Marsh, 2013), pancreatic cancer (Jia et al., 2010; Mayr & Schmid, 2010), coronary heart disease (Kubzansky & Kawachi, 2000), and myocardial infarction (Martens, Hoen, Mittelhauser, de Jonge, & Denollet, 2010) are also associated with depressive symptoms. Neurological findings suggest that cerebrovascular disease (particularly ischemic small-vessel disease) may be related to the onset of late-life depression (Rapp et al., 2005), although it is unclear whether these illnesses directly cause depression or whether the depression is the result of the negative life changes brought on by the illness. Recovery from these diseases (when possible), or stabilization, often helps to alleviate depressive symptoms.

Drug and Alcohol Use and Abuse

The next step in establishing a diagnosis is to determine to what extent the person drinks alcohol or uses drugs (including prescription medication and nonprescribed or illicit drugs). Often substance abuse or dependence disorders (now referred to in the *DSM-5* as *substance-related and addictive disorders*) are strongly associated with depressive symptoms (Gunnarsdottir et al., 2000; Merikangas & Avenevoli, 2000; Ostacher, 2007). Scientists have debated whether depressive symptoms are a consequence of substance abuse and the problems related to this disorder, or whether the substance use is a means of self-medicating depressive symptoms. The psychiatric and substance abuse fields are moving toward the co-management of depression and substance abuse, and while abstaining from substances does frequently clarify the diagnostic picture, it is often very unlikely that someone who is abusing substances and has depression will be able to abstain without treatment. Therefore, when these two conditions present together, clinicians generally ascribe a dual diagnosis and attempt to untangle which disorder was apparent first through gathering a thorough diagnostic history.

In determining the best course of action regarding treatment, it is crucial to get a list of all medications (both prescribed and over-the-counter) that the person uses, given that the side-effects of many medications can cause or contribute to the depressive symptoms observed (referred to as substance/medication-induced depressive disorder). This is particularly true with older adults, who are more vulnerable to the side-effects of medication. For example, in a review of late-life depression, Dick, Gallagher-Thompson, and Thompson (1996) note that some medications, such as antihistamines, antihypertensives, some antiparkinsonian drugs, and some pain medications, commonly cause symptoms of depression. In addition, diuretics, synthetic hormones, and benzodiazepines have also been noted to contribute to depressive symptomatology (Cooper, Peters, & Andrews, 1998). The APA (2013) notes that other prescription medications, such as steroids, chemotherapy drugs, and antibiotics, may also induce depressive symptoms (refer to Table 8.2). The higher the number of drugs the person takes, the higher the risk for medication side-effects and drug–drug interactions—a situation that emphasizes the need for a thorough assessment of drug regimens.

GRIEF AND BEREAVEMENT

Grief over the loss of a special person, the presence of a major life stressor, or significant changes in one's life can also complicate attempts to diagnose depressive disorders. Although *bereavement* may produce a grief response that mimics symptoms of depression, it was previously an exclusion for a diagnosis of MDD. This exclusion was originally intended to prevent misdiagnosing "normal" grief as depression (Maj, 2008). Therefore, the removal of the bereavement exclusion has created controversies in the field; some clinicians criticized that bereavement was the only psychosocial stressor to exclude an individual from an MDE diagnosis (Wakefield, Schmitz, First, & Horwitz, 2007), whereas others conceptualize grief as a normal reaction to loss and are loath to pathologize it.

The *DSM-5* recognizes that a significant psychosocial stressor, such as a loss of a loved one, can trigger a depressive episode. Because of the overlap between "normal" grieving and depression, careful consideration is given to delineate what is a normal or appropriate response, with consideration given to the person's history and cultural norms. In making this distinction, clinicians must use their judgment to decide whether symptoms (e.g., sadness, weight loss) are appropriate for the loss or whether the symptoms more resemble those associated with a depressive episode. For example, grieving is typically classified by feelings of emptiness and loss, whereas depression is associated with a persistent sadness and an inability to experience pleasure or happiness. Also, grief is often experienced in waves of dysphoria, longing, and/or yearning, typically brought on by reminders of the deceased. These pangs of grief might also include positive emotions associated with these memories. In contrast, the unhappiness of depression is persistent and pervasive and not associated with specific thoughts or memories.

Although it is possible that those with uncomplicated bereavement or adjustment disorder can develop a depressive disorder, little is known about the extent to which grief can develop into a depressive disorder (Boelen, van de Schoot, van den Hout, de Keijser, & van den Bout, 2010; Wellen, 2010). However, when bereavement and a depressive episode co-occur, the individual often experiences more severe functional impairment and a worse prognosis (Shear et al., 2011; Zisook et al., 2010) than bereavement not accompanied by a depressive disorder. Individuals with other risk factors for depression (e.g., poor social support, trauma history, increased stressors, previous MDEs) may be more apt to experience an MDE with bereavement (Ellifritt, Nelson, & Walsh, 2003; Shear et al., 2011; Zisook et al., 2012).

DEPRESSION DUE TO OTHER PSYCHIATRIC DISORDERS

Adults with other psychiatric disorders can have co-occurring depressive symptoms, and thus establishing a differential rule-out for these other disorders is often important and necessary. For instance, people with anxiety disorders, particularly generalized anxiety disorder, report feelings of sadness and hopelessness (Hopko et al., 2000). Co-occurring mood and anxiety disorders are also more commonly reported in middle-aged and older women than in men (Byers et al., 2009). When under stress, people with personality disorders often report significant symptoms of depression (Petersen et al., 2002). In fact, they can become quite acutely depressed, which may predominate the clinical presentation, often obscuring the underlying personality disorder. Specifically, depressive episodes are most prevalent with avoidant, borderline, and obsessive-compulsive personality disorders (Rossi et al., 2001). Furthermore, personality disorders have an association with a longer remission onset from a depressive episode (O'Leary & Costello, 2001). Finally, depression is common in prodromal phases of schizophrenia and is a recurrent feature in bipolar disorder.

LATE-LIFE DEPRESSION

Depression, although not a natural consequence of aging, is one of the most common mental health disorders that older adults experience. Prevalence rates differ depending on the population surveyed and the settings observed (see the "Epidemiology" section). Older adults present differently than younger populations in that they are less likely to report feeling sad or depressed (Fiske, Wetherell, & Gatz, 2009) or symptoms of guilt (Gallagher et al., 2010) and may instead report more anhedonia, memory problems (in the absence of dementia), and somatic symptoms such as fatigue, decreased appetite, and muscle pain (Kim, Shin, Yoon, & Stewart, 2002). In addition, because older adults are more likely to have chronic illnesses, the presence of physical illnesses as well as the side-effects of medications taken to treat these conditions can overshadow or worsen symptoms of depression (Areán & Reynolds, 2005), which can further complicate diagnosis. In older populations, depression is also associated with increased mortality and health service usage, and in many cases is a prodromal sign for an emerging neurocognitive disorder, such as Alzheimer's disease (Segal, Qualls, & Smyer, 2018). These associations highlight the importance of early recognition, differential diagnosis, and treatment of this disabling disorder.

EPIDEMIOLOGY

The patients described in this chapter are representative of a growing number of people in the United States suffering from depressive disorders. Several large-scale epidemiological studies on mental disorders have taken place in the US. The Epidemiological Catchment Area Study (ECA) was conducted in the 1980s (Regier, 1988) and was the first to definitively determine the prevalence of psychiatric problems in the US. However, the generalizability of the ECA was limited, as data were collected at only five sites. The second study, called the National Comorbidity Survey (NCS; Kessler et al., 1994), was carried out on a national sample representative of the US at the time of data collection. The NCS focused specifically on English-speaking adults between the ages of 18 and 65 and was mostly concerned with the prevalence of co-occurring *DSM-III-R* psychiatric disorders in the US. The NCS was replicated a decade later to examine the prevalence for the *DSM-IV* and the *International Classification of Disease, version 10 (ICD-10)* psychiatric disorders and to provide age-of-onset estimates for mental health disorders in a new US sample of 10,000 adults (NCS-R; Kessler et al., 2004; Kessler & Merikangas, 2004).

At the time of writing, the most recent prevalence statistics were drawn from the 2015 National Survey on Drug Use and Health (NSDUH; Center for Behavioral Health Statistics and Quality, 2016). This annual survey of the US noninstitutionalized, civilian population aged 12 years and older began in 1971 and is the primary source of substance use statistical information. The NSDUH also includes questions focused on mental health; beginning in 2004, modules related to MDE were asked of youths (aged 12–17) and adults (aged 18 and older). These modules were adapted from the NCS-R and were derived from *DSM-IV* criteria for MDE; they have not been changed since the emergence of the *DSM-5*. Thus, our understanding of psychiatric epidemiology is largely based on diagnostic criteria that predate the current *DSM-5*. However, since the definition of depressive disorders has undergone only small changes in recent DSM editions, data drawn from past studies still allow for reasonable inferences. Since the data from the NSDUH and the above surveys have consistently demonstrated that the prevalence of depressive disorders varies between populations, the following discussion will present the prevalence of depressive disorders by different populations.

COMMUNITY SAMPLES

Depressive disorders are serious and relatively common. However, it is important to bear in mind that the individuals most severely impaired by depressive disorders are not represented in the population-based surveys that inform much of the epidemiological data of depressive disorders; it is with that caveat that we summarize the surveillance data of depression among community-dwelling adults. Indeed, the most widely cited prevalence estimates continue to be based on NCS-R findings. Using *DSM-IV-TR* criteria, the NCS-R reported *lifetime prevalence*, or the number of persons who have ever experienced any type of mood disorder (as the *DSM-IV-TR* referred to them), to be 20.8% (Kessler et al., 2005). At the time of writing, only one published study (PsyCoLaus study; Vandeleur et al., 2017) had examined the prevalence of depressive disorders based on *DSM-5* criteria. Using semistructured diagnostic interviews with a random sample of urban-dwelling adults in Switzerland, this study found a lifetime prevalence estimate of 54.4% for any *DSM-5* depressive disorder. The use of semistructured rather than structured interviews may have contributed somewhat to this much higher prevalence rate than that previously published by NCS-R. However, 70% of individuals meeting criteria for any *DSM-5* depressive disorder in the PsyCoLaus study reported having sought treatment for depression, which lends credibility to these findings (Vandeleur et al., 2017).

With regard to specific depressive disorder diagnoses, the NCS-R (Kessler et al., 2005) found a lifetime prevalence for an episode of major depression to be 16.6% in a community-dwelling sample, with a 12-month prevalence of 6.6% (Kessler et al., 2003). This is comparable to 1-year MDE prevalence rates of 6.6% and 6.7% from the 2014 and 2015 NSDUH data, respectively (Center for Behavioral Health Statistics and Quality, 2016). Previous estimates of MDE were as low as 5.8% (Regier, 1988) using *DSM-III-R* diagnostic criteria. The high lifetime prevalence of 28.2% for MDD found in the PsyCoLaus study was well above the typical range of these estimates, and may not generalize beyond their sample from an urban setting in Switzerland.

Regarding persistent depressive disorder (dysthymia), the lifetime prevalence is lower than the rates for MDD. According to the NCS and the NCS-R (Kilzieh, Rastam, Ward, & Maziak, 2010), between 2.5% and 6% of the general population have had a period of what the *DSM-IV-TR* labeled dysthymic disorder. To date, no representative prevalence data from the US are yet available for the new *DSM-5* diagnostic label of persistent depressive disorder.

The ECA, NCS, and NSDUH show differential prevalence of depressive disorders by gender. While still based on *DSM-IV-TR* criteria, the most recent prevalence estimates reported in the 2015 NSDUH data suggest that 8.5% of women and 4.7% of men had an MDE during a 12-month span (Center for Behavioral Health Statistics and Quality, 2016). In the ECA studies, lifetime prevalence of affective disorders for adult women average 6.6%, whereas in the NCS, prevalence is significantly higher, at 21.3% (Kessler et al., 1994; Regier, 1988). The lifetime prevalence for men was 8.2% in the ECA and 12.7% in the NCS. Although prevalence for depression varied between studies, a consistent theme emerges: more women than men report having depressive episodes. The most recent nationally representative lifetime prevalence data from the NCS-R found that women are at a 1.5-fold increased risk (compared with their male counter-parts) of developing a mood disorder over their lifetime, and a 1.7-fold increased risk of developing MDD specifically (Kessler et al., 2003, 2005). This difference between men and women has been found repeatedly throughout the world and thus appears to be an accurate reflection of true differences in the prevalence of the disorder between men and women (Kessler, 2003). Although the reasons for these differences are not fully established, some speculate that sex differences in biological makeup, differences in cognitive and behavioral patterns of mood control (Nolen-Hoeksema, Wisco, & Lyubomirsky, 2008), and social influences, including differential expectations for the two genders, account for the difference in prevalence (Kilzieh et al., 2010). However, recent work has critiqued the validity of these sex differences and postulated that men and women differentially express and endorse symptoms of depression, such that men are more likely to report anger, aggression, irritability, and substance abuse than traditional symptoms of dysphoria and social withdrawal (Martin, Neighbors, & Griffith, 2013). Based on their reanalysis of the NCS-R, Martin et al. found that sex differences in prevalence of depression disappeared when accounting for alternative depressive symptom expression. Clearly, further work is needed to refine our conceptualization and assessment of depression, particularly in light of sociocultural changes and advances in neuroscience.

The prevalence of depressive disorders in the US varies by age, with the NCS-R reporting a peak in 12-month prevalence of MDD between the ages of 18 and 29 years (Kessler et al., 2003). Prevalence in this age group is three-fold higher than the prevalence in individuals 60 years or older; estimates drop to a 1.8-fold and 1.2-fold increased odds of having depression for adults aged 30–44 and 45–59, respectively, relative to their older counter-parts (Kessler et al. 2003). As demonstrated in the NCS-R, NSDUH, and other epidemiological data, prevalence rates of many psychiatric disorders are increasing with each decade, suggesting that disorders like depression may be influenced by cohort effects, including willingness to self-disclose symptoms and differences in assessment across studies (Richards, 2011). However, the information presented by the NCS-R on the differential prevalence rates of depression between younger and older people is limited. Although the NCS-R included individuals over the age of 60 and up to the age of 75, which is an improvement over the demographics in the previous ECA and NCS samples

(Kessler & Merikangas, 2004), it did not include our fastest-growing segment of the population, the "oldest old" (those 85 years old and older). With the preceding caveat in mind, it is important to highlight what is known about the prevalence of depression in older adults.

The prevalence of depression among older adult populations is one of the highest of any mental disorder (Kessler et al., 2005). Age-associated factors such as physical health vulnerabilities, neurobiological changes, and stressors of role transitions and losses may curtail daily activities and increase vulnerability to depressive disorders (Fiske et al., 2009). The NCS-R reports lifetime prevalence of mood disorders for individuals over the age of 60 to be 11.9%, with the majority of these cases accounted for with the diagnosis of MDD (10.6%; Kessler et al., 2005). More recent NSDUH data provide 12-month prevalence estimates (rather than lifetime prevalence) for this age group. These data suggested a slight increase in MDE from 2.8% to 3.0% of adults over the age of 65 from 2014 to 2015 (Center for Behavioral Health Statistics and Quality, 2016). Finally, a meta-analysis of 24 studies reporting age- and gender-specific prevalence of adults aged 75 years and older found a pooled point prevalence of 7.2% (range: 4.6–9.3%) for MDD and 17.1% (range: 4.5–37.4%) for depressive disorders (Luppa et al., 2012). This review estimated the lifetime prevalence of MDD for individuals aged 75 and older to vary between 3.7% and 28.0%. Indeed, even the most rigorous prevalence estimates of depression vary substantially by population studied (e.g., the NCS-R study did not include institutionalized older adults), and is affected by other sociodemographic variables such as gender, socioeconomic status, and race/ethnicity. Also, the difficulties in detecting depression in older adults (see "Late-Life Depression") make this a difficult population from which to obtain precise epidemiological data. However, as the demographics of the US and other countries shift toward an aging population, estimating the prevalence of depression across the life span and into older age is a necessary step in ensuring adequate health care.

PREVALENCE IN RACIAL/ETHNIC MINORITIES

Rates of depression also vary by ethnic group. According to the NCS data, African Americans have rates of depression similar to those of the White population. Approximately 3.1% of African Americans have had an MDD episode, and 3.2% have had persistent depressive disorder, pure dysthymic syndrome (Jackson-Triche et al., 2000). However, Asian Americans have historically had the lowest rates, with only 0.8% reporting that they had experienced an MDE and 0.8% experiencing persistent depressive disorder, pure dysthymic syndrome (Jackson-Triche et al., 2000). Among individuals identifying as Hispanic or Latino, some data have suggested that immigration status moderates the presentation and prevalence of depressive symptoms. According to earlier data, Hispanics/Latinos who recently emigrated from Latin America were less likely to have depression than Hispanics/Latinos who were born and raised in the US (Alderete, Vega, Kolody, & Aguilar-Gaxiola, 1999). Hispanics/Latinos who were US-born had rates of depression much like the estimates for non-Hispanic Whites (3.5% for MDD and 5% for persistent depressive disorder, pure dysthymic syndrome), whereas immigrants reported only half the prevalence of US-born Hispanics (Alderete et al., 1999). Although unconfirmed empirically, Vega, Kolody, Valle, and Hough (1986) posited that *hardiness* among immigrants resulted in lower rates of depression; that is, those who are able to withstand the stress related to immigration are more likely to cope with stress related to depression. However, the evidence has been inconclusive in empirical tests of this "immigrant paradox," and reanalyses of NCS-R suggest that there are variations between Latino groups, with only Mexican immigrants showing a lower rate of mood disorders relative to US-born counterparts (Alegría et al., 2008b).

More recent epidemiological data suggest varying prevalence estimates among racial and ethnic groups, with estimates demonstrating an increase in depressive disorders among all racial groups relative to earlier NCS data. The 2015 NSDUH data reported 12-month prevalence estimates of MDE as highest among multiracial individuals (12.2%), followed by those identifying as American Indian or Alaska Natives (8.9%), relative to non-Latino Whites (7.5%). Other ethnic and racial minority groups fared better compared with their non-Latino White counterparts, with 5.2% of Native Hawaiian or Pacific Islander, 4.9% of African American, 4.8% of Hispanic or Latino, and 4.1% of Asian adults experiencing a MDE in the last year. Other data come from two large studies aimed at addressing the poor representation of racial and ethnic minorities in epidemiological research. First, the National Latino and Asian American Study (NLAAS) is a household survey that includes nationally represented samples of adults from various ethnic groups (i.e., eight different ethnic and subethnic groups including Latinos, Asian Americans, African Americans, and non-Latino Whites) (Alegría et al., 2004). Second, the National Survey of American Life (NSAL) is a household survey of community-dwelling African American and Afro-Caribbean individuals. In a recent study, the data from the NLAAS, the NCS-R, and the NSAL were combined into a single dataset ($n = 8762$). This study found that the 12-month prevalence of depressive disorders was higher than that found in earlier epidemiological studies—5.4% for Asians, 10.8% for Latinos, and 8% for African Americans compared with 11.2% for non-Latino Whites (Alegría et al., 2008a). This study also confirmed that of those with depressive disorders, an alarming number did not receive any kind of mental health treatment or received inadequate treatment, highlighting the need for better assessment and treatment of depression for diverse groups. As the US becomes increasingly diverse, caution is warranted in generalizing all ethnic or racial minority groups, as this may mask differences in vulnerability for depression due to multicultural issues, including immigration status, acculturation, socioeconomic status, access to health care, substance use patterns, and myriad other factors, including anti-immigrant and racial bias and discrimination. Further research is needed to understand risk and protective factors of depression related to these unique sociocultural intersections.

PREVALENCE IN SPECIAL SETTINGS

The extant literature discussed in preceding sections highlights the variability in estimating depression prevalence. To further complicate our understanding of this condition, the prevalence of depression also varies by setting, such as in the case of medical settings relative to the general community. Indeed, primary care has long been labeled the *de facto* mental health services system (Regier, Goldberg, & Taube, 1978). Nationally, 20% of all primary care visits have a clear mental health indication, including depression screening, treatment (psychotherapy, counseling, or prescription of a psychotropic drug), or other mental health reason for visit (Olfson, Kroenke, Wang, & Blanco, 2014). Estimates vary, but experts agree that depression is one of the most common and burdensome health problems encountered in primary care (Unützer & Park, 2012). A cross-sectional survey of 86 general practices in Belgium found that 31% of primary care patients met diagnostic criteria for a unipolar depressive disorder (13.9% for MDD; 12.6% for what was previously labeled dysthymia but referred to as persistent depressive disorder in the *DSM-5*; Ansseau et al., 2004). Another international study evidenced a 9.6% point prevalence of MDD in Spanish primary care patients (Serrano-Blanco et al., 2010). Here in the US, a random sample of primary care clinics in the US Department of Veterans Affairs yielded 12% of patients classified as having probable MDD based on a screening measure (the Patient Health Questionnaire; see the "Psychological Assessment" section following for more information on this measure; Yano et al., 2012). Little is known about prevalence of other unipolar depressive disorders in primary care and other settings. Although subsyndromal depression may be the most common depressive disorder in these settings, the heterogeneity of this presentation may have impeded accurate detection, particularly in screening measures in medical settings. Clearly, ongoing refinement of the assessment and treatment of depressive disorders and other behavioral health conditions in primary care is needed to optimize overall health.

Other settings with high rates for depression include long-term care and palliative settings. A meta-analysis of 24 studies examining 4,007 individuals in palliative care settings across seven countries estimated a point prevalence of MDD of 14.3% using *DSM-IV-TR* criteria (Mitchell et al., 2011). Chronic medical illness is also associated with elevated rates of depression, as seen in patients with chronic kidney disease (28% meeting criteria in a clinical interview; Palmer et al., 2013), congestive heart failure (two to three times higher rate of MDD than the general population; Rustad, Stern, Hebert, & Musselman, 2013), and type 2 diabetes mellitus (up to two times increased odds of depression among patients with diabetes compared with those without; Ali, Stone, Peters, Davies, & Khunti, 2006). Even more staggering estimates suggest that approximately 32% of people living in assisted living facilities experience MDD (Waraich, Goldner, Somers, & Hsu, 2004), with new episodes occurring in 31.6% of patients within the first 12 months of admittance (Hoover et al., 2010). The causes of higher prevalence of depressive disorders in long-term care facilities may vary but most likely include loss of functional independence, loss of familiar surroundings, decreased access to pleasant activities (Feliciano, Steers, Elite-Marcandonatu, McLane, & Areán, 2009) or loved ones, and comorbid physical illnesses. Given the impact that depressive disorders have on rehabilitation, the high rate of these disorders in these settings is cause for concern and necessitates more vigilant and proactive treatment of depression in long-term care.

PSYCHOLOGICAL ASSESSMENT

Assessment of depression has evolved substantially over the past two decades and many approaches and instruments have the benefit of a substantial evidence base. That being said, assessment is often complicated by factors such as ethnicity and culture, aging, substance abuse, and other psychiatric comorbidities. In this section, we focus on the strengths and weaknesses of different methods for assessing depression, ranging from screening instruments to structured clinical interviews.

The most common way to assess for depressive disorders is by conducting in-person interviews with patients. Interviewers, usually a mental health professional or trained clinic worker, ask questions to patients regarding the current episode of depression, including a full accounting of symptoms with which they present, how long they have been experiencing them, what they think caused the symptoms, how they have been coping with the symptoms, and what they would like to do about the symptoms. In addition, intake clinicians will also ask about family and personal history, past and current medical history, previous psychiatric history, and the impact of the depression on day-to-day functioning. All this information is compiled to determine whether patients have a depressive disorder, the type of disorder they have, and the degree to which they are suffering. This information is then used to determine appropriate case disposition and treatment.

Most mental health professionals have their preferred methods of assessment. Some will conduct an open-ended interview that is guided not by any instrumentation, but rather by patients' disclosures and responses to questions. Although this method is most commonly practiced, it also carries the greatest risk of misdiagnosis, particularly if the interviewer is not an expert in depressive disorders. Because of this risk, many mental health organizations prefer to use a combination of an open-ended interview in conjunction with a screening instrument or a guide, such as a semistructured interview, to help remind clinicians to ask for all relevant information. In using a screening instrument or semistructured interview, it is imperative that the instruments chosen have evidence for reliability and validity for the specific population being assessed. Other than a medical examination to rule out physical causes for depressive symptoms, there is no biological test to diagnose depression, so accurate diagnosis rests with clinicians and the instrumentation used to confirm a diagnosis.

SCREENING INSTRUMENTS

In many health settings, practitioners are concerned with identifying as many people as possible who have the disorder so that quick and effective interventions can take place. This tradition comes from medical practice, where physicians routinely conduct medical tests when they suspect a particular illness. These screening tests help the doctor determine whether further tests are needed to make a specific diagnosis. For instance, when a patient sees a doctor about symptoms of fatigue, the physician will likely order blood and urine screens to determine whether the fatigue is due to medical conditions such as anemia, poorly controlled diabetes, or mononucleosis. Standardized screening instruments are used for similar purposes in mental health. In fact, Siu and the US Preventive Services Task Force (2016) recommend the routine screening for depression in US adults, and especially those in high-risk groups, such as pregnant and postpartum women, individuals with chronic illness, and those with other mental disorders. In a sense, depression (and we would argue anxiety as well) are psychological "vital signs" that should be routinely screened and assessed, much like weight and blood pressure are routinely evaluated in medical settings. Screening instruments should be highly sensitive; that is, they should detect depression in everyone with the disorder. Otherwise, their utility is limited. Once someone screens positive for depression, further assessment is required to confirm a diagnosis.

The most common mechanism for screening for depression in adults is through *self-report measures*. The *DSM-5* proposed that one such measure, the Patient Health Questionnaire (PHQ-9; Spitzer, Williams, Kroenke, Hornyak, & McMurray, 2000) be used as an "emerging measure" for future research and clinical evaluation to monitor treatment progress. However, there are numerous other self-report measures that are well represented in the literature and clinical practice, including a two-item, shorter version of the Patient Health Questionnaire (PHQ-2; Arroll et al., 2010), the Beck Depression Inventory-II (BDI-II; Beck, Steer, & Brown, 1996), the Center for Epidemiological Studies—Depression Scale (CES-D; Radloff, 1977), the Hospital Anxiety and Depression Scale (HADS; Zigmond & Snaith, 1983), the Zung Self-Rating Depression Scale (Zung, 1972), the Montgomery Asberg Depression Rating Scale (MADRS-S; Montgomery & Asberg, 1979), and the Profile of Mood States (POMS; Plutchik, Platman, & Fieve, 1968). Because some of these measures contain items that are related to somatic symptoms (e.g., fatigue) and are frequently scored in a depressed direction by older adults who have acute physical or chronic illnesses (Edelstein et al., 2008), some self-report measures have been designed specifically for detecting depression in older adults, such as the Geriatric Depression Scale (GDS; Yesavage et al., 1982). The GDS is the most widely used depression screening measure among older adults and has demonstrated excellent psychometric properties and clinical utility in diverse samples of older adults in the US and in most developed countries (see review by Marty, Pepin, June, & Segal, 2011). Patients complete these instruments and indicate the degree to which they have experienced symptoms over a specified period (e.g., 1 week, 2 weeks), and then the instrument is scored by computer or manually. A patient's score on the instrument reflects the severity of depressive symptoms.

These self-report screening instruments are considered cost-effective and efficient. They are useful in diverse health and mental health settings in making quick assessments, especially when followed by a more nuanced clinical assessment. However, one problem with their usage is the "false-positive" in which individuals screen positive for depression but they actually do not have depression or they have some other mental or physical disorder which is masquerading as depression. Additionally, some health care providers are incorrectly using these instruments for determining a formal diagnosis. One must recognize that these instruments are designed to be screening devices and not diagnostic tools.

Because of the prevalence of depression in primary care medicine, several instruments have been created specifically for use in that environment. These instruments are meant to raise a red flag to the provider so that a more thorough assessment of depression can be conducted. The Primary Care Evaluation of Mental Disorders (PRIME-MD; Spitzer et al., 1994) is a good example. The patient completes a brief questionnaire in which two questions are red flags for depression. If the patient endorses one of the two red flag questions, then the provider asks more specific questions to finalize the diagnosis. The PRIME-MD has satisfactory psychometric properties (Spitzer, Kroenke, & Williams, 1999). The PHQ-9 (Spitzer et al., 2000) is a self-administered depression module adapted from the PRIME-MD. Like the PRIME-MD, it has strong internal reliability in a primary care setting (Cronbach's alpha = 0.89), excellent test–retest reliability, as well as good criterion and construct validity (Kroenke, Spitzer, & Williams, 2001). In addition, the PHQ-9 has validity for use among individuals of different ages and from diverse cultural backgrounds (e.g., Han et al., 2008; Lotrakul et al., 2008).

Another brief self-report questionnaire for medical patients is the Beck Depression Inventory—Primary Care (BDI-PC; Beck, Guth, Steer, & Ball, 1997). This seven-item questionnaire consists of some of the same items from the full BDI and instructs patients to rate symptoms occurring over the past 2 weeks on a four-point scale. In research examining the BDI-PC as a screening measure for MDD, it has been shown to have high internal consistency in primary care outpatient settings (Cronbach's alpha = 0.85; Steer, Cavalieri, Leonard, & Beck, 1999) and in medical inpatients (Cronbach's alpha = 0.86; Parker, Hilton, Hadzi-Pavlovi, & Bains, 2001). When using a cut score of 4 and greater, it yielded excellent sensitivity (97%) and specificity (99%; Steer et al., 1999). Researchers noted that an advantage of the BDI-PC is that it has been found to be unrelated to age, sex, or ethnicity/racial status (Beck et al., 1997; Winter, Steer, Jones-Hicks, & Beck, 1999).

Two additional screening measures for depression are the General Health Questionnaire (GHQ; Goldberg, 1972) and the WHO's Well-Being Index (WHO-5; WHO, 1990b). Both measures are used in community and nonpsychiatric clinical settings, such as primary care. The GHQ is a screening instrument used in primary care and general practice to detect psychiatric disorders. The original scale included 60 questions intended to capture the patient's somatic and psychiatric symptoms in less than 10 minutes. The test creators found a 0.80 correlation between clinical assessment and GHQ score (Goldberg & Blackwell, 1970). More recent modifications of the scale include 12-item,

20-item, 28-item, and 30-item questionnaires. The WHO-5 was adapted from the original 28-item questionnaire of quality of life in patients with diabetes. The five items chosen cover positive mood, vitality, and general interest. Although originally developed as a well-being index, the WHO-5 has been validated as a depression-screening tool for use with older adults (Bonsignore, Barkow, Jessen, & Heun, 2001).

STRUCTURED AND SEMI-STRUCTURED CLINICAL INTERVIEWS

Once a person screens positive for a depressive disorder, the next step is to confirm the diagnosis, which is best done by using a structured or semistructured interview. As stated earlier, most people who are expert in the diagnosis of depressive disorders do not need the assistance of a structured instrument. However, because experts are not always available and using them can be costly, structured and semistructured interviews have been developed for use by less experienced personnel or for use in research protocols. Indeed, structured and semistructured interviews have a rich history in clinical psychology, and are notable for their advantages, namely increased reliability (consistency) and validity (accuracy) of the assessment, and great utility as training tools for less experienced clinicians or trainees (Segal & Williams, 2014). Among the best-known instruments are the Structured Clinical Interview for *DSM-5* Disorders (SCID-5) and the Composite International Diagnostic Interview (CIDI). Another short structured diagnostic interview is the Mini-International Neuropsychiatric Interview (MINI). These are discussed in more detail below.

The Structured Clinical Interview for DSM-5 Disorders   The SCID-5 (First, Williams, Karg, & Spitzer, 2016) is one of the most widely used structured interviews in clinical research, training, and practice, and it includes a full module for depressive disorders. The SCID-5 is semistructured, which allows for flexibility in administration. Although interviewers use the instrument as a guide to structure the interview, the interviewer can also rely on his or her judgment in interpreting a patient's answers to questions. Because there is a reliance on clinical judgment, the SCID functions best when administered by a trained mental health professional. The SCID has been demonstrated to be useful for adults and older adults, with diverse diagnoses including depressive and bipolar disorders (see review by Segal & Williams, 2014).

Composite International Diagnostic Interview   The CIDI was developed by the WHO (1990a) for the purpose of assisting with psychiatric diagnosis in large epidemiological studies, and it has been updated for concordance with *DSM-5*. This structured clinical interview is a fully computerized interview and so is able to attain a complexity and depth of diagnosis with carefully programmed skip patterns and flowcharts. Its great advantage is that it does not require a mental health professional to administer the instrument—in fact, the CIDI can be used as a patient-only-administered instrument, although it is also common for a researcher to administer it. Because the program makes the diagnosis, the researcher giving the interview does not need to make any independent clinical judgments. The obvious benefits of the CIDI are that it is computerized and thus cuts down on costs of training interviewers and of using health practitioners to make diagnoses. There are, however, some drawbacks to the use of the CIDI. The most prominent ones are that it is not sensitive to the context in which respondents experience their symptoms and it is subject to easy falsification if respondents desire to either deny or exaggerate their symptoms.

The Mini-International Neuropsychiatric Interview   The MINI was developed by Sheehan et al. (1998) to assess the most common mental disorders and has been updated for *DSM-5*. It is a brief structured clinical interview that covers 17 common disorders, including MDD. With a 15-minute administration time, the MINI is shorter than the typical interviews used in most clinical and research settings but is more thorough than screening tests. Like the CIDI, the MINI is advantageous in that it does not require a mental health professional to administer the instrument, thus saving costs and freeing time for mental health professionals to focus on other critical issues. The interview items focus largely on current symptoms that are most routinely asked about by clinicians, which allows for a shorter administration time than other interviews which may focus additionally on past episodes of psychopathology. Research testing the validity of the clinician-rated MINI has shown good to very good concordance with other clinician-rated diagnostic interviews (SCID and CIDI), and it has excellent interrater reliability (kappa > 0.79) for all diagnostic categories and good test–retest reliability (kappa > 0.63) for all diagnostic categories except simple phobia and current mania. The MINI also demonstrated very good specificity (>0.86 with SCID; >0.72 with CIDI) and very good positive and negative predictive values for most diagnostic categories (Sheehan et al., 1998).

COMMENT

Determining the presence of a depressive disorder requires skill and effort in gathering information about the depression and its potential causes. The most efficient method to determine the presence of a depressive disorder is, first, to screen the patient and then, if the screening is positive, to perform an in-depth clinical interview or structured interview.

ETIOLOGICAL CONSIDERATIONS

Despite the tremendous prevalence and burden of depressive disorders, the definitive etiology is not fully understood. As a result, it is perhaps the most debated topic in depression research. To date, the majority of research in this area has focused on MDD, with very little research on other unipolar conditions such as persistent depressive disorder or unspecified depressive disorders. Most scientists now believe that the pathogenesis of depressive disorders is multifaceted, resulting from a complex interaction of psychological, social, and biological factors (O'Keane, 2000). For example, stressful life events have been found to increase the risk for developing depression (Vinkers et al., 2014). However, factors such as personality traits (e.g., neuroticism; Vinkers et al., 2014), the person's coping style (Bjørkløf, Engedal, Selbæk, Kouwenhoven, & Helvik, 2013), perceived social support (Liu, Gou, & Zuo, 2016; Rueger, Malecki, Pyun, Aycock, & Coyle, 2016), and genetic makeup (Flint & Kendler, 2014) all mediate the effect that stress has on depression. A person who loses his job but has good social support and coping skills may be less likely to develop a depressive disorder than another individual facing unemployment with limited coping skills and no social support. When conceptualizing depression, clinicians should consider the intermingling of these myriad influences, rather than look to any single factor in determining the emergence of a depressive disorder. In most cases, genetics, biological and neurological differences, psychological factors, and life experiences all work together to cause depression.

FAMILIAL AND GENETIC FACTORS

Some of the most fascinating research on the etiology of depression has been the recent work on the role of genetics in mental health. With the mapping of the human genome, the prospect of clearly identifying the influence of genetics on mental health is within reach. However, with depressive disorders, the contribution of genetics may take longer to uncover than for other disorders that have already demonstrated a clear genetic and biological cause (i.e., schizophrenia). Although past evidence from twin studies has been able to demonstrate some degree of genetic involvement in the pathogenesis of depressive disorders, those links have thus far been weak.

Historically, the principal method for studying the influence of genetics on psychopathology was to compare the concordance of depression in identical twins (MZ; monozygotic twins), who originate from the same fertilized egg and are effectively genetically identical individuals, with that of fraternal twins (DZ; dizygotic), who share only half of their genes and thus are genetically similar to siblings. Because the frequency of twin births is low, genetic researchers also observe the *heritability* of depressive disorder in first-degree relatives (often parents and children). Heritability refers to the proportion of risk of developing a disease that is attributed to genetic variation. An early meta-analysis of high-quality twin studies estimated that the risk of developing MDD was 2.84 times greater among individuals with first-degree relatives with MDD (Sullivan, Neale, & Kendler, 2000). Later, a large-scale study of Swedish twins estimated the heritability of MDD at 38%, with a notable sex difference (42% heritability among women versus 29% among men; Kendler, Gatz, Gardner, & Pedersen, 2006). This suggests that overall, about two-thirds of the variance in developing depression is contributed to environmental (and not genetic) influences. Studies of mental health disorders within families also provided robust demonstrations that mood alterations, such as depressive and bipolar disorders, tend to co-occur. However, early studies of familial aggregation did not differentiate between unipolar and bipolar mood disorders. Recently, a large-scale investigation funded by the National Institute of Mental Health (Merikangas et al., 2014) examined the familial links between bipolar and depressive disorders and found that mania and MDD tend to be independently transmitted in families, suggesting these disorders may have distinct genetic pathways of inheritance.

Despite much interest in the field, identification of the genetic architecture of depression has been a slow process. Identifying a genetic link to mood is a popular idea, as molecular genetics would extend findings from earlier twin and family studies to understand the unique biology of depression, independent of environment influences. Genetics studies are able to compare depressed individuals with nondepressed controls on genetic characteristics associated with depressive disorders. While emerging research has been helpful in confirming a genetic contribution to the development of depressive disorders, to date, no single genetic variation or candidate gene has yielded robust effects for understanding depression (Flint & Kendler, 2014). Early work by Dikeos et al. (1999) studied whether the genetic location of the D3 dopamine receptor differed in patients with MDD as compared with those with no history or current MDD. The investigators observed that genotypes carrying the allele (DNA structure) associated with D3 polymorphisms were found in 75% of the MDD patients and in 50% of the controls, suggesting genetic influences in MDD. Green et al. (2010) later demonstrated an increased risk for recurrent MDD in individuals who have a variation in a gene that provides instructions to cells for making calcium channels. These channels are an important feature of cells, as they are involved in intercellular communication and generating and transmitting electrical signals, although their exact role in brain tissue is still unclear (Splawski et al., 2004). However, many other studies have not yet yielded robust or consistent evidence of a clear genetic variation in depression. Some of the most robust findings to date have been among homogeneous cases with severe forms of recurrent MDD; genetic risk factors for other unipolar depressive disorders may not be entirely the same as those identified in such stringently defined samples (CONVERGE Consortium, 2015). Most recently, Hyde et al. (2016) identified 15 genetic loci associated with MDD among individuals of European descent, and at the time of writing are examining data from a genome-wide association study. While in its infancy, this work will hopefully guide a future understanding of depression that may be used to guide risk identification and develop better treatments.

Other targets in the genetics of depression reflect the understanding that genes likely confer a susceptibility to depression through interactions with the environment. An increasingly popular framework to understand the complicated mechanisms of depression risk is *epigenetics*, which is a field in clinical genetics that seeks to understand how the expression of genes are influenced by environmental factors. Rather than relying on a simple cause-and-effect mechanism, epigenetics seeks to explain how and why certain genes are switched "on" and "off" in response to internal (e.g., stress) and external environmental cues (e.g., chemicals) (Feinberg, 2007). Emerging work has largely centered around DNA methylation, an epigenetic process that impairs gene expression (Lutz & Turecki, 2014). Recent reviews particularly highlight the focus of DNA methylation as a mediator between early adverse experiences (such as childhood maltreatment) and later emergence of depression (Heim & Binder, 2012; Lutz & Turecki, 2014). Recently, attention has been paid to understanding endophenotypes of depression, which are the inherited intermediary markers of depression. For example, one such endophenotype, the personality trait of neuroticism, has been shown to be highly heritable and implicated in the pathogenesis of depression (Goldstein & Klein, 2014). Perhaps one of the most transformative decisions regarding this emphasis was advocated by the former director of the National Institute of Mental Health (NIMH; Insel et al., 2010). The NIMH revealed the Research Domain Criteria (RDoC; https://www.nimh.nih.gov/research-priorities/rdoc/index.shtml) framework, which emphasized research revealing the brain circuitry of basic dimensions of all psychopathology (i.e., positive valence systems, negative valence systems, cognitive style, systems for social processes, and arousal/regulatory systems). Understanding these midpoints between genes and the clinical expression of depression could help scientists better understand both the genes and the pathways that are associated with depression.

The literature on the genetics of depressive disorder is still in its infancy, but has suggested a promising interplay of factors implicated in depression. At best, the literature suggests a propensity to develop these disorders but that this propensity can be offset by learning and environmental influences. Future research is needed to elucidate the specific molecular and genetic mechanisms that confer such a disposition to depression, particularly in light of environmental experiences and developmental trajectories.

NEUROANATOMY AND NEUROBIOLOGY

Recent decades have noted considerable advancement in our understanding of the neuroanatomy and biology of depression, thanks in part to advances in technology such as neuroimaging. In the quest to uncover biological markers of mental disorders, much research effort has gone into determining biological determinants of depression, with a specific focus on the brain structures that appear to be associated with depression, neurocircuitry, and neurotransmitters. However, to date, no single brain region or neurotransmitter has been definitively demonstrated as a principal cause in the pathogenesis of depression. Similarly, no laboratory test has been uncovered as a valid diagnostic tool for depressive disorders.

Neuroanatomy and Neurocircuitry   Research to localize depression in a neuroanatomical region or system is ongoing and to date remains elusive. Current theories of depression argue that several brain systems likely interact to regulate mood in response to stress, and neuroimaging studies over the past 15 or so years have investigated multiple subdivisions of the brain implicated in depression. Although alterations in numerous cortical and subcortical regions have been identified in depressive disorders (Pandya, Altinay, Malone, & Anand, 2012), we highlight four brain regions commonly associated with depression. The first is the *amygdala*, which is responsible for memory of emotional reactions to stimuli. This part of the brain interprets the emotional salience of stimuli, and when there is a threatening stimulus, it produces an emotional reaction that triggers the brain into action. Next is the *orbitofrontal cortex*, which is responsible for cognitive processing and decision-making. This part of the brain is in part responsible for putting logical meaning to the stimulus and for determining what should be done about the stimulus. The *dorsolateral prefrontal cortex* is responsible for affect regulation, planning, decision-making, intentionality, and social judgment. Finally, the *anterior cingulate cortex* is also involved with depression and is responsible for error detection, anticipation of tasks, motivation, and modulation of emotional responses. However, multiple brain structures are implicated in depressive disorders. In addition to these regions, the hippocampus, cerebellum, and basal ganglia, to name a few, have been found to be smaller in individuals with depression (Oakes, Loukas, Oskouian, & Tubbs, 2016), but it is not clear whether these are causes or effects of depression.

In addition to localized structures or regions in the brain, attention must be paid to neural circuits. Neurons do not function in isolation—rather, their complex synaptic connections compose complex circuits in the central nervous system, akin to how the individual components in an electronic device (like a smartphone or computer) work together to allow for complicated outputs. Depression is associated with alterations in the neural circuits within brain structures affected by depression, which may lead to aberrant signaling between neurons in these areas (Price & Drevets, 2010). Depressive disorders are typically characterized by disruptions in the brain's reward circuitry, which normally allow us to attend and react to rewarding and aversive stimuli in the environment. The most important alteration appears to be in the pathway between the ventral tegmental area and the nucleus accumbens, and is associated with depressive symptoms of anhedonia and cognitive distortions (for review, see Russo & Nestler, 2013). An emerging literature is also investigating the structural and functional abnormalities associated with depression in the dorsolateral prefrontal and anterior cingulate cortices. Termed the *cognitive control network*, this circuit is garnishing current attention in characterizing the underlying characteristics of a subtype of depression (i.e., characterized by apathy, difficulties with executive functioning, and pessimism; Alexopoulos et al., 2012).

These neural systems work together to help us navigate our environment. When they work well and in concert, we are able to manage or cope with most problems that come our way. When we are faced with a problem to solve, whether it is social, financial, or environmental, these systems work together to first let us know there is a problem in the environment, to assess the degree of threat the problem presents with, to modulate our emotions in reaction to the problem, to decide among a series of potential solutions to solve the problem, and then to initiate behavior to either cope with or solve the problem. When any of these systems is not working properly, whether due to brain damage, congenital anomalies, or developmental experiences, our chances of developing a depressive disorder are increased. For instance, if the mood regulation systems in the dorsolateral cortex are not working properly, they fail to regulate the emotional reaction to the problem. This failure prevents the orbitofrontal cortex from being able to create an action plan to solve the problem. What results is the tendency to avoid, rather than solve, the problem or to overreact to the problem.

Given the substantial heterogeneity in the biological factors that influence depression risk across the life span, recent attention has been paid to the neuroanatomy and circuitry of a subtype of depression in older adults. The best studied of these is the *vascular depression hypothesis*, which posits that cardiovascular disease and the resultant structural and functional changes in cerebral white matter are implicated in late-life depression (Taylor, Aizenstein, & Alexopolous, 2013). Specifically, cardiovascular disease may *predispose, precipitate,* or *perpetuate* the vulnerability to developing depression through alterations in metabolism and inflammation associated with these microvascular changes. Proponents of this hypothesis recognize that depression is clearly multifactorial, but that this may represent a neuroanatomical vulnerability among older adults with vascular disease.

Several functional imaging studies are beginning to support the role played by these neural structures and circuits in depression, but the work is still very preliminary. However, because depression is a rather heterogeneous disorder (people with the same diagnosis can have very different clinical presentations), there is not yet consensus on which structures and circuits are most pivotal in the development of depression. Furthermore, because the expense of conducting neuroimaging research is so high, the number of research participants in these studies tends to be quite small; given the heterogeneity of the illness, it is no surprise that small sample sizes across studies yield heterogeneous and thus inconclusive results. Finally, although technologies such as fMRI have revolutionized the field, caution is still warranted in interpreting results of this ever-evolving technology (Logothetis, 2008).

Neurochemistry and Transmitters   Some clinicians and researchers initially believed that depression was caused in part by deficiency in the neurotransmitters *norepinephrine, serotonin,* and/or *dopamine* in the central nervous system. Dubbed the *monoamine hypothesis of depression*, this line of thinking dominated pharmacological treatment of depression and largely focused on increasing concentrations of these three substances in the brain, such as through antidepressant medication (Goldberg, Bell, & Pollard, 2014). However, early studies contradicting this causal hypothesis showed that monoamine depletion in healthy individuals without depression did not result in depressive symptoms (Salomon, Miller, Krystal, Heninger, & Charney, 1997), nor did it worsen depression in those with MDD (Berman et al., 2002). Rather, it is more likely that the dysregulation, rather than a frank deficiency of these neurotransmitters, is implicated in depression. While antidepressant medications are widely prescribed, and use has increased over the past decade (Organisation for Economic Co-operation and Development, 2017), only half of those prescribed such medication will respond (Papakostas, 2009). Indeed, even in the largest and most rigorous study of antidepressant use, the Sequenced Treatment Alternatives to Relieve Depression (STAR*D) trial, a carefully regimented antidepressant treatment plan resulted in only 67% of the patients achieving remission, with high relapse rates (Sinyor, Schaffer, & Levitt, 2010). Thus, the exact psychotherapeutic mechanism of such treatment remains unknown. It is further unclear if the alterations in neurotransmitters associated with depression are a cause of depression or an effect of depression or a related mechanism. That is, the causal link between these substrates and clinical symptoms of depression is unclear at this time. Thus, neurotransmitters provide an important but still only partial picture of the biological origin of depression. Nonetheless, new attention is being paid to other neurotransmitters, such as the inhibitory neurotransmitter gamma aminobutyric acid (Goldberg et al., 2014) and the excitatory transmitter glutamate (Newport et al., 2015). Although these neuro-transmitters are being investigated in the development of pharmaceuticals for the treatment of depression, this work is in its infancy. Forthcoming advances in the role of such transmitters in depression will depend on demonstrations of therapeutic benefit and an understanding of the mechanism of action. Finally, growing attention is being paid to *precision medicine* in depression treatment, in which treatments are chosen based on an individual's unique genetic makeup (Bousman et al., 2017). Burgeoning evidence suggests that genetic factors play a role in an individual's response to antidepressant medication (Crisafulli et al., 2011; Tansey et al., 2013); however, the numerous gaps in the empirical evidence for this approach at present limit the clinical utility and no clear recommendations are currently in place to guide these treatment decisions. Accordingly, as research in this domain advances, it is possible that clinicians will soon have the potential to consider genetic evidence in clinical decision-making regarding psycho-pharmacological treatment of depression (for an overview, see Bousman et al. 2017).

Neuroendocrinology also adds to a more complete understanding of the biological causes of depression. The most heavily researched and well-established link in this area over the past 40 years is the overactivation of the *hypothalamic–pituitary–adrenal (HPA) axis* functioning among adults with depression (Stetler & Miller, 2011). The HPA axis is a major part of the neuroendocrine system that regulates bodily processes, including the stress response; not surprisingly, abnormal HPA axis functioning has been implicated in numerous mental disorders, most notably MDD (Zunszain, Anacker, Cattaneo, Car-valho, & Pariante, 2011). Specifically, evidence points to an overabundance of *cortisol* in the systems of patients with depression. Related to the dysregulated HPA axis function-ing of depression, systemic inflammation has been implicated as having a prime role in pathogenesis of depression, at least among a subset of individuals (Kiecolt-Glaser, Derry, & Fagundes, 2015). The relationship between depression and inflammation is likely bidirectional, in which depression contributes to proinflammatory responses (e.g., increased cytokine activity) and persistent inflammation induces depressive symptoms through multiple processes such as altered neural activity and neurotransmitter metab-olism (Kiecolt-Glaser et al., 2015). These dysregulated inflammatory processes also explain in part the relationship between depression and chronic systemic medical conditions such as diabetes mellitus, rheumatoid arthritis, and multiple sclerosis (Iwata, Ota, & Duman, 2013; Renn, Feliciano, & Segal, 2011). Evidence for such abnormalities not only yields a more complete understanding of causation but may also aid in the development of more effective drug treatments. Ultimately, these neurophysiological and genetic models of depression may be most meaningful in regards to how they contribute to alterations in affective regulation (Forest, 2016).

Psychological Factors

In addition to the biological factors reviewed in the preceding sections, behavioral, social, and environmental influences have been strongly implicated in the development of depression. Typically, a biological or psychological vulnerability interacts with exposure to adversity or other stressors to precipitate the onset of a depressive episode, as per the ubiquitous biopsychosocial perspective. Psychological variables are those mechanisms that mediate the interaction of genetic predispositions and adverse experiences in depression. A review of the literature suggests that depressive disorders appear to be related to four psychological variables:

1. People's cognitive appraisals of themselves, their lives, and others (Abramson et al., 1989; Beck, Rush, Shaw, & Emery, 1979).
2. Whether people proactively solve problems or avoid them (D'Zurilla & Nezu, 1999).
3. The degree to which proactive attempts to cope with stress have been successful (Folkman & Lazarus, 1988).
4. An individual's learning history (i.e., life experiences), which could lead to the development of depressive symptoms or serve to maintain depression/dysphoria.

In the above paradigm, people who have negative expectations about their ability to cope with problems generally acquire these expectations through past learning experiences (factor 1 in the list). Uncontrollable stress may lead to repeated failed attempts to effectively solve problems (factor 2). Over time, this may leave a person feeling hopeless and helpless, which may lead to the individual abandoning their usual methods for solving problems, putting them at risk of developing depression (factor #3; Seligman, Weiss, Weinraub, & Schulman, 1980). Taken together, these factors— cognitive attributions, experiences with problem-solving, coping skills, and learned helplessness—all contribute to one's learning history (factor 4) and are predictive of depression.

Cognitive theories of depression posit that maladaptive cognitions, or thought patterns, contribute to the onset and maintenance of depression. Beck et al. (1979) proposed that depression is a result of specific cognitive distortions, which are faulty, incorrect, and/or maladaptive thinking patterns. Notably, Beck (1987) postulated the *cognitive triad of depression* typified by negativistic views about oneself, the world, and the future. It follows that people with negative expectations or cognitive vulnerabilities are more likely to develop depression when faced with a stressor than are people who do not possess such risk factors. Another major cognitive model of depression, the *hopeless model* (Abramson et al., 1989) proposes that depression results after repeated expectations and experiences of a negative outcome of an event. Individuals with a tendency to make negative inferences after such a negative outcome are more prone to depression. Such hopelessness might be a particularly early and potent symptom among certain subgroups of individuals with depression—those with negative inferential styles who experience a negative life event (Iacoviello, Alloy, Abramson, Choi, & Morgan, 2013). Another cognitive style, *upward counterfactual thinking* or the ruminative tendency to compare oneself to an imagined better version of oneself, has recently been subjected to meta-analytic review (Broomhall, Phillips, Hine, & Loi, 2017). This thinking style was found to be reliably associated with depressive symptoms among a wide array of study samples. Taken together, people with negative perceptions of themselves and their environment are at risk for becoming depressed, particularly when faced with repeated experiences of failure or other adversity.

A failure to effectively cope with diverse types of stressors has also been associated with depression. Most research has found that people who use active forms of coping, such as problem-solving, are less likely to develop depression than are people who use passive forms of coping, such as avoidance or emotion-focused coping (e.g., self-blame) (Lazarus, 1991). Much of this research has investigated coping in the context of adjustment to chronic and debilitating physical conditions, such as hemodialysis (Welch & Austin, 2001), diabetes mellitus (Thorpe et al., 2013), and cardiopulmonary disease

(Hundt et al., 2015), and coping has been strongly and consistently linked with outcomes such as depression across a wide variety of physical health conditions (Dempster, Howell, & McCorry, 2015). Among adults aged 60 years and older, active and religious coping strategies have demonstrated a consistent protective association in relation to depression, contributing to fewer symptoms of depression in this population (Bjørkløf et al., 2013). At the opposite end of the life span, teenagers with depression appear to engage in slightly less problem-solving than their nondepressed peers, but rely much more heavily on maladaptive avoidant and emotion-focused coping (Horwitz, Hill, & King, 2011). Although the literature is replete with the benefits of active coping and the depressogenic associations with emotional/avoidant styles of coping, new research is shifting to emphasize the role of *coping flexibility*, rather than specific coping strategies *per se*, on the risk of depressive symptoms (Kato, 2015). This flexibility refers to one's ability to rely on diverse coping strategies in response to stressful life changes. By allowing the individual to better adapt to an ever-changing environment, this variability in coping behaviors is thought to promote psychological adjustment and perhaps protect against the onset of depressive symptoms in response to external events.

Related to coping, *rumination*, a repetitive pattern of thoughts and behaviors focused on one's depressed state, has been consistently linked with the onset and maintenance of depression (Watkins & Nolen-Hoeksema, 2014). This cognitive process is akin to problem-solving gone awry, such that it becomes difficult to find good solutions to problems and may lead to avoidance or even immobilization. Worse yet, this process can result in a depressogenic cycle, in which people who become depressed begin to ruminate, which further exacerbates their symptomatology and interferes with their thinking and problem-solving. Longitudinal evidence supports this pattern, with rumination put forth as a robust mechanism linking stressful life events with the onset of depressive symptoms (Michl, McLaughlin, Shepherd, & Nolen-Hoeksema, 2013).

An interaction between cognitive styles, adverse events, and one's repertoire of coping behaviors likely precipitate and/or aggravate depression. Several studies have supported this interaction in learned helplessness (Seligman & Maier, 1967). Originally, these theories were tested in animal models, where unsolvable problems were presented to animals and all attempts to solve the problem were met with unpleasant consequences, such as an electric shock. After repeated attempts to solve the problem failed, these animals would exhibit depressogenic behavior—withdrawal, acting as if they were in pain—and, even after a solution was presented to them, the animals would refuse to try the solution (Altenor, Volpicelli, & Seligman, 1979). Over the last four decades, scientists have been able to draw a relationship between learned helplessness and depression in research with people (Maier & Seligman, 2016; Seligman, 1974; Simson & Weiss, 1988). For example, patients who had suffered a stroke were more likely to have clinically significant depressive symptoms if they reported helplessness associated with their physical condition (van Mierlo, van Heugten, Post, de Kort, & Visser-Meily, 2015).

Behavioral mechanisms and environmental contingencies may also play a role in the development of depression. Since the 1970s there has been a tremendous amount of interest in investigating the role that behavioral principles play in the development of depression. Ferster's (1973) functional analysis of depressive behaviors postulated that individuals with depression did not engage in enough positive and fulfilling activities, thus leading to insufficient positive reinforcement for those activities. The individual with depression may even avoid activities or responsibilities. Lewinsohn (1974) expanded upon this theory, emphasizing depression as the result of low levels of positive reinforcement. This lack of reinforcement may be due to loss of reinforcement effectiveness, or because the reinforcer is no longer available or accessible to the individual. This loss of reinforcement that a person would usually obtain from a goal-directed behavior leads to less engagement in those types of behaviors in the future, eventually leading to withdrawal and isolation. According to this model, depression results from either a decrease in pleasant events or an increase in unpleasant events and speaks to the importance of considering context in the development of depression (Jacobson, Martell, & Dimidjian, 2001).

Jacobson et al. (2001) developed the behavioral activation model (which grew from these theories and further developed them), emphasizing that when life is less rewarding or stressful, people sometimes pull away from the world around them and find that basic routines in their life become disrupted. This disruption in routines can increase depressive symptoms and make it difficult to solve life problems effectively. In turn, this can lead to secondary problems (e.g., difficulties in relationships or occupational duties), which maintain or further exacerbate depression. Support for these models is strong and can be found in the depression treatment literature.

LIFE EVENTS

The literature is replete with data indicating that stressful life events contribute to the development of a depressive episode. Indeed, depression rarely, if ever, develops when one is on a pleasant vacation, with no particular environmental stress. Although not everyone who faces difficult problems develops depression, it is evident to many clinicians that prolonged exposure to psychosocial stress can precipitate a depressive episode. In fact, cumulative exposure to stress, ranging from childhood maltreatment, to major life events, to daily hassles, has been empirically linked to depressive symptoms and MDD in adulthood (Vinkers et al., 2014). Several studies have found that most depressive episodes are preceded by a severe life event or difficulty in the 6 months before onset of the episode (Kendler & Gardner, 2010). However, earlier exposure to such adversity can have long-lasting consequences. The Adverse Childhood Experience (ACE) study, conducted by the Centers for Disease Control and Prevention and Kaiser Permanente health organization, was one of the largest investigations of childhood abuse, neglect, and other adverse events. Such data, from over 17,000 individuals, demonstrated a tremendous association, such that 54% of the population attributable risk of a current episode of depression was attributable to childhood maltreatment (Felitti & Anda, 2014). Put more simply, current cases of depression would decrease by more than half if exposure to this risk factor were eliminated. Such early adversity not only influences onset of depression, but has deleterious effects for prognosis. For example, adults with MDD were found to have a less favorable course of depression if they had experienced childhood emotional and/or physical neglect, independent of sociodemographic variables (Paterniti, Sterner, Caldwell, & Bisserbe, 2017). Our current understanding of this phenomenon is that, in part, early experiences interact dynamically with the developing brain to actually modify neural architecture (Fox, Levitt, & Nelson, 2010).

In addition to the sensitive period in childhood development, there are also life stages that are differentially associated with onset of depression. Pregnancy is an increased time of vulnerability for developing a depressive disorder. While hormonal and other physiologic changes are inherent in the ante- and perinatal periods, the life changes associated with pregnancy seem to impart a particularly vulnerable time for onset or remission of depressive disorder. While exact risk factors are still unknown, a recent review of the extant literature suggests that psychosocial factors, such as lack of social support, personal history of abuse, an unplanned or unwanted pregnancy, adverse events and/or high perceived stress, and pregnancy complications or loss, are associated with a greater likelihood of antenatal depression (Biaggi, Conroy, Pawlby, & Pariante, 2016). At the end of their reproductive years, mounting evidence has also suggested that women experience an increased vulnerability to MDD during and immediately after menopause that is not accounted for by changes in reproductive hormones (Bromberger et al., 2011).

As discussed in detail in the section on "Psychological Factors", the interaction of negative life events, coping skills, and attributions about coping skills influences whether a person will experience depression. Referred to as the *diathesis-stress model* (Robins & Block, 1989), a person with a predisposing vulnerability to developing depression (e.g., family history of depression) will be more likely to experience a depressive episode when experiencing a significant stressor than an individual without such diathesis. Because depression is a multifaceted disorder, it is difficult to pinpoint the specific role life events have on the development of a depressive disorder. Most people will have to face severe life stress at some point in their lives, yet not everyone develops depression. How individuals view severe life events and the perceived amount of control they have over the situation both play an important role in determining their vulnerability to depression. Furthermore, social well-being and social support likely serve as a buffer against adverse reactions to stressful life events. The literature consistently demonstrates that greater perceived social support is associated with few depressive symptoms, but it is difficult to determine if poor social support is a cause or effect of depression (and the resultant strain on interpersonal relationships; Ibarra-Rovillard & Kuiper, 2011). Nonetheless, support systems give an individual external support when internal coping skills are put to the test. Without the external support, however, an individual must rely exclusively on his or her own internal resources, which under severe duress might not be entirely effective. Therefore, although negative life events do influence the occurrence of depressive disorders, the social and psychological resources available to the person facing the stressful life event generally mediate the impact on mood.

Gender, Race, and Ethnicity

Many researchers have been trying to determine the reasons for the discrepant rates of depressive disorders across gender and racial-ethnic lines. Are the reasons genetic or biological? Is it that these populations are exposed to more stress and have fewer resources to cope with stress and therefore are more vulnerable than socially privileged groups in the US, such as men and those of European descent? Or is depression presented differently across these groups, meaning that the estimates in the prevalence for depressive disorders in these populations are inaccurate? Mental health researchers are still struggling with these questions and have only been able to give a partial explanation of why the discrepancy exists.

Some theorists believe that the reason racial and ethnic minorities have differing rates of depressive disorder is that they present symptoms of depression differently than do White Americans (Haroz et al., 2017). Many researchers have spent years trying to discern the most appropriate way to assess depression in different cultures. Although research from the WHO indicates that depression is similar across cultures, how people from one culture report the symptoms and their cultural attitude about mental health (and its treatment) can cloud diagnoses. Screening instruments and scales that were developed for White populations can be problematic if they are simply translated without regard to translation bias. Additionally, many studies have found that the factor structures and reliabilities of these instruments tend to differ across ethnic groups, indicating that groups vary in their reports of depressive symptoms (Azocar, Areán, Miranda, & Muñoz, 2001). For instance, lower rates of depression in Asian Americans may be attributable to their tendency to under-report affective symptoms of depression and to rely more on somatic presentation (Kalibatseva, Leong, & Ham, 2014). Similarly, adult Hispanic primary care patients with both depression and co-occurring chronic disease were found to endorse high levels of somatic complaints, suggesting that these symptoms may cloud one's ability to detect depression in this population (Chong, Reinschmidt, & Moreno, 2010).

The epidemiological data suggest that ethnic and racial minorities evidence lower rates of depressive disorders than non-Hispanic White individuals (see the "Epidemiology" section). However, this has been called a paradox, given the differential exposure to stressors among these minority groups compared with Whites. Ethnic and racial minority groups, such as African Americans and Hispanics/Latinos, are more likely to be impoverished and to have to cope with financial and urban stress (Alexopoulos, 2005). Studies have demonstrated that socioeconomic status and exposure to trauma related to racism, urban living, and financial strain are correlated with depression and other mental disorders such as anxiety and substance abuse (Caron & Liu, 2010; Gottlieb, Waitzkin, & Miranda, 2011; Kiima & Jenkins, 2010; Rhodes et al., 2010). However, other studies have found that the rates for depression in middle-class and affluent racial/ethnic minorities are more similar to the national rates of depression than to those of middle-class and affluent White Americans. These studies suggest there may be complex risk and protective factors at play, including the intersection of racial and ethnic identity with socioeconomic status and community, cultural, and sociopolitical factors (e.g., social support, religiosity, immigration policies, health-seeking norms and stigma). The question remains whether marginalized populations, such as those with lower socioeconomic status or who identify as racial/ethnic minorities, truly have lower rates of depressive disorder. Perhaps this paradox is a reflection of systemic biases in our prevalence estimates, including differential symptom presentation (e.g., somatic, rather than affective symptoms), lower utilization rates of both mental and general health care, or other sampling artifacts (e.g., reliance on noninstitutionalized populations). It is critical that more research with these marginalized groups is conducted to inform practice and policy, particularly as the US becomes increasingly diverse.

The differing rate of depressive disorders between men and women is an interesting yet complicated finding. Researchers initially thought that the different prevalence rates resulted from reluctance on the part of men to admit feelings of depression, as well as men's tendency to cope with stress through substance use (Shorey et al., 2011). Others suggest that the increased prevalence of depression in women is because women tend to be victims of sexual abuse and therefore suffer a significant psycho-social stressor that is not as common in men (Gaudiano & Zimmerman, 2010; Ghassemi, Sadeghi, Asadollahi, Yousefy, & Mallik, 2010; Plaza et al., 2010). Still others suggest that the greater willingness of women versus men to seek treatment services might account for the difference in prevalence (Fikretoglu, Liu, Pedlar, & Brunet, 2010; Pattyn, Verhaeghe, & Bracke, 2015). However, because the discrepancy between men and women seems to be universal, others claim that hormonal and biological differences account for the differential prevalence rates. Whatever the differential effect, the fact remains that depression is more commonly reported in women than in men, and this issue still needs to be resolved.

COURSE AND PROGNOSIS

Research has begun to identify variables that can help to predict better or worse course and outcome for depressive disorders, but a great deal of uncertainty still exists. Here we present the descriptive data regarding length, severity, and prognosis of depressive disorders.

COURSE

Beyond the basic diagnostic criteria, MDD has several delineating features. Early-onset depression tends to appear before age 20 and has a more malignant course than late-onset depression (Devanand et al., 2004; Papakostas, Crawford, Scalia, & Fava, 2007). It is also associated with a family history of depression (Bergemann & Boles, 2010). Late-onset depression tends to emerge in the mid-to-late-30s and is associated with fewer recurrent episodes, comorbid personality disorders, and substance abuse disorders relative to early-onset depression (Chui, Cheung, & Lam, 2011; Vandeleur et al., 2017). However, there is a much greater variation in the age of onset with depression than in disorders such as schizophrenia. For example, in a recent study by Vandeleur et al. (2017), the age of onset was found to be tied to whether the person has had a single episode or recurrent episodes, such that single episodes seemed to be tied to a later onset (average age: $M = 38.6$, $SD = 11.0$ years), whereas recurrent episodes seem to have a significantly earlier onset (average age: $M = 27.6$, $SD = 10.7$ years). Second, the course of MDD tends to be time-limited. The average episode lasts 6 months, although this varies greatly from person to person (Rhebergen et al., 2010). Third, MDD tends to be a recurrent disorder. Patients who have one MDE have a 36.7% chance of experiencing a second; those who have two previous episodes have a 48% chance of developing a third episode. With each additional episode, chances for another additional episode increase by approximately 15% (Seemuller et al., 2010).

Persistent depressive disorder is a more chronic, long-lasting disorder. The mean duration of what was previously referred to as dysthymic disorder in the *DSM-IV* is 30 years. Given that the symptom presentation for persistent depressive disorder has not changed much, it is thought that this statistic still holds for the newer persistent depressive disorder category. Almost half of those patients who were previously classified as having dysthymic disorder will develop an MDE in their lifetimes (Rhebergen et al., 2010). Those with persistent depressive disorder (pure dysthymic syndrome) have been found to have worse clinical prognosis than people with either MDD or depressive disorder, not otherwise specified (NOS, now classified as other specified or unspecified depressive disorder) and are as disabled as those with MDD (Griffiths, Ravindran, Merali, & Anisman, 2000). Thankfully, persistent depressive disorder (pure dysthymic syndrome) is responsive to both psychotherapy and medication treatment, at least in the short term, with some studies suggesting that the most robust intervention is a combination of psychotherapy and medication (Barrett et al., 2001). However, some data suggest that few people with persistent depressive disorder ever receive treatment. Fewer than half will ever receive any kind of mental health treatment unless they have also experienced an MDE (Rhebergen et al., 2010). Notably, these rates may be shifting, as Vandeler et al. (2017) reported that 68.5% of their sample of those diagnosed with persistent depressive disorder with pure dysthymia were treatment-seeking and 82.5% of those with persistent depressive disorder with persistent MDE were treatment-seeking.

PROGNOSIS

Early diagnosis and treatment with psychotherapy or medication, or both, result in a better chance of recovery from MDD, persistent depressive disorder (pure dysthymic syndrome or with persistent MDE), and other specified or unspecified depressive disorder (depression NOS) (Rhebergen et al., 2010). The ease of recovery from depression, however, is related to several factors. Prognosis is best when the person is facing few stressful life events (Sherrington, Hawton, Fagg, Andrew, & Smith, 2001) and has a solid support network on which to rely (Rubenstein et al., 2007). Furthermore, individuals with an initial early recovery are less likely to develop recurring symptoms. Early improvements indicate that the patient has access to coping mechanisms that allow for a quick recovery, and this often suggests an overall positive long-term prognosis. The prognosis for persistent depressive disorder (pure dysthymic syndrome) is less certain. For example, Ciechanowski et al. (2004) demonstrated a 50% reduction at the end of a 12-month period in depressive symptoms and functional improvement using problem-solving therapy in home-based intervention for older adults with medical illnesses, minor depression, and persistent depressive disorder (pure dysthymic syndrome). However, Klein, Shankman, & Rose (2006) found that adults with persistent depressive disorder (pure dysthymic syndrome) improved at a much slower rate and were more symptomatic at a 10-year follow-up than were individuals with MDD. As of this writing, few treatment studies have demonstrated any long-lasting positive effect of any intervention for persistent depressive disorder (pure dysthymic syndrome).

Comorbidity is another important factor in the prognosis of depressive disorders, and as previously noted, comorbidity usually complicates the diagnosis, treatment, and recovery process. For example, persistent depressive disorder with persistent MDE has been found to be highly comorbid with anxiety disorders and substance abuse/dependence. This comorbidity was more frequently observed in those with persistent depressive disorder with persistent MDE than in those diagnosed with either a single episode of MDE or any of the other specified depressive disorders (Vandaleur et al., 2017). The prognosis of those with dual diagnoses is much poorer than those with single disorders.

Another factor involved in the prognosis for both MDD and persistent depressive disorder is level of self-esteem. A higher self-esteem predicts an increasingly positive prognosis (Sherrington et al., 2001). Poor self-esteem, on the other hand, predicts a longer and more delayed recovery. The prognosis of depressive disorders is poor when they have an early onset, there is a premorbid personality disorder, and there has been a previous episode (Ryder, Quilty, Vachon, & Bagby, 2010). More intensive and extended treatment can improve the remission and maintenance of remission from MDD episodes, even with high severity of the depression, although the evidence on persistent depressive disorder is limited.

In general, the extant data suggest that a host of pharmacological treatments (called antidepressant medications) and a variety of psychotherapies are effective in treating depression. The next section briefly summarizes the available treatments.

TREATMENT

Most people seeking mental health care prefer psychosocial interventions (e.g., psychotherapy, case management; McHugh, Whitton, Peckham, Welge, & Otto, 2013), including vulnerable or traditionally underserved populations such as older adults (Raue, Weinberger, Sirey, Meyers, & Bruce, 2011), military veterans (Quiñones et al., 2014), and Hispanic individuals (Fernandez y Garcia, Franks, Jerant, Bell, & Kravitz, 2011). Such interventions have a robust evidence base for treating depressive disorders and have demonstrated effectiveness across decades of study, with no difference across treatments (see the following for reviews: Cuijpers, 2017; Cuijpers et al., 2014a; Renn & Areán, 2017). Although evidence-based psychotherapy demonstrates equivalent outcomes in depression, many theoretical perspectives have offered their own psychological framework for understanding the emergence of depressive disorders and a corresponding model of psychotherapy.

The behavioral mechanisms discussed in the section on "Etiology", along with Beck's cognitive theory, provide the foundation for modern-day cognitive behavioral therapy (CBT; Beck, 2011) and related treatments such as behavioral activation (BA; Jacobson et al., 2001) and so-called "third-wave" CBT models such as acceptance and commitment therapy (ACT; Hayes, Strosahl, & Wilson, 2012). In addition to cognitive and behavioral frameworks of depression, discussed earlier, other psychotherapies have demonstrated efficacy and inform the evidence base for improving depression. It is worth noting the particular effectiveness of interpersonal therapy (IPT; Klerman, Weissman, Rounsaville, & Chevron, 1984) and problem-solving treatment (PST; D'Zurilla & Goldfried, 1971) as structured, short-term approaches to treating depression. IPT draws on psychodynamic and attachment theory and focuses specifically on interpersonal issues thought to contribute to depression. Combined with biological and other biopsychosocial vulnerabilities, IPT conceptualizes the genesis of depression as arising from an interaction of acute interpersonal crisis and inadequate social support. PST is another short-term treatment based on the belief that depression arises from ineffective problem-solving, which results in negative emotions and loss of self-efficacy. Finally, models of psychoanalytic and psychodynamic psychotherapies highlight the role of early developmental factors and unconscious processes. For example, an excessive neediness and dependence resulting from early developmental difficulties may predispose an individual to depression in response to a loss of relationship (Freud, 1905). More contemporary psychodynamic models of depression assert that the heart of depressive symptoms lies in the loss of a goal or relationship, and/or a painful gap between the ideal and actual self (Freud, 1914). Coupled with insufficient or exhausted coping or defense mechanisms, depression is a universal reaction in the face of such helplessness (Luyten & Blatt, 2012). Psychodynamic models of depression have garnered increasing attention, with a surge in the number of randomized controlled trials demonstrating the efficacy of these treatment approaches (e.g., short-term psychodynamic psychotherapy for depression; Driessen et al., 2015).

While a thorough review of treatment of depression is beyond the scope of this chapter, suffice it to say that psychological and biological mechanisms are strongly implicated in the genesis, maintenance, and treatment of depressive disorders (see Simon & Ciechanowski, 2015, for a review of treatment of unipolar major depression in adults). Work is ongoing to inform the most efficacious and effective treatments based on these key mechanisms. In addition to psychotherapy, a host of pharmacological treatments, namely two classes of antidepressant medications (selective serotonin reuptake inhibitors [SSRIs] and serotonin–norepinephrine reuptake inhibitors [SNRIs]), are also known to have reasonable effectiveness for MDD (Khan et al., 2012), and many newer medications are under development (e.g., ketamine; see Kirby, 2015 for overview). Psychotherapy is about as effective as pharmacotherapy for depression (Cuijpers, 2017); however, combined treatment is superior to either psychotropic medication or psychotherapy alone for MDD (Cuijpers et al., 2014b). With the advent of new technologies to support both our understanding of the genesis of depression, and to improve the implementation and reach of effective treatments for depression, the future of the treatment of depressive disorders remains optimistic.

CASE STUDIES

Major Depression

Case Identification   Rowena (a pseudonym) was a single, 32-year-old, obese African American woman who self-referred to mental health services for what she called a "depression, like a dark cloud hanging over me."

Presenting Complaints   Before seeking services, Rowena had contemplated getting gastric bypass surgery and was extremely unhappy with her employment. She was managing several large projects for the company she worked for and thought that she was the only member of her staff who was doing any work. She further perceived that she was not trusted to do her job, was not respected for the work she did, and was being taken for granted. She was also concerned about getting the surgery, because she would need recovery time and would be unable to care for her family members. Her symptoms included feeling dysphoric nearly all day, every day, for the past 12 months; feeling a lack of interest in her usual activities (in this case walking and attending a weight-loss program); and increased irritability. For the past 12 months, she also reported experiencing insomnia, increased appetite, feelings of worthlessness, and hopelessness about the future. She reported feelings of guilt, believed that she was being punished, and constantly worried that she was not doing enough for her family. In addition, she reported having difficulty concentrating and making decisions. Although she had occasionally felt that she would be better off dead, she was not actively suicidal. She did not feel that suicide was an option and had no plan to harm herself.

History   Rowena was the younger of two female siblings from the northwestern region of the US. As a child, she did not have time for friends, because she was often caring for her sick mother. She was a good student but had dropped out of high school to care for her mother. Her father had left her mother and moved out of state shortly before her mother became ill. Rowena had a large extended family but felt the loss of a father figure acutely. Her uncle had problems with drugs and was incarcerated. Subsequently, Rowena took on the care of her younger niece and nephews. As an adult, Rowena had success in school (she was able to achieve her GED and was successfully taking college courses) and in her work, but remained socially isolated. She believed that she had suffered from depression twice before in her adult life but had always been able to overcome the depression on her own. However, she had often turned to food for comfort and was suffering from obesity. She explained that she had never sought help for her depression before because she was busy caring for her family and did not take time for herself. Furthermore, she indicated that it was not like her to talk with someone about her feelings. She believed her mother was depressed following the loss of her husband and subsequent medical problems but was unsure of these facts, because these issues were never discussed.

Assessment   Rowena presents with several interesting issues related to depression. First, she reports having all nine of the classic symptoms of depression, six of them for more than a year; she also reports having these symptoms nearly every day and that they are impairing her ability to function at work and socially. Rowena also indicates having had two previous depressive episodes that remitted without active treatment, and that her mother may have suffered from depression as well. Based on this assessment, Rowena met criteria for major depressive disorder, recurrent type.

PERSISTENT DEPRESSIVE DISORDER

Case Identification   Bill was a retired, 55-year-old non-Hispanic White man who sought services for depression after a doctor recommended he talk to a mental health professional.

Presenting Complaints   Bill stated that for the past 3 years, he occasionally felt worthless, depressed, and irritable. He reported that on some days, he found it difficult to get himself going to complete his chores for the day but would somehow manage to do so. He indicated that he was unsure of whether he needed treatment, because he had "good days," but upon further probing he reported that these days were infrequent (no more than 1 or 2 days per week). Although he said he and his wife did not have marital problems, he felt guilty that she worked and he did not. The primary symptoms he complained about were sadness, lack of energy, and feelings of worthlessness and guilt.

History   Bill was the oldest of five children in his family and was currently married with three children, all of whom were grown and living in other parts of the country. He completed high school and trade school afterward. He had been employed with one construction company his entire adult life. He had no serious health problems other than chronic pain resulting from a back injury. Bill retired because the back injury prevented him from performing his job. Three years ago, his wife took on a part-time job to make extra money, and Bill began looking after the house, although he really can't do much physically. Prior to this visit, he had never sought mental health services, nor had he ever felt significantly depressed.

Assessment   Bill presents with some classic symptoms of persistent depressive disorder (dysthymia). He reports having a depressed mood more days than not for more than the required 2-year period. He denied a history of manic episodes and did not meet criteria for an MDE during this 2-year period. He also met the two or more additional symptom requirements, which included his symptoms of lack of energy and low self-esteem. Although Bill reported brief periods in which he felt "good," these symptom-free periods only occurred, on average, 1–2 days per week, and therefore he met the additional specification of not having been symptom-free for more than 2 months at a time during the current episode. Based on our assessment, Bill met criteria for a diagnosis of persistent depressive disorder, late onset, with pure dysthymic syndrome.

UNSPECIFIED DEPRESSIVE DISORDER

Case Identification   Tia was a 40-year-old Mexican American woman who was referred by her physician for treatment of depression. According to the physician, Tia was struggling with placing her mother in a nursing home, and this struggle made Tia quite depressed. The physician indicated that Tia had a recent diagnosis of hyperthyroidism and was being treated with medication.

Presenting Complaints   Tia stated that she had been feeling "down in the dumps" for several months, ever since her mother had become more frail and Tia began trying to find a nursing home for her. Her primary complaints were feeling dysphoric nearly all day, every day; feeling slowed down; and having trouble with concentration. She also indicated that having had a recent diagnosis of hyperthyroidism complicated matters for her and that she had been unable to take her medication regularly.

History   Tia was an only child who was living with her mother at the time of referral. She had a college education and had been employed as an administrative assistant for 10 years. She was divorced with no children. Tia indicated that she had been her mother's caregiver for most of her life and that they had a "love/hate" relationship. Her mother was reportedly being verbally abusive to Tia regarding the placement, making Tia feel guilty. Tia indicated that she would normally be able to let her mother's abuse roll off her back, having long ago accepted that her mother was a difficult person. However, the last 4 months were hard to cope with, even though she had a good caseworker helping her, and her mother would be placed in a pleasant assisted-living facility within the next month.

Assessment/Treatment   After consideration of her symptoms, Tia's symptoms did not appear to meet full criteria for MDD, but it was clear to the clinician that a depressive disorder was present. What was unclear was whether the depression was primary, whether her medical symptoms were the cause of the depression, or whether the client's depressive symptoms were related to a psychosocial stressor. Thus, a diagnosis of unspecified depressive disorder was assigned.

Tia was encouraged to start taking her medication for hyperthyroidism and was educated about the known link between thyroid problems and depressive symptoms. Tia and her clinician agreed to meet again in 2 weeks. At that meeting, Tia reported that her mother had been placed in the assisted-living facility and that while Tia felt guilty for a few days, she found that her mother was actually quite happy at the facility, getting the assistance and attention she needed. She also reported taking the medication regularly and stated she already felt much better ("like my old self"), although she was still somewhat symptomatic with occasional sadness and poor energy. Now that her mother had been successfully placed, Tia indicated that she would like to work on rebuilding her social life.

SUMMARY

Depressive disorders are common and widely studied. Given the extent of our knowledge of MDD and what was previously classified as dysthymic disorder, research continues to address the best means of recognizing depression, how to treat depression in different settings, across different age groups and in different cultures, and further clarification of the etiology of these disorders. The causes and symptoms of depressive disorders are extremely variable and multifaceted. The causes include varying combinations of biopsychosocial factors, and the expressions of depression vary from short, severe episodes to chronic symptomatology. Because of the immense complexity of the depressive disorders, further research will aid in the ability to tailor diagnosis and treatment to each particular manifestation, to better address these disorders with medical comorbidities, and to explore cross-cultural concerns in assessment and treatment.

REFERENCES

Abramson, L. Y., Metalsky, G. I., & Alloy, L. B. (1989). Hopelessness depression: A theory-based subtype of depression. *Psychological Review*, 96(2), 358–372.

Alderete, E., Vega, W. A., Kolody, B., & Aguilar-Gaxiola, S. (1999). Depressive symptomatology: Prevalence and psychosocial risk factors among Mexican migrant farmworkers in California. *Journal of Community Psychology*, 27(4), 457–471.

Aldao, A., Nolen-Hoeksema, S., & Schweizer, S. (2010). Emotion-regulation strategies across psychopathology: A meta-analytic review. *Clinical Psychology Review, 30*, 217–237.

Alegría, M., Canino, G., Shrout, P. E., Woo, M., Duan, N., Vila, D., . . . Meng, X. L. (2008a). Prevalence of mental illness in immigrant and non-immigrant US Latino groups. *American Journal of Psychiatry, 165*(3), 359–369.

Alegría, M., Chatterji, P., Wells, K., Cao, Z., Chen, C., Takeuchi, D., . . . Meng, X. (2008b). Disparity in depression treatment among racial and ethnic minority populations in the United States. *Psychiatric Services, 59*(11), 1264–1272.

Alegría, M., Takeuchi, D., Canino, G., Duan, N., Shrout, P., Meng, X. L., . . . Gong, F. (2004). Considering context, place, and culture: The National Latino and Asian American Study. *International Journal of Methods in Psychiatric Research, 13*(4), 208–220.

Alexopoulos, G. S. (2005). Depression in the elderly. *Lancet, 365*(9475), 1961–1970.

Alexopoulos, G. S., Hoptman, M. J., Kanellopoulos, D., Murphy, C. F., Lim, K. O., & Gunning, F. M. (2012). Functional connectivity in the cognitive control network and the default mode network in late-life depression. *Journal of Affective Disorders, 139*(1), 56–65.

Ali, S., Stone, M. A., Peters, J. L., Davies, M. J., & Khunti, K. (2006). The prevalence of co-morbid depression in adults with Type 2 diabetes: A systematic review and meta-analysis. *Diabetic Medicine, 23*(11), 1165–1173.

Alloy, L. B., Abramson, L. Y., Whitehouse, W. G., Hogan, M. E., Tashman, N. A., Steinberg, D. L., . . . Donovan, P. (2000). The Temple-Wisconsin Cognitive Vulnerability to Depression Project: Lifetime history of axis I psychopathology in individuals at high and low cognitive risk for depression. *Abnormal Psychology, 109*(3), 403–418.

Altenor, A., Volpicelli, J. R., & Seligman, M. E. (1979). Debilitated shock escape is produced by both short- and long-duration inescapable shock: Learned helplessness versus learned inactivity. *Bulletin of the Psychomonic Society, 14*(5), 337–339.

American Psychiatric Association. (2000). *Diagnostic and statistical manual of mental disorders* (4th ed., text rev.). Washington, DC: Author.

American Psychiatric Association. (2013). *Diagnostic and statistical manual of mental disorders* (5th ed.). Arlington, VA: American Psychiatric Publishing.

Andrus, B. M., Blizinsky, K., Vedell, P. T., Dennis, K., Shukla, P. K., Schaffer, D. J., . . . Redei, E. E. (2012). Gene expression patterns in the hippocampus and amygdala of endogenous depression and chronic stress models. *Molecular Psychiatry, 17*, 49–61.

Ansseau, M., Dierick, M., Buntinkx, F., Cnockaert, P., De Smedt, J., Van Den Haute, M., & Vander Mijnsbrugge, D. (2004). High prevalence of mental disorders in primary care. *Journal of Affective Disorders, 78*(1), 49–55.

Areán, P. A., & Reynolds, C. F., 3rd. (2005). The impact of psychosocial factors on late-life depression. *Biological Psychiatry, 58*(4), 277–282.

Arroll, B., Goodyear-Smith, F., Crengle, S., Gunn, J., Kerse, N., Fishman, T., . . . Hatcher, S. (2010). Validation of PHQ-2 and PHQ-9 to screen for major depression in the primary care population. *Annals of Family Medicine, 8*(4), 348–353.

Azocar, F., Areán, P., Miranda, J., & Muñoz, R. F. (2001). Differential item functioning in a Spanish translation of the Beck Depression Inventory. *Journal of Clinical Psychology, 57*(3), 355–365.

Barrett, J. E., Williams, J. W., Jr., Oxman, T. E., Frank, E., Katon, W., Sullivan, M., . . . Sengupta, A. S. (2001). Treatment of dysthymia and minor depression in primary care: A randomized trial in patients aged 18 to 59 years. *Journal of Family Practice, 50*(5), 405–412.

Barros-Loscertales, A., Ventura-Campos, N., Sanjuan-Tomas, A., Belloch, V., Parcet, M. A., & Avila, C. (2010). Behavioral activation system modulation on brain activation during appetitive and aversive stimulus processing. *Social Cognitive and Affective Neuroscience, 5*(1), 18–28.

Beck, A. T. (1961). A systematic investigation of depression. *Comprehensive Psychiatry, 2*, 163–170.

Beck, A. T. (1987). Cognitive therapy. In J. K. Zeig (Ed.), *The evolution of psychotherapy* (pp. 149–178). New York, NY: Brunner/Mazel.

Beck, A. T., Guth, D., Steer, R. A., & Ball, R. (1997). Screening for major depression disorders in medical inpatients with the Beck Depression Inventory for Primary Care. *Behaviour Research and Therapy, 35*(8), 785–791.

Beck, A. T., Rush, A. J., Shaw, B. F., & Emery, G. (1979). *Cognitive therapy of depression.* New York, NY: Guilford Press.

Beck, A. T., Steer, R. A., & Brown, G. K. (1996). *Manual for the Beck Depression Inventory–II.* San Antonio, TX: Psychological Corporation/Pearson.

Beck, J. S. (2011). *Cognitive behavior therapy: Basics and beyond* (2nd ed.). New York, NY: Guilford Press.

Bergemann, E. R., & Boles, R. G. (2010). Maternal inheritance in recurrent early-onset depression. *Psychiatric Genetics, 20*(1), 31–34.

Berman, R. M., Sanacora, G., Anand, A., Roach, L. M., Fasula, M. K., Finkelstein, C. O., . . . Charney, D. S. (2002). Monoamine depletion in unmedicated depressed subjects. *Biological Psychiatry, 51*(6), 469–473.

Biaggi, A., Conroy, S., Pawlby, S., & Pariante, C. M. (2016). Identifying the women at risk of antenatal anxiety and depression: A systematic review. *Journal of Affective Disorders, 191*, 62–77.

Bjørkløf, G. H., Engedal, K., Selbæk, G., Kouwenhoven, S. E., & Helvik, A. S. (2013). Coping and depression in old age: A literature review. *Dementia and Geriatric Cognitive Disorders, 35*(3–4), 121–154.

Boelen, P. A., van deSchoot, R., van denHout, M. A., deKeijser, J., & van denBout, J. (2010). Prolonged grief disorder, depression, and posttraumatic stress disorder are distinguishable syndromes. *Journal of Affective Disorders, 125*(1–3), 374–378.

Bolton, J. M., Pagura, J., Enns, M. W., Grant, B., & Sareen, J. (2010). A population-based longitudinal study of risk factors for suicide attempts in major depressive disorder. *Journal of Psychiatric Research, 44*(13), 817–826.

Bonsignore, M., Barkow, K., Jessen, F., & Heun, R. (2001). Validity of the five-item WHO Well-Being Index (WHO-5) in an elderly population. *European Archives of Psychiatry and Clinical Neuroscience, 251*(Suppl. 2), II27–II31.

Bostwick, J. M., & Pankratz, V. S. (2000). Affective disorders and suicide risk: A reexamination. *American Journal of Psychiatry, 157*, 1925–1932.

Bousman, C. A., Forbes, M., Jayaram, M., Eyre, H., Reynolds, C. F., Berk, M., . . . Ng, C. (2017). Antidepressant prescribing in the precision medicine era: a prescriber's primer on pharmacogenetic tools. *BMC Psychiatry, 17*(1), 60.

Bromberger, J. T., Kravitz, H. M., Chang, Y. F., Cyranowski, J. M., Brown, C., & Matthews, K. A. (2011). Major depression during and after the menopausal transition: Study of Women's Health Across the Nation (SWAN). *Psychological Medicine, 41*(09), 1879–1888.

Broomhall, A. G., Phillips, W. J., Hine, D. W., & Loi, N. M. (2017). Upward counterfactual thinking and depression: A meta-analysis. *Clinical Psychology Review, 55*, 56–73.

Byers, A. L., Levy, B. R., Stanislav, V. K., Bruce, M. L., Allore, H. G., Caap-Ahlgren, M., & Dehlin, O. (2009). Heritability of depressive symptoms: A case study using a multilevel approach. *International Journal of Methods in Psychiatric Research, 18*(4), 287–296.

Cacioppo, J. T., Hawkley, L. C., & Thisted, R. A. (2010). Perceived social isolation makes me sad: 5-year cross-lagged analyses of loneliness and depressive symptomatology in the Chicago Health, Aging, and Social Relations Study. *Psychology and Aging, 25*(2), 453–463.

Calmes, C. A., & Roberts, J. E. (2007). Repetitive thought and emotional distress: Rumination and worry as prospective predictors of depressive and anxious symptomatology. *Cognitive Therapy and Research, 31*(3), 343–356.

Caron, J., & Liu, A. (2010). A descriptive study of the prevalence of psychological distress and mental disorders in the Canadian population: Comparison between low-income and non-low-income populations. *Chronic Diseases in Canada, 30*(3), 84–94.

Center for Behavioral Health Statistics and Quality. (2016). *2015 National survey on drug use and health: Detailed tables.* Rockville, MD: Substance Abuse and Mental Health Services Administration.

Chapman, D. P., & Perry, G. S. (2008). Depression as a major component of public health for older adults. *Preventing Chronic Disease, 5,* 1–9.

Charney, D. S., Reynolds, C. F., Lewis, L., Lebowitz, B. D., Sunderland, T., Alexopoulos, G. S., . . . Young, R. C. (2003). Depression and bipolar support alliance consensus statement on the unmet needs in diagnosis and treatment of mood disorders in late life. *Archives of General Psychiatry, 60,* 664–672.

Chentsova-Dutton, Y., & Hanley, K. (2010). The effects of anhedonia and depression on hedonic responses. *Psychiatry Research, 179*(2), 176–180.

Chong, J., Reinschmidt, K. M., & Moreno, F. A. (2010). Symptoms of depression in a Hispanic primary care population with and without chronic medical illnesses. *Primary Care Companion to the Journal of Clinical Psychiatry, 12.* (3).

Chui, W. W., Cheung, E. F., & Lam, L. C. (2011). Neuropsychological profiles and short-term outcome in late-onset depression. *International Journal of Geriatric Psychiatry, 26*(5), 458–465.

Ciechanowski, P., Wagner, E., Schmaling, K., Schwartz, S., Williams, B., Diehr, P., . . . LoGerfo, J. (2004). Community-integrated home-based depression treatment in older adults: A randomized controlled trial. *Journal of the American Medical Association, 291*(13), 1569–1577.

Conti, D. J., & Burton, W. N. (1995). The cost of depression in the workplace. *Behavioral Health Care Tomorrow, 4*(4), 25–27.

CONVERGE, Consortium. (2015). Sparse whole genome sequencing identifies two loci for major depressive disorder. *Nature, 523*(7562), 588–591.

Cooper, L., Peters, L., & Andrews, G. (1998). Validity of the Composite International Diagnostic Interview (CIDI) psychosis module in a psychiatric setting. *Journal of Psychiatric Research, 32*(6), 361–368.

Corruble, E., Falissard, B., & Gorwood, P. (2011). DSM bereavement exclusion for major depression and objective cognitive impairment. *Journal of Affective Disorders, 130*(1–2), 113–117.

Coryell, W., & Young, E. A. (2005). Clinical predictors of suicide in primary major depressive disorder, *Journal of Clinical Psychiatry, 66,* 412–417.

Crisafulli, C., Fabbri, C., Porcelli, S., Drago, A., Spina, E., De Ronchi, D., & Serretti, A. (2011). Pharmacogenetics of antidepressants. *Frontiers in Pharmacology, 2*(6).

Cuijpers, P. (2017). Four decades of outcome research on psychotherapies for adult depression: An overview of a series of meta-analyses. *Canadian Psychology/Psychologie Canadienne, 58*(1), 7–19.

Cuijpers, P., Karyotaki, E., Pot, A. M., Park, M., & Reynolds, C. F. (2014a). Managing depression in older age: Psychological interventions. *Maturitas, 79,* 160–169.

Cuijpers, P., Sijbrandij, M., Koole, S. L., Andersson, G., Beekman, A. T., & Reynolds, C. F. (2014b). Adding psychotherapy to antidepressant medication in depression and anxiety disorders: A meta-analysis. *World Psychiatry, 13*(1), 56–67.

de Groot, M., Jacobson, A. M., Samson, J. A., & Welch, G. (1999). Glycemic control and major depression in patients with type 1 and type 2 diabetes mellitus. *Journal of Psychosomatic Research, 46*(5), 425–435.

Dempster, M., Howell, D., & McCorry, N. K. (2015). Illness perceptions and coping in physical health conditions: A meta-analysis. *Journal of Psychosomatic Research, 79*(6), 506–513.

Devanand, D. P., Adorno, E., Cheng, J., Burt, T., Pelton, G. H., Roose, S. P., & Sackheim, H. A. (2004). Late onset dysthymic disorder and major depression differ from early onset dysthymic disorder and major depression in elderly outpatients. *Journal of Affective Disorders, 78*(3), 259–267.

Dichter, G. S., Felder, J. N., & Smoski, M. J. (2010). The effects of Brief Behavioral Activation Therapy for Depression on cognitive control in affective contexts: An fMRI investigation. *Journal of Affective Disorders, 126*(1–2), 236–244.

Dick, L. P., Gallagher-Thompson, D., & Thompson, L. W. (1996). Cognitive-behavioral therapy. In R. T. Woods (Ed.), *Handbook of the clinical psychology of ageing* (pp. 509–544). Oxford, England: Wiley.

Dikeos, D. G., Papadimitriou, G. N., Avramopoulos, D., Karadima, G., Daskalopoulou, E. G., Souery, D., & Stefanis, C. N. (1999). Association between the dopamine D3 receptor gene locus (DRD3) and unipolar affective disorder. *Psychiatric Genetics, 9*(4), 189–195.

Driessen, E., Hegelmaier, L. M., Abbass, A. A., Barber, J. P., Dekker, J. J., Van, H. L., . . . Cuijpers, P. (2015). The efficacy of short-term psychodynamic psychotherapy for depression: A meta-analysis update. *Clinical Psychology Review, 42,* 1–15.

Druss, B. G., Rosenheck, R. A., & Sledge, W. H. (2000). Health and disability costs of depressive illness in a major U.S. corporation. *American Journal of Psychiatry, 157*(8), 1274–1278.

D'Zurilla, T. J., & Goldfried, M. R. (1971). Problem solving and behavior modification. *Journal of Abnormal Psychology, 78*(1), 107–26.

D'Zurilla, T. J., & Nezu, A. M. (1999). *Problem-solving therapy: A social competence approach to clinical intervention.* New York, NY: Springer.

Edelstein, B. A., Woodhead, E. L., Segal, D. L., Heisel, M. J., Bower, E. H., Lowery, A. J., & Stoner, S. A. (2008). Older adult psychological assessment: Current instrument status and related considerations. *Clinical Gerontologist, 31*(3), 1–35.

Ejaz, S. M., Khawaja, I. S., Bhatia, S., & Hurwitz, T. D. (2011), Obstructive sleep apnea and depression: A review. *Innovations in Clinical Neurosocience, 8*(8), 17–25.

Ellifritt, J., Nelson, K. A., & Walsh, D. (2003). Complicated bereavement: A national survey of potential risk factors. *American Journal of Hospice and Palliative Medicine, 20*(2), 114–120.

Feinberg, A. P. (2007). Phenotypic plasticity and the epigenetics of human disease. *Nature, 447* (7143), 433–440.

Feliciano, L., Steers, M. E., Elite-Marcandonatou, A., McLane, M., & Areán, P. A. (2009). Applications of preference assessment procedures in depression and agitation management in elders with dementia. *Clinical Gerontologist, 32*(3), 239–259.

Felitti, V. J., & Anda, R. F. (2014). The relationship of adverse childhood experiences to adult health status. Retrieved from https://www.acf.hhs.gov/sites/default/files/cb/nccan14_opening_plenary.pdf

Fernandez y Garcia, E., Franks, P., Jerant, A., Bell, R. A., & Kravitz, R. L. (2011). Depression treatment preferences of Hispanic individuals: Exploring the influence of ethnicity, language, and explanatory models. *The Journal of the American Board of Family Medicine, 24*(1), 39–50.

Ferster, C. B. (1973). A functional analysis of depression. *American Psychologist, 28,* 857–870.

Flint, J., & Kendler, K. S. (2014). The genetics of major depression. *Neuron, 81,* 484–503.

Fikretoglu, D., Liu, A., Pedlar, D., & Brunet, A. (2010). Patterns and predictors of treatment delay for mental disorders in a nationally representative, active Canadian military sample. *Medical Care, 48*(1), 10–17.

First, M. B., Williams, J. B. W., Karg, R. S., & Spitzer, R. L. (2016). *Structured Clinical Interview for DSM-5 Disorders: Clinician Version (SCID-5-CV)* Arlington, VA: American Psychiatric Association Publishing.

Fisher, L., Glasgow, R. E., & Strycker, L. A. (2010a). The relationship between diabetes distress and clinical depression with glycemic control among patients with type 2 diabetes. *Diabetes Care, 33*(5), 1034–1036.

Fisher, L., Mullan, J. T., Areán, P., Glasgow, R. E., Hessler, D., & Masharani, U. (2010b). Diabetes distress but not clinical depression or depressive symptoms is associated with glycemic control in both cross-sectional and longitudinal analyses. *Diabetes Care, 33*(1), 23–28.

Fiske, A., Wetherell, J. L., & Gatz, M. (2009). Depression in older adults. *Annual Review of Clinical Psychology, 5,* 363–389.

Folkman, S., & Lazarus, R. S. (1986). Stress-processes and depressive symptomatology. *Journal of Abnormal Psychology, 95*(2), 107–113.

Folkman, S., & Lazarus, R. S. (1988). The relationship between coping and emotion: Implications for theory and research. *Social Science and Medicine, 26*(3), 309–317.

Forest, D. (2016). Is an anatomy of melancholia possible? Brain processes, depression, and mood regulation. In J. C. Wakefield & S. Demazeux (Eds.), *Sadness or depression? International perspectives on the depression epidemic and its meaning* (pp. 95–107). Dordrecht, NLD: Springer.

Fox, S. E., Levitt, P., Nelson, C. A. (2010). How the timing and quality of early experiences influence the development of brain architecture. *Child Development, 81*(1), 28–40.

Freud, S. (1905). *Three essays on the theory of sexuality.* Reprinted (1953–1974) in the Standard Edition of the Complete Psychological Works of Sigmund Freud (trans. And ed. J Strachey), vol 7, pp. 125–243. London, UK: Hogarth Press.

Freud, S. (1914). *The history of the psychoanalytic movement* (trans. A. A. Brill) Washington, DC: Nervous and Mental Disease Publishing Co.

Gallagher, D., Mhaolain, A. N., Greene, E., Walsh, C., Denihan, A., Bruce, I., . . . Lawlor, B. A. (2010). Late life depression: A comparison of risk factors and symptoms according to age of onset in community dwelling older adults. *International Journal of Geriatric Psychiatry, 25*(10), 981–987.

Gaudiano, B. A., & Zimmerman, M. (2010). The relationship between childhood trauma history and the psychotic subtype of major depression. *Acta Psychiatrica Scandinavica, 121*(6), 462–470.

Ghassemi, G. R., Sadeghi, S., Asadollahi, G. A., Yousefy, A. R., & Mallik, S. (2010). Early experiences of abuse and current depressive disorders in Iranian women. *East Mediterranean Health Journal, 16*(5), 498–504.

Goldberg, D. P. (1972). *The detection of psychiatric illness by questionnaire: A technique for the identification and assessment of non-psychotic psychiatric illness.* London, England: Oxford University Press.

Goldberg, D. P., & Blackwell, B. (1970). Psychiatric illness in general practice: A detailed study using a new method of case identification. *British Medical Journal, 2*(5707), 439–443.

Goldberg, J. S., Bell Jr, C. E., & Pollard, D. A. (2014). Revisiting the monoamine hypothesis of depression: A new perspective. *Perspectives in Medicinal Chemistry, 6*, 1–8.

Goldstein, B. L., & Klein, D. N. (2014). A review of selected candidate endophenotypes for depression. *Clinical Psychology Review, 34*(5), 417–427.

Gonzalez, J. S., Fisher, L., & Polonsky, W. H. (2011). Depression in diabetes: Have we been missing something important? *Diabetes Care, 34*(1), 236–239.

Gottlieb, L., Waitzkin, H., & Miranda, J. (2011). Depressive symptoms and their social contexts: A qualitative systematic literature review of contextual interventions. *International Journal of Social Psychiatry, 57*(4), 402–417.

Green, E. K., Grozeva, D., Jones, I., Jones, L., Kirov, G., Caesar, S., . . . Craddock, N. (2010). The bipolar disorder risk allele at CACNA1C also confers risk of recurrent major depression and of schizophrenia. *Molecular Psychiatry, 15*, 1016–1022.

Greenberg, P. E., Kessler, R. C., Birnbaum, H. G., Leong, S. A., Lowe, S. W., Berglund, P. A., & Corey-Lisle, P. K. (2003). The economic burden of depression in the United States: How did it change between 1990 and 2000? *Journal of Clinical Psychiatry, 64*(12), 1465–1475.

Griffiths, J., Ravindran, A. V., Merali, Z., & Anisman, H. (2000). Dysthymia: A review of pharmacological and behavioral factors. *Molecular Psychiatry, 5*(3), 242–261.

Gunnarsdottir, E. D., Pingitore, R. A., Spring, B. J., Konopka, L. M., Crayton, J. W., Milo, T., & Shirazi, P. (2000). Individual differences among cocaine users. *Addictive Behaviors, 25*(5), 641–652.

Gupta, A., Bahadur, I., Gupta, K. R., & Bhugra, D. (2006). Self-awareness of depression and life events in three groups of patients: Psychotic depression, obsessive-compulsive disorder and chronic medical illness in North India. *Indian Journal of Psychiatry, 48*(4), 251–253.

Gruber, J., Eidelman, P., Johnson, S. L., Smith, B., & Harvey, A. G. (2011). Hooked on a feeling: Rumination about positive and negative emotion in inter-episode bipolar disorder. *Journal of Abnormal Psychology, 120*(4), 956–961.

Han, C., Jo, S. A., Kwak, J. H., Pae, C. U., Steffens, D., Jo, I., & Park, M. H. (2008). Validation of the Patient Health Questionnaire-9 Korean version in the elderly population: The Ansan geriatric study. *Comprehensive Psychiatry, 49*(2), 218–223.

Haroz, E. E., Ritchey, M., Bass, J. B., Kohrt, B., Augustinavicius, J., Michalopoulous, L., . . . Bolton, P. (2017). How is depression experienced around the world? A systematic review of qualitative literature. *Social Science & Medicine, 183*, 151–162.

Hayes, S. C., Strosahl, K. D., & Wilson, K. G. (2012). *Acceptance and commitment therapy: the process and practice of mindful change* (2nd ed.). New York, NY: Guilford Press.

Heim, C., & Binder, E. B. (2012). Current research trends in early life stress and depression: Review of human studies on sensitive periods, gene–environment interactions, and epigenetics. *Experimental Neurology, 233*(1), 102–111.

Ho, Y. C., & Wang, S. (2010). Adult neurogenesis is reduced in the dorsal hippocampus of rats displaying learned helplessness behavior. *Neuroscience, 171*(1), 153–161.

Hoover, D. R., Siegel, M., Lucas, J., Kalay, E., Gaboda, D., Devanand, D. P., & Crystal, S. (2010). Depression in the first year of stay for elderly long-term nursing home residents in the U. S. A. *International Psychogeriatrics, 22*(7), 1161–1171.

Hopko, D. R., Bourland, S. L., Stanley, M. A., Beck, J. G., Novy, D. M., Averill, P. M., & Swann, A. C. (2000). Generalized anxiety disorder in older adults: Examining the relation between clinician severity ratings and patient self-report measures. *Depression and Anxiety, 12*(4), 217–225.

Horwitz, A. G., Hill, R. M., & King, C. A. (2011). Specific coping behaviors in relation to adolescent depression and suicidal ideation. *Journal of Adolescence, 34*(5), 1077–1085.

Huffziger, S., Reinhard, I., & Kuehner, C. (2009). A longitudinal study of rumination and distraction in formerly depressed inpatients and community controls. *Journal of Abnormal Psychology, 118*(4), 746–756.

Hundt, N. E., Bensadon, B. A., Stanley, M. A., Petersen, N. J., Kunik, M. E., Kauth, M. R., & Cully, J. A. (2015). Coping mediates the relationship between disease severity and illness intrusiveness among chronically ill patients. *Journal of Health Psychology, 20*(9), 1186–1195.

Hyde, C. L., Nagle, M. W., Tian, C., Chen, X., Paciga, S. A., Wendland, J. R., . . . Winslow, A. R. (2016). Identification of 15 genetic loci associated with risk of major depression in individuals of European descent. *Nature Genetics, 48*(9), 1031–1036.

Iacoviello, B. M., Alloy, L. B., Abramson, L. Y., Choi, J. Y., & Morgan, J. E. (2013). Patterns of symptom onset and remission in episodes of hopelessness depression. *Depression and Anxiety, 30* (6), 564–573.

Ibarra-Rovillard, M. S., & Kuiper, N. A. (2011). Social support and social negativity findings in depression: perceived responsiveness to basic psychological needs. *Clinical Psychology Review, 31*(3), 342–352.

Insel, T., Cuthbert, B., Garvey, M., Heinssen, R., Pine, D. S., Quinn, K., . . . Wang, P. (2010). Research domain criteria (RDoC): Toward a new classification framework for research on mental disorders. *American Journal of Psychiatry, 167*(7), 748–751.

Isaacowitz, D. M., & Seligman, M. E. (2001). Is pessimism a risk factor for depressive mood among community-dwelling older adults? *Behavior Research and Therapy, 39*(3), 255–272.

Iwata, M., Ota, K. T., & Duman, R. S. (2013). The inflammasome: Pathways linking psychological stress, depression, and systemic illnesses. *Brain, Behavior, and Immunity, 31*, 105–114.

Jackson-Triche, M. E., Greer Sullivan, J., Wells, K. B., Rogers, W., Camp, P., & Mazel, R. (2000). Depression and health-related quality of life in ethnic minorities seeking care in general medical settings. *Journal of Affective Disorders, 58*(2), 89–97.

Jacobson, N., Martell, C., & Dimidjian, S. (2001). Behavioral activation treatment for depression: Returning to contextual roots. *Clinical Psychology: Science and Practice, 8*, 255–270.

Jakupcak, M., Wagner, A., Paulson, A., Varra, A., & McFall, M. (2010). Behavioral activation as a primary care-based treatment for PTSD and depression among returning veterans. *Journal of Traumatic Stress, 23*(4), 491–495.

Jia, L., Jiang, S. M., Shang, Y. Y., Huang, Y. X., Li, Y. J., Xie, D. R., . . . Ji, F. C. (2010). Investigation of the incidence of pancreatic cancer-related depression and its relationship with the quality of life of patients. *Digestion, 82*(1), 4–9.

Kalibatseva, Z., Leong, F. T. L., & Ham, E. H. (2014). A symptom profile of depression among Asian Americans: Is there evidence for differential item functioning of depressive symptoms? *Psychological Medicine, 44*(12), 2567–2578.

Kato, T. (2015). The impact of coping flexibility on the risk of depressive symptoms. *PLoS One, 10*(5), e0128307.

Katon, W. J. (2003). Clinical and health services relationships between major depression, depressive symptoms, and general medical illness. *Biological Psychiatry, 54*(3), 216–226.

Kendler, K. S., & Gardner, C. O. (2010). Dependent stressful life events and prior depressive episodes in the prediction of major depression: The problem of causal inference in psychiatric epidemiology. *Archives of General Psychiatry, 67*(11), 1120–1127.

Kendler, K. S., Gatz, M., Gardner, C. O., & Pedersen, N. L. (2006). Personality and major depression: A Swedish longitudinal, population-based twin study. *Archives of General Psychiatry, 63*(10), 1113–1120.

Kendler, K. S., Hettema, J. M., Butera, F., Gardner, C. O., & Prescott, C. A. (2003). Life event dimensions of loss, humiliation, entrapment, and danger in the prediction of onsets of major depression and generalized anxiety. *Archives of General Psychiatry, 60*(8), 789–796.

Kessler, R. C. (2003). Epidemiology of women and depression. *Journal of Affective Disorders, 74*(1), 5–13.

Kessler, R. C., Barber, C., Birnbaum, H. G., Frank, R. G., Greenberg, P. E., Rose, R. M., . . . Wang, P. (1999). Depression in the workplace: Effects on short-term disability. *Health Affairs, 18*(5), 163–171.

Kessler, R. C., Berglund, P., Chiu, W. T., Demler, O., Heeringa, S., Hiripi, E., . . . Zheng, H. (2004). The US National Comorbidity Survey Replication (NCS-R): Design and field procedures. *International Journal of Methods in Psychiatric Research, 13*(2), 69–92.

Kessler, R.C., Berglund, P., Demler, O., Jin, R., Koretz, D., Merikangas, K.R., . . . Wang, P.S. (2003). The epidemiology of major depressive disorder: Results from the National Comorbidity Survey Replication (NCS-R). *Journal of the American Medical Association, 289*(23), 3095–3105.

Kessler, R. C., Berglund, P., Demler, O., Jin, R., Merikangas, K. R., & Walters, E. E. (2005). Lifetime prevalence and age-of-onset distributions of DSM-IV disorders in the National Comorbidity Survey Replication. *Archives of General Psychiatry, 62*(6), 593–602.

Kessler, R. C., & Frank, R. G. (1997). The impact of psychiatric disorders on work loss days. *Psychological Medicine, 27*(4), 861–873.

Kessler, R. C., McGonagle, K. A., Nelson, C. B., Hughes, M., Swartz, M., & Blazer, D. G. (1994). Sex and depression in the National Comorbidity Survey. II: Cohort effects. *Journal of Affective Disorders, 30*(1), 15–26.

Kessler, R. C., McGonagle, K. A., Zhao, S., Nelson, C. B., Hughes, M., Eshleman, S., . . . Kendler, K. S. (1994). Lifetime and 12-month prevalence of DSM-II-R psychiatric disorders in the United States. Results from the National Comorbidity Survey. *Archives of General Psychiatry, 51*(1), 8–19.

Kessler, R. C., & Merikangas, K. R. (2004). The National Comorbidity Survey Replication (NCS-R): Background and aims. *International Journal of Methods in Psychiatric Research, 13*(2), 60–68.

Khan, A., Faucett, J., Lichtenberg, P., Kirsch, I., & Brown, W. A. (2012). A systematic review of comparative efficacy of treatments and controls for depression. *PLoS ONE, 7*(7), e41778.

Kiecolt-Glaser, J. K., Derry, H. M., & Fagundes, C. P. (2015). Inflammation: depression fans the flames and feasts on the heat. *American Journal of Psychiatry, 172*(11), 1075–1091.

Kiima, D., & Jenkins, R. (2010). Mental health policy in Kenya: An integrated approach to scaling up equitable care for poor populations. *International Journal of Mental Health Systems, 4*, 19.

Kilzieh, N., Rastam, S., Ward, K. D., & Maziak, W. (2010). Gender, depression and physical impairment: An epidemiologic perspective from Aleppo, Syria. *Social Psychiatry and Psychiatric Epidemiology, 45*(6), 595–602.

Kim, J. M., Shin, I. S., Yoon, J. S., & Stewart, R. (2002). Prevalence and correlates of late-life depression compared between urban and rural populations in Korea. *International Journal of Geriatric Psychiatry, 17*(5), 409–415.

King-Kallimanis, B., Gum, A. M., & Kohn, R. (2009) Comorbidity of depressive and anxiety disorders for older Americans in the National Comorbidity Survey Replication. *American Journal of Geriatric Psychiatry, 17*(9), 782–792.

Kirby, T. (2015). Ketamine for depression: The highs and lows. *The Lancet Psychiatry, 2*(9), 783–784.

Klein, D. N., Shankman, S., & Rose, S. (2006). Ten-year prospective follow-up study of the naturalistic course of dysthymic disorder and double depression. *American Journal of Psychiatry, 163*(5), 872–880.

Klerman, G. L., Weissman, M. M., Rounsaville, B. J., & Chevron, E. S. (1984). *Interpersonal psychotherapy of depression.* New York, NY: Basic Books.

Kroenke, K., Spitzer, R. L., & Williams, J. B. W. (2001). The PHQ-9: Validity of a brief depression severity measure. *Journal of General Internal Medicine, 16*(9), 606–613.

Kubzansky, L. D., & Kawachi, I. (2000). Going to the heart of the matter: Do negative emotions cause coronary heart disease? *Journal of Psychosomatic Research, 48*(4–5), 323–337.

Lazarus, R. S. (1991). *Stress and emotion: A new synthesis.* New York, NY: Springer.

Lewinsohn, P. M. (1974). A behavioral approach to depression. In R. J. Friedman & M. M. Katz (Eds.), *The psychology of depression: Contemporary theory and research.* Oxford, England: Wiley.

Liu, L., Gou, Z., & Zuo, J. (2016). Social support mediates loneliness and depression in elderly people. *Journal of Health Psychology, 21*(5), 750–758.

Logothetis, N. K. (2008). What we can do and what we cannot do with fMRI. *Nature, 453*(7197), 869–878.

Lotrakul, M., Sumrithe, S., Saipanish, R., Lotrakul, M., Sumrithe, S., & Saipanish, R. (2008). Reliability and validity of the Thai version of the PHQ-9. *BMC Psychiatry, 8*, 46.

Luppa, M., Sikorski, C., Luck, T., Ehreke, L., Konnopka, A., Wiese, B., . . . Riedel-Heller, S. G. (2012). Age-and gender-specific prevalence of depression in latest-life–systematic review and meta-analysis. *Journal of Affective Disorders, 136*(3), 212–221.

Lutz, P. E., & Turecki, G. (2014). DNA methylation and childhood maltreatment: from animal models to human studies. *Neuroscience, 264*, 142–156.

Luyten, P., & Blatt, S. J. (2012). Psychodynamic treatment of depression. *Psychiatric Clinics of North America, 35*(1), 111–129.

Maier, S. F., & Seligman, M. E. (2016). Learned helplessness at fifty: Insights from neuroscience. *Psychological Review, 123*(4), 349.

Maj, M. (2008). Depression, bereavement, and "understandable" intense sadness: Should the DSM-IV approach be revised? *American Journal of Psychiatry, 165*, 1373–1375.

Marsh, L. (2013). Depression and Parkinson's disease: Current knowledge. *Current Neurology and Neuroscience Reports, 13*(12), 1–17.

Martens, E. J., Hoen, P. W., Mittelhaeuser, M., de Jonge, P., & Denollet, J. (2010). Symptom dimensions of post-myocardial infarction depression, disease severity and cardiac prognosis. *Psychological Medicine, 40*(5), 807–814.

Martin, C. E., Renn, B. N., Winderman, K. E., Hundt, N., Petersen, N. J., Naik, A. D., & Cully, J. A. (2017). Classifying diabetes-burden: A factor analysis of the Problem Areas in Diabetes Scale. *Journal of Health Psychology,* epub ahead of print. doi: 10.1177/1359105316678667.

Martin, L. A., Neighbors, H. W., & Griffith, D. M. (2013). The experience of symptoms of depression in men vs women: analysis of the National Comorbidity Survey Replication. *JAMA Psychiatry*, *70*(10), 1100–1106.

Marty, M. A., Pepin, R., June, A., & Segal, D. L. (2011). Geriatric depression scale. In M. Abou-Saleh, C. Katona, & A. Kumar (Eds.), *Principles and practice of geriatric psychiatry* (3rd ed., pp. 152–156). New York: Wiley.

Mathers, C. D., & Loncar, D. (2006). Projections of global mortality and burden of disease from 2002 to 2030. *PLoS Medicine*, *3*(11), e442.

Mayr, M., & Schmid, R. M. (2010). Pancreatic cancer and depression: Myth and truth. *BMC Cancer*, *10*, 569.

Mazzucchelli, T. G., Kane, R. T., & Rees, C. S. (2010). Behavioral activation interventions for well-being: A meta-analysis. *Journal of Positive Psychology*, *5*(2), 105–121.

McHugh, R. K., Whitton, S. W., Peckham, A. D., Welge, J. A., & Otto, M. W. (2013). Patient preference for psychological vs. pharmacological treatment of psychiatric disorders: A meta-analytic review. *The Journal of Clinical Psychiatry*, *74*(6), 595–602.

Merikangas, K. R., & Avenevoli, S. (2000). Implications of genetic epidemiology for the prevention of substance use disorders. *Addictive Behaviors*, *25*(6), 807–820.

Merikangas, K. R., Cui, L., Heaton, L., Nakamura, E., Roca, C., Ding, J., . . . Angst, J. (2014). Independence of familial transmission of mania and depression: Results of the NIMH family study of affective spectrum disorders. *Molecular Psychiatry*, *19*(2), 214–219.

Michl, L. C., McLaughlin, K. A., Shepherd, K., & Nolen-Hoeksema, S. (2013). Rumination as a mechanism linking stressful life events to symptoms of depression and anxiety: Longitudinal evidence in early adolescents and adults. *Journal of Abnormal Psychology*, *122*(2), 339–352.

Mitchell, A. J., Chan, M., Bhatti, H., Halton, M., Grassi, L., Johansen, C., & Meader, N. (2011). Prevalence of depression, anxiety, and adjustment disorder in oncological, haematological, and palliative-care settings: A meta-analysis of 94 interview-based studies. *The Lancet Oncology*, *12*(2), 160–174.

Montgomery, S. A., & Asberg, M. (1979). A new depression scale designed to be sensitive to change. *British Journal of Psychiatry*, *134*, 382–389.

Newport, D. J., Carpenter, L. L., McDonald, W. M., Potash, J. B., Tohen, M., & Nemeroff, C. B. (2015). Ketamine and other NMDA antagonists: early clinical trials and possible mechanisms in depression. *American Journal of Psychiatry*, *172*(10), 950–966.

Nezu, A. M. (1986). Cognitive appraisal of problem solving effectiveness: Relation to depression and depressive symptoms. *Journal of Clinical Psychology*, *42*(1), 42–48.

Nock, M. K., Borges, G., Bromet, E. J., Alonso, J., Angermeyer, M., Beautrais, A., . . . Williams, D. (2008). Cross-national prevalence and risk factors for suicidal ideation, plans and attempts. *The British Journal of Psychiatry*, *192*, 98–105.

Nolen-Hoeksema, S. (1991). Reponses to depression and their effects on the duration of depressive episodes. *Journal of Abnormal Psychology*, *100*(4), 569–582.

Nolen-Hoeksema, S., Larson, J., & Grayson, C. (1999). Explaining the gender difference in depressive symptoms. *Journal of Personality and Social Psychology*, *77*(5), 1061–1072.

Nolen-Hoeksema, S., Wisco, B. E., & Lyubomirsky, S. (2008). Rethinking rumination. *Perspectives on Psychological Science*, *3*(5), 400–424.

Nutt, D. J., Davidson, J. R., Gelenberg, A. J., Higuchi, T., Kanba, S., Karamustafalioglu, O., . . . Zhang, M. (2010). International consensus statement on major depressive disorder. *Journal of Clinical Psychiatry*, *71*(Suppl. E1), E08.

Oakes, P., Loukas, M., Oskouian, R. J., & Tubbs, R. S. (2016). The neuroanatomy of depression: A review. *Clinical Anatomy*, *30*(44–49).

O'Keane, V. (2000). Evolving model of depression as an expression of multiple interacting risk factors. *British Journal of Psychiatry*, *177*, 482–483.

O'Leary, D., & Costello, F. (2001). Personality and outcome in depression:;1; An 18-month prospective follow-up study. *Journal of Affective Disorders, 63*(1–3), 67–78.

Olatunji, B. O., Naragon-Gainey, K., & Wolitzky-Taylor, K. B. (2013). Specificity of rumination in anxiety and depression: A multimodal meta-analysis. *Clinical Psychology: Science and Practice, 20,* 225–257.

Olfson, M., Kroenke, K., Wang, S., & Blanco, C. (2014). Trends in office-based mental health care provided by psychiatrists and primary care physicians. *The Journal of Clinical Psychiatry, 75*(3), 247–253.

Organisation for Economic Cooperation and Development (2017), "Pharmaceutical market", *OECD Health Statistics* (database). doi: http://dx.doi.org/10.1787/data-00545-en

Ostacher, M. J. (2007). Comorbid alcohol and substance abuse dependence in depression: Impact on the outcome of antidepressant treatment. *Psychiatric Clinics of North America, 30*(1), 69–76.

Palmer, S., Vecchio, M., Craig, J. C., Tonelli, M., Johnson, D. W., Nicolucci, A., . . . Strippoli, G. F. (2013). Prevalence of depression in chronic kidney disease: systematic review and meta-analysis of observational studies. *Kidney International, 84*(1), 179–191.

Pandya, M., Altinay, M., Malone Jr, D. A., & Anand, A. (2012). Where in the brain is depression? *Current Psychiatry Reports, 14*(6), 634–642.

Papakostas, G. I. (2009). The efficacy, tolerability, and safety of contemporary antidepressants. *The Journal of Clinical Psychiatry, 71*(Supp E), e03.

Papakostas, G. I., Crawford, C. M., Scalia, M. J., & Fava, M. (2007). Timing of clinical improvement and symptom resolution in the treatment of major depressive disorder. A replication of findings with the use of a double-blind, placebo-controlled trial of Hypericum perforatum versus fluoxetine. *Neuropsychobiology, 56*(2–3), 132–137.

Parker, G., Hilton, T., Hadzi-Pavlovic, D., & Bains, J. (2001). Screening for depression in the medically ill: The suggested utility of a cognitive-based approach. *Australian and New Zealand Journal of Psychiatry, 35*(4), 474–480.

Paterniti, S., Sterner, I., Caldwell, C., & Bisserbe, J. C. (2017). Childhood neglect predicts the course of major depression in a tertiary care sample: A follow-up study. *BMC Psychiatry, 17*(1), 113.

Pattyn, E., Verhaeghe, M., & Bracke, P. (2015). The gender gap in mental health service use. *Social Psychiatry and Psychiatric Epidemiology, 50*(7), 1089–1095.

Petersen, T., Hughes, M., Papakostas, G. I., Kant, A., Fava, M., Rosenbaum, J. F., & Nierenberg, A. A. (2002). Treatment-resistant depression and Axis II comorbidity. *Psychotherapy and Psychosomatics, 71*(5), 269–274.

Pincus, H. A., & Pettit, A. R. (2001). The societal costs of chronic major depression. *Journal of Clinical Psychiatry, 62*(Suppl. 6), 5–9.

Plaza, A., Garcia-Esteve, L., Ascaso, C., Navarro, P., Gelabert, E., Halperin, I., . . . Martín-Santos, R. (2010). Childhood sexual abuse and hypothalamus-pituitary-thyroid axis in postpartum major depression. *Journal of Affective Disorders, 122*(1–2), 159–163.

Plutchik, R., Platman, S. R., & Fieve, R. R. (1968). Repeated measurements in the manic depressive illness: Some methodological problems. *Journal of Psychology, 70,* 131–137.

Price, J. L., & Drevets, W. C. (2010). Neurocircuitry of mood disorders. *Neuropsychopharmacology, 35,* 192–216.

Quiñones, A. R., Thielke, S. M., Beaver, K. A., Trivedi, R. B., Williams, E. C., & Fan, V. S. (2014). Racial and ethnic differences in receipt of antidepressants and psychotherapy by veterans with chronic depression. *Psychiatric Services, 65*(2), 193–200.

Radloff, L. S. (1977). The CES-D Scale: A self-report depression scale for research in the general population. *Applied Psychological Measurement, 1*(3), 385–401.

Rapp, M. A., Dahlman, K., Sano, M., Grossman, H. T., Haroutunian, V., & Gorman, J. M. (2005). Neuropsychological differences between late-onset and recurrent geriatric major depression. *American Journal of Psychiatry, 162*(4), 691–698.

Raue, P. J., Weinberger, M. I., Sirey, J. A., Meyers, B. S., & Bruce, M. L. (2011). Preferences for depression treatment among elderly home health care patients. *Psychiatric Services*, *62*(5), 532–537.

Regier, D. A. (1988). The NIMH depression awareness, recognition, and treatment program: Structure, aims, and scientific basis. *American Journal of Psychiatry*, *145*(11), 1351–1357.

Regier, D. A., Goldberg, I. D., & Taube, C. A. (1978). The de facto US mental health services system: A public health perspective. *Archives of General Psychiatry*, *35*(6), 685–693.

Renn, B. N., & Areán, P. A. (2017). Psychosocial treatment options for major depressive disorder in older adults. *Current Treatment Options in Psychiatry*, *4*(1), 1–12.

Renn, B.N., Feliciano, L., & Segal, D.L. (2011) The bidirectional relationship of depression and diabetes: A systematic review. *Clinical Psychology Review*, *31*, 1239–1246.

Renn, B. N., Steers, M. E., Jay, A. A., & Feliciano, L. (2013). Prevalence of depressive symptoms among low-income adults with impaired glucose tolerance. *Annals of Behavioral Medicine*, *45*(2), s203.

Rhebergen, D., Beekman, A. T., deGraaf, R., Nolen, W. A., Spijker, J., Hoogendijk, W. J., & Penninx, B. W. (2010). Trajectories of recovery of social and physical functioning in major depression, dysthymic disorder and double depression: A 3-year follow-up. *Journal of Affective Disorders*, *124* (1–2), 148–156.

Rhodes, J., Chan, C., Paxson, C., Rouse, C. E., Waters, M., & Fussell, E. (2010). The impact of hurricane Katrina on the mental and physical health of low-income parents in New Orleans. *American Journal of Orthopsychiatry*, *80*(2), 237–247.

Richards, D. (2011). Prevalence and clinical course of depression: A review. *Clinical Psychology Review*, *31*(7), 1117–1125.

Robins, C. J., & Block, P. (1989). Cognitive theories of depression viewed from a diathesis-stress perspective: Evaluations of the models of Beck and of Abramson, Seligman, and Teasdale. *Cognitive Therapy and Research*, *13*(4), 297–313.

Rossi, A., Marinangeli, M. G., Butti, G., Scinto, A., DiCicco, L., Kalyvoka, A., & Petruzzi, C. (2001). Personality disorders in bipolar and depressive disorders. *Journal of Affective Disorders*, *65*(1), 3–8.

Rubenstein, L. V., Rayburn, N. R., Keeler, E. B., Ford, D. E., Rost, K. M., & Sherbourne, C. D. (2007). Predicting outcomes of primary care patients with major depression: Development of a Depression Prognosis Index. *Psychiatric Services*, *58*(8), 1049–1056.

Rueger, S. Y., Malecki, C. K., Pyun, Y., Aycock, C., & Coyle, S. (2016). A meta-analytic review of the association between perceived social support and depression in childhood and adolescence. *Psychological Bulletin*, *142*(10), 1017–1067.

Russo, S. J., & Nestler, E. J. (2013). The brain reward circuitry in mood disorders. *Nature Reviews Neuroscience*, *14*(9), 609–625.

Rustad, J. K., Stern, T. A., Hebert, K. A., & Musselman, D. L. (2013). Diagnosis and treatment of depression in patients with congestive heart failure: A review of the literature. *Primary Care Companion for CNS Disorder*, *15*(4), 13r01511.

Ryder, A. G., Quilty, L. C., Vachon, D. D., & Bagby, R. M. (2010). Depressive personality and treatment outcome in major depressive disorder. *Journal of Personality Disorders*, *24*(3), 392–404.

Sagen, U., Finset, A., Moum, T., Morland, T., Vik, T. G., Nagy, T., & Dammen, T. (2010). Early detection of patients at risk for anxiety, depression and apathy after stroke. *General Hospital Psychiatry*, *32*(1), 80–85.

Salomon, R. M., Miller, H. L., Krystal, J. H., Heninger, G. R., & Charney, D. S. (1997). Lack of behavioral effects of monoamine depletion in healthy subjects. *Biological Psychiatry*, *41*(1), 58–64.

Seemuller, F., Riedel, M., Obermeier, M., Bauer, M., Adli, M., Kronmuller, K., . . . Möller, H. J. (2010). Outcomes of 1014 naturalistically treated inpatients with major depressive episode. *European Neuropsychopharmacology*, *20*(5), 346–355.

Segal, D. L., Qualls, S. H., & Smyer, M. A. (2018). *Aging and mental health* (3rd ed.). Hoboken, NJ: Wiley.

Segal, D. L. & Williams, K. N. (2014). Structured and semistructured interviews for differential diagnosis: Fundamental issues, applications, and features. In D. C. Beidel, B. C. Frueh, & M. Hersen (Eds.), *Adult psychopathology and diagnosis* (7th ed., pp. 103–129). Hoboken, NJ: Wiley.

Seligman, M. E. (1974). *Depression and learned helplessness.* John Wiley & Sons.

Seligman, M. E., & Csikszentmihalyi, M. (2000). Positive psychology. An introduction. *American Psychology, 55*(1), 5–14.

Seligman, M. E. P., & Maier, S. F. (1967). Failure to escape traumatic shock. *Journal of Experimental Psychology, 74*(1), 1–9.

Seligman, M. E., Steen, T. A., Park, N., & Peterson, C. (2005). Positive psychology progress: Empirical validation of interventions. *American Psychology, 60*(5), 410–421.

Seligman, M. E., Weiss, J., Weinraub, M., & Schulman, A. (1980). Coping behavior: Learned helplessness, physiological change and learned inactivity. *Behavior Research and Therapy, 18*(5), 459–512.

Serrano-Blanco, A., Palao, D. J., Luciano, J. V., Pinto-Meza, A., Luján, L., Fernández, A., . . . Haro, J. M. (2010). Prevalence of mental disorders in primary care: results from the diagnosis and treatment of mental disorders in primary care study (DASMAP). *Social Psychiatry and Psychiatric Epidemiology, 45*(2), 201–210.

Shear, M. K., Simon, N., Wall, M., Zisook, S., Neimeyer, R., Duan, N., . . . Keshaviah, A. (2011). Complicated grief and related bereavement issues for DSM-5. *Depression and Anxiety, 28*(2), 103–117.

Sheehan, D. V., Lecrubier, Y., Harnett-Sheehan, K., Amorim, P., Janavs, J., Weiller, E., Hergueta, T., Baker, R., & Dunbar, G. (1998). The Mini-International Neuropsychiatric Interview (MINI): The development and validation of a structured diagnostic psychiatric interview for DSM-IV and ICD-10. *Journal of Clinical Psychiatry, 59*(Suppl. 20), 22–33.

Sherrington, J. M., Hawton, K., Fagg, J., Andrew, B., & Smith, D. (2001). Outcome of women admitted to hospital for depressive illness: Factors in the prognosis of severe depression. *Psychological Medicine, 31*(1), 115–125.

Shorey, R. C., Sherman, A. E., Kivisto, A. J., Elkins, S. R., Rhatigan, D. L., & Moore, T. M. (2011). Gender differences in depression and anxiety among victims of intimate partner violence: The moderating effect of shame proneness. *Journal of Interpersonal Violence, 26*(9), 1834–1850.

Simon, G. E., & Ciechanowski, P. (2015). Unipolar major depression in adults: Choosing initial treatment. In P. P. Roy-Byrne & D. Solomon (Eds.), *UpToDate.* Retrieved from http://www.uptodate.com/contents/unipolar-depression-in-adults-and-initial-treatment-general-principles-and-prognosis

Simon, G. E., Revicki, D., Heiligenstein, J., Grothaus, L., VonKorff, M., Katon, W. J., & Hylan, T. R. (2000). Recovery from depression, work productivity, and health care costs among primary care patients. *General Hospital Psychiatry, 22*(3), 153–162.

Simon, G. E., VonKorff, M., & Lin, E. (2005). Clinical and functional outcomes of depression treatment in patients with and without chronic medical illness. *Psychological Medicine, 35*(2), 271–279.

Simson, P. E., & Weiss, J. M. (1988). Altered activity of the locus coeruleus in an animal model of depression. *Neuropsychopharmacology, 1*(4), 287–295.

Sin, N. L., & Lyubomirsky, S. (2009). Enhancing well-being and alleviating depressive symptoms with positive psychology interventions: A practice-friendly meta-analysis. *Journal of Clinical Psychology, 65*(5), 467–487.

Sinyor, M., Schaffer, A., & Levitt, A. (2010). The sequenced treatment alternatives to relieve depression (STAR*D) trial: A review. *Canadian Journal of Psychiatry, 55*(3), 126–135.

Siu, A. L., and the US Preventive Services Task Force (USPSTF). (2016). Screening for depression in adults: US Preventive Services Task Force Recommendation Statement. *Journal of the American Medical Association, 315,* 380–387.

Spitzer, R. L., Kroenke, K., & Williams, J. B. (1999). Validation and utility of a self-report version of PRIME-MD: The PHQ primary care study. Primary Care Evaluation of Mental Disorders. Patient Health Questionnaire. *Journal of the American Medical Association, 282*(18), 1737–1744.

Spitzer, R. L., Williams, J. B., Kroenke, K., Hornyak, R., & McMurray, J. (2000). Validity and utility of the PRIME-MD patient health questionnaire in assessment of 3000 obstetric- gynecologic patients: The PRIME-MD Patient Health Questionnaire Obstetrics-Gynecology Study. *American Journal of Obstetrics and Gynecology, 183*(3), 759–769.

Spitzer, R. L., Williams, J. B., Kroenke, K., Linzer, M., deGruy, F. V. 3rd, Hahn, S. R., . . . Johnson, J. G. (1994). Utility of a new procedure for diagnosing mental disorders in primary care: The PRIME-MD 1000 study. *Journal of the American Medical Association, 272*(22), 1749–1756.

Splawski, I., Timothy, K. W., Sharpe, L. M., Decher, N., Kumar, P., Bloise, R., . . . Keating, M. T. (2004). Ca(V)1.2 calcium channel dysfunction cause a multisystem disorder including arrhythmia and autism. *Cell, 119*(1), 19–31.

Steer, R. A., Cavalieri, T. A., Leonard, D. M., & Beck, A. T. (1999). Use of the Beck Depression Inventory for Primary Care to screen for major depression disorders. *General Hospital Psychiatry, 21*(2), 106–111.

Stetler, C., & Miller, G. E. (2011). Depression and hypothalamic-pituitary-adrenal activation: a quantitative summary of four decades of research. *Psychosomatic Medicine, 73*(2), 114–126.

Stover, E., Fenton, W., Rosenfeld, A., & Insel, T. R. (2003). Depression and comorbid medical illness: The National Institute of Mental Health perspective. *Biological Psychiatry, 54*(3), 184–186.

Sullivan, P. F., Neale, M. C., & Kendler, K. S. (2000). Genetic epidemiology of major depression: Review and meta-analysis. *American Journal of Psychiatry, 157*(10), 1552–1562.

Tansey, K. E., Guipponi, M., Hu, X., Domenici, E., Lewis, G., Malafosse, A., . . . Uher, R. (2013). Contribution of common genetic variants to antidepressant response. *Biological Psychiatry, 73*(7), 679–682.

Taylor, W. D., Aizenstein, H. J., & Alexopoulos, G. S. (2013). The vascular depression hypothesis: mechanisms linking vascular disease with depression. *Molecular Psychiatry 18*, 963–974.

Thorpe, C. T., Fahey, L. E., Johnson, H., Deshpande, M., Thorpe, J. M., & Fisher, E. B. (2013). Facilitating healthy coping in patients with diabetes: A systematic review. *The Diabetes Educator, 39*(1), 33–52.

Trivedi, M. H., Clayton, A. H., & Frank, E. (2007). Treating depression complicated by comorbid medical illness or anxiety. *Journal of Clinical Psychiatry, 68*(1), e01.

Unützer, J., & Park, M. (2012). Strategies to improve the management of depression in primary care. *Primary Care: Clinics in Office Practice, 39*(2), 415–431.

Vandeleur, C. L., Fassassi, S., Castelao, E., Glaus, J., Strippoli, M. F., Lasserre, A. M., . . . Preisig, M. (2017). Prevalence and correlates of DSM-5 major depressive and related disorders in the community. *Psychiatry Research, 250*, 50–58.

Van Mierlo, M. L., Van Heugten, C. M., Post, M. W., De Kort, P. L., & Visser-Meily, J. M. (2015). Psychological factors determine depressive symptomatology after stroke. *Archives of Physical Medicine and Rehabilitation, 96*(6), 1064–1070.

Vega, W. A., Kolody, B., Valle, R., & Hough, R. (1986). Depressive symptoms and their correlates among immigrant Mexican women in the United States. *Social Science and Medicine, 22*(6), 645–652.

Verplanken, B., Friborg, O., Wang, C. E., Trafimow, D., & Woolf, K. (2007). Mental habits: Metacognitive reflection on negative self-thinking. *Journal of Personality and Social Psychology, 92*(3), 526–554.

Viinamaki, H., Tanskanen, A., Honkalampi, K., Koivumaa-Honkanen, H., Antikainen, R., Haatainen, K., & Hintikka, J. (2000). Effect of somatic comorbidity on alleviation of depressive symptoms. *Australian and New Zealand Journal of Psychiatry, 34*(5), 755–761.

Vinkers, C. H., Joëls, M., Milaneschi, Y., Kahn, R. S., Penninx, B. W., & Boks, M. P. (2014). Stress exposure across the life span cumulatively increases depression risk and is moderated by neuroticism. *Depression and Anxiety, 31*(9), 737–745.

Wakefield, J. C., Schmitz, M. F., First, M. B., & Horwitz, A. V. (2007). Extending the bereavement exclusion for major depression to other losses: Evidence from the National Comorbidity Survey. *Archives of General Psychiatry, 64*(4), 433–440.

Waraich, P., Goldner, E. M., Somers, J. M., & Hsu, L. (2004). Prevalence and incidence studies of mood disorders: A systematic review of the literature. *Canadian Journal of Psychiatry, 49*(2), 124–138.

Watkins, E. R., & Nolen-Hoeksema, S. (2014). A habit-goal framework of depressive rumination. *Journal of Abnormal Psychology, 123*(1), 24–34.

Welch, J. L., & Austin, J. K. (2001). Stressors, coping and depression in haemodialysis patients. *Journal of Advanced Nursing, 33*(2), 200–207.

Wellen, M. (2010). Differentiation between demoralization, grief, and anhedonic depression. *Current Psychiatry Reports, 12*(3), 229–233.

Winter, L. B., Steer, R. A., Jones-Hicks, L., & Beck, A. T. (1999). Screening for major depression disorders in adolescent medical outpatients with the Beck Depression Inventory for Primary Care. *Journal of Adolescent Health, 24*(6), 389–394.

World Health Organization (1990a). *Composite International Diagnostic Interview, Version 1.0* Geneva: World Health Organization.

World Health Organization (WHO), Regional Office for Europe and the International Diabetes Federation, Europe. (1990b). Diabetes mellitus in Europe: A problem at all ages and in all countries. A model for prevention and self care. *Giornale Italiano Diabetologia e Metabolismo, 10*(Supplement), 1–140.

World Health Organization (2017). *Depression: Fact sheet.* Retrieved from http://www.who.int/mediacentre/factsheets/fs369/en/

Yano, E. M., Chaney, E. F., Campbell, D. G., Klap, R., Simon, B. F., Bonner, L. M., . . . Rubenstein, L. V. (2012). Yield of practice-based depression screening in VA primary care settings. *Journal of General Internal Medicine, 27*(3), 331–338.

Yesavage, J. A., Brink, T. L., Rose, T. L., Lum, O., Huang, V., Adey, M., & Leirer, V. O. (1982). Development and validation of a geriatric depression screening scale: A preliminary report. *Journal of Psychiatric Research, 17*(1), 37–49.

Zigmond, A. S., & Snaith, R. P. (1983). The Hospital Anxiety and Depression Scale. *Acta Psychiatrica Scandinavica, 67*(6), 361–370.

Zisook, S., Corruble, E., Duan, N., Iglewicz, A., Karam, E. G., Lanuoette, N., . . . Young, H. T. (2012). The bereavement exclusion and DSM-5. *Depression and Anxiety, 29*, 425–443.

Zisook, S., Simon, N. M., Reynolds, C. F. 3rd, Pies, R., Lebowitz, B., Young, I. T., . . . Shear, M. K. (2010). Bereavement, complicated grief, and DSM, part 2: Complicated grief. *Journal of Clinical Psychiatry, 71*(8), 1097–1098.

Zung, W. W. (1972). The Depression Status Inventory: An adjunct to the Self-Rating Depression Scale. *Journal of Clinical Psychology, 28*(4), 539–543.

Zunszain, P. A., Anacker, C., Cattaneo, A., Carvalho, L. A., & Pariante, C. M. (2011). Glucocorticoids, cytokines and brain abnormalities in depression. *Progress in Neuropsychopharmacology and Biological Psychiatry, 35*(3), 722–729.

CHAPTER 9

Anxiety Disorders

JANET WOODRUFF-BORDEN, ANGELA LEE, and COLETTE GRAMSZLO

A NXIETY DISORDERS ARE commonly diagnosed in the United States, with almost one-third of individuals meeting criteria for at least one of the anxiety disorders at some time in their lives (Aalto-Setälä, Marttunen, Tuulio-Henriksson, & Lönnqvist, 2001; Beekman et al., 1998; Kessler et al., 1994; Steel et al., 2014). In addition to their prevalence, the anxiety disorders are also associated with decreased quality of life (Olatunji, Cisler, & Tolin, 2007) and substantial interference, including poor educational outcomes (Kessler, Foster, Saunders, & Stang, 1995), under-employment or unemployment (Goisman et al., 1994), decreased work productivity and school performance (Liebowitz, Gorman, Fyer, & Klein, 1985; Turner, Beidel, Dancu, & Keys, 1986; van Ameringen, Mancini, & Streiner, 1993; Wittchen & Beloch, 1996; Zhang, Ross, & Davidson, 2004), and increased use of services, particularly primary health care (Wittchen, 2002). Anxiety disorders create a large societal burden, with annual costs estimated at $42.3 billion, or $1,542 per individual meeting the criteria for an anxiety disorder (Greenberg et al., 1999). In this chapter, we review descriptions of each of the anxiety disorders in the *Diagnostic and Statistical Manual of Mental Disorders*, fifth edition (*DSM-5*; American Psychiatric Association [APA], 2013), and their epidemiology, assessment, treatment, and etiology.

DESCRIPTION OF THE DISORDERS

PANIC DISORDER

Panic attacks are defined as discrete periods of intense fear or discomfort that begin abruptly and reach their peak within 10 minutes. The *DSM-5* requires that at least four of the following 13 symptoms be present: palpitations, pounding heart, or accelerated heart rate; sweating; trembling or shaking; sensations of shortness of breath or smothering; feelings of choking; chest pain or discomfort; nausea or abdominal distress; feeling dizzy, unsteady, lightheaded, or faint; derealization or depersonalization; fear of losing control or going crazy; fear of dying; paresthesias; and chills or hot flushes.

Panic attacks can be expected (i.e., cued), as well as unexpected (i.e., uncued). Anyone, including individuals with no panic disorder (PD) diagnoses, can experience expected or

Adult Psychopathology and Diagnosis, Eighth Edition. Edited by Deborah C. Beidel and B. Christopher Frueh.
© 2018 John Wiley & Sons, Inc. Published 2018 by John Wiley & Sons, Inc.
Companion website: www.wiley.com/go/beidel/psychopathology8e

unexpected panic attacks. Expected panic attacks often occur in the context of many psychiatric conditions, especially anxiety disorders. For example, the acute fear responses that individuals with specific phobias experience in the presence of feared objects or situations (e.g., spider phobics' responses to spiders) sometimes meet the criteria for a panic attack. When a panic attack is triggered by exposure to or anticipation of a feared object or situation, it is considered to be an expected or cued panic attack. Expected panic attacks occur in nonclinical populations, with about 6.3% of a community sample reporting having experienced a full-blown panic attack at some time during their lives (Craske et al., 2010; Norton, Zvolensky, Bonn-Miller, Cox, & Norton, 2008). Due to the ubiquitous nature of panic attacks, they have been designated as a potential specifier for any *DSM* disorder in the *DSM-5* (APA, 2013).

Unlike cued panic attacks, uncued panic attacks seemingly have no cue or trigger, and happen during unexpected times. The diagnosis of PD requires recurrent and unexpected (uncued) panic attacks, followed by at least 1 month of concern about (a) additional attacks or the implications of the attack, or (b) changes in behavior (APA, 2013). The *DSM-5* does not recognize subtypes of PD (e.g., respiratory, nocturnal, nonfearful, cognitive, and vestibular subtypes), although some investigators have explored the possibility of categorizing PD in this way (see Kircanski, Craske, Epstein, & Wittchen, 2010). Individuals with PD appear to have heightened awareness of and sensitivity to bodily sensations of arousal (e.g., Zoellner & Craske, 1999). One factor theorized to maintain PD is interoceptive conditioning, or the conditioned fear of internal bodily cues (e.g., elevated heart rate), due to their connections to negative effects of panic (e.g., fear or distress). Low levels of somatic sensations of arousal become conditioned to elicit large reactions of anxiety or panic (Dworkin & Dworkin, 1999). The second factor is the catastrophic misappraisal of bodily sensations; the physiological sensations associated with panic attacks are misinterpreted as signs of losing one's mind, death, etc.

One issue that should be considered when diagnosing PD is that symptom frequency appears to vary cross-culturally (Lewis-Fernández et al., 2010). Cultural syndromes, which include systems of affiliated bodily sensations, may help to explain why non-*DSM* physiological arousal symptoms are prominent during panic attacks in different cultures. For example, 53% of *ataques de nervios* (attack of nerves) among Latin Americans are characterized by a sense of heat rising in the chest (Guarnaccia, Rivera, Franco, & Neighbors, 1996). This may not be appropriately captured by the *DSM-5* phrase "hot flushes", which indicates a sensation throughout the entire body. Similarly, although panic attacks are commonly considered to peak within 10 minutes, various cultures consider panic attacks to stem from worry episodes. Thus, one should consider cultural context when utilizing reports of panic attack duration as a means of discerning for PD.

AGORAPHOBIA

Agoraphobia is a fear of being in public places or situations in which escape might be difficult or in which help may be unavailable if a panic attack occurred. Patients with agoraphobia avoid (or endure with marked distress) certain situations, including large stores; open or crowded public spaces; traveling on buses, trains, or in cars; and being far or away from home (APA, 2013).

The *DSM-III-R* (APA, 1987) viewed agoraphobia as primary and panic attacks as a frequent but secondary feature. It included the diagnostic categories of "agoraphobia with panic attacks" and "agoraphobia without panic attacks." Subsequent revisions of the *DSM* have reversed this view and have included diagnostic categories of "panic disorder with agoraphobia," "panic disorder without agoraphobia," and an infrequently used category of "agoraphobia without panic disorder." This last category is used for patients who deny or have an unclear history of panic attacks, or who merely report histories of panic-like experiences (e.g., limited symptom panic attacks). Such cases may be difficult to differentiate from specific phobias, obsessive-compulsive disorder, and post-traumatic stress disorder (PTSD). Although agoraphobia was seen as a frequent but secondary feature of PD in the *DSM-III-R* and *DSM-IV* (APA, 2000), the view that it is a distinctive condition independent of PD (Wittchen, Gloster, Beesdo-Baum, Fava, & Craske, 2010) is now incorporated into the *DSM-5*.

GENERALIZED ANXIETY DISORDER

Generalized anxiety disorder (GAD) is characterized by worry (APA, 2013), which is typically defined as repetitive thinking about potential future threat, imagined catastrophes, uncertainties, and risks (Watkins, 2008). Individuals with GAD spend an excessive amount of time worrying and feeling anxious about a variety of topics, and they find it difficult to control the worry. The diagnosis also requires three or more of the following six symptoms: (1) restlessness or feeling keyed up or on edge; (2) being easily fatigued; (3) difficulty concentrating or mind going blank; (4) irritability; (5) muscle tension; and (6) sleep disturbance. Finally, the worry and anxiety are not confined to another disorder (e.g., worry about social evaluation only in the context of social anxiety disorder), and they lead to significant distress or impairment.

The diagnosis of GAD first appeared in the *DSM-III* (APA, 1980), but it was poorly defined, unreliable, and assigned only in the absence of other disorders (Mennin, Heimberg, & Turk, 2004). With publication of the *DSM-III-R* (APA, 1987), the diagnostic criteria for GAD were revised to include worry as the primary feature and to allow for primary diagnoses of GAD in the presence of other disorders. Despite these improvements, diagnostic reliability remained poor due to overly broad criteria for associated symptoms (Marten et al., 1993). The *DSM-IV* (APA, 1994) added the uncontrollability criterion and reduced the set of associated symptoms to reflect empirical findings and to improve specificity. As a result, diagnostic reliability improved but remained low relative to most of the other anxiety disorders (Brown, Di Nardo, Lehman, & Campbell, 2001). The *DSM-5* continues to use the same diagnostic criteria.

Although worry is the primary diagnostic and clinical feature of GAD, the majority of high worriers do not meet criteria for the disorder (Ruscio, 2002). However, compared with high worriers without GAD, high worriers with GAD report greater distress and impairment associated with worry, indicating that worry is more harmful at clinical levels. High worriers with GAD are also more likely to perceive their worry as uncontrollable (Ruscio & Borkovec, 2004). Individuals who do not meet the "excessiveness of worry" criterion may present a milder form of GAD; they are less symptomatic overall and report fewer comorbid disorders compared with individuals with full GAD (Ruscio et al., 2005).

Several theoretical conceptualizations of GAD converge on the idea that worry serves an avoidant function. These conceptualizations include the avoidance theory, the intolerance of uncertainty model, the metacognitive model, and emotion regulation models (for a detailed review, see Behar, DiMarco, Hekler, Mohlman, & Staples, 2009).

The avoidance theory (Borkovec, Alcaine, & Behar, 2004) holds that the verbal-linguistic properties of worry preclude emotional processing. Worry is primarily verbal-linguistic as opposed to imagery-based in nature (Behar, Zuellig, & Borkovec, 2005; Borkovec & Inz, 1990; Stöber, Tepperwien, & Staak, 2000), and it inhibits somatic arousal during a subsequent anxiety-inducing task (Borkovec & Hu, 1990; Borkovec, Lyonfields,

Wiser, & Deihl, 1993; Peasley-Miklus & Vrana, 2000). Moreover, worry is associated with decreased anxious affect during subsequent periods of trauma recall (Behar et al., 2005) and depressive rumination (McLaughlin, Borkovec, & Sibrava, 2007). Lastly, individuals with GAD often report that worry serves as a distraction from more emotional topics (Borkovec & Roemer, 1995). Thus, it seems that worry precludes the somatic and emotional activation required for habituation to anxiety-provoking stimuli. Moreover, worry may be negatively reinforced via the removal of aversive and evocative images and emotional experiences (Borkovec et al., 2004). Intolerance of uncertainty (IU) is defined as the tendency to respond negatively to uncertain situations in terms of cognition, affect, and behavior (Dugas, Buhr, & Ladouceur, 2004). IU is further defined as a schema through which an individual with GAD perceives the environment; for the individual with GAD, uncertain situations are unacceptable and distressing and may lead to worry (Dugas et al., 2004). Individuals with GAD consistently report greater levels of IU compared with nonclinical controls (Dugas, Gagnon, Ladouceur, & Freeston, 1998; Ladouceur, Blais, Freeston, & Dugas, 1998) and individuals with other anxiety disorders (Dugas, Marchand, & Ladouceur, 2005; Ladouceur et al., 1999). Finally, worry partially statistically mediates the relationship between IU and anxiety (Yook, Kim, Suh, & Lee, 2010).

The premise of the metacognitive model of GAD is that individuals with GAD experience two types of worry: type 1 worry refers to worry about external threats and noncognitive internal triggers (e.g., physical symptoms), whereas type 2 worry refers to meta-worry, or worry about worry (Wells, 1995, 2004). Positive beliefs about worry (e.g., that worrying will help avoid a catastrophe) give rise to type 1 worry, whereas negative beliefs about worry (e.g., the belief that worry is uncontrollable) prompt type 2 worry. Negative beliefs about worry may be more specific to GAD compared with positive beliefs about worry. Individuals with GAD perceive worry as more dangerous and uncontrollable than do individuals with other anxiety disorders and controls, even when controlling for type 1 worry (Davis & Valentiner, 2000; Wells & Carter, 2001). Type 2 worry, on the other hand, may not be specific to GAD; individuals with GAD do not report greater positive beliefs about worry compared with anxious nonworriers (Davis & Valentiner, 2000), high worriers without GAD (Ruscio & Borkovec, 2004), and individuals with other anxiety disorders (Wells & Carter, 2001).

Emotion dysregulation models propose that individuals with GAD have difficulties understanding and modulating their emotions, and they may instead rely on suppression and control strategies (e.g., worry; Mennin, Heimberg, Turk, & Fresco, 2002). The model further describes specific components of emotion dysregulation in GAD, including heightened intensity of emotions (both positive and negative, but particularly negative; Turk, Heimberg, Luterek, Mennin, & Fresco, 2005), poor understanding of emotions, negative reactivity to emotions, and maladaptive management of emotions (Mennin, Heimberg, Turk, & Fresco, 2005; Mennin, Holaway, Fresco, Moore, & Heimberg, 2007). Both analogue and clinical GAD samples report higher emotion dysregulation compared with nonanxious participants, although individuals with depression report similar deficits. Moreover, self-reported emotion dysregulation predicts severity of trait worry and analogue GAD status when controlling for negative affect (Salters-Pedneault, Roemer, Tull, Rucker, & Mennin, 2006). The acceptance-based model also posits difficulties with emotional experiences in GAD, but instead focuses on fear and avoidance of internal experiences (Roemer, Salters, Raffa, & Orsillo, 2005). Indeed, deficits in mindfulness account for unique variance in GAD symptom severity, even after controlling for emotion regulation and depressive and anxious symptoms (Roemer et al., 2009).

Social Anxiety Disorder

Social anxiety disorder (SAD) is a marked and persistent fear of social or performance situations in which embarrassment may occur. Exposure to or anticipation of the feared social situation almost invariably provokes anxiety or fear. Acute fear responses can take the form of situationally bound or predisposed panic attacks. Feared situations include performing certain activities in the presence of others (such as speaking, eating, drinking, or writing), or fearing that one may do something that will cause humiliation or embarrassment, such as saying something stupid or not knowing what to say, behaving inappropriately, or appearing overly anxious. The diagnosis requires that these feared situations are either avoided or endured with significant distress (APA, 2013). The insight criterion found in previous versions of the *DSM* (i.e., that the individual recognizes that the fear is irrational) has been replaced with the criterion that the clinician judges the fear to be out of proportion to actual danger (APA, 2013). Cultural factors are likely to affect the assessment of this requirement, as it implies a comparison to the patient's social reference group (Lewis-Fernández et al., 2010).

If an individual fears many or most social interactions, the generalized subtype should be specified. Generalized SAD overlaps considerably with avoidant personality disorder, so much so that they there has been debate as to whether the latter should be removed as a classification, and family studies have shown that the two co-aggregate in the same families (Chavira, Shipon-Blum, Hitchcock, Cohen, & Stein, 2007; Isomura et al., 2015; Stein & Stein, 2008). Individuals not assigned to the generalized subtype are commonly viewed as belonging to a nongeneralized or specific subtype. Compared with the nongeneralized subtype, the generalized subtype is associated with greater comorbidity, earlier age of onset, greater heritability, and is generally an indicator of greater severity, as is the overlapping diagnosis of avoidant personality disorder (Bögels et al., 2010).

Social anxiety disorder may subsume three other possible disorders. First, the separate diagnostic category of selective mutism may be an expression of SAD during childhood (Bögels et al., 2010). This conceptualization of selective mutism treats the refusal to talk as a form of social avoidance. Second, the *DSM-5* recognizes a culturally bound syndrome, Taijin Kyofusho, found mainly in Japan and Korea. This condition appears to be a cultural form of anthropophobia, a condition recognized in the *ICD-10* (World Health Organization, 1992). These conditions involve a fear of offending and making others uncomfortable, such as through poor manners or bad odors, and have also been documented in Western cultures (Choy, Schneier, Heimberg, Oh, & Liebowitz, 2008; Kim, Rapee, & Gaston, 2008; McNally, Cassiday, & Calamari, 1990). Lewis-Fernández et al. (2010) have suggested that the definition of SAD could be broadened to subsume Taijin Kyofusho and equivalent conditions. Third, the *DSM-5* does not recognize test anxiety as a separate disorder but subsumes it within SAD. LeBeau et al. (2010) suggested that one form of test anxiety may be a form of SAD in that it involves social evaluative concerns and acute fear reactions, whereas a second form may be a form of GAD in that it involves anticipatory anxiety and worry. The *DSM-5* requires a specification when "performance anxiety only" applies, implying that there may be two distinct conditions within the diagnostic category of SAD.

Specific Phobias

Specific phobias are marked and persistent fears of clearly discernible, circumscribed objects or situations. Exposure or anticipation of exposure to the feared object or situation almost invariably provokes anxiety or fear. Acute fear responses can take the form of expected (situationally bound or cued) panic attacks. Five subtypes of specific phobia are recognized by the *DSM-5* and are specified based on the type of object or situation that is feared: animals (e.g., dogs, snakes, spiders), natural environment (e.g., storms, water, heights), blood-injection-injury (BII; e.g., seeing blood, getting an injection with a syringe), situations (e.g., elevators, flying), and other (e.g., situations related to choking, vomiting, illness, falling without means of physical support). The diagnosis requires that these feared situations are either avoided or endured with significant distress (APA, 2013).

Although many individuals meet criteria for a specific phobia, very few seek treatment (Barlow, DiNardo, Vermilyea, Vermilyea, & Blanchard, 1986), although individuals with comorbid diagnoses might be more likely to seek treatment (Barlow, 1988). Animal phobia and height phobia are the most frequently diagnosed forms (Curtis, Magee, Eaton, Wittchen, & Kessler, 1998; Stinson et al., 2007). Although subtypes of specific phobia appear to have relatively distinctive ages of onset (Öst, 1987), they are generally accepted as constituting a single category. An exception is the BII subtype, which may be or may subsume a disorder with distinct features and etiological factors (LeBeau et al., 2010; Page, 1994). A primary distinction between BII and other subtypes is its unique physiological profile, including initial heart rate acceleration and subsequent deceleration, and consequent associations with vasovagal fainting. In a factor analysis of specific phobia symptoms, Wittchen, Beesdo, and Gloster (2009) found that while animal, situational and natural environment phobia loaded onto the same factor, BII phobia was not consistently associated with any one factor, further distinguishing the separation of the subtype from others.

DIAGNOSTIC CONSIDERATIONS

With its emphasis on clinical utility, previous editions of the *DSM* have utilized a strictly categorical model: either the *DSM* criteria for a mental illness are met, and the illness is considered present, or they are not met, and the illness is absent. A benefit of using categorical models is high predictive power—clinicians can expect similar behaviors, and make treatment decisions accordingly. A drawback to this system is that an individual may still exhibit significant disorder symptomatology, while not technically meeting criteria for diagnosis. Thus, existing treatments have mostly only been empirically validated with individuals who meet full *DSM* criteria, as extant literature has also been guided by categorical models of disorders. Some researchers have suggested that dimensional methods may more accurately model the nature of these problems (Krueger, 1999; Watson, 2005). While all of the disorders in the *DSM-5* remain in categories, certain amendments move the system towards a dimensional model. For example, four categorical disorders were combined to form autism spectrum disorder. Dimensional models allow researchers and clinicians the flexibility to assess severity of conditions along a continuum, without imposing a concrete boundary between normalcy and pathology. This may be particularly appropriate for anxiety disorders, which show considerable overlap and high rates of comorbidity, and continuously span the spectrum from clinical to nonclinical levels.

In diagnosing anxiety disorders, it is important to consider typical versus pathological anxiety. It is normal to feel anxious under certain situations, and is often an appropriate response to threatening or stressful situations. It is important to assess whether the experienced anxiety is excessive or impairs the individual's day-to-day functioning. Consequently, one should also consider differential diagnosis for anxiety.

Due to the natural response of anxiety in the face of uncertainty, many symptoms of anxiety, such as panic, rumination, and worry, can be present in a variety of other psychopathologies. Indeed, there are high rates of comorbidity between the different types of anxiety disorders, as well as between anxiety disorders and other disorders, such as major depressive disorder (MDD) and personality disorders (e.g., Friborg, Martinussen, Kaiser, Øvergård, & Rosenvinge, 2013). Further, it is important to rule out medical reasons for bodily sensations that mimic physiological arousal symptoms indicative of anxiety disorders. For example, withdrawal symptoms after substance abuse are very similar to symptoms for certain anxiety disorders, including irritability, anxiety, restlessness, sweating and hot flashes, and altered appetite (National Institute on Drug Abuse, 2016).

EPIDEMIOLOGY

PANIC DISORDER

Prevalence　The lifetime prevalence rate of PD is estimated to be between approximately 1.5% and 5%, whereas the 12-month prevalence rate is estimated to be between approximately 1% and 3.7% (Bandelow & Michaelis, 2015; Barlow, 2002; Grant et al., 2006; Kessler et al., 2005a; Kessler, Chiu, Demler, & Walters, 2005b; Kessler, Petukhova, Sampson, Zaslavsky, & Wittchen, 2012).

Gender　The incidence rate of PD is approximately two-fold higher in women than in men (Barlow, 2002; Bland, Orn, & Newman, 1988; Mathews, Gelder, & Johnson, 1981; Wittchen, Essau, von Zerssen, Krieg, & Zaudig, 1992). Different hypotheses have been proposed to account for observed gender differences in relation to the incidence of PD. For example, it is possible that women are simply more likely to report fear, or it is possible that men are more likely than women to engage in self-medication for their anxiety and, thus, are less likely to report problems with panic (Barlow, 2002). Factor structure analyses suggest that gender differences among anxiety disorders more generally may reflect a latent tendency for women to experience internalizing symptoms, while men are more likely to experience externalizing symptoms (Eaton et al., 2013).

Age of Onset　The average age of onset for PD is 26.5 years (range = 19.7–32) (Burke, Burke, Regier, & Rae, 1990; Grant et al., 2006; McNally, 2001; Öst, 1987). PD typically first appears during adulthood, although it may also appear in prepubescent children and older adults (Barlow, 2002).

Comorbidity　Approximately half of individuals currently suffering from PD also suffer from a comorbid psychological disorder, with comorbidity estimates ranging from 51% to 60% (Brown, Antony, & Barlow, 1995; Brown, Campbell, Lehman, Grisham, & Mancill, 2001). Among the most commonly co-occurring disorders, approximately 59% of individuals with PD are diagnosed with a comorbid mood or anxiety disorder and 46% with a comorbid anxiety disorder alone. Among specific disorders, approximately 23% of individuals with PD experience co-occurring MDD, 16% co-occurring GAD, 15% co-occurring SAD, and 15% co-occurring specific phobia (SpP; Brown et al., 2001). PD is also often accompanied by substance use disorders (Barlow, 2002), and this comorbidity appears to reflect attempts at self-medication, and, to a lesser degree, common genetic vulnerability (Kushner, Abrams, & Borchardt, 2000).

Clinical Course   The clinical course for PD is chronic and disabling without treatment. The 12-month remission rate for PD is estimated to be approximately 17%, while the 5-year remission rate is estimated to be approximately 39% (Keller et al., 1994; Yonkers et al., 1998). PD is also associated with substantial social, occupational, and physical disability, including especially high rates of medical utilization (Barlow, 2002).

Agoraphobia

Prevalence   Because most current, nationally representative epidemiological studies were conducted prior to the publication of the *DSM-5*, agoraphobia has been primarily measured in the context of PD. The lifetime prevalence rate of agoraphobia with or without PD is estimated to be between 0.08% and 2.6%, while the 12-month prevalence rate is between 0.01% and 1.7% (Bandelow & Michaelis, 2015; Kessler et al., 2012).

Gender   Lifetime prevalence of agoraphobia is nearly twice as high for women. This gender gap is significant for individuals 64 years and younger. Though women over 65 report agoraphobia more than do men, the gender gap is closed somewhat in this age group (Kessler et al., 2012).

Age of Onset   The average age of onset among individuals diagnosed with agoraphobia is 27 years (Tibi et al., 2015) with diagnosis before age 14 being very rare (Copeland, Angold, Shanahan, & Costello, 2014). There is recent evidence of an older-adult subtype of agoraphobia. In an epidemiological survey of adults 65 and older, as much as 10% of the population met for a current diagnosis of agoraphobia, and 11% of those followed over a 4-year period experienced their first agoraphobic episode in that time period (Ritchie, Norton, Mann, Carriere, & Ancelin, 2013).

Comorbidity   Agoraphobia is highly comorbid with other psychiatric disorders, with 88% of those diagnosed with agoraphobia experiencing another disorder as well. Results of the National Comorbidity Study indicate that agoraphobia is most frequently comorbid with social phobia (46.5%) followed closely by MDD (45.9%) and other phobias (45.6%). Though agoraphobia has historically been diagnosed in the context of PD, only 21.6% of those with agoraphobia also meet criteria for PD. Approximately one-third of individuals with agoraphobia also experience a substance use disorder, most commonly alcohol use disorder (Magee, Eaton, Wittchen, McGonagle, & Kessler, 1996).

Clinical Course   Agoraphobia rarely remits without intervention. Over a 6-year period, about 12% of individuals diagnosed with agoraphobia experienced symptomatic improvement, while the remainder experienced persistence or deterioration, including 14.8% experiencing severe deterioration. Agoraphobia is thought to be particularly intractable because individuals with agoraphobia experience a particularly high level of avoidance, reducing opportunities to decrease anxiety without treatment (Spinhoven et al., 2016).

Generalized Anxiety Disorder

Prevalence   The lifetime prevalence rate of GAD is between 2.8% and 6.2%, whereas the 12-month prevalence rate is between 0.9% and 2.9% (Bandelow & Michaelis, 2015; Kessler et al., 2005a,b, 2012).

Gender Generalized anxiety disorder is more prevalent among women. In a nationally representative sample, women were approximately twice as likely as men to report lifetime and 12-month diagnoses of GAD, and reported greater disability from GAD (Vesga-López et al., 2008). Given that the genetic contribution to GAD is equivalent among men and women, gender differences in prevalence are likely due to cognitive and environmental influences (Hettema, Prescott, & Kendler, 2001). Finally, although prevalence and severity differ between genders, rates of relapse and remission are similar (Yonkers, Bruce, Dyck, & Keller, 2003).

Age of Onset Generalized anxiety disorder is associated with a later age of onset compared with the other anxiety disorders, with 50% of lifetime cases beginning by age 31 (Kessler et al., 2005a), though recent studies suggest that the age of onset may be closer to adolescence or young adulthood (McGorry, Purcell, Goldstone, & Amminger, 2011).

Comorbidity Correctly classifying GAD may be particularly difficult due to high rates of comorbidity and symptom overlap with other disorders, especially MDD (Kessler et al., 2005b). GAD and MDD have the highest rate of comorbidity of any anxiety and mood disorders. Indeed, 67% of those with lifetime GAD retrospectively reported MDD, while 20% of those with MDD reported experiencing GAD at some point (Zbozinek, 2012). Twenty-six percent of those with a primary diagnosis of GAD also meet criteria for current MDD (Brown et al., 2001). In a longitudinal birth-cohort study, Moffitt et al. (2007) found that 12% of the sample had lifetime diagnoses of both GAD and MDD. Among those comorbid cases, 37% reported that GAD temporally preceded MDD, whereas 32% reported that MDD temporally preceded GAD. Despite substantial comorbidity between GAD and MDD, a recent study found evidence that GAD was more like other anxiety disorders than it was to depression with respect to risk factors and temporal patterns (Beesdo, Pine, Lieb, & Wittchen, 2010). Furthermore, a substantial proportion of GAD diagnoses occur without comorbid depression, and levels of impairment between the two disorders are comparable (Kessler, DuPont, Berglund, & Wittchen, 1999). Thus, although GAD and MDD overlap considerably, evidence suggests that they occur independently and likely represent unique syndromes.

Clinical Course A naturalistic longitudinal study found that 42% of participants who were diagnosed with GAD at baseline were still symptomatic at a 12-year follow-up (Bruce et al., 2005). Although cognitive-behavioral therapy (CBT) is effective for treating GAD (Borkovec & Ruscio, 2001) only 50% of patients achieve high end-state functioning following treatment (Borkovec, Newman, Pincus, & Lytle, 2002).

SOCIAL ANXIETY DISORDER

Prevalence The lifetime prevalence rate of SAD is estimated to be between 5.0% and 13.3%, whereas the 12-month prevalence rate is estimated to be between 2.8% and 7.4% (Grant et al., 2005; Kessler et al., 1994, 2005a,b, 2014).

Gender The incidence rate of SAD is relatively equally represented between women and men, with the sex ratio (1.4:1) only somewhat favoring women relative to men (Kessler et al., 2005a).

Age of Onset   The average age of onset for SAD is approximately 15 years of age, with a median age of onset of approximately 12.5 years of age (Grant et al., 2005). SAD is typically especially prevalent among young adults between the ages of 18 and 29 (Kessler et al., 2005a).

Comorbidity   Approximately 70% of adults diagnosed with SAD will develop a comorbid psychiatric disorder (Clauss & Blackford, 2012). Among the most commonly co-occurring disorders, approximately 45% of individuals with SAD present with a comorbid mood or anxiety disorder, and approximately 28% of individuals with a comorbid anxiety disorder alone. Among specific disorders, approximately 14% of individuals with SAD suffer from co-occurring MDD, and 13% of individuals from co-occurring GAD (Brown et al., 2001). Other commonly comorbid disorders include substance use disorders (Grant et al., 2005).

Clinical Course   The clinical course for SAD is chronic and disabling without treatment. The 12-month remission rate for SAD is estimated to be approximately 7%, and the 5-year remission rate is estimated to be approximately 27% (Yonkers et al., 2003). SAD is also associated with substantial social, occupational, and physical disability, including especially high levels of scholastic difficulties (Stein & Kean, 2000).

SPECIFIC PHOBIA

Prevalence   The lifetime prevalence rate for specific phobia is estimated to be between 2% and 15.6%, whereas the 12-month prevalence rate is estimated to be between 1.8% and 12.1% (Bland et al., 1988; Eaton, Dryman, & Weissman, 1991; Kessler et al., 2005a,b, 2014; Lindal & Stefansson, 1993; Stinson et al., 2007; Wittchen, Nelson, & Lachner, 1998). Among the specific phobias, animal phobia and height phobia are the most frequently diagnosed forms (Curtis et al., 1998; Stinson et al., 2007).

Gender   Specific phobia is approximately four times more common in women than in men (Kessler et al., 2005a). However, research indicates that the incidence of phobias of heights, flying, injections, dentists, and injury do not differ significantly between women and men (Fredrikson, Annas, Fischer, & Wik, 1996). Different hypotheses have been put forth to account for observed gender differences in relation to the incidence of specific phobia. These hypotheses include differences in the reporting of fear between men and women, as well as differences in emotion socialization (Barlow, 2002).

Age of Onset   The average age of onset for specific phobia is between 9.1 and 16.1 years of age (Stinson et al., 2007; Thyer, Parrish, Curtis, Nesse, & Cameron, 1985), with a median age of onset of approximately 15 years (Magee et al., 1996). Results suggest that particular specific phobias may have differential ages of onset. For example, animal phobia and BII phobia tend to begin in childhood, whereas situational phobia and height phobia tend to develop in adolescence or adulthood (e.g., Antony, Brown, & Barlow, 1997; Barlow, 2002; Himle, McPhee, Cameron, & Curtis, 1989; Marks & Gelder, 1966; Öst, 1987).

Comorbidity   Specific phobias are likely to co-occur with other specific phobias, with only 24.4% of phobic individuals having a single specific phobia (Curtis et al., 1998). However, other findings suggest that the presence of multiple specific phobias is relatively rare (Fredrikson et al., 1996). Approximately 34% of individuals currently suffering from a specific phobia meet the criteria for an additional psychiatr, with mood and anxiety disorders being the most commonly comorbid disord ___ ___wn et al., 2001). Among mood and anxiety disorders, some research has found especially high rates of co-occurring PD in individuals suffering from specific phobias (Stinson et al., 2007). Other data suggest that specific phobias are rarely the principal diagnosis when they co-occur with other disorders, but they are often a secondary diagnosis (Barlow, 2002; Sanderson, Di Nardo, Rapee, & Barlow, 1990).

Clinical Course   The clinical course for specific phobia is relatively chronic and disabling without treatment. The 15-month full remission rate is estimated to be approximately 19% (Trumpf, Becker, Vriends, Meyer, & Margraf, 2009). Specific phobia is also often associated with substantial social, occupational, and physical disability, including avoidance of medical procedures (Wolitzky-Taylor, Horowitz, Powers, & Telch, 2008).

ASSESSMENT

Multimodal approaches are generally recommended in the assessment of anxiety disorders. These approaches often include the use of a clinical interview, self-report measures, and behavioral tests (e.g., see Antony, 1997; Barlow, 2002; Grös & Antony, 2006). In addition, the emergence of biological assessments may lead to enhanced knowledge of these conditions in the future.

CLINICAL INTERVIEWS

Clinical interviews provide detailed information relating to an individual's psychiatric history and current functioning. Clinical interviews can differ with respect to their format: some clinical interviews are highly structured and directive, whereas other clinical interviews use an unstructured and conversational approach. When seeking a diagnosis, the use of structured clinical interviews is recommended due to their increased standardization and reliability (Summerfeldt, Kloosterman, & Antony, 2010).

Two of the most commonly used semistructured clinical interviews for diagnosing anxiety disorders are the Anxiety Disorders Interview Schedule for *DSM-5* (ADIS-5; Brown & Barlow, 2013) and the Structured Clinical Interview for *DSM-5* (SCID-5; First, Williams, Karg & Spitzer, 2016). These interviews both assess criteria of anxiety disorders specified in the *DSM-5* (APA, 2013). The ADIS-5 informs diagnostic assessment through distress and interference ratings, which comprise an overall Clinician Severity Rating. The SCID-5 relies on a binary rating scale of the presence or absence of symptoms, thus restricting the depth of information collected during the interview, but allowing for a somewhat broader range of diagnoses to be assessed. No psychometric data are currently available for the SCID-5 or the ADIS-5 but previous versions of these tools yielded adequate reliability and validity (Brown et al., 2001). The ADIS-IV demonstrates good interrater reliability ($r = 0.76$–0.90). The SCID also demonstrates fair to excellent interrater reliability, with kappa values between 0.60 and 0.83 (Lobbestael, Leurgans, & Arntz, 2011).

Despite the ADIS-5 and the SCID-5 providing standardized, systematic, and valid assessments, both interviews require training and can be time-consuming to administer. Nonetheless, the use of such interviews is recommended when assessing for these disorders. Other semistructured clinical interviews assess a wider range of *DSM-5* disorders, along with anxiety disorders. These interviews include the Mini International

Neuropsychiatric Interview (MINI-5; Sheehan, 2015), a briefer version of the SCID-5, the Alcohol Use Disorder and Associated Disabilities Interview Schedule—*DSM-5* (AUDADIS-5; Hasin et al., 2015) and the Diagnostic Interview for Anxiety, Mood, and OCD and Related Neuropsychiatric Disorders (DIAMOND; Tolin et al., 2016).

SELF-REPORT MEASURES

Self-report measures provide an efficient and cost-effective method to assess for anxiety disorders, as well as their associated symptoms. For PD, well-validated and frequently used self-report measures include the Panic Disorder Severity Scale (PDSS; Shear et al., 1997) and the Panic and Agoraphobia Scale (PAS; Bandelow, 1999). The Anxiety Sensitivity Index-3 (ASI-3; Taylor et al., 2007) is frequently used to measure anxiety focused on physical sensations, while the Body Sensations Questionnaire focuses more specifically on feared bodily sensations (Chambless, Caputo, Bright, & Gallagher, 1984). Two self-report measures used in the assessment of agoraphobia include the Agoraphobia Cognitions Questionnaire, which assesses for misappraisals of physical sensations, and the Mobility Inventory, which prompts individuals to rate avoidance of agoraphobic situations (Chambless, Caputo, Gracely, Jasin, & Williams, 1985). For GAD, the most commonly used self-report measure is the Generalized Anxiety Disorder Questionnaire—*DSM-IV* (GAD-Q-IV; Newman et al., 2002). The GAD-Q-IV is a nine-item self-report measure of the symptoms of GAD as outlined in the *DSM-IV-TR* and *DSM-5*. The GAD-7 is a similar measure which has demonstrated optimized sensitivity and specificity in screening for GAD (Spitzer, Kroenke, Williams, & Lowe, 2006). Worry, the central symptom dimension underlying GAD, can also be assessed with existing self-report measures, most notably the Penn State Worry Questionnaire (PSWQ; Meyer, Miller, Metzger, & Borkovec, 1990). The PSWQ is a 16-item self-report trait measure of the frequency and intensity of worry. The PSWQ has demonstrated high internal consistency and good retest reliability (Meyer et al., 1990), correlates well with diagnostic measures of GAD (Behar et al., 2005), is distinct from measures of anxiety and depression in clinical samples (Meyer et al., 1990), and discriminates individuals with GAD from those with other anxiety disorders (Brown, Antony, & Barlow, 1992). For SAD, well-validated and frequently used self-report measures include the Social Phobia and Anxiety Inventory (SPAI; Turner, Beidel, Dancu, & Stanley, 1989), the Social Interaction Anxiety Scale (SIAS; Mattick & Clarke, 1998), and the Social Phobia Scale (SPS; Mattick & Clarke, 1998). The Brief Fear of Negative Evaluation Scale (BFNES; Leary, 1983a) is a frequently used self-report measure to assess for the core cognition purported to underlie SAD. For specific phobias, the Fear Survey Schedule (FSS-II; Geer, 1965) is well validated and commonly used, although other promising self-report measures exist as well (e.g., Phobic Stimuli Response Scales; Cutshall & Watson, 2004). Whereas the FSS-II assesses a broad range of specific phobias, self-report measures designed to assess certain types of specific phobias exist as well (e.g., Fear of Spider Questionnaire [Szymanski & O'Donohue, 1995]; Blood-Injection Symptom Scale [Page, Bennett, Carter, Smith, & Woodmore, 1997]).

BEHAVIORAL ASSESSMENTS

Although less frequently used in clinical practice, behavioral assessment strategies offer unique insights into the nature and expression of an individual's symptoms. The chief goal of behavioral assessments is to evaluate an individual's distress during exposure to and avoidance of his/her feared stimulus. Such an assessment is commonly referred to as a behavioral approach test (BAT). BATs can differ in their orientations, with multiple-task BATs (i.e., BATs that require individuals to complete several fear-related tasks) generally being favored relative to single-task BATs. BATs are idiographic in nature, such that the feared stimulus is chosen based on an individual's specific symptom profile. For example, an individual with spider phobia would likely be exposed to different stimuli relating to spiders, whereas an individual with SAD would likely be exposed to situations relating to social or performance situations. In the case of PD, behavioral assessments include physiological symptom inductions that trigger anxiety or fear. Subjective units of distress are often assessed during BATs, with higher units indicating higher levels of distress (e.g., Antony, 1997; Barlow, 2002; Grös & Antony, 2006).

Self-monitoring is another behavioral assessment strategy that is important in the assessment of anxiety disorders. Self-monitoring involves recording thoughts, emotions, and behaviors in response to specific situations. In PD, self-monitoring typically entails recording the time of onset, intensity, antecedents, consequences, and location of panic attacks, as well as cognitions experienced during the attacks. If accompanied by agoraphobia, additional information might include the frequency and duration of excursions from home, distance traveled, escape behaviors, safety behaviors, and level of anxiety (Barlow, 2002). In GAD, self-monitoring entails recording levels of anxiety and associated behaviors and cognitions at many points throughout the day; the resulting enhanced awareness is then used to help clients catch the anxiety spiral early enough to intervene using prescribed interventions before anxiety becomes excessive (e.g., Behar & Borkovec, 2005, 2009). In SAD, self-monitoring typically includes recording the frequency and duration of social interactions, antecedents and consequences of these interactions, cognitions during the interactions, and level of anxiety experienced (e.g., Heimberg, Madsen, Montgomery, & McNabb, 1980). In specific phobia, self-monitoring entails recording thoughts, behaviors, and fear levels upon coming into contact with the feared stimulus. Self-monitoring may also have therapeutic value by helping individuals become more aware of the automatic cognitions and behaviors that maintain their disorders.

Despite the potentially useful information that accompanies behavioral assessment strategies, it is important to note that such strategies have been broadly criticized for poorer reliability and validity relative to structured clinical interviews and self-report measures. Moreover, behavioral assessment strategies can be prone to bias (e.g., observer bias, confirmation bias; Groth-Marnat, 2003).

BIOLOGICAL ASSESSMENT

The pathophysiology of anxiety disorders has been indexed through use of startle reflexes, heart rate reactivity, electrodermal reactivity and facial electromyographic reactions (Lang, McTeague, & Bradley, 2016). Though primarily used for research purposes, these measures are predictive of negative affectivity among individuals with anxiety disorders. Similarly, neuroanatomical assessment techniques are a promising area of research. Though their diagnostic value is limited at present, structural and functional neuroanatomy differences have been identified among anxious individuals (Donzuso, Cerasa, Gioia, Caracciolo, & Quattrone, 2014).

Structural and functional brain differences have been identified among those with anxiety disorders through the use of magnetic resonance imagining (MRI) and functional MRI (fMRI), respectively. Individuals with anxiety disorders evidence reduced gray matter volume in the right ventral anterior cingulate gyrus and the left inferior frontal gyrus (Shang et al., 2014). While individual anxiety disorders demonstrate individual neuroimaging differences, hyperactivity of the amygdala consistently emerges as a shared trait among anxiety disorders (Spoormaker, Vermetten, Czisch, & Frank, 2014). This bottom-up amygdala reactivity is coupled with weak top-down control of such fear responses due to hypoactivity of the ventromedial prefrontal cortex and the anterior cingulate cortex (Taylor & Whalen, 2015). Further, during rest, anxious individuals show decreased connectivity between amygdala areas and the salience network, and increased connectivity between amygdala areas and the central executive network (Peterson, Thome, Frewen, & Lanius, 2014).

TREATMENT

PHARMACOLOGICAL TREATMENTS

Panic Disorder　Many pharmacological agents have been used for the treatment of PD with and without agoraphobia, including benzodiazepines, selective serotonin reuptake inhibitors (SSRIs), serotonin norepinephrine reuptake inhibitors (SNRIs), monoamine oxidase inhibitors (MAOIs), and tricyclic antidepressants (TCAs) (e.g., Ballenger et al., 1988; Barlow, Gorman, Shear, & Woods, 2000; Kjernisted & McIntosh, 2010; Marks et al., 1993; Mavissakalian & Perel, 1999; Nardi et al., 2010; Tesar et al., 1991; van Vliet, Westenberg, & den Boer, 1993). Among these agents, a growing body of research suggests that SSRIs and SNRIs should be considered the front-line pharmacological agents for the treatment of PD, due to the increased levels of tolerance and decreased risks of dependence associated with these drugs (Hoffman & Mathew, 2008; McHugh, Smits, & Otto, 2009; Mochcovitch & Nardi, 2010; Pollack et al., 2007). Although benzodiazepines and TCAs have been shown to be effective in the treatment of panic, they are coupled with increased risks of dependence and side-effects (Bakker, van Balkom, & Spinoven, 2002; Doble & Martin, 2000; Nardi et al., 2005). Thus, they are considered second-choice pharmacological agents for PD (Freire, Cosci, & Nardi, 2011).

Generalized Anxiety Disorder　A host of pharmacological interventions have been used in the treatment of GAD, including benzodiazepines, SSRIs, SNRIs, and TCAs (Baldwin, Waldman, & Allgulander, 2011; Hidalgo, Tupler, & Davidson, 2007; Katzman, 2009; Mitte, Noack, Steil, & Hautzinger, 2005; Mula, Pini, & Cassano, 2007; Rickels & Rynn, 2002). Evidence-based guidelines currently recommend initial treatment with an SSRI or SNRI, based on their proven efficacy in acute and long-term treatment of GAD (Hartford et al., 2007; Koponen et al., 2007; Nicolini et al., 2009). Benzodiazepines have been shown to have short-term efficacy in the treatment of GAD, but are also associated with increased abuse potential and higher drop-out rates (Martin et al., 2007). While benzodiazepines are effective in providing relief from somatic symptoms, the use of an SSRI or SNRI is generally recommended for its larger effect on affective symptom relief, particularly when GAD is comorbid with depression (Davidson, 2009; Olatunji et al., 2008; Mitte et al., 2005).

Social Anxiety Disorder　Efficacious pharmacological agents for the treatment of SAD include benzodiazepines, SSRIs, SNRIs, and MAOIs (e.g., Blackmore, Erwin, Heimberg, Magee, & Fresco, 2009; Blanco et al., 2003; Clark et al., 2003; Davidson et al., 2004; Gerlernter et al., 1991; Kobak, Greist, Jefferson, & Katzelnick, 2002; Ledley & Heimberg, 2005; Otto et al., 2000). Given the noted concerns surrounding benzodiazepines, SSRIs and SNRIs are considered the first-line pharmacological agents for the treatment of SAD, as they are generally well tolerated and efficacious (Jorstad-Stein & Heimberg, 2009). While MAOIs have been shown to be effective, and are usually well tolerated, the accompanying low tyramine diet is an inconvenience for many individuals (Blanco, Bragdon, Schneier, & Liebowitz, 2013). Benzodiazepines may be useful to utilize on an as-needed basis to reduce somatic arousal in response to performance anxiety elicited by social situations, but are not recommended as a long-term treatment.

Specific Phobia Extant data supporting the use of pharmacological agents, such as benzodiazepines and sedatives, in the treatment of specific phobias is limited. While some literature suggests that the use of benzodiazepines may reduce somatic symptomatology during exposure, it also resulted in a greater relapse at follow-up when compared with psychotherapeutic treatments (Choy, Fyer, & Lipsitz, 2007). Moreover, there is a paucity of data relating to the efficacy of antidepressant medications as they relate to the treatment of specific phobias (Grös & Antony, 2006; Hamm, 2009). Two studies examining the efficacy of SSRIs in treating specific phobia produced only modest treatment gains when compared with placebo (Almay et al., 2008; Benjamin et al., 2000). Pharmacological agents are not standard treatments for specific phobias, and many individuals with specific phobia do not seek medical treatment, especially if they are able to manage their fears by avoiding the feared stimulus or situation (Bandelow et al., 2012).

COGNITIVE-BEHAVIORAL TREATMENTS

Panic Disorder Often considered to be a first-line treatment, Cognitive Behavioral Therapy (CBT) that incorporates psychoeducation, interoceptive and *in vivo* exposures, and cognitive restructuring has been shown to be efficacious, with 80–90% of patients showing marked improvement (e.g., Barlow et al., 2000; Clark et al., 2003; Hofmann & Smits, 2008; McHugh et al., 2009; Olatunji, Cisler, & Deacon, 2010; Öst, Thulin, & Ramnero, 2004; Penava, Otto, Maki, & Pollack, 1998; Telch et al., 1993). CBT in both group and individual settings positively benefits individuals with PD and agoraphobia, and the literature has shown that internet-based CBT programs can also have comparable effects to those of face-to-face CBT in the treatment of panic (Kiropoulos et al., 2007; Newman et al., 1997; Sharp et al., 2004) Exposure experiments are coupled with cognitive restructuring, where individuals identify and restructure panic-related threat appraisals. Interoceptive exposures entail provoking feared arousal-related sensations in order to facilitate habituation of fear and disconfirmation of feared catastrophic outcomes of such sensations. In order to keep the level of arousal manageable, a hierarchy of feared situations and sensations is developed and exposure experiments begin with lower-ranked situations (i.e., those that elicit relatively less anxiety), and gradually move up to situations provoking a high amount of anxiety. Treatment gains associated with CBT for PD have shown excellent maintenance, including at 2 years post-treatment (e.g., Craske, Brown, & Barlow, 1991).

Generalized Anxiety Disorder Cognitive-behavioral therapy is also an effective treatment for GAD (Borkovec & Ruscio, 2001). Contemporary approaches to treating GAD emphasize the function of worry, a cardinal feature of GAD, in maintaining anxiety via avoidance of internal experiences (Behar et al., 2009). Treatments combine components such as targeting nonadaptive patterns of behavior and cognition, exposure experiments, and teaching relaxation and problem-solving strategies (Behar & Borkovec,

2005, 2009; Borkovec et al., 2002; Newman et al., 2011). A recent meta-analysis found that CBT treatments have large effects on worrying, anxiety, and depression in adults with GAD, as compared with waitlist control groups. These effects persisted regardless of whether outcome variables were measured with self-report questionnaires or clinician-rated instruments (Cuijpers et al., 2014). Comparisons for differences in modalities showed larger effect sizes for individual therapy than for group therapy. However, in follow-up data, individuals who participated in group therapy showed continued reduction of worry at both 6 and 12 months while individual therapy showed little change post-treatment.

Social Anxiety Disorder   Cognitive-behavioral therapy for SAD includes engagement in psychoeducation, exposure to feared social-evaluative situations, social skills training, and cognitive restructuring in an attempt to modify appraisals and reactions to social situations. A recent meta-analysis showed the benefits of combining exposure and cognitive restructuring, above and beyond either intervention on its own (Ougrin, 2011). As used in the treatment of PD, hierarchically constructed social exposure experiments allow for habituation of fear and disconfirmation of feared catastrophes in the absence of maladaptive responses such as escape and avoidance (e.g., see Clark & Wells, 1995). CBT for SAD has been shown to be efficacious in both individual and group formats (Clark et al., 2006; Feske & Chambless, 1995; Goldin et al., 2014; Heimberg & Becker, 2002; Jorstad-Stein & Heimberg, 2009; Ledley et al., 2009; Olatunji, Cisler, & Deacon 2010; Ponniah & Hollon, 2008; Powers, Sigmarsson, & Emmelkamp, 2008). Moreover, treatment gains associated with CBT for SAD show excellent maintenance, including at 5 years post-treatment (e.g., Heimberg, Salzman, Holt, & Blendell, 1993). Newer formulations of CBT (e.g., Clark, 2001; Clark & Wells, 1995; Hofmann & Otto, 2008) incorporate manipulation of self-focused attention, elimination of safety behaviors, reevaluation of social costs, and change in self-perceptions.

Specific Phobia   Cognitive-behavioral therapy for specific phobia typically involves exposure to feared stimuli in a systematic manner, preventing avoidance responses. In the absence of avoidance, such exposure allows for habituation of fear and disconfirmation of the expected catastrophes associated with encountering feared stimuli (e.g., Antony & Swinson, 2000). Cognitive-behavioral treatments for specific phobia have been shown to be efficacious (e.g., Choy et al., 2007; Hamm, 2009; Muhlberger, Herrmann, Wiedemann, Ellgring, & Pauli, 2001; Olatunji, Cisler, & Deacon 2010; Öst, 1989; Rothbaum, Hodges, Smith, Lee, & Price, 2000; Van Gerwen, Spinhoven, Diekstra, & Van Dyck, 2002; Wolitzky-Taylor et al., 2008). One version of this treatment, delivered during a single session lasting 2–4 hours, has been shown to be highly effective, with about 90% of patients showing marked improvement (Öst, 1989). Notably, *in vivo* exposures have been shown to outperform other active types of treatments, including exposure, relaxation, and cognitive therapy (Wolitzky-Taylor et al., 2008). A variation of *in vivo* exposure therapy that is growing in popularity is virtual reality (VR) and computer-assisted exposure therapy. These types of platforms are helpful when the feared stimuli or situations are difficult to access *in vivo* (e.g., flying phobia). However, there is also preliminary evidence that the appeal of VR-based exposure for participants may be the reduced anticipatory anxiety for people with specific phobia (Garcia-Palacios et al., 2007). Overall, treatment gains associated with CBT for specific phobia have shown excellent maintenance, including at 14 months post-treatment (e.g., Choy et al., 2007).

OTHER PSYCHOLOGICAL TREATMENTS

Acceptance and commitment therapy (ACT) is one of the third-wave cognitive-behavioral therapies that have garnered recent interest as a potential treatment for anxiety disorders (Hayes, Luoma, Bond, Masuda, & Lillis, 2006). An extension of traditional CBT, third-wave treatments also utilize traditional cognitive-behavioral interventions, but additionally place a relatively greater emphasis on the experiential aspects of psychological experiences. Broadly speaking, ACT seeks to reduce the extent to which individuals respond to thoughts and inner experiences in rigid ways that maintain and exacerbate emotional distress, by increasing psychological flexibility. ACT-based treatments have been examined for GAD, PD, and SAD (Avdagic, Morrissey, & Boschen, 2014; Dalrymple & Herbert, 2007; Lopez & Salas, 2009). Preliminary data indicate that ACT is an efficacious treatment for reducing anxiety symptoms in comparison to control conditions (Öst, 2008; Powers et al., 2009, Ruiz, 2010). Findings are more variable when comparing the efficacy of ACT with existing evidence-based therapies, such as CBT. A recent study utilizing sequential meta-analysis techniques showed that there is currently insufficient evidence to confidently conclude that ACT is a more efficacious treatment than CBT for anxiety, although some previous meta-analyses and individual studies have found that ACT was comparable to, or outperformed, CBT (Bluett et al., 2014; Hacker, Stone, & MacBeth, 2016; Ruiz, 2012).

Mindfulness-based interventions (MBIs) have also received increased attention, particularly in the treatment of GAD. Mindfulness is defined as "paying attention in a particular way, on purpose, in the present moment, and nonjudgmentally" (Kabat-Zinn, 1994, p. 4) and "bringing one's complete attention to the present experience on a moment-to-moment basis" (Marlatt & Kristeller, 1999, p. 68). It has been utilized to create interventions such as Mindfulness-Based-Stress Reduction, and has also been incorporated with existing CBT techniques to form Mindfulness-Based Cognitive Therapy. Mindfulness-based treatments aim to increase clients' awareness and acceptance through practicing mindfulness of internal and external experiences, nonjudgmental observation of those experiences, relaxation, meditation, and a focus on the present moment, thereby interrupting the automatic cognitive processes that often maintain anxiety (Roemer, Salters-Pedneault, & Orsillo, 2006). MBIs have been effective in reducing anxiety symptoms in both clinical and nonclinical populations (Hoffman, Sawyer, Witt, & Oh, 2010; Roemer, Orsillo, & Salters-Pedneault, 2008; Vøllestad, Nielsen, & Nielsen, 2012); however, the existing literature has demonstrated mixed results in comparing the effects of MBIs and traditional cognitive-behavioral interventions (e.g., Faucher, Koszycki, Bradwejn, Merali, & Bielajew, 2016; Goldin et al., 2016; Wong et al., 2016). Thus, further research is necessary to better determine whether CBT or MBIs are more efficacious in the treatment of anxiety disorders.

Other psychological treatments that have garnered some interest in the treatment of PD, GAD, SAD, and specific phobias include interpersonal therapy (IPT), psychoanalytic psychotherapy, and eye movement desensitization and reprocessing (EMDR) therapy. High-quality randomized and controlled clinical trials have generally not yet been conducted, or have found no support for treating these disorders with these alternative psychological approaches. For example, an examination of the efficacy of EMDR in the treatment of PD with agoraphobia indicated that EMDR was not significantly different from a credible attention placebo condition (e.g., Goldstein, de Beurs, Chambless, & Wilson, 2000). There has been considerable interest in utilizing IPT, which addresses problematic interpersonal behavior patterns, for the treatment of anxiety. In a study comparing IPT with cognitive therapy, results showed that both cognitive therapy and

IPT led to considerable improvements that were maintained a year later (Stangier, Schramm, Heidenreich, Berger, & Clark, 2011). However, cognitive therapy performed significantly better than IPT in the reduction of social anxiety symptoms. Another study explored the potential augmentation of GAD treatment by integrating IPT with CBT (Newman et al., 2011). Results showed that there were no differences between the CBT condition and the CBT+IPT condition, suggesting that interpersonal and emotional processing techniques may not augment CBT. Overall, due to the lack of current empirical support in favor of these alternate psychological approaches in lieu of CBT, these treatments are not widely considered to be first-line treatments (Hamm, 2009; Jorstad-Stein & Heimberg, 2009; McHugh et al., 2009).

COMBINED PHARMACOLOGICAL AND PSYCHOLOGICAL TREATMENTS

Several studies have examined the combined effects of traditional pharmacological agents and CBT for PD (e.g., Azhar, 2000; Barlow et al., 2000; Berger et al., 2004; Spinhoven, Onstein, Klinkhamer, & Knoppert-van der Klein, 1996; Stein, Norton, Walker, Chartier, & Graham, 2000). In a review of such studies, Furukawa, Watanabe, and Churchill (2006) concluded that combined traditional pharmacological and psychological treatments in the treatment of PD is modestly more efficacious relative to either pharmacological treatment or CBT for PD alone. However, such a combined approach is associated with greater dropouts and side-effects relative to CBT alone for PD (e.g., Barlow et al., 2000). Further, some evidence suggests that while combined treatment may be superior to monotherapies in acute-phase treatment, follow-up measures indicate that combined therapy is equally as effective as psychotherapy (Furukawa, Watanabe, & Churchill, 2008).

Likewise, only a few investigations have examined the efficacy of a combined treatment approach for GAD. Power et al. (1990) failed to find superiority of a combined CBT+ diazepam approach over CBT alone, and Crits-Cristoph et al. (2011) failed to find superiority of a combined CBT+venlafaxine approach over venlafaxine alone, suggesting that combination treatments are not superior to monotherapies in the treatment of GAD. Several studies have found considerable effect sizes of combined treatments when comparing pre–post data, but further investigation would be necessary to determine long-term maintenance of treatment gains beyond those of monotherapies (Bandelow, Seidler-Brandler, Becker, Wedekind, & Rüther, 2007; Bandelow et al., 2015).

Results from studies examining whether a combined approach is efficacious for SAD have been mixed. One study found the combination of pharmacotherapy and cognitive behavioral group therapy to be superior to either approach alone (Blanco et al., 2010), while another found that a combined approach was not superior to either monotherapy (Davidson et al., 2004). In a recent study comparing the efficacy of cognitive therapy, SSRIs, and the combination of both, cognitive therapy was the most effective for SAD both immediately post-treatment and at the 12-month follow-up, compared with both the combined treatment, and pharmacotherapy conditions (Nordahl et al., 2016).

No known studies have examined the efficacy of a combined approach in the treatment of specific phobias, although advantages of such an approach have been posited (e.g., Cottraux, 2004). Some researchers view the use of medications, particularly benzodiazepines, as antithetical to the mechanisms of change in CBT if they are used to reduce feared somatic sensation; clients may attribute treatment gains to the use of medication, which may lead to greater relapse post-treatment (Bruce, Spiegel, & Hegel, 1999; Deacon & Abramowitz, 2005; Moscovitch, Antony, & Swinson, 2009). An exception appears to be the use of D-cycloserine (DCS) as a supplement to traditional CBT for anxiety disorders. DCS, an N-methyl-D-aspartic acid agonist, has been shown to augment learning and memory by facilitating conditioned fear extinction and post-treatment memory consolidation in clinical animal and human studies (Ledgerwood, Richardson, & Cranney, 2003; Norberg, Krystal, & Tolin, 2008; Schwartz, Hashtroudi, Herting, Schwartz, & Deutsch, 1996; Tsai, Falk, Gunther, & Coyle, 1999; Walker, Ressler, Lu, & Davis, 2002). Such evidence led investigators to examine whether DCS might enhance the effects of exposure-based cognitive-behavioral interventions in a host of anxiety disorders (e.g., Guastella et al., 2008; Hofmann et al., 2006; Norberg et al., 2008; Ressler et al., 2004). Thus far, evidence indicates that DCS does indeed enhance the effects of CBT for PD, SAD, and specific phobias at post-treatment and follow-up.

PREDICTORS OF TREATMENT OUTCOME

A host of variables may predict enhanced or compromised response to treatment across anxiety disorders. One commonly examined predictor of treatment outcome is symptom severity. In PD, higher baseline levels of agoraphobia and panic symptoms are associated with poorer CBT treatment outcome (e.g., Cowley, Flick, & Roy-Byrne, 1996; Kampman et al., 2008; Warshaw, Massion, Shea, Allsworth, & Keller, 1997). However, in GAD, the evidence is mixed. Some investigations have shown that patients with more severe anxiety at pretreatment respond less well to therapy (Butler, 1993; Butler & Anastasiades, 1988; Yonkers, Dyck, Warshaw, & Keller, 2000), whereas others have failed to find such relationships (e.g., Barlow, Rapee, & Brown, 1992; Biswas & Chattopadhyay, 2001; Durham, Allan, & Hackett, 1997). In SAD, greater severity of social anxiety symptoms at baseline has been found to be negatively associated with post-treatment measures of symptom severity, as well as remission rates (Hoyer et al., 2016; Mululo, Menezes, Vigne, & Fontenelle, 2012).

Overall, there are mixed findings regarding the impact of comorbid conditions on treatment outcome. For example, some research indicates that individuals with PD who have comorbid MDD evidence poorer treatment outcome (Cowley et al., 1996), whereas other research has found that it does not negatively impact treatment outcome in panic (Kampman et al., 2008; McLean, Woody, Taylor, & Koch, 1998; Tsao, Mystkowski, Zucker, & Craske, 2002). Similarly, in GAD, some findings have suggested that comorbidity is unrelated to the persistence of the disorder (e.g., Kessler et al., 2007), while other studies have found effects of comorbid conditions on treatment of GAD (Bruce et al., 2001, 2005). For example, some evidence suggests that the presence of a comorbid disorder generally, and comorbid dysthymia or PD specifically, predicts relapse of symptoms (Durham et al., 1997; Tyrer, Seivewright, Simmonds, & Johnson, 2001). In specific phobias, the presence of additional comorbid anxiety disorders does not seem to affect treatment outcome (Ollendick, Öst, Reuterskiöld, & Costa, 2010). Personality traits have also been associated with poorer response to cognitive therapy and self-help treatments among GAD patients, but not in other anxiety disorders (Harte & Hawkins, 2016; Kampman et al., 2008; Tyrer, Seivewright, Ferguson, Murphy, & Johnson, 1993).

Finally, several treatment process variables (e.g., therapeutic alliance, treatment compliance) have also been examined as predictors of treatment outcome (Kim et al., 2015; Patterson, Uhlin, & Anderson, 2008). The degree to which patients expect to change seems to be especially important (Jorstad-Stein & Heimberg, 2009; Price & Anderson, 2012). For example, research indicates that lower levels of treatment expectancy are related to poorer outcome in SAD (Chambless, Tran, & Glass, 1997).

ETIOLOGY

Behavioral Genetics

Behavioral genetic studies (e.g., studies of identical twins, studies of adopted siblings) estimate that about 30–50% of the variance in PD, SAD, and specific phobias is attributable to genetic factors (e.g., Hettema, Neale, & Kendelr 2001; Scaini et al., 2012, 2014). Family studies show that the risk of anxiety disorders is approximately four to six times higher in first-degree relatives of affected individuals than in relatives of unaffected individuals (Hettema et al., 2001). Although some behavioral genetics studies have resulted in higher estimates of the contribution of heritable genetics (perhaps as high as 40–65% when correcting for measurement error; Kendler, Karkowski, & Prescott, 1999; Kendler, Myers, Prescott, & Neale, 2001), compared with other psychological conditions, anxiety disorders appear to be relatively less influenced by heritable genetics and more influenced by environment and gene–environment interactions. A notable exception to these findings is that the BII subtype of specific phobia appears to be relatively more heritable (Kendler et al., 1999, 2001). In addition, when SAD subtypes are examined, the generalized subtype appears to involve somewhat greater heritable genetic risk than does the nongeneralized subtype (Mannuzza et al., 1995; Stein et al., 1998).

The two largest sources of twin data for most anxiety disorders are the Virginia Adult Twin Study of Psychiatric and Substance Use Disorders (VATSPSUD) and the Vietnam Era Twin (VET) Registry, both consisting of about 9,000 twins. Estimates of heritability of PD from these two studies are between 30% and 40% (Chantarujikapong et al., 2001; Hettema et al., 2001). A series of analyses in the VATSPSUD examining phobic fears found that genetic factors explain 30–60% of individual differences between agoraphobia, SAD, and specific phobia. The studies also supported familial aggregation of GAD, finding that genetic factors account for approximately 32% of the variance in liability to GAD.

While many family studies of anxiety disorders report relative specificity of disorder type in familial aggregation, twin studies have suggested that genetic factors are shared across many anxiety disorders, as well as other commonly comorbid disorders (Roberson-Nay et al., 2012; Smoller, 2015). For example, there is considerable overlap in genetic liability for GAD and MDD, 25% of which is accounted for by neuroticism (Kendler, Gardner, Gatz, & Pedersen, 2007). In another study, GAD was linked to the same genetic factor as PD and agoraphobia, whereas a different genetic factor was associated with situational and animal phobias (Hettema, Prescott, Myers, Neale, & Kendler, 2005). Additionally, in line with the dimensional model of psychopathology, genetic contributions have been observed for temperamental traits that have been identified as risk factors for multiple internalizing disorders, such as neuroticism (Hettema, Neale, Myers, Prescott, & Kendler, 2006), anxiety sensitivity (Stein, Lang, & Livesley, 1999), and behavioral inhibition (Hirschfield-Becker, Biederman, & Rosenbaum, 2004).

Biological Considerations

Hypothalamic–Pituitary–Adrenal Axis Anxiety disorders are often marked by excessive fear and avoidance of certain stimuli or environments in the absence of real threat. Thus, the neuroanatomy, neurochemistry, and endocrinology underlying normal fear processes have been studied extensively (e.g., Meaney, LeDoux, & Liebowitz, 2008). Normal fear and panic responses are often understood as part of the hypothalamic–pituitary–adrenal (HPA) axis, a complex physical system involving endocrinological, circulatory, muscular, and behavioral systems, stemming from the examination of the neurocircuitry associated with fear responses. This fight-or-flight system is designed to prevent or avoid physical danger and harm, and involves a fast and efficient response. Perceptions of immediate danger trigger a cascade of physical reactions that begin in the amygdala, which projects to the hypothalamus. The hypothalamus releases corticotropin-releasing factor (CRF), which triggers the pituitary to release adrenocorticotropic hormone (ACTH), which in turn triggers the adrenal cortex to release hormones, including cortisol. These hormones play a central role in regulating the body's preparation for stress. The hypothalamus also activates the sympathetic nervous system, resulting in a variety of bodily changes, including the release of glucose from the liver; increases in heart rate, breathing, and blood pressure; a pattern of vasodilation and vasoconstriction that increases blood flow to the major muscles; and other changes associated with preparation for the fight-or-flight response. These physiological changes constitute the physical symptoms of panic attacks. Numbing and tingling in the fingers and toes, and sensations in the stomach (nausea) and bladder are sometimes experienced as less blood reaches these nonvital areas; shaking and trembling are by-products of the readiness of the major muscles to expend energy; sweating releases heat in preparation for physical exertion. Alterations of the HPA axis have been found among the anxiety disorders. For example, Vreeburg et al. (2010) found that anxious patients had a significantly higher 1-hour cortisol awakening response, especially in individuals with PD with agoraphobia, as well as anxious individuals with comorbid depression. Consistent with this view, for example, no abnormalities in the cardiovascular and vestibular systems have been consistently established for PD (Jacob, Furman, Durrant, & Turner, 1996; Kathol et al., 1980; Shear, Devereaux, Kranier-Fox, Mann, & Frances, 1984).

Although we consider panic attacks and acute fear responses in the context of anxiety disorders to reflect pathology, the pathology does not appear to be due to the manner in which the HPA axis system is carrying out its function. Rather, the pathology appears to be due to the inappropriate triggering of the HPA axis, which typically works well to avoid physical danger and harm, even in individuals with PD, SAD, and specific phobias.

Autonomic Inflexibility The autonomic flexibility-neurovisceral integration model, a psychophysiological model of anxiety disorders, proposes that individuals with anxiety disorders display inflexible autonomic responses in both the presence and absence of stress (Friedman, 2007). GAD, in particular, has been characterized by autonomic inflexibility; chronic tension and anxiety may lead to a restricted range of autonomic responses to environmental triggers (Thayer, Friedman, & Borkovec, 1996). For example, GAD is associated with decreased vagal tone (an index of parasympathetic activity) and heart rate (Lyonfields, Borkovec, & Thayer, 1995; Thayer et al., 1996). Importantly, physiological variables differ among individuals with GAD; only those high in baseline sympathetic arousal displayed reduced sympathetic response to a laboratory stressor (Fisher, Granger, & Newman, 2010).

Autonomic inflexibility has also been linked to PD and SAD (Hoehn-Saric, Schlund, & Wong, 2004; Schmitz, Krämer, Tuschen-Caffier, Heinrichs, & Blechert, 2011). Nonetheless, research suggests that the physiological profile of GAD is related to a physiological-inhibitory effect of worry, the primary feature of the disorder. Relative to neutral thinking or relaxation, worrying prior to exposure to a phobic image is associated with decreased heart rate response during that subsequent image (Borkovec & Hu, 1990; Borkovec et al., 1993). Moreover, compared with neutral thinking, experimentally induced worry is also associated with decreased vagal tone, heart rate, and heart rate variability among individuals with and without GAD (Lyonfields et al., 1995; Thayer et al., 1996). Worry is also associated with decreased heart rate response during subsequent anxiety-eliciting tasks (increased heart rate during exposure is a marker of emotional processing; Foa & Kozak, 1986) while increasing subjective distress (e.g., Borkovec & Hu, 1990).

Neurological Considerations

Panic Disorder   Neuroimaging studies have shown that individuals with PD show hyperactivation in the amygdala in response to panic-related words, as well as neutral faces (Pillay et al., 2007; van den Heuvel et al., 2005). There is also evidence for elevated activity in other structures that are a part of the fear network, including the hippocampus and brain stem structures (Sakai et al., 2005; Uchida et al., 2008). In conjunction, the frontal cortex fails to provide inhibitory input to the amygdala, leading to hyper-amygdala activation, and activation of the entire fear network and response in the absence of real threat (Gorman, Kent, Sullivan, & Coplan, 2000).

Social Anxiety Disorder   Hyperactivity in the amygdala has been observed in contexts such as public speaking or anticipation of public speaking, negative comments, negative and threatening facial expressions, and other socially relevant stimuli (Fouche, Wee, Roelofs, & Stein, 2012; Lorberaum et al., 2004; Shah & Angstadt, 2009; Stein, Goldin, Sareen, Zorrilla, & Brown, 2002). Additionally, amygdala response has been positively associated with self-reported severity of social anxiety symptoms (Blair et al., 2008; Evans et al., 2008). Individuals with the short allele of the serotonin transporter had greater amygdala activation during public speaking tasks when compared with individuals with long alleles (Furmark et al., 2004). The insular cortex also appears to be hyperactive in individuals with SAD, where increased activation is seen while anticipating public speaking, and responding to emotional expressions, although a few studies have found decreased activation during public speaking (Lorberbaum et al., 2004; Tillfors et al., 2001; Yoon, Fitzgerald, Angstadt, McCarron, & Phan, 2007).

Specific Phobia   Similar to PD and SAD, increased amygdala activation has been observed in individuals with specific phobias, in response to the stimuli related to their phobia (e.g., Wendt et al., 2008). However, it should be noted that other studies have associated conflicting findings, potentially due to methodological differences (Hermann et al., 2007; Wright et al., 2003). The dorsal anterior cingulate cortex, whose functions include error detection and anticipation of tasks, has also been shown to be hyperactive in response to both phobia-related stimuli and anticipation of such stimuli (Goossens, Schruers, Peeters, Griez, & Sunaert, 2007; Straube, Mentzel, & Miltner, 2007).

Generalized Anxiety Disorder   Patterns of connectivity among the amygdala, the medial prefrontal cortices, and other associated areas suggest the engagement of a compensatory, cognitive control system among individuals with GAD (Etkin, Prater, Schatzberg, Menon, & Greicius, 2009). Moreover, individuals with GAD fail to use the pregenual anterior cingulate to dampen amygdala activity and regulate emotions during laboratory emotional conflict tasks (Etkin, Prater, Hoeft, Menon, & Schatzberg, 2010). Interestingly, the medial prefrontal and anterior cingulate regions are associated with worry both in individuals with GAD and in normal controls, but only individuals with GAD show persistent activation in these areas following experimental worry periods (Paulesu et al., 2010). GAD is also associated with increased brain activity in response to both neutral and worry-related verbal statements, and reductions in that increased activity correspond to reductions in anxiety during treatment with citalopram (Hoehn-Saric et al., 2004). The amygdala has also been implicated in GAD, but the findings are not entirely clear. For example, individuals with GAD show increased activity in the amygdala in response to neutral and aversive pictures (relative to healthy controls; Nitschke et al., 2009). In response to fearful faces, however, individuals with GAD show decreased amygdala activity (relative to individuals with SAD and healthy controls; Blair et al., 2008).

SPECIFIC GENES

Most of the genetic association studies of anxiety disorders have been in the form of candidate gene studies, which test specific genes or markers for their contribution to a phenotype. Currently, a majority of candidate gene studies have focused on a few key genes often involved in the development of the brain structures associated with fear and fear learning: catechol-O-methyltransferase (*COMT*), which is involved in the inactivation of dopamine in the prefrontal cortex appears (Meaney et al., 2008), specific alleles of the serotonin transporter (*5HTT*) gene, which appear to play an important role in fear learning (Risbrough & Geyer, 2008), and brain-derived neurotropic factor (*BDNF*). Of the anxiety disorders, PD has received the most attention in candidate gene studies. A meta-analysis utilizing more than 350 candidate gene findings for PD concluded that most of these results were inconsistent, negative or not clearly replicated (Maron et al., 2010). Genome-wide association studies (GWAS), which provide an unbiased survey of common genetic variation without the need for an *a priori* hypothesis for gene selection, have also been used to investigate the molecular underpinnings of anxiety disorders. While an initial GWAS with PD cases conducted in a Japanese population reported multiple potential loci for susceptibility to PD, the results were not replicated in a follow-up study with a larger sample (Otowa et al., 2009, 2010). Fewer candidate gene studies and no GWAS have been conducted for SAD, phobic disorders, and GAD. Small studies have found nominally significant associations between social anxiety and *COMT*, and between GAD and serotonin transporter monoamine oxidase A (*MAOA*) (Hettema et al., 2015; Tadic et al., 2003).

Due to the overlapping nature of anxiety disorders, as well as dimensional hypotheses that anxiety disorders are the manifestation of extreme levels of certain traits, a significant portion of genetic studies have focused on anxiety-related traits such as behavioral inhibition (BI) and neuroticism (Smoller, 2015). For example, small studies have shown an association between genetic variants of *RSG2* and BI in childhood, as well as introversion and neural responses to emotional faces in adults (Smoller et al., 2008; Yalcin et al., 2004). *RSG2* has also been associated with pathological anxiety in individuals with GAD, PD, and SAD, although it should be noted that there have been conflicting results reported in other studies (Amstadter et al., 2009; Hettema et al., 2015; Hohoff et al., 2015; Leygraf et al., 2006).

As anxiety disorders are likely highly polygenic, an additional approach to investigating genetic associations and their impact on behavior is studying gene–environment (G×E) interactions. For example, in individuals who are carriers of particular alleles of *5HTT*, the experience of current daily stress or childhood maltreatment may lead to high levels of anxiety sensitivity (Gunthert et al., 2007; Stein, Schork, & Gelernter, 2008). However, there have been very few G×E studies thus far, and existing studies have had limited power and reported conflicting results (e.g., Amstadter et al., 2010; Choe et al., 2013; Reinelt et al., 2014).

Personality and Temperament

Anxiety Sensitivity   Anxiety sensitivity is a dispositional trait that is characterized by a fear of autonomic arousal and the physical sensations associated with anxious states (e.g., increased heart rate, dizziness, nausea, shortness of breath; Reiss & McNally, 1985; Reiss, Peterson, Gursky, & McNally, 1986). Anxiety sensitivity, sometimes called fear of fear, is conceptualized as the key feature of PD (McNally, 1990; Taylor, 1999). Anxiety sensitivity contains three factors: cognitive concerns, physical concerns and social concerns (Wheaton, Deacon, McGrath, Berman, & Abramowitz, 2012).

Several investigations have indicated that individuals with PD evidence high levels of anxiety sensitivity (e.g., Rapee, Brown, Antony, & Barlow, 1992), and individuals with PD seem to have higher levels of comorbid anxiety disorders than do individuals with other anxiety disorders (Taylor, Koch, & McNally, 1992). It is important to note, however, that anxiety sensitivity is not unique to PD; it has been identified among those with PTSD (McNally et al., 1987), depression (Schmidt, Lerew, & Jackson, 1997), and other anxiety disorders (Taylor et al., 1992), including agoraphobia (Reiss et al., 1986). A meta-analysis of anxiety sensitivity studies found that, among anxiety disorders, individuals with PD and GAD reported the highest levels of anxiety sensitivity. A path analysis of anxiety sensitivity and disorder-specific symptoms found that anxiety sensitivity is more strongly related to distress disorders, such as GAD, than to fear disorders, such as specific phobia (Naragon-Gainey, 2010).

Anxiety sensitivity has also been identified as a risk factor for the development of anxiety disorders (Mattis & Ollendick, 1997). Anxiety sensitivity intensifies anxious experiences, as individuals experience anxiety coupled with reactivity to that affective experience. This increases the risk of developing an anxiety disorder. It is hypothesized that specific anxiety sensitivity factors (i.e., cognitive, physical or social concerns) differentially contribute to anxiety disorders (i.e., GAD, panic or SAD, respectively). Finally, anxiety sensitivity may interact with emotional regulation to predict the emergence of anxiety disorder symptoms, as individuals who are highly sensitive to anxiety may make more attempts to suppress or avoid anxiety, thereby prolonging the experience (Olatunji & Wolitzky-Taylor, 2009).

Behavioral Inhibition and Shy Temperament   Behavioral inhibition is defined as the temperamental style of fearful reactivity to novel situations or unfamiliar individuals (Kagan, Reznick, & Snidman, 1987), and thus has obvious conceptual similarities to both shyness and social anxiety. Behavioral inhibition during the first few years of life predicts inhibited behavior with peers later in childhood (Aksan & Kochanska, 2004) and SAD in adolescence (Chronis-Tuscan et al., 2009; Hayward, Killen, Kraemer, & Taylor, 1998; Schwartz, Snidman, & Kagan, 1999) and adulthood (Kagan & Snidman, 1999). While behavioral inhibition is primarily associated with SAD, high levels of behavioral inhibition have been identified among individuals with PD, agoraphobia (Fox, Henderson, Marshall, Nichols, & Ghera, 2005) and GAD (Whitmore, Kim-Spoon, & Ollendick, 2013).

The relative stability of socially inhibited behavior from the first years of life until adulthood is consistent with the view of SAD as rooted in relatively unchangeable, biologically based behavioral tendencies (i.e., temperament). It is notable, however, that a substantial number of children classified as having behavioral inhibition do not go on to develop SAD (Hayward et al., 1998; Kagan & Snidman, 1999; Schwartz et al., 1999; Wittchen, Stein, & Kessler, 1999). Behavioral inhibition and temperamental shyness likely interact with higher-order cognitive factors to predict anxiety disorder symptoms.

Individuals who are highly behaviorally inhibited are more likely to develop an anxiety disorder if they also have difficulty with inhibitory control and attentional shifting (White, McDermott, Degnan, Henderson, & Fox, 2011). Behavioral inhibition in early childhood affects the neural correlates of cognitive control processes in adulthood as well (Jarcho et al., 2013). A dual-processing model of behavioral inhibition hypothesizes that because early behavioral inhibition causes increased orienting toward threat, exaggerated top-down neural responses to such threat cues must develop to regulate attention, thus further potentiating the risk for developing an anxiety disorder (Henderson, Pine, & Fox, 2014).

BEHAVIORAL CONSIDERATIONS

Classical Conditioning Studies of fear conditioning have informed models of fear acquisition and extinction among individuals with anxiety disorders (Dymond, Dunsmoor, Vervliet, Roche, & Hermans, 2015). Drawing upon the observation that fears can be acquired through a repeated process of paired learning, early behaviorists proposed that fears are acquired through classical conditioning (Mowrer, 1947). An early and famous demonstration of this approach involves the story of Little Albert, a 4-year-old boy who was conditioned to fear white rabbits after only a few conditioning trials (Watson & Rayner, 1920). Classical conditioning is a learning process in which a conditioned stimulus (CS) is paired with a biologically potent unconditioned stimulus (US), which causes an unconditioned response (UR). After sufficient trials, the UR is elicited by the CS itself, and is then referred to as a conditioned response (CR; Duits et al., 2015). In studies of conditioned fear responses, a neutral CS (CS+; i.e. a picture of a large ring) is paired with an aversive US (i.e. a mild shock), while another distinct but perceptually similar CS (CS−; i.e. a picture of a small ring) is not, allowing this second CS to serve as a safety signal (Lissek & Grillon, 2010). Fear acquisition studies typically quantify behavioral responses to the CS+ and CS− by measuring fear potentiated startle responses, perceived risk, response times and self-reported anxiety (Lissek et al., 2014).

Conditioning research has informed developmental models of anxiety disorders through the use of generalization paradigms. Generalization describes the process through which an individual comes to fear stimuli that resemble a CS (Dymond et al., 2015). For instance, an individual who has been attacked by a large dog in a park may develop anxiety when exposed to any dog or in any situation where dogs may be present. In the case of PD, panic attacks can be viewed as a highly generalized fear response, in which one interoceptive stimulus (e.g., accelerated heart rate) may be sufficient to trigger an acute fear reaction even in the absence of any specific external stimulus. Individuals with anxiety disorders show less steep generalization gradients than do individuals without anxiety disorders, indicating decreased discrimination between CS+ and CS− and thus a facilitated process of fear generalization (Lissek et al., 2008). In contrast, during extinction paradigms, where a CS+ is no longer paired with an aversive US, individuals with anxiety disorders show increased discrimination between the CS+ and CS−, indicating a reduced ability to learn extinction (Duits et al., 2015).

Operant Conditioning Mowrer (1947) proposed that whereas fear is acquired via classical conditioning, it is maintained via operant conditioning. Operant conditioning refers to the modification of behavior through reinforcement or punishment (Skinner, 1963). Specifically, Mowrer posited that the avoidance and escape behaviors that accompany fear are maintained through a process of negative reinforcement in that they remove or prevent negative affective states. This position is influential in treatment models for anxiety disorders, providing a compelling rationale for the reduction or elimination of avoidance and safety behaviors across anxiety disorders (e.g., Bennet-Levy et al., 2004). Escape and avoidance behaviors are thought to maintain fear either through their prevention of fear activation (which is theorized to be a necessary precursor to habituation; Foa & Kozak, 1986) or through their prevention of disconfirmation of erroneous threat beliefs. In addition to escape from and avoidance of feared situations, subtle in-situation avoidance behaviors (also known as safety behaviors) have been identified as an important feature of these disorders (Helbig-Lang & Petermann, 2010).

Vicarious Conditioning   Vicarious conditioning (sometimes called observational learning or learning by modeling) also facilitates learned associations, functionally equivalent to learning by classical conditioning. Fears may be acquired simply by watching someone behave fearfully in a specific situation (Mineka & Zinbarg, 2006). The anxious response of another person (US) to a neutral stimuli (CS) leads the observer to experience an anxious response (UR), which is subsequently experienced again later in the presence of the CS alone (CR), thus facilitating the development of anxiety (Askew & Field, 2008). For example, children who watch their parents act anxiously before a stressful task experience higher levels of anxiety and report a stronger desired avoidance than children whose parents behave in a relaxed and confident manner (Burstein & Ginsburg, 2010).

Informational Acquisition   Rachman (1977) suggested that fears may also be learned through informational acquisition. Information acquisition involves the development of a fear after receiving negative information, such as from a parent or doctor. Recent research suggests that information has an additive effect on fear learning, such that individuals who receive information about the presence of a feared stimulus before exposure to that stimulus experience a more exaggerated fear response, and have more difficulty with extinction of the CR (Javanbakht et al., 2016). Thus, information acquisition may strengthen or facilitate the relation between the CS and the CR.

Preparedness Theory   Common fears are not randomly distributed but are more frequently associated with stimuli that are objectively evolutionarily dangerous. To account for this observation, Seligman (1971) proposed the "preparedness theory," which posits that during the Paleolithic period of the evolution of the human species, survival and reproductive fitness were increased by fear and avoidance of objects and situations that were dangerous. Drawing upon preparedness theory, Mineka and Öhman (2001, 2002) proposed that humans are prepared to fear stimuli that are relevant to survival because we have evolved a module for fear learning that is encapsulated and relatively independent of cognitive processing. This view proposes that fears of survival-relevant stimuli are relatively automatic and involve central brain regions. There is evidence for several aspects of this model (see Mineka & Öhman, 2001; Mineka & Zinbarg, 2006), including evidence of increased fear response to survival-relevant stimuli in infants (Thrasher & LoBue, 2016), slower extinction to survival-relevant stimuli and limited penetrability to conscious cognitive control for fear of stimuli that are relevant to survival (Öhman & Soares, 1998).

COGNITIVE CONSIDERATIONS

Cognitive differences have often been noted in individuals diagnosed with anxiety disorders. These phenomena are usually described using an information-processing framework (Lang, 1979) for understanding pathological fear (Foa & Kozak, 1986; Rachman, 1980). Studies of these biases can be divided into those that focus on content (e.g., beliefs, expectancies, appraisals) and those that focus on process (e.g., attention, interpretation, memory). A key task in evaluating cognitive approaches to understanding the etiology of these disorders is to identify which biases play a causal role and which are simply features or by-products of the disorders.

Content-Specific Cognitions and Related Variables   Approaches to understanding cognitive biases can be further divided into those that emphasize relatively enduring factors and situation-specific cognitions. Enduring factors include anxiety sensitivity, core beliefs, fear of negative evaluation and IU. Anxiety sensitivity, as elaborated earlier, can be viewed as a tendency to overly attend to experiences of anxiety and react negatively to these experiences (McNally, 1990). Core beliefs are the latent variables that interact with situational variables to produce automatic cognitions, which are proximal determinants of fear, anxiety, and avoidance behavior (Beck & Emery, 2005). Fear of negative evaluation (Leary, 1983b) is defined as the tendency to overestimate the likelihood and importance of being negatively evaluated when in a social situation, and has become the axiomatic dimension associated with SAD.

Intolerance of uncertainty is defined as negative reactivity toward or fear of uncertain situations (Carleton, 2016). IU comprises two factors: inhibitory and prospective IU. Inhibitory IU describes difficulty acting or making decisions under uncertainty, while prospective IU is the tendency to worry about future situations when uncertainty is present (Hong & Lee, 2015). While IU is a cognitive factor associated with many emotional disorders, it shares a specific relationship with anxiety disorders (Boswell, Thompson-Hollands, Farchione & Barlow, 2013). IU was originally linked to worry (Freeston et al., 1994), but now appears to be related to all types of negative repetitive thought (McEvoy & Mahoney, 2013) and reductions in IU during therapy are associated with reductions in cognitive perseveration (McEvoy & Erceg-Hurn, 2016). It is not yet clear whether IU is a risk factor which predisposes individuals to the development of anxiety disorders, or if anxious individuals become less tolerant of uncertainty over time.

Regarding situation-specific cognitions, anxiety disorders have been characterized by overestimations of fear and danger. Examining situation-specific cognitions under a variety of names (including expectancies, concerns, automatic thoughts, catastrophic thoughts, and catastrophic misinterpretations), researchers have generally found that situation-specific cognitions are predictors of fear, anxiety, and avoidance behavior. For example, expectancies appear to be proximal cognitive determinants of fear and fear behavior (e.g., Valentiner, Telch, Petruzzi, & Bolte, 1996). The types of expectancies and concerns that are most important vary depending on feared stimuli: acrophobia is believed to involve expectances of falling (Menzies & Clarke, 1995), whereas claustrophobia is believed to involve expectancies of suffocation and entrapment (Radomsky, Rachman, Thordarson, McIsaac, & Teachman, 2001; Valentiner et al., 1996). Panic attacks in the context of PD are believed to involve misinterpretation of bodily sensations, resulting in catastrophic thoughts related to heart dysfunction, suffocation, and mental control (Cox, 1996).

Another situation-specific cognitive variable that has been implicated for the anxiety disorders is self-efficacy, which is conceptualized as a higher-order cognitive process that incorporates estimates of one's coping capacities and expectancies of anxiety and danger (Bandura & Adams, 1977). Although there are methodological concerns about how the self-efficacy construct is typically operationalized, there is some evidence for self-efficacy as a unique predictor of fear and fear behavior for PD (Cho, Smits, Powers, & Telch, 2007) and specific phobias (Valentiner et al., 1996). Furthermore, individuals with GAD overestimate the likelihood of negative future events and underestimate their ability to cope with negative outcomes should they occur (Borkovec, Hazlett-Stevens, & Diaz, 1999).

Situation-specific cognitions and individual differences in the tendency to engage in situation-specific cognitions have proven to be useful in understanding anxiety disorders. These content variables predict changes in functioning over time and during treatment (e.g., Hoffman, 2004; Wilson & Rapee, 2005), and manipulations that target these cognitions appear to improve the ability of behavioral treatment techniques in reducing symptoms of PD (e.g., Murphy, Michelson, Marchione, Marchione, & Testa, 1998), SAD (e.g., Kim, 2005), GAD (Borkovec et al., 2002), and specific phobias (e.g., Kamphuis & Telch, 2000).

A cognitive content variable that appears to be particularly relevant to social anxiety is that of self-focused attention, or the tendency for socially anxious individuals to attend to internal stimuli rather than external, social stimuli. These internal stimuli are believed to include both interoceptive sensations (e.g., racing heart) and negative images of the self and behavior. Consistent with the SAD model proposed by Clark and Wells (1995; see also Clark, 2001), self-focused attention when in social situations appears to be an important cognitive feature of the disorder, as well as an important factor in the maintenance of social anxiety (Bögels & Mansell, 2004), leading to an increased awareness of anxiety responses (Alden & Mellings, 2004) and a disruption of the realistic processing of the situation and other people's behaviors (Bögels & Lamers, 2002). Targeting self-focused attention appears to improve outcomes during exposure-based treatment for SAD (Wells & Papageorgiou, 1998).

Cognitive Processes and Related Variables   Attention has emerged as a cognitive process especially relevant to anxiety disorders (Bar-Haim, Lamy, Pergamin, Bakermans-Kranenburg, & van IJzendoorn, 2007). Anxiety has been found to be associated with biases in various attentional processes, namely orienting, engagement, and disengagement (see Ouimet, Gawronski, & Dozois, 2009). Attentional biases have been identified in all anxiety disorders (see Cisler & Koster, 2010), including PD (e.g., Buckley, Blanchard, & Hickling, 2002), SAD (e.g., Amir, Elias, Klumpp, & Przeworski, 2003), GAD (e.g., Bradley, Mogg, White, Groom, & de Bono, 1999) and specific phobias (e.g., Watts, McKenna, Sharrock, & Trezise, 1986).

While attentional biases are present across anxiety disorders, they appear to demonstrate content specificity (Pergamin-Hight, Naim, Bakermans-Kranenburg, van IJzendoorn, & Bar-Haim, 2015). For example, individuals with spider phobia show attentional biases to spiders (Watts et al., 1986), and individuals with SAD show attentional biases to negative or angry faces (Staugaard, 2010). Attentional bias involves increased orienting toward threatening stimuli evident early in the attentional process, followed by difficulty disengaging from threatening stimuli, and then later avoidance of threatening stimuli (Cisler & Koster, 2010). Retraining of attentional biases may reduce fear and avoidance (Amir, Weber, Beard, Bomyea, & Taylor, 2008; Bar-Haim, 2010). This emerging approach is attractive because relatively brief interventions that modify attention biases may undermine the development or maintenance of anxiety conditions. Thus, attention bias modification might be delivered as an adjunct to enhance exposure-based treatments or as stand-alone approaches for prevention in high-risk populations (Bar-Haim, 2010). However, evidence is limited that these bias modifications are sustained after training, and current bias modifications do not appear to effect higher-order attentional inhibition or control (Heeren, Mogoase, McNally, Schmitz, & Philippot, 2015).

Interpretation bias is a related but distinct cognitive process that may maintain anxiety symptoms. Interpretation bias refers to the tendency of anxious individuals to interpret ambiguous information in a negative or threatening way (Brosan, Hoppitt, Shelfer, Sillence, & MacKintosh, 2011) and anxious individuals are more likely to interpret neutral words in a threatening manner (Eysenck, Mogg, May, Richards, & Mathews, 1991). Interpretation biases also demonstrate content specificity. For example, individuals with SAD tend to interpret neutral faces as angry (Amir, Beard, & Bower, 2005), while individuals with PD tend to interpret bodily sensations as signaling a health emergency (Dash, Engledew, Meeten, & Davey, 2015).

Repetitive negative thought (i.e., worry and rumination) is an important diagnostic component of many anxiety disorders. Worry is described as perseverative thought pertaining to anticipated, future threat, which is used to avoid the unpleasant physiological arousal associated with anxiety (Borkovec et al., 2004). Though elevated levels of worry are characteristic of GAD, worry has been identified across anxiety disorders (Kertz, Bigda-Peyton, Rosmarin, & Björgvinsson, 2012). Worry likely maintains anxiety symptoms by amplifying the perceived likelihood of threat and preventing processing of emotions (Olatunji, Wolitzky-Taylor, Sawchuk, & Ciesielski, 2010). Rumination is defined as perseverative thought pertaining to one's current situation or mood and comparison to some unachieved standard. Research concerning rumination and anxiety disorders has focused specifically on SAD (Brozovich et al., 2015). During SAD-specific rumination one's social performance is reconstructed and distorted to be consistent with the pathological beliefs underlying social anxiety (see Brozovich & Heimberg, 2008). Similar processes may be involved in the development of PD and specific phobias, and Davey and Matchett (1994) have demonstrated that mental rehearsal of a conditioning trial can enhance conditioned fears.

SOCIALIZATION AND THE SOCIAL ENVIRONMENT

Most literature concerning the role of socialization in anxiety disorders focuses on parenting and childhood anxiety. There is little evidence linking specific family factors to adult psychopathology, but the trajectory of anxiety disorders suggests that early childhood family factors may impact the development of anxiety symptoms, which persist into adulthood (Rapee, 2012). Parenting style is one of the most researched family factors, with parents of anxious children being more overcontrolling and less emotionally supportive than parents of nonanxious children (Brumariu & Kerns, 2015; Lewis-Morrarty et al., 2012; Rork & Morris, 2009). Some have modeled parenting as a mediator, with early temperamental shyness and emotional negativity in children predicting later anxiety symptoms through parental control (van der Bruggen, Stams, Bogels, & Paulussen-Hoogeboom, 2010). A number of recent studies now suggest that low warmth and sensitivity may increase the likelihood that at-risk children will later develop anxiety symptoms (Davis, Votruba-Drzal, & Silk, 2015). Though children of parents with anxiety disorders are more likely to develop an anxiety disorder, a large longitudinal study found that parental anxiety status only predicted child anxiety status if children were temperamentally inhibited (Wichstrøm, Belsky, & Berg-Nielsen, 2013). Compared with control participants, individuals with GAD report a history of rejection and neglect from their mothers, along with more frequent role-reversed/enmeshed relationships (in which the child must take care of the mother), as well as current feelings of vulnerability toward their mothers (Cassidy, Lichtenstein-Phelps, Sibrava, Thomas, & Borkovec, 2009). Together these findings suggest that parenting interacts with other child vulnerability factors to predict the development of anxiety.

Messages that parents give to their children about the meaning and importance of their emotions may play a role in the development of anxiety disorders. Parents of children with anxiety disorders show more nonsupportive reactions to children's negative emotions, which in turn contribute to anxious children's own emotion regulation difficulties (Hurrell, Hudson, & Schniering, 2015). Interventions aimed at teaching parents emotional communication skills have effectively reduced internalizing symptoms in young people (Kehoe, Havighurst, & Harley, 2014). Parents may also convey messages to their children about the meaning of physiological experiences, further reinforcing anxious reactions to these experiences. For example, interoceptive sensations, through parental reinforcement of illness behavior, may play a role in the development of panic attacks and PD. A retrospective study by Stewart et al. (2001) provides evidence that childhood learning experiences with respect to arousing-reactive symptoms (e.g., racing heart, shortness of breath, etc.) but not arousing-nonreactive symptoms (e.g., colds, aches, rashes, etc.) contributed to the frequency and intensity of panic attacks. This effect appeared to be partially mediated by anxiety sensitivity.

Social factors also appear to play an important role in the development and course of anxiety disorders. Children who are victimized by peers are more likely to have an anxiety disorder in young adulthood, even after accounting for the effects of childhood psychopathology and general family hardship (Copeland, Wolke, Angold, & Costello, 2013). Peer victimization in childhood prospectively predicts anxiety symptoms in late adolescence (Schwartz, Lansford, Dodge, Pettit, & Bates, 2015) but individuals with anxiety disorders also go on to experience poorer social relationships in childhood (Alden & Taylor, 2004) and adulthood (Lampe, Slade, Issakidis, & Andrews, 2003; Whisman, Sheldon, & Goering, 2000). The social deficits associated with SAD and shyness include peer neglect (Gazelle & Ladd, 2003), fewer positive responses (Spence, Donovan, & Brechman-Toussaint, 2000), and peer victimization (Hawker & Boulton, 2000; La Greca & Harrison, 2005; McCabe, Antony, Summerfeldt, Liss, & Swinson, 2003; Siegel, La Greca, & Harrison, 2009; Storch & Masia-Warner, 2004). Social deficits, such as peer rejection, appear to be mediated by poor social skills (Greco & Morris, 2005), although individuals with SAD do not always show poor social skills (e.g., Beidel, Turner, & Jacob, 1989). Early temperamental factors, such has behavioral inhibition, may interact with parenting style to predict later peer rejection (Guyer et al., 2015). It should also be noted that peer victimization may be both a cause (Bond, Carlin, Thomas, Rubin, & Patton, 2001) and a consequence of social anxiety, as social anxiety predicts subsequent victimization (Siegel et al., 2009).

CULTURE

Large-scale epidemiological studies have found that White Americans are more likely to be diagnosed with an anxiety disorder than are African Americans, Hispanic Americans, and Asian Americans (Asnaani, Richey, Dimaite, Hinton, & Hofmann, 2010; Grant et al., 2005). These studies suggest that the methodology involved in measuring disorder prevalence may not capture cultural differences in anxiety experience and expression. Disorder-specific symptom expression may also vary by culture (Lewis-Fernandez et al., 2010). For instance, in the case of GAD, cross-cultural differences have been identified in the expression of apprehensive expectation, the definition of excessiveness, and the focus on worry versus somatic symptoms associated with the disorder (Hoge et al., 2006).

The *DSM-5* lists several culturally specific concepts of distress related to anxiety. *Ataque de nervios* ("attack of the nerves"; ADN) refers to an acute set of symptoms and behaviors that shares some similarities with a panic attack, although they are typically experienced in response to a stressful family event and incorporate a volitional behavior component (APA, 2013). It is not clear whether this and other culture-specific anxiety conditions represent an inapplicability of our nosological system to Latin American and Caribbean cultures, a culture-specific expression of known anxiety disorders such as PD, or something else (Guarnaccia, Lewis-Fernández, & Marano, 2003). Some studies have found no difference in prevalence between Hispanic and non-Hispanic adults (Fernandes, Hashmi, & Essau, 2015). In addition, the definitional requirement that panic attacks reach a peak within 10 minutes and the duration of panic attacks may vary as a function of culture (Lewis-Fernández et al., 2010). Individuals with ADN may be more likely to experience emotionally triggered asthma attacks (Vazquez, Sandler, Interian, & Feldman, 2017). As in the case of other anxiety disorders, parenting appears to play a mediating role between early risk factors and later development of ataques (Felix, You, & Canino, 2015).

Taijin kyofusho ("interpersonal fear disorder" in Japanese) is a syndrome whose primary features are anxiety about and avoidance of interpersonal situations. Though related to SAD, individuals with taijin kyofusho tend to fear that their appearance or actions in social settings will be offensive to others, rather than fearing they will embarrass themselves, as in SAD (APA, 2013). The underlying structure of taijin kyofusho appears to show cultural variation, with IU mediating taijin kyofusho symptoms for Japanese but not for Chinese individuals (Zhou et al., 2014). There are four subtypes of taijin kyofusho, varying by the content of the individual's fear: fear of blushing, fear of deformed body, fear of eye contact and fear of foul body odor (Hofmann & Hinton, 2014). Studies suggest that individuals are more likely to develop taijin kyofusho symptoms if they see themselves as low on independence but high on interdependence within their communities (Krieg & Xu, 2015).

LIFE EVENTS

Stress, including life events and chronic conditions such as maltreatment during childhood, appears to increase risk for a variety of mental disorders, including anxiety disorders (Allen, Rapee, & Sandberg, 2008; Kessler, Davis, & Kendler, 1997; Phillips, Hammen, Brennan, Najman, & Bor, 2005). Past traumatic events may contribute to feelings of anxious apprehension and the perception that the world is a dangerous place (Borkovec et al., 2004). Stressful events also impact the maintenance and course of PD (Craske, Rapee, & Barlow, 1988), agoraphobia (Rachman, 1984), GAD (Roemer, Molina, Litz, & Borkovec, 1997), SAD (Mineka & Zinbarg, 1996), and specific phobias (Craske, 1991). Individuals with GAD are more likely to have experienced the death of a parent before the age of 16 compared with individuals with PD and controls (Torgersen, 1986). Furthermore, life events that contribute to GAD may differ from those that contribute to depression; events characterized by loss and danger may confer specific vulnerability to noncomorbid GAD, whereas loss and humiliation may be more specific to MDD (Kendler, Hettema, Butera, Gardner, & Prescott, 2003).

Consistent with a conditioning model, individuals with SAD retrospectively report greater incidence of traumatic social events than do healthy controls, and this greater incidence appears to be higher for those with the nongeneralized subtype compared with the generalized subtype (Stemberger, Turner, Beidel, & Calhoun, 1995).

Early studies suggest that onset of anxiety disorders is sometimes triggered by the occurrence of a stressful life event. Longitudinal studies suggest that this relation is mediated by rumination, such that stressful life events increase perseverative negative thinking about the event, which then increases the risk of developing an anxiety disorder

(Michl, McLaughlin, Shepherd, & Nolen-Hoeksema, 2013). More recent evidence has found no greater rates of stressful life events prior to anxiety disorder onset than at other times (Calkins et al., 2009), indicating that stressful events increase risk but are not necessary for the development of an anxiety disorder.

The phenomenon of latent inhibition, in which prior benign (nonfearful) exposure to a stimulus inhibits fear acquisition, is a well-established finding in the animal literature that informs how we think about fear learning in humans (see Mineka & Zinbarg, 2006). Prior exposure also reduces generalization of fear (Vervliet, Kindt, Vansteenwegen, & Hermans, 2010), an observation that may be especially relevant to the development of PD, which is sometimes viewed as involving highly generalized fear responses (Gorman et al., 2001). Related to these ideas, positive control experiences early in life appear to provide protection or resilience against fear conditioning and the development of anxiety disorders (see Chorpita & Barlow, 1998).

REFERENCES

Aalto-Setälä, T., Marttunen, M., Tuulio-Henriksson, A., & Löennqvist, J. (2001). One month prevalence of depression and other DSM-IV disorders among young adults. *Psychological Medicine, 31*, 791–801.

Aksan, N., & Kochanska, G. (2004). Links between systems of inhibition from infancy to preschool years. *Child Development, 75*, 1477–1490.

Alden, L. E., & Mellings, T. M. B. (2004). Generalized social phobia and social judgments: The salience of self- and partner-information. *Journal of Anxiety Disorders, 18*, 143–157.

Alden, L. E., & Taylor, C. T. (2004). Interpersonal processes in social phobia. *Clinical Psychology Review, 24*, 857–882.

Allen, J. L., Rapee, R. M., & Sandberg, S. (2008). Severe life events and chronic adversities as antecedents to anxiety in children: A matched control study. *Journal of Abnormal Child Psychology, 236*, 1047–1056.

Almay, S., Zhang, W., Varia, I., Davidson, J. R. T., & Connor, K. M. (2008). Escitalopram in specific phobia: Results of a placebo-controlled pilot trial. *Journal of Psychopharmacology, 22*, 157–161.

American Psychiatric Association. (1980). *Diagnostic and statistical manual of mental disorders* (3rd ed.). Washington, DC: Author.

American Psychiatric Association. (1987). *Diagnostic and statistical manual of mental disorders* (3rd ed., rev.). Washington, DC: Author.

American Psychiatric Association. (1994). *Diagnostic and statistical manual of mental disorders* (4th ed.). Washington, DC: Author.

American Psychiatric Association. (2000). *Diagnostic and statistical manual of mental disorders* (4th ed., text rev.). Washington DC: Author.

American Psychiatric Association. (2013). *Diagnostic and statistical manual of mental disorders* (5th ed.). Arlington, VA: American Psychiatric Publishing.

Amir, N., Beard, C., & Bower, E. (2005). Interpretation bias and social anxiety. *Cognitive Therapy and Research, 29*(4), 433–443.

Amir, N., Elias, J., Klumpp, J., & Przeworski, A. (2003). Attentional bias to threat in social phobia: Facilitated processing of threat or difficulty disengaging attention from threat? *Behaviour Research and Therapy, 41*, 1325–1335.

Amir, N., Weber, G., Beard, C., Bomyea, J., & Taylor, C. T. (2008). The effect of a single- session attention modification program on response to a public-speaking challenge in socially anxious individuals. *Journal of Abnormal Psychology, 117*, 860–868.

Amstadter, A. B., Koenen, K. C., Ruggiero, K. J., Acierno, R., Galea, S., Kilpatrick, D. G., & Gelernter, J. (2010). NPY moderates the relation between hurricane exposure and generalized anxiety disorder in an epidemiologic sample of hurricane-exposed adults. *Depression and anxiety, 27*(3), 270–275.

Amstadter, A. B., Nugent, N. R., & Koenen, K. C. (2009). Genetics of PTSD: fear conditioning as a model for future research. *Psychiatric annals, 39*(6), 358.

Antony, M. M. (1997). Assessment and treatment of social phobia. *Canadian Journal of Psychiatry, 42*, 826–834.

Antony, M. M., Brown, T. A., & Barlow, D. H. (1997). Heterogeneity among specific phobia types in DSM-IV. *Behaviour Research and Therapy, 35*, 1089–1100.

Antony, M. M., & Swinson, R. P. (2000). *Phobic disorders and panic in adults: A guide to assessment and treatment.* Washington, DC: American Psychological Association.

Askew, C., & Field, A. P. (2008). The vicarious learning pathway to fear 40 years on. *Clinical Psychology Review, 28*(7), 1249–1265.

Asnaani, A., Richey, J. A., Dimaite, R., Hinton, D. E., & Hofmann, S. G. (2010). A cross-ethnic comparison of lifetime prevalence rates of anxiety disorders. *Journal of Nervous and Mental Disease, The, 198*(8), 551–555.

Avdagic, E., Morrissey, S. A., & Boschen, M. J. (2014). A randomised controlled trial of acceptance and commitment therapy and cognitive-behaviour therapy for generalised anxiety disorder. *Behaviour Change, 31.02*, 110–130.

Azhar, M. Z. (2000). Comparison of fluvoxamine alone, fluvoxamine and cognitive psycho-therapy and psychotherapy alone in the treatment of panic disorder in Kelantan— Implications for management by family doctors. *Medical Journal of Malaysia, 55*, 402–408.

Bakker, A., Van Balkom, A. J. L. M., & Spinhoven, P. (2002). SSRIs vs. TCAs in the treatment of panic disorder: a meta-analysis. *Acta Psychiatrica Scandinavica, 106*(3), 163–167.

Baldwin, D. S., Waldman, S., & Allgulander, C. (2011). Evidence-based pharmacological treatment of generalized anxiety disorder. *International Journal of Neuropsychopharmacology, 14*(5), 697–710.

Ballenger, J. C., Burrows, G. D., DuPont, R. L. Jr., Lesser, I. M., Noyes, R. Jr., Pecknold, J. C., . . . Swinson, R. P. (1988). Alprazolam in panic disorder and agoraphobia: Results from a multicenter trial, I: Efficacy in short-term treatment. *Archives of General Psychiatry, 45*, 413–422.

Bandelow, B. (1999). *Panic and Agoraphobia Scale (PAS)*. Seattle, WA: Hogrefe & Huber.

Bandelow, B., & Michaelis, S. (2015). Epidemiology of anxiety disorders in the 21st century. *Dialogues in Clinical Neuroscience, 17*(3), 327–335.

Bandelow, B., Reitt, M., Röver, C., Michaelis, S., Görlich, Y., & Wedekind, D. (2015). Efficacy of treatments for anxiety disorders: a meta-analysis. *International Clinical Psychopharmacology, 30*(4), 183–192.

Bandelow, B., Seidler-Brandler, U., Becker, A., Wedekind, D., & Rüther, E. (2007). Meta-analysis of randomized controlled comparisons of psychopharmacological and psychological treatments for anxiety disorders. *The World Journal of Biological Psychiatry, 8*(3), 175–187.

Bandelow, B., Sher, L., Bunevicius, R., Hollander, E., Kasper, S., Zohar, J., & Möller, H. J. (2012). Guidelines for the pharmacological treatment of anxiety disorders, obsessive-compulsive disorder and posttraumatic stress disorder in primary care. *International Journal of Psychiatry in Clinical Practice, 16*(2), 77–84.

Bandura, A., & Adams, N. E. (1977). Analysis of self-efficacy theory of behavioral change. *Cognitive Therapy and Research, 1*, 287–310.

Bar-Haim, Y. (2010). Research review: Attention bias modification (ABM): A novel treatment for anxiety disorders. *Journal of Child Psychology and Psychiatry, 51*(8), 859–870.

Bar-Haim, Y., Lamy, D., Pergamin, L., Bakermans-Kranenburg, M. J., & van IJzendoorn, M. H. (2007). Threat-related attentional bias in anxious and nonanxious individuals: A meta-analytic study. *Psychological Bulletin, 133*(1), 1.

Barlow, D. H. (1988). *Anxiety and its disorders*. New York, NY: Guilford Press.

Barlow, D. H. (2002). *Anxiety and its disorders: The nature and treatment of anxiety and panic* (2nd ed.). New York, NY: Guilford Press.

Barlow, D. H., DiNardo, P. A., Vermilyea, B. B., Vermilyea, J. A., & Blanchard, E. B. (1986). Comorbidity and depression among the anxiety disorders: Issues in diagnosis and classification. *Journal of Nervous and Mental Disease, 174*, 63–72.

Barlow, D. H., Gorman, J. M., Shear, M. K., & Woods, S. W. (2000). Cognitive-behavioral therapy, imipramine, or their combination for panic disorder: A randomized controlled trial. *Journal of the American Medical Association, 283*, 2529–2536.

Barlow, D. H., Rapee, R. M., & Brown, T. A. (1992). Behavioral treatment of generalized anxiety disorder. *Behavior Therapy, 23*, 551–570.

Beck, A. T., & Emery, G. (2005). *Anxiety disorders and phobias: A cognitive perspective*. New York, NY: Basic Books.

Beekman, A. T., Bremmer, M. A., Deeg, D. J., vanBalkom, A. J., Smith, J. H., deBeurs, E., . . . Tilburg, W. (1998). Anxiety disorders in later life: A report from the Longitudinal Aging Study Amsterdam. *International Journal of Geriatric Psychiatry, 13*, 717–726.

Beesdo, K., Pine, D. S., Lieb, R., & Wittchen, H.-U. (2010). Incidence and risk patterns of anxiety and depressive disorders and categorization of generalized anxiety disorder. *Archives of General Psychiatry, 67*(1), 47–57.

Behar, E., & Borkovec, T. D. (2005). The nature and treatment of generalized anxiety disorder. In B. O. Rothbaum (Ed.), *The nature and treatment of pathological anxiety: Essays in honor of Edna B. Foa* (pp. 181–196). New York, NY: Guilford Press.

Behar, E., & Borkovec, T. D. (2009). Avoiding treatment failures in generalized anxiety disorder. In M. W. Otto & S. Hofmann (Eds.), *Avoiding treatment failures in the anxiety disorders* (pp. 185–208). New York, NY: Springer.

Behar, E., DiMarco, I. D., Hekler, E., Mohlman, J., & Staples, A. (2009). Current theoretical models of generalized anxiety disorder (GAD): Conceptual review and treatment implications. *Journal of Anxiety Disorders, 23*, 1011–1023.

Behar, E., Zuellig, A. R., & Borkovec, T. D. (2005). Thought and imaginal activity during worry and trauma recall. *Behavior Therapy, 36*, 157–168.

Beidel, D. C., Turner, S. M., & Jacob, R. G. (1989). Assessment of social phobia: Reliability of an impromptu speech task. *Journal of Anxiety Disorders, 1*(3), 149–158.

Bennet-Levy, J., Butler, G., Fennell, M., Hackmann, A., Mueller, M., & Westbrook, D. (2004). *Oxford guide to behavioural experiments in cognitive therapy*. New York, NY: Oxford University Press.

Benjamin, J., Ben-Zion, I. Z., Karbofsky, E., & Dannon, P. (2000). Double-blind placebo-controlled pilot study of paroxetine for specific phobia. *Psychopharmacology, 149*, 194–196.

Berger, P., Sachs, G., Amering, M., Holzinger, A., Bankier, B., & Katschnig, H. (2004). Personality disorder and social anxiety predict delayed response in drug and behavioral treatment of panic disorder. *Journal of Affective Disorders, 80*, 75–78.

Biswas, A., & Chattopadhyay, P. K. (2001). Predicting psychotherapeutic outcomes in patients with generalised anxiety disorder. *Journal of Personality and Clinical Studies, 17*, 27–32.

Blackmore, M., Erwin, B. A., Heimberg, R. G., Magee, L., & Fresco, D. M. (2009). Social anxiety disorder and specific phobias. In M. G. Gelder, J. J. Lopez-Ibor, N. C. Andreason, & J. Geddes (Eds.), *New Oxford textbook of psychiatry* (2nd ed., pp. 739–750). Oxford, England: Oxford University Press.

Blair, K., Shaywitz, J., Smith, B. W., Rhodes, R., Geraci, M., Jones, M., . . . Jacobs, M. (2008). Response to emotional expressions in generalized social phobia and generalized anxiety disorder: evidence for separate disorders. *American Journal of Psychiatry, 165*(9), 1193–1202.

Blanco, C., Bragdon, L. B., Schneier, F. R., & Liebowitz, M. R. (2013). The evidence-based pharmacotherapy of social anxiety disorder. *International Journal of Neuropsychopharmacology, 16*(1), 235–249.

Blanco, C., Heimberg, R. G., Schneier, F. R., Fresco, D. M., Chen, H., Turk, C. L., . . . Liebowitz, M. R. (2010). A placebo-controlled trial of phenelzine, cognitive behavioral group therapy and their combination for social anxiety disorder. *Archives of General Psychiatry, 67,* 286–295.

Blanco, C., Schneier, F. R., Schmidt, A., Blanco-Jerez, C. R., Marshall, R. D., Sanchez-Lacay, A., & Liebowitz, M. R. (2003). Pharmacological treatment of social anxiety disorder: A meta- analysis. *Depression and Anxiety, 18,* 29–40.

Bland, R. C., Orn, H., & Newman, S. C. (1988). Lifetime prevalence rates of psychiatric disorders in Edmonton. *Acta Psychiatrica Scandinavica, 77*(Suppl. 338), 24–32.

Bluett, E. J., Homan, K. J., Morrison, K. L., Levin, M. E., & Twohig, M. P. (2014). Acceptance and commitment therapy for anxiety and OCD spectrum disorders: An empirical review. *Journal of anxiety disorders, 28*(6), 612–624.

Bögels, S. M., Alden, L., Beidel, D. C., Clark, L. A., Pine, D., Stein, M. B., & Voncken, M. (2010). Social anxiety disorder: Questions and answers for the DSM-V. *Depression and Anxiety, 27,* 168–189.

Bögels, S. M., & Lamers, C. T. J. (2002). The causal role of self-awareness in blushing-anxious, socially-anxious and social phobic individuals. *Behaviour Research and Therapy, 40,* 1367–1384.

Bögels, S. M., & Mansell, W. (2004). Attention processes in the maintenance and treatment of social phobia: Hypervigilance, avoidance, and self-focused attention. *Clinical Psychology Review, 24,* 827–856.

Bond, L., Carlin, J. B., Thomas, L., Rubin, K., & Patton, G. (2001). Does bullying cause emotional problems? A prospective study of young teenagers. *British Medical Journal, 323,* 480–484.

Borkovec, T. D., Alcaine, O., & Behar, E. (2004). Avoidance theory of worry and generalized anxiety disorder. In R. G. Heimberg, C. L. Turk, & D. S. Mennin (Eds.), *Generalized anxiety disorder: Advances in research and practice* (pp. 77–108). New York, NY: Guilford Press.

Borkovec, T. D., Hazlett-Stevens, H., & Diaz, M. L. (1999). The role of positive beliefs about worry in generalized anxiety disorder and its treatment. *Clinical Psychology and Psychotherapy, 6,* 126–138.

Borkovec, T. D., & Hu, S. (1990). The effect of worry on cardiovascular response to phobic imagery. *Behaviour Research and Therapy, 28*(1), 69–73.

Borkovec, T. D., & Inz, J. (1990). The nature of worry in generalized anxiety disorder: A predominance of thought activity. *Behaviour Research and Therapy, 28,* 153–158.

Borkovec, T. D., Lyonfields, J. D., Wiser, S. L., & Deihl, L. (1993). The role of worrisome thinking in the suppression of cardiovascular response to phobic imagery. *Behaviour Research and Therapy, 31*(3), 321–324.

Borkovec, T. D., Newman, M. G., Pincus, A. L., & Lytle, R. (2002). A component analysis of cognitive behavioral therapy for generalized anxiety disorder and the role of interpersonal problems. *Journal of Consulting and Clinical Psychology, 70,* 288–298.

Borkovec, T. D., & Roemer, L. (1995). Perceived functions of worry among generalized anxiety disorder subjects: Distractions from more emotionally distressing topics? *Journal of Behavior Therapy and Experimental Psychiatry, 26*(1), 25–30.

Borkovec, T. D., & Ruscio, A. M. (2001). Psychotherapy for generalized anxiety disorder. *Journal of Clinical Psychiatry, 62*(11), 37–42.

Boswell, J. F., Thompson-Hollands, J., Farchione, T. J., & Barlow, D. H. (2013). Intolerance of uncertainty: A common factor in the treatment of emotional disorders. *Journal of Clinical Psychology, 69*(6), 630–645.

Bradley, B. P., Mogg, K., White, J., Groom, C., & de Bono, J. (1999). Attentional bias for emotional faces in generalized anxiety disorder. *British Journal of Clinical Psychology, 38,* 267–278.

Brosan, L., Hoppitt, L., Shelfer, L., Sillence, A., & MacKintosh, B. (2011). Cognitive bias modification for attention and interpretation reduces trait and state anxiety in anxious patients referred to an out-patient service: Results from a pilot study. *Journal of Behavior Therapy and Experimental Psychiatry, 42*(3), 258–264.

Brown, T. A., Antony, M. M., & Barlow, D. H. (1992). Psychometric properties of the Penn State Worry Questionnaire in a clinical anxiety disorders sample. *Behaviour Research and Therapy, 30*(1), 33–37.

Brown, T. A., Antony, M. M., & Barlow, D. H. (1995). Long-term outcome in cognitive- behavioral treatment of panic disorder: Clinical predictors and alternative strategies for assessment. *Journal of Consulting and Clinical Psychology, 63*, 754–765.

Brown, T. A., Campbell, L. A., Lehman, C. C., Grisham, J. R., & Mancill, R. B. (2001). Current and lifetime comorbidity of the DSM-IV anxiety and mood disorders in a large clinical sample. *Journal of Abnormal Psychology, 110*, 49–58.

Brown, T. A., & Barlow, D. H. (2013). *Anxiety and related disorders interview schedule for DSM-5, adult and lifetime version: Clinician manual.* Oxford University Press.

Brown, T. A., Di Nardo, P. A., Lehman, C. L., & Campbell, L. A. (2001). Reliability of DSM-IV anxiety and mood disorders: Implications for the classification of emotional disorders. *Journal of Abnormal Psychology, 110*, 49–58.

Brozovich, F. A., Goldin, P., Lee, I., Jazaieri, H., Heimberg, R. G., & Gross, J. J. (2015). The effect of rumination and reappraisal on social anxiety symptoms during cognitive-behavioral therapy for social anxiety disorder. *Journal of Clinical Psychology, 71*(3), 208–218.

Brozovich, F., & Heimberg, R. G. (2008). An analysis of post-event processing in social anxiety disorder. *Clinical Psychology Review, 28*, 891–9903.

Bruce, S. E., Machan, J. T., Dyck, I., & Keller, M. B. (2001). Infrequency of "pure" GAD: impact of psychiatric comorbidity on clinical course. *Depression and Anxiety, 14*(4), 219–225.

Bruce, T. J., Spiegel, D. A., & Hegel, M. T. (1999). Cognitive-behavioral therapy helps prevent relapse and recurrence of panic disorder following alprazolam discontinuation: A long-term follow-up of the Peoria and Dartmouth studies. *Journal of Consulting and Clinical Psychology, 67*, 151–56.

Bruce, S. E., Yonkers, K. A., Otto, M. W., Eisen, J. L., Weisberg, R. B., Pagano, M., . . . Keller, M. B. (2005). Influence of psychiatric comorbidity on recovery and recurrence in generalized anxiety disorder, social phobia, and panic disorder: A 12-year prospective study. *American Journal of Psychiatry, 162*(6), 1179–1187.

Brumariu, L. E., & Kerns, K. A. (2015). Mother–child emotion communication and childhood anxiety symptoms. *Cognition and Emotion, 29*(3), 416–431.

Buckley, T. C., Blanchard, E. B., & Hickling, E. J. (2002). Automatic and strategic processing of threat stimuli: A comparison of PTSD, panic disorder, and non-anxiety controls. *Cognitive Therapy and Research, 26*, 97–115.

Burke, K. C., Burke, J. D. Jr., Regier, D. A., & Rae, D. S. (1990). Age of onset of selected mental disorders in five community populations. *Archives of General Psychiatry, 47*, 511–518.

Burstein, M., & Ginsburg, G. S. (2010). The effect of parental modeling of anxious behaviors and cognitions in school-aged children: An experimental pilot study. *Behaviour Research and Therapy, 48*(6), 506–515.

Butler, G. (1993). Predicting outcome after treatment for generalized anxiety disorder. *Behaviour Research and Therapy, 31*, 211–213.

Butler, G., & Anastasiades, P. (1988). Predicting response to anxiety management in patients with generalised anxiety disorders. *Behaviour Research and Therapy, 26*, 531–534.

Calkins, A. W., Otto, M. W., Cohen, L. S., Soares, C. N., Vitonis, A. F., Hearon, B. A., & Harlow, L. (2009). Psychosocial predictors of the onset of anxiety disorders in women: Results of a prospective 3-year longitudinal study. *Journal of Anxiety Disorders, 23*, 1165–1169.

Carleton, R. N. (2016). Into the unknown: A review and synthesis of contemporary models involving uncertainty. *Journal of Anxiety Disorders, 39*, 30–43.

Cassidy, J., Lichtenstein-Phelps, J., Sibrava, N. J., Thomas, C. L. J., & Borkovec, T. D. (2009). Generalized anxiety disorder: Connections with self-reported attachment. *Behavior Therapy, 40*, 23–38.

Chambless, D. L., Caputo, G. C., Bright, P., & Gallagher, R. (1984). Assessment of "fear of fear" in agoraphobics: The Body Sensations Questionnaire and the Agoraphobic Cognitions Questionnaire. *Journal of Consulting and Clinical Psychology, 52*, 1090–1097.

Chambless, D. L., Caputo, G. C., Jasin, S. E., Gracely, E. J., & Williams, C. (1985). The mobility inventory for agoraphobia. *Behaviour research and therapy, 23*(1), 35–44.

Chambless, D. L., Tran, G. Q., & Glass, C. R. (1997). Predictors of response to cognitive- behavioral group therapy for social phobia. *Journal of Anxiety Disorders, 11*, 221–240.

Chantarujikapong, S. I., Scherrer, J. F., Xian, H., Eisen, S. A., Lyons, M. J., Goldberg, J., . . . True, W. R. (2001). A twin study of generalized anxiety disorder symptoms, panic disorder symptoms and post-traumatic stress disorder in men. *Psychiatry Research, 103*(2), 133–145.

Chavira, D. A., Shipon-Blum, E., Hitchcock, C., Cohan, S., & Stein, M. B. (2007). Selective mutism and social anxiety disorder: all in the family?. *Journal of the American Academy of Child & Adolescent Psychiatry, 46*(11), 1464–1472.

Cho, Y., Smits, J. A. Jr., Powers, M. B., & Telch, M. J. (2007). Do changes in panic appraisal predict improvement in clinical status following cognitive-behavioral treatment of panic disorder? *Cognitive Therapy and Research, 31*, 695–707.

Choe, D. E., Olson, S. L., & Sameroff, A. J. (2013). Effects of early maternal distress and parenting on the development of children's self-regulation and externalizing behavior. *Development and Psychopathology, 25*(02), 437–453.

Chorpita, B. F., & Barlow, D. H. (1998). The development of anxiety: The role of control in the early environment. *Psychological Bulletin, 124*, 3–21.

Choy, Y., Fyer, A. J., & Lipsitz, J. D. (2007). Treatment of specific phobia in adults. *Clinical Psychology Review, 27*, 266–286.

Choy, Y., Schneier, F. R., Heimberg, R. G., Oh, K.-S., & Liebowitz, M. R. (2008). Features of the offensive subtype of Taijin-Kyofu-Sho in US and Korean patients with DSM-IV social anxiety disorder. *Depression and Anxiety, 25*(3), 230–240.

Chronis-Tuscan, A., Degnan, K. A., Pine, D. S., Perea-Edgar, K., Henderson, H. A., Diaz, Y., . . . Fox, N. A. (2009). Stable early maternal report of behavioral inhibition predicts lifetime social anxiety disorder in adolescence. *Journal of the American Academy of Child & Adolescent Psychiatry, 48*, 928–935.

Cisler, J. M., & Koster, E. H. W. (2010). Mechanisms underlying attentional biases towards threat: An integrative review. *Clinical Psychology Review, 30*, 203–216.

Clark, D. M. (2001). A cognitive perspective on social phobia. In R. Crozier & L. E. Alden (Eds.), *International handbook of social anxiety: Concepts, research and interventions relating to the self and shyness* (pp. 405–430). Oxford, England: Wiley.

Clark, D. M., Ehlers, A., Hackmann, A., McManus, F., Fennell, M., Grey, N., . . . Wild, J. (2006). Cognitive therapy versus exposure and applied relaxation in social phobia: A randomized controlled trial. *Journal of Consulting and Clinical Psychology, 74*, 568–578.

Clark, D. M., Ehlers, A., McManus, F., Hackmann, A., Fennell, M., Campbell, H., . . . Louis, B. (2003). Cognitive therapy vs. fluoxetine in generalized social phobia: A randomized placebo-controlled trial. *Journal of Consulting and Clinical Psychology, 71*, 1058–1067.

Clark, D. M., & Wells, A. (1995). A cognitive model of social phobia. In R. Heimberg, M. Liebowitz, D. A. Hope, & F. Schneier (Eds.), *Social phobia: Diagnosis, assessment and treatment* (pp. 69–93). New York, NY: Guilford Press.

Clauss, J., & Blackford, J. (2012). Behavioral Inhibition and Risk for Developing Social Anxiety Disorder: A Meta-Analytic Study. *Journal of the American Academy of Child and Adolescent Psychiatry, 51*(10), 1–13.

Copeland, W. E., Angold, A., Shanahan, L., & Costello, E. J. (2014). Longitudinal Patterns of Anxiety From Childhood to Adulthood: The Great Smoky Mountains Study. *Journal of the American Academy of Child and Adolescent Psychiatry, 53*(1), 21–33.

Copeland, W. E., Wolke, D., Angold, A., & Costello, E. J. (2013). Adult psychiatric outcomes of bullying and being bullied by peers in childhood and adolescence. *JAMA Psychiatry, 70*(4), 419–26.

Cottraux, J. (2004). Combining psychological and pharmacological treatment for specific phobias. *Psychiatry, 3,* 87–89.

Cowley, D. S., Flick, S. N., & Roy-Byrne, P. P. (1996). Long-term course and outcome in panic disorder: A naturalistic follow-up study. *Anxiety, 2,* 13–21.

Cox, B. J. (1996). The nature and assessment of catastrophic thoughts in panic disorder. *Behaviour Research and Therapy, 34,* 363–374.

Craske, M. G. (1991). Phobic fear and panic attacks: The same emotional state triggered by different cues? *Clinical Psychology Review, 11,* 599–620.

Craske, M. G., Brown, T. A., & Barlow, D. H. (1991). Behavioral treatment of panic: A two-year follow-up. *Behavior Therapy, 22,* 289–304.

Craske, M. G., Kircanski, K., Epstein, A., Wittchen, H.-U., Pine, D. S., Lewis-Fernández, R., & Hinton, D. (2010). Panic disorder: A review of DSM-IV panic disorder and proposals for DSM-V. *Depression and Anxiety, 27,* 93–112.

Craske, M. G., Rapee, R. M., & Barlow, D. H. (1988). The significance of panic expectancy for individual patterns of avoidance. *Behavior Therapy, 19,* 577–592.

Crits-Christoph, P., Newman, M. G., Rickels, K., Gallop, R., Gibbons, M. B. C., Hamilton, L., . . . Pastva, A. M. (2011). Combined medication and cognitive therapy for generalized anxiety disorder. *Journal of Anxiety Disorders, 25,* 1087–1094.

Cuijpers, P., Sijbrandij, M., Koole, S., Huibers, M., Berking, M., & Andersson, G. (2014). Psychological treatment of generalized anxiety disorder: a meta-analysis. *Clinical Psychology Review, 34*(2), 130–140.

Curtis, G. C., Magee, W. J., Eaton, W. W., Wittchen, H.-U., & Kessler, R. C. (1998). Specific fears and phobias: Epidemiology and classification. *British Journal of Psychiatry, 173,* 212–217.

Cutshall, C., & Watson, D. (2004). The phobic stimuli response scales: A new self-report measure of fear. *Behaviour Research and Therapy, 42,* 1193–1201.

Dalrymple, K. L., & Herbert, J. D. (2007). Acceptance and Commitment Therapy for generalized social anxiety disorder: A pilot study. *Behavior Modification, 31,* 543–568.

Dash, S. R., Engledew, Z., Meeten, F., & Davey, G. C. L. (2015). Interpretation of Ambiguous Bodily Sensations: The Roles of Mood and Perseveration. *Journal of Social and Clinical Psychology, 34*(2), 95–116.

Davey, G. C. L., & Matchett, G. (1994). Unconditioned stimulus rehearsal and the retention and enhancement of differential "fear" conditioning: Effects of trait and state anxiety. *Journal of Abnormal Psychology, 103,* 708–718.

Davidson, J. R. (2009). First-line pharmacotherapy approaches for generalized anxiety disorder. *Journal of Clinical Psychiatry, 70,* 25–31.

Davidson, J. R., Foa, E. B., Huppert, J. D., Keefe, F. J., Franklin, M. E., Compton, J. S., . . . Gadde, M. (2004). Fluoxetine, comprehensive cognitive behavioral therapy, and placebo in generalized social phobia. *Archives of General Psychiatry, 61,* 1005–1013.

Davis, R. N., & Valentiner, D. P. (2000). Does meta-cognitive theory enhance our understanding of pathological worry and anxiety? *Personality and Individual Differences, 29*(3), 513–526.

Davis, S., Votruba-Drzal, E., & Silk, J. S. (2015). Trajectories of Internalizing Symptoms From Early Childhood to Adolescence: Associations With Temperament and Parenting. *Social Development, 24*(3), 501–520.

Deacon, B. J., & Abramowitz, J. S. (2005). Patients' perceptions of pharmacological and cognitive-behavioral treatment for anxiety disorders. *Behavior Therapy, 36*, 139–145.

Doble, A., & Martin, I. (2000). Insights into the mechanisms of benzodiazepine dependence. *European Neuropsychopharmacology, 10*, 169.

Donzuso, G., Cerasa, A., Gioia, M. C., Caracciolo, M., & Quattrone, A. (2014). The neuroanatomical correlates of anxiety in a healthy population: Differences between the state-trait anxiety inventory and the Hamilton anxiety rating scale. *Brain and Behavior, 4*(4), 504–514.

Dugas, M. J., Buhr, K., & Ladouceur, R. (2004). The role of intolerance of uncertainty in etiology and maintenance. In R. G. Heimberg, C. L. Turk, & D. S. Mennin (Eds.), *Generalized anxiety disorder: Advances in research and practice* (pp. 143–163). New York, NY: Guilford Press.

Dugas, M. J., Gagnon, F., Ladouceur, R., & Freeston, M. H. (1998). Generalized anxiety disorder: A preliminary test of a conceptual model. *Behaviour Research and Therapy, 36*(2), 215–226.

Dugas, M. J., Marchand, A., & Ladouceur, R. (2005). Further validation of a cognitive-behavioral model of generalized anxiety disorder: Diagnostic and symptom specificity. *Journal of Anxiety Disorders, 19*(3), 329–343.

Duits, P., Cath, D. C., Lissek, S., Hox, J. J., Hamm, A. O., Engelhard, I. M., . . . Baas, J. M. P. (2015). Updated meta-analysis of classical fear conditioning in the anxiety disorders. *Depression and Anxiety, 32*(4), 239–253.

Durham, R. C., Allan, T., & Hackett, C. A. (1997). On predicting improvement and relapse in generalized anxiety disorder following psychotherapy. *British Journal of Clinical Psychology, 36*, 101–119.

Dworkin, B. R., & Dworkin, S. (1999). Heterotopic and homotopic classical conditioning of the baroreflex. *Integrative Physiological and Behavioral Science, 34*(3), 158–176.

Dymond, S., Dunsmoor, J. E., Vervliet, B., Roche, B., & Hermans, D. (2015). Fear Generalization in Humans: Systematic Review and Implications for Anxiety Disorder Research. *Behavior Therapy, 46*(5), 561–582.

Eaton, W. W., Dryman, A., & Weissman, M. M. (1991). Panic and phobia. In L. N. Robins & D. A. Regier (Eds.), *Psychiatric disorders in America: The Epidemiological Catchment Area study*. New York, NY: Free Press.

Eaton, N. R., Keyes, K. M., Krueger, R. F., Balsis, S., Andrew, E., Markon, K. E., . . . Hasin, D. S. (2013). An Invariant Dimensional Liability Model of Gender Differences in Mental Disorder Prevalence : Evidence from a National Sample, *121*(1), 282–288.

Etkin, A., Prater, K. E., Hoeft, F., Menon, V., & Schatzberg, A. F. (2010). Failure of anterior cingulate activation and connectivity with the amygdala during implicit regulation of emotional processing in generalized anxiety disorder. *American Journal of Psychiatry, 167*(5), 545–554.

Etkin, A., Prater, K. E., Schatzberg, A. F., Menon, V., & Greicius, M. D. (2009). Disrupted amygdalar subregion functional connectivity and evidence of a compensatory network in generalized anxiety disorder. *Archives of General Psychiatry, 66*(12), 1361–1372.

Evans, K. C., Wright, C. I., Wedig, M. M., Gold A. L., Pollack M. H., & Rauch S. L. (2008). A functional MRI study of amygdala responses to angry schematic faces in social anxiety disorder. *Depression and Anxiety 25*, 496–505.

Eysenck, M. W., Mogg, K., May, J., Richards, A., & Mathews, A. (1991). Bias in interpretation of ambiguous sentences related to threat in anxiety. *Journal of Abnormal Psychology, 100*(2), 144–150.

Faucher, J., Koszycki, D., Bradwejn, J., Merali, Z., & Bielajew, C. (2016). Effects of CBT versus MBSR treatment on social stress reactions in social anxiety disorder. *Mindfulness, 7*(2), 514–526.

Felix, E. D., You, S., & Canino, G. (2015). Family Influences on the Relationship Between Hurricane Exposure and Ataques de Nervios. *Journal of Child and Family Studies, 24*(8), 2229–2240.

Fernandes, B., Hashmi, S. I., & Essau, C. A. (2015). Ataque de Nervios. *The Encyclopedia of Clinical Psychology*, (January), 1–3.

Feske, U., & Chambless, D. L. (1995). Cognitive behavioral versus exposure only treatment for social phobia: A meta-analysis. *Behavior Therapy, 26*, 695–720.

First, M. B., Williams, J. B., Karg, R. S., & Spitzer, R. L. (2016). *Structured Clinical Interview for DSM-5 Disorders: SCID-5-CV Clinician Version*. American Psychiatric Association Publishing.

Fisher, A. J., Granger, D. A., & Newman, M. G. (2010). Sympathetic arousal moderates self-reported physiological arousal symptoms at baseline and physiological flexibility in response to a stressor in generalized anxiety disorder. *Biological Psychology, 83*, 191–200.

Foa, E. B., & Kozak, M. J. (1986). Emotional processing of fear: Exposure to corrective information. *Psychological Bulletin, 99*, 20–35.

Fouche, J. P., Wee, N. J., Roelofs, K., & Stein, D. J. (2012). Recent advances in the brain imaging of social anxiety disorder. *Human Psychopharmacology: Clinical and Experimental, 28*(1), 102–105.

Fox, N. A., Henderson, H. A., Marshall, P. J., Nichols, K. E., & Ghera, M. M. (2005). Behavioral Inhibition: Linking Biology and Behavior within a Developmental Framework. *Annual Review of Psychology, 56*(1), 235–262.

Fredrikson, M., Annas, P., Fischer, H., & Wik, G. (1996). Gender and age differences in the prevalence of specific fears and phobias. *Behaviour Research and Therapy, 26*, 241–244.

Freeston, M. H., Rhéaume, J., Letarte, H., Dugas, M. J., & Ladouceur, R. (1994). Why do people worry? *Personality and individual differences, 17*(6), 791–802.

Freire, R. C., Cosci, F., & Nardi, A. E. (2011). Update on pharmacological treatment of panic disorder. *Minerva Psichiatrica, 52*(3), 145–155.

Friborg, O., Martinussen, M., Kaiser, S., Øvergârd, K. T., & Rosenvinge, J. H. (2013). Comorbidity of personality disorders in anxiety disorders: a meta-analysis of 30 years of research. *Journal of Affective Disorders, 145*(2), 143–155.

Friedman, B. H. (2007). An autonomic flexibility-neurovisceral integration model of anxiety and cardiac vagal tone. *Biological Psychology, 74*(2), 185–199.

Furmark, T., Tillfors, M., Garpenstrand, H., Marteinsdottir, I., Långström, B., Oreland, L., & Fredrikson, M. (2004). Serotonin transporter polymorphism related to amygdala excitability and symptom severity in patients with social phobia. *Neuroscience letters, 362*(3), 189–192.

Furukawa, T. A., Watanabe, N., & Churchill, R. (2006). Psychotherapy plus antidepressant for panic disorder with and without agoraphobia: Systematic review. *British Journal of Psychiatry, 188*, 305–312.

Furukawa, T. A., Watanabe, N., & Churchill, R. (2008). Psychotherapy Plus Antidepressant for Panic Disorder With or Without Agoraphobia: Systematic Review. *FOCUS, 6*(4), 528–538.

Garcia-Palacios, A., Botella, C., Hoffman, H., & Fabregat, S. (2007). Comparing acceptance and refusal rates of virtual reality exposure vs. in vivo exposure by patients with specific phobias. *Cyberpsychology & behavior, 10*(5), 722–724.

Gazelle, H., & Ladd, G. W. (2003). Anxious solitude and peer exclusion: A diathesis-stress model of internalizing trajectories in childhood. *Child Development, 74*, 257–278.

Geer, J. H. (1965). The development of a scale to measure fear. *Behaviour Research and Therapy, 3*, 45–53.

Gerlernter, C. S., Uhde, T. W., Cimbolic, P., Arnkoff, D. B., Vittone, B. J., Tancer, M. E., & Bartko, J. J. (1991). Cognitive-behavioral and pharmacological treatments of social phobia: A controlled study. *Archives of General Psychiatry, 48*, 938–945.

Goisman, R. M., Warshaw, M. G., Peterson, L. G., Rogers, M. P., Cuneo, P., Hunt, M. E., . . . Kellar, M. B. (1994). Panic, agoraphobia, and panic disorder with agoraphobia: Data from a multicenter anxiety disorders study. *Journal of Nervous and Mental Disease, 182*, 72–79.

Goldin, P. R., Lee, I., Ziv, M., Jazaieri, H., Heimberg, R. G., & Gross, J. J. (2014). Trajectories of change in emotion regulation and social anxiety during cognitive-behavioral therapy for social anxiety disorder. *Behaviour research and therapy, 56*, 7–15.

Goldin, P. R., Morrison, A., Jazaieri, H., Brozovich, F., Heimberg, R., & Gross, J. J. (2016). Group CBT versus MBSR for social anxiety disorder: A randomized controlled trial. *Journal of Consulting and Clinical Psychology, 84*(5), 427–437.

Goldstein, A. J., de Beurs, E., Chambless, D. L., & Wilson, K. A. (2000). EMDR for panic disorder with agoraphobia: Comparison with waiting list and credible attention placebo control conditions. *Journal of Consulting and Clinical Psychology, 68*, 947–956.

Goossens, L., Schruers, K., Peeters, R., Griez, E., & Sunaert, S. (2007). Visual presentation of phobic stimuli: amygdala activation via an extrageniculostriate pathway? *Psychiatry Res 155*: 113–120.

Gorman, J. M., Kent, J. M., Martinez, J. M., Browne, S. T., Coplan, J. D., & Papp, L. A. (2001). Physiological changes during carbon dioxide inhalation in patients with panic disorder, major depression, and premenstrual dysphoric disorder: Evidence for a central fear mechanism. *Archives of General Psychiatry, 58*, 125–131.

Gorman, J. M., Kent, J. M., Sullivan, G. M., & Coplan, J. D. (2000). Neuroanatomical hypothesis of panic disorder, revised. *American Journal of Psychiatry, 157*(4), 493–505.

Grant, B. F., Hasin, D. S., Blanco, C., Stinson, F. S., Chou, P., Goldstein, R. B., . . . Huang, B. (2005). The epidemiology of social anxiety disorder in the United States: Results from the National Epidemiologic Survey on Alcohol and Related Conditions. *Journal of Clinical Psychiatry, 66*, 1351–1361.

Grant, B. F., Hasin, D. S., Stinson, F. S., Dawson, D. A., Goldstein, R. B., Smith, S. M., . . . Huang, B. (2006). The epidemiology of DSM-IV panic disorder and agoraphobia in the United States: Results from the National Epidemiologic Survey on Alcohol and Related Conditions. *Journal of Clinical Psychiatry, 67*, 363–374.

Grant, B. F., Hasin, D. S., Stinson, F. S., Dawson, D. A., June Ruan, W., Goldstein, R. B., . . . Huang, B. (2005). Prevalence, correlates, co-morbidity, and comparative disability of DSM-IV generalized anxiety disorder in the USA: Results from the National Epidemiologic Survey on Alcohol and Related Conditions. *Psychological Medicine, 35*(12), 1747–1759.

Greco, L. A., & Morris, T. L. (2005). Factors influencing the link between social anxiety and peer acceptance: Contributions of social skills and close friendships during middle childhood. *Behavior Therapy, 36*, 197–205.

Greenberg, P. E., Sisitsky, T., Kessler, R. C., Finkelstein, S. N., Berndt, E. R., Davidson, J. R., . . . Fyer, A. J. (1999). The economic burden of anxiety disorders in the 1990s. *Journal of Clinical Psychiatry, 60*, 427–435.

Grös, D. F., & Antony, M. M. (2006). The assessment and treatment of specific phobias: A review. *Current Psychiatry Reports, 8*, 298–303.

Groth-Marnat, G. (2003). *Handbook of psychological assessment* (4th ed.). Hoboken, NJ: Wiley.

Guarnaccia, P. J., Lewis-Fernandez, R., & Marano, M. R. (2003). Toward a Puerto Rican popular nosology: Nervios and ataque de nervios. *Culture, Medicine, and Psychiatry, 27*, 339–366.

Guarnaccia, P. J., Rivera, M., Franco, F., & Neighbors, C. (1996). The experiences of ataques de nervios: towards an anthropology of emotions in Puerto Rico. *Culture, Medicine and Psychiatry, 20*(3), 343–367.

Guastella, A. J., Richardson, R., Lovibond, P. F., Rapee, R. M., Gaston, J. E., Mitchell, P., & Dadds, M. R. (2008). A randomized controlled trial of D-cycloserine enhancement of exposure therapy for social anxiety disorder. *Biological Psychiatry, 63*, 544–549.

Gunthert, K. C., Conner, T. S., Armeli, S., Tennen, H., Covault, J., & Kranzler, H. R. (2007). Serotonin transporter gene polymorphism (5-HTTLPR) and anxiety reactivity in daily life: A daily process approach to gene-environment interaction. *Psychosomatic medicine, 69*(8), 762–768.

Guyer, A. E., Jarcho, J. M., Pérez-Edgar, K., Degnan, K. A., Pine, D. S., Fox, N. A., & Nelson, E. E. (2015). Temperament and Parenting Styles in Early Childhood Differentially Influence Neural Response to Peer Evaluation in Adolescence. *Journal of Abnormal Child Psychology, 43*(5), 863–874.

Hacker, T., Stone, P., & MacBeth, A. (2016). Acceptance and commitment therapy–do we know enough? Cumulative and sequential meta-analyses of randomized controlled trials. *Journal of affective disorders*, *190*, 551–565.

Hamm, A. O. (2009). Specific phobias. *Psychiatric Clinics of North America*, *32*, 577–591.

Harte, C. B., & Hawkins, R. C. I. (2016). Impact of personality disorder comorbidity on cognitive-behavioral therapy outcome for mood and anxiety disorders: Results from a university training clinic. *Research in Psychotherapy: Psychopathology, Process and Outcome*, *19*(2), 114–125.

Hartford, J., Kornstein, S., Liebowitz, M., Pigott, T., Russell, J., Detke, M., . . . Erickson, J. (2007). Duloxetine as an SNRI treatment for generalized anxiety disorder: results from a placebo and active-controlled trial. *International Clinical Psychopharmacology*, *22*(3), 167–174.

Hasin, D. S., Greenstein, E., Aivadyan, C., Stohl, M., Aharonovich, E., Saha, T., . . . Grant, B. F. (2015). The Alcohol Use Disorder and Associated Disabilities Interview Schedule–5 (AUDADIS-5): Procedural validity of substance use disorders modules through clinical re-appraisal in a general population sample. *Drug and Alcohol Dependence*, *148*, 40–46.

Hawker, D. S. Jr., & Boulton, M. J. (2000). Twenty years' research on peer victimization and psychosocial maladjustment: A meta-analytic review of cross-sectional studies. *Journal of Child Psychology and Psychiatry*, *41*, 441–455.

Hayes, S. C., Luoma, J. B., Bond, F. W., Masuda, A., & Lillis, J. (2006). Acceptance and commitment therapy: Model, processes, and outcomes. *Behaviour Research and Therapy*, *44*, 1–26.

Hayward, C., Killen, J. D., Kraemer, H. C., & Taylor, C. B. (1998). Linking self-reported childhood behavioral inhibition to adolescent social phobia. *Journal of the American Academy of Child & Adolescent Psychiatry*, *37*, 1308–1316.

Heeren, A., Mogoase, C., McNally, R. J., Schmitz, A., & Philippot, P. (2015). Does attention bias modification improve attentional control? A double-blind randomized experiment with individuals with social anxiety disorder. [References]. *Journal of Anxiety Disorders*, *29*(1), 35–42.

Heimberg, R. G., & Becker, R. E. (2002). *Cognitive behavioral group therapy for social phobia: Basic mechanisms and clinical applications*. New York, NY: Guilford Press.

Heimberg, R. G., Madsen, C. H., Montgomery, D., & McNabb, C. E. (1980). Behavioral treatments for heterosocial problems: Effects on daily self-monitored and role played interactions. *Behavior Modification*, *4*, 147–172.

Heimberg, R. G., Salzman, D. G., Holt, C. S., & Blendell, K. A. (1993). Cognitive-behavioral group treatment for social phobia: Effectiveness at five-year follow-up. *Cognitive Therapy and Research*, *17*, 325–339.

Helbig-Lang, S., & Petermann, F. (2010). Tolerate or eliminate?: A systematic review of the effects of safety behavior across anxiety disorders. *Clinical Psychology: Science and Practice*, *17*, 218–233.

Henderson, H. A., Pine, D. S., & Fox, N. A. (2014). Behavioral Inhibition and Developmental Risk: A Dual-Processing Perspective. *Neuropsychopharmacology : Official Publication of the American College of Neuropsychopharmacology*, *40*(1), 1–63.

Hermann, A., Schäfer, A., Walter, B., Stark, R., Vaitl, D., & Schienle, A. (2007). Diminished medial prefrontal cortex activity in blood-injection-injury phobia. *Biological psychology*, *75*(2), 124–130.

Hettema, J. M., Chen, X., Sun, C., & Brown, T. A. (2015). Direct, indirect and pleiotropic effects of candidate genes on internalizing disorder psychopathology. *Psychological medicine*, *45*(10), 2227–2236.

Hettema, J. M., Neale, M. C., & Kendler, K. S. (2001). A review and meta-analysis of the genetic epidemiology of anxiety disorders. *American Journal of Psychiatry*, *158*, 1568–1578.

Hettema, J. M., Neale, M. C., Myers, J. M., Prescott, C. A., & Kendler, K. S. (2006). A population-based twin study of the relationship between neuroticism and internalizing disorders. *American Journal of Psychiatry*, *163*, 857–864.

Hettema, J. M., Prescott, C. A., & Kendler, K. S. (2001). A population-based twin study of generalized anxiety disorder in men and women. *Journal of Nervous and Mental Disease, 189,* 413–420.

Hettema, J. M., Prescott, C. A., Myers, J. M., Neale, M. C., & Kendler, K. S. (2005). The structure of genetic and environmental risk factors for anxiety disorders in men and women. *Archives of General Psychiatry, 62,* 182–189.

Hidalgo, R. B., Tupler, L. A., & Davidson, J. R. T. (2007). An effect-size analysis of pharmacologic treatments for generalized anxiety disorder. *Journal of Psychopharmacology, 21,* 864–872.

Himle, J. A., McPhee, K., Cameron, O. G., & Curtis, G. C. (1989). Simple phobia: Evidence for heterogeneity. *Psychiatry Research, 28,* 25–30.

Hirschfield-Becker, D. R., Biederman, J., & Rosenbaum, J. F. (2004). Behavioral inhibhition. In T. L. Morris & J. S. March (Eds.), *Anxiety disorders in children and adolescents* (pp. 27–58). New York, NY: Guilford Press.

Hoehn-Saric, R., Schlund, M. W., & Wong, S. H. Y. (2004). Effects of citalopram on worry and brain activation in patients with generalized anxiety disorder. *Psychiatry Research: Neuro- imaging, 131,* 11–21.

Hoffman, S. G. (2004). Cognitive mediation of treatment change in social phobia. *Journal of Consulting and Clinical Psychology, 72,* 392–399.

Hofmann, S. G., & Hinton, D. E. (2014). Cross-cultural aspects of anxiety disorders. *Current Psychiatry Reports, 16*(6), 450.

Hoffman, E. J., & Mathew, S. J. (2008). Anxiety disorders: A comprehensive review of pharma-cotherapies. *Mount Sinai Journal of Medicine, 75,* 248–262.

Hofmann, S. G., Meuret, A. E., Smits, J. A., Simon, N. M., Pollack, M. H., Eisenmenger, K., . . . Otto, M. W. (2006). Augmentation of exposure therapy with D-cycloserine for social anxiety disorder. *Archives of General Psychiatry, 63,* 298–304.

Hofmann, S. G., & Otto, M. W. (2008). *Cognitive-behavior therapy of social phobia: Evidence-based and disorder specific treatment techniques.* New York, NY: Routledge.

Hofmann, S. G., Sawyer, A. T., Witt, A. A., & Oh, D. (2010). The effect of mindfulness-based therapy on anxiety and depression: A meta-analytic review. *Journal of Consulting and Clinical Psychology, 78*(2), 169–183.

Hofmann, S. G., & Smits, J. A. (2008). Cognitive-behavioral therapy for adult anxiety disorders: A meta-analysis of randomized placebo-controlled trials. *Journal of Clinical Psychiatry, 69,* 621–632.

Hoge, E. A., Tamrakar, S. M., Christian, K. M., Mahara, N., Nepal, M. K., Pollack, M. H., & Simon, N. M. (2006). Cross-cultural differences in somatic presentation in patients with generalized anxiety disorder. *Journal of Nervous and Mental Disease, 194*(12), 962–966.

Hohoff, C., Weber, H., Richter, J., Domschke, K., Zwanzger, P. M., Ohrmann, P., . . . Klauke, B. (2015). RGS2 genetic variation: association analysis with panic disorder and dimensional as well as intermediate phenotypes of anxiety. *American Journal of Medical Genetics Part B: Neuro-psychiatric Genetics, 168*(3), 211–222.

Hong, R. Y., & Lee, S. S. (2015). Further clarifying prospective and inhibitory intolerance of uncertainty: Factorial and construct validity of test scores from the Intolerance of Uncertainty Scale. *Psychological assessment, 27*(2), 605.

Hoyer, J., Wiltink, J., Hiller, W., Miller, R., Salzer, S., Sarnowsky, S., . . . Leibing, E. (2016). Baseline patient characteristics predicting outcome and attrition in cognitive therapy for social phobia: Results from a large multicentre trial. *Clinical Psychology & Psychotherapy, 23*(1), 35–46.

Hurrell, K. E., Hudson, J. L., & Schniering, C. A. (2015). Parental reactions to children's negative emotions: Relationships with emotion regulation in children with an anxiety disorder. *Journal of Anxiety Disorders, 29*(2015), 72–82.

Isomura, K., Boman, M., Rück, C., Serlachius, E., Larsson, H., Lichtenstein, P., & Mataix-Cols, D. (2015). Population-based, multi-generational family clustering study of social anxiety disorder and avoidant personality disorder. *Psychological Medicine, 45*(8), 1581–1589.

Jacob, R. G., Furman, J. M., Durrant, J. D., & Turner, S. M. (1996). Panic, agoraphobia, and vestibular dysfunction. *American Journal of Psychiatry, 153,* 503–512.

Jarcho, J. M., Fox, N. A., Pine, D. S., Etkin, A., Leibenluft, E., Shechner, T., & Ernst, M. (2013). The neural correlates of emotion-based cognitive control in adults with early childhood behavioral inhibition. *Biological Psychology, 92*(2), 306–314.

Javanbakht, A., Duval, E. R., Cisneros, M. E., Taylor, S. F., Kessler, D., & Liberzon, I. (2016). Instructed fear learning, extinction, and recall: additive effects of cognitive information on emotional learning of fear. *Cognition and Emotion, 9931*(May), 1–8.

Jorstad-Stein, E. C., & Heimberg, R. G. (2009). Social phobia: An update on treatment. *Psychiatric Clinics of North America, 32,* 641–663.

Kabat-Zinn, J. (1994). *Mindfulness meditation for everyday life.* New York: Hyperion.

Kagan, J., Reznick, J. S., & Snidman, N. (1987). The physiology and psychology of behavioral inhibition in children. *Child Development, 58,* 1459–1473.

Kagan, J., & Snidman, N. (1999). Early childhood predictors of adult anxiety disorders. *Biological Psychiatry, 46,* 1536–1541.

Kagan, J., & Snidman, N. (2013). Early Childhood Predictors of Adult Anxiety Disorders. *Fear and Anxiety: The Science of Mental Health, 10,* 76.

Kamphuis, J. H., & Telch, M. J. (2000). Effects of distraction and guided threat reappraisal on fear reduction during exposure-based treatments for specific fears. *Behaviour Research and Therapy, 38,* 1163–1181.

Kampman, M., Keijsers, G. P., Hoogduin, C. A., & Hendriks, G. J. (2008). Outcome prediction of cognitive behaviour therapy for panic disorder: Initial symptom severity is predictive for treatment outcome, comorbid anxiety or depressive disorder, cluster C personality disorders and initial motivation are not. *Behavioural and Cognitive Psychotherapy, 36*(01), 99–112.

Kathol, R. G., Noyes, R., Slyman, D. J., Crowe, R. R., Clancy, J., & Kerber, R. E. (1980). Propranolol in chronic anxiety disorders. *Archives of General Psychiatry, 37,* 1361–1365.

Katzman, M. A. (2009). Current considerations in the treatment of generalized anxiety disorder. *CNS Drugs, 23*(2), 103–120.

Kehoe, C. E., Havighurst, S. S., & Harley, A. E. (2014). Tuning in to Teens: Improving Parent Emotion Socialization to Reduce Youth Internalizing Difficulties. *Social Development, 23*(2), 413–431.

Keller, M. B., Yonkers, K. A., Warshaw, M. G., Pratt, L. A., Golan, J., Mathews, A. O., . . . Lavori, P. (1994). Remission and relapse in subjects with panic disorder and agoraphobia: A prospective short interval naturalistic follow-up. *Journal of Nervous and Mental Disorders, 182,* 290–296.

Kendler, K. S., Gardner, C. O., Gatz, M., & Pedersen, N. L. (2007). The sources of co-morbidity between major depression and generalized anxiety disorder in a Swedish national twin sample. *Psychological Medicine, 37,* 453–462.

Kendler, K. S., Hettema, J. M., Butera, F., Gardner, C. O., & Prescott, C. A. (2003). Life event dimensions of loss, humiliation, entrapment, and danger in the prediction of onsets of major depression and generalized anxiety. *Archives of General Psychiatry, 60,* 789–796.

Kendler, K., Karkowski, L., & Prescott, C. (1999). Fears and phobias: Reliability and heritability. *Psychological Medicine, 29,* 539–553.

Kendler, K., Myers, J., Prescott, C., & Neale, M. C. (2001). The genetic epidemiology of irrational fears and phobias in men. *Archives in General Psychiatry, 58,* 257–265.

Kendler, K. S., Prescott, C. A., Myers, J., & Neale, M. C. (2003). The structure of genetic and environmental risk factors for common psychiatric and substance use disorders in men and women. *Archives of General Psychiatry, 60,* 929–937.

Kertz, S. J., Bigda-Peyton, J. S., Rosmarin, D. H., & Björgvinsson, T. (2012). The importance of worry across diagnostic presentations: Prevalence, severity and associated symptoms in a partial hospital setting. *Journal of Anxiety Disorders, 26*(1), 126–133.

Kessler, R. C., Berglund, P., Demler, O., Jin, R., Merikangas, K., & Walters, E. E. (2005a). Lifetime prevalence and age-of-onset distributions of DSM-IV disorders in the National Comorbidity Survey Replication. *Archives of General Psychiatry, 62,* 593–602.

Kessler, R. C., Chiu, W. T., Demler, O., & Walters, E. E. (2005b). Prevalence, severity, and comorbidity of 12-month DSM-IV disorders in the National Comorbidity Survey Replication. *Archives of General Psychiatry, 62,* 617–627.

Kessler, R. C., Davis, C. G., & Kendler, K. S. (1997). Childhood adversity and adult psychiatric disorder in the US National Comorbidity Survey. *Psychological Medicine, 27,* 1101–1119.

Kessler, R. C., DuPont, R. L., Berglund, P., & Wittchen, H.-U. (1999). Impairment in pure and comorbid generalized anxiety disorder and major depression at 12 months in two national surveys. *American Journal of Psychiatry, 156,* 1915–1923.

Kessler, R. C., Foster, C. L., Saunders, W. B., & Stang, P. E. (1995). Social consequences of psychiatric disorders, I: Education attainment. *American Journal of Psychiatry, 152,* 1026–1032.

Kessler, R. C., Gruber, M., Hettema, J. M., Hwang, I., Sampson, N., & Yonkers, K. A. (2007). Major depression and generalized anxiety disorders in the National Comorbidity Survey Follow-up Survey. *Paper presented at the American Psychological Association DSM-IV Workshop on Depression and GAD, London, England.*

Kessler, R. C., McGonagle, K. A., Zhao, S., Nelson, C. B., Hughes, M., Eshleman, S., . . . Kendler, K. S. (1994). Lifetime and 12-month prevalence of DSM-III-R psychiatric disorders in the United States: Results from the National Comorbidity Survey. *Archives of General Psychiatry, 51,* 8–19.

Kessler, R. C., Petukhova, M., Sampson, N. A., Zaslavsky, A. M., & Wittchen, H. (2012). Twelve-month and lifetime prevalence and lifetime morbid risk of anxiety and mood disorders in the United States. *International Journal of Methods in Psychiatric Research, 21*(3), 169–184.

Kim, E. J. (2005). The effect of the decreased safety behaviors on anxiety and negative thoughts in social phobics. *Journal of Anxiety Disorders, 19,* 69–86.

Kim, J., Rapee, R. M., & Gaston, J. E. (2008). Symptoms of offensive type Taijin-Kyofusho among Australian social phobics. *Depression and Anxiety, 25,* 601–608.

Kim, S., Roth, W. T., & Wollburg, E. (2015). Effects of therapeutic relationship, expectancy, and credibility in breathing therapies for anxiety. *Bulletin of the Menninger Clinic, 79*(2), 116–130.

Kircanski, K., Craske, M. G., Epstein, A. M., & Wittchen, H.-U. (2010). Subtypes of panic attacks: A critical review of the empirical literature. *Depression and Anxiety, 26,* 878–887.

Kiropoulos, L. A., Klein, B., Austin, D. W., Gilson, K., Pier, C., Mitchell, J., & Ciechomski, L. (2008). Is internet-based CBT for panic disorder and agoraphobia as effective as face-to-face CBT? *Journal of Anxiety Disorders, 22*(8), 1273–1284.

Kjernisted, K., & McIntosh, D. (2007). Venlafaxine extended release (XR) in the treatment of panic disorder. *Therapeutics and Clinical Risk Management, 3*(1), 59.

Kobak, K. A., Greist, J. H., Jefferson, J. W., & Katzelnick, D. J. (2002). Fluoxetine in social phobia: A double-blind, placebo-controlled pilot study. *Journal of Clinical Psychopharmacology, 22,* 257–262.

Koponen, H., Allgulander, C., Erickson, J., Dunayevich, E., Pritchett, Y., Detke, M. J., . . . Russell, J. M. (2007). Efficacy of duloxetine for the treatment of generalized anxiety disorder: implications for primary care physicians. *Primary Care Companion to the Journal of Clinical Psychiatry, 9*(2), 100.

Krieg, A., & Xu, Y. (2015). Ethnic differences in social anxiety between individuals of Asian heritage and European heritage: A meta-analytic review. *Asian American Journal of Psychology, 6*(1), 66–80.

Krueger, R. F. (1999). The structure of common mental disorders. *Archives of General Psychiatry, 56,* 921–926.

Kushner, M. G., Abrams, K., & Borchardt, C. (2000). The relationship between anxiety disorders and alcohol use disorders: A review of major perspectives and findings. *Clinical Psychology Review, 20,* 149–171.

Ladouceur, R., Blais, F., Freeston, M. H., & Dugas, M. J. (1998). Problem solving and problem orientation in generalized anxiety disorder. *Journal of Anxiety Disorders, 12*(2), 139–152.

Ladouceur, R., Dugas, M. J., Freeston, M. H., Rheaume, J., Blais, F., Boisvert, J. M., . . . Thibodeau, N. (1999). Specificity of generalized anxiety disorder symptoms and processes. *Behavior Therapy, 30*, 191–207.

La Greca, A. M., & Harrison, H. M. (2005). Adolescent peer relations, friendships, and romantic relationships: Do they predict social anxiety and depression? *Journal of Clinical Child and Adolescent Psychology, 34*, 49–61.

Lampe, L., Slade, T., Issakidis, C., & Andrews, G. (2003). Social phobia in the Australian National Survey of Mental Health and Well-Being (NSMHWB). *Psychological Medicine, 33*, 637–646.

Lang, P. J. (1979). A bio-informational theory of emotional imagery. *Psychophysiology, 16*, 495–512.

Lang, P. J., McTeague, L. M., & Bradley, M. M. (2016). RDoC, DSM, and the reflex physiology of fear: A biodimensional analysis of the anxiety disorders spectrum. *Psychophysiology, 53*(3), 336–347.

Leary, M. R. (1983a). A brief version of the Fear of Negative Evaluation Scale. *Personality and Social Psychology Bulletin, 9*, 371–375.

Leary, M. R. (1983b). *Understanding social anxiety: Social, personality, and clinical perspectives.* Beverly Hills, CA: Sage.

LeBeau, R. T., Glenn, D., Liao, B., Wittchen, H.-U., Beesdo-Baum, K., Ollendick, T., & Craske, M. G. (2010). Specific phobia: A review of DSM-IV specific phobia and preliminary recommendations for DSM-V. *Depression and Anxiety, 27*, 148–167.

Ledgerwood, L., Richardson, R., & Cranney, J. (2003). Effects of D-cycloserine on extinction of conditioned freezing. *Behavioral Neuroscience, 117*, 341–349.

Ledley, D. R., & Heimberg, R. G. (2005). Social anxiety disorder. In M. M. Antony, D. R. Ledley, & R. G. Heimberg (Eds.), *Improving outcomes and preventing relapse in cognitive-behavioral therapy* (pp. 38–76). New York, NY: Guilford Press.

Ledley, D. R., Heimberg, R. G., Hope, D. A., Hayes, S. A., Zaider, T. I., Van Dyke, M., . . . Fresco, D. M. (2009). Efficacy of a manualized and workbook-driven individual treatment for social anxiety disorder. *Behavior Therapy, 40*(4), 414–424.

Lewis-Fernández, R., Hinton, D. E., Laria, A. J., Patterson, E. H., Hofmann, S. G., Craske, M. G., Liao, B. (2010). Culture and the anxiety disorders: recommendations for DSM-V. *Depression and Anxiety, 27*(2), 212–229.

Lewis-Morrarty, E., Degnan, K. A., Chronis-Tuscano, A., Rubin, K. H., Cheah, C. S. L., Pine, D. S., . . . Fox, N. A. (2012). Maternal over-control moderates the association between early childhood behavioral inhibition and adolescent social anxiety symptoms. *Journal of Abnormal Child Psychology, 40*(8), 1363–1373.

Leygraf, A., Hohoff, C., Freitag, C., Willis-Owen, S. A. G., Krakowitzky, P., Fritze, J., . . . Deckert, J. (2006). Rgs 2 gene polymorphisms as modulators of anxiety in humans?. *Journal of Neural Transmission, 113*(12), 1921–1925.

Liebowitz, M. R., Gorman, J. M., Fyer, A. J., & Klein, D. R. (1985). Social phobia. *Archives of General Psychiatry, 42*, 729–736.

Lindal, E., & Stefansson, J. G. (1993). The lifetime prevalence of anxiety disorders in Iceland as estimated by the US National Institute of Mental Health Diagnostic Interview Schedule. *Acta Psychiatrica Scandinavica, 88*, 29–34.

Lissek, S., Biggs, A. L., Rabin, S. J., Cornwell, B. R., Alvarez, R. P., Pine, D. S., & Grillon, C. (2008). Generalization of Conditioned Fear-Potentiated Startle in Humans. *Behaviour Research and Therapy, 46*(5), 678–687.

Lissek, S., & Grillon, C. (2010). Overgeneralization of Conditioned Fear in the Anxiety Disorders: Putative Memorial Mechanisms. *Journal of Psychology, 218*(2), 146–148.

Lissek, S., Kaczkurkin, A. N., Rabin, S., Geraci, M., Pine, D. S., & Grillon, C. (2014). Generalized anxiety disorder is associated with overgeneralization of classically conditioned-fear. *Biological Psychiatry, 75*(11), 909–915.

Lobbestael, J., Leurgans, M., & Arntz, A. (2011). Inter-rater reliability of the Structured Clinical Interview for DSM-IV Axis I disorders (SCID I) and Axis II disorders (SCID II). *Clinical Psychology & Psychotherapy, 18*(1), 75–79.

Lopez, F. J. C., & Salas, S. V. (2009). Acceptance and Commitment Therapy (ACT) in the treatment of panic disorder: Some considerations from the research on basic processes. *International Journal of Psychology and Psychological Theory, 9*, 299–315.

Lorberbaum, J. P., Kose, S., Johnson, M. R., Arana, G. W., Sullivan, L. K., Hamner, M. B., & George, M. S. (2004). Neural correlates of speech anticipatory anxiety in generalized social phobia. *Neuroreport, 15*(18), 2701–2705.

Lyonfields, J. D., Borkovec, T. D., & Thayer, J. F. (1995). Vagal tone in generalized anxiety disorder and the effects of aversive imagery and worrisome thinking. *Behavior Therapy, 26*, 457–466.

Magee, W. J., Eaton, W. W., Wittchen, H.-U., McGonagle, K. A., & Kessler, R. C. (1996). Agoraphobia, simple phobia, and social phobia in the National Comorbidity Survey. *Archives of General Psychiatry, 53*, 159–168.

Mannuzza, S., Schneier, F. R., Chapman, T. F., Liebowitz, M. R., Klein, D. F., & Fyer, A. J. (1995). Generalized social phobia: Reliability and validity. *Archives of General Psychiatry, 52*, 230–237.

Marks, I. M., & Gelder, M. G. (1966). Different ages of onset in varieties of phobia. *American Journal of Psychiatry, 123*, 218–221.

Marks, I. M., Swinson, R. P., Basoglu, M., Kuch, K., Noshirvani, H., O'Sullivan, G., . . . Wickwire, K. (1993). Alprazolam and exposure alone and combined in panic disorder with agoraphobia. A controlled study in London and Toronto. *British Journal of Psychiatry, 162*, 776–787.

Marlatt, G. A., & Kristeller, J. L. (1999). Mindfulness and meditation. In W. R. Miller (Ed.), *Integrating spirituality into treatment: Resources for practitioners* (pp. 67–84). Washington, DC: American Psychological Association.

Maron, E., Tõru, I., Tasa, G., Must, A., Toover, E., Lang, A., . . . Shlik, J. (2008). Association testing of panic disorder candidate genes using CCK-4 challenge in healthy volunteers. *Neuroscience Letters, 446*, 88–92.

Marten, P. A., Brown, T. A., Barlow, D. H., Borkovec, T. D., Shear, M. K., & Lydiard, R. B. (1993). Evaluating of the ratings comprising the associated symptom criteria of DSM-III-R generalized anxiety disorder. *Journal of Nervous and Mental Disease, 181*(11), 676–682.

Martin, J. L. R., Sainz-Pardo, M., Furukawa, T. A., Martin-Sanchez, E., Seoane, T., & Galan, C. (2007). Benzodiazepines in generalized anxiety disorder: Heterogeneity of outcomes based on a systematic review and meta-analysis of clinical trials. *Journal of Psychopharmacology, 21*, 774–782.

Mathews, A. M., Gelder, M. G., & Johnston, D. W. (1981). *Agoraphobia: Nature and treatment.* New York, NY: Guilford Press.

Mattick, R. P., & Clarke, J. C. (1998). Development and validation of measures of social phobia scrutiny fear and social interaction anxiety. *Behaviour Research and Therapy, 36*, 455–470.

Mattis, S. G., & Ollendick, T. H. (1997). Panic in children and adolescents: A developmental analysis. *Advances in Clinical Child Psychology, 19*, 74.

Mavissakalian, M. R., & Perel, J. M. (1999). Long-term maintenance and discontinuation of imipramine therapy in panic disorder with agoraphobia. *Archives of General Psychiatry, 56*, 821–827.

McCabe, R. E., Antony, M. M., Summerfeldt, L. J., Liss, A., & Swinson, R. P. (2003). Preliminary examination of the relationship between anxiety disorders in adults and self-reported history of teasing or bullying experiences. *Cognitive and Behaviour Therapy, 32*, 187–193.

McEvoy, P. M., & Erceg-Hurn, D. M. (2016). The search for universal transdiagnostic and trans-therapy change processes: Evidence for intolerance of uncertainty. *Journal of anxiety disorders, 41*, 96–107.

McEvoy, P. M., & Mahoney, A. E. (2013). Intolerance of uncertainty and negative metacognitive beliefs as transdiagnostic mediators of repetitive negative thinking in a clinical sample with anxiety disorders. *Journal of Anxiety Disorders, 27*(2), 216–224.

McGorry, P. D., Purcell, R., Goldstone, S., & Amminger, G. P. (2011). Age of onset and timing of treatment for mental and substance use disorders: implications for preventive intervention strategies and models of care. *Current opinion in psychiatry, 24*(4), 301–306.

McHugh, R. K., Smits, J. A. Jr., & Otto, M. W. (2009). Empirically supported treatments for panic disorder. *Psychiatric Clinics of North America, 32*, 593–610.

McLaughlin, K. A., Borkovec, T. D., & Sibrava, N. J. (2007). The effects of worry and rumination on affect states and cognitive activity. *Behavior Therapy, 38*, 23–38.

McLean, P. D., Woody, S., Taylor, S., & Koch, W. J. (1998). Comorbid panic disorder and major depression: Implications for cognitive-behavioral therapy. *Journal of Consulting and Clinical Psychology, 66*, 240–247.

McNally, R. J. (1990). Psychological approaches to panic disorder: A review. *Psychological Bulletin, 108*, 403–419.

McNally, R. J. (2001). Vulnerability to anxiety disorders in adulthood. In R. E. Ingram & J. M. Price (Eds.), *Vulnerability to psychopathology: Risk across the lifespan* (pp. 304–321). New York, NY: Guilford Press.

McNally, R. J., Cassiday, K. L., & Calamari, J. E. (1990). Taijin-kyofu-sho in a black American woman: Behavioral treatment of a "culture-bound" anxiety disorder. *Journal of Anxiety Disorders, 4*, 83–87.

McNally, R. J., Luedke, D. L., Besyner, J. K., Peterson, R. A., Bohm, K., & Lips, O. J. (1987). Sensitivity to stress-relevant stimuli in posttraumatic stress disorder. *Journal of Anxiety Disorders, 1*, 105–116.

Meaney, M. J., LeDoux, J. E., & Liebowitz, M. L. (2008). Neurobiology of anxiety disorders. In A. Tasman, J. Kay, J. A. Lieberman, M. B. First, & M. May (Eds.), *Psychiatry* (3rd ed., pp. 317–328). Hoboken, NJ: Wiley.

Mennin, D. S., Heimberg, R. G., & Turk, C. L. (2004). Clinical presentation and diagnostic features. In R. G. Heimberg, C. L. Turk, & D. S. Mennin (Eds.), *Generalized anxiety disorder: Advances in research and practice* (pp. 3–28). New York, NY: Guilford Press.

Mennin, D. S., Heimberg, R. G., Turk, C. L., & Fresco, D. M. (2002). Applying an emotion regulation framework to integrative approaches to generalized anxiety disorder. *Clinical Psychology Science and Practice, 9*, 85–90.

Mennin, D. S., Heimberg, R. G., Turk, C. L., & Fresco, D. M. (2005). Preliminary evidence for an emotion dysregulation model of generalized anxiety disorder. *Behaviour Research and Therapy, 43*, 1281–1310.

Mennin, D. S., Holaway, R. M., Fresco, D. M., Moore, M. T., & Heimberg, R. G. (2007). Delineating components of emotion and its dysregulation in anxiety and mood psychopathology. *Behavior Therapy, 38*, 284–302.

Menzies, R. G., & Clarke, J. C. (1995). Danger expectancies and insight in acrophobia. *Behaviour Research and Therapy, 33*, 215–221.

Meyer, T. J., Miller, M. L., Metzger, R. L., & Borkovec, T. D. (1990). Development and validation of the Penn State Worry Questionnaire. *Behaviour Research and Therapy, 28*(6), 487–495.

Michl, L. C., McLaughlin, K. A., Shepherd, K., & Nolen-Hoeksema, S. (2013). Rumination as a mechanism linking stressful life events to symptoms of depression and anxiety: longitudinal evidence in early adolescents and adults. *Journal of Abnormal Psychology, 122*(2), 339–52.

Mineka, S., & Öhman, A. (2001). Fears, phobias, and preparedness: Toward an evolved module of fear learning. *Psychological Review, 108*, 483–522.

Mineka, S., & Öhman, A. (2002). Phobias and preparedness: The selective, automatic, and encapsulated nature of fear. *Biological Psychiatry, 15*, 927–937.

Mineka, S., & Zinbarg, R. (1996). Conditioning and ethological models of anxiety disorders. In D. A. Hope (Ed.), *Nebraska Symposium on Motivation, Volume 43: Perspectives on anxiety, panic, and fear: Current theory and research in motivation* (pp. 135–201). Lincoln: University of Nebraska Press.

Mineka, S., & Zinbarg, R. (2006). A contemporary learning theory perspective on the etiology of anxiety disorders: it's not what you thought it was. *The American Psychologist, 61*(1), 10–26.

Mitte, K., Noack, P., Steil, R., & Hautzinger, M. (2005). A meta-analytic review of the efficacy of drug treatment in generalized anxiety disorder. *Journal of Clinical Psychopharmacology, 25*, 141–150.

Mochcovitch, M. D., & Nardi, A. E. (2010). Selective serotonin-reuptake inhibitors in the treatment of panic disorder: a systematic review of placebo-controlled studies. *Expert review of neurotherapeutics, 10*(8), 1285–1293.

Moffitt, T. E., Harrington, H., Caspi, A., Kim-Cohen, J., Goldberg, D., Gregory, A. M., & Poulton, R. (2007). Depression and generalized anxiety disorder: Cumulative and sequential comorbidity in a birth cohort followed prospectively to age 32 years. *Archives of General Psychiatry, 64*, 651–660.

Moscovitch, D. A., Antony, M. M., & Swinson, R. P. (2009). Exposure-based treatments for anxiety disorders: Theory and process. In M. M. Antony & M. B. Stein (Eds.), *Oxford handbook of anxiety and related disorders* (pp. 461–475). New York: Oxford University Press.

Mowrer, O. H. (1947). On the dual nature of learning: A re-interpretation of "conditioning" and "problem-solving." *Harvard Educational Review, 17*, 102–148.

Muhlberger, A., Herrmann, M. J., Wiedemann, G. C., Ellgring, H., & Pauli, P. (2001). Repeated exposure of flight phobics to flights in virtual reality. *Behaviour Research and Therapy, 39*, 1033–1050.

Mula, M., Pini, S., & Cassano, G. B. (2007). The role of anticonvulsant drugs in anxiety disorders: A critical review of the evidence. *Journal of Clinical Psychopharmacology, 27*, 263–272.

Mululo, S. C. C., Menezes, G. B. de, Vigne, P., & Fontenelle, L. F. (2012). A review on predictors of treatment outcome in social anxiety disorder. *Revista Brasileira de Psiquiatria, 34*(1), 92–100.

Murphy, M. T., Michelson, L. K., Marchione, K., Marchione, N., & Testa, S. (1998). The role of self-directed in vivo exposure in combination with cognitive therapy, relaxation training, or therapist-assisted exposure in the treatment of panic disorder with agoraphobia. *Journal of Anxiety Disorders, 12*, 117–138.

Naragon-Gainey, K. (2010). Meta-analysis of the relations of anxiety sensitivity to the depressive and anxiety disorders. *Psychological Bulletin, 136*, 128–150.

Nardi, A. E., Lopes, F. L., Valença, A. M., Freire, R. C., Nascimento, I., Veras, A. B., & Grivet, L. O. (2010). Double-blind comparison of 30 and 60 mg tranylcypromine daily in patients with panic disorder comorbid with social anxiety disorder. *Psychiatry Research, 175*(3), 260–265.

Nardi, A. E., Valença, A. M., Nascimento, I., Lopes, F. L., Mezzasalma, M. A., Freire, R. C., & Versiani, M. (2005). A three-year follow-up study of patients with the respiratory subtype of panic disorder after treatment with clonazepam. *Psychiatry Research, 137*(1), 61–70.

National Institute on Drug Abuse (2016, January 1). Commonly Abused Drugs Charts. Retrieved from https://www.drugabuse.gov/drugs-abuse/commonly-abused-drugs-charts, March 21, 2017.

Newman, M. G., Castonguay, L. G., Borkovec, T. D., Fisher, A. J., Boswell, J. F., Szkodny, L. E., & Nordberg, S. S. (2011). A randomized controlled trial of cognitive-behavioral therapy for generalized anxiety disorder with integrated techniques from emotion-focused and interpersonal therapies. *Journal of Consulting and Clinical Psychology, 79*, 171–181.

Newman, M. G., Kenardy, J., Herman, S., & Taylor, C. B. (1997). Comparison of Palmtop-computer-assisted Brief Cognitive–behavioral Treatment to Cognitive–behavioral Treatment for Panic Disorder. *Journal of Consulting and Clinical Psychology, 65*(1), 178–183.

Newman, M. G., Zuellig, A. R., Kachin, K. E., Constantino, M. J., Przeworski, A., Erickson, T., & Cashman-McGrath, L. (2002). Preliminary reliability and validity of the generalized anxiety disorder questionnaire–IV: A revised self-report diagnostic measure of generalized anxiety disorder. *Behavior Therapy, 33*, 215–233.

Nicolini, H., Bakish, D., Duenas, H., Spann, M., Erickson, J., Hallberg, C., . . . Russell, J. M. (2009). Improvement of psychic and somatic symptoms in adult patients with generalized anxiety disorder: examination from a duloxetine, venlafaxine extended-release and placebo-controlled trial. *Psychological medicine, 39*(02), 267–276.

Nitschke, J. B., Sarinopoulos, I., Oathes, D. J., Johnstone, T., Whalen, P. J., Davidson, R. J., & Kalin, N. H. (2009). Anticipatory activation in the amygdala and anterior cingulate in generalized anxiety disorder and prediction of treatment response. *American Journal of Psychiatry, 166*(3), 302–310.

Norberg, M. M., Krystal, J. H., & Tolin, D. F. (2008). A meta-analysis of D-cycloserine and the facilitation of fear extinction and exposure therapy. *Biological Psychiatry, 63,* 1118–1126.

Nordahl, H. M., Vogel, P. A., Morken, G., Stiles, T. C., Sandvik, P., & Wells, A. (2016). Paroxetine, cognitive therapy or their combination in the treatment of social anxiety disorder with and without avoidant personality disorder: A randomized clinical trial. *Psychotherapy and Psychosomatics, 85*(6), 346–356.

Norton, P. J., Zvolensky, M. J., Bonn-Miller, M. O., Cox, B. J., & Norton, R. (2008). Use of the Panic Attack Questionnaire-IV to assess non-clinical panic attacks and limited symptom panic attacks in student and community samples. *Journal of Anxiety Disorders, 22,* 1159–1171.

Öhman, A., & Soares, J. J. F. (1998). Emotional conditioning to masked stimuli: Expectancies for aversive outcomes following nonrecognized fear-irrelevant stimuli. *Journal of Experimental Psychology: General, 127,* 69–82.

Olatunji, B. O., Cisler, J. M., & Deacon, B. J. (2010). Efficacy of cognitive behavioral therapy for anxiety disorders: A review of meta-analytic findings. *Psychiatric Clinics of North America, 33,* 557–577.

Olatunji, B. O., Cisler, J. M., & Tolin, D. T. (2007). Quality of life in the anxiety disorders: A meta-analytic review. *Clinical Psychology Review, 27,* 572–581.

Olatunji, B., Feldman, G., Smits, J. A. J., Christian, K. M., Zalta, A. K., Pollack, M. H., & Simon, N. M. (2008). Examination of the decline in symptoms of anxiety and depression in generalized anxiety disorder: Impact of anxiety sensitivity on response to pharmacotherapy. *Depression and Anxiety, 25,* 167–171.

Olatunji, B. O., & Wolitzky-Taylor, K. B. (2009). Anxiety sensitivity and the anxiety disorders: meta-analytic review and synthesis. *Psychological Bulletin, 135,* 974–999.

Olatunji, B. O., Wolitzky-Taylor, K. B., Sawchuk, C. N., & Ciesielski, B. G. (2010). Worry and the anxiety disorders: A meta-analytic synthesis of specificity to GAD. *Applied and Preventive Psychology, 14*(1–4), 1–24.

Ollendick, T. H., Öst, L. G., Reuterskiöld, L., & Costa, N. (2010). Comorbidity in youth with specific phobias: Impact of comorbidity on treatment outcome and the impact of treatment on comorbid disorders. *Behaviour Research and Therapy, 48,* 827–831.

Otowa, T., Yoshida, E., Sugaya, N., Yasuda, S., Nishimura, Y., Inoue, K., . . . Tokunaga, K. (2009). Genome-wide association study of panic disorder in the Japanese population. *Journal of human genetics, 54*(2), 122–126.

Öst, L. G. (1987). Age of onset in different phobias. *Journal of Abnormal Psychology, 96,* 223–229.

Öst, L. G. (1989). One-session treatment for specific phobias. *Behaviour Research and Therapy, 27,* 1–7.

Öst, L. G. (2008). Efficacy of the third wave of behavioral therapies: A systematic review and meta-analysis. *Behaviour Research and Therapy, 46,* 296–321.

Öst, L. G., Thulin, U., & Ramnero, J. (2004). Cognitive behavior therapy vs. exposure in vivo in the treatment of panic disorder with agoraphobia. *Behaviour Research and Therapy, 42,* 1105–1127.

Otowa, T., Tanii, H., Sugaya, N., Yoshida, E., Inoue, K., Yasuda, S., . . . Umekage, T. (2010). Replication of a genome-wide association study of panic disorder in a Japanese population. *Journal of human genetics, 55*(2), 91–96.

Otto, M. W., Pollack, M. H., Gould, R. A., Worthington, J. J., McArdle, E. T., & Rosenbaum, J. F. (2000). A comparison of the efficacy of clonazepam and cognitive-behavioral group therapy for the treatment of social phobia. *Journal Anxiety Disorders, 14*, 345–358.

Ougrin, D. (2011). Efficacy of exposure versus cognitive therapy in anxiety disorders: systematic review and meta-analysis. *BMC psychiatry, 11*(1), 200.

Ouimet, A. J., Gawronski, B., & Dozois, D. J. A. (2009). Cognitive vulnerability to anxiety: A review and an integrative model. *Clinical Psychology Review, 29*, 459–470.

Page, A. C. (1994). Blood-injury phobia. *Clinical Psychology Review, 14*, 443–461.

Page, A. C., Bennett, K. S., Carter, O., Smith, J., & Woodmore, K. (1997). The Blood-Injection Symptom Scale (BISS): Assessing a structure of phobic symptoms elicited by blood and injections. *Behaviour Research and Therapy, 35*, 457–464.

Patterson, C. L., Uhlin, B., & Anderson, T. (2008). Clients' pretreatment counseling expectations as predictors of the working alliance. *Journal of Counseling Psychology, 55*(4), 528.

Paulesu, E., Sambugaro, E., Torti, T., Danelli, L., Ferri, F., Scialfa, G., . . . Sassaroli, S. (2010). Neural correlates of worry in generalized anxiety disorder and in normal controls: A functional MRI study. *Psychological Medicine, 40*, 117–124.

Peasley-Miklus, C., & Vrana, S. R. (2000). Effect of worrisome and relaxing thinking on fearful emotional processing. *Behaviour Research and Therapy, 38*, 129–144.

Penava, S. J., Otto, M. W., Maki, K. M., & Pollack, M. H. (1998). Rate of improvement during cognitive-behavioral group treatment for panic disorder. *Behaviour Research and Therapy, 36*, 665–673.

Pergamin-Hight, L., Naim, R., Bakermans-Kranenburg, M. J., van IJzendoorn, M. H., & Bar-Haim, Y. (2015). Content specificity of attention bias to threat in anxiety disorders: A meta-analysis. *Clinical Psychology Review, 35*(November), 10–18.

Peterson, A., Thome, J., Frewen, P., & Lanius, R. A. (2014). Resting-State neuroimaging studies: A new way of identifying differences and similarities among the anxiety disorders? *Canadian Journal of Psychiatry, 59*(6), 294–300.

Phillips, N. K., Hammen, C. L., Brennan, P. A., Najman, J. M., & Bor, W. (2005). Early adversity and the prospective prediction of depressive and anxiety disorders in adolescents. *Journal of Abnormal Child Psychology, 33*, 13–24.

Pillay, S. S., Rogowska, J., Gruber, S. A., Simpson, N., & Yurgelun-Todd, D. A. (2007). Recognition of happy facial affect in panic disorder: an fMRI study. *Journal of Anxiety Disorders, 21*(3), 381–393.

Pollack, M., Mangano, R., Entsuah, R., Tzanis, E., Simon, N. M., & Zhang, Y. (2007). A randomized controlled trial of venlafaxine ER and paroxetine in the treatment of outpatients with panic disorder. *Psychopharmacology, 194*, 233–242.

Ponniah, K., & Hollon, S. D. (2008). Empirically supported psychological interventions for social phobia in adults: A qualitative review of randomized controlled trials. *Psychological Medicine, 38*, 3–14.

Power, K. G., Simpson, R. J., Swanson, V., Wallace L. A., Feistner, A. T. C., & Sharp, D. (1990). A controlled comparison of cognitive behavior therapy, diazepam, and placebo, alone and in combination, for the treatment of generalized anxiety disorder. *Journal of Anxiety Disorders, 4*, 267–292.

Powers, M. B., Sigmarsson, S. R., & Emmelkamp, P. M. G. (2008). A meta-analytic review of psychological treatments for social anxiety disorder. *International Journal of Cognitive Therapy, 1*, 94–113.

Powers, M. B., Zum Vorde Sive Vording, M. B., & Emmelkamp M. P. (2009). Acceptance and Commitment Therapy: A meta-analytic review. *Psychotherapy and Psychosomatics, 78*, 73–80.

Price, M., & Anderson, P. L. (2012). Outcome expectancy as a predictor of treatment response in cognitive behavioral therapy for public speaking fears within social anxiety disorder. *Psychotherapy, 49*(2), 173.

Rachman, S. (1977). The condition theory of fear acquisition: A critical examination. *Behaviour Research and Therapy, 15,* 375–387.

Rachman, S. (1980). Emotional processing. *Behaviour Research and Therapy, 18,* 51–60.

Rachman, S. (1984). Agoraphobia: Safety signal perspective. *Behavioral Research and Therapy, 22,* 59–70.

Radomsky, A. S., Rachman, S., Thordarson, D. S., McIsaac, H. K., & Teachman, B. A. (2001). The claustrophobia questionnaire. *Journal of Anxiety Disorders, 15,* 287–297.

Rapee, R. M. (2012). Family Factors in the Development and Management of Anxiety Disorders. *Clinical Child and Family Psychology Review, 15*(1), 69–80.

Rapee, R. M., Brown, T. A., Antony, M. M., & Barlow, D. H. (1992). Response to hyperventilation and inhalation of 5.5% carbon dioxide-enriched air across the DSM-III-R anxiety disorders. *Journal of Abnormal Psychology, 101,* 538–552.

Reinelt, E., Aldinger, M., Stopsack, M., Schwahn, C., John, U., Baumeister, S. E., . . . Barnow, S. (2014). High social support buffers the effects of 5-HTTLPR genotypes within social anxiety disorder. *European Archives of Psychiatry and Clinical Neuroscience, 264*(5), 433–439.

Reiss, S., & McNally, R. (1985). Expectancy model of fear. In S. Reiss & R. R. Bootzin (Eds.), *Theoretical issues in behavior therapy* (pp. 107–122). New York, NY: Academic Press.

Reiss, S., Peterson, R. A., Gursky, D. M., & McNally, R. J. (1986). Anxiety sensitivity, anxiety frequency and the prediction of fearfulness. *Behaviour Research and Therapy, 24,* 1–8.

Ressler, K. J., Rothbaum, B. O., Tannenbaum, L., Anderson, P., Graap, K., Zimand, E., . . . David, M. (2004). Cognitive enhancers as adjuncts to psychotherapy: Use of D-cycloserine in phobic individuals to facilitate extinction of fear. *Archives of General Psychiatry, 61,* 1136–1144.

Rickels, K., & Rynn, M. (2002). Pharmacotherapy of generalized anxiety disorder. *Journal of Clinical Psychiatry, 63,* 9–16.

Risbrough, V. B., & Geyer, M. A. (2008). Preclinical approaches to understanding anxiety disorders. In M. Antony (Ed.), *Oxford handbook of anxiety and related disorders* (pp. 75–86). New York, NY: Oxford University Press.

Ritchie, K., Norton, J., Mann, A., Carriere, I., & Ancelin, M. L. (2013). Late-onset agoraphobia: General population incidence and evidence for a clinical subtype. *American Journal of Psychiatry, 170*(7), 790–798.

Roberson-Nay, R., Eaves, L. J., Hettema, J. M., Kendler, K. S., & Silberg, J. L. (2012). Childhood separation anxiety disorder and adult onset panic attacks share a common genetic diathesis. *Depression and Anxiety, 29*(4), 320–327.

Roemer, L., Lee, J. K., Salters-Pedneault, K., Erisman, S. M., Orsillo, S. M., & Mennin, D. S. (2009). Mindfulness and emotion regulation difficulties in generalized anxiety disorder: Preliminary evidence for independent and overlapping contributions. *Behavior Therapy, 40,* 142–154.

Roemer, L., Molina, S., Litz, B. T., & Borkovec, T. D. (1997a). Preliminary investigation of the role of previous exposure to potentially traumatic events in generalized anxiety disorder. *Depression and Anxiety, 4,* 134–138.

Roemer, L., Orsillo, S. M., & Salters-Pedneault, K. (2008). Efficacy of an acceptance-based behavior therapy for generalized anxiety disorder: Evaluation in a randomized controlled trial. *Journal of Consulting and Clinical Psychology, 76,* 1083–1089.

Roemer, L., Salters, K., Raffa, S. D., & Orsillo, S. M. (2005). Fear and avoidance of internal experiences in GAD: Preliminary tests of a conceptual model. *Cognitive Therapy and Research, 29*(1), 71–88.

Roemer, L., Salters-Pedneault, K., & Orsillo, S. M. (2006). Incorporating mindfulness- and acceptance-based strategies in the treatment of generalized anxiety disorder. In R. A. Baer (Ed.), *Mindfulness-based treatment approaches: Clinician's guide to evidence base and applications* (pp. 51–74). San Diego, CA: Elsevier Academic Press.

Rork, K. E., & Morris, T. L. (2009). Influence of Parenting Factors on Childhood Social Anxiety: Direct Observation of Parental Warmth and Control. *Child & Family Behavior Therapy, 31*(March 2015), 220–235.

Rothbaum, B. O., Hodges, L., Smith, S., Lee, J. H., & Price, L. (2000). A controlled study of virtual reality exposure therapy for the fear of flying. *Journal of Consulting and Clinical Psychology, 68,* 1020–1026.

Ruiz, F. J. (2012) Acceptance and commitment therapy: a meta-analytic review. *Psychother. Psychosom., 78*(2) (2009), pp. 73–80.

Ruscio, A. M. (2002). Delimiting the boundaries of generalized anxiety disorder: Differentiating high worriers with and without GAD. *Journal of Anxiety Disorders, 16,* 377–400.

Ruscio, A. M., & Borkovec, T. D. (2004). Experience and appraisal of worry among high worriers with and without generalized anxiety disorder. *Behaviour Research and Therapy, 42,* 1469–1482.

Ruscio, A. M., Lane, M., Roy-Byrne, P., Stang, P. E., Stein, D. J., Wittchen, H.-U., & Kessler, R. C. (2005). Should excessive worry be required for a diagnosis of generalized anxiety disorder? Results from the US National Comorbidity Survey Replication. *Psychological Medicine, 35,* 1761–1772.

Sakai, Y., Kumano, H., Nishikawa, M., Sakano, Y., Kaiya, H., Imabayashi, E., & Diksic, M. (2005). Cerebral glucose metabolism associated with a fear network in panic disorder. *Neuroreport, 16*(9), 927–931.

Salters-Pedneault, K., Roemer, L., Tull, M. T., Rucker, L., & Mennin, D. S. (2006). Evidence of broad deficits in emotion regulation associated with chronic worry and generalized anxiety disorder. *Cognitive Therapy and Research, 30,* 469–480.

Sanderson, W. C., Di Nardo, P. A., Rapee, R. M., & Barlow, D. H. (1990). Syndrome comorbidity in patients diagnosed with a DSM-III-R anxiety disorder. *Journal of Abnormal Psychology, 99,* 308–312.

Scaini, S., Belotti, R., & Ogliari, A. (2014). Genetic and environmental contributions to social anxiety across different ages: A meta-analytic approach to twin data. *Journal of anxiety disorders, 28*(7), 650–656.

Scaini, S., Ogliari, A., Eley, T. C., Zavos, H., & Battaglia, M. (2012). Genetic and environmental contributions to separation anxiety: A meta-analytic approach to twin data. *Depression and anxiety, 29*(9), 754–761.

Schmidt, N. B., Lerew, D. R., & Jackson, R. J. (1997). The role of anxiety sensitivity in the pathogenesis of panic: Prospective evaluation of spontaneous panic attacks during acute distress. *Journal of Abnormal Psychology, 106,* 355–364.

Schmidt, N. B., Lerew, D. R., & Jackson, R. J. (1999). Prospective evaluation of anxiety sensitivity in the pathogenesis of panic: Replication and extension. *Journal of Abnormal Psychology, 108,* 532–537.

Schmitz, J., Krämer, M., Tuschen-Caffier, B., Heinrichs, N., & Blechert, J. (2011). Restricted autonomic flexibility in children with social phobia. *Journal of Child Psychology and Psychiatry, 52*(11), 1203–1211.

Schwartz, B. L., Hashtroudi, S., Herting, R. L., Schwartz, P., & Deutsch, S. I. (1996). D-cycloserine enhances implicit memory in Alzheimer patients. *Neurology, 46*(2), 420–424.

Schwartz, D., Lansford, J. E., Dodge, K. A., Pettit, G. S., & Bates, J. E. (2015). Peer victimization during middle childhood as a lead indicator of internalizing problems and diagnostic outcomes in late adolescence. *Journal of Clinical Child and Adolescent Psychology, 53,* 44(3), 393–404.

Schwartz, C. E., Snidman, N., & Kagan, J. (1999). Adolescent social anxiety as an outcome of inhibited temperament in childhood. *Journal of the American Academy of Child & Adolescent Psychiatry, 38,* 1008–1015.

Seligman, M. (1971). Phobias and preparedness. *Behavior Therapy*, 2, 307–320.

Shah, S. G., & Angstadt, M. (2009). Amygdala and insula response to emotional images in patients with generalized social anxiety disorder. *Journal of Psychiatry & Neuroscience: JPN*, 34(4), 296.

Shang, J., Fu, Y., Ren, Z., Zhang, T., Du, M., Gong, Q., . . . Zhang, W. (2014). The common traits of the ACC and PFC in anxiety disorders in the DSM-5: Meta-analysis of voxel-based morphometry studies. *PLoS ONE*, 9(3).

Sharp, D. M., Power, K. G., & Swanson, V. (2004). A comparison of the efficacy and acceptability of group versus individual cognitive behaviour therapy in the treatment of panic disorder and agoraphobia in primary care. *Clinical Psychology & Psychotherapy*, 11(2), 73–82.

Shear, M. K., Brown, T. A., Sholomskas, D. E., Barlow, D. H., Gorman, J. M., Woods, S. W., & Cloitre, M. (1997). *Panic Disorder Severity Scale (PDSS)*. Pittsburgh, PA: Department of Psychiatry, University of Pittsburgh School of Medicine.

Shear, M. K., Devereux, R. B., Kranier-Fox, R., Mann, J. J., & Frances, A. (1984). Low prevalence of mitral valve prolapse in patients with panic disorder. *American Journal of Psychiatry*, 141, 302–303.

Sheehan, D. V. (2015). *Mini International Neuropsychiatric Interview 7.0*. Jacksonville, FL: Medical Outcomes Systems.

Siegel, R. S., LaGreca, A. M., & Harrison, H. M. (2009). Peer victimization and social anxiety in adolescents: Prospective and reciprocal relationships. *Journal of Youth and Adolescence*, 38, 1096–1109.

Skinner, B. F. (1963). Operant Behavior. *American Psychologist*, 18(8), 503.

Smoller, J. W. (2015). The genetics of stress-related disorders: PTSD, depression, and anxiety disorders. *Neuropsychopharmacology*

Smoller, J. W., Paulus, M. P., Fagerness, J. A., Purcell, S., Yamaki, L. H., Hirshfeld-Becker, D., . . . Stein, M. B. (2008). Influence of RGS2 on anxiety-related temperament, personality, and brain function. *Archives of General Psychiatry*, 65(3), 298–308.

Spence, S. H., Donovan, C., & Brechman-Toussaint, M. (2000). The treatment of childhood social phobia: The effectiveness of a social skills training-based, cognitive-behavioral intervention, with and without parental involvement. *Journal of Child Psychology and Psychiatry*, 41(6), 713–726.

Spinhoven, P., Batelaan, N., Rhebergen, D., van Balkom, A., Schoevers, R., & Penninx, B. W. (2016). Prediction of 6-yr symptom course trajectories of anxiety disorders by diagnostic, clinical and psychological variables. *Journal of Anxiety Disorders*, 44, 92–101.

Spinhoven, P., Onstein, E. J., Klinkhamer, R. A., & Knoppert-van der Klein, E. A. M. (1996). Panic management, trazodone and a combination of both in the treatment of panic disorder. *Clinical Psychology and Psychotherapy*, 3, 86–92.

Spitzer, R., Kroenke, K., Williams, J., & Lowe, B. (2006). A brief measure for assessing generalized anxiety disorder: The GAD-7. *Archives of Internal Medicine*, 166, 1092–1097.

Spoormaker, V. I., Vermetten, E., Czisch, M., & Frank, H. W. (2014). Functional Neuroimaging of Anxiety Disorders. *MRI in Psychiatry*, 249–274.

Stangier, U., Schramm, E., Heidenreich, T., Berger, M., & Clark, D. M. (2011). Cognitive therapy vs interpersonal psychotherapy in social anxiety disorder: A randomized controlled trial. *Archives of General Psychiatry*, 68(7), 692–700.

Staugaard, S. R. (2010). Threatening faces and social anxiety: A literature review. *Clinical Psychology Review*, 30(6), 669–690.

Steel, Z., Marnane, C., Iranpour, C., Chey, T., Jackson, J. W., Patel, V., & Silove, D. (2014). The global prevalence of common mental disorders: a systematic review and meta-analysis 1980–2013. *International Journal of Epidemiology*, 43(2), 476–493.

Stein, M. B., Chartier, M. J., Hazen, A. L., Kozak, M. V., Tancer, M. E., Lander, S., . . . Walker, J. R. (1998). A direct-interview family study of generalized social phobia. *American Journal of Psychiatry*, 155, 90–97.

Stein, M. B., Goldin, P. R., Sareen, J., Zorrilla, L. T. E., & Brown, G. G. (2002). Increased amygdala activation to angry and contemptuous faces in generalized social phobia. *Archives of general psychiatry, 59*(11), 1027–1034.

Stein, M. B., & Kean, Y. M. (2000). Disability and quality of life in social phobia: Epidemiologic findings. *American Journal of Psychiatry, 157,* 1606–1613.

Stein, M. B., Lang, K. L., & Livesley, W. J. (1999). Heritability of anxiety sensitivity: A twin study. *American Journal of Psychiatry, 156,* 246–251.

Stein, M. B., Norton, R. G., Walker, J. R., Chartier, M. J., & Graham, R. (2000). Do selective serotonin re-uptake inhibitors enhance the efficacy of very brief cognitive-behavioral therapy for panic disorder? A pilot study. *Psychiatry Research, 94,* 191–200.

Stein, M. B., Schork, N. J., & Gelernter, J. (2008). Gene-by-environment (serotonin transporter and childhood maltreatment) interaction for anxiety sensitivity, an intermediate phenotype for anxiety disorders. *Neuropsychopharmacology, 33,* 312–319.

Stein, M. B., & Stein, D. J. (2008). Social anxiety disorder. *The Lancet, 371*(9618), 1115–1125.

Stemberger, R., Turner, S. M., Beidel, D. C., & Calhoun, K. S. (1995). Social phobia: An analysis of possible developmental factors. *Journal of Abnormal Psychology, 104,* 526–531.

Stewart, S. H., Taylor, S., Lang, K. L., Box, B. J., Watt, M. C., Fedroff, I. C., & Borger, S. C. (2001). Causal modeling of relations among learning history, anxiety sensitivity, and panic attacks. *Behaviour Research and Therapy, 39,* 443–456.

Stinson, F. S., Dawson, D. A., Chou, S. P., Smith, S., Goldenstein, R. B., Ruan, W. J., & Grant, B. F. (2007). The epidemiology of DSM-IV specific phobia in the USA: Results from the National Epidemiologic Survey on Alcohol and Related Conditions. *Psychological Medicine, 37,* 1047–1059.

Stöber, J., Tepperwien, S., & Staak, M. (2000). Worrying leads to reduced concreteness of problem elaboration: Evidence for the avoidance theory of worry. *Anxiety, Stress, and Coping, 13,* 217–227.

Storch, E. A., & Masia-Warner, C. (2004). The relationship of peer victimization to social anxiety and loneliness in adolescent females. *Journal of Adolescence, 27,* 351–362.

Straube, T., Mentzel, H. J., & Miltner, W. H. (2007). Waiting for spiders: brain activation during anticipatory anxiety in spider phobics. *Neuroimage, 37*(4), 1427–1436.

Summerfeldt, L. J., Kloosterman, P. H., & Antony, M. M. (2010). Structured and semistructured diagnostic interviews. In M. M. Antony & D. H. Barlow (Eds.), *Handbook of assessment and treatment planning for psychological disorders* (pp. 95–137). New York, NY: Guilford Press.

Szymanski, J., & O'Donohue, W. (1995). Fear of Spiders Questionnaire. *Journal of Behavior Therapy and Experimental Psychiatry, 26,* 31–34.

Tadic, A., Rujescu, D., Szegedi, A., Giegling, I., Singer, P., Möller, H. J., & Dahmen, N. (2003). Association of a MAOA gene variant with generalized anxiety disorder, but not with panic disorder or major depression. *American Journal of Medical Genetics and Neuropsychiatric Genetics, 117B*(1), 1–6.

Taylor, S. (1999). *Anxiety sensitivity: Theory, research, and treatment of the fear of anxiety.* Mahwah, NJ: Erlbaum.

Taylor, S., Koch, W. J., & McNally, R. J. (1992). How does anxiety sensitivity vary across the anxiety disorders? *Journal of Anxiety Disorders, 6,* 249–259.

Taylor, J. M., & Whalen, P. J. (2015). Neuroimaging and anxiety: the neural substrates of pathological and non-pathological anxiety. *Current Psychiatry Reports, 17*(6), 49.

Taylor, S., Zvolensky, M. J., Cox, B. J., Deacon, B., Heimberg, R. G., Ledley, D. R., & Cardenas, S. J. (2007). Robust dimensions of anxiety sensitivity: Development and initial validation of the Anxiety Sensitivity Index–3. *Psychological Assessment, 19,* 176–188.

Telch, M. J., Lucas, J. A., Schmidt, N. B., Hanna, H. H., Jaimez, T. L., & Lucas, R. A. (1993). Group cognitive-behavioral treatment of panic disorder. *Behaviour Research and Therapy, 31,* 279–287.

Tesar, G. E., Rosenbaum, J. F., Pollack, M. H., Otto, M. W., Sachs, G. S., Herman, J. B., . . . Spier, S. A. (1991). Double-blind, placebo-controlled comparison of clonazepam and alprazolam for panic disorder. *Journal of Clinical Psychiatry, 52,* 69–76.

Thayer, J. F., Friedman, B. H., & Borkovec, T. D. (1996). Autonomic characteristics of generalized anxiety disorder and worry. *Biological Psychiatry, 39,* 255–266.

Thrasher, C., & LoBue, V. (2016). Do infants find snakes aversive? Infants' physiological responses to "fear-relevant" stimuli. *Journal of Experimental Child Psychology, 142*(October), 382–390.

Thyer, B. A., Parrish, R. T., Curtis, G. C., Nesse, R. M., & Cameron, O. G. (1985). Ages of onset of DSM-III anxiety disorders. *Comprehensive Psychiatry, 26,* 113–122.

Tibi, L., Van Oppen, P., Aderka, I. M., Van Balkom, A. J. L. M., Batelaan, N. M., Spinhoven, P., . . . Anholt, G. E. (2015). An admixture analysis of age of onset in agoraphobia. *Journal of Affective Disorders, 180*(April), 112–115.

Tillfors, M., Furmark, T., Marteinsdottir, I., Fischer, H., Pissiota, A., Långström, B., & Fredrikson, M. (2001). Cerebral blood flow in subjects with social phobia during stressful speaking tasks: a PET study. *American Journal of Psychiatry, 158*(8), 1220–1226.

Tolin, D. F., Gilliam, C., Wootton, B. M., Bowe, W., Bragdon, L. B., Davis, E., . . . Hallion, L. S. (2016). Psychometric properties of a structured diagnostic interview for DSM-5 anxiety, mood, and obsessive-compulsive and related disorders. *Assessment,* 1073191116638410.

Torgersen, S. (1986). Childhood and family characteristics in panic and generalized anxiety disorders. *American Journal of Psychiatry, 143,* 630–632.

Trumpf, J., Becker, E. S., Vriends, N., Meyer, A. H., & Margraf, J. (2009). Rates and predictors of remission in young women with specific phobia: A prospective community study. *Journal of Anxiety Disorders, 23,* 958–964.

Tsai, G. E., Falk, W. E., Gunther, J., & Coyle, J. T. (1999). Improved cognition in Alzheimer's disease with short-term D-cycloserine treatment. *American Journal of Psychiatry, 156*(3), 467–469.

Tsao, J. C. I., Mystkowski, J. L., Zucker, B. G., & Craske, M. G. (2002). Effects of cognitive-behavioral therapy for panic disorder on comorbid conditions: Replication and extension. *Behavior Therapy, 33,* 493–509.

Turk, C. L., Heimberg, R. G., Luterek, J. A., Mennin, D. S., & Fresco, D. M. (2005). Emotion dysregulation in generalized anxiety disorder: A comparison with social anxiety disorder. *Cognitive Therapy and Research, 29*(1), 89–106.

Turner, S. M., Beidel, D. C., Dancu, C. V., & Keys, D. J. (1986). Psychopathology of social phobia and comparison to avoidant personality disorder. *Journal of Abnormal Psychology, 95,* 389–394.

Turner, S. M., Beidel, D. C., Dancu, C. V., & Stanley, M. A. (1989). An empirically derived inventory to measure social fears and anxiety: The Social Phobia and Anxiety Inventory. *Psychological Assessment, 1,* 35–40.

Tyrer, P., Seivewright, N., Ferguson, B., Murphy, S., & Johnson, A. L. (1993). The Nottingham study of neurotic disorder: Effect of personality status on response to drug treatment, cognitive therapy and self-help over two years. *British Journal of Psychiatry, 162,* 219–226.

Tyrer, P., Seivewright, H., Simmonds, S., & Johnson, T. (2001). Prospective studies of cothymia (mixed anxiety-depression): How do they inform clinical practice? *European Archives of Psychiatry and Clinical Neuroscience, 251*(2), 53–56.

Uchida, R. R., Del-Ben, C. M., Busatto, G. F., Duran, F. L., Guimarães, F. S., Crippa, J. A., & Graeff, F. G. (2008). Regional gray matter abnormalities in panic disorder: a voxel-based morphometry study. *Psychiatry Research: Neuroimaging, 163*(1), 21–29.

Valentiner, D. P., Telch, M. J., Petruzzi, D. C., & Bolte, M. C. (1996). Cognitive mechanisms in claustrophobia: An examination of Reiss and McNally's expectancy model and Bandura's self-efficacy theory. *Cognitive Therapy and Research, 20,* 593–612.

van Ameringan, M., Mancini, C., & Streiner, D. (1993). Fluoxetine efficacy in social phobia. *Journal of Clinical Psychiatry, 54,* 27–32.

van den Heuvel, O. A., Veltman, D. J., Groenewegen, H. J., Witter, M. P., Merkelbach, J., Cath, D. C., . . . van Dyck, R. (2005). Disorder-specific neuroanatomical correlates of attentional bias in obsessive-compulsive disorder, panic disorder, and hypochondriasis. *Archives of General Psychiatry, 62*(8), 922–933.

van der Bruggen, C., Stams, G., Bogels, S., & Paulussen-Hoogeboom, M. (2010). Parenting Behavior as a Mediator between Young Children's Negative Emotionality and their Anxiety/Depression. *Infant and Child Development, 19*(January), 354–365.

van Gerwen, L. J., Spinhoven, P., Diekstra, R. F. W., & Van Dyck, R. (2002). Multicomponent standardized treatment program for fear of flying. Description and effectiveness. *Cognitive and Behavioral Practice, 9*, 138–149.

van Vliet, I. M., Westenberg, H. G., & den Boer, J. A. (1993). MAO inhibitors in panic disorder: Clinical effects of treatment with brofaromine. A double-blind placebo-controlled study. *Psychopharmacology, 112*, 483–489.

Vazquez, K., Sandler, J., Interian, A., & Feldman, J. M. (2017). Emotionally triggered asthma and its relationship to panic disorder, ataques de nervios, and asthma-related death of a loved one in Latino adults. *Journal of Psychosomatic Research, 93*, 76–82.

Vervliet, B., Kindt, M., Vansteenwegen, D., & Hermans, D. (2010). Fear generalization in humans: Impact of prior non-fearful experiences. *Behaviour Research and Therapy, 48*, 1078–1084.

Vesga-López, O., Schneier, F. R., Wang, S., Heimberg, R. G., Liu, S. M., Hasin, D. S., & Blanco, C. (2008). Gender differences in generalized anxiety disorder from the National Epidemiological Survey on Alcohol and Related Conditions (NESARC). *Journal of Clinical Psychiatry, 69*(10), 1606–1616.

Vøllestad, J., Nielsen, M. B., & Nielsen, G. H. (2012). Mindfulness- and acceptance-based interventions for anxiety disorders: A systematic review and meta-analysis. *British Journal of Clinical Psychology, 51*(3), 239–260.

Vreeburg, S. A., Zitman, F. G., van Pelt, J., DeRijk, R. H., Verhagen, J. C., van Dyck, R., . . . Penninx, B. W. (2010). Salivary cortisol levels in persons with and without different anxiety disorders. *Psychosomatic medicine, 72*(4), 340–347.

Walker, D. L., Ressler, K. J., Lu, K. T., & Davis, M. (2002). Facilitation of conditioned fear extinction by systemic adminstration of intra-amygdala infusions of D-cycloserine as assessed with fear-potentiated startle in rats. *Journal of Neuroscience, 22*, 2343–2351.

Warshaw, M. G., Massion, A. O., Shea, M. T., Allsworth, J., & Keller, M. B. (1997). Predictors of remission in patients with panic with and without agoraphobia: Prospective 5-year follow- up data. *Journal of Nervous and Mental Disease, 185*, 517–519.

Watkins, E. R. (2008). Constructive and unconstructive repetitive thought. *Psychological Bulletin, 134*(2), 163–206.

Watson, D. (2005). Rethinking the mood and anxiety disorders: A quantitative hierarchical model for DSM-V. *Journal of Abnormal Psychology, 114*, 522–536.

Watson, J. B., & Rayner, R. (1920). Conditioning emotional reacionts. *Journal of Experimental Psychology, 3*, 1–14.

Watts, F. N., McKenna, F. P. Sharrock, R., & Trezise, L. (1986). Color naming of phobia-related words. *British Journal of Psychology, 77*, 97–108.

Wells, A. (1995). Meta-cognition and worry: A cognitive model of generalized anxiety disorders. *Behavioural and Cognitive Psychotherapy, 6*, 86–95.

Wells, A. (2004). A cognitive model of GAD: Metacognitions and pathological worry. In R. G. Heimberg, C. L. Turk, & D. S. Mennin (Eds.), *Generalized anxiety disorder: Advances in research and practice* (pp. 164–186). New York, NY: Guilford Press.

Wells, A., & Carter, K. (2001). Further tests of a cognitive model of generalized anxiety disorder: Metacognitions and worry in GAD, panic disorder, social phobia, depression, and non-patients. *Behavior Therapy, 32*(1), 85–102.

Wells, A., & Papageorgiou, C. (1998). Social phobia: Effects of external attention on anxiety, negative beliefs, and perspective taking. *Behavior Therapy, 29*, 357–370.

Wendt, J., Lotze, M., Weike, A. I., Hosten, N., & Hamm, A. O. (2008). Brain activation and defensive response mobilization during sustained exposure to phobia-related and other affective pictures in spider phobia. *Psychophysiology, 45*(2), 205–215.

Wheaton, M. G., Deacon, B. J., McGrath, P. B., Berman, N. C., & Abramowitz, J. S. (2012). Dimensions of anxiety sensitivity in the anxiety disorders: Evaluation of the ASI-3. *Journal of Anxiety Disorders, 26*(3), 401–408.

Whisman, M. A., Sheldon, C. T., & Goering, P. (2000). Psychiatric disorders and dissatisfaction with social relationships: Does type of relationship matter? *Journal of Abnormal Psychology, 109*, 803–808.

White, L. K., McDermott, J. M., Degnan, K. A., Henderson, H. A., & Fox, N. A. (2011). Behavioral inhibition and anxiety: The moderating roles of inhibitory control and attention shifting. *Journal of Abnormal Child Psychology, 39*(5), 735–747.

Whitmore, M. J., Kim-Spoon, J., & Ollendick, T. H. (2013). Generalized Anxiety Disorder and Social Anxiety Disorder in Youth: Are They Distinguishable? *Child Psychiatry & Human Development, 45*(4), 456–63.

Wichstrøm, L., Belsky, J., & Berg-Nielsen, T. S. (2013). Preschool predictors of childhood anxiety disorders: A prospective community study. *Journal of Child Psychology and Psychiatry and Allied Disciplines, 54*(12), 1327–1336.

Wilson, J. K., & Rapee, R. M. (2005). The interpretation of negative social events in social phobia: Changes during treatment and relationship to outcome. *Behaviour Research and Therapy, 43*, 373–389.

Wittchen, H.-U. (2002). Generalized anxiety disorder: Prevalence, burden, and cost to society. *Depression and Anxiety, 16*(4), 162–171.

Wittchen, H. U., Beesdo, K., & Gloster, A. T. (2009). The position of anxiety disorders in structural models of mental disorders. *Psychiatric Clinics of North America, 32*(3), 465–481.

Wittchen, H.-U., & Beloch, E. (1996). The impact of social phobia on quality of life. *International Clinical Psychopharmacology, 11*(Suppl. 3), 15–23.

Wittchen, H.-U., Essau, C. A., von Zerssen, D., Krieg, J. C., & Zaudig, M. (1992). Lifetime and six-month prevalence of mental disorders in the Munich follow-up study. *European Archives of Psychiatry and Clinical Neuroscience, 241*, 247–258.

Wittchen, H.-U., Gloster, A. T., Beesdo-Baum, K., Fava, G. A., & Craske, M. G. (2010). Agoraphobia: A review of the diagnostic classificatory position and criteria. *Depression and Anxiety, 27*, 113–133.

Wittchen, H.-U., Nelson, C. B., & Lachner, G. (1998). Prevalence of mental disorders and psychosocial impairments in adolescents and young adults. *Psychological Medicine, 28*, 109–126.

Wittchen, H.-U., Stein, M. B., & Kessler, R. C. (1999). Social fears and social phobia in a community sample of adolescents and young adults: Prevalence, risk factors, and comorbidity. *Psychological Medicine, 29*, 309–323.

Wolitzky-Taylor, K. B., Horowitz, J. D., Powers, M. B., & Telch, M. J. (2008). Psychological approaches in the treatment of specific phobias: A meta-analysis. *Clinical Psychology Review, 28*, 1021–1037.

Wong, S. Y. S., Yip, B. H. K., Mak, W. W. S., Mercer, S., Cheung, E. Y. L., Ling, C. Y. M., . . . Ma, H. S. W. (2016). Mindfulness-based cognitive therapy v. group psychoeducation for people with generalised anxiety disorder: Randomised controlled trial. *The British Journal of Psychiatry, 209*(1), 68–75.

World Health Organization. (1992). *The ICD-10 classification of mental and behavioral disorders: Clinical descriptions and diagnostic guidelines*. Geneva, Switzerland: Author.

Wright, C. I., Martis, B., McMullin, K., Shin, L. M., & Rauch, S. L. (2003). Amygdala and insular responses to emotionally valenced human faces in small animal specific phobia. *Biological psychiatry*, *54*(10), 1067–1076.

Yalcin, B., Willis-Owen, S. A., Fullerton, J., Meesaq, A., Deacon, R. M., Rawlins, J. N. P., . . . Mott, R. (2004). Genetic dissection of a behavioral quantitative trait locus shows that Rgs2 modulates anxiety in mice. *Nature Genetics*, *36*(11), 1197–1202.

Yonkers, K. A., Bruce, S. E., Dyck, I. R., & Keller, M. B. (2003). Chronicity, relapse, and illness—Course of panic disorder, social phobia, and generalized anxiety disorder: Findings in men and women from 8 years of follow-up. *Depression and Anxiety*, *17*, 173–179.

Yonkers, K. A., Dyck, I. R., Warshaw, M., & Keller, M. B. (2000). Factors predicting the clinical course of generalised anxiety disorder. *British Journal of Psychiatry*, *176*, 544–549.

Yonkers, K. A., Zlotnik, C., Allsworth, J., Warshaw, M., Shea, T., & Keller, M. B. (1998). Is the course of panic disorder the same in men and women? *American Journal of Psychiatry*, *155*, 596–602.

Yook, K., Kim, K.-H., Suh, S. Y., & Lee, K. S. (2010). Intolerance of uncertainty, worry, and rumination in major depressive disorder and generalized anxiety disorder. *Journal of Anxiety Disorders*, *24*, 623–628.

Yoon, K. L., Fitzgerald, D. A., Angstadt, M., McCarron, R. A., & Phan, K. L. (2007). Amygdala reactivity to emotional faces at high and low intensity in generalized social phobia: a 4-Tesla functional MRI study. *Psychiatry Research: Neuroimaging*, *154*(1), 93–98.

Zbozinek, T. (2012). Diagnostic overlap of generalized anxiety disorder and major depressive disorder in a primary care sample. *Depression and Anxiety*, *29*(12), 1065–1071.

Zhang, W., Ross, J., & Davidson, J. R. T. (2004). Social anxiety disorder in callers to the Anxiety Disorders Association of America. *Depression and Anxiety*, *20*, 101–107.

Zhou, B., Lacroix, F., Sasaki, J., Peng, Y., Wang, X., & Ryder, A. G. (2014). Unpacking cultural variations in social anxiety and the offensive- type of taijin kyofusho through the indirect effects of intolerance of uncertainty and self-construals. *Journal of Cross-Cultural Psychology*, *45*(10), 1561–1578.

Zoellner, L. A., & Craske, M. G. (1999). Interoceptive accuracy and panic. *Behaviour Research and Therapy*, *37*(12), 1141–1158.

CHAPTER 10

Obsessive-Compulsive and Related Disorders

SANDRA M. NEER, MICHAEL A. GRAMLICH, and KATIE A. RAGSDALE

O BSESSIVE-COMPULSIVE AND RELATED disorders (OCRDs) were introduced as a new chapter in the fifth edition of the *Diagnostic and Statistical Manual of Mental Disorders* (*DSM-5*; American Psychiatric Association [APA], 2013) and include obsessive-compulsive disorder (OCD), body dysmorphic disorder (BDD), hoarding disorder (HD), trichotillomania (TTM), and excoriation (skin-picking) disorder (ED). The chapter includes disorders previously categorized elsewhere within the *DSM-IV-TR* (APA, 2000) (e.g., anxiety disorders [OCD], somatoform disorders [BDD], and impulse-control disorders not elsewhere classified [TTM]), as well as two new diagnoses (HD and ED). The disorders were reclassified within this new chapter to reflect their diagnostic and clinical relatedness (APA, 2013).

Diagnostically, OCD is characterized by obsessions and/or compulsions that consume more than 1 hour per day or cause clinically significant distress or impairment (APA, 2013). Obsessions include recurrent and persistent thoughts, urges, or images (e.g., thoughts of contamination or urges to kill someone) of an intrusive or unwanted nature, which individuals attempt to suppress, ignore, or neutralize (e.g., by performing a compulsion). Compulsions are repetitive behaviors or mental acts (e.g., counting or washing) that individuals engage in to prevent or reduce anxiety or distress. Compulsions do not need to be logically connected to the obsessions they are attempting to neutralize, though they often are. Specifiers of the diagnosis include level of insight and presence of past or current tic disorder.

Body dysmorphic disorder is characterized by an excessive preoccupation with a slight or imagined defect related to an individual's physical appearance that is not apparent to others (APA, 2013). The *DSM-5* requires that an individual with BDD endorse a history of performing repetitive behaviors (e.g., excessive grooming, reassurance checking) or mental checking (e.g., comparing his or her physical appearance with that of others) due to the perceived physical flaw(s). Repetitive behaviors commonly include camouflaging areas of concern (e.g., using makeup or clothing items such as sunglasses, scarves, or hats) in effort to conceal perceived imperfections. While the perceived defects cannot be accounted for by weight or body fat concerns associated with eating disorders, preoccupation with body build can be specified. The *DSM-5* muscle dysmorphia specifier describes an individual who perceives his or her muscles as insufficiently lean or inadequate when in reality they appear normal or excessively muscular. Lastly, the *DSM-5* requires clinicians to specify an individual's degree of insight to capture how convinced the individual is of their appearance-related defects.

Hoarding disorder reflects persistent difficulty in parting with possessions, to the point that it causes clinically significant distress or impairment (APA, 2013). Difficulty discarding an item is unrelated to the item's actual value; rather, it is related to both the distress associated with discarding the item and a perceived need to save it. As a result, accumulation of possessions causes congestion and clutter in living areas, which substantially compromises their intended uses. Unlike HD, normative collecting does not involve significant disorganization or clutter, distress, or impairment. In addition, individuals who excessively acquire additional possessions which are not needed or for which there is no room would meet criteria for the specification of HD with excessive acquisition.

Trichotillomania (hair-pulling disorder) is defined by recurrent hair pulling that results in hair loss. Although hair pulling typically results in visible hair loss, individuals who widely pull hair from various body regions may not evidence this clinical marker (APA, 2013). The scalp, eyelids, and eyebrows are the most common sites; however, hair pulling may occur at any region of the body where hair grows. In addition to hair pulling, individuals suffering from TTM repeatedly attempt to decrease or stop hair pulling, and endorse significant associated distress or impairment.

Excoriation disorder (skin-picking disorder) is characterized by recurrent skin picking which results in skin lesions (APA, 2013). Skin picking commonly occurs on the face, arms, and hands; however, individuals may pick multiple body regions (APA, 2013). Although individuals typically use fingernails to pick, other objects (e.g., tweezers) and techniques (e.g., squeezing or rubbing) may be used. Individuals may pick at a variety of sites, including healthy skin, scabs, or skin irregularities, and repeatedly attempt to decrease or stop skin picking. As with all other psychiatric disorders, individuals must experience clinically significant distress or impairment to meet diagnostic criteria.

CLINICAL FEATURES

Obsessive-compulsive disorder is a clinically heterogeneous disorder with various presentations of obsessions and/or compulsions. Although individuals only need to endorse either obsessions or compulsions to meet diagnostic criteria (APA, 2013), studies suggest that nearly all individuals with OCD experience both obsessions and compulsions (Foa & Kazak, 1995; Leonard & Riemann, 2012). Contamination and checking are the most commonly reported obsession and compulsion, respectively (Foa & Kazak, 1995; Pinto, Mancebo, Eisen, Pagano, & Rasmussen, 2006); however, most individuals with OCD endorse multiple obsessions and compulsions (Pinto et al., 2006). Obsessions and compulsions may often appear functionally related (e.g., contamination obsessions accompanied by cleaning compulsions); however, other presentations are less specific (e.g., checking compulsions related to a variety of obsessions) (Bloch, Landeros-Weisenberger, Rosario, Pittenger, & Leckman, 2008).

Research investigating subtypes of OCD have typically identified four to five symptom dimensions (e.g., Brakoulias et al., 2013; Bloch et al., 2008; Stewart et al., 2008). A meta-analysis of factor analytic studies of OCD symptom categories resulted in four factors, which explained nearly 80% of the variance in 17 studies of adults with OCD (Bloch et al., 2008). The four factors included: (1) symmetry (symmetry obsessions and repeating, counting, and ordering compulsions); (2) cleaning (contar and cleaning compulsions); (3) forbidden thoughts (aggressive, re obsessions); and (4) hoarding (hoarding obsessions and compul hoarding is now classified as a separate disorder in the *DSM-5* (Ar examining OCD symptom dimensions using updated diagnostic criteria is needed.

Obsessive-compulsive disorder is a debilitating disorder with significant functional impairment and reduced quality of life (Norberg, Calamari, Cohen, & Riemann, 2008; Subramaniam, Soh, Vaingankar, Picco, & Chong, 2013). In fact, a recent review found that quality of life in OCD is significantly lower than quality of life in community controls and individuals with other psychiatric and medical disorders (Macy et al., 2013). Unfortunately, despite the associated impairment and distress, few individuals with the disorder initiate treatment (Levy, McLean, Yadin, & Foa, 2013).

Individuals with BDD are typically concerned with five to seven body areas, most commonly involving skin, hair, nose, stomach, and teeth (Phillips, Menard, Fay, & Weisberg, 2005). Phillips (2005) reported that preoccupations typically last at least 1 hour per day with an average length of 3–8 hours per day (as cited by Bjornsson, Didie, & Phillips, 2010). Common repetitive behaviors are as follows: comparing disliked body areas with those of others (95%), camouflaging (92%), mirror checking (90%), grooming (69%), touching body areas (59%), seeking reassurance related to physical appearance (58%), changing clothes (46%), skin picking to improve appearance (44%), dieting (38%), tanning (25%), and excessive exercising (22%; Phillips et al., 2005). Motivations for mirror gazing are often complex, uncontrollable, and masochistic, with documented cases of severe disappointment that "nothing has changed" (Silver & Farrants, 2016). Another key behavioral feature of BDD involves camouflage checking, which ranges from masking the perceived defect in public to hiding its visibility to themselves in private (e.g., due to high disgust; Veale et al., 1996). Individuals with BDD may avoid physical contact or public situations altogether, which may result in them becoming housebound (Phillips, Menard, & Fay, 2006a). A pathway analysis study revealed anxiety, but not shame, elevated risk of being housebound in BDD and OCD groups (Weingarden, Renshaw, Wilhelm, Tangney, & DiMauro, 2016). Approximately 30% of individuals with BDD endorse appearance-related symmetry concerns, most commonly focusing on hair, breast/chest, eyes, eyebrows, nose, and lips (Hart & Phillips, 2013). For instance, a patient with BDD may report uneven hair or one eyebrow disproportionate in size.

Typically, rituals of BDD are performed to provide a sense of comfort. For example, a patient may repeatedly gaze in the mirror to examine their makeup until it feels "just right." However, patients often feel more distress after mirror gazing than before gazing (Baldock, Anson, & Veale, 2012). Additionally, individuals with BDD exhibit a stable motivational trait to reduce imperfection known as "incompleteness," which has been found to predict symptom severity of the disorder (Summerfeldt, 2004; Summers, Matheny, & Cougle, 2017). "Not just right" experiences and feelings of incompleteness are evident among BDD-related *in vivo* stressor tasks (e.g., face photos) and visual sensory stimuli in general (Summers et al., 2017). This urge to engage in rituals until it feels just right or to diminish perceptions of incompleteness may extend to interventions such as exposure and response prevention (ERP).

Individuals with muscle dysmorphia endorse poorer quality of life and higher frequency of suicide attempts and substance use disorders (SUDs; Pope et al., 2005), as well as a higher number of perceived physical defects compared with those with BDD alone (mean of 7.6 vs. 4.8, respectively; Pope et al., 2005). Furthermore, individuals with muscle dysmorphia endorse a higher frequency of anabolic steroid use, which may increase risk of premature death and cardiovascular dysfunctions, amongst other ᵧmptoms (Pope et al., 2014). Often, patients avoid disclosing use of anabolic steroids—as such, this specifier requires further assessment to prevent adverse health consequences (Pope, Khalsa, & Bhasin, 2017).

Poor insight related to physical appearance defects is a prominent feature attributed to BDD. Individuals with BDD are more likely to exhibit delusional beliefs connected to their symptoms compared with individuals with OCD (32% vs. 2.4%, respectively; Phillips et al., 2012). Examples of delusional beliefs include complete conviction that others agree with their beliefs (e.g., appearance is ugly) or that their symptoms are not caused by psychiatric illness. Consistent findings have shown level of insight associated with symptom severity of BDD (Phillips, Hart, Simpson, & Stein, 2014b). Although clinicians found degree of insight correlated with severity of OCD, the majority of individuals suffering from OCD exhibit good insight, whereas the majority of individuals with BDD show poor or delusional insight (Phillips et al., 2012). Delusional thinking related to BDD is correlated with poorer social functioning and increased likelihood of suicidal ideation or attempts and SUD. Conversely, individuals with and without delusional insight endorsed similar age of BDD onset (mean ages 16.4 vs. 16.5 years, respectively), quality of life, and probability of remission at 1 year follow-up (Phillips, Menard, Pagano, Fay, & Stout, 2006b). As reviewed by Phillips et al. (2014b), delusional versus nondelusional beliefs may exhibit dissimilar impairment that is better accounted for by greater symptom severity. Nonetheless, clinicians should assess for degree of insight to monitor severity of BDD and further case conceptualization during treatment.

Suicidality is a common risk present among individuals with BDD. The lifetime prevalence rates of suicidal ideation or attempts are 71.2–81.3% and 25.8–28.4%, respectively (Phillips et al., 2005). Within a given year, the approximate annual rate of suicidal ideation is 57.8%, that of suicide attempt is 2.6%, and that of completed suicide is 0.3% (Phillips & Menard, 2006). Individuals with BDD are four times more likely to exhibit suicidal ideation and 2.6 times more likely to attempt suicide compared with healthy controls and individuals diagnosed with other psychiatric disorders (e.g., OCD or any other anxiety disorder; Angelakis, Gooding, & Panagioti, 2016). Lifetime comorbidity of major depressive disorder and functional impairment due to BDD predicted suicidal ideation, whereas lifetime history of post-traumatic stress disorder (PTSD), functional impairment due to BDD, and BDD-related restrictive food intake predicted suicidal attempts (Witte, Didie, Menard, & Phillips, 2012). A path analysis study found shame as a risk factor for suicidality in OCD and BDD groups; however, only shame predicted depression for BDD (Weingarden et al., 2016). A recent study of a nonclinical sample found that depressive symptoms fully mediated the relationship between severity of BDD and a novel construct termed suicidal desire (i.e., feelings of burdensomeness and disconnect from others; Shaw, Hall, Rosenfield, & Timpano, 2016). Future research should examine other potential mediators that increase risk of suicidal ideation or attempts in this population.

The typical clinical presentation of HD involves an individual who has significant difficulty parting with possessions and associated distress and/or impairment. Over two-thirds of individuals with the disorder may also exhibit excessive acquisition of items. Excessive acquisition has been found to be a clinical predictor of distress and/or impairment (Timpano et al., 2011), and greater severity of the following: OCD (non-hoarding) symptoms, perfectionism or uncertainty, and other HD symptoms (e.g., difficultly discarding or clutter; Frost, Rosenfield, Steketee, & Tolin, 2013). Individuals with the disorder most frequently accumulate items through purchase (64.4%) and obtaining free things (53.4%); however, a subsample of those who engage in excessive acquisition may also steal (25.3%; Timpano et al., 2011). Approximately 70% of individuals who did not meet current criteria for the excessive acquisition specifier reported acquisition difficulties in the past, and no significant differences emerged between current and past acquisition groups on avoidance of acquiring triggers (e.g., places or store aisles; Frost et al., 2013). This suggests the urge to acquire items may still exist even if an individual denies acquiring behaviors. Among HD cases encountered by social services, professionals estimated that individuals hoard both inanimate objects and animals (51%); however, hoarding of animals only is rarer than inanimate objects alone (2% vs. 47%, respectively; McGuire, Kaercher, Park, & Storch, 2013). Clinically significant hoarding may lead to work impairment and is a significant public health burden (Tolin, Frost, Steketee, Gray, & Fitch, 2008). HD may result in clutter removal fees (estimated to be $3,700 per case), eviction from the home, living alone and/or removal of others from the home (McGuire et al., 2013; Tolin et al., 2008).

The hallmark symptom of TTM is clinically significant hair pulling. Individuals usually pull hair from multiple sites, most frequently the scalp, followed by eyelashes, eyebrows, and pubic hair (Flessner, Woods, Franklin, Keuthen, & Piacentini, 2009). In a recent study, Grzesiak, Reich, Szepietowski, Hadrys, & Pacan (2017) reported that half (50%) of the individuals with TTM in their sample pulled hair from the scalp, 37.5% pulled from the eyebrows, 25% pulled the eyelashes, and one patient pulled from the abdominal area. Although it is not necessary for diagnosis, many adults with the disorder report an urge, need, or drive to pull hair, as well as a sense of gratification or relief during or after pulling (Lochner et al., 2012). Most individuals pull out single hairs (68%); however, some may pull out clumps (5%), or a combination of single hairs and clumps (27%; Christenson, MacKenzie, & Mitchell, 1991). Additionally, individuals may target specific types of hair based on thickness, texture, or color and may manipulate hair after it is pulled (e.g., suck on hairs or scrape off roots; Walsh & McDougle, 2001). Bottesi, Cerea, Ouimet, Sica, & Ghisi (2016) reported that almost 70% of their Italian TTM sample pulled more than once per day, 20% more than once a week, 5.6% once a day, and 4.5% once a week. Finally, individuals with TTM may express associated negative affective states, including perceived unattractiveness (87%), secretiveness (83%), shame (75%), irritability (71%), low self-esteem (77%), and depressed mood (81%; Stemberger, Thomas, Mansueto, & Carter, 2000). Bottesi et al. (2016) also reported affective correlates across the hair pulling cycle, with increased levels of shame, sadness, and frustration from pre- to post-pulling and decreased levels of calmness after hair pulling episodes in an Italian sample.

Excoriation disorder describes clinically significant picking of the skin that results in skin lesions. An examination of 60 individuals with pathologic skin picking suggests that the disorder is time-consuming and associated with various complications, such as scarring, ulcerations, and infections (Odlaug & Grant, 2008). Results of this study also suggest that individuals often begin picking in response to triggers, such as feel (55%) or sight (26.7%) of the skin, boredom/downtime (25%), and stress (20%). The face and head (60%) are the most common sights for picking, followed by the legs and feet (33.3%), arms (30%), torso (23.3%), and hands and fingers (21.7%). Most individuals (68.8%) pick from multiple sites of the body, often switching areas in order for other sites to heal. In fact, 35% of this sample experienced infections requiring antibiotics as a result of skin picking.

DIAGNOSTIC CONSIDERATIONS

Studies show that upwards of 90% of individuals with OCD meet criteria for an additional disorder at some point in their lifetime (Pinto et al., 2006; Ruscio, Stein, Chiu, & Kessler, 2010; Torres et al., 2016). Within the National Comorbidity Survey

Replication (NCS-R; Kessler et al., 2004), the most common comorbid disorders for individuals with a lifetime diagnosis of OCD were anxiety disorders (75.8%), followed by mood disorders (63.3%), impulse-control disorders (55.9%), and finally SUDs (38.6%). Within anxiety disorders, the highest comorbidity rates were found for lifetime social phobia (43.5%), specific phobia (42.7%), and separation anxiety disorder (37.1%); whereas major depressive disorder (40.7%) was the most frequent comorbid mood disorder. Other studies corroborate high rates of anxiety and depression comorbidity (Hofmeijer-Sevink et al., 2013; Pinto et al., 2006; Torres et al., 2016), as well as high rates of lifetime comorbid obsessive-compulsive personality disorder (Bulli, Melli, Cavalletti, Stopani, & Carraresi, 2016; Pinto et al., 2006).

Body dysmorphic disorder has high lifetime comorbidity with major depressive disorder (75.4% in treated and 72.7% in untreated samples), SUD (50.0% and 43.9%, respectively), social anxiety disorder (40.3% and 34.8%, respectively), OCD (38.8% and 21.2%, respectively), and PTSD (9.0% and 9.1%, respectively; Phillips et al., 2005). In addition, BDD is highly comorbid with personality disorders (47.9% in treated and 39.0% in untreated samples), with the highest prevalence among avoidant personality disorder (26.9% and 22.0%, respectively; Phillips et al., 2005). Similar to BDD, "not just right" experiences and feelings of incompleteness are evident among symptoms of OCD such as checking or ordering objects (Belloch et al., 2016; Taylor et al., 2014); however, BDD should be diagnosed if symptoms of obsessions and compulsions primarily concern physical features.

Literature on the comorbidity rates of HD is sparse, likely due to its introduction as a stand-alone disorder in the *DSM-5*. However, one study examined current comorbidity of HD (defined by the then-proposed *DSM-5* criteria) in 217 individuals with the diagnosis (Frost, Steketee, & Tolin, 2011). Major depression was the most common comorbid mood disorder (50.7%); however, comorbidity rates were also high for attention deficit hyper-activity disorder (ADHD) inattentive type (27.8%), generalized anxiety disorder (24.4%), social phobia (23.5%), and OCD (18%). An investigation of the clinical correlates of HD found 42% as "noncomorbid," 42% as hoarding with depression, and 16% as hoarding with depression and inattention (Hall, Tolin, Frost, & Steketee, 2013). Although this investigation relied on self-report measures of hoarding behavior, this study concluded that HD is not secondary to other disorders (e.g., OCD) and that a substantial percentage of individuals with HD also suffer from depression and inattention.

Research examining comorbidities of TTM suggests that mood, anxiety, and SUDs are the most commonly identified comorbidities (Duke, Keeley, Geffken, & Storch, 2010). In a large, nationally representative sample of TTM patients, 75.5% of patients with TTM had another psychiatric comorbid disorder (Gupta, Gupta, & Knapp, 2015). More specifically, 37.8% had comorbid depressive disorder, 35.1% had OCD, 21% had other anxiety disorders, 15.4% had attention deficit disorder and only 2% had drug or alcohol dependence. However, the mean age of the sample was 24 years old, with 20% of the sample under the age of 12, so drug and alcohol problems may not have been prevalent.

Trichotillomania is also related to skin picking disorder (Grant et al., 2016). In a sample of 421 participants with primary TTM, 14.5% had co-occurring ED. Of 124 patients with ED, 16.9% had comorbid TTM. Participants with primary TTM and comorbid ED had significantly more severe TTM symptoms and were more likely to have major depressive disorder than those with TTM alone. Participants with primary ED and comorbid TTM reported significantly more severe skin picking symptoms than those who had ED only. In an earlier study, with a smaller sample, the comorbidity of TTM and ED was somewhat higher, with an average of 20.8% of TTM outpatient samples endorsing skin picking, with a similar rate of 15.5% of ED outpatient samples endorsing TTM

(Snorrason, Belleau, & Woods, 2012). Both studies indicate relatedness between the two disorders.

EPIDEMIOLOGY

Due to the recent advent of the *DSM-5*, current epidemiological studies reflect diagnoses largely based on *DSM-IV* and *DSM-IV-TR* criteria. Diagnostic changes introduced in the *DSM-5*, as well as inclusion of new disorders, will continue to generate new research that may elucidate changes in prevalances reflective of new diagnostic criteria. Thus, epidemiological data reflected here are based on *DSM-IV* or *DSM-IV-TR* criteria and in samples of United States adults, unless otherwise noted.

Although over one-fourth of individuals report experiencing obsessions or compulsions at some point in their lives, meeting diagnostic criteria for OCD occurs in a much smaller percentage of individuals (Ruscio et al., 2010). Specifically, the 12-month prevalence of OCD is 1.2% and the lifetime prevalence is 2.3%. Notably, rates vary based on the population and setting examined. For instance, rates appear lower in veteran primary care settings (1.9%; Gros, Magruder, & Frueh, 2013) and may be attenuated in treatment-seeking populations as well (Levy et al., 2013).

The estimated point prevalence of BDD among adults in the community ranges from 1.7% to 2.4% (Koran, Abujaoude, Large, & Serpe, 2008; Rief, Buhlmann, Wilhelm, Borkenhagen, & Brähler, 2006), with updated *DSM-5* criteria finding similar rates in the general population (2.9%; Schieber, Kollei, de Zwaan, & Martin, 2015). The rate of individuals screening positive for BDD varies across settings: 5.8% of outpatients, 7.4–16% of psychiatric inpatients, 11.3% of dermatology patients, 13.2% of general cosmetic surgery patients, and 20% of rhinoplasty patients (Conroy et al., 2008; Veale, Gledhill, Christodoulou, & Hodsoll, 2016). The estimated prevalence of muscle dysmorphia is approximately 22% of the BDD population and is predominately found among males (Phillips et al., 2010; Pope et al., 2005). Patients are often reluctant to disclose symptoms related to BDD due to feelings of shame; as such, clinicians should regularly screen for BDD during intake evaluations (Conroy et al., 2008; Grant, Kim, & Crow, 2001).

Prior investigations on the point prevalence of HD found estimates at approximately 5.8% (Timpano et al., 2011), whereas more recent epidemiological studies using *DSM-5* criteria reported lower estimates of 1.5–2.1% (Cath, Nizar, Boomsma, & Mathews, 2016; Nordsletten et al., 2013c). Importantly, age is a key factor when considering the prevalence of HD. For instance, Cath et al. (2016) found that the diagnosis of HD increased by 20% with every 5 years of age. This study found that, among individuals 70 years or older, the point prevalence of HD reached more than 6%. With regard to the prevalence of animal hoarding, there is a lack of epidemiological data. A recent investigation among treatment-seeking adults with HD found little evidence of animal hoarding behaviors and, therefore, further inquiry is necessary due to the health risks for both humans and animals (Ung, Dozier, Bratiotis, & Ayers, 2016a).

In a community sample, 0.6% of individuals met *DSM-IV-TR* criteria for TTM; however, the prevalence increased to 1.2% when the prior diagnostic criteria of building tension or release were ignored (Duke, Bodzin, Tavares, Geffken, & Storch, 2009), suggesting that the *DSM-5* criteria may be less restrictive and produce larger prevalence rates. Among a psychiatric inpatient sample, the point prevalence of TTM was 3.4% and the lifetime prevalence was 4.4% (Grant, Levine, Kim, & Potenza, 2005). Interestingly, a similar rate of TTM (3.9%) was found for a sample of college students; however, the college sample rate was based on a modified self-report measure of the clinical interview administered to the inpatient sample (Odlaug & Grant, 2010). In a recent study of TTM prevalence in young adults, 3.5% reported hair pulling during their lifetime, with only 2.4% meeting diagnostic criteria for current TTM (Grzesiak et al., 2017).

Although ED was not an official diagnosis within the *DSM-IV-TR* (APA, 2000), prevalence rates based on various diagnostic criteria do exist. For instance, in nonclinical community samples, 1.4–5.4% of individuals endorsed clinically significant skin picking with associated distress or impairment (Grant et al., 2012; Hayes, Storch, & Berlanga, 2009). In a study examining prevalence based on (then proposed) *DSM-5* criteria, 4.2% of college students met diagnostic criteria for ED (Odlaug et al., 2013). In a study based on 2,513 telephone interviews, Keuthen, Koran, Aboujaoude, Large, & Serpe (2010a) found that 1.4% met all *DSM-5* criteria for ED.

PSYCHOLOGICAL AND BIOLOGICAL ASSESSMENT

Various clinician-administered measures for the assessment of OCD exist, some of which have recently been updated to reflect changes introduced in the *DSM-5* (APA, 2013). For instance, the Anxiety and Related Disorders Interview Schedule for *DSM-5* (ADIS-5)–Lifetime Version (ADIS-5L; Brown & Barlow, 2014) and the Structured Clinical Interview for *DSM-5* Disorders–Clinician Version (SCID-5-CV; First, Spitzer, Williams, & Karg, 2015) are semistructured diagnostic interviews that assess for OCD and other disorders. The ADIS-5L provides clinician-rated interference and distress ratings to track progress throughout the course of treatment. Additionally, the Yale-Brown Obsessive-Compulsive Scale (Y-BOCS; Goodman et al., 1989a,b) is considered the "gold standard" for assessing OCD symptom severity and now includes a revised second edition (Y-BOCS-II; Storch et al., 2010b). The Y-BOCS-II is a semistructured, clinician-administered measure that assesses for the frequency and severity of OCD symptoms over the past week, with good to excellent psychometric properties (Storch et al., 2010a,b).

Although OCD is typically assessed using semistructured clinical interviews, various self-report measures with established reliability and validity exist, including the Y-BOCS-Self Report (Baer, Brown-Beasley, Sorce, & Henriques, 1993; Steketee, Frost, & Bogart, 1996) and Obsessive-Compulsive Inventory–Revised (OCI-R; Foa et al., 2002). Finally, behavioral avoidance tests (BATs), or observational tasks in which individuals are exposed to feared stimuli while rating their distress, have recently been used to assess OCD (Grabill et al., 2008). BATs are often administered before treatment to assess the severity of avoidance and distress, and after treatment to assess functional change. BATs are generally considered an adjunct to traditional clinical interviewing and provide particularly helpful information for development of exposure hierarchies. For comprehensive reviews of assessment measures for OCD, see Benito and Storch (2011), Grabill et al. (2008), and Rapp, Bergman, Piacentini, and McGuire (2016).

With regard to BDD, the ADIS-5L (Brown & Barlow, 2014) is a clinician-administered interview that diagnoses BDD based on *DSM-5* diagnostic criteria. Other validated diagnostic assessments and screeners exist, including the Body Dysmorphic Diagnostic Module and Body Dysmorphic Disorder Questionnaire (as reviewed by Phillips, 2005); however, to our knowledge, *DSM-5* revisions are still pending. Furthermore, the Y-BOCS modified for Body Dysmorphic Disorder (BDD-YBOCS; Phillips, Hollander, Rasmussen, & Aronowitz, 1997) is a 12-item semistructured clinician interview that assesses the severity of BDD. The BDD-YBOCS is sensitive to change (Phillips, Hart, & Menard, 2014a), has strong internal consistency, excellent interrater and test–retest reliability, and good convergent (e.g., BDD Examination, $r = 0.82$; Rosen & Reiter, 1996) and divergent validity (e.g., Duke Brief Social Phobia Scale, $r = 0.24$; Davidson et al., 1997; Phillips et al.,

2014a). Finally, the Brown Assessment of Beliefs Scale (BABS; Eisen et al., 1998) is a semistructured interview that includes detailed assessment of delusional and nondelusional beliefs of pathology, with higher scores indicating poorer insight (total score of ≥18 indicates delusional). Among individuals with BDD, the BABS demonstrated excellent interrater and test–retest reliability, and sensitivity to change (Phillips, Hart, Menard, & Eisen, 2013).

The Structured Interview for Hoarding Disorder (SIHD; Nordsletten et al., 2013a) is a semistructured interview based on *DSM-5* criteria. The SIHD demonstrates excellent interrater reliability for HD criteria and specifiers, and appropriate convergent and divergent validity to other hoarding measures or alternative conditions (Nordsletten et al., 2013a). Another widely used diagnostic interview for the presence of HD includes the Hoarding Rating Scale-Interview (HRS-I; Tolin, Frost, & Steketee, 2010). The HRS-I exhibits excellent reliability, is sensitive to treatment changes, and can distinguish individuals with hoarding from both OCD patients without hoarding and community controls (Tolin et al., 2010). Additionally, the UCLA Hoarding Severity Scale (UHSS; Saxena et al., 2007) is a 10-item clinician-administered interview, which assesses the symptom severity and associated features of HD. The UHSS exhibits good internal consistency, strong convergent and divergent validity, and appropriate discrimination between individuals who meet *DSM-5* criteria for HD and healthy controls (Saxena, Ayers, Dozier, & Maidment, 2015).

With regard to self-reports measures, the Saving Inventory–Revised (SI-R; Frost, Steketee, & Grisham, 2004) is a 23-item self-report measure that assesses for clutter, difficulty discarding, and excessive acquisition, and exhibits appropriate reliability and validity. While an investigation found that the SI-R is a reliable and valid measure in geriatric populations for hoarding severity, the subscales require continued research before use in the community (Ayers, Dozier, & Mayes, 2016). Secondary sources that may benefit clinicians assessing HD include home visits and consultation with family members and friends (Kress, Stargell, Zoldan, & Paylo, 2016). However, a discrepancy in HD symptomatology may occur between individuals with the disorder underreporting and family members or friends over-reporting due to the negative impact loved ones experience (DiMauro, Tolin, Frost, & Steketee, 2013). Photographs from patients' homes may also assist clinicians in determining the presence of HD when home visits are not possible (Fernández de la Cruz, Nordsletten, Billotti, & Mataix-Cols, 2013).

Recent research has improved differential diagnosis of TTM and other scalp diseases. Rakowska, Slowinska, Olszewska and Rudnicka (2014) used trichoscopy (hair and scalp dermoscopy) to determine characteristics of TTM and found 100% of TTM patients had irregularly broken hairs. In addition, flame hairs (defined as semitransparent, wavy and cone-shaped hair residues) were found to be specific for TTM (compared with alopecia and tinea capitis). They also identified other types of broken hair features (v-sign hairs, tulip hairs, and hair powder) that were highly characteristic of patients with TTM. Given the secrecy and denial of hair pulling characteristic of this disorder, new methods to diagnose TTM, such as trichoscopy, are needed. Although no gold standard psychological assessment for TTM exists, there are some measures designed to assess for the disorder (Stargell, Kress, Paylo, & Zins, 2016). Measures with properties include the Massachusetts General Hospital Hairpulling Scale (MGH-HPS; Keuthen et al., 1995; O'Sullivan et al., 1995), a seven-item self-report scale, and the Milwaukee Inventory for Subtypes of Trichotillomania-Adult Version (MIST-A; Flessner, Woods, Franklin, Cashin, & Keuthen, 2008), a 15-item scale that provides two distinct scale scores (i.e., automatic pulling and focused pulling scores). The ADIS-5L (Brown & Barlow, 2014) also includes a screening question for TTM with added prompts for clinicians to acquire further information, such as nature of symptoms, onset, and frequency.

There does not appear to be an assessment measure yet developed for the *DSM-5* diagnosis of ED; however, some measures do assess for factors related to earlier conceptualizations of skin picking. For instance, the Skin Picking Scale (SPS; Keuthen et al., 2001) is a six-item self-report measure modeled after the original Y-BOCS (Goodman et al., 1989a,b); however, the measure only assesses for severity of skin picking. Furthermore, similar to the MIST-A (Flessner et al., 2008), the Milwaukee Inventory for the Dimensions of Adult Skin Picking (MIDAS; Walther, Flessner, Conelea, & Woods, 2009) is a reliable and valid assessment of automatic and focused skin picking for individuals who engage in the behavior. Finally, the Skin Picking Impact Scale (SPIS; Keuthen et al., 2001) has been revised to a shorter version (SPIS-S; Snorrason, Stein, & Woods, 2013). These measures assess the impact of ED on social life, associated embarrassment, consequences of picking, and the perception of unattractiveness (Snorrason et al., 2012). The ADIS-5L (Brown & Barlow, 2014) also includes a screening question for ED with added prompts for clinicians to acquire further information such as nature of symptoms, onset, and frequency. A functional analysis approach may also be used to assess ED (LaBrot, Dufrene, Ness, & Mitchell, 2014) in which interviews are used to determine antecedents to and consequences of the skin picking behavior.

ETIOLOGICAL CONSIDERATIONS

Behavioral and Molecular Genetics

Obsessive-compulsive disorder has a complex etiology involving both genetic and environmental factors. Evidence from family, twin, and segregation studies shows that heredity plays a major role in the etiology of OCD (Pauls, 2010). In fact, a recent review reported odds ratios of 12–30 in childhood-onset OCD and an odds ratio of approximately 5 in adult OCD (Pauls, Abramovitch, Rauch, & Geller, 2014). Furthermore, a meta-analysis found an average prevalence rate of 8.2% for first-degree relatives of OCD probands, compared with 2% in comparison relatives, supporting the heritability of the disorder (Hettema, Neale, & Kendler, 2001).

Twin studies of OCD patients also support the presence of significant genetic influence, with estimates of 45–65% in children, and 27–47% in adults (Jonnal, Gardner, Prescott, & Kendler, 2000). For instance, in a large twin study examining heritability of OCD dimensions (e.g., rumination, contamination, and checking), genetic factors accounted for 36% of the variance, whereas the remaining 64% was explained by environmental factors (van Grootheest, Boomsma, Hettema, & Kendler, 2008). Similarly, five major symptom dimensions (checking, hoarding, obsessing, ordering, and washing) were analyzed in a sample of female twins (Iervolino, Rijsdijk, Cherkas, Fullana, & Mataix-Cols, 2011) and no single underlying factor could explain the heterogeneity of OCD. However, the majority of the genetic variance was due to shared genetic factors (62.5–100%), whereas the nonshared environmental variance was due to dimension-specific factors. Interestingly, meta-analysis of twin studies examining the etiology of obsessions and compulsions found that additive genetic effects and nonshared environment accounted for the majority of the variance in obsessive-compulsive symptoms, whereas shared environment and nonadditive genetics accounted for minimal to no variance (Taylor, 2011b). Future research is needed to help identify specific genetic and environmental factors underlying the dimensions of this heterogeneous disorder.

The specific genetic markers for OCD are largely unknown; however, genetic linkage, genome-wide association, and candidate gene studies have been conducted in attempt to identify regions that may contain vulnerability genes for OCD (see Pauls et al., 2014 for review). Studies suggest that regions containing chromosomes 9 (Hanna et al., 2002; Willour et al., 2004) and 15 (Ross et al., 2011; Shugart et al., 2006) may be of particular importance (Pauls et al., 2014). Although these results are far from definitive, it is interesting to note that several studies have reported an association between OCD and a glutamate transporter gene (SLC1A1), which is located in the area of chromosome 9p (Chakrabarty, Bhattacharyya, Christopher, & Khanna, 2005; Rotge et al., 2010; Stewart et al., 2013; Ting & Feng, 2008; Willour et al., 2004). More recently, however, Mathews et al. (2012) conducted a genome-wide linkage analysis using 33 families that had two or more individuals with childhood-onset OCD. Authors identified five areas of interest on chromosomes, with the strongest result on chromosome 1p36. In summary, OCD is genetically heterogeneous disorder, and environmental factors appear to play a large role in the manifestation of the disorder (Pauls et al., 2014).

A family study investigating over 300 individuals for probable OCRDs revealed that 8% of individuals with BDD have a first-degree relative with a lifetime diagnosis of BDD, which is approximately three times greater than prevalence rates among adults in the community (Bienvenu et al., 2000; Koran et al., 2008). Examining large samples of monozygotic and dizygotic twins, genetics contributed to approximately 44% of the variance of BDD, whereas unique environmental factors generally accounted for the remaining 56% (López-Solà et al., 2014; Monzani et al., 2012; Monzani, Rijsdijk, Harris, & Mataix-Cols, 2014). Furthermore, the clinical disorders of OCD, HD, and BDD shared a common latent genetic factor, whereas TTM and excoriation disorder ED shared a separate latent genetic factor (Monzani et al., 2014). This finding reflects the higher similarity of symptoms among OCD, HD, and BDD (i.e., primarily "cognitive" OCRDs; Phillips et al., 2010) and greater symptom agreement between TTM and ED (i.e., primarily "body-focused" OCRDs; Stein et al., 2010). Preliminary evidence supports identification of candidate genes of serotonin and GABA systems within a sample of individuals with BDD; however, the findings were likely limited due to small sample size and require further investigation (Phillips et al., 2015).

Given the recent inclusion of hoarding as a diagnostic category, information has primarily derived from research on patients with OCD who have been divided into hoarding or nonhoarding subgroups. For instance, using data from a large collaborative genetics study of OCD, Samuels et al. (2007) found significant linkage of compulsive hoarding to chromosome 14 in families with OCD. These investigators also found that hoarding and indecision were more prevalent in relatives of hoarding than nonhoarding OCD patients. Steketee et al. (2015) interviewed 443 individuals using the HRS-I (Tolin et al., 2010) and reported higher rates of hoarding symptoms among first-degree relatives of HD participants (57.1%) compared with OCD (30.0%) and control (26.0%) groups. Specifically, this study found higher rates of hoarding symptoms among female than among male first-degree relatives. Given the high rate of hoarding symptoms among first-degree relatives, these findings suggest further examination of genetics and vicarious learning is warranted.

In a study of monozygotic and dizygotic twins from the UK twin registry (Monzani et al., 2014), hoarding was determined by completion of the Hoarding Rating Scale–Self Report (HRS-SR, modified from the HRS-I; Tolin et al., 2010). The authors found that heritability of hoarding in female twins was associated with both genetic (51%) and nonshared environmental factors (49%; as well as measurement error). Shared environmental factors did not contribute to the liability. Another investigation found lower rates of heritability for HD among male (25%) and female (39%) Australian monozygotic twins (33% overall; López-Solà et al., 2014). Conversely, a Netherlands-based twin registry investigation found similar genetic correlations for hoarding among male and female monozygotic twins (36% overall; Mathews, Delucchi, Cath, Willemsen, & Boomsma, 2014). Taken together, the non-UK twin registry studies found lower overall rates of genetic factors accounting for hoarding; however, this discrepancy may result from the lack of older adults collected in the López-Solà et al. (2014) and Mathews et al. (2014) samples compared with the Monzani et al. (2014) UK twin registry. With regard to symptoms, among UK female monozygotic twins, genetic correlations were associated with difficulty discarding (43%) and excessive acquisition (50%), with a shared genetic linkage between these hallmark features (59%; Nordsletten et al., 2013b). Nonetheless, this study indicated that a large portion of nonshared factors explained both HD behaviors (41%) and further investigation of unique environmental conditions may inform tailored intervention strategies.

Overall, the genetics of TTM are complex and not well understood; however, a recent population-based twin study administered the MGH-HPS (Keuthen et al., 1995; O'Sullivan et al., 1995) to determine the heritability for TTM (Monzani et al., 2014). Results indicated genetics accounted for 31.6% of TTM, while the nonshared environment accounted for the remaining variance. Early genetic research indicates that hair-pulling behavior occurs at increased rates (5–8%) in family members of TTM probands relative to normal controls (Christenson, Mackenzie, & Reeve, 1992; Lenane et al., 1992). Heritability has also been suggested by results of a twin study in which concordance rate for TTM (as defined by *DSM-IV-TR* criteria) was 38.1% for monozygotic twins compared with 0% for dizygotic twins (Novak, Keuthen, Stewart, & Pauls, 2009). The etiology of TTM for any particular patient is most likely an interaction between biological, psychological, and social factors (Diefenbach, Reitman, & Williamson, 2000); however, these studies suggest heritability is an important component in the etiology of TTM.

Excoriation disorder also appears to have a familial component. In a study with 60 patients with skin picking disorder, Odlaug and Grant (2012) found that 28.3% of first-degree family members also met criteria for the disorder. Another study found that 43% of 40 patients with ED had first-degree relatives with skin picking symptoms (Neziroglu, Rabinowitz, Breytman, & Jacofsky, 2008). Further in support of a heritability component in the etiology of ED, Monzani et al. (2012) used the SPS assessment and found that clinically significant skin picking was reported by 1.2% of twins, with higher concordance for monozygotic than for dizygotic twins. Within this female sample, genetic factors accounted for 40% of the variance, with the remaining variance attributable to nonshared environmental factors. A more recent estimate among adult female twins found the heritability of ED up to 47% (Monzani et al., 2014). Future studies are needed with homogenous samples, diagnosed with *DSM-5* criteria, to establish heritability of ED.

NEUROANATOMY AND NEUROBIOLOGY

Extant literature supports an association between OCD and impairments of the brain's corticostriatal systems, which include organized neural circuits that connect the basal ganglia, thalamus, and cortex. For instance, functional magnetic resonance imaging (fMRI) findings suggest that patients with OCD exhibit impairments in functional connectivity of both the ventral and dorsal corticostriatal systems, with a direct link between ventral corticostriatal connectivity and symptom severity (Harrison et al., 2009). Although authors were able to demonstrate system-wide differences in connectivity, the sample size was too small to determine the effects of specific symptom dimensions. A recent study, however, examined the influence of OCD symptom dimensions on brain corticostriatal functional systems (Harrison et al., 2013). Results found a shared connectivity involving the ventral striatum and orbitofrontal cortex (OFC) related to specific symptom dimensions. Specifically, aggression symptoms moderated connectivity in the ventral striatum, amygdala, and ventromedial frontal cortex, and sexual/religious symptoms affected ventral striatal-insular connectivity. These recent data suggest common pathophysiological changes in orbitofrontal-striatal regions across various forms of OCD.

Furthermore, Beucke et al. (2013) examined abnormal connectivity in the OFC in medicated and nonmedicated OCD patients and matched normal controls. Consistent with previous research, the OFC and the basal ganglia showed greater connectivity in unmedicated OCD patients, suggesting that antidepressant medication may reduce brain connectivity in OCD patients (Beucke et al., 2013). Interestingly, a recent review of studies that examined brain alterations following psychotherapy for OCD (with and without concurrent pharmacological intervention), indicated that individuals with OCD experience various brain changes following treatment, suggesting that successful treatment may lead to neurobiological recovery (Thorsen, van den Heuvel, Hansen, & Kvale, 2015).

While the corticostriatal (also referred to as the cortico-striato-thalamo-cortical) model of OCD has been the leading model underlying OCD pathophysiology (Pauls et al., 2014), recent meta-analytic review suggests that brain regions outside of this circuit (i.e., the cerebellum and parietal cortex) are likely implicated in the disorder (Eng, Sim, & Chen, 2015). As such, future research is needed to more comprehensively understand the pathophysiological underpinnings of OCD.

Individuals with BDD may exhibit disruptions of the serotonergic and dopaminergic systems. Specifically, one study revealed an abnormality of presynaptic serotonin (5-HT) transporters (Marazziti et al., 1999) and another reported lower dopamine D2/3 receptor binding potential in the putamen and caudate nucleus (Vulink, Planting, Figee, Booij, & Denys, 2016). These findings corroborate interventions of selective serotonin reuptake inhibitors (SSRIs) alleviating symptoms of BDD (e.g., Phillips, Albertini, & Rasmussen, 2002; Phillips et al., 2016).

Studies using fMRI among individuals with BDD demonstrated abnormalities during visual processing of other faces (Feusner, Townsend, Bystritsky, & Bookheimer, 2007), own face (Feusner et al., 2010a), and nonface objects (e.g., houses; Feusner, Hembacher, Moller, & Moody, 2011). With regard to faces, these studies revealed hyperactivity of brain activation in the left frontal, parietal, and temporal regions (e.g., left OFC or left caudate) associated with detailed or local processing in the BDD groups, whereas healthy controls displayed greater activity in the right hemisphere related to global or holistic processing of visual information. Greater activity in the frontostriatal regions in BDD participants occurred while viewing faces and not during pictures of nonface objects, which suggests this activation correlates with aversion (Feusner et al., 2010b, 2011). Compared with healthy control and anorexia nervosa groups, individuals with BDD displayed greater connection between the anterior occipital and fusiform face areas while viewing faces of others (Moody et al., 2015). Additionally, individuals with BDD displayed hypoactivation of primary and secondary visual systems (e.g., left occipital cortex or left parahippocampal gyrus) during processing of holistic or low detailed visual information (Feusner et al., 2010b, 2011). This finding suggests that individuals with BDD experience abnormalities of visual processing systems outside of face-related physical features that extend primarily to holistic or global processing.

Recent neuroimaging studies measured white matter intensity (i.e., diffusion tensor imaging; DTI) between BDD and healthy control groups. Individuals with BDD displayed reductions in white matter tracts in areas such as the corpus callosum and uncinate fasciculus, which are attributed to global information processing and threat perception, respectively (Buchanan et al., 2013). Although no differences emerged between BDD and healthy control groups, worse insight related to BDD and greater white matter fiber dispersion (e.g., fiber crossing or disorganization) was associated in visual and emotional processing systems (Feusner et al., 2013). Further investigation of functional and white matter abnormalities in visual processing systems is needed.

With regard to HD, preliminary evidence suggests that hoarding symptoms may have a different neural substrate than OCD. Electroencephalography studies found unique neurological patterns in hoarding symptoms during error monitoring compared with OCD and control participants (Baldwin, Whitford, & Grisham, 2016; Mathews et al., 2016). These studies revealed distinct neurobiological findings associated with younger age, greater intolerance of uncertainty, and possession-related tasks.

Studies of animal hoarding and hoarding due to brain damage or dementia have implicated the subcortical limbic structures and the ventromedial prefrontal cortex (VMPFC) as important in hoarding behavior (see Mataix-Cols, Pertusa, & Snowdon, 2011 for a review). Recent fMRI studies of humans with compulsive hoarding have focused on the same brain areas and found similar results. Hough et al. (2016) compared fMRI brain activation across HD, OCD, and control groups during computerized executive functioning tasks. Participants with HD demonstrated greater activity during conflict monitoring and response inhibition in the right dorsolateral prefrontal cortex (DLPFC) compared with both OCD and control participants, whereas greater activity in the anterior cingulate cortex (ACC) was seen relative to control participants only. Furthermore, the HD group displayed greater activity during evaluation of the value of stimuli (i.e., salience network) relative to OCD and control participants in the anterior insula, OFC, and striatum regions; and compared with the control group only, the HD participants showed greater activation of the ACC. In summary, individuals with HD may experience heightened awareness during error processing and value-based decision-making of stimuli.

Furthermore, brain activity of hoarding and nonhoarding OCD patients was compared with normal controls in a symptom-provocation study (An et al., 2009). During an fMRI assessment, subjects were asked to imagine throwing away objects that belonged to them while being shown pictures of the items. The OCD patients with hoarding symptoms showed more reactivity in the VMPFC than did the other groups. In an exploratory study, Tolin, Kiehl, Worhunsky, Book, and Maltby (2009) conducted fMRI assessment of a small group of severe hoarders ($n = 12$; only two with OCD diagnosis) and normal controls. When deciding whether to keep or discard real personal items, individuals with hoarding symptoms showed greater activity in the left lateral OFC and parahippocampal gyrus compared with controls.

In a more recent discarding-related study, neural activity was measured by fMRI in patients with well-defined primary HD (as proposed for *DSM-5* in Mataix-Cols et al., 2010) and compared with patients with OCD and normal controls (Tolin et al., 2012). The task involved real-time, binding decisions that had to be made about whether to keep or abandon actual belongings compared with control items. The HD group discarded significantly fewer personal items than did the OCD and control groups, with no differences in decisions to discard control items. With regard to neural activity, the HD group differed from OCD and normal controls in relation to the ACC and the left and right insular cortex. A recent case study of HD applied repetitive transcranial magnetic stimulation (rTMS) to the right DLPFC to improve activation between the DLPFC, VMPFC, and amygdala (Diefenbach et al., 2015). Following rTMS treatment, the study found the patient no longer met criteria for HD at follow-up and the patient discarded more items during a computerized simulation task at post-treatment (83% discarded) compared with baseline (57% discarded). Future controlled trials should attempt to replicate this rTMS outcome. Taken together, these studies suggest that the ventromedial prefrontal/cingulate and medial temporal regions may be involved in hoarding behavior.

Imaging studies of TTM have been somewhat inconsistent. Early studies of hair pulling (then defined as an impulse control disorder not otherwise specified [NOS] in *DSM-IV*) found evidence of frontostriatal abnormalities (Keuthen et al., 2007; O'Sullivan et al., 1997) and frontostriatal-thalamic pathways (Chamberlain et al., 2008). Structural abnormalities implicated increased gray matter densities in extensive areas, including the prefrontal lobe, ACC, striatum, amygdala, and hippocampus (Chamberlain et al., 2008). In a subsequent study, Chamberlain et al. (2010) looked at white matter integrity, rather than gray matter abnormalities, using DTI. Results indicated a disruption in white matter integrity in the ACC, OFC, presupplementary motor areas, and temporal lobe compared with normal controls. These findings are, in part, similar to the findings in OCD patients described previously. White matter integrity was explored in patients with TTM and normal controls (Roos, Fouche, Stein, & Lochner, 2013). Although there were no differences between patients with TTM and controls on DTI measures, these investigators reported increased mean density (global average of all diffusion directions) in white matter tracts of the frontostriatal-thalamic pathway in patients with longer hair-pulling duration and increased TTM severity. Odlaug, Chamberlin, Derbyshire, Leppink, and Grant (2014) found significantly increased cortical thickness in TTM patients and their unaffected first-degree relatives compared with control subjects. The thickness was observed in areas controlling response inhibition, specifically the right inferior/middle frontal gyri, left superior temporal cortex, left precuneus, and the right lingual gyrus. Finally, a recent review of 13 studies regarding the neurobiology of TTM (Johnson & El-Alfy, 2016) suggests that a variety of brain regions are implicated in the pathology of TTM, including the cerebral cortex, basal ganglia, thalamus, hippocampus, amygdala, and hypothalamus. Clearly, more studies are needed for a clearer understanding of the neurobiology of this disorder.

White matter abnormalities have also been shown in ED. Neurocognitive findings indicate that ED is related to impairment in prepotent motor responses and that this function is dependent on the integrity of the right frontal gyrus and the ACC as well as the white matter tracts that connect them. To examine whether these regions are impaired, Grant, Odlaug, Hampshire, Schreiber, and Chamberlain (2013) conducted a DTI study with 13 subjects meeting the proposed *DSM-5* criteria for ED. Results were as expected, with patients with ED showing significantly reduced fractional anisotropy in tracts distributed bilaterally, which included the ACC. The findings support disorganization of white matter tracts involved in motor generation and suppression in the pathophysiology of excoriation in patients with ED. In a recent study comparing brain volume and cortical thickness in TTM and ED, female ED patients demonstrated greater ventral striatum volume (bilaterally) and reduced cortical thickness in right hemisphere frontal areas compared with patients with TTM and controls (Roos, Grant, Fouche, Stein, & Lochner, 2015). They also found greater thickness of the cuneus (bilaterally) in ED versus TTM and controls. These results suggest greater involvement of the reward system in ED relative to TTM and controls. In a recent fMRI study, Odlaug, Hampshire, Chamberlain and Grant (2016) found functional underactivation in a cluster involving the bilateral dorsal striatum, bilateral ACC and right medial regions. These results suggest abnormalities in regions related to habit formation, action monitoring, and inhibition.

LEARNING, MODELING, AND LIFE EVENTS

While there is some evidence that trauma may be associated with increased likelihood of OCD (Bomyea et al., 2013; Gothelf, Aharonovsky, Horesh, Carty, & Apter, 2004), another study found that adverse childhood experiences were not associated with increased OCD symptom severity or chronicity (Visser et al., 2014). This later study (Visser et al., 2014), coupled with research by Hofmeijer-Sevink et al. (2013), suggests that childhood trauma may be a vulnerability factor not for OCD, but rather for comorbidity in OCD. Conversely, a large twin study indicated that some specific life events (i.e., "abuse and family disruption" and "sexual abuse") were significantly associated with symptom severity, even after adjusting for current depressive symptoms (Vidal-Ribas et al., 2015). Other life events associated with OCD onset include accidents and serious mistakes (e.g., accidentally harming someone or a financial mistake at work; Rheaume, Freeston, Leger, & Ladouceur, 1998), strokes (Cumming, Blomstrand, Skoog, & Linden, 2016), and pregnancy and childbirth (Wisner, Peindl, Gigliotti, & Hanusa, 1999; Zambaldi et al., 2009).

Retrospective investigations have reported higher rates of physical or sexual abuse among individuals with BDD compared with healthy controls (e.g., Buhlmann, Marques, & Wilhelm, 2012). Low self-esteem is endorsed among individuals with BDD and is negatively associated with overall symptom severity (Boroughs, Krawczyk, & Thompson, 2010; Buhlmann, Teachman, Naumann, Fehlinger, & Rief, 2009). Early social interactions may also affect the development of BDD. For instance, after accounting for social anxiety, appearance-related teasing from adolescent peers correlates with BDD symptoms over other peer-related victimization (Webb et al., 2015). This effect was prominent for cross-sex over same-sex teasing, which may be associated with the start of heightened perceptions of opposite sex evaluations between ages 10 and 13 years.

A retrospective study found appearance-based teasing to be an independent risk factor for severity of BDD but not OCD severity (Weingarden & Renshaw, 2016). Among individuals with BDD, ratings for appearance-based rejection sensitivity were higher than personal-based rejection and contributed more to severity of BDD (Kelly, Didie, & Phillips, 2014). Appearance-based rejection sensitivity mediated the relationship between appearance-related teasing and BDD symptoms (Lavell, Zimmer-Gembeck, Farrell, & Webb, 2014). A longitudinal study among adolescents revealed a bidirectional model: (a) peer victimization (e.g., made fun of) influences symptoms of BDD; and (b) severity of BDD negatively affects perceptions of peer relationships (Webb, Zimmer-Gembeck, & Mastro, 2016). Perceived teasing may cause symptoms of BDD that lead to greater social isolation and, subsequently, higher pathology in the future.

Furthermore, maladaptive social comparisons concerning their own physical features may be associated with BDD. When evaluating appearances of others, individuals with BDD displayed a higher focus on specific features they were most concerned about, compared with overall appearance, and rated greater dissatisfaction with self-appearance (Anson, Veale, & Miles, 2015). Compared with anorexia nervosa and healthy control groups, individuals with BDD were more likely to think of their own faces while rating facial attractiveness of others (Moody et al., 2017). Eye-tracking studies demonstrated that individuals with BDD spend more time focusing on unattractive features of their own face than do healthy controls; however, mixed findings revealed discrepancies between BDD samples. When given 40 seconds to view their own face, individuals with BDD spent more time attending to unattractive self-features, whereas during 10-second presentations, an equal amount of time was allotted to attractive and unattractive self-features (Greenberg, Reuman, Hartmann, Kasarskis, & Wilhelm, 2014; Kollei, Horn-dasch, Erim, & Martin, 2017). Additionally, during 40-second presentations, individuals with BDD focused on unattractive features of others, while, conversely, attending to attractive features during 10-second time frames (Greenberg et al., 2014; Kollei et al., 2017). These results suggest allowing more time for face viewing (self or others) could add a cognitive component of negative bias to over-focus on unattractive areas. This visual selective attention towards negative physical features could maintain BDD-related symptoms and interfere with holistic viewing that includes positive features. Taken together, the higher frequency of comparisons to someone perceived as good-looking found in individuals with BDD may produce negative appearance evaluations and body dissatisfaction. Future research should investigate whether over-focus on specific physical details is an atypical predisposition or a learned behavior due to constant concern with body features.

It has been suggested that HD may develop as a conditioned emotional response related to thoughts or beliefs concerning items or possessions (Grisham & Barlow, 2005). Anxiety experienced with discarding and decision-making is avoided by acquisition and hoarding of items. Qualitative research has found animal hoarders attribute more human characteristics to their pets than do non-HD animal collectors (Steketee et al., 2011). A recent investigation found that waste avoidance and aesthetic motives predicted acquiring, whereas only saving to avoid waste (for information or emotional reasons) predicted difficulty discarding items (Frost, Steketee, Tolin, Sinopoli, & Ruby, 2015). Aesthetic motives include acquiring an item due to shape or color, rather than utility.

Researchers have found that induced negative emotions are associated with greater severity of hoarding symptoms. Intense emotional reactivity during imagined discarding predicted greater overall severity of HD, difficulty discarding, and acquiring, but not clutter (Shaw, Timpano, Steketee, Tolin, & Frost, 2015). Specifically, this study found that fear of decision-making predicted the interaction between emotional reactivity and difficulty discarding, whereas poor confidence in memory predicted acquisition. Furthermore, recent investigations have found intolerance uncertainty as a significant predictor of HD symptom severity (Mathes et al., 2017; Wheaton, Abramowitz, Jacoby, Zwerling, & Rodriguez, 2016). Intolerance uncertainty may be an underlying factor of HD (e.g., "What if I get rid of this and need it again?"; Mathes et al., 2017). Overall, these findings indicate faulty learning or maladaptive thinking processes in HD, which may require remediation through cognitive-behavioral intervention.

Trichotillomania and ED may have similar environmental risk factors. Lack of stimulation or boredom has been suggested as a factor in both experimental (Teng, Woods, Marcks, & Twohig, 2004) and self-report studies (Shusterman, Feld, Baer, & Keuthen, 2009; Snorrason, Smári, & Olafsson, 2010). Early case reports also suggested that severe activity restriction may be implicated in the development of TTM and ED (Evans, 1976; Gupta, Gupta, & Haberman, 1986). Furthermore, a number of case studies have suggested a relationship between history of trauma and skin picking/hair pulling; however, longitudinal data are needed to determine whether traumatic events play a causal role in these disorders (Snorrason et al., 2012). Family factors have also been suggested as having a critical role in the onset and maintenance of psychiatric disorders. Keuthen et al. (2013) examined family environment variables in adolescents with TTM and matched controls. The TTM group expressed significantly more anger, aggression, and conflict in their families, and less family support, compared with controls. The significance of family history was also evaluated in a recent study of both TTM and ED participants, pooled as "body focused repetitive behavior disorders" (BFRBs; Redden, Leppink, & Grant, 2016). Almost 30% of participants had a first-degree family member with a BFRB, but the more interesting finding is that 22.2% had a first-degree family member with an SUD. In addition, severity of the BFRB in the participant (amount of time spent picking or pulling) was higher among those with a first-degree relative with an SUD. Although there were no significant cognitive differences based on family history, there were higher rates of ADHD and higher depressive symptom scores in those with a positive family history of an SUD. More studies are necessary to understand the role that family plays in the development and maintenance of TTM and ED.

COGNITIVE INFLUENCES

A cognitive model of OCD (Rachman, 1997) proposes that it is not the content of the intrusive thought *per se*, but the interpretation of the thought that leads to preoccupation and anxiety in patients with OCD. In this model, dysfunctional beliefs about the inability to tolerate the negative emotions associated with the intrusive thoughts are thought to lead to the development and maintenance of OCD. Three types of dysfunctional beliefs have been proposed to contribute to OCD: (1) overestimated responsibility and exaggerated threat; (2) perfectionism and intolerance of uncertainty; and (3) over-importance of thoughts and need to control thoughts (Calkins, Berman, & Wilhelm, 2013).

In a large, nonclinical sample, Taylor et al. (2010) used structural equation modeling and found that responsibility and threat estimation beliefs predicted all six OCD symptom types examined (i.e., checking, hoarding, neutralizing, obsessing, ordering, and washing) above and beyond the other two types of beliefs. Wheaton, Abramowitz, Berman, Riemann, and Hale (2010) examined these relationships in a clinical sample and found that beliefs related to overestimated responsibility and exaggerated threat predicted both the contamination- and harm-causing dimensions. However, other symptom dimensions were predicted by other beliefs, with each dimension of OCD uniquely predicted by a single belief domain. More recently, Brakoulias et al. (2014) used the Y-BOCS (Goodman et al., 1989a,b) to investigate relationships between beliefs and OCD symptoms and found various associations; however, no relationship existed between responsibility and threat beliefs and contamination. These findings, along with other studies indicating that intolerance of uncertainty predicts obsessive-compulsive symptoms (Boelen & Carleton, 2012; Carleton et al., 2012; Sarawgi, Oglesby, & Cougle, 2013) highlight the importance of investigating OCD as a multidimensional, heterogeneous disorder.

Neurocognitive performance in OCD patients has received considerable attention, with impairment in executive functioning a common finding. Early examples of executive dysfunction include studies that showed decreased cognitive flexibility and set shifting (Henry, 2006; Lawrence et al., 2006) and impaired decision-making and planning (Shin et al., 2004). Memory impairments in tests requiring implicit organization have also been demonstrated (Greisberg & McKay, 2003). In a recent study, Kashyap, Kumar, Kandavel, and Reddy (2013) tested neuropsychological functions in 150 patients with OCD compared with 205 healthy control subjects. Patients with OCD showed deficits in scanning, planning time, concept formation, decision-making, and encoding of non-verbal memory. Thus, these results confirm executive dysfunction, with particular difficulties in strategizing and organizing. Of note, the neuropsychological profile identified in this study involves the prefrontal cortex and striatum, suggesting that OCD may not be just an orbito frontostriatal disorder. Overall, while executive dysfunction is a common finding in neuropsychological studies of individuals with OCD, a recent review indicates that neuropsychological investigations of OCD have largely produced mixed results (Abramovitch & Cooperman, 2015), highlighting the heterogeneity of the disorder.

Cognitive abnormalities found in BDD are associated with defects in executive functioning and holistic processing (i.e., ability to perceive global features of visual information). Prior neuropsychological studies of executive functioning found that individuals with BDD focus more on specific details rather than on larger organizational features and exhibit more errors and slower processing on tasks related to planning, mental manipulation, and organization of information compared with healthy controls (Deckersbach et al., 2000; Dunai, Labuschagne, Castle, Kyrios, & Rossell, 2010; Kerwin, Hovav, Hellemann, & Feusner, 2014). This executive dysfunction may contribute to increased focus on specific details opposed to overall appearance when looking in the mirror. One method researchers use to examine detailed versus holistic processing is through recognition of inverted faces. Accurate and faster response times indicate a higher preference of evaluation of a few specific details, whereas a slower strategy indicates processing the image as a whole. Overall, individuals with BDD display greater accuracy and faster response times at recognizing inverted faces compared with healthy controls (Feusner et al., 2010a; Jefferies, Laws, & Fineberg, 2012), suggesting individuals with BDD typically perform detailed rather than holistic processing; however, some investigations revealed no differences between groups (e.g., Monzani, Krebs, Anson, Veale, & Mataix-Cols, 2013). These discrepancies may be due to whether sufficient time duration of stimulus presentation occurred to allow visual abnormalities or, perhaps, due to different testing conditions (e.g., Jefferies et al. [2012] used pictures of celebrities, whereas Monzani et al. [2013] used a stock male photograph).

Furthermore, misinterpretations of social situations may perpetuate cognitive biases among individuals with BDD. During ambiguous scenarios concerning the participants, individuals high in BDD symptoms endorsed more negative appearance-related thoughts (e.g., people are laughing because of my appearance), whereas individuals low in BDD were less likely to make these conclusions (Clerkin & Teachman, 2008). This study found no differences between those high- and low-BDD groups when ambiguous scenarios concerned others. Individuals with BDD may show difficulty in interpreting others' thoughts and intentions compared with individuals with OCD and healthy controls (Buhlmann, Wacker, & Dziobek, 2015). One study found preliminary support for modifying interpretation biases in reducing BDD symptoms (Summers & Cougle, 2016). With regard to emotion recognition, individuals with BDD viewed neutral expressions as being contemptuous or angry during self-referent scenarios, but not other-referent scenarios, when compared with healthy controls (Buhlmann, Etcoff, & Wilhelm, 2006). The findings are mixed among individuals with BDD in terms of reading the emotional states of others, with some studies finding worse emotion recognition (e.g., Jefferies et al., 2012) and others finding similar performances (e.g., Buhlmann, Winter, & Kathmann, 2013). Individuals with BDD may not have a universal deficit in emotion recognition, but rather a negative bias when directed toward themselves.

Extant findings have indicated that individuals with BDD show stronger implicit associations between physical "attractiveness/competence" (Buhlmann et al., 2009) and "attractiveness/importance" (Buhlmann, Teachman, & Kathmann, 2011), whereas other implicit investigations did not corroborate these findings (e.g., Hartmann et al., 2015). Perhaps different implicit biases exist for BDD. For instance, individuals with BDD displayed greater body-relevant implicit shame, whereas individuals with OCD endorsed greater shame connected to obsessive thoughts (Clerkin, Teachman, Smith, & Buhlmann, 2014). Additional investigations of implicit biases may reveal further differences between OCRDs. Nonetheless, there is evidence to suggest that individuals with BDD attribute more explicit meaning and consequences to attractiveness, which may be an underlying target to be addressed by intervention.

Several aspects of cognition are implicated in HD. Individuals endorsing current excessive acquisition reported more inhibited self-control and cognitive failures compared with both past and nonacquiring hoarders (Frost et al., 2013). Grisham, Norberg, Williams, Ceroma, and Kadib (2010) used a well-standardized neuropsychological battery to assess severe hoarders, matched anxious, and matched normal controls. In this study, severe hoarders showed deficits on only a planning/problem-solving task and did not differ on tasks of decision-making, cognitive flexibility, or response inhibition. Conversely, Carbonella and Timpano (2016) found deficits of cognitive flexibility in participants with high versus low hoarding symptom severity, regardless of hoarding or nonhoarding contexts. Challenges in cognitive flexibility suggest that individuals with this disorder may experience challenges ignoring irrelevant details and shifting focus between changing conditions; however, further replication is necessary due to limited and mixed findings. Raines, Timpano, and Schmidt (2014) found an association between hoarding symptom severity and difficulties in sustained attention; however, these deficits were not context-dependent (i.e., clutter or nonclutter condition). Future research should examine cognitive flexibility and sustained attention between global and hoarding-specific contexts.

Furthermore, Frost, Tolin, Steketee, and Oh (2011) examined indecisiveness in a large sample of adults who self-referred as having severe hoarding. Interestingly, they also examined hoarding in adult children and spouses of these individuals. Individuals with hoarding problems reported more decision-making problems than did their children or spouses and substantially more than normal controls. In addition, adult children reported more indecisiveness than spouses, suggesting a familial characteristic. Moshier et al. (2016) compared findings between self-report and objective neuropsychological impairments. This study found higher self-reported impairments of attention and memory among the HD group, but no clinically meaningful differences were detected on corresponding objective measures, as compared with participants with OCD or OCD with hoarding symptoms. This finding was corroborated by another study which found that self-reported confidence in attention and memory abilities predicted severity of hoarding symptoms in a nonclinical sample (Timpano, Rasmussen, Exner, Rief, & Wilhelm, 2014). Overall, the individuals with HD had a lower concordance rate between self and objective measures of neuropsychological deficits compared with individuals with OCD; however, further replication is necessary because the samples were treatment-seeking and no comparisons with healthy controls were conducted.

Memory problems and inattentive symptoms of ADHD have also been implicated in this population. Tolin et al. (2011) found decreased ability to sustain attention and poorer adaptive memory strategies in patients with HD than in those with OCD and normal controls. The authors note that true impairment on any neuropsychological task was rather low across all groups; however, 67% of hoarders (compared with 58% of those with OCD and 42% of normal controls) scored in the impaired range on at least one measure. Similarly, Hall et al. (2013) found that individuals with clinically elevated inattentive symptoms of ADHD and depression endorsed greater impairment due to HD (e.g., difficulties in activities of daily living, stress, living in squalor) compared with a comorbid depression-HD type alone. Importantly, a recent investigation found that poorer memory performance, excessive saving of possessions, and clutter fully mediated the effect of inattention on functional impairment due to HD (Hallion, Diefenbach, & Tolin, 2015). This mediation model accounted for over 90% of the variance in impairment and it is recommended that future research continue to explore underlying mechanisms through mediation models.

Finally, executive functioning has been assessed in older adults with HD. Matched for age with healthy controls, older adults showed significantly more executive dysfunction, including working memory, mental control, inhibition, and set shifting (Ayers et al., 2013). A recent study found that the severity of executive functioning (operationalized as Wisconsin Card Sorting Test perseverative errors) predicted greater severity of HD (i.e., Clutter Image Rating score; Ayers, Dozer, Wetherell, Twamley, & Schiesher, 2016). Another investigation revealed that older adults with HD demonstrated a few impairments of executive functioning and lower performance in daily functioning (e.g., planning and communication) compared with younger adults with HD (Dozier, Wetherell, Twamley, Schiehser, & Ayers, 2016b). More research is needed to replicate these findings with homogeneous groups under similar conditions. Nonetheless, older adults with HD may require cognitive rehabilitation or behavioral treatments (e.g., exposure to discarding and nonacquiring) in comparison to cognitive-focused interventions because of impaired executive functioning.

Most research in TTM and ED has focused on emotion regulation theory rather than on cognitive influences. However, cognitive inflexibility has been suggested in a subset of patients with ED as evidenced by selective impairment in attentional set shifting (Grant, Odlaug, Chamberlain, & Kim, 2010a). In addition, the cognitive component of habit reversal training (i.e., awareness of pulling or picking) has been shown to be effective in the treatment of these disorders. In cognitive-behavioral treatment for ED and TTM, patients are often asked to record dysfunctional thoughts that precede picking or pulling and then taught to restructure the thoughts to be more rational (e.g., "I can tolerate stressful situations and I don't have to pick or pull"; Kress & Paylo, 2015). Additionally, obsessive thoughts about skin imperfections and anxiety over not picking in ED patients can be temporarily relieved by completing the behavior (e.g., picking; Capriotti, Ely, Snorrason, & Woods, 2015), which likely reinforces the behavior and perpetuates the disorder. More research is needed to further elucidate the cognitive influences in TTM and ED.

SEX AND RACIAL-ETHNIC CONSIDERATIONS

Most studies indicate that males and females are equally likely to suffer from OCD; however, males tend to experience an earlier age of onset. In fact, males account for nearly two-thirds of childhood-onset cases (de Mathis et al., 2011), and meta-analysis suggests that earlier onset is associated with greater symptom severity (Taylor, 2011a). In a recent comprehensive cross-sectional study conducted in Brazil, phenomenological characteristics of men and women with OCD were evaluated (Torresan et al., 2013). The sample included 504 women (58.7%) and 354 men (41.3%) with a mean age of 35.4 years old (range 18–77). Men were found to be younger, more frequently single, and with symptom interference occurring at a younger age. In addition to these differences, the obsessional content in men was more likely to encompass sexual/religious themes, whereas women were more likely to present with symptoms related to aggression, contamination/cleaning, and hoarding. Results of this study are similar to results found in studies conducted in Italy (Lensi et al., 1996), India (Cherian et al., 2014; Khandelwal, Aggarwal, Garg, & Jiloha, 2009), and Turkey (Tükel, Polat, Genc, Bozkurt, & Atlı, 2004).

Contamination and checking are OCD themes most consistently found across cultures (Matsunaga & Seedat, 2007). Other specific themes or content of OCD symptoms may be more prevalent in certain cultures, such as fear of leprosy among those who live in Africa (Steketee & Barlow, 2002) or religious themes among those from the Middle East (Fontenelle, Mendlowicz, Marques, & Versiani, 2004). Evidence suggests that cultural differences can impact treatment-seeking barriers and behaviors (Fernández de la Cruz et al., 2016), leading to an under-representation of minorities in treatment settings. Furthermore, an under-representation of minorities in clinical trials of evidence-based treatments suggests that efficacy in non-White populations is not known (Williams, Powers, Yun, & Foa, 2010).

Women have a higher prevalence of BDD in adult community (ratio women:men, 1.27:1), psychiatric inpatient (1.71:1), and psychiatric outpatient (1.41:1) settings; however, the sex ratio flips in general cosmetic surgery (0.71:1) and rhinoplasty (0.91:1) settings (Veale et al., 2016). Men are more likely to be single, have a comorbid SUD, and endorse preoccupations with thinning hair, small body build, and their genitals. Conversely, women are more likely to pick their skin, camouflage with clothes and makeup, check mirrors, have a comorbid eating disorder, and be preoccupied with their breasts, weight, stomach, buttocks, thighs, legs, and hips (Phillips et al., 2006a). These findings emerged in a Pakistani sample showing higher likelihoods of men being preoccupied with head hair and being too thin, and women endorsing more concern with being overweight (Taqui et al., 2008). These differences between sexes may be affected by expectations delivered via media or popular culture. Additionally, men are more likely to be unemployed and receive disability compensation due to BDD (Phillips et al., 2006a). A recent twin study investigating heritability found qualitative sex differences that suggest distinct biological risk factors in developing BDD-related symptoms in men and women (López-Solà et al., 2014). In summary, the nature and prevalence of BDD differs between men and women, which should be acknowledged in research and clinical settings.

The rates of screening positive for BDD in the general community were approximately 1.9% for Australia and Germany (López-Solà et al., 2014; Veale et al., 2016) and 2.4% for the US (Koran et al., 2008). Rates found in student populations were 3.3% in Germany (Veale et al., 2016), 5.1% in South Africa (Dlagnikova & van Niekerk, 2015), and 5.8% in Pakistan (Taqui et al., 2008). In a US prevalence study, African American women endorsed fewer symptoms of BDD than did Caucasian and Latina women (Boroughs et al., 2010). African American, Latino/a, and Caucasian ethnic groups reported similar body parts of concern (i.e., hair, skin, and nose) and rituals (i.e., comparing with others, checking mirrors, and grooming); however, differences emerged between Caucasian and Asian ethnicities. Specifically, Asians were more likely to endorse concerns about skin tone being too dark or hair too straight, whereas Caucasians indicated more dissatisfaction with shape-related concerns (e.g., stomach). Additionally, Asians were less likely to engage in grooming or camouflaging and more likely to exercise excessively compared with Caucasians (Marques et al., 2011). These findings were corroborated among a British multicultural sample measuring skin tone dissatisfaction which revealed that British South Asians preferred a lighter skin tone than White and African Caribbean groups, whereas White individuals favored a darker skin tone (Swami, Henry, Peacock, Roberts-Dunn, & Porter, 2013). There is a paucity of research related to sexual orientation and BDD symptomatology. One investigation found that homosexual women had the highest severity of BDD, whereas heterosexual men had the lowest severity (Boroughs et al., 2010). Based on limited research, cultural characteristics appear to affect preoccupations and rituals related to BDD; however, further investigation is needed due to the potential of cultural integration enhancing treatment (e.g., Weingarden et al., 2011).

Although studies of HD demonstrate an over-representation of women, recent epidemiological research has found no difference in prevalence between sexes (Cath et al., 2016; Nordsletten et al., 2013c). This discrepancy is uncertain; however, it may be accounted for by a willingness among women to seek treatment for hoarding behaviors (Tolin, Frost, Steketee, & Muroff, 2015) or, perhaps, higher response rates among men for large community-based surveys compared with referrals by mental health clinics. Additionally, an exploratory investigation of animal hoarding found higher rates among women; however, further research is warranted due to limited sample size and recruitment strategy (i.e., complaints via animal protection services; Steketee et al., 2011). Furthermore, a retrospective study found that men endorsed a greater severity of clutter symptoms early in life compared with women, whereas no differences emerged for difficulty discarding or saving (Dozier et al., 2016b). This study also reported that all symptoms of hoarding increased more slowly over time among men compared with women. With regard to motives in HD behavior, men were more likely to endorse acquiring to avoid waste, whereas no differences were found between sexes for saving motives (Frost et al., 2015). Future research should determine whether findings apply equally to men, as the majority of samples predominately included women with HD.

Recent investigations have examined cross-cultural hoarding behaviors. A study in Italy found the prevalence of hoarding disorder to be 3.7–6.0% (Bulli et al., 2014); however, this estimation may be inflated due to the nature of self-report compared with recent epidemiological research using clinician interviews (e.g., Nordsletten et al., 2013c). Although cross-culture prevalence studies using semistructured interviews are scarce in the literature, validation studies of self-report measures found elevated hoarding symptoms outside of European and US cultures such as Singapore, China, Turkey, Brazil, and Iran (Fontenelle et al., 2010; Mohammadzadeh, 2009; Ong et al., 2016; Timpano et al., 2015; Yorulmaz & Dermihan, 2015). Timpano et al. (2015) found attitudes of wastefulness and usefulness as primary motivations to save in the Chinese hoarding sample, whereas the US hoarding sample endorsed additional motivations such as emotional attachment or aesthetic qualities. Future research should continue to examine culture-specific contributors that influence the development and maintenance of HD.

The existing literature indicates that 88–94% of patients with TTM are female (Odlaug, Kim, & Grant, 2010). The reason for this large gender bias is unclear, but may be related to societal values of beauty, and related distress, and greater drive to seek help due to hair loss in women. There is very little research regarding racial/ethnic differences in TTM. In a survey of American college students, there was no difference found between African American and non-African American students (McCarley, Spirrison, & Ceminsky, 2002). In a more recent study, ethnic differences in TTM symptoms were evaluated among minority and Caucasian participants (Neal-Barnett et al., 2010). Overall, results indicate that the minority sample was less likely to report pulling from eyebrows and eyelashes, and also less likely to report tension prior to pulling. There was also a difference in interference, in which minorities reported more problems with home management related to pulling, and Caucasians reported more interference with academic endeavors. In addition, Caucasians reported more daily stress and treatment utilization, although treatment efficacy did not differ among ethnic groups. ED is more frequent in females with higher rates of co-occurring grooming disorders (Grant et al., 2012). The clinical characteristics have been shown to be the same across age ranges as well as cultures (Bohne, Keuthen, Wilhelm, Deckersbach, & Jenike, 2002; Lochner, Simeon, Niehaus, & Stein, 2002).

Course and Prognosis

The development of OCD usually begins gradually between late adolescence and early adulthood. The mean age of onset is 19.5 years and onset after the early 30s is rare (Ruscio et al., 2010). Symptoms of OCD are typically stable over time, with changes occurring within symptom dimensions rather than between symptom dimensions (Mataix-Cols et al., 2002). OCD is a chronic and disabling disorder that rarely remits without treatment; however, meta-analysis of long-term outcome of psychopharmacological and/or cognitive-behavioral treatment for OCD found a pooled remission rate of 53% (Sharma, Thennarasu, & Reddy, 2014). Studies suggest that early onset, long duration of illness, (Dell'Osso et al., 2013; Sharma et al., 2014), and male gender are negative predictors of long-term outcome (Sharma et al., 2014).

Both biological and behavioral therapies have been shown to be effective in the treatment of OCD. Positive treatment outcome has been shown with SSRIs (such as Prozac or Zoloft) as well as cognitive-behavioral therapy (CBT), such as ERP (NICE, 2006). In a recent meta-analysis, Olatunji, Davis, Powers, and Smits (2013) evaluated 16 randomized controlled trials (RCTs) of CBT for OCD and found that CBT outperformed control conditions (placebo and/or waitlist) across studies. Of greater interest, perhaps, is the fact that few moderator variables affected efficacy. Specifically, outcome was not associated with greater severity of OCD or level of depression at pretreatment. There were smaller effect sizes for adult RCTs and older age, suggesting greater efficacy in younger patients with OCD. A later meta-analysis, which included RCTs with active treatments as control conditions, supported the efficacy of CBT for OCD (Öst, Havnen, Hansen, & Kvale, 2015). Overall, results suggest that CBT should be a first-line treatment for OCD.

The mean age of BDD onset is approximately 16.5 years and the mode is 13 years; most individuals endorse a continuous course (Phillips et al., 2005, 2012). Overall, the clinical severity, psychosocial functioning, and quality of life for early- and late-onset BDD appear similar (Bjornsson et al., 2013). This finding is contrary to OCD, for which early age of onset is associated with greater OCD severity (e.g., Millet et al., 2004; Taylor, 2011a). However, individuals with early-onset BDD are more likely to endorse gradual onset, lifetime history of suicidal attempts, and greater comorbidity compared with late-onset BDD (Bjornsson et al., 2013).

Cognitive-behavioral therapy is an empirically supported intervention for BDD. Specific interventions for BDD include cognitive restructuring, mindfulness-based therapy, perceptual retraining, and ERP (e.g., Wilhelm et al., 2014). A recent investigation conducted a systematic review of RCTs delivering CBT for BDD (Harrison, Fernández de la Cruz, Enander, Radua, & Mataix-Cols, 2016). This study found large and medium effect sizes for reduction of BDD and depressive symptoms, respectively, and treatment responses maintained 2–4 months at follow-up. Harrison et al. (2016) included treatments delivered in various formats such as Internet-based CBT (i.e., stepped care approach; Enander et al., 2016) and group CBT (cost-effective approach; Rosen, Reiter, & Orosan, 1995). Unfortunately, prior investigations reported that 71–76% of individuals with BDD seek ineffective treatments such as cosmetic surgery (Crerand, Phillips, Menard, & Fay, 2005; Phillips, Grant, Siniscalchi, & Albertini, 2001). A review of cosmetic treatment outcomes for BDD found 72–91% of individuals reported no improvement in symptoms (Bowyer, Krebs, Mataix-Cols, Veale, & Monzani, 2016).

Pharmacotherapy (e.g., SSRIs) is another effective treatment intervention for reducing symptoms of BDD (e.g., Phillips et al., 2002). A recent meta-analysis of RCTs using pharmacotherapy and CBT found improvement of BDD symptoms (Phillipou, Rossell, Wilding, & Castle, 2016). Specifically, CBT and medications related to serotonin (e.g., SSRIs) reduced symptoms of BDD (even with delusional beliefs or depression; e.g., Veale et al., 2014). Further investigations addressing the following variables are warranted:

dismantling studies (e.g., implementation of a purely behavioral intervention), larger samples of BDD, longer follow-up, stronger comparisons (e.g., SSRIs alone or combined with CBT), and predictors of successful treatment outcome.

It has been suggested that HD may develop in response to early deprivation, both emotional and material, but this has not been largely supported (Frost & Gross, 1993). Studies have shown abnormally high levels of trauma or stressful life events that, in some cases, occur prior to the onset or worsening of symptoms (Cromer, Schmidt, & Murphy, 2007; Samuels et al., 2008). However, hoarding is a chronic disorder and there is no evidence that hoarding can be explained as a response to stressors or losses (Mataix-Cols et al., 2010). The course of compulsive hoarding is typically chronic, with hoarding behavior beginning decades before symptoms reach a clinical level (Samuels et al., 2008). No prospective studies have been completed, but retrospective data suggest that hoarding symptoms begin in childhood or early adolescence and begin interfering with daily life by the mid-30s (Dozier et al., 2016b). Difficulty discarding or clutter emerges by middle adolescence to early 20s, whereas excessive acquisition typically onsets around the mid-20s and reaches peak severity around the early 40s (Frost et al., 2013; Grisham, Frost, Steketee, Kim, & Hood, 2006). As mentioned previously, Cath et al. (2016) reported that the point prevalence of HD increased by 20% every 5 years after age 30, whereas OCD displayed a U-shaped trajectory. Epidemiological research found that the severity of hoarding disorder increased by age, with greater difficulty discarding as the primary contributor rather than excessive acquisition (Cath et al., 2016). Difficulty discarding appears to be a core feature of HD, especially among older adults. Given the associations between cognitive impairment and geriatric HD, further research should address the etiology or maintenance of difficulty discarding through executive functioning (e.g., impaired decision-making) or perhaps stronger emotional attachment to possessions over time.

With regard to treatment, most patients with hoarding symptoms respond to medications affecting serotonin (e.g., serotonin-reuptake inhibitors; Brakoulias, Eslick, & Starcevic, 2015). CBT for HD typically involves psychoeducation, motivational interviewing, exposure to discarding items or acquiring cues, and practice in decision-making (e.g., sorting), and is generally thought of as the treatment of choice for HD (Williams & Viscusi, 2016). Given HD's recent inclusion as a stand-alone diagnosis, most extant controlled group designs delivered cognitive-behavioral interventions for patients within OCD. A systematic review of treatment outcomes for OCD found that responses to interventions were worse for patients with hoarding symptoms than for those without hoarding symptoms, regardless of treatment modality (i.e., behavioral, pharmacotherapy, or combination; Bloch et al., 2014). Additionally, Williams and Viscusi (2016) found that hoarding symptoms responded less favorably to ERP than did primary symptoms of OCD (e.g., contamination).

A recent meta-analysis examined RCTs that delivered CBT in patients with primary hoarding symptomatology as opposed to another psychiatric disorder (e.g., OCD; Tolin et al., 2015). Large effect sizes were found for reductions in difficulty discarding, clutter, acquiring, and overall symptom severity of HD; however, the percentage of reliable and clinically significant changes in patients were between 25% and 40% across outcomes. This suggests that although patients are likely to experience substantial pre- to post-treatment improvements, most individuals still fall within the clinical range at termination. Several predictors of successful treatment outcomes were identified, including more home visits, younger age, female gender, and use of psychiatric medication. However, these predictors may be confounded due to higher pretreatment severity allowing greater room for reduction between time intervals.

Taken together, approximately one-third of patients receiving traditional CBT demonstrate clinically meaningful changes in hoarding symptoms. However, treatment of compulsive hoarding has been described as challenging, due to low levels of insight, little motivation for treatment, and impaired cognitive functioning (Grisham & Barlow, 2005). In patients with OCD, the presence of hoarding symptoms is typically associated with refusal of treatment and higher dropout rates (Williams & Viscusi, 2016). Further research should reduce complications associated with HD such as high comorbidity with depression, low motivation, or higher number of sessions than typically received by ERP for OCD (Frost, Steketee, et al., 2011; Williams & Viscusi, 2016). Potential directions may include incorporating well-established interventions for depression (e.g., Behavioral Activation; Mazzucchelli, Kane, & Rees, 2010), contingency management to address low motivation in HD (Worden, Bowe, & Tolin, 2017), or novel platforms that provide access to booster sessions (e.g., web-based therapy).

Trichotillomania may occur at any age, from infancy through later life. Most research, however, indicates an average age of onset at 12.9 years (Cohen et al., 1995; Grant, Odlaug, & Kim, 2010b; Lochner, Seedat, & Stein, 2010; Odlaug & Grant, 2008). TTM may interfere with social relationships, family life, and work, and has been associated with significant impairment (Woods et al., 2006a). Although there are studies on the long-term course of the disorder, most data suggest that the course is chronic, with waxing and waning symptom severity (Snorrason et al., 2012). With regard to treatment, Flessner, Penzel, and Keuthen (2010) have identified CBT as the treatment of choice for TTM. Although habit reversal training (Azrin, Nunn, & Frantz, 1980) was initially posited as effective for TTM, failure to achieve greater symptom reduction, with longer-lasting effects, has led researchers to look at inner experiences that may trigger hair pulling. Experiential avoidance has been associated with more severe hair pulling and fear of negative evaluation (Norberg, Wetterneck, Woods, & Conelea, 2007). Woods and colleagues have evaluated the addition of acceptance and commitment therapy (ACT) to traditional habit reversal and have shown significant reductions in hair pulling that persisted to 3-month follow-up (Twohig & Woods, 2004; Woods, Wetterneck, & Flessner, 2006b). Affective dysregulation has also been evaluated as playing a role in TTM (Shusterman et al., 2009). Dialectical behavior therapy (DBT; Linehan, 1993a,b) has also been combined with habit reversal training with positive results. In a series of trials, Keuthen and colleagues have demonstrated an inverse relationship between hair-pulling severity and emotional regulation that has persisted at both 3- and 6-month follow-ups (Keuthen et al., 2010a, 2011, 2012). Given these promising results, DBT-enhanced CBT for TTM should be evaluated against other credible treatment interventions and at longer follow-up.

Research suggests that the age of onset for skin picking varies considerably, with onset from childhood through adulthood. Most research has shown an age of onset from 12 to 16 years, with an average age across studies of 13.5 years (Flessner & Woods, 2006; Grant et al., 2010a; Grant, Odlaug, & Kim, 2007; Lochner et al., 2002). Symptoms appear to be similar regardless of age and no differences have been reported in different cultures (Grant et al., 2012). The course of the disorder is also variable, with most cases being chronic in nature with fluctuating intensity. Patients usually pick on a daily basis, often for a significant amount of time, and severity tends to vary with life stressors (Snorrason et al., 2013). Skin problems may occur, including bleeding and soreness, with possibility of infection or permanent skin damage.

Individuals with ED may experience mild to severe impairment in social, academic, or occupational functioning. Treatment has largely focused on cognitive-behavioral interventions and pharmacology (SSRIs). Habit reversal training has been used (Deckersbach,

Wilhelm, Keuthen, Baer, & Jenike, 2002), as well as habit reversal combined with ACT (Siev, Reese, Timpano, & Wilhelm, 2012; Woods et al., 2006b), both with promising results. Emotion dysregulation has been suggested to be a factor in ED, which may lead to future research on treatment using DBT procedures in conjunction with traditional CBT.

CASE STUDIES

Obsessive-Compulsive Disorder

Identifying Information and Presenting Problem Ann is a 34-year-old female who is consumed by thoughts of germs, contamination, and sickness. She is constantly fearful that she may encounter bacteria or a virus that will cause her to become ill and ultimately lead to her death. She experiences intrusive images of herself lying in a hospital bed and of her own funeral. Despite attempting to disregard these thoughts and images, Ann is unable to control her need to clean and sterilize her surroundings to ensure she does not come into contact with germs. Ann spends hours each day cleaning and disinfecting her home, often re-cleaning areas she has just cleaned. She no longer allows friends or family to enter the home in an effort to protect herself. Ann rarely leaves the house, except to purchase cleaning supplies or go to medical appointments. She is no longer able to work and has little to no social life. Ann was beginning to deplete what was left of her financial savings and hoped to obtain gainful employment, which ultimately drove her to seek help.

Assessment and Treatment Ann presented for assessment and treatment at a local university's doctoral program clinic. At the clinic, Ann and her clinician completed a diagnostic assessment that included the SCID-5-CV (First et al., 2015), Y-BOCS-II (Storch et al., 2010a,b), and various self-report measures. Results of the assessment confirmed that Ann met *DSM-5* (APA, 2013) criteria for OCD with good or fair insight. Ann was predominately engaged in obsessional thoughts and images related to fears of contamination, germs, and illness. Her compulsions included cleaning and sterilizing her home, excessive handwashing and bathing, and frequent silent prayers related to fear of illness or death due to contamination. Ann was engaged in significant avoidance behavior which generally kept her homebound. Following the assessment, Ann's clinician provided psychoeducation on OCD, including information on ERP. Ann and her clinician agreed to begin ERP and together developed a treatment plan. Treatment goals included: (a) a reduction or elimination of obsessions and compulsions; (b) increased social activity and other valued behaviors; and (c) ultimately, achieving gainful employment.

Components of Ann's treatment included self-monitoring of her symptoms, in-session and at-home exposures to thoughts, images, objects, or situations that trigger obsessions in the absence of ritualized behavior, and behavioral activation. Examples of her exposures in session included touching surfaces in a therapy room (e.g., table surface, tissue box, and door knob) and shaking hands with confederates, all while resisting the urge to engage in handwashing, prayers, or any other behavior that may reduce her anxiety. At home, Ann worked to resist compulsive behaviors by agreeing to various rules (e.g., one 15-minute shower every other day), engaged in self-led exposures with response prevention (e.g., holding items she believed to be contaminated or allowing her mother to come visit, all while resisting compulsive behaviors). Overall, the goal of Ann's treatment was to behaviorally challenge her fears so she could learn that typical living (e.g., exposure to potential contamination in the absence of compulsive behaviors) would not result in significant danger or death. Once she began to make treatment gains and experienced a reduction in anxiety and distress (as evidenced by continual monitoring of symptoms and progress), Ann began engaging in behaviors aimed at obtaining gainful employment (e.g., updating her résumé, searching job advertisements, calling and/or visiting potential places of employment, and eventually interviews). Prior to termination, Ann and her clinician engaged in discharge planning which included specific identification of various relapse prevention behaviors and strategies.

Body Dysmorphic Disorder

Identifying Information and Presenting Problem   Tanya is a 22-year-old female who is preoccupied with the shape of her face. She recently received her undergraduate degree in English, is unemployed, and is currently living at home with her parents. She spends hours per day gazing into the mirror, criticizing the odd shape of her face, mentally commenting on the asymmetrical angles of her cheekbones, the sharp point of her chin, and the uneven hairline above her forehead. Friends and family are aware of her preoccupation and believe that she is an ordinary, even attractive, looking female. Aside from spending hours critiquing herself in the mirror, Tanya is constantly comparing her facial features to others around her, noting how pronounced her perceived defects are compared with the perfection of others' facial shapes. Despite her attempts to hide the perceived flaws using hairstyles, scarves, and makeup, she stated that she sometimes avoids social activities or job interviews due to preoccupation with mirror checking or with thoughts that she cannot handle others evaluating her defects. Feeling hopeless about her future, Tanya begins to experience passive suicidal ideation.

Assessment and Treatment   Tanya presented with hallmark features of BDD. First, she reported repetitive behaviors (e.g., mirror checking) and mental checking (e.g., comparing her physical appearance to others) due to perceived defects of her face. She endorsed camouflaging areas of concern, which is characteristic among individuals with this disorder. The therapist who interviewed Tanya administered the ADIS-5L (Brown & Barlow, 2014), which captured the *DSM-5* diagnostic criteria for BDD. Similar to her family and friends, the therapist agreed that her perceived flaws appear to be unsubstantiated by her actual appearance. Tanya reported occasionally seeking reassurance about her physical appearance from her family; however, she reported that her family does not corroborate her imperfections simply because, "I look ugly and they are trying to be nice." In the ADIS-5L, the therapist also assessed for depressive disorders due to her passive suicidal ideation. Tanya told the therapist, "I have moments when I want my imperfections to all go away, but I just don't know how to make them disappear unless I'm no longer here. I have no intention or plan of hurting myself." Tanya endorsed occasional sadness after engaging with BDD-related thoughts or rituals; however, she denied any other depression-related symptoms. While she did not meet diagnostic criteria for any depressive disorders at her initial visit, the therapist will monitor suicidal ideation and depressive symptoms throughout the course of treatment. In addition to the clinical interview, the therapist administered the BDD-YBOCS (Phillips et al., 1997) to assess the severity, insight, and avoidance of BDD. Her total score was 40 out of 48, which fell within the severe range of BDD severity. Furthermore, the therapist administered the BABS (Eisen et al., 1998), which examines the degree of delusional beliefs of her pathology. Tanya's total score on the BABS was 19 out of 24, which indicated delusional insight. Taken together, Tanya met diagnostic criteria for BDD with absent insight/delusional beliefs.

Tanya and her therapist outlined the following treatment goals: (a) reduce repetitive behaviors (e.g., mirror checking, reassurance checking, and camouflaging) and mental checking (e.g., comparing her physical appearance to others); (b) reduce distress related to appearance concerns; (c) increase social activities and value-driven hobbies (e.g., write poetry); and (d) increase overall functioning and occupational pursuits (e.g., obtain employment). The therapist structured a CBT plan which started with psychoeducation and self-monitoring forms. The self-monitoring forms included functional analysis to inform Tanya on the antecedents and consequences of her maladaptive BDD-related behaviors and adaptive replacement strategies (e.g., deep breathing or writing activities). Additionally, the therapist had Tanya track the frequency or duration of engaging in adaptive and maladaptive behaviors. The goal of the self-monitoring forms was to assess her change in symptoms over time, increase her awareness of problem behaviors, and reduce their frequency. The next component of treatment included ERP, which involved imaginal exposure in the absence of BDD-related rituals (e.g., mirror checking or seeking reassurance from others). At the initial imaginal exposure sessions, the therapist encouraged Tanya to refrain from rituals for at least 2 hours after exposures terminated. Once Tanya habituated to imaginal exposure, the therapist conducted perceptual retraining by having Tanya evaluate herself objectively in a full-length mirror without focusing exclusively on "hot spots," or using critical language. The therapist incorporated role-play scenarios with Tanya to practice mock job interviews to increase her confidence in facing in-person evaluations. Furthermore, the therapist encouraged Tanya to engage in more social activities and valued hobbies, which were tracked using self-monitoring forms. Lastly, the therapist reviewed the components of ERP and discussed relapse prevention strategies with Tanya before services terminated.

HOARDING DISORDER

Identifying Information and Presenting Problem   Jack is a 67-year-old retired, widowed male. He spends the majority of his time shopping at garage sales, exploring dumpsters for what he calls "treasures," and shopping online. Despite an excessive accumulation of items, Jack is unable to discard anything in his home to make room for his new purchases. In fact, he experiences such difficulty parting with items, even boxes, newspapers, and broken tools, that he has little room left in his home to live. Despite the urging of his family to de-clutter his home and curb his shopping, he is unable to make the necessary changes due to the distress he experiences attempting to make them. As a result, Jack is experiencing significant strain in his familial relationships and is at risk of losing his home due to his inability to maintain city health codes. He endorsed mild depressive symptoms of "crying spells" when thinking about how severe his clutter has become and losing touch with friends and relatives over many years. Jack recognizes his hoarding behaviors are problematic and expresses strong desire to seek help.

Assessment and Treatment   Jack's clinical presentation was characteristic of HD. During the initial clinical interview, the therapist administered the SIHD (Nordsletten et al., 2013a) and UHSS (Saxena et al., 2007) to determine the presence, severity, and degree of impairment due to hoarding behaviors. He reported that he did not need the items; however, he endorsed significant distress with the notion of discarding or sorting items. Jack met *DSM-5* criteria for HD with good or fair insight. In addition, as a result of having no available space and excessive acquiring of items (e.g., buying online), Jack met criteria for the *DSM-5* specifier with excessive acquisition. His total score on UHSS was 28 out of a possible 40, which fell within the clinical cut-off range denoting the presence of HD.

Based on the therapist's request, Jack brought in photographs from his home to assist the therapist in conceptualizing the severity of clutter. Based on the clinical interview and photographs, approximately 80–90% of his living space was filled with clutter. Items such as old newspapers, magazines, and clothing were collected in the middle of the rooms or on furniture in piles (e.g., kitchen, garage, back porch, tables, chairs, couches, and floors). His kitchen sink was broken; however, he reported he couldn't let the plumber inside due to fear of letting others see how dirty his living space had become. Each photograph displayed a clear lack of organization, with only enough space to navigate through rooms using trails. He demonstrated an inability to judge the most important features of possessions. Specifically, he endorsed keeping items based primarily on the aesthetics of the items, such as shape and color.

Jack and his therapist outlined the following treatment goals: (a) increase sorting and discarding behaviors; (b) reduce excessive acquiring; and (c) improve quality of life and overall functioning (e.g., invite people to his home and complete house repairs). The initial component of treatment included psychoeducation (e.g., maladaptive vs. adaptive sorting) and a functional analysis to increase his awareness of what antecedents and consequences accompanied hoarding behaviors. Typically, motivational interviewing or contingency management may serve as a beneficial aspect during initial stages of treatment; however, his level of motivation was satisfactory from the start. Before initiating exposure, the therapist reviewed with Jack organizing and making decisions related to discarding and clutter. The next component of treatment was a graduated, home-based delivery of ERP. This phase of ERP began with discussion of the rationale of exposure-based interventions and creation of a hierarchy of least to most coveted items. Additionally, an "ERP contract" was agreed upon between the therapist and Jack, which instructed him to resist urges to acquire items after exposure sessions ended.

During exposures, the therapist monitored Jack's fear using the subjective units of distress scale (SUDS), which ranged from 0 (no distress) to 8 (extreme distress). Each ERP continued until within-session habituation occurred (i.e., at least a 50% reduction of fear activation or return to baseline SUDS). The initial ERP sessions typically lasted 2.5 hours per session. The exposures consisted of sorting through items at his home, and only Jack touched or discarded objects. The aim was to reduce his clutter from covering 80–90% to less than 10% of his home. After Jack habituated to discarding and sorting his hoarding-related items at home, the therapist introduced Jack to exposure in situations which triggered acquiring behaviors. These situations included visiting garage sales, dumpsters, and online shopping websites without obtaining items.

After 6 weeks of ERP, the therapist outlined homework assignments for Jack to reconnect with friends and family members such as by calling or emailing. Furthermore, the therapist assigned Jack to call service repair companies to fix appliances (e.g., his kitchen sink). After 9 weeks of treatment, Jack's "crying spells" disappeared and he planned social activities at his home to celebrate his progress during the course of treatment. At the termination of treatment, the therapist reviewed ERP and outlined relapse prevention strategies to maintain his progress.

Trichotillomania

Identifying Information and Presenting Problem　Jess is a 29-year-old female who works as a dental hygienist in a busy urban practice. She presented to her primary care doctor when several coworkers noticed and commented on spots of hair loss on her scalp. During the physician visit, Jess admitted pulling the occasional hair from her scalp during times of high stress, but denied pulling frequently enough to cause the hair loss. Her doctor noticed that Jess had very thin eyebrows and that some of her eyelashes were also missing. She recommended a consultation with a behavior health specialist who made a provisional diagnosis of TTM and recommended baseline monitoring of hair pulling in a functional analysis format (antecedent–behavior–consequence; A–B–C). Specifically, Jess was asked to monitor episodes of hair pulling (B) while noting the antecedent (what was happening before the pulling) and the consequence of pulling (thoughts and feelings after pulling as well as physical changes).

Assessment and Treatment   Self-monitoring indicated a higher rate of hair pulling than Jess had initially reported. The monitoring was consistent with the amount of hair loss. She endorsed hiding areas of hair loss, which is characteristic among individuals with this disorder. The therapist who interviewed Jess administered the ADIS-5L (Brown & Barlow, 2014), which confirmed the *DSM-5* diagnosis of TTM. No other psychiatric diagnoses were made, but Jess did endorse family history of OCD in her mother and maternal grandmother. In addition to the clinical interview, the therapist administered the MGH-HPS (Keuthen et al., 1995; O'Sullivan et al., 1995), a seven-item self-report scale, and the MIST-A (Flessner et al., 2008), a 15-item scale that provides two distinct scale scores (i.e., automatic pulling and focused pulling scores). On the MGH-HPS, Jess obtained a score of 23 out of 28, indicating significant hair pulling with moderate–severe urges to pull and moderate–severe distress regarding pulling. On the MIST-A, Jess scored higher on focused pulling which is consistent with the level of urges seen on the MGH-HPS.

Jess and her therapist determined the following treatment goals: (a) reduce number of hair pulling episodes; (b) reduce distress related to hair pulling; and (c) increase competing activities (e.g., writing). The therapist structured a treatment plan that started with psychoeducation regarding TTM and continuation of self-monitoring forms. The goal of the self-monitoring forms was to assess change in symptoms over time, increase awareness of problem behaviors, and reduce their frequency. The treatment included an evidence-based treatment that included relaxation, habit reversal training, contingencies, thought monitoring, and cognitive restructuring (Keuthen, Stein, & Christenson, 2001). Jess was compliant with all aspects of treatment and within 9 weeks had regrown hair on most bald spots on the scalp and had completely stopped pulling hair from her brows and her lashes. On follow-up at 3 months, there was evidence of one spot of hair loss on the scalp. Jess admitted to pulling when she experienced the loss of her brother. Booster sessions were provided and Jess was free of hair loss at the next 3-month follow-up appointment.

EXCORIATION (SKIN-PICKING) DISORDER

Identifying Information and Presenting Problem   Tim is an 18-year-old male who attends community college in a rural area of the Midwest. He lives with his family on a farm and helps with chores on a daily basis. He has very dry skin that is made worse by his allergy to hay. He has seen numerous dermatologists due to the frequency of open sores on his arms and legs. He denies excessive picking but his parents report that he is always "picking something." His girlfriend has threatened to break up if he doesn't stop picking.

During a clinical interview, Tim reported that he remembered picking at an ingrown hair on his leg when he was 7 or 8 years old. He admitted that he felt an urge to pick at it when he was watching TV or lying in bed at night. Although he felt a sense of relief after picking, the resultant skin damage made him feel frustrated and ashamed. He could not remember when he started picking at normal skin, but by the time he presented for treatment he had lesions and scabs all over his body. Initially, Tim used his fingernails to pick, but began using tweezers, toothpicks, and even knives. Although he feels embarrassed by the scars, some of which are infected, Tim feels as though he is unable to stop picking.

Assessment and Treatment   The ADIS-5L (Brown & Barlow, 2014) was administered to confirm the *DSM-5* diagnosis of ED and to assess for comorbid disorders. Although Tim endorsed feelings of sadness and low self-esteem, he did not meet criteria for a depressive disorder. The Skin Picking Scale (Keuthen et al., 2001) was administered and Tim obtained a score of 21, indicating severe ED. He completed self-monitoring of skin picking for 1 week, which was augmented by photos that he agreed to take of three identified lesions on his legs. This baseline monitoring was useful to increase awareness of the skin picking as well as a baseline for treatment response.

The first step in treatment was dermatologic assessment of the skin. Antibiotic ointment was prescribed for infected areas and a moisturizer was prescribed for all areas of dry skin. Tim was also apprised of the potential benefits of pharmacotherapy but he declined. An acceptance-enhanced behavior therapy for excoriation (Capriotti et al., 2015) was utilized. This treatment utilizes habit reversal training with the addition of mindfulness to increase awareness. The focus is on increased distress tolerance and acceptance of urges (Kress & Paylo, 2015). Tim worked hard to resist the urges to pick and had clearer skin in as little as 3 weeks. He complied with the treatment recommendations and was symptom-free by 6 months.

REFERENCES

Abramovitch, A., & Cooperman, A. (2015). The cognitive neuropsychology of obsessive-compulsive disorder: A critical review. *Journal of Obsessive-Compulsive and Related Disorders, 5,* 524–536.

American Psychiatric Association. (2000). *Diagnostic and statistical manual of mental disorders* (4th ed., text rev.). Washington, DC: American Psychiatric Association.

American Psychiatric Association. (2013). *Diagnostic and statistical manual of mental disorders* (5th ed.). Arlington, VA: American Psychiatric Association.

An, S., Mataix-Cols, D., Lawrence, N., Wooderson, S., Giampietro, V., Speckens, A., . . . Phillips, M. (2009). To discard or not to discard: The neural basis of hoarding symptoms in obsessive-compulsive disorder. *Molecular Psychiatry, 14*(3), 318–331.

Angelakis, I., Gooding, P. A., & Panagioti, M. (2016). Suicidality in body dysmorphic disorder (BDD): A systematic review with meta-analysis. *Clinical Psychology Review, 49,* 55–66.

Anson, M., Veale, D., & Miles, S. (2015). Appearance comparison in individuals with body dysmorphic disorder and controls. *Body Image, 15,* 132–140.

Ayers, C. R., Dozier, M. E., & Mayes, T. L. (2016). Psychometric evaluation of the saving inventory-revised in older adults. *Clinical Gerontologist,* 1–6.

Ayers, C. R., Dozier, M. E., Wetherell, J. L., Twamley, E. W., & Schiehser, D. M. (2016). Executive functioning in participants over age of 50 with hoarding disorder. *The American Journal of Geriatric Psychiatry, 24*(5), 342–349.

Ayers, C. R., Wetherell, J. L., Schiehser, D., Almklov, E., Golshan, S., & Saxena, S. (2013). Executive functioning in older adults with hoarding disorder. *International Journal of Geriatric Psychiatry, 28*(11), 1175–1181.

Azrin, N. H., Nunn, R. G., & Frantz, S. E. (1980). Treatment of hairpulling (trichotillomania): A comparative study of habit reversal and negative practice training. *Journal of Behavior Therapy & Experimental Psychiatry, 11,* 13–20.

Baer, L., Brown-Beasley, M. W., Sorce, J., & Henriques, A. I. (1993). Computer-assisted telephone administration of a structured interview for obsessive-compulsive disorder. *The American Journal of Psychiatry, 150*(11), 1737–1738.

Baldock, E., Anson, M., & Veale, D. (2012). The stopping criteria for mirror-gazing in body dysmorphic disorder. *British Journal of Clinical Psychology, 51*(3), 323–344.

Baldwin, P. A., Whitford, T. J., & Grisham, J. R. (2016). The Relationship between hoarding symptoms, intolerance of uncertainty, and error-related negativity. *Journal of Psychopathology and Behavioral Assessment,* 1–9.

Belloch, A., Fornés, G., Carrasco, A., López-Solá, C., Alonso, P., & Menchón, J. M. (2016). Incompleteness and not just right experiences in the explanation of obsessive-compulsive disorder. *Psychiatry Research, 236,* 1–8.

Benito, K., & Storch, E. (2011). Assessment of obsessive-compulsive disorder: Review and future directions. *Expert Review of Neurotherapeutics, 11*(2), 287–298.

Beucke, J. C., Sepulcre, J., Talukdar, T., Linnman, C., Zschenderlein, K., Endras, T., . . . Kathmann, N. (2013). Abnormally high degree connectivity of the orbitofrontal cortex in obsessive-compulsive disorder. *Journal of American Medical Association Psychiatry, 70*(6), 619–629.

Bienvenu, O., Samuels, J. F., Riddle, M. A., Hoehn-Saric, R., Liang, K., Cullen, B. M., . . . Nestadt, G. (2000). The relationship of obsessive-compulsive disorder to possible spectrum disorders: Results from a family study. *Biological Psychiatry, 48*(4), 287–293.

Bjornsson, A. S., Didie, E. R., Grant, J. E., Menard, W., Stalker, E., & Phillips, K. A. (2013). Age at onset and clinical correlates in body dysmorphic disorder. *Comprehensive Psychiatry, 54*(7), 893–903.

Bjornsson, A. S., Didie, E. R., & Phillips, K. A. (2010). Body dysmorphic disorder. *Dialogues in Clinical Neuroscience, 12*(2), 221–232.

Bloch, M. H., Bartley, C. A., Zipperer, L., Jakubovski, E., Landeros-Weisenberger, A., Pittenger, C., & Leckman, J. F. (2014). Meta-analysis: Hoarding symptoms associated with poor treatment outcome in obsessive-compulsive disorder. *Molecular Psychiatry, 19*(9), 1025–1030.

Bloch, M. H., Landeros-Weisenberger, A., Rosario, M. C., Pittenger, C., & Leckman, J. F. (2008). Meta-analysis of the symptom structure of obsessive-compulsive disorder. *The American Journal of Psychiatry, 165*(12), 1532–1542.

Boelen, P. A., & Carleton, R. N. (2012). Intolerance of uncertainty, hypochondriacal concerns, obsessive-compulsive symptoms, and worry. *Journal of Nervous and Mental Diseases, 200,* 208–213.

Bohne, A., Keuthen, N. J., Wilhelm, S., Deckersbach, T., & Jenike, M. A. (2002). Prevalence of symptoms of body dysmorphic disorder and its correlates: A cross-cultural comparison. *Psychosomatics, 43*(6), 486–490.

Bomyea, J., Lang, A. J., Golinelli, D., Craske, M. G., Chavira, D. A., Sherbourne, C. D., . . . Stein, M. B. (2013). Trauma exposure in anxious primary care patients. *Journal of Psychopathology and Behavioral Assessment, 35*(2), 254–263.

Boroughs, M. S., Krawczyk, R., & Thompson, J. K. (2010). Body dysmorphic disorder among diverse racial/ethnic and sexual orientation groups: Prevalence estimates and associated factors. *Sex Roles, 63*(9), 725–737.

Bottesi, G., Cerea, S., Ouimet, A. J., Sica, C., & Ghisis, M. (2016). Affective correlates of trichotillomania across the hair pulling cycle: Findings from an Italian sample of self-identified hair-pullers. *Psychiatry Research, 246,* 606–611.

Bowyer, L., Krebs, G., Mataix-Cols, D., Veale, D., & Monzani, B. (2016). A critical review of cosmetic treatment outcomes in body dysmorphic disorder. *Body Image, 19,* 1–8.

Brakoulias, V., Eslick, G. D., & Starcevic, V. (2015). A meta-analysis of the response of pathological hoarding to pharmacotherapy. *Psychiatry Research, 229*(1), 272–276.

Brakoulias, V., Starcevic, V., Berle, D., Milicevic, D., Hannan, A., & Martin, A. (2014). The relationships between obsessive-compulsive symptom dimensions and cognitions in obsessive-compulsive disorder. *Psychiatric Quarterly*, 85(2), 133–142.

Brakoulias, V., Starcevic, V., Berle, D., Sammut, P., Milicevic, D., Moses, K., . . . Martin, A. (2013). Further support for five dimensions of obsessive-compulsive symptoms. *Journal of Nervous and Mental Disease*, 201(6), 452–459.

Brown, T. A., & Barlow, D. H. (2014). *Anxiety and Related Disorders Interview Schedule for DSM-5 (ADIS-5L) - Lifetime Version*. Oxford, England: Oxford University Press.

Buchanan, B. G., Rossell, S. L., Maller, J. J., Toh, W. L., Brennan, S., & Castle, D. J. (2013). Brain connectivity in body dysmorphic disorder compared with controls: A diffusion tensor imaging study. *Psychological Medicine*, 43(12), 2513–2521.

Buhlmann, U., Etcoff, N. L., & Wilhelm, S. (2006). Emotion recognition bias for contempt and anger in body dysmorphic disorder. *Journal of Psychiatric Research*, 40(2), 105–111.

Buhlmann, U., Marques, L. M., & Wilhelm, S. (2012). Traumatic experiences in individuals with body dysmorphic disorder. *The Journal of Nervous and Mental Disease*, 200(1), 95–98.

Buhlmann, U., Teachman, B. A., & Kathmann, N. (2011). Evaluating implicit attractiveness beliefs in body dysmorphic disorder using the go/no-go association task. *Journal of Behavior Therapy and Experimental Psychiatry*, 42(2), 192–197.

Buhlmann, U., Teachman, B. A., Naumann, E., Fehlinger, T., & Rief, W. (2009). The meaning of beauty: Implicit and explicit self-esteem and attractiveness beliefs in body dysmorphic disorder. *Journal of Anxiety Disorders*, 23(5), 694–702.

Buhlmann, U., Wacker, R., & Dziobek, I. (2015). Inferring other people's states of mind: Comparison across social anxiety, body dysmorphic, and obsessive-compulsive disorders. *Journal of Anxiety Disorders*, 34, 107–113.

Buhlmann, U., Winter, A., & Kathmann, N. (2013). Emotion recognition in body dysmorphic disorder: Application of the reading the mind in the eyes task. *Body Image*, 10(2), 247–250.

Bulli, F., Melli, G., Carraresi, C., Stopani, E., Pertusa, A., & Frost, R. O. (2014). Hoarding behaviour in an Italian non-clinical sample. *Behavioural and Cognitive Psychotherapy*, 42(03), 297–311.

Bulli, F., Melli, G., Cavalletti, V., Stopani, E., & Carraresi, C. (2016). Comorbid personality disorders in obsessive-compulsive disorder and its symptom dimensions. *Psychiatric Quarterly*, 87(2), 365–376.

Calkins, A. W., Berman, N. C., & Wilhelm, S. (2013). Recent advances in research on cognition and emotion in OCD: A review. *Current Psychiatry Reports*, 15(5), 357–363.

Capriotti, M. R., Ely, L. J., Snorrason, I., & Woods, D. W. (2015). Acceptance-enhanced behavior therapy for excoriation (skin picking) disorder in adults: A clinical case series. *Cognitive and Behavioral Practice*, 22(2), 230–239.

Carbonella, J. Y., & Timpano, K. R. (2016). Examining the link between hoarding symptoms and cognitive flexibility deficits. *Behavior Therapy*, 47(2), 262–273.

Carleton, R., Mulvogue, M., Thibodeau, M., McCabe, R., Antony, M., & Asmundson, G. (2012). Increasingly certain about uncertainty: Intolerance of uncertainty across anxiety and depression. *Journal of Anxiety Disorders*, 26(3), 468–479.

Cath, D. C., Nizar, K., Boomsma, D., & Mathews, C. A. (2016). Age-specific prevalence of hoarding and obsessive compulsive disorder: A population-based study. *The American Journal of Geriatric Psychiatry*, 25(3), 245–255.

Chakrabarty, K., Bhattacharyya, S., Christopher, R., & Khanna, S., (2005). Glutamatergic dysfunction in OCD. *Neuropsychopharmacology*, 30, 1735–1740.

Chamberlain, S. R., Hampshire, A., Menzies, L. A., Garyfallidis, E., Grant, J. E., Odlaug, B. L., . . . Sahakian, B. J. (2010). Reduced brain white matter integrity in trichotillomania: A diffusion tensor imaging study. *Archives of General Psychiatry*, 67, 965–971.

Chamberlain, S. R., Menzies, L. A., Fineberg, N. A., del Campo, N., Suckling, J., Craig, K., . . . Sahakian, B. J. (2008). Grey matter abnormalities in trichotillomania: Morphometric magnetic resonance imaging study. *British Journal of Psychiatry, 193*(3), 216–221.

Cherian, A. V., Narayanaswamy, J. C., Viswanath, B., Guru, N., George, C. M., Bada Math, S., . . . Janardhan Reddy, Y. C. (2014). Gender differences in obsessive-compulsive disorder: Findings from a large Indian sample. *Asian Journal of Psychiatry,* 917–921.

Christenson, G. A., Mackenzie, T., & Mitchell, J. (1991). Characteristics of 60 adult chronic hair pullers. *American Journal of Psychiatry, 148*(3), 365–370.

Christenson, G. A., Mackenzie, T. B., & Reeve, E. A. (1992). Familial trichotillomania. [Letter to the editor]. *American Journal of Psychiatry, 149,* 283.

Clerkin, E. M., & Teachman, B. A. (2008). Perceptual and cognitive biases in individuals with body dysmorphic disorder symptoms. *Cognition and Emotion, 22*(7), 1327–1339.

Clerkin, E. M., Teachman, B. A., Smith, A. R., & Buhlmann, U. (2014). Specificity of implicit-shame associations comparison across body dysmorphic, obsessive-compulsive, and social anxiety disorders. *Clinical Psychological Science, 2*(5), 560–575.

Cohen, L. J., Stein, D. J., Simeon, D., Spadaccini, E., Rosen, J. J., Aronowitz, B. B., & Hollander, E. E. (1995). Clinical profile, comorbidity, and treatment history in 123 hair pullers: A survey study. *Journal of Clinical Psychiatry, 56*(7), 319–326.

Conroy, M., Menard, W., Fleming-Ives, K., Modha, P., Cerullo, H., & Phillips, K. A. (2008). Prevalence and clinical characteristics of body dysmorphic disorder in an adult inpatient setting. *General Hospital Psychiatry, 30*(1), 67–72.

Crerand, C. E., Phillips, K. A., Menard, W., & Fay, C. (2005). Nonpsychiatric medical treatment of body dysmorphic disorder. *Psychosomatics, 46*(6), 549–555.

Cromer, K. R., Schmidt, N. B., & Murphy, D. L. (2007). Do traumatic events influence the clinical expression of compulsive hoarding? *Behavior Research and Therapy, 45,* 2581–2592.

Cumming, T. B., Blomstrand, C., Skoog, I., & Linden, T. (2016). The high prevalence of anxiety disorders after stroke. *The American Journal of Geriatric Psychiatry, 24*(2), 154–160.

Davidson, J. R., Miner, C. M., De Veaugh-Geiss, J., Tupler, L. A., Colket, J. T., & Potts, N. L. S. (1997). The Brief Social Phobia Scale: A psychometric evaluation. *Psychological Medicine, 27,* 161–166.

de Mathis, M. A., de Alvarenga, P., Funaro, G., Torresan, R. C., Moraes, I., Torres, A. R., . . . Hounie, A. G. (2011). Gender differences in obsessive-compulsive disorder: A literature review. *Revista Brasileira De Psiquiatria, 33*(4), 390–399.

Deckersbach, T., Savage, C. R., Phillips, K. A., Wilhelm, S., Buhlmann, U., Rauch, S. L., . . . Jenike, M. A. (2000). Characteristics of memory dysfunction in body dysmorphic disorder. *Journal of the International Neuropsychological Society, 6*(06), 673–681.

Deckersbach, T., Wilhelm, S., Keuthen, N. J., Baer, L., & Jenike, M. A. (2002). Cognitive- behavior therapy for self-injurious skin picking: A case series. *Behavior Modification, 26*(3), 361–377.

Dell'Osso, B., Benatti, B., Buoli, M., Altamura, A., Marazziti, D., Hollander, E., . . . Zohar, J. (2013). The influence of age at onset and duration of illness on long-term outcome in patients with obsessive-compulsive disorder: A report from the International College of Obsessive Compulsive Spectrum Disorders (ICOCS). *European Neuropsychopharmacology, 23*(8), 865–871.

Diefenbach, G. J., Reitman, D., & Williamson, D. A. (2000). Trichotillomania: A challenge to research and practice. *Clinical Psychology Review, 20,* 289–309.

Diefenbach, G. J., Tolin, D. F., Hallion, L. S., Zertuche, L., Rabany, L., Goethe, J. W., & Assaf, M. (2015). A case study of clinical and neuroimaging outcomes following repetitive transcranial magnetic stimulation for hoarding disorder. *American Journal of Psychiatry, 172*(11), 1160–1162.

DiMauro, J., Tolin, D. F., Frost, R. O., & Steketee, G. (2013). Do people with hoarding disorder under-report their symptoms? *Journal of Obsessive-Compulsive and Related Disorders, 2*(2), 130–136.

Dlagnikova, A., & van Niekerk, R. L. (2015). The prevalence of body dysmorphic disorder among South African university students. *South African Journal of Psychiatry*, 21(3), 104–106.

Dozier, M. E., Porter, B., & Ayers, C. R. (2016a). Age of onset and progression of hoarding symptoms in older adults with hoarding disorder. *Aging & Mental Health*, 20(7), 736–742.

Dozier, M. E., Wetherell, J. L., Twamley, E. W., Schiehser, D. M., & Ayers, C. R. (2016b). The relationship between age and neurocognitive and daily functioning in adults with hoarding disorder. *International Journal of Geriatric Psychiatry*, 31(12), 1329–1336.

Duke, D., Bodzin, D., Tavares, P., Geffken, G., & Storch, E. (2009). The phenomenology of hair pulling in a community sample. *Journal of Anxiety Disorders*, 23(8), 1118–1125.

Duke, D., Keeley, M., Geffken, G., & Storch, E. (2010). Trichotillomania: A current review. *Clinical Psychology Review*, 30(2), 181–193.

Dunai, J., Labuschagne, I., Castle, D. J., Kyrios, M., & Rossell, S. L. (2010). Executive function in body dysmorphic disorder. *Psychological Medicine*, 40(9), 1541–1548.

Eisen, J. L., Phillips, K. A., Baer, L., Beer, D. A., Atala, K. D., & Rasmussen, S. A. (1998). The Brown Assessment of Beliefs Scale: Reliability and validity. *American Journal of Psychiatry*, 155(1), 102–108.

Enander, J., Andersson, E., Mataix-Cols, D., Lichtenstein, L., Alström, K., Andersson, G., . . . Rück, C. (2016). Therapist guided internet based cognitive behavioural therapy for body dysmorphic disorder: Single blind randomised controlled trial. *British Medical Journal*, 352, i241.

Eng, G. K., Sim, K., & Chen, S. A. (2015). Meta-analytic investigations of structural grey matter, executive domain-related functional activations, and white matter diffusivity in obsessive compulsive disorder: An integrative review. *Neuroscience and Biobehavioral Reviews*, 52, 233–257.

Evans, B. (1976). A case of trichotillomania in a child treated in a home token program. *Journal of Behavior Therapy and Experimental Psychiatry*, 7, 197–198.

Fernández de la Cruz, L., Kolvenbach, S., Vidal-Ribas, P., Jassi, A., Llorens, M., Patel, N., . . . Mataix-Cols, D. (2016). Illness perception, help-seeking attitudes, and knowledge related to obsessive-compulsive disorder across different ethnic groups: A community survey. *Social Psychiatry and Psychiatric Epidemiology*, 51(3), 455–464.

Fernández de la Cruz, L., Nordsletten, A. E., Billotti, D., & Mataix-Cols, D. (2013). Photograph-aided assessment of clutter in hoarding disorder: Is a picture worth a thousand words? *Depression and Anxiety*, 30(1), 61–66.

Feusner, J. D., Arienzo, D., Li, W., Zhan, L., GadElkarim, J., Thompson, P. M., & Leow, A. D. (2013). White matter microstructure in body dysmorphic disorder and its clinical correlates. *Psychiatry Research*, 211(2), 132–140.

Feusner, J. D., Hembacher, E., Moller, H., & Moody, T. D. (2011). Abnormalities of object visual processing in body dysmorphic disorder. *Psychological Medicine*, 41(11), 2385–2397.

Feusner, J. D., Moller, H., Altstein, L., Sugar, C., Bookheimer, S., Yoon, J., & Hembacher, E. (2010a). Inverted face processing in body dysmorphic disorder. *Journal of Psychiatric Research*, 44(15), 1088–1094.

Feusner, J. D., Moody, T., Hembacher, E., Townsend, J., McKinley, M., Moller, H., & Bookheimer, S. (2010b). Abnormalities of visual processing and frontostriatal systems in body dysmorphic disorder. *Archives of General Psychiatry*, 67(2), 197–205.

Feusner, J. D., Townsend, J., Bystritsky, A., & Bookheimer, S. (2007). Visual information processing of faces in body dysmorphic disorder. *Archives of General Psychiatry*, 64(12), 1417–1425.

First, M. B., Spitzer, R. L., Williams, J. B. W., & Karg, R. S. (2015). *Structured Clinical Interview for DSM-5 Disorders (SCID-5-CV): Clinician Version*. Arlington, VA: American Psychiatric Publishing Incorporated.

Flessner, C. A., Penzel, F., & Keuthen, N. J. (2010). Current treatment practices for children and adults with trichotillomania: Consensus among experts. *Cognitive & Behavioral Practice*, 17(3), 290–300.

Flessner, C. A., & Woods, D. W. (2006). Phenomenological characteristics, social problems, and the economic impact associated with chronic skin picking. *Behavior Modification, 30,* 944–963.

Flessner, C. A., Woods, D. W., Franklin, M. E., Cashin, S. E., & Keuthen, N. J. (2008). The Milwaukee Inventory for Subtypes of Trichotillomania-Adult Version (MIST-A): Development of an instrument for the assessment of "focused" and "automatic" hair pulling. *Journal of Psychopathology and Behavioral Assessment, 30*(1), 20–30.

Flessner, C. A., Woods, D. W., Franklin, M. E., Keuthen, N. J., & Piacentini, J. (2009). Cross- sectional study of women with trichotillomania: A preliminary examination of pulling styles, severity, phenomenology, and functional impact. *Child Psychiatry and Human Development, 1,* 153–167.

Foa, E. B., Huppert, J. D., Leiberg, S., Langner, R., Kichic, R., Hajcak, G., & Salkovskis, P. M., (2002). The Obsessive–Compulsive Inventory: Development and validation of a short version. *Psychological Assessment, 14,* 485–496.

Foa, E. B., & Kozak, M. J. (1995). *DSM-IV* field trial: Obsessive-compulsive disorder. *American Journal of Psychiatry, 152,* 90–96.

Fontenelle, L. F., Mendlowicz, M. V., Marques, C., & Versiani, M. (2004). Trans-cultural aspects of obsessive-compulsive disorder: A description of a Brazilian sample and a systematic review of international studies. *Journal of Psychiatric Research, 38,* 403–411.

Fontenelle, I. S., Rangé, B. P., Prazeres, A. M., Borges, M. C., Versiani, M., & Fontenelle, L. F. (2010). The Brazilian Portuguese version of the Saving Inventory–Revised: Internal consistency, test-retest reliability, and validity of a questionnaire to assess hoarding. *Psychological Reports, 106*(1), 279–296.

Frost, R. O., & Gross, R. C. (1993). The hoarding of possessions. *Behavior Research and Therapy, 31,* 367–381.

Frost, R. O., Rosenfield, E., Steketee, G., & Tolin, D. F. (2013). An examination of excessive acquisition in hoarding disorder. *Journal of Obsessive-Compulsive and Related Disorders, 2*(3), 338–345.

Frost, R. O., Steketee, G., & Grisham, J. (2004). Measurement of compulsive hoarding: Saving Inventory Revised. *Behavior Research and Therapy, 42*(10), 1163–1182.

Frost, R. O., Steketee, G., & Tolin, D. F. (2011). Comorbidity in hoarding disorder. *Depression and Anxiety, 28*(10), 876–884.

Frost, R. O., Steketee, G., Tolin, D. F., Sinopoli, N., & Ruby, D. (2015). Motives for acquiring and saving in hoarding disorder, OCD, and community controls. *Journal of Obsessive-Compulsive and Related Disorders, 4,* 54–59.

Frost, R. O., Tolin, D. F., Steketee, G., & Oh, M. (2011). Indecisiveness and hoarding. *International Journal of Cognitive Therapy, 4*(3), 253–262.

Goodman, W. K., Price, L., Rasmussen, S., Mazure, C., Delgado, P., Heninger, G., & Charney, D. (1989a). The Yale-Brown Obsessive Compulsive Scale, II. Validity. *Archives of General Psychiatry, 46*(11), 1012–1016.

Goodman, W. K., Price, L. H., Rasmussen, S. A., Mazure, C., Fleischmann, R. L., Hill, C. L., . . . Charney, D. S. (1989b). The Yale-Brown Obsessive Compulsive Scale, I: Development, use, and reliability. *Archives of General Psychiatry, 46*(11), 1006–1011.

Gothelf, D., Aharonovsky, O., Horesh, N., Carty, T., & Apter, A. (2004). Life events and personality factors in children and adolescents with obsessive-compulsive disorder and other anxiety disorders. *Comprehensive Psychiatry, 45*(3), 192–198.

Grabill, K., Merlo, L., Duke, D., Harford, K., Keeley, M. L., Geffken, G. R., & Storch, E. A. (2008). Assessment of obsessive-compulsive disorder: A review. *Journal of Anxiety Disorders, 22*(1), 1–17.

Grant, J. E., Kim, S. W., & Crow, S. J. (2001). Prevalence and clinical features of body dysmorphic disorder in adolescent and adult psychiatric inpatients. *The Journal of Clinical Psychiatry, 62*(7), 517–522.

Grant, J. E., Leppink, E. W., Tsai, J., Chamberlain, S. R., Redden, S. A., Curley, E. E., . . . Keuthen, N. J. (2016). Does comorbidity matter in body-focused repetitive behavior disorders? *Annals of Clinical Psychiatry, 28*(3), 175–181.

Grant, J. E., Levine, L., Kim, D., & Potenza, M. (2005). Impulse control disorders in adult psychiatric inpatients. *American Journal of Psychiatry, 162*(11), 2184–2188.

Grant, J. E., Odlaug, B. L., Chamberlain, S. R., Keuthen, N. J., Lochner, C., & Stein, D. J. (2012). Skin-picking disorder. *American Journal of Psychiatry, 169*, 1143–1149.

Grant, J. E., Odlaug, B. L., Chamberlain, S. R., & Kim, S. W. (2010a). A double-blind, placebo-controlled trial of lamotrigine for pathological skin picking: Treatment efficacy and neuro-cognitive predictors of response. *Journal of Clinical Psychopharmacology, 30*, 396–403.

Grant, J. E., Odlaug, B. L., Hampshire, A., Schreiber, L. R. N., & Chamberlain, S. R. (2013). White matter abnormalities in skin-picking disorder: A diffusion tensor imaging study. *Neuropsychopharmacology, 38*(5), 763–769.

Grant, J. E., Odlaug, B. L., & Kim, S. W. (2007). Lamotrigine treatment of pathologic skin picking: An open label study. *Journal of Clinical Psychology, 68*, 1384–1391.

Grant, J. E., Odlaug, B. L., & Kim, S. W. (2010b). A clinical comparison of pathologic skin picking and obsessive-compulsive disorder. *Comprehensive Psychiatry, 51*, 347–352.

Greenberg, J. L., Reuman, L., Hartmann, A. S., Kasarskis, I., & Wilhelm, S. (2014). Visual hot spots: An eye tracking study of attention bias in body dysmorphic disorder. *Journal of Psychiatric Research, 57*, 125–132.

Greisberg, S., & McKay, D. (2003). Neuropsychology of obsessive-compulsive disorder: A review and treatment implications. *Clinical Psychology Review, 23*(1), 95–117.

Grisham, J. R., & Barlow, D. H. (2005). Compulsive hoarding: Current research and therapy. *Journal of Psychopathology and Behavioral Assessment, 27*(1), 45–52.

Grisham, J. R., Frost, R. O., Steketee, G., Kim, H., & Hood, S. (2006). Age of onset of compulsive hoarding. *Journal of Anxiety Disorders, 20*(5), 675–686.

Grisham, J. R., Norberg, M. M., Williams, A. D., Ceroma, S. P., & Kadib, R. (2010). Categorization and cognitive deficits in compulsive hoarding. *Behaviour Research and Therapy, 48*(9), 866–872.

Gros, D. F., Magruder, K. M., & Frueh, B. C. (2013). Obsessive compulsive disorder in veterans in primary care: Prevalence and impairment. *General Hospital Psychiatry, 35*(1), 71–73.

Grzesiak, M., Reich, A., Szepietowski, J. C., Hadryś, T., & Pacan, P. (2017). Trichotillomania among young adults: Prevalence and comorbidity. *Acta Dermato-Venereologica, 97*, 1–4.

Gupta, M. A., Gupta, A. K., & Haberman, H. F. (1986). Neurotic excoriations: A review and some new perspectives. *Comprehensive Psychiatry, 27*, 381–386.

Gupta, M. A., Gupta, A. K., & Knapp, K. (2015). Trichotillomania: Demographic and clinical features from a nationally representative US sample. *Skinmed, 13*(6), 455–460.

Hall, B. J., Tolin, D. F., Frost, R. O., & Steketee, G. (2013). An exploration of comorbid symptoms and clinical correlates of clinically significant hoarding symptoms. *Depression and Anxiety, 30*(1), 67–76.

Hallion, L. S., Diefenbach, G. J., & Tolin, D. F. (2015). Poor memory confidence mediates the association between inattention symptoms and hoarding severity and impairment. *Journal of Obsessive-Compulsive and Related Disorders, 7*, 43–48.

Hanna, G., Veenstra-VanderWeele, J., Cox, N., Boehnke, M., Himle, J., Curtis, G., . . . Cook, E. (2002). Genome-wide linkage analysis of families with obsessive-compulsive disorder ascertained through pediatric probands. *American Journal of Medical Genetics, 114*(5), 541–552.

Harrison, A., Fernández de la Cruz, L., Enander, J., Radua, J., & Mataix-Cols, D. (2016). Cognitive-behavioral therapy for body dysmorphic disorder: A systematic review and meta-analysis of randomized controlled trials. *Clinical Psychology Review, 48*, 43–51.

Harrison, B. J., Pujol, J., Cardoner, N., Deus, J., Alonso, P., López-Solà, M., . . . Soriano-Mas, C. (2013). Brain corticostriatal systems and the major clinical symptom dimensions of obsessive-compulsive disorder. *Biological Psychiatry, 73*, 321–328.

Harrison, B. J., Soriano-Mas, C., Pujol, J., Ortiz, H., López-Solà, M., Hernández-Ribas, R., . . . Cardoner, N. (2009). Altered corticostriatal functional connectivity in obsessive-compulsive disorder. *Archives of General Psychiatry, 66*(11), 1189–1200.

Hart, A. S., & Phillips, K. A. (2013). Symmetry concerns as a symptom of body dysmorphic disorder. *Journal of Obsessive-Compulsive and Related Disorders, 2*(3), 292–298.

Hartmann, A. S., Thomas, J. J., Greenberg, J. L., Elliott, C. M., Matheny, N. L., & Wilhelm, S. (2015). Anorexia nervosa and body dysmorphic disorder: A comparison of body image concerns and explicit and implicit attractiveness beliefs. *Body Image, 14*, 77–84.

Hayes, S., Storch, E., & Berlanga, L. (2009). Skin picking behaviors: An examination of the prevalence and severity in a community sample. *Journal of Anxiety Disorders, 23*(3), 314–319.

Henry, J. (2006). A meta-analytic review of Wisconsin Card Sorting Test and verbal fluency performance in obsessive-compulsive disorder. *Cognitive Neuropsychiatry, 11*(2), 156–176.

Hettema, J. M., Neale, M. C., & Kendler, K. S. (2001). A review and meta-analysis of the genetic epidemiology of anxiety disorders. *American Journal of Psychiatry, 158*, 1568–1578.

Hofmeijer-Sevink, M. K., van Oppen, P., van Megen, H. J., Batelaan, N. M., Cath, D. C., van der Wee, N. A., . . . van Balkom, A. J. (2013). Clinical relevance of comorbidity in obsessive compulsive disorder: The Netherlands OCD association study. *Journal of Affective Disorders, 150*(3), 847–854.

Hough, C. M., Luks, T. L., Lai, K., Vigil, O., Guillory, S., Nongpiur, A., . . . Mathews, C. A. (2016). Comparison of brain activation patterns during executive function tasks in hoarding disorder and non-hoarding OCD. *Psychiatry Research: Neuroimaging, 255*, 50–59.

Iervolino, A. C., Rijsdijk, F. V., Cherkas, L., Fullana, M., & Mataix-Cols, D. (2011). A multivariate twin study of obsessive-compulsive symptom dimensions. *Archives of General Psychiatry, 68*(6), 637–644.

Jefferies, K., Laws, K. R., & Fineberg, N. A. (2012). Superior face recognition in body dysmorphic disorder. *Journal of Obsessive-Compulsive and Related Disorders, 1*(3), 175–179.

Johnson, J., & El-Alfy, A. T. (2016). Review of the available studies of neurobiology and pharmacotherapeutic management of trichotillomania. *Journal of Advanced Research, 7*, 169–184.

Jonnal, A. H., Gardner, C. O., Prescott, C. A., & Kendler, K. S. (2000). Obsessive and compulsive symptoms in a general population sample of female twins. *American Journal of Medical Genetics, 96*(6), 791–796.

Kashyap, H., Kumar, J. K., Kandavel, T., & Reddy, Y. C. J. (2013). Neuropsychological functioning in obsessive-compulsive disorder: Are executive functions the key deficit? *Comprehensive Psychiatry, 54*, 533–540.

Kelly, M. M., Didie, E. R., & Phillips, K. A. (2014). Personal and appearance-based rejection sensitivity in body dysmorphic disorder. *Body Image, 11*(3), 260–265.

Kerwin, L., Hovav, S., Hellemann, G., & Feusner, J. D. (2014). Impairment in local and global processing and set-shifting in body dysmorphic disorder. *Journal of Psychiatric Research, 57*, 41–50.

Kessler, R. C., Berglund, P., Chiu, W., Demler, O., Heeringa, S., Hiripi, E., . . . Zheng, H. (2004). The US National Comorbidity Survey Replication (NCS-R): Design and field procedures. *International Journal of Methods in Psychiatric Research, 13*(2), 69–92.

Keuthen, N. J., Deckersbach, T., Wilhelm, S., Engelhard, I., Forker, A., O'Sullivan, R. L., . . . Baer, L. (2001). The Skin Picking Impact Scale (SPIS): Scale development and psychometric analyses. *Psychosomatics: Journal of Consultation Liaison Psychiatry, 42*(5), 397–403.

Keuthen, N. J., Fama, J., Altenberger, E. M., Allen, A., Raff, A., & Pauls, D. (2013). Family environment in adolescent trichotillomania. *Journal of Obsessive-Compulsive and Related Disorders, 2*, 366–374.

Keuthen, N. J., Koran, L. M., Aboujaoude, E., Large, M. D., & Serpe, R. T. (2010a). The prevalence of pathologic skin picking in US adults. *Comprehensive Psychiatry, 51*(2), 183–186.

Keuthen, N. J., Makris, N., Schlerf, J. E., Martis, B., Savage, C. R., McMullin, K., . . . Rauch, S. L. (2007). Evidence for reduced cerebellar volumes in trichotillomania. *Biological Psychiatry, 61*(3), 374–381.

Keuthen, N. J., O'Sullivan, R., Ricciardi, J., Shera, D., Savage, C., Borgmann, A., . . . Baer, L. (1995). The Massachusetts General Hospital (MGH) Hairpulling Scale: 1. Development and factor analyses. *Psychotherapy and Psychosomatics, 64*(3–4), 141–145.

Keuthen, N. J., Rothbaum, B. O., Falkenstein, M. J., Meunier, S., Timpano, K. R., Jenike, M. A., & Welch, S. S. (2011). DBT-enhanced habit reversal treatment for trichotillomania: 3- and 6-month follow-up results. *Depression and Anxiety, 28*(4), 310–313.

Keuthen, N. J., Rothbaum, B. O., Fama, J., Altenburger, E., Falkenstein, M. J., Sprich, S. E., . . . Welch, S. S. (2012). DBT-enhanced cognitive-behavioral treatment for trichotillomania: A randomized controlled trial. *Journal of Behavioral Addictions, 1*(3), 106–114.

Keuthen, N. J., Rothbaum, B. O., Welch, S. S., Taylor, C., Falkenstein, M., Heekin, M., . . . Jenike, M. A. (2010b). Pilot trial of dialectical behavior therapy-enhanced habit reversal for trichotillomania. *Depression and Anxiety, 27*(10), 953–959.

Keuthen, N. J., Stein, D. J., & Christenson, G. A. (2001). Help for hair pullers: Understanding and coping with trichotillomania. Oakland, CA: New Harbinger Publications, Inc.

Khandelwal, A., Aggarwal, A., Garg, A., & Jiloha, R. C. (2009). Gender differences in phenomenology of patients with obsessive-compulsive disorder. *Delhi Psychiatry Journal, 12*(1), 8–17.

Kollei, I., Horndasch, S., Erim, Y., & Martin, A. (2017). Visual selective attention in body dysmorphic disorder, bulimia nervosa and healthy controls. *Journal of Psychosomatic Research, 92*, 26–33.

Koran, L. M., Abujaoude, E., Large, M. D., & Serpe, R. T. (2008). The prevalence of body dysmorphic disorder in the United States adult population. *CNS Spectrums, 13*(04), 316–322.

Kress, V. E., & Paylo, M. J. (2015). *Treating those with mental disorders: A comprehensive approach to case conceptualization and treatment.* Upper Saddle River, NJ: Pearson.

Kress, V. E., Stargell, N. A., Zoldan, C. A., & Paylo, M. J. (2016). Hoarding disorder: Diagnosis, assessment, and treatment. *Journal of Counseling & Development, 94*(1), 83–90.

LaBrot, Z., Dufrene, B. A., Ness, E., & Mitchell, R. (2014). Functional assessment and treatment of trichotillomania and skin-picking: A case study. *Journal of Obsessive-Compulsive and Related Disorders, 3*(3), 257–264.

Lavell, C. H., Zimmer-Gembeck, M. J., Farrell, L. J., & Webb, H. (2014). Victimization, social anxiety, and body dysmorphic concerns: Appearance-based rejection sensitivity as a mediator. *Body Image, 11*(4), 391–395.

Lawrence, N. S., Wooderson, S., Mataix-Cols, D., David, R., Speckens, A., & Phillips, M. L. (2006). Decision-making and set shifting impairments are associated with distinct symptom dimensions in obsessive-compulsive disorder. *Neuropsychology, 20*(4), 409–419.

Lenane, M. C., Swedo, S. E., Rapoport, J. L., Leonard, H., Sceery, W., & Guroff, J. J. (1992). Rates of obsessive compulsive disorder in first degree relatives of patients with trichotillomania: A research note. *Child Psychology & Psychiatry & Allied Disciplines, 33*(5), 925–933.

Lensi, P., Cassano, G. B., Correddu, G., Ravagli, S., Kunovac, J. L., & Akiskal, H. S. (1996). Obsessive-compulsive disorder: Familial developmental history, symptomatology, comorbidity and course with special reference to gender-related differences. *The British Journal of Psychiatry, 169*, 101–107.

Leonard, R. C., & Riemann, B. C. (2012). The co-occurrence of obsessions and compulsions in OCD. *Journal of Obsessive-Compulsive and Related Disorders, 1*, 211–215.

Levy, H. C., McLean, C. P., Yadin, E., & Foa, E. B. (2013). Characteristics of individuals seeking treatment for obsessive-compulsive disorder. *Behavior Therapy, 44*(3), 408–416.

Linehan, M. M. (1993a). *Cognitive-behavioral treatment of borderline personality disorder.* New York, NY: Guilford Press.

Linehan, M. M. (1993b). *Skills training manual for treating borderline personality disorder*. New York, NY: Guilford Press.

Lochner, C., Grant, J. E., Odlaug, B. L., Woods, D. W., Keuthen, N. J., & Stein, D. J. (2012). DSM-5 field survey: Hair-pulling disorder (trichotillomania). *Depression and Anxiety*, 29(12), 1025–1031.

Lochner, C., Seedat, S., & Stein, D. J. (2010). Chronic hair pulling: Phenomenology-based subtypes. *Journal of Anxiety Disorders*, 24, 196–202.

Lochner, C., Simeon, D., Niehaus, D. H., & Stein, D. J. (2002). Trichotillomania and skin-picking: A phenomenological comparison. *Depression and Anxiety*, 15(2), 83–86.

López-Solà, C., Fontenelle, L. F., Alonso, P., Cuadras, D., Foley, D. L., Pantelis, C., . . . Menchón, J. M. (2014). Prevalence and heritability of obsessive-compulsive spectrum and anxiety disorder symptoms: A survey of the Australian twin registry. *American Journal of Medical Genetics Part B: Neuropsychiatric Genetics*, 165(4), 314–325.

Macy, A., Theo, J., Kaufmann, S., Ghazzaoui, R., Pawlowski, P., Fakhry, H., . . . IsHak, W. (2013). Quality of life in obsessive compulsive disorder. *CNS Spectrums*, 18(1), 21–33.

Marazziti, D., Dell'Osso, L., Presta, S., Pfanner, C., Rossi, A., Masala, I., . . . Cassano, G. B. (1999). Platelet [3 H] paroxetine binding in patients with OCD-related disorders. *Psychiatry Research*, 89(3), 223–228.

Marques, L., LeBlanc, N., Weingarden, H., Greenberg, J. L., Traeger, L. N., Keshaviah, A., & Wilhelm, S. (2011). Body dysmorphic symptoms: Phenomenology and ethnicity. *Body Image*, 8(2), 163–167.

Mataix-Cols, D., Frost, R. O., Pertusa, A., Clark, L. A., Saxena, S., Leckman, J. F., . . . Wilhelm, S. (2010). Hoarding disorder: A new diagnosis for DSM-V? *Depression and Anxiety*, 27(6), 556–572.

Mataix-Cols, D., Pertusa, A., & Snowden, J. (2011). Neuropsychological and neural correlates of hoarding: A practice-friendly review. *Journal of Clinical Psychology: In Session*, 67(5), 467–476.

Mataix-Cols, D., Rauch, S., Baer, L., Eisen, J., Shera, D., Goodman, W., . . . Jenike, M. (2002). Symptom stability in adult obsessive-compulsive disorder: Data from a naturalistic two-year follow-up study. *The American Journal of Psychiatry*, 159(2), 263–268.

Mathes, B. M., Oglesby, M. E., Short, N. A., Portero, A. K., Raines, A. M., & Schmidt, N. B. (2017). An examination of the role of intolerance of distress and uncertainty in hoarding symptoms. *Comprehensive Psychiatry*, 72, 121–129.

Mathews, C. A., Badner, J. A., Andresen, J. M., Sheppard, B., Himle, J. A., Grant, J. E., . . . Hanna, G. L. (2012). Genome-wide linkage analysis of obsessive-compulsive disorder implicates chromosome 1p36. *Biological Psychiatry*, 72(8), 629–636.

Mathews, C. A., Delucchi, K., Cath, D. C., Willemsen, G., & Boomsma, D. I. (2014). Partitioning the etiology of hoarding and obsessive-compulsive symptoms. *Psychological Medicine*, 44(13), 2867–2876.

Mathews, C. A., Perez, V. B., Roach, B. J., Fekri, S., Vigil, O., Kupferman, E., & Mathalon, D. H. (2016). Error-related brain activity dissociates hoarding disorder from obsessive-compulsive disorder. *Psychological Medicine*, 46(02), 367–379.

Matsunaga, H., & Seedat, S. (2007). Obsessive-compulsive spectrum disorders: Cross-national and ethnic issues. *CNS Spectrums*, 12(5), 392–400.

Mazzucchelli, T. G., Kane, R. T., & Rees, C. S. (2010). Behavioral activation interventions for well-being: A meta-analysis. *The Journal of Positive Psychology*, 5(2), 105–121.

McCarley, N. G., Spirrison, C. L., & Ceminsky, J. L. (2002). Hair pulling behavior reported by African American and non-African American college students. *Journal of Psychopathology and Behavioral Assessment*, 24(3), 139–144.

McGuire, J. F., Kaercher, L., Park, J. M., & Storch, E. A. (2013). Hoarding in the community: A code enforcement and social service perspective. *Journal of Social Service Research*, 39(3), 335–344.

Millet, B., Kochman, F., Gallarda, T., Krebs, M. O., Demonfaucon, F., Barrot, I., . . . Hantouche, E. G. (2004). Phenomenological and comorbid features associated in obsessive-compulsive disorder: Influence of age of onset. *Journal of Affective Disorders*, 79(1), 241–246.

Mohammadzadeh, A. (2009). Validation of Saving Inventory-Revised (SI-R): Compulsive hoarding measure. *Iranian Journal of Psychiatry and Clinical Psychology*, *15*(1), 33–41.

Monzani, B., Krebs, G., Anson, M., Veale, D., & Mataix-Cols, D. (2013). Holistic versus detailed visual processing in body dysmorphic disorder: Testing the inversion, composite and global precedence effects. *Psychiatry Research*, *210*(3), 994–999.

Monzani, B., Rijsdijk, F., Anson, M., Iervolino, A. C., Cherkas, L., Spector, T., & Mataix-Cols, D. (2012). A twin study of body dysmorphic concerns. *Psychological Medicine*, *42*(9), 1949–1955.

Monzani, B., Rijsdijk, F., Harris, J., & Mataix-Cols, D. (2014). The structure of genetic and environmental risk factors for dimensional representations of DSM-5 obsessive-compulsive spectrum disorders. *Journal of the American Medical Association Psychiatry*, *71*(2), 182–189.

Moody, T. D., Sasaki, M. A., Bohon, C., Strober, M. A., Bookheimer, S. Y., Sheen, C. L., & Feusner, J. D. (2015). Functional connectivity for face processing in individuals with body dysmorphic disorder and anorexia nervosa. *Psychological Medicine*, *45*(16), 3491–3503.

Moody, T. D., Shen, V. W., Hutcheson, N. L., Henretty, J. R., Sheen, C. L., Strober, M., & Feusner, J. D. (2017). Appearance evaluation of others' faces and bodies in anorexia nervosa and body dysmorphic disorder. *International Journal of Eating Disorders*, *50*(2), 127–138.

Moshier, S. J., Wootton, B. M., Bragdon, L. B., Tolin, D. F., Davis, E., DiMauro, J., & Diefenbach, G. J. (2016). The relationship between self-reported and objective neuropsychological impairments in patients with hoarding disorder. *Journal of Obsessive-Compulsive and Related Disorders*, *9*, 9–15.

National Institute for Health and Clinical Excellence (NICE). (2006). *Obsessive-compulsive disorder: Core interventions in the treatment of obsessive-compulsive disorder and body dysmorphic disorder*. Leicester, England & London, England: The British Psychological Society & the Royal College of Psychiatrists. Retrieved from https://www.ncbi.nlm.nih.gov/pubmedhealth/PMH0015812/pdf/PubMedHealth_PMH0015812.pdf.

Neal-Barnett, A., Flessner, C., Franklin, M., Woods, D., Keuthen, N., & Stein, D. (2010). Ethnic differences in trichotillomania: Phenomenology, interference, impairment, and treatment efficacy. *Journal of Anxiety Disorders*, *24*(6), 553–558.

Neziroglu, F., Rabinowitz, D., Breytman, A., & Jacofsky, M. (2008). Skin picking phenomenology and severity comparison. *Journal of Clinical Psychiatry*, *10*, 306–312.

Norberg, M. M., Calamari, J. E., Cohen, R. J., & Riemann, B. C. (2008). Quality of life in obsessive-compulsive disorder: An evaluation of impairment and a preliminary analysis of the ameliorating effects of treatment. *Depression and Anxiety*, *25*(3), 248–259.

Norberg, M. M., Wetterneck, C. T., Woods, D. W., & Conelea, C. A. (2007). Experiential avoidance as a mediator of relationships between cognitions and hair-pulling severity. *Behavior Modification*, *31*(4), 367–381.

Nordsletten, A. E., Fernández de la Cruz, L., Pertusa, A., Reichenberg, A., Hatch, S. L., & Mataix-Cols, D. (2013a). The Structured Interview for Hoarding Disorder (SIHD): Development, usage and further validation. *Journal of Obsessive-Compulsive and Related Disorders*, *2*(3), 346–350.

Nordsletten, A. E., Monzani, B., Fernández de la Cruz, L., Iervolino, A. C., Fullana, M. A., Harris, J., . . . Mataix-Cols, D. (2013b). Overlap and specificity of genetic and environmental influences on excessive acquisition and difficulties discarding possessions: Implications for hoarding disorder. *American Journal of Medical Genetics Part B: Neuropsychiatric Genetics*, *162*(4), 380–387.

Nordsletten, A. E., Reichenberg, A., Hatch, S. L., Fernández de la Cruz, L., Pertusa, A., Hotopf, M., & Mataix-Cols, D. (2013c). Epidemiology of hoarding disorder. *The British Journal of Psychiatry*, 1–8.

Novak, C. E., Keuthen, N. J., Stewart, E. S., & Pauls, D. L. (2009). A twin concordance study of trichotillomania. *American Journal of Medical Genetics*, *150*, 944–949.

Odlaug, B. L., Chamberlain, S. R., Derbyshire, K. L., Leppink, E. W., & Grant, J. E. (2014). Impaired response inhibition and excess cortical thickness as candidate endophenotypes for trichotillomania. *Psychiatric Research*, *59*, 167–173.

Odlaug, B. L., & Grant, J. E. (2008). Trichotillomania and pathological skin picking: Clinical comparison with an examination of comorbidity. *Annals of Clinical Psychiatry, 20,* 57–63.

Odlaug, B. L., & Grant, J. E. (2010). Impulse-control disorders in a college student sample: Results from the self-administered Minnesota Impulse Disorders Interview (MIDI). *Primary Care Companion Journal of Clinical Psychiatry, 12*(2), PCC.09m00842.

Odlaug, B. L., & Grant, J. E. (2012). Pathological skin picking. In J. E. Grant, D. J. Stein, D. W. Woods, & N. J. Keuthen (Eds.), *Trichotillomania, skin picking, and other body-focused repetitive behaviors* (pp. 21–41). Washington, DC: American Psychiatric Publishing.

Odlaug, B. L., Hampshire, A., Chamberlain, S. R., & Grant, J. E. (2016). Abnormal brain activation in excoriation (skin-picking) disorder: Evidence from an executive planning fMRI study. *The British Journal of Psychiatry, 208,* 168–174.

Odlaug, B. L., Kim, S. W., & Grant, J. E. (2010). Quality of life and clinical severity in pathological skin picking and trichotillomania. *Journal of Anxiety Disorders, 24,* 823–829.

Odlaug, B. L., Lust, K., Schreiber, L. R. N., Christenson, G., Derbyshire, K., & Grant, J. E. (2013). Skin picking disorder in university students: Health correlates and gender differences. *General Hospital Psychiatry, 35*(2), 168–173.

Olatunji, B. O., Davis, M. L., Powers, M. B., & Smits, J. A. J. (2013). Cognitive-behavioral therapy for obsessive-compulsive disorder: A meta-analysis of treatment outcome and moderator variables. *Journal of Psychiatric Research, 47,* 33–41.

Ong, C., Sagayadevan, V., Lee, S. P., Ong, R., Chong, S. A., Frost, R. O., & Subramaniam, M. (2016). Hoarding among outpatients seeking treatment at a psychiatric hospital in Singapore. *Journal of Obsessive-Compulsive and Related Disorders, 8,* 56–63.

Öst, L., Havnen, A., Hansen, B., & Kvale, G. (2015). Cognitive behavioral treatments of obsessive-compulsive disorder. A systematic review and meta-analysis of studies published 1993–2014. *Clinical Psychology Review, 40,* 156–169.

O'Sullivan, R. L., Keuthen, N. J., Hayday, C. F., Ricciardi, J. N., Buttolph, M. L., Jenike, M. A., & Baer, L. (1995). The Massachusetts General Hospital (MGH) Hairpulling Scale: 2. Reliability and validity. *Psychotherapy and Psychosomatics, 64*(3–4), 146–148.

O'Sullivan, R. L., Rauch, S. L., Breiter, H. C., Grachev, I. D., Baer, L., Kennedy, D. N., . . . Jenike, M. A. (1997). Reduced basal ganglia volumes in trichotillomania measured via morphometric magnetic resonance imaging. *Biological Psychiatry, 42*(1), 39–45.

Pauls, D. L. (2010). The genetics of obsessive-compulsive disorder: A review. *Dialogues in Clinical Neuroscience, 12*(2), 149–163.

Pauls, D. L., Abramovitch, A., Rauch, S. L., & Geller, D. A. (2014). Obsessive-compulsive disorder: An integrative genetic and neurobiological perspective. *Nature Reviews Neuroscience, 15*(6), 410–424.

Phillipou, A., Rossell, S. L., Wilding, H. E., & Castle, D. J. (2016). Randomised controlled trials of psychological & pharmacological treatments for body dysmorphic disorder: A systematic review. *Psychiatry Research, 245,* 179–185.

Phillips, K. A. (2005). *The broken mirror: Understanding and treating body dysmorphic disorder* (2nd ed., revised) New York, NY: Oxford University Press, Inc.

Phillips, K. A., Albertini, R. S., & Rasmussen, S. A. (2002). A randomized placebo-controlled trial of fluoxetine in body dysmorphic disorder. *Archives of General Psychiatry, 59*(4), 381–388.

Phillips, K. A., Grant, J., Siniscalchi, J., & Albertini, R. S. (2001). Surgical and nonpsychiatric medical treatment of patients with body dysmorphic disorder. *Psychosomatics, 42*(6), 504–510.

Phillips, K. A., Hart, A. S., & Menard, W. (2014a). Psychometric evaluation of the Yale–Brown Obsessive-Compulsive Scale modified for body dysmorphic disorder (BDD-YBOCS). *Journal of Obsessive-Compulsive and Related Disorders, 3*(3), 205–208.

Phillips, K. A., Hart, A. S., Menard, W., & Eisen, J. L. (2013). Psychometric evaluation of the Brown Assessment of Beliefs Scale in body dysmorphic disorder. *The Journal of Nervous and Mental Disease, 201*(7), 640–643.

Phillips, K. A., Hart, A. S., Simpson, H. B., & Stein, D. J. (2014b). Delusional versus nondelusional body dysmorphic disorder: Recommendations for DSM-5. *CNS Spectrums, 19*, 10–20.

Phillips, K. A., Hollander, E., Rasmussen, S. A., & Aronowitz, B. R. (1997). A severity rating scale for body dysmorphic disorder: Development, reliability, and validity of a modified version of the Yale-Brown Obsessive Compulsive Scale. *Psychopharmacology Bulletin, 33*(1), 17–22.

Phillips, K. A., Keshaviah, A., Dougherty, D. D., Stout, R. L., Menard, W., & Wilhelm, S. (2016). Pharmacotherapy relapse prevention in body dysmorphic disorder: A double-blind, placebo-controlled trial. *American Journal of Psychiatry, 173*(9), 887–895.

Phillips, K. A., & Menard, W. (2006). Suicidality in body dysmorphic disorder: A prospective study. *American Journal of Psychiatry, 163*(7), 1280–1282.

Phillips, K. A., Menard, W., & Fay, C. (2006a). Gender similarities and differences in 200 individuals with body dysmorphic disorder. *Comprehensive Psychiatry, 47*(2), 77–87.

Phillips, K. A., Menard, W., Fay, C., & Weisberg, R. (2005). Demographic characteristics, phenomenology, comorbidity, and family history in 200 individuals with body dysmorphic disorder. *Psychosomatics, 46*(4), 317–325.

Phillips, K. A., Menard, W., Pagano, M. E., Fay, C., & Stout, R. L. (2006b). Delusional versus nondelusional body dysmorphic disorder: Clinical features and course of illness. *Journal of Psychiatric Research, 40*(2), 95–104.

Phillips, K. A., Pinto, A., Hart, A. S., Coles, M. E., Eisen, J. L., Menard, W., & Rasmussen, S. A. (2012). A comparison of insight in body dysmorphic disorder and obsessive-compulsive disorder. *Journal of Psychiatric Research, 46*(10), 1293–1299.

Phillips, K. A., Wilhelm, S., Koran, L. M., Didie, E. R., Fallon, B. A., Feusner, J., & Stein, D. J. (2010). Body dysmorphic disorder: Some key issues for DSM-V. *Depression and Anxiety, 27*(6), 573–591.

Phillips, K. A., Zai, G., King, N. A., Menard, W., Kennedy, J. L., & Richter, M. A. (2015). A preliminary candidate gene study in body dysmorphic disorder. *Journal of Obsessive-Compulsive and Related Disorders, 6*, 72–76.

Pinto, A., Mancebo, M. C., Eisen, J. L., Pagano, M. E., & Rasmussen, S. A. (2006). The Brown longitudinal obsessive compulsive study: Clinical features and symptoms of the sample at intake. *Journal of Clinical Psychiatry, 67*(5), 703–711.

Pope, H. G., Khalsa, J. H., & Bhasin, S. (2017). Body image disorders and abuse of anabolic-androgenic steroids among men. *Journal of the American Medical Association, 317*(1), 23–24.

Pope, C. G., Pope, H. G., Menard, W., Fay, C., Olivardia, R., & Phillips, K. A. (2005). Clinical features of muscle dysmorphia among males with body dysmorphic disorder. *Body Image, 2*(4), 395–400.

Pope, H. G., Wood, R. I., Rogol, A., Nyberg, F., Bowers, L., & Bhasin, S. (2014). Adverse health consequences of performance-enhancing drugs: An endocrine society scientific statement. *Endocrine Reviews, 35*(3), 341–375.

Rachman, S. A. (1997). A cognitive theory of obsessions. *Behaviour Research & Therapy, 35*, 793–802.

Raines, A. M., Timpano, K. R., & Schmidt, N. B. (2014). Effects of clutter on information processing deficits in individuals with hoarding disorder. *Journal of Affective Disorders, 166*, 30–35.

Rakowska, A., Slowinska, M., Olszewska, M., & Rudnicka, L. (2014). New trichoscopy findings in trichotillomania: Flame hairs, V-sign, hook hairs, hair powder, tulip hairs. *Acta Dermato-Venereologica, 94*(3), 303–306.

Rapp, A. M., Bergman, R. L., Piacentini, J., & McGuire, J. F. (2016). Evidence-based assessment of obsessive-compulsive disorder. *Journal of Central Nervous System Disease, 8*, 13–29.

Redden, S. A., Leppink, E. W., & Grant, J. E. (2016). Body focused repetitive behavior disorders: Significance of family history. *Comprehensive Psychiatry, 66*, 187–192.

Rheaume, J., Freeston, M. H., Leger, E., & Ladouceur, R. (1998). Bad luck: An underestimated factor in the development of obsessive-compulsive disorder. *Clinical Psychology & Psychotherapy, 5*, 1–12.

Rief, W., Buhlmann, U., Wilhelm, S., Borkenhagen, A. D. A., & Brähler, E. (2006). The prevalence of body dysmorphic disorder: A population-based survey. *Psychological Medicine, 36*(06), 877–885.

Roos, A., Fouche, J. P., Stein, D. J., & Lochner, C. (2013). White matter integrity in hair-pulling disorder (trichotillomania). *Psychiatry Research: Neuroimaging, 211,* 246–250.

Roos, A., Grant, J. E., Fouche, J. P. Stein, D. J., & Lochner, C. (2015). A comparison of brain volume and cortical thickness in excoriation (skin picking) disorder and trichotillomania (hair pulling disorder) in women. *Behavioural Brain Research, 279,* 255–258.

Rosen, J. C., Reiter, J., & Orosan, P. (1995). Cognitive-behavioral body image therapy for body dysmorphic disorder. *Journal of Consulting and Clinical Psychology, 63*(2), 263–268.

Rosen, J. C., & Reiter, J. (1996). Development of the body dysmorphic disorder examination. *Behaviour Research and Therapy, 34*(9), 755–766.

Ross, J., Badner, J., Garrido, H., Sheppard, B., Chavira, D. A., Grados, M., . . . Mathews, C. A. (2011). Genomewide linkage analysis in Costa Rican families implicates chromosome 15q14 as a candidate region for OCD. *Human Genetics, 130*(6), 795–805.

Rotge, J. Y., Aouizerate, B., Tignol, J., Bioulac, B., Burbaud, P., & Guehl, D. (2010). The glutamate-based genetic immune hypothesis in obsessive-compulsive disorder: An integrative approach from genes to symptoms. *Neuroscience, 165,* 408–417.

Ruscio, A., Stein, D., Chiu, W., & Kessler, R. (2010). The epidemiology of obsessive-compulsive disorder in the national comorbidity survey replication. *Molecular Psychiatry, 15*(1), 53–63.

Samuels, J., Bienvenu, O., Grados, M., Cullen, B., Riddle, M., Liang, K., . . . Nestadt, G. (2008). Prevalence and correlates of hoarding behavior in a community-based sample. *Behaviour Research and Therapy, 46*(7), 836–844.

Samuels, J., Shugart, Y., Grados, M. A., Willour, V. L., Bienvenu, O., Greenberg, B. D., . . . Nestadt, G. (2007). Significant linkage to compulsive hoarding on chromosome 14 in families with obsessive-compulsive disorder: Results from the OCD collaborative genetics study. *American Journal of Psychiatry, 164*(3), 493–499.

Sarawgi, S., Oglesby, M. E., & Cougle, J. R. (2013). Intolerance of uncertainty and obsessive-compulsive symptom expression. *Journal of Behavior Therapy and Experimental Psychiatry, 44*(4), 456–462.

Saxena, S., Ayers, C. R., Dozier, M. E., & Maidment, K. M. (2015). The UCLA Hoarding Severity Scale: Development and validation. *Journal of Affective Disorders, 175,* 488–493.

Saxena, S., Brody, A. L., Maidment, K. M., & Baxter, L. R. (2007). Paroxetine treatment of compulsive hoarding. *Journal of Psychiatric Research, 41*(6), 481–487.

Schieber, K., Kollei, I., de Zwaan, M., & Martin, A. (2015). Classification of body dysmorphic disorder – what is the advantage of the new DSM-5 criteria? *Journal of Psychosomatic Research, 78*(3), 223–227.

Sharma, E., Thennarasu, K., & Reddy, Y. J. (2014). Long-term outcome of obsessive-compulsive disorder in adults: A meta-analysis. *The Journal of Clinical Psychiatry, 75*(9), 1019–1027.

Shaw, A. M., Hall, K. A., Rosenfield, E., & Timpano, K. R. (2016). Body dysmorphic disorder symptoms and risk for suicide: The role of depression. *Body Image, 19,* 169–174.

Shaw, A. M., Timpano, K. R., Steketee, G., Tolin, D. F., & Frost, R. O. (2015). Hoarding and emotional reactivity: The link between negative emotional reactions and hoarding symptomatology. *Journal of Psychiatric Research, 63,* 84–90.

Shin, M., Park, S., Kim, M., Lee, Y., Ha, T., & Kwon, J. (2004). Deficits of organizational strategy and visual memory in obsessive-compulsive disorder. *Neuropsychology, 18*(4), 665–672.

Shugart, Y., Samuels, J., Willour, V., Grados, M., Greenberg, B., Knowles, J., . . . Nestadt, G. (2006). Genomewide linkage scan for obsessive-compulsive disorder: Evidence for susceptibility loci on chromosomes 3q, 7p, 1q, 15q, and 6q. *Molecular Psychiatry, 11*(8), 763–770.

Shusterman, A., Feld, L., Baer, L., & Keuthen, N. (2009). Affective regulation in trichotillomania: Evidence from a large-scale internet survey. *Behaviour Research & Therapy, 47,* 637–644.

Siev, J., Reese, H. E., Timpano, K. R., & Wilhelm, S. (2012). Assessment and treatment of pathological skin picking. In J. E. Grant & M. N. Potenza (Eds.), *The Oxford handbook of impulse control disorders* (pp. 360–374). New York, NY: Oxford University Press.

Silver, J., & Farrants, J. (2016). 'I once stared at myself in the mirror for eleven hours.' Exploring mirror gazing in participants with body dysmorphic disorder. *Journal of Health Psychology, 21*(11), 2647–2657.

Snorrason, I., Belleau, E. L., & Woods, D. W. (2012). How related are hair pulling disorder (trichotillomania) and skin-picking disorder? A review of evidence for comorbidity, similarities and shared etiology. *Clinical Psychology Review, 32*(7), 618–629.

Snorrason, I., Smári, J., & Olafsson, R. (2010). Emotion regulation in pathological skin picking: Findings from a non-treatment seeking sample. *Journal of Behavior Therapy and Experimental Psychiatry, 41*(3), 238–245.

Snorrason, I., Stein, D., & Woods, D. (2013). Classification of excoriation (skin picking) disorder: Current status and future directions. *Acta Psychiatrica Scandinavica, 128*, 406–407.

Stargell, N. A., Kress, V. E., Paylo, M. J., & Zins, A. (2016). Excoriation disorder: Assessment, diagnosis and treatment. *The Professional Counselor, 6*(1), 50–60.

Stein, D. J., Grant, J. E., Franklin, M. E., Keuthen, N., Lochner, C., Singer, H. S., & Woods, D. W. (2010). Trichotillomania (hair pulling disorder), skin picking disorder, and stereotypic movement disorder: Toward DSM-V. *Depression and Anxiety, 27*(6), 611–626.

Steketee, G., & Barlow, D. H. (2002). Obsessive compulsive disorder. In D. H. Barlow (Ed.), *Anxiety and its disorders: The nature and treatment of anxiety and panic* (2nd ed., pp. 516–550). New York: Guilford Press.

Steketee, G., Frost, R., & Bogart, K. (1996). The Yale-Brown Obsessive Compulsive Scale: Interview versus self-report. *Behaviour Research and Therapy, 34*(8), 675–684.

Steketee, G., Gibson, A., Frost, R. O., Alabiso, J., Arluke, A., & Patronek, G. (2011). Characteristics and antecedents of people who hoard animals: An exploratory comparative interview study. *Review of General Psychology, 15*(2), 114–124.

Steketee, G., Kelley, A. A., Wernick, J. A., Muroff, J., Frost, R. O., & Tolin, D. F. (2015). Familial patterns of hoarding symptoms. *Depression and Anxiety, 32*(10), 728–736.

Stewart, S. E., Mayerfeld, C., Arnold, P. D., Crane, J. R., O'Dushlaine, C., Fagerness, J. A., . . . Mathews, C. A. (2013). Meta-analysis of association between obsessive-compulsive disorder and the 3' region of neuronal glutamate transporter gene SLC1A1. *American Journal of Medical Genetics Part B: Neuropsychiatric Genetics, 162*(4), 367–379.

Stewart, S. E., Rosario, M. C., Baer, L., Carter, A. S., Brown, T. A., Scharf, J. M., . . . Rasmussen, S. (2008). Four-factor structure of obsessive-compulsive disorder symptoms in children, adolescents, and adults. *Journal of the American Academy of Child & Adolescent Psychiatry, 47*(7), 763–772.

Stemberger, R., Thomas, A., Mansueto, C. S., & Carter, J. (2000). Personal toll of trichotillomania: Behavioral and interpersonal sequelae. *Journal of Anxiety Disorders, 14*(1), 97–104.

Storch, E. A., Larson, M., Price, L., Rasmussen, S. A., Murphy, T., & Goodman, W. (2010a). Psychometric analysis of the Yale-Brown Obsessive-Compulsive Scale Second Edition Symptom Checklist. *Journal of Anxiety Disorders, 24*(6), 650–656.

Storch, E. A., Rasmussen, S. A., Price, L. H., Larson, M. J., Murphy, T. K., & Goodman, W. K. (2010b). Development and psychometric evaluation of the Yale–Brown Obsessive-Compulsive Scale-Second Edition. *Psychological Assessment, 22*(2), 223–232.

Subramaniam, M., Soh, P., Vaingankar, J. A., Picco, L., & Chong, S. A. (2013). Quality of life in obsessive-compulsive disorder: Impact of the disorder and of treatment. *CNS Drugs, 27*(5), 367–383.

Summerfeldt, L. J. (2004). Understanding and treating incompleteness in obsessive-compulsive disorder. *Journal of Clinical Psychology, 60*(11), 1155–1168.

Summers, B. J., & Cougle, J. R. (2016). Modifying interpretation biases in body dysmorphic disorder: Evaluation of a brief computerized treatment. *Behaviour Research and Therapy, 87*, 117–127.

Summers, B. J., Matheny, N. L., & Cougle, J. R. (2017). 'Not just right' experiences and incompleteness in body dysmorphic disorder. *Psychiatry Research, 247*, 200–207.

Swami, V., Henry, A., Peacock, N., Roberts-Dunn, A., & Porter, A. (2013). "Mirror, mirror . . . ." A preliminary investigation of skin tone dissatisfaction and its impact among British adults. *Cultural Diversity and Ethnic Minority Psychology, 19*(4), 468–476.

Taqui, A. M., Shaikh, M., Gowani, S. A., Shahid, F., Khan, A., Tayyeb, S. M., . . . Ganatra, H. A. (2008). Body dysmorphic disorder: Gender differences and prevalence in a Pakistani medical student population. *Bio Med Central Psychiatry, 8*(20), 1–10.

Taylor, S. (2011a). Early versus late onset obsessive-compulsive disorder: Evidence for distinct subtypes. *Clinical Psychology Review, 31*(7), 1083–1100.

Taylor, S. (2011b). Etiology of obsessions and compulsions: A meta-analysis and narrative review of twin studies. *Clinical Psychology Review, 31*(8), 1361–1372.

Taylor, S., Coles, M. E., Abramowitz, J. S., Wu, K. D., Olatunji, B. O., Timpano, K. R., . . . Tolin, D. F. (2010). How are dysfunctional beliefs related to obsessive-compulsive symptoms? *Journal of Cognitive Psychotherapy, 24*(3), 165–176.

Taylor, S., McKay, D., Crowe, K. B., Abramowitz, J. S., Conelea, C. A., Calamari, J. E., & Sica, C. (2014). The sense of incompleteness as a motivator of obsessive-compulsive symptoms: An empirical analysis of concepts and correlates. *Behavior Therapy, 45*(2), 254–262.

Teng, E. J., Woods, D. W., Marcks, B. A., & Twohig, M. P. (2004). Body-focused repetitive behaviors: The proximal and distal effects of affective variables on behavioral expression. *Journal of Psychopathology and Behavioral Assessment, 26*(1), 55–64.

Thorsen, A. L., van den Heuvel, O. A., Hansen, B., & Kvale, G. (2015). Neuroimaging of psychotherapy for obsessive-compulsive disorder: A systematic review. *Psychiatry Research, 233*(3), 306–313.

Timpano, K. R., Çek, D., Fu, Z. F., Tang, T., Wang, J. P., & Chasson, G. S. (2015). A consideration of hoarding disorder symptoms in China. *Comprehensive Psychiatry, 57*, 36–45.

Timpano, K. R., Exner, C., Glaesmer, H., Rief, W., Keshaviah, A., Brahler, E., & Wilhelm, S. (2011). The epidemiology of the proposed DSM-5 hoarding disorder: Exploration of the acquisition specifier, associated features, and distress. *Journal of Clinical Psychiatry, 72*(6), 780–786.

Timpano, K. R., Rasmussen, J. L., Exner, C., Rief, W., & Wilhelm, S. (2014). The association between metacognitions, the obsessive compulsive symptom dimensions and hoarding: A focus on specificity. *Journal of Obsessive-Compulsive and Related Disorders, 3*(2), 188–194.

Ting, J. T., & Feng, G. (2008). Glutamatergic synaptic dysfunction and obsessive-compulsive disorder. *Current Chemical Genomics, 2*, 62–75.

Tolin, D. F., Frost, R. O., & Steketee, G. (2010). A brief interview for assessing compulsive hoarding: The Hoarding Rating Scale-Interview. *Psychiatry Research, 178*(1), 147–152.

Tolin, D. F., Frost, R. O., Steketee, G., Gray, K. D., & Fitch, K. E. (2008). The economic and social burden of compulsive hoarding. *Psychiatry Research, 160*(2), 200–211.

Tolin, D. F., Frost, R. O., Steketee, G., & Muroff, J. (2015). Cognitive behavioral therapy for hoarding disorder: A meta-analysis. *Depression and Anxiety, 32*(3), 158–166.

Tolin, D. F., Kiehl, K. A., Worhunsky, P., Book, G. A., & Maltby, N. (2009). An exploratory study of the neural mechanisms of decision making in compulsive hoarding. *Psychological Medicine, 39*, 325–336.

Tolin, D. F., Stevens, M. C., Villavicencio, A. L., Norberg, M. M., Calhoun, V. D., Frost, R. O., . . . Pearlson, G. D. (2012). Neural mechanisms of decision making in hoarding disorder. *Archives of General Psychiatry, 69*(8), 832–841.

Tolin, D. F., Villavicencio, A., Umbach, A., & Kurtz, M. M. (2011). Neuropsychological functioning in hoarding disorder. *Psychiatry Research, 189*, 413–418.

Torres, A. R., Fontenelle, L. F., Shavitt, R. G., Ferrão, Y. A., do Rosário, M. C., Storch, E. A., & Miguel, E. C. (2016). Comorbidity variation in patients with obsessive-compulsive disorder according to symptom dimensions: Results from a large multicentre clinical sample. *Journal of Affective Disorders, 190*, 508–516.

Torresan, R. C., Ramos-Cerqueiraa, A. T., Shavitt, R. G., Conceicao do Rosario, M., de Mathis, M. A., Miguel, E. C., & Torres, A. R. (2013). Symptom dimensions, clinical course and comorbidity in men and women with obsessive-compulsive disorder. *Psychiatry Research, 209*(2), 186–195.

Tükel, R., Polat, A., Genç, A., Bozkurt, O., & Atlı, H. (2004). Gender-related differences among Turkish patients with obsessive-compulsive disorder. *Comprehensive Psychiatry, 45*(5), 362–366.

Twohig, M. P., & Woods, D. W. (2004). A preliminary investigation of acceptance and commitment therapy as a treatment for trichotillomania. *Behavior Therapy, 35*, 803–820.

Ung, J. E., Dozier, M. E., Bratiotis, C., & Ayers, C. R. (2016). An exploratory investigation of animal hoarding symptoms in a sample of adults diagnosed with hoarding disorder. *Journal of Clinical Psychology*, 1–12.

van Grootheest, D. S., Boomsma, D. I., Hettema, J. M., & Kendler, K. S. (2008). Heritability of obsessive-compulsive symptom dimensions. *American Journal of Medical Genetics Part B: Neuropsychiatric Genetics, 147*(4), 473–478.

Veale, D., Anson, M., Miles, S., Pieta, M., Costa, A., & Ellison, N. (2014). Efficacy of cognitive behaviour therapy versus anxiety management for body dysmorphic disorder: A randomised controlled trial. *Psychotherapy and Psychosomatics, 83*(6), 341–353.

Veale, D., Gledhill, L. J., Christodoulou, P., & Hodsoll, J. (2016). Body dysmorphic disorder in different settings: A systematic review and estimated weighted prevalence. *Body Image, 18*, 168–186.

Veale, D., Gournay, K., Dryden, W., Boocock, A., Shah, F., Willson, R., & Walburn, J. (1996). Body dysmorphic disorder: A cognitive behavioural model and pilot randomised controlled trial. *Behaviour Research and Therapy, 34*(9), 717–729.

Vidal-Ribas, P., Stringaris, A., Rück, C., Serlachius, E., Lichtenstein, P., & Mataix-Cols, D. (2015). Are stressful life events causally related to the severity of obsessive-compulsive symptoms? A monozygotic twin difference study. *European Psychiatry, 30*(2), 309–316.

Visser, H. A., van Minnen, A., van Megen, H., Eikelenboom, M., Hoogendoorn, A. W., Kaarsemaker, M., . . . van Oppen, P. (2014). The relationship between adverse childhood experiences and symptom severity, chronicity, and comorbidity in patients with obsessive-compulsive disorder. *The Journal of Clinical Psychiatry, 75*(10), 1034–1039.

Vulink, N. C., Planting, R. S., Figee, M., Booij, J., & Denys, D. (2016). Reduced striatal dopamine D 2/3 receptor availability in body dysmorphic disorder. *European Neuropsychopharmacology, 26*(2), 350–356.

Walsh, K., & McDougle, C. (2001). Trichotillomania. Presentation, etiology, diagnosis and therapy. *American Journal of Clinical Dermatology, 2*(5), 327–333.

Walther, M. R., Flessner, C. A., Conelea, C. A., & Woods, D. W. (2009). The Milwaukee Inventory for the Dimensions of Adult Skin Picking (MIDAS): Initial development and psychometric properties. *Journal of Behavior Therapy and Experimental Psychiatry, 40*(1), 127–135.

Webb, H. J., Zimmer-Gembeck, M. J., & Mastro, S. (2016). Stress exposure and generation: A conjoint longitudinal model of body dysmorphic symptoms, peer acceptance, popularity, and victimization. *Body Image, 18*, 14–18.

Webb, H. J., Zimmer-Gembeck, M. J., Mastro, S., Farrell, L. J., Waters, A. M., & Lavell, C. H. (2015). Young adolescents' body dysmorphic symptoms: Associations with same-and cross-sex peer teasing via appearance-based rejection sensitivity. *Journal of Abnormal Child Psychology, 43*(6), 1161–1173.

Weingarden, H., Marques, L., Fang, A., LeBlanc, N., Buhlmann, U., Phillips, K. A., & Wilhelm, S. (2011). Culturally adapted cognitive behavioral therapy for body dysmorphic disorder: Case examples. *International Journal of Cognitive Therapy, 4*(4), 381–396.

Weingarden, H., & Renshaw, K. D. (2016). Body dysmorphic symptoms, functional impairment, and depression: The role of appearance-based teasing. *The Journal of Psychology, 150*(1), 119–131.

Weingarden, H., Renshaw, K. D., Wilhelm, S., Tangney, J. P., & DiMauro, J. (2016). Anxiety and shame as risk factors for depression, suicidality, and functional impairment in body dysmorphic disorder and obsessive compulsive disorder. *The Journal of Nervous and Mental Disease, 204*(11), 832–839.

Wheaton, M. G., Abramowitz, J. S., Berman, N. C., Riemann, B. C., & Hale, L. R. (2010). The relationship between obsessive beliefs and symptom dimensions in obsessive-compulsive disorder. *Behaviour Research and Therapy, 48*(10), 949–954.

Wheaton, M. G., Abramowitz, J. S., Jacoby, R. J., Zwerling, J., & Rodriguez, C. I. (2016). An investigation of the role of intolerance of uncertainty in hoarding symptoms. *Journal of Affective Disorders, 193*, 208–214.

Wilhelm, S., Phillips, K. A., Didie, E., Buhlmann, U., Greenberg, J. L., Fama, J. M., . . . Steketee, G. (2014). Modular cognitive-behavioral therapy for body dysmorphic disorder: A randomized controlled trial. *Behavior Therapy, 45*(3), 314–327.

Williams, M., Powers, M., Yun, Y., & Foa, E. (2010). Minority participation in randomized controlled trials for obsessive-compulsive disorder. *Journal of Anxiety Disorders, 24*(2), 171–177.

Williams, M., & Viscusi, J. A. (2016). Hoarding disorder and a systematic review of treatment with cognitive behavioral therapy. *Cognitive Behaviour Therapy, 45*(2), 93–110.

Willour, V., Yao Shugart, Y., Samuels, J., Grados, M., Cullen, B., Bienvenu, O., . . . Nestadt, G. (2004). Replication study supports evidence for linkage to 9p24 in obsessive-compulsive disorder. *American Journal of Human Genetics, 75*(3), 508–513.

Wisner, K. L., Peindl, K. S., Gigliotti, T., & Hanusa, B. H. (1999). Obsessions and compulsions in women with postpartum depression. *Journal of Clinical Psychiatry, 60*, 176–189.

Witte, T. K., Didie, E. R., Menard, W., & Phillips, K. A. (2012). The relationship between body dysmorphic disorder behaviors and the acquired capability for suicide. *Suicide and Life-Threatening Behavior, 42*(3), 318–331.

Woods, D. W., Flessner, C. A., Franklin, M. E., Keuthen, N. J., Goodwin, R. D., Stein, D. J., & Walther, M. R. (2006a). The Trichotillomania Impact Project (TIP): Exploring phenomenology, functional impairment, and treatment utilization. *Journal of Clinical Psychiatry, 67*, 1877–1888.

Woods, D. W., Wetterneck, C. T., & Flessner, C. A. (2006b). A controlled evaluation of acceptance and commitment therapy plus habit reversal for trichotillomania. *Behaviour Research & Therapy, 44*, 639–656.

Worden, B. L., Bowe, W. M., & Tolin, D. F. (2017). An open trial of cognitive behavioral therapy with contingency management for hoarding disorder. *Journal of Obsessive-Compulsive and Related Disorders, 12*, 78–86.

Yorulmaz, O., & Dermihan, N. (2015). Cognitive correlates of hoarding symptoms: An exploratory study with a non-Western community sample. *Journal of Obsessive-Compulsive and Related Disorders, 7*, 16–23.

Zambaldi, C. F., Cantilino, A., Montenegro, A. C., Paes, J. A., de Albuquerque, T. C., & Sougey, E. B. (2009). Postpartum obsessive-compulsive disorder: Prevalence and clinical characteristics. *Comprehensive Psychiatry, 50*(6), 503–509.

CHAPTER 11

Trauma and Stressor-Related Disorders: Post-traumatic Stress Disorder, Acute Stress, and Adjustment Disorders

ANOUK L. GRUBAUGH

THE *DIAGNOSTIC AND Statistical Manual of Mental Disorders*, fifth edition (*DSM-5*; American Psychiatric Association [APA], 2013) includes a chapter titled "Trauma and Stress-Related Disorders," which contains post-traumatic stress disorder (PTSD), acute stress disorder (ASD), and the adjustment disorders. Both PTSD and ASD were previously classified under the "Anxiety Disorders" chapter of the *DSM-IV*, whereas adjustment disorders were classified separately as a residual diagnostic category (APA, 1994). PTSD is characterized as a psychiatric disorder resulting from a life-threatening event and requires a history of exposure to a traumatic event (criterion A) that results in a minimum threshold of symptoms across four symptom clusters: intrusion, avoidance, negative alterations in cognitions and mood, and alterations in arousal and reactivity (criteria B–E). Additional criteria concern duration of symptoms (criterion F), functioning (criterion G), and differential diagnosis due to a substance or other co-occurring condition (criterion H).

For criterion A, an event associated with PTSD must include actual or threatened death, serious injury, or sexual violation resulting from one or more of the following scenarios:

- Directly experiencing the traumatic event.
- Witnessing the traumatic event in person.
- Experiencing the actual or threatened death of a close family member or friend that is either violent or accidental.
- Directly experiencing repeated and extreme exposure to aversive details of the event (i.e., the types of exposure frequently encountered by police officers and first responders).

With regard to criteria B–E, an individual must report symptoms from each of the four symptom clusters. *Intrusion symptoms* (criterion B) include repetitive, involuntary, and

---

Adult Psychopathology and Diagnosis, Eighth Edition. Edited by Deborah C. Beidel and B. Christopher Frueh.
© 2018 John Wiley & Sons, Inc. Published 2018 by John Wiley & Sons, Inc.
Companion website: www.wiley.com/go/beidel/psychopathology8e

intrusive memories of the event; traumatic nightmares; dissociative reactions (i.e., flashbacks) along a broad continuum; intense prolonged distress after exposure to reminders of the trauma; and heightened physiological reactivity to reminders of the trauma. *Avoidance symptoms* (criterion C) include avoidance of trauma-related thoughts or feelings; and avoidance of people, places, activities, and so forth that cue distressing thoughts or feelings about the traumatic event. *Negative alterations in cognitions and mood symptoms* (criterion D) include a persistent and distorted sense of self or the world; blame of self or others; persistent trauma-related emotions such as anger, guilt, shame; feeling estranged or detached from others; marked lack of interest in pre-trauma activities; restricted range of affect; and difficulty or inability remembering important parts of the traumatic event. Finally, *alterations in arousal and reactivity symptoms* (criterion E) include irritability and aggressiveness, self-destructive or reckless behaviors, sleep difficulties, hypervigilance, marked startle response, concentration difficulties, and sleep disturbance.

For a diagnosis of PTSD, an individual must exhibit at least one symptom from criterion B, one symptom from criterion C, two symptoms from criterion D, and two symptoms from criterion E, and the symptoms endorsed in categories B through E must be present for 1 month or longer (criterion F). The symptoms must also be accompanied by significant distress or impairment in social, occupational, or other important life domains (criterion G), and symptoms cannot be better explained by another medical or psychiatric illness (criterion H).

The *DSM-5* includes two additional specifiers or associated features that can be added to a PTSD diagnosis: "with dissociated symptoms" and "with delayed expression." The dissociated symptoms specifier includes either *depersonalization* (i.e., experience of being an outside observer to one's experience or feeling detached from oneself) or *derealization* (i.e., experience of unreality or distortion) in response to trauma-related cues. The delayed onset specifier includes an onset of symptoms that can occur immediately after the trauma, but that may not meet full criteria for PTSD until at least 6 months after the trauma.

Some notable changes were made to the diagnostic criteria for PTSD from *DSM-IV* (APA, 1994) to *DSM-5*. In addition to the inclusion of specifiers for depersonalization and derealization, the *DSM-5* provides greater specification regarding what events constitute a traumatic event (i.e., what events constitute a criterion A event); and excludes the need for an individual to have experienced intense fear, helplessness, or horror at the time of the trauma due to its lack of predictive utility. Additionally, the avoidance/numbing symptom cluster found in the *DSM-IV* is divided into two distinct clusters in the *DSM-5*: *avoidance* and *negative alterations in cognitions and mood*. The second of these clusters retain most of the *DSM-IV* numbing symptoms while also including a broader range of emotional reactions. Last, criterion E, alterations in arousal and reactivity, retains the majority of *DSM-IV* arousal symptoms but also includes additional symptoms regarding aggressive or reckless behavior.

A diagnosis of ASD requires an antecedent event (criterion A event) in which the person:

- experienced an event or events that involved a threat of death, actual or threatened serious injury, or actual or threatened physical or sexual violation;
- witnessed an event or events that involved the actual or threatened death, serious injury, or physical or sexual violation of others;
- learned of such harm coming to a close relative or friend;
- experienced repeated or extreme exposure to aversive details of unnatural death, serious injury, or serious assault or sexual violation of others that were not limited to electronic media, television, video games, and so forth.

Individuals must then exhibit a minimum of nine out of 14 symptoms across a broad spectrum of post-traumatic reactions (criterion B). This spectrum includes symptoms related to negative mood, intrusive thoughts, dissociation, avoidance, and anxiety. Aside from a greater emphasis on dissociative symptoms, the other criterion B symptoms for ASD largely mirror the criteria B–E symptoms for PTSD. Additional criteria for ASD concern duration of symptoms (criterion C), functioning (criterion D), and differential diagnosis due to a substance or other co-occurring condition (criterion E).

Changes to the diagnostic criteria of ASD from *DSM-IV* to *DSM-5* include less emphasis on dissociative criteria (i.e., feeling detached from one's body, emotions, or the world). Rather than being required for a diagnosis, as was the case in the *DSM-IV*, dissociative symptoms in *DSM-5* are viewed as one of several possible post-traumatic reactions that an individual may experience. Comparable to changes to the diagnostic criteria for PTSD, the *DSM-5* provides more specification regarding the qualifying traumatic event for ASD; and the criterion requiring a subjective reaction to the trauma (i.e., fear, helplessness, horror) was eliminated.

Adjustment disorders are classified in the *DSM-5* as a range of stress response syndromes. This differs from the *DSM-IV* in which adjustment disorders were part of a residual category for individuals experiencing clinically significant distress that did not fit diagnostic criteria for other psychiatric disorders. Specific *DSM-5* criteria for an adjustment disorder include: (a) the development of emotional or behavioral problems in response to an identifiable stressor occurring within 3 months of exposure to the stressor (this feature is considered the core feature of adjustment disorders; (b) symptoms or behaviors are clinically significant and out of proportion to the severity of the stressor once cultural and contextual factors are taken into account. Additionally, the stress response (a) cannot be better accounted for by another disorder and is not an exacerbation of a pre-existing condition; (b) is not indicative of normal bereavement (if this is the precipitating event); and (c) once the stressor is removed, the symptoms do not persist for more than an additional 6 months. Diagnostic specifiers for the adjustment disorders include depressed mood, anxiety, mixed anxiety and depressed mood, disturbance of conduct, mixed disturbance of emotions and conduct, and unspecified.

Whereas PTSD and ASD emphasize fear and anxiety responses, adjustment disorders can accommodate a broader range of stress reactions. Second, although there is an explicit potential for ASD to predict subsequent impairment (i.e., to predict the development of PTSD), an adjustment disorder is typically viewed as a discrete disorder that has a fairly immediate onset and is relatively short in duration. A third distinction between PTSD, ASD, and adjustment disorders regards the timing of diagnosis. Adjustment disorders can be diagnosed immediately after the event, ASD can be diagnosed from 2 days up to 1 month after the event, and PTSD can be diagnosed from 1 month to several years after the trauma.

CLINICAL FEATURES

The clinical expression of PTSD can vary significantly in terms of severity. Although the diagnosis is categorical, there is evidence of a dimensional structure to PTSD (Broman-Fulks et al., 2006; Forbes, Haslam, Williams, & Creamer, 2005). An implication of this dimensional structure is that milder symptoms of PTSD may cause significant distress and impairment. A recent meta-analytic review found that individuals with subthreshold PTSD experienced worse psychological and behavioral impairment than did individuals without PTSD, but less impairment relative to those with full PTSD

(Brancu et al., 2016). Several of the studies cited also reported an increased risk of suicidality and hopelessness as well as higher health care utilization among those with subthreshold PTSD relative to those without PTSD.

Suicidality is elevated among individuals with PTSD (Bentley et al., 2016; McKinney et al., 2017), and particular types of trauma, such as childhood abuse, military sexual trauma, and combat, may be more strongly associated with suicidality than others (Kimerling et al., 2016; McLean et al., 2017). Additionally, increased risk of suicidality is uniquely associated with PTSD (McKinney et al., 2017). That is, this association is not solely accounted for by the presence of other psychiatric conditions commonly found with PTSD. Of course, an increased risk of suicidality is present in a number of other psychiatric conditions to a comparable or greater degree than that found in PTSD (Nock, Hwang, Sampson, & Kessler, 2010).

The clinical picture of ASD is similar to that of PTSD. Additionally, a review on the topic found that at least half of trauma survivors with ASD subsequently met criteria for PTSD (Bryant, Friedman, Spiegel, Ursano, & Starin, 2011). A more recent evaluation using *DSM-V* criteria found that 43% of individuals with ASD developed PTSD at 3 months and 42% of individuals with ASD developed PTSD at 12 months (Bryant et al., 2015). This study also found that *DSM-V* criteria for ASD were better than *DSM-IV* criteria for predicting PTSD. These findings suggest that individuals with ASD are, in fact, at higher risk of subsequently developing PTSD, and that *DSM-V* may yield more predictive validity for PTSD than earlier versions of the *DSM*.

Due to the conceptualization of adjustment disorders as fairly time-limited, as well as their history as a nebulous catch-all diagnostic category they have not been well studied in the psychiatric literature. The findings that do exist consist largely of non-US samples, focus on children or adolescents, and/or were published in the 1980s and early 1990s. Some commonly agreed-upon emotional signs of adjustment disorder are sadness, hopelessness, lack of enjoyment, crying spells, nervousness, anxiety, worry, trouble sleeping, difficulty concentrating, feeling overwhelmed, and thoughts of suicide. Some behavioral signs of disorders include fighting, reckless behaviors, neglecting important tasks or responsibilities, and avoiding family or friends. Although the presence of an adjustment disorder has been linked to increased suicidal ideation and risk of suicide in a review of the topic (e.g., Appart et al., 2017), they are often considered less severe than other psychiatric disorders. Supporting this view, one study found that adjustment disorders range in severity between no psychiatric disorder and the presence of a mood or anxiety disorder (Fernandez et al., 2012).

DIAGNOSTIC CONSIDERATIONS

Comorbidity is common with PTSD. Large, nationally representative samples have found that PTSD is significantly correlated with the majority of mood and anxiety disorders, as well as alcohol use disorders (National Comorbidity Survey Replication [NCS-R]; Kessler, Chiu, Demler, & Walters, 2005; National Comorbidity Survey [NCS]; Kessler, Sonnega, Bromet, Hughes, & Nelson, 1995). Data from the NCS-R found that approximately half of those who met criteria for PTSD also met criteria for at least three additional psychiatric diagnoses (Kessler et al., 1995). Although there is some degree of symptom overlap between PTSD and other psychiatric diagnoses (e.g., sleep and concentration difficulties and diminished interest in activities are common to both depression and PTSD), this overlap does not account for the high rate of comorbidity (Elhai, Grubaugh, Kashdan, & Frueh, 2008). When comorbid with mood disorders, PTSD is more likely to be primary, whereas it is more likely to be secondary when comorbid with anxiety disorders (Kessler et al., 1995). Importantly, PTSD and comorbid diagnoses may change over time within a given individual. A study of trauma survivors found that half of those who reported PTSD only at 3-month follow-up reported depression only at 12-month follow-up; likewise, half of those with depression only at 3-month follow-up reported PTSD only at 12-month follow-up (O'Donnell, Creamer, & Pattison, 2004).

Due to the lack of epidemiological studies specific to ASD or the adjustment disorders, there are few reliable data on the clinical comorbidity associated with these disorders. Given the conceptual overlap between ASD and PTSD, it is likely that individuals with ASD experience high rates of mood, anxiety, and substance disorders relative to the general population, as well as an increased risk of suicidality. As noted elsewhere, adjustment disorders in the *DSM-IV* served as a residual "catch-all" diagnostic category once other psychiatric conditions were ruled out. As such, they are seldom diagnosed with other psychiatric conditions. With this restriction in mind and the lack of studies using *DSM-V* criteria, adjustment disorders have most often been linked in adult samples to a comorbid diagnosis of a personality disorder or certain personality profiles and increased suicidality (Appart et al., 2017).

EPIDEMIOLOGY

In the general population, the 12-month and lifetime prevalence rates of PTSD are 3.5% and 6.8%, respectively (Kessler, Burglund, Demler, et al., 2005; Kessler et al., 2005). Point prevalence of PTSD among US combat veterans is estimated to be between 2% and 17%, depending on the characteristics of the sample and the measurement strategies that were used (Richardson, Frueh, & Acierno, 2010). There are different conditional probabilities of developing PTSD by trauma type. For example, combat exposure and physical and sexual abuse are more often associated with PTSD than are other types of trauma. Despite this variability, the symptom expression of PTSD remains fairly consistent regardless of the type of trauma experienced.

Little is known about the prevalence of ASD and the adjustment disorders in the general population. Large-scale epidemiological studies, such as the World Health Organization (WHO) Mental Health Epidemiologic Survey, the Epidemiologic Catchment Area study, and the National Comorbidity Survey Replication, did not report on these disorders. Rates of ASD in community and clinical samples range from 7% to as high as 28%, with a mean rate of 13% (Bryant et al., 2011), and rates of ASD are typically higher among victims of violent versus nonviolent traumas. When subsyndromal cases of ASD are included, estimates of the disorder increase from 10% to 32% with a mean rate of 23% (Bryant et al., 2011).

There are few reliable findings on the prevalence of adjustment disorders. This gap in our knowledge is likely influenced by the poor delineation between adjustment disorders and normal or adaptive stress responses, as well as the use of adjustment disorders as a residual "last resort" diagnostic category in the *DSM-IV*. One epidemiological study, the European Outcome of Depression International Network, found a 1% prevalence of adjustment disorder with depressed mood (ODIN; Ayuso-Mateos et al., 2001). More circumscribed samples of adults suggest that adjustment disorders are more common in hospital psychiatric consultation settings (12%; Strain et al., 1998; 18.5%; Foster & Oxman, 1994) and among psychiatric inpatient admissions (Koran et al., 2002). A recent meta-analysis found prevalence rates of 15.4% and 19.4% in palliative care and oncology settings, respectively (Mitchell et al., 2011).

PSYCHOLOGICAL AND BIOLOGICAL ASSESSMENT

There are a number of diagnostic measures for assessing PTSD. The Clinician-Administered PTSD Scale (CAPS; Weathers, Keane, & Davidson, 2001) is the most common interviewer-based instrument for PTSD and has robust psychometric properties (Weathers et al., 2001). The CAPS was revised for *DSM-V* and includes a detailed assessment of each traumatic event, a combined frequency and severity rating for each symptom, and overall distress and impairment ratings. Other interview measures include the PTSD Symptom Scale–Interview (PSS-I for DSM-V; Foa et al., 2016), the Structured Clinical Interview for PTSD (SCID; First et al., 2015), and the Anxiety Disorders Interview Schedule for DSM-V (ADIS-V; Brown & Barlow, 2014).

Self-report questionnaires may also be used to assess PTSD. Commonly used measures include the PTSD Checklist for *DSM-V* (Weathers et al., 2013b), the Posttraumatic Diagnostic Scale for *DSM-V* (PDS; Foa, 2016), and the Life Events Checklist for *DSM-V* (LEC-5; Weathers et al., 2013a). A more extensive list of measures used to assess PTSD is available from the National Center for PTSD (www.ptsd.va.gov). Not all of these measures have been updated to reflect changes in PTSD criteria from *DSM-IV* to *DSM-V*.

Aside from interview and self-report measures of PTSD, several physiological variables have been found to distinguish current PTSD from lifetime PTSD and the absence of PTSD. These include an increased resting heart rate, an increased response to non-trauma-related stressors, and increased heart rate, skin conductance, and diastolic blood pressure in response to trauma cues (Shvil et al., 2013). However, the diagnostic utility of these physiological variables is limited in that they tend to be less accurate than interview-based and self-report assessments in predicting PTSD.

There are few empirically validated diagnostic measures for ASD or adjustment disorders. Measures designed specifically for ASD include the Acute Stress Disorder Interview (ASDI) and the Acute Stress Disorder Scale (ASDS), both developed by the same group of investigators (Bryant, Harvey, Dang, Sackville, & Basten, 1998). The SCID-V contains an optional module for ASD, as well as a section on adjustment disorders that specifies that the diagnosis should not be made if the criteria for any other psychiatric disorders are met (First et al., 2015). With regard to physiological measures, there are some data indicating that individuals who subsequently develop PTSD have higher heart and respiration rates immediately post-trauma as compared with those who do not (Bryant et al., 2011). However, these data are not limited to individuals with ASD, and are likely hampered by the same classification precision of these measures for PTSD.

ETIOLOGICAL CONSIDERATIONS

A number of causal mechanisms have been implicated in the development of PTSD. These include genetic factors, brain structure and neurochemical abnormalities, pre- and post-trauma life events, cognitive appraisals and attentional biases, and sociodemographic variables such as gender.

BEHAVIORAL AND MOLECULAR GENETICS

Increasing data support the role of gene–environment interactions in PTSD (Mehta & Binder 2012). Among Vietnam era veterans, the risk of developing PTSD has been explained by (a) a genetic factor common to alcohol use and PTSD, (b) a genetic factor associated with PTSD but not with alcohol use, and (c) unique environmental effects (Xian et al., 2000). Yet another twin study of Vietnam-era veterans found that the genetic factors that accounted for the relationship between combat exposure and PTSD also accounted for the relationship between combat exposure and alcohol use (McLeod et al., 2001). Genetic factors contributed more to the relationship between combat exposure and PTSD as compared with environmental factors, whereas genetic and environmental factors contributed equally to the relationship between combat exposure and alcohol use. Interestingly, the genetic factors that account for the presence of PTSD may also influence exposure to certain types of traumatic events. Concordance of both interpersonal violence and PTSD is higher among monozygotic twins than among dizygotic twins, whereas other types of trauma (i.e., natural disasters, motor vehicle accidents) are not accounted for by genetic factors (Stein, Jang, Taylor, Vernon, & Livesley, 2002).

In terms of specific genetic markers, the 5-HTTLPR polymorphism has been associated with an increased risk of developing PTSD in specific groups of trauma survivors, including hurricane survivors with a high degree of exposure (Kilpatrick et al., 2007) and individuals reporting a traumatic event in childhood as well as adulthood (Xie et al., 2009). A similar interaction has been reported for variants of polymorphisms in the FK506 binding protein 5 (FKBP5) gene, which is involved in regulating the intracellular effects of cortisol. Individuals with these variants, who reported severe child abuse, were found to be at increased risk for developing PTSD after experiencing a traumatic event in adulthood (Binder et al., 2008; Xie et al., 2009). This gene was under-expressed among survivors of the September 11, 2001 attacks on the World Trade Center who developed PTSD compared with those who did not (Yehuda et al., 2009). There is evidence for candidate genes in other systems (e.g., the dopamine system), but findings have been limited or inconsistent (Broekman, Olff, & Boer, 2007; Koenen, 2007; Nugent, Amstadter, & Koenen, 2008). Genetic research on the trauma and stress-related disorders of the DSM-5 are limited to PTSD.

NEUROANATOMY AND NEUROBIOLOGY

Several brain structures have been implicated in PTSD, including the amygdala, the medial prefrontal cortex, and the hippocampus. First, PTSD is associated with increased activation in the amygdala in response to trauma-related stimuli (Francati, Vermetten, & Bremner, 2007). This increased activity likely represents the neural substrates of exaggerated fear acquisition and expression and may explain the salience of trauma memories in PTSD (Rauch, Shin, & Phelps, 2006). Importantly, hyperactivity in the amygdala is not unique to PTSD; increased activity in response to disorder-related stimuli has also been noted in specific phobia and social anxiety disorder (Etkin & Wagner, 2007; Shin & Liberzon, 2010). Second, PTSD is associated with deficient functioning in the medial prefrontal cortex (Francati et al., 2007; Shin & Liberzon, 2010). This deficiency is thought to underlie inadequate top-down modulation of the amygdala (Rauch et al., 2006). Moreover, the medial prefrontal cortex is thought to regulate processes that are important for habituation and extinction of fear responses, including emotional appraisal (Liberzon & Sripada, 2008). Third, PTSD is associated with abnormalities in the hippocampus. These abnormalities may underlie difficulties contextualizing memories (e.g., recognizing that certain contexts are safe; Liberzon & Spirada, 2008; Rauch et al., 2006). A meta-analysis concluded that increased PTSD severity is associated with decreased volume of the hippocampus, as well as decreased volume in the amygdala and the anterior cingulate, a structure in the medial prefrontal cortex (Karl et al., 2006).

Decreased hippocampal volume likely represents a risk factor for developing PTSD, as opposed to a neurobiological effect of trauma (McNally, 2003). Consistent with this, hippocampal volume does not change over time following trauma exposure (Bonne et al., 2001). Moreover, a study of veteran twin pairs discordant for combat exposure and PTSD found that PTSD severity among affected twins was negatively correlated with not only their own hippocampal volume but also that of their nonexposed twin (Gilbertson et al., 2002).

The neurochemical underpinnings of PTSD likely involve catecholamines (epinephrine, norepinephrine, and dopamine) and cortisol, a hormone involved in the neuro-endocrine response to stress, as well as a variety of other neurotransmitters (Yehuda, 2006). PTSD may also be characterized by disturbance of the hypothalamic–pituitary–adrenal axis, arising primarily from hypersensitivity of glucocorticoid (i.e., cortisol) receptors (Yehuda et al., 2009). This may represent a risk factor, although the research findings are not yet clearly integrated into a cohesive model.

There are few data specifically reporting on neurobiological models of ASD or adjustment disorders. When viewed as a stress reaction conceptually related to PTSD, ASD in particular may also involve a dysregulation of the neurotransmitter and neuroendocrine systems implicated in PTSD. In addition, ASD may quite possibly involve deficits in certain brain regions such as the hippocampus, which are implicated as a risk factor for PTSD.

LEARNING, MODELING, AND LIFE EVENTS

Clearly, traumatic life events contribute to PTSD. Less clear is whether trauma exposure and PTSD share a dose–response relationship in which frequency and/or intensity of trauma correspond with symptom severity. Rates of PTSD vary based on the type of traumatic event, with assaultive violence and sexual assault being associated with the highest rates (Breslau et al., 1998; Norris, 1992). Furthermore, rates of PTSD among veterans roughly correspond to degree of combat exposure (Dohrenwend et al., 2006). However, PTSD severity has not been found to correspond to severity of exposure in other trauma samples such as motor vehicle accident survivors and political prisoners (Başoğlu et al., 1994; Schnyder, Moergeli, Klaghofer, & Buddeberg, 2001). Importantly, a dose–response relationship between trauma exposure and PTSD may be nonlinear. That is, after a certain degree of trauma exposure, symptom exacerbation may reach a plateau (McNally, 2003).

Post-traumatic stress disorder may also be related to degree of trauma exposure prior to the traumatic event. Exposure to childhood physical or sexual abuse is associated with an increased risk of future trauma exposure, as well as the development of PTSD in response to those subsequent traumas (Koenen, Moffitt, Poulton, Martin, & Caspi, 2007). In addition to previous childhood abuse or neglect, meta-analyses on the topic have identified other pre-trauma risk factors for PTSD, such as level of prior psychological adjustment and/or the presence of a previous personal or family history of psychiatric illness. Post-trauma risk factors include a lack of social support and additional life stressors (Brewin, Andrews, & Valentine, 2000; Keane, Marshall, & Taft, 2006; Ozer, Best, Lipsey, & Weiss, 2008).

Few studies have examined risk factors specifically in relation to the development of ASD or adjustment disorders. However, given the conceptual overlap between PTSD and ASD, they likely share similar pre- and post-trauma risk factors. Supporting this line of reasoning, one study found that individuals with a previous history of trauma exposure or PTSD and those with more psychiatric dysfunction were at greater risk for developing ASD when experiencing a new trauma (Barton, Blanchard, & Hickling, 1996).

Cognitive Influences

Cognitive influences of PTSD include maladaptive beliefs that one holds about the meaning of the traumatic event that is experienced (e.g., self-blame, guilt). Consistent with this view, cognitive processing therapy (CPT) emphasizes the importance of identifying and revising maladaptive beliefs about the trauma and promoting a more balanced integration of the traumatic event (Resick & Schnicke, 1993). Other possible cognitive mechanisms of PTSD include attentional or memory related biases toward threat-related stimuli or trauma-related material, which may specifically reflect a cognitive vulnerability to developing PTSD (Brewin & Homes, 2003; Fani et al., 2012; Weber, 2008). PTSD may also be influenced by perceived seriousness of threat, which in turn may be influenced by cognitive variables such as poor contextualization of autobiographical memory (Ehlers & Clark, 2000). Although not specific to ASD, a number of studies have found that maladaptive or negative appraisals and beliefs predict the subsequent development of PTSD (Bryant, Salmon, Sinclair, & Davidson, 2007; Mayou, Bryant, & Ehlers, 2001).

Sex and Racial-Ethnic Considerations

Epidemiological surveys suggest that women are more likely to report sexual assault or child molestation and men are more likely to report physical assault, combat exposure, or being threatened or attacked with a weapon (Norris, 1992). Prevalence studies of PTSD further indicate that women are more likely to develop PTSD relative to men (at a 2:1 ratio) given exposure to a traumatic event (Norris et al., 1992). That is, women have a higher conditional risk of developing PTSD relative to men. Traumas associated with ASD are similar to those for PTSD. However, systematic efforts are needed to confirm whether gender differences in rates of ASD are comparable to those associated with PTSD.

Findings regarding the interplay among trauma exposure, PTSD, and race/ethnicity are often mixed (Pole, Gone, & Kulkarni, 2008). Overall, however, most studies have found comparable rates of PTSD between African Americans and Caucasians. The few studies that have found significant racial/ethnic differences report higher base rates of PTSD among African Americans relative to Caucasians that largely disappear once severity of trauma exposure is controlled for. The most consistent findings regarding PTSD and race/ethnicity pertain to Hispanics. Relative to non-Hispanic Caucasians, Hispanics often have higher rates of PTSD in both community and clinical samples (Pole et al., 2008). Cultural context may influence some aspects of PTSD, but the disorder generally presents as a coherent group of symptoms across cultures. Parallel efforts to study the relationship between race/ethnicity and both ASD and adjustment disorders are lacking.

COURSE, PROGNOSIS, AND TREATMENT

According to the *DSM-5*, symptoms consistent with a diagnosis of PTSD may begin immediately following or long after a traumatic event, and there is sufficient evidence that PTSD can persist for several years after the index trauma. The diagnostic specifier "with delayed expression" allows for a diagnosis of PTSD when all of the criteria for the disorder are not met for 6 months or longer after the traumatic event. A review on the occurrence of delayed-onset PTSD revealed an average prevalence of 5.6% (Utzon-Frank et al., 2014). The proportion of delayed-onset PTSD cases relative to all PTSD cases was 24.5%, with significant variation in rates across studies. It was further noted that delayed-onset PTSD was almost always preceded by subthreshold PTSD symptoms. Data show that delayed-onset PTSD in the absence of prior symptoms is exceedingly rare (Andrews, Brewin, Philpott, & Stewart, 2007; Frueh, Grubaugh, Yeager, & Magruder, 2009). These and other findings suggest that delayed-onset PTSD is likely due to an exacerbation of prior symptoms over time.

Post-traumatic stress disorder symptoms can persist over time. Findings from the National Vietnam Veterans Longitudinal Study found that 4.5% of male veterans met criteria for *DSM-V* PTSD 40 years after the Vietnam War (Marmar et al., 2015). In a national sample of Vietnam-era male twins, 3.65% of theatre veterans retained their PTSD diagnosis 20 years later (Magruder et al., 2016). Studies using civilian samples likewise suggest that PTSD can be a chronic condition but report much shorter time frames from the baseline to follow-up.

Parallel with its theoretical underpinnings, clinical practice guidelines generally recommend cognitive behavioral interventions as the most effective treatment approach for PTSD (DVA, 2010; Foa, Keane, & Friedman, 2009; IOM, 2007; NICE, 2005). Treatments that fall under this umbrella typically include elements of psychoeducation, stress reduction, exposure to trauma-related cues and memories, and cognitive restructuring, with the latter two components being considered the "active ingredients" for PTSD symptom reduction.

Although there are a number of interventions that emphasize exposure and/or cognitive restructuring, the empirical data weigh heavily in support of two specific manualized treatments for adults with PTSD: prolonged exposure (PE—an exposure-based intervention; Foa, Hembree, & Rothbaum, 2007) and CPT (predominantly a cognitive restructuring intervention that includes elements of exposure; Resick & Schnicke, 1993). The focus in PE is on habituation to graded fear exposures, whereas the focus in CPT is on modification of maladaptive trauma-related beliefs (e.g., denial or self-blame). However, CPT often includes exposure exercises, and PE often includes elements of cognitive restructuring. Adding cognitive restructuring to PE does not appear to increase its efficacy (Foa et al., 2005), nor does adding writing exposure exercises to CPT (Resick et al., 2008), indicating that the therapies are efficacious in both their combined and component forms.

Reviews on the topic suggest the average patient receiving PE or CPT fares better than 86–90% of patients who are assigned to a control group (i.e., do not receive what is considered an active treatment) (Bradley, Greene, Russ, Dutra, & Westen, 2005; Powers, Halpern, Ferenschak, Gillihan, & Foa, 2010). Despite the overall efficacy of PTSD interventions, 18–35% of individuals who complete treatment retain the diagnosis at follow-up, with civilians showing dramatically greater improvement than military veterans (Bradley et al., 2005). Disability incentives to remain ill have been posited as one possible reason why veterans evidence less clinical improvement than civilians (Frueh, Grubaugh, Elhai, & Buckley, 2007), as have other characteristics unique to veteran populations (e.g., nature of combat trauma). Additionally, treatment dropout rates hover around 30% across clinical populations (Cloitre, 2009). Recently, multi-component interventions combining exposure therapy and other cognitive-behavioral interventions (e.g., behavioral activation, anger management, social skills) have been demonstrated to be effective in treating the range of symptoms associated with the PTSD syndrome (e.g., Acierno et al., 2016; Beidel, Frueh, Uhde, Wong, & Mentrikoski, 2011). Multicomponent interventions have also been shown to have special promise when delivered in an intensive outpatient program format (Beidel, Frueh, Neer, & Lejuez, 2017).

Reflecting neurobiological models of the disorder, pharmacological treatments for PTSD act primarily on the neurotransmitters associated with fear and anxiety, which include serotonin, norepinephrine, GABA, and dopamine. Selective serotonin reuptake inhibitors (SSRIs) are generally considered the pharmacological treatment of choice for PTSD (DVA, 2010; Hoskins et al., 2015; Stein, Ipser, & McAnda, 2009), and this class of drugs include the only two medications that are currently FDA-approved for the treatment of PTSD—sertraline (Zoloft) and paroxetine (Paxil). Although there is some support for the efficacy of psychotropic medications for the treatment of PTSD, not all practice guidelines support their use. For example, after a review of 37 PTSD pharmaco-therapy trials, the Institute of Medicine determined that there was insufficient evidence in support of any psychotropic medications for PTSD including SSRIs (IOM, 2007). A more recent review found that SSRIs were superior to placebo in reducing PTSD symptoms but the effect size was small (Hoskins et al., 2015). Additionally, psychotropic medications do not typically alleviate all the symptoms associated with this disorder and it is generally recommended that patients take medications in conjunction with a psychotherapy specifically developed to treat PTSD, particularly with more complex symptom presentations.

Brief cognitive behavioral interventions immediately post-trauma have yielded prom-ising results in terms of preventing the subsequent development of PTSD among those with ASD (Bryant, Moulds, Nixon, & Basten, 2003; Echeburua, deCorral, Sarasua, & Zubizarreta, 1996; Gidron et al., 2001). These interventions generally consist of education about symptoms, relaxation training, exposure exercises, and cognitive therapy. In contrast, psychological debriefing interventions, which were sometimes used in the aftermath of traumatic events like natural disasters, have failed to demonstrate sufficient efficacy and are generally contraindicated with more severe traumas or post-traumatic reactions (Forneris et al., 2013; North & Pfefferbaum, 2013).

Due to the acute nature of most adjustment disorders, they often do not require treatment, or require limited treatment. Additionally, however, the high degree of variability in the symptom expression of adjustment disorders has likely complicated the development of standardized treatment approaches. Consistent with this, systematic investigations on the efficacy of specific interventions for adjustment disorders are limited to two randomized controlled trials, one targeting adjustment disorder with depressed mood secondary to myocardial infarction (Gonzales-Jaimes & Turnbull-Plaza, 2003) and another targeting adjustment disorder resulting in occupational dysfunction (van der Klink, Blonk, Schene, & van Dijk, 2003). Both of these interventions were tailored for a specific target population and anticipated deficits, with the first demonstrating efficacy of the intervention in terms of symptom reduction and the latter in terms of decreasing absenteeism but not symptom reduction. Pharmacotherapy trials for the treatment of adjustment disorders are likewise few in number and have not established the superiority of antidepressants versus placebo for symptom reduction (Casey, 2009; Casey et al., 2013). Less systematic efforts and clinical wisdom would suggest that psychosocial treatments for adjustment disorders should be relatively brief in duration, and focus on decreasing or removing the stressor as well as improving the patient's adaptation and coping skills.

CASE STUDIES

POST-TRAUMATIC STRESS DISORDER

Paul is a 26-year-old African American Iraq War veteran who presented to his local VA primary care clinic due to feelings of anxiety. Paul served two tours of duty in Iraq and witnessed multiple roadside bombings in which members of his unit were injured and killed. His final tour ended 2 years ago. He reports symptoms that began shortly after the first roadside bombing he witnessed while overseas, and an increase in the severity and frequency of these symptoms since his return to the US. He experiences frequent nightmares and intrusive memories about Iraq, including nightmares and unwanted thoughts related to a bombing in which he witnessed the death of two of his comrades with whom he was particularly close. Paul questions in his mind why he lived while his comrades died and feels certain that he should have been able to prevent what happened. He avoids internal and external reminders of the event, which include thinking about the bombings and other graphic scenes from his service, as well as driving. Last, he is experiencing marked irritability, anger, and hypervigilance, especially while driving. Paul often catches himself gripping the steering wheel of his car, anticipating an improvised explosive device. Because of his symptoms, Paul's relationships have suffered, most notably his relationship with his girlfriend of several years, who has made a number of comments to him about him having changed since coming back from Iraq and not being the same "easygoing" guy she met. Paul is enrolled in college under the GI Bill and is having difficulty studying due to problems concentrating and a persistent lack of sleep. He fears he may have to withdraw from the semester.

Paul's experiences in Iraq are consistent with the definition of a traumatic event, and his symptoms reflect chronic PTSD with acute onset.

ADJUSTMENT DISORDER

Susan is a 42-year-old Caucasian woman who presented to her primary care physician for her annual appointment. During the course of the appointment, Susan admits to her physician that she has been struggling emotionally since the end of her marriage (2 months prior) and the loss of her job (9 months prior). After both of these events, but to a much greater extent since her son moved out of the home, Susan describes feeling a mixture of depression and sadness about her failed marriage and lack of new job prospects, as well as general feelings of anxiety and fear about her future. She reports feeling at a loss as to how to manage her time and feels overwhelming sadness at being 45 and alone, with few friends or family to rely on. She acknowledges calling in sick from work a few times a month for the past few months and then ruminating about the potential consequences of having not gone in to work. She reports watching television several hours a day followed by periods of anxious and somewhat obsessive house-cleaning. She also reports having crying spells "over just about anything" and is tearful while discussing her symptoms during her primary care appointment.

Susan's clinical presentation is consistent with a diagnosis of adjustment disorder with mixed anxiety and depressed mood.

SUMMARY

Post-traumatic stress disorder, ASD, and adjustment disorders are classified in the *DSM-5* as trauma- and stress-related disorders that were precipitated by a stressful or traumatic event. The value of classifying these disorders together will enable clinicians to better differentiate normal and mild stress reactions from more severe and pathological stress reactions. It also more clearly highlights the temporal and symptom requirement distinctions between PTSD, ASD, and adjustment disorders. Whereas PTSD and ASD emphasize fear and anxiety responses, adjustment disorder symptoms can accommodate a broader range of stress reactions. Second, although there is an explicit potential for ASD to predict subsequent impairment (i.e., to predict PTSD), an adjustment disorder is typically viewed as a discrete disorder that has a fairly immediate and time-limited symptom duration. A third distinction between PTSD, ASD, and adjustment disorders regards the timing of diagnosis. Adjustment disorders can be diagnosed immediately after the event, ASD can be diagnosed from 2 days up to 1 month after the event, and PTSD can be diagnosed from 1 month to several years after the trauma.

In conclusion, based on being linked to a clear precipitating stressful or traumatic event, PTSD, ASD, and adjustment disorders are viewed as stress reactions along a continuum that are differentiated by the severity of the initial stressor, an anxiety-focused or broader set of symptoms in reaction to the event, and the onset and duration of the symptoms. PTSD and ASD share many of the same symptoms, with ASD being limited in duration to 1 month, and in some but not all cases predicting the subsequent development of PTSD. The relationship among adjustment disorders, PTSD, and ASD is poorly understood as there has been little systematic study on the topic. The placement of adjustment disorders in the same chapter as PTSD and ASD in the *DSM-5* will likely prompt a better understanding of the unique and overlapping features of this disorder in relation to PTSD and ASD. Future studies will likely shed light on the similarities and differences between these three disorders with regard to prevalence, diagnosis, clinical presentation, correlates, and treatment.

REFERENCES

Acierno, R., Gros, D. F., Ruggiero, K. J., Hernandez-Tejada, M. B. A., Knapp, R. G., Lejuez, C. W., . . . Tuerk, P. W. (2016). Behavioral activation and therapeutic exposure for post-traumatic stress disorder: A non-inferiority trial of treatment delivered in person vs home-based telehealth. *Depression & Anxiety, 33*, 415–423.

American Psychiatric Association. (1994). *Diagnostic and statistical manual of mental disorders* (4th ed.). Washington, DC: Author.

American Psychiatric Association. (2013). *Diagnostic and statistical manual of mental disorders* (5th ed.). Arlington, VA: American Psychiatric Publishing.

Andrews, B., Brewin, C. R., Philpott, R., & Stewart, L. (2007). Delayed-onset posttraumatic stress disorder: A systematic review of the evidence. *American Journal of Psychiatry, 164*, 1319–1326.

Appart, A., Lange, A. K., Sievert, I., Bihain, F., & Tordeurs, D. (2017). Adjustment disorder and DSM-V: A review. *Encephale, 43*, 41–46.

Ayuso-Mateos, J. L., Vazquez-Barquero, J. L., Dowrick, C., Lehtinen, V., Dalgard, O. S., Casey, P., . . . ODIN Group. (2001). Depressive disorders in Europe: Prevalence figures from the ODIN study. *British Journal of Psychiatry, 179*, 308–316.

Barton, K. A., Blanchard, E. B., & Hickling, E. J. (1996). Antecedents and consequences of acute stress disorder among motor vehicle accident victims. *Behaviour Research and Therapy, 34*, 805–813.

Başoğlu, M., Paker, M., Paker, O., Özmen, E., Marks, I., Incesu, D., . . . Sarımurat, N. (1994). Psychological effects of torture: A comparison of tortured with non-tortured political activists in Turkey. *American Journal of Psychiatry, 151*, 76–81.

Beidel, D. C., Frueh, B. C., Neer, S., & Lejuez, C. (2017). The efficacy of Trauma Management Therapy: A controlled pilot investigation of a three-week intensive outpatient program for combat-related PTSD. *Journal of Anxiety Disorders, 50,* 23–32.

Beidel, D. C., Frueh, B. C., Uhde, T., Wong, N., & Mentrikoski, J. (2011). Multicomponent behavioral treatment for chronic combat-related posttraumatic stress disorder: A randomized controlled trial. *Journal of Anxiety Disorders, 25,* 224–231.

Bentley, K. H., Franklin, J. C., Ribeiro, J. D., Kleiman, E. M., Fox, K. R., & Nock, M. K. (2016). Anxiety and its disorders as risk factors for suicidal thoughts and behaviors: A meta-analytic review. *Clinical Psychology Review, 43,* 30–46.

Binder, E. B., Bradley, R. G., Liu, W., Epstein, M. P., Deveau, T. C., Mercer, K. B., . . . Ressler, K. J. (2008). Association of FKBP5 polymorphisms and childhood abuse with risk of posttraumatic stress disorder symptoms in adults. *Journal of the American Medical Association, 299,* 1291–1305.

Bonne, O., Brandes, D., Gilboa, A., Gomori, J. M., Shenton, M. E., Pitman, R. K., & Shalev, A. Y. (2001). Longitudinal MRI study of hippocampal volume in trauma survivors with PTSD. *American Journal of Psychiatry, 158,* 1248–1251.

Bradley, R., Greene, J., Russ, E., Dutra, L., & Westen, D. (2005). A multidimensional meta- analysis of psychotherapy for PTSD. *American Journal of Psychiatry, 162,* 214–227.

Brancu, M., Mann-Wrobel, M., Beckham, J. C., Wagner, H. R., Elliot, A., Robbins, A. T., . . . Runnals, J. J. (2016). Subthreshold posttraumatic stress disorder: a meta-analytic review of DSM-IV prevalence and a proposed DSM-5 approach to measurement. *Psychological Trauma, 8,* 222–232.

Brewin, C. R., Andrews, B., & Valentine, J. D. (2000). Meta-analysis of risk factors for post-traumatic stress disorder in trauma-exposed adults. *Journal of Consulting and Clinical Psychology, 68,* 748–766.

Brewin, C. R., & Holmes, E. A. (2003). Psychological theories of posttraumatic stress disorder. *Clinical Psychology Review, 23,* 339–376.

Breslau, N., Kessler, R. C., Chilcoat, H. D., Schultz, L. R., Davis, G. C., & Andreski, P. (1998). Trauma and posttraumatic stress disorder in the community: The 1996 Detroit Area Survey of Trauma. *Archives of General Psychiatry, 55,* 626–632.

Broekman, B. F. P., Olff, M., & Boer, F. (2007). The genetic background to PTSD. *Neuroscience and Biobehavioral Reviews, 31,* 348–362.

Broman-Fulks, J. J., Ruggiero, K. J., Green, B. A., Kilpatrick, D. G., Danielson, C. K., Resnick, H. S., & Saunders, B. E. (2006). Taxometric investigation of PTSD: Data from two nationally representative samples. *Behavior Therapy, 37,* 364–380.

Brown, T. A., & Barlow, D. H. (2014). Anxiety and Related Disorders Interview Schedule for DSM-IV (ADIS-5)-Adult and Lifetime Version Kits. OUP.

Bryant, R. A., Creamer, M., O'Donnell, M., Silove, D., McFarlane A. C., & Forbes, D. (2015). A comparison of the capacity of DSM-IV and DSM-V acute stress disorder definitions to predict posttraumatic stress disorder and related disorders. *Journal of Clinical Psychiatry, 76,* 391–397.

Bryant, R. A., Friedman, M. J., Speigel, D., Ursano, R., & Starin, J. (2011). A review of acute stress disorder in DSM-V. *Depression and Anxiety, 28,* 802–817.

Bryant, R. A., Harvey, A. G., Dang, S. T., Sackville, T., & Basten, C. (1998). Treatment of acute stress disorder: A comparison of cognitive behavioral therapy and supportive counseling. *International Journal of Psychophysiology, 20,* 209–213.

Bryant, R. A., Moulds, M. L., Nixon, R. V., & Basten, C. (2003). Cognitive behavioral therapy of acute stress disorder: A four year follow-up study. *Behavior Research & Therapy, 41,* 489–494.

Bryant, R. A., Salmon, K., Sinclair, E., & Davidson, P. A. (2007). A prospective study of appraisals in childhood posttraumatic stress disorder. *Behavior Research & Therapy, 45,* 2502–2507.

Casey, P. (2009). Adjustment disorder. *CNS Drugs, 23,* 927–938.

Casey, P., Pillay, D., Wilson, L., Maercker, A., Rice, A., & Kelly, B. (2013). Pharmacological interventions for adjustment disorders in adults. *Cochrane Database of Systematic Reviews, 2013*(6), CD010530.

Cloitre, M. (2009). Effective psychotherapies for posttraumatic stress disorder: A review and critique. *CNS Spectrums, 14* (Suppl. 1), 32–43.

Department of Veterans Administration. (2010). *Programs for veterans with PTSD* (VHA Handbook no. 1160.03).

Dohrenwend, B. P., Turner, J. B., Turse, N. A., Adams, B. G., Koenen, K. C., & Marshall, R. (2006). The psychological risks of Vietnam for U. S. veterans: A revisit with new data and methods. *Science, 313*, 979–982.

Echeburua, E., deCorral, P., Sarasua, B., & Zubizarreta, I. (1996). Treatment of acute post-traumatic stress disorder in rape victims: An experimental study. *Journal of Anxiety Disorders, 10*, 185–199.

Ehlers, A., & Clark, D. M. (2000). A cognitive model of posttraumatic stress disorder. *Behaviour Research and Therapy, 38*, 319–345.

Elhai, J. D., Grubaugh, A. L., Kashdan, T. B., & Frueh, B. C. (2008). Empirical examination of a proposed refinement to DSM-IV posttraumatic stress disorder symptom criteria using the National Comorbidity Survey Replication data. *Journal of Clinical Psychiatry, 69*, 597–602.

Etkin, A. & Wagner, T. D. (2007). Functional neuroimaging of anxiety: A meta-analysis of emotional processing in PTSD, social anxiety disorder, and specific phobia. *American Journal of Psychiatry, 164*, 1476–1488.

Fani, N., Jovanovic, T., Ely, T. D., Bradley, B., Gutman, D. Tone, E. B., . . . Ressler, K. J. (2012). Neural correlates of attention bias to threat in post-traumatic stress disorder. *Biological Psychology, 90*, 134–142.

Fernandez A., Medive, J. M., Salvador-Carulla, L., Rubio-Valera, M., Luciano, J. V., Pinto-Meza, A., . . . DASMAP investigators. (2012). Adjustment disorders in primary care: Prevalence, recognition, and use of services. *British Journal of Psychiatry, 201*, 137–142.

First, M. B., Williams. J. B. W., Karg, R. S., & Spitzer, R. L. (2015). *Structured Clinical Interview for DSM-5 Disorders, Clinician Version (SCID-5-CV)*. American Psychiatric Association: Arlington, VA.

Foa, E. B., Hembree, E. A., Cahill, S. P. Rauch, S. A., Riggs, D. S., Feeny, N. C., & Yadin, E. (2005). *Journal of Consulting & Clinical Psychology, 73*, 953–964.

Foa, E. B., Hembree, E. A., & Rothbaum, B. O. (2007). *Prolonged exposure therapy for PTSD: Therapist guide*. New York, NY: Oxford University Press.

Foa, E. B., Keane, T. M., & Friedman, M. J. (2009). *Effective treatments for PTSD: Practice guidelines from the International Society for Traumatic Stress Studies (1–388)*. New York, NY: Guilford Press.

Foa, E. B., McLean, C. P., Zang, Y., Zhong, J., Powers, M. B., Kauffman, B. Y., . . . Knowles, K. (2016). Psychometric properties of the Posttraumatic Stress Disorder Symptom Scale for DSM-V (PSSI-5). *Psychological Assessment, 28*, 1159–1165.

Foa, E. B., McLean, C. P., Zang, Y., Zhong, J., Powers, M. B., Kauffman, B. Y., . . . Knowles, K. (2016). Psychometric properties of the Posttraumatic Stress Disorder Diagnostic Scale for DSM-V (PDS-5). *Psychological Assessment, 28*, 1166–1171.

Foa, E. B., Riggs, D. S., Dancu, C. V., & Rothbaum, B. O. (1993). Reliability and validity of a brief instrument for assessing post-traumatic stress disorder. *Journal of Traumatic Stress, 6*, 459–473.

Forbes, D., Haslam, N., Williams, B. J., & Creamer, M. (2005). Testing the latent structure of posttraumatic stress disorder: A taxometric study of combat veterans. *Journal of Traumatic Stress, 18*, 647–656.

Forneris, C. A., Gartlehner, G., Brownley, K. A., Gaynes, B. N., Sonis, J., Coker-Schwimmer, E., . . . Lohr, K. N. (2013). Interventions to prevent post-traumatic stress disorder: A systematic review. *American Journal of Preventive Medicine, 44*, 635–650.

Foster, P., & Oxman, T. A. (1994). Descriptive study of adjustment disorder diagnosis in general hospital patients. *Irish Journal of Psychological Medicine, 11*, 153–157.

Francati, V., Vermetten, E., & Bremner, J. D. (2007). Functional neuroimaging studies in posttraumatic stress disorder: Review of current methods and findings. *Depression and Anxiety, 24*, 202–218.

Frueh, B. C., Grubaugh, A. L., Elhai, J. D., & Buckley, T. C. (2007). U. S. Department of Veterans Affairs disability policies for PTSD: Administrative trends and implications for treatment, rehabilitation, and research. *American Journal of Public Health, 97*, 2143–2145.

Frueh, B. C., Grubaugh, A. L., Yeager, D. E., & Magruder, K. M. (2009). Delayed-onset posttraumatic stress disorder among veterans in primary care clinics. *British Journal of Psychiatry, 194*, 515–520.

Gidron, Y., Gal, R., Freedman, S. A., Twiser, I., Lauden, A., Snir, Y., & Benjamin, J. (2001). Translating research findings to PTSD prevention: Results of a randomized-controlled pilot study. *Journal of Traumatic Stress, 14*, 773–780.

Gilbertson, M. W., Shenton, M. E., Ciszewski, A., Kasai, K., Lasko, N. B., Orr, S. P., & Pitman, R. K. (2002). Smaller hippocampal volume predicts pathologic vulnerability to psychological trauma. *Nature Neuroscience, 5*, 1242–1247.

Gonzales-Jaimes, E. I., & Turnbull-Plaza, B. (2003). Selection of psychotherapeutic treatment for adjustment disorder with depressive mood due to acute myocardial infarction. *Archives of Medical Research, 34*, 298–304.

Hoskins, M., Pearce, J., Bethell, A., Dankova, L., Barbui, C., Tol, W. A., . . . Bisson, J. I. (2015). Pharmacotherapy for post-traumatic stress disorder: Systematic review and meta-analysis. *British of Journal Psychiatry, 206*, 93–100.

Institute of Medicine & the National Research Council. (2007). *Treatment of PTSD: An assessment of the evidence*. Washington, DC: National Academies Press.

Karl, A., Schaefer, M., Malta, L. S., Dörfel, D., Rohleder, N., & Werner, A. (2006). A meta-analysis of structural brain abnormalities in PTSD. *Neuroscience and Biobehavioral Reviews, 30*, 1004–1031.

Keane, T. M., Marshall, A. D., & Taft, C. T. (2006). Posttraumatic stress disorder: Etiology, epidemiology, and treatment outcome. *Annual Review Clinical Psychology, 2*, 161–97.

Kessler, R. C., Berglund, P., Demler, O., Jin, R., Merikangas, K. R., & Walters, E. E. (2005). Lifetime prevalence and age-of-onset distributions of *DSM-IV* disorders in the National Survey Replication. *Archives of General Psychiatry, 62*, 593–602.

Kessler, R. C., Chiu, W. T., Demler, O., & Walters, E. E. (2005). Prevalence, severity, and comorbidity of 12-month *DSM-IV* disorders in the National Comorbidity Survey Replication. *Archives of General Psychiatry, 62*, 617–627.

Kessler, R. C., Sonnega, A., Bromet, E., Hughes, M., & Nelson, C. B. (1995). Posttraumatic stress disorder in the National Comorbidity Survey. *Archives of General Psychiatry, 52*, 1048–1060.

Kilpatrick, D. G., Koenen, K. C., Ruggiero, K. J., Acerino, R., Galea, S., Resnick, R., . . . Gelernter, J. (2007). The serotonin transporter genotype and social support and moderation of posttraumatic stress disorder and depression in hurricane-exposed adults. *American Journal of Psychiatry, 164*, 1693–1699.

Kimerling, R., Makin-Byrd, K., Louzon, S., Ignacio, R. V., & McCarthy, J. F. (2016). Military sexual trauma and suicide mortality. *American Journal of Preventive Medicine, 50*, 684–691.

Koenen, K. C. (2007). Genetics of posttraumatic stress disorder: Review and recommendations for future studies. *Journal of Traumatic Stress, 20*, 737–750.

Koenen, K. C., Moffitt, T. E., Poulton, R., Martin, J., & Caspi, A. (2007). Early childhood factors associated with the development of post-traumatic stress disorder: Results from a longitudinal birth cohort. *Psychological Medicine, 37*, 181–192.

Koran, I. M., Sheline, Y., Imai, K., Kelsey, T. G., Freedland, K. E., & Mathews, J. (2002). Medical disorders among patients admitted to a public-sector psychiatric inpatient unit. *Psychiatric Services, 53*, 1623–1625.

Liberzon, I., & Sripada, C. S. (2008). The functional neuroanatomy of PTSD: A critical review. *Progress in Brain Research, 167*, 151–169.

Magruder, K. M., Goldberg, J., Forsberg, C. W., Friedman, M. J., Litz, B. T., Vaccarino, V., . . . Smith, N. L. (2016). Long-term trajectories of PTSD in Vietnam-era veterans: The course and consequence of PTSD in twins. *Journal of Traumatic Stress, 29*, 5–16.

Marmar, C. R., Schlenger, W., Henn-Haase, C., Qian, M., Purchia, E., Li, M., . . . Kulka, R. A. (2015). Course of posttraumatic stress disorder 40 years after the Vietnam War: Findings from the National Vietnam Veterans Longitudinal Study. *JAMA Psychiatry, 72*, 875–881.

Mayou, R. A., Bryant, B., & Ehlers, A. (2001). Prediction of psychological outcomes one year after a motor vehicle accident. *American Journal of Psychiatry, 158*, 1231–1238.

McKinney, J. M., Hirsch, J. K., & Britton, P. C. (2017). PTSD symptoms and suicide risk in veterans: Serial and indirect effects via depression and anger. *Journal of Affective Disorders, 214*, 100–107.

McLean, C. P., Zang, Y., Zandberg, L., Bryan, C. J., Gay, N., Yarvis, J. S., . . . Foa, E. B. (2017). Predictors of suicidal ideation among active duty military personnel with posttraumatic stress disorder. *Journal of Affective Disorders, 208*, 392–398.

McLeod, D. S., Koenen, K. C., Meyer, J. M., Lyons, M. J., Eisen, S., True, W., & Goldberg, J. (2001). Genetic and environmental influences on the relationship among combat exposure, post-traumatic stress disorder symptoms, and alcohol use. *Journal of Traumatic Stress, 14*, 259–275.

McNally, R. J. (2003). Progress and controversy in the study of posttraumatic stress disorder. *Annual Review of Psychology, 54*, 229–252.

Mehta, D. & Binder, E. B. (2012). Gene X environment vulnerability factors for PTSD: The HPA-axis. *Neuropharmacology, 62*, 654–662.

Mitchell, A. J., Chan, M., Bhatti, H., Halton, M., Grassi, L., Johansen, C., & Meader, N. 2011. Prevalence of depression, anxiety, and adjustment disorder in oncological, haematological, and palliative-care settings: A meta-analysis of 94 interview based studies. *Lancet Oncology, 12*, 160–174.

National Institute for Clinical Excellence. (2005). *Clinical Guideline 26. PTSD: The management of PTSD in adults & children in primary & secondary care.* London, England: National Collaborating Centre for Mental Health.

Nock, M. K., Hwang, I., Sampson, N. A., & Kessler, R. C. (2010). Mental disorders, comorbidity and suicidal behavior: Results from the National Comorbidity Survey Replication. *Molecular Psychiatry, 15*, 868–876.

Norris, F. H. (1992). Epidemiology of trauma: Frequency and impact of different potentially traumatic events on different demographic groups. *Journal of Consulting & Clinical Psychology, 60*, 409–418.

North, C. C., & Pfefferbaum, B. (2013). Mental health response to community disasters: A systematic review. *Journal of the American Medical Association, 310*, 507–518.

Nugent, N. R., Amstadter, A. B., & Koenen, K. C. (2008). Genetics of posttraumatic stress disorder: Informing clinical conceptualizations and promoting future research. *American Journal of Medical Genetics C Seminar Medical Genetics, 148C*, 127–132.

O'Donnell, M. L., Creamer, M., & Pattison, P. (2004). Posttraumatic stress disorder and depression following trauma: Understanding comorbidity. *American Journal of Psychiatry, 161*, 1390–1396.

Ozer, E. J., Best, S. R., Lipsey, T. L., & Weiss, D. S. (2008). Predictors of posttraumatic stress disorder and symptoms in adults: A meta-analysis. *Psychological Trauma: Theory, Research, Practice, and Policy, 1*, 3–36.

Pole, N. (2007). The psychophysiology of posttraumatic stress disorder: A meta-analysis. *Psychological Bulletin, 133*, 725–746.

Pole, N., Gone, J. P., & Kulkarni, M. (2008). Posttraumatic stress disorder among ethnoracial minorities in the United States. *Clinical Psychology: Science and Practice, 51*, 35–61.

Powers, M. B., Halpern, J. M., Ferenschak, M. P., Gillihan, S. J., & Foa, E. B. (2010). A meta-analytic review of prolonged exposure for posttraumatic stress disorder. *Clinical Psychology Review, 30*, 635–641.

Rauch, S. L., Shin, L. M., & Phelps, E. A. (2006). Neurocircuitry models of posttraumatic stress disorder and extinction: Human neuroimaging research—past, present, and future. *Biological Psychiatry, 60,* 376–382.

Resick, P. A., Galovski, T. E., O'Brien Uhlmansiek, M., Scher, C. D., Clum, G. A., & Young-Xu, Y. (2008). A randomized clinical trial to dismantle components of cognitive processing therapy for posttraumatic stress disorder in female victims of interpersonal violence. *Journal of Consulting and Clinical Psychology, 76,* 243–258.

Resick, P. A., & Schnicke, M. K. (1993). *Cognitive processing therapy for rape victims: A treatment manual.* Newbury Park, CA: Sage.

Richardson, L. K., Frueh, B. C., & Acierno, R. (2010). Prevalence estimates of combat-related posttraumatic stress disorder: A critical review. *Australian and New Zealand Journal of Psychiatry, 44,* 4–19.

Schnyder, U., Moergeli, H., Klaghofer, R., & Buddeberg, C. (2001). Incidence and prediction of posttraumatic stress disorder symptoms in severely injured accident victims. *American Journal of Psychiatry, 158,* 594–599.

Shin, L. M., & Liberzon, I. (2010). The neurocircuitry of fear, stress, and anxiety disorders. *Neuropsychopharmacology Reviews, 35,* 169–191.

Shvil, E., Rusch, H. L., Sullivan, G. M., & Neria, Y. (2013). Neural, psychophysiological, and behavioral markers of fear processing in PTSD: A review of the literature. *Current Psychiatry Reports, 15,* 358.

Stein, D. J., Ipser, J., & McAnda, N. (2009). Pharmacotherapy of posttraumatic stress disorder: A review of meta-analyses and treatment guidelines. *CNS Spectrums, 1*(Suppl. 1), 25–31.

Stein, M. B., Jang, K. L., Taylor, S., Vernon, P. A., & Livesley, W. J. (2002). Genetic and environmental influences on trauma exposure and posttraumatic stress disorder symptoms: A twin study. *American Journal of Psychiatry, 159,* 1675–1681.

Strain, J. J., Smith, G. C., Hammer, J. S., McKenzie, D. P., Blumenfield, M., Muskin, P., . . . Schleifer. (1998). Adjustment Disorder: A multi-site study of its utilization and interventions in the consultation-liaison psychiatry setting. *General Hospital Psychiatry, 20,* 139–149.

Utzon-Frank, N., Breinegaard, N., Bertelsen, M., Borritz, M., Eller, N. H., Nordentoft, M., . . . Bonde, J. P. (2014). Occurrence of delayed onset posttraumatic stress disorder: A systematic review and meta-analysis of prospective studies. *Scandinavian Journal of Work, Environment & Health, 40,* 215–229.

van der Klink, J. J. L., Blonk, R. W. B., Schene, A. H., & van Dijk, F. J. H. (2003). Reducing long-term sickness absence by an activating intervention in adjustment disorders: A cluster randomized controlled design. *Occupational & Environmental Medicine, 60,* 429–437.

Weathers, F. W., Blake, D. D., Schnurr, P. P., Kaloupek, D. G., Marx, B. P., & Keane, T. M. (2013a). *The Life Events Checklist for DSM-5 (LEC-5).* Instrument available from the National Center for PTSD at www.ptsd.va.gov.

Weathers, F. W., Keane, T. M., & Davidson, J. R. T. (2001). Clinician-Administered PTSD Scale: A review of the first ten years of research. *Depression & Anxiety, 13,* 132–156.

Weathers, F. W., Litz, B. T., Keane, T. M., Palmieri, P. A., Marx, B. P., & Schnurr, P. P. (2013b). The PTSD Checklist for *DSM-5* (PCL-5). Scale available from the National Center for PTSD at www.ptsd.va.gov.

Weber, D. L. (2008). Information processing bias in post-traumatic stress disorder. *Open Neuroimaging Journal, 2,* 29–51.

Xian, H., Chantarujikapong, S., Scherrer, J. F., Eisen, S. A., Lyons, M. J., Goldberg, J., . . . True, W. R. (2000). Genetic and environmental influences on posttraumatic stress disorder, alcohol and drug dependence in twin pairs. *Drug and Alcohol Dependence, 61,* 95–102.

Xie, P., Kranzler, H. R., Poling, J., Stein, M. B., Anton, R. F., Brady, K., . . . Gelernter, J. (2009). Interactive effect of stressful life events and the serotonin transporter 5-HTTLPR genotype on posttraumatic stress disorder diagnosis in two independent populations. *Archives of General Psychiatry, 66*, 1201–1209.

Yehuda, R. (2006). Advances in understanding neuroendocrine alterations in PTSD and their therapeutic implications. *Annals of the New York Academy of Sciences, 1071*, 137–166.

Yehuda, R., Cai, G., Golier, J. A., Sarapas, C., Galea, S., Ising, M., . . . Buxbaum, J. D. (2009). Gene expression patterns associated with posttraumatic stress disorder following exposure to the World Trade Center attacks. *Biological Psychiatry, 66*, 708–711.

CHAPTER 12

Somatic Symptom and Related Disorders

GORDON J. G. ASMUNDSON and DANIEL M. LeBOUTHILLIER

DESCRIPTION OF THE DISORDERS

The somatic symptom and related disorders were introduced in the *Diagnostic and Statistical Manual of Mental Disorders*, fifth edition (*DSM-5*; American Psychiatric Association [APA], 2013) and replaced the *Diagnostic and Statistical Manual of Mental Disorders*, fourth edition, text revision (*DSM-IV-TR*; APA, 2000) somatoform disorders. Changes were made in an effort to eliminate overlap and clarify boundaries between diagnosable disorders and to recognize that people meeting diagnostic criteria for one of these disorders may or may not have an identifiable medical condition; however, as noted later, there is continuing debate as to the validity of the changes made. The somatic symptom and related disorders include somatic symptom disorder, illness anxiety disorder, conversion disorder (functional neurological symptom disorder), psychological factors affecting other medical conditions, factitious disorder, other specified somatic symptom and related disorder, and unspecified somatic symptom and related disorder.

SPECIFIC DISORDERS

The common feature of the somatic symptom and related disorders is prominent somatic sensations (e.g., dyspnea, pain) or changes (e.g., subcutaneous lumps, rash)—called "symptoms" in *DSM-5* terminology—that are associated with significant emotional distress and functional impairment and often interpreted by the person as being symptomatic of some disease process or physical anomaly. Bodily sensations and changes are a ubiquitous experience, and they typically remit without medical attention; however, about 25% of the population seeks medical attention when these sensations and changes persist (Kroenke, 2003). Up to 30% of those seeking medical attention will exhibit clinically significant distress about having an unidentified disease when there is no medical explanation for presenting "symptoms" (Fink, Sørensen, Engberg, Holm, & Munk-Jørgensen, 1999); yet many remain distressed despite identifiable medical explanation (APA, 2013; Taylor & Asmundson, 2004). This distress is associated with

Adult Psychopathology and Diagnosis, Eighth Edition. Edited by Deborah C. Beidel and B. Christopher Frueh.
© 2018 John Wiley & Sons, Inc. Published 2018 by John Wiley & Sons, Inc.
Companion website: www.wiley.com/go/beidel/psychopathology8e

substantial impairment of personal, social, and professional functioning as well as considerable costs to health care (Hessel, Geyer, Hinz, & Brahier, 2005), even after controlling for medical and psychiatric comorbidity (Barsky, Orav, & Bates, 2005).

Despite the prevalence and cost of distressing somatic sensations and changes, as well as a substantive increase in empirical attention during the past decade, understanding of their presentation remains limited. Likewise, although there are some data on the validity, reliability, and clinical utility of the diagnoses of somatic symptom disorder and illness anxiety disorder (Bailer et al., 2016; Dimsdale et al., 2013; van Dessel, van der Wouden, Dekker, & van der Horst, 2016), there have been few studies on the diagnostic category as a whole. In the sections that follow, we provide an overview of the general clinical profile, diagnostic considerations, and epidemiology of the somatic symptom and related disorders. Assessment, etiological considerations, and course and prognosis are also considered. In each of these latter sections, we touch on issues germane to the collective category as well as its specific disorders. In the case study, we focus more specifically on an illustration of uncomplicated somatic symptom disorder. There are currently few data on epidemiology, etiology, course, prognosis, assessment, or treatment of the somatic symptom and related disorders; therefore, much of the data presented below are borrowed from pre-*DSM-5* knowledge of related conditions and disorders.

CLINICAL PICTURE

The clinical profile for each somatic symptom and related disorder is unique, although each disorder is predicated on the prominence of somatic sensations or changes associated with distress and impairment. A brief overview of the clinical profile of each somatic symptom disorder is provided, along with reference to *DSM-5* diagnostic criteria.

Somatic Symptom Disorder

Somatic symptom disorder is the cornerstone diagnosis of the somatic symptom and related disorders category. The main feature of somatic symptom disorder is the presence of one or more somatic symptoms or features that cause distress and impairment in daily living (criterion A). The concern ranges from highly specific (e.g., "This pain in my gut is so bad. I must have stomach cancer") to vague and diffuse (e.g., "My whole body is aching. What could it be? Maybe it's ALS"). Individuals with somatic symptom disorder exhibit excessive thoughts, feelings, or behaviors related to their somatic symptoms (criterion B). An individual meets criterion B if he or she: (a) exhibits disproportionate thoughts about the seriousness of their symptoms, (b) experiences persistently high levels of anxiety regarding their symptoms or about their health, or (c) devotes an excessive amount of time to their health (e.g., seeking reassurance from health professionals, doing research about their somatic sensations or changes, perusing body parts to find potential lumps). Excessive somatic concerns must persist for at least 6 months (criterion C), although somatic symptoms do not need to be present for this entire period. Individuals with somatic symptom disorder may often resist the idea that they are suffering from a mental health disorder and may come to rely on reassurance-seeking (e.g., deriving comfort from assurances by significant others that everything is okay) and checking behaviors (e.g., palpating subcutaneous lumps, searching for information about disease in medical textbooks and on the Internet) to placate concerns about having a serious disease. Although these behaviors can be effective in providing short-term relief, they perpetuate the condition in the long term (Taylor & Asmundson, 2004).

There are several diagnostic specifiers that can accompany somatic symptom disorder. When somatic complaints revolve largely around pain, the "with predominant pain" specifier can be applied. This specifier replaces the pain disorder diagnosis from *DSM-IV*. The persistent specifier applies in cases where severe symptoms and impairment last for longer than 6 months. Finally, severity can be specified as mild, moderate, or severe when an individual meets one, two, or three of the criterion B symptoms, respectively. For example, a moderate severity specifier is assigned to an individual who reports debilitating anxiety due to bodily symptoms and who checks their body for hours a day to ensure no new blemishes have appeared.

ILLNESS ANXIETY DISORDER

Illness anxiety disorder involves preoccupation with having or acquiring a serious illness (criterion A). For example, an individual may fear contracting HIV or having recently contracted the virus. Illness anxiety disorder differs from somatic symptom disorder in that somatic symptoms are not present or are only minor (criterion B). If minor somatic symptoms are present (e.g., light pain, minor bruising), the individual's distress is clearly out of proportion to the actual threat and focuses more on the meaning of the symptoms (e.g., consequences of having diabetes) rather than on the somatic symptoms themselves. Individuals with illness anxiety disorder experience a great deal of distress rooted in their disease-related preoccupations and are easily alarmed about health-related matters (criterion C). To illustrate, an individual with illness anxiety disorder may be excessively distressed when learning that a colleague or family member has been diagnosed with cancer. Individuals with illness anxiety disorder participate in excessive behaviors aimed at reducing their anxiety (criterion D), often bodily checking (e.g., looking for lesions that could be signs of an infection), reassurance-seeking (e.g., repeatedly seeking medical testing), health-related research (e.g., reading about HIV on the Internet), and avoidance (e.g., avoiding hospitals as these could house harmful germs). These behaviors may placate concerns in the short term but, ultimately, serve to reinforce disease-related preoccupation (Taylor & Asmundson, 2004). A diagnosis of illness anxiety disorder is contingent on illness anxiety lasting at least 6 months (criterion E), although the focus of the anxiety may change during this time (e.g., from HIV to syphilis). Finally, the symptoms of illness anxiety disorder must not be better explained by another diagnosis (criterion F), such as somatic symptom disorder, panic disorder, or obsessive-compulsive disorder. There are two contrasting specifiers that can accompany illness anxiety disorder. The care-seeking type specifier is applied when individuals frequently seek medical care, whereas the care-avoidant type specifier is applied when individuals rarely use medical care.

CONVERSION DISORDER (FUNCTIONAL NEUROLOGICAL SYMPTOM DISORDER)

Conversion disorder involves the manifestation of altered voluntary motor or sensory functioning (criterion A). Motor symptoms can include paralysis, paresthesia, tremors, convulsions, and abnormal movements or posture. Sensory symptoms can include blindness, altered or reduced hearing, unusual or inconsistent skin sensations, and altered speech patterns. The hallmark of conversion disorder is a lack of correspondence between signs and symptoms and medical understanding of the possible neurological condition (criterion B). For example, an individual may display symptoms very consistent with epileptic seizures, but lack electrical activity in the brain consistent with epilepsy. Such an inconsistency is needed for a diagnosis. A lack of neurological evidence for reported or observed symptoms is not sufficient (e.g., trembling without any apparent brain damage). Symptoms of conversion disorder must not be better explained by another mental health or medical disorder (criterion C) and the symptoms must cause clinically significant distress or impairment or warrant medical evaluation (criterion D).

People with conversion disorder are often unaware of psychological factors associated with their condition, and many report an inability to control their symptoms. Although not a criterion for diagnosis, lack of worry or concern about symptoms (i.e., la belle indifference) is mentioned in the *DSM-5* list of associated features; however, the extant literature fails to support the use of la belle indifference as a means of discriminating between conversion disorder and symptoms of organic pathology (Stone, Smyth, Carson, Warlow, & Sharpe, 2006).

Observed signs and symptoms of conversion disorder often appear to represent patient beliefs about how neurological deficits should present, rather than how neuro-logical diseases actually function (Hurwitz, 2004). Onset typically follows a period of distress, such as that stemming from trauma (McFarlane, Atchison, Rafalowicz, & Papay, 1994; Roelofs, Keijsers, Hoogduin, Naring, & Moene, 2002; Van der Kolk et al., 1996) or physical injury (Stone et al., 2009). There are several specifiers that can accompany conversion disorder, including with psychological stressor or without psychological stressor and acute episode (i.e., when symptoms present for less than 6 months) or persistent (i.e., when symptoms present for more than 6 months).

PSYCHOLOGICAL FACTORS AFFECTING OTHER MEDICAL CONDITIONS

A diagnosis of psychological factors affecting other medical conditions is given to individuals who suffer from a medical condition (criterion A) that is adversely affected by psychological or behavioral factors (criterion B). The effects on the medical condition can increase the odds of suffering, disability, or death. Psychological or behavioral factors can be deemed as detrimental if meeting one of the following conditions: (a) the psychological or behavioral factors preceded the development or worsening of the medical condition, or delayed recovery from the condition (e.g., repeatedly exacerbating an injury following discharge from hospital); (b) the factors interfere with treatment; (c) the factors are well established health risks; or (d) the factors influence medical pathology, thereby exacerbating symptoms or requiring medical attention. Psychological or behavioral factors can include distress, maladaptive interpersonal patterns, and poor treatment adherence. The psychological or behavioral factors must not be subsumed within another mental disorder (criterion C); thus, worsening of a medical condition due to panic disorder or due to substance abuse would not meet criteria for psychological factors affecting other medical conditions. The degree of influence of psychological factors on a medical condition can be specified as mild (increases medical risk), moderate (aggravates medical condition), severe (results in hospitalization or emergency attention), or extreme (life-threatening risk).

FACTITIOUS DISORDER

Factitious disorder imposed on self is a condition wherein an individual acts as if they have physical or psychological signs of an illness by producing, feigning, or exaggerating symptoms (criterion A). The individual must present as ill or impaired (criterion B) and a diagnosis is contingent on identifying that the individual is actively misrepresenting their condition. Moreover, the deceptive behavior must occur without any obvious external rewards (criterion C), such as monetary compensation or reduced responsibilities. A diagnosis of factitious disorder can be assigned to individuals who have a medical condition, but, in such cases, the deceptive behavior is intended to make the person appear even more ill. The deceptive behavior cannot be better explained by another disorder, such as schizophrenia or delusional disorder (criterion D). Individuals with factitious disorder may produce or exaggerate symptoms by consuming drugs (e.g., insulin, hallucinogens), injecting themselves with noxious substances (e.g., bacteria), contaminating blood and urine samples, or reporting symptoms that have never occurred (e.g., seizures). A specifier of recurrent episodes is applied in cases where the individual has exhibited deceptive behavior more than once.

A separate diagnosis, referred to as factitious disorder imposed on another, can also be assigned. The criteria for this diagnosis are the same as factitious disorder, but a person other than the victim conducts the deceptive behavior. For example, a parent may tamper with the urine sample of his or her child to misrepresent the child's health status. In this case, the parent would be assigned the diagnosis, not the child.

OTHER SPECIFIED SOMATIC SYMPTOM AND RELATED DISORDER AND UNSPECIFIED SOMATIC SYMPTOM AND RELATED DISORDER

Other specified somatic symptom and related disorder applies to individuals who present with distressing or impairing symptoms that are similar to one of the somatic symptom and related disorders but that do not fully satisfy the criteria for a diagnosis. The *DSM-5* presents four specific disorders that can be used with the other specified disorder diagnosis. These include brief somatic symptom disorder, which can be assigned when an individual meets diagnostic criteria for somatic symptom disorder, but for less than 6 months; brief illness anxiety disorder, which can be assigned when symptoms of illness anxiety disorder last for less than 6 months; illness anxiety disorder without excessive health-related behaviors, which can be assigned when an individual meets all criteria for illness anxiety disorder except criterion D; and, pseudocyesis, which can be assigned in individuals with a false belief of being pregnant that is associated with objective and reported signs of pregnancy (e.g., morning sickness, breast tenderness). A diagnosis of unspecified somatic symptom and related disorder is applied when an individual presents with distressing or impairing symptoms that are similar to a somatic symptom and related disorder, but that do not meet the diagnostic criteria for any of the somatic symptom and related disorders.

DIAGNOSTIC CONSIDERATIONS (INCLUDING DUAL DIAGNOSIS)

To qualify for a *DSM-IV-TR* somatoform disorder diagnosis, somatic signs and symptoms were required to be medically unexplained (i.e., they could not be explained by organic pathology or physical deficit). Suggesting that diagnoses based on the absence of medically explained symptoms promoted stigma, the Somatic Symptom Workgroup noted that the reliability of establishing that somatic symptoms are not due to a general medical condition is low (Dimsdale et al., 2013; also see Sykes, 2006). As a consequence, *DSM-5* somatic symptom disorder is defined on the basis of positive symptoms (i.e., distressing somatic symptoms that present along with "observable" cognitions, emotions, and behaviors in response to the somatic symptoms). It is, therefore, possible for people presenting with and without a diagnosable general medical condition to satisfy diagnostic criteria for the disorder. Medically unexplained symptoms only remain relevant to conversion disorder and other specified somatic symptom and related disorder (i.e., pseudocyesis), where it is possible to demonstrate inconsistency between presenting symptoms and medical pathology.

In arriving at a diagnosis of one of the somatic symptom and related disorders it is important to consider that there are multiple sources of distressing somatic sensation and changes. First, a number of mental health disorders are characterized by somatic symptoms (e.g., depression, panic disorder, post-traumatic stress disorder) and may either account for or accompany the somatic symptoms. In the former case, a somatic symptom and related disorder diagnosis would not be warranted, whereas in the latter case, a dual diagnosis would be warranted. Likewise, given that distressing somatic symptoms often occur in response to a general medical condition, such as cancer or multiple sclerosis, considerable care is warranted in establishing whether the response is psychopathological in nature. Some critics of the *DSM-5* are concerned that diagnostic thresholds have been loosened to the point where clinicians will be challenged in distinguishing normal from psychopathological responses in those with distressing somatic symptoms stemming from a medical condition, resulting in overdiagnosis of somatic symptom disorders (Frances, 2013). There are also concerns about the validity of the new diagnostic criteria, particularly somatic symptom disorder (Rief & Martin, 2014). It is also important to recognize that many benign physical factors can give rise to somatic signs and symptoms. Consider, for example, physical deconditioning. People concerned by somatic sensations often avoid physical exertion, including aerobic and anaerobic exercise, for fear that it will have harmful consequences (Taylor & Asmundson, 2004). As a result, they become physically deconditioned. Physical deconditioning is associated with postural hypotension, muscle atrophy, and exertion-related breathlessness and fatigue, all of which can promote further inactivity and reinforce beliefs that one is ill.

According to the APA (2013), somatic symptom disorder encapsulates approximately 75% of individuals who previously met diagnostic criteria for hypochondriasis, and likely represents the most prevalent of the somatic symptom and related disorders. Emerging evidence on validity of the new classification of somatic symptom and related disorders suggests that only approximately half of individuals who meet *DSM-IV-TR* criteria for a somatoform disorder also meet criteria for a *DSM-5* diagnosis of somatic symptom disorder (van Dessel, van der Wouden, Dekker, & van der Horst, 2016), although other research has found similar or slightly greater rates of diagnosis for somatic symptom disorder compared with *DSM-IV-TR* somatoform disorder (Voigt et al., 2012). Nonetheless, those who meet the *DSM-5* criteria appear to have greater symptom severity and lower physical functioning, supporting the clinical utility of the diagnosis (van Dessel et al., 2016). There is criticism regarding splitting of new diagnoses; indeed, research on hypochondriasis suggests that about three-quarters of individuals diagnosed meet *DSM-5* criteria for somatic symptom disorder and one-quarter for illness anxiety disorder, but that the two groups have few differences in terms of attitudes, behaviors, and physical symptoms (Bailer et al., 2016). Further research is required to determine whether the modifications made in the *DSM-5* facilitate accuracy of diagnoses relative to that attainable with the *DSM-IV-TR* somatoform disorders. The importance of diagnosis cannot be overstated, as any diagnosis carries significant implications for individuals receiving the diagnosis and their related experiences (e.g., stigmatization, interpretation of symptoms, nature of treatment, response to treatment). As Kirmayer and Looper (2007) have noted, diagnosis is a form of intervention and, as such, is a crucial element in shaping treatment and outcome.

EPIDEMIOLOGY

Somatic symptom and related disorders are often associated with true or perceived organic pathology; consequently, this class of disorders is a challenge to diagnose and to study from an epidemiological standpoint due to difficulties in thoroughly assessing the mind and body. Given the substantial changes in diagnostic criteria between the *DSM-III* and *DSM-5*, providing precise epidemiological prevalence rates for somatic symptom and related disorders is extremely challenging. Indeed, the somatoform disorders were not included in the large-scale national comorbidity surveys based on *DSM-III-R* (Kessler, 1994) and *DSM-IV-TR* criteria (Kessler, Chiu, Demler, Merikangas, & Walters, 2005), nor were they examined in the World Health Organization World Mental Health Surveys initiative (Kessler & Üstün, 2008), which further limits inferences regarding the somatic symptom and related disorders. Moreover, epidemiological researchers have often paired somatoform disorders with other disorders (e.g., anxiety disorders; Bland, Orn, & Newman, 1988) or have excluded specific disorders from analyses due to low or high base rates or differences in classification methodologies (Leiknes, Finset, Moum, & Sandanger, 2008). Consequently, the prevalence of somatic symptom and related disorders as a class of disorders remains understudied and our knowledge at this time can only be extrapolated from earlier research on the somatoform disorders.

As noted earlier, the somatic symptom and related disorders are substantially different from the somatoform disorders described in *DSM-IV-TR*; however, some of the broader epidemiological findings likely still hold true. For example, presentation of somatic concerns that do not meet diagnostic criteria for a somatoform disorder or medical condition account for approximately half of all physician visits (Nimnuan, Hotopf, & Wessely, 2001), suggesting that subsyndromal somatic symptom presentations are highly prevalent and costly (Barsky et al., 2005; Kirmayer & Robbins, 1991). Somatic symptom and related disorders are likely more common in women (Wittchen & Jacobi, 2005), with perhaps the exception of somatic symptom disorder, which appears to have similar prevalence in both genders based on the rates of hypochondriasis (Asmundson, Taylor, Sevgur, & Cox, 2001; Bleichhardt & Hiller, 2007). People with a somatic symptom and related disorder are also very likely to frequently experience co-occurring mood disorders (Leiknes et al., 2008), anxiety disorders (Lowe et al., 2008), personality disorders (Bornstein & Gold, 2008; Sakai, Nestoriuc, Nolido, & Barsky, 2010), as well as other somatic symptom and related disorders (Leiknes et al., 2008).

Somatic symptom disorder has a prevalence of approximately 5–7% in the general population (APA, 2013), which is consistent with the 12-month prevalence rate of 4.5% for hypochondriasis (Faravelli et al., 1997). Research on hypochondriasis suggests that somatic symptom disorder is likely more common in primary care settings. Reported prevalence rates of hypochondriasis in primary care settings have varied considerably based on methodology. Studies using diagnostic interviews have reported a point prevalence of 3% (Escobar et al., 1998) and a 12-month prevalence of 0.8% (Gureje, Üstün, & Simon, 1997), whereas a study using cutoff scores from self-report measures followed by interviews suggests a 12-month prevalence of 8.5% (Noyes et al., 1993). The inclusion of the with predominant pain specifier to somatic symptom disorder, which subsumes a portion of the *DSM-IV* pain disorder diagnosis, may increase the prevalence of somatic symptom disorder beyond the prevalence of hypochondriasis.

The prevalence of illness anxiety disorder is relatively unknown, but can be estimated based on other phenomena. The 1- to 2-year prevalence of health anxiety and disease conviction (i.e., the belief that one has a disease) in community-based samples ranges from 1.3% to 10% (APA, 2013). A strong fear of contracting a disease, which is relatively similar to illness anxiety disorder, has a point prevalence of approximately 3–4% (Agras, Sylvester, & Oliveau, 1969; Malis, Hartz, Doebbeling, & Noyes, 2002). Together these findings suggest that illness anxiety disorder is relatively common. The point and 12-month prevalence rates of conversion disorder in the general population are less than 0.1% (Akagi & House, 2001). Point prevalence rates in neurology and primary care settings have been reported as 1% (Smith, Clarke, Handrinos, Dunsis, & McKenzie, 2000) and 0.2% (de Waal, Arnold, Eekhof, & van Hemert, 2004), respectively. Despite low prevalence of conversion disorder, medically unexplained neurological symptoms are present in approximately 11–35% of neurology patients (Carson et al., 2000; Snijders, de Leeuw, Klumpers, Kappelle, & van Gijn, 2004), suggesting that subsyndromal conversion may be more common than almost all neurological diseases. The prevalence of other somatic symptom and related disorders are unknown, partially because they are new diagnoses (e.g., psychological factors affecting other medical conditions) and are very difficult to study (e.g., factitious disorder, unspecified somatic symptom and related disorder).

PSYCHOLOGICAL AND BIOLOGICAL ASSESSMENT

Individuals with somatic symptom and related disorders will typically present in primary care and other medical (nonpsychiatric) clinics rather than in mental health settings; indeed, they may often refuse a mental health referral because of a belief that their condition is purely organic. Cooperation between medical and mental health professionals aids the referral process and, due to the complexity of the factors involved (e.g., possibility of co-occurring organic pathology), is typically necessary in making an accurate diagnosis. Throughout the course of assessing a person with a possible somatic symptom and related disorder, the mental health professional must seek to establish and maintain rapport and should clearly relay an understanding that, although a disease process may or may not be present, the symptoms are real and not feigned or "in the head" (Taylor & Asmundson, 2004). The general goals of assessment for the somatic symptom and related disorders are to rule out organic pathology-based, substance-based, or other psychopathology-based explanations of presenting signs and symptoms, to determine the type and severity of signs and symptoms, and to facilitate appropriate treatment planning.

Ruling out organic pathology is no longer requisite to diagnosis of somatic symptom and related disorders, as it was in the *DSM-IV-TR* somatoform disorders. This aspect of the diagnostic process was considered problematic for two primary reasons. First, it relied heavily on the exclusion of general medical conditions, and 100% certainty was rarely, if ever, possible (Taylor & Asmundson, 2004; Woolfolk & Allen, 2007). Second, diagnosis is not usually based on the absence of something but, rather, according to the presence of positive features of a condition (Dimsdale et al., 2013). Gathering a detailed history of somatic complaints, past and current medical conditions, and medical professionals consulted is a crucial part of a comprehensive diagnostic process and may provide insight regarding the nature of the presenting condition. A consult with the family physician may be necessary to determine the need for further medical assessments; however, caution is warranted, because further assessments may reinforce maladaptive coping (e.g., reassurance-seeking) while also increasing the costs and potential risks associated with medical care.

Structured clinical interviews have proven to be the gold standard in the diagnosis of mental disorders, and will likely remain so for the somatic symptom and related disorders. Broad structured interviews that include sections on numerous mental disorders are the most commonly utilized. The Structured Clinical Interview for the *DSM-IV* (First, Spitzer, Gibbon, & Williams, 1996) and the Composite International Diagnostic Interview (CIDI; World Health Organization, 1990) based on the *International Statistical Classification of Diseases*, 10th edition, criteria (ICD-10; World Health Organization, 2007) were both used widely and demonstrated efficacy and reliability in diagnosing somatoform disorders. Other useful structured interviews for diagnosing somatoform disorders included the Somatoform Disorders Schedule (World Health Organization, 1994), the Schedules for Clinical Assessment in Neuropsychiatry (Wing et al., 1990), and the Diagnostic Interview Schedule (Robins, Helzer, Croughan, & Ratcliff, 1981). The majority of these structured interviews have not been updated for *DSM-5* somatic symptom and related disorders, with the exception of the Structured Clinical Interview for *DSM-5* (First, Williams, Karg, & Spitzer, 2015), which queries somatic symptom disorder and illness anxiety disorder. Additionally, the Health Preoccupation Diagnostic Interview (Axelsson, Andersson, Ljótsson, Wallhed Finn, & Hedman, 2016) is a newly developed instrument for the diagnosis of *DSM-5* somatic symptom disorder and illness anxiety disorder that has preliminary evidence for its reliability.

Structured clinical interviews can be supplemented with diarized monitoring of catastrophic thinking and maladaptive coping behaviors as well as information gleaned from standardized self-report measures. Self-report measures are efficient and effective screening tools that can provide invaluable information for case conceptualization and regular monitoring of treatment progress. The Screening for Somatoform Symptoms (Rief, Hiller, & Heuser, 1997), the Symptom Checklist-90, Revised (Derogatis, 1975), or the Patient Health Questionnaire-15 (Kroenke, Spitzer, & Williams, 2002) have been used to assess a broad range of somatic symptoms. More specific information can be derived from a wide array of self-report measures that have been developed to assess the severity of specific somatic symptoms. It is beyond the scope of this chapter to provide a comprehensive list of these measures; examples include the Health Attitude Survey (Noyes, Langbehn, Happel, Sieren, & Muller, 1999), for use in assessing attitudes and perceptions associated with multiple somatic symptoms; the Health Anxiety Questionnaire (Lucock & Morley, 1996), for use in assessing reassurance-seeking behavior and the extent to which symptoms interfere with a person's life; the Whiteley Index (Pilowsky, 1967), for use in assessing cognitions associated with health anxiety; and the Short Health Anxiety Inventory (Salkovskis, Rimes, Warwick, & Clark, 2002), to assess health anxiety in both medical and nonmedical populations. Instruments developed in relation to the *DSM-5* classification include the Somatic Symptom Scale–8 (Gierk et al., 2014; an abbreviated version of the Patient Health Questionnaire-15 developed for *DSM-5* somatic symptom disorder field trials), as well as the Somatic Symptom Disorder-B Criteria Scale (Toussaint et al., 2015, 2017). Medical service utilization and visual analogue scales pertaining to distressing thoughts and maladaptive coping behaviors can also be used to assess emotional and functional impact and to monitor treatment progress. Finally, measures of mood and anxiety can be useful in case conceptualization and monitoring and might include the Beck Depression Inventory-II (Beck, Steer, & Brown, 1996), the Beck Anxiety Inventory (Beck & Steer, 1993), and the Anxiety Sensitivity Index-3 (Taylor et al., 2007).

ETIOLOGICAL CONSIDERATIONS

Behavioral Genetics and Molecular Genetics

Heritability of somatoform disorders has been suggested by findings from behavioral (e.g., Kendler et al., 2011; Torgersen, 1986) and molecular (e.g., Hennings, Zill, & Rief, 2009) genetics studies. Somatic symptom concordance rates between monozygotic twins are higher than between dizygotic twins, even when controlling for co-occurring psychiatric symptoms (Lembo, Zaman, Krueger, Tomenson, & Creed, 2009). Although mood and somatoform disorders share common genetic factors (e.g., deregulation of serotonergic pathways), there are numerous genetic features unique to somatoform disorders (e.g., immunological deregulation, hypothalamic–pituitary–adrenal [HPA] axis responses; Rief, Hennings, Riemer, & Euteneuer, 2010). The role of specific genetic markers in the development of somatic symptoms remains unclear; however, research in this area is ongoing, and genetic factors are now being considered within the context of psychological models of various somatoform disorders (e.g., Taylor, Jang, Stein, & Asmundson, 2008; Veale, 2004). Whether these findings generalize to the somatic symptom and related disorders remains to be determined.

Neuroanatomy and Neurobiology

Neurological research on the *DSM-5* somatic symptom and related disorders remains in its infancy; but, research using *DSM-IV-TR* criteria has demonstrated neurological correlates for conversion disorder (e.g., Vuilleumier, 2005), hypochondriasis (e.g., Atmaca, Sec, Yildirim, Kayali, & Korkmaz, 2010), and other related disorders (e.g., somatization disorder; Hakala, Vahlberg, Niemi, & Karlsson, 2006; pain disorder and fibromyalgia, Wood, Glabus, Simpson, & Patterson, 2009). The HPA axis has been a focus of research in this area. A recent longitudinal study reported preliminary evidence that cortisol deregulation in the HPA axis may predate the development of somatic symptoms in some people (Tak & Rosmalen, 2010). The HPA axis controls glandular and hormonal responses to stress and, when stressors (e.g., chronic pain, anxiety) have a chronic course, may lead to hypocortisolism (i.e., adrenal insufficiency), which induces greater stress and enhances experiences of pain and fatigue (Fries, Hesse, Hellhammer, & Hellhammer, 2005). Increases in these experiences typically exacerbate somatic symptoms or lead to behaviors that exacerbate or maintain them (Taylor & Asmundson, 2004). The second somatosensory area (SII) of the cerebral cortex, which is involved in the analysis and evaluation of complex patterns of somesthetic input (e.g., perception of pain, sensations from visceral structures, gastric sensations), has also been implicated as a source of the somatic perturbation associated with the somatoform disorders (Miller, 1984); however, despite its appeal as a neural structure underlying this class of disorders, people presenting with concerns about somatic symptoms do not typically show abnormalities in sensory acuity.

Learning, Modeling, and Life Events

Adverse life events (e.g., childhood physical and sexual abuse, neglect) have been associated with increased physician visits during adulthood (Fiddler, Jackson, Kapur, Wells, & Creed, 2004), health anxiety (Reiser, McMillan, Wright, & Asmundson, 2013), hypochondriasis (Barsky, Wool, Barnett, & Cleary, 1994), and unexplained somatic symptoms (Tak, Kingma, van Ockenburg, Ormel, & Rosmalen, 2015). Unfavorable socioeconomic conditions during development may also be associated with unexplained somatic symptoms in adulthood, likely because socioeconomic status may engender a series of social and material difficulties (Jonsson, San Sebastian, Strömsten, Hammar-ström, & Gustafsson, 2016); however, it is noteworthy that increased prevalence of abuse and other stressful life events are characteristic of people with a variety of psychiatric conditions (e.g., panic disorder; Taylor, 2000), not just those presenting with concerns regarding somatic symptoms. Early childhood experiences of illness and perceptions of significant illness in others are associated with the experience of medically unexplained symptoms in adulthood (Hotopf, Wilson-Jones, Mayou, Wadsworth, & Wessely, 2000). Likewise, parents who fear disease, who are preoccupied with their bodies, and who overreact to minor ailments experienced by their children are more likely to have children with the same tendencies, both during childhood and adulthood (Craig, Boardman, Mills, Daly-Jones, & Drake, 1993; Hotopf, Mayou, Wadsworth, & Wessely, 1999; Marshall, Jones, Ramchandani, Stein, & Bass, 2007). That being said, a recent twin study suggests that environmental factors not shared by twins (e.g., an ailment in one of the twins), rather than shared environmental factors (e.g., parental style), seem most important in the development of *DSM-IV-TR*-defined hypochondriasis (Taylor & Asmundson, 2012).

COGNITIVE INFLUENCES

Greater focus on somatic sensations is associated with greater experiences of those sensations (Brown, 2004; Ursin, 2005). When attention is directed to the body, the intensity of perceived sensations increases (Mechanic, 1983; Pennebaker, 1980). People with somatoform disorders have been shown to spend a considerable amount of time focusing on their bodies, thereby increasing their chances of noticing somatic sensations and changes. They also tend to believe that somatic sensations and changes are indicative of disease or are otherwise harmful in some way (Barsky, 1992; Taylor & Asmundson, 2004; Vervoort, Goubert, Eccleston, Bijttebier, & Crombez, 2006). These beliefs increase the attention directed to somatic sensations and changes and, in turn, increase associated distress. It is likely that similar cognitive influences will be identified in the various somatic symptom and related disorders diagnoses.

SEX AND RACIAL-ETHNIC CONSIDERATIONS

As noted in the "Epidemiology" section, the somatoform disorders were more prevalent in women than in men, perhaps with the exception of hypochondriasis. There are several possible explanations for this difference. Because women are more likely to seek medical services (Corney, 1990; Kessler et al., 2008), they may be more prone to diagnostic biases wherein physicians consider somatic symptoms presented by a woman as more likely to be psychological than organic in nature (e.g., Martin, Gordon, & Lounsbury, 1998). Women also tend to experience higher rates of psychopathology (Kessler et al., 2008). Shared etiological or maintenance factors between mental disorders may make it more likely that women are at a higher risk of developing a somatic symptom and related disorder. There is evidence that women tend to focus more on their bodies (Beebe, 1995) and are more fearful of some of their bodily sensations (Stewart, Taylor, & Baker, 1997), further increasing their risk for developing somatic symptom and related disorders. Other putative sex differences have been proposed (e.g., differential experiences of abuse; HPA axis dysregulation) but warrant further empirical scrutiny in the context of their role in somatic symptom and related disorders etiology.

Somatic sensations and changes are common in all cultural groups; however, presentation varies widely depending on sociocultural norms (Kirmayer & Young, 1998). Cultural factors, such as socially transmitted values, beliefs, and expectations, can influence how a person interprets somatic sensations and changes, and whether treatment-seeking is initiated. Some cultures appear to be more distressed by gastrointestinal sensations (e.g., excessive concerns about constipation in the UK), whereas others are more distressed by cardiopulmonary (e.g., excessive concerns about low blood pressure in Germany) and immunologically based (e.g., excessive concerns about viruses and their effects in the USA and Canada) symptoms (Escobar, Allen, Hoyos Nervi, & Gara, 2001). Whether one seeks care for somatic concerns also appears to vary as a function of culture, with those of Chinese, African American, Puerto Rican, and other Latin American descent presenting with more medically unexplained somatic symptoms than those from other groups (Escobar et al., 2001). Whether concern over somatic sensations and changes are excessive needs to be judged in the context of the individual's cultural background.

COURSE AND PROGNOSIS (INCLUDING ISSUES OF TREATMENT)

As a diagnostic category, somatic symptom and related disorders share somatic features and concerns as a prominent aspect of clinical presentation. That said, each disorder does not necessarily share a similar course and prognosis. Like the somatoform disorders, course and prognosis may vary considerably, because the disorders are heterogeneous in presentation and involve substantial comorbidity with mood and anxiety disorders, personality disorders, and, in some cases, general medical conditions. Certain prognostic indicators have been shown to be common across somatoform disorders; for example, comorbidity with other psychiatric disorders contributes to a more chronic and persistent course (e.g., Rief, Hiller, Geissner, & Fichter, 1995). More somatic symptoms, sensitization to bodily sensations and pain, as well as presence of a medical condition all contribute to greater severity and chronic course (APA, 2013). The presence of fewer somatic symptoms, few or no comorbid conditions, identifiable stressors at the time of onset, high intellectual functioning, as well as sound social support networks are typically associated with good prognosis. Also indicative of good prognosis is the development of a strong therapeutic alliance between the patient and care provider, wherein the patient believes that the care provider views the patient's presenting signs and symptoms as legitimate, albeit possibly not due to an organic pathology or physical defect (Taylor & Asmundson, 2004).

Little research on psychological interventions for somatic symptom disorders currently exists. A recent randomized controlled trial found large improvements in individuals with somatic symptom disorder or illness anxiety disorder engaged in Internet cognitive-behavioral therapy (CBT), unguided Internet CBT, and unguided bibliotherapy compared with a waitlist (Hedman, Axelsson, Andersson, Lekander. & Ljotsson, 2016). CBT has also demonstrated efficacy across the *DSM-IV-TR* somatoform disorders. The treatment is superior to standard medical care in reducing health-related anxiety (Barsky & Ahern, 2004) and improving somatic complaints/somatization (Allen, Woolfolk, Escobar, Gara, & Hamer, 2006; Speckens, van Hemert, Bolk, Rooijmans, & Hengeveld, 1996). These findings are echoed by a recent meta-analysis of CBT trials for hypochondriasis and health anxiety (Olatunji, Kauffman, Meltzer, Davis, Smits, & Powers, 2014) as well as more recent health anxiety treatment trials (Weck, Neng, Schwind, & Hofling, 2015). Psychiatric consultation letters to primary-care physicians describing somatization and providing recommendations for primary care have also been shown to significantly improve physical functioning and reduce the cost of medical care (Rost, Kashner, & Smith, 1994). Finally, a stepped care approach, including distinguishing between acutely and nonacutely serious complaints, assessing and treating psychiatric comorbidities, and developing a multimodal approach to managing symptoms, could be an effective way forward in addressing somatic symptom disorders in primary care (Hubley, Uebelacker, & Eaton, 2014; Korenke, 2003).

CASE STUDY

Case Identification

The basic features of this case are undisguised; however, in line with Clifft's (1986) guidelines, identifying information has been altered or omitted to protect confidentiality and privacy.

Jacob is a 37-year-old White male who has been married for 10 years and has a 5-year-old daughter and a 6-month-old son. He currently resides with his wife and children in an upper-middle-class suburban neighborhood. His family is financially secure, and he is not involved in any legal proceedings. Jacob is employed full time as an electrical engineer for a large company, a job he has held for the past 6 years. He enjoys a variety of sports, walking the family dog, and spending time with his family. Until recently, he was active as a competitive triathlete. His job requires that he travel periodically, with absences from home and his family for up to 1 month at a time. He reports that job demands increase in the months prior to extended travel and that his next lengthy trip is fast approaching in 10 weeks.

Presenting Complaints

Jacob was referred by his family physician for assessment and, if appropriate, treatment of increasing anxiety over his physical well-being which was negatively impacting on his work (e.g., spending excessive amounts of time searching medical information on the Internet instead of working) as well as leisure and family functioning (e.g., withdrawing from physical activity and shared leisure activities). These concerns started 9 months ago, when his father died of heart complications associated with amyloidosis, a disease wherein amyloid proteins build up in specific organs and, over time, disrupt organ function and eventually lead to failure of the affected organs. There is a rare form—hereditary amyloidosis—that is most frequently passed from father to son and for which there are no preventive measures other than not having children. There is no cure for amyloidosis, and the effects do not become apparent until later in life (i.e., over the age of 50 years). Beginning shortly after his father's death, Jacob became increasingly aware of and concerned by somatic sensations in his body—heart palpitations and racing, upper body aches and pain, dizziness, and blurred vision—all of which were similar to those initially experienced by his father. He feared that he may also have amyloidosis and might die from it. His fears were exacerbated upon the birth of his son, with specific concerns that he had passed on the condition and that his son would eventually succumb as well.

History

Jacob had no prior history of mental health problems or treatment and, aside from chickenpox and tonsillitis as a child, had been physically healthy throughout his life. The report from his physician indicated that, despite numerous visits regarding various somatic complaints over recent months, there was no evidence of an organic basis for Jacob's concerns. The physician report also indicated that Jacob was physically healthy and that he and his son had a pending appointment for genetic testing to rule out the genetic profile for hereditary amyloidosis. Jacob reported having a loving and supportive relationship with his wife, although she was becoming increasingly concerned by his condition and, at times, annoyed at his growing reluctance to actively play with their children. Until recently, he was exercising five or six times per week and had competed in numerous triathlons; however, because of growing concerns about his health, he had significantly cut down his frequency of training and was not competing in order to "avoid physical exertion" for fear that his heart would "explode." In place of training, he was spending hours checking the Internet for medical information.

Assessment (Related To *DSM-5* Criteria)

Jacob was assessed using the Structured Clinical Interview for the *DSM-5* and a battery of self-report questionnaires, including (a) the Beck Depression Inventory-II, a measure of depression over the past 2 weeks (Beck et al., 1996), (b) the Beck Anxiety Inventory, a measure of general anxiety over the past week (Beck & Steer, 1993), (c) the Anxiety Sensitivity Index-3 (Taylor et al., 2007), a measure of the fear of arousal-related bodily sensations, and (d) the Whiteley Index (Pilowsky, 1967), a measure of the core features of health anxiety, including disease fear, disease conviction, and bodily pre-occupation. The structured interview and self-report measures provided detailed data regarding general features of Jacob's distress, as well as specific features of his health-related concerns.

Jacob met the *DSM-5* diagnostic criteria for somatic symptom disorder. He presented with several specific concerns, including daily worry that somatic changes and sensations (e.g., heart palpitations and racing, upper body aches and pain, dizziness, blurred vision) were signs of physical disease as well as increasing inability to focus on work-related tasks and to be involved in family activities (somatic symptom disorder criterion A). He also presented with considerable worry and anxiety about his personal health and the future-oriented health and well-being of his 6-month-old son, and reported spending hours on the Internet checking medical information (somatic symptom disorder criterion B). His concerns had, as noted previously, begun around the time of his father's death 9 months prior and had persisted since then (somatic symptom disorder criterion C).

Given that the effects of amyloidosis are typically not evident until later in life, and that Jacob was in his mid-30s, it was deemed unlikely that amyloid deposits were responsible for the bodily sensations he was experiencing; however, since Jacob (and his son) had not yet completed genetic testing and did not know whether they had the genetic profile for hereditary amyloidosis at the time of assessment, we remained cautious in our opinion as to whether his thoughts about the seriousness of symptoms were disproportionate. At the time of assessment, Jacob's score on the Whiteley Index was moderate overall (score = 8; possible range 0–14), characterized by significant disease fear (score = 3; possible range 0–4) and bodily preoccupation (score = 3; possible range 0–3) but little disease conviction (score = 0; possible range 0–3), the latter of which is indicative of good prognosis with treatment (Taylor & Asmundson, 2004). The moderately high levels of health anxiety combined with excessive checking behavior, in our opinion, were sufficient to warrant a moderate severity specifier.

Jacob did not meet diagnostic criteria for other diagnosis. Scores on the Beck Depression Inventory (score = 13; possible range 0–63) and Beck Anxiety Inventory (score = 26; possible range 0–63) suggested a mildly depressed mood and moderate general anxiety, respectively. The absence of comorbid diagnoses, along with depression and general anxiety in the mild to moderate range, are also indicative of good prognosis with treatment (Taylor & Asmundson, 2004). His score on the Anxiety Sensitivity Index-3 (score = 33; possible range 0–72) indicated strong beliefs that arousal-related bodily sensations have harmful consequences, which, when considered in the context of his significant disease fear and bodily preoccupation, suggest that attention-focusing exercises (e.g., Furer, Walker, & Stein, 2007; Wells, 1997) and interoceptive exposure (Taylor & Asmundson, 2004) may prove to be particularly beneficial additions to treatment.

SUMMARY

Conditions characterized by significant concern over somatic signs and symptoms, often presenting as medically unexplainable, are associated with significant emotional distress, cognitions characterized by catastrophic thinking, maladaptive coping behaviors typically manifest as excessive checking and reassurance-seeking, limitations in social and occupational functioning, and excessive use of health care resources. These conditions are represented by the disorders subsumed under the *DSM-5* somatic symptom and related disorders. While it is generally agreed that changes to the former *DSM* conceptualizations of the somatoform disorders were warranted, it remains to be determined whether the changes set forth in the *DSM-5* somatic symptom and related disorders will promote more accurate diagnosis of people concerned and functionally disabled by somatic sensations and changes and, if so, whether this will direct appropriate treatment resources to optimize outcomes. It also remains unclear if, or how, the changes to classification will facilitate efforts to identify underlying mechanisms. The burden on the health care system and the personal distress associated with somatic symptoms highlight the need for appropriate reconceptualization of disorders characterized by somatic symptom presentation; however, some investigators have suggested that there was insufficient empirical evidence to warrant change, that important evidence may have been overlooked, and that the changes in the *DSM-5* may have been premature (Taylor, 2009; Sirri & Fava, 2013; Starcevic, 2013) or lacking in precision and clarity (Rief & Martin, 2014), and that the new changes will increase, rather than decrease, diagnostic misclassification (Frances, 2013). Answers to these questions await the accumulation of empirical evidence based on the *DSM-5* diagnostic criteria. Efforts such as the EURONET-SOMA initiative (Weigel et al., 2017), which is bringing leading European experts in the field together to work on research agendas, diagnostic issues, and treatment, hold promise in providing answers to the many questions that remain.

REFERENCES

Agras, S., Sylvester, D., & Oliveau, D. (1969). The epidemiology of common fears and phobia. *Comprehensive Psychiatry, 10,* 151–156.

Akagi, H., & House, A. (2001). The epidemiology of hysterical conversion. In P. Halligan, C. Bass, & J. Marshall (Eds.), *Contemporary approaches to the study of hysteria.* Oxford, England: Oxford University Press.

Allen, L. A., Woolfolk, R. L., Escobar, J. I., Gara, M. A., & Hamer, R. M. (2006). Cognitive-behaviour therapy for somatization disorder. *Psychosomatic Medicine, 63,* 93–94.

American Psychiatric Association. (2000). *Diagnostic and statistical manual of mental disorders* (4th ed., text rev.) Washington, DC: Author.

American Psychiatric Association. (2013). *Diagnostic and statistical manual of mental disorders* (5th ed.). Arlington, VA: American Psychiatric Publishing.

Asmundson, G. J. G., Taylor, S., Sevgur, S., & Cox, B. J. (2001). Health anxiety: Classification and clinical features. In G. J. G. Asmundson, S. Taylor, & B. J. Cox (Eds.), *Health anxiety: Clinical and research perspectives on hypochondriasis and related disorders* (pp. 3–21). New York, NY: Wiley.

Atmaca, M., Sec, S., Yildirim, H., Kayali, A., & Korkmaz, S. (2010). A volumetric MRI analysis of hypochondriac patients. *Bulletin of Clinical Psychopharmacology, 20,* 293–299.

Axelsson, E., Andersson, E., Ljótsson, B., Wallhed Finn, D., & Hedman, E. (2016). The health preoccupation diagnostic interview: Inter-rater reliability of a structured interview for diagnostic assessment of DSM-5 somatic symptom disorder and illness anxiety disorder. *Cognitive Behaviour Therapy, 45,* 259–269.

Bailer, J., Kerstner, T., Witthöft, M., Diener, C., Mier, D., & Rist, F. (2016). Health anxiety and hypochondriasis in the light of *DSM-5*. *Anxiety, Stress, & Coping, 29,* 219–239.

Barsky, A. J. (1992). Amplification, somatization, and the somatoform disorders. *Psychosomatics, 33,* 28–34.

Barsky, A. J., & Ahern, D. K. (2004). Cognitive behaviour therapy for hypochondriasis: A randomized controlled trial. *Journal of the American Medical Association, 291,* 1464–1470.

Barsky, A. J., Orav, E. J., & Bates, D. W. (2005). Somatization increases medical utilization and costs independent of psychiatric and medical comorbidity. *Archives of General Psychiatry, 62,* 903–910.

Barsky, A., Wool, C., Barnett, M., & Cleary, P. (1994). Histories of childhood trauma in adult hypochondriacal patients. *American Journal of Psychiatry, 151,* 397–401.

Beck, A. T., & Steer, R. A. (1993). *Manual for the Beck Anxiety Inventory.* San Antonio, TX: Psychological Corporation.

Beck, A. T., Steer, R. A., & Brown, G. K. (1996). *Manual for the Beck Depression Inventory-II.* San Antonio, TX: Psychological Corporation.

Beebe, D. W. (1995). The Attention of Body Shape Scale: A new measure of body focus. *Journal of Personality Assessment, 65,* 486–501.

Bland, R. C., Orn, H., & Newman, S. C. (1988). Lifetime prevalence of psychiatric disorders in Edmonton. *Acta Psychiatrica Scandinavica, 77,* 24–32.

Bleichhardt, G., & Hiller, W. (2007). Hypochondriasis and health anxiety in the German population. *British Journal of Health Psychology, 12,* 511–523.

Bornstein, R. F., & Gold, S. H. (2008). Comorbidity of personality disorders and somatization disorder: A meta-analytic review. *Journal of Psychopathology and Behavioral Assessment, 30,* 154–161.

Brown, R. J. (2004). Psychological mechanisms of medically unexplained symptoms: An integrative conceptual model. *Psychological Bulletin, 130,* 793–812.

Carson, A. J., Ringbauer, B., Stone, J., McKenzie, L., Warlow, C., & Sharpe, M. (2000). Do medically unexplained symptoms matter? A prospective cohort study of 300 new referrals to neurology outpatient clinics. *Journal of Neurology Neurosurgery and Psychiatry, 68,* 207–210.

Clifft, M. A. (1986). Writing about psychiatric patients. Guidelines for disguising case material. *Bulletin of the Menninger Clinic, 50,* 511–524.

Corney, R. H. (1990). Sex differences in general practice attendance and help seeking for minor illness. *Journal of Psychosomatic Research, 34,* 525–534.

Craig, T. K., Boardman, A. P., Mills, K., Daly-Jones, O., & Drake, H. (1993). The South London Somatisation Study, I: Longitudinal course and the influence of early life experiences. *British Journal of Psychiatry, 163,* 579–588.

de Waal, M. W. M., Arnold, I. A., Eekhof, J. A. H., & van Hemert, A. M. (2004). Somatoform disorders in general practice: Prevalence, functional impairment and comorbidity with anxiety and depressive disorders. *British Journal of Psychiatry, 184,* 470–476.

Derogatis, L. R. (1975). *SCL-90-R: Administration, scoring and procedures manual-II for the revised version and other instruments of the psychopathology rating scale series*. Towson, MD: Clinical Psychometric Research.

Dimsdale, J. E., Creed, F., Escobar, J., Sharpe, M., Wulsin, L., Barsky, A., . . . Levenson, J. (2013). Somatic symptom disorder: An important change in DSM. *Journal of Psychosomatic Research, 75,* 223–228.

Escobar, J. I., Allen, L. A., Hoyos Nervi, C., & Gara, M. A. (2001). General and cross-cultural considerations in a medical setting for patients presenting with medically unexplained symptoms. In G. J. G. Asmundson, S. Taylor, & B. J. Cox (Eds.), *Health anxiety: Clinical and research perspectives on hypochondriasis and related conditions* (pp. 220–245). New York, NY: Wiley.

Escobar, J. I., Gara, M., Waitzkin, H., Silver, R. C., Holman, A., & Compton, W. (1998). *DSM-IV* hypochondriasis in primary care. *General Hospital Psychiatry, 20,* 155–159.

Faravelli, C., Salvatori, S., Galassi, F., Aiazzi, L., Drei, C., & Cabras, P. (1997). Epidemiology of somatoform disorders: A community survey in Florence. *Social Psychiatry and Psychiatric Epidemiology, 32,* 24–29.

Fiddler, M., Jackson, J., Kapur, N., Wells, A., & Creed, F. (2004). Childhood adversity and frequent medical consultations. *General Hospital Psychiatry, 26,* 367–377.

Fink, P., Sørensen, L., Engberg, M., Holm, M., & Munk-Jørgensen, P. (1999). Somatization in primary care: Prevalence, health care utilization, and general practitioner recognition. *Psychosomatics, 40,* 330–338.

First, M. B., Spitzer, R. L., Gibbon, M., & Williams, J. B. W. (1996). *Structured clinical interview for DSM-IV axis I disorders—Patient edition*. New York, NY: State Psychiatric Institute, Biometrics Research Department.

First M. B., Williams J. B. W., Karg R. S., Spitzer R. L. (2015). *Structured Clinical Interview for DSM-5 Disorders, Clinician Version (SCID-5-CV)*. Arlington, VA: American Psychiatric Association.

Frances, A. (2013). The new somatic symptom disorder in DSM-5 risks mislabeling many people as mentally ill. *BMJ, 346,* f1580.

Fries, E., Hesse, J., Hellhammer, J., & Hellhammer, D. H. (2005). A new view on hypocortisolism. *Psychoneuroendocrinology, 30,* 1010–1016.

Furer, P., Walker, J. R., & Stein, M. B. (2007). *Treating health anxiety and fear of death*. New York, NY: Springer.

Gierk, B., Kohlmann, S., Kroenke, K., Spangenberg, L., Zenger, M., Brähler, E., & Löwe, B. (2014). The Somatic Symptom Scale–8 (SSS-8). *JAMA Internal Medicine, 174,* 399.

Gureje, O., Üstün, T. B., & Simon, G. E. (1997). The syndrome of hypochondriasis: A cross- national study in primary care. *Psychological Medicine, 27,* 1001–1010.

Hakala, M., Vahlberg, T., Niemi, P. M., & Karlsson, H. (2006). Brain glucose metabolism and temperament in relation to severe somatization. *Psychiatry and Clinical Neurosciences, 60,* 669–675.

Hedman, E., Axelsson, E., Andersson, E., Lekander, M., & Ljótsson, B. (2016). Exposure-based cognitive-behavioural therapy via the internet and as bibliotherapy for somatic symptom disorder and illness anxiety disorder: Randomised controlled trial. *British Journal of Psychiatry, 209,* 407–413.

Hennings, A., Zill, P., & Rief, W. (2009). Serotonin transporter gene promoter polymorphism and somatoform symptoms. *Journal of Clinical Psychiatry, 70,* 1536–1539.

Hessel, A., Geyer, M., Hinz, A., & Brahier, E. (2005). Utilization of the health care system due to somatoform complaints: Results of a representative survey. *Zeitschrift fur Psychosomatische Medizin und Psychotherapie, 51,* 38–56.

Hotopf, M., Mayou, R., Wadsworth, M., & Wessely, S. (1999). Childhood risk factors for adults with medically unexplained symptoms: Results from a national birth cohort study. *American Journal of Psychiatry, 156,* 1796–1800.

Hotopf, M., Wilson-Jones, C., Mayou, R., Wadsworth, M., & Wessely, S. (2000). Childhood predictors of adult medically unexplained hospitalisations: Results from a national birth cohort study. *British Journal of Psychiatry, 176,* 273–280.

Hubley, S., Uebelacker, L., & Eaton, C. (2014). Managing medically unexplined symptoms in primary care: A narrative review and treatment. *American Journal of Lifestyle Medicine, 10,* 109–119.

Hurwitz, T. A. (2004). Somatization and conversion disorder. *Canadian Journal of Psychiatry, 49,* 172–178.

Jonsson, F., San Sebastian, M., Strömsten, L. M. J., Hammarström, A., & Gustafsson, P. E. (2016). Life course pathways of adversities linking adolescent socioeconomic circumstances and functional somatic symptoms in mid-adulthood: A path analysis study. *PLOS One, 11,* e0155963.

Kendler, K., Aggen, S. H., Knudsen, G. P., Røysamb, E., Neale, M. C., & Reichborn-Kjennerud, T. (2011). The structure of genetic and environmental risk factors for syndromal and subsyndromal common *DSM*-IV axis I and all axis II disorders. *American Journal of Psychiatry, 168,* 29–39.

Kessler, R. C. (1994). The National Comorbidity Survey of the United States. *International Review of Psychiatry, 6,* 365–376.

Kessler, R. C., Berglund, P. A., Chiu, W.-T., Demler, O., Glantz, M., Lane, M. C., . . . Wells, K. B. (2008). The National Comorbidity Survey Replication (NCS-R): Cornerstone in improving mental health and mental health care in the United States. In R. C. Kessler & T. B. Üstün (Eds.), *The WHO World Mental Health Surveys: Global perspectives on the epidemiology of mental disorders* (pp. 165–209). New York, NY: Cambridge University Press.

Kessler, R. C., Chiu, W. T., Demler, O., Merikangas, K. R., & Walters, E. E. (2005). Prevalence, severity, and comorbidity of 12-month DSM-IV disorders in the national comorbidity survey replication. *Archives of General Psychiatry, 62,* 617–627.

Kessler, R. C., & Üstün, T. B. (2008). *The WHO World Mental Health Surveys: Global perspectives on the epidemiology of mental disorders.* New York, NY: Cambridge University Press.

Kirmayer, L. J., & Looper, K. J. (2007). Somatoform disorders. In M. Hersen, S. Turner, & D. Beidel (Eds.), *Adult psychopathology* (5th ed., pp. 410–472). Hoboken, NJ: Wiley.

Kirmayer, L. J., & Robbins, J. M. (1991). Three forms of somatization in primary care: Prevalence, co-occurrence, and sociodemographic characteristics. *Journal of Nervous and Mental Disease, 179,* 647–655.

Kirmayer, L. J., & Young, A. (1998). Culture and somatization: Clinical, epidemiological, and ethnographic perspectives. *Psychosomatic Medicine, 60,* 420–430.

Kroenke, K. (2003). Patients presenting with somatic complaints: Epidemiology, psychiatric co-morbidity and management. *International Journal of Methods in Psychiatric Research, 12,* 34–43.

Kroenke, K., Spitzer, R. L., & Williams, J. B. W. (2002). The PHQ-15: Validity of a new measure for evaluating the severity of somatic symptoms. *Psychosomatic Medicine, 64,* 258–266.

Leiknes, K. A., Finset, A., Moum, T., & Sandanger, I. (2008). Overlap, comorbidity, and the use of and stability of somatoform disorders current versus lifetime criteria. *Psychosomatics, 49,* 152–162.

Lembo, A. J., Zaman, M., Krueger, R. F., Tomenson, B. M., & Creed, F. H. (2009). Psychiatric disorder, irritable bowel syndrome, and extra-intestinal symptoms in a population-based sample of twins. *American Journal of Gastroenterology, 104,* 686–694.

Lowe, B., Spitzer, R. L., Williams, J. B. W., Mussell, M., Schellberg, D., & Kroenke, K. (2008). Depression, anxiety and somatization in primary care: Syndrome overlap and functional impairment. *General Hospital Psychiatry, 30,* 191–199.

Lucock M. P., & Morley, S. (1996). The health anxiety questionnaire. *British Journal of Health Psychology, 1,* 597–602.

Malis, R. W., Hartz, A. J., Doebbeling, C. C., & Noyes, R. Jr. (2002). Specific phobia of illness in the community. *General Hospital Psychiatry, 24*, 135–139.

Marshall, T., Jones, D. P. H., Ramchandani, P. G., Stein, A., & Bass, C. (2007). Intergenerational transmission of health beliefs in somatoform disorders: Exploratory study. *The British Journal of Psychiatry, 191*, 449–50.

Martin, R., Gordon, E. E., & Lounsbury, P. (1998). Gender disparities in the attribution of cardiac-related symptoms: Contribution of common sense models of illness. *Health Psychology, 17*, 346–357.

McFarlane, A. C., Atchison, M., Rafalowicz, E., & Papay, P. (1994). Physical symptoms in posttraumatic stress disorder. *Journal of Psychosomatic Research, 38*, 715–726.

Mechanic, D. (1983). Adolescent health and illness behavior: Review of the literature and a new hypothesis for the study of stress. *Journal of Human Stress, 9*, 4–13.

Miller, L. (1984). Neuropsychological concepts of somatoform disorders. *International Journal of Psychiatry in Medicine, 14*, 31–46.

Nimnuan, C., Hotopf, M., & Wessely, S. (2001). Medically unexplained symptoms: An epidemiological study in seven specialities. *Journal of Psychosomatic Research, 51*, 361–367.

Noyes, R., Kathol, R. G., Fisher, M. M., Phillips, B. M., Suelzer, M. T., & Holt, C. S. (1993). The validity of DSM-III-R hypochondriasis. *Archives of General Psychiatry, 50*, 961–970.

Noyes, R., Langbehn, D. R., Happel, R. L., Sieren, L. R., & Muller, B. A. (1999). Health Attitude Survey: A scale for assessing somatizing patients. *Psychosomatics, 40*, 470–478.

Olatunji, B. O., Kauffman, B. Y., Meltzer, S., Davis, M. L., Smits, J. A. J., & Powers, M. B. (2014). Cognitive-behavioral therapy for hypochondriasis/health anxiety: A meta-analysis of treatment outcome and moderators. *Behaviour Research and Therapy, 58*, 65–74.

Pennebaker, J. W. (1980). Perceptual and environmental determinants of coughing. *Basic and Applied Social Psychology, 1*, 83–91.

Pilowsky, I. (1967). Dimensions of hypochondriasis. *The British Journal of Psychiatry, 113*, 89–93.

Rief W., & Martin, A. (2014). How to use the new DSM-5 Somatic Symptom Disorder diagnosis in research and practice: A critical evaluation and a proposal for modifications. *Annual Review Clinical Psychology, 10*, 339–367.

Reiser, S. J., McMillan, K. A., Wright, K. D., & Asmundson, G. J. G. (2014). Adverse childhood experiences and health anxiety in adulthood. *Child Abuse and Neglect, 38*, 407–413.

Rief, W., Hennings, A., Riemer, S., & Euteneuer, F. (2010). Psychobiological differences between depression and somatization. *Journal of Psychosomatic Research, 68*, 495–502.

Rief, W., Hiller, W., Geissner, E., & Fichter, M. M. (1995). A two-year follow-up study of patients with somatoform disorders. *Psychosomatics, 36*, 376–386.

Rief, W., Hiller, W., & Heuser, J. (1997). *SOMS—Screening für somatoforme Störungen. Manual Zum Fragebogen (SOMS—the Screening for Somatoform Symptoms—Manual)*. Berne, Switzerland: Huber.

Robins, L. N., Helzer, J. E., Croughan, J., & Ratcliff, K. S. (1981). National Institute of Mental Health diagnostic interview schedule: Its history, characteristics, and validity. *Archives of General Psychiatry, 38*, 381–389.

Roelofs, K., Keijers, G. P. J., Hoogduin, C. A. L., Naring, G. W. B., & Moene, F. C. (2002). Childhood abuse in patients with conversion disorder. *American Journal of Psychiatry, 159*, 1908–1913.

Rost, K., Kashner, T. M., & Smith, G. R. Jr. (1994). Effectiveness of psychiatric intervention with somatization disorder patients: Improved outcomes at reduced cost. *General Hospital Psychiatry, 16*, 381–387.

Sakai, R., Nestoriuc, Y., Nolido, N. V., & Barsky, A. J. (2010). The prevalence of personality disorders in hypochondriasis. *Journal of Clinical Psychiatry, 71*, 41–47.

Salkovskis, P. M., Rimes, K. A., Warwick, H. M. C., & Clark, D. M. (2002). The Health Anxiety Inventory: development and validation of scales for the measurement of health anxiety and hypochondriasis. *Psychological Medicine, 32*(5), 843–853.

Sirri, L., & Fava, G. A. (2013). Diagnostic criteria for psychosomatic research and somatic symptom disorders. *Review of Psychiatry, 25*, 19–30.

Smith, C. G., Clarke, D. M., Handrinos, D., Dunsis, A., & McKenzie, D. P. (2000). Consultation-liaison psychiatrists' management of somatoform disorders. *Psychosomatics, 41*, 481–489.

Snijders, T. J., de Leeuw, F. E., Klumpers, U. M. H., Kappelle, L. J., & van Gijn, J. (2004). Prevalence and predictors of unexplained neurological symptoms in an academic neurology outpatient clinic: An observational study. *Journal of Neurology, 251*, 66–71.

Speckens, A. E., van Hemert, A. M., Bolk, J. H., Rooijmans, H. G. M., & Hengeveld, M. W. (1996). Unexplained physical symptoms: Outcome, utilization of medical care and associated factors. *Psychological Medicine, 26*, 745–752.

Starcevic, V. (2013). Hypochondriasis and health anxiety: Conceptual challenges. *British Journal of Psychiatry, 202*, 7–8.

Stewart, S. H., Taylor, S., & Baker, J. M. (1997). Gender differences in dimensions of anxiety sensitivity. *Journal of Anxiety Disorders, 11*, 179–200.

Stone, J., Carson, A., Aditya, H., Presscott, R., Zaubi, M., Warlow, C., & Sharpe, M. (2009). The role of physical injury in motor and sensory conversion symptoms: A systematic and narrative review. *Journal of Psychosomatic Research, 66*, 383–390.

Stone, J., Smyth, R., Carson, A., Warlow, C., & Sharpe, M. (2006). La belle indifference in conversion symptoms and hysteria. *British Journal of Psychiatry, 188*, 204–209.

Sykes, R. (2006). Somatoform disorders in *DSM-IV*: Mental or physical disorders? *Psychosomatic Research, 60*, 341–344.

Tak, L. M., Kingma, E. M., van Ockenburg, S. L., Ormel, J., & Rosmalen, J. G. M. (2015). Age- and sex-specific associations between adverse life events and functional bodily symptoms in the general population. *Journal of Psychosomatic Research, 79*, 112–116.

Tak, L. M., & Rosmalen, J. G. M. (2010). Dysfunction of stress responsive systems as a risk factor for functional somatic syndromes. *Journal of Psychosomatic Research, 68*, 461–468.

Taylor, S. (2000). *Understanding and treating panic disorder*. New York, NY: Wiley.

Taylor, S. (2009). Is it time to revise the classification of somatoform disorders? [Review of *Somatic presentations of mental disorders: Refining the research agenda for DSM-V*, by Dimsdale et al. (Eds.).] *PsycCRITIQUES, 54*(36), Article 7 (http://psycnet.apa.org/record/2009-11099-001).

Taylor, S., & Asmundson, G. J. G. (2004). *Treating health anxiety: A cognitive-behavioral approach*. New York, NY: Guilford Press.

Taylor, S., & Asmundson, G. J. G. (2012). Etiology of hypochondriasis: A preliminary behavioral-genetic investigation. *International Journal of Genetics and Gene Therapy, 2*, 1–5.

Taylor, S., Jang, K. L., Stein, M. B., & Asmundson, G. J. G. (2008). A behavioral-genetic analysis of health anxiety: Implications for the cognitive-behavioral model of hypochondriasis. *Journal of Cognitive Psychotherapy, 22*, 143–153.

Taylor, S., Zvolensky, M. J., Cox, B. J., Deacon, B., Heimberg, R. G., Ledley, D. R., . . . Cardenas, S. J. (2007). Robust dimensions of anxiety sensitivity: Development and initial validation of the Anxiety Sensitivity Index–3. *Psychological Assessment, 19*(2), 176–188.

Torgersen, S. (1986). Genetics of somatoform disorders. *Archives of General Psychiatry, 43*, 502–505.

Toussaint, A., Lowe, B., Brahler, E., & Jordan, P. (2017). The Somatic Symptom Disorder – B Criteria Scale (SSD-12): Factorial structure, validity, and population-based norms. *Journal of Psychosomatic Research, 97*, 9–17.

Toussaint, A., Murray, A. M., Voigt, K., Herzog, A., Gierk, B., Kroenke, K., . . . Lowe, B. (2015). Development and Validation of the Somatic Symptom Disorder-B Criteria Scale (SSD-12). *Psychosomatic Medicine, 78*, 1–8.

Ursin, H. (2005). Press stop to start: The role of inhibition for choice and health. *Psychoneuroendoc-rinology, 30,* 1059–1065.

Van der Kolk, B. A., Pelcovitz, D., Roth, S., Mandel, F. S., McFarlane, A., & Herman, J. L. (1996). Dissociation, somatization, and affect dysregulation: The complexity of adaptation to trauma. *American Journal of Psychiatry, 153,* 83–93.

van Dessel, N. C., van der Wouden, J. C., Dekker, J., & van der Horst, H. E. (2016). Clinical value of *DSM* IV and *DSM* 5 criteria for diagnosing the most prevalent somatoform disorders in patients with medically unexplained physical symptoms (MUPS). *Journal of Psychosomatic Research, 82,* 4–10.

Veale, D. (2004). Advances in a cognitive behavioural model of body dysmorphic disorder. *Body Image, 1,* 113–125.

Vervoort, T., Goubert, L., Eccleston, C., Bijttebier, P., & Crombez, G. (2006). Catastrophic thinking about pain is independently associated with pain severity, disability, and somatic complaints in school children and children with chronic pain. *Journal of Pediatric Psychology, 31,* 674–683.

Voigt, K., Wollburg, E., Weinmann, N., Herzog, A., Meyer, B., Langs, G., & Löwe, B. (2012). Predictive validity and clinical utility of *DSM-5* Somatic Symptom Disorder – Comparison with *DSM-IV* somatoform disorders and additional criteria for consideration. *Journal of Psychosomatic Research, 73,* 345–350.

Vuilleumier, P. (2005). Hysterical conversion and brain function. *Progress in Brain Research, 150,* 309–329.

Weck, F., Neng, J. M. B., Schwind, J., & Hofling, V. (2015). Exposure therapy changes dysfunctional evaluations of somatic symptoms in patients with hypochondriasis (health anxiety): A randomized controlled trial. *Journal of Anxiety Disorders, 34,* 1–7.

Weigel, A., Husing, P., Kohlmann, S., Lehman, M., Shedden-Mora, M., Toussaint, A., Lowe, B., & EURONET-SOMA Group. (in press). A European research network to improve diagnosis, treatment, and care for patients with persistent somatic symptoms: Work report of the EURO-NET-SOMA conference series. *Journal of Psychosomatic Research, 97,* 136–138.

Wells, A. (1997). *Cognitive therapy for anxiety disorders.* New York, NY: Wiley.

Wing, J. K., Babor, T., Brugha, T., Burke, J., Cooper, J. E., Giel, R., & Sartorius, N. (1990). SCAN: Schedules for Clinical Assessment in Neuropsychiatry. *Archives of General Psychiatry, 47,* 589–593.

Wittchen, H. U., & Jacobi, F. (2005). Size and burden of mental disorders in Europe: A critical review and appraisal of 27 studies. *European Neuropsychopharmacology, 15,* 357–376.

Wood, P. B., Glabus, M. F., Simpson, R., & Patterson, J. C. (2009). Changes in gray matter density in fibromyalgia: Correlation with dopamine metabolism. *The Journal of Pain, 10,* 609–618.

Woolfolk, R. L., & Allen, L. A. (2007). *Treating somatization: A cognitive-behavioral approach.* New York, NY: Guilford Press.

World Health Organization. (1990). *The composite international diagnostic interview (CIDI).* Geneva, Switzerland: Author.

World Health Organization. (1994). *Somatoform disorders schedule (SDS).* Geneva, Switzerland: Author.

World Health Organization. (2007). *International statistical classification of diseases and related health problems,* 10th revision. Geneva, Switzerland: Author.

CHAPTER 13

Dissociative Disorders

STEVEN JAY LYNN, JOANNA M. BERG, SCOTT O. LILIENFELD, HARALD
MERCKELBACH, TIMO GIESBRECHT, DALENA VAN-HEUGTEN-VAN DER KLOET,
MICHELLE ACCARDI-RAVID, COLLEEN MUNDO, and CRAIG P. POLIZZI

THE MOST RECENT edition of the *Diagnostic and Statistical Manual of Mental Disorders* (*DSM-5*; American Psychiatric Association [APA], 2013) defines dissociative disorders as conditions marked by a disruption of and/or discontinuity in the normal integration of consciousness, memory, identity, emotion, perception, body representation, motor control, and behavior" (p. 291). The presentation of dissociative disorders is often dramatic, perplexing, and highly variable, both within and across individuals. The hallmarks of dissociation are profound and often unpredictable shifts in consciousness, the sense of self, and perceptions of the environment.

DSM-5 asserts that the dissociative disorders share a common feature: They are frequently manifested in the wake of trauma and are influenced by their proximity to trauma (p. 291). Later in the chapter, we contrast the post-traumatic theory that is firmly embedded in the *DSM-5* account of dissociation with a competing theory that does not conceptualize trauma as a necessary precursor to dissociation. In the course of our discussion, we will present a case study that illustrates the treatment of a patient with dissociative identity disorder (DID) and highlight controversies that have dogged the field of dissociation since the time of Janet's seminal writings on the topic (Janet, 1889/ 1973).

The *DSM-5* (APA, 2013) identifies three major dissociative disorders that we discuss in turn—dissociative amnesia, depersonalization/derealization, and DID. We then present an overview of dissociation in general, followed by a more detailed discussion of diagnostic considerations, prevalence, assessment, and etiology specific to each of the dissociative disorders.

1. *Dissociative amnesia* is marked by an inability to recall important autobiographical information, usually of a traumatic or stressful nature inconsistent with ordinary forgetting. This condition most often "consists of localized or selective amnesia for a specific event or events, or generalized amnesia for identity and life history" (APA, 2013, p. 298).

Adult Psychopathology and Diagnosis, Eighth Edition. Edited by Deborah C. Beidel and B. Christopher Frueh.
© 2018 John Wiley & Sons, Inc. Published 2018 by John Wiley & Sons, Inc.
Companion website: www.wiley.com/go/beidel/psychopathology8e

2. *Depersonalization/derealization disorder (DDD)*, formerly known as depersonalization disorder, is diagnosed on the basis of symptoms of persistent depersonalization, derealization, or both. Depersonalization symptoms include experiences of unreality; feelings of detachment or being an outside observer of one's thoughts, feelings, sensations, or actions; an unreal or absent sense of self; physical and emotional numbing; and time distortion. In contrast, derealization experiences involve feelings of unreality or detachment with respect to one's surroundings that include the experience of individuals or objects as unreal, dreamlike, foggy, visually distorted, or lifeless.

3. *Dissociative identity disorder* (DID; formerly called multiple personality disorder) is marked by a disruption of identity characterized by two or more distinct personality states and recurrent gaps in the recall of everyday events, personal information, and/or traumatic events that are inconsistent with ordinary forgetting (APA, 2013, p. 292).

DSM-5 also includes a fourth category of other specified dissociative disorder, for patients who do not meet full criteria for any dissociative disorder. The essential features here are chronic and recurrent clusters of mixed dissociative symptoms, identity disturbance due to prolonged and intense coercive persuasion, acute dissociative reactions to stressors, and dissociative trance. Additionally, *DSM-5* includes a fifth category of unspecified dissociative disorder in which criteria are not met for a specific dissociative disorder and there is insufficient information to make a more specific diagnosis. Finally, *DSM-5* currently describes a dissociative subtype of post-traumatic stress disorder (PTSD) in which persistent or recurring feelings of depersonalization and/or derealization are manifested in reaction to trauma-related stimuli. *DSM-5* requires that the symptoms of all dissociative disorders must cause significant distress, impairment of functioning in major aspects of daily life, or both, and must not be attributable to the effects of a substance or another medical condition.

Some epidemiological studies among psychiatric inpatients and outpatients have reported prevalence rates of dissociative disorders exceeding 10% (Ross, Anderson, Fleischer, & Norton, 1991; Sar, Tutkun, Alyanak, Bakim, & Barai, 2000; Tutkun, Sar, Yargiç, Özpulat, Yank, & Kiziltan, 1998), and a study among community women in Turkey even reported a prevalence rate of 18.3% for lifetime diagnoses of a dissociative disorder (Sar, Akyüz, & Dogan, 2007). In contrast, many authors would take issue with these high prevalence rates in both clinical and nonclinical samples. Indeed, as our discussion will reveal, estimates of the prevalence of dissociative disorders vary widely and are surrounded by considerable controversy.

Although many authors regard symptoms of depersonalization/derealization and dissociative amnesia as core features of dissociation, the concept of dissociation is semantically open and lacks a precise and generally accepted definition (Giesbrecht, Lynn, Lilienfeld, & Merckelbach, 2008). This definitional ambiguity is related, in no small measure, to the substantial diversity of experiences that fall under the rubric of "dissociation." Dissociative symptoms range in their manifestation from common cognitive failures (e.g., lapses in attention), to nonpathological absorption and daydreaming, to more pathological manifestations of dissociation, as represented by the dissociative disorders (Holmes et al., 2005).

This variability raises the possibility that some of these symptoms are milder manifestations of the same etiology or have different etiologies and biological substrates, raising questions about whether dissociation is a unitary conceptual domain (Hacking, 1995; Holmes et al., 2005; Jureidini, 2003). Indeed, van der Hart, Nijenhuis, Steele, and

Brown (2004, 2006) have distinguished ostensibly trauma-related or pathological dissociation, which they term structural dissociation of the personality, from nonpathological dissociative experiences (e.g., altered sense of time, absorption). Structural dissociation, in turn, can be subdivided into levels that encompass primary dissociation, which is thought to involve one purportedly apparently normal part of the personality (ANP) and one emotional part of the personality (EP), secondary structural dissociation, supposedly associated with a single ANP and further division of the EP, and tertiary dissociation, ostensibly limited to DID and characterized by several ANPs and EPs. Nevertheless, as our review will demonstrate, researchers' attempts to discriminate pathological from nonpathological dissociative experiences psychometrically have been subject to criticism and have been less than uniformly successful (Giesbrecht et al., 2008; Modestin & Erni, 2004; Waller, Putnam, & Carlson, 1996; Waller & Ross, 1997).

Other researchers (Allen, 2001; Cardeña, 1994; Holmes et al., 2005) have proposed two distinct forms of dissociation: detachment and compartmentalization. Detachment consists of depersonalization and derealization, which we describe in some detail later, and related phenomena, like out-of-body experiences. Psychopathological conditions, which reflect symptoms of detachment, include depersonalization disorder and feelings of detachment that occur during flashbacks in PTSD. Compartmentalization, in contrast, ostensibly encompasses dissociative amnesia, marked by extensive forgetting of autobiographical material, and somatoform dissociation, such as sensory loss and "unexplained" neurological symptoms (Nijenhuis, Spinhoven, Van Dyck, Van der Hart, & Vanderlinden, 1998). The core feature of compartmentalization is a deficit in deliberate control of processes or actions that would normally be amenable to control, as is evident in DID or somatization disorder. Although clinicians may find it helpful to subdivide dissociative symptoms into two different symptom clusters (Bernstein-Carlson & Putnam, 1993), attempts to differentiate such clusters on a psychometric basis have not been consistently successful (see, for an example, Ruiz et al., 2008).

Dissociation is often presumed to reflect a splitting of consciousness, although it must be distinguished from the superficially similar but much debated concept of Freudian repression. Specifically, dissociation can be described as a "horizontal" split; that is, consciousness is split into two or more parts that operate in parallel. In contrast, repression is more akin to a "vertical" split, in which consciousness is arranged in levels, and traumatic or otherwise undesirable memories are ostensibly pushed downwards and rendered more or less inaccessible.

Although the existence of dissociation as a clinical symptom is not much in dispute, dissociative disorders are among the most controversial psychiatric diagnoses. Disagreement generally centers on the etiology of these disorders, with advocates often arguing for largely trauma-based origins (e.g., Dalenberg et al., 2012; 2014; Gleaves, 1996). In this light, dissociative symptoms are regarded as manifestations of a coping mechanism that serves to mitigate the impact of highly aversive or traumatic events (Gershuny & Thayer, 1999; Nijenhuis, van der Hart, & Steel, 2010). In contrast, skeptics often emphasize the role of social influences, including cultural expectancies and inadvertent therapist cueing of symptoms (e.g., Lilienfeld et al., 1999; Lynn et al., 2015; McHugh, 2008). As we will learn later in the chapter, the controversies stemming from etiology and classification of dissociative disorders extend to their assessment and treatment. We will focus our discussion on chronic dissociative symptoms, rather than dissociation at the time of a highly aversive event (i.e., peritraumatic dissociation). Also, we will not elaborate on the dissociative subtype of PTSD described in *DSM-5* (see, for a critical analysis, Dutra & Wolf, 2017). However, we will present a number of "state" measures of dissociation because researchers not infrequently consider temporary changes in dissociation in the context of research on more chronic presentations of dissociation.

DISSOCIATIVE AMNESIA

The diagnosis of dissociative amnesia requires that the memory loss is extensive and not attributable to substance use or to a neurological or other medical condition such as age-related cognitive loss, complex partial seizures, or closed-head brain injury and that the symptoms are not better explained by DID, PTSD, acute stress disorder, somatic symptom disorder, or major or mild neurocognitive disorder (APA, 2013, p. 298). This disorder, formerly referred to as psychogenic amnesia, often presents as retrospective amnesia for some period or series of periods in a person's life, frequently involving a traumatic experience.

DSM-5 lists several subtypes of dissociative amnesia. In localized amnesia, the individual cannot recall any information from a specific period of time, such as total forgetting of a holiday week. Selective amnesia involves the loss of memories for some, but not all, events from a specific period of time. In generalized amnesia, individuals cannot recall anything about their entire lives, and in continuous amnesia, individuals forget each new event as it occurs. Finally, systematized amnesia consists of the "loss of memory for specific categories of information" (e.g., sexual abuse, a particular person). These last three types of dissociative amnesia—generalized, continuous, and systematized—are much less common than the others, and may be manifestations of more complex dissociative disorders, such as DID rather than dissociative amnesia alone.

Lynn et al. (2014a) argued that the central diagnostic criterion for dissociative amnesia is vague and subjective in stipulating that one or more episodes of inability to recall important information must be ". . . inconsistent with ordinary forgetting" (APA, 2013, p. 298). The reliability of judgments of what constitutes "ordinary forgetfulness" is questionable, and what is "ordinary" hinges on a variety of factors, including the situational context and presence of comorbid conditions. A similar point was raised by Read and Lindsay (2000), who demonstrated that when people are encouraged to remember more about a selected target event, they report their forgetting to be more extensive, compared with individuals who are asked to simply reminisce about a target event.

Epidemiology

Because rates of reporting vary so widely, it is difficult to obtain reliable epidemiological information regarding dissociative amnesia. Questions concerning the validity of dissociative amnesia as a diagnostic entity are fueled by markedly different prevalence rates in the general population across cultures: 0.2% in China, 0.9% and 7.3% in Turkey, and 3.0% in Canada (Dell, 2009). These varying prevalence estimates could reflect genuine cultural differences, but they could just as plausibly reflect different interviewer criteria for evaluating amnesia.

The *DSM-5* states that dissociative amnesia can present in any age group, although it is more difficult to diagnose in younger children due to their difficulty in answering questions about periods of forgetting and possible confusion with a number of other disorders and conditions, including inattention, anxiety, oppositional behavior, and learning disorders. There may be just one episode of amnesia, or there may be multiple episodes, with each episode lasting anywhere from minutes to decades. Other sources (e.g., Coons, 1998) suggest that most cases occur in individuals in their 30s or 40s, and that 75% of cases last between 24 hours and 5 days. The prevalence of dissociative amnesia is approximately equal between genders. Still others argue that the scientific evidence for the existence of dissociative amnesia is unconvincing, and that barring brain injury or substance abuse or dependence, individuals who have experienced trauma do not forget those events (e.g., McNally, 2003; Pope, Hudson, Bodkin, & Oliva, 1998).

Certain cases of purported traumatic amnesia are in fact attributable to organic or other nondissociative causes. For example, when critiquing a "convincing demonstration of dissociative amnesia" (Brown, Scheflin, & Hammond, 1997), McNally (2004) discussed a study (Dollinger, 1985) of two children who witnessed a playmate struck and killed by lightning, and who were later diagnosed with dissociative amnesia. Yet as McNally noted, this diagnosis was clearly mistaken, because the children had also been struck by lightning and knocked unconscious.

Amusingly, and perhaps tellingly, Pope, Poliakoff, Parker, Boynes, and Hudson (2007) offered a reward of $1,000 to "the first individual who could find a case of dissociative amnesia for a traumatic event in any fictional or nonfictional work before 1800" (p. 225) on the basis that, whereas the vast majority of psychological symptoms can be found in literature or records dating back centuries, dissociative amnesia appears only in more modern literature beginning in the late 1800s. Over 100 individuals came forward with examples, but none met the diagnostic criteria for the disorder (although the prize later went to someone who discovered a case of dissociative amnesia in a 1786 opera, *Nina*, by the French composer Nicholas Dalayrac). Although Pope and colleagues' challenge does not "prove" anything regarding the validity of the disorder, its relative scarcity, and apparently recent (perhaps after the late 18th century) development, raise troubling questions about its existence as a natural category or entity.

A special form of dissociative amnesia is crime-related amnesia. Many perpetrators of violent crimes claim to experience great difficulty remembering the essential details of the crime they committed (Moskowitz, 2004). Memory loss for crime has been reported in 25–40% of homicide cases and severe sex offenses. Nevertheless, skeptics believe that genuine dissociative amnesia in these cases is rare. They have pointed out that trauma victims (e.g., concentration camp survivors) almost never report dissociative amnesia (Merckelbach, Dekkers, Wessel, & Roefs, 2003). For example, Rivard, Dietz, Matell, and Widawski (2002) examined a large sample of police officers involved in critical shooting incidents and found no reports of amnesia.

Also, recent laboratory research shows that when participants encode information while in a "survival mode," this manipulation yields superior memory effects (Nairne & Pandeirada, 2008). This finding is difficult to reconcile with the idea of dissociative amnesia while committing a crime. Thus, it is likely that feigning underlies most claims of crime-related amnesia (Van Oorsouw & Merckelbach, 2010), and the recent literature provides detailed case studies illustrating this point (Marcopolus, Hedjar, & Arredondo, 2016).

DISSOCIATIVE FUGUE

Dissociative fugue (previously called psychogenic fugue) is arguably the most controversial dissociative phenomenon after DID. In *DSM-IV-TR*, dissociative fugue (i.e., short-lived reversible amnesia for personal identity, involving unplanned travel or wandering) was listed as a separate diagnosis. In *DSM-5*, dissociative fugue—defined therein as apparently purposeful travel or bewildered wandering associated with amnesia for identity or other important autobiographical information—is no longer diagnosed as a disorder in its own right, but is instead coded as a condition that can accompany dissociative amnesia. In a fugue ("fugue" has the same etymology as the word "fugitive") episode, amnesia for identity may be so extreme that a person physically escapes his or her present surroundings and adopts an entirely new identity. If and when this identity develops, it is often characterized by higher levels of extraversion than the individual displayed pre-fugue, and he or she usually presents as well integrated and nondisordered.

Periods of fugue vary considerably across individuals, both in duration and in distance traveled. In some cases, the travel can be a brief and relatively short trip, whereas, in more extreme cases, it can involve traveling thousands of miles and even crossing national borders. While in the dissociative fugue state, individuals often appear to be devoid of psychopathology; if they attract attention at all, it is usually because of amnesia or confusion about personal identity. Again, it is doubtful that fugues constitute a fixed and cross-cultural diagnostic category. Hacking (1995) provides a detailed historical and critical analysis of fugue showing that they first appeared in the 19th century and since that time fluctuated in apparent prevalence and acceptance by the psychiatric community.

DIAGNOSTIC CONSIDERATIONS

Although *DSM-5* notes that dissociative fugue, with travel, is not uncommon in DID, dissociative fugue may manifest with other symptoms, including depression, anxiety, dysphoria, grief, shame, guilt, stress, and aggressive or suicidal impulses (APA, 2013). Reportedly, the condition often develops as a result of traumatic or stressful events, which has led to controversy and ambiguity regarding the relation between dissociative fugue and PTSD. Precipitants associated with the development of dissociative fugue include war or natural disasters, as well as the avoidance of various stressors, such as marital discord or financial or legal problems (Coons, 1998). Such avoidance suggests that clinicians must be certain to rule out malingering and factitious disorders before diagnosing dissociative fugue. Staniliou and Markowitsch (2014) discuss basic memory mechanisms that might be involved in fugue states.

Certain culture-bound syndromes exhibit similar symptoms to dissociative fugue. These include *amok*, present in Western Pacific cultures (which has given rise to the colloquialism "running amok"), *pibloktok*, which is present in native cultures of the Arctic, and Navajo "frenzy" witchcraft, all of which are marked by "a sudden onset of a high level of activity, a trancelike state, potentially dangerous behavior in the form of running or fleeing, and ensuing exhaustion, sleep, and amnesia" for the duration of the episode (APA, 2000, p. 524; Simons & Hughes, 1985).

EPIDEMIOLOGY

DSM-IV-TR places the population prevalence estimate of dissociative fugue at 0.02%, with the majority of cases occurring in adults (APA, 2000, p. 524). Ross (2009b) observed that in the approximately 3,000 individuals he treated in his trauma program over a 12-year period, he encountered fewer than 10 individuals with pure dissociative amnesia or pure dissociative fugue, although he noted that symptoms of amnesia and fugue were common in the patients he admitted.

DEPERSONALIZATION/DEREALIZATION DISORDER

Depersonalization/derealization disorder (DDD) is one of the most common dissociative disorders and perhaps the least controversial. In DDD, reality testing remains intact (APA, 2013, p. 302): Individuals are aware that the sensations are not real and that they are not experiencing a break from reality akin to psychosis. In a departure from *DSM-IV*, in which depersonalization and derealization were diagnosed separately, *DSM-5* created a new diagnostic category of DDD. This "lumping" of formerly separate conditions is supported by findings (Simeon, 2009a) that individuals with derealization symptoms do not differ significantly from those with depersonalization accompanied by derealization in salient respects (e.g., illness characteristics, comorbidity, demographics).

Greatly contributing to our knowledge about depersonalization symptoms has been the development of well-validated screening instruments, notably the Cambridge Depersonalization Scale (CDS; Sierra & Berrios, 2000; Sierra, Baker, Medford, & David, 2005). Depersonalization episodes are not uncommonly triggered by intense stress and are often associated with high levels of interpersonal impairment (Simeon et al., 1997).

Episodes of depersonalization or derealization are also frequently associated with panic attacks, unfamiliar environments, perceived threatening social interactions, the ingestion of hallucinogens, depression, and PTSD (Simeon, Knutelska, Nelson, & Guralnik, 2003). Individuals with DDD are also more likely than healthy individuals to report a history of emotional abuse. In contrast, general dissociation scores are better predicted by a history of combined emotional and sexual abuse (Simeon, Guralnik, Schmeidler, Sirof, & Knutelska, 2001).

DIAGNOSTIC CONSIDERATIONS

Nearly 50% of adults have experienced at least one episode of depersonalization in their lifetimes, usually in adolescence, although a single episode is not sufficient to meet criteria for the disorder (Aderibigbe, Bloch, & Walker, 2001). Because depersonalization and derealization are common, DDD should be diagnosed only if these symptoms are persistent or recurrent and are severe enough to cause distress or impairment in functioning, or both. The distress associated with DDD may be extreme, with sufferers reporting they feel robotic, unreal, and "unalive." They may fear becoming psychotic, losing control, and suffering permanent brain damage (Simeon, 2009a). Individuals with DDD may perceive an alteration in the size or shape of objects around them. Other people may appear mechanical or unfamiliar, and affected individuals may experience a disturbance in their sense of time (Simeon & Abugel, 2006).

Although symptoms of depersonalization often occur in the presence of psychotic symptoms (e.g., Gonzalez-Torres et al., 2010; Goren et al., 2012; Vogel, Braungardt, Grabe, Schneider, & Klauer, 2013), a diagnosis of DDD requires that the symptoms do not occur exclusively in the course of another mental disorder, nor can they be attributable to substance abuse or dependence or to a general medical condition. Furthermore, DDD should not be diagnosed solely in the context of meditative or trance practices.

Symptoms of other disorders, such as anxiety disorders, major depression, somatoform disorders, substance use disorders, and certain personality disorders (especially avoidant, borderline, and obsessive-compulsive), may also be present in the context of DDD (Belli, Ural, Vardar, Yesilyrt, & Oncu, 2012; Lynn et al., 2014b; Simeon et al., 1997). Depersonalization and derealization symptoms are also commonly part of the symptom picture of acute stress disorder (ASD; APA, 2013), which is often a precursor to PTSD.

EPIDEMIOLOGY

DSM-5 estimates the lifetime prevalence of DDD in the United States at 2%, with a range of 0.8– 2.8% (see also Ross, 1991), suggesting that DDD might be as common as or more common than schizophrenia and bipolar disorder. DDD is diagnosed almost equally in women and men (Simeon et al., 2003). It frequently presents for treatment in adolescence or adulthood, even as late as the 40s, though its onset may be earlier. Estimates of the age of onset of DDD range from 16.1 (Simeon et al., 1997) to 22 years (Baker et al., 2003).

The onset and course of DDD vary widely across individuals. Some people experience a sudden onset and others a more gradual onset; some experience a chronic form of the disorder, whereas others experience it episodically. In about two-thirds of people with DDD, the course is chronic, and symptoms of depersonalization are present most of the time, if not continually. Episodes of depersonalization may last from hours to weeks or months, and in more extreme cases, years or decades (Simeon, 2009a).

DISSOCIATIVE IDENTITY DISORDER

According to *DSM-5*, "the defining feature of DID is the presence of two or more distinct personality states or experiences of possession" (APA, 2013, p. 292). Thus, the requirement that people diagnosed with DID must experience distinct identities that recurrently take control over one's behavior is no longer present. Importantly, in *DSM-5* "distinct personality states" replaces the term *identities*. The diagnostic language in *DSM-5* represents a marked departure from *DSM-II* (APA, 1968), which used the term multiple personalities, and from *DSM-IV* (APA, 1994), which labeled the condition DID to underscore alterations in identity, rather than fixed and/or complete "personalities."

These shifts in diagnostic criteria may prove to be problematic and result in changes in the prevalence rates of DID. For example, what constitutes a personality state or an experience of possession may be open to greater interpretation compared with previous iterations of *DSM*. Moreover, in *DSM-5*, signs and symptoms of personality alteration may be not merely "observed by others," but also "reported by the individual" (APA, 2013; p. 292), further expanding opportunities for the diagnosis of DID. In cases in which alternate personality states are not witnessed, in *DSM-5* it is still possible to diagnose the disorder when there are "sudden alterations or discontinuities in sense of self or agency . . . and recurrent dissociative amnesias" (APA, 2013; p. 293), creating even more latitude and subjectivity in the diagnosis of DID. Moreover, amnesia is no longer restricted to traumatic events and may now be diagnosed in relation to everyday events, which may also increase the base rates of diagnosed DID. Although *DSM-5* no longer defines DID in terms of "distinct identities that recurrently take control of the individual's behavior" (*DSM-IV*, p. 519), in the remainder of the chapter, we will not refrain from using the terms *personalities* and *identities,* insofar as these terms (a) continue to be widely used in the extant literature and (b) encompass "personality states."

DIAGNOSTIC CONSIDERATIONS

To meet diagnostic criteria for DID, an individual's symptoms cannot be attributable to substance use or to a medical condition, and the "disturbance is not a normal part of a broadly accepted cultural or religious practice" (APA, 2013; p. 292). When the disorder is assessed in children, the symptoms must not be confused with imaginary play. To recognize cultural variants of dissociative phenomena, *DSM-5* refers to a "possession form" of DID, which is "typically manifest as behaviors that appear as if a 'spirit,' supernatural being, or outside person has taken control, such that the individual begins speaking or acting in a distinctly different manner" (APA, 2013, p. 293). Because such manifestations are not uncommon in different cultures (see, for a discussion of trance/possession phenomena, Cardeña, van Duijl, Weiner, & Terhune, 2009), to warrant a diagnosis of DID, the identities must be present recurrently, be unwanted or involuntary, engender significant distress or impairment, and not be a part of accepted cultural/religious practices. Some authors have questioned clinicians' ability to discriminate between pathological and nonpathological forms of possession (see, for a discussion, Delmonte, Lucchetti, Moreira-Almeida, & Farias, 2016).

In nonpossession forms of DID, there is typically considerable variation in the presentation of symptoms. Nevertheless, the primary identity or personality state in an individual with DID often carries the individual's given name and tends to be "passive, dependent, guilty, and depressed." Other personalities, often called "alters," may be assertive or even aggressive and hostile, and these more dominant identities usually possess more complete memories regarding the individual's actions and history. Within one individual, there can often be anywhere between two and 100 or more personalities, with approximately 50% of individuals reporting 10 or fewer distinct identities, although extreme cases of many as 4,500 alters have been reported (Acocella, 1999). Reported identities are usually just "regular" people, but more extreme and bizarre cases exist. There have been reports of identities claiming to be Mr. Spock from *Star Trek*, the rock star Madonna, the bride of Satan, and even a lobster.

Researchers have documented substantial comorbidity of DID with other disorders. For example, Ellason, Ross, and Fuchs (1996) reported that DID patients met criteria for an average of eight Axis I disorders and 4.5 Axis II disorders. One-half to two-thirds of patients with DID meet diagnostic criteria for borderline personality disorder (BPD; Coons, Bowman, & Milstein, 1988; Horevitz & Braun, 1984). Conversely, Sar, Akyuz, Kugu, Ozturk, and Ertem-Vehid (2006) found that 72.5% of patients screened for BPD had a dissociative disorder. In one study, researchers (Kemp, Gilbertson, & Torem, 1988) reported no significant differences between BPD and DID patients on measures of personality traits, cognitive and adaptive functioning, and clinician ratings, suggesting noteworthy commonalities between the two conditions. Histories of sexual and physical abuse are also commonly reported in both patient groups, and BPD patients score well above general population norms on measures of dissociation (Lauer, Black, & Keen, 1993). High levels of dissociation among BPD patients exacerbate cognitive performance deficits (Krause-Utz et al., 2017; Winter et al., 2015). Although Lauer et al. (1993) suggested that DID is an epiphenomenon of the combination of BPD with high suggestibility, Brand et al. (2016) argued that DID and BPD are distinct disorders.

Individuals with DID often experience additional symptoms, including self-mutilation; suicidal or aggressive behavior; as well as major depression, substance abuse, and sexual, eating, and sleep disorders (Fullerton et al., 2000; North, Ryall, Ricci, & Wetzel, 1993; Ross, 1997). Accordingly, some clinicians have argued that the DID diagnosis really is a severity marker identifying extreme variants of a host of other disorders (for an extensive discussion see North et al., 1993).

Many DID patients meet the criteria for schizoaffective disorder (Lauer et al., 1993), and as many as half have received a previous diagnosis of schizophrenia (Ross & Norton, 1988). Indeed, auditory and visual hallucinations are common in both DID and schizophrenia. However, patients with DID commonly report that hallucinated voices originate inside their heads, whereas patients with schizophrenia tend to perceive the origin of voices outside their heads and possess less insight into the nature of their symptoms (Coons, 1998; Kluft, 1993).

Chiu et al. (2016a) reported that among acute psychiatric patients, symptoms of psychosis and dissociation were associated with an altered sense of individuality. DID patients have been reported to endorse more positive symptoms (e.g., delusions, hallucinations, and suspiciousness) and Schneiderian first-rank symptoms, which include themes of passivity, than do schizophrenic patients (Ellason & Ross, 1995; Steinberg, Rounsaville, & Cichetti, 1990). Ellason and Ross (1995) argued that the presence of positive symptoms can be used to formulate an accurate differential diagnosis between the two disorders, although further research regarding this possibility is necessary (for further diagnostic considerations see Steinberg & Siegel, 2008).

Post-traumatic stress disorder is one of the most commonly comorbid conditions with DID (Loewenstein, 1991). Moreover, PTSD patients are more likely to present with symptoms of dissociation (e.g., numbing, amnesia, flashback phenomena) than are patients with major depression, schizophrenia, and schizoaffective disorder (Bremner, Steinberg, Southwick, Johnson, & Charney, 1993).

DSM-5 lists a number of differential conditions that clinicians should consider before diagnosing a patient with DID. Two of these are malingering and factitious disorder in which individuals intentionally fabricate symptoms. For those who want to fabricate illness, the odd, unusual, and highly subjective experiences that are inherent to dissociative symptoms are ideal because they signal so clearly to other people that one suffers from a disease (Kuperman, 2006). Recent studies have drawn attention to the overlap between dissociative symptoms and feigning tendencies (Merckelbach, Boskovic, Pesy, Dalsklev, & Lynn, 2017) and, given this state of affairs, clinicians are well advised to look into the possibility of feigning with so-called symptom validity tests (see later) when psychometrically evaluating the nature and intensity of dissociative symptoms.

EPIDEMIOLOGY

Dissociative identity disorder may be episodic or continuous, and in some cases may remit after the late 40s (APA, 2000). There are documented cases of DID extending decades, and the concept of fragmented or multiple personalities is an ancient one. That said, the number of cases has increased exponentially in the past few decades. Prior to 1970, there were approximately 80 reported cases, but by 1986 that number had ballooned to approximately 6,000. As of 1998, there were approximately 40,000 cases (Lilienfeld & Lynn, 2015).

Population prevalence estimates vary widely, from extremely rare (e.g., Piper, 1997; Rifkin, Ghisalbert, Dimatou, Jin, & Sethi, 1998) to rates approximating that of schizophrenia (1–2%; Coons, 1998; Ross, 1997). Estimates of DID in inpatient settings range from 1% to 9.6% (Rifkin et al., 1998; Ross, Duffy, & Ellason, 2002). In addition to the dramatic increase in DID's prevalence over the past few decades, there has been an increase in the number of "alters" reported, from only two or three separate identities to an average of approximately 16 (interestingly, the exact number reported by the movie Sybil; see later) by 1990.

Dissociative identity disorder is between three and nine times more common in women than men, and women also tend to have more identities (an average of 15, as compared with the male average of eight; APA, 2000). Nevertheless, this imbalanced sex ratio may be an artifact of selection and referral biases (Lynn, Fassler, Knox, & Lilienfeld, 2009). In particular, a larger proportion of males with DID may end up in prisons (or other forensic settings) than in clinical settings (Putnam & Loewenstein, 2000).

Dissociative identity disorder is the most controversial dissociative disorder, and easily among the most controversial disorders in *DSM-5*. Skeptics of the disorder (Paris, 2012; Piper & Merskey, 2004) argue that its proliferation is in part a function of media exposure. In 1976, the movie *Sybil* was released, documenting the real-life story of a woman who had supposedly experienced severe child abuse and later developed 16 personalities (but see the "Etiological Considerations" section for evidence calling into question significant details of the *Sybil* case). In addition to the number of cases increasing after the release of this movie, the number of individuals reporting child abuse as a cause of DID also rose drastically (Lilienfeld & Lynn, 2015; Spanos, 1996). In contrast, proponents of the disorder respond that clinicians are now simply better equipped to identify the disorder (Gleaves, May, & Cardeña, 2001) and continue to maintain that dissociative disorders are massively underdiagnosed (Brand et al., 2016). We elaborate on this etiological debate later in the chapter.

PSYCHOLOGICAL ASSESSMENT

A variety of assessment instruments are available to evaluate dissociation and dissociative disorders. In this section, we review commonly used structured interview and self-report measures.

Structured Interview Measures

The Structured Clinical Interview for *DSM-IV* (SCID-D; Steinberg, 1985) and its revision (SCID-D-R; Steinberg, 1994) are semistructured interviews that systematically assess five core symptoms of dissociation: amnesia, depersonalization, derealization, identity confusion, and identity alteration. The SCID-D incorporates the *DSM-IV* criteria for dissociative disorders. The full 250-item administration may take 2–3 hours for psychiatric patients with dissociative symptoms; however, nondissociative psychiatric patients may complete the interview in 30–90 minutes, and nonpsychiatric participants in 30 minutes. The severity of each of the five core symptoms is scored in terms of distress, dysfunctionality, frequency, duration, and course. The revised scale was administered in National Institute of Mental Health field trials that encompassed 350 interviews of dissociative and nondissociative adults. Reports from the field trials ($N = 141$ mixed psychiatric patients) revealed that the interexaminer and temporal reliability of the SCID-D-R ranges from adequate to excellent (weighted kappa $= 0.77$–0.86) for both the presence and extent of dissociative symptoms over three time periods. For type of dissociative disorder, inter-examiner agreement ranged from 0.72 to 0.86, and test–retest reliability for the overall presence of a dissociative disorder was good (0.88 over 7-day period). The SCID-D-R possesses good convergent validity and is capable of distinguishing DID patients from patients with anxiety disorders, substance abuse, personality disorders, eating disorders, and psychotic disorders (Cardeña, 2008). The SCID-D-R may be helpful in discriminating DID from feigning. It also appears to distinguish DID from schizophrenia (Wellburn et al., 2003). Nevertheless, Kihlstrom (2005, p. 3) countered that "even with relatively strict criteria in place, it can be difficult to discriminate between dissociative disorders and bipolar disorder, borderline personality disorder, and even schizophrenia."

The Dissociative Disorders Interview Schedule (DDIS; Ross et al., 1989) is a structured interview used to assist in the diagnosis of dissociative disorders, as well as conditions that often co-occur with it, including somatization disorder, major depressive disorder, and borderline personality disorder. The interview has been used for clinical and research purposes and consists of 16 sections with a total of 131 questions. The interview is highly structured to minimize interviewer confirmation bias and sequenced so that indirect questions about secondary features of DID precede increasingly specific questions.

In the original validation study, 80 psychiatric patients from specialized research clinics were interviewed. Patients diagnosed with DID ($n = 20$) were compared with patients with panic disorder ($n = 20$), eating disorder ($n = 20$), and schizophrenia ($n = 20$). For DID, the DDIS yielded a sensitivity of 90% and a specificity of 100% [see also Ross et al. (1992) who demonstrated high agreement (94.1%) of DDIS classification using the DDIS with independent clinical evaluation]. The authors reported that interrater reliability was adequate ($r = 0.68$; Ross et al., 1989). The DDIS has demonstrated good convergent validity, as indexed by high correlations of DID diagnosis scores with the Dissociative Experiences Scale (DES; $r = 0.67–0.78$; Cardeña, 2008). Nevertheless, the authors (Ross et al., 1989) cautioned that depersonalization disorder cannot be reliably diagnosed using the DDIS (interrater reliability = 0.56).

The Clinician Administered Dissociation State Scale (CADSS; Bremner et al., 1998) was developed to assess dissociative states. The clinician verbally administers 19 "subject-rated" items on a Likert-type scale ranging from 0 (not at all) to 4 (extremely). Three subscales subsume the subject-rated items: amnesia, depersonalization, and derealization. The clinician also observes the participant's behavior during the interview and rates eight behaviors presumed to indicate the presence of a dissociative state on the same Likert-type scale as the subject-rated items.

In the original study, the CADSS was administered to patients with combat-related PTSD and a comorbid dissociative disorder (PTSD/dissociative) ($n = 68$). These patients were compared with patients with schizophrenia ($n = 22$), mood disorders ($n = 15$), healthy comparison individuals ($n = 8$), and combat veterans without PTSD ($n = 11$). The CADSS discriminated between patients with PTSD and comorbid dissociative disorders (86% of cases) and patients with the comparison conditions. Furthermore, the CADSS detected changes in dissociative symptoms before and after patients with PTSD participated in a traumatic memories group. These patients showed a significant increase in symptoms compared with baseline, suggesting that the CADSS may be sensitive enough to capture changes in repeated measures designs. Interrater reliability was excellent for the total scale (intraclass correlation coefficient, ICC = 0.92) and for the subject-rated portion (ICC = 0.99), but was markedly lower for the observer ratings (ICC = 0.34). The internal consistency of the CADSS was good to excellent for the total scale ($\alpha = 0.94$), subjective portion ($\alpha = 0.94$), observer ratings ($\alpha = 0.90$), and the individual subscales ($\alpha = 0.74–.90$). Recently, Condon and Lynn (2014) reported that the CADSS correlated at $r = 0.63$ with the revised DES (DES-II) and reported the internal consistency of the CADSS to be $\alpha = 0.80$ in a sample of undergraduates.

SELF-REPORT MEASURES

The DES (Bernstein & Putnam, 1986) and the DES-II (Bernstein-Carlson & Putnam, 1993) are brief self-report measures of dissociation that can be used in both research and clinical settings to assess individuals within normal and psychiatric populations. Participants rate 28 items pertaining to dissociation in terms of the frequency at which they are experienced, from 0% to 100%. In the original sample, the test–retest reliability among 192 participants was 0.84 over a period of 4–8 weeks, and split half reliability coefficients ranged from 0.71 to 0.96, indicating good internal consistency. In addition, DES scores differentiated participants with a dissociative disorder (e.g., DID) from those without a dissociative disorder (e.g., nonsymptomatic adults, late adolescent college students, people with alcohol problems, and people with phobias) A cutoff of 30 correctly identified 74% of patients with DID and 80% of subjects without DID in a multicenter study (Carlson et al., 1991b).

The DES is the most frequently used self-report measure of dissociation (Brand, Armstrong, & Loewenstein, 2006). Nevertheless, researchers have questioned whether the scale is unidimensional, as would be expected of a factorially pure measure of dissociation. Carlson et al. (1991a) reported a three-factor solution—amnesia, absorption (related to openness to experience), and depersonalization (also see Ross, Ellason, & Anderson, 1995; Sanders & Green, 1994)—and others (Ray & Faith, 1994) have identified four factors. In contrast, Waller (1995) reanalyzed Carlson et al.'s (1991a) data and concluded that their three-factor solution could reflect the skewed distribution of the items, and thus might be a statistical artifact reflecting the presence of difficulty factors (that is, factors induced by similar levels of skewness across the items; see also Holmes et al., 2005; Wright & Loftus, 1999).

Waller, Putnam, and Carlson (1996) responded to criticisms that the DES contains a substantial number of nonpathological items that tap absorption (e.g., "Some people find that when they are watching television or a movie they become so absorbed in the story that they are unaware of other events happening around them") by developing the DES-Taxon (DES-T) scale. This eight-item scale contains items from the original DES that measure pathological dissociation, including derealization, depersonalization, psychogenic amnesia, and identity alteration. Waller and Ross (1997) estimated that the general population base rate of pathological dissociation is 3.3%. Of course, being classified as a taxon member (i.e., distinct type or latent class) cannot be equated with DID (Modestin & Erni, 2004), as the prevalence of DID in the general population is almost certainly much lower than 3%. Although the resulting scale was stricter in the criteria for establishing evidence of pathologic dissociation, the data supporting its validity are mixed. Simeon et al. (1998) found that the DES-T sum score is superior to the standard DES at distinguishing patients with depersonalization disorders (DDD) from comparison subjects. Nevertheless, later studies revealed that the DES-T: (a) classified only 64% of patients with DDD as having a dissociative disorder (Simeon et al., 2003), (b) produced high false-positive rates (Giesbrecht, Merckelbach, & Geraerts, 2007b; Modestin & Erni, 2004), and (c) lacked temporal stability for taxon membership probability (Watson, 2003). Nevertheless, many studies have documented significant differences between people who score high versus low on both the DES and the DES-T with respect to a variety of measures of memory and cognition (Giesbrecht et al., 2008).

The Adolescent Dissociative Experiences Scale (A-DES; Armstrong, Putnam, Carlson, Libero, & Smith, 1997) is a 30-item self-report measure designed exclusively for use with adolescent populations. The scale is intended to serve as a screening tool for dissociative disorders among adolescents and traces the developmental trajectories of normal and pathological dissociation over time. The A-DES items are rated on an 11-point Likert-type scale, and they comprise the following subscales: dissociative amnesia, absorption and imaginative involvement, passive influence, and depersonalization and derealization. The A-DES was normed using a group of healthy adolescents in junior-high and high school populations (Smith & Carlson, 1996) and a group of adolescent clinical patients (Armstrong et al., 1997). The authors reported excellent internal consistency for the total score ($\alpha = 0.93$) and subscales ($\alpha = 0.72-85$). Nevertheless, there are questions concerning the A-DES's convergent validity. In a sample of 331 nonreferred youths, Muris,

Merckelbach, and Peeters (2003) reported that A-DES scores are significantly related not only to PTSD symptoms and fantasy proneness, but also to other anxiety symptoms.

The Multidimensional Inventory of Dissociation (MID 5.0; Dell, 2006) is a self-report measure created to assess the symptom domain of DID and the phenomenological domain of dissociation. The MID 5.0 contains 168 dissociation items and 50 validity items rated on a 0–10 Likert-type scale. The validity items measure response sets (e.g., careless, inattentive responding, which is a feature that other self-report instruments measuring dissociativity (e.g., the DES) lack. The MID shows promising convergent validity with other psychiatric diagnoses (e.g., it distinguishes among individuals with DID, dissociative disorder not otherwise specified, mixed psychiatric, and nonclinical adults; Dell, 2002) and self-report measures (e.g., correlations with the DES = 0.90; Dell, 2006), as well as structural validity (e.g., factor analyses isolated a single overarching factor of pathological dissociation; see Dell, 2006). Nevertheless, these findings have yet to be replicated by independent research groups, and Kruger and Fletcher (2017) have described one first attempt with encouraging results. The authors reported good-to-excellent internal consistency of the 23 dissociation scales ($\alpha = 0.84$–0.96) and temporal stability (4- to 8-week test–retest interval; $r = 0.82$–0.97) in a large clinical sample. These latter results were replicated in Israel and Germany (see Dell, 2006).

The Somatoform Dissociation Questionnaire (SDQ-20; Nijenhuis, Spinhoven, Van Dyck, Van der Hart, & Vanderlinden, 1996) is a self-report measure designed to evaluate the presence of somatoform responses associated with dissociative states that cannot be medically explained. Participants rate items on a five-point Likert-type scale. Twenty of the 75 original items discriminated outpatients with dissociative disorders from non-dissociative psychiatric outpatients and comprised the final scale. The authors reported excellent internal consistency ($\alpha = 0.95$) and higher scores among patients with DID compared with patients with dissociative disorder not otherwise specified. The authors also reduced the SDQ-20 to a five-item screen for dissociative disorders (SDQ-5; Nijenhuis, Spinhoven, Van Dyck, Van der Hart, & Vanderlinden, 1997). For dissociative disorders among psychiatric patients, the SDQ-5 exhibited a sensitivity of 94% and a specificity of 98% (Nijenhuis et al., 1998). A study in which DES, MID, and SDQ-20 were compared with SCID-D outcomes in psychiatric outpatients found that these self-report instruments have comparable diagnostic accuracy and are equivalently suitable as screening tools for dissociative disorders (Mueller-Pfeiffer et al., 2013).

The Dissociation Questionnaire (DIS-Q; Vanderlinden, Van Dyck, Vandereycken, & Vertommen, 1991) was developed to account for sociocultural differences in European populations as well as to assess a broad spectrum of dissociative experiences. The authors generated items from existing dissociation questionnaires and clinical experience. Participants rate items on a 1–5 Likert-type scale; the final 63-item scale was normed on 374 participants from the general population in Belgium and the Netherlands. Four factors constitute the DIS-Q (i.e., identity confusion, loss of control, amnesia, and absorption). Internal consistency of the subscales ($\alpha = 0.67$–0.94) and the overall scale ($\alpha = 0.96$) was adequate to excellent, as was test–retest reliability over a period of 3–4 weeks. The authors report successful discrimination of patients with dissociative disorders and nondissociative disorders with the exception of PTSD. Within the dissociative disorders, the DIS-Q successfully discriminated DID from dissociative disorder–not otherwise specified.

The State Scale of Dissociation (SSD; Kruger & Mace, 2002) is a self-report inventory designed to detect changes in dissociative states, rather than traits. The SSD was developed using existing scales, the *DSM-IV* and the *ICD-10*, along with the aid of clinical experts. The 56-item scale is scored on a Likert-type scale from 0 to 9 and broken down into seven subscales: derealization, depersonalization, identity confusion, identity alteration, conversion, amnesia, and hypermnesia (remembering things too well). In the original study, the SSD was administered to 130 patients with major depression ($n = 19$), schizophrenia ($n = 18$), alcohol withdrawal ($n = 20$), dissociative disorders ($n = 10$), and healthy controls ($n = 63$). A score of > 3.9 nearly doubled the certainty of a diagnosis of a dissociative disorder, although an important limitation is the small sample of dissociative patients. The internal consistency of the SSD was good to excellent for the total scale ($\alpha = 0.97$), and correlation between the SSD and the DES among people with a dissociative disorder was $r = 0.81$, and in healthy controls, $r = 0.57$. Following a brief grounding activity (53 minutes, during which participants completed a number of other scales), the SSD scores among all participants decreased significantly on retest, suggesting that the SSD is sensitive to short-term changes in dissociative states across diagnostic groups.

The *Cambridge Depersonalization Scale* (CDS; Sierra & Berrios, 2000) consists of 29 items that ask respondents to rate recent depersonalization symptoms on a five-point frequency scale (anchors: $0 =$ never; $4 =$ all the time) and a six-point duration scale (anchors: $1 =$ few seconds; $6 =$ more than a week). The scale differentiates patients with DDD from other patient groups (e.g., patients with epilepsy, anxiety disorders) and from healthy controls (Sierra & Berrios, 2000). Sierra and Berrios (2000, 2001) reported sound internal consistency for the CDS (e.g., $\alpha = 0.89$). An exploratory factor analysis identified four factors that accounted for 73.3% of the variance: anomalous body experience, emotional numbing, anomalous subjective recall, and alienation from surroundings (Sierra et al., 2005).

Apart from those that have already been mentioned, there are other self-report measures of dissociative symptoms (e.g., the Multi-scale Dissociation Inventory; MDI; Briere, Weathers, & Runtz, 2005). What is currently missing is a thorough analysis of how these various instrument relate to one another and what aspects of dissociation they are particularly sensitive to. Also, with the exception of the MID, none of these instruments contain validity scales, i.e., items with which inattentive responding or symptom exaggeration can be detected. These response sets may artificially increase dissociative symptom reports. To detect and exclude such artefacts, diagnostic assessment procedures in this domain should include symptom validity tests geared to identify overreporting (see, for examples, Merckelbach et al., 2017).

Assessment is often an ongoing process in psychotherapy, and much information can be gleaned in the absence of standardized tests of dissociative experiences and symptoms. In this regard, a number of caveats are in order. Less formal assessment procedures that even subtly suggest a history of abuse or validate the manifestation of alters with separate histories (e.g., personality "system mapping" to establish contact with non-forthcoming alters, providing names to alters, prompting or suggesting the emergence or appearance of alters) should be avoided. A concern is that therapists who repeatedly ask leading questions such as "Is it possible that there is another part of you with whom I haven't yet spoken?" may elicit via suggestion imagined-believed-in alter personalities that ostensibly account for their clients' otherwise enigmatic behaviors (e.g., self-mutilation, and rapid and intense mood shifts). The point here is that clinicians are positioned to shape the illness beliefs of their patients in such way that misinformation about symptoms may set into motion symptom escalation (see also Merckelbach et al., 2011). Repeated questioning about historical events is not helpful, as it can lead patients to mistakenly believe that they have significant gaps (e.g., amnesia) in their autobiographical memories of childhood (Belli, Winkielman, Read, Schwartz, & Lynn, 1998; Read & Lindsay, 2000). Assessors should also eschew the use of hypnosis to recover allegedly dissociated or repressed memories given that hypnosis does not enhance the overall accuracy of memories and is associated with a heightened risk for confabulation (Lynn, Knox, Fassler, Lilienfeld, & Loftus, 2004).

CASE EXAMPLE

CASE IDENTIFICATION AND PRESENTING COMPLAINTS

The patient, a 47-year old Caucasian female, first presented with dissociative symptoms to a health professional during a routine pelvic examination (see Colletti, Lynn, & Laurence, 2010 for a more complete description). During the exam, she exhibited dramatic changes in her demeanor. In quick succession, her emotions vacillated unpredictably, from calm and composed, to scared and vulnerable, to angry and aggressive. The physician referred her for psychotherapy, insofar as her histrionic presentation was at sharp variance with what he observed during prior office visits.

HISTORY

When the patient reinstated treatment with a psychotherapist, she insisted that her problems were the product of stress at work related to serious medical concerns (e.g., lupus, peripheral neuralgia, among others) that interfered with her job performance. Nevertheless, the therapist, a graduate student at a psychological clinic, noted that her mood and behavior fluctuated dramatically both within and between sessions, with episodes of anger and anxiety flaring up frequently and unpredictably within sessions. Over the next 2 years, the patient recounted a history of sexual assault 7 years prior to treatment, the death of a sibling, intense and sometimes unstable interpersonal relationships, and sexual abuse in childhood. Emotional outbursts during sessions escalated; seemingly innocuous statements by the therapist could trigger memories of highly aversive events. The patient began to experience more frequent crises in and out of sessions as well as emotional lability, often alternating between speaking in a childlike voice and that of an angry adult, only to later apologize and express deep regret. Her memory for what transpired when she appeared to be enacting different "identities" was spotty and at times devoid of meaningful content.

After 2 years of treatment, the graduate student transferred the case to his supervisor, who witnessed increased irritability, vitriolic anger, and flashback-like experiences in sessions that were followed by amnesia, depersonalization, derealization, and problems in focusing attention. The patient reported feeling "spaced out" in session, and reported that she often was aware of "missing time" at home, and experienced difficulties recalling anything beyond the gist of the previous session. At the start of treatment with her second therapist, she met the criteria for borderline personality disorder, and DID was considered a rule-out diagnosis. She reported hearing "voices in my head" and experienced herself as "splitting off" into an angry "adult protector" or defender of others and childlike aspects of herself that required protection. One major diathesis for her dissociative symptoms appeared to be a history of fantasy versus reality-based coping originating in childhood. She became aware of this style of coping when her sister died when the patient was 5 years old, and she experienced guilt for not somehow preventing her death. She stated that she began, from that time forward, to think of herself as split into angry and protective "parts." As therapy progressed, she reported more frequent episodes of depersonalization and disturbing episodes of amnesia, as well as disorientation at times of high stress. She also reported more incidents of abuse during childhood, and her therapist felt her presentation now met criteria for DID.

At this time, Steven Jay Lynn, one of the authors of this chapter, was invited to serve as a consultant and co-therapist. The therapists conveyed the consistent message that although at times she felt as if she housed distinct personalities, she truly embodied only one personality. The therapists implemented a multifaceted treatment that included: (a) elements of affect management and problem-solving to contend with anger; (b) cognitive-behavioral therapy (CBT techniques including activity scheduling for depressed mood, progressive muscle and hypnosis-based relaxation, and rational disputation of maladaptive thoughts); (c) mindfulness-based techniques for detaching from negative and self-deprecating cognitions and moods; and (d) affect containment methods derived from dialectical behavior therapy. After 4 years of treatment, the patient exhibited no signs of "personality split" and only occasional episodes of depersonalization, with improved functioning and mood stabilization.

Assessment

The patient met all the diagnostic criteria for DID, including her enacting distinct "identities" during sessions and reports of such alterations outside of sessions. She also reported amnesia associated with dissociative episodes, and she was troubled by her failure to recall key interpersonal interactions that others remembered well. The patient was not assessed at the outset of treatment, although when SJL came onboard, she was evaluated with the DES and scored in the clinical range (i.e., 39) and met diagnostic criteria for DID based on the SCID-D (Steinberg, 1994).

ETIOLOGICAL CONSIDERATIONS

Behavioral Genetics

Limited research is available on the behavioral genetics of dissociative disorders. The evidence indicates that DID co-aggregates within biological families (APA, 1994), although data on intact family members are indeterminate with regard to genetic versus shared environmental causation. Using twin registry data, Jang, Paris, Zweig, Frank, and Livesley (1998) reported that 48% of the variability in DES-T scores is attributable to genes, and that the other 52% of the variance can be attributed to nonshared environments. When the researchers considered nonpathological dissociation scores, excluding taxon items, genetic influences accounted for 55% of the variance, whereas nonshared environmental influences accounted for 45% of the variance. Similarly, a study of children and adolescents found a substantial genetic (59% genes, 41% nonshared environments) contribution to dissociation scores (Becker-Blease et al., 2004). In contrast, a study based on 280 identical twins and 148 fraternal twins (Waller & Ross, 1997) found no evidence of genetic influences. Approximately 45% of the variance on a measure of pathological dissociation (DES-T) was attributable to shared environmental influences, with the remaining variance due to nonshared environmental influences. A Polish study of 83 monozygotic and 65 dizygotic twins estimated the heritability of dissociativity at 62% and concluded that the propensity to dissociate is highly heritable (Domozych & Dragen, 2017). Researchers have begun to explore how traumatic experiences may interact with genetic vulnerabilities to produce dissociative symptoms; variations in the FK506 binding protein 5 gene, which is involved in the regulation of the body's stress system, are an intriguing target for this type of gene × environment research (Yaylaci, Cicchetti, Rogosch, Bulut, & Hertzel, 2017). Adoption studies would help to clarify the extent to which the familial clustering of dissociative disorders is due to genes, shared environment, or both.

Biology

Drugs, notably low doses of the anesthetic ketamine, often produce dream-like states and dissociative symptoms, suggesting that dissociative experiences need not necessarily arise in the aftermath of trauma. Krystal et al. (1994) found that ketamine produces alterations in the perception of time (i.e., slowing) and alterations in the vividness, form, and context of sensory experiences, all possibly attributable to diminished N-methyl-D-aspartate (NMDA)-related neurotransmission (Simeon, 2004). Interestingly, cannabinoids, including marijuana, which induce dissociative experiences, may similarly affect NMDA receptors (Simeon et al., 2003). The fact that hallucinogens (e.g., LSD), which frequently elicit depersonalization reactions in healthy participants, are agonists of serotonin 5-HT2A and 5-HT2C receptors, implies that serotonin also may mediate dissociation (Simeon, 2004). Research that establishes links between drugs that produce dissociative symptoms in conjunction with changes in specific neurotransmitter systems hold the potential to shed light on the neurobiological basis of these dissociative symptoms (Giesbrecht et al., 2008). For example, a recent study showed that MDMA, cannabis, and cocaine all induce acute dissociative symptoms (Van Heugten-van der Kloet et al., 2015). The pharmacological study of dissociation is important because it may shed light on the paradoxical phenomenon that detoxified opiate users exhibit higher dissociation scores than do patients who are on a methadone maintenance regimen (Somer, Altus, & Ginzburg, 2010). One possible explanation for this pattern is the chemical dissociation hypothesis, that is, the notion that substance abuse patients achieve dissociative-like states through chemicals (e.g., alcohol, opiates), and in the absence of chemicals, they feel compelled to produce the dissociative symptoms themselves (see, for a recent discussion, Wegen, van Kijke, Aalbers, & Zedlitz, in press). This line of reasoning is consistent with pilot data suggesting that the opioid-blocking drug naloxone is effective in reducing depersonalization experiences (Nuller, Morozova, Kushnir, & Hamper, 2001; but see Somer, Amos-Williams, & Stein, 2013).

Studies examining daytime EEG activity in highly dissociative individuals have generally found evidence that dissociative experiences are related to parameters signaling reduced attentional control (e.g., attenuated P300, Kirino, 2006; decreased theta activity; Krüger, Bartel, & Fletcher, 2013). Sleep EEG recordings obtained in insomnia patients found suggestive evidence that dissociative psychopathology is related to extended REM sleep (van der Kloet et al., 2013). It is tempting to relate lack of attentional control and extended REM to structural sleep disturbances, as suggested later in our discussion.

Simeon et al. (2000) used positron emission tomography (PET) and magnetic resonance imaging (MRI) of the brain to compare eight participants with DDD with 24 healthy participants. The researchers found that depersonalization is associated with functional abnormalities in sequential hierarchical areas—secondary and cross-modal—of the sensory cortex (visual, auditory, and somatosensory), as well as areas responsible for integrated body schemas. Specifically, DDD patients showed lower metabolic activity in right Brodmann areas 21 and 22 of the superior and middle temporal gyri, and higher metabolism in parietal Brodmann areas 7B and 39 and left occipital Brodmann area 19. The researchers contended that these findings are compatible with the phenomenological conceptualization of depersonalization as a dissociation of perceptions, as well as with the subjective symptoms of DDD.

In a fascinating study, Sang, Jáuregui-Renaud, Green, Bronstein, and Gresty (2006) showed that disorienting vestibular stimulation produced by caloric irrigation of the ear labyrinths engendered depersonalization in healthy participants and symptoms (e.g., feeling spaced out, body feels strange/not in control of self) similar to those experienced by patients with vestibular disease. The researchers suggested that depersonalization/derealization experiences may "occur because distorted vestibular signals mismatch with sensory input to create an incoherent frame of spatial reference which makes the patient feel that he or she is detached or separated from the world" (p. 760).

In a later study, the researchers (Jáuregui-Renaud, Sang, Gresty, Green, & Bronstein, 2008b) found that patients with peripheral vestibular disease reported a higher prevalence of depersonalization/derealization symptoms and greater errors on a body rotation test of updating spatial orientation compared with healthy comparison participants. The investigators claimed that their findings support their theory that DDD symptoms sometimes reflect a mismatch between disordered vestibular input and other sensory signals of orientation. This claim was supported in a study in which patients with vestibular disease, and patients with retinal disease reported more symptoms of depersonalization than did patients with hearing loss and healthy participants (Jáuregui-Renaud, Ramos-Toledo, Aguilar-Bolaños, Montaño-Velazquez, & Pliego-Maldonado, 2008a). Depersonalization and derealization experiences may well be the product of mismatches or lack of integration between multisensory inputs (e.g., vestibular, visual, proprioceptive) which produces dysfunctional neural representations that, in turn, generate an altered sense of self and reality (Aspell & Blanke, 2009).

Out-of-body experiences (OBEs), which are intimately related to depersonalization, are increasingly being studied in the laboratory (e.g., Ehrsson, 2007; Lenggenhager, Tadi, Metzinger, & Blanke, 2007) and are coming to be understood in terms of the scrambling of the senses (e.g., touch and vision) when people's usual experience of their physical body becomes disrupted. In addition, scientists are identifying the brain location of OBEs by stimulating the vestibular cortex, the superior temporal gyrus, and the place where the brain's right temporal and parietal lobes join (Blanke, Ortigue, Landis, & Seeck, 2002; Blanke & Thut, 2007; Cheyne & Girard, 2009; De Ridder, Van Laere, Dupont, Menovsky, & Van de Heyning, 2007; Persinger, 2001).

Ehrrson (2007) provided participants with goggles that permitted them to view a video display of themselves relayed by a camera placed behind them. This setup created the illusion that their bodies, viewed from the rear, were standing in front of them. Ehrrson touched participants with a rod on the chest while he used cameras to make it appear that the visual image was being touched at the same time. Participants reported the eerie sensation that their video double was also being touched. In short, they reported that they could experience the touch in a location outside their physical bodies (see also Aspell, Lenggenhager, & Blanke, 2009; Lenggenhager et al., 2007). When visual sensory impressions combine with physical sensations, they can deceive people into believing that their physical selves are separate from their bodies (Cheyne & Girard, 2009; Terhune, 2009), suggesting a physiological genesis of at least some depersonalization experiences. Relatedly, disruptions in somatosensory signals may explain why some people experience OBEs during sleep paralysis (Nelson, Mattingly, Lee, & Schmitt, 2006) and during general anesthesia when they retain partial awareness (Bunning & Blanke, 2005). Nevertheless, researchers have little understanding of how stressors and other precipitants of depersonalization and derealization create and maintain the symptoms of dissociative disorders.

Researchers have devoted considerable attention to describing physiological differences among alters in DID and have reported inter-identity differences in heart rates, voice pitch, eyeglass prescriptions, handedness, handwriting, allergies, or pain tolerance (see Lilienfeld & Lynn, 2015). Nevertheless, it is unclear whether such differences validate the existence of alters, as many of these differences may merely reflect differences in mood or differences stemming from the unconscious role-playing of different identities, or both. Also, some authors have pointed out that one may obtain similar intraindividual differences when healthy actors are instructed to role-play alters (Boysen & Van Bergen, 2014; Merckelbach, Devilly & Rassin, 2002a). Moreover, Allen and Movius (2000) suggested that some of these apparent differences might reflect type I errors, given the large number of psychophysiological variables analyzed in many of these studies.

Tsai, Condie, Wu, and Chang (1999) used MRI with a 47-year-old female with DID in an attempt to corroborate a history of childhood abuse. The authors drew upon previous investigations that had reported a reduction in hippocampal volume following combat trauma (e.g., Bremner, Randall, Scott, & Bronen, 1995) and early abuse (Bremner, Randall, Vermetten, & Staib, 1997; Stein, Koverola, Hanna, & Torchia, 1997) to hypothesize that DID patients—given their presumed history of early abuse—would similarly exhibit decreased hippocampal volume. As predicted, they found significant bilateral reductions in hippocampal volume in their patient with DID. Nevertheless, this finding must be interpreted cautiously for two major reasons (Lilienfeld & Lynn, 2015). First, because it is based on only one patient, its generalizability to other individuals with DID is unclear. Second, decreased hippocampal volume is not specific to PTSD or to other conditions secondary to trauma, and has also been reported in schizophrenia (Nelson, Saykin, Flashman, & Riordan, 1988) and depression (Bremner et al., 2000). Consequently, decreased hippocampal volume may be a nonspecific marker of long-term stress (Sapolsky, 2000) that is present in many psychiatric conditions.

More recent neuroimaging studies have focused on brain activation patterns during the different identity states of people with DID. For example, in one study, researchers (Reinders et al., 2014) confronted DID patients ($n = 11$) and matched DID-simulating healthy comparison subjects ($n = 16$) with autobiographic script-driven imagery while brain activation was monitored using PET. According to the authors, their results are in line with the idea that DID involves alternations between a hypoaroused identity state with overmodulation of emotional regulation that activates the prefrontal cortex, cingulate, posterior association areas, and parahippocampal gyri, and a hyperaroused identity state with undermodulated emotion regulation that activates the amygdala and insula as well as the dorsal striatum.

LEARNING, MODELING AND LIFE EVENTS

Some cases of (mis)diagnosed dissociative disorders are probably the product of malingering. Estimates suggest that malingering or other forms of feigning (e.g., the faking seen in factitious disorders) account for 2–10% of diagnoses of inpatient dissociative disorders (Friedl & Draijer, 2000). There is widespread agreement that DID can be successfully malingered. For example, Kenneth Bianchi, one of the two Hillside Strangler murderers, is widely believed to have faked DID to escape criminal responsibility (Orne, Dinges, & Orne, 1984). In one survey, experienced neuropsychologists estimated the prevalence of feigned dissociative symptoms in cases involved in litigation to be about 10% (Mittenberg, Patton, Canyock, & Condit, 2002). Nevertheless, cases of malingered DID are believed to be quite rare outside of forensic settings, and the substantial majority of individuals with this condition do not appear to be intentionally fabricating their symptoms. Malingerers strive for advantages (e.g., financial, legal), but dissociative disorders are known to be associated with functional impairments that are so severe that they qualify as serious and often debilitating mental illnesses (Mueller-Pfeiffer et al., 2012).

THE POST-TRAUMATIC VERSUS THE SOCIOCOGNITIVE MODELS OF DISSOCIATION

There is little dispute that some individuals meet the diagnostic criteria for DID, display unpredictable and sometimes bizarre shifts in mood and behavior, and are convinced that they house compartmentalized "personalities" engendered by severe early physical abuse, sexual abuse, or both. Nevertheless, over the past 25 years, controversy has swirled around the question of whether the symptoms of DID are naturally occurring responses to early trauma (Dalenberg et al., 2012; Gleaves, 1996), as the post-traumatic model (PTM) of dissociation holds, or are largely socially constructed and culturally influenced, as the sociocognitive model (SCM)—called by some the fantasy model (Dalenberg et al., 2012)—of dissociation holds (Spanos, 1994). One commentator (Paris, 2012) has gone so far as to claim that DID is a fad that is now declining in interest in the psychiatric community, whereas others have vigorously challenged this assertion (Brand, Loewenstein, & Spiegel, 2013b; Martinez-Taboas, Dorahy, Sar, Middleton, & Krüger, 2013).

Proponents of the PTM (Gleaves, 1996; Gleaves et al., 2001; Ross, 1997) argue that DID is a post-traumatic condition that arises primarily from a history of severe physical and/or sexual abuse in childhood. Advocates of the PTM contend that such abuse is a crucial contributor to DID: The child compartmentalizes the abuse so that he or she feels as though it is happening to someone else (Ross, 1997). Moreover, alters or ego states supposedly arise as a means of coping with the intense emotional pain of the trauma (see Lilienfeld & Lynn [2015], for an explanation and critique). PTM theories variously emphasize the effects of childhood abuse and early traumatic experiences on producing (a) patterns of disorganized interpersonal attachment (Liotti, 1999, 2009) that engender dissociation; (b) structural dissociation (i.e., the development of different "parts" of the personality to handle different functions in "defense" and everyday life; Steele, van der Hart, Nijenhuis, 2009); (c) disturbances in the self-system that integrates "identity-mind-body-world-time" into a coherent whole—in this view, alters are conceptualized as "younger self-systems (ego-states) that are 'trapped' in a past trauma" (Beere, 2009, p. 283); (d) developmental deficits that degrade self-regulation and promote fragmentation of the self (Carlson, Yates, & Sroufe, 2009); and (e) a dissociative information processing style related to feelings of being betrayed by a trusted caregiver (Barlow & Freyd, 2009; Freyd, 1996).

These diverse theories are ostensibly supported by very high rates—sometimes exceeding 90%—of reported histories of severe child abuse among patients diagnosed with DID and other severe dissociative disorders (Dalenberg et al., 2012; Gleaves, 1996). Nevertheless, critics of the PTM (see Giesbrecht et al., 2008, 2010; Lilienfeld et al., 1999; Lynn et al., 2014b; Merckelbach & Muris, 2001; Spanos, 1994, 1996) have questioned the notion that DID is invariably linked to child abuse or maltreatment for the following six reasons:

1. Many studies that purport to confirm this association lack objective corroboration of child abuse (e.g., Coons, Bowman, & Milstein, 1988). For example, Sanders and Giolas (1991) found a correlation of $r = 0.44$ between the DES and scores on a child-abuse questionnaire. Yet when a psychiatrist (unaware of the dissociative status of participants) provided more objective ratings of trauma based on hospital records, the authors found a nonsignificant *negative* correlation between ratings of traumatic experiences and dissociation ($r = -0.21$).
2. Correlations between dissociation and highly aversive events are highly variable, ranging between $r = -0.013$ (not significant) to $r = 0.44$ ($P < 0.001$) in nonclinical

samples, and from $r = 0.14$ (not significant) to $r = 0.63$ in clinical samples (see Dalenberg et al., 2012; Patihis & Lynn, 2017). Additionally, 40% of the correlations have been below 0.30 (Dalenberg et al., 2012). Consistent substantive moderators of these marked correlational differences have yet to be identified (although see no. 6 for a potential methodological moderator). Briere et al. (2005) found in their heterogeneous sample of $N > 1300$ participants that the percentage of unique dissociation variance accounted for by trauma exposure was only 4.4%, with an effect size (d) of approximately 0.41. The authors concluded that "trauma exposure may be only a relatively small aspect in the genesis of dissociative responses" (Briere et al., 2005, p. 229).

3. The overwhelming majority of studies investigating the link between self-reported trauma and dissociation are based on cross-sectional designs that do not permit causal inferences (Merckelbach & Muris, 2001) and that are subject to retrospective biases. Prospective studies that circumvent the pitfalls of retrospective reporting often fail to substantiate a consistent link between childhood abuse and dissociation in adulthood (Dutra, Bureau, Holmes, Lyubchik, & Lyons-Ruth, 2009; Noll, Trickett, & Putnam, 2003; Ogawa, Sroufe, Weinfield, Carlson, & Egeland, 1997; but see Bremner, 2010; Dalenberg et al., 2012).

4. Researchers rarely control for potentially comorbid psychopathological syndromes and symptoms known to be related to dissociative disorders (e.g., anxiety/obsessive-compulsive, eating, personality disorders, impulsivity, schizotypal traits; see Giesbrecht et al., 2008; Lynn et al., 2014b; Soffer-Dudek, 2014).

5. The reported high levels of child abuse among DID patients may be attributable to selection and referral biases common in psychiatric samples. For example, patients who are abused are more likely than other patients to enter treatment (Pope & Hudson, 1995).

6. Correlations between abuse and psychopathology tend to decrease substantially or disappear when (a) participants' perception of family pathology is controlled statistically (Nash, Hulsey, Sexton, Harralson, & Lambert, 1993) and (b) measures of trauma and dissociation are administered in separate test contexts, suggesting that the trauma-dissociation link may be, in part, an artifact of the way trauma and dissociation are measured (Lemons & Lynn, 2016). Based on these six points of contention, Lilienfeld and Lynn (2015) noted that the available evidence provides little or no warrant for concluding that abuse is a necessary causal antecedent of DID (see also Lynn et al., 2014b), although it may be one nonspecific influence among many others in the causal matrix. In contrast to the PTM, proponents of the SCM (Spanos, 1994, 1996; see also Aldridge-Morris, 1989; Lilienfeld et al., 1999; 2014; Lynn & Pintar, 1997; McHugh, 1993; Merskey, 1992; Sarbin, 1995) contend that DID results from inadvertent therapist cueing (e.g., suggestive questioning regarding the existence of possible alters, hypnosis, sodium amytal), a tendency to fantasize and suggestibility (see a more extended discussion below in the context of cognitive mechanisms), media influences (e.g., television and film portrayals of DID, such as *Sybil*), and broader sociocultural expectations regarding the presumed clinical features of DID.

Advocates of the SCM cite the following findings (Lilienfeld et al., 1999; Lilienfeld & Lynn, 2015) as consistent with the SCM or as challenges to the PTM:

1. The number of patients with DID, along with the number of alters per DID individual, have increased dramatically over the past few decades (Elzinga, van

Dyck, & Spinhoven, 1998; North et al., 1993), although the number of alters at the time of initial diagnosis appears to have remained constant (Ross, Norton, & Wozney et al., 1989).

2. The massive increase in reported cases of DID followed closely upon the release of the best-selling book *Sybil* (Schreiber, 1973) in the mid-1970s, which told the story of a young woman with 16 personalities who reported a history of severe child abuse at the hands of her mother. As noted earlier, in 1976, this book was turned into a widely viewed television film starring Sally Fields. Interestingly, however, a well-known psychiatrist who was involved closely with the Sybil case later contended that Sybil's presentation of DID was largely or entirely the product of therapeutic suggestion. Herbert Spiegel, who served as a backup therapist for Sybil, maintained that Sybil's primary therapist, Cornelia Wilbur, frequently encouraged her to develop and display different personalities in therapy. According to Rieber (2006), who possessed tapes of conversations between Sybil and Cornelia Wilbur, Spiegel referred to Sybil as a "brilliant hysteric," with multiple identities fabricated to please the all too credulous Wilbur. Spiegel further maintained that Cornelia Wilbur and Flora Schreiber, who authored the best-selling book about Sybil, insisted that Sybil be described in the book as a "multiple" to make the book more appealing (Acocella, 1999). Rieber concluded "the three women—Wilbur, Schreiber, and Sybil—are responsible for shaping the modern myth of multiple personality disorder" (Rieber, 2006, p. 109). In short, increases in the diagnosis of DID and the number of alters per DID patient coincide with dramatically increased therapist and public awareness of the major features of DID (Fahy, 1988).

3. Mainstream treatment techniques for DID often reinforce patients' displays of multiplicity (e.g., asking questions like, "Is there another part of you with whom I have not spoken?"), reify alters as distinct personalities (e.g., therapists calling different alters by different names, mapping their "personality systems"), and encourage patients to establish contact and dialogue with presumed latent alters (Spanos, 1994, 1996). A case in point is the $N = 1$ within-subject study by Kohlenberg (1973), who showed that the behavioral displays of alter personalities can depend on reinforcement contingencies: The patient's alters soon "disappeared" after hospital staff stopped attending to them.

4. Many or most DID patients show few or no clear-cut signs of this condition (e.g., alters) prior to psychotherapy (Kluft, 1984).

5. The number of alters per DID individual tends to increase substantially over the course of DID-oriented psychotherapy (Piper, 1997), and there are indications that this type of therapy might exacerbate symptoms (Fetkewicz, Sharma, & Merskey, 2000).

6. Therapists who use hypnosis tend to have more DID patients in their caseloads than do psychotherapists who do not use hypnosis (Powell & Gee, 1999).

7. The majority of diagnoses of DID derive from a relatively small number of psychotherapists, many of whom are specialists in DID (Mai, 1995), and from a relatively small number of people in treatment (Boysen, 2011; Boysen & Van Bergen, 2013; but see Brand, Loewenstein, & Spiegel, 2013b; Brand et al., 2016 for a rebuttal).

8. Laboratory studies suggest that nonclinical participants who are provided with appropriate cues and prompts can reproduce many of the overt features of DID (Spanos, Weekes, & Bertrand, 1985; Stafford & Lynn, 2002).

9. Until 20 years ago, diagnoses of DID were limited largely to North America, where the condition has received widespread media publicity (Spanos, 1996), although DID is now being diagnosed with considerable frequency in some countries (e.g., the Netherlands) in which it has become more widely publicized since the 1990s.

Manifestations of DID symptoms also vary across cultures. For example, in India, the transition period during which the individual shifts between alter personalities is typically preceded by sleep, a presentation that reflects common media portrayals of DID in India (North et al., 1993). There are indications that both research interest in DID and media coverage of the condition are waning, and so it will be interesting to see whether this change heralds a drop in prevalence rates (Pope, Barry, Bodkin & Hudson, 2006).

10. Laboratory research summarized in the following discussion challenges the assertion that consciousness can be separated into multiple streams by amnesic barriers to form independently functioning alter personalities (Huntjens, Verschuere, & McNally, 2012; Kong, Allen, & Glisky, 2008; Lynn et al., 2004).

These 10 sources of evidence do not imply that DID can typically be created *in vacuo* by iatrogenic (therapist-induced) or sociocultural influences. SCM theorists acknowledge that iatrogenic and sociocultural influences typically operate on a backdrop of preexisting psychopathology, and exert their impact primarily on individuals who are seeking a causal explanation for their instability, identity problems, and impulsive and seemingly inexplicable behaviors. Indeed, the SCM is entirely consistent with findings, reviewed earlier, that many or most patients with DID meet criteria for borderline personality disorder, a condition marked by extremely labile behaviors. Still, many of the tenets of the SCM have been vigorously challenged by advocates of the trauma-dissociation perspective (e.g., Brand et al., 2016; Dalenberg et al., 2012, 2014; Gleaves, 1996), ensuring that theoretical tensions are unlikely to abate in the foreseeable future.

Cognitive Mechanisms of Dissociation

Despite subjective reports of profound cognitive disturbances like amnesia, feelings of unreality, and identity alterations, researchers have found evidence for only relatively subtle and specific cognitive deficits in highly dissociative individuals. Such individuals usually fall within the normative range on tests of intellectual ability and standard neuropsychological tests (Giesbrecht et al. 2008; Schurle, Ray, Bruce, Arnett, & Carlson, 2007). Indeed, whereas most studies, with few exceptions (but see Prohl, Resch, Parzer, & Brunner, 2001), fail to report any link between dissociation and working memory capacity, some report that dissociative individuals exhibit *superior* verbal working memory capacity or verbal memory performance (Giesbrecht et al., 2008; McKinnon et al., 2016).

When cognitive deficits in dissociative patients are identified, they tend to be quite specific. For example, Guralnik, Schmeidler, and Simeon (2000) found that DDD patients exhibited deficits in visual perception and visual-spatial reasoning for both two- and three-dimensional stimuli. Patients' visual and verbal short-term memory capacity was also compromised, for both abstract and meaningful information, especially under information overload conditions. DDD participants experienced difficulty with early stimulus-encoding tasks under conditions of heightened distraction, to which they responded with more omission errors. Accordingly, DDD appears to be characterized by vulnerability in early information processing at the level of perception and attention (for replications, see Guralnik, Giesbrecht, Knutelska, Sirroff, & Simeon, 2007; Quaedflieg et al., 2012).

Simeon, Hwu, and Knutelska (2007) found evidence for a relation between the dissociative symptoms of DDD patients, temporal disintegration (i.e., problems in memory regarding the chronology and dating of events), and total DES scores. They concluded that the dissociative dimension of absorption is a significant predictor of temporal disintegration.

The relative absence of a measurable general neuropsychological deficit in the dissociative disorders is noteworthy, as it differentiates them from most other severe psychiatric disorders, such as schizophrenia and bipolar disorder. These other conditions overlap with the dissociative disorders, but unlike them, are marked by a wide range of neuropsychological deficits (Heinrichs & Zakzanis, 1998). In addition, different dissociative disorders appear related to different cognitive deficiencies. DID is characterized mainly by performance fluctuations (e.g., increased scatter on the Wechsler Adult Intelligence Scale [Wechsler, 1981]; Rossini, Schwartz, & Braun, 1996; reduced P300 amplitudes, but only during acute dissociative episodes in DID patients; Kirino, 2006), whereas DDD is associated with disruptions in early stages of information processing (Guralnik et al., 2000). Nevertheless, few investigations have controlled for general distress and psychopathology, or for scores on openness to experience, which is moderately associated with both dissociative tendencies (Kihlstrom, Glisky, & Angiulo, 1994) and with crystallized intelligence (DeYoung, Peterson, & Higgins, 2005). Interestingly, as we have noted earlier, dissociative individuals sometimes exhibit a performance advantage relative to nondissociative individuals (e.g., Chiu, Yeh, Huang, Wu, & Chiu, 2009), such as the ability to shift attention (Chiu et al., 2016b).

Some of the literature on cognitive mechanisms of dissociation is arguably more consistent with the SCM than with the PTM. As already noted, proponents of the PTM typically argue that individuals who undergo horrific trauma in early life often dissociate or compartmentalize their personalities into discrete alters, segregated by amnesic barriers, as a means of coping with the intense emotional pain of the trauma. However, studies of amnesia among patients with DID have generally not reported findings commensurate with the existence of true amnesia among so-called alter personalities (Giesbrecht et al., 2010). For example, researchers have found little or no evidence for inter-identity amnesia using objective measures (e.g., behavioral tasks or event-related potentials) of memory (e.g., Allen & Movius, 2000; Huntjens et al., 2006, 2012; Huntjens, Peters, Woertman, van der Hart, & Postma, 2007; Kong et al., 2008).

If dissociative symptoms attenuate the impact of traumatic events, individuals with heightened levels of dissociation should exhibit slower or impaired processing of threat-related information. Nevertheless, patients with DID and other "high dissociators" display *better* memory for to-be-forgotten sexual words in directed forgetting tasks (Elzinga, de Beurs, Sergeant, Van Dyck, & Phaf, 2000; see also Cloitre, Cancienne, Brodsky, Dulit, & Perry, 1996), a finding strikingly discrepant with the presumed defensive function of dissociation. Research on nonclinical samples (e.g., Candel, Merckelbach, & Kuijpers, 2003) showing that dissociation is not associated with inferior memory performance has been replicated in patients with DDD (Montagne et al., 2007). Studies of cognitive inhibition in high dissociative clinical (Dorahy, Irwin, & Middleton, 2002; Dorahy, Middleton, & Irwin, 2005; Dorahy, McCusker, Loewenstein, Colbert, & Mulholland, 2006) and nonclinical (Giesbrecht, Merckelbach, & Smeets, 2006) samples typically find a breakdown in such inhibition, which stands in sharp contrast with the widespread idea that amnesia (i.e., extreme inhibitory effect on memory) is a core feature of dissociation (Anderson et al., 2004). Research also finds mixed support at best for the contention that highly dissociative individuals are superior to low dissociators in dividing their attention. In two samples, Devilly et al. (2007) failed to replicate DePrince and Freyd's (2001) findings of superior forgetting of trauma-related words in high- versus low-dissociator college students in a divided attention task (see also Giesbrecht & Merckelbach, 2009). Giesbrecht et al. (2010) contended that the findings we have reviewed challenge the widespread assumption that dissociation is related to avoidant information processing and suggested that apparent gaps in memory in inter-identity amnesia, or dissociative amnesia more generally, could reflect intentional failures to report (McNally, 2003; Pope et al., 2006).

Giesbrecht and colleagues (Giesbrecht et al., 2008, 2010) further argued that dissociation is marked by a propensity toward pseudomemories, possibly mediated by heightened levels of suggestibility, fantasy proneness, and cognitive failures. They noted that at least 10 studies from diverse laboratories have confirmed a link between dissociation and fantasy proneness (Giesbrecht, Merckelbach, Kater, & Sluis, 2007c), and that heightened levels of fantasy proneness are associated with both the tendency to over-report autobiographical memories (Merckelbach, Muris, Horselenberg, & Stougie, 2000a) and the false recall of aversive memory material (Giesbrecht, Geraerts, & Merckelbach, 2007a).These authors contended that the relation between dissociation and fantasy proneness may explain why individuals with high levels of dissociation are more prone than other individuals to develop false memories of emotional childhood events (e.g., a severe animal attack; Porter, Birt, Yuille, & Lehman, 2000), and further pointed to data revealing links between hypnotizability, dissociative symptoms (Frischholz, Lipman, Braun, & Sachs, 1992), and high scores on the Gudjonsson Suggestibility Scale (GSS; Gudjonsson, 1984; Merckelbach, Muris, Rassin, & Horselenberg, 2000b; Wofradt & Meyer, 1998). Similarly, some researchers have shown that dissociation increases the risk of commission (e.g., confabulations/false positives, problems discriminating perception from vivid imagery, errors in response to misleading questions) rather than omission memory errors; the latter type of error is presumably associated with dissociative amnesia (Giesbrecht et al., 2008; Holmes et al., 2005). Nevertheless, findings pertinent to the relation between trait dissociation and false memory susceptibility are often mixed and not invariably strong in magnitude (see Dalenberg et al., 2012; Lynn et al., 2014b).

Taken together with research demonstrating a consistent link between dissociation and cognitive failures (Merckelbach, Horselenberg, & Schmidt, 2002b; Merckelbach, Muris, & Rassin, 1999; Wright & Osborne, 2005) and the tendency to over-report eccentric or rare symptoms of any kind (Merckelbach, Boskovic, Pesy, Dalsklev, & Lynn, 2017), the aforementioned findings point to a heightened risk of inaccurate reporting, confabulation, and possibly pseudomemories, which raise questions regarding the accuracy of retrospective reports of traumatic experiences. In addition, these findings limit the inferences that we can draw from studies that rely exclusively on self-reports to establish a connection between trauma and dissociation (Merckelbach & Jelicic, 2004; Merckelbach et al., 2000a). Still, these findings do not exclude some role for trauma in the genesis of dissociation and dissociative disorders. Suggestibility, cognitive failures, and fantasy proneness might contribute to an overestimation of a genuine, although perhaps weak or modest, link between dissociation and trauma. Alternatively, early trauma might predispose individuals to develop high levels of fantasy proneness (Lynn, Rhue, & Green, 1988), absorption (Tellegen & Atkinson, 1974), or related traits. In turn, such traits may render individuals susceptible to the iatrogenic and cultural influences posited by the SCM, thereby increasing the likelihood that they will develop DID following exposure to these influences. This and even more sophisticated etiological models of DID have yet to be subjected to direct empirical tests. In the next section, we examine a theory that provides a possible basis of rapprochement between the PTM and the SCM.

Sleep, Memory, and Dissociation: Possibilities for Theoretical Integration

A theory originally formulated by Watson (2001) linking sleep, memory failure, and dissociation may provide a conceptual bridge between the PTM and the SCM. In a review of 19 studies, van der Kloet, Merckelbach, Giesbrecht, and Lynn (2012) concluded that the extant research provides strong support for a link between dissociative experiences and a labile sleep–wake cycle that is evident across a range of phenomena, including waking dreams, nightmares, and hypnagogic (occurring while falling asleep) and hypnopompic (occurring after falling sleep) hallucinations. Studies that offered evidence for a link between dissociative experiences and sleep disturbances relied on clinical and nonclinical samples, and, with only one exception, yielded correlations in the range of 0.30–0.55, suggesting that unusual sleep experiences and dissociation are discriminable yet related constructs. Moreover, researchers (Giesbrecht, Smeets, Leppink, Jelicic, & Merckelbach, 2007d) have shown that sleep loss induced in the laboratory intensifies dissociative symptoms (see also van Heugten-van der Kloet, Giesbrecht, & Merckelbach, 2015), suggesting a possible causal link between sleep experiences and dissociation.

These findings suggest an intriguing interpretation of the link between dissociative symptoms and deviant sleep phenomena (see also Watson, 2001). Individuals with a labile sleep–wake cycle—perhaps associated with a genetic propensity or perhaps a byproduct of intrusions of trauma-related memories—experience intrusions of sleep phenomena (e.g., dream-like experiences) into waking consciousness, which in turn foster fantasy proneness, depersonalization, derealization, and a tendency to hyperassociate in response to emotional stimuli (Lynn et al., 2015; van Heugten-van der Kloet, Merckelbach, & Lynn, 2013). Researchers (Lynn et al., 2015; Van Heugten-van der Kloet, Cosgrave, Merckelbach, Haines, Golodetz, & Lynn, 2015) have hypothesized that the tendency to hyperassociate is a key feature of the sleep–dissociaton link and may account for rapid shifts in mental set that render it difficult for dissociative individuals to maintain a coherent sense of self and to recall autobiographical memories (Chiu, Lin, Yeh, Hwu, 2011; Chiu et. al., 2016b). Not only do dream-like experiences infiltrate everyday consciousness, but Soffer-Dudek (2017) hypothesized that daytime experiences of arousal may penetrate sleep states and engender unusual nocturnal experiences (e.g., sleep paralysis) that disturb sleep and produce difficulties in maintaining focus in response to distracting stimuli in the daytime (Soffer-Dudek, 2014). Disruptions of the sleep–wake cycle thus degrade memory (Hairston & Knight, 2004) and attentional control (Williamson, Feyer, Mattick, Friswell, & Finlay-Brown, 2001), which may account for, or contribute to, the attention deficits and cognitive failures evidenced by highly dissociative individuals (Giesbrecht, Merckelbach, Geraerts, & Smeets, 2004) and dissociative patients (Dorahy et al., 2006; Guralnik et al., 2007).

Accordingly, the sleep–dissociation perspective may explain both (a) how highly aversive events disrupt the sleep cycle and increase vulnerability to dissociative symptoms, and (b) why dissociation, trauma, fantasy proneness, and cognitive failures overlap. Thus, the sleep–dissociation perspective is commensurate with the possibility that trauma mediated by sleep disturbances plays a pivotal role in the genesis of dissociation, and suggests that previously competing theoretical perspectives may be amenable to integration. The SCM holds that patients become convinced they possess separate indwelling identities as a byproduct of suggestive media, sociocultural, and psychotherapeutic influences. These patients' sensitivity to suggestive influences may arise from their propensity to fantasize, memory errors, increased salience of negative memories, and difficulties in distinguishing fantasy and reality brought about by disruptions in the sleep cycle.

SIGNS OF THEORETICAL CONVERGENCE

Signs are emerging of a modicum of convergence or rapprochement between competing theoretical perspectives. On the one hand, adherents of the PTM (Dalenberg et al., 2012) acknowledge that (a) "DID is a disorder of self-understanding" (p. 568) and that "those with DID have the inaccurate idea that they are more than one person" (p. 568); (b) the potential effects of trauma on dissociation are difficult to completely parcel out from harms caused by a pathogenic family environment; (c) biological vulnerabilities, psychiatric history, social support, and prenatal factors probably contribute to the genesis of dissociation; and (d) fantasy proneness may lead to inaccurate trauma reports. On the other hand, proponents of the SCM (Lynn et al., 2014b) currently acknowledge that (a) trauma may play a nonspecific role in dissociation (e.g., by increasing stress levels); (b) laboratory support for the link between false memories and dissociation is mixed and not consistently impressive in magnitude; (c) traumatic events may produce the subjective sense of memory fragmentation, although objective indications of fragmentation are largely absent (Crespo & Fernández-Lansac, 2016); and (d) therapeutic approaches to treat dissociation may be helpful, although the mechanisms by which improvement occurs have yet to be delineated and isolated from nonspecific effects of psychotherapy in the context of randomized clinical trials. The fact that divergent perspectives concur that multiple causal antecedents, and not merely early trauma, need to be considered to provide a comprehensive account of dissociation and dissociative disorders is a welcome development.

TREATMENT

Depersonalization and Derealization The available research evidence provides few guidelines for the treatment of dissociative disorders. Pharmacological treatments have proven to be of little help in improving symptoms of DDD or other dissociative disorders (Somer, Amos-Williams, & Stein, 2013). For example, only a small proportion of people with DDD exhibit a clinically meaningful or even partial response to selective serotonin reuptake inhibitors or benzodiazepines. Although stimulant medications may improve concentration in individuals with DDD, they have little effect on the core symptoms of depersonalization (Simeon, et al., 1997, 2003). Moreover, the symptoms of depersonalization are no more responsive to fluoxetine (Simeon, Guralnik, Schmeidler, & Knutelska, 2004) or lamotrigine (Sierra, Phillips, Krystal, & David, 2003) than they are to a placebo. According to Simeon (2009b), the well-documented lack of response to anxiolytics or mood stabilizers among DDD patients suggests that this condition cannot be reduced to a mood or anxiety spectrum disorder, "despite being often triggered by, or co-occurring with, the latter" (p. 439). Nevertheless, the fact that treatment response differs across disorders does not necessarily preclude commonalities in etiology.

The literature on psychotherapy with patients with DDD is similarly scant. An open study conducted by Hunter, Baker, Phillips, Sierra, and David (2005) examined the effects of CBT in DDD. The investigators taught patients to interpret their symptoms in a nonthreatening way. Although there were dramatic improvements in the patient sample, and follow-up results were on the whole promising, the results must be interpreted with caution given the absence of a randomized control group. More rigorous trials are needed to confirm the merits of CBT and other psychotherapeutic approaches in patients with DDD. Recent studies on the beneficial effects of behavioral interventions on DDD symptoms that accompany anxiety disorders (e.g., social anxiety) indicate that this is a promising area of research (e.g., Schweden et al., 2016; see also Cathey & Zettle, 2016).

Dissociative Identity Disorder Individuals with DID typically are in treatment for an average of 6–7 years before being diagnosed with this condition (Gleaves, 1996). Advocates of the PTM see this finding as evidence that individuals with DID are underdiagnosed, whereas advocates of the SCM see it as evidence that patients who are later diagnosed with DID typically enter treatment with few or no symptoms of the disorder. The treatment outcome literature for DID is sparse. According to Brand, Classen, McNary, and Zaveri (2009a), only eight studies have examined treatment outcomes for DID and other dissociative disorders. Brand's research team (Brand et al., 2009b) reported a naturalistic study of DID and DD-NOS treatment by community clinicians and recently reported promising 30-month treatment and follow-up findings (Brand et al., 2013c). Nevertheless, there are no randomized controlled trials on DID. Furthermore, studies do not permit an evaluation of the extent to which symptom reduction in dissociative patients is due to regression to the mean, the passage of time, placebo effects, or other artifacts that are unrelated to the treatment (see Lilienfeld, Ritschel, Lynn, Cautin, & Latzman, 2014). Other methodological problems include variability in treatments offered to patients (e.g., Choe & Kluft, 1995), lack of controls for nonspecific effects (e.g., Ellason & Ross, 1997), dropout rates as high as 68% (Gantt & Tinnin, 2007), and the failure to evaluate purported mediators of treatment gains and consistently document clinically meaningful changes following treatment (Maxwell, Merckelbach, Lilienfeld, & Lynn, 2018). As a consequence, one cannot draw confident conclusions regarding treatment efficacy from the extant literature.

Importantly, some literature suggests that patients treated with commonly used DID interventions that involve identifying alters, addressing "parts," and recovering memories deteriorate significantly over the course of treatment (see Brand, Loewenstein, & Spiegel, 2014; Brand et al., 2016 for a contrary perspective). In one study, the majority of patients developed "florid posttraumatic stress disorder during treatment" (Dell & Eisenhower, 1990, p. 361). Moreover, after treatment commences, patients have reported increased suicide attempts (Fetkewicz et al., 2000), hallucinations, severe dysphoria, and chronic crises (Piper & Merskey, 2004). Nevertheless, Brand and Loewenstein (2014; see also Brand, Loewenstein, & Spiegel, 2014) contended that their analysis of treatment outcomes indicates that DID treatment, including interacting with "dissociated self-states," improves clinical outcomes, particularly when treatment guidelines are followed, and that depriving DID patients of treatment may cause "iatrogenic harm." Studies that compare negative sequelae across DID and conventional therapies are a clear priority.

Assuming that future studies establish that certain sleep deviations serve as causal antecedents of dissociative symptoms, it will be imperative to examine the effects of treatment interventions focused on sleep normalization in dissociative patients (Hamner, Broderick, & Labbate, 2001; Merckelbach & Giesbrecht, 2006). Previous studies that have explored the effectiveness of sleep medication in PTSD (Van Liempt, Vermetten, Geuze, & Westenberg, 2006), DID (Loewenstein, Hornstein, & Farber, 1988), and sleep hygiene protocols to reduce dissociative symptoms in a mixed inpatient group (van der Kloet, Giesbrecht, Lynn, Merckelbach, & de Zutter, 2012) and in a college sample (van der Kloet, Giesbrecht, Merckelbach, & Soontiens, 2015) have yielded promising results.

Dissociative symptoms and sleep disturbances overlap with alexithymia ("no words for feelings"), an impairment in the ability to accurately evaluate internal states and experiences (Bauermann, Parker, & Tayler, 2008; Merckelbach et al., 2017). Such impairment may contribute to a highly labile symptom presentation, as a lack of accurate evaluation of internal states may exacerbate both difficulties regulating emotions (Brady, Bujarski, Feldner, & Pyne, 2017) and the tendency of dissociative individuals to switch from one attentional set to another (Chiu et al., 2009). Because alexithymia may be reduced by interventions that encourage recognition and verbalization of feelings, which may also be promising in treating dissociative symptoms (Korzekwa, Dell, & Pain, 2009;

Ogrodniczuk, Sochting, Piper, & Joyce, 2012), addressing alexityhmia may play a more prominent role in treating dissociation in the future (Maxwell et al., 2018).

CONCLUSION

Dissociative disorders and conditions, especially DID and dissociative fugue, are among the most controversial in all of descriptive psychopathology, and for good reason. Although dissociation is unquestionably a genuine subjective experience, serious questions remain concerning the assessment, etiology, and treatment of most dissociative disorders. Etiological issues are a particular sticking point, and appear no closer to resolution with the publication of *DSM-5*. Although some authors (e.g., Dalenberg et al., 2012; Gleaves, 1996) maintain that DID and perhaps other dissociative disorders stem primarily from early child abuse and maltreatment, others (e.g., Spanos, 1994) maintain that these conditions are largely socially and culturally influenced products that are aided and abetted by therapist prompting and cueing of symptoms—a view that is supported by multiple sources of circumstantial evidence (Lilienfeld et al., 1999). It remains to be seen whether new and promising models, such as those linking sleep deprivation to dissociative symptoms (van der Kloet et al., 2012), may provide common ground between these competing theories of the genesis of dissociative disorders. Scant controversy exists surrounding the idea that people diagnosed with dissociative disorders experience genuine psychological distress. Yet clinicians who work with dissociative patients should bear in mind the powerful historical lesson imparted by the literature on DID: In their well-meaning efforts to unearth psychopathology, assessors and therapists may inadvertently end up creating it (Lilienfeld et al., 1999).

REFERENCES

Acocella, J. (1999). *Creating hysteria: Women and multiple personality disorder*. San Francisco, CA: Jossey-Bass.

Aderibigbe, Y. A., Bloch, R. M., & Walker, W. R. (2001). Prevalence of depersonalization and derealization experiences in a rural population. *Social Psychiatry and Psychiatric Epidemiology*, *36*, 63–69.

Aldridge-Morris, R. (1989). *Multiple personality: An exercise in deception*. Hillsdale, NJ: Erlbaum.

Allen, J. G. (2001). *Traumatic relationships and serious mental disorders*. New York, NY: Wiley.

Allen, J. J. B., & Movius, H. L., II. (2000). The objective assessment of amnesia in dissociative identity disorder using event-related potentials. *International Journal of Psychophysiology, 38*, 21–41.

American Psychiatric Association. (1968). *Diagnostic and statistical manual of mental disorders* (2nd ed., rev.) Washington, DC: Author.

American Psychiatric Association. (1994). *Diagnostic and statistical manual of mental disorders* (4th ed.). Washington, DC: Author.

American Psychiatric Association. (2000). *Diagnostic and statistical manual of mental disorders* (4th ed., text rev.) Washington, DC: Author.

American Psychiatric Association. (2013). *Diagnostic and statistical manual of mental disorders* (5th ed.). Arlington, VA: American Psychiatric Publishing.

Anderson, M. C., Ochsner, K. N., Kuhl, B., Cooper, J., Robertson, E., Gabrieli, S. W., . . . Gabrieli, J. D. (2004). Neural systems underlying the suppression of unwanted memories. *Science, 303*, 232–235.

Armstrong, J., Putnam, F., Carlson, E., Libero, D., & Smith, S. (1997). Development and validation of a measure of adolescent dissociation: The Adolescent Dissociative Experiences Scale. *Journal of Nervous and Mental Disorders, 185*, 491–497.

Aspell, J. E., & Blanke, O. (2009) Understanding the out-of-body experience from a neuroscientific perspective. In C. Murray (Ed.), *Psychological and scientific perspectives on out-of-body and near death experiences*. New York, NY: Nova Science.

Aspell, J. E., Lenggenhager, B., & Blanke, O. (2009). Keeping in touch with one's self: Multisensory mechanisms of self-consciousness. *PLoS ONE*, 4(8), e6488. doi: 10.1371/journal. pone.0006488

Baker, D., Hunter, E., Lawrence, E., Medford, N., Patel, M., Senior, C., . . . David, A. S. (2003). Depersonalisation disorder: Clinical features of 204 cases. *British Journal of Psychiatry*, 182, 428–433.

Barlow, M. R., & Freyd, J. J. (2009). Adaptive dissociation: Information processing and response to betrayal. In P. F. Dell & J. A. O'Neil (Eds.), *Dissociation and the dissociative disorders* (pp. 93–105). New York, NY: Routledge/Taylor Francis.

Bauermann, T. M., Parker, J. D., & Taylor, G. J. (2008). Sleep problems and sleep hygiene in young adults with alexithymia. *Personality and Individual Differences*, 45(4), 318–322.

Becker-Blease, K. A., Deater-Deckard, K., Eley, T., Freyd, J. J., Stevenson, J., & Plomin, R. (2004). A genetic analysis of individual differences in dissociative behaviors in childhood and adolescence. *Journal of Child Psychology and Psychiatry and Allied Disciplines*, 45, 522–532.

Beere, D. B. (2009). The self-system as a mechanism for the dissociative disorders: An extension of the perceptual theory of dissociation. In P. F. Dell & J. A. O'Neil (Eds.), *Dissociation and the dissociative disorders* (pp. 277–286). New York, NY: Routledge/Taylor Francis.

Belli, R. F., Winkielman, P., Read, J. D., Schwarz, N., & Lynn, S. J. (1998). Recalling more childhood events leads to judgments of poorer memory: Implications for the recovered/false memory debate. *Psychonomic Bulletin & Review*, 5, 318–323.

Belli, H., Ural, C., Vardar, M. K., Yesilyurt, S., & Oncu, F. (2012). Dissociative symptoms and dissociative disorder comorbidity in patients with obsessive-compulsive disorder. *Comprehensive Psychiatry*, 53(7), 975–80.

Bernstein, E. M., & Putnam, F. W. (1986). Development, reliability, and validity of a dissociation scale. *Journal of Nervous and Mental Disease*, 174, 727–735.

Bernstein-Carlson, E., & Putnam, F. W. (1993). An update on the Dissociative Experiences Scale. *Dissociation*, 6, 19–27.

Blanke, O., Ortigue, S., Landis, T., & Seeck, M. (2002). Neuropsychology: Stimulating illusory own-body perceptions. *Nature*, 419(6904), 269–270.

Blanke, O., & Thut, G. (2007). Inducing out of body experiences. In G. Della Sala (Ed.), *Tall tales*. Oxford, England: Oxford University Press.

Boysen, G. A. (2011). The scientific status of childhood dissociative identity disorder: A review of published research. *Psychotherapy and Psychosomatics*, 80(6), 329–334.

Boysen, G. A., & Van Bergen, A. (2013). A review of published research on adult dissociative identity disorder: 2000–2010. *Journal of Nervous and Mental Disease*, 201(1), 5–11.

Boysen, G., & Van Bergen, A. (2014). The simulation of multiple personalities: A review of research comparing diagnosed and simulated dissociative identity disorder. *Clinical Psychology Review*, 34(1), 14–28.

Brady, R. E., Bujarski, S. J., Feldner, M. T., & Pyne, J. M. (2017). Examining the effects of alexithymia on the relation between posttraumatic stress disorder and over-reporting. *Psychological Trauma: Theory, Research, Practice, and Policy*, 9(1), 80.

Brand, B. L., Armstrong, J. G., & Loewenstein, R. J. (2006). Psychological assessment of patientswith dissociative identity disorder. *Psychiatric Clinics of North America*, 29, 145–168.

Brand, B., Classen, C. C., McNary, S. W., & Zaveri, P. (2009a). A review of dissociative disorders treatment studies. *Journal of Nervous and Mental Disease*, 197, 646–694.

Brand, B., Classen, C., Lanius, R., Loewenstein, R., McNary, S., Pain, C., & Putnam, F. W. (2009b). A naturalistic study of dissociative identity disorder and dissociative disorder not otherwise specified patients treated by community physicians. *Psychological Trauma: Theory, Research, Practice, and Policy, 1,* 153–171.

Brand, B., & Loewenstein, R. J. (2014). Does phasic trauma treatment make patients with dissociative identity disorder treatment more dissociative? *Journal of Trauma & Dissociation, 15*(1), 52–65.

Brand, B., Loewenstein, R. J., & Spiegel, D. (2013a). Disinformation about dissociation: Dr. Joel Paris's notions about dissociative identity disorder. *Journal of Nervous and Mental Disease, 201*(4), 354–356.

Brand, B., Loewenstein, R., & Spiegel, D. (2013b). Patients with DID are found and researched more widely than Boysen and VanBergen recognized. *Journal of Nervous and Mental Disease, 201*(5), 440.

Brand, B. L., Loewenstein, R. J., & Spiegel, D. (2014). Dispelling myths about dissociative identity disorder treatment: An empirically based approach. *Psychiatry: Interpersonal and Biological Processes, 77*(2), 169–189.

Brand, B. L., McNary, S. W., Myrick, A. C., Classen, C. C., Lanius, R., Loewenstein, R. J., . . . Putnam, F. W. (2013c). A longitudinal naturalistic study of patients with dissociative disorders treated by community clinicians. *Psychological Trauma: Theory, Research, Practice, and Policy, 5*(4), 301.

Brand, B. L., Sar, V., Stavropoulos, P., Krüger, C., Korzekwa, M., Martínez-Taboas, A., & Middleton, W. (2016). Separating fact from fiction: an empirical examination of six myths about dissociative identity disorder. *Harvard Review of Psychiatry, 24*(4), 257–270.

Bremner, J. D. (2010). Cognitive processes in dissociation: Comment on Giesbrecht et al. (2008). *Psychological Bulletin, 136*(1), 1–6.

Bremner, J. D., Krystal, J. H., Putnam, F. W., Southwick, S. M., Marmar, C., Charney, D. S., & Mazure, C. M. (1998). Measurement of dissociative states with the Clinician Administered Dissociative States Scale (CADSS). *Journal of Traumatic Stress, 11,* 125–136.

Bremner, J. D., Narayan, M., Anderson, E. R., Staib, L. H., Miller, H. L., & Charney, D. S. (2000). Hippocampal volume reduction in major depression. *American Journal of Psychiatry, 157,* 115–117.

Bremner, J. D., Randall, P., Scott, T. M., & Bronen, R. (1995). MRI-based measurement of hippocampal volume in patients with combat-related posttraumatic stress disorder. *American Journal of Psychiatry, 152,* 973–981.

Bremner, J. D., Randall, P., Vermetten, E., & Staib, L. (1997). Magnetic resonance imagingbased measurement of hippocampal volume in posttraumatic stress disorder related to childhood physical and sexual abuse: A preliminary report. *Biological Psychiatry, 41,* 23–32.

Bremner, J. D., Steinberg, M., Southwick, S. M., Johnson, D. R., & Charney, D. S. (1993). Use of the Structured Clinical Interview for DSM-IV-Dissociative Disorders for systematic assessment of dissociative symptoms in posttraumatic stress disorder. *American Journal of Psychiatry, 150,* 1011–1014.

Briere, J., Weathers, F. W., & Runtz, M. (2005). Is dissociation a multidimensional construct? Data from the Multiscale Dissociation Inventory. *Journal of Traumatic Stress, 18,* 221–231.

Brown, D. P., Scheflin, A. W., & Hammond, D. C. (1997). *Memory, trauma, treatment, and the law.* New York, NY: W. W. Norton.

Bunning, S., & Blanke, O. (2005). The out-of-body experience: Precipitating factors and neural correlates. *Progress in Brain Research, 150,* 331–350.

Candel, I., Merckelbach, H., & Kuijpers, M. (2003). Dissociative experiences are related to commissions in emotional memory. *Behaviour Research and Therapy, 41,* 719–725.

Cardeña, E. (1994). The domain of dissociation. In S. J. Lynn, & J. W. Rhue (Eds.), *Dissociation: Clinical and theoretical perspectives* (pp. 15–31). New York, NY: Guilford Press.

Cardeña, E. (2008). Dissociative disorders measures. In A. J. Rush, M. First, & D. Blacker (Eds.), *Handbook of psychiatric measures* (2nd ed., pp. 677–690). Washington, DC: American Psychiatric Publishing.

Cardeña, E., van Duijl, M., Weiner, L. A., & Terhune, D. (2009). Possession/trance phenomena. In P. F. Dell & J. A. O'Neil (Eds.), *Dissociation and the dissociative disorders: DSM-V and beyond* (pp. 171–181). New York, NY: Routledge/Taylor & Francis.

Carlson, E. B., Putnam, F. W., Ross, C. A., Anderson, G., Clark, P., Torem, M., . . . Braun, B. G. (1991a). Factor analysis of the Dissociative Experiences Scale: A multicenter study. In B. G. Braun & E. B. Carlson (Eds.), *Proceedings of the eighth international conference on multiple personality and dissociative states.* Chicago, IL: Rush.

Carlson, E. B., Putnam, F. W., Ross, C. A., Torem, M., Coons, P., Bowman, E. S., Braun, B. G. (1991b). Validity of the Dissociative Experiences Scale in screening for multiple personality disorder: A multicenter study. *American Journal of Psychiatry, 150*(7), 1030–1036.

Carlson, E. A., Yates, T. M., & Sroufe, L. A. (2009). Dissociation and development of the self. In P. F. Dell & J. A. O'Neil (Eds.), *Dissociation and the dissociative disorders* (pp. 39–52). New York, NY: Routledge/Taylor Francis.

Cathey, A. J., & Zettle, R. D. (2016). The development of novel interoceptive exposure methods for inducing derealization and depersonalization symptoms. *Journal of Cognitive Psychotherapy, 30,* 223–234.

Cheyne, J. A., & Girard, T. A. (2009). The body unbound: Vestibular-motor hallucinations and out-of-body experiences. *Cortex, 45*(2), 201–215.

Chiu, C. D., Lin, C. C., Yeh, Y. Y., & Hwu, H. G. (2012). Forgetting the unforgotten affective autobiographical memories in nonclinical dissociators. *Emotion, 12*(5), 1102.

Chiu, C. D., Tseng, M. C. M., Chien, Y. L., Liao, S. C., Liu, C. M., Yeh, Y. Y., & Hwu, H. G. (2016a). Misattributing the source of self-generated representations related to dissociative and psychotic symptoms. *Frontiers in Psychology, 7,* 541.

Chiu, C. D., Tseng, M. C. M., Chien, Y. L., Liao, S. C., Liu, C. M., Yeh, Y. Y., & Hwu, H. G. (2016b). Switch function and pathological dissociation in acute psychiatric inpatients. *PloS One, 11*(4), e0154667.

Chiu, C. D., Yeh, Y. Y., Huang, Y. M., Wu, Y. C., & Chiu, Y. C. (2009). The set switching function of nonclinical dissociators under negative emotion. *Journal of Abnormal Psychology, 118*(1), 214–222.

Choe, B. M., & Kluft, R. P. (1995). The use of the DES in studying treatment outcome with dissociative identity disorder: A pilot study. *Dissociation, 8,* 160–164.

Cloitre, M., Cancienne, J., Brodsky, B., Dulit, R., & Perry, S. W. (1996). Memory performance among women with parental abuse histories: Enhanced directed forgetting or directed remembering? *Journal of Abnormal Psychology, 105,* 204–211.

Colletti, G., Lynn, S. J., & Laurence, J.-R. (2010). Hypnosis and the treatment of dissociative identity disorder. In S. J. Lynn, I. Kirsch, & J. W. Rhue (Eds.), *Handbook of clinical hypnosis* (2nd ed., pp. 433–452). Washington, DC: American Psychological Association.

Condon, L., & Lynn, S. J. (2014). State and trait dissociation: Evaluating convergent and discriminant validity. *Imagination, Cognition, and Personality 34*(1), 25–37.

Coons, P. M. (1988). Schneiderian first rank symptoms in schizophrenia and multiple personality disorder. *Acta Psychiatrica Scandinavica, 77,* 235.

Coons, P. M. (1998). The dissociative disorders: Rarely considered and underdiagnosed. *Psychiatric Clinics of North America, 21,* 637–648.

Coons, P. M., Bowman, E. S., & Milstein, V. (1988). Multiple personality disorder: A clinical investigation of 50 cases. *Journal of Nervous and Mental Disease, 176,* 519–527.

Crespo, M., & Fernández-Lansac, V. (2016). Memory and narrative of traumatic events: A literature review. *Psychological Trauma: Theory, Research, Practice, and Policy, 8,* 149.

Dalenberg, C. J., Brand, B. L., Gleaves, D. H., Dorahy, M. J., Loewenstein, R. J., Cardeña, E., . . . Spiegel, D. (2012). Evaluation of the evidence for the trauma and fantasy models of dissociation. *Psychological Bulletin, 138*(3), 550–558.

Dalenberg, C. J., Brand, B. L., Loewenstein, R. J., Gleaves, D. H., Dorahy, M. J., Cardeña, E., . . . & Spiegel, D. (2014). Reality versus fantasy: reply to Lynn et al. (2014). *Psychological Bulletin, 140*(3), 911–920.

Dell, P. F. (2002). Dissociative phenomenology of dissociative identity disorder. *Journal of Nervous and Mental Disease, 190*(1), 10–15.

Dell, P. F. (2006). The Mulitdimensional Inventory of Dissociation (MID): A comprehensive measure of pathological dissociation. *Journal of Trauma and Dissociation, 7*(2), 77–106.

Dell, P. F. (2009). The long struggle to diagnose multiple personality disorder (MPD): Partial MPD. In P. F. Dell & J. A. O'Neil (Eds.), *Dissociation and the dissociative disorders: DSM-5 and beyond* (pp. 403–428). New York, NY: Routledge/Taylor & Francis.

Dell, P. F., & Eisenhower, J. W. (1990). Adolescent multiple personality disorder: A preliminary study of eleven cases. *Journal of the Academy of Child & Adolescent Psychiatry, 29*, 359–366.

Delmonte, R., Lucchetti, G., Moreira-Almeida, A., & Farias, M. (2016). Can the DSM-5 differentiate between nonpathological possession and dissociative identity disorder? A case study from an Afro-Brazilian religion. *Journal of Trauma & Dissociation, 17*, 322–337.

DePrince, A. P., & Freyd, J. J. (2001). Memory and dissociative tendencies: The roles of attentional context and word meaning in a directed forgetting task. *Journal of Trauma and Dissociation, 2*, 67–82.

De Ridder, D., Van Laere, K., Dupont, P., Menovsky, T., & Van de Heyning, P. (2007). Visualizing out-of-body experience in the brain. *New England Journal of Medicine, 357*(18), 1829–1833.

Devilly, G. J., Ciorciari, J., Piesse, A., Sherwell, S., Zammit, S., Cook, F., & Turton, C. (2007). Dissociative tendencies and memory performance on directed forgetting tasks. *Psychological Science, 18*, 212–217.

DeYoung, C. G., Peterson, J. B., & Higgins, D. M. (2005). Sources of openness/intellect: Cognitive and neuropsychological correlates of the fifth factor of personality. *Journal of Personality, 73*, 825–858.

Dollinger, S. J. (1985). Lightning strike disaster among children. *British Journal of Medical Psychology, 58*, 375–383.

Domozych, W., & Dragan, W. Ł. (2016). Genetic and Environmental Basis of the Relationship Between Dissociative Experiences and Cloninger's Temperament and Character Dimensions–Pilot Study. *Polish Psychological Bulletin, 47*, 412–420.

Dorahy, M. J., Irwin, H. J., & Middleton, W. (2002). Cognitive inhibition in dissociative identity disorder (DID): Developing an understanding of working memory function in DID. *Journal of Trauma and Dissociation, 3*, 111–132.

Dorahy, M. J., McCusker, C. G., Loewenstein, R. J., Colbert, K., & Mulholland, C. (2006). Cognitive inhibition and interference in dissociative identity disorder: The effects of anxiety on specific executive functions. *Behaviour Research and Therapy, 44*, 749–764.

Dorahy, M. J., Middleton, W., & Irwin, H. J. (2005). The effect of emotional context on cognitive inhibition and attentional processing in dissociative identity disorder. *Behaviour Research and Therapy, 43*, 555–568.

Dutra, L., Bureau, J. F., Holmes, B., Lyubchik, A., & Lyons-Ruth, K. (2009). Quality of early care and childhood trauma: A prospective study of developmental pathways to dissociation. *Journal of Nervous and Mental Disease, 197*(6), 383–390.

Dutra, S. J., & Wolf, E. J. (2017). Perspectives on the conceptualization of the dissociative subtype of PTSD and implications for treatment. *Current Opinion in Psychology, 14*, 35–39.

Ehrsson, H. (2007). The experimental induction of out-of-body experiences. *Science, 317*(5841), 1048.

Ellason, J. W., & Ross, C. A. (1995). Positive and negative symptoms in dissociative identity disorder and schizophrenia: A comparative analysis. *Journal of Nervous and Mental Disease*, *183*(4), 236–241.

Ellason, J. W., & Ross, C. A. (1997). Two-year follow-up of inpatients with dissociative identity disorder. *American Journal of Psychiatry*, *154*, 832–839.

Ellason, J. W., Ross, C. A., & Fuchs, D. L. (1996). Lifetime Axis 1 and II comorbidity and childhood trauma history in dissociative identity disorder. *Psychiatry*, *59*, 255–261.

Elzinga, B. M., de Beurs, E., Sergeant, J. A., Van Dyck, R., & Phaf, R. H. (2000). Dissociative style and directed forgetting. *Cognitive Therapy and Research*, *24*, 279–295.

Elzinga, B. M., van Dyck, R., & Spinhoven, P. (1998). Three controversies about dissociative identity disorder. *Clinical Psychology and Psychotherapy*, *5*, 13–23.

Fahy, T. A. (1988). The diagnosis of multiple personality disorder: A critical review. *British Journal of Psychiatry*, *153*, 597–606.

Fetkewicz, J., Sharma, V., & Merskey, H. (2000). A note on suicidal deterioration with recovered memory treatment. *Journal of Affective Disorders*, *58*, 155–159.

Freyd, J. J. (1996). *Betrayal trauma theory: The logic of forgetting childhood abuse*. Cambridge, MA: Harvard University Press.

Friedl, M. C., & Draijer, N. (2000). Dissociative disorders in Dutch psychiatric inpatients. *American Journal of Psychiatry*, *157*, 1012–1013.

Frischholz, E. J., Lipman, L. S., Braun, B. G., & Sachs, R. G. (1992). Psychopathology, hypnotizability and dissociation. *American Journal of Psychiatry*, *149*, 1521–1525.

Fullerton, C., Ursano, R., Epstein, R., Crowley, B., Vance, K., Kao, T.-C., & Baum, A. (2000). Posttraumatic dissociation following motor vehicle accidents: Relationship to prior trauma and prior major depression. *Journal of Nervous and Mental Disease*, *188*(5), 267–272.

Gantt, L., & Tinnin, L. W. (2007). Intensive trauma therapy of PTSD and dissociation: An outcome study. *The Arts in Psychotherapy*, *34*, 69–80.

Gershuny, B. S., & Thayer, J. F. (1999). Relations among psychological trauma, dissociative phenomena, and trauma-related distress: A review and integration. *Clinical Psychology Review*, *19*, 631–637.

Giesbrecht, T., Geraerts, E., & Merckelbach, H. (2007a). Dissociation, memory commission errors, and heightened autonomic reactivity. *Psychiatry Research*, *150*, 277.

Giesbrecht, T., Lynn, S. J., Lilienfeld, S., & Merckelbach, H. (2008). Cognitive processes in dissociation: An analysis of core theoretical assumptions. *Psychological Bulletin*, *134*, 617–647.

Giesbrecht, T., Lynn, S. J., Lilienfeld, S., & Merckelbach, H. (2010). Cognitive processes, trauma, and dissociation: Misconceptions and misrepresentations (Reply to Bremner, 2009). *Psychological Bulletin*, *136*, 7–11.

Giesbrecht, T., & Merckelbach, H. (2009). Betrayal trauma theory of dissociative experiences: Stroop and directed forgetting findings. *American Journal of Psychology*, *122*, 337–348.

Giesbrecht, T., Merckelbach, H., & Geraerts, E. (2007b). The dissociative experiences taxon is related to fantasy proneness. *Journal of Nervous and Mental Disease*, *195*, 769–772.

Giesbrecht, T., Merckelbach, H., Geraerts, E., & Smeets, E. (2004). Disruptions in executive functioning and dissociation in undergraduate students. *Journal of Nervous and Mental Disease*, *192*, 567–569.

Giesbrecht, T., Merckelbach, H., Kater, M., & Sluis, A. F. (2007c). Why dissociation and schizotypy overlap—The joint influence of fantasy proneness, cognitive failures, and childhood trauma. *Journal of Nervous and Mental Disease*, *195*, 812–818.

Giesbrecht, T., Merckelbach, H., & Smeets, E. (2006). Thought suppression, dissociation, and context effects. *Netherlands Journal of Psychology*, *62*, 73–80.

Giesbrecht, T., Smeets, T., Leppink, J., Jelicic, M., & Merckelbach, H. (2007d). Acute dissociation after 1 night of sleep loss. *Journal of Abnormal Psychology*, *116*, 599–606.

Gleaves, D. H. (1996). The sociocognitive model of dissociative identity disorder: A reexamination of the evidence. *Psychological Bulletin, 120,* 142–159.

Gleaves, D. H., May, M. C., & Cardeña, E. (2001). An examination of the diagnostic validity of dissociative identity disorder. *Clinical Psychology Review, 21,* 577–608.

Gonzalez-Torres, M. A., Inchausti, L., Aristegui, M., Ibañez, B., Diez, L., Fernandez-Rivas, A., . . . Mingo, A. (2010). Depersonalization in patients with schizophrenia spectrum disorders, first-degree relatives and normal controls. *Psychopathology, 43*(3), 141–149.

Goren, J., Phillips, L., Chapman, M., & Salo, B. (2012). Dissociative and psychotic experiences of adolescents admitted to a psychiatric inpatient unit. *Journal of Trauma & Dissociation, 13*(5), 554–567.

Gudjonsson, G. H. (1984). A new scale of interrogative suggestibility. *Personality and Individual Differences, 5,* 303–314.

Guralnik, O., Giesbrecht, T., Knutelska, M., Sirroff, B., & Simeon, D. (2007). Cognitive functioning in depersonalization disorder. *Journal of Nervous and Mental Disease, 195,* 983–988.

Guralnik, O., Schmeidler, J., & Simeon, D. (2000). Feeling unreal: Cognitive processes in depersonalization. *American Journal of Psychiatry, 157,* 103–109.

Hacking, I. (1995). *Rewriting the soul: Multiple personality and the sciences.* Princeton, NJ: Princeton University Press.

Hairston, I. S., & Knight, R. T. (2004). Neurobiology—Sleep on it. *Nature, 430,* 27–28.

Hamner, M. B., Broderick, P. S., & Labbate, L. S. (2001). Gabapentin in PTSD: A retrospective clinical series of adjunctive therapy. *Annals of Clinical Psychiatry, 13,* 141–146.

Heinrichs, R. W., & Zakzanis, K. K. (1998). Neurocognitive deficit in schizophrenia: A quantitative review of the evidence. *Neuropsychology, 12,* 426–445.

Holmes, E. A., Brown, R. J., Mansell, W., Fearon, R., Hunter, E. C. M., Frasquilho, F., & Oakley, D. A. (2005). Are there two qualitatively distinct forms of dissociation? A review and some clinical implications. *Clinical Psychology Review, 25,* 1–23.

Horevitz, R. P. & Braun, B. G. (1984). Are multiple personalities borderline? *Psychiatric Clinics of North America, 7,* 69–87.

Hunter, E. C. M., Baker, D., Phillips, M. L., Sierra, M., & David, A. S. (2005). Cognitive-behaviour therapy for depersonalization disorder: An open study. *Behaviour Research and Therapy, 43,* 1121–1130.

Huntjens, R. J. C., Peters, M. L., Woertman, L., Bovenschen, L. M., Martin, R. C., & Postma, A. (2006). Inter-identity amnesia in dissociative identity disorder: A simulated memory impairment? *Psychological Medicine, 36,* 857–863.

Huntjens, R. J. C., Peters, M. L., Woertman, L., van der Hart, O., & Postma, A. (2007). Memory transfer for emotionally valenced words between identities in dissociative identity disorder. *Behaviour Research and Therapy, 45,* 775–789.

Huntjens, R. J. C., Verschuere, B., & McNally, R. J. (2012). Inter-identity autobiographical amnesia in patients with dissociative identity disorder. *PLoS ONE, 7*(7), e40580. doi: 10.1371/journal.pone. 0040580

Janet, P. (1973). *L'automatisme psychologique.* Paris, France: Société Pierre Janet. (Original work published 1889).

Jang, K. L., Paris, J., Zweig-Frank, H., & Livesley, W. J. (1998). Twin study of dissociative experiences. *Journal of Abnormal Psychology, 186,* 345–351.

Jáuregui-Renaud, K., Ramos-Toledo, V., Aguilar-Bolaños, M., Montaño-Velazquez, B., & Pliego-Maldonado, A. (2008a). Symptoms of detachment from the self or from the environment in patients with an acquired deficiency of the special senses. *Journal of Vestibular Research, 18,* 129–137.

Jáuregui-Renaud, K., Sang, F. Y., Gresty, M. A., Green, D. A., & Bronstein, A. M. (2008b). Depersonalization/derealization symptoms and updating orientation in patients with vestibular disease. *Journal of Neurology, Neurosurgery, and Psychiatry, 79*(3), 276–283.

Jureidini, J. (2003). Does dissociation offer a useful explanation for psychopathology? *Psychopathology, 37,* 259–265.

Kemp, K., Gilbertson, A. D., & Torem, M. (1988). The differential diagnosis of multiple personality disorder from borderline personality disorder. *Dissociation, 1,* 41–46.

Kihlstrom, J. F. (2005). Dissociative disorders. *Annual Review of Clinical Psychology, 1,* 1–27.

Kihlstrom, J. F., Glisky, M. L., & Angiulo, M. J. (1994). Dissociative tendencies and dissociative disorders. *Journal of Abnormal Psychology, 103,* 117–124.

Kirino, E. (2006). P300 is attenuated during dissociative episodes. *Journal of Nervous and Mental Disease, 194,* 83–90.

Kluft, R. P. (1984). Treatment of multiple personality disorders: A study of 33 cases. *Psychiatric Clinics of North America, 7,* 9–29.

Kluft, R. P. (1993). Multiple personality disorders. In D. Spiegel (Ed.), *Dissociative disorders: A clinical review* (pp. 14–44). Lutherville, MD: Sidran Press.

Kohlenberg, R. J. (1973). Behavioristic approach to multiple personality: A case study. *Behavior Therapy, 4,* 137–140.

Kong, L. L., Allen, J. J. B., & Glisky, E. L. (2008). Interidentity memory transfer in dissociative identity disorder. *Journal of Abnormal Psychology, 117,* 686–692.

Korzekwa, M. I., Dell, P. F., & Pain, C. (2009). Dissociation and borderline personality disorder: An update for clinicians. *Current Psychiatry Reports, 11*(1), 82–88.

Krause-Utz, A., Winter, D., Schriner, F., Chiu, C. D., Lis, S., Spinhoven, P., . . . Elzinga, B. M. (2017). Reduced amygdala reactivity and impaired working memory during dissociation in borderline personality disorder. *European Archives of Psychiatry and Clinical Neuroscience,* 1–15.

Krüger, C., Bartel, P., & Fletcher, L. (2014). Dissociative mental states are canonically associated with decreased temporal theta activity on spectral analysis of the EEG. *Journal of Trauma and Dissociation, 14*(4), 473–491.

Krüger, C., & Fletcher, L. (2017). Predicting a dissociative disorder from type of childhood maltreatment and abuser–abused relational tie. *Journal of Trauma & Dissociation, 18*(3), 356–372.

Kruger, C., & Mace, C. J. (2002). Psychometric validation of the State Scale of Dissociation (SSD). *Psychology and Psychotherapy: Theory, Research, and Practice, 75,* 33–51.

Krystal, J. H., Karper, L. P., Seibyl, J. P., Freeman, G. K., Delaney, R., Bremner, J. D., . . . Charney, D. S. (1994). Subanesthetic effects of the noncompetitive NMDA antagonist, ketamine, in humans. Psychotomimetic, perceptual, cognitive, and neuroendocrine responses. *Archives of General Psychiatry, 51,* 199–214.

Kuperman, V. (2006). Narratives of psychiatric malingering in works of fiction. *Medical Humanities, 32,* 67–72.

Lauer, J., Black, D. W., & Keen, P. (1993). Multiple personality disorder and borderline personality disorder: Distinct entities or variations on a common theme? *Annals of Clinical Psychiatry, 5,* 129–134.

Lemons, P., & Lynn, S. J. (2016). Self-reports of trauma and dissociation: An examination of context effects. *Consciousness and Cognition, 44,* 8–19.

Lenggenhager, B., Tadi, T., Metzinger, T., & Blanke, O. (2007). Video ergo sum: Manipulating bodily self-consciousness. *Science, 317*(5841), 1096–1099.

Lilienfeld, S. O., & Lynn, S. J. (2015). Dissociative identity disorder: Multiple personalities, multiple controversies. In S. O. Lilienfeld, S. J. Lynn, & J. M. Lohr (Eds.), *Science and pseudoscience in clinical psychology* (2nd ed.) (pp. 115–154). New York, NY: Guilford Press.

Lilienfeld, S. O., Lynn, S. J., Kirsch, I., Chaves, J., Sarbin, T., Ganaway, G., & Powell, R. (1999). Dissociative identity disorder and the sociocognitive model: Recalling the lessons of the past. *Psychological Bulletin, 125,* 507–523.

Lilienfeld, S. O., Ritschel, L. A., Lynn, S. J., Cautin, R. L., & Latzman, R. D. (2014). Why ineffective psychotherapies can appear to work: A taxonomy of causes of spurious therapeutic effectiveness. *Perspectives on Psychological Science,* 9(4), 355–387.

Liotti, G. (1999). Understanding the dissociative processes: The contribution of attachment theory. *Psychoanalytic Inquiry,* 19, 757–783.

Liotti, G. (2009). Attachment and dissociation. In P. F. Dell & J. A. O'Neil (Eds.), *Dissociation and the dissociative disorders* (pp. 53–66). New York, NY: Routledge/Taylor Francis.

Loewenstein, R. J. (1991). An office mental status examination for complex chronic dissociative symptoms and multiple personality disorder. In R. J. Loewenstein (Ed.), *Psychiatric clinics of North America* (Vol. 14, pp. 567–604). Philadelphia, PA: W. B. Saunders.

Loewenstein, R. J., Hornstein, N., & Farber, B. (1998). Open trial of clonazepam in the treatment of posttraumatic stress symptoms in MPD. *Dissociation,* 1, 3–12.

Lynn, S. J., Berg, J., Lilienfeld, S. O., Merckelbach, H., Giesbrecht, T., Accardi, M., & Cleere, C. (2014a). Dissociative disorders. In M. Hersen, S. Turner, & D. Beidel (Eds.). *Adult psychopathology and diagnosis* (7th ed., pp. 406–450). New York: Wiley.

Lynn, S. J., Fassler, O., Knox, J., & Lilienfeld, S. O. (2009). Dissociation and dissociative identity disorder: Treatment guidelines and cautions. In J. Fisher & W. O'Donohue (Eds.), *Practitioner's guide to evidence based psychotherapy* (pp. 248–257). New York, NY: Springer.

Lynn, S. J., Knox, J., Fassler, O., Lilienfeld, S. O., & Loftus, E. (2004). Trauma, dissociation, and memory. In J. Rosen (Ed.), *Posttraumatic stress disorder: Issues and controversies.* Hoboken, NJ: Wiley.

Lynn, S. J., Lilienfeld, S. O., Merckelbach, H., Giesbrecht, T., McNally, R., Loftus, E., . . . Malaktaris, A. (2014b). The trauma model of dissociation: Inconvenient truths and stubborn fictions: Comment on Dalenberg et al. (2012). *Psychological Bulletin,* 140, 896–910.

Lynn, S. J., Lilienfeld, S. O., Merckelbach, H., Maxwell, R., Baltman, J,. & Giesbrecht, T. (2015). Dissociative Disorders. In J. E. Maddux, & B. A. Winstead (Eds.). *Psychopathology: Foundations for a contemporary understanding* (pp. 298–318). London: Routledge.

Lynn, S. J., & Pintar, J. (1997). A social narrative model of dissociative identity disorder. *Australian Journal of Clinical and Experimental Hypnosis,* 25, 1–7.

Lynn, S. J., Rhue, J., & Green, J. (1988). Multiple personality and fantasy-proneness: Is there an association or dissociation? *British Journal of Experimental and Clinical Hypnosis,* 5, 138–142.

Mai, F. M. (1995). Psychiatrists' attitudes to multiple personality disorder: A questionnaire study. *Canadian Journal of Psychiatry,* 40, 154–157.

Marcopulos, B. A., Hedjar, L., & Arredondo, B. C. (2016). Dissociative Amnesia or Malingered Amnesia? A Case Report. *Journal of Forensic Psychology Practice,* 16, 106–117.

Martnez-Taboas, A., Dorahy, M., Sar, V., Middleton, W., & Krüger, C. (2013). Growing not dwindling: International research on the worldwide phenomenon of dissociative disorders. *Journal of Nervous and Mental Disease,* 201, 353.

Maxwell, R., Merckelbach, H., Lilienfeld, S. O., & Lynn, S. J. (2018) The treatment of dissociation: An evaluation of effectiveness and potential mechanisms. In D. David, S. J. Lynn, & G. Montgomery (Eds.), *Evidence-based psychotherapy: The state of the science and practice.* New York: Wiley Blackwell.

McHugh, P. R. (1993). Multiple personality disorder. *Harvard Mental Health Newsletter,* 10(3), 4–6.

McHugh, P. R. (2008). *Try to remember: Psychiatry's clash over meaning.* New York, NY: Dana Press.

McKinnon, M. C., Boyd, J. E., Frewen, P. A., Lanius, U. F., Jetly, R., Richardson, J. D., & Lanius, R. A. (2016). A review of the relation between dissociation, memory, executive functioning and social cognition in military members and civilians with neuropsychiatric conditions. *Neuropsychologia,* 90, 210–234.

McNally, R. J. (2003). Recovering memories of trauma: A view from the laboratory. *Current Directions in Psychological Science,* 12, 32–35.

McNally, R. J. (2004). The science and folklore of traumatic amnesia. *Clinical Psychology: Science and Practice, 11*, 29–33.

Merckelbach, H., Boskovic, I., Pesy, D., Dalsklev, M., & Lynn, S. J. (2017). Symptom overreporting and dissociative experiences: A qualitative review. *Consciousness and Cognition, 49*, 132–144.

Merckelbach, H., Dekkers, T., Wessel, I., & Roefs, A. (2003). Dissociative symptoms and amnesia in Dutch concentration camp survivors. *Comprehensive Psychiatry, 44*, 65–69.

Merckelbach, H., Devilly, G. J., & Rassin, E. (2002a). Alters in dissociative identity disorder: Metaphors or genuine entities? *Clinical Psychology Review, 22*, 481–497.

Merckelbach, H., & Giesbrecht, T. (2006). Subclinical dissociation, schizotypy, and traumatic distress. *Personality and Individual Differences, 40*, 365–374.

Merckelbach, H., Horselenberg, R., & Schmidt, H. (2002b). Modeling the connection between self-reported trauma and dissociation in a student sample. *Personality and Individual Differences, 32*, 695–705.

Merckelbach, H., & Jelicic, M. (2004). Dissociative symptoms are related to endorsement of vague trauma items. *Comprehensive Psychiatry, 45*, 70–75.

Merckelbach, H., Jelicic, M., & Pieters, M. (2011). Misinformation increases symptom reporting: a test–retest study. *JRSM short reports, 2*, 1–6.

Merckelbach, H. & Muris, P. (2001). The causal link between self-reported trauma and dissociation: A critical review. *Behaviour Research and Therapy, 39*, 245–254.

Merckelbach, H., Muris, P., Horselenberg, R., & Stougie, S. (2000a). Dissociative experiences, response bias, and fantasy proneness in college students. *Personality and Individual Differences, 28*, 49–58.

Merckelbach, H., Muris, P., & Rassin, E. (1999). Fantasy proneness and cognitive failures as correlates of dissociative experiences. *Personality and Individual Differences, 26*, 961–967.

Merckelbach, H., Muris, P., Rassin, E., & Horselenberg, R. (2000b). Dissociative experiences and interrogative suggestibility in college students. *Personality and Individual Differences, 29*, 1133–1140.

Merskey, H. (1992). The manufacture of personalities: The production of multiple personality disorder. *British Journal of Psychiatry, 160*, 327–340.

Mittenberg, W., Patton, C., Canyock, E. M., & Condit, D. C. (2002). Base rates of malingering and symptom exaggeration. *Journal of Clinical and Experimental Neuropsychology, 24*, 1094–1102.

Modestin, J. & Erni, T. (2004). Testing the dissociative taxon. *Psychiatry Research, 126*, 77–82.

Montagne, B., Sierra, M., Medford, N., Hunter, E. C. M., Baker, D., Kessels, R. P. C., . . . David, S. (2007). Emotional memory and perception of emotional faces in patients suffering from depersonalization disorder. *British Journal of Psychology, 98*, 517–527.

Moskowitz, A. (2004). Dissociation and violence: A review of the literature. *Trauma, Violence, and Abuse, 5*, 21–46.

Mueller-Pfeiffer, C., Rufibach, K., Perron, N., Wyss, D., Kuenzler, C., Prezewowsky, C., . . . Rufer, M. (2012). Global functioning and disability in dissociative disorders. *Psychiatry Research, 200*, 475–481.

Mueller-Pfeiffer, C., Rufibach, K., Wyss, D., Perron, N., Pitman, R. K., & Rufer, M. (2013). Screening for dissociative disorders in psychiatric outand day care-patients. *Journal of Psychopathology & Behavioral Assessment, 35*, 592–602.

Muris, P., Merckelbach, H., & Peeters, E. (2003). The links between the adolescent Dissociative Experiences Scale (A-DES), fantasy proneness, and anxiety symptoms. *Journal of Nervous and Mental Disease, 191*, 18–24.

Nairne, J. S., & Pandeirada, J. N. S. (2008). Adaptive memory: Remembering with a stone-age brain. *Current Directions in Psychological Science, 17*, 239–243.

Nash, M. R., Hulsey, T. L., Sexton, M. C., Harralson, T. L., & Lambert, W. (1993). Long-term sequelae of childhood sexual abuse: Perceived family environment, psychopathology, and dissociation. *Journal of Consulting and Clinical Psychology, 61*, 276–283.

Nelson, K. R., Mattingly, M., Lee, S. A., & Schmitt, F. A. (2006). Does the arousal system contribute to near death experience? *Neurology, 66*(7), 1003–1009.

Nelson, M. D., Saykin, A. J., Flashman, L. A., & Riordan, H. J. (1988). Hippocampal volume reduction as assessed by magnetic resonance imaging: A meta-analytic study. *Archives of General Psychiatry, 55*, 433–440.

Nijenhuis, E. R., Spinhoven, P., Van Dyck, R., Van der Hart, O., & Vanderlinden, J. (1996). The development and psychometric characteristics of the Somatoform Dissociation Questionnaire (SDQ-20). *Journal of Nervous and Mental Disease, 184*, 688–694.

Nijenhuis, E. R. S., Spinhoven, P., Van Dyck, R., Van der Hart, O., & Vanderlinden, J. (1997). The development of the Somatoform Dissociation Questionnaire (SDQ 5) as a screening instrument for dissociative disorders. *Acta Psychiatrica Scandinavica, 96*, 311–318.

Nijenhuis, E. R. S., Spinhoven, P., Van Dyck, R., Van der Hart, O., & Vanderlinden, J. (1998). Psychometric characteristics of the Somatoform Dissociation Questionnaire: A replication study. *Psychotherapy and Psychosomatics, 67*, 17–23.

Nijenhuis, E., van der Hart, O., & Steel, C. (2010). Trauma-related structural dissociation of the personality. *Activitas Nervosa Superior, 52*, 1–23.

Noll, J., Trickett, P., & Putnam, F. W. (2003). A prospective investigation of the impact of childhood sexual abuse on the development of sexuality. *Journal of Consulting and Clinical Psychology, 71*(3), 575–586.

North, C. S., Ryall, J. M., Ricci, D. A., & Wetzel, R. D. (1993). *Multiple personalities, multiple disorders: Psychiatric classification and media influence.* Oxford, England: Oxford University Press.

Nuller, Y. L., Morozova, M. G., Kushnir, O. N., & Hamper, N. (2001). Effect of naloxone therapy on depersonalization: A pilot study. *Journal of Psychopharmacology, 15*, 93–95.

Ogawa, J. R., Sroufe, L. A., Weinfield, N. S., Carlson, E. A., & Egeland, B. (1997). Development and the fragmented self: Longitudinal study of dissociative symptomatology in a nonclinical sample. *Development and Psychopathology, 9*, 855–879.

Ogrodniczuk, J. S., Sochting, I., Piper, W. E., & Joyce, A. S. (2012). A naturalistic study of alexithymia among psychiatric outpatients treated in an integrated group therapy program. *Psychology and Psychotherapy: Theory, Research and Practice, 85*(3), 278–291.

Orne, M. T., Dinges, D. F., & Orne, E. C. (1984). On the differential diagnosis of multiple personality in the forensic context. *International Journal of Clinical and Experimental Hypnosis, 32*, 118–169.

Paris, J. (2012). The rise and fall of dissociative identity disorder. *Journal of Nervous and Mental Disease, 200*(12), 1076–1079.

Patihis, L., & Lynn, S. J. (2017). Psychometric comparison of the Dissociative Experiences Scale II and C: Evaluating the trauma-dissociation link. *Applied Cognitive Psychology.* doi: 10.1002/acp.3337.

Persinger, M. M. (2001). The neuropsychiatry of paranormal experiences. *Neuropsychiatric Practice and Opinion, 13*, 521–522.

Piper, A. (1997). *Hoax and reality: The bizarre world of multiple personality disorder.* Northvale, NJ: Jason Aronson.

Piper, A., & Merskey, H. (2004). The persistence of folly: Critical examination of dissociative identity disorder. Part II. The defence and decline of multiple personality or dissociative identity disorder. *Canadian Journal of Psychiatry, 49*, 678–683.

Pope, H. G., Barry, S., Bodkin, A., & Hudson, J. I. (2006). Tracking scientific interest in the dissociative disorders: A study of scientific publication output 1984–2003. *Psychotherapy & Psychosomatics, 75*, 19–24.

Pope, H. G., & Hudson, J. I. (1995). Does childhood sexual abuse cause adult psychiatric disorders? Essentials of methodology. *Journal of Psychiatry & Law, 12,* 363–381.

Pope, H. G., Hudson, J. I., Bodkin, J. A., & Oliva, P. (1998). Questionable validity of "dissociative amnesia" in trauma victims: Evidence from prospective studies. *British Journal of Psychiatry, 172,* 210–215.

Pope, H. G., Poliakoff, M. B., Parker, M. P., Boynes, M., & Hudson, J. I. (2007). Is dissociative amnesia a culture-bound syndrome? Findings from a survey of historical literature. *Psychological Medicine, 37,* 225–233.

Porter, S., Birt, A. R., Yuille, J. C., & Lehman, D. R. (2000). Negotiating false memories: Interviewer and rememberer characteristics relate to memory distortion. *Psychological Science, 11,* 507–510.

Powell, R. A., & Gee, T. L. (1999). The effects of hypnosis on dissociative identity disorder: A reexamination of the evidence. *Canadian Journal of Psychiatry, 44,* 914–916.

Prohl, J., Resch, F., Parzer, P., & Brunner, R. (2001). Relationship between dissociative symptomatology and declarative and procedural memory in adolescent psychiatric patients. *Journal of Nervous and Mental Disease, 198,* 602–607.

Putnam, F. W., & Lowenstein, R. J. (2000). Dissociative identity disorder. In B. J. Sadock & V. A. Sadock (Eds.), *Kaplan and Sadock's comprehensive textbook of psychiatry* (7th ed., Vol. 1, pp. 1552–1564). Philadelphia, PA: Lippincott, Williams, & Wilkins.

Quaedflieg, C. W., Giesbrecht, T., Meijer, E., Merckelbach, H., de Jong, P. J., Thorsteinsson, H., . . . Simeon, D. (2012). Early emotional processing deficits in depersonalization: An exploration with event-related potentials in an undergraduate sample. *Psychiatry Research: Neuroimaging, 212,* 223–229.

Ray, W., & Faith, M. (1994). Dissociative experiences in a college age population. *Personality and Individual Differences, 18,* 223–230.

Read, J. D., & Lindsay, D. S. (2000). "Amnesia" for summer camps and high school graduation: Memory work increases reports of prior periods of remembering less. *Journal of Traumatic Stress, 13,* 129–147.

Reinders, A. A., Willemsen, A. T., den Boer, J. A., Vos, H. P., Veltman, D. J., & Loewenstein, R. J. (2014). Opposite brain emotion-regulation patterns in identity states of dissociative identity disorder: A PET study and neurobiological model. *Psychiatry Research: Neuroimaging, 223,* 236–243.

Rieber, R. W. (2006). *The bifurcation of the self: The history and theory of dissociation and its disorders.* New York, NY: Springer.

Rifkin, A., Ghisalbert, D., Dimatou, S., Jin, C., & Sethi, M. (1998). Dissociative identity disorder in psychiatric inpatients. *American Journal of Psychiatry, 155,* 844–845.

Rivard, J. M., Dietz, P., Matell, D., & Widawski, M. (2002). Acute dissociative responses in law enforcement officers involved in critical shooting incidents. *Journal of Forensic Sciences, 47,* 1093–1100.

Ross, C. A. (1991). High and low dissociators in a college student population. *Dissociation: Progress in the Dissociative Disorders, 4*(3), 147–151.

Ross, C. A. (1997). *Dissociative identity disorder: Diagnosis, clinical features, and treatment of multiple personality.* New York, NY: Wiley.

Ross, C. A. (2009a). The theory of a dissociative subtype of schizophrenia. In P. Dell, & J. A. O'Neil (Eds.), *Dissociation and the dissociative disorders: DSM-V and beyond* (pp. 557–568). New York, NY: Routledge/Taylor & Francis.

Ross, C. A. (2009b). Dissociative amnesia and dissociative fugue. In P. Dell & J. A. O'Neil (Eds.), *Dissociation and the dissociative disorders: DSM-V and beyond* (pp. 429–434). New York, NY: Routledge/Taylor & Francis.

Ross, C. A., Anderson, G., Fleisher, W. P., & Norton, G. R. (1991). The frequency of multiple personality disorder among psychiatric inpatients. *American Journal of Psychiatry, 148,* 1717–1720.

Ross, C. A., Anderson, G., Fraser, G. A., Reagor, P., Bjornson, L., & Miller, S. D. (1992). Differentiating multiple personality disorder and dissociative disorder not otherwise specified. *Dissociation, 5*, 88–91.

Ross, C. A., Duffy, C. M. M., & Ellason J. W. (2002). Prevalence, reliability and validity of dissociative disorders in an inpatient setting. *Journal of Trauma & Dissociation, 3*, 7–17.

Ross, C. A., Ellason, J. W., & Anderson, G. (1995). A factor analysis of the dissociative experiences scale (DES) in dissociative identity disorder. *Dissociation, 8*, 229–235.

Ross, C. A., Heber, S., Norton, G. R., Anderson, D., Anderson, G., & Barchet, P. (1989). The Dissociative Disorders Interview Schedule: A structured interview. *Dissociation, 2*, 169–189.

Ross, C. A., & Norton, G. R. (1988). Multiple personality patients with a past diagnosis of schizophrenia. *Dissociation, 1*(2), 39–42.

Ross, C. A., Norton, G. R., & Wozney, K. (1989). Multiple personality disorder: An analysis of 236 cases. *Canadian Journal of Psychiatry, 34*, 413–418.

Rossini, E. D., Schwartz, D. R., & Braun, B. G. (1996). Intellectual functioning of inpatients with dissociative identity disorder and dissociative disorder not otherwise specified. Cognitive and neuropsychological aspects. *Journal of Nervous and Mental Disease, 184*, 289–294.

Ruiz, M. A., Poythress, N. G., Lilienfeld, S. O., Douglas, K. S. (2008). Factor structure and correlates of the dissociative experiences scale in a large offender sample. *Assessment, 15*, 511–521.

Sanders, B., & Green, A. (1994). The factor structure of dissociative experiences in college students. *Dissociation, 7*, 23–27.

Sanders, B., & Giolas, M. H. (1991). Dissociation and childhood trauma in psychologically disturbed adolescents. *American Journal of Psychiatry, 148*, 50–54.

Sang, F. Y. P., Jáuregui-Renaud, K., Green, D. A., Bronstein, A. M., & Gresty, M. A. (2006). *Journal of Neurology, Neurosurgery, and Psychiatry, 77*, 760–766.

Sapolsky, R. M. (2000). Glucocorticoids and hippocampal atrophy in neuropsychiatric disorders. *Archives of General Psychiatry, 57*, 925–935.

Sar, V., Akyüz, G., & Dogan, O. (2007). Prevalence of dissociative disorders among women in the general population. *Psychiatry Research, 149*(1–3), 169–176.

Sar, V., Akyüz, G., Kugu, N., Ozturk, E., & Ertem-Vehid, H. (2006). Axis I dissociative disorder comorbidity in borderline personality disorder and reports of childhood trauma. *Journal of Clinical Psychiatry, 67*(10), 1583–1590.

Sar, V., Tutkun, H., Alyanak, B., Bakim, B., & Barai, I. (2000). Frequency of dissociative disorders among psychiatric outpatients in Turkey. *Comprehensive Psychiatry, 41*, 216–222.

Sarbin, T. R. (1995). On the belief that one body may be host to two or more personalities. *International Journal of Clinical and Experimental Hypnosis, 43*, 163–183.

Schreiber, F. R. (1973). *Sybil*. New York, NY: Warner.

Schurle, B. A., Ray, W. J., Bruce, J. M., Arnett, P. A., & Carlson, R. A. (2007). The relationship between executive functioning and dissociation. *Journal of Clinical and Experimental Neuropsychology, 29*, 626–633.

Schweden, T. L., Pittig, A., Bräuer, D., Klumbies, E., Kirschbaum, C., & Hoyer, J. (2016). Reduction of depersonalization during social stress through cognitive therapy for social anxiety disorder: A randomized controlled trial. *Journal of Anxiety Disorders, 43*, 99–105.

Sierra, M., Baker, D., Medford, N., & David, A. S. (2005). Unpacking the depersonalization syndrome: An exploratory factor analysis on the Cambridge Depersonalization Scale (CDS). *Psychological Medicine, 35*, 1523–1532.

Sierra, M., & Berrios, G. E. (2000). The Cambridge Depersonalisation Scale: A new instrument for the measurement of depersonalization. *Psychiatry Research, 93*, 163–164.

Sierra, M., & Berrios, G. E. (2001). The phenomenological stability of depersonalization: Comparing the old with the new. *Journal of Nervous and Mental Disease, 189*, 629–636.

Sierra, M., Phillips, M. L., Krystal, J., & David, A. S. (2003). A placebo-controlled, crossover trial of lamotrigine in depersonalization disorder. *Journal of Psychopharmacology, 17,* 103–105.

Simeon, D. (2004). Depersonalization disorder: A contemporary overview. *CNS Drugs, 18,* 343–354.

Simeon, D. (2009a). Depersonalization disorder. In P. F. Dell & J. A. O'Neil (Eds.), *Dissociation and dissociative disorders: DSM-5 and beyond* (pp. 435–446). New York, NY: Routledge/Taylor & Francis.

Simeon, D. (2009b). Neurobiology of depersonalization disorder. In P. F. Dell & J. A. O'Neil (Eds.), *Dissociation and dissociative disorders: DSM-5 and beyond* (pp. 367–372). New York, NY: Routledge/Taylor & Francis.

Simeon, D., & Abugel, J. (2006). *Feeling unreal: Depersonalization disorder and the loss of the self.* New York, NY: Oxford University Press.

Simeon, D., Gross, S., Guralnik, O., Stein, D. J., Schmeidler, J., & Hollander, E. (1997). Feeling unreal: 30 cases of DSM-III-R depersonalization disorder. *American Journal of Psychiatry, 154,* 1107–1113.

Simeon, D., Guralnik, O., Gross, S., Stein, D. J., Schmeidler, J., & Hollander, E. (1998). The detection and measurement of depersonalization disorder. *Journal of Nervous and Mental Disease, 186,* 536–542.

Simeon, D., Guralnik, O., Hazlett, E. A., Spiegel-Cohen, J., Hollander, E., & Buchsbaum, M. S. (2000). Feeling Unreal: A PET study of depersonalization disorder. *American Journal of Psychiatry, 157,* 1782–1788.

Simeon, D., Guralnik, O., Schmeidler, J., & Knutelska, M. (2004). Fluoxetine therapy in depersonalization disorder: Randomized clinical trial. *British Journal of Psychiatry, 185,* 31–36.

Simeon, D., Guralnik, O., Schmeidler, J., Sirof, B., & Knutelska, M. (2001). The role of childhood interpersonal trauma in depersonalization disorder. *American Journal of Psychiatry, 158,* 1027–1033.

Simeon, D., Hwu, R., & Knutelska, M. (2007). Temporal disintegration in depersonalization disorder. *Journal of Trauma & Dissociation, 8*(1), 11–24.

Simeon, D., Knutelska, M., Nelson, D., & Guralnik, O. (2003). Feeling unreal: A depersonalization disorder update of 117 cases. *Journal of Clinical Psychiatry, 64,* 990–997.

Simons, R. C., & Hughes, C. C. (Eds.). (1985). *The culture-bound syndromes: Folk illnesses of psychiatric and anthropological interest.* Dordrecht, the Netherlands: D. Reidel.

Smith, S. R., & Carlson, E. B. (1996). Reliability and validity of the Adolescent Dissociative Experiences Scale. *Dissociation 9,* 125–129.

Soffer-Dudek, N. (2014). Dissociation and dissociative mechanisms in panic disorder, obsessive–compulsive disorder, and depression: A review and heuristic framework. *Psychology of Consciousness: Theory, Research, and Practice, 1*(3), 243–70.

Soffer-Dudek, N. (2017). Arousal in nocturnal consciousness: How dream-and sleep experiences may inform us of poor sleep quality, stress, and psychopathology. *Frontiers in Psychology, 8,* 733.

Somer, E., Altus, L., & Ginzburg, K. (2010). Dissociative psychopathology among opioid use disorder patients: Exploring the chemical dissociation hypothesis. *Comprehensive Psychiatry, 51,* 419–425.

Somer, E., Amos-Williams, T., & Stein, D. J. (2013). Evidence-based treatment for depersonalisation-derealisation disorder (DPRD). *BMC Psychology, 1,* 20.

Spanos, N. P. (1994). Multiple identity enactments and multiple personality disorder: A socio-cognitive perspective. *Psychological Bulletin, 116,* 143–165.

Spanos, N. P. (1996). *Multiple identities and false memories: A sociocognitive perspective.* Washington, DC: American Psychiatric Association.

Spanos, N. P., Weekes, J. R., & Bertrand, L. D. (1985). Multiple personality: Asocial psychological perspective. *Journal of Abnormal Psychology, 94,* 362–376.

Stafford, J., & Lynn, S. J. (2002). Cultural scripts, childhood abuse, and multiple identities: A study of role-played enactments. *International Journal of Clinical & Experimental Hypnosis, 50,* 67–85.

Staniloiu, A., & Markowitsch, H. J. (2014). Dissociative amnesia. *The Lancet Psychiatry, 1*(3), 226–241.

Steele, K., van der Hart, O., & Nijenhuis, E. (2009). The trauma-related structural dissociation of the personality. In P. F. Dell & J. A. O'Neil (Eds.), *Dissociation and the dissociative disorders* (pp. 239–258). New York, NY: Routledge/Taylor & Francis.

Stein, M. B., Koverola, C., Hanna, C., & Torchia, M. G. (1997). Hippocampal volume in women victimized by childhood sexual abuse. *Psychological Medicine, 27*, 951–959.

Steinberg, M. (1985). *Structured clinical interview for DSM-III-R dissociative disorders (SCID-D)*. New Haven, CT: Yale University School of Medicine.

Steinberg, M. (1994). *Structured clinical interview for DSM-IV dissociative disorders revised (SCID-D-R)*. Washington, DC: American Psychiatric Press.

Steinberg, M., Rounsaville, B., & Cichetti, D., (1990). The Structured Clinical Interview for DSM-III-R dissociative disorders: Preliminary report on a new diagnostic instrument. *American Journal of Psychiatry, 147*, 76–82.

Steinberg, M., & Siegel, H. D. (2008). Advances in assessment. The differential diagnosis of dissociative identity disorder and schizophrenia. In A. Moskowitz, I. Schäfer, & M. J. Dorahy (Eds.), *Psychosis, trauma, and dissociation: Emerging perspectives on severe psychopathology* (pp. 177–189). Chichester, UK: Wiley.

Tellegen, A., & Atkinson, G. (1974). Openness to absorbing and self-altering experiences ("absorption"), a trait related to hypnotic susceptibility. *Journal of Abnormal Psychology, 83*, 268–277.

Terhune, D. B. (2009). The incidence and determinants of visual phenomenology during out-of-body experiences. *Cortex, 45*(2), 236–242.

Tsai, G. E., Condie, D., Wu, M.-T., & Chang, I.-W. (1999). Functional magnetic resonance imaging of personality switches in a woman with dissociative identity disorder. *Harvard Review of Psychiatry, 72*, 119–122.

Tutkun, H., Sar, V., Yargic, L. L., Özpulat, T., Yank, M., & Kiziltan, E. (1998). Frequency of dissociative disorders among psychiatric inpatients in a Turkish University Clinic. *American Journal of Psychiatry, 155*, 800–805.

van der Hart, O., Nijenhuis, E., Steele, K., & Brown, D. (2004). Trauma-related dissociation: Conceptual clarity lost and found. *Australian and New Zealand Journal of Psychiatry 38*, 906–914.

van der Hart, O., Nijenhuis, E., Steele, K., & Brown, D. (2006). *The haunted self: Structural dissociation and the treatment of chronic traumatization*. New York, NY: W. W. Norton.

van der Kloet, D., Giesbrecht, T., Franck, E., Gastel, V., de Volder, I., Eede, V. D., . . . Merckelbach, H. (2013). Dissociative symptoms and sleep parameters: An all-night polysomnography study in patients with insomnia. *Comprehensive Psychiatry, 54*, 658–664.

van der Kloet, D., Giesbrecht, T., Lynn, S. J., Merckelbach, H., & de Zutter, A. (2012). Sleep normalization and decrease in dissociative experiences: Evaluation in an inpatient sample. *Journal of Abnormal Psychology, 121*, 140–150.

van der Kloet, D., Giesbrecht, T., Merckelbach, H., & Soontiens, F. (2015). *Decreasing dissociative symptoms using sleep hygiene recommendations: An exploratory study*. Manuscript submitted for publication.

van der Kloet, D., Merckelbach, H., Giesbrecht, T., & Lynn, S. J. (2012). Fragmented sleep, fragmented mind: The role of sleep in dissociative symptoms. *Perspectives on Psychological Science, 7*, 159–175.

Vanderlinden, J., Van Dyck, R., Vandereycken, W., & Vertommen, H. (1991). Dissociative experiences in the general population in the Netherlands and Belgium: A study with the Dissociative Questionnaire (DIS-Q). *Dissociation: Progress in the Dissociative Disorders, 4*, 180–184.

van Heugten-van der Kloet, D., Cosgrave, J., Merckelbach, H., Haines, R., Golodetz, S., & Lynn, S. J. (2015). Imagining the impossible before breakfast: the relation between creativity, dissociation, and sleep. *Frontiers in Psychology, 6*, 324.

van Heugten-van der Kloet, D., Giesbrecht, T., & Merckelbach, H. (2015). Sleep loss increases dissociation and affects memory for emotional stimuli. *Journal of Behavior Therapy and Experimental Psychiatry, 47*, 9–17.

van Heugten-van der Kloet, D., Giesbrecht, T., van Wel, J., Bosker, W. M., Kuypers, K. P., Theunissen, E. L., Spronk, D. B., Verkes, R. J., Merckelbach, H., & Ramaekers, J. G., (2015). MDMA, cannabis, and cocaine produce acute dissociative symptoms. *Psychiatry Research, 228*, 907–912.

van Heugten-van der Kloet, D., Merckelbach, H., & Lynn, S. J. (2013). Dissociative symptoms and sleep. *Behavioral and Brain Sciences, 36*(6), 630–631.

Van Liempt, S., Vermetten, E., Geuze, E., & Westenberg, H. (2006). Pharmacotherapeutic treatment of disordered sleep in posttraumatic stress disorder: A systematic review. *International Journal of Clinical Psychopharmacology, 21*(4), 193–202.

Van Oorsouw, K., & Merckelbach, H. (2010). Detecting malingered memory problems in the civil and criminal arena. *Legal and Criminological Psychology, 15*, 97–114.

Vogel, M., Braungardt, T., Grabe, H. J., Schneider, W., & Klauer, T. (2013). Detachment, compartmentalization, and schizophrenia: Linking dissociation and psychosis by subtype. *Journal of Trauma & Dissociation, 14*(3), 273–287.

Waller, N. G. (1995). *The Dissociative Experiences Scale. The 12th mental measurements yearbook* (pp. 317–318). Lincoln, NE: The Buros Institute of Mental Measurements.

Waller, N. G., Putnam, F. W., & Carlson, E. B. (1996). Types of dissociation and dissociation and dissociative types: A taxometric analysis of dissociative experiences. *Psychological Methods, 1*, 300–321.

Waller, N. G., & Ross, C. A. (1997). The prevalence and biometric structure of pathological dissociation in the general population: Taxometric and behavior genetic findings. *Journal of Abnormal Psychology, 106*, 499–510.

Watson, D. (2001). Dissociations of the night: Individual differences in sleep-related experiences and their relation to dissociation and schizotypy. *Journal of Abnormal Psychology, 110*, 526–535.

Watson, D. (2003). Investigating the construct validity of the dissociative taxon: Stability analysis of normal and pathological dissociation. *Journal of Abnormal Psychology, 112*, 298–305.

Wechsler, D. (1981). *Wechsler Adult Intelligence Scale–Revised*. San Antonio, TX: Psychological Corporation.

Wegen, K. S., van Dijke, A., Aalbers, A., & Zedlitz, A. M. (in press). Dissociation and under-regulation of affect in patients with posttraumatic stress disorder with and without a co-morbid substance use disorder. *European Journal of Trauma & Dissociation*.

Welburn, K. R., Fraser, G. A., Jordan, S. A., Cameron, C., Webb, L. M., & Raine, D. (2003). Discriminating dissociative identity disorder from schizophrenia and feigned dissociation on psychological tests and structured interview. *Journal of Trauma & Dissociation, 4*(2), 109–130.

Williamson, A. M., Feyer, A. M., Mattick, R. P., Friswell, R., & Finlay-Brown, S. (2001). Developing measures of fatigue using an alcohol comparison to validate the effects of fatigue on performance. *Accident Analysis and Prevention, 33*, 313–326.

Winter, D., Krause-Utz, A., Lis, S., Chiu, C. D., Lanius, R. A., Schriner, F., . . . Schmahl, C. (2015). Dissociation in borderline personality disorder: disturbed cognitive and emotional inhibition and its neural correlates. *Psychiatry Research: Neuroimaging, 233*(3), 339–351.

Wolfradt, U., & Meyer, T. (1998). Interrogative suggestibility, anxiety and dissociation among anxious patients and normal controls. *Personality and Individual Differences, 25*, 425–432.

Wright, D. B., & Loftus, E. F. (1999). Measuring dissociation: Comparison of alternative forms of the dissociative experiences scale. *American Journal of Psychology, 112*, 497–519.

Wright, D. B., & Osborne, J. E. (2005). Dissociation, cognitive failures, and working memory. *American Journal of Psychology, 118*, 103–113.

Yaylaci, F. T., Cicchetti, D., Rogosch, F. A., Bulut, O., & Hetzel, S. R. (2017). The interactive effects of child maltreatment and the FK506 binding protein 5 gene (FKBP5) on dissociative symptoms in adolescence. *Development and Psychopathology, 29*(3), 1105–1117.

CHAPTER 14

Feeding and Eating Disorders

CYNTHIA M. BULIK, LAUREN BREITHAUPT, ZEYNEP YILMAZ, RACHEL W. GOW,
SARA E. TRACE, SUSAN C. KLEIMAN, and SUZANNE E. MAZZEO

DESCRIPTION OF THE DISORDERS

Eating disorders represent a category of partially overlapping syndromes, all of which have some clinical features marked by eating dysregulation. We will focus our discussion on anorexia nervosa (AN), bulimia nervosa (BN), and binge-eating disorder (BED), which represent the primary eating disorders listed in *DSM-5*. Feeding disorders, such as pica, rumination disorder, and avoidant/restrictive food intake disorder—all more common in, but not exclusive to, children—will not be covered in this chapter. Eating disorders are serious mental illnesses that are influenced by both genetic and environmental factors. The syndromes are partially overlapping, as considerable diagnostic flux occurs over time, with individuals migrating from one clinical presentation to another, and because several diagnostic features are shared across disorders. Nonetheless, pure forms of each of the presentations also exist.

CLINICAL PICTURE

Anorexia nervosa, the most visible eating disorder, is a serious psychiatric illness characterized by an inability to maintain a normal healthy body weight or, in individuals who are still growing, failure to make expected increases in weight (and often height) and bone density. Despite increasing weight loss and frank emaciation, individuals with AN strive for additional weight loss, see themselves as fat even when they are severely underweight, and often engage in unhealthy weight-loss behaviors (e.g., purging, dieting, excessive exercise, and fasting).

Anorexia nervosa is characterized by low weight; however, the definition of "low weight" is somewhat complicated. *DSM-5* highlights restriction of energy intake relative to requirements, leading to a significantly low body weight, and embeds that in the context of the individual's age, sex, developmental trajectory, and physical health. Even when at low weight, people with AN experience an intense fear of gaining weight or of becoming fat, or they engage in persistent behavior that interferes with weight gain. The behavior and cognitions of individuals with AN vigorously defend low body weight.

Adult Psychopathology and Diagnosis, Eighth Edition. Edited by Deborah C. Beidel and B. Christopher Frueh.
© 2018 John Wiley & Sons, Inc. Published 2018 by John Wiley & Sons, Inc.
Companion website: www.wiley.com/go/beidel/psychopathology8e

Other aspects of the diagnostic criteria include a three-part criterion, of which only one component is necessary: disturbance in the way in which one's body weight or shape is experienced, undue influence of body weight or shape on self-evaluation, or persistent lack of recognition of the seriousness of the current low body weight.

In the past, amenorrhea of 3 months' or longer duration was a diagnostic criterion for AN. Wisely, this has been eliminated, as there are no meaningful differences between individuals with AN who do and do not menstruate (Gendall et al., 2006; Watson & Andersen, 2003). Although not diagnostic, cessation of menstruation can be a useful indicator of severity, and resumption of menses is a factor in determining recovery. AN presents either as the restricting subtype, in which low weight is achieved and maintained through energy restriction and increased physical activity only, or as the binge-eating/purging subtype, in which the individual has been regularly engaging in binge-eating or purging behavior (i.e., self-induced vomiting or the misuse of laxatives, diuretics, or enemas) over the past 3 months.

Bulimia nervosa is characterized by recurrent binge-eating episodes, defined as eating an unusually large amount of food in a short period of time (~2 hours) while experiencing a sense of loss of control over the eating episode. In addition, bulimia includes recurrent inappropriate compensatory behaviors (e.g., self-induced vomiting, laxative, diuretic, or other medication misuse, fasting, or excessive exercise). In individuals with BN, self-evaluation is unduly influenced by body shape and weight. Binge eating and compensatory episodes occur on average once a week for at least 3 months. BN is only diagnosed if AN criteria are not met. Thus, to be diagnosed with BN, individuals should have a body mass index (BMI) greater than 18.5 kg/m^2 in adults (i.e., the lower bound of normal weight according to the World Health Organization [WHO, 1992] and the Centers for Disease Control).

Bulimia nervosa onset most frequently occurs in adolescence or early adulthood, although it can occur at any point across the life span (American Psychiatric Association [APA], 2013). BN can also occur at any body weight (with the exception of the requirement to diagnose AN binge-eating/purging type if criteria for AN are met). BN tends to be over-represented in women; however, it has been argued that BN diagnostic criteria are gender-biased, leading to under-detection in men. Men who seek treatment for BN tend to manifest a greater reliance on nonpurging forms of compensatory behavior, such as excessive exercise (Anderson & Bulik, 2004; Lewinsohn, Seeley, Moerk, & Striegel-Moore, 2002). It is important to consider such gender differences in the clinical presentation of BN to revise prevalence estimates of this diagnosis (Anderson & Bulik, 2004).

In *DSM-5*, BED received recognition as a stand-alone disorder after years of being categorized as a disorder "worthy of further study." Binge eating was first noted in a subset of obese individuals by Stunkard (1959). BED has had a slow and controversial evolution in the psychiatric nosology for eating disorders (Fairburn, Welch, & Hay, 1993; Spitzer et al., 1993; Walsh, 1992).

Binge-eating disorder is marked by recurrent binge eating (at least weekly for 3 months, as in BN) and a sense of lack of control over eating during the episode, but in the absence of regular compensatory behaviors. Unlike BN, the diagnostic criteria for BED include descriptions of the binge experience. To meet criteria, an individual must experience distress regarding the binge eating as well as at least three of the following: eating much more rapidly than normal, eating until feeling uncomfortably full, eating large amounts of food when not feeling physically hungry, eating alone because of feeling embarrassed by how much one is eating, or feeling disgusted with oneself, depressed, or very guilty afterward. It remains a curiosity as to why these descriptors remained in the BED criteria when they are not in the BN criteria; presumably, this was related to ensuring that individuals who simply overeat were not misdiagnosed as having BED. BED can occur at any body weight and is only diagnosed if neither AN nor BN criteria are met.

Other specified feeding or eating disorder (OSFED) is a new category in *DSM-5*, which replaces the historical eating disorder not otherwise specified (EDNOS). The reorganization in *DSM-5* occurred in part because BED became a stand-alone diagnosis and in part because, historically, far too many individuals with eating disorders received a diagnosis of EDNOS, rendering it the most frequently diagnosed eating disorder. This alerted many researchers and clinicians to the fact that the diagnostic system was in need of revision so that a greater number of individuals could be captured under the hallmark categories of AN, BN, and BED. OSFED applies to presentations with symptoms characteristic of a feeding and eating disorder, but full diagnostic criteria are not met. Research suggests that these changes to the diagnostic schema yield fewer residual diagnoses. More specifically, applying *DSM-5* diagnostic criteria, in comparison to *DSM-IV* criteria, increased diagnoses of AN by 3–7% (Brownley, Peat, La Via, & Bulik, 2015; Yilmaz, Hardaway, & Bulik, 2015; Yilmaz et al., 2014), BN by 0–4.5% (Mancuso et al., 2015; Vo, Accurso, Goldschmidt, & Le Grange, 2016), with ~3–13% meeting BED criteria (Austin et al., 2011; Brandys et al., 2013; Grilo et al., 2012; Mancuso et al., 2015). In parallel, *DSM 5* criteria reduced residual diagnoses (OSFED and UFED) by 8.6–28% (Mancuso et al., 2015; Thomas et al., 2015; Vo et al., 2016). Additional research is needed to clarify further whether *DSM-5* criteria affect eating disorder treatment.

Other specified feeding or eating disorder includes a useful category of atypical AN, in which an individual meets all criteria for AN except that his/her weight falls within or above the normal weight range. This would capture, for example, an individual who was obese who precipitously lost a large amount of weight and exhibited all of the psychological features of AN, but, because of the weight at which the weight loss started, still fell within the normal weight range. Other presentations under OSFED include BN and BED of low frequency or limited duration, purging disorder (i.e., purging behavior in the absence of binge eating), and night eating syndrome, in which individuals report recurrent episodes of night eating, marked by eating after awakening from sleep or by excessive food consumption after the evening meal.

Based on previous research with EDNOS, it is not expected that individuals diagnosed with OSFED category have less serious symptomatology. The severity of pathology and psychosocial impairment is comparable among individuals with EDNOS, AN, and BN (Fairburn & Bohn, 2005; Keel, Gravener, Joiner, & Haedt, 2010). Clinical descriptions of EDNOS are consistent in stating that most cases have features similar to AN and BN (Crow, Agras, Halmi, Mitchell, & Kraemer, 2002; Waller, 1993; Walsh & Garner, 1997). Three studies (Fairburn & Cooper, 2007; Ricca et al., 2001; Turner & Bryant-Waugh, 2004) using the Eating Disorder Examination (EDE; Cooper & Fairburn, 1987) found that individuals with EDNOS presented with significant cognitive symptomatology related to eating, shape, and weight, suggesting that these syndromes are clinically significant. A recent study applying *DSM-5* criteria found residual eating disorders (OSFED and UFED) are also clinically significant (Wu et al., 2016).

DIAGNOSTIC CONSIDERATIONS

With the publication of *DSM-5* in 2013, investigation of the validity of the new classification system is an important research focus. Some advances of the *DSM-5* system include attention to stages of illness. In the past, for example, if someone had met criteria for AN and then began to recover, she or he might have received a new diagnosis of EDNOS. In *DSM-5*, there is now the option to include the specifier of "in partial remission" if, after having met full criteria, weight has normalized but the psychological features remain, and "full remission" if, after having met full criteria, no criteria have been met for a sustained period of time. In addition, severity specifiers also exist, and are currently based on BMI, with mild AN being $\geq 17\,kg/m2$, moderate $16–16.99\,kg/m2$, severe $15–15.99\,kg/m2$, and extreme $<15\,kg/m^2$.

In addition to the core diagnostic features, individuals with AN often manifest a specific cluster of personality traits, including perfectionism, obsessionality, anxiety, harm avoidance, and low self-esteem (Cassin & von Ranson, 2005; Fassino, Amianto, Gramaglia, Facchini, & Abbate Daga, 2004; Klump et al., 2000). Furthermore, both these personality characteristics and anxiety disorders often precede AN onset (Bulik, Sullivan, Fear, & Joyce, 1997; Kaye, Bulik, Thornton, Barbarich, & Masters, 2004). Major depression and anxiety disorders frequently co-occur with AN (Bulik et al., 1997; Fernandez-Aranda et al., 2007; Godart, Flament, Perdereau, & Jeammet, 2002; Godart, Flament, Lecrubier, & Jeammet, 2000; Kaye et al., 2004), and longitudinal research suggests that depression often persists following recovery from AN (Sullivan, Bulik, Fear, & Pickering, 1998).

Some personality features common among individuals with AN are also manifested by many women with BN, such as high harm avoidance, perfectionism, and low self-esteem. However, other personality features appear more specific to BN, including elevated novelty-seeking and impulsivity, low self-directedness, and low cooperative-ness (Bulik, Sullivan, Joyce, & Carter, 1995; Fassino et al., 2004; Steiger et al., 2004). Further refinements of the components of impulsivity suggest that negative urgency, or the tendency to act rashly when distressed, is the facet of impulsivity most strongly associated with bulimia (Fischer, Smith, & Cyders, 2008).

Comorbid psychiatric disorders are very common among individuals with BN, occurring among nearly 80% of patients (Fichter & Quadflieg, 1997). These comorbidities include anxiety disorders, major depression, dysthymia, substance use, and personality disorders (Braun et al., 1994; Brewerton et al., 1995; Bulik et al., 2004; Perez, Joiner, & Lewinsohn, 2004).

Finally, BED also commonly co-occurs with numerous other psychiatric diagnoses, including mood, anxiety, and substance abuse disorders (Grucza, Przybeck, & Cloninger, 2007; Johnson, Spitzer, & Williams, 2001; Marcus, 1995; Striegel-Moore et al., 2001; Wilfley, Friedman, et al., 2000). Data from the National Comorbidity Survey Replication (Hudson, Hiripi, Pope Jr, & Kessler, 2007) indicate that BED is a chronic condition associated with significant impairment in daily functioning. Global data from the World Health Organization World Mental Health Surveys indicate that BED and BN are associated with significantly increased education in women. Early-onset BED predicted reduced odds of marriage in women and reduced odds of employment in men, while early-onset BN predicted increased odds of current work disability in both sexes. Both BED and BN were associated with significantly increased days of role impairment, although much of the role impairment was accounted for by the presence of comorbid disorders (Kessler et al., 2013).

Finally, those individuals with BED who are overweight or obese are at risk for medical complications (Hudson et al., 2007). Yet, the negative psychological impact of BED does not appear to be attributable to obesity. Obese individuals with BED report substantially poorer psychological functioning than do obese individuals without BED (Grucza et al., 2007), and normal-weight and overweight individuals with BED report equivalent psychological features of disordered eating and depression (Dingemans & van Furth, 2012).

EPIDEMIOLOGY

Most available epidemiologic data on eating disorders reflect *DSM-IV* diagnostic criteria; data based on the *DSM-5* are slowly emerging. Thus, in this review, *DSM-5* data are included where possible. Lifetime prevalence estimates of *DSM-5* AN, BN, and BED by over age 20 are 0.8–1.7%, 0.08–2.6%, 2.3–3% in women (Brandys et al., 2012, 2013), and 0.1%, 0.1%, and 0.7% in men, respectively (Smink, Hoeken, Oldehinkel, & Hoek, 2014). The prevalence of subthreshold AN, defined as at least one criterion short of threshold, is greater and ranges from 0.37% to 1.3% (Hoek, 1991); *DSM-5's* atypical AN is 2.8% (Brandys et al., 2013). The gender ratio (women:men) for AN is approximately 9:1 (Association, 1994). Awareness of these disorders has increased; however, the data on changing incidence are conflicting. Some studies report increasing incidence of AN or increases in disordered eating behavior (such as strict dieting or fasting for weight or shape control) that are associated with AN (e.g., Eagles, Johnston, Hunter, Lobban, & Millar, 1995; Hay, Mond, Buttner, & Darby, 2008; Jones, Fox, Babigian, & Hutton, 1980; Lucas, Crowson, O'Fallon, & Melton, 1999; Møller-Madsen & Nystrup, 1992), whereas others describe stable prevalence (e.g., Currin, Schmidt, Treasure, & Jick, 2005; Hall & Hay, 1991; Hoek, 2006; Hoek et al., 1995; Pawluck & Gorey, 1998; Smink, van Hoeken, & Hoek, 2012). The peak age of onset for AN is between 15 and 19 years (Lucas, Beard, O'Fallon, & Kurland, 1988), However, reports suggest new-onset cases in mid-life and late life (Beck, Casper, & Andersen, 1996; Gagne et al., 2012; Inagaki et al., 2002; Mangweth-Matzek et al., 2006). A recent study of middle age women estimated lifetime eating disorder prevalence as 3.64% for AN, 2.15% for BN, and 1.96% for BED (Shea et al., 2012). Reports also suggest increasing presentations in children (Rosen, 2010).

The prevalence of BN in the United States is estimated to be 1.5% for women and 0.5% for men (Hudson et al., 2007). The prevalence of subthreshold behaviors is considerably higher, with 4.9% of women and 4% of men endorsing any binge eating. Similar to AN, reports suggest that more children and older adults are presenting with BN (Marcus, Bromberger, Wei, Brown, & Kravitz, 2007; Rosen, 2010).

The prevalence of BED among adults (>18 years) in the United States based on *DSM-5* criteria has been estimated at 3.6% for women and 2.1% for men (Duncan et al., 2016; Hudson et al., 2007) while community surveys across 12 countries estimate the lifetime prevalence across both genders at 1.9% (Kessler et al., 2013). In a population-based study of female twins, 37% of obese women (BMI ≥ 30) reported binge eating (Bulik, Sullivan, & Kendler, 2002), 2.7% of the female population studied. Community studies of obese individuals have found a prevalence of BED of between 5% and 8% (Bruce & Agras, 1992; Bruce & Wilfley, 1996). The sex distribution in BED is more equal than in AN or BN (Duncan et al., 2016; Hudson et al., 2007), with few differences in prevalence across races or ethnic groups (Alegria et al., 2007; Marcus et al., 2007).

PSYCHOLOGICAL AND BIOLOGICAL ASSESSMENT

Careful and accurate assessment of eating disorders, which are frequently complex and have multiple presentations, is critical for effective treatment and research. The general goal of psychological assessment is to elicit information that accurately describes symptomatology, accurately characterizes diagnostic profile, and indicates appropriate treatment recommendations (Peterson, 2005). Assessing individuals with eating disorders is often challenging secondary to denial of the illness and hidden signs and symptoms (Palmer, 2003; Schacter, 1999; Túry, Güleç, & Kohls, 2010; Vitousek, Daly, & Heiser, 1991). The use of active listening skills is important for developing rapport (Keel, 2001), and motivational interviewing techniques (Miller & Rollnick, 2002), which encourage rolling with resistance, avoiding arguments, and expressing empathy, are often helpful for conducting a successful assessment.

Clinical interviews in eating disorders are used to elicit the patient's perspective of the development of his or her difficulties and frequently include the reason for the assessment/primary complaint, history of present illness, medical complications, treatment history, and coexisting conditions (Peterson, 2005). A combination of structured interviews, self-report measures, and medical assessments might also be employed to obtain a more complete clinical picture. In the case of minors, corroborating information, such as reports from parents or school officials, is additionally informative (Lock, LeGrange, Agras, & Dare, 2001).

STRUCTURED INTERVIEWS

Structured interviews are essential for clarifying differential diagnostic issues and assessing psychiatric comorbidity. Structured interviews are advantageous in that they allow for active involvement of the interviewer, who can help to clarify concepts or answer questions that may arise during the assessment. Obvious drawbacks to structured interviews include greater financial cost and clinician burden (Grilo, 2005).

For untrained interviewers, the two dominant instruments for assessing Axis I pathology are the Diagnostic Interview Schedule (DIS; Robins, Helzer, Croughan, & Ratcliff, 1981) and the Composite International Diagnostic Interview (CIDI; Organization, 1992). However, these have not been updated for DSM-5 (Culbert, Racine, & Klump, 2015). The various versions of the Structured Clinical Interview for DSM-IV (SCID; First, Spitzer, Gibbon, & Williams, 1997) and DSM-5 (Frank, Shott, Riederer, & Pryor, 2016) have excellent validity and reliability (Grilo, 2005; Zanarini et al., 2000) and are recommended for assessing Axis I pathology in adults by trained interviewers.

To assess eating disorder symptomatology specifically, several clinician-based structured or semistructured interviews have been developed. The EDE (Cooper & Fairburn, 1987) is well established (Wilfley, Schwartz, Spurrell, & Fairburn, 2000) and widely used. It has been updated for DSM-5 (EDE-17.0;Frank, 2015) and includes 33 items that measure behavioral and psychological traits in AN and BN. With the exception of the diagnostic items, the EDE focuses on the 28 days preceding the assessment. Items are rated on a seven-point scale, with higher scores indicating greater pathology, and comprise the following scales: dietary restraint, eating concern, weight concern, and shape concern. The EDE has high interrater reliability (Cooper & Fairburn, 1987; Grilo, Masheb, Lozano-Blanco, & Barry, 2004; Rizvi, Peterson, Crow, & Agras, 2000), adequate internal consistency (Beumont, Kopec-Schrader, Talbot, & Touyz, 1993; Cooper, Cooper, & Fairburn, 1989), and good discriminative validity for distinguishing those with eating disorders from healthy individuals (Cooper et al., 1989; Wilson & Smith, 1989). The updated version (EDE-17.0; Frank, 2015) includes the same items as in previous versions; however, there are no skip logic rules, which helps to capture subthreshold features (Hardaway, Crowley, Bulik, & Kash, 2015). Other popular structured interviews for assessing disordered eating include the Interview for Diagnosis of Eating Disorders (IDED; Williamson, 1990) and the Structured Interview for Anorexic and Bulimic Disorders (SIAB-EX; Fichter, Herpertz, Quadflieg, & Herpertz-Dahlmann, 1998). However, these have not been updated for DSM-5 criteria. The Eating Disorders Assessment for DSM-5 (EDA-5; Fonville, Giampietro, Williams, Simmons, & Tchanturia, 2014) is a new semistructured interview developed to assess DSM-5 feeding and eating disorders (Fonville et al., 2014). For a full review of these and other structured interviews in eating disorders, see Grilo (2005).

The IDED-IV (Kutlesic, Williamson, Gleaves, Barbin, & Murphy-Eberenz, 1998) is another semistructured interview primarily used for differential diagnosis of *DSM-IV* AN, BN, and EDNOS. The IDED-IV differs from the EDE in that it does not focus on frequency and severity data, but rather on differential diagnosis. Four studies support the psychometric properties of this instrument (Kutlesic et al., 1998).

The current version of the SIAB-EX (Fichter et al., 1998) assesses specific criteria for AN and BN (including subtypes), consistent with both the *DSM-IV* and the *ICD-10*. There is also an algorithm that allows the data to be used to generate the BED research diagnosis and other eating disorder syndromes under the EDNOS category. The SIAB-EX has demonstrated good internal consistency, factor structure, interrater reliability, and convergent and discriminant construct validity (Fichter & Quadflieg, 2000, 2001). Overall, the EDE and the SIAB-EX have been shown to produce generally similar findings. However, areas of divergence do exist, many of which could be attributable to the differences in criteria and time frames for assessment (Fichter & Quadflieg, 2001).

The EDA-5 (Fonville et al., 2014) is a recently developed semistructured interview that assesses for all *DSM-5* feeding and eating disorder diagnoses. Strengths of the EDA-5 include its brief administration time (approximately 15 minutes), web-based application, allowing for greater access and portability, and less intensive training required to administer as the application calculates BMI, enforces skip rules, and generates diagnoses (Sysko et al., 2015). However, the limitations of skip rules might inadvertently underestimate symptoms (Culbert et al., 2015). Initial validity and reliability for *DSM-5* eating disorder diagnoses (AN, BN, and BED) were supported; however, additional psychometric data are needed (Sysko et al., 2015; Thomas & Roberto, 2015).

SELF-REPORTS

Many self-report measures are available for assessing disordered eating in both research and clinical settings. Self-report assessments can be used for a variety of purposes, including identifying clinical features, quantifying symptoms, and verifying diagnoses. They are particularly useful for assessing change over time and are time- and cost-effective because they can be completed independently by the patient (Peterson & Mitchell, 2005). Two of the most widely used self-report questionnaires for assessing disordered eating include the Eating Disorder Inventory (EDI) and the Eating Disorder Examination–Questionnaire (EDE-Q).

The EDI (Garner, Olmsted, & Polivy, 1983, 1984), which assesses eating disorder symptoms and associated psychological traits, is useful for differentiating levels of eating disorder severity and for assessing treatment outcome (Williamson, Anderson, Jackman, & Jackson, 1995). This assessment is described by the authors as "investigator-based," emphasizing that it is the investigator's job to make final judgments about what symptoms and behaviors are present (e.g., to determine what constitutes a binge). The EDI has 64 questions answered on a six-point scale and comprises the following eight subscales: drive for thinness, bulimia, body dissatisfaction, ineffectiveness, perfectionism, interpersonal distress, interoceptive awareness, and maturity fears. A revised version of the EDI, the EDI-2, was published in 1991 and includes 27 additional questions. The eight scales from the EDI were retained, and three additional scales—asceticism, impulse regulation, and social insecurity—were incorporated (Garner, 1991).

The third version of the scale, EDI-3 (Garner, 2004), retained the same items as the EDI-2 but has a slightly different factor structure (Garner, Olmsted, & Polivy, 2008). It contains 91 items rated on a 0–4 point scoring system. The three subscales assessing eating pathology added in the EDI-2 (drive for thinness, bulimia, and body dissatisfaction) remain largely unchanged, and the general psychology subscales include low self-esteem, personal alienation, interpersonal insecurity, interpersonal alienation, interoceptive deficits, emotional dysregulation, perfectionism, asceticism, and maturity fears. Scoring for the EDI-3 includes six composite scores – (1) eating disorder risk, (2) ineffectiveness, (3) interpersonal problems, (4) affective problems, (5) over-control, and (6) general psychological maladjustment – as well as infrequency and negative impression scores. The EDI-3 has yielded reliable and valid scores (Garner, 2004). The EDE-Q (Fairburn & Beglin, 1994), another widely used self-report measure of eating disorder symptoms, assesses severity of eating pathology and associated disturbances over the past 28 days. It is most often used in research, but it can be applied in clinical settings as well (Peterson & Mitchell, 2005). The EDE-Q was adapted from the structured interview EDE (Cooper & Fairburn, 1987), and, like the EDE, it consists of 33 items and four subscales (restraint, eating concern, shape concern, and weight concern). The subscales and total scores are based on averages from 0 to 6, with higher scores indicating greater pathology. The EDE-Q has been described as an accurate method for assessing binge eating (Wilson, Nonas, & Rosenblum, 1993) and shows acceptable reliability and validity (Fairburn & Cooper, 1993).

There are numerous other self-report assessments for eating disorders, including the Multiaxial Assessment of Eating Disorder Symptoms (MAEDS; Anderson, Williamson, Duchmann, Gleaves, & Barbin, 1999), the Stirling Eating Disorder Scales (SEDS; Williams et al., 1994), the Anorexia Nervosa Inventory for Self-Rating (ANIS; Fichter & Keeser, 1980), the Three Factor Eating Questionnaire (TFEQ; Stunkard & Messick, 1985), the Binge Eating Scale (BES; Gormally, Black, Daston, & Rardin, 1982), and the Questionnaire for Eating and Weight Patterns-Revised (QEWP-R; Yanovski, 1993). A full review of these and other self-report measures for assessing disordered eating can be found in Peterson and Mitchell (2005) or Túry et al. (2010).

MEDICAL ASSESSMENT

Careful medical assessment, both initially and as indicated throughout the duration of eating disorder treatment, is critical for effective treatment (Crow, 2005). It is also important for emergency medicine physicians to be able to screen for and recognize patients with eating disorders, and to be aware of their medical complications and psychiatric comorbidities, in order to carry out a successful therapeutic intervention (Mascolo, Trent, Colwell, & Mehler, 2012; Trent, Moreira, Colwell, & Mehler, 2013). Documentation of medical complications is imperative, not only for treatment planning but also for service authorization by insurance companies. Although all eating disorder presentations require medical monitoring, low-weight patients, individuals with purging behaviors, and obese individuals with binge-eating behavior (or a combination of these behaviors) are typically at greatest risk for medical complications (e.g., Crow, Salisbury, Crosby, & Mitchell, 1997; Harris & Barraclough, 1998; Kohn, Golden, & Shenker, 1998).

Low-weight individuals are particularly vulnerable to medical morbidity and mortality (Harris & Barraclough, 1998). A BMI < 13 is associated with less favorable outcome (Hebebrand et al., 1997), and low weight is associated with increased likelihood of sudden cardiac death. AN, BN, and EDNOS are all associated with increased mortality

(Crow et al., 2009). Evidence of medical complications might also encourage otherwise resistant patients to enter treatment. A standard initial assessment for low-weight individuals should include a complete blood count, an electrolyte battery (including phosphorus, calcium, and magnesium), an electrocardiogram, liver function tests, and a dual-energy X-ray absorptiometry (DEXA) scan (Crow, 2005). Blood pressure and pulse should also be documented, as dehydration can lead to orthostatic hypotension. The patient should be monitored carefully through the re-feeding process, because provision of adequate calories may lead to a drop in serum phosphorus, which is associated with mortality (Kohn et al., 1998) in both hospital (Ornstein, Golden, Jacobson, & Shenker, 2003) and outpatient settings (Winston & Wells, 2002).

Electrolyte disturbance is the most commonly recognized complication of purging behaviors (Crow et al., 1997). Although not sensitive to vomiting frequency, hypokalemia is a marker of vomiting behavior (Crow et al., 1997). Another common complication of self-induced vomiting is parotid hypertrophy, or painless swelling of the parotid glands, which may persist for months following cessation of purging (Ogren, Huerter, Pearson, Antonson, & Moore, 1987). Dental complications, including dental enamel erosion on the lingual surfaces of teeth (Little, 2002), may occur in individuals who vomit frequently, and thus continued dental monitoring is important. A smaller number of individuals with purging behaviors report gastrointestinal symptoms, including intestinal bleeding, hematemesis (vomiting blood), the passing of melanotic stools, or blood in the stools. Although rare, esophageal tears, gastric erosions, hemorrhoids, and gastric rupture may also occur (Cuellar, Kaye, Hsu, & Van Thiel, 1988; Cuellar & Van Thiel, 1986). Abuse of laxatives and emetics are also associated with significant medical morbidity. The use of syrup of Ipecac should signal a medical and cardiac evaluation, as it is associated with severe cardiac effects.

Binge-eating disorder, which is among the most common of eating disorder presentations, is often associated with co-occurring conditions (Crow, 2005), including type II diabetes mellitus and obesity. There is some evidence to suggest that obese individuals with type II diabetes mellitus who also binge-eat experience worse outcomes than their non-binge-eating peers (Goodwin, Hoven, & Spitzer, 2003; Mannucci et al., 2002). Binge eating appears to be associated with medical problems independent of obesity (Bulik et al., 2002). Moreover, BED may confer a risk of developing metabolic syndrome (a cluster of related risk factors for atherosclerotic cardiovascular disease, including abdominal obesity, dyslipidemia, hypertension, and abnormal glucose metabolism) beyond the risk attributable to obesity alone (Hudson et al., 2010). It is critical to remember that not all individuals with BED are overweight or obese. We await further data on the health impact of BED in normal-weight individuals.

The growing interest in eating disorders over the past 20 years has resulted in the development of numerous assessment tools for research and clinical purposes. Accurate assessment of individuals with disordered eating requires a multidisciplinary approach to address both the psychological and biological factors underlying etiology.

ETIOLOGICAL CONSIDERATIONS

Although numerous psychological, social, and biological factors have been implicated as potential causes of eating disorders, few specific risk factors have been consistently identified across studies, and the etiology of these disorders is not fully understood (Jacobi, Hayward, de Zwaan, Kraemer, & Agras, 2004; Striegel-Moore & Bulik, 2007). Common risk factors across eating disorders include female sex, race, or ethnicity, childhood eating and gastrointestinal problems, elevated concerns about shape and weight, negative self-evaluation, prior history of sexual abuse and other adverse events, and presence of additional psychiatric diagnoses (Jacobi et al., 2004). Developmentally, prematurity, smallness for gestational age, and cephalohematoma have been identified as possible risk factors for AN (Cnattingius et al., 1999).

Current studies suggest that eating disorders are caused by a variety of factors, including both genetic (e.g., Bulik, Slof-Op't Landt, van Furth, & Sullivan, 2007; Trace, Baker, Peas-Lled, & Bulik, 2013) and environmental influences (e.g., Becker & Hamburg, 1996; Garner & Garfinkel, 1980; Striegel-Moore & Bulik, 2007). Contemporary understanding of eating disorders incorporates both genetic and environmental factors into causal models. Previously, an overemphasis on sociocultural factors ignored the fact that, although social pressures toward thinness are ubiquitous, only a fraction of individuals exposed to these factors develop eating disorders. Therefore, a clearer understanding of vulnerability has led to the model that individuals who are more genetically predisposed to eating disorders are those who are also more vulnerable to environmental triggers of illness—typically ones that result in dieting, drive for thinness, and persistent negative energy balance.

Environmental influences that might serve as eating disorder triggers include the media's idealization of the thin body ideal and pressure to achieve an unrealistically thin body type (Irving, 1990; Levine & Harrison, 2004). Sociocultural models of disordered eating (e.g., Polivy & Herman, 1985; Striegel-Moore, Silberstein, & Rodin, 1986) suggest that the perception of a discrepancy between the self and the thin ideal leads to psychological discomfort. In turn, a desire to ameliorate this discomfort might result in eating-disordered behavior. Striegel-Moore and Bulik (2007) report that cultural models of eating disorders are supported by the following: (a) the high percentage of female cases of disordered eating; (b) the increase in incidence of eating disorders in women coinciding with the decreasing body-weight ideal for women; (c) the reported higher incidence of eating disorders in cultures that emphasize thinness; and (d) the significant association between thin ideal internalization and disordered eating. Fairburn et al. (1998) found significant differences in exposure to risk factors between women with BED and healthy controls, but surprisingly few differences between women with BED and BN. Specifically, compared with controls, women with BED reported more adverse childhood experiences, parental depression, personal vulnerability to depression, and exposure to negative comments about weight, shape, and eating.

Other studies have indicated that environmental factors, including parental and peer behaviors, contribute to both risk and protection from eating pathology (Enten & Golan, 2009; Twamley & Davis, 1999). For example, Twamley and Davis reported that low family pressures to control weight moderated the relation between exposure to thin norms and internalization of these messages. In addition, other environmental variables, including social pressure, could amplify or mitigate the risk of eating disorders (Striegel-Moore et al., 1986). For example, individuals exposed to peer teasing might be more likely to develop disordered eating (Thompson, Coovert, Richards, Johnson, & Cattarin, 1995; Thompson & Heinberg, 1993). Similarly, individuals from higher social classes might be more prone to develop disordered eating, as they presumably have more time, attention, and resources available to focus on the achievement of cultural beauty ideals (Striegel-Moore & Bulik, 2007). Although these factors might influence eating disorder etiology, they are likely not solely responsible for their development (Striegel-Moore & Bulik, 2007). Personality traits such as perfectionism, as well as social anxiety, elevated weight, and high impulsivity, might also play important etiological roles. These sociocultural and environmental factors likely combine with genetic influences

(Strober, Freeman, Lampert, Diamond, & Kaye, 2000) to contribute to the development of disordered eating, as is described in the next section.

BEHAVIORAL GENETICS AND MOLECULAR GENETICS

The conceptualization of eating disorders has evolved rather radically across time (Vemuri & Steiner, 2007). Previously dominant sociocultural and psychodynamic theories have been supplanted by a biopsychosocial model. This evolution can be attributed in part to a systematic series of family twin and molecular genetics investigations of eating disorders, which have supported the role of familial and genetic factors in liability to eating disorders (Bulik et al., 2006; Klump, Miller, Keel, McGue, & Iacono, 2001). In this section, we review results of family, twin, and molecular genetic studies (for a more thorough review, see Trace et al., 2013).

Family studies investigate the degree to which a particular trait runs in families. Although they are a valuable tool, family studies cannot tell us why a trait runs in families—whether due to genetic factors, environmental factors, or some combination of both. The familial nature of AN is well established. For example, first-degree relatives of patients with AN (parents, children, and siblings) are 11 times more likely to have AN during their lifetime than are first-degree relatives of individuals who have never had AN (Strober et al., 2000). Population-based twin studies have provided additional support for the familiarity of AN.

Twin studies allow us to examine familial components of disordered eating by comparing similarities and differences in eating problems between monozygotic (MZ) and dizygotic (DZ) twins. MZ twins are generally assumed to share 100% of their genetic material, whereas DZ twins, on average, share 50% of their genetic material (like brothers and sisters). Variance in liability to a disorder can be dissected into additive genetic factors, shared environmental factors, and unique environmental factors. Additive genetic factors refer to the cumulative effects of many genes, each of which makes a small to moderate contribution. Shared environmental factors reflect environmental influences that affect both members of a twin pair and are believed to make twins more similar. Unique environmental factors (including measurement error), on the other hand, reflect environmental factors that only one twin is exposed to. Unique environmental factors are believed to make twins dissimilar. Twin studies have yielded heritability estimates between 28% and 74% for AN, with the remaining variability largely attributed to unique environmental factors (Bulik et al., 2006; Klump et al., 2001; Kortegaard, Hoerder, Joergensen, Gillberg, & Kyvik, 2001). Although twin studies can reveal the proportion of individual differences in a disorder that are due to genetic factors, they are unable to identify which specific genes are involved.

Molecular genetic studies have the potential to provide greater clarity regarding which genes influence risk for a trait or disorder. Association studies examine a genetic variant's association with a trait; if the variant and trait are correlated, there is said to be an association between the two. Association studies that involve a single gene or set of genes that have a hypothesized association with the trait under study are referred to as candidate gene studies. Molecular genetic designs that do not focus on one particular gene or set of genes include linkage and genome-wide association studies (GWAS). Linkage studies identify chromosomal regions that house predisposing or protective genes and allow us to narrow the search from the entire human genome to specific regions. GWAS examine millions of genetic markers scattered across the genome, comparing cases with the trait against controls. If a genetic variant is significantly more frequent in cases, the variant is said to be associated with the trait.

GWAS represent an agnostic search of the human genome and, as such, is a genetic discovery tool.

Decades of candidate gene association studies for AN have primarily examined genes involved in the serotonergic, catecholaminergic, and dopaminergic systems and those affecting appetite and weight regulation. The practice of preselecting a single gene based on presumed biological involvement has fallen out of favor, and has given way to genome-wide approaches (described next). More detailed information on candidate gene association studies in AN and other eating disorders can be found elsewhere (Yilmaz et al., 2015).

Historically, using candidate gene approaches, serotonergic, dopaminergic, and neurotrophic system genes received significant attention, and results regarding its importance to eating disorders are inconclusive. For instance, meta-analyses of studies investigating 5-HTTLPR—a 43 base-pair repeat polymorphism in the promoter region of SLC6A4—and AN have yielded conflicting findings for the potential involvement of that short allele in AN risk (Calati, De Ronchi, Bellini, & Serretti, 2011; Solmi et al., 2016). In a similar fashion, meta-analyses of studies examining brain-derived neurotrophic factor (BDNF) and catechol-O-methyl transferase (COMT) also failed to confirm the associations reported by previous studies with small sample sizes (Brandys et al., 2012, 2013).

Linkage studies identified chromosomes 1, 4, 11, 13, and 15 as possible regions of interest in AN (Bacanu et al., 2005; Devlin et al., 2002; Grice et al., 2002). A follow-up study of candidate genes on chromosome 1 revealed associations with the serotonergic (5-HTR1D) and opioidergic (OPRD1) neurotransmitter system (Bergen et al., 2003). Chromosome 1 was also implicated in AN in a small genome-wide microsatellite study (Kazuhiko et al., 2009), but these finding have yet to be replicated. The first GWAS for AN was conducted by Wang et al. (2010), in 1,033 female AN cases and 3,733 pediatric controls. However, no single nucleotide polymorphism (SNP) reached genome-wide significance, which is typical for studies with small sample sizes. A GWAS conducted under the auspices of the Wellcome Trust Case Control Consortium 3, which was also underpowered, failed to identify genome-wide significant SNPs associated with AN (Boraska et al., 2014). However, 76% of the variants prioritized for replication were in the same direction in the replication sample as the discovery sample, which is a promising sign that true genetic signals exist for AN, but larger sample sizes are required to detect them. The most recent AN GWAS was carried out under the umbrella of the Eating Disorders Working Group of the Psychiatric Genomics Consortium (PGC-ED) and comprised updated versions of the previous two GWAS cohorts. In a sample of 3,495 AN cases and 10,982 controls, the first genome-wide significant locus for AN was identified (Duncan et al., 2016). This locus—located on chromosome 12—is multigenic, overlapping six genes with six additional genes located nearby. Although the index SNP has not been directly associated with a phenotype or trait in the literature, some of the other variants in high linkage disequilibrium (LD) with the index SNP have previously yielded significant GWAS associations with type I diabetes, asthma, polycystic ovary syndrome, rheumatoid arthritis, and height (Duncan et al., 2016). Of note, none of the candidate genes with previous reports of significant associations with AN reached genome-wide significance, which has also been the case for other psychiatric disorders. Large global efforts are under way and projected to boost sample sizes to over 25,000 AN cases over the next few years in order to identify more genetic variants that influence risk for AN (Yilmaz et al., 2015).

Cross-disorder analyses have provided strong evidence for shared etiology among psychiatric disorders (Cross-Disorder Group of the Psychiatric Genomics, 2013; Lee et al., 2013). Through the application of LD Score Regression—a computational method which accounts for LD for each genomic variant while estimating heritability and co-heritability (Bulik-Sullivan et al., 2015)—to the PGC-ED AN GWAS data and various publicly available consortia GWAS summary statistics, statistically significant positive genetic correlations were reported between AN and psychiatric phenotypes such as neuroticisim, schizophrenia, and results from a meta-analysis across the original PGC psychiatric phenotypes (i.e., schizophrenia, bipolar disorder, major depressive disorder, autism spectrum disorder, and attention-deficit/hyperactivity disorder; Duncan et al., 2016). These results mean that the common variants cumulatively associated with these psychiatric phenotypes also increase risk for AN, highlighting their shared genetic architectures. In addition to psychiatric disorders, positive genetic correlations between AN and educational attainment phenotypes (i.e., years of education and college attendance) have also been reported (Duncan et al., 2016). Outside of psychiatric traits, significant negative genetic correlations have been observed for AN with metabolic phenotypes such as high BMI, obesity, and low-density lipoprotein cholesterol, while high-density lipoprotein cholesterol has yielded a positive genetic correlation with AN (Duncan et al., 2016). Taken together, these results suggest a potential role for metabolic risk factors in the etiology of AN, and if replicated, may have important implications for the reconceptualization of AN as a psychiatric disorder with considerable metabolic involvement.

Like AN, BN runs in families. First-degree relatives of individuals with BN are four to 10 times more likely to have the disorder themselves (Lilenfeld et al., 1998). In studies of female twins, the estimated heritability of BN ranges between 54% and 83% in females (see Slof-Op't Landt et al., 2005, for a review). As is the case in AN, molecular genetic studies of BN have generally focused on the serotonergic, dopaminergic, catecholaminergic, and appetite systems.

Several meta-analyses (Calati et al., 2011; Lee & Lin, 2010; Polsinelli, Levitan, & De Luca, 2012) have examined the association between *5-HTTLPR* polymorphisms and BN, with the large majority suggesting no significant association between *5-HTTLPR* polymorphisms and BN. Investigations exploring associations between other serotonin receptor genes and BN have also yielded mixed results (see Scherag, Hebebrand, & Hinney, 2010, for a review).

Studies investigating genes within the dopamine and catecholamine systems and genes involved in appetite regulation have also yielded inconsistent findings. Nisoli et al. (2007) examined the prevalence of TaqA1 polymorphisms of the *ANKK1* gene (rs1800497) in individuals with eating disorders, including BN, and in controls. No significant associations were found between the A1+ allele in BN for either the A1/A1 or A1/A2 genotypes. Sporadic associations were reported by small studies for BN and the dopamine transporter gene (*SLC6A3*; also referred to as *DAT1*) (Shinohara et al., 2004), *COMT* (Mikołajczyk, Grzywacz, & Samochowiec, 2010), preproghrelin (Miyasaka et al., 2006) and *BDNF*; however, these results failed to replicate in other studies (see Yilmaz et al., 2015, for a review; Yilmaz et al., 2014).

Only one linkage study has been conducted for BN, which examined 308 multiplex families identified through a patient with BN. Significant linkage was found on chromosome 10, and another region on chromosome 14 met criteria for genome- wide-suggestive linkage (Bulik et al., 2003). No GWAS of BN have been conducted to date. In sum, results of molecular genetic studies of BN remain inconclusive and are limited by the use of small samples, which provide relatively low power.

The study of BED has burgeoned in the past decade. However, as the disorder has been operationalized more recently than AN and BN, less research on the genetics of BED has emerged. Nonetheless, extant family, twin, and molecular research largely suggests that familial and genetic factors influence risk for BED. A small number of family studies have been conducted (Fowler & Bulik, 1997; Hudson et al., 2006; Lee et al., 1999). With the exception of the Lee et al. (1999) investigation, these studies suggest that BED is familial. This has been further corroborated by twin studies. Two population-based twin studies have examined the heritability of BED (Javaras et al., 2008; Mitchell et al., 2010) and reported heritability estimates ranging from 39% to 45%.

Candidate gene association studies of binge eating and BED have focused on serotonin and dopamine neurotransmitter systems, as well as genetic variants implicated in appetite regulation and obesity. One small case–control investigation, reported an association between the long-allele of the 5-HTTLPR polymorphism and BED (Monteleone, Tortorella, Castaldo, & Maj, 2006). While these results may suggest a role of the 5-HTTLPR polymorphism in BED, they should be considered preliminary, as the study was underpowered. Several investigations have also examined the role of dopamine polymorphisms, and particularly polymorphisms of the DRD2 gene, in BED (Davis et al., 2008, 2009, 2012). Overall, studies exploring the association between BED and polymorphisms of the DRD2 gene have been inconsistent, likely due to small sample sizes and a lack of statistical power.

Genes associated with obesity have also been investigated for their potential role in BED, given the positive correlation between these conditions. MC4R (which is associated with obesity) was examined as an early candidate for BED (Branson et al., 2003), although this finding is not consistently replicated across studies (Hebebrand et al., 2004). Positive associations with SLC6A3, BDNF, and ghrelin have also been identified in BED (Davis et al., 2007; Monteleone, Tortorella, Castaldo, Di Filippo, & Maj, 2007; Monteleone et al., 2006; Shinohara et al., 2004); however, these results require confirmation and replication as there have not been any meta-analyses of genetic studies carried out in BED, and, importantly, the field awaits more comprehensive genome-wide approaches.

NEUROANATOMY AND NEUROBIOLOGY

Neurobiological vulnerabilities contribute to eating disorder pathogenesis (Culbert et al., 2015; Kaye, 2008; Kaye, Wierenga, Bailer, Simmons, & Bischoff-Grethe, 2013; Treasure & Campbell, 1994), and brain structural and functional abnormalities are consistently found in individuals with eating disorders (Fonville et al., 2014; Frank, 2015; Frank, Bailer, Henry, Wagner, & Kaye, 2004; Kaye, Fudge, & Paulus, 2009). In addition, numerous behavioral traits associated with AN, including premorbid anxiety, obsessive behaviors, negative emotionality, impaired cognitive flexibility, increased harm avoidance and perfectionism, and altered interoceptive awareness, are hypothesized to be related to underlying abnormalities or alterations in brain structure and function (Kaye et al., 2013). Neuroimaging studies have consistently shown that the reward pathway may play a central role in ED pathophysiology (Frank, 2015; Wu et al., 2016). Frank et al. (2016) reported evidence of structural and functional differences within the energy-homeostasis and food reward-regulating circuitry of individuals with both AN and BN. Individuals with BN and AN tasted varying intensity of sucrose solutions paired with a visual stimulus while in the MRI. This paradigm allowed the researchers to look at reward circuitry patterns. They suggested that functional connectivity pattern provides a possible biological correlate that individuals with ED are able to override homeostatic signals.

Brain structural abnormalities in eating disorders have been investigated using computed tomography (CT) and magnetic resonance imaging (MRI). Functional imaging studies, including positron emission tomography (PET), single photon emission computer tomography (SPECT), and functional magnetic resonance imaging (fMRI), have also been employed to provide information about the cerebral activity of a system or receptor being studied. Improvements in technology over the last decade, particularly in neuroimaging and genetics, have greatly enhanced our ability to characterize the complex neuronal systems involved in disordered eating (Kaye, 2008; Kaye et al., 2013). However, these techniques are still relatively new, and our understanding of the relation between biological vulnerabilities and subsequent changes in brain pathways contributing to disordered eating are limited. Neurobiological investigations of disordered eating are further complicated by state-related effects from changes in diet and weight, which impact neuronal processes. One advancement in the field of neuroscience is the shift from focusing on isolated brain regions to focusing on neural circuits (Insel, 2009). Neurocircuitry is assessed using multimodal MRI to look at both structural and functional activity patterns of the brain, providing a better understanding of the molecular mechanism associated with brain function. Using longitudinal and multimodal MRI, Cha et al. (2016) studied connectivity between the nucleus accumbens and the orbitofrontal cortex (OFC), structures implicated in reward processing, using resting-state images in AN before and after weight restoration. The AN group showed an effective connectivity direction from the OFC to the nucleus accumbens, as well as greater anatomical connectivity strength using probabilistic tractography between two regions of interest (Cha et al., 2016). The findings suggest that hyperconnectivity in reward circuitry may be an important neural substrate in AN and may not fully resolve with weight restoration.

Brain imaging is not yet at a point where it can be used diagnostically; however, with the refinement of imaging hardware and improved models of the neurobiology and genetics of psychiatric illness, scientists are hopeful that in the future, imaging will allow us to untangle the complexities of eating disorders, predicting illness development, treatment response, and long-term prognosis (Frank, 2013, 2015). At present, central nervous system (CNS) dysregulation of neuropeptides (Bailer & Kaye, 2003) and monoamines (Bailer et al., 2007; Kaye, 2008), as well as brain structural abnormalities (Artmann, Grau, Adelmann, & Schleiffer, 1985; Heinz, Martinez, & Haenggeli, 1977; Joos et al., 2010; Krieg, Lauer, & Pirke, 1989), are implicated in the neurobiology of disordered eating.

Neuropeptides   Neuropeptides involve a complicated interplay between the peripheral system and the CNS (Morton, Cummings, Baskin, Barsh, & Schwartz, 2006), and opioid peptides, corticotropin-releasing hormone (CRH), vasopressin, oxytocin, neuropeptide-Y (NPY), peptide YY (PYY), cholecystokinin (CCK), leptin, ghrelin, and gastrin-releasing peptides are reported to play an important role in the regulation of feeding behavior (Akio et al., 2012; Bailer & Kaye, 2003; Monteleone, 2011). A growing body of literature documents alterations in neuropeptides in individuals with eating disorders (for a recent in-depth review, see Monteleone & Maj, 2013). Briefly, individuals with AN have state-dependent altered levels of CRH (Licinio, Wong, & Gold, 1996), NPY, beta-endorphin, and leptin that normalize with weight restoration (Bailer & Kaye, 2003; Kaye, 2008), whereas individuals with BN demonstrate state-related reductions in CCK response (Brewerton, Lydiard, Laraia, Shook, & Ballenger, 1992; Hannon-Engel, 2012; Kaye et al., 1987; Lesem, Berrettini, Kaye, & Jimerson, 1991) and beta-endorphin levels.

A number of the CNS neuropeptides implicated in AN and BN are also involved in regulating cognitive functioning, mood, the autonomic nervous system, and hormone secretion (Jimerson & Wolfe, 2006). While abnormalities in neuropeptide systems typically remit following recovery from AN and BN, malnutrition in combination with neuropeptide alterations can exaggerate symptoms of increased satiety and dysphoric mood, which might perpetuate eating-disordered behavior (see Bailer & Kaye, 2003; Monteleone & Maj, 2013 for full reviews of how neuropeptides influence AN and BN).

Neuropeptides are also implicated in BED, and both human and animal studies suggest that binge eating alters the endogenous opioid system (Bencherif et al., 2005; Blasio, Steardo, Sabino, & Cottone, 2014; Munsch, Biedert, Meyer, Herpertz, & Beglinger, 2009). Individuals with BED have higher meal-induced levels of CCK and PYY than controls (Munsch et al., 2009). Furthermore, both obese and nonobese women with binge eating demonstrate decreased levels of ghrelin in the morning, compared with nonobese healthy women and obese non-binge-eating women (Monteleone et al., 2005). However, these findings have not been consistently replicated across studies (Geliebter, Hashim, & Gluck, 2008; Munsch et al., 2009).

Monoamines   The monoamine system, including serotonin (5-HT), dopamine, and norepinephrine (NE), has also been implicated in the development and maintenance of disordered eating (Hildebrandt, Alfano, Tricamo, & Pfaff, 2010; Kaye et al., 2009; Steiger, 2004; Vaz-Leal, Rodríguez-Santos, García-Herráiz, & Ramos-Fuentes, 2011). The 5-HT system is critical in regulating appetite, anxiety, and impulse control (Fairbanks, Melega, Jorgensen, Kaplan, & McGuire, 2001), and the effects of 5-HT manipulation on eating behaviors have been demonstrated in both animal and human models (e.g., Blundell, 1986; Hardaway et al., 2015; Mancilla-Díaz, Escartín-Pérez, López-Alonso, & Cruz-Morales, 2002).

Studies of individuals with eating disorders document alterations in 5-HT metabolism, receptor sensitivity, and transporter activity (Bailer et al., 2011; Frank & Kaye, 2005; Kaye, 2008). As a general trend, decreased 5-HT is associated with increased feeding (Brewerton, 1995), leading to the expectancy that AN would coincide with increased 5-HT.

At first glance, individuals with AN appear to contradict expectation with regard to levels of 5-HT. Individuals with AN have significant reductions in cerebral spinal fluid 5-hydroxyindoleacetic acid (CSF 5-HIAA) compared with controls (Kaye et al., 2009), suggesting reduced 5-HT activity. However, CSF 5-HIAA levels are elevated following long-term recovery from AN (Kaye, 2008), indicating that AN may correspond to a primary state of increased 5-HT and that diminished 5-HT activity may be a result of malnutrition, rather than a trait-related feature.

Positron emission tomography and SPECT have been used to investigate the role of the 5-HT1A and 5-HT2A receptors in AN (Bailer & Kaye, 2011). Although studies have not been entirely consistent, most have shown that both ill and weight-restored individuals with AN have reduced binding of 5-HT2A (Bailer et al., 2004; Frank et al., 2002; Kaye et al., 2001) and increased binding of 5-HT1A (Bailer et al., 2005, 2011). In an animal model, interactions between 5-HT1A and 5-HT2A in the medial prefrontal cortex have been implicated in anxiety, attention, impulsivity, and compulsive behavior (Carli, Baviera, Invernizzi, & Balducci, 2006; Krebs-Thomson & Geyer, 1998; Winstanley et al., 2003). This is an interesting finding given that these traits have been implicated in AN, and particularly AN binge-purge type (AN-BP).

Findings in acute BN are generally compatible with a low 5-HT hypothesis (decreased 5-HT promotes increased feeding). Individuals with BN demonstrate decreased CSF 5-HIAA levels (Kaye, 2008) that are inversely related to binging and purging frequency (Jimerson, Lesem, Kaye, & Brewerton, 1992), platelet binding of 5-HT uptake inhibitors, reduced availability of central transporters, and decreased neuroendocrine responses to

5-HT precursors and 5-HT agonists/partial agonists. However, similar to individuals with AN, following recovery, they have elevated levels of CSF 5-HIAA compared with controls (Kaye, 2008). Abnormalities in 5- HT have also been implicated in binge eating (Akkermann, Nordquist, Oreland, & Harro, 2010) and in the frequency of binge eating for individuals with BN (Jimerson et al., 1992; Monteleone, Brambilla, Bortolotti, Ferraro, & Maj, 1998). Decreased 5-HT responses are hypothesized to contribute to blunted satiety, which may increase propensity for binge eating (Chiodo et al., 1986).

Further support of the role of 5-HT in eating disorders is provided by studies indicating that selective serotonin reuptake inhibitors (SSRIs) are fairly efficacious in treating BN and BED (see Brownley et al., 2015, 2016 for reviews). Fluoxetine is the only Food and Drug Administration (FDA)-approved medication for the treatment of AN and BN. Vyvanse was approved by the FDA for the treatment of BED in 2015. Fewer investigations have examined the effectiveness of SSRIs in treating AN, and in the small number of available studies, results were mixed (Attia, Haiman, Walsh, & Flater, 1998; Ferguson, La Via, Crossan, & Kaye, 1999; Kaye et al., 2001; Rosenblum & Forman, 2003; Vaswani, Linda, & Ramesh, 2003; Walsh et al., 2006).

In summary, there is significant evidence to suggest an overall dysregulation of 5-HT in eating disorders (Kaye et al., 2013; Steiger, 2004), which persists following recovery. Together, these results suggest that patterns of 5-HT dysregulation might vary by eating disorder subtype, suggesting that underlying pathophysiology might differ across varying eating disorder presentations (Bailer et al., 2013; Frank, 2015; Kaye, 2008).

Dopamine is another monoamine hypothesized to contribute to disordered eating (Bailer et al., 2013; Bello & Hajnal, 2010; Frank & Kaye, 2005; Jimerson et al., 1992; Kaye, Frank, & McConaha, 1999), and it is known to be involved in the reward and motivational aspects of feeding behavior (Erlanson-Albertsson, 2005; Szczypka, Rainey, & Palmiter, 2000). Individuals in recovery from restricting-type AN (AN-R) show lower CSF levels of the dopamine metabolite homovanillic acid (HVA; Kaye et al., 1999), which is typically considered an indicator of reduced dopamine function and reduced dopamine turnover (dopamine:HVA ratio). Individuals recovered from AN-R and AN-BP also demonstrate increased binding of D2/D3 receptors in the anteroventral striatum (Bailer et al., 2013; Frank et al., 2005), including the nucleus accumbens, a brain region implicated in the response to reward stimuli (Delgado, Nystrom, Fissell, Noll, & Fiez, 2000; Montague, Hyman, & Cohen, 2004).

Individuals with BN, particularly those with high binge frequency, also have significantly lower HVA levels (Jimerson et al., 1992; Kaplan, Garfinkel, Warsh, & Brown, 1989; Kaye et al., 1990). However, Jimerson et al. (1992) found that after weight restoration and normalization of food intake, individuals who recovered from BN did not differ significantly from controls on HVA concentrations, suggesting that abnormalities in the dopamine system in BN might be state-dependent. Lastly, dopamine has also been hypothesized to play a role in BED by modulating reward pathways (Bello & Hajnal, 2010; Mathes, Brownley, Mo, & Bulik, 2009; O'Hara, Campbell, & Schmidt, 2015).

Norepinephrine transmission in the medial prefrontal cortex is also implicated in food-related motivational behavior in animal models (Ventura, Latagliata, Morrone, La Mela, & Puglisi-Allegra, 2008; Ventura, Morrone, & Puglisi-Allegra, 2007). Although few investigations have specifically examined the role of NE in disordered eating, it plays a central role in CNS modulation of energy balance, which has downstream effects on satiety, hunger, and feeding behavior (Hainer, Kabrnova, Aldhoon, Kunesova, & Wagenknecht, 2006).

Overall, the field is embracing more complex systems and pathway-driven models of disease to understand the complicated way in which monoamines and other neurotransmitters are implicated in disease etiology (Kaye, 2008; Kaye et al., 2009). Further, there is evidence to suggest that these neurotransmitter systems likely act in concert, contributing to behaviors associated with disordered eating. For example, a recent study by Bailer et al. (2013) using PET showed that an interaction between the 5-HT transporter and striatal dopamine D2/D3 receptor radioligand binding measures was associated with harm avoidant symptoms in women who had recovered from eating disorders. Based on this finding, authors hypothesize that interactions between the 5-HT and dopamine systems may contribute to eating disorder symptoms.

Structural Abnormalities   Neuroimaging studies with CT show neuroanatomical changes in individuals with AN, including cerebral atrophy and enlarged ventricles (Artmann et al., 1985; Heinz et al., 1977; Krieg et al., 1989; Lankenau, Swigar, Bhimani, Quinlan, & Luchins, 1985; Nussbaum, Shenker, Marc, & Klein, 1980; Titova, Hjorth, Schiöth, & Brooks, 2013). A 2012 systematic review by Van Den Eynde et al. (2012) reported that the eight studies they included found reduced gray matter volume in AN in the insula, frontal operculum, and occipital, medial temporal, or cingulate cortex. MRI studies in AN also demonstrate increased volumes of CSF in association with deficits in both total gray matter and total white matter volumes (Castro-Fornieles et al., 2010; Joos et al., 2010; Katzman et al., 1996; Titova et al., 2013) and enlarged ventricles (Golden et al., 1996). There is much debate over whether these changes persist after successful treatment and weight restoration. Several investigations have reported that neuroanatomical changes persist following normalization of weight (Artmann et al., 1985; Krieg et al., 1989), whereas other studies have found that brain tissue may increase with weight restoration in AN (Roberto et al., 2011) and that structural brain abnormalities are reversible after long-term recovery (Golden et al., 1996; Wagner et al., 2006) but not short-term recovery (Friederich et al., 2012). A 2015 study used a more sensitive measure of cortical thickness, surface-based morphometry (Hogstrom, Westlye, Walhovd, & Fjell, 2013), and found that the cortical thinning and decreased subcortical volume in AN are largely state-dependent and due to malnutrition (King et al., 2015). Although definitive conclusions cannot be drawn, if lasting brain abnormalities in AN do occur, they might represent residual damage to the brain or persistent abnormal metabolism (Husain et al., 1992). They could also represent under-developed areas that originally contributed to the eating pathology (Artmann et al., 1985).

Findings regarding structural abnormalities are mixed (Frank, 2013). Several studies support structural changes in BN, including cerebral atrophy and decreased ventricle size (Hoffman et al., 1989; Krieg et al., 1989). Other studies suggest normal or increased localized gray matter in the orbitofrontal cortex and striatum (Joos et al., 2010). A 2010 study by Schäfer, Vaitl, and Schienle (2010) found that individuals with BN had greater medial orbitofrontal cortex volume relative to controls. Further, in individuals with BN who had increased ventral striatum volumes, purging severity and BMI were correlated with striatal gray matter volume, suggesting a potential correlation between behavioral and neuroanatomical findings. Reductions in inferior frontal regions correlated inversely with symptom severity, age, and Stroop interference scores in the BN group. Marsh et al. (2015) reported significant reductions, in 34 adolescent and adult patients with BN relative to healthy controls, of local volumes on the brain surface in frontal and temporoparietal areas in the BN participants. The authors suggested that this difference could be related to deficits in self-regulation seen in BN. Other studies, however, have found no evidence for neuroanatomical abnormalities in BN (Husain et al., 1992; Joos et al., 2010). Taken together, results from these studies indicate that neuroanatomical abnormalities often occur in individuals with eating disorder, particularly AN.

Additional prospective studies are needed to understand whether these abnormalities are a cause or an effect of the disordered eating behavior.

LEARNING, MODELING, AND LIFE EVENTS

As noted previously, biology only accounts for part of the liability to developing an eating disorder. It is hypothesized that environment, via channels such as learning, modeling, and life events, can contribute to eating disorder risk either directly or indirectly through their influence on genetic expression.

Life Events   Stressful life events have long been hypothesized to play an important role in eating disorder etiology (Klump, Wonderlich, Lehoux, Lilenfeld, & Bulik, 2002; Pike et al., 2006; Schmidt, Troop, & Treasure, 1999). However, research in this area is fraught with methodological challenges. Many studies have included exclusively clinical samples of individuals with eating disorder symptomatology, did not include controls, and assessed life events retrospectively (Berge, Loth, Hanson, Croll-Lampert, & Neumark-Sztainer, 2012; Degortes et al., 2014; Raffi, Rondini, Grandi, & Fava, 2000; Schmidt et al., 1999).

Nonetheless, one investigation that did include a community-recruited sample of women with BN and matched controls suggested that individuals with BN were more likely than controls to experience certain stressful life events (e.g., a major move, illness, pregnancy, physical abuse, and sexual abuse) during the year prior to the beginning of their illness (Welch, Doll, & Fairburn, 1997). There was no association between BN status and the occurrence of other life events (e.g., bereavement, illness of a close relative, friend, or partner, and beginning or ending a romantic relationship) in the last year. In addition, 29% of women with BN experienced none of the life events assessed in the 12 months prior to the onset of their diagnosis.

Adverse life events were also associated with BED risk (in the year prior to the onset of the disorder; Pike et al., 2006), in a study comparing women with BED with psychiatric and nonclinical controls. Specifically, individuals with BED were most likely to report significant changes in life circumstances and relationships during the previous year. Furthermore, compared with the nonclinical controls, women with BED more commonly reported specific adverse events, including physical abuse, perceived risk of physical abuse, safety concerns, stress, and experiences of weight- and shape-related criticism. A major limitation of both the Welch et al. (1997) and Pike et al. (2006) studies, as well as many others (e.g., Berge et al., 2012; Mitchell, Mazzeo, Schlesinger, Brewerton, & Smith, 2012; Raffi et al., 2000; Reyes-Rodríguez et al., 2011; Schmidt et al., 1999), is that they relied on participants' retrospective recall of stressful life events, and thus are vulnerable to memory biases.

A small number of studies of community samples have used a longitudinal approach to investigate the potential role of stressful life events in the onset of disordered eating. For example, Loth, van den Berg, Eisenberg, & Neumark-Sztainer (2008) evaluated these constructs in a sample of adolescents and emerging adults enrolled in Project EAT. Respondents reported whether they had experienced a broad range of stressful events within the year prior to assessment. Participants also reported their engagement in "extreme weight control behaviors" (defined as laxative diuretic or diet pill use, and vomiting), and binge eating (assessed via a single item) at both time 1 (approximately 5 years earlier) and time 2 (when the sample had a mean age of 20.4 years).

This study is relatively unique in its inclusion of men and women. The most common stressful life event among men was "excessive credit card debt" (reported by 17.8% of men and 19.3% of women). Among women, the most commonly reported stressor was "termination of a long personal relationship" (reported by 22.9% of women and 17.2% of men). For both men and women, the number of stressful life events was positively associated with binge eating and extreme weight control behaviors. This study adds to the literature because of its longitudinal approach, use of a community sample, and inclusion of men and women. It also assessed stressors not often evaluated in other studies (and not typically considered traumas), such as financial concerns.

The relative influence of both major and minor (i.e., daily) life stressors on eating disorder symptomatology was also evaluated in a recent study of college students (Woods, Racine, & Klump, 2010). Major stressors were assessed for the 12 months prior to the study. Results suggested that daily stress moderated the link between restraint and binge eating, but only in the context of high levels of major life stress. Interestingly, the link between restraint and binge eating was not significant under conditions of high major life stress and low daily stress. The authors concluded that the cumulative effects of both major and daily stressors might overwhelm individuals' coping resources, and lead to eating disturbances, consistent with many prominent theories of eating disorder etiology (e.g., Heatherton & Baumeister, 1991). This study's cross-sectional design is a limitation; however, it does highlight the importance of considering daily stressors when evaluating life events and coping resources, and suggests this is an important construct to consider in future clinical and research efforts.

Smyth, Heron, Wonderlich, Crosby, & Thompson (2008) investigated the influence of traumatic events on young adults' eating disorder symptomatology during their transition to college. Participants reported not only whether they had *experienced* each trauma in their lifetime, but also *its perceived severity* (rated on a five-point scale). Thus, this study incorporated cognitive appraisal of stressors, an important construct discussed further in the following section. Traumas were assessed at time 1 only. Trauma severity was positively associated with increases in both restrictive eating and binge-eating symptomatology over the course of the first semester of college. There were some differences in the specific types of trauma associated with binge and restrictive eating, respectively. For example, nonpersonal traumas were the only specific trauma type associated with increases in restrictive eating. In contrast, several trauma types (e.g., death of a loved one, parents' separation/divorce) were associated with increases in binge eating over the first semester. A study by Bodell, Smith, Holm-Denoma, Gordon, & Joiner (2011) also found that the number of life stressors experienced by college students between the fall and spring semesters was associated with some eating disorder symptoms (as measured by the EDI-Bulimia subscale) but not others (restrictive eating, as measured by the EDI-Drive for thinness subscale). This study also assessed a range of stressors, including some especially relevant to college students, such as academic performance.

The influence of stressful life events on relapse following remission from BN and EDNOS was investigated in a 6-year longitudinal study (Grilo et al., 2012). Both the total number of stressful life events and specific types of stressors, such as social and work-related issues, were positively associated with relapse. These findings suggest that some stressful life events might increase susceptibility to eating disorder symptomatology, but this risk is not uniform and is likely mediated by cognitive processes, such as appraisal distress tolerance, and general coping ability, which are discussed in the following section.

Eating disorder symptomatology might also influence both perceptions of stress and the likelihood that stressful events occur. Bodell et al. (2011) investigated this possibility in a study with undergraduates, and found that eating disorder symptomatology (bulimic symptoms and drive for thinness) was not associated with negative life events beyond that accounted for by depression. However, in a subsequent study, with a similar sample, dietary restraint was predictive of the occurrence of negative life events between the two data collection points. Nonetheless, other eating disorder symptoms (i.e., body dissatisfaction, weight concern, bulimic symptoms, eating concern, and shape concern) were not associated with negative life events. Thus, one must be cautious in interpreting this finding, which could be spurious given the number of tests conducted. Yet it does suggest that future research should investigate whether specific eating disorder-related behaviors might put individuals at particular risk for stress.

Distress Tolerance   Perhaps one reason for the somewhat inconsistent findings regarding the impact of stressful life events on eating disorder symptomatology is that the impact of these experiences is influenced by the way in which they are appraised and how well individuals cope in response to them. Numerous studies have documented the link between cognitive appraisal and psychological outcomes (Folkman, Lazarus, Dunkel-Schetter, Delongis, & Gruen, 1986a; Folkman, Lazarus, Gruen, & Delongis, 1986b). More recently, the construct of distress tolerance has received attention in the area of eating disorders. This construct seems especially relevant to individuals with eating disorders, as emotion regulation difficulties have long been identified in affected individuals and across eating disorder subtypes (Brockmeyer et al., 2012; de Zwaan, Biener, Bach, Wiesnagrotzki, & Stacher, 1996; Harrison, Sullivan, Tchanturia, & Treasure, 2009; Heatherton & Baumeister, 1991), and research has linked poor distress tolerance and eating disorder symptomatology (Anestis, Selby, Fink, & Joiner, 2007). There is also significant comorbidity between eating disorders and post-traumatic stress disorder (PTSD; Mitchell et al., 2012; Reyes-Rodríguez et al., 2011). In addition, a recent study found that the link between PTSD and eating disorder severity was mediated by psychological distress (Isomaa, Backholm, & Birgegård, 2015). Gene–environment inter-actions also likely play an important role in the relations among adverse events, coping, and eating disorder outcomes. In one of the few studies in this area, Akkermann et al. (2012) investigated the role of the 5-HTTLPR genotype and environmental stressors on eating disorder symptoms. The short (*s*) allele of the 5-HTT polymorphic region is positively associated with several mental health outcomes, including neuroticism (Sen et al., 2004). Akkerman et al.'s (2012) sample included girls from the longitudinal Estonian Children Personality, Behaviour and Health Study. Two assessment points were used in the analyses (time 1, mean age = 14.8; time 2, mean age = 17.8). Participants reported the lifetime occurrence of specific life events at time 1; eating disorder symptoms (EDI- Bulimia and EDI-Drive for thinness) were assessed at time 2. Results indicated that the 5-HTTLPR genotype was not significantly associated with eating disorder symp-tomatology; however, this polymorphism interacted with life events to predict higher scores on the EDI-Bulimia subscale at time 2. Individuals with both this genotype and more negative life events by age 15 were more likely than their peers to report bulimic symptoms at age 18. There was no significant main or interaction effect between genotype and drive for thinness.

Mixed results were obtained in related study investigating interactions between genetic influences and a specific life stressor, parental divorce, in a sample of female twins (Suisman, Alexandra Burt, McGue, Iacono, & Klump, 2011). Parental divorce was not associated with most forms of eating disorder symptomatology measured (binge eating, weight preoccupation, and total disordered eating); however, it was associated with body dissatisfaction. A limitation of both the Akkermann et al. (2012) and Suisman et al. (2011) studies is that it is unclear when the stressor(s) occurred in relation to the precise onset of eating disorder symptomatology. Nonetheless, these two studies extend the prior literature on life events, eating disorders, and the stress response, and highlight the complexity of these relations.

A more recent investigation (Fairweather-Schmidt & Wade, 2015) looked at the impact of genetic influences, weight-related teasing, and negative life events (occurring during the 12 months prior to data collection) on eating disorder symptoms in twins using longitudinal data from early and late adolescence. Parents completed the measure of negative life events; adolescents completed the other measures. Negative life events were not associated with eating pathology in late adolescence. However, weight-related teasing did significantly contribute to eating disorder symptomatology. A limitation of the negative life events measure used in this study is that it included only those events occurring in the prior 12 months. Further, parents completed this measure and might not be aware of all of their daughters' experiences. It is also important to note that, in this study, genetic factors accounted for a substantial proportion of variance in disordered eating symptomatology. The authors concluded that these findings suggest a potential interaction between a critical period genetic risk and a specific environmental stressor, weight teasing, in the development of eating disorders during mid-to-late adolescence.

COGNITIVE FUNCTIONING

The possibility that there is CNS dysfunction in affected individuals has been explored through a variety of mechanisms, including neuropsychological performance (Duchesne et al., 2004; Jáuregui-Lobera, 2013; Weider, Indredavik, Lydersen, & Hestad, 2015). Cognitive functions implicated in AN include decreased attentional capability (Ferraro, Wonderlich, & Jocic, 1997; Giel et al., 2011; Green, Elliman, Wakeling, & Rogers, 1996; Jones, Duncan, Brouwers, & Mirsky, 1991) memory (Kingston, Szmukler, Andrewes, Tress, & Desmond, 1996; Mathias & Kent, 1998), visuo-spatial construction (Thompson & Spana, 1991), learning capacity (Witt, Ryan, & Hsu, 1985), and executive functioning (Kingston et al., 1996; Szmukler et al., 1992). Cognitive functioning in BN and BED has been less extensively studied and has largely focused on decreased attention and executive functioning (Aloi et al., 2015; Manasse et al., 2015; Weider et al., 2015).

Various deficits in executive functioning have been noted in the eating disorder literature (Cooper, Anastasiades, & Fairburn, 1992; Fassino et al., 2002; Jáuregui-Lobera, 2013; Kemps, Tiggemann, & Marshall, 2005; Koba, Horie, & Nabeta, 2002; Tchanturia et al., 2012, 2004; Zastrow et al., 2009). Executive functioning is an umbrella term that refers to a set of neuropsychological processes in the frontal lobe of the brain that govern higher-level, goal directed behavior (Miyake et al., 2000). A set of systematic reviews and meta-analyses provides strong evidence that deficits in set shifting, central coherence, and working memory are present within ED diagnostic groups (Lang, Lopez, Stahl, Tchanturia, & Treasure, 2014a; Lang, Stahl, Espie, Treasure, & Tchanturia, 2014b; Lopez, Tchanturia, Stahl, & Treasure, 2008b; Roberts, Tchanturia, Stahl, Southgate, & Treasure, 2007; Wu et al., 2014). Furthermore, the magnitude of impairment appears to be similar across BN and AN subtypes (Lang et al., 2014b; Roberts et al., 2007). Set shifting, or the ability to move back and forth between tasks or mental sets, is an important component of executive functioning (Miyake et al., 2000). Set-shifting ability is essential for cognitive and behavioral flexibility, allowing an individual to adapt his or her behavior to meet the changing demands of the environment. Problems in set shifting might manifest in a variety of forms of cognitive inflexibility (e.g., rigid approaches to problem-solving) or response inflexibility (e.g., perseverative or stereotyped behavior; Roberts et al., 2007). Recent research has suggested that set-shifting difficulties might be related to the development of disordered eating (Danner et al., 2012; Kanakam, Raoult,

Collier, & Treasure, 2013; Roberts et al., 2007; Steinglass, Walsh, & Stern, 2006; Tchanturia et al., 2004; Wu et al., 2014; Zastrow et al., 2009).

For example, individuals with EDs perform poorly on set-shifting tasks compared with controls. A 2014 systematic review and meta-analysis (Wu et al. 2014) examined set shifting in eating disorders and obesity (for the scope of this chapter, we review only the ED findings). A total of 64 eating disorder papers that administered at least one of the seven set-shifting tasks—including the Wisconsion Trail Making Task (TMT; Halstead, 1947; Reitan, 1958), Wisconsin Card Sorting Test (WCST; Heaton, Chelune, Talley, Kay, & Curtis, 1993), Verbal Fluency Test (VFT; Delis, Kaplan, & Kramer, 2001), the Intra-Dimensional/Extra-Dimensional (ID/ED) set-shifting tasking (Robbins et al., 1998), the Brixton spatial anticipation test (Burgess & Shallice, 1997), the Object Alternation Test (OAT; Freedman, 1990) and Weigl's Sorting Test (WST; Weigl, 1941)—were reviewed (for obesity/overweight findings see Wu et al., 2014). A significant deficit was found across the whole spectrum of EDs, AN, BED, and BN, regardless of age, with small to medium effect sizes across assessment measures used. This is consistent with a 2007 systematic review and meta-analysis (Roberts et al., 2007) finding a similar deficit in set shifting that traversed diagnoses, state of illness, and the majority of the set-shifting assessment measures used. Although this study employed a limited amount of data from recovered/weight-restored subgroups of individuals with AN, preliminary results suggest that deficits in set shifting, particularly as measured by the TMT, the Haptic Illusion, and the CatBat, remain following weight restoration (Roberts et al., 2007).

A study by Tchanturia et al. (2004) examined whether suboptimal set shifting was state- or trait-related by examining set shifting in individuals with current or past AN. The association of these deficits with obsessive-compulsive behaviors and traits was also explored. The authors compared set-shifting abilities in females with current AN (AN-R, $n = 20$; AN-BP, $n = 14$) prior to receiving treatment, individuals with past AN in long-term recovery ($n = 18$, stable body mass for minimum of a year, regular menses for a year, and no psychotropic medication for a year), and healthy controls ($n = 36$). Participants were given a battery of neuropsychological tests assessing various facets of set shifting and executive functioning. A computerized version of the TMT (Kravariti, Morris, Rabe-Hesketh, Murray, & Frangou, 2003; Reitan, 1958) assessed rapid simple alternation between mental sets; the Brixton Test (Burgess & Shallice, 1997), the Set Flexibility Picture Test (Surguladze, 1995), and the CatBat Task were used to assess problem-solving and set shifting. The Uznadze Illusion Task (Uznadze, 1966) was used to assess perceptual set shifting. Lastly, a verbal fluency test (as described in Lezak, Howieson, & Loring, 2004) assessed cognitive retrieval and flexibility in cognitive search options. In addition, a semistructured interview evaluated obsessive-compulsive traits in childhood and adulthood.

Scores of individuals with current AN-R or AN-BP on several set-shifting tasks (e.g., including the TMT and the Brixton Illusion) were significantly lower than those of the recovered and control groups. Individuals recovered from AN had significantly more illusions on the Uznadze Illusion Task and made more errors on the Set Flexibility Picture Test, relative to the control group. Overall, the individuals who had recovered from AN obtained scores that were between those of individuals with current AN and healthy controls, suggesting that nutritional status might play some role but is not entirely responsible for the mental inflexibility associated with AN.

To better understand the relationship between starvation and set-shifting deficits, recent studies assessing set shifting in adolescents with AN have begun to emerge. Conducting neuropsychological investigations in younger populations increases the chances that the change in set shifting is more likely related to the illness rather than to starvation, as the duration of the illness is shorter. In a preliminary systematic review and meta-analysis, children with AN typically showed poorer performance on set shifting compared with health controls, although this finding was nonsignificant (Lang et al., 2014b). The results from the preliminary meta-analysis suggest that set-shifting inefficiencies are less pronounced in children/adolescents than in adults; however, more research is needed to clarify the neuropsychological profile of children and adolescents with AN.

Although less research has examined executive functioning deficits in BN and BED, there is some emerging evidence of cognitive flexibility deficits in BN (Wu et al., 2014) and BED (Aloi et al., 2015; Wu et al., 2014). However, it is unknown if theses deficits persist after recovery in BN or BED. Familial data provide some evidence for a trait-related dysfunction in BN. For example, nonaffected biological sisters of individuals with BN demonstrated problems with cognitive flexibility compared with controls (Tchanturia et al., 2012).

Weak central coherence refers to an emphasis on small details and weak ability to integrate information globally (Happé & Booth, 2008) and is one of the three main neurocognitive theories of autism to explain its characteristic behavioral impairments (Oldershaw, Treasure, Hambrook, Tchanturia, & Schmidt, 2011). Weak central coherence has been observed in AN and BN (Aloi et al., 2015; Lopez et al., 2008a,b; Lopez, Tchanturia, Stahl, & Treasure, 2008c; Southgate, Tchanturia, & Treasure, 2008) and there is some evidence that this deficit persists after recovery (Lopez, Tchanturia, Stahl, & Treasure, 2009). In a 2014 systematic review and meta-analysis, Lang et al. found that individuals with EDs display a bias towards detail at the expense of global integration, providing support for a weak central-coherence hypothesis. A bias towards details over the global "gist" was consistently demonstrated with all studies using the Group/Embedded Figures Task (G/EFT), with medium effect sizes, across ED diagnosis (Lang et al., 2014b). Very few studies have looked specifically at BED central coherence specifically. However, when comparing AN with BED subjects and healthy controls, weak central coherence characterizes AN patients, while poor attention is the distinctive trait of BED patients (Aloi et al., 2015).

Across studies, findings suggest that executive functioning deficits might be related to an underlying biological vulnerability to EDs. Neurobiological deficits in set shifting and central coherence found among individuals with AN might mirror the behavioral and personality characteristics, such as rigidity and inflexibility, observed within this diagnostic group (see reviews by Braun & Chouinard, 1992; Jáuregui-Lobera, 2013; Lauer, 2002), whereas poor inhibitory control best typifies the EDs characterized by binge eating.

Effortful control may represent one domain that differs clearly between the restricting subtype of AN, in which it is presumed that individuals use high levels of cognitive control, especially in relation to eating (van Elburg & Treasure, 2013), and those with eating disorders characterized by binge eating or purging, which may represent a deficit in top-down control of biological reactivity to reward and emotion (Claes, Mitchell, & Vandereycken, 2012).

Finally, many individuals with AN also appear to have social cognitive deficits (van Elburg & Treasure, 2013; Zucker et al., 2007). Some patients report long-standing interpersonal discomfort even premorbidly, and long-term outcome studies of AN suggest a higher proportion of individuals with traits characteristic of the autism spectrum (see Zucker et al., 2007 for a comprehensive review). Of course, all studies of cognitive function in eating disorders must carefully consider the impact of nutritional state on functioning. Planned and ongoing investigations of high-risk cohorts, unaffected relatives, and long-term recovered individuals have the potential to disambiguate state from trait deficits.

RACIAL-ETHNIC CONSIDERATIONS

For many years, eating disorders were often considered illnesses that affected White women nearly exclusively (Becker, Franko, Speck, & Herzog, 2003). This cultural stereotype appears to have influenced clinicians as well, as studies show that women of color are less likely to be identified as having an eating disorder (even when their symptoms are consistent with diagnosis) or referred for eating disorder treatment (Becker et al., 2003).

As noted previously, lifetime prevalence estimates of *DSM-IV* AN, BN, and BED from a nationally representative population sample of women over age 18 are 0.9%, 1.5%, and 3.5%, respectively (Hudson et al., 2007). Prevalence estimates vary across racial and ethnic groups, however. The lifetime prevalence of eating disorders among African American adult females from a US population-based survey is 0.14% for AN, 1.90% for BN, 2.36% for BED, and 5.82% for any binge-eating behavior (Taylor, Caldwell, Baser, Faison, & Jackson, 2007). Other studies have reported slightly lower prevalence estimates in African American women (Striegel-Moore et al., 2003). One set of lifetime prevalence estimates among Latinas are 0.12% for AN, 1.91% for BN, 2.31% for BED, and 5.80% for any binge eating (Alegria et al., 2007). Relatively similar estimates were obtained in a more recent population-based sample (Marques et al., 2010).

The prevalence of eating disorders among Asian women has been estimated to be 0.12% for AN, 1.42% for BN, 2.67% for BED, and 4.71% for any binge eating (Nicdao, Hong, & Takeuchi, 2007). Further, more recent research (Lee-Winn, Mendelson, & Mojtabai, 2014) found a significant discrepancy between rates of BED and all binge eating in Asian women in a national sample of adults in the US. Asian Americans were less likely than Whites to report experiencing distress related to binge eating, or loss of control. However, rates of lifetime BED were similar among Whites and Asian Americans. The authors of this report conclude that rates of threshold BED are likely underestimated, due to potential cultural differences in the interpretation of loss of control eating and distress in response to this behavior.

African American women's risk for binge eating and BED may indeed be equal to, or possibly even greater than, that of White women (Striegel-Moore et al. 2000b). For example, Taylor et al. (2007) found that BED was not only more common than either AN or BN among African American women, but also was the most chronic eating disorder diagnosis, with a mean duration of over 7 years. These findings are consistent with those of other studies with respect to the clinical significance and prevalence of binge-eating behaviors among African American adults (Marcus et al., 2007; Striegel-Moore et al., 2000b). Another significant concern regarding eating disorders among African Americans is that rates of treatment-seeking for eating disorders are significantly lower among this group than among White women (Becker et al., 2003; Cachelin, Veisel, Barzegarnazari, & Striegel-Moore, 2000; Marques et al., 2010). These findings suggest that many African American women with clinically significant binge-eating behaviors remain untreated.

The few extant studies on eating disorders in Latinos suggest prevalence estimates on a par with Whites in the United States (Alegria et al., 2007; Reyes-Rodríguez et al., 2010). A few investigations have suggested that Latinas were more likely than White women to report eating disorder symptomatology (Austin et al., 2011; Fitzgibbon et al., 1998; Marques et al., 2010). Other research has found that BED is the most common eating disorder within this ethnic group (Alegria et al., 2007).). Studies suggest eating pathology and related attitudes are a significant concern among Latinas. Pumariega (1986) found that 20% of young Hispanic urban high school students scored at or above the clinical screening threshold on the Eating Attitudes Test. Binge eating has also been reported to be more severe in Latinas than in Whites or African Americans (Fitzgibbon et al., 1998). Latina girls report greater body dissatisfaction than do White girls (Robinson et al., 1996) and more disturbed eating attitudes and behaviors than do African American girls (Vander Wal & Thomas, 2004).

Although research is emerging regarding the prevalence of eating disorders across racial and ethnic groups, much less is known about the treatment of eating disorders in diverse populations. The majority of studies constituting the evidence base have been conducted primarily on White samples. This is especially concerning, as results of one recent study indicated that African Americans were more likely than Whites to drop out of treatment for BED (Thompson-Brenner et al., 2013).

Further, a qualitative investigation of Latina women with eating disorder histories found that multiple factors, including systemic (e.g., health insurance, availability of bilingual services) and cultural (e.g., emphasis on family privacy, fatalism) barriers, influenced treatment-seeking and retention. In addition, women in this study reported encountering the perception that individuals from their cultural group do not experience eating disorders, which also discouraged treatment-seeking (Reyes-Rodríguez, Ramírez, Davis, Patrice, & Bulik, 2013). A few small studies have investigated the feasibility of adapting existing evidence-based eating disorder treatments, such as cognitive-behavioral therapy (CBT) for Latina populations. One pilot trial (Cachelin et al., 2014) involved a sample of 31 Mexican American women diagnosed with either BN, BED, or recurrent binge eating. All were enrolled in guided self-help CBT treatment. This treatment was specifically adapted for this ethnic group based on the results of prior qualitative research conducted with Mexican American women (Shea et al., 2012). Results of the pilot trial indicated that the adapted intervention was effective; binge eating was significantly reduced, and participants rated the intervention as helpful. Attrition rates were comparable to those of other studies, but were, nonetheless, a bit high (35% dropout after enrollment). Participants with less education and those with BN were more likely to drop out, highlighting the importance of offering a range of interventions in subsequent clinical trials.

Research testing the appropriateness of standard eating disorder treatments and the optimal approaches to cultural adaptation of treatments for diverse populations remains urgently needed.

COURSE AND PROGNOSIS

Anorexia nervosa has serious medical and psychological consequences, many of which persist even after recovery. In addition to the eating-related symptomatology, many other comorbidities of this disorder, including depression, anxiety, social withdrawal, heightened self-consciousness, fatigue, and multiple medical complications, cause considerable impairment (Berkman, Lohr, & Bulik, 2007). For example, the social toll of AN interferes with normal adolescent development (Bulik, 2002). Across psychiatric disorders, the highest risks of premature death, from both natural and unnatural causes, are from substance abuse and eating disorders (Harris & Barraclough, 1998).

Anorexia nervosa history is further associated with reproductive problems (Bulik et al., 1999; Micali, Simonoff, & Treasure, 2007; Micali & Treasure, 2009), osteoporosis (Mehler & Mackenzie, 2009), continued low BMI (Sullivan et al., 1998), and major depression (Fernandez-Aranda et al., 2007). Given the high morbidity and mortality associated with AN, it is critical to develop effective treatments. Initial treatment typically includes a comprehensive medical evaluation and nutritional counseling. Less medically compromised cases of AN are most often treated on an outpatient basis by mental health providers, with primary-care physicians managing medical issues.

Treatment guidelines or position papers outlining recommended AN treatment have been developed by numerous professional organizations, including the American Psychiatric Association (APA, 2006), the National Institute for Clinical Excellence (NICE, 2004), the Society for Adolescent Medicine (Golden et al., 2003), the American Academy of Pediatrics (AAP, 2003) and the Royal Australian and New Zealand College of Psychiatrists (Beumont et al., 2004).

Anorexia nervosa treatment also typically involves psychotherapeutic intervention. Individual, family, and group psychotherapy for AN are conducted from a multitude of theoretical perspectives (e.g., cognitive-behavioral, interpersonal, behavioral, and psychodynamic). For children, family-based therapy has received considerable attention, and it is generally suggested that family members be included in treatment, when feasible and sensible. The current evidence base for treatment of AN suggests some benefit for family-based treatment for young people and recommends a combination of renourishment and psychotherapy (specialist supportive clinical management, CBT, or interpersonal therapy [IPT]) for adults (Watson & Bulik, 2013). Adults with AN have typically been treated entirely on an individual basis, often leaving partners unsure about how best to assist. A new intervention currently being studied, Uniting Couples in the treatment of Anorexia Nervosa (UCAN), leverages the power of interpersonal relationships by incorporating the partner into treatment using a cognitive-behavioral couple therapy approach. UCAN explores several domains (core AN symptoms, body image, affection, sexuality, relapse, and recovery) and helps partners learn to provide support for the patient and reinforce appropriate eating and healthy behaviors, while also improving general relationship functioning (Bulik, Baucom, Kirby, & Pisetsky, 2011).

The APA Working Group on Eating Disorders recommends hospitalization for individuals below 75% of ideal body weight (APA, 2006). However, in addition to weight, parameters such as medical complications, suicidality, previous treatment success, psychiatric comorbidities, social support, role impairment, and availability of other treatment options should all be considered in level-of-care decisions (APA, 2006). Currently, no medications are effective in the treatment of AN (Bulik, Berkman, Brownley, Sedway, & Lohr, 2007). Although commonly prescribed, SSRIs tend to be ineffective in the underweight state, especially in the absence of dietary tryptophan to subsidize the synthesis of serotonin. All treatment commonly involves highly specialized multidisciplinary teams, including psychologists, psychiatrists, internists or pediatricians, dietitians, social workers, and nurse specialists.

Among individuals hospitalized for AN, lengths of stay are much shorter in the United States compared with those in Europe and New Zealand. For example, Striegel-Moore et al. (2000a) found the average length of stay within the United States was 26 days (according to an insurance database of approximately 4 million individuals) (Striegel-Moore, Leslie, & Petrill, 2000a). This is substantially shorter than stays found in other countries, including New Zealand (72 days; McKenzie & Joyce, 1992) and Europe, which ranges from 40.6 days (Finland) to 135.8 days (Switzerland) (Matthias, 2005). Moreover, AN treatment costs in the United States were higher than those for obsessive-compulsive disorder and comparable to those for schizophrenia, both of which occur at similar rates to AN (Striegel-Moore et al., 2000a).

Patients with BN report physical symptoms such as fatigue, lethargy, bloating, and gastrointestinal problems. Frequent vomiting is associated with electrolyte abnormalities, metabolic alkalosis, erosion of dental enamel, swelling of the parotid glands, and scars and calluses on the backs of their hands (Mitchell & Crow, 2006). Laxative misuse often causes edema, fluid loss and subsequent dehydration, electrolyte abnormalities, metabolic acidosis, and potentially permanent loss of normal bowel function (Mitchell & Crow, 2006).

In the United States, most BN treatment is conducted on an outpatient basis. A comprehensive medical evaluation is typically recommended, given the frequency of medical and nutritional complications within this patient population. If significant medical complications related to BN are present, or if the affected individual is pregnant or unable to bring her or his binge-purge behaviors under control in outpatient treatment, partial hospitalization or inpatient treatment may be warranted.

Once medical issues are assessed and under control, psychotherapy (individual and/or group) is typically the primary treatment for BN. As is the case with AN, the theoretical perspectives used in these psychotherapeutic interventions can vary; however, CBT and IPT are commonly used. In 1996, the FDA approved fluoxetine for the treatment of BN. Currently, this is the only FDA-approved medication for the treatment of any eating disorder.

Given that BED has only recently entered the psychiatric nomenclature, minimal population-based data are available regarding the morbidity and mortality related to this diagnosis. However, most adults with BED are obese and, thus, are at risk for medical complications associated with overweight (Hudson et al., 2007; Hudson et al., 2010; Striegel-Moore et al., 2001). Global community surveys suggest that the majority of individuals with a lifetime BED diagnosis (79.0%) also meet diagnostic criteria for at least one additional psychiatric disorder (including mood, anxiety, behavioral, and substance use disorders). BED also predicts subsequent onset of arthritis, chronic back/neck pain, chronic headaches, diabetes, hypertension, and ulcers (Kessler et al., 2013). Many adults with BED report that their symptoms began in childhood (Abbott et al., 1998). Thus, it seems important that future research investigate further the correlates of binge eating in childhood. Within the United States, BED treatment is typically conducted on an outpatient basis. Psychological and nutritional interventions aim to reduce binge eating and control weight (Brownley, Berkman, Sedway, Lohr, & Bulik, 2007). Common psychotherapeutic approaches include CBT and IPT; nutritional approaches include behavioral self-management strategies and facilitating hunger and satiety awareness (Brownley et al., 2007). Pharmacotherapy that targets both the core symptom of binge eating and weight loss (when appropriate) is also available as an off-label intervention (Brownley et al., 2007; Peat, Brownley, Berkman, & Bulik, 2012).

CASE STUDY

Referral

Wendy was a 35-year-old married White female who was referred for treatment for an eating disorder after passing out at the finish line of a half marathon.

Presenting Complaints

The emergency room discharge note indicated that Wendy was 5 feet 6 inches tall and weighed 90 pounds (BMI 14.5 kg/m^2). She was severely dehydrated, her potassium was

2.5 (normal range 3.5–5 mEq/L), and her EKG indicated a prolonged QT interval. Pulse and blood pressure were low. The emergency room physician was vigilant and noted scrapes on her knuckles (Russell's sign) and bloodshot eyes, both indicative of purging.

HISTORY

Wendy was a competitive runner with hopes of qualifying for the Olympics. Two years ago, while on a training run on trails, she was attacked by a man who tried to rape her. She screamed and fought and managed to get away by running out of the forest as fast as she could, but she continued to have flashbacks to this attack every day when she was training on the streets or trails. Prior to the attack, all her attention was on training. She had been a healthy eater, she was always focused on performance rather than appearance, and adhered strictly to the recommendations of her trainer and sports dietitian. After the attack, she became increasingly anxious, had difficulty sleeping, and had trouble keeping up her training schedule. Her race times were getting slower and she was gaining weight. She often found herself eating mindlessly in front of the pantry—sometimes not even being aware of what she was eating. Wendy lost two races to one of her main competitors, and when she saw a picture in the newspaper of herself coming in second in the paper, she became fixated on her weight. She was up to 125 pounds, which was higher than she had ever been before. She started cutting back on calories, which she found easy to do. Wendy stated, "I was training hard and pushing through pain to get through marathons, so dealing with hunger is a piece of cake in comparison."

One evening she went out for a post-run pizza and beer with her husband and some friends. She went to the restroom and was overcome by anxiety about how much she had eaten. Although she had never done it before, she decided to vomit and even though she was horrified at what she had done, she felt a huge sense of relief and felt much less anxious afterward. She didn't intend for it to become a habit, but soon the urge to vomit after she ate became overwhelming, and it seemed to be the only way she could control her anxiety. At first she was just vomiting after dinner, but within a few months, she was doing it up to five to 10 times a day. She started vomiting even if she hadn't eaten anything. Her weight continued to drop and her race times kept getting slower. Her coach and trainer were worried about her health, but she denied any problems. She started having difficulty concentrating at work, was sleeping poorly, and withdrew almost completely from her family and friends. She also withdrew from her husband. Even though they had been talking about starting a family, she became less and less interested in having sex and would pull away whenever he tried to touch her. She spent hours in the bathroom scrutinizing her body—checking to see if her shape had changed, pinching the skin on her waist to make sure her shape wasn't changing, and weighing herself—sometimes 10 times per day. She became convinced that the only way to start winning races again was to get below 90 pounds. She was limiting her intake to about 800 calories per day, restricting how much she drank, and continued to vomit several times per day. Wendy made it through the half marathon on sheer will, but passing out at the finish line was the final event that brought her into treatment.

ASSESSMENT

On clinical interview, Wendy demonstrated significant weight loss below 85% of expected weight for her age and sex. She presented with clear drive for thinness, fear of weight gain, and a failure to recognize the seriousness of her underweight state. Her body image was distorted, as she continued to see herself as fat, even though she was 90 pounds and 5 feet 6 inches tall. There were no other medical explanations for her weight loss. She denied objective binge eating (eating unusually large amounts of food and feeling out of control) but endorsed subjective binge eating (feeling out of control when eating regular or small amounts of food). She also admitted to regular purging via self-induced vomiting. She had not menstruated for the previous 6 months. Wendy met the diagnostic criteria for anorexia nervosa, binge-purge subtype.

Clinical interview also indicated that she experienced post-traumatic stress symptoms secondary to the attack while running. She completed three self-report forms—the Eating Disorders Inventory (EDI) and the Beck Depression and Anxiety Inventories (BDI, BAI). Results indicated high scores on drive for thinness, body dissatisfaction, and perfectionism on the EDI. Her BDI scores indicated mild depression and no suicidal ideation, and a BAI score of 38 indicated high anxiety consistent with her clinical interview.

SUMMARY

Our understanding of eating disorders continues to advance. We know that both genetic and environmental factors contribute to their etiology. After vulnerable individuals start to lose weight, even if it is voluntary, the illness often takes on a life of its own and the weight loss becomes uncontrollable. Advances in neurobiological and genetic research are helping us understand why some individuals are more vulnerable to eating disorders than others. Ironically, the thorough study of biology may provide the biggest boost for our understanding of the role of environment as causal in eating disorders. This work may also assist in identifying environmental risk factors, which will fuel prevention efforts.

As work in the eating disorders field is additionally challenged by the new-world context of escalating obesity, eating disorder researchers must partner with obesity researchers to share findings and ensure that prevention and treatment efforts in one area do not increase the risk for development of pathology in the other area. For example, obesity prevention efforts cannot inadvertently lead to more disordered eating behavior in attempts to control weight. Similarly, eating disorder treatment should not inadvertently increase the risk for the development of obesity. Animal models of component features of eating disorders (e.g., driven physical activity, binge eating) are also shedding valuable light on underlying neurobiological processes that initiate and maintain dysregulated eating and activity behavior. The integration of research findings from cell to population is required to complete the complex picture of these perplexing disorders that stand at the intersection of psyche and soma.

REFERENCES

Abbott, D. W., de Zwaan, M., Mussell, M. P., Raymond, N. C., Seim, H. C., Crow, S. J., . . . Mitchell, J. E. (1998). Onset of binge eating and dieting in overweight women: implications for etiology, associated features and treatment. *Journal of Psychosomatic Research, 44*, 367–374.

Akio, I., Shouichi, M., Akihiro, A., Hirotaka, U., Haruka, A., & Takakazu, Y. (2012). The role of ghrelin, salivary secretions, and dental care in eating disorders. *Nutrients, 4*(8), 967–989.

Akkermann, K., Kaasik, K., Kiive, E., Nordquist, N., Oreland, L., & Harro, J. (2012). The impact of adverse life events and the serotonin transporter gene promoter polymorphism on the development of eating disorder symptoms. *Journal of Psychiatric Research, 46*, 38–43.

Akkermann, K., Nordquist, N., Oreland, L., & Harro, J. (2010). Serotonin transporter gene promoter polymorphism affects the severity of binge eating in general population. *Progress in Neuro-Psychopharmacology and Biological Psychiatry, 34,* 111–114.

Alegria, M., Woo, M., Cao, Z., Torres, M., Meng, X.-l., & Striegel-Moore, R. (2007). Prevalence and correlates of eating disorders in Latinos in the United States. *International Journal of Eating Disorders, 40,* S15–S21.

Aloi, M., Rania, M., Caroleo, M., Bruni, A., Palmieri, A., Cauteruccio, M. A., . . . Segura-García, C. (2015). Decision making, central coherence and set-shifting: a comparison between binge eating disorder, anorexia nervosa and healthy controls. *BMC Psychiatry, 15,* 1–10.

American Academy of Pediatrics (AAP). (2003). Identifying and treating eating disorders. *Pediatrics, 111,* 204–211.

American Psychiatric Association (APA). (1994). *Diagnostic and statistical manual of mental disorders.* Washington, DC: APA.

American Psychiatric Association. (2013) *Diagnostic and statistical manual of mental disorders* (5th ed.). Washington, DC: American Psychiatric Association.

American Psychiatric Association (APA). (2006). *Practice guideline for the treatment of patients with eating disorders.* Washington, DC: APA.

Anderson, C. B., & Bulik, C. M. (2004). Gender differences in compensatory behaviors, weight and shape salience, and drive for thinness. *Eating Behaviors, 5*(1), 1–11.

Anderson, D. A., Williamson, D. A., Duchmann, E. G., Gleaves, D. H., & Barbin, J. M. (1999). Development and validation of a multifactorial treatment outcome measure for eating disorders. *Assessment, 6,* 7–20.

Anestis, M. D., Selby, E. A., Fink, E. L., & Joiner, T. E. (2007). The multifaceted role of distress tolerance in dysregulated eating behaviors. *International Journal of Eating Disorders, 40,* 718–726.

Artmann, H., Grau, H., Adelmann, M., & Schleiffer, R. (1985). Reversible and non-reversible enlargement of cerebrospinal fluid spaces in anorexia nervosa. *Neuroradiology, 27,* 304–312.

Attia, E., Haiman, C., Walsh, B. T., & Flater, S. R. (1998). Does fluoxetine augment the inpatient treatment of anorexia nervosa? *American Journal of Psychiatry, 155,* 548–551.

Austin, S. B., Spadano-Gasbarro, J., Greaney, M. L., Richmond, T. K., Feldman, H. A., Osganian, S. K., . . . Peterson, K. E. (2011). Disordered weight control behaviors in early adolescent boys and girls of color: An under-recognized factor in the epidemic of childhood overweight. *Journal of Adolescent Health, 48*(1), 109–112.

Bacanu, S.-A., Bulik, C. M., Klump, K. L., Fichter, M. M., Halmi, K. A., Keel, P., . . . Devlin, B. (2005). Linkage analysis of anorexia and bulimia nervosa cohorts using selected behavioral phenotypes as quantitative traits or covariates. *American Journal of Medical Genetics Part B: Neuropsychiatric Genetics, 139B,* 61–68.

Bailer, U., & Kaye, W. (2003). A review of neuropeptide and neuroendocrine dysregulation in anorexia and bulimia nervosa. *Current Drug Target -CNS & Neurological Disorders, 2,* 53–59.

Bailer, U. F., Bloss, C. S., Frank, G. K., Price, J. C., Meltzer, C. C., Mathis, C. A., . . . Kaye, W. H. (2011). 5-HT1A receptor binding is increased after recovery from bulimia nervosa compared to control women and is associated with behavioral inhibition in both groups. *International Journal of Eating Disorders, 44,* 477–487.

Bailer, U. F., Frank, G. K., Henry, S. E., Price, J. C., Meltzer, C. C., Mathis, C. A., . . . Kaye, W. H. (2007). Exaggerated 5-HT1A but normal 5-HT2A receptor activity in individuals Ill with anorexia nervosa. *Biological Psychiatry, 61,* 1090–1099.

Bailer, U. F., Frank, G. K., Henry, S. E., Price, J. C., Meltzer, C. C., Weissfeld, L., . . . J., T. (2005). Altered brain serotonin 5HT1A receptor binding after recovery from anorexia nervosa measured by positron emission tomography and [carbonyl11C]WAY-100635. *Archives of General Psychiatry, 62,* 1032–1041.

Bailer, U. F., Frank, G. K., Price, J. C., Meltzer, C. C., Becker, C., Mathis, C. A., . . . Kaye, W. H. (2013). Interaction between serotonin transporter and dopamine D2/D3 receptor radioligand measures is associated with harm avoidant symptoms in anorexia and bulimia nervosa. *Psychiatry Research: Neuroimaging, 211*, 160–168.

Bailer, U. F., Price, J. C., Meltzer, C. C., Mathis, C. A., Frank, G. K., Weissfeld, L., . . . Kaye, W. H. (2004). Altered 5-HT(2A) receptor binding after recovery from bulimia-type anorexia nervosa: relationships to harm avoidance and drive for thinness. *Neuropsychopharmacology, 29*, 1143–1155.

Beck, D., Casper, R., & Andersen, A. (1996). Truly late onset of eating disorders: A study of 11 cases averaging 60 years of age at presentation. *International Journal of Eating Disorders, 20*, 389–395.

Becker, A. E., Franko, D. L., Speck, A., & Herzog, D. B. (2003). Ethnicity and differential access to care for eating disorder symptoms. *International Journal of Eating Disorders, 33*, 205–212.

Becker, A. E., & Hamburg, P. (1996). Culture, the Media, and Eating Disorders. *Harvard Review of Psychiatry, 4*, 163–167.

Bello, N. T., & Hajnal, A. (2010). Dopamine and binge eating behaviors. *Pharmacology Biochemistry and Behavior, 97*, 25–33.

Bencherif, B., Guarda, A. S., Colantuoni, C., Ravert, H. T., Dannals, R. F., & Frost, J. J. (2005). Regional mu-opioid receptor binding in insular cortex is decreased in bulimia nervosa and correlates inversely with fasting behavior. *Journal of nuclear medicine: official publication, Society of Nuclear Medicine, 46*, 1349–1351.

Berge, J. M., Loth, K., Hanson, C., Croll-Lampert, J., & Neumark-Sztainer, D. (2012). Family life cycle transitions and the onset of eating disorders: a retrospective grounded theory approach. *Journal of Clinical Nursing, 21*, 1355–1363.

Bergen, A. W., van den Bree, M. B. M., Yeager, M., Welch, R., Ganjei, J. K., Haque, K., . . . Kaye, W. H. (2003). Candidate genes for anorexia nervosa in the 1p33-36 linkage region: serotonin 1D and delta opioid receptor loci exhibit significant association to anorexia nervosa. *Molecular Psychiatry, 8*, 397–406.

Berkman, N. D., Lohr, K. N., & Bulik, C. M. (2007). Outcomes of eating disorders: A systematic review of the literature. *International Journal of Eating Disorders, 40*, 293–309.

Beumont, P., Hay, P., Beumont, D., Birmingham, L., Derham, H., Jordan, A., Royal Australian and New Zealand College of Psychiatrists Clinical Practice Guidelines Team for Anorexia Nervosa. (2004). Australian and New Zealand clinical practice guidelines for the treatment of anorexia nervosa. *The Australian and New Zealand Journal of Psychiatry, 38*, 659–670.

Beumont, P. J. V., Kopec-Schrader, E. M., Talbot, P., & Touyz, S. W. (1993). Measuring the specific psychopathology of eating disorder patients. *Australian & New Zealand Journal of Psychiatry, 27*, 506–511.

Blasio, A., Steardo, L., Sabino, V., & Cottone, P. (2014). Opioid system in the medial prefrontal cortex mediates binge-like eating. *Addiction Biology, 19*, 652–662.

Blundell, J. E. (1986). Serotonin manipulations and the structure of feeding behaviour. *Appetite, 7*, 39–56.

Bodell, L. P., Smith, A. R., Holm-Denoma, J. M., Gordon, K. H., & Joiner, T. E. (2011). The impact of perceived social support and negative life events on bulimic symptoms. *Eating Behaviors, 12*, 44–48.

Boraska, V., Franklin, C. S., Floyd, J. A. B., Thornton, L. M., Huckins, L. M., Southam, L., . . . Bulik, C. M. (2014). A genome-wide association study of anorexia nervosa. *Molecular Psychiatry, 19*(10), 1085–1094.

Brandys, M. K., Kas, M. J. H., Van Elburg, A. A., Ophoff, R., Slof-Op'T Landt, M. C. T., Middeldorp, C. M., . . . Adan, R. A. H. (2013). The Val66Met polymorphism of the BDNF gene in anorexia nervosa: New data and a meta-analysis. *The World Journal of Biological Psychiatry, 14*(6), 441–451.

Brandys, M. K., Slof-Op't Landt, M. C. T., van Elburg, A. A., Ophoff, R., Verduijn, W., Meulenbelt, I., . . . Adan, R. A. H. (2012). Anorexia nervosa and the Val158Met polymorphism of the COMT gene: meta-analysis and new data. *Psychiatric Genetics, 22*(3), 130–136.

Branson, R., Potoczna, N., Kral, J. G., Lentes, K.-U., Hoehe, M. R., & Horber, F. F. (2003). Binge eating as a major phenotype of melanocortin 4 receptor gene mutations. *New England Journal of Medicine, 348*, 1096–1103.

Braun, C. M. J., & Chouinard, M.-J. e. (1992). Is anorexia nervosa a neuropsychological disease? *Neuropsychology Review, 3*, 171–212.

Braun, D. L., Sunday, S. R., Halmi, K. A., Bulik, C. M., Sullivan, P. F., Epstein, L. H., . . . Goodman, S. (1994). Psychiatric comorbidity in patients with eating disorders. *Psychological Medicine, 24*, 859.

Brewerton, T. D. (1995). Toward a unified theory of serotonin dysregulation in eating and related disorders. *Psychoneuroendocrinology, 20*, 561–590.

Brewerton, T. D., Bruce, L. R., Herzog, D. B., Brotman, A. W., O'Neil, P. M., & Ballenger, J. C. (1995). Comorbidity of Axis I psychiatric disorders in bulimia nervosa. *The Journal of Clinical Psychiatry, 56*, 77–80.

Brewerton, T. D., Lydiard, R. B., Laraia, M. T., Shook, J. E., & Ballenger, J. C. (1992). CSF beta-endorphin and dynorphin in bulimia nervosa. *The American Journal of Psychiatry, 149*(8), 1086.

Brockmeyer, T., Holtforth, M. G., Bents, H., Kämmerer, A., Herzog, W., & Friederich, H.-C. (2012). Starvation and emotion regulation in anorexia nervosa. *Comprehensive Psychiatry, 53*, 496–501.

Brownley, K., Peat, C., La Via, M., & Bulik, C. (2015). Pharmacological approaches to the management of binge eating disorder. *Drugs, 75*(1), 9–32.

Brownley, K. A., Berkman, N. D., Peat, C. M., & et al. (2016). Binge-eating disorder in adults: A systematic review and meta-analysis. *Annals of Internal Medicine, 165*(6), 409–420.

Brownley, K. A., Berkman, N. D., Sedway, J. A., Lohr, K. N., & Bulik, C. M. (2007). Binge eating disorder treatment: A systematic review of randomized controlled trials. *International Journal of Eating Disorders, 40*, 337–348.

Bruce, B., & Agras, W. S. (1992). Binge eating in females: A population-based investigation. *International Journal of Eating Disorders, 12*, 365–373.

Bruce, B., & Wilfley, D. (1996). Binge eating among the overweight population: A serious and prevalent problem. *Journal of the American Dietetic Association, 96*, 58–61.

Bulik-Sullivan, B., Finucane, H. K., Anttila, V., Gusev, A., Day, F. R., Loh, P.-R., . . . Neale, B. M. (2015). An atlas of genetic correlations across human diseases and traits. *Nature Genetics, 47*(11), 1236.

Bulik, C. M. (2002). Eating disorders in adolescents and young adults. *Child and Adolescent Psychiatric Clinics of North America, 11*, 201–218.

Bulik, C. M., Baucom, D. H., Kirby, J. S., & Pisetsky, E. (2011). Uniting couples (in the treatment of) anorexia nervosa (UCAN). *International Journal of Eating Disorders, 44*, 19–28.

Bulik, C. M., Berkman, N. D., Brownley, K. A., Sedway, J. A., & Lohr, K. N. (2007). Anorexia nervosa treatment: A systematic review of randomized controlled trials. *International Journal of Eating Disorders, 40*, 310–320.

Bulik, C. M., Devlin, B., Bacanu, S.-A., Thornton, L., Klump, K. L., Fichter, M. M., . . . Kaye, W. H. (2003). Significant linkage on chromosome 10p in families with bulimia nervosa. *The American Journal of Human Genetics, 72*, 200–207.

Bulik, C. M., Klump, K. L., Thornton, L., Kaplan, A. S., Devlin, B., Fichter, M. M., . . . Kaye, W. H. (2004). Alcohol use disorder comorbidity in eating disorders: A multicenter study. *Journal of Clinical Psychiatry, 65*(7), 1000–1006.

Bulik, C. M., Slof-Op't Landt, M. C., van Furth, E. F., & Sullivan, P. F. (2007). The genetics of anorexia nervosa. *Annual Review of Nutrition, 27*, 263–275.

Bulik, C. M., Sullivan, P. F., Fear, J. I., & Joyce, P. R. (1997). Eating disorders and antecedent anxiety disorders: a controlled study. *Acta Psychiatrica Scandinavica, 96*, 101–107.

Bulik, C. M., Sullivan, P. F., Fear, J. L., Pickering, A., Dawn, A., & McCullin, M. (1999). Fertility and reproduction in women with a history of anorexia nervosa: A controlled study. *The Journal of Clinical Psychiatry, 60*, 130–135.

Bulik, C. M., Sullivan, P. F., Joyce, P. R., & Carter, F. A. (1995). Temperament, character, and personality disorder in bulimia nervosa. *Journal of Nervous and Mental Disorders, 183*(9), 593–598.

Bulik, C. M., Sullivan, P. F., & Kendler, K. S. (2002). Medical and psychiatric morbidity in obese women with and without binge eating. *International Journal of Eating Disorders, 32*, 72–78.

Bulik, C. M., Sullivan, P. F., Tozzi, F., Furberg, H., Lichtenstein, P., Pedersen, N. L., . . . DE., G. (2006). Prevalence, heritability, and prospective risk factors for anorexia nervosa. *Archives of General Psychiatry, 63*, 305.

Burgess, P., & Shallice, T. (1997). *The Hayling and Brixton tests.* Bury St Edmunds, UK: Thames Valley Test Company.

Cachelin, F. M., Shea, M., Phimphasone, P., Wilson, G. T., Thompson, D. R., & Striegel, R. H. (2014). Culturally adapted cognitive behavioral guided self-help for binge eating: A feasibility study with Mexican Americans. *Cultural Diversity and Ethnic Minority Psychology, 20*(3), 449–457.

Cachelin, F. M., Veisel, C., Barzegarnazari, E., & Striegel-moore, R. H. (2000). Disordered eating, acculturation, and treatment-seeking in a community sample of Hispanic, Asian, Black, and White women. *Psychology of Women Quarterly, 24*(3), 244–253.

Calati, R., De Ronchi, D., Bellini, M., & Serretti, A. (2011). The 5-HTTLPR polymorphism and eating disorders: A meta-analysis. *International Journal of Eating Disorders, 44*, 191–199.

Carli, M., Baviera, M., Invernizzi, R. W., & Balducci, C. (2006). Dissociable contribution of 5-HT1A and 5-HT2A receptors in the medial prefrontal cortex to different aspects of executive control such as impulsivity and compulsive perseveration in rats. *Neuropsychopharmacology, 31*, 757–767.

Cassin, S. E., & von Ranson, K. M. (2005). Personality and eating disorders: A decade in review. *Clinical Psychology Review, 25*, 895–916.

Castro-Fornieles, J., Caldú, X., Andrés-Perpiñá, S., Lázaro, L., Bargalló, N., Falcón, C., . . . Junqué, C. (2010). A cross-sectional and follow-up functional MRI study with a working memory task in adolescent anorexia nervosa. *Neuropsychologia, 48*, 4111–4116.

Cha, J., Ide, J. S., Bowman, F. D., Simpson, H. B., Posner, J., & Steinglass, J. E. (2016). Abnormal reward circuitry in anorexia nervosa: A longitudinal, multimodal MRI study. *Human Brain Mapping, 37*(11), 3835–3846.

Chiodo, J., Latimer, P. R., Holt, S., Ford, M. J., Grant, S., Heading, R. C., . . . Cozolino, L. (1986). Hunger perceptions and satiety responses among normal-weight bulimics and normals to a high-calorie, carbohydrate-rich food. *Psychological Medicine, 16*, 343.

Claes, L., Mitchell, J. E., & Vandereycken, W. (2012). Out of control?: Inhibition processes in eating disorders from a personality and cognitive perspective. *International Journal of Eating Disorders, 45*, 407–414.

Cnattingius, S., Hultman, C. M., Dahl, M., Sparén, P., M, S., AH, C., . . . I, C. (1999). Very preterm birth, birth trauma, and the risk of anorexia nervosa among girls. *Archives of General Psychiatry, 56*, 634.

Cooper, M. J., Anastasiades, P., & Fairburn, C. G. (1992). Selective processing of eating-, shape-, and weight-related words in persons with bulimia nervosa. *Journal of Abnormal Psychology, 101*, 352–355.

Cooper, Z., Cooper, P. J., & Fairburn, C. G. (1989). The validity of the eating disorder examination and its subscales. *The British Journal of Psychiatry, 154.*

Cooper, Z., & Fairburn, C. G. (1987). The eating disorders examination: A semi-structured interview for the assessment of the specific psychopathology of eating disorders. *International Journal of Eating Disorders, 6*, 1–8.

Cross-Disorder Group of the Psychiatric Genomics, C. (2013). Genetic Risk Outcome of Psychosis (GROUP) Consortium. Identification of risk loci with shared effects on five major psychiatric disorders: a genome-wide analysis. *The Lancet., 381*(9875), 1371.

Crow, S. (2005). Medical complications of eating disorders. In S. Wonderlich, J. Mitchell, M. deZwann, & H. Steiger (Eds.), *Eating disorders review, Part I* (pp. 127–136). Milton Keynes, England: Radcliffe.

Crow, S. J., Agras, W., Halmi, K., Mitchell, J. E., & Kraemer, H. C. (2002). Full syndromal versus subthreshold anorexia nervosa, bulimia nervosa, and binge eating disorder: A multicenter study. *International Journal of Eating Disorders, 32,* 309–318.

Crow, S. J., Peterson, C. B., Swanson, S. A., Raymond, N. C., Specker, S., Eckert, E. D., & Mitchell, J. E. (2009). Increased mortality in bulimia nervosa and other eating disorders. *American Journal of Psychiatry, 166,* 1342–1346.

Crow, S. J., Salisbury, J. J., Crosby, R. D., & Mitchell, J. E. (1997). Serum electrolytes as markers of vomiting in bulimia nervosa. *International Journal of Eating Disorders, 21,* 95–98.

Cuellar, R. E., Kaye, W. H., Hsu, L. K. G., & Van Thiel, D. H. (1988). Upper gastrointestinal tract dysfunction in bulimia. *Digestive Diseases and Sciences, 33,* 1549–1553.

Cuellar, R. E., & Van Thiel, D. H. (1986). Gastrointestinal consequences of the eating disorders: Anorexia nervosa and bulimia. *Digestive Diseases and Sciences, 33,* 1549–1553.

Culbert, K. M., Racine, S. E., & Klump, K. L. (2015). Research Review: What we have learned about the causes of eating disorders – a synthesis of sociocultural, psychological, and biological research. *Journal of Child Psychology and Psychiatry, 56*(11), 1141–1164.

Currin, L., Schmidt, U. H., Treasure, J., & Jick, H. (2005). Time trends in eating disorder incidence. *The British Journal of Psychiatry, 186,* 132–135.

Danner, U. N., Sanders, N., Smeets, P. A. M., van Meer, F., Adan, R. A. H., Hoek, H. W., & van Elburg, A. A. (2012). Neuropsychological weaknesses in anorexia nervosa: Set-shifting, central coherence, and decision making in currently ill and recovered women. *International Journal of Eating Disorders, 45,* 685–694.

Davis, C., Levitan, R. D., Kaplan, A. S., Carter, J., Reid, C., Curtis, C., . . . Kennedy, J. L. (2008). Reward sensitivity and the D2 dopamine receptor gene: A case-control study of binge eating disorder. *Progress in Neuro-Psychopharmacology and Biological Psychiatry, 32,* 620–628.

Davis, C., Levitan, R. D., Kaplan, A. S., Carter, J., Reid, C., Curtis, C., . . . Kennedy, J. L. (2007). Dopamine transporter gene (DAT1) associated with appetite suppression to methylphenidate in a case-control study of binge eating disorder. *Neuropsychopharmacology, 32,* 2199–2206.

Davis, C., Levitan, R. D., Yilmaz, Z., Kaplan, A. S., Carter, J. C., & Kennedy, J. L. (2012). Binge eating disorder and the dopamine D2 receptor: Genotypes and sub-phenotypes. *Progress in Neuro-Psychopharmacology and Biological Psychiatry, 38,* 328–335.

Davis, C. A., Levitan, R. D., Reid, C., Carter, J. C., Kaplan, A. S., Patte, K. A., . . . Kennedy, J. L. (2009). Dopamine for "wanting" and opioids for "liking": A comparison of obese adults with and without binge eating. *Obesity, 17,* 1220–1225.

Degortes, D., Santonastaso, P., Zanetti, T., Tenconi, E., Veronese, A., & Favaro, A. (2014). Stressful life events and binge eating disorder. *European Eating Disorders Review, 22*(5), 378–382.

Delgado, M. R., Nystrom, L. E., Fissell, C., Noll, D. C., & Fiez, J. A. (2000). Tracking the hemodynamic responses to reward and punishment in the striatum. *Journal of Neurophysiology, 84.*

Delis, D. C., Kaplan, E., & Kramer, J. H. (2001). *Delis-Kaplan Executive Function System (D-KEFS).* Psychological Corporation.

Devlin, B., Bacanu, S.-A., Klump, K. L., Bulik, C. M., Fichter, M. M., Halmi, K. A., . . . Kaye, W. H. (2002). Linkage analysis of anorexia nervosa incorporating behavioral covariates. *Human Molecular Genetics, 11,* 689–696.

de Zwaan, M., Biener, D., Bach, M., Wiesnagrotzki, S., & Stacher, G. (1996). Pain sensitivity, alexithymia, and depression in patients with eating disorders: Are they related? *Journal of Psychosomatic Research, 41*, 65–70.

Dingemans, A. E., & van Furth, E. F. (2012). Binge eating disorder psychopathology in normal weight and obese individuals. *International Journal of Eating Disorders, 45*, 135–138.

Duchesne, M., Mattos, P., Fontenelle, L. F., Veiga, H., Rizo, L., & Appolinario, J. C. (2004). Neuropsychology of eating disorders: A systematic review of the literature. *Revista Brasileira de Psiquiatria, 26*, 107–117.

Duncan, L., Yilmaz, Z., Walters, R., Goldstein, J., Antilla, V., Bulik-Sullivan, B., . . . Bulik, C. (2016). Genome-wide association study reveals first locus for anorexia nervosa and metabolic correlations. *Molecular Psychiatry, 19*, 1085–1094.

Eagles, J., Johnston, M., Hunter, D., Lobban, M., & Millar, H. (1995). Increasing incidence of anorexia nervosa in the female population of northeast Scotland. *American Journal of Psychiatry, 152*, 1266–1271.

Enten, R. S., & Golan, M. (2009). Parenting styles and eating disorder pathology. *Appetite, 52*(3), 784–787.

Erlanson-Albertsson, C. (2005). How palatable food disrupts appetite regulation. *Basic Clinical Pharmacology and Toxicology, 97*, 61–73.

Fairbanks, L. A., Melega, W. P., Jorgensen, M. J., Kaplan, J. R., & McGuire, M. T. (2001). Social impulsivity inversely associated with CSF 5-HIAA and fluoxetine exposure in vervet monkeys. *Neuropsychopharmacology, 24*(4), 370–378.

Fairburn, C. G., & Beglin, S. J. (1994). Assessment of eating disorders: Interview or self-report questionnaire. *International Journal of Eating Disorders, 16*, 363–370.

Fairburn, C. G., & Bohn, K. (2005). Eating disorder NOS (EDNOS): an example of the troublesome "not otherwise specified" (NOS) category in DSM-IV. *Behaviour Research and Therapy, 43*(6), 691–701.

Fairburn, C. G., & Cooper, Z. (1993). The eating disorders examination. In C. G. Fairburn & G. T. Wilson (Eds.), *Binge-eating: Nature, assessment, and treatment* (12th ed., pp. 317–360). New York, NY: Guilford Press.

Fairburn, C. G., & Cooper, Z. (2007). Thinking afresh about the classification of eating disorders. *International Journal of Eating Disorders, 40 Suppl*, S107–110.

Fairburn, C. G., Doll, H. A., Welch, S. L., Hay, P. J., Davies, B. A., & O'Connor, M. E. (1998). Risk factors for binge eating disorder: A community-based, case-control study. *Archives of General Psychiatry, 55*(5), 425–432.

Fairburn, C. G., Welch, S. L., & Hay, P. J. (1993). The classification of recurrent overeating: the "binge eating disorder" proposal. *International Journal of Eating Disorders, 13*(2), 155–159.

Fairweather-Schmidt, A. K., & Wade, T. D. (2015). Changes in genetic and environmental influences on disordered eating between early and late adolescence: a longitudinal twin study. *Psychological Medicine, 45*(15), 3249–3258.

Fassino, S., Amianto, F., Gramaglia, C., Facchini, F., & Abbate Daga, G. (2004). Temperament and character in eating disorders: ten years of studies. *Eating and Weight Disorders-Studies on Anorexia, Bulimia and Obesity, 9*(2), 81–90.

Fassino, S., Pieró, A., Daga, G. A., Leombruni, P., Mortara, P., & Rovera, G. G. (2002). Attentional biases and frontal functioning in anorexia nervosa. *International Journal of Eating Disorders, 31*(3), 274–283.

Ferguson, C. P., La Via, M. C., Crossan, P. J., & Kaye, W. H. (1999). Are serotonin selective reuptake inhibitors effective in underweight anorexia nervosa? *International Journal of Eating Disorders, 25*(1), 11–17.

Fernandez-Aranda, F., Pinheiro, A. P., Tozzi, F., Thornton, L. M., Fichter, M. M., Halmi, K. A., . . . Bulik, C. M. (2007). Symptom profile of major depressive disorder in women with eating disorders. *Australian and New Zealand Journal of Psychiatry, 41*(1), 24–31.

Ferraro, F. R., Wonderlich, S., & Jocic, Z. (1997). Performance variability as a new theoretical mechanism regarding eating disorders and cognitive processing. *Journal of Clinical Psychology*, 53(2), 117.

Fichter, M., & Keeser, W. (1980). The anorexia nervosa inventory for self-rating (ANIS). *Archiv für Psychiatrie und Nervenkrankheiten*, 228(1), 67–89.

Fichter, M., & Quadflieg, N. (2001). The structured interview for anorexic and bulimic disorders for DSM-IV and ICD-10 (SIAB-EX): reliability and validity. *European Psychiatry*, 16(1), 38–48.

Fichter, M. M., Herpertz, S., Quadflieg, N., & Herpertz-Dahlmann, B. (1998). Structured interview for anorexic and bulimic disorders for DSM-IV and ICD-10: Updated (third) revision. *International Journal of Eating Disorders*, 24(3), 227–249.

Fichter, M. M., & Quadflieg, N. (1997). Six-year course of bulimia nervosa. *International Journal of Eating Disorders*, 22(4), 361.

Fichter, M. M., & Quadflieg, N. (2000). Comparing self- and expert rating: a self-report screening version (SIAB-S) of the Structured Interview for Anorexic and Bulimic Syndromes for DSM-IV and ICD-10 (SIAB-EX). *European Archives of Psychiatry and Clinical Neuroscience*, 250(4), 175–185.

First, M., Spitzer, R. L., Gibbon, M., & Williams, G. (1997). *Structured Clinical Interview for DSM-IV Axis I Disorders (SCID-I), Clinican Version*. Washington, DC.: American Psychiatric Press.

Fischer, S., Smith, G. T., & Cyders, M. A. (2008). Another look at impulsivity: A meta-analytic review comparing specific dispositions to rash action in their relationship to bulimic symptoms. *Clinical Psychology Review*, 28, 1413–1425.

Fitzgibbon, M. L., Spring, B., Avellone, M. E., Blackman, L. R., Pingitore, R., & Stolley, M. R. (1998). Correlates of binge eating in Hispanic, Black, and White women. *International Journal of Eating Disorders*, 24, 43–52.

Folkman, S., Lazarus, R., Gruen, R., & Delongis, A. (1986a). Appraisal, coping, health status, and psychological symptoms. *Journal of Personality and Social Psychology*, 50(3), 571.

Folkman, S., Lazarus, R. S., Dunkel-Schetter, C., Delongis, A., & Gruen, R. J. (1986b). Dynamics of a stressful encounter: Cognitive appraisal, coping, and encounter outcomes. *Journal of Personality and Social Psychology*, 50(5), 992–1003.

Fonville, L., Giampietro, V., Williams, S. C. R., Simmons, A., & Tchanturia, K. (2014). Alterations in brain structure in adults with anorexia nervosa and the impact of illness duration. *Psychological Medicine*, 44(9), 1965–1975.

Fowler, S. J., & Bulik, C. M. (1997). Family environment and psychiatric history in women with binge-eating disorder and obese controls. *Behavior Change*, 14, 106–112.

Frank, G. (2013). Altered brain reward circuits in eating disorders: Chicken or egg? *Current Psychiatry Reports*, 15(10), 1–7.

Frank, G. K., Bailer, U. F., Henry, S., Wagner, A., & Kaye, W. H. (2004). Neuroimaging studies in eating disorders. *CNS Spectrums*, 9(7), 539–548.

Frank, G. K., Bailer, U. F., Henry, S. E., Drevets, W., Meltzer, C. C., Price, J. C., . . . Kaye, W. H. (2005). Increased dopamine D2/D3 receptor binding after recovery from anorexia nervosa measured by positron emission tomography and [11c]raclopride. *Biological Psychiatry*, 58(11), 908–912.

Frank, G. K., & Kaye, W. H. (2005). Positron emission tomography studies in eating disorders: Multireceptor brain imaging, correlates with behavior and implications for pharmacotherapy. *Nuclear Medicine & Biology*, 32(7), 755–761.

Frank, G. K., Kaye, W. H., Meltzer, C. C., Price, J. C., Greer, P., McConaha, C., & Skovira, K. (2002). Reduced 5-HT2A receptor binding after recovery from anorexia nervosa. *Biological Psychiatry*, 52(9), 896–906.

Frank, G. K. W. (2015). Advances from neuroimaging studies in eating disorders. *CNS Spectrums*, 20(4), 391.

Frank, G. K. W., Shott, M. E., Riederer, J., & Pryor, T. L. (2016). Altered structural and effective connectivity in anorexia and bulimia nervosa in circuits that regulate energy and reward homeostasis. *Translational Psychiatry*, 6(11), e932.

Freedman, M. (1990). Object alternation and orbitofrontal system dysfunction in Alzheimer's and Parkinson's disease. *Brain and Cognition, 14*(2), 134–143.

Friederich, H.-C., Walther, S., Bendszus, M., Biller, A., Thomann, P., Zeigermann, S., . . . Herzog, W. (2012). Grey matter abnormalities within cortico-limbic-striatal circuits in acute and weight-restored anorexia nervosa patients. *NeuroImage, 59*(2), 1106–1113.

Gagne, D. A., Von Holle, A., Brownley, K. A., Runfola, C. D., Hofmeier, S., Branch, K. E., & Bulik, C. M. (2012). Eating disorder symptoms and weight and shape concerns in a large web-based convenience sample of women ages 50 and above: Results of the gender and body image (GABI) study. *International Journal of Eating Disorders, 45*(7), 832–844.

Garner, D., Olmsted, M., & Polivy, J. (1984). *Eating disorder inventory manual*. New York, NY: Psychological Assessment Resources.

Garner, D. M. (1991). *Eating Disorder Inventory 2*. Odessa, FL: Psychological Assessment Resources.

Garner, D. M. (2004). *Eating Disorder Inventory-3*. New York, NY: Psychological Assessment Resources.

Garner, D. M., & Garfinkel, P. E. (1980). Socio-cultural factors in the development of anorexia nervosa. *Psychological Medicine, 10*, 647–656.

Garner, D. M., Olmsted, M. P., & Polivy, J. (1983). Development and validation of a multi-dimensional Eating Disorder Inventory for anorexia and bulimia. *International Journal of Eating Disorders, 2*, 15–34.

Garner, D. M., Olmsted, M. P., & Polivy, J. (2008). Eating Disorder Inventory-3 (EDI-3). In A. J. Rush, M. B. First& D. Blacker (Eds.), *Handbook of Psychiatric Measures*. Washington, DC: American Psychiatric Publishing.

Geliebter, A., Hashim, S. A., & Gluck, M. E. (2008). Appetite-related gut peptides, ghrelin, PYY, and GLP-1 in obese women with and without binge eating disorder (BED). *Physiology & Behavior, 94*(5), 696–699.

Gendall, K. A., Joyce, P. R., Carter, F. A., McIntosh, V. V., Jordan, J., & Bulik, C. M. (2006). The psychobiology and diagnostic significance of amenorrhea in patients with anorexia nervosa. *Fertil Steril, 85*(5), 1531–1535.

Giel, K. E., Friederich, H.-C., Teufel, M., Hautzinger, M., Enck, P., & Zipfel, S. (2011). Attentional processing of food pictures in individuals with anorexia nervosa—An eye-tracking study. *Biological Psychiatry, 69*(7), 661–667.

Godart, N., Flament, M., Perdereau, F., & Jeammet, P. (2002). Comorbidity between eating disorders and anxiety disorders: A review. *International Journal of Eating Disorders, 32*, 253–270.

Godart, N. T., Flament, M. F., Lecrubier, Y., & Jeammet, P. (2000). Anxiety disorders in anorexia nervosa and bulimia nervosa: Co-morbidity and chronology of appearance. *European Psychiatry, 15*(1), 38–45.

Golden, N. H., Ashtari, M., Kohn, M. R., Patel, M., Jacobson, M. S., Fletcher, A., & Shenker, I. R. (1996). Reversibility of cerebral ventricular enlargement in anorexia nervosa, demonstrated by quantitative magnetic resonance imaging. *The Journal of Pediatrics, 128*(2), 296–301.

Golden, N. H., Katzman, D. K., Kreipe, R. E., Stevens, S. L., Sawyer, S. M., Rees, J., . . . Rome, E. S. (2003). Eating disorders in adolescents: position paper of the Society for Adolescent Medicine. *Journal of Adolescent Health, 33*(6), 496–503.

Goodwin, R. D., Hoven, C. W., & Spitzer, R. L. (2003). Diabetes and eating disorders in primary care. *International Journal of Eating Disorders, 33*(1), 85–91.

Gormally, J., Black, S., Daston, S., & Rardin, D. (1982). The assessment of binge eating severity among obese persons. *Addictive Behaviors, 7*, 47–55.

Green, M. W., Elliman, N. A., Wakeling, A., & Rogers, P. J. (1996). Cognitive functioning, weight change and therapy in anorexia nervosa. *Journal of Psychiatric Research, 30*(5), 401–410.

Grice, D. E., Halmi, K. A., Fichter, M. M., Strober, M., Woodside, D. B., Treasure, J. T., . . . Berrettini, W. H. (2002). Evidence for a susceptibility gene for anorexia nervosa on chromosome 1. *American Journal of Human Genetics, 70*(3), 787–792.

Grilo, C. M. (2005). Structured instruments. In J. E. Mitchell & C. B. Peterson (Eds.), *Assessment of eating disorders* (pp. 79–97). New York, NY: Guilford Press.

Grilo, C. M., Masheb, R. M., Lozano-Blanco, C., & Barry, D. T. (2004). Reliability of the Eating Disorder Examination in patients with binge eating disorder. *International Journal of Eating Disorders, 35*(1), 80–85.

Grilo, C. M., Pagano, M. E., Stout, R. L., Markowitz, J. C., Ansell, E. B., Pinto, A., . . . Skodol, A. E. (2012). Stressful life events predict eating disorder relapse following remission: Six-year prospective outcomes. *International Journal of Eating Disorders, 45*(2), 185–192.

Grucza, R. A., Przybeck, T. R., & Cloninger, C. R. (2007). Prevalence and correlates of binge eating disorder in a community sample. *Journal of Comparative Psychology, 48*(2), 124–131.

Hainer, V., Kabrnova, K., Aldhoon, B., Kunesova, M., & Wagenknecht, M. (2006). Serotonin and norepinephrine reuptake inhibition and eating behavior. *Annals of the New York Academy of Sciences, 1083*(1), 252–269.

Hall, A., & Hay, P. J. (1991). Eating disorder patient referrals from a population region 1977–1986. *Psychological Medicine, 21*(3), 697–701.

Halstead, W. C. (1947). *Brain and intelligence; a quantitative study of the frontal lobes.* Chicago, IL, US: University of Chicago Press.

Hannon-Engel, S. (2012). Regulating satiety in bulimia nervosa: The role of cholecystokinin. *Perspectives in Psychiatric Care, 48*(1), 34–40.

Happé, F. G. E., & Booth, R. D. L. (2008). The power of the positive: Revisiting weak coherence in autism spectrum disorders. *The Quarterly Journal of Experimental Psychology, 61*(1), 50–63.

Hardaway, J. A., Crowley, N. A., Bulik, C. M., & Kash, T. L. (2015). *Integrated circuits and molecular components for stress and feeding: implications for eating disorders* (vol. 14, pp. 85–97). Oxford, UK.

Harris, E. C., & Barraclough, B. (1998). Excess mortality of mental disorder. *British Journal of Psychiatry, 173*, 11–53.

Harrison, A., Sullivan, S., Tchanturia, K., & Treasure, J. (2009). Emotion recognition and regulation in anorexia nervosa. *Clinical Psychology & Psychotherapy, 16*(4), 348–356.

Hay, P. J., Mond, J., Buttner, P., & Darby, A. (2008). Eating disorder behaviors are increasing: findings from two sequential community surveys in South Australia. *PLoS One, 3*(2), e1541.

Heatherton, T. F., & Baumeister, R. F. (1991). Binge eating as escape from self-awareness. *Psychological bulletin, 110*(1), 86.

Heaton, R. K., Chelune, G. J., Talley, J. L., Kay, G. G., & Curtiss, G. (1993): *Wisconsin Card Sorting Test Manual: Revised and Expanded.* Odessa, FL: Psychological Assessment Resources.

Hebebrand, J., Geller, F., Dempfle, A., Heinzel-Gutenbrunner, M., Raab, M., Gerber, G., . . . Hinney, A. (2004). Binge-eating episodes are not characteristic of carriers of melanocortin-4 receptor gene mutations. *Molecular Psychiatry, 9*(8), 796–800.

Hebebrand, J., Himmelmann, G. W., Herzog, W., Herpertz-Dahlmann, B. M., Steinhausen, H. C., Amstein, M., . . . Schäfer, H. (1997). Prediction of low body weight at long-term follow-up in acute anorexia nervosa by low body weight at referral. *American Journal of Psychiatry, 154*(4), 566.

Heinz, E. R., Martinez, J., & Haenggeli, A. (1977). Reversibility of cerebral atrophy in anorexia nervosa and Cushing's syndrome. *Journal of Computer Assisted Tomography, 1*(4), 415.

Hildebrandt, T., Alfano, L., Tricamo, M., & Pfaff, D. W. (2010). Conceptualizing the role of estrogens and serotonin in the development and maintenance of bulimia nervosa. *Clinical Psychology Review, 30*(6), 655–668.

Hoek, H. W. (1991). The incidence and prevalence of anorexia nervosa and bulimia nervosa in primary care. *Psychological Medicine, 21*(2), 455–460.

Hoek, H. W. (2006). Incidence, prevalence and mortality of anorexia nervosa and other eating disorders. *Current Opinion in Psychiatry*, *19*(4), 389–398.

Hoek, H. W., Bartelds, A. I., Bosveld, J. J., van Der Graaf, Y., Limpens, V. E., Maiwald, M., & Spaaij, C. J. (1995). Impact of urbanization on detection rates of eating disorders. *American Journal of Psychiatry*, *152*(9), 1272.

Hoffman, G. W., Ellinwood, E. H., Rockwell, W., Herfkens, R. J., Nishita, J., & Guthrie, L. F. (1989). Cerebral atrophy in bulimia. *Biological Psychiatry*, *25*(7), 894–902.

Hogstrom, L. J., Westlye, L. T., Walhovd, K. B., & Fjell, A. M. (2013). The Structure of the Cerebral Cortex Across Adult Life: Age-Related Patterns of Surface Area, Thickness, and Gyrification. *Cerebral Cortex*, *23*(11), 2521–2530.

Hudson, J. I., Hiripi, E., Pope Jr, H. G., & Kessler, R. C. (2007). The prevalence and correlates of eating disorders in the National Comorbidity Survey Replication. *Biological Psychiatry*, *61*(3), 348–358.

Hudson, J. I., Lalonde, J. K., Berry, J. M., Pindyck, L. J., Bulik, C. M., Crow, S. J., . . . Pope, H. G., Jr. (2006). Binge-eating disorder as a distinct familial phenotype in obese individuals. *Archives of General Psychiatry*, *63*(3), 313–319.

Hudson, J. I., Lalonde, J. K., Coit, C. E., Tsuang, M. T., McElroy, S. L., Crow, S. J., . . . Pope, H. G. (2010). Longitudinal study of the diagnosis of components of the metabolic syndrome in individuals with binge-eating disorder. *The American Journal of Clinical Nutrition*, *91*(6), 1568.

Husain, M. M., Black, K. J., Murali Doraiswamy, P., Shah, S. A., Kenneth Rockwell, W. J., Ellinwood, E. H., & Ranga Rama Krishnan, K. (1992). Subcortical brain anatomy in anorexia and bulimia. *Biological Psychiatry*, *31*(7), 735–738.

Inagaki, T., Horiguchi, J., Tsubouchi, K., Miyaoka, T., Uegaki, J., & Seno, H. (2002). Late onset anorexia nervosa: two case reports. *International Journal of Psychiatry in Medicine*, *32*(1), 91.

Insel, T. R. (2009). Disruptive insights in psychiatry: transforming a clinical discipline. *The Journal of clinical investigation*, *119*(4), 700–705.

Irving, L. (1990). Mirror images: Effects of the standard of beauty on the self- and body-esteem of women exhibiting varying levels of bulimic symptoms. *Journal of Social and Clinical Psychology*, *9*(2), 230–242.

Isomaa, R., Backholm, K., & Birgegård, A. (2015). Posttraumatic stress disorder in eating disorder patients: The roles of psychological distress and timing of trauma. *Psychiatry Research*, *230*(2), 506–510.

Jacobi, C., Hayward, C., de Zwaan, M., Kraemer, H., & Agras, W. (2004). Coming to terms with risk factors for eating disorder: Application of risk terminology and suggestions for a general taxonomy. *Psychological Bulletin*, *130*, 19–65.

Jáuregui-Lobera, I. (2013). Neuropsychology of eating disorders: 1995–2012. *Neuropsychiatric Disease and Treatment*, *9*, 415.

Javaras, K. N., Laird, N. M., Reichborn-Kjennerud, T., Bulik, C. M., Pope, H. G., Jr. & Hudson, J. I. (2008). Familiality and heritability of binge eating disorder: results of a case-control family study and a twin study. *International Journal of Eating Disorders*, *41*(2), 174–179.

Jimerson, D. C., Lesem, M. D., Kaye, W. H., & Brewerton, T. D. (1992). Low serotonin and dopamine metabolite concentrations in cerebrospinal fluid from bulimic patients with frequent binge episodes. *Archives of General Psychiatry*, *49*(2), 132–138.

Jimerson, D. C., & Wolfe, B. E. (2006). Psychobiology of eating disorders. In S. A. Wonderlich, J. Mitchell, M. deZwann& H. Steiger (Eds.), *Annual Review of Eating Disorders, Part 2* (pp. 1–15). Abingdon: Radcliffe Publishing.

Johnson, J. G., Spitzer, R. L., & Williams, J. B. (2001). Health problems, impairment and illnesses associated with bulimia nervosa and binge eating disorder among primary care and obstetric gynaecology patients. *Psychological Medicine*, *31*(8), 1455–1466.

Jones, B. P., Duncan, C. C., Brouwers, P., & Mirsky, A. F. (1991). Cognition in eating disorders. *Journal of Clinical and Experimental Neuropsychology, 13*(5), 711–728.

Jones, D. J., Fox, M. M., Babigian, H. M., & Hutton, H. E. (1980). Epidemiology of anorexia nervosa in Monroe County, New York: 1960–1976. *Psychosomatic Medicine, 42*(6), 551.

Joos, A., Klöppel, S., Hartmann, A., Glauche, V., Tüscher, O., Perlov, E., . . . van Elst, L. T. (2010). Voxel-based morphometry in eating disorders: Correlation of psychopathology with grey matter volume. *Psychiatry Research: Neuroimaging, 182*(2), 146–151.

Kanakam, N., Raoult, C., Collier, D., & Treasure, J. (2013). Set shifting and central coherence as neurocognitive endophenotypes in eating disorders: A preliminary investigation in twins. *The World Journal of Biological Psychiatry, 14*(6), 464–475.

Kaplan, A. S., Garfinkel, P. E., Warsh, J. J., & Brown, G. M. (1989). Clonidine challenge test in bulimia nervosa. *International Journal of Eating Disorders, 8*(4), 425–435.

Katzman, D. K., Lambe, E. K., Mikulis, D. J., Ridgley, J. N., Goldbloom, D. S., & Zipursky, R. B. (1996). Cerebral gray matter and white matter volume deficits in adolescent girls with anorexia nervosa. *The Journal of Pediatrics, 129*(6), 794–803.

Kaye, W. (2008). Neurobiology of anorexia and bulimia nervosa. *Physiology & Behavior, 94*(1), 121–135.

Kaye, W. H., Ballenger, J. C., Lydiard, R. B., Stuart, G. W., Laraia, M. T., O'Neil, P., . . . Hsu, G. (1990). CSF monoamine levels in normal-weight bulimia: evidence for abnormal noradrenergic activity. *American Journal of Psychiatry, 147*(2), 225–229.

Kaye, W. H., Berrettini, W. H., Gwirtsman, H. E., Chretien, M., Gold, P. W., George, D. T., . . . Ebert, M. H. (1987). Reduced cerebrospinal fluid levels of immunoreactive pro-opiomelano-cortin related peptides (including beta-endorphin) in anorexia nervosa. *Life Science, 41*(18), 2147–2155.

Kaye, W. H., Bulik, C. M., Thornton, L., Barbarich, N., & Masters, K. (2004). Comorbidity of anxiety disorders with anorexia and bulimia nervosa. *American Journal of Psychiatry, 161*(2), 2215–2221.

Kaye, W. H., Frank, G. K., & McConaha, C. (1999). Altered dopamine activity after recovery from restricting-type anorexia nervosa. *Neuropsychopharmacology, 21*(4), 503–506.

Kaye, W. H., Frank, G. K., Meltzer, C. C., Price, J. C., McConaha, C. W., Crossan, P. J., . . . Rhodes, L. (2001). Altered serotonin 2A receptor activity in women who have recovered from bulimia nervosa. *American Journal of Psychiatry, 158*(7), 1152–1155.

Kaye, W. H., Fudge, J. L., & Paulus, M. (2009). New insights into symptoms and neurocircuit function of anorexia nervosa. *Nature Reviews Neuroscience, 10*(8), 573–584.

Kaye, W. H., Wierenga, C. E., Bailer, U. F., Simmons, A. N., & Bischoff-Grethe, A. (2013). Nothing tastes as good as skinny feels: the neurobiology of anorexia nervosa. *Trends in Neurosciences, 36*(2), 110–120.

Kazuhiko, N., Gen, K., Atsushi, T., Tetsuya, A., Mayuko, I., Junko, N., . . . Senji, S. (2009). Identification of novel candidate loci for anorexia nervosa at 1q41 and 11q22 in Japanese by a genome-wide association analysis with microsatellite markers. *Journal of Human Genetics, 54*(9), 531.

Keel, P. K. (2001). Basic counseling techniques. In J. E. Mitchell (Ed.), *The Outpatient Treatment of Eating Disorders: A Guide for Therapists, Dietitians, and Physicians* (pp. 119–143). Minneapolis, MN: University of Minnesota Press.

Keel, P. K., Gravener, J. A., Joiner, T. E., & Haedt, A. A. (2010). Twenty-year follow-up of bulimia nervosa and related eating disorders not otherwise specified. *International Journal of Eating Disorders, 43*(6), 492–497.

Kemps, E., Tiggemann, M., & Marshall, K. (2005). Relationship between dieting to lose weight and the functioning of the central executive. *Appetite, 45*(3), 287–294.

Kessler, R. C., Berglund, P. A., Chiu, W. T., Deitz, A. C., Hudson, J. I., Shahly, V., . . . Benjet, C. (2013). The prevalence and correlates of binge eating disorder in the World Health Organization World Mental Health Surveys. *Biological Psychiatry.*

King, J. A., Geisler, D., Ritschel, F., Boehm, I., Seidel, M., Roschinski, B., . . . Ehrlich, S. (2015). Global cortical thinning in acute anorexia nervosa normalizes following long-term weight restoration. *Biological Psychiatry, 77*(7), 624–632.

Kingston, K., Szmukler, G., Andrewes, D., Tress, B., & Desmond, P. (1996). Neuropsychological and structural brain changes in anorexia nervosa before and after refeeding. *Psychological Medicine, 26*(1), 15–28.

Klump, K. L., Bulik, C. M., Pollice, C., Halmi, K. A., Fichter, M. M., Berrettini, W. H., . . . Kaye, W. H. (2000). Temperament and character in women with anorexia nervosa. *Journal of Nervous & Mental Disorders, 188*(9), 559–567.

Klump, K. L., Miller, K. B., Keel, P. K., McGue, M., & Iacono, W. G. (2001). Genetic and environmental influences on anorexia nervosa syndromes in a population-based twin sample. *Psychological Medicine, 31*, 737–740.

Klump, K. L., Wonderlich, S., Lehoux, P., Lilenfeld, L. R., & Bulik, C. M. (2002). Does environment matter? A review of nonshared environment and eating disorders. *International Journal of Eating Disorders, 31*(2), 118–135.

Koba, T., Horie, S., & Nabeta, Y. (2002). Impaired performance on Wisconsin card sorting test in patients with eating disorders: A preliminary study. *Seishin Igaku, 44*, 681–683.

Kohn, M. R., Golden, N. H., & Shenker, I. R. (1998). Cardiac arrest and delirium: Presentations of the refeeding syndrome in severely malnourished adolescents with anorexia nervosa. *Journal of Adolescent Health, 22*(3), 239–243.

Kortegaard, L. S., Hoerder, K., Joergensen, J., Gillberg, C., & Kyvik, K. O. (2001). A preliminary population-based twin study of self-reported eating disorder. *Psychological Medicine, 31*(2), 361–365.

Kravariti, E., Morris, R. G., Rabe-Hesketh, S., Murray, R. M., & Frangou, S. (2003). The Maudsley early onset schizophrenia study: cognitive function in adolescents with recent onset schizophrenia. *Schizophrenia Research, 61*(2), 137–148.

Krebs-Thomson, K., & Geyer, M. A. (1998). Evidence for a functional interaction between 5-HT1A and 5-HT2 receptors in rats. *Psychopharmacology, 140*(1), 69–74.

Krieg, J.-C., Lauer, C., & Pirke, K.-M. (1989). Structural brain abnormalities in patients with bulimia nervosa. *Psychiatry Research, 27*(1), 39–48.

Kutlesic, V., Williamson, D. A., Gleaves, D. H., Barbin, J. M., & Murphy-Eberenz, K. P. (1998). The Interview for the Diagnosis of Eating Disorders--IV: Application to DSM-IV Diagnostic Criteria. *Psychological Assessment, 10*(1), 41–48.

Lang, K., Lopez, C., Stahl, D., Tchanturia, K., & Treasure, J. (2014a). Central coherence in eating disorders: an updated systematic review and meta-analysis. *The World Journal of Biological Psychiatry, 15*(8), 586.

Lang, K., Stahl, D., Espie, J., Treasure, J., & Tchanturia, K. (2014b). Set shifting in children and adolescents with anorexia nervosa: An exploratory systematic review and meta-analysis. *International Journal of Eating Disorders, 47*(4), 394–399.

Lankenau, H., Swigar, M. E., Bhimani, S., Quinlan, D. M., & Luchins, D. (1985). Cranial CT scans in eating disorder patients and controls. *Comprehensive Psychiatry, 26*(2), 136–147.

Lauer, C. J. (2002). Neuropsychological findings in eating disorders. In H. D'Haenen, J. A. den Boer & P. Willner (Eds.), *Biological Psychiatry* (pp. 1167–1172). Swansea, UK: Wiley.

Lee, S. H., Ripke, S., Neale, B. M., Faraone, S. V., Purcell, S. M., Perlis, R. H., . . . Asherson, P. (2013). Genetic relationship between five psychiatric disorders estimated from genome-wide SNPs. *Nature Genetics, 45*(9), 984–994.

Lee, Y., & Lin, P. Y. (2010). Association between serotonin transporter gene polymorphism and eating disorders: A meta-analytic study. *International Journal of Eating Disorders, 43*(6), 498–504.

Lee, Y. H., Abbott, D. W., Seim, H., Crosby, R. D., Monson, N., Burgard, M., & Mitchell, J. E. (1999). Eating disorders and psychiatric disorders in the first-degree relatives of obese probands with binge eating disorder and obese non-binge eating disorder controls. *International Journal of Eating Disorders, 26*(3), 322–332.

Lesem, M. D., Berrettini, W. H., Kaye, W. H., & Jimerson, D. C. (1991). Measurement of CSF dynorphin A 1–8 immunoreactivity in anorexia nervosa and normal-weight bulimia. *Biological Psychiatry, 29*(3), 244–252.

Levine, M. P., & Harrison, K. (2004). The role of mass media in the perpetuation and prevention of negative body image and disordered eating. *Handbook of Eating Disorders and Obesity* (pp. 695–717). Hoboken, NJ: John Wiley & Sons Inc.

Lee-Winn, A., Mendelson, T., & Mojtabai, R. (2014). Racial/ethnic disparities in binge eating: Disorder prevalence, symptom presentation, and help-seeking among Asian Americans and non-Latino Whites. *American Journal of Public Health, 104*(7), 1263–1265.

Lewinsohn, P. M., Seeley, J. R., Moerk, K. C., & Striegel-Moore, R. H. (2002). Gender differences in eating disorder symptoms in young adults. *International Journal of Eating Disorders, 32*(4), 426–440.

Lezak, M. D., Howieson, D. B., & Loring, D. W. (2004). *Neuropsychological Assessment*, Fourth Edition. New York: Oxford University Press.

Licinio, J., Wong, M.-L., & Gold, P. W. (1996). The hypothalamic-pituitary-adrenal axis in anorexia nervosa. *Psychiatry Research, 62*(1), 75–83.

Lilenfeld, L. R., Kaye, W. H., Greeno, C. G., Merikangas, K. R., Plotnicov, K., Pollice, C., . . . Nagy, L. (1998). A controlled family study of anorexia nervosa and bulimia nervosa: psychiatric disorders in first-degree relatives and effects of proband comorbidity. *Archives of General Psychiatry, 55*(7), 603–610.

Little, J. W. (2002). Eating disorders; Dental implications. *Oral Surg Oral Med Oral Pathol Oral Radiol Endod, 93*, 138–43.

Lock, J., LeGrange, D., Agras, W. S., & Dare, C. (2001). *Treatment manual for anorexia nervosa: A family-based approach*. New York, NY: Guilford Press.

Lopez, C., Tchanturia, K., Stahl, D., Booth, R., Holliday, J., & Treasure, J. (2008a). An examination of the concept of central coherence in women with anorexia nervosa. *International Journal of Eating Disorders, 41*(2), 143–152.

Lopez, C., Tchanturia, K., Stahl, D., & Treasure, J. (2008b). Central coherence in eating disorders: a systematic review. *Psychological Medicine, 38*(10), 1393–1404.

Lopez, C., Tchanturia, K., Stahl, D., & Treasure, J. (2009). Weak central coherence in eating disorders: A step towards looking for an endophenotype of eating disorders. *Journal of Clinical and Experimental Neuropsychology, 31*(1), 117–125.

Lopez, C. A., Tchanturia, K., Stahl, D., & Treasure, J. (2008c). Central coherence in women with bulimia nervosa. *International Journal of Eating Disorders, 41*(4), 340–347.

Loth, K., van den Berg, P., Eisenberg, M. E., & Neumark-Sztainer, D. (2008). Stressful life events and disordered eating behaviors: findings from Project EAT. *Journal of Adolescent Health, 43*(5), 514–516.

Lucas, A. R., Beard, C. M., O'Fallon, W. M., & Kurland, L. T. (1988). Anorexia nervosa in Rochester, Minnesota: A 45-year study. *Mayo Clinic Proceedings, 63*(5), 433–442.

Lucas, A. R., Crowson, C. S., O'Fallon, W. M., & Melton, L. J. (1999). The ups and downs of anorexia nervosa. *International Journal of Eating Disorders, 26*(4), 397–405.

Manasse, S. M., Forman, E. M., Ruocco, A. C., Butryn, M. L., Juarascio, A. S., & Fitzpatrick, K. K. (2015). Do executive functioning deficits underpin binge eating disorder? A comparison of overweight women with and without binge eating pathology. *International Journal of Eating Disorders, 48*(6), 677–683.

Mancilla-Díaz, J. M., Escartín-Pérez, R. E., López-Alonso, V. E., & Cruz-Morales, S. E. (2002). Effect of 5-HT in mianserin-pretreated rats on the structure of feeding behavior. *European Neuropsychopharmacology, 12*(5), 445–451.

Mancuso, S. G., Newton, J. R., Bosanac, P., Rossell, S. L., Nesci, J. B., & Castle, D. J. (2015). Classification of eating disorders: Comparison of relative prevalence rates using DSM-IV and DSM-5 criteria. *The British Journal of Psychiatry, 206*(6), 519.

Mangweth-Matzek, B., Rupp, C. I., Hausmann, A., Assmayr, K., Mariacher, E., Kemmler, G., . . . Biebl, W. (2006). Never too old for eating disorders or body dissatisfaction: A community study of elderly women. *International Journal of Eating Disorders, 39*, 583–586.

Mannucci, E., Tesi, F., Ricca, V., Pierazzuoli, E., Barciulli, E., Moretti, S., . . . Rotella, C. M. (2002). Eating behavior in obese patients with and without type 2 diabetes mellitus. *International Journal of Obesity, 26*(6), 848–853.

Marcus, M. D. (1995). Cognitive treatment of binge eating versus behavioral weight control in the treatment of binge eating disorder. *Annals of Behavioral Medicine, 17*, S090.

Marcus, M. D., Bromberger, J. T., Wei, H. L., Brown, C., & Kravitz, H. M. (2007). Prevalence and selected correlates of eating disorder symptoms among a multiethnic community sample of midlife women. *Annals of Behavioral Medicine, 33*(3), 269–277.

Marques, L., Alegria, M., Becker, A. E., Chen, C., Fang, A., Chosak, A., & Diniz, J. B. (2010). Comparative prevalence, correlates of impairment, and service utilization for eating disorder across US ethnic groups: Implications for reducing ethnic disparities in health care access for eating disorders. *International Journal of Eating Disorders, 44*(5), 412–420.

Marsh, R., Stefan, M., Bansal, R., Hao, X., Walsh, B. T., & Peterson, B. S. (2015). Anatomical characteristics of the cerebral surface in bulimia nervosa. *Biological Psychiatry, 77*(7), 616.

Mascolo, M., Trent, S., Colwell, C., & Mehler, P. S. (2012). What the emergency department needs to know when caring for your patients with eating disorders. *International Journal of Eating Disorders, 45*(8), 977–981.

Mathes, W. F., Brownley, K. A., Mo, X., & Bulik, C. M. (2009). The biology of binge eating. *Appetite, 52*(3), 545–553.

Mathias, J. L., & Kent, P. S. (1998). Neuropsychological consequences of extreme weight loss and dietary restriction in patients with anorexia nervosa. *Journal of Clinical and Experimental Neuropsychology, 20*(4), 548–564.

Matthias, R. (2005). Care provision for patients with eating disorders in Europe: what patients get what treatment where? *European Eating Disorders Review, 13*(3), 159–168.

McKenzie, J. M., & Joyce, P. R. (1992). Hospitalization for anorexia nervosa. *International Journal of Eating Disorders, 11*(3), 235–241.

Mehler, P. S., & Mackenzie, T. D. (2009). Treatment of osteopenia and osteoporosis in anorexia nervosa: A systematic review of the literature. *International Journal of Eating Disorders, 42*(3), 195–201.

Micali, N., Simonoff, E., & Treasure, J. (2007). Risk of major adverse perinatal outcomes in women with eating disorders. *The British Journal of Psychiatry, 190*, 255.

Micali, N., & Treasure, J. (2009). Biological effects of a maternal ED on pregnancy and foetal development: a review. *European Eating Disorders Review, 17*(6), 448–454.

Mikołajczyk, E., Grzywacz, A., & Samochowiec, J. (2010). The association of catechol- O-methyltransferase genotype with the phenotype of women with eating disorders. *Brain Research, 1307*, 142–148.

Miller, W. R., & Rollnick, S. (2002). *Motivational interviewing: Preparing people for change.* New York, NY: Guilford Press.

Mitchell, J. E., & Crow, S. (2006). Medical complications of anorexia nervosa and bulimia nervosa. *Current Opinion in Psychiatry, 19*(4), 438.

Mitchell, K. S., Mazzeo, S. E., Schlesinger, M. R., Brewerton, T. D., & Smith, B. N. (2012). Comorbidity of partial and subthreshold ptsd among men and women with eating disorders in the national comorbidity survey-replication study. *International Journal of Eating Disorders, 45*(3), 307–315.

Mitchell, K. S., Neale, M. C., Bulik, C. M., Aggen, S. H., Kendler, K. S., & Mazzeo, S. E. (2010). Binge eating disorder: A symptom-level investigation of genetic and evnironmental influences on liability. *Psychological Medicine, 40,* 1899–1906.

Miyake, A., Friedman, N. P., Emerson, M. J., Witzki, A. H., Howerter, A., & Wager, T. D. (2000). The unity and diversity of executive functions and their contributions to complex "Frontal Lobe" tasks: a latent variable analysis. *Cognitive Psychology, 41,* 49–100.

Miyasaka, K., Hosoya, H., Sekime, A., Ohta, M., Amono, H., Matsushita, S., . . . Funakoshi, A. (2006). Association of ghrelin receptor gene polymorphism with bulimia nervosa in a Japanese population. *Journal of Neural Transmission, 113*(9), 1279–1285.

Møller-Madsen, S., & Nystrup, J. (1992). Incidence of anorexia nervosa in Denmark. *Acta Psychiatrica Scandinavica, 86*(3), 197–200.

Montague, P. R., Hyman, S. E., & Cohen, J. D. (2004). Computational roles for dopamine in behavioural control. *Nature, 431*(7010), 760.

Monteleone, P. (2011). New frontiers in endocrinology of eating disorders. *Current Topics in Behavioral Neuroscience, 6,* 189–208.

Monteleone, P., Brambilla, F., Bortolotti, F., Ferraro, C., & Maj, M. (1998). Plasma prolactin response to d -fenfluramine is blunted in bulimic patients with frequent binge episodes. *Psychological Medicine, 28*(4), 975–983.

Monteleone, P., Fabrazzo, M., Tortorella, A., Martiadis, V., Serritella, C., & Maj, M. (2005). Circulating ghrelin is decreased in non-obese and obese women with binge eating disorder as well as in obese non-binge eating women, but not in patients with bulimia nervosa. *Psychoneuroendocrinology, 30*(3), 243–250.

Monteleone, P., & Maj, M. (2013). Dysfunctions of leptin, ghrelin, BDNF and endocannabinoids in eating disorders: Beyond the homeostatic control of food intake. *Psychoneuroendocrinology, 38*(3), 312–330.

Monteleone, P., Tortorella, A., Castaldo, E., Di Filippo, C., & Maj, M. (2007). The Leu72Met polymorphism of the ghrelin gene is significantly associated with binge eating disorder. *Psychiatric Genetics, 17*(1), 13–16.

Monteleone, P., Tortorella, A., Castaldo, E., & Maj, M. (2006). Association of a functional serotonin transporter gene polymorphism with binge eating disorder. *American Journal of Medical Genetics Part B, 141B*(1), 7–9.

Morton, G. J., Cummings, D. E., Baskin, D. G., Barsh, G. S., & Schwartz, M. W. (2006). Central nervous system control of food intake and body weight. *Nature, 443*(7109), 289.

Munsch, S., Biedert, E., Meyer, A. H., Herpertz, S., & Beglinger, C. (2009). CCK, ghrelin, and PYY responses in individuals with binge eating disorder before and after a cognitive behavioral treatment (CBT). *Physiology & Behavior, 97*(1), 14–20.

Nicdao, E. G., Hong, S., & Takeuchi, D. T. (2007). Prevalence and correlates of eating disorders among Asian Americans: results from the National Latino and Asian American Study. *International Journal of Eating Disorders, 40 Suppl,* S22–26.

NICE. (2004). *Eating disorders: Core interventions in the treatment and management of anorexia nervosa, bulimia nervosa and related eating disorders* (Vol CG9). London: National Institute for Health and Clinical Excellence.

Nisoli, E., Brunani, A., Borgomainerio, E., Tonello, C., Dioni, L., Briscini, L., . . . Carruba, M. (2007). D2 dopamine receptor (DRD2) gene Taq1A polymorphism and the eatingrelated psychological traits in eating disorders (anorexia nervosa and bulimia) and obesity. *Official Journal of the Italian Society for the Study of Eating Disorders (SISDCA), 12*(2), 91–96.

Nussbaum, M., Shenker, I. R., Marc, J., & Klein, M. (1980). Cerebral atrophy in anorexia nervosa. *The Journal of Pediatrics*, 96(5), 867–869.

O'Hara, C. B., Campbell, I. C., & Schmidt, U. (2015). A reward-centred model of anorexia nervosa: A focussed narrative review of the neurological and psychophysiological literature. *Neuroscience and Biobehavioral Reviews*, 52, 131–152.

Ogren, F. P., Huerter, J. V., Pearson, P. H., Antonson, C. W., & Moore, G. F. (1987). Transient salivary gland hypertrophy in bulimics. *Laryngoscope*, 97(8), 951–953.

Oldershaw, A., Treasure, J., Hambrook, D., Tchanturia, K., & Schmidt, U. (2011). Is anorexia nervosa a version of autism spectrum disorders? *European Eating Disorders Review*, 19(6), 462–474.

Ornstein, R. M., Golden, N. H., Jacobson, M. S., & Shenker, I. R. (2003). Hypophosphatemia during nutritional rehabilitation in anorexia nervosa: implications for refeeding and monitoring. *Journal of Adolescent Health*, 32(1), 83–88.

Palmer, R. L. (2003). Death in anorexia nervosa. *The Lancet*, 361(9368), 1490–1490.

Pawluck, D. E., & Gorey, K. M. (1998). Secular trends in the incidence of anorexia nervosa: integrative review of population-based studies. *The International Journal of Eating Disorders*, 23(4), 347.

Peat, C. M., Brownley, K. A., Berkman, N. D., & Bulik, C. M. (2012). Binge eating disorder: Evidence-based treatments. *Current Psychiatry*, 11(5), 32–39.

Perez, M., Joiner, T. E., & Lewinsohn, P. M. (2004). Is major depressive disorder or dysthymia more strongly associated with bulimia nervosa? *International Journal of Eating Disorders*, 36(1), 55–61.

Peterson, C. B. (2005). Conducting the diagnostic interview. In J. E. Mitchell & C. B. Peterson (Eds.), *Assessment of eating disorders* (pp. 98–119). New York, NY: Guilford Press.

Peterson, C. B., & Mitchell, J. E. (2005). Self-report measures. In J. E. Mitchell & C. B. Peterson (Eds.), *Assessment of eating disorders* (pp. 98–119). New York: The Guilford Press.

Pike, K. M., Wilfley, D., Hilbert, A., Fairburn, C. G., Dohm, F. A., & Striegel-Moore, R. H. (2006). Antecedent life events of binge-eating disorder. *Psychiatry Research*, 142(1), 19–29.

Polivy, J., & Herman, C. P. (1985). Dieting and binging. A causal analysis. *American Psychologist*, 40(2), 193–201.

Polsinelli, G. N., Levitan, R. N., & De Luca, V. (2012). 5-HTTLPR polymorphism in bulimia nervosa: a multiple-model meta-analysis. *Psychiatric Genetics*, 22(5), 219.

Pumariega, A. J. (1986). Acculturation and eating attitudes in adolescent girls: A comparative and correlational study. *Journal of the American Academy of Child Psychiatry*, 25(2), 276–279.

Raffi, A. R., Rondini, M., Grandi, S., & Fava, G. A. (2000). Life events and prodromal symptoms in bulimia nervosa. *Psychological Medicine*, 30(3), 727.

Reitan, R. M. (1958). Validity of the Trail Making Test as an indicator of organic brain damage. *Perceptual and Motor Skills*, 8(3), 271–276.

Reyes-Rodríguez, M. L., Ramírez, J., Davis, K., Patrice, K., & Bulik, C. M. (2013). Exploring barriers and facilitators in eating disorders treatment among Latinas in the United States. *Journal of Latina/o Psychology*, 1(2), 112–131.

Reyes-Rodríguez, M. L., Von Holle, A., Ulman, T. F., Thornton, L. M., Klump, K. L., Brandt, H., . . . Huber, T. (2011). Posttraumatic stress disorder in anorexia nervosa. *Psychosomatic Medicine*, 73(6), 491–497.

Reyes-Rodríguez, M. L., Franko, D. L., Matos-Lamourt, A., Bulik, C. M., Von Holle, A., Cámara-Fuentes, L. R., . . . Suárez-Torres, A. (2010). Eating disorder symptomatology: Prevalence among Latino college freshmen students. *Journal of Clinical Psychology*, 66(6), 666–679.

Ricca, V., Mannucci, E., Mezzani, B., Bernardo, M., Zucchi, T., Paionni, A., . . . Faravelli, C. (2001). Psychopathological and clinical features of outpatients with an eating disorder not otherwise specified. *Official Journal of the Italian Society for the Study of Eating Disorders (SISDCA)*, 6(3), 157–165.

Rizvi, S. L., Peterson, C. B., Crow, S. J., & Agras, W. S. (2000). Test-retest reliability of the eating disorder examination. *International Journal of Eating Disorders, 28*(3), 311.

Robbins, T. W., James, M., Owen, A. M., Sahakian, B. J., Lawrence, A. D., McInnes, L., & Rabbitt, P. M. A. (1998). A study of performance on tests from the CANTAB battery sensitive to frontal lobe dysfunction in a large sample of normal volunteers: Implications for theories of executive functioning and cognitive aging. *Journal of the International Neuropsychological Society, 4*(5), 474–490.

Roberto, C. A., Mayer, L. E. S., Brickman, A. M., Barnes, A., Muraskin, J., Yeung, L.-K., . . . Walsh, B. T. (2011). Brain tissue volume changes following weight gain in adults with anorexia nervosa. *The International Journal of Eating Disorders, 44*(5), 406.

Roberts, M. E., Tchanturia, K., Stahl, D., Southgate, L., & Treasure, J. (2007). A systematic review and meta-analysis of set-shifting ability in eating disorders. *Psychological Medicine, 37*(8), 1075.

Robins, L. N., Helzer, J. E., Croughan, J., & Ratcliff, K. S. (1981). National Institute of Mental Health diagnostic interview schedule: Its history, characteristics, and validity. *Archives of General Psychiatry, 38*(4), 381.

Robinson, T. N., Killen, J. D., Litt, I. F., Hammer, L. D., Wilson, D. M., Haydel, K. F., . . . Taylor, C. B. (1996). Ethnicity and body dissatisfaction: Are Hispanic and Asian girls at increased risk for eating disorders. *Journal of Adolescent Health, 19*(6), 384–393.

Rosen, D. S. (2010). Identification and management of eating disorders in children and adolescents. *Pediatrics, 126*(6), 1240.

Rosenblum, J., & Forman, S. F. (2003). Management of anorexia nervosa with exercise and selective serotonergic reuptake inhibitors. *Current Opinion in Pediatrics, 15*(3), 346.

Schacter, D. L. (1999). The seven sins of memory. Insights from psychology and cognitive neuroscience. *The American Psychologist, 54*(3), 182–203.

Schäfer, A., Vaitl, D., & Schienle, A. (2010). Regional grey matter volume abnormalities in bulimia nervosa and binge-eating disorder. *Neuorimage, 50,* 639–643.

Scherag, S., Hebebrand, J., & Hinney, A. (2010). Eating disorders: the current status of molecular genetic research. *European Child & Adolescent Psychiatry, 19*(3), 211–226.

Schmidt, U. H., Troop, N. A., & Treasure, J. L. (1999). Events and the onset of eating disorders: Correcting an "age old" myth. *International Journal of Eating Disorders, 25*(1), 83–88.

Sen, S., Villafuerte, S., Nesse, R., Stoltenberg, S. F., Hopcian, J., Gleiberman, L., . . . Burmeister, M. (2004). Serotonin transporter and GABA(A) alpha 6 receptor variants are associated with neuroticism. *Biological Psychiatry, 55*(3), 244–249.

Shea, M., Cachelin, F., Uribe, L., Striegel, R. H., Thompson, D., & Wilson, G. T. (2012). Cultural adaptation of a cognitive behavior therapy guided self-help program for Mexican American women With binge eating disorders. *Journal of Counseling & Development, 90*(3), 308–318.

Shinohara, M., Mizushima, H., Hirano, M., Shioe, K., Nakazawa, M., Hiejima, Y., . . . Kanba, S. (2004). Eating disorders with binge-eating behaviour are associated with the s allele of the 3'-UTR VNTR polymorphism of the dopamine transporter gene. *Journal of Psychiatry and Neuroscience, 29*(2), 134–137.

Slof-Op't Landt, M. C. T., van Furth, E. F., Meulenbelt, I., Slagboom, P. E., Bartels, M., Boomsma, D. I., & al., e. (2005). Eating disorders: From twin studies to candidate genes and beyond. *Twin Research and Human Genetics, 8,* 467–482.

Smink, F., van Hoeken, D., & Hoek, H. (2012). Epidemiology of eating disorders: Incidence, prevalence and mortality rates. *Current Psychiatry Reports, 14*(4), 406–414.

Smink, F. R. E., Hoeken, D., Oldehinkel, A. J., & Hoek, H. W. (2014). Prevalence and severity of DSM-5 eating disorders in a community cohort of adolescents. *International Journal of Eating Disorders, 47*(6), 610–619.

Smyth, J. M., Heron, K. E., Wonderlich, S. A., Crosby, R. D., & Thompson, K. M. (2008). The influence of reported trauma and adverse events on eating disturbance in young adults. *International Journal of Eating Disorders, 41*(3), 195–202.

Solmi, M., Gallicchio, D., Collantoni, E., Correll, C. U., Clementi, M., Pinato, C., . . . Favaro, A. (2016). Serotonin transporter gene polymorphism in eating disorders: Data from a new biobank and META-analysis of previous studies. *The World Journal of Biological Psychiatry, 17*(4), 244–257.

Southgate, L., Tchanturia, K., & Treasure, J. (2008). Information processing bias in anorexia nervosa. *Psychiatry Research, 160*(2), 221–227.

Spitzer, R. L., Stunkard, A., Yanovski, S., Marcus, M. D., Wadden, T., Wing, R., . . . Hasin, D. (1993). Binge eating disorder should be included in DSM-IV: A reply to Fairburn et al.'s "The classification of recurrent overeating: The binge eating disorder proposal". *International Journal of Eating Disorders, 13*(2), 161–169.

Steiger, H. (2004). Eating disorders and the serotonin connection: state, trait and developmental effects. *Journal of Psychiatry and Neuroscience, 29*(1), 20.

Steiger, H., Gauvin, L., Israel, M., Kin, N. M., Young, S. N., & Roussin, J. (2004). Serotonin function, personality-trait variations, and childhood abuse in women with bulimia-spectrum eating disorders. *Journal of Clinical Psychiatry, 65*(6), 830–837.

Steinglass, J. E., Walsh, B. T., & Stern, Y. (2006). Set shifting deficit in anorexia nervosa. *Journal of the International Neuropsychological Society, 12*(03), 431–435.

Striegel-Moore, R. H., & Bulik, C. M. (2007). Risk factors for eating disorders. *American Psychologist, 62*(3), 181–198.

Striegel-Moore, R. H., Cachelin, F. M., Dohm, F. A., Pike, K. M., Wilfley, D. E., & Fairburn, C. G. (2001). Comparison of binge eating disorder and bulimia nervosa in a community sample. *International Journal of Eating Disorders, 29*(2), 157–165.

Striegel-Moore, R. H., Dohm, F. A., Kraemer, H. C., Taylor, C. B., Daniels, S., Crawford, P. B., & Schreiber, G. B. (2003). Eating disorders in White and Black women. *American Journal of Psychiatry, 160*(7), 1326–1331.

Striegel-Moore, R. H., Leslie, D., & Petrill, S. A. (2000a). One-year use and cost of inpatient and outpatient services among female and male patients with an eating disorder: Evidence from a national database of health insurance claims. *International Journal of Eating Disorders, 27,* 381–389.

Striegel-Moore, R. H., Silberstein, L. R., & Rodin, J. (1986). Toward an understanding of risk factors for bulimia. *American Psychology, 41*(3), 246–263.

Striegel-Moore, R. H., Wilfley, D. E., Pike, K. M., Dohm, F. A., & Fairburn, C. G. (2000b). Recurrent binge eating in Black American women. *Archives of Family Medicine, 9,* 83–87.

Strober, M., Freeman, R., Lampert, C., Diamond, J., & Kaye, W. (2000). Controlled family study of anorexia nervosa and bulimia nervosa: Evidence of shared liability and transmission of partial syndromes. *American Journal of Psychiatry, 157,* 393–401.

Stunkard, A. (1959). Eating patterns and obesity. *Psychiatric Quarterly, 33*(2), 284–295.

Stunkard, A. J., & Messick, S. (1985). Three-factor eating questionnaire to measure dietary restraint, disinhibition and hunger. *Journal of Psychosomatic Research, 29*(1), 71–83.

Suisman, J. L., Alexandra Burt, S., McGue, M., Iacono, W. G., & Klump, K. L. (2011). Parental divorce and disordered eating: An investigation of a gene-environment interaction. *International Journal of Eating Disorders, 44*(2), 169–177.

Sullivan, P. F., Bulik, C. M., Fear, J. L., & Pickering, A. (1998). Outcome of anorexia nervosa: a case-control study. *American Journal of Psychiatry, 155*(7), 939–946.

Surguladze, S. (1995). Insight and characteristics of fixed set in patients with schizophrenia. *Journal of Georgian Medicine, 2,* 59–60.

Sysko, R., Glasofer, D. R., Hildebrandt, T., Klimek, P., Mitchell, J. E., Berg, K. C., . . . Walsh, B. T. (2015). The eating disorder assessment for DSM-5 (EDA-5): Development and validation of a structured interview for feeding and eating disorders. *International Journal of Eating Disorders*, *48*(5), 452–463.

Szczypka, M. S., Rainey, M. A., & Palmiter, R. D. (2000). Dopamine is required for hyperphagia in Lepob/ob mice. *Nature Genetics*, *25*(1), 102.

Szmukler, G. I., Andrewes, D., Kingston, K., Chen, L., Stargatt, R., & Stanley, R. (1992). Neuropsychological impairment in anorexia nervosa: Before and after refeeding. *Journal of Clinical and Experimental Neuropsychology*, *14*(2), 347–352.

Taylor, J. Y., Caldwell, C. H., Baser, R. E., Faison, N., & Jackson, J. S. (2007). Prevalence of eating disorders among Blacks in the National Survey of American Life. *International Journal of Eating Disorders*, *40*, 10–14.

Tchanturia, K., Davies, H., Roberts, M., Harrison, A., Nakazato, M., Schmidt, U., . . . Morris, R. (2012). Poor cognitive flexibility in eating disorders: Examining the evidence using the Wisconsin Card Sorting Task. *PLoS One*, *7*(1), e28331.

Tchanturia, K., Morris, R., Anderluh, M. B., Collier, D. A., Nikolaou, V., & Treasure, J. (2004). Set shifting in anorexia nervosa: An examination before and after weight gain, in full recovery and relationship to childhood and adult OCPD traits. *Journal of Psychiatric Research*, *38*(5), 545–552.

Thomas, J. J., Eddy, K. T., Murray, H. B., Tromp, M. D. P., Hartmann, A. S., Stone, M. T., . . . Becker, A. E. (2015). The impact of revised DSM-5 criteria on the relative distribution and inter-rater reliability of eating disorder diagnoses in a residential treatment setting. *Psychiatry Research*, *229*(1–2), 517–523.

Thomas, J. J., & Roberto, C. A. (2015). Assessment measures, then and now. In B. T. Walsh, E. Attia, D. R. Glasofer & R. Sysko (Eds.), *Handbook of assessment and treatment of eating disorders*. Arlington, VA: American Psychiatric Association.

Thompson-Brenner, H., Franko, D. L., Thompson, D. R., Grilo, C. M., Boisseau, C. L., Roehrig, J. P., . . . Wilson, G. T. (2013). Race/ethnicity, education, and treatment parameters as moderators and predictors of outcome in binge eating disorder. *Journal of Consulting and Clinical Psychology*, *81*(4), 710–721.

Thompson, J. K., Coovert, M. D., Richards, K. J., Johnson, S., & Cattarin, J. (1995). Development of body image, eating disturbance, and general psychological functioning in female adolescents: Covariance structure modeling and longitudinal investigations. *International Journal of Eating Disorders*, *18*, 221–236.

Thompson, J. K., & Heinberg, L. J. (1993). Preliminary test of two hypotheses of body image disturbance. *International Journal of Eating Disorders*, *14*(1), 59–63.

Thompson, J. K., & Spana, R. E. (1991). Visuospatial ability, accuracy of size estimation, and bulimic disturbance in a noneating-disordered college sample: a neuropsychological analysis. *Perceptual and Motor Skills*, *73*(1), 335.

Titova, O. E., Hjorth, O. C., Schiöth, H. B., & Brooks, S. J. (2013). Anorexia nervosa is linked to reduced brain structure in reward and somatosensory regions: a meta-analysis of VBM studies. *BMC Psychiatry*, *13*, 110–110.

Trace, S. E., Baker, J. H., Peas-Lled, E., & Bulik, C. M. (2013). The genetics of eating disorders. *Annual Review of Clinical Psychology*, *9*, 589–620.

Treasure, J., & Campbell, I. (1994). The case for biology in the aetiology of anorexia nervosa. *Psychological Medicine*, *24*, 3–8.

Trent, S. A., Moreira, M. E., Colwell, C. B., & Mehler, P. S. (2013). ED management of patients with eating disorders. *The American Journal of Emergency Medicine*, *31*(5), 859.

Turner, H., & Bryant-Waugh, R. (2004). Eating disorder not otherwise specified (EDNOS): profiles of clients presenting at a community eating disorder service. *European Eating Disorders Review*, *12*(1), 18–26.

Túry, F., Güleç, H., & Kohls, E. (2010). Assessment methods for eating disorders and body image disorders. *Journal of Psychosomatic Research*, *69*(6), 601–611.

Twamley, E. W., & Davis, M. C. (1999). The sociocultural model of eating disturbances in young women: The effects of personal attributes and family environment. *Journal of Social and Clinical Psychology, 18*(4), 467–489.

Uznadze, D. N. (1966). *The psychology of set.* New York, NY: Consultants' Bureau.

Van Den Eynde, F., Samarawickrema, N., Kenyon, M., Dejong, H., Lavender, A., Startup, H., & Schmidt, U. (2012). A study of neurocognition in bulimia nervosa and eating disorder not otherwise specified–bulimia type. *Journal of Clinical and Experimental Neuropsychology, 34*(1), 67–77.

van Elburg, A., & Treasure, J. (2013). Advances in the neurobiology of eating disorders. *Current Opinion in Psychiatry, 26*(6), 556–561.

Vander Wal, J. S., & Thomas, N. (2004). Predictors of body image dissatisfaction and disturbed eating attitudes and behaviors in African American and Hispanic girls. *Eating Behaviors, 5*(4), 291–301.

Vaswani, M., Linda, F. K., & Ramesh, S. (2003). Role of selective serotonin reuptake inhibitors in psychiatric disorders: a comprehensive review. *Progress in Neuropsychopharmacology & Biological Psychiatry, 27*(1), 85–102.

Vaz-Leal, F. J., Rodríguez-Santos, L., García-Herráiz, M. A., & Ramos-Fuentes, M. I. (2011). Neurobiological and psychopathological variables related to emotional instability: a study of their capability to discriminate patients with bulimia nervosa from healthy controls. *Neuropsychobiology, 63*(4), 242.

Vemuri, M., & Steiner, H. (2007). Historical and current conceptualizations of eating disorders: A developmental perspective. In T. Jaffa & B. McDermott (Eds.), *Eating disorders in children and adolescents* (pp. 3–11). Cambridge, UK: Cambridge University Press.

Ventura, R., Latagliata, E. C., Morrone, C., La Mela, I., & Puglisi-Allegra, S. (2008). Prefrontal norepinephrine determines attribution of "high" motivational salience. *PLoS One, 3*(8), e3044.

Ventura, R., Morrone, C., & Puglisi-Allegra, S. (2007). Prefrontal/accumbal catecholamine system determines motivational salience attribution to both reward- and aversion-related stimuli. *Proceedings of the National Academy of Sciences, 104*(12), 5181.

Vitousek, K. B., Daly, J., & Heiser, C. (1991). Reconstructing the internal world of the eating-disordered individual: Overcoming denial and distortion in self-report. *International Journal of Eating Disorders, 10*(6), 647–666.

Vo, M., Accurso, E. C., Goldschmidt, A. B., & Le Grange, D. (2016). The impact of DSM-5 on eating disorder diagnoses. *International Journal of Eating Disorders.*

Wagner, A., Greer, P., Bailer, U. F., Frank, G. K., Henry, S. E., Putnam, K., . . . Kaye, W. H. (2006). Normal brain tissue volumes after long-term recovery in anorexia and bulimia nervosa. *Biological Psychiatry, 59*(3), 291–293.

Waller, G. (1993). Association of sexual abuse and borderline personality disorder in eating disordered women. *International Journal of Eating Disorders, 13*(3), 259–263.

Walsh, B. T. (1992). Diagnostic criteria for eating disorders in DSM-IV: Work in progress. *International Journal of Eating Disorders, 11*(4), 301–304.

Walsh, B. T., & Garner, D. M. (1997). Diagnostic issues. In D. M. Garner & P. E. Garfinkel (Eds.), *Handbook of treatment for eating disorders* (2nd ed., pp. 25–33). New York, NY: Guilford Press.

Walsh, B. T., Kaplan, A. S., Attia, E., Olmsted, M., Parides, M., Carter, J. C., . . . Rockert, W. (2006). Fluoxetine after weight restoration in anorexia nervosa: a randomized controlled trial. *Journal of the American Medical Association, 295*(22), 2605.

Wang, K., Zhang, H., Bloss, C. S., Duvvuri, V., Kaye, W., Schork, N. J., . . . Hakonarson, H. (2010). A genome-wide association study on common SNPs and rare CNVs in anorexia nervosa. *Molecular Psychiatry, 16*(9), 949.

Watson, H. J., & Bulik, C. M. (2013). Update on the treatment of anorexia nervosa: review of clinical trials, practice guidelines and emerging interventions. *Psychological Medicine, 43*(12), 2477.

Watson, T. L., & Andersen, A. E. (2003). A critical examination of the amenorrhea and weight criteria for diagnosing anorexia nervosa. *Acta Psychiatrica Scandinavica, 108*(3), 175–182.

Weider, S., Indredavik, M. S., Lydersen, S., & Hestad, K. (2015). Neuropsychological function in patients with anorexia nervosa or bulimia nervosa. *International Journal of Eating Disorders, 48*(4), 397–405.

Weigl, E. (1941). On the psychology of so-called processes of abstraction. *The Journal of Abnormal and Social Psychology, 36*(1), 3–33.

Welch, S. L., Doll, H. A., & Fairburn, C. G. (1997). Life events and the onset of bulimia nervosa: a controlled study. *Psychological Medicine, 27*(3), 515–522.

Wilfley, D. E., Friedman, M. A., Dounchis, J. Z., Stein, R. I., Welch, R. R., & Ball, S. A. (2000). Comorbid psychopathology in binge eating disorder: Relation to eating disorder severity at baseline and following treatment. *Journal of Consulting and Clinical Psychology, 68*(4), 641.

Wilfley, D. E., Schwartz, M. B., Spurrell, E. B., & Fairburn, C. G. (2000). Using the eating disorder examination to identify the specific psychopathology of binge eating disorder. *International Journal of Eating Disorders, 27*(3), 259–269.

Williams, G. J., Power, K. G., Miller, H. R., Freeman, C. P., Yellowlees, A., Dowds, T., . . . Parry-Jones, W. L. (1994). Development and validation of the stirling eating disorder scales. *International Journal of Eating Disorders, 16*(1), 35–43.

Williamson, D. A. (1990). *Assessment of eating disorders: Obesity, anorexia, and bulimia nervosa.* New York, NY: Pergamon Press.

Williamson, D. A., Anderson, D. A., Jackman, L. P., & Jackson, S. R. (1995). Assessment of eating disordered thoughts, feelings, and behaviours. In D. B. Allison (Ed.), *Handbook of assessment methods for eating behaviours and weight related problems. Measures, theory and research* (pp. 347–386). London, England: Sage.

Wilson, G. T., Nonas, C. A., & Rosenblum, G. D. (S). Assessment of binge eating in obese patients. *International Journal of Eating Disorders, 13*(1), 25–33.

Wilson, T. G., & Smith, D. (1989). Assessment of bulimia nervosa: An evaluation of the eating disorders examination. *International Journal of Eating Disorders, 8*(2), 173–179.

Winstanley, C. A., Chudasama, Y., Dalley, J. W., Theobald, D. E. H., Glennon, J. C., & Robbins, T. W. (2003). Intra-prefrontal 8-OH-DPAT and M100907 improve visuospatial attention and decrease impulsivity on the five-choice serial reaction time task in rats. *Psychopharmacology, 167*(3), 304–314.

Winston, A. P., & Wells, F. E. (2002). Hypophosphatemia following self-treatment for anorexia nervosa. *International Journal of Eating Disorders, 32*(2), 245–248.

Witt, D. E., Ryan, K. G. C., & Hsu, K. G. L. (1985). Learning deficits in adolescents with anorexia nervosa. *The Journal of Nervous and Mental Disease, 173*(3), 182–184.

Woods, A. M., Racine, S. E., & Klump, K. L. (2010). Examining the relationship between dietary restraint and binge eating: Differential effects of major and minor stressors. *Eating Behaviors, 11*(4), 276–280.

World Health Organization. (1992). *International statistical classification of diseases and related health problems* (10th ed.). Geneva, Switzerland.

World Health Organization (1992). *Composite International Diagnostic Interview (CIDI).* Geneva, Switzerland.

Wu, M., Brockmeyer, T., Hartmann, M., Skunde, M., Herzog, W., & Friederich, H.-C. (2016). Reward-related decision making in eating and weight disorders: A systematic review and meta-analysis of the evidence from neuropsychological studies. *Neuroscience and Biobehavioral Reviews, 61*, 177–196.

Wu, M., Brockmeyer, T., Hartmann, M., Skunde, M., Herzog, W., & Friederich, H. C. (2014). Set-shifting ability across the spectrum of eating disorders and in overweight and obesity: a systematic review and meta-analysis. *Psychological Medicine, 44*(16), 3365–3385.

Yanovski, S. Z. (1993). Binge eating disorder: Current knowledge and future directions. *Obesity Research, 1*(4), 306.

Yilmaz, Z., Hardaway, J., & Bulik, C. M. (2015). Genetics and epigenetics of eating disorders. *Advances in Genomics and Genetics,* 2015(default), 131–150.

Yilmaz, Z., Kaplan, A. S., Tiwari, A. K., Levitan, R. D., Piran, S., Bergen, A. W., . . . Kennedy, J. L. (2014). The role of leptin, melanocortin, and neurotrophin system genes on body weight in anorexia nervosa and bulimia nervosa. *Journal of Psychiatric Research, 55,* 77–86.

Zanarini, M. C., Skodol, A. E., Bender, D., Dolan, R., Sanislow, C., Schaefer, E., . . . Gunderson, J. G. (2000). The Collaborative Longitudinal Personality Disorders Study: Reliability of Axis I and II diagnoses. *Journal of Personality Disorders, 14*(4), 291–299.

Zastrow, A., Kaiser, S., Stippich, C., Walther, S., Herzog, W., Tchanturia, K., . . . Friederich, H.-C. (2009). Neural correlates of impaired cognitive-behavioral flexibility in anorexia nervosa. *The American Journal of Psychiatry, 166*(5), 608–616.

Zucker, N. L., Losh, M., Bulik, C. M., LaBar, K. S., Piven, J., & Pelphrey, K. A. (2007). Anorexia nervosa and autism spectrum disorders: guided investigation of social cognitive endophenotypes. *Psychological bulletin, 133*(6), 976–1006.

CHAPTER 15

Sleep Disorders

JOANNE L. BOWER and CANDICE A. ALFANO

INTRODUCTION

Sleep complaints are common in the general population and highly prevalent among individuals seeking mental health services. The most recent edition of the *Diagnostic and Statistical Manual of Mental Disorders* (*DSM-5*; American Psychiatric Association [APA], 2013) categorizes sleep disorders into 10 disorders or disorder groups, including: (1) insomnia disorder; (2) hypersomnolence disorder; (3) narcolepsy; (4) breathing-related sleep disorders; (5) circadian rhythm sleep–wake disorders; (6) nonrapid eye movement (non-REM) sleep arousal disorder; (7) nightmare disorder; (8) rapid eye movement (REM) sleep behavior disorder; (9) restless legs syndrome; and (10) substance/medication-induced sleep disorder. Notably, the "Sleep–wake Disorders" section included in *DSM-5* represent a considerable expansion in contrast to the previous *DSM* edition (*DSM-IV-TR*; APA, 2000), which included only four broad sleep disorder categories. *DSM-5* also pays more attention to coexisting conditions, emphasizing the need for sleep-directed clinical intervention even when a comorbid medical or mental disorder is present. These significant changes are reflective of the abundance of sleep-focused research conducted within the past decade.

Although mental health researchers and practitioners tend to be most familiar with *DSM* classifications, the *International Classification of Sleep Disorders*, 3rd edition (*ICSD-3*; American Academy of Sleep Medicine [AASM], 2014) is commonly used within the field of sleep medicine. The *ICSD-3* provides characteristics and diagnostic criteria for over 60 sleep disorders organized into six major categories. In addition to a greater breadth of conditions than provided by the *DSM-5*, the *ICSD-3* also provides information on validated assessments and treatments.

As the focus of this chapter is to highlight sleep disorders relevant to mental health professionals, our review focuses on *DSM-5* sleep–wake disorders most likely to present in clinical practice. We begin with a brief introduction to healthy sleep and its measurement followed by presentation of six specific sleep disorders: insomnia, hypersomnolence, circadian rhythm disorders, non-REM sleep disorders, nightmare disorder, and REM sleep behavior disorder. Information is provided regarding diagnostic criteria,

Adult Psychopathology and Diagnosis, Eighth Edition. Edited by Deborah C. Beidel and B. Christopher Frueh.
© 2018 John Wiley & Sons, Inc. Published 2018 by John Wiley & Sons, Inc.
Companion website: www.wiley.com/go/beidel/psychopathology8e

epidemiology, etiology, and comorbid medical and psychological factors. We conclude with a diagnostic case example of a patient experiencing both nightmares and insomnia.

FEATURES OF HEALTHY SLEEP

Sleep is a reversible condition of lowered consciousness, decreased reactivity to external stimuli, and reduced motor activity that occupies approximately one-third of the human life span. Sleep–wake periods are cyclical, with most adults experiencing one main night-time sleep period during the 24-hour day. This cycle arises through the interplay of two independent processes: a homeostatic sleep drive and circadian rhythms (Borbély, Daan, Wirz-Justice, & Deboer, 2016). Homeostatic sleep pressure increases as time since the previous sleep period lengthens, and dissipates once sleep is initiated. Homeostatic sleep drive greatly influences sleep intensity and structure, which is described in greater detail below.

Circadian rhythms last approximately 24 hours and primarily control the timing of sleep. They are unaffected by previous sleep duration and contribute to sleep–wake timing through the release of melatonin, a hormone produced by the pineal gland. Individuals can be broadly classified as either morning or evening chronotypes, indicating their time preference for carrying out activities (Horne & Ostberg, 1976). Extreme preference for mornings or evenings can be indicative of circadian rhythm disorder.

Genes, age, and environmental factors have important influence over both homeostatic and circadian processes (Dijk, Duffy, Riel, Shanahan, & Czeisler, 1999; Martin & Eastman, 1998; Pace-Schott & Hobson, 2002). Homeostatic processes are also strongly affected by the consumption of certain substances, such as caffeine, which delay the onset of sleepiness by blocking key neurotransmitter receptors (Landolt, Werth, Borbély, & Dijk, 1995). Circadian rhythms are endogenous; however, they can be reset using environmental cues known as "zeitgebers." The most important zeitgeber is light, which suppresses the release of melatonin, in turn delaying the onset of sleep.

SLEEP STAGES

Sleep does not occur uniformly throughout the night. Instead, it can be divided into two major types: REM and non-REM sleep. Cortical activity during REM sleep closely resembles wakefulness, and is often referred to as "paradoxical" or "active" sleep. REM brainwaves are of low voltage and high frequency, and can be distinguished from wake by the presence of muscle atonia and rapid eye movements. During REM sleep, muscle activity is at its lowest, with only the heart, respiratory muscles and eyes maintaining waking functioning. It is also the sleep stage from which dreams are most frequently and vividly recalled upon awakening. REM sleep also appears to be critical for emotional learning and memory (Nishida, Pearsall, Buckner, & Walker, 2009; Walker & van Der Helm, 2009).

Non-REM sleep can be divided into three stages representing increasing depths of sleep from lightest to deepest (N1, N2, and N3 respectively). N1 denotes the transition from wakefulness to sleep, and is characterized by rolling eye movements and a reduction in alpha brain waves. N2 occupies the greatest portion of sleep in adults and is associated with theta waves and the appearance of sleep spindles and K-complex wave forms. N3 is the deepest stage of sleep, comprising predominantly delta waves. Older publications commonly refer to non-REM stage 4, which was combined with N3 by the AASM in 2007. N3 is now used to refer all "slow wave" or "delta" sleep.

SLEEP ARCHITECTURE

Sleep architecture refers to the overall progression of sleep stages throughout the night. In healthy adults, approximately 15–20 minutes of sleep is required to achieve N2 sleep; deep sleep (N3) occurs after approximately 30–60 minutes. After a period of deep sleep, there is a transition back toward lighter (N2) sleep followed by a period of REM sleep. This ultradian cycle repeats itself, with shorter periods of N3 and longer REM periods as the night progresses. Each ultradian sleep cycle lasts approximately 90–120 minutes, with four to five cycles occurring during an 8-hour sleep period. A healthy adult spends, on average, 25% of sleep in REM and 75% in non-REM sleep (N1 [5%], N2 [45–55%], N3 [15–25%]). Abnormalities in the timing, distribution, and/or proportion of different types and phases of sleep are prevalent in various sleep disorders and in some psychiatric conditions (e.g., increased REM sleep in depression).

SLEEP MEASUREMENT

Sleep measurement can be conducted using a variety of methods, including self-report instruments, actigraphy, and polysomnography (PSG). In clinical settings, the selection of evaluation method depends on the suspected sleep disorder; self-report assessments are sufficient for diagnosing some disorders, whereas objective measurement of movement or brain activity is necessary for others.

SELF-REPORT MEASURES

Sleep diaries are the most common self-report sleep measure, used either alone or in conjunction with actigraphy or PSG. They should ideally be completed prior to bedtime and first thing upon awakening for a minimum of 1 week. Although there is no standard format for sleep diaries, they typically include bed and wake times, time taken to fall asleep, total sleep time, number and duration of night-time awakenings, alertness upon awakening, and activities/substances that might impact sleep (e.g., ingestion of caffeine, exercise, use of electronics within the hour before bed). Sleep diaries can be useful in detecting sleep patterns over time and in cases where the information provided by objective measures is inadequate (e.g., perceived sleep quality, nightmares).

ACTIGRAPHY

Actigraphy estimates sleep–wake parameters by using a small watch-like device to measure movement. Activity data are collected 24 hours per day over extended periods (up to several weeks) and then analyzed using software algorithms validated for detecting sleep versus wake periods. Actigraphs often include event markers which individuals use to indicate when they get into bed/are trying to initiate sleep and upon final awakening in the morning. This enables calculation of sleep-onset latency in addition to time in bed. Other common variables derived from actigraphy include total sleep time, wake time after sleep onset, and sleep efficiency (i.e., the proportion of time in bed that is spent asleep). In healthy adults, actigraphy-based estimates of sleep correlate highly with PSG-based sleep estimates. However, as sleep becomes more disturbed, actigraphy parameters become less reliable. Actigraphy is nonetheless highly useful in the diagnosis and management of several sleep disorders. It is recommended by the AASM for diagnosing insomnia, hypersomnia and circadian-rhythm disorders in adults and older adults and for monitoring treatment outcomes for these conditions.

POLYSOMNOGRAPHY

Polysomnography is the gold standard measurement for sleep and can be conducted in a sleep laboratory or at home using ambulatory equipment. The procedure includes placing electrodes on the scalp, face and body. PSG encompasses measurement of cortical activity (electroencephalography [EEG]), eye movements (electro-oculography [EOG]) and muscle tone (electromyography [EMG]) during sleep. Heart rate (EKG) and other body sensors (e.g. respiration belts, leg movement sensors, pulse oximetry) can also be used for the diagnosis of certain sleep disorders.

Polysomnography recordings are necessary for identifying sleep stages and characteristics of cortical activity during sleep (e.g., spectral analysis of EEG waveforms to calculate sleep density). PSG is also necessary for detecting abnormal breathing, limb movements, and other sleep problems using sensors measuring heart rate, respiration, oxygen saturation and leg movements. The most common disorders requiring diagnosis via PSG include obstructive sleep apnea and periodic limb movement disorder.

MULTIPLE SLEEP LATENCY TEST (MSLT)

The Multiple Sleep Latency Test (MSLT) was designed by Carskadon and Dement (1977) and uses PSG to measure daytime sleepiness. The test consists of four to five 20-minute nap opportunities separated by 2-hour intervals. During nap periods the patient lies down in a comfortable, dark room in a sleep laboratory and is asked to try to nap. The first nap period begins within 3 hours of awakening from the previous night's sleep (which should be monitored with PSG). Variables of interest during an MSLT include the number of nap opportunities that result in sleep, sleep onset latency, and the presence of REM sleep during naps. The MSLT is an objective measure of daytime sleep propensity; the appearance of REM sleep during naps is suggestive, though not diagnostic, of narcolepsy.

SLEEP DISORDERS

INSOMNIA DISORDER

Unlike previous editions, the *DSM-5* classifies insomnia as a distinct disorder, encouraging specific treatment, even when it arises alongside other medical or psychological illnesses. Insomnia disorder is a predominantly subjective complaint, whereby individuals experience one of more of the following: delayed sleep onset (early insomnia), difficulty maintaining sleep (i.e. several night-time awakenings; middle insomnia), or early termination of sleep (late insomnia), even when given adequate sleep opportunity. To meet criteria for insomnia, these symptoms must occur alongside daytime impairment (e.g., fatigue, cognitive difficulties, mood change) and be present for three or more nights per week for at least 3 months. A diagnosis of episodic insomnia may also be given if symptoms exist for between 1 and 3 months.

Epidemiology Insomnia is the most common sleep disorder, with approximately 30% of the general population reporting at least one insomnia symptom (APA, 2013; Roth, 2007) and 6–10% meeting criteria for an insomnia diagnosis (Morin & Benca, 2012; Morin &

Jarrin, 2013). It is more prevalent in females (Zhang & Wing, 2006), older patients (Ohayon, 2002), and shift workers (Roth, 2007), with prevalence rates varying greatly across countries (Morin & Jarrin, 2013).

Etiology   Prominent etiologic models implicate physiological and cognitive hyperarousal, as causal factors of insomnia (Perlis, Smith, & Pigeon, 2005; Roth, 2007). Predisposing behavioral, genetic, and environmental influences also increase individual risk (Miller, Espie, & Kyle, 2014). Additionally, acute episodes of insomnia, such as those following stressful or traumatic events, can be worsened and/or prolonged by resulting psychological and behavioral factors. For example, problems sleeping can induce anxiety and negative cognitions regarding sleep, which in turn increase arousal and worsen insomnia. Similar reciprocal relationships also exist between insomnia and physical health problems. For example, Nordin and Kaplan (2010) found that complaints of sleep initiation or maintenance predicted significant weight gain over the course of several decades. Onset of insomnia in childhood is also prognostic for later mental illness and sleep problems in adulthood (Ford & Kamerow, 1989; Ohayon, Caulet, & Lemoine, 1998).

Diagnosis   Insomnia is most commonly diagnosed from self-reports and sleep diaries, though actigraphy may also be used. There is, however, a lack of consensus regarding quantitative criteria for diagnosis. The combination of multiple sleep parameters has been suggested, including total sleep time, sleep onset latency, and number of awakenings longer than 5 minutes (e.g., Natale, Plazzi, & Martoni, 2009). The *DSM-5* criteria for diagnosis includes: sleep latency of 20–30 minutes or more (early insomnia), night-time awakenings totaling >20 minutes (middle insomnia) or awakening > 30 minutes before scheduled wake-up time, with total sleep time also below 6.5 hours (APA, 2013). However a considerable proportion of insomniacs experience "paradoxical insomnia," where sleep complaints tend to be exaggerated in comparison to objective indices of sleep disturbance. Paradoxical insomnia is notoriously difficult to both assess and treat (Edinger & Krystal, 2003). Unlike previous editions, the *DSM-5* no longer includes nonrestorative sleep as a diagnostic criterion for insomnia as poor-quality sleep has multiple origins.

It is important to distinguish insomnia from other sleep disorders that disrupt or limit sleep, particularly circadian rhythm disorders, breathing-related sleep disorders, and restless legs syndrome/periodic limb movement disorder. Insomnia can be distinguished from a circadian rhythm disorder on the basis of sleep timing rather than sleep quality and duration. That is, if sleep difficulties only occur when an individual tries to maintain socially acceptable sleep times, then a diagnosis of circadian rhythm disorder may be more appropriate.

Breathing-related sleep disorders are serious conditions in which air flow is not maintained due to either obstruction (obstructive sleep apnea) or lack of respiratory effort (centralized sleep apnea). These respiratory events can result in multiple arousals or awakenings during the night. Breathing-related sleep disorders are most common in males and individuals who are obese (Young, Peppard, & Gottlieb, 2002), although they can also occur in normal or underweight individuals. Both insomnia and breathing-related sleep disorders can result excessive daytime sleepiness, but the latter is also typically characterized by loud snoring or gasping during sleep, dry mouth upon waking, and recurrent headaches.

Individuals with restless legs syndrome typically complain of uncomfortable sensations in their legs that are temporarily relieved only by movement. Symptoms of restless legs syndrome tend to worsen at night and commonly disrupt sleep onset. A large proportion of patients with restless legs syndrome also suffer from periodic limb movement disorder characterized by muscle twitches/jerks of the legs or arms every 20–40 seconds during sleep. These movements may occur hundreds of times throughout the night and can result in arousals and/or awakenings from sleep.

Comorbid Medical and Psychological Factors   To ensure proper treatment, *DSM-5* criteria for insomnia disorder include co-occurring medical, psychiatric, and/or other sleep disorders as unique specifiers (rather than exclusions for diagnosis as specified in *DSM-IV*). It is nonetheless important to determine whether sleep complaints are caused by or related to other conditions. This can be difficult to determine with certainty as so many disease entities can negatively impact sleep.

Insomnia is highly correlated with mental health problems, with at least 50% of insomnia patients meeting criteria for depression or an anxiety disorder (Ford & Kamerow, 1989; Ohayon et al., 1998). Among the anxiety disorders, generalized anxiety disorder (GAD) is most commonly associated with insomnia; roughly 70% of patients report problems initiating and/or maintaining sleep (Alfano & Mellman, 2010; Monti & Monti, 2000). The severity and nature of insomnia symptoms in GAD patients also closely match those of patients with insomnia disorder, including worry about obtaining sufficient sleep at night. Symptoms of hyperarousal and difficulty concentrating are also common in both disorders.

Insomnia is highly prevalent among patients seeking treatment from primary care physicians. Insomniacs are at greater risk of medical disorders than the general population (Roth, 2007) and increased mortality rates are associated with chronic insomnia (Kripke, Garfinkel, Wingard, Klauber, & Marler, 2002). Consistent with the latter finding, chronic insomnia that is associated with objectively verified short sleep duration independently elevates risk for hypertension, beyond the effects of age, race, obesity, diabetes, alcohol consumption, and smoking (Vgontzas et al., 2009). Thus, objective measures of sleep duration may be useful markers of the physiological impact of the disorder.

HYPERSOMNOLENCE DISORDER

The term "hypersomnolence" broadly includes symptoms of excessive sleep quantity, deteriorated quality of wakefulness, and sleep inertia (i.e., a period of impaired performance or reduce vigilance following awakening from a regular sleep episode). Hypersomnolence disorder is characterized by the presence of excessive sleepiness despite nocturnal sleep duration of 7 hours or more. Sleepiness can take the form of long sleep periods (which in extreme cases can last up to 20 hours), nonrestorative nighttime sleep, or increased daytime sleepiness. Upon awakening from sleep, sleep inertia can last from several minutes to several hours.

Prolonged nocturnal sleep and difficulty awakening in the morning can significantly impair occupational, academic, and personal functioning. As with insomnia, hypersomnolence must be present for at least 3 months and be accompanied by significant distress or daytime impairment for diagnosis to be appropriate (APA, 2013). In contrast to the *DSM-5*, *ICSD-3* describes numerous hypersomnia disorders, including narcolepsy, Kleine–Levin syndrome, insufficient sleep syndrome, and idiopathic hypersomnia. Although not identical, *ICSD-3* idiopathic hypersomnia is most similar to *DSM-5* hypersomnolence disorder.

Epidemiology   The prevalence of hypersomnolence disorder is difficult to determine, due to studies commonly utilizing various symptoms of hypersomnia to estimate the incidence of hypersomnolence disorder (or idiopathic hypersomnia). A recent review suggests prevalence rates to be between 0.002% and 0.01% (Sowa, 2016), whereas reports of daytime hypersomnolence are found in up to 16% of the population (Decker, Lin, Tabassum, & Reeves, 2008). However, the extent to which such reports might capture other sleep pathologies such as obstructive sleep apnea and circadian rhythm disorders is unclear. Still, approximately 5–10% of patients who seek treatment for excessive daytime sleepiness suffer from hypersomnolence disorder (APA, 2013).

Etiology   Hypersomnolence is influenced by genetics. One study found 37% of patients with hypersomnolence disorder had at least one family member who suffered with hypersomnolence (Ali, Auger, Slocumb, & Morgenthaler, 2009). Genome-wide association studies have also identified several candidate genes for susceptibility to hypersomnolence (Billiard & Sonka, 2016; Miyagawa et al., 2009).

Various physiological pathways are implicated in hypersomnolence disorder. For example, the cerebral spinal fluid (CSF) of hypersomnia patients has been found to contain an agent that augments the response of $GABA_A$ receptors, creating increased levels of sleepiness (Rye et al., 2012). Reduced CSF histamine (a natural stimulant) and differences in levels of IgG4 (a type of antibody protein) between individuals with idiopathic hypersomnia and healthy controls have also been reported (Sowa, 2016; Tanaka & Honda, 2010). Viral infections, including infectious mononucleosis, can sometimes produce hypersomnolence in the months following infection (APA, 2013). Hypersomnia can also emerge in the months following a head trauma.

Diagnosis   Hypersomnolence can be detected through a combination of sleep diaries, actigraphy, and/or PSG assessment. In addition, self-report measures of daytime sleepiness such as the Epworth Sleepiness Scale (Johns, 1991) are valuable tools for assessing hypersomnia. PSG monitoring will typically show decreased sleep onset latency for the main sleep period and daytime naps (< 10 minutes). During an MSLT, sleep onset latencies below 8 minutes are common. Increased total sleep time, (including increased duration of slow wave sleep [N3]) and difficulty becoming fully awake after abrupt awakenings may also be observed.

As distinguishing hypersomnolence disorder from other causes of daytime sleepiness is often challenging, it is essential that nocturnal causes of daytime sleepiness (e.g., obstructive sleep apnea) be ruled out prior to diagnosing hypersomnolence disorder. It is equally important to consider subtypes of *ICSD-3* hypersomnia disorders, including narcolepsy and Kleine–Levin hypersomnia, which require more distinct treatment approaches.

Narcolepsy is characterized by a sudden onset of extreme sleepiness, with an irrepressible urge to sleep irrespective of setting. Narcoleptic patients also experience sleep-onset REM, whereby REM sleep periods typically occur abnormally within 15 minutes of initiating sleep. Kleine–Levin syndrome is characterized by recurring periods of hypersomnolence lasting several weeks or months. Other features of the disorder may include compulsive eating (polyphagia) and hypersexual behaviors (e.g., public masturbation) during episodes of hypersomnolence. Between episodes, individuals with Kleine–Levin syndrome show largely normal cognitive, emotional, and behavioral functions.

Comorbid Medical and Psychological Factors   Among all psychiatric disorders, hypersomnolence is most closely associated with mood disorders, occurring in about 15% of depressed patients (Tsuno, Besset, & Ritchie, 2005). Associations between mood and hypersomnia are thought to be bidirectional. Daytime sleepiness is common in prodromal and residual phases of depression (Franzen & Buysse, 2008; Roberts, Shema, Kaplan, & Strawbridge, 2000) and 15–20% of patients with idiopathic hypersomnia report depressive symptoms (Dauvilliers, Lopez, Ohayon, & Bayard, 2013).

Hypersomnolence also co-occurs with a wide range of medical conditions, including diabetes, multiple sclerosis, and autoimmune, kidney and heart disease (Ohayon et al., 2012). In such patients, hypersomnia is often considered a secondary rather than a primary diagnosis.

Circadian Rhythm Disorders

Circadian rhythm sleep disorders involve misalignment of the endogenous circadian rhythm with an individual's preferred or required sleep–wake schedule. Thus, circadian rhythm disorders can be distinguished from other sleep disorders on the basis of sleep timing rather than sleep quality and duration. Sleep disruption caused by these disorders can produce a range of symptoms and impairments, including excessive sleepiness and interference in occupational and academic functioning. There are several types of circadian rhythm disorders, ranging from those with temporary, self-resolving symptoms (e.g., jetlag) to those characterized by sustained and pronounced shifts in sleep timing, such as advanced sleep phase disorder (ASPD) and delayed sleep phase disorder (DSPD). In ASPD, the sleep period occurs significantly earlier than desired. Conversely, in DSPD, the sleep period is significantly delayed. Circadian rhythm sleep–wake disorders are also subspecified into episodic, persistent, or recurrent.

Epidemiology   The most common circadian rhythm sleep–wake disorder is DSPD with a reported prevalence of between 0.13% and 0.17% (Okawa & Uchiyama, 2007). However, prevalence rates fluctuate depending on the diagnostic criteria used, population sampled, and study design (Micic et al., 2016). DSPD is most common in adolescence and in early adults, when prevalence rates are closer to 7% (APA, 2013). Conversely, ASPD is most commonly seen in older adults and the elderly (Zisapel, 2001). Many older adults experience some degree of phase advance (i.e., earlier bed and wake times) with varying levels of accompanying daytime impairment (Neikrug & Ancoli-Israel, 2010). However, the estimated prevalence of ASPD is 1%.

Etiology   Interplay between genetic, physiological, and environmental influences underlies circadian rhythm sleep–wake disorders. Several genes have been identified as potential "clock" genes that influence chronotype and, in turn, elevate risk for circadian disorders. For example, the hPER2 gene is critical for the re-setting effect of light on the circadian clock, with some evidence regarding its potential contribution to ASPD (Sack et al., 2007). Similarly there is mixed evidence regarding the relationship between variants of the PER3 gene and links to DSPD (Archer et al., 2003). However, studies conducted across different cultures and geographical latitudes have produced conflicting results (e.g., Pereira et al., 2005), suggesting that environmental factors such as light exposure produce important modulating effects of these genotypes.

Physiological factors such as melatonin secretion, sensitivity to light entrainment and natural length of the circadian rhythm may also contribute to development of circadian rhythm sleep–wake disorders. Rather than being exactly 24 hours, the endogenous circadian rhythm length varies across individuals. Individuals who have particularly short or long circadian rhythms may be more susceptible to ASPD or DSPD, respectively.

Similarly, individuals vary in the timing of melatonin secretion and in the extent to which their circadian phase is aligned with environmental cues (known as phase angle). Carskadon and colleagues have shown pubertal development to predict a reliable phase delay observed during adolescence (e.g., Carskadon, Vieira, & Acebo, 1993; Crowley, Acebo, & Carskadon, 2007).

In terms of environmental factors, ill-timed exposure to bright light (especially blue wavelength light) is also implicated in the development and maintenance of phase advances and delays. Bright light exposure in the evening, for example, suppresses the secretion of melatonin and promotes wakefulness, resulting in a phase delay (Chang, Aeschbach, Duffy, & Czeisler, 2015; Lovato & Lack, 2016). Blue wavelength light is most closely associated with arousal and is produced by smartphones, tablets, and televisions, which have become ubiquitous during the last decade.

Diagnosis The endogenous circadian rhythm is most accurately estimated by measuring dim light melatonin onset (via blood, saliva or urine), which peaks shortly after habitual bedtime. However, the time and cost of such measurement are prohibitive in most settings. Circadian rhythm disorders are therefore most commonly diagnosed via sleep diaries and/or actigraphy. Sleep typically occurs several hours earlier or later than desired. Chronotype questionnaires such as the Munich Chronotype Questionnaire (Roenneberg, Wirz-Justice, & Merrow, 2003) and the Morningness – Eveningness Questionnaire (Horne & Ostberg, 1976) can also provide useful information, but are not sufficient to diagnose circadian rhythm sleep–wake disorders. As sleep architecture in circadian rhythm disorders is typically normal, PSG is neither required nor useful for confirming diagnosis.

Individuals with circadian rhythm sleep–wake disorders have similar complaints to patients with insomnia (e.g., prolonged sleep onset latency) and hypersomnolence disorders (e.g., excessive daytime sleepiness), which often complicates diagnosis. Practitioners must closely consider the timing of sleep and the individual's desired sleep–wake pattern in relation to occupational, academic, familial, and social requirements. Individuals with DSPD almost always report extreme difficulty waking in the morning, whereas those with ASPD report difficulty maintaining wakefulness during the evening hours. In contrast to other sleep–wake disorders, if allowed to sleep according to their natural body clock, patients with circadian rhythm disorders generally experience restorative sleep.

Comorbid Medical and Psychological Factors Circadian rhythm disturbances are strongly associated with affective disorders. Approximately 18% of adolescents and young adults with major depression (Glozier et al., 2014) and 62% with bipolar illness (Robillard et al., 2013) show a delayed sleep phase, though rates of DSPD may be somewhat lower. Of adolescents diagnosed with DSPD, 35% report depressive symptoms (Saxvig et al., 2012). Among individuals with seasonal affective disorder, which arises from a failure to properly adapt to light changes in the environment, seasonal alterations in melatonin secretion patterns have been found (Danilenko, Putilov, Russkikh, & Ebbesson, 1994; Wehr et al., 2001). Emerging research also supports a relationship between delayed sleep phase and obsessive compulsive disorder (e.g., Schubert & Coles, 2013; Mukhopadhyay et al. 2008). These collective data are indicative of a robust connection between mood dysregulation and circadian misalignment.

Relationships between circadian rhythm sleep–wake disorder and mental health conditions are, in most cases, likely to be bidirectional. For example, avoidance of work and/or social activities due to depression can also produce changes in circadian timing. Conversely, functional impairments imposed by misaligned sleep–wake schedules (e.g., absenteeism, missed social events) increases risk of mood disturbances.

NIGHTMARE DISORDER

Nightmare disorder is characterized by repeated occurrences of lengthy and realistic sequences of dream imagery, eliciting anxiety, fear, and other negative emotions. As nightmares emerge almost exclusively from REM sleep, they predominantly occur during the second half of the night-time sleep period. Typically, the content/theme of nightmares includes threat of imminent harm (e.g., being chased, attacked). Nightmares that follow traumatic experiences/events often involve at least some part of the original trauma. Once awakened, the individual quickly becomes oriented, alert, and remembers the dream in detail. However, resulting negative emotions can persist and contribute to subsequent problems initiating or maintaining sleep. As with other sleep disorders, nightmares must be accompanied by significant distress or impairment in daytime functioning in order to warrant a diagnosis of nightmare disorder. *DSM-5* also specifies duration (acute, <1 month; subacute, 1–6 months; persistent, >6 months) and severity (mild, < one episode a week; moderate, multiple times a week; severe, nightly) of the diagnosis.

Epidemiology   There are several challenges associated with accurately estimating the prevalence of nightmare disorder. First, everyone experiences occasional bad dreams or nightmares but many studies do not report actual dream frequency, making it difficult to fully separate the occurrence of nightmares from nightmare disorder. Second, many studies do not distinguish between idiopathic nightmares and those that develop in relation to a traumatic event. Nightmares that occur in the context of *DSM-5* post-traumatic stress disorder (PTSD) or acute stress disorder may not warrant a separate diagnosis of nightmare disorder.

Frequent or chronic nightmares occur in up to 8% of the general population (AASM, 2014), with an estimated 4% of the adults meeting criteria for nightmare disorder (Aurora et al., 2010). Women are at least twice as likely as men to experience nightmares (Ohayon et al., 1997). The peak ages for experiencing "distressing" nightmares are 10–29 years for women and 30–49 years for men (Nielsen, 2010). Prevalence of nightmares is much higher in psychiatric populations, particularly those with PTSD.

Etiology   Much of the etiological research regarding nightmares has focused on childhood and suggests an interaction between genetic and environmental factors (King, Hamilton, & Ollendick, 1988). Genetic factors account for an estimated 45% of the phenotypic variance in childhood nightmares and 37% of the variance in adult nightmares (Hublin, Kapiro, Partinen, & Koskenvuo, 1999). Traumatic events, psychological distress, and other sleep disturbances also contribute to the onset and maintenance of nightmares.

Several theories regarding the etiology of idiopathic nightmares have been proposed, though most have limited empirical support (Nadorff, Lambdin, & Germain, 2014). One theory incorporates advances in cognitive neuroscience, sleep neurophysiology, and fear conditioning to describe a multilevel model of disturbing dreams (Levin & Nielsen, 2007, 2009). The AMPHAC/AND model includes a neurophysiologic branch (including the amygdala [A], medial prefrontal cortex [MP], hippocampus [H], and anterior cingulate cortex [AC]), and a cognitive branch termed the affect network dysfunction (AND). Broadly, this model theorizes nightmares to represent a failure in emotion regulation, whereby the typical fear-extinction and emotional processing that occurs during sleep becomes disrupted.

Diagnosis   Nightmare disorder is predominantly diagnosed via patient report or sleep diaries. The experience of several nightmares is not itself indicative of nightmare disorder and/or the need for treatment. Nightmares must be accompanied by distress or functional impairment for a diagnosis of nightmare disorder to be considered. PSG assessment is not necessary for diagnosis. Patients with recurrent nightmares tend to experience decreased frequency and severity of nightmares when studied in the sleep laboratory environment, which is attributed to the positive impact of safety cues (i.e., being monitored by staff and physicians). Studies have not found differences in most PSG parameters (e.g. sleep onset latency) compared with healthy controls (Germain & Nielsen, 2003), though increased gross motor activity has been observed in individuals with frequent nightmares (Germain & Nielsen, 2003).

Trauma-related nightmares differ from their idiopathic counterparts not only in terms of content (i.e., thematic or literal replay of the traumatic event), but are more likely to occur in any sleep stage (as contrasted with idiopathic nightmares, which occur predominantly in REM sleep). Consequently, trauma-related nightmares may also occur earlier in the night and include a greater number of body movements.

Nightmare disorder is commonly confused with other parasomnias, including sleep paralysis and sleep terrors. Compared to sleep paralysis, nightmares are easily identified as unreal events. Also unlike nightmares, individuals experiencing sleep terrors will have no recollection of these events upon awakening. Frequent nightmares, particularly if they are coupled with full awakenings and delayed return to sleep, can also produce insomnia.

Comorbid Medical and Psychological Factors   Epidemiological research suggests that individuals who experience frequent nightmares are at least five times more likely to meet criteria for a psychiatric disorder than are those who do not report nightmares (Li, Zhang, Li, & Wing, 2010). Anxiety disorders and PTSD are most closely associated with nightmares (Nadorff et al., 2014). Among patients with PTSD, upwards of 80% experience nightmares (Aurora et al., 2010) which can persist after the disorder has remitted.

Recent research also documents a link with borderline personality disorder (BPD). One study found that 49% of patients diagnosed with BPD met criteria for nightmare disorder (Semiz, Basoglu, Ebrinc, & Cetin, 2008). Patients with BPD and nightmare disorder were more clinically severe than BPD patients without nightmare disorder but also more likely to have suffered some form of abuse or neglect in childhood. Thus, a history of trauma rather than personality disturbance may explain elevated rates of nightmare disorder in this population.

REM SLEEP BEHAVIOR DISORDER

Rapid eye movement sleep behavior disorder (RBD) occurs due to an absence of muscle atonia (i.e., paralysis) normally present during this sleep stage, leading to the enactment of dream content. RBD results in episodes of arousal which typically include vocalizations and/or complex motor behaviors (APA, 2013). Motor behaviors range from mild hand movements or facial expressions to complex actions. There is often strong emotion (e.g., rage, anger) associated with RBD episodes, reflective of responses to dream content. Thus, while behaviors often appear bizarre to observers, they are more easily understood within the context of the co-occurring dream. Unlike non-REM sleep arousal disorders, individuals experiencing RBD are usually able to recall dream content upon awakening.

Epidemiology   Rapid eye movement sleep behavior disorder is most common among adults aged 50 or above, although it can appear at any age. Prevalence estimates indicate 0.38–0.5% of individuals are affected (Aurora et al., 2010). There is a strong male predominance, with the vast majority of injurious or potentially lethal behaviors occurring in men (Schenck, Lee, Bornemann, & Mahowald, 2009). When the diagnosis is made in younger individuals, particularly those without coexisting neurological problems, a gender ratio closer to a 1:1 is observed.

Etiology   Findings from animal and human studies reveal that dysfunction of motor control circuitry in pontomedullary brain structures causes RBD. Progressive degeneration of these structures explains the presence of RBD episodes years and sometimes decades earlier than the onset of various neurogenerative diseases (Boeve et al., 2007). Selective lesions of subnuclei in the reticular formation and the locus coeruleus, as well as pure pontine infarctions in humans, are known to produce REM sleep behaviors without atonia. Collectively, findings implicate brain stem abnormalities in the pathophysiology of RBD. At least 50% of individuals with RBD go on to develop neurodegenerative disorders, including multiple system atrophy, Parkinson's disease, and dementia with Lewy bodies (Siclari et al., 2010).

Diagnosis   In severe cases, RBD is only noticed when it causes injury or potential danger to the patient, their bed partner, or others they encounter. Thus, an important aspect of diagnosis and management of RBD is education about the disorder, including the need for safety precautions. At present there is no genetic test for RBD, either as a primary condition or as a complication of other medical conditions.

Diagnosis of RBD requires PSG confirmation of REM sleep without atonia, unless Parkinson's disease, dementia with Lewy bodies, or multiple system atrophy has already been diagnosed. Symptoms tend to emerge during the second half of the sleep cycle when REM sleep predominates. PSG should be combined with careful video monitoring to confirm presence of RBD. Because only select muscles may be associated with activity or movement (e.g., arms but not legs), extra EMG leads should be placed on different muscle groups.

Rapid eye movement sleep behavior disorder can be confused with other parasomnias, including non-REM sleep arousal disorders such as sleepwalking. In patients exhibiting sexual behaviors during sleep, a differential diagnosis of Kleine–Levin syndrome along with a possible seizure disorder should be ruled out (Nickell & Uhde, 1991). In elderly populations, the "sun-downing" phenomenon (i.e., disorientation and/or aimless wandering during evening hours) should also be considered. Finally, the possibility of malingering should be considered in cases where the patient has been charged with a crime and/or has a history of violent or sociopathic behaviors.

Comorbid Medical and Psychological Factors   As noted earlier, as many as 50% of patients with RBD have or will develop a neurodegenerative disorder. Onset of RBD may either precede or follow the onset of these conditions, though the former is more common.

One of the first studies to document this relationship reported that Parkinson's develops in 11 out of 29 (38%) men, on average 12.7 years after RBD symptom onset (Schenck, Bundlie, & Mahowald, 1996). Seven years later, the proportion of patients that developed Parkinson's and/or dementia increased to 65% (Schenck, Bundlie, & Mahowald, 2003). These and other findings underscore a need to closely follow patients with RBD.

Elevated levels of anxiety and depressive symptoms have been found in patients with RBD (Lee, Choi, Lee, & Jeong, 2016; Molano et al., 2008). However, rates of actual affective disorders are less clear and temporal relationships are rarely documented. In one study of more than 200 patients diagnosed with RBD, 30% had previously received a depression diagnosis, and depression preceded the onset of RBD symptoms in approximately 50% of these patients (Fernández-Arcos, Iranzo, Serradell, Gaig, & Santamaria, 2016).

Narcolepsy is comorbid in approximately 30% of RBD cases and, consistent with the demographic profile of narcolepsy, these patients tend to be younger in age than the typical RBD patient.

Non-REM Sleep Arousal Disorders

Non-REM sleep arousal disorders arise from partial awakenings from non-REM sleep. They typically occur during the first third of the night-time sleep episode. Arousals are recurrent but usually brief (e.g., less than 10 minutes), although some episodes may last longer. Non-REM arousals most commonly take the form of sleepwalking or sleep terrors, with many individuals experiencing both.

Sleep terrors (also called night terrors) are characterized by arousals from sleep in which individuals seem frightened, and may yell, scream or cry. Sleepwalking involves complex motor behaviors including getting out of bed, walking around, eating, or sexual behaviors. During sleepwalking episodes, which may last from a few minutes to 30–45 minutes, the individual often stares blankly, without awareness of his/her surroundings, and is not easily awakened. Upon full awakening, individuals rarely recall these night-time episodes. Diagnosis of a non-REM arousal disorder is only given when episodes are accompanied by significant clinical distress or impairment.

Epidemiology   Non-REM sleep arousal disorders are relatively common in the general population with the highest prevalence rates in children. A recent meta-analysis estimated the lifetime prevalence of sleepwalking as 1.5% in adults (Stallman & Kohler, 2016). The estimated prevalence of night terrors in adults is 2.2% (Ohayon, Guilleminault, & Priest, 1999). Developmental differences in the occurrence of these disorders may be explained in part by a normal decline in the percentage of non-REM sleep across the life span. Also, individuals who develop sleep terrors before the age of 10 are more likely to suffer from sleep terrors as adults.

Etiology   Sleep terrors and sleepwalking both have a strong genetic basis (Kales et al., 1980; Ohayon, Mahowald, Dauvilliers, Krystal, & Leger, 2012) and may represent clinical variants of a common diathesis. This view is supported by the following: (a) high rates of comorbidity among those who sleepwalk and experience sleep terrors; (b) children with sleep terrors often become adult sleepwalkers; and (c) sleep terrors and sleepwalking often co-occur as part of the same episode.

Physiologic and environmental factors also appear to increase risk, including sleep deprivation/fragmentation, stressful life events/changes, high fevers, and light or noise in the environment. However, specific mechanisms are not well understood and some data suggest that associations between parasomnias and sleep deprivation/fragmentation may be better explained by the presence of co-occurring breathing-related sleep disorders (Ohayon et al., 2012). There are several case reports of sedative medications inducing sleepwalking and other non-REM parasomnias.

Consistent with the frequent occurrence of parasomnias and nocturnal seizures, both nocturnal phenomena may arise from differential activation of innate motor behaviors via central pattern generators (Tassinari et al., 2005). Other researchers have speculated that non-REM parasomnias in childhood may be replaced by nocturnal frontal lobe epilepsy in adulthood because both phenomena share a common (possibly genetic) pathophysiological substrate involving a defective arousal system (Tinuper, 2007).

Diagnosis Sleep terrors and sleepwalking are most commonly detected via self-report or reports from bed partners or family members. PSG with video monitoring can be used for detection purposes, though it is often difficult to capture these events in the sleep laboratory setting. EEG changes associated with sleepwalking or sleep terrors may not always be observable. Because the individual may sit up in bed with their eyes open, sleep terrors can be mistaken for nightmares. However, unlike a nightmare, sleep terrors are followed by amnesia for the event the following day.

Non-REM sleep arousal disorders can include a range of sexual behaviors (e.g., masturbation, intercourse). These behaviors are typically abrupt in onset, seemingly occur without motivation, and are uncharacteristic of the individual in comparison to his or her typical behavior. Actions tend to develop early in the sleep period (e.g., 1 hour after sleep onset). Similar to RBD, differential diagnoses of Kleine–Levin disorder and malingering should also be considered.

Sleep terrors may be confused with sleep panic attacks, which also occur during the first half of the sleep period (Craske & Barlow, 1989; Mellman & Uhde, 1988). Sleep panic attacks are abrupt awakenings from sleep that can last for several minutes. They almost always emerge during the transition from N2 to N3 sleep (Mellman & Uhde, 1988; Uhde, 2000). Contrary to sleep terrors, however, sleep panic patients have full and accurate recall of the sleep panic attacks upon awakening and physiological hyperarousal (e.g., tachycardia, increased respiratory rate) is less pronounced than that observed in sleep terror disorder.

Comorbid Medical and Psychological Factors A higher proportion of adult-onset sleep-walkers are found among psychiatric samples than in the general population. Alcohol abuse/dependence, major depressive disorder, and obsessive-compulsive disorder are among the most common psychiatric comorbidities found in adults (Ohayon et al., 2012). Comorbid sleep disorders are also common, including obstructive sleep apnea, circadian rhythm sleep disorders, and insomnia. Sleepwalking and sleep terrors can also coexist, sometimes within the same episode.

Additionally, non-REM parasomnias can co-occur with epileptic disorders. One investigation reported the presence of parasomnias among 34% of adult patients with nocturnal frontal lobe epilepsy (Bisulli et al., 2005). Nocturnal seizures are often mistaken for non-REM parasomnias, and distinguishing these night-time episodes can be particularly challenging, as EEG findings are not always helpful. Most experts agree that definite diagnosis should rest on nocturnal video-PSG findings or at least on video recordings of these events.

CASE STUDY

BACKGROUND AND HISTORY

Richard is a 25-year-old, single, healthy, Caucasian male who has experienced significant sleep problems for more than 1 year, following a car accident that nearly killed his best friend. On the night of the accident, Richard was driving to a local concert with his friend seated in the passenger seat. The two were joking and laughing on the way to the event and Richard consequently did not see a stop sign at a busy intersection. After failing to stop, his vehicle was struck on the passenger's side by an oncoming car. Richard and the other driver sustained minor injuries and were treated at the scene. His friend was less fortunate. He suffered internal injuries and was medevaced for emergency care. He remained in the hospital for 2 weeks and underwent several surgeries before making a recovery.

Despite a history of good-quality sleep, Richard began having nightmares depicting the accident almost immediately. Nightmares woke Richard from sleep, usually drenched in sweat and hyperventilating, and prevented him from returning back to sleep. During the daytime, Richard experienced significant symptoms of hypervigilance and anxiety mixed with anger and guilt. His generally elevated level of arousal combined with fear of having graphic nightmares also produced significant problems with sleep initiation (i.e., prolonged sleep onset), sleep maintenance (i.e., night-time awakenings) and overall nonrestful sleep. Although he returned to his job in construction approximately 1 week after the accident, Richard's anxiety, irritable mood, and inability to sustain attention for long periods rendered him a hazard to himself and others at the job site. He was laid off within the month.

Over the next year, Richard's functioning continued to decline. The frequency of his nightmares decreased from nearly every night to a few times a month. They occasionally wake him from sleep, but he no longer fears their occurrence. His insomnia symptoms have, however, significantly worsened. At present, his anxiety level begins to increase as soon as the sun sets and he now avoids driving during the night-time hours. At home, he engages in several maladaptive habits to feel more relaxed at night, including drinking many beers, always having the TV turned on, and keeping all the lights on in his apartment. Richard generally stays awake watching TV on the sofa until he can barely keep his eyes open before going to bed. However, when he gets into bed, he feels wide awake and is unable to initiate sleep. He will sometimes stay in his bed feeling frustrated and try to "force" himself to fall asleep, whereas other nights he gets out of bed, consumes more alcohol, and repeats the same behavioral pattern. Richard's sleep problems have produced considerable impairments in his daytime functioning. He is unable to keep a steady job due to excessive daytime somnolence, being chronically late for work after oversleeping, and falling asleep during lunch breaks. He often cancels social plans because he is feeling too tired and irritable and/or because it would require him to drive at night.

DIAGNOSTIC CONCEPTUALIZATION

Nightmares are common in the aftermath of trauma and commonly, though not always, depict the original traumatic event. In most cases, nightmares remit over subsequent days and weeks. In other cases, however, nightmares can lead to significant distress and feelings of hyperarousal at night that interfere with sleep (Neylan et al., 1998). A growing body of evidence implicates persistent sleep disruption, including nightmares, in the pathophysiology of PTSD. Both subjective reports of nightmares as well as disruption/

fragmentation of REM sleep periods (i.e., when nightmares occur) following trauma exposure pose increased risk for developing PTSD (Germain, Buysse, & Nofzinger, 2008; Mellman & Hipolito, 2006). Moreover, inadequate sleep can exacerbate other symptoms of the disorder (e.g., irritability, anxiety) and contribute to poor clinical outcomes. Thus, while sleep disturbances represent prominent symptoms of and *DSM-5* criteria for PTSD, sleep–trauma relationships are multifaceted and complex.

In Richard's case, the presence of distressing nightmares depicting the accident in the aftermath of the traumatic event constitute one risk factor for a poor prognosis (Mellman et al., 1995, 2001). His resultant fear of experiencing additional nightmares and heightened level of arousal at night also contribute to his risk profile by interfering with his ability to both fall and stay asleep. Thus, even though the frequency of Richard's nightmares has decreased over time, the severity of his insomnia has worsened, due in part to a conditioned increase in anxiety/arousal at night. The maladaptive coping behaviors he has adopted in response, such as consuming alcohol, exposing himself to bright light at night, and lying in bed for long periods while awake ensure the persistence of his insomnia; and as is often the case among patients with chronic insomnia, his daytime functioning is significantly impacted by his poor sleep.

We do not have adequate information to definitively determine whether a PTSD diagnosis is appropriate in this case. However, the emergence of severe insomnia subsequent to a trauma is among the strongest prognosticators of PTSD (Wright et al., 2011), consistent with other findings showing hyperarousal symptoms to predict the longitudinal course of PTSD (Schell, Marshall, & Jaycox, 2004). Still, insomnia can develop in the absence of the disorder, and even when PTSD is in remission, insomnia often remains a distressing residual symptom that poses increased risk for relapse (Boe, Holgersen, & Holen, 2010). In Richard's case, hyperarousal at night, poor sleep hygiene, and maladaptive coping behaviors contribute to inadequate total sleep and functional impairments. Thus, irrespective of a PTSD diagnosis, a diagnosis of *DSM-5* insomnia disorder (780.52) is appropriate and his insomnia warrants direct clinical intervention.

What about a diagnosis of *DSM-5* nightmare disorder (307.47)? According to *DSM-5* criteria, nightmares that occur a few times a month would be considered "mild" but still adequate for a diagnosis of nightmare disorder. However, Richard is no longer experiencing fear/distress related to his nightmares, which only wake him from sleep occasionally. It is also unclear that his nightmares directly interfere with his functioning, a criterion for diagnosis. Nightmares are included as potential *DSM-5* PTSD intrusion symptoms which may well account for Richard's occasional nightmares. Even if PTSD criteria are not met, nightmares are common, long-term sequelae of trauma exposure that do necessarily warrant formal diagnosis or treatment. Thus, a diagnosis of nightmare disorder would not be appropriate at present in Richard's case.

SUMMARY

A considerably expanded list of sleep disorders in *DSM-5* reflects the wealth of sleep-focused research that has emerged in recent years. These changes also represent efforts to enhance the clinical utility of definitions and diagnostic criteria for clinicians. Some specific changes are particularly noteworthy. First, removal of two previous diagnoses, namely, sleep disorder related to another mental disorder and sleep disorder related to another medical condition, underscores a need for clinical attention to be directed towards sleep specifically. Along these lines, the change from primary insomnia (*DSM-IV*) to insomnia disorder (*DSM-5*) was specifically intended to avoid a primary versus secondary designation of the disorder when it co-occurs with other conditions.

The current chapter focuses on a few specific conditions, but the full range of sleep–wake disorders differ greatly in presentation, course, detection method, and underlying pathophysiology. Comprehensive assessment should always include a detailed patient history, along with physical examination, completion of questionnaires and sleep diaries, and/or objective sleep measures as necessary. Effective treatments are similarly varied and may include behavioral and/or pharmacologic treatments in combination with medical care. Given the bidirectional associations between sleep and virtually all aspects of health, one of the greatest challenges encountered by clinicians can be in determining the cause of different sleep problems. High rates of co-occurring conditions often serve to further cloud a complicated picture. Thus, it is important that patients be referred to a sleep specialist when appropriate.

Multiple methods are available for assessing sleep but the clinical interview remains one of the most valuable tools for understanding the etiology, symptoms, and course of a sleep disorder. A detailed history can reveal relationships among major life events, medical illnesses, emotional disturbances, and sleep symptoms that directly inform both diagnosis and treatment. The selection of additional methods of assessment should directly depend on the suspected sleep diagnosis.

REFERENCES

Alfano, C. A., & Mellman, T. (2010). Sleep in anxiety disorders. In J. W. Winkelman & D. T. Plante (Eds.), *Foundations of Psychiatric Sleep Medicine*. Cambridge University Press; New York, NY.

Ali, M., Auger, R. R., Slocumb, N. L., & Morgenthaler, T. I. (2009). Idiopathic hypersomnia: clinical features and response to treatment. *Journal of Clinical Sleep Medicine, 5*, 562–568.

American Academy of Sleep Medicine. (2014). *International classification of sleep disorders* (3rd ed.). Darien, IL: American Academy of Sleep Medicine.

American Psychiatric Association. (2000). *Diagnostic and statistical manual of mental disorders* (4th ed., rev.). Washington, DC: Author.

American Psychiatric Association. (2013). *Diagnostic and statistical manual of mental disorders* (5th ed.). Arlington, VA: American Psychiatric Publishing.

Archer, S. N., Robilliard, D. L., Skene, D. J., Smits, M., Williams, A., Arendt, J., & von Schantz, M. (2003). A length polymorphism in the circadian clock gene Per3 is linked to delayed sleep phase syndrome and extreme diurnal preference. *Sleep, 26*(4), 413–415.

Aurora, R. N., Zak, R. S., Auerbach, S. H., Casey, K. R., Chowdhuri, S., Karippot, A., . . . Lamm, C. I. (2010). Best practice guide for the treatment of nightmare disorder in adults. *Journal Clinical Sleep Medicine, 6*(4), 389–401.

Billiard, M., & Sonka, K. (2016). Idiopathic hypersomnia. *Sleep Medicine Reviews, 29*, 23–33.

Bisulli, F., Vignatelli, L., Naldi, I., Licchetta, L., Provini, F., Plazzi, G., . . . Tinuper, P. (2010). Increased frequency of arousal parasomnias in families with nocturnal frontal lobe epilepsy: a common mechanism? *Epilepsia, 51*, 1852–1860.

Boe, H. J., Holgersen, K. H., & Holen, A. (2010). Reactivation of posttraumatic stress in male disaster survivors: The role of residual symptoms. *Journal of Anxiety Disorders, 24*, 397–402.

Boeve, B. F., Silber, M. H., Saper, C. B., Ferman, T. J., Dickson, D. W., Parisi, J. E., . . . Tippman-Peikert, M. (2007). Pathophysiology of REM sleep behaviour disorder and relevance to neurodegenerative disease. *Brain, 130*, 2770–2788.

Borbély, A. A., Daan, S., Wirz-Justice, A., & Deboer, T. (2016). The two-process model of sleep regulation: a reappraisal. *Journal of Sleep Research, 25*, 131–143.

Carskadon, M. A., & Dement, W. C. (1997). Sleep tendency: An objective measure of sleep loss. *Sleep Research, 6*, 940.

Carskadon, M. A., Vieira, C., & Acebo, C. (1993). Association between puberty and delayed phase preference. *Sleep*, *16*, 258–258.

Chang, A. M., Aeschbach, D., Duffy, J. F., & Czeisler, C. A. (2015). Evening use of light-emitting eReaders negatively affects sleep, circadian timing, and next-morning alertness. *Proceedings of the National Academy of Sciences*, *112*(4), 1232–1237.

Craske, M. G., & Barlow, D. H. (1989). Nocturnal panic. *Journal of Nervous and Mental Disease*, *177*, 160–168.

Crowley, S. J., Acebo, C., & Carskadon, M. A. (2007). Sleep, circadian rhythms, and delayed phase in adolescence. *Sleep Medicine*, *8*(6), 602–612.

Danilenko, K. V., Putilov, A. A., Russkikh, G. S., Duffy, L. K., & Ebbesson, S. O. (1994). Diurnal and seasonal variations of melatonin and serotonin in women with seasonal affective disorder. *Arctic Medical Research*, *53*, 137–145.

Dauvilliers, Y., Lopez, R., Ohayon, M., & Bayard, S. (2013). Hypersomnia and depressive symptoms: methodological and clinical aspects. *BMC Medicine*, *11*, 78–87.

Decker, M. J., Lin, J. M. S., Tabassum, H., & Reeves, W. C. (2009). Hypersomnolence and sleep-related complaints in metropolitan, urban, and rural Georgia. *American Journal of Epidemiology*, *169*, 435–443.

Dijk, D. J., Duffy, J. F., Riel, E., Shanahan, T. L., & Czeisler, C. A. (1999). Ageing and the circadian and homeostatic regulation of human sleep during forced desynchrony of rest, melatonin and temperature rhythms. *The Journal of Physiology*, *516*, 611–627.

Edinger, J. D. and Krystal, A. D. (2003) Subtyping primary insomnia: is sleep state misperception a distinct clinical entity? *Sleep Medicine Reviews*, *7*, 203–214.

Fernández-Arcos, A., Iranzo, A., Serradell, M., Gaig, C., & Santamaria, J. (2016). The clinical phenotype of idiopathic rapid eye movement sleep behavior disorder at presentation: a study in 203 consecutive patients. *Sleep*, *39*, 121–132.

Ford D. E., & Kamerow D. B. (1989). Epidemiologic study of sleep disturbances and psychiatric disorders: An opportunity for prevention? *Journal of the American Medical Association*, *262*(11): 1479–1484.

Franzen, P. L., & Buysse, D. J. (2008). Sleep disturbances and depression: risk relationships for subsequent depression and therapeutic implications. *Dialogues in Clinical Neuroscience*, *10*, 473–481.

Germain, A., Buysse, D. J., & Nofzinger, E. (2008). Sleep-specific mechanisms underlying post-traumatic stress disorder: integrative review and neurobiological hypotheses. *Sleep Medicine Reviews*, *12*, 185–195.

Germain, A., & Nielsen, T. A. (2003). Sleep pathophysiology in posttraumatic stress disorder and idiopathic nightmare sufferers. *Biological Psychiatry*, *54*, 1092–1098.

Glozier, N., O'Dea, B., McGorry, P. D., Pantelis, C., Amminger, G. P., Hermens, D. F., . . . Hickie, I. B. (2014). Delayed sleep onset in depressed young people. *BMC Psychiatry*, *14*, 33.

Horne, J. A., & Ostberg, O. (1976). A self-assessment questionnaire to determine morningness-eveningness in human circadian rhythms. *International journal of chronobiology*, *4*(2), 97–110.

Hublin, C., Kaprio, J., Partinen, M., & Koskenvuo, M. (1999). Nightmares: familial aggregation and association with psychiatric disorders in a nationwide twin cohort. *American Journal of Medical Genetics*, *88*(4): 329–336.

Johns, M. W. (1991). A new method for measuring daytime sleepiness: the Epworth sleepiness scale. *Sleep*, *14*, 540–545.

Kales, J. D., Kales, A., Soldatos, C. R., Caldwell, A. B., Charney, D. S., & Martin, E. D. (1980). Night terrors: Clinical characteristics and personality patterns. *Archives of General Psychiatry*, *37*(12), 1413–1417.

King, N. J., Hamilton, D. I., & Ollendick, T. H. (1988). *Children's fears and phobias: A behavioral perspective*. Chichester, UK: John Wiley & Sons.

Kripke, D. F., Garfinkel, L., Wingard, D. L., Klauber, M. R., & Marler, M. R. (2002). Mortality associated with sleep duration and insomnia. *Archives of General Psychiatry, 59*, 131–136.

Landolt, H. P., Werth, E., Borbély, A. A., & Dijk, D. J. (1995). Caffeine intake (200 mg) in the morning affects human sleep and EEG power spectra at night. *Brain Research, 675*, 67–74.

Lee, H. G., Choi, J. W., Lee, Y. J., & Jeong, D. U. (2016). Depressed REM sleep behavior disorder patients are less likely to recall enacted dreams than non-depressed ones. *Psychiatry Investigation, 13*, 227–231.

Levin, R., & Nielsen, T. A. (2007). Disturbed dreaming, posttraumatic stress disorder, and affect distress: a review and neurocognitive model. *Psychological Bulletin, 133*, 482–528.

Levin, R., & Nielsen, T. (2009). Nightmares, bad dreams, and emotion dysregulation a review and new neurocognitive model of dreaming. *Current Directions in Psychological Science, 18*, 84–88.

Li, S. X., Zhang, B., Li, A. M., & Wing, Y. K. (2010). Prevalence and correlates of frequent nightmares: a community-based 2-phase study. *Sleep, 33*, 774–780.

Lovato, N., & Lack, L. (2016). Circadian phase delay using the newly developed re-timer portable light device. *Sleep and Biological Rhythms, 14*, 157–164.

Martin, S. K., & Eastman, C. I. (1998). Medium-intensity light produces circadian rhythm adaptation to simulated night-shift work. *Sleep, 21*, 154–166.

Mellman, T. A., David, D., Bustamante, V., Torres, J., & Fins, A. (2001). Dreams in the acute aftermath of trauma and their relationship to PTSD. *Journal of Traumatic Stress, 14*, 241–247.

Mellman, T. A., Kulick-Bell, R., Ashlock, L. E., & Nolan, B. (1995). Sleep events among veterans with combat-related posttraumatic stress disorder. *The American Journal of Psychiatry, 152*, 110–115.

Mellman, T. A., & Hipolito, M. M. (2006). Sleep disturbances in the aftermath of trauma and posttraumatic stress disorder. *CNS Spectrum, 11*, 611–615.

Mellman, T. A., & Uhde, T. W. (1988). Electroencephalographic sleep in panic disorder: A focus on sleep-related panic attacks. *Archives of General Psychiatry, 46*, 178–184.

Micic, G., Lovato, N., Gradisar, M., Ferguson, S. A., Burgess, H. J., & Lack, L. C. (2016). The etiology of delayed sleep phase disorder. *Sleep Medicine Reviews, 27*, 29–38.

Miller, C. B., Espie, C. A., & Kyle, S. D. (2014). Cognitive behavioral therapy for the management of poor sleep in insomnia disorder. *Depression, 9*, 99–107.

Miyagawa, T., Honda, M., Kawashima, M., Shimada, M., Tanaka, S., Honda, Y., & Tokunaga, K. (2009). Polymorphism located between CPT1B and CHKB, and HLA-DRB1* 1501-DQB1* 0602 haplotype confer susceptibility to CNS hypersomnias (essential hypersomnia). *PLoS One, 4*, e5394.

Molano, J. E., Mihci, B., Boeve, et al., (2008). Anxiety and apathy are associated with probable REM sleep behavior disorder among cognitively normal elderly subjects: The Mayo Clinic Study of Aging. *Neurology 70* A146.

Monti, J. M., & Monti, D. (2000). Sleep disturbance in generalized anxiety disorder and its treatment. *Sleep Medicine Review, 4*, 263–276.

Morin, C. M., & Benca, R. (2012). Chronic insomnia. *The Lancet, 379*, 1129–1141.

Morin, C. M., & Jarrin, D. C. (2013). Epidemiology of insomnia: prevalence, course, risk factors, and public health burden. *Sleep Medicine Clinics, 8*, 281–297.

Mukhopadhyay, S., Fineberg, N. A., Drummond, L. M., Turner, J., White, S., Wulff, K., & Ghodse, H. (2008). Delayed sleep phase in severe obsessive-compulsive disorder: a systematic case-report survey. *CNS Spectrums, 13*, 406–413.

Nadorff, M. R., Lambdin, K. K., & Germain, A. (2014). Pharmacological and non-pharmacological treatments for nightmare disorder. *International Review of Psychiatry, 26*(2), 225–236.

Natale, V., Plazzi, G., & Martoni, M. (2009) Actigraphy in the assessment of Insomnia: A quantitative approach. *Sleep, 32*(6): 767–771.

Neikrug, A. B., & Ancoli-Israel, S. (2009). Sleep disorders in the older adult – A mini-review. *Gerontology, 56*(2), 181–189.

Neylan, T. C., Marmar, C. R., Metzler, T. J., Weiss, D. S., Zatzick, D. F., Delucchi, K. L., . . . Schoenfeld, F. B. (1998). Sleep disturbances in the Vietnam generation: findings from a nationally representative sample of male Vietnam veterans. *American Journal of Psychiatry*, *155*, 929–933.

Nickell, P. V., & Uhde, T. W. (1991). Anxiety disorders and epilepsy. In O. Devinsky & W. H. Theodore (Eds.), *Epilepsy and behavior* (pp. 67–84). New York, NY: Wiley-Liss.

Nielsen, T. (2010). Nightmares associated with the eveningness chronotype. *Journal of Biological Rhythms*, *25*, 53–62.

Nishida, M., Pearsall, J., Buckner, R. L., & Walker, M. P. (2009). REM sleep, prefrontal theta, and the consolidation of human emotional memory. *Cerebral Cortex*, *19*, 1158–1166.

Nordin, M., & Kaplan, R. M. (2010). Sleep discontinuity and impaired sleep continuity affect transition to and from obesity over time: Results from the Alameda county study. *Scandinavian Journal of Public Health*, *38*: 200–207.

Ohayon, M. M. (2002). Epidemiology of insomnia: what we know and what we still need to learn. *Sleep Medicine Reviews*, *6*, 97–111.

Ohayon, M. M., Caulet, M., & Lemoine, P. (1998). Comorbidity of mental and insomnia disorders in the general population. *Comprehensive Psychiatry*, *39*, 185–197.

Ohayon, M. M., Guilleminault, C., & Priest, R. G. (1999). Night terrors, sleepwalking, and confusional arousals in the general population: their frequency and relationship to other sleep and mental disorders. *Journal of Clinical Psychiatry*, *60*(4), 268.

Ohayon, M. M., Mahowald, M. W., Dauvilliers, Y., Krystal, A. D., & Leger, D. (2012). Prevalence and comorbidity of nocturnal wandering in the US adult general population. *Neurology*, *78*, 1583–1589.

Okawa, M., & Uchiyama, M. (2007). Circadian rhythm sleep disorders: characteristics and entrainment pathology in delayed sleep phase and non-24 sleep–wake syndrome. *Sleep Medicine Reviews*, *11*(6), 485–496.

Pace-Schott, E. F., & Hobson, J. A. (2002). The neurobiology of sleep: genetics, cellular physiology and subcortical networks. *Nature Reviews Neuroscience*, *3*, 591–605.

Pereira, D. S., Tufik, S., Louzada, F. M., Benedito-Silva, A. A., Lopez, A. R., Lemos, N. A., . . . Pedrazzoli, M. (2005). Association of the length polymorphism in the human Per3 gene with the delayed sleep-phase syndrome: does latitude have an influence upon it. *Sleep*, *28*(1), 29–32.

Perlis, M. L., Smith, M. T., & Pigeon, W. R. (2005). Etiology and pathophysiology of insomnia. *Principles and Practice of Sleep Medicine*, *4*, 714–725.

Roberts, R. E., Shema, S. J., Kaplan, G. A., & Strawbridge, W. J. (2000). Sleep complaints and depression in an aging cohort: a prospective perspective. *American Journal of Psychiatry*, *157*, 81–88.

Robillard, R., Naismith, S. L., Rogers, N. L., Ip, T. K., Hermens, D. F., Scott, E. M., & Hickie, I. B. (2013). Delayed sleep phase in young people with unipolar or bipolar affective disorders. *Journal of Affective Disorders*, *145*, 260–263.

Roenneberg, T., Wirz-Justice, A., & Merrow, M. (2003). Life between clocks: daily temporal patterns of human chronotypes. *Journal of Biological Rhythms*, *18*(1), 80–90.

Roth, T. (2007). Insomnia: definition, prevalence, etiology, and consequences. *Journal of Clinical Sleep Medicine*, *3*, S7–S10.

Rye, D. B., Bliwise, D. L., Parker, K., Trotti, L. M., Saini, P., Fairley, J., . . . Jenkins, A. (2012). Modulation of vigilance in the primary hypersomnias by endogenous enhancement of GABAA receptors. *Science Translational Medicine*, *4*, 161ra151.

Sack, R. L., Auckley, D., Auger, R. R., Carsakadon, M. A., Wright, K. P., & Vitiello, M. V. (2007). Circadian rhythm sleep disorders: part 11, advanced sleep phase disorder, free-running disorder, and irregular sleep-wake rhythm. *Sleep*, *30*, 1484–501.

Saxvig, I. W., Pallesen, S., Wilhelmsen-Langeland, A., Molde, H., & Bjorvatn, B. (2012). Prevalence and correlates of delayed sleep phase in high school students. *Sleep Medicine*, *13*, 193–199.

Schell, T. L., Marshall, G. N., & Jaycox, L. H. (2004). All symptoms are not created equal: the prominent role of hyperarousal in the natural course of posttraumatic psychological distress. *Journal of Abnormal Psychology*, *113*, 189.

Schenck, C. H., Bundlie, S. R., & Mahowald, M. W. (1996). Delayed emergence of a parkinsonian disorder in 38% of 29 older men initially diagnosed with idiopathic rapid eye movement sleep behavior disorder. *Neurology, 46*, 388–393.

Schenck, C. H., Bundlie, S. R., & Mahowald, M. W. (2003). REM behavior disorder (RBD): delayed emergence of parkinsonism and/or dementia in 65% of older men initially diagnosed with idiopathic RBD, and an analysis of the minimum & maximum tonic and/or phasic electro-myographic abnormalities found during REM sleep. *Sleep 26*, A316–A316.

Schenck, C. H., Lee, S. A., Bornemann, M. A. C., & Mahowald, M. W. (2009). Potentially lethal behaviors associated with rapid eye movement sleep behavior disorder: review of the literature and forensic implications. *Journal of Forensic Sciences, 54*(6), 1475–1484.

Schubert, J. R., & Coles, M. E. (2013). Obsessive-compulsive symptoms and characteristics in individuals with delayed sleep phase disorder. *The Journal of Nervous and Mental Disease, 201*, 877–884.

Semiz, U. B., Basoglu, C., Ebrinc, S., & Cetin, M. (2008). Nightmare disorder, dream anxiety, and subjective sleep quality in patients with borderline personality disorder. *Psychiatry and Clinical Neurosciences, 62*, 48–55.

Siclari, F., Khatami, R., Urbaniok, F., Nobili, L., Mahowald, M. W., Schenck, C. H., & Bassetti, C. L. (2010). Violence in sleep. *Brain, 133*, 3494–3509.

Sowa, N. A. (2016). Idiopathic hypersomnia and hypersomnolence disorder: A systematic review of the literature. *Psychosomatics, 57*, 152–164.

Stallman, H. M., & Kohler, M. (2016). Prevalence of sleepwalking: a systematic review and meta-analysis. *PloS One, 11*, e0164769.

Tanaka, S., & Honda, M. (2010). IgG abnormality in narcolepsy and idiopathic hypersomnia. *PLoS One, 5*, e9555.

Tassinari, C. A., Rubboli, G., Gardella, E., Cantalupo, G., Calandra-Buonaura, G., Vedovello, M., . . . Meletti, S. (2005). Central pattern generators for a common semiology in fronto-limbic seizures and in parasomnias. A neuroethologic approach. *Neurological Sciences, 26*, s225–s232.

Tinuper, P., Provini, F., Bisulli, F., Vignatelli, L., Plazzi, G., Vetrugno, R., . . . Lugaresi, E. (2007). Movement disorders in sleep: guidelines for differentiating epileptic from non-epileptic motor phenomena arising from sleep. *Sleep Medicine Reviews, 11*, 255–267.

Tsuno, N., Besset, A., & Ritchie, K. (2005). Sleep and depression. *The Journal of Clinical Psychiatry, 66*, 1254–1269.

Uhde, T. W. (2000). The anxiety disorders. In M. H. Kryger, T. Roth, & W. Dement (Eds.), *Principles and practice in sleep medicine* (3rd ed., pp. 1123–1139). Philadelphia, PA: W. B. Saunders.

Vgontzas, A. N., Liao, D., Bixler, E. O., Chrousos, G. P., & Vela-Bueno, A. (2009). Insomnia with objective short sleep duration is associated with a high risk for hypertension. *Sleep, 32*, 491–497.

Walker, M. P., & van Der Helm, E. (2009). Overnight therapy? The role of sleep in emotional brain processing. *Psychological Bulletin, 135*, 731–748.

Wehr, T. A., Duncan, W. C., Sher, L., Aeschbach, D., Schwartz, P. J., Turner, E. H., . . . Rosenthal, N. E. (2001). A circadian signal of change of season in patients with seasonal affective disorder. *Archives of General Psychiatry, 58*, 1108–1114.

Wright, K. M., Britt, T. W., Bliese, P. D., Adler, A. B., Picchioni, D., & Moore, D. (2011). Insomnia as predictor versus outcome of PTSD and depression among Iraq combat veterans. *Journal of Clinical Psychology, 67*, 1240–1258.

Young, T., Peppard, P. E., & Gottlieb, D. J. (2002). Epidemiology of obstructive sleep apnea: a population health perspective. *American Journal of Respiratory and Critical Care Medicine, 165*, 1217–1239.

Zhang, B., & Wing, Y. (2006). Sex differences in insomnia: a meta-analysis. *Sleep, 29*, 85–93.

Zisapel, N. (2001). Circadian rhythm sleep disorders. *CNS Drugs, 15*(4), 311–328.

CHAPTER 16

Sexual Dysfunctions and Paraphilic Disorders

NATALIE O. ROSEN, LORI A. BROTTO, and KENNETH J. ZUCKER

THE SEXUAL AND GENDER IDENTITY DISORDERS are classified in separate chapters of the *Diagnostic and Statistical Manual of Mental Disorders*, fifth edition (*DSM-5*; American Psychiatric Association [APA], 2013). This represents a change from the *Diagnostic and Statistical Manual of Mental Disorders*, fourth edition, text-revision (*DSM-IV-TR*; APA, 2000) in which the (1) sexual dysfunctions, (2) paraphilias, and (3) gender identity disorders were housed within the same chapter. This chapter focuses on sexual dysfunctions, which characterize sexual problems related to desire, arousal, orgasm and pain, as well as the paraphilias, which are recurrent, sexually arousing fantasies, urges, or behaviors involving nonconventional or nonconsenting persons and/ or objects. Gender identity disorder, renamed gender dysphoria in the *DSM-5*, is covered in a separate chapter.

Part I: Sexual Dysfunctions Description of Sexual Disorders

Nearly 20 years have passed since the approval and subsequent widespread availability of the oral treatments for male sexual dysfunction (e.g., sildenafil, vardenafil, tadalafil, and avanafil); as a result, research exploring the pathophysiology, epidemiology, assessment, and treatment of sexual dysfunctions has had an unprecedented surge. Methodological sophistication has soared, particularly in the area of neural imaging for low desire and genetic studies of orgasmic dysfunction and genito-pelvic pain. With the publication of the *DSM-5* (APA, 2013) and the upcoming 11th edition of the *International Classification of Diseases* (*ICD-11*; due May 2018), there has also been an intensified examination of the reliability and validity of these categories of sexual disorders.

The *DSM-5* abandoned the linear model of sexual response, which categorized the sexual dysfunctions according to which phase of Masters and Johnson's (1966) four-stage human sexual response cycle was disrupted. This change was the result of long-standing dissatisfaction with the linear model's ability to account for the variability in sexual response across individuals. In brief, the sexual dysfunctions in previous editions of the *DSM* were separated into disorders of desire, arousal, and orgasm (and pain), which fit

Adult Psychopathology and Diagnosis, Eighth Edition. Edited by Deborah C. Beidel and B. Christopher Frueh.
© 2018 John Wiley & Sons, Inc. Published 2018 by John Wiley & Sons, Inc.
Companion website: www.wiley.com/go/beidel/psychopathology8e

with Masters and Johnson's conceptualization of the human sexual response cycle—that is, linear stages from sexual desire to arousal to orgasm. As has been noted (e.g., Binik, 2005, 2010a,b), the sexual pain disorders were added as a fourth category of sexual dysfunction, although "pain" was not considered to be part of the human sexual response cycle. Over the past 15 years there have been concerted efforts to redefine these categories given numerous criticisms about the linear response cycle. In particular, concerns about the lack of generalizability of the sexual response cycle for women were that: (a) it is based on the sexual response patterns of men; (b) it assumes a linear progression of sexual experience from desire to arousal to orgasm, although healthy sexual experiences can progress in any order and do not need to proceed in this sequence for satisfaction to occur; (c) many of the experiences that are considered normal parts of female sexual response (e.g., fantasizing) are not reported in all women, yet they remain sexually satisfied; (d) characteristics of the sample on which the human sexual response cycle were based are considered biased; and (e) it decontextualized the sexual experience (Hill & Preston, 1996; Klusmann, 2002; Regan & Berscheid, 1996).

Another system for classifying sexual dysfunctions as "problems" was proposed by the New View Task Force, led by sexologist Leonore Tiefer. The resulting "New View Document" (Kaschak & Tiefer, 2002; Tiefer, 2001) was a radical departure from the DSM classification system and suggested that sexual problems in women have been over-diagnosed and medicalized. This alternate system focused on causes instead of symptoms and concluded that such difficulties can be a result of sociocultural, political, or economic factors; partner and relationship status; psychological factors; or medical factors. The New View nosology fervently rejected the biological emphasis of sexual complaints that was inherent in the DSM, and the associated "medicalization of sex" that resulted. Empirical support for the New View system is sparse; however, some data suggest the usefulness of this classification scheme in that 98% of the sexual issues in one sample of British women could be classified using the New View framework (Nicholls, 2008).

In the absence of a universally agreed upon underlying model of sexual response, the sexual dysfunctions in the DSM-5 are listed in alphabetical order. This represents a radical departure from past DSMs and has generated significant controversy (Balon & Clayton, 2014; Clayton, DeRogatis, Rosen, & Pyke, 2012a, b; DeRogatis, Clayton, Rosen, Sand, & Pyke, 2011). Collectively, sexual dysfunctions are defined by the DSM-5 as "a heterogeneous group of disorders that are typically characterized by a clinically significant disturbance in a person's ability to respond sexually or to experience sexual pleasure" (APA, 2013, p. 497). The definition also emphasizes the need for the clinician to exercise clinical judgment when deciding if the difficulty is due to lack of adequate sexual stimulation, in which case a diagnosis of a mental illness is clearly not appropriate.

The DSM-5 (APA, 2013) list of sexual dysfunctions includes delayed ejaculation, erectile disorder, female orgasmic disorder (FOD), female sexual interest/arousal disorder (FSIAD), genito-pelvic pain/penetration disorder, male hypoactive sexual desire disorder, premature (early) ejaculation, substance/medication-induced sexual dysfunction, other specified sexual dysfunction, and unspecified sexual dysfunction. Like previous editions of the DSM, each sexual dysfunction in the DSM-5 can be specified as being either lifelong (i.e., the problem has existed since the individual first became sexually active) or acquired (i.e., the problem is new in onset), and generalized (i.e., the problem is not limited to certain types of stimulation, situations, or partners) or situational (i.e., the problem occurs only with select types of stimulation, situations, or partners). The DSM-5 also has a new severity specifier in which the clinician is asked to rate the level of distress as mild, moderate, or severe.

Also new to *DSM-5* is a list of five associated features that the clinician should be mindful of during assessment. These are features that may play a role in etiology and/or maintenance of the sexual difficulty and include: (1) partner factors (e.g., a partner's sexual dysfunction); (2) relationship factors (e.g., problematic communication patterns); (3) individual vulnerability factors (e.g., depression or other associated psycho-pathology); (4) cultural/religious factors (e.g., attitudinal prohibitions against sex); and (5) medical factors (e.g., chronic pain or fatigue). During assessment, the clinician is asked to assess each of these domains, taking into account the extent to which each may account for the current presenting complaint. These issues may then be addressed in the course of managing the sexual difficulty. Whereas criterion A for each of the sexual dysfunctions outlines the diagnostic criteria, criterion B for each delineates the duration criterion in that symptoms must be present for a minimum duration of at least 6 months. The addition of this criterion to *DSM-5* is intended to reduce the probability that temporary or otherwise adaptive changes in sexual functioning may be diagnosed as a sexual dysfunction. Also required for a diagnosis across the sexual dysfunctions is the presence of clinically significant distress in the individual (criterion C).

The range of factors that would exclude the diagnosis of a sexual dysfunction has also been expanded from previous editions of the *DSM*. For example, in addition to the rule-outs due to the presence of another psychiatric disorder, a medication, or a medical condition that completely accounts for the presenting sexual problems, a diagnosis of sexual dysfunction is not made if the symptoms are the result of severe relationship distress (such as domestic violence) or significant stressors.

A group of sexual medicine experts, most of whom have ties to pharmaceutical advisory boards, have protested against the revisions made in the *DSM-5*, and, in particular, the expanded criteria for low sexual interest and arousal. The argument is frequently made that the co-occurrence of diagnoses (e.g., that of hypoactive sexual desire disorder and female sexual arousal disorder) does not warrant the merging of these separate diagnoses into a single syndrome. There has also been marked concern about the 6-month duration criterion, noting that it "raises the bar" for a diagnosis to be made. As such, the International Society of Women's Sexual Health (ISSWSH) sponsored a meeting for these experts to convene and come up with a new nomenclature that would be better able to support clinical care, research, and regulatory use in female sexual dysfunction (Parish et al., 2016). The committee recommended that health care providers continue using the former diagnosis of hypoactive sexual desire disorder (HSDD), even though the diagnosis no longer exists in the *DSM-5*. They declared transparently in their consensus document that a return to the former HSDD would allow for continuity in guiding endpoints for clinical trials (Parish et al., 2016, p. 1889). In addition, they recommended that experts consider adopting a new disorder, "female genital arousal disorder" (FGAD), defined as "an inability to develop or maintain adequate genital response including vulvovaginal lubrication, engorgement of the genitalia, and sensi-tivity of the genitalia associated with sexual activity for a minimum of 6 months" (p. 1895). They created subcategories such that FGAD may be associated with vascular injury/dysfunction, and/or neurologic injury or dysfunction. Insufficient arousal due to inadequate stimulation would not be diagnosed. They add that the diagnosis requires a clinical history plus a physical examination. Given that the *DSM* is a document used largely by mental health providers who do not carry out physical exams, it is unclear how most psychiatrists, psychologists, and social workers will be able to make a diagnosis of FGAD.

The ISSWSH-sponsored committee also recommended a number of other additions to the nomenclature for women's sexual dysfunction. They recommended the inclusion of persistent genital arousal disorder, when there is "persistent or recurrent, unwanted or intrusive, distressing feelings of genital arousal or being on the verge of orgasm (genital dysesthesia) not associated with concomitant sexual interest" (Parish et al., 2016, pp. 1897–1898). Although there has been a moderate amount of research done on this condition, it was deemed to be insufficient to justify its inclusion in the *DSM-5*.

The ISSWSH classification committee made a number of recommendations to the orgasm disorders in the *DSM-5*. Though they lauded the inclusion of difficulties with frequency and intensity of orgasm in the *DSM-5*, they argued that many women also experience problems with orgasm timing. Specifically, they recommended that orgasms occurring too early or too late, or those occurring without subjective pleasure, should be included under the heading of female orgasmic disorder (Parish et al., 2016). In addition, the committee recommended a new disorder, "female orgasmic illness syndrome," which reflects peripheral and/or central aversive symptoms that occur with orgasm. The symptoms may include disorientation, confusion, impaired judgment, etc. They acknowledged that very little research exists to support this new condition.

The *ICD* is also undergoing revision, and will be available in May 2018. A preliminary report from the committee assigned to sexual and gender disorders indicates that there will likely be a new section in the *ICD-11* entitled "Conditions Related to Sexual Health" which combines the previous separate sections of the "organic" and "non-organic" sexual dysfunctions in the *ICD-10* (Reed et al., 2016a). Similar to the *DSM-5*, the diagnosis allows for a number of "etiological qualifiers", which are defined as being relevant and contributory. These will include: associated with disorder or disease classified elsewhere, injury or surgical treatment; associated with a medication or substance; associated with lack of knowledge; associated with psychological or behavioral factors; associated with relationship factors; and associated with cultural factors. The term "hypoactive sexual desire dysfunction" will be retained, as well as "female sexual arousal dysfunction", both of which align with categories in the former *DSM-IV-TR*. Unlike the *DSM-5*, which excludes diagnosis of a sexual dysfunction in the case of a medication or medical disorder, these will be permitted in the *ICD-11*, given that the latter is a "classification of all health conditions" (Reed et al., 2016a, p. 209).

On the one hand, the existence of multiple different nomenclatures, with some overlapping but not identical disorders, criteria sets, and descriptions, speaks to the field's lack of understanding on the precise nature of sexual desire, arousal, and orgasm functioning, and dysfunction. On the other hand, this type of diagnostic debate fuels additional research, which will ultimately reveal the true nature of the sexual response.

CLINICAL PICTURE

DELAYED EJACULATION

Delayed or retarded ejaculation is defined as either a marked delay in ejaculation or the marked infrequency or absence of ejaculation. The difficulty must occur on the majority (approximately 75% or more) of partnered sexual encounters, and take place without the man desiring the delay. Importantly, the symptoms must not be the result of inadequate sexual stimulation. Because the delay leads to extended sexual activity, some have suggested that it provides a prolonged period of penetration, thus enhancing a female partner's potential for pleasure. Although this may be true, delayed ejaculation is associated with significant distress in both the man and his partner. In some instances, partners may report feeling less attractive due to their partner's inability to ejaculate.

ERECTILE DISORDER

Erectile disorder (ED) has been the topic of considerable research and academic interest for many decades, but particularly since the oral phosphodiesterase type 5 inhibitors sildenafil, tadalafil, vardenafil, and avanafil have been approved and readily available. ED is defined by the *DSM-5* as the presence of at least one of the three following symptoms, 75–100% of the time: (1) marked difficulty in obtaining an erection during sexual activity; (2) marked difficulty in maintaining an erection until the completion of sexual activity; or (3) marked decrease in erectile rigidity (APA, 2013). Despite the view among some researchers that erectile difficulties warrant the diagnosis of dysfunction regardless of whether the man is distressed or not, the *DSM-5* requires the presence of clinically significant distress in the individual. Often associated with ED is behavioral avoidance of sexual activities, alterations in self-confidence or mood, and marked anxiety over future sexual encounters.

FEMALE ORGASMIC DISORDER

The *DSM-5* defines FOD as the presence (on 75–100% of occasions of sexual activity) of either (1) marked delay in, marked infrequency of, or absence altogether of orgasm, or (2) markedly reduced intensity of orgasmic sensations (APA, 2013). As women show wide variability in the factors and types of stimulation that elicit orgasm, the clinician must exercise judgment in determining if the difficulty connotes a sexual dysfunction. Women who are able to reach orgasm via clitoral stimulation only and not through vaginal penetration should not be diagnosed as having FOD.

FEMALE SEXUAL INTEREST/AROUSAL DISORDER

The diagnosis of FSIAD is new to *DSM-5* and represents an expansion of the previous diagnosis of HSDD in women, with the addition of a criterion pertaining to inadequate or absent genital sensations. Low sexual desire in women has been the focus of intense research and media attention, given the promising findings of pharmaceutical agents for women's complaints of absent desire. However, the finding that low sexual desire in women is both highly prevalent and usually multifactorial, suggests that this diagnosis may be especially difficult to treat. Even though the Food and Drug Administration (FDA) in the United States has now approved the centrally acting medication, Addyi (flibanserin), for premenopausal women with clinically low desire, sales of the medication are extremely low, its efficacy is meager, and it is completely contraindicated with alcohol (Gao, Yang, Yu, & Cui, 2015; Jaspers et al., 2016; Saadat et al., 2017). Among a number of other reasons, the finding that sexual desire and arousal overlap significantly in women (Brotto, 2010a; Graham, 2010), and that women endorse multiple different models of sexual response (Nowosielski, Wróbel, & Kowalczyk, 2016) led to the expansion of the previous diagnosis of low desire, and the deletion of female sexual arousal disorder (FSAD) from the *DSM-5*.

A major change in this diagnosis from previous editions of the *DSM* is the introduction of a polythetic diagnosis in which a woman may experience any three of six possible symptoms in order to meet diagnostic criteria. In brief, these six criteria include: (1) absent or reduced interest in sex; (2) absent or reduced erotic thoughts or fantasies; (3) difficulties with initiation of sexual activity and receptivity to sex; (4) lack of sexual excitement/ pleasure during sex (75–100% of the time); (5) lack of sexual interest/arousal in response to any sexual triggers (e.g., erotica); and (6) lack of genital or nongenital sensations during sex (75–100% of the time). The use of polythetic criteria means that two women can have different symptom profiles and still both meet diagnostic criteria for FSIAD. Although criticized by some researchers, the new criteria reflect the wide variability across women in the ways that their sexual desire is expressed, and the finding that women do not adhere to a single model of sexual excitement (Giraldi, Kristensen, & Sand, 2015; Nowosielski et al., 2016). It is important for clinicians to note that the mere presence of inadequate vaginal lubrication is not grounds for a sexual dysfunction diagnosis, despite the fact that vulvovaginal atrophy is a common problem and often the focus of gynecological care (Reed et al., 2016a).

Genito-Pelvic Pain/Penetration Disorder

Binik (2005, 2010a,b) has provided compelling arguments for moving the sexual pain disorders from the "Sexual Dysfunctions" section of the *DSM* to the "Pain Disorders" category. In summary, the reasoning is that dyspareunia (previously defined as pain with intercourse in the *DSM-IV-TR*) shares many more similarities to other pain disorders than it does with other sexual dysfunctions. However, this proposal was rejected for *DSM-5*. Nonetheless, this category did undergo a major revision in that the previous diagnoses of dyspareunia and vaginismus (the latter previously defined by significant tension or spasm of the pelvic floor muscles, not due to a structural/physical abnormality, which prevents penetration of the vagina) were merged into a single diagnosis newly titled "genito-pelvic pain/penetration disorder" (GPPPD). Furthermore, sexual pain in men was removed from the *DSM-5* due to insufficient data. Men's pain during sexual activity is not an uncommon experience and deserves further study (Herbenick, Schick, Sanders, Reece, & Fortenberry, 2015).

Genito-pelvic pain/penetration disorder is diagnosed when a woman experiences persistent or recurrent difficulties for a minimum duration of six months in any one of the following areas: (1) during vaginal penetration, (2) marked pain with attempted or actual penetration, (3) marked fear or anxiety about vaginal pain, or (4) marked tensing of the pelvic floor muscles during attempted penetration. In some women, the symptoms may lead to extreme avoidance of any attempt at vaginal penetration, whereas in other women, sexual activity may continue despite the presence of symptoms or pain. To adequately assess the fourth criterion of pelvic floor hypertonicity, a skilled pelvic floor physiotherapist or a gynecologist with expertise in vulvovaginal disorders should conduct the assessment. Since there are no valid physiological measures of these symptoms, the diagnosis is made entirely based on the woman's self-report.

Male Hypoactive Sexual Desire Disorder

A proposal to extend the diagnostic criteria for sexual interest/arousal disorder to men (Brotto, 2010b) was rejected on the grounds of insufficient evidence. Thus, disorders of sexual desire are separated by gender in the *DSM-5*, with most of the previous diagnostic criteria for HSDD (*DSM-IV-TR*; APA, 2000) being retained in the diagnosis of male hypoactive sexual desire disorder (MHSDD). Thus, a man may meet criteria for MHSDD if he experiences deficient or absent sexual thoughts/fantasies and deficient or absent desire for sex, as long as the symptoms occur for a minimum of 6 months and produce clinically significant distress. Instances of desire discrepancy in a couple, whereby the man experiences significantly lower levels of sexual desire compared with his partner, are not always indicative of a problem in that individual. Thus, clinical judgment that takes into account age, relationship duration, and other contextual factors must be exercised when making this diagnosis.

Premature (Early) Ejaculation

The *DSM-5* defines premature (early) ejaculation (PE), as a persistent or recurrent pattern (i.e., on at least 75–100% of partnered sexual activities) of ejaculation occurring less than 1 minute following the onset of vaginal penetration, and occurs despite the man's wish. Considerable research has led to the 1-minute criterion, and this definition is also accepted internationally by other sexual medicine societies. The *DSM-5* notes that although ejaculation may occur earlier than desired during other, nonintercourse sexual activities, precise duration criteria have not been established. Reports of lack of control over the impending ejaculation and associated anxiety are commonplace among men with this disorder. PE has an impact on the man's partner, given that the defining criterion is that ejaculation takes place before, on, or shortly after penetration with a partner. In fact, men with PE report fulfilling a partner's needs as being very important to their own rating of sexual satisfaction. Rowland et al. (2004) and Symonds, Roblin, Hart, and Althof (2003) found that 50% of men reported distressing effects of their PE on either finding new relationships or on not satisfying a current partner.

Substance/Medication-Induced Sexual Dysfunction

In the *DSM-5* (APA, 2013), a diagnosis of sexual dysfunction is not made in instances in which the sexual symptoms are attributable to the effects of a substance (e.g., alcohol) or medication (e.g., selective serotonin reuptake inhibitors [SSRIs]). Interestingly, in the forthcoming *ICD-11*, sexual dysfunction associated with substances, medications, or medical conditions can still be diagnosed, but a qualifier indicating the likely source of the sexual problems is to be identified. However, when there is evidence of both sexual difficulties developing during or soon after substance intoxication or medication withdrawal, and knowledge that the given substance or medication is capable of producing sexual symptoms, then a diagnosis of substance/medication-induced sexual dysfunction is made. The sexual difficulties must not be due to a separate sexual dysfunction that is not associated with a substance or medication, and must not take place during a state of delirium.

Other Specified Sexual Dysfunction and Unspecified Sexual Dysfunction

The categories of "Other Specified Sexual Dysfunction" and "Unspecified Sexual Dysfunction" have replaced the previous *DSM-IV-TR* category of "Sexual Dysfunction Not Otherwise Specified". In the case of "other specified," this diagnosis is made when there are symptoms characteristic of a sexual dysfunction that cause significant distress; however, the symptoms do not meet full criteria for a sexual dysfunction or are not captured by the present definitions of sexual dysfunctions. For example, symptoms of sexual aversion or persistent genital arousal might be considered as another specified sexual dysfunction. This category is used when the clinician wishes to indicate the specific reason that the symptoms do not meet full criteria for a disorder. The diagnosis of unspecified sexual dysfunction is reserved for instances in which the clinician chooses not to indicate the reason that the criteria are not met for a specific sexual dysfunction or when there is insufficient information to allow the clinician to make a diagnosis.

DIAGNOSTIC CONSIDERATIONS

Primary care providers are often the first point of contact for individuals with sexual concerns. Adequate assessment requires a thorough biopsychosocial approach, including attention to early family history, relationship and sexual history, and psychiatric status and history, and may require the assistance of a sexual health expert. In some cases, pre-existing and confounding contributors may be directly responsible for the sexual issues. For example, relationship factors can mask sexual dysfunction, as these constructs are highly correlated (e.g., Dennerstein, Lehert, Guthrie, & Burger, 2007). Problems in the relationship can directly impact sexual functioning, and difficulties expressing one's sexual needs can negatively impact sexual desire. In general, men have more difficulty than women with discussing emotional and sexual issues (Banmen & Vogel, 1985). It is important to note that some decline in sexual function is normative with age and relationship duration (Klusmann, 2002) and should not be considered a sexual dysfunction. Cases in which a lack of adequate sexual stimulation accounts for the sexual problems should not be diagnosed as a dysfunction. The clinician is advised to take into account factors that affect sexual function, such as age, novelty of the sexual partner or situation, and recent frequency of sexual activity, before making a sexual diagnosis. Also of note, the comorbidity of sexual dysfunctions other than the presenting one is very common (Hendrickx, Gijs, & Enzlin, 2014). A problem at any stage of sexual response frequently engenders difficulties at other stages.

Sometimes a sexual difficulty may be an adaptive reaction to a stressful or aversive situation. For example, in homosexuals who are ashamed or insecure about their sexual orientation and who are, thus, in heterosexual relationships, sexual desire may be low in response to individuals of the opposite sex but may be satisfactory toward individuals of the desired sex (Sandfort & de Keizer, 2001). In this case, a diagnosis of sexual desire disorder would not be warranted. The list of associated features for each sexual dysfunction allows a clinician to determine whether individual vulnerability factors, including stress, are contributing to the sexual complaints. This would orient treatment to the stressor and may reduce the likelihood of prematurely resorting to pharmacological aids.

EPIDEMIOLOGY

In the last two decades, there have been several international surveys aimed at determining the prevalence of sexual dysfunction. Early epidemiological studies, such as the National Health and Social Life Survey, a population-based study of 3,159 American men and women between the ages of 18 and 59, found a total prevalence for sexual difficulties of 43% in women and 31% in men (Laumann, Paik, & Rosen, 1999; Laumann, Gagnon, Michael, & Michaels, 1994). Similarly, the Global Study of Sexual Behaviors, which surveyed 13,882 women and 13,618 men aged 40–80 years across 29 countries, reported prevalence rates ranging from 7.7% to 43.45% in women and 2.9% to 30.5% in men, depending on the region and the problem (Laumann et al., 2005). However, critics raised concerns about the accuracy of these figures and the potential medicalization of sexual problems, noting that personal distress over the problem was not accounted for, and that a sexual difficulty is not necessarily a dysfunction if such a large proportion of the population experiences it (Tiefer, 2002). Shifren et al. (2008) assessed the extent to which sexual difficulties in 31,581 American women aged 18 or older were associated with distress about the sexual relationship and one's own sexuality. They found that 43% of women reported a sexual problem, 22% experienced sexual distress, and 12% of the sample experienced a sexual problem that evoked distress. Further, the positive relationship between low desire and age has been found to disappear when distress is taken into account (Hayes, Dennerstein, Bennett, & Fairley, 2008). And the majority of sexual problems with a 1-month duration do not persist to 6 months (Mercer et al., 2003). Finally, several studies have found a high prevalence of sexual satisfaction despite the presence of sexual symptoms (e.g., Cain et al., 2003). Clearly the presence of distress and persistence are critical to an accurate estimation of the prevalence of sexual dysfunction.

In addition to Shifren et al. (2008), two other studies (Bancroft, Loftus, & Long, 2003; Witting et al., 2008) reported the prevalence rates of women's sexual difficulties over the past 4 weeks and accounting for distress to be 24% and 7–23%, respectively (rates varied depending on the specific sexual difficulty and age group). Two recent studies have examined the prevalence of sexual dysfunctions in both men and women. Christensen et al. (2011) found that 11% of men and 11% of women reported at least one distressing sexual problem over the past year, and Hendrickx et al. (2014) found that 11.3% of men and 20.2% of women had at least one distressing sexual problem over the previous 4 weeks. It is notable that the prevalence of sexual problems may vary considerably across cultures, further highlighting the importance of contextual factors (Laumann et al., 2005).

Probably the best population-based estimates available for sexual dysfunction come from Britain's third National Survey of Sexual Attitudes and Lifestyles (Natsal-3; Mitchell et al., 2016). The Natsal-3 consisted of a stratified probability sample of 15,162 British men and women between the ages of 16 and 74, had a good response rate (57.7%), and used a combination of face-to-face interviews and questionnaires (Mitchell et al., 2016). The researchers inquired about sexual dysfunctions based on the *DSM-5* diagnostic criteria. The following dysfunctions were examined: delayed ejaculation, ED, FOD, FSIAD, GPPPD, MHSDD, and PE. Of all sexually active men and women reporting one or more of the sexual function problems lasting 3 months or more in the last year, 11.1% of men and 16% of women reported at least one problem that met all three *DSM-5* morbidity criteria (i.e., symptom persistence of 6 months or longer, always or often symptomatic, and fairly/very distressing). The specific prevalence rates for each sexual dysfunction in men and women are presented in Tables 16.1 and 16.2, respectively. The tables include the prevalence rate of the population reporting the problem, in addition to the rate meeting the *DSM-5* morbidity criteria. The prevalence rates stratified by age are those that meet the *DSM-5* morbidity criteria. It should be noted that these rates represent individuals who were sexually active with one or more partner in the previous year. Thus, these rates exclude sexually inactive people, some of who may in fact be avoiding sexual activity due to sexual dysfunction. The *DSM-5* now recognizes the contribution of biological, psychological, and social factors (termed "associated features" in the *DSM-5*). In the Natsal-3, several factors were associated with sexual problems regardless of whether or not problems met morbidity criteria. Medical factors (e.g., other chronic health conditions, use of medications with sexual side-effects), intraindividual factors (e.g., symptoms of depression and anxiety), as well as interpersonal factors (e.g., sexual incompatibility with a partner, poor sexual communication) were associated with higher rates of sexual difficulties. In terms of gender differences, unemployment was associated with male but not female dysfunction, and experiencing nonvolitional sex was more strongly associated with women's than with men's sexual dysfunction (Mitchell et al., 2016).

Delayed ejaculation is less prevalent than premature or early ejaculation, with a prevalence according to the Natsal-3 of 9%, and of 0.5% when accounting for morbidity

Table 16.1

Prevalence (%) of Sexual Difficulties According to Age in Men Aged 16–74 (*n* = 4840) in the National Survey of Sexual Attitudes and Lifestyles (Mitchell et al., 2016), Rounded to the Nearest 0.5%

Sexual Difficulty	Population Reporting Problem (%)	Population Meeting DSM-5 Morbidity Criteria (%)[1]	Age (years)					
			16–24	25–34	35–44	45–54	55–64	65–74
Difficulty in reaching climax	9	0.5	0	0.5	0.5	0.5	0.5	1.5
Trouble getting or keeping an erection	13	2	0.5	0.5	1	2	4.5	5
Lacked interest in having sex	15	1	0	1	1	1	1.5	1
Reached climax more quickly than you would like	15	1.5	1.5	2	2	1.5	1	1
Experienced one or more of these problems	38	4	2	3.5	3.5	4	6.5	7.5

[1]*DSM-5* morbidity criteria are: (1) symptoms have persisted for a minimum duration of approximately 6 months; (2) symptoms have been experienced in almost all or all (approximately 75–100%) sexual encounters or have been persistent/recurrent; and (3) symptoms have caused the individual clinically significant distress.

criteria. Hendrickx et al. (2014), who surveyed 17,598 heterosexual Flemish men, found similar prevalence rates; the rate of distressing retrograde ejaculation was 0.2% and lack of a forceful propulsive ejaculation had a rate of 0.6%. Previous research has shown that prevalence rates might be higher in Southeast Asia than in Europe (Laumann et al., 2005); however, no studies that have included distress have made this comparison.

According to the Natsal-3, the prevalence of ED is 13%, but when meeting the *DSM-5* morbidity criteria, it drops to 0.5–2.0% in men aged 16–54, and 4.5–5.0% in men

Table 16.2

Prevalence (%) of Sexual Difficulties According to Age in Women Aged 16–74 (*n* = 6669) in the National Survey of Sexual Attitudes and Lifestyles (Mitchell et al., 2016), Rounded to the Nearest 0.5%

Sexual Difficulty	Population Reporting Problem (%)	Population Meeting DSM-5 Morbidity Criteria (%)[1]	Age					
			16–24	25–34	35–44	45–54	55–64	65–74
Difficulty in reaching climax	16.5	2	3	2.5	1	2	1.5	0
Lacked interest and arousal	6.5	0.5	0.5	1	0.5	0.5	1	0
Felt physical pain as a result of sex	7.5	2	1.5	2	1.5	1	4	1
Experienced one or more of these problems	23	3.5	4.5	4	3	3	5.5	1.5

[1]*DSM-5* morbidity criteria are: (1) symptoms have persisted for a minimum duration of approximately 6 months; (2) symptoms have been experienced in almost all or all (approximately 75–100%) sexual encounters or have been persistent/recurrent; and (3) symptoms have caused the individual clinically significant distress.

aged 55–74. These numbers are in line with two other recent studies examining erectile difficulties. Christensen et al. (2011), who included 2,120 sexually active Danish men in their study, found that 5% of the men reported erectile difficulties meeting the *DSM-IV-TR* sexual dysfunction criteria. Hendrickx et al. (2014) also found that 4.8% of men reported erectile difficulties meeting the *DSM-IV-TR* criteria. Additionally, although the prevalence and severity of ED appears to increase with age, older men are often less distressed when compared with middle-aged or younger men (Rosen, Miner, & Wincze, 2014b).

The prevalence of FOD in the Natsal-3 was 16.5%, and 2% when accounting for morbidity, making it the most common female sexual dysfunction. Other studies, primarily of Caucasian or Black/African American women from North America or Northern Europe have found the prevalence of orgasmic dysfunction to range between 3.1% and 21.1% (Bancroft et al., 2003; Christensen et al., 2011; Hendrickx et al., 2014; Shifren et al., 2008; Witting et al., 2008). Orgasmic difficulties are more common among younger women, perhaps due to a lack of sexual skill and high partner turnover. Rates of anorgasmia may also be culturally determined, with higher prevalence in women from Southeast Asia (Laumann et al., 2005).

In the Natsal-3, 6.5% of women lacked sexual interest and arousal. This rate dropped to 0.5% when accounting for morbidity. Other recent studies have found the prevalence of dysfunction in desire and/or arousal to range from 2.5% to 37.7%, although these studies measured desire and arousal separately based on the *DSM-IV-TR* disorders (Bancroft et al., 2003; Christensen et al., 2014; Hendrickx et al., 2014; Shifren et al., 2008; Witting et al., 2008). The prevalence rates for women's low desire and arousal in the Natsal-3 are strikingly lower than prior estimates, possibly a reflection of the more stringent methods and criteria of this study. The British Natsal-3 sample was also primarily Caucasian and heterosexual, limiting its generalizability. There is some evidence to suggest that difficulties with desire and arousal may be higher in women aged 40–80 from the Middle East and Southeast Asia (Laumann et al., 2005).

Pain elicited from sexual activity was reported by 7.5% of the women in the Natsal-3, and 2% met morbidity criteria. Notably, the proportion reporting distress was twice as high among women with pain compared with the other two sexual problems. Other recent studies have found the prevalence rates to range from 0.4% to 11.3%, although some of these studies measured pain based on differing criteria (Bancroft et al., 2003; Christensen et al., 2011; Hendrickx et al., 2014; Witting et al., 2008). The rates of pain are highest among postmenopausal women, likely related to the vulvovaginal atrophy that is common during this time.

Based on the findings from the Natsal-3, low desire in men occurs in approximately 15%, or 1.0% when meeting the morbidity criteria. These numbers are in line with those other studies that included distress as a criterion; both Bancroft et al. (2003) and Hendrickx et al. (2014) found the prevalence of hypoactive sexual desire to be 1.6% in men. It is important to note that men may be reticent to report low desire for numerous reasons, including an adherence to cultural norms (Meana & Steiner, 2014).

Premature (early) ejaculation affects approximately 15% of men, and 1.5% when meeting the morbidity criteria in the Natsal-3. Hendrickx et al. (2014) found the prevalence of PE among men aged 16–74 to be 5.7%, and Christensen et al. (2011) reported a rate of 7% among men aged 16–94. However, these studies based their criteria on the *DSM-IV-TR*, which did not include the new *DSM-5* requirement that ejaculation occur within 1 minute of penetration to be considered premature.

PSYCHOLOGICAL AND BIOLOGICAL ASSESSMENT

A thorough biopsychosocial interview is foundational in the assessment of sexual difficulties. An important aspect in assessing sexual dysfunction is determining whether the problem is related to a psychological or a biological/organic etiology, or both. It is also important for the clinician to distinguish lifelong (primary) versus acquired (secondary), and generalized versus situational difficulties, as these may point to important etiological factors. For example, clinicians should inquire about morning erections to gain a sense of the degree to which ED is situational or generalized. Complete loss of morning erections suggests a vascular or neurological component to the ED, and a referral to a qualified urologist is indicated.

Assessment involves face-to-face interviews of the presenting person, ideally together with and separately from the partner, covering known and supposed predisposing, precipitating, and perpetuating issues relevant to the sexual difficulty, as well as potential protective factors that could be capitalized upon in treatment. These include assessments of mood and general psychiatric status, medications and medical comorbidities, psychosexual history, and personal history. Although many self-report questionnaires are available, these can only serve to complement and not replace a thorough clinical interview (Brotto et al., 2016a).

Accurate assessment of medical factors often requires physical and laboratory examinations. In men, testosterone that is free, bound to albumin, and bound to sex hormone binding globulin (SHBG) should be measured first thing in the morning. A thorough assessment of sexual interest/arousal disorder in women involves separately assessing for difficulties in mental sexual arousal and interest versus genital excitement. It is important to bear in mind that the experience of sexual desire may emerge following sexual arousal initiated by a sexually meaningful stimulus, rather than always preceding arousal (Laan & Both, 2008).

Assessment of GPPPD may include a physical examination of the level of voluntary control of the pelvic floor muscles, pelvic floor muscle tonus, presence of vaginal wall prolapse, signs of vaginal atrophy, size of introitus, presence of discharge, evidence of infection (acute or chronic), epithelial disorders, and/or pain by a qualified health professional (usually a gynecologist or primary care provider with specialized training in vulvovaginal disorders). To assess for the criterion of marked vulvovaginal pain, the physician can use the cotton swab test in which the vestibule is palpated with a cotton swab and the woman reports areas of particular tenderness or pain. During such an assessment, it is important for the clinician to elicit as much information as possible regarding the qualities of pain (onset, location, quality, duration, and intensity). Because the elicitation of pain may evoke distressing emotions for the woman, it is important for the clinician to be sensitive to the woman's emotional state and only conduct the genital examination with sufficient explanation and preparation. As pelvic floor muscle spasms have been found to be an unreliable indicator of GPPPD, the diagnosis is largely based on the patient's self-report of pain during the examination as well as difficulties with intercourse, including anticipation of pain, anxiety, and phobic avoidance.

Assessment of PE in clinical trials has adopted the stopwatch technique, in which the duration of time between penetration and ejaculation is monitored, usually by the man's partner. Studies using this methodology have led to the current recommendation that 1 minute be used as the threshold for determining when early ejaculation might constitute a sexual dysfunction. However, this additional layer of performance anxiety may artificially inflate the man's dysfunction, making this technique suboptimal, particularly when making a diagnosis of PE. Accurate assessment can also be confounded by embarrassment (Symonds et al., 2003). Grenier and Byers (2001) found marked differences in the prevalence of PE depending on the operational definition of "rapid." They concluded that a multifaceted approach should include assessment of behavior, affect, self-efficacy, and the degree of severity of different dimensions of PE. Perelman (2006) has also stressed the importance of assessing whether the patient is able to detect premonitory sensations (bodily changes reflecting arousal/impending ejaculation), as this is central for control over the decision to ejaculate.

ETIOLOGICAL CONSIDERATIONS

As implied in the previous section on assessment, all of the sexual dysfunctions are considered to be biopsychosocial in their etiology. Although previous editions of the *DSM* included the specifier of "due to psychological factors" or "due to combined factors," this has been eliminated from the *DSM-5* due to the recognition that this level of delineation is rarely possible. Even in cases when there is a clear biological or medical etiology to the sexual symptoms, sexual functioning typically involves an integration of all organ systems of the body, the vascular system, muscles, and the brain, and it is experienced in an intrapersonal, interpersonal, and cultural context, making multifactorial etiology the norm rather than the exception.

DELAYED EJACULATION

The most common physiological etiologies for delayed ejaculation include certain disease processes associated with aging, such as heart disease and benign prostatic hyperplasia/lower urinary tract symptoms. Genetic factors including aberrations in the serotonergic system, such as hyperactivity at the 5-HT2C receptor and hypoactivity at the 5-HT1A receptor, have been found, in rodent studies, to be related to delayed ejaculation. Pelvic surgeries, diabetes, neurological disturbances, antidepressants, and alpha-blockers have been linked to delayed ejaculation. Injury to the lumbar sympathetic ganglia (i.e., such as from multiple sclerosis) may also delay ejaculation. Possible psychosocial etiologic pathways include fear, performance anxiety, hostility, guilt, low desire for the partner, lack of confidence, and inadequate stimulation (Rowland et al., 2010). One chart review has suggested that idiosyncratic masturbatory style (e.g., using rapid stimulation or pressure in a manner that is not easily duplicated by partnered sexual activity), as well as using a variant sexual fantasy (e.g., fantasy about sadism and masochism [S&M]), act as predisposing factors for delayed ejaculation (Perelman, 2006).

ERECTILE DISORDER

Vascular and neurological diseases or damage, as well as lifestyle behaviors (e.g., smoking, alcohol abuse, inactivity) that affect the vascularization and innervation necessary for erection and/or the stamina to sustain the physical exertion of penetration, are associated with ED (Rosen et al., 2014b). Some antidepressants, antihypertensives, and drugs that block the conversion of testosterone into dihydro-testosterone, which are commonly used to treat male pattern hair loss and benign prostatic hyperplasia (Shamloul & Ghanem, 2013), have also been implicated. Hypothyroidism, hypogonadism, and hyperprolactinemia are also associated with ED (Morales et al., 2004). Radical genital or pelvic surgeries, such as prostate cancer surgery (Bolt, Evans, & Marshall, 1987;

Stanford et al., 2000), can result in a sudden loss of erectile function, especially if the procedure did not involve nerve-sparing techniques. Among men treated for diabetes, the prevalence of ED is 28% (Feldman, Goldstein, Hatzichristou, Krane, & McKinlay, 1994). Overall, any medical condition that causes blood vessel damage will likely have a negative impact on erectile function.

When a man can regularly obtain and maintain an erection in some circumstances (e.g., morning erections, masturbation) but not others (partnered intercourse), then it is reasonable to assume that psychological factors are playing an important role. There are many cases of ED where psychological factors are responsible but go unrecognized. For example, distinguishing ED that is secondary to depression from ED that is a result of antidepressant use (Ferguson, 2001) is an important consideration. Performance anxiety is also strongly associated with erectile dysfunction, whether it is primarily an organic or psychological problem. Anxiety or stress may activate the sympathetic nervous system, which can both increase smooth muscle tone and interfere with signals from the sacral spinal cord. The man with no prior history of ED who fails to reach an erection one time due to stress or other factors may become concerned about his future erectile ability such that his ED is maintained by performance anxiety. Implicit in this example is the phenomenon that factors that maintain a sexual dysfunction may not be the same factors that initially triggered the complaint.

Female Orgasmic Disorder

The same organic factors implicated in delayed ejaculation in men have been associated with FOD in women (e.g., neurologic injury, use of SSRIs, alcohol). There may also be a genetic aspect to orgasmic difficulties in women, given the finding of higher correlations between orgasmic frequency during masturbation and orgasmic frequency during sexual intercourse in monozygotic twins versus dizygotic twins (Dunne et al., 1997). In addition, the heritability for orgasm problems with intercourse is 31–34%, and the rate for orgasm problems in masturbation is 37–45% (Dunn, Cherkas, & Spector, 2005). Psychological factors found to be associated with anorgasmia in women include lower educational levels, high religiosity, fear of losing control, communication difficulties with a partner, and sex guilt (Graham, 2014; Laumann et al., 1999). Although sexual abuse has been associated with anorgasmia in some studies, other studies have failed to find such a relationship. There does not appear to be a correlation between relationship satisfaction and orgasmic ability, given that many women are sexually satisfied with their partners despite not consistently, or perhaps ever, attaining orgasm with intercourse (Basson, 2004).

Female Sexual Interest / Arousal Disorder

Low desire in both men and women is considered to result from a combination of organic and psychological factors. In women, relationship duration, age, feelings for one's partner, and depression have all been associated with sexual desire disorder (Brotto, Bitzer, Laan, Leiblum, & Luria 2010). In fact, 27–62% of women with low desire also meet criteria for a depressive disorder (Hartmann, Heiser, Ruffer-Hesse, & Kloth, 2002; Phillips & Slaughter, 2000). Interestingly, a few studies report that depressed mood is associated with increased frequency of masturbation (Cyranowski et al., 2004; Frolich & Meston, 2002)—one potential index of sexual desire. Low testosterone and testosterone metabolites have not been found to significantly differentiate women with and without

HSDD (Reed, Nemer, & Carr, 2016b), although the latter are found to have lower levels of the androgen precursor, dihydroepiandrosterone (DHEA; Basson, Brotto, Petkau, & Labrie, 2010). Women with HSDD show different patterns of neural activation particularly in neural circuits involved with encoding arousing stimuli, retrieval of past erotic situations, or both (Arnow et al., 2009).

The *DSM-5* includes cultural and religious factors as a specifier to consider before making a diagnosis of any sexual dysfunction (APA, 2013). Studies on cultural influences in low desire have shown women of East Asian heritage to have lower levels of desire compared with women of European descent. Moreover, among the East Asian women, those with higher levels of mainstream (i.e., Westernized) acculturation had higher sexual desire than those who retained their culture or heritage (Woo, Brotto, & Gorzalka, 2011). Interestingly, studies in Middle Eastern countries find that anorgasmia and difficulties with penetration due to pelvic floor tightness are more common than complaints of low sexual desire (Atallah et al., 2016). As such, the most recent International Consultation on Sexual Medicine recommended that sexual desire, as with other sexual complaints, be considered in the context of the individual's culture, and that caution be exercised when using assessment measures validated in Western samples.

Vaginal photoplethysmography as a measure of genital vagocongestion has not been able to differentiate women with versus those without significant sexual arousal concerns (Laan, van Driel, & van Lunsen, 2008). For this reason, it is assumed that impairments in genital blood flow do not underlie genital arousal complaints of women. The reasons for women's lower levels of concordance (i.e., association between genital and self-reported sexual response) compared with men (Chivers, Seto, Lalumière, Laan, & Grimbos, 2010) have become the focus of several lines of research, because it may shed light on different models of sexual responding between the sexes. Regardless of the cause, it is essential for the clinician to tease apart true FSIAD from desire that is simply lower than what a partner wishes, or society idealizes.

GENITO-PELVIC PAIN/PENETRATION DISORDER

Pelvic or vulvar surgeries, chemotherapy, and radiation have all been associated with genito-pelvic pain, as have nonspecific inflammatory or nerve dysfunctions (Bergeron, Corsini-Munt, Aerts, Rancourt, & Rosen, 2015). Menopausal changes due to loss of estrogen and subsequent loss of elasticity in the vaginal tissues can also lead to this pain. In one type of genital pain, provoked vestibulodynia (PVD), biological etiological factors have included yeast infections, use of oral contraceptives, early menarche, a genetic predisposition, human papillomavirus, and urethral conditions or infections (Bergeron et al., 2015). Assessment with functional magnetic resonance imaging (fMRI) indicates that women with PVD have a more general hypersensitivity to touch and pain compared with unaffected women (Pukall et al., 2005). Additionally, women who suffer from sexual, physical or psychological abuse have an increased likelihood of developing genito-pelvic pain (Harlow & Stewart, 2005).

Although psychological factors are not considered primary causes of GPPPD, personality and psychiatric symptoms can exacerbate pain as well as pain-induced affect and other sexual and relational consequences. Among the many psychological factors correlated with greater genital pain are anxiety, depression, fear of and hypervigilance to pain, somatization, and pain catastrophization (as summarized in Bergeron et al., 2015). Recently, researchers have identified several interpersonal factors that are associated with greater pain and poorer psychosexual adjustment, such as partner response to the pain, intimacy, and couple communication (Rosen et al., 2014a). Male partners of women with PVD report more erectile difficulties compared with controls (Pazmany, Bergeron, & Verhaeghe, 2014; Smith & Pukall, 2014).

Dysfunctions of the pelvic floor also play a role in the experience of genito-pelvic pain. Some women exhibit a protective, defensive reaction of the pelvic floor muscles (PFM) during attempted vaginal penetration as well as other PFM abnormalities when in a resting state (Bergeron, Rosen, & Morin, 2011; Gentilcore-Saulnier, McLean, Goldfinger, Pukall, & Chamberlain, 2010; Reissing, Binik, Khalifé, Cohen, & Amsel, 2004; Reissing, Brown, Lord, Binik, & Khalifé, 2005). Together, these factors may close the vaginal opening and trigger vestibular sensory changes and inflammation (Zoloun et al., 2006). Ultrasound studies have also shown that women with genito-pelvic pain experience deficits in their PFM contractile capacities, including reductions in strength and endurance, compared with controls (Morin, Bergeron, Khalifé, Mayrand, & Binik, 2014). Physiotherapy with biofeedback is a key treatment approach for addressing PFM dysfunctions.

MALE HYPOACTIVE SEXUAL DESIRE DISORDER

Adherence to social or cultural norms may play a role in MHSDD such that men may be reluctant to report low desire (Meana & Steiner, 2014). The most frequently cited biological factor implicated in MHSDD has been hormones. Androgen deprivation and hyperprolactinemia seem to play a more pertinent role in men than in women (Brotto, 2010b). Hyperprolactinemia may result from antipsychotic medications or prolactin-secreting tumors. With respect to androgen deprivation, as men age, SHBG levels increase, thereby decreasing the level of free testosterone. Similarly, bioavailable testosterone begins to decline when men are in their 30s and 40s, and continues to decline throughout the life span (Seidman, 2003). A syndrome known as androgen deficiency in the aging male (ADAM) or partial ADAM can include fatigue, depression, reduced sex drive, ED, and changes in mood and cognition (Morales, Heaton, & Carson, 2000).

As for psychosocial factors, negative early life experiences, shame, cognitive distractions, performance anxiety, depression and anxiety, and relationship factors may play a role (Carvalho & Nobre, 2011). Specifically, beliefs related to restrictive attitudes toward sexuality, erection concerns, and lack of erotic thoughts in a sexual context had a significant direct effect on reduced sexual desire. Moreover, this set of cognitive-emotional factors also mediated the relationship between medical problems, age, and sexual desire. There is significant comorbidity between ED and HSDD in men such that men experiencing erectile difficulties eventually have reduced levels of desire, and low levels of desire may be hidden under erectile problems.

PREMATURE (EARLY) EJACULATION

The precise etiology of PE is unknown, but a combination of psychological, biological, and behavioral components likely contribute. Much of the research exploring etiology in PE is based on rodent studies in which serotonergic disruption is the primary etiological factor. Stimulation of 5-HT1A receptors in rats leads to rapid ejaculation, whereas hyposensitivity at the 5-HT2C receptor shortens ejaculation time (Waldinger, 2002). Studies in rodents have led Waldinger, a leading authority on PE, to formulate the

Ejaculation Threshold Hypothesis, which posits that men with PE have a lower ejaculatory setpoint (threshold) due to low serotonin neurotransmission, leading them to tolerate only a very low amount of sexual arousal prior to ejaculation (Waldinger, 2005). There is also evidence of a genetic predisposition to PE, given the finding that 71% of first-degree relatives of men with PE also have the condition (Waldinger, Rietschel, Nothen, Hengeveld, & Olivier, 1998).

Acquired and/or situational PE may suggest a psychological etiology related to early sexual experiences, low frequency of sexual activity, or poor ejaculatory control techniques. Among men with PE, 50% of the female partners meet criteria for anorgasmia and 54% meet criteria for hypoactive sexual desire (Fugl-Meyer & Sjogren Fugl-Meyer, 1999), suggesting a reciprocal relationship between PE and women's sexual complaints. Masters and Johnson (1970) forwarded the possibility that performance anxiety leads to loss of ejaculatory control, but more recent research suggests that high anxiety, if present, may be the consequence, rather than the cause, of PE (Strassberg, Kelly, Carroll, & Kircher, 1987). Other psychosocial factors hypothesized to contribute to PE include negative mood states, unrealistic expectancies, sexual misinformation, poor sexual skills and sensory awareness, maladaptive arousal patterns, and relational problems (Althof 2014; Perelman, 2006).

COURSE, PROGNOSIS, AND TREATMENT

As implied in the section on etiology, there has been a pendulum shift in the last two decades, with much research attention focused on finding effective pharmacological treatments for the most prevalent sexual complaints (low desire in women, erectile and ejaculation difficulties in men). As a result, there has been a recent dearth of randomized controlled trials (RCTs) of psychological treatments, and much of the information on efficacy of psychological treatments is based on studies conducted in the 1970s and 1980s. However, the most recent international consultation on sexual medicine continued to recommend that psychological treatments are effective and needed, and deserving of additional research (Brotto et al., 2016a).

Delayed Ejaculation

In cases of an organic etiology, amelioration of the underlying biological factors is an important first line of treatment. This may include switching the patient to a different antidepressant, androgen administration, or attempts to control diabetic neuropathy. Delayed ejaculation is the only male sexual disorder for which there is currently no safe, effective medication. Current approaches usually integrate behavioral masturbatory training within sex therapy with the aim of moving from neutral to pleasurable sensations and removing the "demand" aspects of performance. Addressing cognitions that interfere with arousal is also important. In the case of delayed ejaculation during partnered intercourse, men should be counseled to temporarily refrain from masturbation and noncoital orgasm while using fantasy and movements with their partner that approximate the thoughts and sensations during masturbation (Perelman, 2016). In addition, couple therapy may be warranted if there are perpetuating interpersonal factors. The known efficacy of treatment for delayed ejaculation is limited by small samples, uncontrolled, nonrandomized methods, and lack of validated outcome measures.

ERECTILE DISORDER

Sildenafil citrate (Viagra, Pfizer Inc.) is a phosphodiesterase type-5 (PDE5) inhibitor that has become a first-line treatment for ED since its approval in 1998. All PDE5 inhibitors work by inhibiting the action of PDE5, a molecule in the corpus cavernosum of the penis that is involved in detumescence (loss of erection). There are over 2,000 published studies in various subgroups of men with ED ranging in age from 19 to 87 years. The drug, in 20, 50, or 100 mg doses, is taken 1 hour before planned sexual activity with a low-fat meal and must be combined with subjective or mechanical sexual stimulation. Its effectiveness ranges from 43% for men with radical prostatectomy, to 59% of those with diabetes, and 84% for men with ED due to psychological causes (Osterloh & Riley, 2002).

Tadalafil (Cialis, Lilly ICOS LLC.) is a PDE5 inhibitor with a 17.5-hour half-life which promotes greater sexual spontaneity—an important factor for some couples. A large analysis of 2,100 men taking tadalafil found that the drug was significantly more effective than placebo among all subgroups of men studied, including those with diabetes, hypertension, cardiovascular disease, hyperlipidemia, depression, and benign prostatic hyperplasia, and across ethnocultural groups (Lewis et al., 2005). Vardenafil (Levitra, Bayer) is another PDE5 inhibitor that has been found to be particularly effective for two difficult-to-treat groups: namely, men with diabetes and men who have undergone a radical prostatectomy. More than 70% of men in both groups responded to vardenafil with improved erections (Brock et al., 2001; Goldstein, Fischer, Taylor, & Thibonnier, 2002). The most recent PDE5 inhibitor is avanafil (Stendra, Vivus), which has a more rapid onset of action (30 minutes; Goldstein et al., 2012). Patient preference is typically the guiding principle for which drug to try first. Importantly, success with a PDE5 inhibitor improves self-confidence and relationship satisfaction as well (Althof et al., 2006).

Before the approval of the PDE5 inhibitors, injectable and intraurethral treatments were considered the mainstay of ED treatment. Traditionally reserved for men with an organic basis to their ED, these techniques involve intracavernosal injection of alprostadil (prostaglandin E1) directly into the penis, and, unlike the oral medications, sexual stimulation is not necessary for an erection. Although these treatments were found to be highly effective in 87% of men (Linet & Ogrinc, 1996), the side-effects of penile pain or prolonged erections interfere with their use. Alprostadil can also be delivered directly into the urethra as MUSE (medicated urethral system for erection) for men who cannot tolerate oral medications or injections. Approximately 70% of men respond positively to MUSE (Padma-Nathan et al., 1997), which requires some training from a sexual health clinician for proper insertion. Testosterone therapy, both alone (Isidori et al., 2005) and in combination with a PDE5 inhibitor (Shabsigh, 2005), has also been found effective in the treatment of ED.

Vacuum constriction devices (VCDs) and constriction rings are also available for ED and do not require administration/ingestion of a medication. A VCD is a cylindrical tube that is placed over the flaccid penis, and a vacuum draws blood into the penis either manually or with a battery-operated motor. A constriction ring is then typically placed over the base of the penis to sustain the erection for intercourse. This approach requires a certain degree of manual dexterity and is not suitable for men with sickle cell disease, leukemia, or those who are using anticoagulation treatments (Wylie & MacInnes, 2005).

Despite their efficacy and safety, a substantial portion of men with ED discontinue the use of medications, possibly due to lack of education on their use, fear of side-effects, partner concerns, or failed expectations (Rosen et al., 2004). Such findings underscore the importance of combined psychological and medical approaches. Psychological techniques can be essential for couples in which relationship discord and difficulties in communication are related to the ED. Such techniques might include sensate focus (focus on nonintercourse sexual activities and pleasure, rather than the man's erection) challenging unrealistic beliefs and expectations, and expanding or adjusting sexual scripts. Considerably less research has examined the efficacy of psychological therapies for men with ED, although multiple case reports indicate benefit from combined oral medications plus cognitive behavioral therapies (Schmidt, Munder, Gerger, Frühauf, & Barth, 2014). As ED also impacts the sexual functioning of a female partner (Fisher, Rosen, Eardley, Sand, & Goldstein, 2005), a couple-based psychological approach could be beneficial, though one has yet to be developed or tested.

Female Orgasmic Disorder

Psychological treatments have been the mainstay for effective treatment of FOD. Directed masturbation exercises (Masters & Johnson, 1970) are designed to teach women to focus on sexually erotic cues, not focus on distracting nonsexual cues, and apply graded stimulation to the clitoris in an effort to become orgasmic with masturbation. The self-help book *Becoming Orgasmic: A Sexual Growth Program for Women* recommends these exercises (Heiman & LoPiccolo, 1987) and has an approximately 90% efficacy rate.

Because anxiety may act as a cognitive distraction, thereby distracting the woman away from sexual cues, anxiety reduction is often a target in treatment. Uncontrolled studies have found that mindfulness interventions, which enable women to shift their attention to "being in the moment without judgment", may be a promising adjunct to cognitive-behavioral interventions for FOD. More controlled trials are needed (Laan, Rellini, & Barnes, 2013). Sensate focus involves having a partner touch the woman, with her verbal guidance, while she focuses on relaxation (Masters & Johnson, 1970). In controlled studies, sensate focus combined with directed masturbation was more effective than sensate focus alone for FOD (Heiman, 2002).

The coital alignment technique (CAT) was developed for heterosexual partners engaging in penile–vaginal intercourse, with the aim of increasing the woman's orgasmic ability during intercourse. In CAT, the man is in the superior position and shifts forward such that the base of his penis makes direct contact with the woman's clitoris. This ensures constant clitoral stimulation and results in improved coital orgasmic ability in approximately 56% of women with primary anorgasmia (Hurlbert & Apt, 1995). Currently, one product has been approved by the FDA for the treatment of FSAD: the EROS Clitoral Therapy Device (CTD; Urometrics, St. Paul, MN). It is a small, hand-held, battery-operated device that is placed over the clitoris and increases blood flow through gentle suction. In trials for women with loss of arousal, the EROS-CTD has also been found to significantly improve orgasmic ability in women with FOD (Billups et al., 2001).

Several placebo-controlled studies have examined the efficacy of pharmacologic treatments for FOD. For example, pre- and postmenopausal women with low arousal and anorgasmia showed significant improvements with sildenafil (Basson & Brotto, 2003; Caruso, Intelisano, Lupo, & Agnello, 2001). In a double-blind trial of 100 mg sildenafil versus placebo for women with SSRI-induced FOD, there were significantly fewer sexual side-effects in the sildenafil group (Nurnberg et al., 2008). However, given the study's highly selective inclusion criteria and the difficulties in recruiting participants to the trial, the generalizability of these findings remains tentative, and there have been no published studies on the efficacy of sildenafil for SSRI-induced anorgasmia since the 2008 paper by Nurnberg and colleagues.

FEMALE SEXUAL INTEREST/AROUSAL DISORDER

Given that FSIAD is a relatively new addition to the *DSM* nomenclature, most of the existing literature has been based on women diagnosed with the *DSM-IV-TR* conditions of HSDD and FSAD, and there is only an emerging literature evaluating treatments specifically for women meeting criteria for FSIAD. In terms of pharmacological treatments for low sexual desire in women, research is ongoing with respect to finding an effective dose and method of administration of testosterone, and several randomized, placebo-controlled trials investigating a transdermal testosterone patch for improving desire in postmenopausal women receiving estrogen replacement have shown a benefit (e.g., Davis et al., 2006; Kroll et al., 2004). However, given a concern over the lack of long-term safety data, particularly with the possible link of testosterone and breast cancer (Tworoger et al., 2005), and the finding that serum testosterone levels do not differ between women with and without sexual desire concerns (Reed et al., 2016b), the testosterone patch remains unapproved by the FDA and, therefore, continues to be prescribed "off-label". Nonetheless, the most recent International Consultation on Sexual Medicine still concluded that high physiologic doses of transdermal testosterone are effective for treating low desire in postmenopausal women (Davis, Worsley, Miller, Parish, & Santoro, 2016).

The only approved medication in the United States for the treatment of premenopausal HSDD is the serotonin-1A receptor agonist/2A antagonist and dopamine-4 receptor partial agonist, flibanserin (Addyi). A number of clinical trials have evaluated flibanserin against a placebo, with some inconsistency across the findings. Three meta-analyses have been published that highlight these inconsistencies, with one meta-analysis based on four published studies finding statistically superior effects of flibanserin over placebo on sexually satisfying events, sexual desire, and sex-related distress (Gao et al., 2015). A second meta-analysis based on five studies, including unpublished RCTs, demonstrated a less positive outcome, with flibanserin producing a mean increase in only one sexually satisfying event for every 2 months, compared with placebo, as well as clinically significant risk of dizziness, somnolence, nausea, and fatigue (Jaspers et al., 2016). A more recent third meta-analysis (Saadat et al., 2017) based on six published and four unpublished studies on a total of 8,345 women concluded that although flibanserin was associated with significant increases in sexual desire, the magnitude of this increase did not differ from the effect of placebo (Saadat et al., 2017). If prescribing patterns are any indication of its popularity, flibanserin is not likely to make monumental shifts in improving sexual desire for women, given that only a few hundred prescriptions were made for flibanserin during the same period of time that a half million prescriptions for Viagra (sildenafil) were written for men (Edney & Colby, 2015).

With the approval of flibanserin for women, some have viewed this as paving the way for other sexual pharmaceuticals. For example, the melanocortin agonist, bremelanotide, has been under intense study over the past decade, showing promising results in early studies when administered intranasally (Diamond et al., 2011). However, concerns about the impact of bremelanotide on blood pressure led the company, Palatin Technologies Inc., to explore other routes of administration. Clayton et al. (2016) led a study in which women diagnosed with HSDD or FSAD, or both, self-administered three different doses of bremelanotide at home through subcutaneous route. Women receiving 1.25 and 1.75 mg bremelanotide (but not 0.75 mg) had an increase of 0.7 sexually satisfying events per month, compared with an increase of 0.2 in the placebo group. Sexual distress also decreased more in the bremelanotide (–11.1) compared with the placebo (–6.8) group.

Significantly more women in the bremelanotide arm (24%) compared with the placebo arm (7%) experienced injection site reactions such as irritation, rash, and swelling.

The synthetic hormone tibolone, which has estrogenic, androgenic, and progestogenic effects, has also been of great interest due to its effect on significantly increasing sexual desire, frequency of sexual fantasies, and sexual arousability in a randomized, double-blind study of postmenopausal women free of sexual complaints (Laan, van Lunsen, & Everaerd, 2001); however, although it is licensed for the treatment of menopausal symptoms in Europe, it does not have FDA approval in the United States. Moreover, a Cochrane review found that tibolone was associated with increased risk of breast cancer among women with a prior history of breast cancer (Formoso et al., 2016).

Another hormone of intense interest is DHEA, a precursor for extragonadal biosynthesis of E1 and testosterone. Although DHEA was found to be lower in women with HSDD than in controls (Davis, Davison, Donath, & Bell, 2005), a meta-analysis found no evidence that DHEA improved sexual desire (Elraiyah et al., 2014).

Finally, there have been initial promising results from two new agents, Lybrido and Lybridos, for improving sexual desire among women who are considered to be relatively insensitive to cues for sexual desire or to be prone to sexual inhibition. Lybrido is a combination of 0.5 mg testosterone in a cyclodextrin carrier and 50 mg sildenafil citrate in a powder-filled gelatin capsule. Among women with low desire due to a relatively insensitive system for sexual cues ($n = 29$), Lybrido led to a significantly greater genital arousal response to a sexual fantasy (but not to sexual films), and significantly higher sexual desire and satisfaction during sexual events compared with placebo (Poels et al., 2013). Lybrido had no effect on women with low desire who were highly sensitive to sexual cues. Lybridos, on the other hand, is a combination of 0.5 mg testosterone in a cyclodextrin carrier and 10 mg buspirone in a powder-filled gelatin capsule. Among 28 women who were considered to be "high inhibitors" (i.e., those with high acute serotonergic inhibitory control), treatment significantly increased genital arousal response to a fantasy (but not to sexual films) as well as subjective reports of desire and satisfaction during sex compared with placebo (van Rooij et al., 2013). Lybridos had no effect on women with low desire and who had low inhibitory mechanisms.

Cognitive-behavioral therapies (CBT) for low desire have very good empirical support, and include behavioral skill training to improve communication between partners, increase sexual skills and reduce sexual and performance anxiety; anxiety reduction, and cognitive challenging. Trudel et al. (2001) compared the effects of CBT to a waitlist control in 74 couples in which women met the criteria for HSDD. Treatment included psychoeducation, skills and emotional training, and couple assignments in a group format. After 12 weeks, 74% of women no longer met diagnostic criteria for HSDD, and this stabilized to 64% after 1-year follow-up. In addition to significantly improved sexual desire, women also reported improved quality of marital life and perception of sexual arousal. Interestingly, CBT addressing a different aspect of the sexual response cycle—namely, orgasm—is also effective in increasing sexual desire in women (Hurlbert, 1993) and provides additional evidence that components of sexual response are highly correlated. Several studies including both members of the couple, which tested the efficacy of marital therapy for women's low desire, have also found promising effects on sexual desire (Fish, Busby, & Killian, 1994; MacPhee, Johnson, & Van der Veer, 1995). A meta-analysis of controlled studies evaluating CBT for women with low desire found an overall effect size of $d = 0.91$ for the primary endpoint of low desire, corresponding to a large effect size, and a moderate effect on improving sexual satisfaction, $d = 0.51$ (Frühauf, Gerger, Schmidt, Munder, & Barth 2013).

Over the past decade, there has been increasing interest in mindfulness-based interventions for women with low desire (Brotto & Goldmeier, 2015), with mindfulness focused on guiding participants to notice breath, body, sound, and thought sensations, moment by moment, and in a nonjudgmental manner. To date there has been only one waitlist controlled study of mindfulness for women with low desire, and four sessions of group mindfulness-based therapy significantly improved sexual desire and elicited a moderate effect size ($d = 0.56$) (Brotto & Basson, 2014). The change in sex-related distress was also significantly greater than the control arm, and associated with a more modest effect size ($d = -0.31$). Though researchers are now focused on more intensive, eight-session interventions, with very promising findings (Paterson, Handy, & Brotto, 2016), controlled trials have yet to be conducted.

Female sexual interest/arousal disorder has one criterion pertaining to absent or reduced genital or nongenital sensations during sexual activity; however, we are not aware of any studies evaluating this single criterion within a treatment outcome study. Past studies on women with FSAD have focused largely on pharmacologic agents. The dopaminergic agonist apomorphine SL was found to significantly improve sexual arousal, desire, orgasm, satisfaction, and enjoyment when taken daily at 2–3 mg doses but not when taken on an as-needed basis (Caruso et al., 2004). Phentolamine mesylate, commonly used to treat ED, significantly improved self-reported lubrication and tingling sensations, but had no effect on physiological sexual arousal, subjective pleasure, or arousal in postmenopausal women when administered orally (Rosen, Phillips, Gendrano, & Ferguson, 1999). In a much larger, double-blind replication of the study, vaginally applied phentolamine significantly increased physiological arousal in postmenopausal women receiving hormone replacement (Rubio-Aurioles et al., 2002). Sildenafil (Viagra) has also been studied in a variety of different populations of women (Basson & Brotto, 2003; Basson, McInnes, Smith, Hodgson, & Koppiker, 2002; Berman et al., 2003; Caruso et al., 2001), but the lack of consistent positive effects led the drug's maker, Pfizer Inc., to halt its program in women's sexuality.

The EROS-CTD, described earlier, has been found to significantly improve all measures of sexual response and satisfaction in women with FSAD (Billups et al., 2001) and in women with arousal complaints secondary to radiation therapy for cervical cancer (Schroder et al., 2005), but lack of a control condition and the fact that women were required to use the device several times per week for the duration of the study makes it difficult to ascertain whether positive effects were due to the suction, *per se* (in which case a vibrator might suffice), or to nonspecific attentional factors.

GENITO-PELVIC PAIN/PENETRATION DISORDER

In the past, empirically tested treatments have either focused on dyspareunia or vaginismus (*DSM-IV-TR*) and not on GPPPD. There are four general categories of treatment for PVD, a type of GPPPD and the most common cause of pain during intercourse in premenopausal women: (1) medical, (2) physical, (3) surgical, and (4) psychological. Among the medical treatments for PVD, current treatment algorithms recommend nightly applications of topical lidocaine (Mandal et al., 2010; Mariani, 2002; Reed, 2006; Ventolini, 2011). Failing pain relief, a systemic treatment of low dose trycyclic antidepressants can be tried. Foster et al. (2010) conducted a randomized, double-blind, placebo-controlled trial in which they compared the antidepressant desipramine to lidocaine. Neither the desipramine nor the lidocaine arm had significantly greater pain reductions than the placebo, but all treatment arms demonstrated decreased pain (Foster et al., 2010).

There is also evidence to support the efficacy of a corticosteroid cream (Bergeron, Khalifé, Dupuis, & McDuff, 2016).

Physiotherapy with pelvic floor biofeedback has been found to be effective for PVD (Bergeron et al., 2002; Goldfinger, Pukall, Gentilcore-Saulnier, McLean, & Chamberlain, 2009). Surgery, usually in the form of vestibulectomy, involves excision of the hymen and sensitive areas of the vestibule. Studies have demonstrated a high degree of efficacy (73–90%; Gaunt, Good, & Stanhope, 2003; Lavy, Lev-Sagie, Hamani, Zacut, & Ben-Chetrit, 2005); however, results are poorer for women with acquired PVD, who also have a higher rate of recurrence (Rettenmaier, Brown, & Micha, 2003).

Cognitive-behavioral therapy is the most studied psychological treatment to date. The advantage of a psychological approach to GPPPD is that it targets multiple aspects of the genito-pelvic pain beyond the pain itself, including sexual, relationship, and psychological distress. In the first randomized, comparison of 12-week group CBT, pelvic floor physiotherapy, and vestibulectomy ($N=78$ women), all groups experienced a significant reduction in pain at post-treatment and at 6-month follow-up, with the vestibulectomy group showing the greatest degree of improvement (Bergeron et al., 2001). All groups also significantly improved on measures of psychological and sexual function. At a 2.5-year follow-up, the ratings of pain during intercourse in the CBT group were equivalent to those of women having undergone a vestibulectomy, and gains in pain and sexuality outcomes were also maintained (Bergeron, Khalifé, Glazer, & Binik, 2008). In another randomized clinical trial comparing a corticosteroid cream to a 13-week group CBT, both groups improved in pain and sexual function at post-treatment and 6-month follow-up, although the CBT group reported significantly more improvements at the 6-month follow-up (Bergeron et al., 2016). Recently, preliminary effectiveness and feasibility of a 12-session cognitive-behavioral couple therapy were established in nine couples coping with PVD (Corsini-Munt et al., 2014). Finally, there is evidence of a four-session group mindfulness-based treatment for improving pain and reducing catastrophizing and pain hypervigilance in women with PVD from pre- to post-treatment (Brotto, Basson, Driscoll, Smith, & Sadownik, 2015).

Behavioral treatments for women who show a high phobic anxiety and avoidance of penetration, sometimes to the extent that there is a defensive reaction of the pelvic floor muscles, making penetration impossible (i.e., women who may previously have received a diagnosis of vaginismus), have included sex therapy, pelvic floor physical therapy and cognitive-behavioral pain management. An RCT examining cognitive-behavioral sex therapy for vaginismus yielded a low success rate of only 15%, highlighting the limits of this 'talk therapy' approach (van Lankveld et al., 2006). However, a more recent RCT of intensive therapist-aided exposure showed that 89% of women were able to achieve vaginal intercourse at post-treatment, and that treatment outcome was mediated by a reduction in catastrophic pain penetration beliefs (ter Kuile, Melles, de Groot, Tuijnman-Raasveld, & van Lankveld, 2013).

MALE HYPOACTIVE SEXUAL DESIRE DISORDER

Treatment for MHSDD largely depends on the presumed etiology and can involve any combination of psychotherapy (either alone or with the partner), medications, or hormonal therapy. Psychological therapy may involve exploration of couple issues, including anger, trust, exploration of an affair, and feelings of attractiveness. Treatment may also include identifying and challenging maladaptive thoughts and restricted sexual scripts, and encouraging the use of fantasies, erotic stimuli, and other forms of sexual activity besides intercourse. Unfortunately, there are no controlled publications on the efficacy of psychological treatment without concomitant medication treatment for HSDD in men (Meuleman & van Lankveld, 2005).

Among the pharmacological treatments for low desire, bupropion (marketed as the antidepressant Wellbutrin) is a norepinephrine and dopamine agonist that has been found to have an efficacy rate of approximately 86% in nondepressed men with HSDD (Crenshaw, Goldberg, & Stern, 1987). Testosterone replacement has been the primary hormonal treatment studied for MHSDD and is administered as an injection, a patch, or a gel. Administration of exogenous testosterone has been found to enhance desire in hypogonadal men with erectile dysfunction; however, increased testosterone also positively impacts energy and mood, which may improve desire (Khera et al., 2011). It is unlikely that testosterone replacement would enhance desire in eugonadal men (Meana & Steiner, 2014).

PREMATURE (EARLY) EJACULATION

Seman's Squeeze technique is an effective behavioral treatment for PE. The method requires the man to provide direct feedback to his partner when he feels an ejaculatory urge. The couple discontinues sexual stimulation, and the partner applies pressure to the glans of the penis until the urge is reduced (Masters & Johnson, 1970; Semans, 1956). The technique can be used during masturbation before attempting it with a partner. The efficacy of the Squeeze technique is approximately 60% (Metz, Pryor, Nesvacil, Abuzzahab, & Koznar, 1997). The Stop-Pause approach is very similar but, because it involves a reduction in penile stimulation as the man nears ejaculatory inevitability, it better simulates natural behaviors during intercourse (Kaplan, 1989). Sexual stimulation is resumed once the man feels control over his ejaculation. Although early studies by Masters and Johnson and Kaplan found efficacy rates nearing 100%, more recent controlled trials find efficacy in the range of 64% (Hawton, Catalan, Martin, & Fagg, 1986). In one of the few high-quality treatment studies, De Carufel and Trudel (2006) showed an eight-fold increase in intravaginal ejaculatory latency time (IELT) as well as higher sexual satisfaction among men treated with behavioral techniques compared with a waitlist control at post-treatment and 3 months later.

Based on the hypothesis that a low ejaculatory setpoint due to low serotonin neurotransmission may underlie some forms of PE, SSRIs have become a mainstay of pharmacological treatment. This SSRI effect takes advantage of one of the negative side-effects of SSRI use, namely delayed orgasm. Several dozen trials examining the efficacy of SSRIs (daily or on-demand) in PE have been conducted, and a meta-analysis of daily SSRI use showed paroxetine to have the greatest efficacy in delaying ejaculation (Kara et al., 1996). Approved in some countries, dapoxetine is a rapid-acting and short-half-life SSRI that can be used as an on-demand treatment. In RCTs, dapoxetine taken 1–2 hours before intercourse resulted in a 2.5–3.0-fold increase in IELT, increased ejaculatory control, decreased distress, and increased satisfaction, compared with placebo (McMahon et al., 2011).

Pharmacological treatment for PE may also include topical local anesthetics such as lidocaine and/or prilocaine applied to the penis as a cream, gel or spray. Clinical trials have shown this treatment to result in increased IELTs, with associated improvements in perceived control over ejaculation and sexual satisfaction (Dinsmore & Wylie, 2009; Carson & Wylie, 2010). Finally, combining behavior therapy with pharmacological treatment has been found to be superior to pharmacotherapy alone (Tang, Ma, Zhao, Liu, & Chen, 2004).

CASE STUDIES

HYPOACTIVE SEXUAL DESIRE DISORDER IN A MAN

Robert is a 64-year-old married, Caucasian, heterosexual man. He and his wife, Cecile, age 58, have been married for 36 years and have three adult children ages 35, 31, and 28. Robert presented to his primary-care doctor with complaints of "lost libido," which he thought might be due to a "hormonal imbalance." Robert's physician conducted a brief but focused assessment of his loss of desire, focusing on how Robert defined desire, the impact on his self-esteem and relationship, and an exploration of other contributing factors in Robert's (and Cecile's) lives. The physician ordered a complete hormone profile, focusing on Robert's levels of bioavailable testosterone. Robert reported that in the past 5 years he became less interested in sex, thought about sex less than once per week (previously he would think about it daily), and only very reluctantly initiated sexual activity. He became quite anxious about sex in the evenings, which was typically when sexual activity would occur. Although Cecile was not present during this appointment, Robert noted that Cecile had also experienced a reduction in sexual interest, and that she had increased vaginal dryness over the past few years coinciding with menopause.

When asked what steps Robert and Cecile had taken on their own to improve Robert's desire for sex, he stated that they were unsure, and this is what prompted their speaking to the physician. Robert noted that there had also been recent problems with his erectile capacity. He was unable to reach an erection in approximately 50% of his sexual attempts. Robert concluded the appointment by stating that these changes were quite distressing to him, and he worried about becoming less attractive to Cecile. Therefore, he was quite motivated for treatment. The physician referred Robert and Cecile to a sex therapist to provide some educational information on normative sexual function changes with age and relationship duration, and to discuss with Robert and Cecile sexual skills (e.g., sensate focus) that might improve the quality of their sexual interactions. The sex therapist could also address Robert's anxiety, as well as perform a more thorough assessment of mood and lifestyle factors. Although the physician suggested examining Robert's hormonal profile, he knew that Robert was otherwise "hormonally healthy" and showed no clinical signs of hypogonadism.

A COUPLE-BASED APPROACH TO GENITO-PELVIC PAIN/PENETRATION DISORDER

Alanna is a warm, introverted woman in her late 20s who has suffered from pain during intercourse ever since her first sexual experience in her late teens. She also reports severe pain during attempts at a Pap test or when any kind of pressure is placed on the vestibule (e.g., inserting a tampon). A physical examination ruled out vulvovaginal atrophy and other painful dermatological conditions. Over time, intercourse has become increasingly painful such that she hardly has any desire for sexual activity anymore. When she does have sex, it is on her partner, Jack's, (rare) initiation to which she agrees because of concern over losing him, and feelings of guilt and shame that she is not a good "partner." Alanna had always been an anxious person, which contributed to her hypervigilance to bodily symptoms and especially any indication of genital pain. At the outset of therapy, she was visibly uncomfortable talking about sex and genitals. She could not recall any conversations about healthy sexuality as a child, having always avoided the topic of sex, and Jack rarely broached the topic for fear of upsetting Alanna. Their mutual avoidance further fueled anxieties and associated negative cognitions (e.g., "Talking about sex is awful", "My genitals are gross", "I can't describe my pain and he won't understand anyways", "She'll feel pressure to have sex if I touch her"), which reinforced further avoidance. Their lack of communication about the pain and sexuality had also, over time, generalized to avoidance of any form of touch and displays of affection.

On the one hand, having Jack present in the therapy increased Alanna's anxiety because she worried that he would interpret her negative attitudes toward sex as a rejection of him. On the other hand, Alanna was quickly surprised by how easily Jack was able to talk about sex and what it means to him – including his own feelings of frustration and guilt – which encouraged her to confront her own avoidance. Psychoeducation about genito-pelvic pain and the role of anxiety validated Alanna's experience, and provided her with the language to describe her pain to Jack. Alanna was taught relaxation strategies for managing her anxiety, which has consequences for arousal and pelvic floor muscle dysfunction, and therefore, her pain. The therapist increased Alanna's and Jack's awareness of their mutual avoidance of both painful sensations and all forms of sexual intimacy, and helped them develop enhanced communication and assertiveness skills to accommodate both of their needs. They were also given couple breathing exercises as a way to approach intimacy, and were later introduced to sensate focus, a stepped approach to physical intimacy that involves giving and receiving pleasure in a nondemanding context. Cognitive defusion techniques were also helpful for addressing both Alanna's and Jack's anticipatory anxiety and preoccupying thoughts about the pain and sex (e.g., pain catastrophizing, worry that sex is too complicated or won't be pleasurable). For Alanna and Jack, approaching their mutual avoidance through enhanced communication about both sex and the pain, and experimenting with pain-free intimate sexual and nonsexual behaviors were integral steps toward reducing Alanna's pain and re-establishing their sexual relationship. Importantly, attending the therapy together diminished their feelings of isolation and validated that this was a problem that they were both impacted by, and could work together to manage.

SUMMARY OF SEXUAL DYSFUNCTIONS

The past 20 years have seen an unprecedented increase in research aimed at understanding the etiology, pathophysiology, prevalence, diagnostic features of, and treatments for sexual dysfunction. The increased presence of the pharmaceutical industry's interests in this field has led to greater research funding, but this boom has also been associated with caution and criticism for fear of medicalizing conditions that many argue are largely influenced (and created) by sociopolitical and psychological pressures. In recent years and since the "age of Viagra," there has been a much-needed shift toward the study of female sexual function and the development of novel psychological treatment approaches for women's sexual difficulties, but we must be careful not to ignore the complexity of male sexual function. With the *DSM-5* now published and widely available, it is incumbent upon the field of sex therapy and research to generate new data as to the pathophysiology, assessment, and treatment of the current roster of sexual dysfunctions. Furthermore, given the challenges inherent to designing controlled treatment outcome studies when evaluating psychological interventions (Brotto et al., 2016b; Chivers, Basson, Brotto, Graham, & Stephenson, 2017), it is imperative that researchers consider the specific as well as non-specific agents of change in such treatments, and incorporate these into designing studies.

Part II: Paraphilic Disorders

DESCRIPTION OF PARAPHILIAS

The paraphilias, as defined in the *DSM-5* (APA, 2013), refer to "any intense and persistent sexual interest other than sexual interest in genital stimulation or preparatory fondling with phenotypically normal, physically mature, consenting human partners" (p. 685). The paraphilias cluster into two main types: the first involves anomalous activity preferences (courtship disorders, which resemble distorted components of human courtship behavior, or algolagnic disorders, which involve pain and suffering); the second involves anomalous target preferences, which are either directed at other humans or elsewhere.

Over 90 years ago, Stekel (1923) coined the term paraphilia, which translates into love (philia) beyond the usual (para) (Money, 1984). Although paraphilias are often associated with sexual offending, the two terms are not synonymous. As Krueger and Kaplan (2001) point out, paraphilias often refer to a type of mental disorder. In contrast, "sexual offender" is a psycholegal term that denotes individuals who have been convicted of a sexual offense. Nevertheless, many sexual offenders do meet diagnostic criteria for a paraphilic disorder and some individuals diagnosed with a paraphilic disorder have committed sexual offenses; thus, the two phenomena are by no means mutually exclusive (Seto, 2009).

As a result of the association between paraphilic disorders and sexual offending, much of the research on paraphilias has been based on samples of convicted sexual offenders, although some recent studies have assayed adults with paraphilic interests who have not acted on them (e.g., Beier et al., 2015). The more common approach, unfortunately, has led to three major confounds. First, many sexual offenders were never formally diagnosed with a paraphilic disorder. Second, the generalizability of the samples to all individuals with paraphilic disorders is suspect, because individuals convicted of a sexual offense often represent the more severe end of the spectrum. Third, the veracity of self-reports by sexual offenders needs to be considered, because these individuals often have high motivations to appear less "deviant" in their sexual interests. As a result, they may under- and over-report certain fantasies and experiences. As a consequence of these issues, there is an increasing call for more research based on noncriminological samples (e.g., Kramer, 2011; Okami & Goldberg, 1992).

CLINICAL PICTURE

EXHIBITIONISTIC DISORDER

Exhibitionism pertains to recurrent and intense sexual arousal from the exposure of one's genitals to an unsuspecting person, over a period of at least 6 months. It is one of the most commonly reported paraphilias (Firestone, Kingston, Wexler, & Bradford, 2006; Långström, 2010; Långström & Seto, 2006). Exhibiting may consist of showing the genitals to, and/or actively masturbating in front of, a stranger. Often, the victim's shock is sexually arousing to the perpetrator and, in most cases, there is no other contact. To meet *DSM-5* criteria, the individual must either have acted on the sexual urges or fantasies or have experienced marked distress or interpersonal difficulty as a result of the sexual interest (APA, 2013).

Although primarily a disorder of men, female exhibitionism has been reported (e.g., Bader, Schoeneman-Morris, Scalora, & Casady, 2008; Fedoroff, Fishell, & Fedoroff, 1999).

The majority of victims of exhibitionism are females, including both children and adolescents (Bader et al., 2008) although exhibitionists who prefer to expose themselves to children may have a different disorder from those who prefer to expose themselves to adults (Murphy & Page, 2008). Exhibitionists are a heterogeneous group whose education, intelligence, and socioeconomic status do not differ from the general population. Initial investigations found high rates of shy and nonassertive personalities (Ellis & Brancale, 1956), but later studies utilizing more standardized assessment instruments did not find abnormal or specific personality patterns (Langevin, Paitich, Freeman, Mann, & Handy, 1978; Langevin et al., 1979; Smukler & Schiebel, 1975) nor did they find that psychopathology symptoms differed from other sexual or nonsexual offenders (Murphy, Haynes, & Worley, 1991; Murphy & Peters, 1992). Moreover, the majority of exhibitionists are married or in common-law relationships and enjoy nonpathological sexual relationships with their partners (Langevin & Lang, 1987; Maletzky, 1991). Cox and Maletzky (1980) found that, in comparison to those with other paraphilias, exhibitionists were least likely to see their behavior as harmful to their victims—a factor likely to influence both motivations for, and success of, treatment. Relatedly, they are more likely to under-report or minimize their exhibitionistic and other paraphilic fantasies and behaviors (McConaghy, 1993; McConaghy, Blaszczyzynski, & Kidson, 1988) and, among all individuals with paraphilias, exhibitionists were most likely to have committed other sexual offenses (Freund & Blanchard, 1986; Langevin & Lang, 1987).

FETISHISTIC DISORDER

Fetishism pertains to recurrent and intense sexual arousal from either the use of nonliving objects or a highly specific focus on nongenital body part(s), present for at least 6 months and accompanied by clinically significant distress or impairment (APA, 2013). The objects are not limited to female clothing used in cross-dressing or to devices specifically designed for tactile genital stimulation, such as vibrators (Kafka, 2010). In the *DSM-5*, the object can be specified as either body parts or nonliving objects (or both).

Fetish objects can take many forms, including clothing (particularly underwear and stockings), footwear, diapers, gloves, and certain fabrics or materials such as rubber and leather. Sexual arousal may take the form of looking at, fondling, smelling, licking, sucking, cutting, burning, stealing, or seeing someone else dressed in the fetish objects (Chalkley & Powell, 1983). As with exhibitionism and, in fact, all the paraphilias, fetishism is largely a disorder found in men, although there are a few reports of women engaged in this behavior (Zavitzianos, 1971).

FROTTEURISTIC DISORDER

Frotteurism pertains to recurrent and intense sexual arousal from touching or rubbing against a nonconsenting person, over a period of at least 6 months. Unlike fetishism, but similar to exhibitionism, clinically significant distress or impairment is not required if the individual has acted on the urges (APA, 2013). Although numerous researchers (e.g., Freund, 1990; Freund, Seto, & Kuban, 1996) include both touching and rubbing under the definition of frotteurism, others have differentiated frotteurism from toucherism (e.g., Kafka, 2010). The latter refers to sexual arousal from touching exclusively with the hands, rather than touching with, for example, the groin.

Frotteurism generally takes place in crowded places, such as on public transportation or on busy sidewalks, where escape for the frotteur is feasible (APA, 2000). Although engaging in frotteuristic activities, the frotteur "usually fantasizes an exclusive, caring relationship with the victim" (APA, 2000, p. 570). Frotteurism, as with most paraphilias, appears to occur mainly in men, although a few cases of frotteurism in women have been reported (Fedoroff et al., 1999; Kar & Koola, 2007). Krueger and Kaplan (1997) noted that "men who engage in frotteurism have large numbers of victims, are not often arrested, and, when apprehended, do not serve long sentences" (p. 145). Very little published data exist on frotteurism. For example, Krueger and Kaplan (1997) found only 17 studies published on the topic between 1966 and 1997 on PsychLit and Medline. Our own PubMed search from 1997 to 2017 yielded only an additional 18 publications.

PEDOPHILIC DISORDER

Pedophilia pertains to recurrent, intense sexually arousing fantasies, sexual urges, or behaviors involving sexual activity with a prepubescent child or children (generally age 13 years or younger) over a period of at least 6 months. To meet criteria, the individual must either have experienced consequent distress or interpersonal difficulty or have acted on the urges. Moreover, the individual must be at least 16 years of age and at least 5 years older than the prepubescent target of arousal (APA, 2013).

Unlike the other paraphilic disorders in the *DSM-5*, the Board of Trustees of the American Psychiatric Association did not accept the recommended changes to the diagnostic criteria for pedophilia (other than the name change from "Pedophilia" to "Pedophilic Disorder"). For example, the recommendation to have specifiers pertaining to the stage of puberty of the child for whom the patient has an erotic preference (e.g., Tanner stage 1 [prepubertal or pedophilia], Tanner stages 2–3 [early puberty or hebephilia] or both [pedohebephilia]) were not approved, despite rather substantive evidence for the distinction between an erotic preference for prepubertal versus peripubertal children (e.g., Blanchard, 2010a; Blanchard et al., 2012; Cantor & McPhail, 2015; Stephens, Seto, Goodwill, & Cantor, 2017; for a meta-analytic review, see McPhail et al., 2017). The Board of Trustees also chose not to include this proposed change in Section III of the manual, in the section "Conditions for Further Study." It is of note that the Board of Trustees has never made public the reason for their decision to decline the recommendations made by the Paraphilias subworkgroup of the Sexual and Gender Identity Disorders Work Group (Zucker, 2013) and the decision was rather quickly subjected to a charge of "politics" (Balon, 2014). The reason that this change had been proposed is that there are now many children under the age of 13 years who are in early puberty, and the introduction of this specifier would have more accurately acknowledged this empirical fact (see Blanchard, 2010a, 2013). One recent judicial ruling—a so-called Frye hearing (People of the State of Illinois vs. Nicholas Bauer, 2017)—was extremely critical of the secrecy behind the Board of Trustees' decision and extremely supportive of the proposed revision to the pedophilic diagnostic criteria that would have been able to characterize men with an erotic preference for early-pubertal children under the age of 13. Indeed, the judicial ruling concluded that the State was under no obligation to adhere to the *DSM-5* in considering psycholegal issues.

Pedophilia is a term that is often incorrectly used interchangeably with child molestation. Although they can overlap, similar to the terms paraphilia and sexual offender, pedophilic disorder describes the diagnostic criteria for a mental disorder diagnosis, whereas child molester refers to any individual who has engaged in sexual activity with a prepubescent or pubescent child. As Barbaree and Seto (1997) point out, some pedophiles who have recurrent sexual fantasies or urges involving prepubescent children but without action would not be considered child molesters; conversely, individuals who have engaged in sexual activity with a minor once or even on occasion, but who do not experience recurrent fantasies, urges, or behaviors over a 6-month period, would not be diagnosed with pedophilia.

Individuals with pedophilia may be sexually aroused by girls, boys, both girls and boys, and even to both adults and children (APA, 2013). Furthermore, sexual arousal may be specific to children of particular ages. Although pedophilia involving girl victims is more frequent, the average number of victims is higher in pedophiles attracted to boys (Abel & Osborn, 1992). In addition, the rate of recidivism of male-preferential pedophilia is higher than that of female-preferential pedophilia (Abel & Osborn, 1992). Although originally believed to be a disorder specific to males, child sexual molestation by women has been reported in the literature (e.g., Wijkman, Bijleveld, & Hendriks, 2010).

Compared with other paraphilias, an extensive literature exists for pedophilia (although much is based on child molesters who were never formally diagnosed with the disorder). A relatively high proportion of convicted child molesters experienced sexual abuse as children (50% vs. 20% in nonsex offenders; Dhawan & Marshall, 1996), as well as nonsexual abuse and neglect (Finkelhor, 1979, 1984; Marshall, Hudson, & Hodkinson, 1993). A meta-analysis by Jesperson, Lalumière, and Seto (2009) found a higher prevalence of a sexual abuse history among adult sex offenders than among nonsex offenders. Interestingly, this was stronger among those who had offended against children than among those who had offended against adults. In contrast to the studies noted earlier, there was no evidence of a differential rate of a physical abuse history between the sex and nonsex offenders. Child molesters apparently do not suffer from higher rates of psychopathology or personality disturbances than do nonmolesters (Abel, Rouleau, & Cunningham-Rathner, 1986; Mohr, Turner, & Jerry, 1964). Finkelhor (1984) proposed that child molesters may suffer from a lack of empathy toward their victims that disinhibits restrictions the individual would otherwise have against offending. This finding has some support (Fernandez, Marshall, Lightbody, & O'Sullivan, 1999), although empathy toward adults and children more generally (i.e., not victims) does not differ from that of nonoffenders (Fernandez et al., 1999; Marshall, Hudson, Jones, & Fernandez, 1995). Thus, child molesters may push away empathic feelings toward their victims (see Babchishin, Hanson, & VanZuylen, 2015), but they do not suffer from any pervasive empathy deficits.

SEXUAL MASOCHISM DISORDER

Sexual masochism pertains to recurrent and intense sexual arousal from the act of being humiliated, beaten, bound, or otherwise made to suffer over a period of at least 6 months, and the person must suffer consequent distress or impairment in at least one important area of functioning. Furthermore, the sexual arousal must be in response to actual, not simulated, humiliation, bondage, or beatings, although the use of pornography is sometimes an associated feature of the disorder (APA, 2013). In the DSM-5, asphyxiophilia can be denoted as a specifier (Coluccia et al., 2016; Hucker, 2011).

Although pain through being slapped, spanked, or whipped is considered sexually arousing by most sexual masochists (Baumeister, 1989; Moser & Levitt, 1987), many sexual masochists use little or no pain (Baumeister & Butler, 1997), instead becoming aroused through loss of control by being bound or becoming aroused by carrying out humiliating acts such as wearing diapers, licking their partner's shoes, or having to display themselves while naked. Other masochistic activities include the use of electrical shocks, piercing (infibulation), being urinated or defecated on, being subjected to verbal abuse, self-mutilation, and oxygen deprivation (hypoxyphilia). Although many sexual masochists appear to practice these activities with safety in mind—by, for example, prearranging a signal with their partners to indicate when to stop (Weinberg & Kamel, 1983)—masochistic behaviors can lead to serious injuries and death (e.g., Hucker, 1985; Roma, Pazzelli, Pompili, Girardi, & Ferracuti, 2013). This is particularly true for activities involving oxygen deprivation, such as hanging or the use of ligatures, plastic bags, scarves, and chemicals.

The ratio of men to women who meet the criteria for this disorder is much smaller than that of the other paraphilias, with approximately 20 men having the disorder for every woman (APA, 2000). In community samples, the percentage of males who report masochistic sexual activities is higher than the percentage of females (2.2% vs. 1.3%) (APA, 2013). Gender differences in preferences for various masochistic activities reveal that pain and humiliation are the preferred forms of masochism for women; however, women prefer less severe forms of pain than men (Baumeister, 1989). Being forced to be a slave and anal penetration have been found to be somewhat equally enjoyed by both sexes (Baumeister, 1989). Interestingly, sexual masochism seems to be fairly modern when compared with the other paraphilias and also appears to be limited to Western cultures (Baumeister, 1989). Furthermore, it has been associated with increased socio-economic functioning, with community samples of individuals who practice sexual masochism evidencing a higher level of education, higher income, and higher occupational status as compared with norms for the general population (for a review, see Weinberg, 2006). These findings have been corroborated by the demographics of those involved in S&M (sadism and masochism) organizations (Moser & Levitt, 1987; Spengler, 1977).

In line with the correlation between sexual masochism and socioeconomic status, it has been found that sexual masochists are well-adjusted individuals who are often quite successful and above norms on measures of mental health (Cowan, 1982; Moser & Levitt, 1987; Spengler, 1977; Weinberg, 2006). In fact, one study that measured hormone levels before and after participation in consensual, sadomasochistic activities revealed reductions in cortisol following the activities, indicating reduced physiological stress with this behavior (Sagarin, Cutler, Cuther, Lawler-Sagarin, & Matuszewich, 2009). Furthermore, this study also found that indices of relationship closeness increased following engagement in positively experienced sadomasochistic activities. Some investigators have examined whether masochistic individuals enjoy pain, humiliation, and/or loss of control outside of sexual activity; however, there appears to be no relationship between sexual masochism and nonsexual forms of masochism (i.e., self-defeating behaviors or enjoyment of nonsexual painful behaviors such as going to the dentist; Baumeister, 1989, 1991; Baumeister & Scher, 1988; Berglas & Baumeister, 1993; Friedman, 1991; Weinberg, Williams, & Moser, 1984). In general, studies of individuals who engage in consensual sadomasochism have been important in demarcating the line between a paraphilic behavior and a paraphilic disorder (see Graham, Butler, McGraw, Cannes, & Smith, 2016). This argument is also consistent with the general recognition that consensual masochism is a quite common fantasy among women, as exemplified, for example, in the success of *Fifty Shades* fiction (Altenburger, Carotta, Bonomi, & Snyder, 2017).

Sexual Sadism Disorder

Sexual sadism, in some ways the complementary opposite of sexual masochism, pertains to recurrent and intense sexual arousal from the physical or psychological suffering of another person over a period of at least 6 months. The urges and/or fantasies must have been carried out, must be distressing, or must cause interpersonal difficulty (APA, 2013).

As with sexual masochism, many individuals with sexual sadism engage in this behavior consensually and take precautions to ensure that their behavior does not exceed a certain threshold of pain or injury. However, sexual sadism can lead to serious injury or death, particularly when individuals with sexual sadism have a comorbid diagnosis of antisocial personality disorder (APA, 2013). Although the lay public often associates torture and cruelty with sexual sadism, it should be noted that these violent behaviors are not always accompanied by sexual arousal (Dietz, Hazelwood, & Warren, 1990; Hazelwood, Dietz, & Warren, 1992). Furthermore, it has been suggested that a sexual interest in power, and not the infliction of pain, is at the core of sexual sadism (Cross & Matheson, 2006). As with all the paraphilias, sexual sadism appears to be more common in men than in women (e.g., Breslow, Evans, & Langley, 1995).

TRANSVESTIC DISORDER

Transvestic disorder pertains to recurrent and intense sexual arousal from cross-dressing, as manifested by fantasies, urges, or behaviors of at least 6 months' duration and is accompanied by significant distress or impairment (APA, 2013). Specifiers for this disorder are with fetishism or with autogynephilia (sexual arousal related to thoughts or images of self as female) (for a review of the term autogynephilia, see Lawrence, 2013, 2017). Although in theory transvestic disorder can be present in both men and women, in practice, it is virtually never observed in women. Thus, the diagnostic criteria and the *DSM-5* text reflect this clinical reality. Moreover, the vast majority of males with transvestic disorder self-identify as heterosexual, although some homosexual men have also been found to report sexual arousal to cross-dressing, albeit to a significantly lesser extent than heterosexual men (Blanchard & Collins, 1993; Docter & Prince, 1997).

Transvestic disorder can be associated with gender dysphoria and a desire to transition to the female gender role, particularly when it is associated with autogynephilia (Blanchard, 2005, 2010b; Lawrence, 2013, 2017). The gender-related childhood and adolescent behaviors of men with transvestic disorder are consistent with those of other heterosexual men and unlike the childhood and adolescent behaviors often seen in gay men (Buhrich & McConaghy, 1985; Doorn, Poortinga, & Verschoor, 1994; Zucker & Bradley, 1995). Similarly, as adults, men with transvestic disorder generally have masculine occupations and hobbies (Chung & Harmon, 1994).

Transvestic disorder must be distinguished from transvestic behavior. Although the former involves sexual arousal in response to cross-dressing, this is not necessarily the case in the latter. Nonsexual transvestic behaviors can be found, for example, in men who cross-dress for entertainment purposes (colloquially referred to as "drag queens").

VOYEURISTIC DISORDER

Voyeurism pertains to recurrent and intense sexual arousal from observing an unsuspecting person who is naked, in the process of disrobing, or engaging in sexual activity as manifested by fantasies, urges, or behaviors. As with the other paraphilias, the *DSM-5* diagnostic criteria require the behavior to cause significant distress or interpersonal difficulty, or to be present in the form of actual voyeuristic activities (APA, 2013; Långström, 2010). Abel et al. (1986) and Marshall and Eccles (1991) examined interpersonal skills and sexual functioning in voyeurs and found that these individuals had deficits in social and assertiveness skills as well as sexual knowledge, and that they also had higher rates of sexual dysfunctions and difficulties with intimacy than nonvoyeurs.

Nevertheless, approximately half have been found to be involved in marital relationships (Gebhard, Gagnon, Pomeroy, & Christenson, 1965).

OTHER SPECIFIED PARAPHILIC DISORDER

This category applies to presentations in which symptoms of a paraphilic disorder are present, but the full criteria are not met for any of the disorders in the paraphilic disorders diagnostic class. It allows the clinician to communicate the specific reason why the individual does not meet criteria for a paraphilic disorder and record the specific reason, including the presence of a relatively uncommon paraphilia. Examples given in the *DSM-5* include telephone scatalogia, necrophilia, zoophilia, coprophilia, klismaphilia, and urophilia.

UNSPECIFIED PARAPHILIC DISORDER

This diagnostic category is also used when the individual does not meet the full criteria for a paraphilic disorder and may be given in situations in which there is insufficient information to make a more specific diagnosis.

DIAGNOSTIC CONSIDERATIONS

In the *DSM-5*, a more formal distinction was made between the definition of a paraphilia (as earlier) and a paraphilic disorder. The latter requires that a paraphilia causes distress or impairment to the individual or a paraphilia whose satisfaction has entailed personal harm, or risk of harm, to others. Thus, a paraphilia is a necessary but not sufficient condition for having a paraphilic disorder, and a paraphilia by itself does not necessarily justify or require clinical intervention. The distinction between the ascertainment of a paraphilia and the diagnosis of a paraphilic disorder has already been applied in legal situations. The National Coalition for Sexual Freedom has documented that parents who engage in consensual bondage and discipline or sadomasochism are no longer being sanctioned for this conduct in child custody hearings (Wright, 2014).

In addition to this change, the *DSM-5* has introduced two specifiers that cut across all the paraphilias: in a controlled environment (noting that there may be some environments in which the opportunity to enact a paraphilia is restricted), and in full remission (for at least 5 years while in an uncontrolled environment). The only exception to this pertains to pedophilic disorder: because the Board of Trustees preserved the diagnostic criteria as they appeared in *DSM-IV-TR*, these specifiers were not added (for a critique, see Balon, 2014).

Paraphilias must be distinguished not only from nonpathological sexual interests, but also from each other. For example, transvestic disorder must be distinguished from fetishistic disorder and sexual masochism disorder. Both transvestic disorder and fetishistic disorder can involve articles of feminine clothing, making it necessary to distinguish between a sexual interest in cross-dressing (necessary for a diagnosis of transvestic disorder) and a sexual interest in the articles of clothing themselves (necessary for a diagnosis of fetishistic disorder). Similarly, sexual masochism can involve humiliation via dressing in women's clothing, and thus must be distinguished from transvestic disorder and fetishistic disorder by the fact that the interest in cross-dressing seen in sexual masochism is specific to the humiliation felt while engaging in this behavior.

Distinguishing among the paraphilias can be complicated by the fact that the presence of one paraphilia is associated with an elevated risk of having additional paraphilias (e.g., Kafka & Hennen, 1999; Price, Gutheil, Commons, Kafka, & Dodd-Kimmey, 2001). For example, transvestic disorder has been associated with autoerotic asphyxia—a form of sexual masochism—(Blanchard & Hucker, 1991), as well as with exhibitionism, voyeurism, and pedophilia (e.g., Långström & Zucker, 2005). Similarly, significant comorbidity has been found among exhibitionism, voyeurism, and frotteurism (Freund, 1990; Långström, 2010; Långström & Seto, 2006). In fact, in one study, only 10.4% of 561 non-incarcerated paraphiliacs had only one paraphilia (Abel, Becker, Cunningham-Rathner, Mittelman, & Rouleau, 1988).

Finally, paraphilic disorders need to be distinguished from other nonparaphilic disorders. For example, significant overlap can exist between transvestic disorder and gender dysphoria, whereby individuals may meet the criteria exclusively for either of these two diagnoses, but where it is also possible for individuals to meet criteria for both (APA, 2013).

As the *DSM-5* notes, other disorders that must be differentiated from the paraphilias include intellectual disability, dementia, personality disorders, personality change due to a general medical condition, substance intoxication, mania, and schizophrenia.

EPIDEMIOLOGY

Epidemiological study of the paraphilias has been challenging. In part, this is because of their secretive, stigmatizing, and often illegal nature (regarding stigma and pedophilia, see, for example, Imhoff, 2015; Jahnke, Imhoff, & Hoyer, 2015). Therefore, prevalence estimates are generally based either on nonrepresentative samples of convicted sexual offenders or on general population samples (mostly nonrandom samples) that ask about paraphilic interests and behaviors. However, it is crucial to bear in mind that most of these studies do not use *DSM* criteria, so this must be recognized in appraising the various claims about prevalence. A good example of this general point comes from a recent study by Joyal and Carpentier (2017), who surveyed 1,040 adults in Quebec and found that the percentage of men who self-reported at least one paraphilic behavior/experience ranged from 7.8% for exhibitionism to 50.3% for voyeurism; among women, the percentage ranged from 2.7% for exhibitionism to 23.7% for masochism. However, the prevalence rates drop considerably once intensity or persistence were taken into account, as one would expect (see also Ahlers et al., 2011).

As previously noted, exhibitionism is one of the most common paraphilias and may be the most common sexual offense (e.g., Bartosh, Garby, Lewis, & Gray, 2003; Firestone et al., 2006). With respect to prevalence, studies have found that exhibitionism accounts for between one-third and two-thirds of all sexual offenses reported to police in Canada, the United States, and Europe (e.g., Gebhard et al., 1965; Smukler & Schiebel, 1975). Although estimates have varied, up to 20% of women may be victims of exhibitionism (Kaplan & Krueger, 1997; Meyer, 1995). Corroborating this high number of victims, Abel and Rouleau (1990) found that 25% of offenders in their outpatient clinics had a history of exhibitionism and that these 142 offenders reported a total of 72,074 victims. In one nonoffender study, 2% admitted to a history of exhibitionism (Templeman & Stinnett, 1991); however, in a more recent study involving a nationally representative sample of 2,450 adults in Sweden, more than 4% of males and 2% of females reported a history of at least one instance of exhibitionistic behavior for the purposes of sexual arousal (Långström & Seto, 2006).

Fetishism is a rare condition (APA, 2013). Chalkley and Powell (1983) reported that 0.8% of patients seen in three psychiatric hospitals over a period of 20 years met the criteria, and Curren (1954) found that only five out of 4,000 clients seen in private practice had a primary diagnosis of fetishism; however, as Mason (1997) noted, clinicians likely see only a small minority of the total number of individuals with fetishistic interests considering the wide proliferation of organizations and materials catering to these individuals. Nevertheless, it is unlikely that the majority of these individuals meet *DSM-5* criteria for fetishism, given that many do not experience distress or impairment.

Abel et al. (1988) interviewed 561 nonincarcerated paraphiliacs and found that 62 (11%) had a primary diagnosis of frotteurism, leading them to conclude that frottage was not the uncommon paraphilic act it has sometimes been touted to be. These rates are in line with other studies (Bradford, Boulet, & Pawlak, 1992; Kafka & Hennen, 2002), although even higher rates were found by Templeman and Stinnett (1991), who asked 60 college-aged men about frotteuristic activities and found that 35% indicated that they had engaged in frottage (see also Clark, Jeglic, Calkins, & Tatar, 2016). Interestingly, a study of 33 adult men and 28 adult women in India revealed higher rates of reported sexual interests in frotteurism in women (14.3%) than in men (9.1%) (Kar & Koola, 2007); this finding is very surprising given that paraphilias are generally considered to be very uncommon in women, with the exception of sexual masochism. From an epidemiological perspective, however, virtually nothing is known regarding its prevalence, because the few studies that have been conducted did not employ formal diagnostic criteria (Johnson, Ostermeyer, Sikes, Nelsen, & Coverdale, 2014).

Although a substantial amount of research has been conducted on pedophilia, its prevalence is unknown. Seto (2009, 2017) conjectured that the upper limit for the prevalence of pedophilia was likely around 5%. This is based on the fact that several surveys with men have revealed rates of between 3% and 9% for self-reported sexual fantasies or sexual contact involving prepubescent children (e.g., Templeman & Stinnett, 1991; Wurtele, Simons, & Moreno, 2014), but also on the fact that these rates are likely to overestimate the prevalence of pedophilia because these surveys did not assess the intensity, persistence, or presence of distress/impairment related to the sexual fantasies/behaviors. An important study by Dombert et al. (2016) found that, among 8,718 German men recruited online, 4.1% reported sexual fantasies involving prepubescent children and 3.2% reported having sexually offended against such children, but only 0.1% reported a pedophilic erotic preference.

Baumeister (1989) estimated that between 5% and 10% of the population has engaged in some form of masochistic activities based on a literature review of findings from other studies. He further hypothesized that double this number have had fantasies about sexual masochism but that less than 1% of the population likely engages in masochistic sexual activities on a regular basis. Since Baumeister's (1989) review, studies have been conducted with both clinical and nonclinical populations. In studies with sexual offenders, the rates of sexual masochism have ranged from 2% (Becker, Stinson, Tromp, & Messer, 2003) to just over 5% (Hill, Habermann, Berner, & Briken, 2006). Higher percentages—but still in line with the review by Baumeister (1989)—have been found in studies of outpatient males seeking treatment for paraphilic or paraphilia-related disorders, with between 9% and 11% of the samples meeting criteria for sexual masochism (Kafka & Hennen, 2002, 2003; Kafka & Prentky, 1994). With respect to nonclinical populations, an Australian study that assessed participation in bondage, discipline, sadomasochism, dominance, or submission via telephone survey revealed that 2.0% of men and 1.4% of women acknowledged having engaged in these activities at some point in their lives (Richters, Grulich, de Visser, Smith, & Rissel, 2003). In line with the notion that sexual masochism is not specific to males, one review of studies that have assessed women's rape fantasies revealed that between 31% and 57% of women have had sexual fantasies involving forced sexual activities, and that, of these women, 9–17% reported that these fantasies were either their most frequent or their most preferred fantasies (Critelli & Bivona, 2008).

Several studies have been conducted on the extent of sexual sadism in clinical and nonclinical samples. Of studies with convicted sexual offenders, rates of sexual sadism have ranged substantially, from 4% to 9% in some studies (e.g., Becker et al., 2003; Elwood, Doren, & Thornton, 2010; Levenson, 2004) to upwards of 35% in other studies (e.g., Berger, Berner, Bolterauer, Gutierrez, & Berger, 1999; Hill et al., 2006). In a study of 561 adult males seeking outpatient treatment for possible paraphilias, 28 (5%) of participants met the criteria for sexual sadism (Abel et al., 1987, 1988), consistent with a more recent study with 120 outpatient males with paraphilias or paraphilia-related disorders, 60 of whom were sex offenders (Kafka & Hennen, 2002, 2003). Another study of 63 outpatient males found 12% of the sample meeting criteria for sexual sadism (Kafka & Prentky, 1994). With respect to nonclinical samples, Hunt (1974) surveyed both men and women on their sexual experiences and found that 5% of men and 2% of women endorsed becoming sexually aroused to inflicting pain on others. Crepault and Couture (1980) assessed rates of sexually sadistic fantasies in a community sample of men and found that 11% had fantasies of beating up a woman and 15% had fantasies of humiliating a woman. Arndt, Foehl, and Good (1985) found that half of their sample of men and one-third of their sample of women indicated having had prior fantasies of tying up their partners.

Along with exhibitionism, voyeurism is one of the most common paraphilias and one of the most common sexual offenses (e.g., Bradford et al., 1992; Långström & Seto, 2006). In the study by Långström and Seto (2006), involving 2,450 adult men and women from a nationally representative sample in Sweden, 12% of men and 4% of women acknowledged at least one instance of sexual arousal in response to viewing unsuspecting individuals engaging in sexual activities. Much higher rates were found in a study of 33 adult men and 28 adult women in India (Kar & Koola, 2007), where 55% of the men and 25% of the women in the sample had engaged in voyeuristic activities. Furthermore, 3% of these men reported that voyeurism was a necessary component for sexual gratification. These high rates are in line with at least one study of 60 male college students in the United States, in which 42% engaged in voyeuristic activities and 53% reported an interest in voyeurism (Templeman & Stinnett, 1991). Meyer (1995) has posited that up to 20% of women have been targeted by voyeurs.

In a population-based study on transvestic fetishism, Långström and Zucker (2005) found that 2.8% of 1,279 Swedish men and 0.4% of 1,171 Swedish women reported sexual arousal in response to cross-dressing. The percentage for men is consistent with a subsequent study, which also found that 3% of a small sample of men ($n = 33$) acknowledged engaging in cross-dressing for sexual purposes (Kar & Koola, 2007). Interestingly, this latter study found a higher rate of transvestism (7.1%) in the 28 women in the sample.

PSYCHOLOGICAL AND BIOLOGICAL ASSESSMENT

Assessment strategies include questionnaires and self-report measures, as well as objective, physiological measures, such as the plethysmograph, the polygraph, and measures of visual reaction time. Two challenges inherent in measuring paraphilic interests are: (1) the fact that sexuality is typically a private matter and many individuals are uncomfortable discussing their interests and/or behaviors that carry a social stigma; and (2) the ethical aspects of assessment, whereby some techniques are invasive and/or involve the presentation of potentially disturbing sexual stimuli. All of these techniques suffer from problems with reliability, validity, and vulnerability to dissimulation to varying degrees. Therefore, no one technique should be used in isolation.

SELF-REPORT MEASURES

One of the most widely used self-report measures is the Clarke Sexual History Questionnaire for Males (Paitich, Langevin, Freeman, Mann, & Handy, 1977), a 190-item questionnaire that assesses a wide range of sexual experiences, including paraphilic experiences, their frequency, and their age of onset. Another self-report measure, the Multiphasic Sex Inventory (Nichols & Molinder, 1992), assesses paraphilic sexual preferences, sexual knowledge, and sexual dysfunction. The Wilson Sex Fantasy Questionnaire (Wilson, 1978) is a further standardized, commonly used instrument. Unfortunately, all these measures have the potential for biased or dishonest responses. Card-sort techniques contain rating scales composed of pictorial or written sexual stimuli that individuals are asked to view and then rate according to the degree of sexual arousal elicited. Examples include the Sexual Interest Questionnaire (Holland, Zolondek, Abel, Jordan, & Becker, 2000) and Laws' (1986) Sexual Deviance Card Sort.

Card Sort. Clinicians can also develop their own card sorts specific to what they know about a client or they can ask their clients to record their daily sexual fantasies and urges and then rate the corresponding degree of sexual arousal (Maletzky, 1997). A review by Schiavi, Derogatis, Kuriansky, O'Connor, and Sharpe (1979) of 50 self-report instruments used with sexual offenders found little evidence for their validity; however, their usefulness may lie in their ability to be used in conjunction with historical information that allows examination of inconsistencies (Kaplan & Krueger, 1997) or bias (Abel & Rouleau, 1990).

More recently, there have been some important advances in the use of rating scales and clinical chart data in the assessment of paraphilias, For example, with regard to sexual interest in children, the Screening Scale for Pedophilic Interests, a rating scale based on four child victim characteristics (e.g, age, number of victims, etc.), has been used as a method to identify men with a sexual arousal pattern for children, with promising findings (see, e.g., Helmus, Ó Ciardha, & Seto, 2015; Seto, Harris, Rice, & Barbaree, 2004; Seto, Sandler, & Freeman, 2017a; Seto, Stephens, Lalumière, & Cantor, 2017b). With regard to sexual sadism, one study relied on clinical chart data and crime scene information to identify dimensionality (severity) of sexual sadism among sex offenders (Mokros, Schilling, Weiss, Nitschke, & Eher, 2014; see also Longpré, Proulx, & Brouillette-Alarie, 2016).

PSYCHOPHYSIOLOGICAL MEASURES

Because of the difficulties with self-report, many clinicians and researchers depend on objective measures. Of these, phallometric assessment is considered to be the most reliable and valid and the least prone to dissimulation (Blanchard et al., 2009, 2012; Seto, 2001; Seto et al., 2016; Seto, Kingston, & Bourget, 2014). This technique involves the psychophysiological recording of sexual arousal through a device that measures either volumetric or circumferential changes in penile tumescence in response to sexual stimuli. The stimuli can take various forms, such as videos, audiotapes, photographs, and written text. Consistent increases in penile tumescence to specific sexual stimuli relative to other sexual and nonsexual stimuli are considered to indicate sexual preferences for those stimuli (Freund, 1963). The use of stimuli depicting individuals of all ages and both sexes, engaged in various sexual and nonsexual activities, reliably discriminates sexual from nonsexual offenders, including child molesters and nonchild molesters (Barbaree & Marshall, 1989; Freund & Blanchard, 1989); rapists and nonrapists (Harris, Rice, Chaplin, & Quinsey, 1999; Lalumière & Quinsey, 1994); men who admit to sadistic fantasies, cross-dress, or expose their genitals in public from men who do not (Freund et al., 1996; Seto & Kuban, 1996; Seto, Lalumière, Harris, & Chivers, 2012); and incest offenders and nonoffenders (Barsetti, Earls, & Lalumière, 1998; Chaplin, Rice, & Harris, 1995). Phallometry also has high predictive power for sexual and violent recidivism (Malcolm, Andrews, & Quinsey, 1993; Rice, Harris, & Quinsey, 1990; Seto, 2001), similar to that of psychopathy diagnoses and criminal history (Hanson & Bussiere, 1998). Sexual interests, as measured through phallometric testing, are considered to be the most consistently identifiable distinguishing characteristics of sexual offenders compared with general psychopathology, empathy, and social skills (Quinsey & Lalumière, 1996; Seto & Lalumière, 2001).

Phallometric testing is not without its criticisms. For example, group discrimination is not perfect, with the distributions of phallometric scores overlapping between sex offenders and nonoffenders (Seto, 2001, 2009). Furthermore, although the specificity of phallometry is very high (i.e., the test is able to accurately identify men who have not committed a sexual offense as nondeviant 90–97.5% of the time), the sensitivity of the test (i.e., the ability of the test to identify men who have committed a sexual offense as deviant) appears to be only between 44% and 50% (Freund & Watson, 1991; Lalumière & Quinsey, 1993). In addition, in 21% of participants assessed with phallometric testing, no clear diagnosis with respect to paraphilic sexual preferences was possible (Freund & Blanchard, 1989). Furthermore, a lack of standardization in stimuli, testing procedures, and data analysis results in considerable variability in procedures, data interpretation, and outcome across phallometric laboratories (Howes, 1995), making it difficult to evaluate the technical adequacy of different phallometric studies, replicate experiments, and account for discrepancies between studies (Schouten & Simon, 1992). There are also ethical concerns because sexual stimuli that depict violent sexual behavior or sexual images of children are usually presented. Finally, although phallometric testing is much less susceptible than self-report to response bias or dissimulation, some participants can alter their physiological responses in a socially desirable direction (for review, see Freund, Watson, & Rienzo, 1988; Lalumière & Earls, 1992), an issue that has an impact on the procedure's sensitivity. Furthermore, the ability of participants to control, or alter, their physiological responses increases with subsequent testing (Quinsey, Rice, & Harris, 1995), suggesting that multiple assessments give participants the opportunity to learn how to alter their responses so they appear less sexually deviant (Lalumière & Harris, 1998; see Babchishin, Curry, Fedoroff, Bradford, & Seto, 2017 for counter-evidence).

The polygraph (also known as the "lie detector") is another psychophysiological assessment technique used with individuals who have been accused or convicted of a sexual offense. However, unlike the plethysmograph, which is used to assess current sexual interests, the polygraph assesses past sexual behaviors and deceitfulness by measuring galvanic skin response, heart rate, blood pressure, and respiration. Changes in arousal are associated with involuntary responses to fear, based on the assumption that when people lie, they fear that their lie will be discovered, leading to measurable physiological increases. As Branaman and Gallagher (2005) indicate, the validity of the polygraph largely depends on the types of questions asked during the assessment. This has led to significant caution, because the implications of incorrectly identifying someone as having committed sexual offenses are numerous and severe. Furthermore, skeptics note that some individuals may feel coerced into admitting to offenses they never committed (Cross & Saxe, 2001). Because of these concerns, the polygraph is not generally admissible in court.

Another objective assessment is visual reaction time (also referred to as viewing time). Similar to phallometric testing, this strategy involves showing pictures of various sexual and nonsexual stimuli. Participants are informed that the technique assesses sexual interests through their self-reported ratings of sexual attractiveness to each picture. However, participants do not know that the procedure involves the unobtrusive recording of the length of time they view each stimulus. The technique is based on findings that individuals view images they find sexually stimulating longer than those they do not (Quinsey, Rice, Harris, & Reid, 1993). Visual reaction time has similar reliability and validity as phallometric testing (Abel, Huffman, Warberg, & Holland, 1998; Letourneau, 2002), with the added advantages of greater efficiency, less intrusiveness, and less technological complexity than phallometry (Abel et al., 1998; Harris, Rice, Quinsey, & Chaplin, 1996). Because the technique is less intrusive and thus less ethically controversial, it has also been used with adolescent sexual offenders with promising results (Abel et al., 2004).

ETIOLOGICAL CONSIDERATIONS

Numerous theories have been proposed to explain how the paraphilias develop; however, empirical evidence is either lacking or contradictory, and, as a result, no individual theory satisfactorily explains the development of paraphilic sexual interests. Nevertheless, knowledge of these theories provides some insight into current thinking about how paraphilic sexual disorders develop and the rationale behind various treatment approaches.

NEUROANATOMY AND NEUROBIOLOGY

Cases in which individuals developed paraphilic sexual interests following brain injuries and degenerative brain diseases (for a review, see Langevin, 1990) have led to hypotheses that the paraphilias may be caused by certain neurological abnormalities, particularly temporal lobe and limbic area abnormalities. Unfortunately, these findings are not uniform and they fail to account for a large number of individuals with paraphilias (Hucker et al., 1988). Further, numerous studies have found that temporal lobe disorders are generally associated with hyposexuality, not hypersexuality (Miller, Darby, Swartz, Yener, & Mena, 1995; Rosenblum, 1974).

New research suggests possible neurobiological underpinnings of paraphilic interests. In particular, research by Cantor et al. (2008), which compared the MRI scans of a sample of 65 pedophiles to a sample of 62 nonsexual offenders, found that pedophilic men had significantly less white matter in the superior fronto-occipital fasciculus and the right arcuate fasciculus regions of the brain (see also Cantor et al., 2015). These regions of the brain, located in the temporal and parietal lobes, are composed of axons that connect to other brain regions, thereby suggesting differences in the connectivity of the various regions of the brain between pedophiles and nonpedophiles. Specifically, Cantor et al. surmised that because the superior fronto-occipital fasciculus and arcuate fasciculus connect those regions of the brain that respond to sexual cues, pedophilia may be the result of a partial disconnection within the network that recognizes sexually relevant stimuli. With regard to gray matter variations, however, the MRI studies to date have yielded inconsistent findings (see Schiffer et al., 2017).

As Cantor et al. (2008) pointed out, it must be acknowledged that it is unknown whether these differences are the cause or the result of pedophilia, or due to an unknown third variable. However, given that these two regions of the brain are not generally associated with changes following environmental stimulation, the possibility that these changes are the result of pedophilia is unlikely. In general, new lines of evidence suggest the presence of a neurodevelopmental vulnerability among men with pedophilia or hebephilia, both prenatally and in childhood, as compared with nonpedophilic men: the presence of minor physical anomalies (Dyshniku, Murray, Fazio, Lykins, & Cantor, 2015), shorter height (Cantor et al., 2007; Fazio, Dyshniku, Lykins, & Cantor, 2017), higher rates of nonright-handedness (Cantor et al., 2004, 2005), higher rates of head injuries that resulted in unconsciousness in childhood (Blanchard et al., 2002, 2003), lower IQs (Blanchard et al., 2007; Cantor, Blanchard, Christensen, Dickey, & Klassen, 2004; Cantor, Blanchard, Robichaud, & Christensen, 2005), poorer visuospatial and verbal memory abilities (Cantor et al., 2004), and higher rates of having failed grades in school or having been placed in special education programs (Cantor et al., 2006).

Learning, Modeling, and Life Events

Behavioral theories of paraphilias have garnered much attention from clinicians and researchers, and have shaped many of the psychotherapeutic approaches used to treat paraphilic interests. Behavioral theories posit that paraphilias develop through operant or classical conditioning in which the object of paraphilic attention becomes paired with sexual arousal, resulting in abnormal arousal patterns (see Hoffmann, 2017). In essence, sexual arousal becomes the conditioned response to the paraphilic target and is reinforced through masturbation and orgasm. Research by Rachman (1966; see also Rachman & Hodgson, 1968) demonstrated that sexual arousal can, in fact, be conditioned; they conditioned a sexual response to a picture of a pair of boots by pairing the picture of the boots with photographs of nude adult women. However, the responses were easily extinguished, leading others to argue that the behavioral theory is not sufficient on its own to explain the maintenance of such behaviors throughout an individual's life (Bancroft, 2009).

Modeling and the effects of early life events have also been hypothesized to play a causal role. The belief that negative and disruptive early childhood and family functioning may lead to paraphilias comes from research indicating high rates of childhood abuse (both sexual and nonsexual), neglect, and disturbed family relations in paraphilic individuals (e.g., Marshall et al., 1993; Saunders, Awad, & White, 1986). However, as noted earlier, Jesperson et al. (2009) found less support for various kinds of abuse among sex offenders against children and pointed to a more specific association with sexual abuse.

Marshall et al. (1993) suggested that these negative experiences serve as templates for future relationships, leading to distrust or ambivalence with appropriate partners and teaching individuals to be abusive toward others. McGuire, Carlisle, and Young (1965) more specifically hypothesized that individuals who experience sexual abuse as children go on to use thoughts of the abuse during masturbation in adolescence, thus pairing abusive thoughts with the pleasure of masturbation, and leading to specific, paraphilic sexual preferences. These hypotheses, however, fail to account for the many individuals who have experienced abuse and dysfunctional family relationships who do not go on to develop paraphilias and, conversely, the many individuals with paraphilias who have no history of familial instability or victimization (Murphy, Haynes, & Page, 1992; Murphy & Smith, 1996).

COGNITIVE INFLUENCES

Cognitive-behavioral theories have emphasized the role of cognitions in the etiology of sexual offending (e.g., Ward, Hudson, & Marshall, 1995). Cognitive distortions include beliefs and ways of thinking that minimize or deny harm and attribute blame to victims or to other external factors, resulting in a lack of empathy toward victims. These distorted beliefs facilitate and justify further sexual offending (Abel, Becker, & Cunningham-Rathner, 1984) and have, thus, become the target of most treatment efforts with sexual offenders. However, evidence is lacking that these cognitions cause paraphilic sexual interests to develop. In fact, even the extent to which they cause initial instances of sexual offending, versus emerging after the fact, remains unclear. Of note is the fact that researchers have found that child molesters are not lacking in general empathy (i.e., they have not been found to be less empathic compared with nonchild molesters), but that they are lacking in specific empathy toward their victims (Marshall, Jones, Hudson, & McDonald, 1994).

COURSE, PROGNOSIS, AND TREATMENT

Paraphilias most commonly first appear in adolescence (e.g., Abel, Osborn, & Twigg, 1993; Zucker & Bradley, 1995), with charges and convictions most frequently occurring in early adulthood (e.g., Berah & Meyers, 1983). The course has generally been found to be chronic (e.g., Gosselin & Wilson, 1980), and, at least in the case of sexual sadism, the severity may increase over time (APA, 2000). Some researchers have argued, however, that pedophilia can, in fact, be treated successfully, which challenges the narrative of chronicity (Müller et al., 2014); however, this study has been strongly critiqued on methodological and statistical grounds (Bailey, 2016; Cantor, 2015; Lalumière, 2015; Mokros & Habermeyer, 2016).

Due to ethical and methodological limitations in conducting empirical investigations of treatment efficacy with paraphilic individuals (such as randomly assigning convicted offenders to a no-treatment control group), and because most paraphilias have extremely low base rates, leading to difficulties with acquiring adequate sample sizes, efficacy rates for the treatment of the paraphilias have not been conclusive. In fact, some professionals have argued that there is currently no empirical basis indicating that treatment for sexual offenders is superior to placebo (e.g., Furby, Weinrott, & Blackshaw, 1989). Treatment of paraphilias with nonoffending individuals is often focused on helping them understand that paraphilias are lifelong and that people do not choose what will interest them sexually. In addition, treatment may focus on how the interests can be managed in ways that do not involve illegal activities or risks to physical health and safety, and in ways that do not affect social and/or occupational functioning. Response prevention programs have attracted considerable interest, particularly the Dunkelfeld Project in Germany (Hillier & Murphy, 2015), in which men with a sexual interest in children (yet who have not acted on these interests) are seen in a therapeutic milieu (Beier et al., 2009).

CASE STUDY

John is a 21-year-old, single, heterosexual, Caucasian male who resides with his parents and two younger siblings. He has a college diploma and is currently employed in the sales industry. John's probation officer referred John to a behavioral sexology clinic following John's conviction for committing an indecent act (also known as "indecent exposure" or "public indecency"). John was charged and convicted of committing an indecent act after he drove his car alongside two females, aged 14 and 20, exposed his penis, and then masturbated to the point of ejaculation before driving away. John has no criminal record for any prior sexual or nonsexual offenses; however, John acknowledged a sexual interest in exhibitionism and a prior history of exposing himself to strangers. He reported that he spontaneously began to have fantasies about exposing himself to unsuspecting women when he was approximately 18 or 19 years of age. His fantasies of exhibitionism involve the unsuspecting woman becoming intrigued and aroused by his exhibitionism and this leading to consensual partnered sexual activities. At the same time, John acknowledged that, although this is his fantasy, he has never actually believed that this would happen in reality.

John reported that he exposed himself for the first time when he was 19 years old. He was driving in his car, with no prior intention of exposing himself, when he drove past an attractive, adult female walking on the street. John reported that he developed a strong urge to expose himself to her. He maneuvered his car in such a way that she walked by him and could see in his window, and he then masturbated to the point of ejaculation. According to John, the female noticed what he was doing but gave no reaction. John felt very guilty after the incident. Nonetheless, he noticed that his fantasies and urges to expose himself increased.

John's second instance of exposing himself occurred when he was in college. He was in the college library when he saw an attractive female studying in a study carrel across from him. John once again exposed his penis and masturbated to the point of ejaculation, after which he ran out of the library and again felt very guilty.

With respect to the incident that resulted in John's conviction and subsequent referral to the behavioral sexology clinic, John reported that he had purposely gotten in his car and driven around searching for an attractive female to expose himself to after experiencing strong urges to do so. He reported that he then saw the two victims, the older of whom he found attractive. He pulled up to them, exposed himself, and masturbated to the point of ejaculation. He then drove away but was contacted by police an hour later.

John expressed a lot of guilt about his exhibitionistic urges and behaviors. He acknowledged that he continues to have urges to expose himself since the index offense but reported that he has been able to refrain from acting out on the urges by reminding himself of his arrest and conviction. At the same time, he expressed concern that thinking of the index offense may not be enough to resist his urges in the future.

With respect to other sexual interests, John reported that he is sexually attracted exclusively to females who are approximately his age. He reported no sexual attraction to prepubescent or pubescent females. He similarly reported that he has no sexual interest in cross-dressing, leather, latex, rough or violent sexual behavior, or being humiliated. He reported no interest in voyeurism beyond viewing "amateur" pornographic videos that advertise that the performers are unaware of being filmed. He reported no concerns pertaining to sexual functioning or gender identity.

Assessment involved a comprehensive psychosexual history, including information about his exhibitionistic fantasies, urges, and behaviors, information about other paraphilic and nonparaphilic interests and behaviors, general mental and physical health, and social and interpersonal functioning. Through this psychosexual history, John met *DSM-IV-TR* criteria for exhibitionism. John did not report any other paraphilic sexual interests; however, given the nature of the referral and the additional fact that one of the two victims of the index offense was 14 years of age, corroborative objective assessment via phallometric testing was deemed appropriate. Phallometric testing was not indicative of a sexual interest in either prepubescent or pubescent children. Thus, John's final diagnosis was exhibitionism, and it was concluded that he could potentially benefit from participation in cognitive-behavioral/relapse prevention treatment for his sexual offending behaviors.

SUMMARY

Often associated with sexual deviance and sexual offending, the paraphilias are one of the most controversial groups of disorders. Indeed, some clinicians have argued that all of the paraphilias should be removed from the *DSM-5* because no one has ever produced unambiguous evidence that they meet the *DSM* definition of a mental disorder (Shindel & Moser, 2011)—distress, for example, is not really "in the person" but more a result of social ostracism, discrimination, etc. They are merely sexual variants. For those paraphilias that are illegal, they should be considered sex crimes, but not mental disorders. In the forthcoming *ICD-11*, it has been proposed to remove from the catalog of paraphilic disorders those that do not affect other persons (e.g., fetishism, fetishistic transvestism, and (consensual) sadomasochism). However, contra Shindel and Moser, it has been recommended to retain the other paraphilias and add others (Krueger et al., 2017).

This controversy is furthered by the limited amount of sound empirical research—particularly epidemiological research—on individuals with these conditions. However, assessment and treatment of the paraphilias have advanced significantly toward more effective, efficient, and ethical techniques.

REFERENCES

Abel, G. G., Becker, J. V., & Cunningham-Rathner, J. (1984). Complications, consent and cognitions in sex between children and adults. *International Journal of Law and Psychiatry, 7*, 89–103.

Abel, G. G., Becker, J. V., Cunningham-Rathner, J., Mittelman, M., & Rouleau, J. (1988). Multiple paraphilic diagnoses among sex offenders. *Bulletin of the American Academy of Psychiatry and the Law, 16*, 153–168.

Abel, G. G., Becker, J. V., Mittelman, M., Cunningham-Rathner, J., Rouleau, J. L., & Murphy, W. D. (1987). Self-reported sex crimes of nonincarcerated paraphiliacs. *Journal of Interpersonal Violence, 2*, 3–25.

Abel, G. G., Huffman, J., Warberg, B., & Holland, C. L. (1998). Visual reaction time and plethysmography as measures of sexual interest in child molesters. *Sexual Abuse: A Journal of Research and Treatment, 10*, 81–95.

Abel, G. G., Jordan, A., Rouleau, J. L., Emerick, R., Barboza-Whitehead, S., & Osborn, C. (2004). Use of visual reaction time to assess male adolescents who molest children. *Sexual Abuse: A Journal of Research and Treatment, 16*, 255–265.

Abel, G. G., & Osborn, C. (1992). The paraphilias: The extent and nature of sexually deviant and criminal behavior. *Clinical Forensic Psychiatry, 15*, 675–687.

Abel, G., Osborn, C., & Twigg, D. (1993). Sexual assault through the life span: Adult offenders with juvenile histories. In H. E. Barbaree, W. L. Marshall, & S. M. Hudson (Eds.), *The juvenile sex offender* (pp. 104–117). New York, NY: Guilford Press.

Abel, G. G., & Rouleau, J. L. (1990). The nature and extent of sexual assault. In W. L. Marshall, D. R. Laws, & H. E. Barbaree (Eds.), *Handbook of sexual assault: Issues, theories, and treatment of the offender* (pp. 9–21). New York, NY: Plenum Press.

Abel, G. G., Rouleau, J. L., & Cunningham-Rathner, J. (1986). Sexually aggressive behavior. In W. J. Curran, A. L. McGarry, & S. Shah (Eds.), *Forensic psychiatry and psychology: Perspectives and standards for interdisciplinary practice* (pp. 289–313). Philadelphia, PA: F. A. Davis.

Ahlers, C. J., Schneider, G. A., Mundt, I. A., Roll, S., Englert, H., Willich, S. N., & Beier, K. M. (2011). How unusual are the contents of the paraphilias? Paraphilia-associated sexual arousal patterns in a community-based sample of men. *Journal of Sexual Medicine, 8,* 1362–1370.

Altenburger, L. E., Carotta, C. L., Bonomi, A. E., & Snyder, A. (2017). Sexist attitudes among emerging adult women readers of *Fifty Shades* fiction. *Archives of Sexual Behavior, 46,* 455–464.

Althof, S. E. (2014). Treatment of premature ejaculation: Psychotherapy, pharmacotherapy, and combined therapy. In Y. M. Binik & K. S. K. Hall (Eds.), *Principles and practice of sex therapy* (5th ed., pp. 112–137). New York, NY: The Guilford Press.

Althof, S. E., O'Leary, M. P., Cappelleri, J. C., Crowley, A. R., Tseng, L., & Collins, S. (2006). Impact of erectile dysfunction on confidence, self-esteem and relationship satisfaction after 9 months of sildenafil citrate treatment. *Journal of Urology, 176,* 2132–2137.

American Psychiatric Association. (2000). *Diagnostic and statistical manual of mental disorders* (4th ed., text revision). Washington, DC: American Psychiatric Association.

American Psychiatric Association. (2013). *Diagnostic and statistical manual of mental disorders* (5th ed.). Arlington, VA: American Psychiatric Association.

Arndt, W., Foehl, J., & Good, F. (1985). Specific sexual fantasy themes: A multidimensional study. *Journal of Personality and Social Psychology, 48,* 472–480.

Arnow, B. A., Millheiser, L., Garrett, A., Lake Polan, M., Glover, G. H., Lightbody, A., . . . Desmond, J. E. (2009). Women with hypoactive sexual desire disorder compared to normal females: A functional magnetic resonance imaging study. *Neuroscience, 158,* 484–502.

Atallah, S., Johnson-Agbakwu, C., Rosenbaum, R., Abdo, C., Byers, E. S., Graham, C. A., . . . Brotto, L. (2016). Ethical and socio-cultural aspects of sexual function and dysfunction in both sexes. *Journal of Sexual Medicine, 13,* 591–606.

Babchishin, K. M., Curry, S. D., Fedoroff, J. P., Bradford, J., & Seto, M. C. (2017). Inhibiting sexual arousal to children: Correlates and its influence on the validity of penile plethysmography. *Archives of Sexual Behavior, 46,* 671–684.

Babchishin, K. M., Hanson, R. K., & VanZuylen, H. (2015). Online child pornography offenders are different: A meta-analysis of the characteristics of online and offline sex offenders against children. *Archives of Sexual Behavior, 44,* 45–66.

Bader, S. M., Schoeneman-Morris, K. A., Scalora, M. J., & Casady, T. K. (2008). Exhibitionism: Findings from a midwestern police contact sample. *International Journal of Offender Therapy and Comparative Criminology, 52,* 270–279.

Bailey, J. M. (2015). A failure to demonstrate changes in sexual interest in pedophilic men: Comment on Müller et al. (2014). *Archives of Sexual Behavior, 44,* 249–252.

Balon, R. (2014). Politics of diagnostic criteria: Specifiers of pedophilic disorder in *DSM-5. Archives of Sexual Behavior, 43,* 1235–1236.

Balon, R., & Clayton, A. H. (2014). DSM-5 female sexual interest/arousal disorder: A diagnosis out of thin air. *Archives of Sexual Behavior, 43,* 1227–1229.

Bancroft, J. (2009). *Human sexuality and its problems* (3rd ed.). Edinburgh, UK: Churchill Livingstone.

Bancroft, J., Loftus, J., & Long, S. J. (2003). Distress about sex: A national survey of women in heterosexual relationships. *Archives of Sexual Behavior, 32,* 193–208.

Banmen, J., & Vogel, N. A. (1985). The relationship between marital quality and interpersonal sexual communication. *Family Therapy, 12,* 45–58.

Barbaree, H. E., & Marshall, W. L. (1989). Erectile responses among heterosexual child molesters, father-daughter incest offenders, and matched non-offenders: Five distinct age preference profiles. *Canadian Journal of Behavioral Science, 21*, 70–82.

Barbaree, H. E., & Seto, M. C. (1997). Pedophilia: Assessment and treatment. In D. R. Laws & W. O'Donohue (Eds.), *Sexual deviance: Theory, assessment, and treatment* (pp. 175–193). New York, NY: Guilford Press.

Barsetti, I., Earls, C. M., & Lalumière, M. L. (1998). The differentiation of intrafamilial and extrafamilial heterosexual child molesters. *Journal of Interpersonal Violence, 13*, 275–286.

Bartosh, D. L., Garby, T., Lewis, D., & Gray, S. (2003). Differences in predictive validity of actuarial risk assessments in relation to sex offender type. *International Journal of Offender Therapy and Comparative Criminology, 47*, 422–438.

Basson, R. (2004). Pharmacotherapy for sexual dysfunction in women. *Expert Opinion in Pharmacotherapy, 5*, 1045–1059.

Basson, R., & Brotto, L. A. (2003). Sexual psychophysiology and effects of sildenafil citrate in oestrogenised women with acquired genital arousal disorder and impaired orgasm: A randomised controlled trial. *British Journal of Obstetrics and Gynaecology, 110*, 1014–1024.

Basson, R., Brotto, L. A., Petkau, J. A., & Labrie, F. (2010). Role of androgens in women's sexual dysfunction. *Menopause, 17*, 962–971.

Basson, R., McInnes, R., Smith, M. D., Hodgson, G., & Koppiker, N. (2002). Efficacy and safety of sildenafil citrate in women with sexual dysfunction associated with female sexual arousal disorder. *Journal of Women's Health and Gender-Based Medicine, 11*, 367–377.

Baumeister, R. F. (1989). *Masochism and the self.* Hillsdale, NJ: Erlbaum.

Baumeister, R. F. (1991). *Escaping the self: Alcoholism, spirituality, masochism, and other flights from the burden of selfhood.* New York, NY: Basic Books.

Baumeister, R. F., & Butler, J. L. (1997). Sexual masochism: Deviance without pathology. In D. R. Laws & W. O'Donohue (Eds.), *Sexual deviance: Theory, assessment, and treatment* (pp. 225–239). New York, NY: Guilford Press.

Baumeister, R. F., & Scher, S. J. (1988). Self-defeating behavior patterns among normal individuals: Review and analysis of common self-destructive tendencies. *Psychological Bulletin, 104*, 3–22.

Becker, J. V., Stinson, J., Tromp, S., & Messer, G. (2003). Characteristics of individuals petitioned for civil commitment. *International Journal of Offender Therapy and Comparative Criminology, 47*, 185–195.

Beier, K. M., Grundmann, D., Kuhle, L. F., Scherner, G., Konrad, A., & Amelung, T. (2015). The German Dunkefeld Project: A pilot study to prevent child sexual abuse and the use of child abusive images. *Journal of Sexual Medicine, 12*, 529–542.

Beier, K. M., Neutze, J., Mundt, I. A., Ahlers, C. J., Goecker, D., Konrad, A., & Schaefer, G. A. (2009). Encouraging self-identified pedophiles and hebephiles to seek professional help: First results of the Prevention Project Dunkelfeld (PPD). *Child Abuse and Neglect, 33*, 545–549.

Berah, E. F., & Meyers, R. G. (1983). The offense records of a sample of convicted exhibitionists. *Bulletin of the American Academy of Psychiatry and the Law, 11*, 365–369.

Berger, P., Berner, W., Bolterauer, J., Gutierrez, K., & Berger, K. (1999). Sadistic personality disorder in sex offenders: Relationship to antisocial personality disorder and sexual sadism. *Journal of Personality Disorders, 13*, 175–186.

Bergeron, S., Binik, Y. M., Khalifé, S., Pagidas, K., Glazer, H. I., Meana, M., & Amsel, R. (2001). A randomized comparison of group cognitive-behavioural therapy, surface electromyographic biofeedback, and vestibulectomy in the treatment of dyspareunia resulting from vulvar vestibulitis. *Pain, 91*, 297–306.

Bergeron, S., Brown, C., Lord, M. J., Oala, M., Binik, Y. M., & Khalifé, S. (2002). Physical therapy for vulvar vestibulitis syndrome: A retrospective study. *Journal of Sex and Marital Therapy, 28*, 183–192.

Bergeron, S., Corsini-Munt, S., Aerts, L., Rancourt, K., & Rosen, N. O. (2015). Female sexual pain disorders: A review of the literature on etiology and treatment. *Current Sexual Health Reports, 7,* 159–169.

Bergeron, S., Khalifé, S., Dupuis, M. J., & McDuff, P. (2016). A randomized clinical trial comparing group cognitive-behavioral therapy and a topical steroid for women with dyspareunia. *Journal of Consulting and Clinical Psychology, 84,* 259–268.

Bergeron, S., Khalifé, S., Glazer, H. I., & Binik, Y. M. (2008). Surgical and behavioral treatments for vestibulodynia: Two-and-one-half year follow-up and predictors of outcome. *Obstetrics and Gynecology, 111,* 159–166.

Bergeron, S., Rosen, N. O., & Morin, M. (2011). Genital pain in women: Beyond interference with intercourse. *Pain, 152,* 1223–1225.

Berglas, S. C., & Baumeister, R. F. (1993). *Your own worst enemy: Understanding the paradox of self-defeating behavior.* New York, NY: Basic Books.

Berman, J. R., Berman, L. A., Toler, S. M., Gill, J., Haughie, S., & Sildenafil Study Group (2003). Safety and efficacy of sildenafil citrate for the treatment of female sexual arousal disorder: A double-blind, placebo controlled study. *Journal of Urology, 170,* 2333–2338.

Billups, K. L., Berman, L., Berman, J., Metz, M. E., Glennon, M. E., & Goldstein, I. (2001). A new non-pharmacological vacuum therapy for female sexual dysfunction. *Journal of Sex and Marital Therapy, 27,* 435–441.

Binik, Y. M. (2005). Should dyspareunia be retained as a sexual dysfunction in DSM-V? A painful classification decision. *Archives of Sexual Behavior, 34,* 11–21.

Binik, Y. M. (2010a). The DSM diagnostic criteria for dyspareunia. *Archives of Sexual Behavior, 39,* 292–303.

Binik, Y. M. (2010b). The DSM diagnostic criteria for vaginismus. *Archives of Sexual Behavior, 9,* 861–873.

Blanchard, R. (2005). Early history of the concept of autogynephilia. *Archives of Sexual Behavior, 34,* 439–446.

Blanchard, R. (2010a). The DSM diagnostic criteria for pedophilia. *Archives of Sexual Behavior, 39,* 304–316.

Blanchard, R. (2010b). The DSM diagnostic criteria for transvestic fetishism. *Archives of Sexual Behavior, 39,* 363–372.

Blanchard, R. (2013). A dissenting opinion on DSM-5 Pedophilic Disorder [Letter to the Editor]. *Archives of Sexual Behavior, 42,* 675–678.

Blanchard, R., Christensen, B. K., Strong, S. M., Cantor, J. M., Kuban, M. E., Klassen, P., . . . Blak, T. (2002). Retrospective self-reports of childhood accidents causing unconsciousness in phallometrically diagnosed pedophiles. *Archives of Sexual Behavior, 31,* 511–526.

Blanchard, R., & Collins, P. (1993). Men with sexual interest in transvestites, transsexuals and she-males. *Journal of Nervous and Mental Disease, 181,* 570–575.

Blanchard, R., & Hucker, S. J. (1991). Age, transvestism, bondage, and concurrent paraphilic activities in 117 fatal cases of autoerotic asphyxia. *British Journal of Psychiatry, 159,* 371–377.

Blanchard, R., Kolla, N. J., Cantor, J. M., Klassen, P. E., Dickey, R., Kuban, M. E., & Blak, T. (2007). IQ, handedness, and pedophilia in adult male patients stratified by referral source. *Sexual Abuse: A Journal of Research and Treatment, 19,* 285–309.

Blanchard, R., Kuban, M. E., Blak, T., Cantor, J. M., Klassen, P. E., & Dickey, R. (2009). Absolute versus relative ascertainment of pedophilia in men. *Sexual Abuse: A Journal of Research and Treatment, 21,* 431–441.

Blanchard, R., Kuban, M. E., Blak, T., Klassen, P. E., Dickey, R., & Cantor, J. M. (2012). Sexual attraction to others: A comparison of two models of alloerotic responding in men. *Archives of Sexual Behavior, 41,* 13–29.

Blanchard, R., Kuban, M. E., Klassen, P., Dickey, R., Christensen, B. K., Cantor, J. M., & Blak, T. (2003). Self-reported head injuries before and after age 13 in pedophilic and non-pedophilic men referred for clinical assessment. *Archives of Sexual Behavior, 32*, 573–581.

Bolt, J. W., Evans, C., & Marshall, V. R. (1987). Sexual dysfunction after prostatectomy. *British Journal of Urology, 59*, 319–322.

Bradford, J., Boulet, J., & Pawlak, A. (1992). The paraphilias: A multiplicity of deviant behaviors. *Canadian Journal of Psychiatry, 37*, 104–108.

Branaman, T. F., & Gallagher, S. N. (2005). Polygraph testing in sex offender treatment: A review of limitations. *American Journal of Forensic Psychology, 23*, 45–64.

Breslow, N., Evans, L., & Langley, J. (1995). On the prevalence and roles of females in sado-masochistic sub culture: Report of an empirical study. *Archives of Sexual Behavior, 14*, 303–317.

Brock, G., Iglesias, J. Toulouse, K., Ferguson, K. M., Pullman, W. E., & Anglin, G. (2001, April). Efficacy and safety of tadalafil (IC351) treatment for ED. Paper presented at the *Congress of the European Association of Urology, Geneva, Switzerland*.

Brotto, L. A. (2010a). The DSM diagnostic criteria for hypoactive sexual desire disorder in women. *Archives of Sexual Behavior, 39*, 221–239.

Brotto, L. A. (2010b). The DSM diagnostic criteria for hypoactive sexual desire disorder in men. *Journal of Sexual Medicine, 7*, 2015–2030.

Brotto, L., Atallah, S., Johnson-Agbakwu, C., Rosenbaum, T., Abdo, C., Byers, S., . . . Wylie, K. (2016a). Psychological and interpersonal dimensions of sexual function and dysfunction. *Journal of Sexual Medicine, 13*, 538–571.

Brotto, L. A., & Basson, R. (2014). Group mindfulness-based therapy significantly improves sexual desire in women. *Behaviour Research and Therapy, 57*, 43–54.

Brotto, L. A., Basson, R., Chivers, M. L., Graham, C. A., Pollock, P., & Stephenson, K. R. (2016b). Challenges in designing psychological treatment studies for sexual dysfunction. *Journal of Sex & Marital Therapy*. Advance online publication. doi: 10.1080/0092623X.2016.1212294.

Brotto, L. A., Basson, R., Driscoll, M., Smith, K. B. S., & Sadownik, L. A. (2015). Mindfulness-based group therapy for women with Provoked Vestibulodynia. *Mindfulness, 6*, 417–432.

Brotto, L. A., Bitzer, J., Laan, E., Leiblum, S., & Luria, M. (2010). Women's sexual desire and arousal disorders. *Journal of Sexual Medicine, 7*, 586–614.

Brotto, L. A., & Goldmeier, D. (2015). Mindfulness interventions for treating sexual dysfunctions: The gentle science of finding focus in a multitask world [Invited Commentary]. *Journal of Sexual Medicine, 12*, 1687–1689.

Buhrich, N., & McConaghy, N. (1985). Preadult feminine behaviors of male transvestites. *Archives of Sexual Behavior, 14*, 413–419.

Cain, V. S., Johannes, C. B., Avis, N. E., Mohr, B., Schocken, M., Skurnick, J., & Ory, M. (2003). Sexual functioning and practices in a multi-ethnic study of midlife women: Baseline results from SWAN. *Journal of Sex Research, 40*, 266–276.

Cantor, J. M. (2015). Purported changes in pedophilia as statistical artefacts: Comment on Müller et al. (2014). *Archives of Sexual Behavior, 44*, 253–254.

Cantor, J. M., Blanchard, R., Christensen, B. K., Dickey, R., & Klassen, P. E. (2004). Intelligence, memory, and handedness in pedophilia. *Neuropsychology, 18*, 3–14.

Cantor, J. M., Blanchard, R., Robichaud, L. K., & Christensen, B. K. (2005). Quantitative reanalysis of aggregate data on IQ in sexual offenders. *Psychological Bulletin, 131*, 555–568.

Cantor, J. M., Kabani, N., Christensen, B. K., Zipursky, R. B., Barbaree, H. E., Dickey, R., . . . Blanchard, R. (2008). Cerebral white matter deficiencies in pedophilic men. *Journal of Psychiatric Research, 42*, 167–183.

Cantor, J. M., Kuban, M. E., Blak, T., Klassen, P. E., Dickey, R., & Blanchard, R. (2006). Grade failure and special education placement in sexual offenders' educational histories. *Archives of Sexual Behavior, 35*, 743–751.

Cantor, J. M., Kuban, M. E., Blak, T., Klassen, P. E., Dickey, R., & Blanchard, R. (2007). Physical height in pedophilic and hebephilic sexual offenders. *Sexual Abuse: A Journal of Research and Treatment*, 19, 395–407.

Cantor, J. M., Lafaille, S., Soh, D. W., Moayedi, M., Mikulis, D. J., & Girard, T. A. (2015). Diffusion tensor imaging of pedophilia. *Archives of Sexual Behavior*, 44, 2161–2712.

Cantor, J. M., & McPhail, I. V. (2015). Sensitivity and specificity of the phallometric test for hebephilia. *Journal of Sexual Medicine*, 12, 1940–1950.

Carson, C., & Wylie, M. (2010). Improved ejaculatory latency, control and sexual satisfaction when PSD502 is applied topically in men with premature ejaculation: Results of a phase III, double-blind, placebo-controlled study. *Journal of Sexual Medicine*, 7, 3179–3189.

Caruso, S., Agnello, C., Intelisano, G., Farina, M., DiMari, L., & Cianci, A. (2004). Placebo-controlled study on efficacy and safety of daily apomorphine SL intake in premenopausal women affected by hypoactive sexual desire disorder and sexual arousal disorder. *Urology*, 63, 955–959.

Caruso, S., Intelisano, G., Lupo, L., & Agnello, C. (2001). Premenopausal women affected by sexual arousal disorder treated with sildenafil: A double-blind, cross-over, placebo-controlled study. *British Journal of Obstetrics and Gynaecology*, 108, 623–628.

Carvalho, J. & Nobre, P. (2011). Predictors of men's sexual desire: The role of psychological cognitive-emotional, relational and medical factors. *Journal of Sex Research*, 48, 254–262.

Chalkley, A. J., & Powell, G. E. (1983). The clinical description of forty-eight cases of sexual fetishism. *British Journal of Psychiatry*, 142, 292–295.

Chaplin, T. C., Rice, M. E., & Harris, G. T. (1995). Salient victim suffering and the sexual responses of child molesters. *Journal of Consulting and Clinical Psychology*, 63, 249–255.

Chivers, M. L., Basson, R., Brotto, L. A., Graham, C. A., & Stephenson, K. R. (2017). Statistical and epistemological issues in the evaluation of treatment efficacy of pharmaceutical, psychological, and combination treatments for women's sexual desire difficulties. *Journal of Sex and Marital Therapy*, 43, 210–217.

Chivers, M. L., Seto, M. C., Lalumière, M. L., Laan, E., & Grimbos, T. (2010). Agreement of self-reported and genital measures of sexual arousal in men and women: A meta-analysis. *Archives of Sexual Behavior*, 39, 5–56.

Christensen, B. S., Grønbæk, M., Osler, M., Pedersen, B. V., Graugaard, C., & Frisch, M. (2011). Sexual dysfunctions and difficulties in Denmark: Prevalence and associated sociodemographic factors. *Archives of Sexual Behavior*, 40, 121–132.

Chung, Y. B., & Harmon, L. W. (1994). The career interests and aspirations of gay men: How sex-role orientation is related. *Journal of Vocational Behavior*, 45, 223–239.

Clark, S. K., Jeglic, E. L., Calkins, C., & Tatar, J. R. More than a nuisance: The prevalence and consequences of frotteurism and exhibitionism. *Sexual Abuse: A Journal of Research and Treatment*, 28, 3–19.

Clayton, A. H., Althof, S. E., Kingsberg, S., DeRogatis, L. R., Kroll, R., Goldstein, I., . . . Portman, D. J. (2016). Bremelanotide for female sexual dysfunctions in premenopausal women: A randomized, placebo-controlled dose-finding trial. *Women's Health*, 12, 325–337.

Clayton, A. H., DeRogatis, L. R., Rosen, R. C., & Pyke, R. (2012a). Intended or unintended consequences? The likely implications of raising the bar for sexual dysfunction diagnosis in the proposed DSM-V revisions: 1. For women with incomplete loss of desire or sexual receptivity. *Journal of Sexual Medicine*, 9, 2027–2039.

Clayton, A. H., DeRogatis, L. R., Rosen, R. C., & Pyke, R. (2012b). Intended or unintended consequences? The likely implications of raising the bar for sexual dysfunction diagnosis in the proposed DSM-V revisions: 2. For women with loss of subjective sexual arousal. *Journal of Sexual Medicine*, 9, 2040–2046.

Coluccia, A., Gabbrielli, M., Gualtieri, G., Ferreyti, E., Pozza, & Fagiolini, A. (2016). Sexual masochism disorder with asphyxiophilia: A deadly yet unrecognized disease. *Case Reports in Psychiatry.* doi: 10.1155/2016/5474862

Corsini-Munt, S., Bergeron, S., Rosen, N., Steben, M., Mayrand, M.-H., Delisle, I., . . . Santerre-Baillargean, M. (2014). A comparison of cognitive-behavioral couple therapy and lidocaine in the treatment of provoked vestibulodynia: Study protocol for a randomized clinical trial. *Trials, 15,* 506.

Cowan, L. (1982). *Masochism: A Jungian view.* Dallas, TX: Spring.

Cox, D. J., & Maletzky, B. M. (1980). Victims of exhibitionism. In D. J. Cox & R. J. Daitzman (Eds.), *Exhibitionism: Description, assessment and treatment* (pp. 289–293). New York, NY: Garland.

Crenshaw, T. L., Goldberg, J. P., & Stern, W. C. (1987). Pharmacologic modification of psychosexual dysfunction. *Journal of Sex and Marital Therapy, 13,* 239–252.

Crepault, E., & Couture, M. (1980). Men's erotic fantasies. *Archives of Sexual Behavior, 9,* 565–581.

Critelli, J. W., & Bivona, J. M. (2008). Women's erotic rape fantasies: An evaluation of theory and research. *Journal of Sex Research, 45,* 57–70.

Cross, P. A., & Matheson, K. (2006). Understanding sadomasochism: An empirical examination of four perspectives. *Journal of Homosexuality, 50,* 133–166.

Cross, T. P., & Saxe, L. (2001). Polygraph testing and sexual abuse: The lure of the magic lasso. *Child Maltreatment, 6,* 195–206.

Curren, D. (1954). Sexual perversion. *Practitioner, 172,* 440–445.

Cyranowski, J. M., Bromberger, J., Youk, A., Matthews, K., Kravitz, H., & Powell, L. H. (2004). Lifetime depression and sexual function in women at midlife. *Archives of Sexual Behavior, 33,* 539–548.

Davis, S. R., Davison, S. L., Donath, S., & Bell, R. J. (2005). Circulating androgen levels and self-reported sexual function in women. *Journal of the American Medical Association, 294,* 91–96.

Davis, S. R., van der Mooren, M. J., van Lunsen, R. H. W., Lopes, P., Ribot, C., Rees, M., . . . Purdie, D. W. (2006). Efficacy and safety of a testosterone patch for the treatment of hypoactive sexual desire disorder in surgically menopausal women: A randomized, placebo-controlled trial. *Menopause, 13,* 387–396.

Davis, S. R., Worsley, R., Miller, K. K., Parish, S. J., & Santoro, N. (2016). Androgens and female sexual function and dysfunction–Findings from the Fourth International Consultation of Sexual Medicine. *Journal of Sexual Medicine, 13,* 168–178.

De Carufel, F. & Trudel, G. (2006). Effects of a new functional sexological treatment for premature ejaculation. *Journal of Sex and Marital Therapy, 32,* 97–114.

Dennerstein, L., Lehert, P., Guthrie, J. R., & Burger, H. G. (2007). Modeling women's health during the menopausal transition: A longitudinal analysis. *Menopause, 14,* 53–62.

DeRogatis, L. R., Clayton, A. H., Rosen, R. C., Sand, M., & Pyke, R. E. (2011). Should sexual desire and arousal disorders in women be merged? *Archives of Sexual Behavior, 40,* 217–219.

Dhawan, S., & Marshall, W. L. (1996). Sexual abuse histories of sexual offenders. *Sexual Abuse: A Journal of Research and Treatment, 8,* 7–15.

Diamond, L. E., Earle, D. C., Heiman, J. R., Rosen, R. C., Perelman, M. A., & Harning, R. (2011). An effect on the subjective sexual response in premenopausal women with sexual arousal disorder by bremelanotide (PT-141), a melanocortin receptor agonist. *Journal of Sexual Medicine, 3,* 628–638.

Dietz, P. E., Hazelwood, R. R., & Warren, J. (1990). The sexually sadistic criminal and his offenses. *Bulletin of the American Academy of Psychiatry and the Law, 18,* 163–178.

Dinsmore, W., & Wylie, M. (2009). PSD502 improves ejaculatory latency, control and sexual satisfaction when applied topically 5 minutes before intercourse in men with premature ejaculation: Results of a phase III, multicentre, double-blind, placebo-controlled study. *BJU International, 103,* 940–949.

Docter, R. F., & Prince, V. (1997). Transvestism: A survey of 1032 cross-dressers. *Archives of Sexual Behavior, 26,* 589–605.

Dombert, B., Schmidt, A. F., Banse, R., Briken, P., Hoyer, J., Neutze, J., & Osterheider, M. (2016). How common is men's self-reported sexual interest in prepubescent children? *Journal of Sex Research, 53,* 214–223.

Doorn, C. D., Poortinga, J., & Verschoor, A. M. (1994). Cross-gender identity in transvestites and male transsexuals. *Archives of Sexual Behavior, 23,* 185–201.

Dunn, K. M., Cherkas, L. F., & Spector, T. D. (2005). Genetic influences on variation in female orgasmic function: A twin study. *Biology Letters, 1,* 260–263.

Dunne, M. P., Martin, N. G., Statham, D. J., Slutskie, W. S., Dinwiddie, S. H., Bucholz, K. K., . . . Heath, A. C. (1997). Genetic and environmental contributions to variance in age at first sexual intercourse. *Psychological Bulletin, 8,* 211–216.

Dyshniku, E., Murray, M. E., Fazio, R. L., Lykins, A. D., & Cantor, J. M. (2015). Minor physical anomalies as a window into the prenatal origins of pedophilia. *Archives of Sexual Behavior, 44,* 2151–2159.

Edney, A., & Colby, L. (2015, November 17). Valeant's newest problem: The female libido pill isn't selling. *The Globe and Mail.* Retrieved from http://www.theglobeandmail.com/report-on-business/valeants-newest-problem-the-female-libido-pill-isnt-selling/article27291467/

Ellis, A., & Brancale, R. (1956). *The psychology of sex offenders.* Springfield, IL: Charles C Thomas.

Elraiyah, T., Sonbol, M. B., Wang, Z., Khairalseed, T., Asi, N., Undavalli, C., . . . Murad, M. H. (2014). The benefits and harms of systematic dehydroepiandrosterone (DHEA) in post-menopausal women with normal adrenal function: A systematic review and meta-analysis. *Journal of Clinical Endocrinology and Metabolism, 99,* 3536–3542.

Elwood, R. W., Doren, D. M., & Thornton, D. (2010). Diagnostic and risk profiles of men detained under Wisconsin's sexually violent person law. *International Journal of Offender Therapy and Comparative Criminology, 54,* 187–196.

Fazio, R. L., Dyshniku, F., Lykins, A. D., & Cantor, J. M. (2017). Leg length versus torso length in pedophilia: Further evidence of atypical physical development early in life. *Sexual Abuse: A Journal of Research and Treatment, 29*(5), 500–514.

Fedoroff, J. P., Fishell, A., & Fedoroff, B. (1999). A case series of women evaluated for paraphilic sexual disorders. *The Canadian Journal of Human Sexuality, 8,* 127–140.

Feldman, H. A., Goldstein, I., Hatzichristou, D. G., Krane, R. J., & McKinlay, J. B. (1994). Impotence and its medical and psychosocial correlates: Results of the Massachusetts male aging study. *Journal of Urology, 151,* 54–61.

Ferguson, J. M. (2001). The effects of antidepressants on sexual functioning in depressed patients: A review. *Journal of Clinical Psychiatry, 62*(Suppl. 3), 22–34.

Fernandez, Y. M., Marshall, W. L., Lightbody, S., & O'Sullivan, C. (1999). The child molester empathy measure: Description and examination of its reliability and validity. *Sexual Abuse: A Journal of Research and Treatment, 11,* 17–32.

Finkelhor, D. (1979). *Sexually victimized children.* New York, NY: Free Press.

Finkelhor, D. (1984). *Child sexual abuse: New theory and research.* New York, NY: Free Press.

Firestone, P., Kingston, D., Wexler, A., & Bradford, J. M. (2006). Long-term follow-up of exhibitionists: Psychological, phallometric, and offense characteristics. *Journal of the American Academy of Psychiatry and the Law, 34,* 349–359.

Fish, L. S., Busby, D., & Killian, K. (1994). Structural couple therapy in the treatment of inhibited sexual desire. *American Journal of Family Therapy, 22,* 113–125.

Fisher, W. A., Rosen, R. C., Eardley, I., Sand, M., & Goldstein, I. (2005). Sexual experience of female partners of men with erectile dysfunction: The Female Experience of Men's Attitudes to Life Events and Sexuality (FEMALES) Study. *Journal of Sexual Medicine, 2,* 675–684.

Formoso, G., Perrone, E., Maltoni, S., Balduzzi, S., Wilkinson, J., Basevi, V., . . . Maestri, E. (2016). Short-term and long-term effects of tibolone in postmenopausal women. *Cochrane Database of Systematic Reviews, 10*, 1–139.

Foster, D. C., Kotok, M. B., Huang, L. S., Watts, A., Oakes, D., Howard, F. M., . . . Dworkin, R. H. (2010). Oral desipramine and topical lidocaine for vulvodynia: A randomized controlled trial. *Obstetrics & Gynecology, 116*, 583–593.

Freund, K. (1963). A laboratory method for diagnosing predominance of homo- or hetero-erotic interest in the male. *Behaviour Research and Therapy, 1*, 85–93.

Freund, K. (1990). Courtship disorders. In W. L. Marshall, D. R. Laws, & H. E. Barbaree (Eds.), *Handbook of sexual assault: Issues, theories, and treatment of the offender* (pp. 195–207). New York, NY: Plenum Press.

Freund, K., & Blanchard, R. (1986). The concept of courtship disorder. *Journal of Sex and Marital Therapy, 12*, 79–92.

Freund, K., & Blanchard, R. (1989). Phallometric diagnosis of pedophilia. *Journal of Consulting and Clinical Psychology, 57*, 100–105.

Freund, K., Seto, M. C., & Kuban, M. (1996). Two types of fetishism. *Behavior Research and Therapy, 34*, 687–694.

Freund, K., & Watson, R. J. (1991). Assessment of the sensitivity and specificity of a phallometric test: An update of phallometric diagnosis of pedophilia. *Psychological Assessment, 3*, 254–260.

Freund, K., Watson, R., & Reinzo, D. (1988). Signs of feigning in the phallometric test. *Behaviour Research and Therapy, 26*, 105–112.

Friedman, R. C. (1991). The depressed masochistic patient: Diagnostic and management considerations—A contemporary psychoanalytic perspective. *Journal of the American Academy of Psychoanalysis, 19*, 9–31.

Frolich, P., & Meston, C. (2002). Sexual functioning and self-reported depressive symptoms among college women. *Journal of Sex Research, 39*, 321–325.

Frühauf, S., Gerger, H., Schmidt, H. M., Munder, T., & Barth, J. (2013). Efficacy of psychological interventions for sexual dysfunction: A systematic review and meta-analysis. *Archives of Sexual Behavior, 42*, 915–933.

Fugl-Meyer, A. R., & Sjogren Fugl-Meyer, K. (1999). Sexual disabilities, problems and satisfaction in 18–74 year old Swedes. *Scandinavian Journal of Sexology, 2*, 79–105.

Furby, L., Weinrott, M. R., & Blackshaw, L. (1989). Sex offender recidivism: A review. *Psychological Bulletin, 105*, 3–30.

Gao, Z., Yang, D., Yu, L., & Cui, Y. (2015). Efficacy and safety of flibanserin in women with hypoactive sexual desire disorder: A systematic review and meta-analysis. *Journal of Sexual Medicine, 12*, 2095–2104.

Gaunt, G., Good, A., & Stanhope, C. R. (2003). Vestibulectomy for vulvar vestibulitis. *Journal of Reproductive Medicine, 48*, 591–595.

Gebhard, P. H., Gagnon, J. H., Pomeroy, W. B., & Christenson, C. V. (1965). *Sex offenders: An analysis of types.* New York, NY: Harper & Row.

Gentilcore-Saulnier, E., McLean, L., Goldfinger, C., Pukall, C. F., & Chamberlain, S. (2010). Pelvic floor muscle assessment outcomes in women with and without provoked vestibulodynia and the impact of a physical therapy program. *Journal of Sexual Medicine, 7*, 1003–1022.

Giraldi, A., Kristensen E., & Sand, M. (2015). Endorsement of models describing sexual response of men and women with a sexual partner: An online survey in a population sample of Danish adults ages 20–65 years. *Journal of Sexual Medicine, 12*, 116–128.

Goldfinger, C., Pukall, C. F., Gentilcore-Saulnier, E., McLean, L., & Chamberlain, S. (2009). A prospective study of pelvic floor physical therapy: Pain and psychosexual outcomes in provoked vestibulodynia. *Journal of Sexual Medicine, 6*, 1955–1968.

Goldstein, I., Fischer, J., Taylor, T., & Thibonnier, M. (2002). Influence of HbA1c on the efficacy and safety of vardenafil for the treatment of erectile dysfunction in men with diabetes. *Diabetes, 51* (*Suppl.* 2), A98.

Goldstein, I., McCullough, A. R., Jones, L. A., Hellstrom, W. J., Bowden, C. H., DiDonato, K., . . . Day, W. W. (2012). A randomized, double-blind, placebo-controlled evaluation of the safety and efficacy of avanafil in subjects with erectile dysfunction. *Journal of Sexual Medicine, 12,* 1122–1133.

Gosselin, C., & Wilson, G. (1980). *Sexual variations.* London, England: Faber & Faber.

Graham, B. C., Butler, S. E., McGraw, R., Cannes, S. M., & Smith, J. (2016). Member perspectives on the role of BDSM communities. *Journal of Sex Research, 53,* 895–909.

Graham, C. A. (2010). The DSM diagnostic criteria for female sexual arousal disorder. *Archives of Sexual Behavior, 39,* 240–255.

Graham, C. A. (2014). Orgasm disorders in women. In Y. M. Binik & K. S. K. Hall (Eds.), *Principles and practice of sex therapy* (5th ed., pp. 89–111). New York, NY: The Guilford Press.

Grenier, G., & Byers, E. S. (2001). Operationalizing early or premature ejaculation. *Journal of Sex Research, 38,* 369–378.

Hanson, P. K., & Bussiere, M. T. (1998). Predicting relapse: A meta-analysis of sexual offender recidivism studies. *Journal of Consulting and Clinical Psychology, 66,* 348–362.

Harlow, B. L., & Stewart, E. G. (2005). Adult-onset vulvodynia in relation to childhood violence victimization. *American Journal of Epidemiology, 161,* 871–880.

Harris, G. T., Rice, M. E., Chaplin, T. C., & Quinsey, V. L. (1999). Dissimulation in phallometric testing of rapists' sexual preferences. *Archives of Sexual Behavior, 28,* 223–232.

Harris, G. T., Rice, M. E., Quinsey, V. L., & Chaplin, T. C. (1996). Viewing time as a measure of sexual interest among child molesters and normal heterosexual men. *Behaviour Research and Therapy, 34,* 389–394.

Hartmann, U., Heiser, K., Ruffer-Hesse, C., & Kloth, G. (2002). Female sexual desire disorders: Subtypes, classification, personality factors and new directions for treatment. *World Journal of Urology, 20,* 79–88.

Hawton, K., Catalan, J., Martin, P., & Fagg, J. (1986). Long-term outcome of sex therapy. *Behaviour Research and Therapy, 24,* 665–675.

Hayes, R. D., Dennerstein, L., Bennett, C. M., & Fairley, C. K. (2008). What is the "true" prevalence of female sexual dysfunctions and does the way we assess these conditions have an impact? *Journal of Sexual Medicine, 5,* 777–787.

Hazelwood, R. R., Dietz, P. E., & Warren, J. (1992). The criminal sexual sadist. *FBI Law Enforcement Bulletin, 61,* 12–20.

Heiman, J. R. (2002). Psychologic treatments for female sexual dysfunction: Are they effective and do we need them? *Archives of Sexual Behavior, 31,* 445–450.

Heiman, J. R., & LoPiccolo, J. (1987). *Becoming orgasmic: A sexual and personal growth program for women* (Revised and expanded ed.). New York, NY: Simon & Schuster.

Helmus, L., Ó Ciardha, C., & Seto, M. C. (2015). The Screening Scale for Pedophilic Interests (SSPI): Construct, predictive, and incremental validity. *Law and Human Behavior, 39,* 35–43.

Hendrickx, L., Gijs, L., & Enzlin, P. (2014). Prevalence rates of sexual difficulties and associated distress in heterosexual men and women: Results from an Internet survey in Flanders. *Journal of Sex Research, 51,* 1–12.

Herbenick, D., Schick, V., Sanders, S. A., Reece, M., & Fortenberry, J. D. (2015). Pain experienced during vaginal and anal intercourse with other-sex partners: Findings from a nationally representative probability study in the United States. *Journal of Sexual Medicine, 12,* 1040–1051.

Hill, A., Habermann, N., Berner, W., & Briken, P. (2006). Sexual sadism and sadistic personality disorders in sexual homicide. *Journal of Personality Disorders, 20,* 671–684.

Hill, C. A., & Preston, L. K. (1996). Individual differences in the experience of sexual motivation: Theory and measurement of dispositional sexual motives. *Journal of Sex Research, 33*, 27–45.

Hillier, B., & Murphy, P. (2015). Preventing sex offences: The Dunkelfeld Project. *British Medical Journal, 350*. doi: 10.1136/bmj.h2648.

Hoffmann, H. L. (2017). Situating human sexual conditioning. *Archives of Sexual Behavior, 46*, 2213–2229.

Holland, L. A., Zolondek, S. C., Abel, G. G., Jordan, A. D., & Becker, J. V. (2000). Psychometric analysis of the sexual interest cardsort questionnaire. *Sexual Abuse: A Journal of Research and Treatment, 12*, 107–122.

Howes, R. J. (1995). A survey of plethysmographic assessment in North America. *Sexual Abuse: A Journal of Research and Treatment, 7*, 9–24.

Hucker, S. J. (1985). Self-harmful sexual behavior. *Psychiatric Clinics of North America, 8*, 323–337.

Hucker, S. J. (2011). Hypoxyphilia. *Archives of Sexual Behavior, 40*, 1323–1326.

Hucker, S., Langevin, R., Dickey, R., Handy, L., Chambers, J., Wright, S., . . . Wortzman, G. (1988). Cerebral damage and dysfunction in sexually aggressive men. *Annals of Sex Research, 1*, 33–47.

Hunt, M. (1974). *Sexual behavior in the 1970's*. New York, NY: Playboy Press.

Hurlbert, D. F. (1993). A comparative study using orgasm consistency training in the treatment of women reporting hypoactive sexual desire. *Journal of Sex and Marital Therapy, 19*, 41–55.

Hurlbert, D. F., & Apt, C. (1995). The coital alignment technique and direct masturbation: A comparison study on female orgasm. *Journal of Sex and Marital Therapy, 21*, 21–29.

Imhoff, R. (2015). Punitive attitudes against pedophiles or persons with sexual interest in children: Does the label matter? *Archives of Sexual Behavior, 44*, 35–44.

Isidori, A. M., Giannetta, E., Gianfrilli, D., Greco, E. A., Bonifacio, V., Aversa, A., . . . Lenzi, A. (2005). Effects of testosterone on sexual function in men: Results of a meta-analysis. *Clinical Endocrinology, 63*, 381–394.

Jahnke, S., Imhoff, R., & Hoyer, J. (2015). Stigmatization of people with pedophilia: Two comparative surveys. *Archives of Sexual Behavior, 44*, 21–34.

Jaspers, L., Feys, F., Bramer, W. M., Franco, O. H., Leusink, P., & Laan, E. T. (2016). Efficacy and safety of flibanserin for the treatment of hypoactive sexual desire disorder in women: A systematic review and meta-analysis. *JAMA Internal Medicine, 176*, 453–462.

Jesperson, A. F., Lalumière, M. L., & Seto, M. C. (2009). Sexual abuse history among adult sex offenders and non-sex-offenders: A meta-analysis. *Child Abuse & Neglect, 33*, 179–192.

Johnson, R. S., Ostermeyer, B., Sikes, K. A., Nelsen, A. J., & Coverdale, J. H. (2014). Prevalence and treatment of frotteurism in the community: A systematic review. *Journal of the American Academy of Psychiatry and the Law, 42*, 478–483.

Joyal, C. C., & Carpentier, J. (2017). The prevalence of paraphilic interests and behaviors in the general population: A provincial survey. *Journal of Sex Research, 54*, 161–171.

Kafka, M. P. (2010). The DSM diagnostic criteria for fetishism. *Archives of Sexual Behavior, 39*, 357–362.

Kafka, M. P., & Hennen, J. (1999). The paraphilia-related disorders: An empirical investigation of nonparaphilic hypersexuality disorders in outpatient males. *Journal of Sex and Marital Therapy, 25*, 305–319.

Kafka, M. P., & Hennen, J. (2002). A DSM-IV Axis I comorbidity study of males (n = 120) with paraphilia-related disorders. *Sexual Abuse: A Journal of Research and Treatment, 14*, 349–366.

Kafka, M. P., & Hennen, J. (2003). Hypersexual desire in males: Are males with paraphilias different from males with paraphilia-related disorders? *Sexual Abuse: A Journal of Research and Treatment, 15*, 307–321.

Kafka, M. P., & Prentky, R. A. (1994). Preliminary observations of DSM-III-R Axis I comorbidity in men with paraphilias and paraphilia-related disorders. *Journal of Clinical Psychiatry, 55*, 481–487.

Kaplan, H. S. (1989). *Premature ejaculation: Overcoming early ejaculation*. New York, NY: Brunner Mazel.

Kaplan, M. S., & Krueger, R. B. (1997). Voyeurism: Psychopathology and theory. In D. R. Laws & W. O'Donohue (Eds.), *Sexual deviance: Theory, assessment, and treatment* (pp. 297–310). New York, NY: Guilford Press.

Kar, N., & Koola, M. M. (2007). A pilot survey of sexual functioning and preferences in a sample of English-speaking adults from a small south Indian town. *Journal of Sexual Medicine, 4*, 1254–1261.

Kara, H., Aydin, S., Yucel, M., Agargun, M. Y., Odabas, O., & Yilmaz, Y. (1996). The efficacy of fluoextine in the treatment of premature ejaculation: A double-blind placebo controlled study. *Journal of Urology, 156*, 1631–1632.

Kaschak, E., & Tiefer, L. (2002). *A new view of women's sexual problems*. Binghamton, NY: Haworth Press.

Khera, M., Bhattacharya, R. K., Blick, G., Kushner, H., Nguyen, D., & Miner, M. M. (2011). Improved sexual function with testosterone replacement therapy in hypogonadal men: Real-world data from the Testim Registry in the United States (TRiUS). *Journal of Sexual Medicine, 8*, 3204–3213.

Klusmann, D. (2002). Sexual motivation and the duration of partnership. *Archives of Sexual Behavior, 31*, 275–287.

Kramer, R. (2011). APA guidelines ignored in development of diagnostic criteria for pedohebephilia. *Archives of Sexual Behavior, 40*, 233–235.

Kroll, R., Davis, S., Moreau, M., Waldbaum, A., Shifren, J., & Wekselman, K. (2004). Testosterone transdermal patch (TTP) significantly improved sexual function in naturally menopausal women in a large phase III study. *Fertility and Sterility, 82*(Suppl. 2), S77–S78.

Krueger, R. B., & Kaplan, M. S. (1997). Frotteurism: Assessment and treatment. In D. R. Laws & W. O'Donohue (Eds.), *Sexual deviance: Theory, assessment, and treatment* (pp. 131–151). New York, NY: Guilford Press.

Krueger, R. B., & Kaplan, M. S. (2001). The paraphilic and hypersexual disorders: An overview. *Journal of Psychiatric Practice, 7*, 391–403.

Krueger, R. B., Reed, G. B., First, M. B., Marais, A., Kismodi, E., & Briken, P. (2017). Proposals for paraphilic disorders in the International Classification of Diseases and Related Health Problems, Eleventh revision (ICD-11). *Archives of Sexual Behavior, 46*, 1529–1545.

Laan, E., & Both, S. (2008). What makes women experience desire? *Feminism & Psychology, 18*, 505–514.

Laan, E., Rellini, A., & Barnes, T. (2013). Standard operating procedures for female orgasmic disorder: Consensus of the International Society for Sexual Medicine. *Journal of Sexual Medcine, 10*, 74–82.

Laan, E., van Driel, E. M., & van Lunsen, R. H. (2008). Genital responsiveness in healthy women with and without sexual arousal disorder. *Journal of Sexual Medicine, 5*, 1424–1435.

Laan, E., van Lunsen, R. H., & Everaerd, W. (2001). The effects of tibolone on vaginal blood flow, sexual desire and arousability in postmenopausal women. *Climacteric, 4*, 28–41.

Lalumière, M. L. (2015). The lability of pedophilic interests as measured by phallometry. *Archives of Sexual Behavior, 44*, 255–258.

Lalumière, M. L., & Earls, C. M. (1992). Voluntary control of penile responses as a function of stimulus duration and instructions. *Behavioral Assessment, 14*, 121–132.

Lalumière, M. L., & Harris, G. T. (1998). Common questions regarding the use of phallometric testing with sexual offenders. *Sexual Abuse: A Journal of Research and Treatment, 10*, 227–237.

Lalumière, M. L., & Quinsey, V. L. (1993). The sensitivity of phallometric measures with rapists. *Annals of Sex Research, 6*, 123–138.

Lalumière, M. L., & Quinsey, V. L. (1994). The discriminability of rapists from non-sex offenders using phallometric measures: A meta-analysis. *Criminal Justice and Behavior, 21*, 150–175.

Langevin, R. (1990). Sexual anomalies and the brain. In W. L. Marshall, D. R. Laws, & H. E. Barbaree (Eds.), *Handbook of sexual assault: Issues, theories, and treatment of the offender* (pp. 103–113). New York, NY: Plenum Press.

Langevin, R., & Lang, R. A., (1987). The courtship disorders. In G. O. Wilson (Ed.), *Variant sexuality: Research and theory* (pp. 202–228). London, England: Croom Helm.

Langevin, R., Paitich, D., Freeman, R., Mann, K., & Handy, L. (1978). Personality characteristics and sexual anomalies in males. *Canadian Journal of Behavioral Science, 10*, 222–238.

Langevin, R., Paitich, D., Ramsey, G., Anderson, C., Kamrad, J., Pope, S., . . . Newman, S. (1979). Experimental studies of the etiology of genital exhibitionism. *Archives of Sexual Behavior, 8*, 307–331.

Långström, N. (2010). The DSM diagnostic criteria for exhibitionism, voyeurism, and frotteurism. *Archives of Sexual Behavior, 39*, 317–324.

Långström, N., & Seto, M. C. (2006). Exhibitionistic and voyeuristic behavior in a Swedish national population survey. *Archives of Sexual Behavior, 35*, 427–435.

Långström, N., & Zucker, K. J. (2005). Transvestic fetishism in the general population. *Journal of Sex & Marital Therapy, 31*, 87–95.

Laumann, E. O., Gagnon, J. H., Michael, R. T., & Michaels, S. (1994). *The social organization of sexuality: Sexual practices in the United States.* Chicago, IL: University of Chicago Press.

Laumann, E. O., Nicolosi, A., Glasser, D. B., Paik, A., Gingell, C., Moreira, E., . . . The GSSAB Investigators' Group (2005). Sexual problems among women and men aged 40–80 years: Prevalence and correlates identified in the Global Study of Sexual Attitudes and Behaviors. *International Journal of Impotence Research, 17*, 39–57.

Laumann, E. O., Paik, A., & Rosen, R. C. (1999). Sexual dysfunction in the United States: Prevalence and predictors. *Journal of the American Medical Association, 281*, 537–544.

Lavy, Y., Lev-Sagie, A., Hamani, Y., Zacut, D., & Ben-Chetrit, A. (2005). Modified vulvar vestibulectomy: Simple and effective surgery for the treatment of vulvar vestibulitis. *European Journal of Obstetric & Gynecology and Reproductive Biology, 120*, 91–95.

Lawrence, A. A. (2013). *Men trapped in men's bodies: Narratives of autogynephilic transsexualism.* New York, NY: Springer.

Lawrence, A. A. (2017). Autogynephilia and the typology of male-to-female transsexualism: Concepts and controversies. *European Psychologist, 22*, 39–54.

Laws, D. R. (1986). *Sexual deviance card sort.* Unpublished manuscript, Florida Mental Health Institute, Tampa, Florida.

Letourneau, E. J. (2002). A comparison of objective measures of sexual arousal and interest: Visual reaction time and penile plethysmography. *Sexual Abuse: A Journal of Research and Treatment, 14*, 207–223.

Levenson, J. S. (2004). Sexual predator civil commitment: A comparison of selected and released offenders. *International Journal of Offender Therapy and Comparative Criminology, 48*, 638–648.

Lewis, R. W., Sadovsky, R., Eardley, I., O'Leary, M., Seftel, A., Wang, W. C., . . . Ahuja, S. (2005). The efficacy of tadalafil in clinical populations. *Journal of Sexual Medicine, 2*, 517–531.

Linet, O. I., & Ogrinc, F. G. (1996). Efficacy and safety of intracavernosal alprostadil in men with erectile dysfunction. *New England Journal of Medicine, 334*, 873–877.

Longpré, N., Proulx, J., & Brouilletter-Alarie, S. (2016). Convergent validity of three measures of sexual sadism: Value of a dimensional measure. *Sexual Abuse: A Journal of Research and Treatment.* doi: 10.1177/1079063216649592.

MacPhee, D. C., Johnson, S. M., & Van der Veer, M. M. (1995). Low sexual desire in women: The effects of marital therapy. *Journal of Sex and Marital Therapy, 21*, 159–182.

Malcolm, P. B., Andrews, D. A., & Quinsey, V. L. (1993). Discriminant and predictive validity of phallometrically measured sexual age and gender preference. *Journal of Interpersonal Violence, 8*, 486–501.

Maletzky, B. M. (1991). *Treating the sexual offender*. Newbury Park, CA: Sage.

Maletzky, B. M. (1997). Exhibitionism: Assessment and treatment. In D. R. Laws & W. O'Donohue (Eds.), *Sexual deviance: Theory, assessment, and treatment* (pp. 40–74). New York, NY: Guilford Press.

Mandal, D., Nunns, D., Byrne, M., McLelland, J., Rani, R., Cullimore, J., . . . Wier, M. (2010). Guidelines for the management of vulvodynia. *British Journal of Dermatology, 162*, 1180–1185.

Mariani, L. (2002). Vulvar vestibulitis syndrome: An overview of non-surgical treatment. *European Journal of Obstetrics, Gynecology, and Reproductive Biology, 101*, 109–112.

Marshall, W. L., & Eccles, A. (1991). Issues in clinical practice with sex offenders. *Journal of Interpersonal Violence, 6*, 68–93.

Marshall, W. L., Hudson, S. M., & Hodkinson, S. (1993). The importance of attachment bonds in the development of juvenile sex offending. In H. E. Barbaree, W. L. Marshall, & S. M. Hudson (Eds.), *The juvenile sex offender* (pp. 164–181). New York, NY: Guilford Press.

Marshall, W. L., Hudson, S. M., Jones, R., & Fernandez, Y. M. (1995). Empathy in sex offenders. *Clinical Psychology Review, 15*, 99–113.

Marshall, W. L., Jones, R., Hudson, S. M., & McDonald, E. (1994). Generalised empathy in child molesters. *Journal of Child Sexual Abuse, 2*, 61–68.

Mason, F. L. (1997). Fetishism: Psychopathology and theory. In D. R. Laws & W. O'Donohue (Eds.), *Sexual deviance: Theory, assessment, and treatment* (pp. 75–91). New York, NY: Guilford Press.

Masters, W. H., & Johnson, V. E. (1966). *Human sexual response*. Boston, MA: Little, Brown.

Masters, W. H., & Johnson, V. E. (1970). *Human sexual inadequacy*. Boston, MA: Little, Brown.

McConaghy, N. (1993). *Sexual Behavior: Problems and management*. New York, NY: Plenum Press.

McConaghy, N., Blaszcyzynski, A., & Kidson, W. (1988). Treatment of sex offenders with imaginal desensitization and/or medroxyprogesterone. *Acta Psychiatrica Scandinavica, 77*, 199–206.

McGuire, R. J., Carlisle, J. M., & Young, B. G. (1965). Sexual deviations as conditioned behavior: A hypothesis. *Behaviour Research and Therapy, 2*, 185–190.

McMahon, C. G., Althof, S. E., Kaufman, J. M., Buvat, J., Levine, S. B., Aquilina, J. W., . . . Porst, H. (2011). Efficacy and safety of dapoxetine for the treatment of premature ejaculation: Integrated analysis of results from five phase 3 trials. *Journal of Sexual Medicine, 8*, 524–539.

McPhail, I. V., Hermann, C. A., Fernane, S., Fernandez, Y. M., Nunes, K. L., & Cantor, J. M. (2017). Validity in phallometric testing for sexual interests in children: A meta-analytic review. *Assessment*. doi: 10.1177/1073191117706139

Meana, M., & Steiner, E. T. (2014). Hidden disorder/hidden desire: Presentations of low sexual desire in men. In Y. M. Binik & K. S. K. Hall (Eds.), *Principles and practice of sex therapy* (5th ed., pp. 42–60). New York, NY: The Guilford Press.

Mercer, C. H., Fenton, K. A., Johnson, A. M., Wellings, K., Macdowall, W., McManus, S., . . . Erens, B. (2003). Sexual function problems and help seeking behaviour in Britain: National probability sample survey. *British Medical Journal, 327*, 426–427.

Metz, M. E., Pryor, J. L., Nesvacil, L. J., Abuzzahab, F., Sr., & Koznar, J. (1997). Premature ejaculation: A psychophysiological review. *Journal of Sex and Marital Therapy, 23*, 3–23.

Meuleman, E. J. H. & van Lankveld, J. J. D. M. (2005). Hypoactive sexual desire disorder: An underestimated condition in men. *BJU International, 95*, 291–296.

Meyer, J. K. (1995). Paraphilias. In H. I. Kaplan & B. J. Sadock (Eds.), *Comprehensive textbook of psychiatry VI* (6th ed., pp. 1334–1347). Baltimore, MD: Williams & Wilkins.

Miller, B. L., Darby, A. L., Swartz, J. R., Yener, G. G., & Mena, I. (1995). Dietary changes, compulsions and sexual behavior in frontotemporal degeneration. *Dementia, 6*, 195–199.

Mitchell, K. R., Jones, K. G., Wellings, K., Johnson, A. M., Graham, C. A., Datta, J., . . . Mercer, C. H. (2016). Estimating the prevalence of sexual function problems: The impact of morbidity criteria. *Journal of Sex Research, 53*, 955–967.

Mohr, J. W., Turner, R. E., & Jerry, M. B. (1964). *Pedophilia and exhibitionism*. Toronto, ON: University of Toronto Press.

Mokros, A., & Habermeyer, E. (2016). Regression to the mean mimicking changes in sexual arousal to child stimuli in pedophiles. *Archives of Sexual Behavior, 45*, 1863–1867.

Mokros, A., Schilling, F., Weiss, K., Nitschke, J., & Eher, R. (2014). Sadism in sexual offenders: Evidence for dimensionality. *Psychological Assessment, 26*, 138–147.

Money, J. (1984). Paraphilias: Phenomenology and classification. *American Journal of Psychotherapy, 38*, 164–179.

Morales, A., Buvat, J., Gooren, L. J., Guay, A. T., Kaufman, J.-M., Tan, H. M., & Torres, L. O. (2004). Endocrine aspects of sexual dysfunction in men. *Journal of Sexual Medicine, 1*, 69–81.

Morales, A., Heaton, J. P. W., & Carson, C. C. III (2000). Andropause: A misnomer for a true clinical entity. *Journal of Urology, 163*, 705–712.

Morin, M., Bergeron, S., Khalifé, S., Mayrand, M. H., & Binik, Y. M. (2014). Morphometry of the pelvic floor muscles in women with and without provoked vestibulodynia using 4D ultrasound. *Journal of Sexual Medicine, 11*, 776–785.

Moser, C., & Levitt, E. E. (1987). An exploratory-descriptive study of a sadomasochistically oriented sample. *Journal of Sex Research, 23*, 322–337.

Müller, K., Curry, S., Ranger, R., Briken, P., Bradford, J., & Fedoroff, J. P. (2014). Changes in sexual arousal as measured by penile plethysmography in men with pedophilic sexual interest. *Journal of Sexual Medicine, 11*, 1221–1229.

Murphy, W. D., Haynes, M. R., & Page, I. J. (1992). Adolescent sex offenders. In W. O'Donohue & J. H. Geer (Eds.), *The sexual abuse of children: Clinical issues* (Vol. 2, pp. 395–429). Hillsdale, NJ: Erlbaum.

Murphy, W. D., Haynes, M. R., & Worley, P. J. (1991). Assessment of adult sexual interest. In R. Hollin & K. Howells (Eds.), *Clinical approaches to sex offenders and their victims* (pp. 77–92). West Sussex, England: Wiley.

Murphy, W., & Page, I. (2008). Exhibitionism: Psychopathology and theory. In D. R. Laws & W. T. O'Donohue (Eds.), *Sexual deviance: Theory, assessment, and treatment* (2nd ed., pp. 61–75). New York, NY: Guilford Press.

Murphy, W. D., & Peters, J. M. (1992). Profiling child sexual abusers: Psychological considerations. *Criminal Justice and Behavior, 19*, 24–37.

Murphy, W. D., & Smith, T. A. (1996). Sex offenders against children: Empirical and clinical issues. In J. Briere, L. Berliner, J. A. Bulkley, C. Jenny, & T. Reid (Eds.), *The APSAC handbook on child maltreatment* (pp. 175–191). Thousand Oaks, CA: Sage.

Nicholls, L. (2008). Putting the New View classification scheme to an empirical test. *Feminism and Psychology, 18*, 515–526.

Nichols, H. R., & Molinder, I. (1992). *The Multiphasic Sex Inventory manual*. Tacoma, WA: Author.

Nowosielski, K., Wróbel, B., & Kowalczyk, R. (2016). Women's endorsement of models of sexual response: Correlates and predictors. *Archives of Sexual Behavior, 45*, 291–302.

Nurnberg, H. G., Hensley, P. L., Heiman, J. R., Croft, H. A., Debattista, C. & Paine, S. (2008). Sildenafil treatment of women with antidepressant-associated sexual dysfunction: A randomized controlled trial. *Journal of the American Medical Association, 300*, 395–404.

Okami, P., & Goldberg, A. (1992). Personality correlates of pedophilia: Are they reliable indicators? *Journal of Sex Research, 29*, 297–328.

Osterloh, I. H., & Riley, A. (2002). Clinical update on sildenafil citrate. *British Journal of Clinical Pharmacology, 53*, 219–223.

Padma-Nathan, H., Hellstrom, W. J., Kaiser, F. E., Labasky, R. F., Lue, T. F., Nolten, W. E., . . . Gesundheit, N. (1997). Treatment of men with erectile dysfunction with transurethral alprostadil. *New England Journal of Medicine, 336*, 1–7.

Paitich, D., Langevin, R., Freeman, R., Mann, K., & Handy, L. (1977). The Clarke Sexual History Questionnaire: A clinical sex history questionnaire for males. *Archives of Sexual Behavior, 6,* 421–435.

Parish, S. J., Goldstein, A. T., Goldstein, S. W., Goldstein, I., Pfaus, J., Clayton, A. H., . . . Whipple, B. (2016). Toward a more evidence-based nosology and nomenclature for female sexual dysfunctions—Part II. *Journal of Sexual Medicine, 13,* 1888–1906.

Paterson, L. Q. P., Handy, A. B., & Brotto, L. A. (2016). A pilot study of eight-session mindfulness-based cognitive therapy adapted for women's sexual interest/arousal disorder. *Journal of Sex Research, 54,* 850–861.

Pazmany, E., Bergeron, S., & Verhaeghe, J. (2014). Sexual communication, dyadic adjustment, and psychosexual well-being in premenopausal women with self-reported dyspareunia and their partners: A controlled study. *Journal of Sexual Medicine, 7,* 1786–1797.

People of the State of Illinois vs. Nicholas Bauer. (2017). In the Circuit Court of the Fifteenth Judicial Circuit Lee County, Illinois.

Perelman, M. A. (2006, March). *Masturbation is a key variable in the treatment of retarded ejaculation by health care professionals.* Poster presented at the annual meeting of the International Society for the Study of Women's Sexual Health, Lisbon, Portugal.

Perelmen, M. A. (2016). Psychosexual therapy for delayed ejaculation based on the Sexual Tipping Point Model. *Translational Andrology and Urology, 5,* 563–575.

Phillips, L., & Slaughter, J. R. (2000). Depression and sexual desire. *American Family Physician, 62,* 782–786.

Poels, S., Bloemers, J., van Rooij, K., Goldstein, I., Gerritsen, J., van Ham, D., . . . Tuiten, A. (2013). Toward personalized sexual medicine (part 2): Testosterone combined with a PDE5 inhibitor increases sexual satisfaction in women with HSDD and FSAD, and a low sensitive system for sexual cues. *Journal of Sexual Medicine, 10,* 810–823.

Price, M., Gutheil, T. G., Commons, M. L., Kafka, M. P., & Dodd-Kimmey, S. (2001). Telephone scatologia: Comorbidity and theories of etiology. *Psychiatric Annals, 31,* 226–232.

Pukall, C. F., Strigo, I. A., Binik, Y. M., Amsel, R., Khalifé, S., & Bushnell, M. C. (2005). Neural correlates of painful genital touch in women with vulvar vestibulitis syndrome. *Pain, 115,* 118–117.

Quinsey, V. L., & Lalumière, M. L. (1996). *Assessment of sexual offenders against children.* Newbury Park, CA: Sage.

Quinsey, V. L., Rice, M. E., & Harris, G. T. (1995). The actuarial prediction of sexual recidivism. *Journal of Interpersonal Violence, 10,* 85–105.

Quinsey, V. L., Rice, M. E., Harris, G. T., & Reid, K. S. (1993). The phylogenetic and ontogenetic development of sexual age preferences in males: Conceptual and measurement issues. In H. Barbaree, W. L. Marshall, & S. M. Hudson (Eds.), *The juvenile sex offender* (pp. 143–163). New York, NY: Guilford Press.

Rachman, S. (1966). Sexual fetishism: An experimental analogue. *Psychological Record, 16,* 293–296.

Rachman, S., & Hodgson, R. J. (1968). Experimentally-induced "sexual fetishism": Replication and development. *Psychological Record, 18,* 25–27.

Reed, B. D. (2006). Vulvodynia: Diagnosis and management. *Canadian Journal of Cardiology, 73,* 1231–1238.

Reed, G. M., Drescher, J., Krueger, R. B., Atalla, E., Cochran, S. D., First, M. B., . . . Saxena, S. (2016a). Disorders related to sexuality and gender identity in the ICD-11: Revising the ICD-10 classification based on current scientific evidence, best clinical practices, and human rights considerations. *World Psychiatry, 15,* 205–221.

Reed, B. G., Nemer, L. B., & Carr, B. R. (2016b). Has testosterone passed the test in premenopausal women with low libido? A systematic review. *International Journal of Women's Health, 2016, 8,* 599–607.

Regan, P., & Berscheid, C. E. (1996). Belief about the state, goals, and objects of sexual desire. *Journal of Sex and Marital Therapy, 22,* 110–120.

Reissing, E. D., Binik, Y. M., Khalifé, S., Cohen, D., & Amsel, R. (2004). Vaginal spasm, pain, and behavior: An empirical investigation of the diagnosis of vaginismus. *Archives of Sexual Behavior, 33,* 5–17.

Reissing, E. D., Brown, C., Lord, M. J., Binik, Y. M., & Khalifé, S. (2005). Pelvic floor muscle functioning in women with vulvar vestibulitis syndrome. *Journal of Psychosomatic Obstetrics and Gynecology, 26,* 107–113.

Rettenmaier, M. A., Brown, J. V., & Micha, J. P. (2003). Modified vestibulectomy is inadequate treatment for secondary vulvar vestibulitis. *Journal of Gynecologic Surgery, 19,* 13–17.

Rice, M. E., Harris, G. T., & Quinsey, V. L. (1990). A follow-up of rapists assessed in a maximum security psychiatric facility. *Journal of Interpersonal Violence, 5,* 435–448.

Richters, J., Grulich, A. E., de Visser, R. O., Smith, A. M. A., & Rissel, C. E. (2003). Sex in Australia: Autoerotic, esoteric and other sexual practices engaged in by a representative sample of adults. *Australian and New Zealand Journal of Public Health, 27,* 180–190.

Roma, P., Pazzelli, F., Pompili, M., Girardi, P., & Ferracuti, S. (2013). Shibari: Double hanging during consensual sexual asphyxia. *Archives of Sexual Behavior, 42,* 895–900.

Rosen, N. O., Bergeron, S., Sadikaj, G., Glowacka, M., Baxter, M. L., & Delisle, I. (2014a). Relationship satisfaction moderates the associations between male partner responses and depression in women with vulvodynia: A dyadic daily experience study. *Pain, 155,* 1374–1383.

Rosen, R. C., Fisher, W. A., Eardley, I., Niederberger, C., Nadel, A., & Sand, M. (2004). The multinational men's attitudes of life events and sexuality (MALES) study: Prevalence of erectile dysfunction and related health concerns in the general population. *Current Medical Research and Opinion, 20,* 607–617.

Rosen, R., Miner, M., & Wincze, J. (2014b). Erectile dysfunction: Integration of medical and psychological approaches. In Y. M. Binik & K. S. K. Hall (Eds.) *Principles and practices of sex therapy* (5th ed., pp. 61–85). New York, NY: The Guilford Press.

Rosen, R. C., Phillips, N. A., Gendrano, N. C. 3rd, & Ferguson, D. M. (1999). Oral phentolamine and female sexual arousal disorder: A pilot study. *Journal of Sex and Marital Therapy, 25,* 137–144.

Rosenblum, J. A. (1974). Human sexuality and the cerebral cortex. *Diseases of the Nervous System, 35,* 268–271.

Rowland, D., McMahon, C. G., Abdo, C., Chen, J., Jannini, E., Waldinger, M. D. & Young Ahn, T. (2010). Disorders of orgasm and ejaculation in men. *Journal of Sexual Medicine, 7,* 1668–1686.

Rowland, D., Perelman, M., Althof, S., Barada, J., McCullough, A., Bull, S., . . . Ho, K. F. (2004). Self-reported premature ejaculation and aspects of sexual functioning and satisfaction. *Journal of Sexual Medicine, 1,* 225–232.

Rubio-Aurioles, E., Lopez, M., Lipezker, M., Lara, C., Ramirez, A., Rampazzo, C., . . . Lammers, P. (2002). Phentolamine mesylate in postmenopausal women with female sexual arousal disorder: A psychophysiological study. *Journal of Sex and Marital Therapy, 28*(Suppl. 1), 205–215.

Saadat, S. H., Panahi, Y., Hosseinialhashemi, M., Kabir, A., Rahmani, K., & Sahebkar, A. (2017). Systematic review and meta-analysis of flibanserin's effects and adverse events in women with hypoactive sexual desire disorder. *Current Drug Metabolism, 18,* 78–85.

Sagarin, B. J., Cutler, B., Cuther, N., Lawler-Sagarin, K. A., & Matuszewich, L. (2009). Hormonal changes and couple bonding in consensual sadomasochistic activity. *Archives of Sexual Behavior, 38,* 186–200.

Sandfort, T. G., & de Keizer, M. (2001). Sexual problems in gay men: An overview of empirical research. *Annual Review of Sex Research, 12,* 93–120.

Saunders, E., Awad, G. A., & White, G. (1986). Male adolescent sexual offenders: The offender and the offense. *Canadian Journal of Psychiatry, 31,* 542–549.

Schiavi, R. C., DeRogatis, L. R., Kuriansky, J., O'Connor, D., & Sharpe, L. (1979). The assessment of sexual function and marital interaction. *Journal of Sex and Marital Therapy, 5*, 169–224.

Schiffer, B., Amelung, T., Pohl, A., Kaergel, C., Tenbergen, G., Gerwinn, H., . . . Walter, H. (2017). Gray matter anomalies in pedophiles with and without a history of child sexual offending. *Translational Psychiatry, 7*, e1129.

Schmidt, H. M., Munder, T., Gerger, H., Frühauf, S., & Barth, J. (2014). Combination of psychological intervention and phosphodiesterase-5 inhibitors for erectile dysfunction: A narrative review and meta-analysis. *Journal of Sexual Medicine, 11*, 1376–1391.

Schouten, P. G. W., & Simon, W. T. (1992). Validity of phallometric measures with sex offenders: Comments on the Quinsey, Laws, and Hall debate. *Journal of Consulting and Clinical Psychology, 60*, 812–814.

Schroder, M., Mell, L. K., Hurteau, J. A., Collins, Y. C., Rotmensch, J., Waggoner, S. E., . . . Mundt, A. J. (2005). Clitoral therapy device for treatment of sexual dysfunction in irradiated cervical cancer patients. *International Journal of Radiation Oncology, Biology, Physics, 61*, 1078–1086.

Seidman, S. N. (2003). Testosterone deficiency and mood in aging men: Pathogenic and therapeutic interactions. *Journal of Clinical Psychiatry, 4*, 14–20.

Semans, J. H. (1956). Premature ejaculation. *Southern Medical Journal, 49*, 353–358.

Seto, M. C. (2001). The value of phallometry in the assessment of male sex offenders. *Journal of Forensic Psychology Practice, 1*, 65–75.

Seto, M. C. (2009). Pedophilia. *Annual Review of Clinical Psychology, 5*, 391–407.

Seto, M. C. (2017). The puzzle of male chronophilias. *Archives of Sexual Behavior, 46*, 3–22.

Seto, M. C., Fedoroff, J. P., Bradford, J. M., Knack, N., Rodriguez, N. C., Curry, S., . . . Ahmed, A. G. (2016). Reliability and validity of the DSM-IV-TR and proposed DSM-5 criteria for pedophilia: Implications for the ICD-11 and the next DSM. *International Journal of Law and Psychiatry, 49*, 98–106.

Seto, M. C., Harris, G. T., Rice, M. E., & Barbaree, H. E. (2004). The Screening Scale for Pedophilic Interests predicts recidivism among adult sex offenders with child victims. *Archives of Sexual Behavior, 33*, 455–466.

Seto, M. C., Kingston, D. A., & Bourget, D. (2014). Assessment of the paraphilias. *Psychiatric Clinics of North America, 37*, 149–161.

Seto, M. C., & Kuban, M. (1996). Criterion-related validity of a phallometric test for paraphilic rape and sadism. *Behavior Research and Therapy, 34*, 175–183.

Seto, M. C., & Lalumière, M. L. (2001). A brief screening scale to identify pedophilic interests among child molesters. *Sexual Abuse: A Journal of Research and Treatment, 13*, 15–25.

Seto, M. C., Lalumière, M. L., Harris, G. T., & Chivers, M. L. (2012). The sexual response of sexual sadists. *Journal of Abnormal Psychology, 121*, 739–753.

Seto, M. C., Sandler, J. C., & Freeman, N. J. (2017a). The Revised Screening Scale for Pedophilic Interests: Predictive and concurrent validity. *Sexual Abuse: A Journal of Research and Treatment, 29*, 636–657.

Seto, M. C., Stephens, S., Lalumière, M. L., & Cantor, J. M. (2017b). The Revised Screening Scale for Pedophilic Interests (SSPI-2): Development and criterion-related validation. *Sexual Abuse: A Journal of Research and Treatment, 29*, 619–635.

Shabsigh, R. (2005). Testosterone therapy in erectile dysfunction and hypogonadism. *Journal of Sexual Medicine, 2*, 785–792.

Shamloul, R., & Ghanem, H. (2013). Erectile dysfunction. *The Lancet, 381*, 153–165.

Shifren, J. L., Monz, B. U., Russo, P. A., Segreti, & Johannes, C. S. (2008). Sexual problems and distress in United States women: Prevalence and correlates. *Obstetrics & Gynecology, 112*, 970–978.

Shindel, A. W., & Moser, C. A. (2011). Why are the paraphilias mental disorders? *Journal of Sexual Medicine, 8*, 927–929.

Smith, K. B. & Pukall, C. F. (2014). Sexual function, relationship adjustment, and the relational impact of pain in male partners of women with provoked vulvar pain. *Journal of Sexual Medicine, 11*, 1283–1293.

Smukler, A. J., & Schiebel, D. (1975). Personality characteristics of exhibitionists. *Diseases of the Nervous System, 36*, 600–603.

Spengler, A. (1977). Manifest sadomasochism of males: Results of an empirical study. *Archives of Sexual Behavior, 6*, 441–456.

Stanford, J. L., Feng, Z., Hamilton, A. S., Gilliland, F. D., Stephenson, R. A., Eley, J. W., . . . Potosky, A. L. (2000). Urinary and sexual function after radical prostatectomy for clinically localized prostate cancer: The Prostate Cancer Outcomes Study. *Journal of the American Medical Association, 283*, 354–360.

Stekel, W. (1923). *Der fetischismus dargestellt für Ärzte und Kriminalogen. Störungen des Trieb- und Affektlebens (die parapathischen Erkrankungen)*. Berlin/Wien: Urban & Schwarzenberg.

Stephens, S., Seto, M. C., Goodwill, A. M., & Cantor, J. M. (2017). Evidence of construct validity in the assessment of hebephilia. *Archives of Sexual Behavior, 46*, 301–309.

Strassberg, D. S., Kelly, M. P., Carroll, C., & Kircher, J. C. (1987). The psychophysiological nature of premature ejaculation. *Archives of Sexual Behavior, 16*, 327–336.

Symonds, T., Roblin, D., Hart, K., & Althof, S. (2003). How does premature ejaculation impact a man's life? *Journal of Sex and Marital Therapy, 29*, 361–370.

Tang, W., Ma, L., Zhao, L., Liu, Y., & Chen, Z. (2004). Clinical efficacy of Viagra with behavior therapy against premature ejaculation. *Zhonghua Nan Ke Xue, 10*, 366–370.

Templeman, T. L., & Stinnett, R. D. (1991). Patterns of sexual arousal and history in a "normal" sample of young men. *Archives of Sexual Behavior, 20*, 137–150.

ter Kuile, M. M., Melles, R. J., Tuijnman-Raasveld, C. C., de Groot, H. E., & van Lankveld, J. J. D. M. (2013). Therapist-aided exposure for women with lifelong vaginismus: Mediators of treatment outcome: A randomized waiting list control trial. *Journal of Sexual Medicine, 12*, 1807–1819.

Tiefer, L. (2001). A new view of women's sexual problems: Why new? Why now? *Journal of Sex Research, 38*, 89–96.

Tiefer, L. (2002). Sexual behaviour and its medicalisation. Many (especially economic) forces promote medicalisation. *British Medical Journal, 325*, 45.

Trudel, G., Marchand, A., Ravart, M., Aubin, S., Turgeon, L., & Fortier, P. (2001). The effect of a cognitive behavioral group treatment program on hypoactive sexual desire in women. *Sexual and Relationship Therapy, 16*, 145–164.

Tworoger, S. S., Missmer, S. A., Barbieri, R. L., Willett, W. C., Colditz, G. A., & Hankinson, R. G. (2005). Plasma sex hormone concentrations and subsequent risk of breast cancer among women using postmenopausal hormones. *Journal of the National Cancer Institute, 97*, 595–602.

van Lankveld, J. J., Ter Kuile, M. M., de Groot, H. E., Melles, R., Nefs, J., & Zandbergen, M. (2006). Cognitive-behavioral therapy for women with lifelong vaginismus: A randomized waiting-list controlled trial of efficacy. *Journal of Consulting and Clinical Psychology, 74*, 168–178.

van Rooij, K., Poels, S., Bloemers, J., Goldstein, I., Gerritsen, J., van Ham, D., . . . Tuiten, A. (2013). Toward personalized sexual medicine (part 3): Testosterone combined with a serotonin 1A receptor agonist increases sexual satisfaction in women with HSDD and FSAD, and dysfunctional activation of sexual inhibitory mechanisms. *Journal of Sexual Medicine, 10*, 824–837.

Ventolini, G. (2011). Measuring treatment outcomes in women with vulvodynia. *Journal of Clinical Medicine Research, 3*, 59–64.

Waldinger, M. D. (2002). The neurobiological approach to early ejaculation. *Journal of Urology, 168*, 2359–2367.

Waldinger, M. D. (2005). Male ejaculation and orgasmic disorders. In R. Balon & R. T. Segraves (Eds.), *Handbook of sexual dysfunction* (pp. 215–248). Boca Raton, FL: Taylor & Francis Group.

Waldinger, M. D., Rietschel, M., Nothen, M. M., Hengeveld, M. W., & Olivier, B. (1998). Familial occurrence of primary premature ejaculation. *Psychiatric Genetics, 8*, 37–40.

Ward, T., Hudson, S. M., & Marshall, W. L. (1995). Cognitive distortions and affective deficits in sex offenders: A cognitive deconstructionist interpretation. *Sexual Abuse: A Journal of Research and Treatment, 7*, 67–83.

Weinberg, T. A. (2006). Sadomasochism and the social sciences: A review of the sociological and social psychological literature. *Journal of Homosexuality, 50*, 17–40.

Weinberg, T., & Kamel, W. L. (Eds.). (1983). *S and M: Studies in sadomasochism*. Buffalo, NY: Prometheus.

Weinberg, T. S., Williams, C. J., & Moser, C. (1984). The social constituents of sadomasochism. *Social Problems, 31*, 379–389.

Wijkman, M., Bijleveld, C., & Hendriks, J. (2010). Women don't do such things! Characteristics of female sex offenders and offender types. *Sexual Abuse: A Journal of Research and Treatment, 22*, 135–156.

Wilson, G. (1978). *The secrets of sexual fantasy*. London, England: Dent.

Witting, K., Santtila, P., Varjonen, M., Jern, P., Johansson, A., vonderPahlen, B., & Sandnabba, K. (2008). Female sexual dysfunction, sexual distress, and compatibility with partner. *Journal of Sexual Medicine, 5*, 2587–2599.

Woo, J. S. T., Brotto, L. A., & Gorzalka, B. B. (2011). The role of sex guilt in the relationship between culture and women's sexual desire. *Archives of Sexual Behavior, 40*, 385–394.

World Health Organization. (forthcoming). *ICD-11: International statistical classification of diseases and related health problems* (11th ed.). New York, NY.

Wright, S. (2014). Kinky parents and child custody: The effect of the DSM-5 differentiation between the paraphilias and paraphilic disorders. *Archives of Sexual Behavior, 43*, 1257–1258.

Wurtele, S. K., Simons, D. A., & Moreno, T. (2014). Sexual interest in children among an online sample of men and women: Prevalence and correlates. *Sexual Abuse: A Journal of Research and Treatment, 26*, 546–568.

Wylie, K., & MacInnes, I. (2005). Erectile dysfunction. In R. Balon & R. T. Segraves (Eds.), *Handbook of sexual dysfunction* (pp. 155–191). Boca Raton, FL: Taylor & Francis Group.

Zavitzianos, G. (1971). Fetishism and exhibitionism in the female and their relationship to psychopathology and kleptomania. *International Journal of Psycho-Analysis, 52*, 297–305.

Zoloun, D., Hartmann, K., Lamvu, G., As-Sanie, S., Maixner, W., & Steege, J. (2006). A conceptual model for the pathophysiology of vulvar vestibulitis syndrome. *Obstetrical & Gynecological Survey, 61*, 395–401.

Zucker, K. J. (2013). DSM-5: Call for commentaries on Gender Dysphoria, Sexual Dysfunctions, and Paraphilic Disorders [Editorial]. *Archives of Sexual Behavior, 42*, 669–674.

Zucker, K. J., & Bradley, S. J. (1995). *Gender identity disorder and psychosexual problems in children and adolescents*. New York, NY: Guilford Press.

CHAPTER 17

Gender Dysphoria

ANNE A. LAWRENCE

DESCRIPTION OF THE DISORDER

The term *gender dysphoria* (GD) denotes discomfort with one's biologic sex or assigned gender. GD is the defining characteristic of a category of psychosexual disorders in which affected persons are "intensely and abidingly uncomfortable in their anatomic and genetic sex and their assigned gender" (Fisk, 1974b, p. 10). The most widely recognized and severe manifestation of GD is *transsexualism*, in which affected persons express an intense and persistent desire to live and be recognized as members of the other sex and to make their bodies resemble those of the other sex through hormonal and surgical treatment. Less severe and less widely known manifestations of GD also exist, however, and are probably more prevalent than transsexualism.

HISTORY AND TERMINOLOGY

Individuals who wish to live and be regarded as members of the other sex have been recognized since antiquity in many different societies worldwide (Green, 1969). The German physicians Krafft-Ebing (1903/1965) and Hirschfeld (1910/1991) described patients who would now be recognized as suffering from GD. Christine Jorgensen's widely reported sex reassignment in 1952 brought the phenomenon of transsexualism to public attention in Western countries (Meyerowitz, 2002), as did Benjamin's (1966) book *The Transsexual Phenomenon*. Starting in the 1960s, academic medical centers in the United States and Western Europe began to offer hormonal and surgical sex reassignment to carefully selected patients. In 1980, conditions involving GD were first recognized as psychiatric diagnoses in the third edition of the *Diagnostic and Statistical Manual of Mental Disorders* (*DSM-III*; American Psychiatric Association [APA], 1980).

Historically, the term GD has been used in several different ways, which has sometimes caused confusion. Fisk, who introduced the term, offered three slightly different definitions: he originally defined GD as discomfort with *both* biologic sex and assigned gender (Fisk, 1974b), but in subsequent definitions focused primarily on either biologic sex ("displeasure with the sex of [one's] genital anatomy, the chromosomes, and the endocrine secretions"; Laub & Fisk, 1974, p. 390) or assigned gender ("dysphoria concerning the individual's gender of assignment or rearing"; Fisk, 1974a,

Adult Psychopathology and Diagnosis, Eighth Edition. Edited by Deborah C. Beidel and B. Christopher Frueh.
© 2018 John Wiley & Sons, Inc. Published 2018 by John Wiley & Sons, Inc.
Companion website: www.wiley.com/go/beidel/psychopathology8e

p. 388). Blanchard's (1993b) definitions of GD sometimes emphasized only discomfort with biologic sex ("persistent discontent with the primary or secondary sexual characteristics of one's body"; p. 70) but at other times also emphasized cross-gender role aspirations ("discontent with one's biological sex, the desire to possess the body of the opposite sex, and the desire to be regarded by others as a member of the opposite sex"; Blanchard, 1993a, p. 301). The *DSM-IV* (APA, 1994) and *DSM-IV-TR* (APA, 2000) stated that intense discomfort with *either* biologic sex or assigned gender role could justify a diagnosis of GD ("persistent aversion toward some or all of those physical characteristics or social roles that connote one's own biological sex"; APA, 2000, p. 823). Note that, in at least some of these definitions, discomfort with biologic sex characteristics alone was considered sufficient to diagnose GD; cross-gender identification was not always explicitly required.

More recent definitions of GD, in contrast, have deemphasized discomfort with biologic sex characteristics and have focused almost exclusively on discordance between assigned sex and *gender identity* ("an individual's identification as male, female, or, occasionally, some category other than male or female"; APA, 2013, p. 451). The World Professional Association for Transgender Health (WPATH), for example, defined GD as "discomfort or distress that is caused by a discrepancy between a person's gender identity and that person's sex assigned at birth (and the associated gender role and/or primary and secondary sex characteristics)" (Coleman et al., 2011, p. 5). Two succinct definitions of GD that occur in the *DSM-5* (APA, 2013) do not even mention biologically based discontent or distress ("affective/cognitive discontent with the assigned gender" and "distress that may accompany the incongruence between one's experienced or expressed gender and one's assigned gender"; APA, 2013, p. 451). Although the term *experienced or expressed gender* is never formally defined in the *DSM-5*, its usage therein suggests that it is synonymous with *gender identity* (e.g., "experienced gender may include gender identities beyond binary stereotypes"; APA, 2013, p. 453).

The *DSM-III*, *DSM-III-R*, *DSM-IV*, and *DSM-IV-TR* all categorized psychosexual disorders involving GD under the overarching category of *gender identity disorders* (GIDs), because an "incongruence between anatomic sex and gender identity" (APA, 1980, p. 261) was considered to be the defining characteristic of these conditions. The *DSM-5* made GD both the overarching category and a specific diagnosis within the category, because "the current term [GD] is more descriptive than the previous *DSM-IV* term *gender identity disorder* and focuses on dysphoria as the clinical problem, not identity per se" (APA, 2013, p. 451). The *DSM-5* makes it clear, however, that a problem involving one's gender identity—now framed as an "incongruence between one's experienced/expressed gender and assigned gender" (APA, 2013, p. 452)—"is the core component of the diagnosis" (p. 453). Thus, the *DSM-5* apparently still conceptualizes GD as a disorder primarily involving gender identity, if not a disorder *of* gender identity.

In all of these *DSM* editions, adult and adolescent psychosexual diagnoses involving GD or GIDs have consisted of one principal or prototypical diagnosis with specific diagnostic criteria and one or more residual diagnoses, sometimes without specific criteria. In the *DSM-III* (APA, 1980), the principal diagnosis was transsexualism and the residual diagnosis was atypical gender identity disorder. In the *DSM-III-R* (APA, 1987), the principal diagnosis remained transsexualism, and the residual diagnoses became gender identity disorder of adolescence or adulthood, nontranssexual type (GIDAANT)—the only residual diagnosis to have specific criteria—and gender identity disorder not otherwise specified (GIDNOS). In the *DSM-IV* (APA, 1994) and *DSM-IV-TR* (APA, 2000), GID became the principal diagnosis and the only residual diagnosis was GIDNOS. The *DSM-5* continues this general pattern: The principal diagnosis is GD and the residual diagnoses are other specified GD and unspecified GD. The principal diagnoses for disorders of gender identity have become progressively more encompassing in successive versions of the *DSM*: many clinical presentations that once would have received a residual diagnosis (e.g., GIDAANT or GIDNOS) would now receive the principal diagnosis, GD.

Although transsexualism is no longer a *DSM* diagnosis, many clinicians continue to use the term, in part because it remains an official diagnosis in the most recent edition of the *International Classification of Diseases* (World Health Organization, 1992). Some experts consider transsexualism to be essentially synonymous with severe GD (e.g., Blanchard, 1993c). The distinction between transsexualism and GD may be of limited practical importance, because much of the research relevant to understanding GD in adults has involved persons who would meet diagnostic criteria for transsexualism by most definitions. Adults with severe GD, especially those who request or have completed sex reassignment, are commonly referred to as male-to-female (MtF) and female-to-male (FtM) transsexuals, or simply as MtFs and FtMs.

The terms *transgender* and *transgenderism* are used informally to describe persons who report or exhibit significant cross-gender or gender-variant identity or behavior, regardless of whether they meet diagnostic criteria for GD or transsexualism. Some of these individuals, including some persons who meet diagnostic criteria for GD, may explicitly identify as transgender persons.

CLINICAL PICTURE

TYPICAL CLINICAL PRESENTATIONS

Dislike for one's primary or secondary sex characteristics, discomfort with one's assigned gender or associated gender role, identification with the other gender, and requests for approval for hormonal and surgical sex reassignment are the most frequent presenting complaints of adult patients with GD. Some adults with GD initially present with other clinical concerns, however, including paraphilias, sexual dysfunctions, depression, or other general psychiatric conditions (Levine, 1993).

Persons with GD usually identify with the other sex; they may want the anatomy, the gender role, or the sexuality of the other sex, or any combination of these (Carroll, 1999). Persons with severe GD or transsexualism typically want both the anatomy and the gender role of the other sex (Deogracias et al., 2007; Singh et al., 2010). As noted earlier, an intense feeling of "wrong embodiment," manifesting as discontent with sexed body characteristics and a strong desire to acquire the anatomy of the other sex, has sometimes been considered the essential feature of severe GD and especially of transsexualism (Blanchard, 1993b; Bower, 2001; Laub & Fisk, 1974; Prosser, 1998). However, not all patients with GD experience intense anatomic dysphoria; some primarily desire to enact the gender role or sexuality of the other sex and are unconcerned or ambivalent about acquiring the anatomic features of the other sex.

LESS COMMON CLINICAL PRESENTATIONS

Rarely, persons with GD may identify with what the *DSM-5* calls "some alternative gender", which corresponds to neither their assigned sex nor the other sex. Examples would include males who desire castration and who identify as *eunuchs* (Johnson, Brett, Roberts, & Wassersug, 2007; Johnson & Wassersug, 2010); persons who want some combination of the secondary sex characteristics of both sexes and identify as *she-males*, *trans* persons, or transgender persons (Davidmann, 2010); and bi-gender persons who identify as both male and female and live at various times in both gender roles (Richards et al., 2016).

In some cases, persons with various *disorders of sex development* (DSDs; formerly known as *intersex* conditions) experience distress due to an incongruence between their gender identity and their assigned gender. These individuals can be given the principal diagnosis of GD in the *DSM-5*, with the assignment of the newly added DSD specifier. In previous editions of the *DSM*, the presence of a DSD or intersex condition was considered an exclusion criterion for the principal GID diagnosis, and gender dysphoric persons with these conditions would receive a residual diagnosis (e.g., GIDNOS). Richter-Appelt and Sandberg (2010) noted, however, that "the etiology, natural history, and response to treatment may be quite different" (p. 98) in gender dysphoric persons with and without DSDs. For example, in persons without DSDs, GD often appears during childhood and is more prevalent in males than in females; in persons with recognized DSDs, GD more commonly appears during adolescence and is more prevalent in female-assigned than in male-assigned persons. Discussion of the prevalence and manifestations of GD in specific DSD syndromes is beyond the purview of this chapter, but useful summaries and reviews exist (e.g., Mazur, Colsman, & Sandburg, 2007; Steensma, Kreukels, de Vries, & Cohen-Kettenis, 2013). It is recognized that GD is rarely if ever reported in conjunction with some DSDs, such as Turner's syndrome and complete androgen insensitivity syndrome but is overrepresented relative to the general population in association with other DSDs, such as congenital adrenal hyperplasia (CAH) and partial androgen insensitivity syndrome (Dessens, Slijper, & Drop, 2005; Mazur, 2005; Mazur et al., 2007). Jordan-Young (2012) argued that the gender-atypical interests and attitudes of females with CAH plausibly reflect a complex set of influences—the general physiological effects of adrenal androgens, the consequences of medical interventions and surveillance, the sexual effects of atypical genital morphology, and altered societal expectations—rather than simply a masculinization of brain gender due to elevated androgen levels. Similar considerations may be relevant to understanding the etiology of GD in other DSD syndromes as well.

Individuals with DSDs who experience GD typically identify as men or women of the gender other than their assigned gender, but some may identify as *intersex, intersexual,* or *epicene* persons (Bearman, 2007; Harper, 2007; Preves, 2003).

Subtypes of GD in Adults

The *DSM-III* described transsexualism as a "heterogeneous disorder" (APA, 1980, p. 261), and subsequent research has confirmed that adults with GD are a diverse population. Recognizable clinical subtypes underlie this diversity; these subtypes have important implications for understanding the etiology, development, clinical course, and effective treatment of GD. Two clinical characteristics—sexual orientation and age of onset of GD symptoms—have been used to formulate most typologies of GD (Lawrence, 2010b). Within each typology, subtypes are applicable to both males and females with GD, but clinical features are usually described separately for each sex because relevant features often differ substantially between sexes.

Subtypes Based on Sexual Orientation   Subtypes based on sexual orientation were first formulated in the 1960s. They are grounded in the theory that sexual orientation is a stable, biologically based characteristic that is determined early in development (Poeppl, Langguth, Rupprecht, Laird, & Eickhoff, 2016). Subtypes based on sexual orientation have substantial descriptive, predictive, and heuristic value (Lawrence, 2010b), and they were used as specifiers for the diagnoses of transsexualism and GID in the *DSM-III*, *DSM-III-R*, *DSM-IV*, and *DSM-IV-TR* (APA, 1980, 1987, 1994, 2000). One limitation of these subtypes is that self-reported sexual orientation often differs from clinician-rated sexual orientation, especially in males (Lawrence, 2017; Nieder et al., 2011). Consequently, subtype assignment based on self-reported sexual orientation can be unreliable.

In adult males with GD, persons who are sexually oriented exclusively to men are described as *androphilic*, whereas those who are sexually oriented to women, women and men, or neither sex are described as *nonandrophilic*. Androphilic and nonandrophilic males with GD differ significantly in clinical presentation (Blanchard, 1985, 1989b; Lawrence, 2010b). These two subtypes appear to represent separate, distinct clinical spectra (Whitam, 1987) and plausibly reflect completely different etiologies (Freund, 1985; Guillamon, Junque, & Gómez-Gil, 2016; Lawrence, 2017; Smith, van Goozen, Kuiper, & Cohen-Kettenis, 2005b).

Androphilic males with GD were usually conspicuously feminine as children and are usually very feminine as adults (Blanchard, 1988; Whitam, 1987, 1997); in particular, they are more feminine in physical appearance than are nonandrophilic males with GD (Smith et al., 2005b; van de Grift et al., 2016). They rarely report any history of sexual arousal with cross-dressing (Blanchard, 1985, 1989b). Whitam (1987) observed that "in most societies these persons regard themselves as homosexuals and are regarded by more masculine homosexuals as a natural part of the homosexual world" (p. 177); clinicians may also find this perspective useful. Androphilic males with GD who seek sex reassignment usually do so in their 20s or early 30s (Blanchard, Clemmensen, & Steiner, 1987; Smith et al., 2005b). In past decades, most males who underwent sex reassignment in Western countries were androphilic, but this is no longer true (Lawrence, 2010c).

Nonandrophilic males now constitute the most prevalent male GD subtype in many Western countries (Lawrence, 2010c; van de Grift et al., 2016; see Table 17.1). They may describe themselves as sexually oriented to women, to women and men, or to neither sex; but in most cases they also are, or once were, sexually aroused by the thought or image of themselves as women, a paraphilic sexual interest called *autogynephilia* ("love of oneself as a woman"; Blanchard, 1989a,b). The most common manifestation of autogynephilia is erotic cross-dressing; most nonandrophilic males with GD have a history of erotic

Table 17.1
Sexual Orientation and Age of Onset in 640 European Adults with Gender Dysphoria

Males (MtFs; $N = 367$)	Early onset, n (%)	Late onset, n (%)	Total, n (%)
Androphilic	88 (24)	38 (10)	74 (34)
Nonandrophilic	102 (28)	139 (38)	241 (66)
Total	190 (52)	177 (48)	367 (100)

Females (FtMs; $N = 273$)	Early onset, n (%)	Late onset, n (%)	Total, n (%)
Gynephilic	193 (71)	26 (10)	219 (80)
Nongynephilic	37 (14)	17 (6)	54 (20)
Total	230 (84)	43 (16)	273 (100)

MtF, male-to-female transsexual; FtM, female-to-male transsexual.
Note: Data are from van de Grift et al. (2016), p. 579. Due to rounding, sums of subgroup percentages may differ from total percentages.

cross-dressing or sexual arousal with cross-gender fantasy (Blanchard, 1985; Blanchard, Racansky, & Steiner, 1986; Lawrence, 2005). Autogynephilia focused on female anatomic features (i.e., sexual arousal to the thought or image of having breasts or a vulva) is especially characteristic of nonandrophilic males who seek surgical sex reassignment (Blanchard, 1993c). It is useful to think of nonandrophilic males with GD as having a paraphilic sexual interest that makes them want to *become what they love* (Lawrence, 2007) by turning their bodies into facsimiles of the females they find sexually desirable (Freund & Blanchard, 1993). Nonandrophilic males with GD often have other paraphilic sexual interests, especially sexual masochism (Bolin, 1988; Lawrence, 2013; Walworth, 1997). Sometimes they develop a secondary sexual interest in men because they are aroused by the idea of taking a woman's sexual role with a man, thereby having their "physical attractiveness as women validated by others" (Blanchard, 1989b, p. 622). Most nonandrophilic males with GD were not overtly feminine as children and often are not especially feminine as adults (Blanchard, 1990; Smith et al., 2005b; Whitam, 1997). Some report mild gender nonconformity during childhood (Buhrich & McConaghy, 1977) but less so than is the case for androphilic males with GD (Zucker et al., 2012). Non-androphilic males with GD typically seek sex reassignment in their mid-30s or later (Blanchard et al., 1987; Gaither et al., 2017; Smith et al., 2005b) and not uncommonly in their 50s or 60s (Lawrence, 2003).

Adult females with GD who are sexually oriented exclusively to women are described as *gynephilic*, whereas those who are sexually oriented to men, women and men, or neither sex are described as *nongynephilic*. Gynephilic and nongynephilic females with GD are similar in some ways; for example, they apply for sex reassignment at roughly similar ages (Smith et al., 2005b). Gynephilic females with GD are the most prevalent female GD subtype (van de Grift et al., 2016). Most gynephilic females with GD were extremely masculine as children (Smith et al., 2005b) and probably would have met diagnostic criteria for GD in childhood. Their sexual attitudes are male-typical in many respects: they display greater sexual than emotional jealousy and report more sexual partners, more interest in visual sexual stimuli, and greater desire for phalloplasty than their nongynephilic counterparts (Chivers & Bailey, 2000). As children, nongynephilic females with GD "may have been girls with neutral interests or with some tomboy characteristics" (Smith et al., 2005b, p. 159), but they were usually less pervasively masculine than their gynephilic counterparts. As adults, their sexual attitudes are less male-typical (Chivers & Bailey, 2000), and they are more likely to have comorbid psychopathology (Smith et al., 2005b), for reasons that are not well understood. Sexual arousal to cross-dressing or cross-gender fantasy does not appear to be a significant factor in the development of nongynephilic GD in females (Smith et al., 2005b). Nongynephilic females with GD were once believed to be rare, but they now comprise about 16% of females with GD in northern European countries (van de Grift et al., 2016; see Table 17.1).

In the past, androphilic males and gynephilic females with GD were usually described as *homosexual* gender dysphoric persons, because their sexual orientation is homosexual relative to their natal sex. Nonandrophilic males and nongynephilic females with GD were similarly described as *nonhomosexual* gender dysphoric persons. These descriptive terms, while technically accurate, are potentially confusing and are considered objectionable by some persons with GD (Cohen-Kettenis & Pfäfflin, 2010). Consequently, these terms have been de-emphasized in contemporary clinical usage.

Subtypes Based on Age of Onset   Subtypes based on age of onset of GD symptoms were first formulated in the 1970s (Lawrence, 2010b). When the *DSM-5* (APA, 2013) eliminated specifiers based on sexual orientation for the diagnosis of GD, it adopted subtypes based on age of onset for descriptive purposes, albeit not as formal specifiers. In the *DSM-5*, adults with GD are considered to be *early onset* (EO) if they met full criteria for the diagnosis of GD during childhood (i.e., they displayed a strong, persistent cross-gender identification and a strong preference for the typical clothing, gender roles, activities, or anatomic characteristics of the other sex). Adults with GD are considered be *late onset* (LO) if they did *not* meet full criteria for the diagnosis of GD during childhood. However, some investigators who have studied age of onset in persons with GD have adopted different category definitions for age of onset (e.g., Nieder et al., 2011; Schneider et al., 2016; van de Grift et al., 2016).

Assignment of an EO or LO subtype in a person with GD typically relies on the person's retrospective recollection of childhood cross-gender wishes and gender non-conformity. Such recollections can be inaccurate, sometimes exaggerating the strength and pervasiveness of childhood cross-gender traits (Lawrence, 2010b). Consequently, accurate assessment of age of onset subtypes can be problematic. Subtypes based on age of onset have less descriptive and predictive value than subtypes based on sexual orientation (Lawrence, 2010b) but have nevertheless become widely utilized in clinical research, especially in northern Europe.

Early-onset males, who, by definition, report more intense GD during childhood than do LO males, also report more intense GD in adulthood (Schneider et al., 2016). EO males present for treatment at younger ages than do LO males (Nieder et al., 2011), and clinicians rate them as more feminine in appearance (van de Grift et al., 2016). EO and LO females, in contrast, appear similar in many respects. Although EO females, by definition, report more intense GD during childhood than do LO females, the two groups report equally intense GD in adulthood (Schneider et al., 2016), and they present for treatment at similar ages (Nieder et al., 2011). Clinicians also rate EO and LO females as about equally masculine in appearance (van de Grift et al., 2016).

Table 17.1 displays the relative prevalence of subtypes based on sexual orientation and age of onset and the relationship between them in a large contemporary sample of European adults with GD.

DIAGNOSTIC CONSIDERATIONS

Diagnosing GD

The defining diagnostic criterion of GD (APA, 2013) is a marked incongruence between gender identity ("experienced/expressed gender") and assigned sex, manifesting as some combination of discomfort with anatomic sex, desire for the anatomy of the other sex, desire to live or be treated as a member of the other sex, or a feeling of psychological similarity to the other sex. There is also a requirement of clinically significant distress or impairment in functioning.

Like past editions of the *DSM*, the *DSM-5* provides one principal diagnosis for these conditions—GD—along with residual diagnoses. The two residual diagnoses in the *DSM-5* are *other specified GD* and *unspecified GD*. Other specified GD is applicable where symptoms of gender dysphoria are present and there is clinically significant distress or impairment but full diagnostic criteria for GD are not met and the clinician wishes to state why the clinical presentation does not meet full criteria for the principal diagnosis. Unspecified GD is applicable in the same circumstances, except that the clinician does not wish to state why full criteria for the principal diagnosis have not been met (APA, 2013).

Differential Diagnosis

The principal differential diagnostic considerations for the diagnosis of GD in adults include transvestic disorder; schizophrenia, bipolar disorder, and other psychotic conditions; dissociative identity disorder; some personality disorders (PDs); body dysmorphic disorder; and gender nonconformity.

Although transvestic disorder is one of the differential diagnoses for GD, the two conditions can and do co-occur (Blanchard, 2010). It is useful, in fact, to think of transvestic disorder and the nonandrophilic subtype of male GD as points on a spectrum of symptomatology, rather than as discrete entities (Lawrence, 2009b). In persons with transvestic disorder, the absence of a marked incongruence between gender identity and assigned sex would exclude the diagnosis of GD. Many cross-dressing men who meet diagnostic criteria for transvestic disorder, however, describe cross-gender identities of some strength (Docter, 1988) and some express a desire to use feminizing hormone therapy (Docter & Prince, 1997).

Patients with schizophrenia, bipolar disorder, and other psychotic disorders sometimes experience delusional beliefs of being or becoming the other sex (Habermeyer, Kamps, & Kawohl, 2003; Manderson & Kumar, 2001); treatment of the psychotic condition usually leads to resolution of this cross-gender identification, but GD and psychotic disorders sometimes co-occur, as both individual case reports (Baltieri & De Andrade, 2009; Haberman, Hollingsworth, Falek, & Michael, 1975) and large cohort studies (Brown & Jones, 2016) demonstrate. Cross-gender ideation sometimes occurs in dissociative identity disorder (Modestin & Ebner, 1995; Saks, 1998); persons with GD display fewer dissociative symptoms than do patients with dissociative disorders (Kersting et al., 2003) but more than nonclinical controls. Persons with antisocial PD have been reported to seek sex reassignment in the absence of GD (Laub & Fisk, 1974). Some theorists (e.g., Lothstein, 1984; Person & Ovesey, 1974) have proposed that the identity diffusion associated with borderline personality disturbances might manifest as GD, implying that borderline PD could be a possible differential diagnostic consideration. Wilkinson-Ryan and Westen (2000) found that patients with borderline PD were more conflicted or unsure about their gender identity than were nonclinical controls, but Singh, McMain, and Zucker (2011) found no individuals meeting criteria for GD among 100 women diagnosed with borderline PD. Pfäfflin (2007) suggested that body dysmorphic disorder focused on the genitals could be mistaken for GD; the absence of a marked incongruence between gender identity and assigned sex would exclude the latter diagnosis (see also Phillips et al., 2010). Persons with gender nonconformity sometimes report significant cross-gender identification or a preference for the gender role of the other sex but may not experience enough distress or functional impairment to meet full diagnostic criteria for GD.

Comorbid Psychiatric Conditions and Dual Diagnoses

Investigators have conducted many studies of comorbid psychopathology in persons with GD, and their reports reveal a wide range of confusing and sometimes contradictory results. Most high-quality studies, however, have found a substantially increased prevalence of associated psychopathology in persons with transsexualism—the most intense and most studied form of GD. Depression and anxiety disorders are especially prevalent comorbid conditions. Two recent methodologically strong investigations illustrate these conclusions.

Dhejne et al. (2011) conducted a longitudinal, population-based follow-up study of 191 MtF and 131 FtMs who underwent sex reassignment surgery (SRS) in Sweden from

1973 through 2003, comparing them with a randomly selected, age-matched control cohort using data from Swedish national health registries. They found that 19% of MtFs and 17% of FtMs had been hospitalized for other psychiatric problems before SRS, compared with 3–4% of controls. After SRS, transsexuals were 2.8 times more likely to have been hospitalized for other psychiatric problems and 19.1 times more likely to have died from suicide, even after adjusting for prior psychiatric conditions. The prevalence of documented attempted suicide in transsexuals was 9%, versus 1.4% for controls.

Heylens et al. (2014) described current and lifetime comorbid psychopathology in 182 MtF and 123 FtM transsexuals from northern European countries, using structured clinical interviews for data collection. Approximately 38% of patients had one or more current *DSM-IV* Axis I disorders and about 69% had one or more lifetime Axis I disorders, with similar prevalence figures in MtFs and FtMs. The most common comorbid conditions were mood disorders (27% current, 60% lifetime) and anxiety disorders (17% current, 28% lifetime). These figures greatly exceed the prevalence of comorbid psychopathology in western European adults: for example, Alonso & Lépine (2007) found a 26% lifetime prevalence of mental disorders in European adults. Most other studies of comorbid pathology that have used structured clinical interviews for data collection have reported similar conclusions (for a review, see Zucker, Lawrence, & Kreukels, 2016), including a recent study of young MtF transgender women in the United States (Reisner et al., 2016). A few reports, however, have not confirmed this general pattern (e.g., Colizzi, Costa, & Todarello, 2014; Fisher et al., 2013).

Recent reviews and case series have focused attention on an increased prevalence of autism spectrum disorder (ASD) in male and female adolescents and adults with GD (e.g., Jones et al., 2012; Pasterski, Gilligan, & Curtis, 2014; van der Miesen, Hurley, & de Vries, 2016). Van der Miesen et al. (2016) concluded that "around 20% of gender identity clinic-assessed individuals reported clinical range features of ASD" (p. 78). These findings are intriguing in light of the theory that ASD reflects an "extreme male brain" developmental pattern (Baron-Cohen, 2002); such a theory seemingly would account for an overrepresentation of ASD in females with GD, but not in males with GD.

Comorbid substance abuse ("dual diagnosis") is sometimes considered separately from other comorbid psychiatric disorders. Substance-related disorders are fairly common in persons with GD. Gómez-Gil, Trilla, Salamero, Godás, and Valdés (2009) found that among 159 MtFs, about 11% had a current or lifetime history of alcohol abuse or dependence, and about 15% and 30% had a current or lifetime history, respectively, of nonalcohol substance abuse or dependence. In a cohort of 298 young MtF transgender adults, Reisner et al. (2016) found 11% and 15% prevalence figures for alcohol dependence and other psychoactive substance dependence. Hepp, Kraemer, Schnyder, Miller, and Delsignore (2005) reported that 50% of MtFs had a lifetime history of substance-related disorders. Among FtMs, substance-related problems are somewhat less prevalent: Gómez-Gil et al. (2009) reported that only 4% of 71 FtMs had a lifetime history of alcohol abuse or dependence and only 11% had a lifetime history of nonalcohol substance abuse or dependence. Hepp et al. (2005) observed a lifetime history of substance abuse or dependence in 36% of FtMs.

Personality disorders (PDs) are also often considered separately from other comorbid conditions. Data on the prevalence of PDs in persons with GD are inconsistent. Heylens et al. (2014) found associated PDs in only 12% of MtF and 18% of FtM transsexuals, comparable to nonclinical populations. Other investigators utilizing structured clinical interviews for data collection have found higher figures, albeit in smaller samples. Madeddu, Prunas, and Hartmann (2009) reported that 59% of MtFs and 38% of FtMs they studied had at least one PD; Hepp et al. (2005) found that 42% of a combined group of

MtFs and FtMs had at least one comorbid PD. In both of the latter studies, cluster B disorders were most prevalent.

Mental disorders tend to be significantly correlated with each other, and having one mental disorder greatly increases the probability of having one or more other mental disorders (Caspi et al. 2014). From this perspective, the increased prevalence of comorbid psychopathology in patients with GD is not surprising. Some theorists suggest that associated psychopathology in GD is largely a consequence of minority stress (Meyer, 2003), resulting from the pervasive discrimination and victimization that many persons with GD experience. Perceived prejudice and discrimination have been shown to be associated with an increased prevalence of mental health problems in ethnic and other minority groups (Pascoe & Smart Richman, 2009; Pieterse, Todd, Neville, & Carter, 2012), albeit with only small-to-medium effect sizes. Direction of effect is difficult to determine, however: prejudice and discrimination might lead to a greater likelihood of persons with GD developing comorbid mental health problems; or comorbid mental health problems in persons with GD might lead to a greater likelihood of their experiencing (or simply perceiving) prejudice and discrimination. Possibly both of these phenomena occur. Heylens et al. (2014a) and Terada et al. (2012) found no significant relationship between age of onset of GD symptoms and comorbid psychopathology, which implies that longer exposure to GD-related prejudice and discrimination is not necessarily associated with more prevalent psychopathology.

EPIDEMIOLOGY

PREVALENCE AND SEX RATIO

Population-based treatment data from European countries provide the best estimates of the prevalence of GD and transsexualism in Western societies. In a meta-analysis of 11 epidemiologic studies published between 1974 and 2014, 10 of which were conducted in Europe, Arcelus et al. (2015) found the prevalence of transsexualism to be 1:14,705 adult males and 1:38,461 adult females. Recent studies from northern Europe reveal still higher prevalence figures in adults: 1:12,900 males and 1:33,800 females in Belgium (De Cuypere et al., 2007); 1:7,750 males and 1:13,120 females in Sweden (Dhejne et al., 2014), and 1:10,154 males and 1:27,668 females in Ireland (Judge et al., 2014). These reports reflect only severe cases of GD, treated with legal, hormonal, or surgical sex reassignment.

Treatment-based studies almost certainly underestimate the true prevalence of GD. Primary-care physicians in Scotland reported a prevalence of GD, treated with cross-sex hormone therapy or SRS, of 1:12,800 adult male patients and 1:52,100 adult female patients, but the overall prevalence of GD, treated or untreated, was higher: 1:7,400 males and 1:31,200 females (Wilson, Sharp, & Carr, 1999). Cross-gender identification, not necessarily indicative of clinically significant GD, is more prevalent still. Based on New Zealand passport data, Veale (2008) found the prevalence of cross-gender identification to be 1:3,630 adult males and 1:22,714 adult females. In a probability sample of over 28,000 male and female adults who participated in a telephone health survey in the US, 0.5% of participants reported a cross-gender identification (Conron, Scott, Stowell, & Landers, 2012). A similar study of over 150,000 US adults also found that 0.5% identified as transgender (Crissman, Berger, Graham, & Dalton, 2017). In yet another large population-based survey of persons 15–70 years old in the Netherlands, 1.1% of males and 0.8% of females reported an incongruent gender identity (stronger identification with the other sex than with their assigned sex; Kuyper & Wijsen, 2014); but respondents who also disliked their sexed body characteristics and desired to change their bodies hormonally or surgically were much less prevalent, only 0.2% of males and 0.05% of females. These last results make it clear that incongruent gender identity does not necessarily imply clinically significant GD or a desire for sex reassignment.

In almost all Western countries, transsexualism, GD, and cross-gender identification are two or three times more prevalent in males than in females (Landén, Wålinder, & Lundström, 1996). Longitudinal data suggest that GD is becoming more prevalent over time. For example, Landén et el. reported a prevalence of transsexualism of 1:37,000 adult males and 1:103,000 adult females in Sweden in the 1960s, roughly one-fifth of current estimates (Dhejne et al., 2014). The observed increase in the prevalence of transsexualism probably reflects a lower threshold at which individuals consider themselves to be appropriate candidates for sex reassignment.

Two surveys revealed that 2.7% and 2.8% of adult males reported having experienced sexual arousal in association with cross-dressing (Ahlers et al., 2011; Långström & Zucker, 2005). These results imply that autogynephilic cross-dressers plausibly constitute the most numerous transgender subgroup. Many of these individuals, however, may not experience their gender identities as incongruent with their assigned sex or identify as transgender persons. Moreover, many probably do not experience sufficient distress or impairment to meet diagnostic criteria for either GD or transvestic disorder.

AGE OF ONSET

In European countries, about 50% of males and 85% of females with GD are categorized as EO, meaning that they met full diagnostic criteria for GD during childhood. Other persons with GD, categorized as LO, did not meet these criteria in full during childhood. Many LO individuals nevertheless report childhood feelings and behaviors that were subthreshold for diagnosis. Some persons with GD describe being aware of transgender feelings from their earliest memories. Most androphilic males, most gynephilic females, and many nongynephilic females with GD report that they displayed overt cross-gender behaviors and interests during early childhood. Nonandrophilic males with GD typically report experiencing their first desire to be the other sex or to change sex in middle childhood, but sometimes as late as adolescence or adulthood (Lawrence, 2005, 2013; Nieder et al., 2011; Zucker et al., 2012).

PSYCHOLOGICAL AND BIOLOGICAL ASSESSMENT

PSYCHOLOGICAL ASSESSMENT

Psychological assessment in cases of known or suspected GD involves evaluation of the presence or absence of GD symptoms, appraisal of their duration and severity, and investigation of possible comorbid psychopathology. In adults, GD is diagnosed primarily on the basis of self-report: "There are no so-called objective tests, either medical or psychological, that serve as proof of the diagnosis" (Pfäfflin, 2007, p. 176). The clinician should obtain information about the patient's psychosexual development, gender identification, sexual orientation, and feelings concerning sexed body characteristics and assigned gender role. Patients sometimes deliberately or inadvertently provide misleading information to caregivers, especially if they are eager to be approved for treatment (Walworth, 1997). Clinicians should not uncritically accept self-reported sexual orientation in male patients with known or suspected GD who have an unequivocal history of sexual attraction to women; some of these individuals develop a secondary sexual attraction to men in connection with their cross-gender identification and subsequently describe themselves as exclusively attracted to men, whereas experienced clinicians often judge otherwise (Nieder et al., 2011).

Self-report questionnaires and scales for the assessment of GD exist but are more commonly employed in research settings than in clinical practice. The Minnesota Multiphasic Personality Inventory–2 (MMPI-2; Butcher et al., 2001; Martin & Finn, 2010), a widely used assessment instrument, includes three gender-related scales (*Mf*, *GM*, and *GF*) that provide quantitative measures of gender-typical or atypical attitudes and interests (see Gómez-Gil, Vidal-Hagemeijer, & Salmero, 2008). The Gender Identity/ GD Questionnaire for Adolescents and Adults (Deogracias et al., 2007; see also Schneider et al., 2016) is a published self-report instrument with good sensitivity and specificity; it has been cross-validated (Singh et al., 2010) and seems destined to achieve widespread clinical acceptance. The Utrecht GD Scale, a similar inventory, was recently described in detail in an English-language publication (Schneider et al., 2016).

The specific focus of GD can vary considerably among patients. GD may involve dissatisfaction with sexed body characteristics or gender role, or both; the specific pattern may affect treatment planning. Intensity of GD not only varies among patients but can also vary over time in the same patient. GD often intensifies following significant crises or losses (Levine, 1993; Lothstein, 1979; Roback, Fellemann, & Abramowitz, 1984) but may moderate or remit when these have resolved.

As noted previously, comorbid mental health problems are prevalent in persons with GD. Treatment of comorbid psychotic, affective, and anxiety disorders may be required before GD can be confidently diagnosed and adequately characterized. According to contemporary treatment guidelines (e.g., Coleman et al., 2011), comorbid mental health problems must be reasonably well controlled before approval for genital SRS.

BIOLOGICAL ASSESSMENT

Physical examination and laboratory testing are of limited value in the assessment of GD. Physical examination could help to ascertain the presence of a DSD, which might lead to assignment of a specifier. Some gender identity clinics routinely perform karyotyping in GD evaluations, but the procedure is expensive and the results will be normal in roughly 97% of patients with known or suspected GD or transsexualism (Auer, Fuss, Stalla, & Athanasoulia, 2013; Bearman, 2007; Inoubli et al., 2011). Non-autosomal positive findings in males will usually represent Kleinfelter syndrome (47, XXY) or an XYY karyotype (Auer et al., 2013; Wylie & Steward, 2008). Bearman (2007) suggested that if karyotyping is performed at all, it should be offered only to male patients with hypogonadism, tall stature, gynecomastia, or learning disorders. There are a few case reports in the literature showing sex chromosome abnormalities in FtM patients (Auer et al., 2013; Turan et al., 2000).

Evidence concerning a possible elevated prevalence of polycystic ovary syndrome (PCOS) in females with GD has been inconsistent. Baba et al. (2007) reported an unexpectedly high figure, 58%, in a Japanese sample; the same investigators subsequently reported a figure of 32% in FtMs who had never used testosterone (Baba et al., 2011). In contrast, a well-controlled study that used a rigorous definition of PCOS found a prevalence of only 11.5% in Dutch FtMs, not significantly different from the 9.6% found in healthy controls (Mueller et al., 2008). Because PCOS may be related to both prenatal and postnatal androgen levels, it should probably be assessed as part of a routine endocrinological evaluation.

CLINICAL COURSE AND TREATMENT

CLINICAL COURSE

The clinical course of GD is variable, not easily predictable, and not well understood, even in persons who have been carefully evaluated and diagnosed (Coleman et al., 2011). There are at least four recognized outcomes of severe GD in adults (Carroll, 1999): (1) unresolved or unknown, (2) acceptance of natal gender, (3) part-time cross-gender expression, and (4) full-time cross-living and sex reassignment.

Unresolved or Unknown Outcomes   As many as half of patients who undergo evaluation or psychotherapy for GD may withdraw from treatment (Carroll, 1999). They may find the process prohibitively expensive, become impatient with a prolonged evaluation, or feel ambivalent or hopeless about achieving a solution to their gender concerns. Some patients who drop out subsequently resume treatment, but otherwise little is known about the natural history of GD in these persons.

Acceptance of Natal Gender   Acceptance of natal gender was once considered the optimal outcome for patients with GD. There have been no convincing demonstrations, however, that any form of psychiatric treatment can eliminate GD symptoms or reliably facilitate acceptance of natal gender in adults with GD. Some adults diagnosed with GD, however, do appear to subsequently accept their natal gender (Marks, Green, & Mataix-Cols, 2000; Shore, 1984). Acceptance of natal gender sometimes occurs in persons who undergo treatment of comorbid psychological problems, who are unwilling to risk losing their employment or their families, who hold religious beliefs that condemn sex reassignment, or who have physical characteristics that make it impossible for them to present convincingly as members of the other sex (Carroll, 1999; Shore, 1984). Nonandrophilic men with GD sometimes successfully postpone treatment until they have completed parental or spousal obligations (Blanchard, 1994). Coleman et al. (2011) described various "options for social support and changes in gender expression" for individuals who decide not to live part- or full-time in a cross-gender role.

Part-Time Cross-Gender Behavior   Persons with GD may decide to live part-time in their preferred gender role and part-time as members of their natal sex. They sometimes use masculinizing or feminizing hormone therapy or undergo surgical procedures to facilitate this process. Docter and Prince (1997) surveyed more than 1,000 heterosexual cross-dressers, none of whom lived full-time as women, and found that 17% would seek sex reassignment if possible, 28% considered their feminine self their preferred gender identity, and nearly 50% were either using feminizing hormones or wanted to do so. Many of these persons presumably experienced some degree of GD, yet decided to live only part-time as women. Adult females with GD sometimes live part-time in the cross-sex gender role as well, but this rarely becomes a focus of clinical attention and has not been as thoroughly documented.

Full-Time Cross-Living and Sex Reassignment   Many patients with a presenting complaint of GD or transsexualism will want to undergo sex reassignment and live full-time as members of the other sex. In reality, full-time and part-time cross-gender behaviors do not represent distinctly demarcated outcomes but rather points on a spectrum of options available to persons with GD, involving many possible choices of presentation, cross-gender role assumption, and anatomic modification. Some persons who live full-time in a cross-gender role do not undergo SRS and may not use cross-sex hormone therapy. Some persons who use cross-sex hormones and undergo SRS do not present themselves unambiguously as members of the other sex, but as gender-ambiguous, androgynous, or openly transgender individuals.

The decision to undertake full-time cross-living and sex reassignment and the process of actualizing this decision typically occurs in stages, similar to the stages of coming out for lesbians and gay men. Several multistage models of transsexual coming out have been proposed (e.g., Devor, 2004; Gagne, Tewksbury, & McGaughey, 1997; Lewins, 1995). These typically involve acknowledging GD, questioning and information gathering, developing a cross-gender identity, disclosing one's feelings to significant others, cross-living, undergoing SRS if desired, and experiencing further evolution of gender identity following transition (Devor, 2004).

TREATMENT

Treatment Guidelines   Treatment of GD in adults has largely become standardized in developed countries, due to the publication of authoritative clinical guidelines. Of these, the *Standards of Care for the Health of Transsexual, Transgender, and Gender-Nonconforming People* (SOC; Coleman et al., 2011), promulgated by WPATH, is the best known and most influential. The SOC and similar guidelines (e.g., Byne et al., 2012; Wylie et al. 2014) reflect the consensus opinions of experienced professionals but rarely a higher quality of evidence (Byne et al., 2012).

The SOC describe four main treatment modalities for GD and transsexualism: counseling and psychotherapy, cross-sex hormone therapy, real-life experience (RLE) in the desired gender role, and SRS. SRS usually denotes feminizing genitoplasty in MtFs but can denote either mastectomy with chest reconstruction or masculinizing genitoplasty in FtM transsexuals. Adults with GD may not always want all of these therapeutic elements (Beek, Kreukels, Cohen-Kettenis, & Steensma, 2015); for example, some individuals are satisfied with cross-sex hormone therapy and living part-time in their preferred gender role. The SOC state that hormone therapy, RLE, and nongenital surgery can be provided separately or in any combination, but that feminizing or masculinizing genitoplasty should ordinarily be provided only to patients who have previously used cross-sex hormone therapy for at least 1 year and have completed at least 1 year of successful, full-time, RLE in their desired gender role (Coleman et al., 2011).

Counseling and Psychotherapy   Counseling and psychotherapy are strongly encouraged for adults with GD (Coleman et al., 2011; see also Bockting, 2008). These therapies are not intended to cure GD but rather to allow patients to explore evolving gender identities, discuss relationship and employment issues, and consider various treatment options. Zucker et al. (2016) proposed that "helping adults with GD find greater acceptance and comfort with their natal sex and assigned gender" (p. 237) was also a legitimate goal of therapy, albeit one that has recently been de-emphasized. Seikowski (2007) argued that psychotherapy was most appropriate for GD patients with some type of personality disorder but was not necessary for most patients. Some persons with GD can benefit from group psychotherapy (Heck, 2017; Stermac, Blanchard, Clemmensen, & Dickey, 1991), which can reduce feelings of isolation, provide opportunities to receive and give support, and facilitate the acquisition of problem-solving skills.

Cross-Sex Hormone Therapy   Cross-sex hormone therapy suppresses or minimizes the secondary sex characteristics of the person's natal sex and promotes the development of the secondary sex characteristics of the other sex. Review articles and expert guidelines describe the recommended management of cross-sex hormone therapy (e.g., Hembree et al., 2009; Unger, 2016; Wylie et al. 2014). The SOC (Coleman et al., 2011) discuss eligibility criteria for cross-sex hormone therapy. Hormone therapy is usually prescribed for persons who seek sex reassignment, but it can also be beneficial for those who do not wish to live full-time in a cross-gender role or do not desire SRS. It is not unusual for adults with GD, especially MtF persons, to use hormone therapy without medical supervision (Gómez-Gil et al., 2009; Simonsen et al., 2015).

Hormone therapy for males with GD (e.g., MtF transsexuals) usually involves a combination of estrogens and antiandrogens (Unger, 2016). These feminizing hormone regimens typically result in breast growth, decreased muscle mass, reduction in the growth of facial and body hair, slowing of scalp hair loss, and decreased sexual interest. MtFs who receive treatment with feminizing hormone therapy report improvements in self-esteem, mood, and quality of life (Gómez-Gil et al., 2012; Gorin-Lazard et al., 2013). Feminizing hormone therapy is reasonably safe for short-term use: Wierckx et al. (2014) detected no serious complications in a prospective study of 53 MtFs who received hormone therapy for 1 year. In a long-term follow-up study, however, Wierckx et al. (2012) reported that 12% of hormone-treated MtFs experienced thromboembolic events (6%) or other serious cardiovascular problems (6%), and about one-quarter displayed significant osteoporosis. Asscheman et al. (2011) found that all-cause mortality in hormone-treated MtFs was 51% higher than in the general population, with most of the increased mortality attributable to suicide, AIDS, cardiovascular disease, and drug abuse.

Hormone therapy for females with GD (e.g., FtM transsexuals) usually involves only testosterone, although synthetic progestins are sometimes added (Gorin-Lazard et al., 2012). Such masculinizing hormone therapy typically results in increased facial and body hair and muscle mass, male pattern scalp hair loss, deepening of the voice, clitoral enlargement, and suppression of menses. Masculinizing hormone therapy also has emotional and psychological effects, including increased aggressiveness and anger-proneness and greater sexual interest and arousal (Costantino et al., 2013; Van Goozen, Cohen-Kettenis, Gooren, Frijda, & Van de Poll, 1995). Hormone therapy in FtMs is associated with improvements in self-esteem, mood, and quality of life (Gómez-Gil et al., 2012; Gorin-Lazard et al., 2013). Asscheman et al. (2011) found that mortality in hormone-treated FtMs was no higher than in the general population, and Wierckx et al. (2012) reported no evidence of significant cardiovascular or other medical complications in a group of FtMs who had used masculinizing hormones for nearly a decade on average.

RLE in the Desired Gender Role   Adults with GD can undertake a full- or part-time RLE without professional help, and some patients will already be living full-time in their desired gender role when clinicians first encounter them. RLE in the desired gender role can help patients decide whether living in this role long-term might offer an improved quality of life. The SOC describe the RLE as a reversible step that, if successful, allows patients and caregivers to consider the irreversible step of genital SRS with greater confidence (Coleman et al., 2011). However, undertaking a full-time RLE in the other gender role may have irreversible social and economic consequences (Zucker et al., 2016).

Being regarded as a person of the other sex during a RLE is usually easier for FtM than MtF transsexuals. Attribution of male status results from observed signs of masculiniza-tion, whereas attribution of female status occurs by a process of exclusion, when few or no signs of masculinization are observed (Kessler & McKenna, 1978). Although it is nearly impossible for either MtFs or FtMs to remove all physical signs of their natal sex, residual signs of maleness in MtFs will often prevent their being regarded as unequivocally female, whereas residual signs of femaleness in FtMs will rarely prevent their being regarded as unequivocally male, assuming they also display visible signs of masculinization.

Although the SOC consider a 1-year, full-time RLE to be a requirement for genital SRS (Coleman et al., 2011), surgical candidates are only required to live in a gender role that is congruent with their gender identity, not as typical members of the other sex. The *DSM-5* diagnosis of GD is applicable to persons who want to live in some "alternative gender different from one's assigned gender" (APA, 2013, p. 452) and such an alternative gender might include elements of both male- and female-typical gender roles. Consequently, persons with GD could theoretically satisfy the SOC eligibility requirement for SRS by living part-time in their original gender role and part-time in the other gender role, effectively rendering the SOC requirement moot (Zucker et al., 2016). Nevertheless, most adults with GD who undertake a RLE typically attempt to live and present themselves full-time as members of the other sex.

Sex Reassignment Surgery   Genital SRS in males with GD yields excellent cosmetic and functional results and a high degree of patient satisfaction (Gijs & Brewaeys, 2007; Giraldo, Mora, Solano, Gonzáles, & Smith-Fernández, 2002). Because all the elements of the sex reassignment process appear to contribute to improvement of GD symptoms in MtFs (Kuiper & Cohen-Kettenis, 1988), it is difficult to determine the specific social and psychological benefits of genital SRS *per se*. In a prospective controlled study of SRS outcomes, MtF patients who received expedited SRS reported better psychosocial outcomes than did waitlist controls (Mate-Kole, Freschi, & Robin, 1990). On the other hand, Udeze et al. (2008) found no difference in pre- and post-SRS psychological adjustment in 40 MtFs, with each patient acting as her own control. Good surgical results and absence of surgical complications are associated with greater subjective satisfaction and better psychosocial outcomes after SRS in MtFs (Lawrence, 2003; Karpel et al., 2015).

Subcutaneous mastectomy with chest reconstruction is the surgical procedure that females with GD most frequently undergo, and it is arguably the most important one (Monstrey, Buncamper, Bouman, & Hoebeke, 2014). It is often performed early in the sex reassignment process, which the SOC explicitly permit. There are no entirely satisfactory genital SRS techniques available to females with GD, and some patients forego this procedure entirely. Phalloplasty using a vascularized tissue flap from the forearm is currently considered the "gold standard" genital SRS technique for FtMs (Monstrey et al., 2014). The resulting neophallus usually allows standing urination. The labia majora are typically fused to create a neoscrotum and silicone testicular prostheses are inserted. An erectile prosthesis is sometimes placed in the neophallus. Complications related to tissue necrosis, urinary leakage or obstruction, and erectile prosthesis problems are not uncommon following phalloplasty. These difficulties notwithstanding, the great majority of FtMs who undergo phalloplasty report being satisfied with the results (Wierckx et al., 2011). Barrett (1998) found no difference in psychological and social functioning between FtMs who had undergone phalloplasty several years earlier and other FtMs who had been approved for but had not yet undergone surgery. An alternative genital SRS technique for females with GD is metoidioplasty, in which the hypertrophied clitoris is used to create a microphallus (Monstrey et al., 2014); this is a much less complex surgical procedure with fewer potential complications.

Outcomes of Sex Reassignment   Most studies of outcomes of the sex reassignment process have involved MtFs who have undergone hormone therapy and genital SRS, and FtMs who have undergone hormone therapy and chest reconstruction. Nearly all such studies have concluded that sex reassignment usually results in substantial relief of GD, high levels of patient satisfaction, and generally favorable, or not worsened, psychosocial outcomes (Gijs & Brewaeys, 2007; Lawrence, 2003; Murad et al., 2010). Dhejne et al. (2014) reported that only 2.2% of Swedish transsexuals who had undergone SRS during the period 1960–2010 subsequently submitted "regret applications" for reversal of their legal sex reassignment, suggesting a low prevalence of overt regret after sex reassignment.

Factors associated with favorable outcomes of sex reassignment involving SRS include careful diagnostic screening of candidates, availability of social support, psychological stability, and freedom from surgical complications. Nevertheless, sex reassignment does not successfully solve all the problems that persons with GD face. As noted previously, Dhejne et al. (2011) found that Swedish MtFs and FtMs who had successfully completed SRS displayed higher mortality rates than age-matched controls of either sex, especially death from suicide; they were also at higher risk for suicide attempts and inpatient psychiatric hospitalization.

ETIOLOGICAL CONSIDERATIONS

It is important to recognize the limitations of current research concerning the etiology of GD and transsexualism in adults. Many studies have addressed the etiology of GD as it manifests in children. Most cases of GD in childhood, however, remit before adulthood (Drummond, Bradley, Badali-Peterson, & Zucker, 2008; Green, 1987; Singh, 2012; Wallien & Cohen-Kettenis, 2008), and many adults with GD are of the LO type and did not meet diagnostic criteria for GD during childhood. Much of the research on the etiology of GD has been conducted in males; females have received less attention. Finally, some researchers have not distinguished between androphilic and nonandrophilic males with GD, or between gynephilic and nongynephilic females with GD, even though these subtypes plausibly reflect different etiologies.

BEHAVIORAL GENETICS AND MOLECULAR GENETICS

Behavioral Genetics   Studies of the co-occurrence of behavioral traits within families and especially within monozygotic (MZ) twin pairs are the usual methods of estimating the influence of genetic factors on behavioral traits, including GD and gender non-conformity. Heylens et al. (2012) conducted an analysis of MZ and dizygotic (DZ) twin pairs in which one twin had been diagnosed with GID; among 23 pairs of MZ twins, nine pairs (39%) were concordant for GID, whereas among 21 pairs of same-sex DZ twins, none were concordant for GID, a statistically significant difference. There have also been two large studies of co-occurring transsexualism or related conditions in first-degree relatives of persons diagnosed with transsexualism. Green (2000) reported 10 instances of co-occurring transsexualism or transvestism in the siblings, parents, or children of roughly 1,500 transsexual probands. Gómez-Gil et al. (2010) reported finding 12 pairs of nontwin siblings among a sample of 995 consecutive transsexual probands; the prevalence of transsexualism in the siblings of transsexuals, 1 in 211, was much higher than the estimated prevalence in the general population.

Coolidge, Thede, and Young (2002) conducted the best-known investigation of the heritability of GID in children. They studied 96 MZ and 61 DZ twin pairs, aged 4–17 years. They assessed GID using a six-item scale based on *DSM-IV* criteria for GID, but none of the twins had been clinically diagnosed with GID. Coolidge et al. found that heritability accounted for 62% of the variance in GID scores, and nonshared environment accounted for 38%. Based on these scores, however, the prevalence of GID in the children was 2.3%, suggesting that the authors' threshold for ascertaining the GID was too low and that their heritability findings addressed childhood gender nonconformity rather than true GID. Two large twin studies that explicitly addressed the heritability of childhood gender nonconformity found different results using different methodologies. Bailey, Dunne, and Martin (2000) reported that heritability accounted for 50% of variance in recalled childhood gender nonconformity among males and 37% among females, with nonshared environment accounting for the rest. Knafo, Iervolino, and Plomin (2005) found that heritability accounted for 27% of variance in parent-reported gender atypicality in boys ages 3–4 years, with shared environment accounting for 57% and nonshared environment accounting for 16%; the comparable figures for girls were heritability 42%, shared environment 43%, and nonshared environment 15%.

Molecular Genetics   Sexual differentiation of the mammalian brain is influenced by prenatal sex hormone activity (Gooren, 2006; Savic, Garcia-Falgueras, & Swaab, 2010). Consequently, researchers have hypothesized that abnormalities in genes that code for sex hormone receptors or enzymes that catalyze the synthesis or metabolism of sex hormones might show associations with GD and transsexualism. Candidate genes include those coding for the androgen receptor (AR), estrogen receptor alpha (ERα), estrogen receptor beta (ERβ), and progesterone receptor (PR), and the enzymes aromatase (CYP19A1), 17-alpha-hydroxylase (CYP17), and 5-alpha-reductase, type II (SRD5A2). Most studies have investigated differences between transsexual patients and same-sex controls in mean repeat numbers of specific polymorphisms in candidate genes or in the frequencies of specific mutant alleles or genotypes. None of these studies have attempted to differentiate between transsexual subtypes.

Henningsson et al. (2005) found no significant differences between MtFs and male controls for the AR or CYP19A1 genes but did find a significant difference for the ERβ gene. Hare et al. (2009) examined the same three candidate genes in MtFs and male controls but obtained different results: no significant differences for the CYP19A1 or ERβ genes, but a significant difference for the AR gene, albeit using a one-tailed test (a two-tailed test would have been nonsignificant). Bentz et al. (2007) reported no differences between MtFs and male controls or FtMs and female controls for the SRD5A2 gene. Bentz et al. (2008) found no differences between MtFs and male controls for CPY17 alleles and genotypes but did find a significant difference between FtMs and female controls. Ujike et al. (2009) detected no significant differences between MtFs and male controls or FtMs and female controls for the AR, ERα, ERβ, PR, or CYP19A1 genes. Fernández et al. (2014a) described similar negative results for the AR, ERβ, and CYP19A1 genes in MtFs; however, the same investigators (Fernández et al., 2014b) reported a significant difference for the ERβ gene in FtMs. Finally, in a study of young MtFs, Lombardo et al. (2013) found no significant associated molecular mutations in candidate genes related to male sexual differentiation (AR, DAX1, SOX9, SRY, and the AZF region of Y). In summary, there is little evidence at present that abnormalities related to molecular genetics account for GD or transsexualism: Most investigations have produced negative results, and the few positive reports in the literature have not been replicated.

NEUROANATOMY AND NEUROBIOLOGY

One influential etiologic hypothesis proposes that GD may reflect abnormal sexual differentiation of the brain during early development (Savic et al., 2010), resulting in sex-atypical brain morphology, connectivity, or function. Investigators have studied these features in adult transsexuals using histologic, neuroimaging, and other techniques. Several detailed summaries of this research are available (e.g., Guillamon et al., 2016; Kreukels & Guillamon, 2016; Smith, Junger, Derntl, & Habel, 2015).

Neuroanatomy: Histological Studies Among the earliest neuroanatomic studies in transsexuals were the postmortem histologic investigations conducted by Swaab and colleagues (e.g., Garcia-Falgueras & Swaab, 2008; Kruijver et al., 2000; Zhou, Hofman, Gooren, & Swaab, 1995). They examined several limbic or hypothalamic nuclei, some of which had been reported to be sexually dimorphic. Their most influential line of research involved the central subdivision of the bed nucleus of the stria terminalis (BSTc): this structure has a larger volume and cell number in males than in females but was discovered to be sex-atypical for these parameters in the brains of six MtFs (Kruijver et al., 2000; Zhou et al., 1995). Interpretation of the Zhou/Kruijver findings was complicated by the possible effects of cross-sex hormone therapy, which all subjects had received. Hulshoff Pol et al. (2006) demonstrated using magnetic resonance imaging (MRI) that hormone therapy in MtFs was associated with significant reductions in the volume of the hypothalamus; this led them to suggest that, in the Zhou/Kruijver studies, "the altered size of the bed nucleus of the stria terminalis could have been due to the exposure of cross-sex hormones in adult life" (p. S108). Again using MRI, Schiltz et al. (2007) found that male pedophiles also had a lower than expected BST volume; noting the similar findings in MtFs, they proposed that "these alterations may not be specific to pedophilia but may rather be a feature of sexual abnormalities in general" (p. 744). Detailed information about the sexual orientation of the six Zhou/Kruijver MtFs, reported by Garcia-Falgueras and Swaab (2008), was consistent with the hypothesis that all were nonandrophilic. Consequently, a sex-reversed BSTc size and neuron number might be a marker for nonandrophilic MtF transsexualism specifically (or for paraphilic male sexuality), rather than for MtF transsexualism generally. Alternatively, the Zhou/Kruijver BSTc findings may be attributable to the effects of hormone therapy; Guillamon et al. (2016) suggested that this explanation was more probable.

Neuroanatomy: Imaging Studies Other investigators have used neuroimaging techniques to examine sexually dimorphic features in the brains of MtF and FtM transsexuals. Because cross-sex hormone therapy is capable of altering brain structure and function (Guillamon et al., 2016; Smith et al., 2015), this review focuses on studies conducted in persons who had not yet undergone hormone therapy. Gray matter in the brain consists primarily of neuronal cell bodies; females generally have larger gray matter volumes than males and typically display greater cortical thickness (CTh), an alternative measure of gray matter volume. In some studies of MtFs who were primarily nonandrophilic (Luders et al., 2009) or exclusively nonandrophilic (Savic & Arver, 2011), investigators found gray matter volumes that were largely typical for natal sex. But Simon et al. (2013) observed gray matter volumes in androphilic MtFs to be sex-atypical in several regions. In a study of CTh in a group of primarily nonandrophilic MtFs, Luders et al. (2012) observed some areas that were comparatively large and sex-atypical. Zubiaurre-Elorza et al. (2013) examined CTh in androphilic MtFs and gynephilic FtMs; they found sex-atypical values in the MtFs, but sex-typical values in the FtMs.

The few imaging studies of the putamen, a large subcortical nucleus, conducted in transsexuals have produced inconsistent results. A recent meta-analysis found that the right putamen is sexually dimorphic in humans, larger in males than in females (Ruigrok et al., 2014), but not all imaging studies in transsexuals have confirmed this in control subjects. Zubiaurre-Elorza et al. (2013), who observed the same direction of sexual dimorphism reported by Ruigrok et al. found that right putamen volume in androphilic MtFs was comparable to that in both male and female controls, but was larger in gynephilic FtMs than in female controls (i.e., more male-typical). Savic & Arver (2011), who also observed the same direction of sexual dimorphism, reported right putamen volume in nonandrophilic MtFs to be smaller than in either male or female controls. Luders et al. (2009), in contrast, found that the right putamen was larger in females than in males, and was largest of all (but in the typical female range) in a group of mostly nonandrophilic MtFs.

White matter (WM) in the brain primarily consists of myelinated nerve fibers; WM structure is usually studied using diffusion tensor imaging (DTI). This technique yields measures of fractional anisotropy (FA), an indicator of WM coherence and organization, and mean diffusivity (MD), a complementary measure, with "high MD values indicating loss of white matter integrity, while a low FA reflects the same" (Guillamon et al., 2016, p. 1618). FA values are generally higher in males than in females for most important WM structures; the pattern is reversed for MD values. Rametti et al. (2011b) observed that androphilic MtFs were intermediate between the males and females on most measures of FA and differed significantly from both. In a parallel investigation, Rametti et al. (2011a) found that gynephilic FtMs were also intermediate on most measures of FA, but more closely matched the male control group. Kranz et al. (2014b) reported that, for FA measurements, neither a group of mostly nonandrophilic MtFs nor a group of mostly gynephilic FtMs differed from either male or female controls; for MD measures, the MtFs and FtMs were intermediate between male and female controls. Using MRI, Hahn et al. (2015) investigated structural connectivity networks in the brains of these same transsexual participants; they found evidence of decreased hemispheric connectivity ratios (the ratios between inter- and intra-hemispheric connections) in subcortical limbic regions in both MtFs and FtMs, but attributable to increased inter-hemispheric connectivity in MtFs and decreased intra-hemispheric connectivity in FtMs.

Neurophysiology   A few investigators have used neuroimaging techniques to conduct neurophysiological studies of transsexuals prior to hormone therapy. Berglund, Lindström, Dhejne-Helmy, and Savic (2008) used positron emission tomography (PET) to study the effect of inhaling odorous steroid compounds on regional cerebral blood flow in the hypothalamus in nonandrophilic MtFs and male and female controls; the MtFs displayed an intermediate activation pattern. Gizewski et al. (2008) employed functional MRI (fMRI) to study patterns of cerebral activation in response to visual erotic stimuli in mostly nonandrophilic MtFs and male and female controls; they found that the MtFs' activation pattern more closely matched that of female controls. Schöning et al. (2010) utilized fMRI to examine cerebral activation patterns during a mental rotation task in MtFs (sexual orientation unspecified) and male controls. Both groups activated the classical cerebral mental rotation network, but with some between-group regional differences. Kranz et al. (2014a) used PET to study regional asymmetries in the serotonin transporter system in the brains of MtFs (androphilic and nonandrophilic in about equal numbers) and male and female controls; all three groups displayed similar regional patterns of leftward and rightward asymmetry except in the midcingulate cortex, where rightward asymmetry was observed in male controls, but not in MtFs or female controls.

Summarizing neuroanatomic and neurophysiologic studies in adults with GD, Guillamon et al. (2016) observed: "The review of the available data seems to support two existing hypotheses: (1) a brain-restricted intersexuality in . . . [androphilic] MtFs and [gynephilic] FtMs and (2) Blanchard's insight on the existence of two brain phenotypes that differentiate 'homosexual' [androphilic] and 'nonhomosexual' [nonandrophilic] MtFs" (p. 1643).

LEARNING, MODELING, AND LIFE EVENTS

Early psychoanalytic theorists viewed parenting behavior as etiologically important in GD. Stoller (1968, 1975) emphasized the importance of maternal parenting style: he believed that the mother's excessive closeness to her son ("blissful symbiosis"; Stoller, 1975, p. 37) was largely responsible for the development of transsexualism in males, whereas the mother's inability to achieve emotional closeness with an "unfeminine" daughter contributed significantly to the development of transsexualism in females. Moberly (1986) similarly proposed that transsexualism reflected a "same-sex developmental deficit" (p. 205) in which a child's inability to identify with the same-sex parent led to a defensive opposite-sex identification.

Although these psychoanalytic formulations are no longer widely accepted, parenting behavior nevertheless may be etiologically important. Zucker and Bradley (1995) observed that the mothers of boys with GD often have a history of significant psychopathology (see also Zucker et al., 2003), which is positively correlated with their reinforcement of feminine behaviors in their sons; they proposed that the mothers of boys who develop GD may be unwilling or unable to limit or discourage their sons' cross-gender behavior. Something similar may occur in girls with GD: maternal psychopathology may again be associated with an inability to limit cross-gender expression (Zucker & Bradley, 1995). Consistent with these observations, Simon, Zsolt, Fogd, and Czobor (2011) reported that, compared with nonclinical controls, adult MtFs and FtMs retrospectively described their mothers as less caring and less affectionate but more controlling. MtFs also described their mothers as more unreliable and abusive yet less demanding; they described their fathers as less caring, reliable, and available.

COGNITIVE INFLUENCES

Cognitive factors appear to play a limited role in the etiology of GD in adults. Most relevant research has focused on a few specific areas: childhood development of cognitive schemas concerning gender, cognitive comparisons of self and others during transgender coming out, and cognitive contributions to cross-gender identity formation in transvestism and nonandrophilic MtF transsexualism.

Children develop cognitive schemas concerning gender identity and gender stereotypes during early and middle childhood (Martin, Ruble, & Szkrybalo, 2002). Some children with GD develop gender schemas that include a cross-gender identity, but the reasons for this are unclear; perhaps these children observe that their behaviors and interests conform to opposite-sex gender stereotypes and mislabel themselves accordingly (Zucker & Bradley, 1995). Although such a cognitive process could explain the mechanism of cross-gender identity formation in children with GD, it does not explain the origins of the sex-atypical behaviors and interests that are the putative objects of cognitive appraisal. Moreover, most children who display gender nonconformity do not go on to experience GD in adulthood.

Cognitive comparisons of self and others concerning gender-related interests and behaviors is a recognized mechanism of identity formation and consolidation in the process of coming out for transsexuals and transgender persons. Devor (2004) observed that transgender persons typically use "a number of techniques of identity comparison to try to determine if there is an identity in which they can comfortably live their lives in their originally assigned gender and sex" (pp. 50–51). They subsequently undertake a similar cognitive process as they try to find an authentic identity within the other gender. Docter's (1988) theory of gender identity formation in transvestism and nonandrophilic MtF transsexualism stressed the importance of fully enacting the cross-gender role through complete cross-dressing and public self-presentation. Implicitly, this is a cognitive process, grounded in self-observation ("I dress and behave like a female; therefore I *am*, in some sense, female"). Docter described the process of reconciling core gender identity and the emergent cross-gender identity as an attempt to resolve cognitive dissonance. He observed that this process could lead to integration of the cross-gender identity into the existing male self-system (i.e., a revised cognitive schema) or reorganization of the self-system to give primacy to the cross-gender identity (i.e., an alternative cognitive schema).

SEX AND ETHNICITY CONSIDERATIONS

As previously noted, biologic sex is a key feature that explains much of the diversity in the phenomenology of GD. GD in adults is two or three times more common in males than in females, perhaps because autogynephilia accounts for many cases of nonandrophilic GD in males, whereas the analogous paraphilia is probably rare in females (Lawrence, 2009a, 2017). Males with GD are quite diverse with respect to sexual orientation, age at clinical presentation, and congruence between physical appearance and desired gender role; females with GD are more homogeneous with respect to these variables. Cross-sex hormone therapy is very effective in masculinizing the appearance of FtMs but is less effective in feminizing the appearance of MtFs. Genital SRS techniques for MtFs are highly refined and generally yield excellent results, whereas many FtMs forego genital SRS altogether for want of a surgical technique that is affordable, has a low rate of significant complications, and predictably yields high-quality results.

The role of ethnicity in accounting for the etiology and clinical manifestations of GD is incompletely understood, but there is a significant association between ethnicity and MtF transsexual typology across national cultures, and probably within national cultures as well. In Asian, Polynesian, and Latin American countries, most MtFs (or, at least, the cultural equivalents of MtFs) are androphilic, whereas in the United States, Canada, and most western European countries, the majority of MtFs are currently nonandrophilic (Lawrence, 2010c). Societal individualism appears to mediate the relationship between ethnicity and MtF transsexual typology: nonandrophilic MtFs are relatively more prevalent in more individualistic societies and less prevalent in less individualistic societies (Lawrence, 2010c). There is also evidence of a significant association between ethnicity and MtF transsexual typology within the United States. Hwahng and Nuttbrock (2007) reported that Black and Hispanic transgender and transsexual males in New York City were more likely than their White counterparts to be androphilic in orientation. In a subsequent, larger study of transgender and transsexual males in New York City, most of whom were Black or Hispanic, the correlation between nonandrophilic orientation and White ethnicity was 0.60 (Nuttbrock et al., 2011; see also Lawrence, 2010a). Kellogg, Clements-Nolle, Dilley, Katz, and McFarland (2001) similarly observed that, in a predominantly (71%) non-White sample of transgender and transsexual men in San Francisco, about 64% were probably androphilic, a much higher percentage than has typically been observed among predominantly White MtFs in the United States (Lawrence, 2010c).

CASE STUDY

The patient is a 58-year-old male who sought consultation because of distress related to his gender identity and dissatisfaction with his sexed body characteristics. He has a history of cross-dressing and medically unsupervised feminizing hormone use, and he is considering undergoing sex reassignment. He is a twice-married and twice-divorced father of two children from his first marriage. He is a college and business school graduate who works as a self-employed designer and manufacturer of specialized electrical equipment.

The patient was the eldest of five children in a lower middle-class family. All of his younger siblings were girls. He was never overtly feminine as a child; he enjoyed typical boys' games and rough-and-tumble play. At around 7 years old, he first became aware of cross-gender feelings, and he began to cross-dress occasionally with the help of his sisters. At age 10, his father caught him wearing his mother's undergarments and beat him, but he continued to cross-dress in secret. Beginning in adolescence, his cross-dressing was associated with sexual arousal and masturbation. As a young adult, he often wore women's undergarments beneath his male outer clothes. He felt confused and ashamed by his cross-gender feelings and the associated sexual arousal he experienced. He married his first wife at age 20; she knew that he sometimes cross-dressed, but they never talked about it. During the marriage, he would occasionally go out in the evenings dressed as a woman. He needed to fantasize that he was a woman in order to achieve sufficient sexual arousal to permit coitus with his wife.

After 18 years of marriage, he and his wife underwent a bitter divorce that left him with little contact with his two children. He married again at age 45 and continued to cross-dress in secret. His wife was aware that he had gender issues, but again they never discussed it. They divorced after 8 years of marriage. He briefly resumed cross-dressing in public and also began sporadic self-treatment with estrogen and antiandrogens, obtained via the Internet. He later stopped cross-dressing publicly so as not to jeopardize his business and his employees if he were discovered. He stated that he would like to take medically prescribed hormone therapy and live full-time as a woman. He doubted, however, that he could preserve his relationships with his business suppliers and customers, some of whom were culturally conservative foreign nationals, if he were to undergo complete sex reassignment. He said that he believed he was a very feminine person inside: he noted that he cried easily, disliked violent movies, and related to children and animals in what he considered an unmasculine way.

Assessment involved a detailed psychological and social history, as well as administration of the MMPI-2. Based on the information obtained, the patient met full *DSM-5* diagnostic criteria for GD: he experienced a marked incongruence between his gender identification and his sex of assignment, resulting in a desire to acquire the primary and secondary sex characteristics of the other sex and to assume a gender role different from that of his assigned gender. He also experienced clinically significant distress and disability because of this incongruence. His GD was of the nonandrophilic, LO type, in that he was sexually attracted only to females and had not met full diagnostic criteria for GD during childhood. A secondary diagnosis was transvestic disorder with autogynephilia, based on his history of intense sexual arousal with cross-dressing, including arousal from the thought or image of himself as female, associated with clinically significant distress.

The patient was referred to a physician for cross-sex hormone therapy and underwent regular psychotherapy for approximately 2 years. These treatments were associated with significant reduction in the patient's GD-related distress. The patient gradually transitioned to a female-typical gender role and social presentation in most domains of life, facilitated by a name change to a female-typical first name and a legal gender change. In a few domains of life, primarily in her business affairs, the patient chose to present herself as an androgynous male rather than unambiguously as a female. Her decision appeared to reflect both pragmatic considerations and the fact that she genuinely valued and enjoyed enacting some elements of the traditional male gender role in business settings.

She was referred to a surgeon for SRS, which she successfully underwent. The therapist's referral letter made it clear that the patient had not been living full-time in a female-typical gender role, but part-time in a female-typical role and part-time as an androgynous male. The therapist explained that WPATH SOC (Coleman et al., 2011) do not require candidates for SRS to live full-time in a cross-gender role, but only "in a gender role that is congruent with their gender identity" (p. 178). The therapist expressed the opinion that the patient had fulfilled both the letter and the spirit of this requirement. The patient's surgeon and her health insurance provider agreed that the patient had complied with the WPATH SOC and were willing to perform SRS and provide insurance coverage for the procedure.

SUMMARY

Gender dysphoria refers to severe discomfort with one's biologic sex or assigned gender, reflecting a marked incongruence between one's gender identity and assigned sex. Biologic sex (male vs. female), sexual orientation, and age of onset define GD subtypes that differ in clinical presentation. Possible outcomes of GD include acceptance of assigned gender, part-time cross-gender expression, or sex reassignment and full-time cross-gender living. Individual and group psychotherapy can benefit some persons with GD. Treatment with cross-sex hormone therapy and SRS can provide significant relief of GD, high levels of patient satisfaction, and favorable psychosocial outcomes.

REFERENCES

Ahlers, C. J., Schaefer, G. A., Mundt, I. A., Roll, S., Englert, H., Willich, S. N., & Beier, K. M. (2011). How unusual are the contents of paraphilias? Paraphilia-associated sexual arousal patterns in a community-based sample of men. *Journal of Sexual Medicine, 8*, 1362–1370.

Alonso, J., & Lépine, J.-P. (2007). Overview of key data from the European Study of the Epidemiology of Mental Disorders (ESEMeD). *Journal of Clinical Psychiatry, 68*(Suppl. 2), 3–9.

American Psychiatric Association. (1980). *Diagnostic and statistical manual of mental disorders* (3rd ed.). Washington, DC: Author.

American Psychiatric Association. (1987). *Diagnostic and statistical manual of mental disorders* (3rd ed., rev.) Washington, DC: Author.

American Psychiatric Association. (1994). *Diagnostic and statistical manual of mental disorders* (4th ed.). Washington, DC: Author.

American Psychiatric Association. (2000). *Diagnostic and statistical manual of mental disorders* (4th ed., text rev.). Washington, DC: Author.

American Psychiatric Association. (2013). *Diagnostic and statistical manual of mental disorders* (5th ed.). Arlington, VA: American Psychiatric Publishing.

Arcelus, J., Bouman, W. P., Van Den Noortgate, W., Claes, L., Witcomb, G., & Fernandez-Aranda, F. (2015). Systematic review and meta-analysis of prevalence studies in transsexualism. *European Psychiatry, 30*, 807–815.

Asscheman, H., Giltay, E. J., Megens, J. A., de Ronde, W. P., van Trotsenburg, M. A., & Gooren, L. J. (2011). A long-term follow-up study of mortality in transsexuals receiving treatment with cross-sex hormones. *European Journal of Endocrinology, 164*, 635–642.

Auer, M. K., Fuss, J., Stalla, G. K., & Athanasoulia, A. P. (2013). Twenty years of endocrinologic treatment in transsexualism: Analyzing the role of chromosomal analysis and hormonal profiling in the diagnostic work-up. *Fertility and Sterility, 100*, 1103–1110.

Baba, T., Endo, T., Honnma, H., Kitajima, Y., Hayashi, T., Ikeda, H., . . . Saito, T. (2007). Association between polycystic ovary syndrome and female-to-male transsexuality. *Human Reproduction, 22*, 1011–1016.

Baba, T., Endo, T., Ikeda, K., Shimizu, A., Honnma, H., Ikeda, H., . . . Saito, T. (2011). Distinctive features of female-to-male transsexualism and prevalence of gender identity disorder in Japan. *Journal of Sexual Medicine, 8*, 1686–1693.

Bailey, J. M., Dunne, M. P., & Martin, N. G. (2000). Genetic and environmental influences on sexual orientation and its correlates in an Australian twin sample. *Journal of Personality and Social Psychology, 78*, 524–536.

Baltieri, A., & De Andrade, A. G. (2009). Schizophrenia modifying the expression of gender identity disorder. *Journal of Sexual Medicine, 6*, 1185–1118.

Baron-Cohen, S. (2002). The extreme male brain theory of autism. *Trends in Cognitive Science, 6*, 248–254.

Barrett, J. (1998). Psychological and social function before and after phalloplasty. *International Journal of Transgenderism, 2*(1).

Bearman, G. (2007). Karyotyping and genetics in the transgendered population. In R. Ettner, Monstrey, & A. E. Eyler (Eds.), *Principles of transgender medicine and surgery* (pp. 223–233). Binghamton, NY: Haworth Press.

Beek, T. F., Kreukels, B. P., Cohen-Kettenis, P. T., & Steensma, T. D. (2015). Partial treatment requests and underlying motives of applicants for gender affirming interventions. *Journal of Sexual Medicine, 12*, 2201–2205.

Benjamin, H. (1966). *The transsexual phenomenon.* New York: Julian Press.

Bentz, E. K., Hefler, L. A., Kaufmann, U., Huber, J. C., Kolbus, A., & Tempfer, C. B. (2008). A polymorphism of the CYP17 gene related to sex steroid metabolism is associated with female-to-male but not male-to-female transsexualism. *Fertility and Sterility, 90*, 56–59.

Bentz, E. K., Schneeberger, C., Hefler, L. A., van Trotsenburg, M., Kaufmann, U., Huber, J. C., & Tempfer, C. B. (2007). A common polymorphism of the SRD5A2 gene and transsexualism. *Reproductive Science, 14*, 705–709.

Berglund, H., Lindström, P., Dhejne-Helmy, C., & Savic, I. (2008). Male-to-female transsexuals show sex-atypical hypothalamus activation when smelling odorous steroids. *Cerebral Cortex, 18*, 1900–1908.

Blanchard, R. (1985). Typology of male-to-female transsexualism. *Archives of Sexual Behavior, 14*, 247–261.

Blanchard, R. (1988). Nonhomosexual gender dysphoria. *Journal of Sex Research, 24*, 188–193.

Blanchard, R. (1989a). The classification and labeling of nonhomosexual gender dysphorias. *Archives of Sexual Behavior, 18*, 315–334.

Blanchard, R. (1989b). The concept of autogynephilia and the typology of male gender dysphoria. *Journal of Nervous and Mental Disease, 177*, 616–623.

Blanchard, R. (1990). Gender identity disorders in adult men. In R. Blanchard & B. Steiner (Eds.), *Clinical management of gender identity disorders in children and adults* (pp. 49–76). Washington, DC: American Psychiatric Press.

Blanchard, R. (1993a). Partial versus complete autogynephilia and gender dysphoria. *Journal of Sex & Marital Therapy, 19*, 301–307.

Blanchard, R. (1993b). The she-male phenomenon and the concept of partial autogynephilia. *Journal of Sex & Marital Therapy, 19*, 69–76.

Blanchard, R. (1993c). Varieties of autogynephilia and their relationship to gender dysphoria. *Archives of Sexual Behavior, 22*, 241–251.

Blanchard, R. (1994). A structural equation model for age at clinical presentation in non-homosexual male gender dysphorics. *Archives of Sexual Behavior, 23*, 311–320.

Blanchard, R. (2010). The DSM diagnostic criteria for transvestic fetishism. *Archives of Sexual Behavior, 39*, 363–372.

Blanchard, R., Clemmensen, L. H., & Steiner, B. W. (1987). Heterosexual and homosexual gender dysphoria. *Archives of Sexual Behavior, 16*, 139–152.

Blanchard, R., Racansky, I. G., & Steiner, B. W. (1986). Phallometric detection of fetishistic arousal in heterosexual male cross-dressers. *Journal of Sex Research, 22*, 452–462.

Bockting, W. O. (2008). Psychotherapy and the real-life experience: From gender dichotomy to gender diversity. *Sexologies, 17*, 211–224.

Bolin, A. (1988). *In search of Eve: Transsexual rites of passage*. New York, NY: Bergin & Garvey.

Bower, H. (2001). The gender identity disorders in the DSM-IV classification: A critical evaluation. *Australian and New Zealand Journal of Psychiatry, 35*, 1–8.

Brown, G. R., & Jones, K. T. (2016). Mental health and medical health disparities in 5135 transgender veterans receiving healthcare in the Veterans Health Administration: A case-control study. *LGBT Health, 3*, 122–131.

Buhrich, N., & McConaghy, N. (1977). Can fetishism occur in transsexuals? *Archives of Sexual Behavior, 6*, 223–235.

Butcher, J. N., Graham, J. R., Ben-Porath, Y. S., Telligen, A., Dahlstrom, W. G., & Kaemmer, B. (2001). *MMPI-2 (Minnesota Multiphasic Personality Inventory-2) manual for administration, scoring, and interpretation* (rev. ed.). Minneapolis: University of Minnesota Press.

Byne, W., Bradley, S. J., Coleman, E., Eyler, A. E., Green, R., Menvielle, E. J., . . . Tompkins, D. A. (2012). Report of the American Psychiatric Association Task Force on Treatment of Gender Identity Disorder. *Archives of Sexual Behavior, 41*, 759–796.

Carroll, R. A. (1999). Outcomes of treatment for gender dysphoria. *Journal of Sex Education and Therapy, 24*, 128–136.

Caspi, A., Houts, R. M., Belsky, D. W., Goldman-Mellor, S. J., Harrington, H., Israel, S., . . . Moffit, T. E. (2014). The p factor: One general psychopathology factor in the structure of psychiatric disorders? *Clinical Psychological Science, 2*, 119–137.

Chivers, M. L., & Bailey, J. M. (2000). Sexual orientation of female-to-male transsexuals: A comparison of homosexual and nonhomosexual types. *Archives of Sexual Behavior, 29*, 259–278.

Cohen-Kettenis, P. T., & Pfäfflin, F. (2010). The DSM diagnostic criteria for gender identity disorder in adolescents and adults. *Archives of Sexual Behavior, 39*, 499–513.

Coleman, E., Bockting, W., Botzer, M., Cohen-Kettenis, P., De Cuypere, G., Feldman, J., . . . Zucker, K. (2011). Standards of care for the health of transsexual, transgender, and gender-nonconforming people, version 7. *International Journal of Transgenderism, 13*, 65–232.

Colizzi, M., Costa, R., & Todarello, O. (2014). Transsexual patients' psychiatric comorbidity and positive effect of cross-sex hormonal treatment on mental health: Results from a longitudinal study. *Psychoneuroendocrinology, 39*, 65–73.

Coolidge, F. L., Thede, L. L., & Young, S. E. (2002). The heritability of gender identity disorder in a child and adolescent twin sample. *Behavior Genetics, 32*, 251–257.

Conron, K. J., Scott, G., Stowell, G. S., & Landers, S. J. (2012). Transgender health in Massachusetts: Results from a household probability sample of adults. *American Journal of Public Health, 102*, 118–122.

Costantino, A., Cerpolini, S., Alvisi, S., Morselli, P. G., Venturoli, S., & Meriggiola, M. C. (2013). A prospective study on sexual function and mood in female-to-male transsexuals during testosterone administration and after sex reassignment surgery. *Journal of Sex & Marital Therapy*, *39*, 321–335.

Crissman, H. P., Berger, M. B., Graham, L. F., & Dalton, V. K. (2017). Transgender demographics: A household probability sample of US adults, 2014. *American Journal of Public Health*, *107*, 213–215.

Davidmann, S. (2010). Beyond borders: Lived experiences of atypically gendered transsexual people. In S. Hines & T. Sanger (Eds.), *Transgender identities: Towards a social analysis of gender diversity* (pp. 186–203). New York, NY: Routledge.

De Cuypere, G., Van Hemelrijck, M., Michel, A., Carael, B., Heylens, G., Rubens, R., . . . Monstrey, S. (2007). Prevalence and demography of transsexualism in Belgium. *European Psychiatry*, *22*, 137–141.

Deogracias, J. J., Johnson, L. L., Meyer-Bahlburg, H. F. L., Kessler, S. J., Schober, J. M., & Zucker, K. J. (2007). The Gender Identity/Gender Dysphoria Questionnaire for Adolescents and Adults. *Journal of Sex Research*, *44*, 370–379.

Dessens, A. B., Slijper, F. M., & Drop, S. L. (2005). Gender dysphoria and gender change in chromosomal females with congenital adrenal hyperplasia. *Archives of Sexual Behavior*, *34*, 389–397.

Devor, A. H. (2004). Witnessing and mirroring: A fourteen stage model of transsexual identity formation. *Journal of Gay & Lesbian Psychotherapy*, *8*(1/2), 41–67.

Dhejne, C., Lichtenstein, P., Boman, M., Johansson, A. L., Långström, N., & Landén, M. (2011). Long-term follow-up of transsexual persons undergoing sex reassignment surgery: Cohort study in Sweden. *PLoS One*, *6*, e16885.

Dhejne, C., Oberg, K., Arver, S., & Landén, M. (2014). An analysis of all applications for sex reassignment surgery in Sweden, 1960–2010: Prevalence, incidence, and regrets. *Archives of Sexual Behavior*, *43*, 1535–1545.

Docter, R. F. (1988). *Transvestites and transsexuals: Toward a theory of cross-gender behavior*. New York, NY: Plenum Press.

Docter, R. F., & Prince, V. (1997). Transvestism: A survey of 1032 cross-dressers. *Archives of Sexual Behavior*, *26*, 589–605.

Drummond, K. D., Bradley, S. J., Badali-Peterson, M., & Zucker, K. J. (2008). A follow-up study of girls with gender identity disorder. *Developmental Psychology*, *44*, 34–45.

Fernández, R., Esteva, I., Gómez-Gil, E., Rumbo, T., Almaraz, M. C., Roda, E., . . . Pásaro E. (2014a). Association study of *ERβ*, *AR*, and *CYP19A1* genes and MtF transsexualism. *Journal of Sexual Medicine*, *11*, 2986–2994.

Fernández, R., Esteva, I., Gómez-Gil, E., Rumbo, T., Almaraz, M. C., Roda, E., . . . Pásaro E. (2014b). The (CA)n polymorphism of *ERβ* gene is associated with FtM transsexualism. *Journal of Sexual Medicine*, *11*, 720–728.

Fisher, A. D., Bandini, E., Casale, H., Ferruccio, N., Meriggiola, M. C., Gualerzi, A., . . . Maggi, M. (2013). Sociodemographic and clinical features of gender identity disorder: An Italian multicentric evaluation. *Journal of Sexual Medicine*, *10*, 408–419.

Fisk, N. (1974a). Gender dysphoria syndrome: The conceptualization that liberalizes indications for total gender reorientation and implies a broadly based multi-dimensional rehabilitative regimen [editorial comment]. *Western Journal of Medicine*, *120*, 386–391.

Fisk, N. (1974b). Gender dysphoria syndrome (the how, what, and why of a disease). In D. R. Laub & P. Gandy (Eds.), *Proceedings of the Second Interdisciplinary Symposium on Gender Dysphoria Syndrome* (pp. 7–14). Stanford, CA: Stanford University Press.

Freund, K. (1985). Cross gender identity in a broader context. In B. W. Steiner (Ed.), *Gender dysphoria: Development, research, management* (pp. 259–324). New York: Plenum Press.

Freund, K., & Blanchard, R. (1993). Erotic target location errors in male gender dysphorics, paedophiles, and fetishists. *British Journal of Psychiatry*, *162*, 558–563.

Gagne, P., Tewksbury, R., & McGaughey, D. (1997). Coming out and crossing over: Identity formation and proclamation in a transgender community. *Gender & Society, 11,* 478–508.

Gaither, T. W., Awad, M. A., Osterberg, E. C., Romero, A., Bowers, M. L., & Breyer, B. N. (2017). Impact of sexual orientation identity on medical morbidities in male-to-female transgender patients. *LGBT Health, 4,* 11–16.

Garcia-Falgueras, A., & Swaab, D. F. (2008). A sex difference in the hypothalamic uncinate nucleus: Relationship to gender identity. *Brain, 131,* 3132–3146.

Gijs, L., & Brewaeys, A. (2007). Surgical treatment of gender dysphoria in adults and adolescents: Recent developments, effectiveness, and challenges. *Annual Review of Sex Research, 18,* 178–224.

Giraldo, F., Mora, M. J., Solano, A., Gonzáles, C., & Smith-Fernández, V. (2002). Male perineogenital anatomy and clinical applications in genital reconstructions and male-to-female sex reassignment surgery. *Plastic and Reconstructive Surgery, 109,* 1301–1310.

Gizewski, E. R., Krause, E., Schlamann, M., Happich, F., Ladd, M. E., Forsting, M., & Senf, W. (2008). Specific cerebral activation due to visual erotic stimuli in male-to-female transsexuals compared with male and female controls: An fMRI study. *Journal of Sexual Medicine, 6,* 440–448.

Gómez-Gil, E., Zubiaurre-Elorza, L., Esteva, I., Guillamon, A., Godás, T., Cruz Almaraz, M., . . . Salamero, M. (2012). Hormone-treated transsexuals report less social distress, anxiety and depression. *Psychoneuroendocrinology, 37,* 66–670.

Gómez-Gil, E., Esteva, I., Almaraz, M. C., Pasaro, E., Segovia, S., & Guillamon, A. (2010). Familiality of gender identity disorder in non-twin siblings. *Archives of Sexual Behavior, 39,* 546–552.

Gómez-Gil, E., Trilla, A., Salamero, M., Godás, T., & Valdés, M. (2009). Sociodemographic, clinical, and psychiatric characteristics of transsexuals from Spain. *Archives of Sexual Behavior, 41,* 378–392.

Gómez-Gil, E., Vidal-Hagemeijer, A., & Salamero, M. (2008). MMPI-2 characteristics of transsexuals requesting sex reassignment: Comparison of patients in prehormonal and presurgical phases. *Journal of Personality Assessment, 90,* 368–374.

Gooren, L. (2006). The biology of human psychosexual differentiation. *Hormones and Behavior, 50,* 589–601.

Gorin-Lazard, A., Baumstarck, K., Boyer, L., Maquigneau, A., Gebleux, S., Penochet, J. C, . . . Bonierbale, M. (2012). Is hormonal therapy associated with better quality of life in transsexuals? A cross-sectional study. *Journal of Sexual Medicine, 9,* 531–41.

Gorin-Lazard, A., Baumstarck, K., Boyer, L., Maquigneau, A., Penochet, J.-C, Pringuey, D., . . . Auquier, P. (2013). Hormonal therapy is associated with better self-esteem, mood, and quality of life in transsexuals. *Journal of Nervous and Mental Disease, 201,* 996–1000.

Green, R. (1969). Mythological, historical, and cross-cultural aspects of transsexualism. In R. Green & J. Money (Eds.), *Transsexualism and sex reassignment* (pp. 13–22). Baltimore, MD: Johns Hopkins Press.

Green, R. (1987). *The "sissy boy syndrome" and the development of homosexuality.* New Haven, CT: Yale University Press.

Green, R. (2000). Family cooccurrence of "gender dysphoria": Ten sibling or parent-child pairs. *Archives of Sexual Behavior, 29,* 499–507.

Guillamon, A., Junque, C., & Gómez-Gil, E. (2016). A review of the status of brain structure research in transsexualism. *Archives of Sexual Behavior, 45,* 1615–1648.

Haberman, M., Hollingsworth, F., Falek, A., & Michael, R. P. (1975). Gender identity confusion, schizophrenia and a 47 XYY karyotype: A case report. *Psychoneuroendocrinology, 1,* 207–209.

Habermeyer, E., Kamps, I., & Kawohl, W. (2003). A case of bipolar psychosis and transsexualism. *Psychopathology, 36,* 168–170.

Hahn, A., Kranz, G. S., Küblböck, M., Kaufmann, U., Ganger, S., Hummer, A., . . . Lanzenberger, R. (2015). Structural connectivity networks of transgender people. *Cerebral Cortex, 25,* 3527–3534.

Hare, L., Bernard, P., Sánchez, F. J., Baird, P. N., Vilain, E., Kennedy, T., & Harley, V. R. (2009). Androgen receptor repeat length polymorphism associated with male-to-female transsexualism. *Biological Psychiatry, 65,* 93–96.

Harper, C. (2007). *Intersex.* New York: Berg.

Heck, N. C. (2017). Group psychotherapy with transgender and gender nonconforming adults: Evidence-based practice applications. *Psychiatric Clinics of North America, 40,* 157–175.

Hembree, W. C., Cohen-Kettenis, P., Delemarre-van de Waal, H. A., Gooren, L. J., Meyer, W. J., Spack, N. P., . . . Montori, V. M. (2009). Endocrine treatment of transsexual persons: An Endocrine Society clinical practice guideline. *Journal of Clinical Endocrinology and Metabolism, 94,* 3132–3154.

Henningsson, S., Westberg, L., Nilsson, S., Lundström, B., Ekselius, L., Bodlund, O., . . . Landén, M. (2005). Sex steroid-related genes and male-to-female transsexualism. *Psychoneuroendocrinology, 30,* 657–664.

Hepp, U., Kraemer, B., Schnyder, U., Miller, N., & Delsignore, A. (2005). Psychiatric comorbidity in gender identity disorder. *Journal of Psychosomatic Research, 58,* 259–261.

Heylens, G., De Cuypere, G., Zucker, K. J., Schelfaut, C., Elaut, E., Vanden Bossche, H., . . . T'Sjoen, G. (2012). Gender identity disorder in twins: A review of the case report literature. *Journal of Sexual Medicine, 9,* 751–757.

Heylens, G., Elaut, E., Kreukels, B. P., Paap, M. C., Cerwenka, S., Richter-Appelt, H., . . . De Cuypere, G. (2014). Psychiatric characteristics in transsexual individuals: Multicentre study in four European countries. *British Journal of Psychiatry, 204,* 151–156.

Hirschfeld, M. (1991). *Transvestites: The erotic drive to cross-dress* (M. A. Lombardi-Nash, Trans.). Buffalo, NY: Prometheus Books. (Original work published 1910).

Hulshoff Pol, H. E., Cohen-Kettenis, P. T., Van Haren, N. E., Peper, J. S., Brans, R. G., Cahn, W., . . . Kahn, R. S. (2006). Changing your sex changes your brain: Influences of testosterone and estrogen on adult human brain structure. *European Journal of Endocrinology, 155*(Suppl. 1), S107–S114.

Hwahng, J. S., & Nuttbrock, L. (2007). Sex workers, fem queens, and cross-dressers: Differential marginalizations and HIV vulnerabilities among three ethnocultural male-to-female transgender communities in New York City. *Sexuality Research & Social Policy, 4*(4), 36–59.

Inoubli, A., De Cuypere, G., Rubens, R., Heylens, G., Elaut, E., Van Caenegem, E., . . . T'Sjoen, G. (2011). Karyotyping, is it worthwhile in transsexualism? *Journal of Sexual Medicine, 8,* 475–478.

Johnson, T. W., Brett, M. A., Roberts, L. F., & Wassersug, R. J. (2007). Eunuchs in contemporary society: Characterizing men who are voluntarily castrated (part I). *Journal of Sexual Medicine, 4,* 930–945.

Johnson, T. W., & Wassersug, R. J. (2010). Gender identity disorder outside the binary: When gender identity disorder-not otherwise specified is not good enough [Letter to the Editor]. *Archives of Sexual Behavior, 39,* 597–598.

Jones, R. M., Wheelwright, S., Farrell, K., Martin E., Green, R., Di Ceglie, D., & Baron-Cohen, S. (2012). Brief report: Female-to- male transsexual people and autistic traits. *Journal of Autism and Developmental Disorders, 42,* 301–306.

Jordan-Young, R. M. (2012). Hormones, context, and "brain gender": A review of evidence from congenital adrenal hyperplasia. *Social Science & Medicine, 74,* 1738–1744.

Judge, C., O'Donovan, C., Callaghan, G., Gaoatswe, G., & O'Shea, D. (2014). Gender dysphoria – prevalence and co-morbidities in an Irish adult population. *Frontiers in Endocrinology, 5,* 87.

Karpel, L., Gardel, B., Revol, M., Brémont-Weil, C., Ayoubi, J.-M., & Cordier, B. (2015). Bien-être psychosocial postopératoire de 207 transsexuels (Psychological and sexual well-being of 207 transsexuals after sex reassignment in France). *Annales Médico-Psychologiques, 173,* 511–519.

Kellogg, T. A., Clements-Nolle, K., Dilley, J., Katz, M. H., & McFarland, W. (2001). Incidence of human immunodeficiency virus among male-to-female transgendered persons in San Francisco. *Journal of Acquired Immune Deficiency Syndromes, 28,* 380–384.

Kersting, A., Reutemann, M., Gast, U., Ohrmann, P., Suslow, T., Michael, N., & Arolt, V. (2003). Dissociative disorders and traumatic childhood experiences in transsexuals. *Journal of Nervous and Mental Disease, 191,* 182–189.

Kessler, S. J., & McKenna, W. (1978). *Gender: An ethnomethodological approach.* Chicago, IL: University of Chicago Press.

Knafo, A., Iervolino, A. C., & Plomin. R. (2005). Masculine girls and feminine boys: Genetic and environmental contributions to atypical gender development in early childhood. *Journal of Personality and Social Psychology, 88,* 400–412.

Krafft-Ebing, R. (1965). *Psychopathia sexualis* (F. S. Klaf, Trans.). New York, NY: Stein and Day (original work published 1903).

Kranz, G. S., Hahn, A., Baldinger, P., Haeusler, D., Philippe, C., Kaufmann, U., . . . Lanzenberger, R. (2014a). Cerebral serotonin transporter asymmetry in females, males and male-to-female transsexuals measured by PET in vivo. *Brain Structure & Function, 219,* 171–183.

Kranz, G. S., Hahn, A., Kaufmann, U., Küblböck, M., Hummer, A., Ganger, S., . . . Lanzenberger, R. (2014b). White matter microstructure in transsexuals and controls investigated by diffusion tensor imaging. *Journal of Neuroscience, 34,* 15466–15475.

Kreukels, B. P., & Guillamon, A. (2016). Neuroimaging studies in people with gender incongruence. *International Review of Psychiatry, 28,* 120–128.

Kruijver, F. P., Zhou, J. N., Pool, C. W., Hofman, M. A., Gooren, L. J., & Swaab, D. F. (2000). Male-to-female transsexuals have female neuron numbers in a limbic nucleus. *Journal of Clinical Endocrinology and Metabolism, 85,* 2034–2041.

Kuiper, B., & Cohen-Kettenis, P. T. (1988). Sex reassignment surgery: A study of 141 Dutch transsexuals. *Archives of Sexual Behavior, 17,* 439–457.

Kuyper, L., & Wijsen, C. (2014). Gender identities and gender dysphoria in the Netherlands. *Archives of Sexual Behavior, 43,* 377–385.

Landén, M., Wålinder, J., & Lundström, B. (1996). Prevalence, incidence, and sex ratio of transsexualism. *Acta Psychiatrica Scandinavica, 93,* 221–223.

Långström, N., & Zucker, K. J. (2005). Transvestic fetishism in the general population: Prevalence and correlates. *Journal of Sex & Marital Therapy, 31,* 87–95.

Laub, D. R., & Fisk, N. M. (1974). A rehabilitation program for gender dysphoria syndrome by surgical sex change. *Plastic and Reconstructive Surgery, 53,* 388–403.

Lawrence, A. A. (2003). Factors associated with satisfaction or regret following male-to-female sex reassignment surgery. *Archives of Sexual Behavior, 32,* 299–315.

Lawrence, A. A. (2005). Sexuality before and after male-to-female sex reassignment surgery. *Archives of Sexual Behavior, 34,* 147–166.

Lawrence, A. A. (2007). Becoming what we love: Autogynephilic transsexualism conceptualized as an expression of romantic love. *Perspectives in Biology and Medicine, 50,* 506–520.

Lawrence, A. A. (2009a). Erotic target location errors: An underappreciated paraphilic dimension. *Journal of Sex Research, 46,* 194–215.

Lawrence, A. A. (2009b). Transgenderism in nonhomosexual males as a paraphilic phenomenon: Implications for case conceptualization and treatment. *Sexual and Relationship Therapy, 24,* 188–206.

Lawrence, A. A. (2010a). A validation of Blanchard's typology: Comment on Nuttbrock et al. (2010) [Letter to the Editor]. *Archives of Sexual Behavior, 39,* 1011–1015.

Lawrence, A. A. (2010b). Sexual orientation versus age of onset as bases for typologies (subtypes) of gender identity disorder in adolescents and adults. *Archives of Sexual Behavior, 39,* 514–545.

Lawrence, A. A. (2010c). Societal individualism predicts prevalence of nonhomosexual orientation in male-to-female transsexualism. *Archives of Sexual Behavior, 39*, 573–583.

Lawrence, A. A. (2013). *Men trapped in men's bodies: Narratives of autogynephilic transsexualism.* New York: Springer.

Lawrence, A. A. (2017). Autogynephilia and the typology of male-to-female transsexualism: Concepts and controversies. *European Psychologist, 22*, 39–54.

Levine, S. B. (1993). Gender-disturbed males. *Journal of Sex & Marital Therapy, 19*, 131–141.

Lewins, F. (1995). *Transsexualism in society: A sociology of male-to-female transsexuals.* South Melbourne, Australia: MacMillan Education Australia.

Lombardo, F., Toselli, L., Grassetti, D., Paoli, D., Masciandaro, P., Valentini, F., . . . Gandini, L. (2013). Hormone and genetic study in male to female transsexual patients. *Journal of Endocrinological Investigation, 36*, 550–557.

Lothstein, L. M. (1979). The aging gender dysphoria (transsexual) patient. *Archives of Sexual Behavior, 8*, 431–444.

Lothstein, L. M. (1984). Psychological testing with transsexuals: A 30-year review. *Journal of Personality Assessment, 48*, 500–507.

Luders, E., Sánchez, F. J., Gaser, C., Toga, A. W., Narr, K. L., Hamilton, L. S., & Vilain, E. (2009). Regional gray matter variation in male-to-female transsexualism. *NeuroImage, 46*, 904–907.

Luders, E., Sánchez, F. J., Tosun, D., Shattuck, D. W., Gaser, C., Vilain, E., & Toga, A. W. (2012). Increased cortical thickness in male-to-female transsexualism. *Journal of Behavioral and Brain Science, 2*, 357–362.

Madeddu, F., Prunas, A., & Hartmann, D. (2009). Prevalence of Axis II disorders in a sample of clients undertaking psychiatric evaluation for sex reassignment surgery. *Psychiatric Quarterly, 80*, 261–267.

Manderson, L., & Kumar, S. (2001). Gender identity disorder as a rare manifestation of schizophrenia. *Australian and New Zealand Journal of Psychiatry, 35*, 546–547.

Marks, I., Green, R., & Mataix-Cols, D. (2000). Adult gender identity disorder can remit. *Comprehensive Psychiatry, 41*, 273–275.

Martin, C. L., Ruble, D. N., & Szkrybalo, J. (2002). Cognitive theories of early gender development. *Psychological Bulletin, 128*, 903–933.

Martin, H., & Finn, S. E. (2010). *Masculinity and femininity in the MMPI-2 and MMPI-A.* Minneapolis: University of Minnesota Press.

Mate-Kole, C., Freschi, M., & Robin, A. (1990). A controlled study of psychological and social change after surgical gender reassignment in selected male transsexuals. *British Journal of Psychiatry, 157*, 261–264.

Mazur, T. (2005). Gender dysphoria and gender change in androgen insensitivity or micropenis. *Archives of Sexual Behavior, 34*, 411–421.

Mazur, T., Colsman, M., & Sandberg, D. E. (2007). Intersex: Definition, examples, gender stability, and the case against merging with transsexualism. In R. Ettner, S. Monstrey, & A. E. Eyler (Eds.), *Principles of transgender medicine and surgery* (pp. 235–259). Binghamton, NY: Haworth Press.

Meyer, I. H. (2003). Prejudice, social stress, and mental health in lesbian, gay, and bisexual populations: Conceptual issues and research evidence. *Psychological Bulletin, 129*, 674–697.

Meyerowitz, J. (2002). *How sex changed: A history of transsexuality in the United States.* Cambridge, MA: Harvard University Press.

Moberly, E. R. (1986). Attachment and separation: The implications for gender identity and for the structuralization of the self: A theoretical model for transsexualism, and homosexuality. *Psychiatric Journal of the University of Ottawa, 11*, 205–209.

Modestin, J., & Ebner, G. (1995). Multiple personality disorder manifesting itself under the mask of transsexualism. *Psychopathology, 28*, 317–321.

Monstrey, S. J., Buncamper, M., Bouman, M.-B., & Hoebeke, P. (2014). Surgical interventions for gender dysphoria. In B. P. C. Kreukels, T. D. Steensma, & A. L. C. de Vries (Eds.), *Gender dysphoria and disorders of sex development: Progress in care and knowledge* (pp. 299–318). New York: Springer.

Mueller, A., Gooren, L. J., Naton-Schöotz, S., Cupisti, S., Beckmann, M., & Dittrich, R. (2008). Prevalence of polycystic ovary syndrome and hyperandrogenemia in female-to-male transsexuals. *Journal of Clinical Endocrinology and Metabolism, 93,* 1408–1411.

Murad, M. H., Elamin, M. B., Garcia, M. A., Mullan, R. J., Murad, A., Erwin, P. J., & Montori, V. M. (2010). Hormonal therapy and sex reassignment: A systematic review and meta-analysis of quality of life and psychosocial outcomes. *Clinical Endocrinology, 72,* 214–231.

Nieder, T. O., Herff, M., Cerwenka, S., Preuss, W. F., Cohen-Kettenis, P. T., De Cuypere, G., . . . Richter-Appelt, H. (2011). Age of onset and sexual orientation in transsexual males and females. *Journal of Sexual Medicine, 8,* 783–791.

Nuttbrock, L., Bockting, W. O., Mason, M., Hwahng, S., Rosenblum, A., Macri, M., & Becker, J. (2011). A further assessment of Blanchard's typology of homosexual versus non-homosexual or autogynephilic gender dysphoria. *Archives of Sexual Behavior, 40,* 247–257.

Pascoe, E. A., & Smart Richman, L. (2009). Perceived discrimination and health: A meta-analytic review. *Psychological Bulletin, 135,* 531–554.

Pasterski, V., Gilligan, L., & Curtis, R. (2014). Traits of autism spectrum disorders in adults with gender dysphoria. *Archives of Sexual Behavior, 43,* 387–393.

Person, E., & Ovesey, L. (1974). The transsexual syndrome in males. I. Primary transsexualism. *American Journal of Psychotherapy, 28,* 4–20.

Pfäfflin, F. (2007). Mental health issues. In R. Ettner, S. Monstrey, & A. E. Eyler (Eds.), *Principles of transgender medicine and surgery* (pp. 169–184). Binghamton, NY: Haworth Press.

Phillips, K. A., Wilhelm, S., Koran, L. M., Didie, E. R., Fallon, B. A., Feusner, J., & Stein, D. J. (2010). Body dysmorphic disorder: Some key issues for DSM-V. *Depression and Anxiety, 27,* 573–591.

Pieterse, A. L., Todd, N. R., Neville, H. A., & Carter, R. T. (2012). Perceived racism and mental health among Black American adults: A meta-analytic review. *Journal of Counseling Psychology, 59,* 1–9.

Poeppl, T. B., Langguth, B., Rupprecht, R., Laird, A. R., & Eickhoff, S. B. (2016). A neural circuit encoding sexual preference in humans. *Neuroscience and Biobehavioral Reviews, 68,* 530–536.

Preves, S. E. (2003). *Intersex and identity: The contested self.* New Brunswick, NJ: Rutgers University Press.

Prosser, J. (1998). *Second skins: The body narratives of transsexuality.* New York, NY: Columbia University Press.

Rametti, G., Carrillo, B., Gómez-Gil, E., Junque, C., Segovia, S., Gomez, A., & Guillamon, A. (2011a). White matter microstructure in female to male transsexuals before cross-sex hormonal treatment. A diffusion tensor imaging study. *Journal of Psychiatric Research, 45,* 199–204.

Rametti, G., Carrillo, B., Gómez-Gil, E., Junque, C., Zubiarre-Elorza, L., Segovia, S., . . . Guillamon, A. (2011b). The microstructure of white matter in male to female transsexuals before cross-sex hormonal treatment. A DTI study. *Journal of Psychiatric Research, 45,* 949–954.

Reisner, S. L., Biello, K. B., White Hughto, J. M., Kuhns, L., Mayer, K. H., Garofalo, R., & Mimiaga, M. J. (2016). Psychiatric diagnoses and comorbidities in a diverse, multicity cohort of young transgender women: Baseline findings from Project LifeSkills. *JAMA Pediatrics, 170,* 481–486.

Richards, C., Bouman, W. P., Seal, L., Barker, M. J., Nieder, T. O., & T'Sjoen, G. (2016). Non-binary or genderqueer genders. *International Review of Psychiatry, 28,* 95–102.

Richter-Appelt, H., & Sandberg, D. E. (2010). Should disorders of sex development be an exclusion criterion for Gender Identity Disorder in DSM-5? *International Journal of Transgenderism, 12,* 94–99.

Roback, H. B., Fellemann, E. S., & Abramowitz, S. I. (1984). The mid-life male sex-change applicant: A multiclinic survey. *Archives of Sexual Behavior, 13,* 141–153.

Ruigrok, A. N., Salimi-Khorshidi, G., Lai, M. C., Baron-Cohen, S., Lombardo, M. V., Tait, R. J., & Suckling, J. (2014). A meta-analysis of sex differences in human brain structure. *Neuroscience and Biobehavioral Reviews*, *39*, 34–50.

Saks, B. M. (1998). Transgenderism and dissociative identity disorder: A case study. *International Journal of Transgenderism*, *2*(2). Retrieved from www.iiav.nl/ezines/web/IJT/97–03/numbers/symposion/ijtc0404.htm.

Savic, I., & Arver, S. (2011). Sex dimorphism of the brain in male-to-female transsexuals. *Cerebral Cortex*, *21*, 2525–2533.

Savic, I., Garcia-Falgueras, & Swaab, D. F. (2010). Sexual differentiation of the human brain in relation to gender identity and sexual orientation. *Progress in Brain Research*, *186*, 41–62.

Schiltz, K., Witzel, J., Northoff, G., Zierhut, K., Gubka, U., Fellmann, H., . . . Bogerts, B. (2007). Brain pathology in pedophilic offenders: Evidence of volume reduction in the right amygdala and related diencephalic structures. *Archives of General Psychiatry*, *64*, 737–746.

Schneider, C., Cerwenka, S., Nieder, T. O., Briken, P., Cohen-Kettenis, P. T., De Cuypere, G., . . . Richter-Appelt, H. (2016). Measuring gender dysphoria: A multicenter examination and comparison of the Utrecht Gender Dysphoria Scale and the Gender Identity/Gender Dysphoria Questionnaire for Adolescents and Adults. *Archives of Sexual Behavior*, *45*, 551–558.

Schöning, S., Engelien, A., Bauer, C., Kugel, H., Kersting, A., Roestel, C., . . . Konrad, C. (2010). Neuroimaging differences in spatial cognition between men and male-to-female transsexuals before and during hormone therapy. *Journal of Sexual Medicine*, *7*, 1858–1867.

Seikowski, K. (2007). Psychotherapy and transsexualism. *Andrologia*, *39*, 248–252.

Shore, E. S. (1984). The former transsexual: A case study. *Archives of Sexual Behavior*, *13*, 277–285.

Simon, L., Kozák, L. R., Simon, V., Czobor, P., Unoka, Z., Szabó, A., & Csukly, G. (2013). Regional grey matter structure differences between transsexuals and healthy controls—A voxel based morphometry study. *PLoS One*, *8*, e83947.

Simon, L., Zsolt, U., Fogd, D., & Czobor, P. (2011). Dysfunctional core beliefs, perceived parenting behavior and psychopathology in gender identity disorder: A comparison of male-to-female, female-to-male transsexual and nontranssexual control subjects. *Journal of Behavior Therapy and Experimental Psychiatry*, *42*, 38–45.

Simonsen, R., Hald, G. M., Giraldi, A., & Kristensen, E. (2015). Sociodemographic study of Danish individuals diagnosed with transsexualism. *Sexual Medicine*, *3*, 109–117.

Singh, D. (2012). *A follow-up study of boys with gender identity disorder*. Unpublished doctoral dissertation, University of Toronto.

Singh, D., Deogracias, J. J., Johnson, L. L., Bradley, S. J., Kibblewhite, S. J., Owen-Anderson, A., . . . Zucker, K. J. (2010). The Gender Identity/Gender Dysphoria Questionnaire for Adolescents and Adults: Further validity evidence. *Journal of Sex Research*, *47*, 49–58.

Singh, D., McMain, S., & Zucker, K. J. (2011). Gender identity and sexual orientation in women with borderline personality disorder. *Journal of Sexual Medicine*, *8*, 447–454.

Smith, E. S., Junger, J., Derntl, B., & Habel, U. (2015). The transsexual brain – A review of findings on the neural basis of transsexualism. *Neuroscience and Biobehavioral Reviews*, *59*, 251–266.

Smith, Y. L. S., van Goozen, S. H. M., Kuiper, A. J., & Cohen-Kettenis, P. T. (2005a). Sex reassignment: Outcomes and predictors of treatment for adolescent and adult transsexuals. *Psychological Medicine*, *35*, 89–99.

Smith, Y. L. S., van Goozen, S. H. M., Kuiper, A. J., & Cohen-Kettenis, P. T. (2005b). Transsexual subtypes: Clinical and theoretical significance. *Psychiatry Research*, *137*, 151–160.

Steensma, T. D., Kreukels, B. P. C., de Vries, A. L. C., & Cohen-Kettenis, P. T. (2013). Gender identity development in adolescence. *Hormones and Behavior*, *64*, 288–297.

Stermac, L., Blanchard, R., Clemmensen, L. H., & Dickey, R. (1991). Group therapy for gender-dysphoric heterosexual men. *Journal of Sex & Marital Therapy*, *17*, 252–258.

Stoller, R. J. (1968). *Sex and gender: On the development of masculinity and femininity*. New York: Science House.

Stoller, R. J. (1975). *Sex and gender: Vol. 2. The transsexual experiment*. New York, NY: Jason Aronson.

Terada, S., Matsumoto, Y., Sato, T., Okabe, N., Kishimoto, Y., & Uchitomi, Y. (2012). Factors predicting psychiatric co-morbidity in gender-dysphoric adults. *Psychiatry Research, 200*, 469–474.

Turan, M. T., Esel, E., Dündar, M., Candemir, Z., Bastürk, M., Sofuoglu, S., & Ozkul, Y. (2000). Female-to-male transsexual with 47, XXX karyotype. *Biological Psychiatry, 48*, 1116–1117.

Udeze, B., Abdelmawla, N., Khoosal, D., & Terry, T. (2008). Psychological functions in male-to-female transsexual people before and after surgery. *Sexual and Relationship Therapy, 23*, 141–145.

Ujike, H., Otani, K., Nakatsuka, M., Ishii, K., Sasaki, A., Oishi, T., . . . Kuroda, S. (2009). Association study of gender identity disorder and sex hormone-related genes. *Progress in Neuro-Psychopharmacology & Biological Psychiatry, 33*, 1241–1244.

Unger, C. A. (2016) Hormone therapy for transgender patients. *Translational Andrology and Urology, 5*, 877–884.

Van de Grift, T. C., Cohen-Kettenis, P. T., Steensma, T. D., De Cuypere, G., Richter-Appelt, H., Haraldsen, I. R., . . . Kreukels, B. P. (2016). Body satisfaction and physical appearance in gender dysphoria. *Archives of Sexual Behavior, 45*, 575–585.

Van der Miesen, A. I., Hurley, H. & de Vries, A. L. (2016). Gender dysphoria and autism spectrum disorder: A narrative review. *International Review of Psychiatry, 28*, 70–80.

Van Goozen, S. H., Cohen-Kettenis, P. T., Gooren, L. J. G., Frijda, N. H., & Van de Poll, N. E. (1995). Gender differences in behaviour: Activating effects of cross-sex hormones. *Psychoneuroendocrinology, 20*, 343–363.

Veale, J. F. (2008). Prevalence of transsexualism among New Zealand passport holders. *Australian and New Zealand Journal of Psychiatry, 42*, 887–889.

Wallien, M. S., & Cohen-Kettenis, P. T. (2008). Psychosexual outcome of gender-dysphoric children. *Journal of the American Academy of Child & Adolescent Psychiatry, 47*, 1413–1423.

Walworth, J. R. (1997). Sex-reassignment surgery in male-to-female transsexuals: Client satisfaction in relation to selection criteria. In B. Bullough, V. L. Bullough, & J. Elias (Eds.), *Gender blending* (pp. 352–369). Amherst, NY: Prometheus Books.

Whitam, F. L. (1987). A cross-cultural perspective on homosexuality, transvestism, and transsexualism. In G. D. Wilson (Ed.), *Variant sexuality: Research and theory* (pp. 176–201). Baltimore, MD: Johns Hopkins University Press.

Whitam, F. L. (1997). Culturally universal aspects of male homosexual transvestites and transsexuals. In B. Bullough, V. L. Bullough, & J. Elias (Eds.), *Gender blending* (pp. 189–203). Amherst, NY: Prometheus Books.

Wierckx, K., Mueller, S., Weyers, S., Van Caenegem, E., Roef, G., Heylens, G., & T'Sjoen, G. (2012). Long-term evaluation of cross-sex hormone treatment in transsexual persons. *Journal of Sexual Medicine, 9*, 2641–2651.

Wierckx, K., Van Caenegem, E., Elaut, E., Dedecker, D., Van de Peer, F., Toye, K., . . . T'Sjoen, G. (2011). Quality of life and sexual health after sex reassignment surgery in transsexual men. *Journal of Sexual Medicine, 8*, 3379–3388.

Wierckx, K., Van Caenegem, E., Schreiner, T., Haraldsen, I., Fisher, A., Toye, K., . . . T'Sjoen, G. (2014). Cross-sex hormone therapy in trans persons is safe and effective at short-time follow-up: Results from the European Network for the Investigation of Gender Incongruence. *Journal of Sexual Medicine, 11*, 1999–2011.

Wilkinson-Ryan, T., & Westen, D. (2000). Identity disturbance in borderline personality disorder: An empirical investigation. *American Journal of Psychiatry, 157*, 528–541.

Wilson, P., Sharp, C., & Carr, S. (1999). The prevalence of gender dysphoria in Scotland: A primary care study. *British Journal of General Practice, 49*, 991–992.

World Health Organization. (1992). *International statistical classification of diseases and related health problems* (10th rev., Vol. 1). Geneva, Switzerland: Author.

Wylie, K., Barrett, J., Besser, M., Bouman, W. P., Bridgman, M., Clayton, A., . . . Ward, D. (2014). Good practice guidelines for the assessment and treatment of adults with gender dysphoria. *Sexual and Relationship Therapy, 29,* 154–214.

Wylie, K. R., & Steward, D. (2008). A consecutive series of 52 transsexual people presenting for assessment and chromosomal analysis at a gender identity clinic. *International Journal of Transgenderism, 10,* 147–148.

Zhou, J. N., Hofman, M. A., Gooren, L. J., & Swaab, D. F. (1995). A sex difference in the human brain and its relation to transsexuality. *Nature, 378,* 68–70.

Zubiaurre-Elorza, L., Junque, C., Gómez-Gil, E., Segovia, S., Carrillo, B., Rametti, G., & Guillamon, A. (2013). Cortical thickness in untreated transsexuals. *Cerebral Cortex, 23,* 2855–2862.

Zucker, K. J., & Bradley, S. J. (1995). *Gender identity disorder and psychosexual problems in children and adolescents.* New York, NY: Guilford Press.

Zucker, K. J., Bradley, S. J., Ben-Dat, D. N., Ho, C., Johnson, L., & Owen, A. (2003). Psychopathology in the parents of boys with gender identity disorder [Letter to the Editor]. *Journal of the American Academy of Child & Adolescent Psychiatry, 42,* 2–4.

Zucker, K. J., Bradley, S. J., Owen-Anderson, A., Kibblewhite, S. J., Wood, H., Singh, D., & Choi, K. (2012) Demographics, behavior problems, and psychosexual characteristics of adolescents with gender identity disorder or transvestic fetishism. *Journal of Sex & Marital Therapy, 38,* 151–189.

Zucker, K. J., Lawrence, A. A., & Kreukels, B. P. C. (2016). Gender dysphoria in adults. *Annual Review of Clinical Psychology, 12,* 217–247.

CHAPTER 18

Substance-Related and Addictive Disorders: Alcohol

ERIC F. WAGNER, MICHELLE M. HOSPITAL, MARK B. SOBELL, and LINDA C. SOBELL

DESCRIPTION OF THE DISORDER

This chapter addresses diagnostic and assessment issues across the continuum of individuals suffering with alcohol use problems. This continuum ranges from risky drinkers ("misusers," with up to three symptoms of disorder), to those with moderate severity disorder (four to five symptoms), to those who are severely dependent on alcohol (more than six symptoms). It is now widely recognized that individuals with less serious alcohol problems—misusers—outnumber those with more severe alcohol problems. Moreover, it now appears that alcohol use problems are best conceptualized as a unitary phenomenon with variation along this severity continuum. Contemporary assessment and treatment approaches for alcohol use disorders have incorporated such a conceptualization into their description of the disorder.

Just what does an alcohol use disorder look like? Descriptively, an alcohol use disorder involves a compulsive desire to use alcohol, combined with difficulties controlling drinking. Individuals suffering from an alcohol use disorder become increasingly consumed with drinking, with drinking soon replacing other pleasures in life. Compulsive drinking quickly becomes excessive drinking, characteristically leading to negative physical, psychological, and social consequences. For some people, their drinking problems eventually lead to physiological addiction to alcohol, and multiple problems across physical, psychological, and social domains. Diagnostically, as per *DSM-5* (American Psychiatric Association, 2013), an alcohol use disorder is defined as a problematic pattern of alcohol use leading to significant impairment or distress as manifested by at least two of the following:

a. using alcohol in larger amounts or for a longer time than intended;
b. a persistent desire or unsuccessful attempts to cut down or control use;
c. significant time being spent to obtain, use or recover from alcohol use;
d. cravings, or strong desires (urges) to use;
e. failure to fulfill obligations;
f. interpersonal problems occur because of persistent use;

Adult Psychopathology and Diagnosis, Eighth Edition. Edited by Deborah C. Beidel and B. Christopher Frueh.
© 2018 John Wiley & Sons, Inc. Published 2018 by John Wiley & Sons, Inc.
Companion website: www.wiley.com/go/beidel/psychopathology8e

g. the individual gives up important activities (work, social interaction) because of alcohol;

h. evidence of tolerance (defined as the need for increasingly amounts of alcohol to achieve intoxication or a markedly diminished effect with continued use of the same amount); or

i. withdrawal (defined as physiological responses that occur after consistent and excessive use).

The foregoing *DSM-5* alcohol use disorder criteria represent a conceptual shift from the now obsolete *DSM-IV* biaxial distinction between alcohol abuse and dependence. *DSM-5* criteria also eliminate the *DSM-IV* legal problems criterion due to its limited clinical utility, and add an alcohol craving criterion, due to its long recognized diagnostic utility (e.g., see Marlatt, 1988). Several studies have supported the *DSM-5* diagnostic revisions, particularly the adoption of a one factor model of alcohol use disorder (e.g., Hagman & Cohn, 2011; Kuerbis, Hagman, & Sacco, 2013; Mewton, Slade, McBride, Grove, & Teesso, 2011). Moreover, it appears that the *DSM-5* criteria are an improvement over the *DSM-IV* criteria for identifying those with low severity alcohol use disorders, and particularly useful with college student (Hagman & Cohn, 2011) and older adult populations (Kuerbis, Hagman, & Sacco, 2013). That said, most studies have found only minimal differences in prevalence rates of alcohol use disorders when comparing the *DSM-IV* and *DSM-5* (e.g., Dawson, Goldstein, & Grant, 2013; Di Giacomo, Zappa, Madeddu, Colmegna, & Clerici, 2017; Edwards, Gillespie, Aggen, & Kendler, 2013).

Current views about alcohol use problems are a grafting of concepts derived from research, clinical anecdotes, and common wisdom. Over the past century and a half, public opinion has softened from viewing those who suffer with alcohol problems as moral reprobates to viewing them as victims of a disease. In the United States, the perspective that alcohol problems are a medical disorder became dominant in the mid-1900s, spurred by (a) the rise of Alcoholics Anonymous (AA), founded in Akron, Ohio, in 1935; (b) the seminal work of E. M. Jellinek from 1940 through 1960; and (c) the proclamation that alcoholism is a disease by the American Medical Association in 1956. The embracing of the disease concept was intended to shift societal responsibility for dealing with alcohol problems from the criminal justice system to the health care system, and helped destigmatize alcohol problems.

Alcoholics Anonymous, the ubiquitous mutual-help approach that emerged in the 1930s, viewed alcoholism as a biological aberration—an "allergy" to alcohol (i.e., with repeated exposure to alcohol, alcoholics would quickly become physically dependent on the substance, and once dependent they would continue to drink to avoid withdrawal symptoms). To explain relapse, AA stated that alcoholics had an "obsession" to drink like normal drinkers. In addition, alcoholism was thought to be a progressive disorder (i.e., if alcoholics continued to drink, their problem would inevitably worsen), and persons who were mildly dependent on alcohol were thought to be in the "early stages" of developing alcoholism. Consequently, even those with mild problems were viewed as needing the same treatment as those who with severe problems.

Jellinek, a scientist, attempted to bridge the gap between lay views and the evidence in support of the disease concept of alcoholism. He and others felt that the medical profession should be responsible for treating alcohol abusers (Jellinek, 1942, 1952, 1960). Although he alluded to genetic components, he did not speculate as to why some drinkers develop alcohol problems but others do not. Jellinek did postulate that alcoholics: (a) use alcohol to cope with emotional problems; (b) over time develop tolerance to alcohol, leading to increased consumption to achieve desired effects; and,

(c) eventually develop "loss of control, " where even small amounts of alcohol initiate physical dependence and trigger more drinking (Jellinek, 1960). Finally, Jellinek proposed that there were many types of alcohol problems, including gamma alcoholism, which he felt was the most common type of alcohol use disorder in the United States and a progressive disorder.

Today, more than half a century later, considerable research has refuted many of these earlier conceptualizations. Although some individuals may be genetically predisposed to develop alcohol problems, a large proportion of individuals with alcohol problems do not have this positive family history, and a large proportion of individuals with a positive family history for alcohol use disorders do not have alcohol problems (Dahl et al., 2005; Humphreys, 2009). Research has consistently shown that genes are responsible for about half of the risk for an alcohol use disorder; environmental factors (including social and cultural factors), as well interactions between genes and environmental factors, are responsible for the remaining half of the risk. Moreover, in most cases of alcohol use problems, the natural history of the disorder is not progressive (Dawson, 1996; Institute of Medicine, 1990); rather, it includes periods of alcohol problems of varying severity, punctuated by periods of either nondrinking or drinking limited quantities without notable problems (Cahalan, 1970; King & Tucker, 2000). Also, natural history studies have found that self-recovery, recovery from alcohol problems in the absence of treatment, is more prevalent than once thought (Bischof et al., 2003; Dawson et al., 2005; Klingemann et al., 2001; Klingemann, Sobell, & Sobell, 2009; Mohatt et al., 2007; Sobell, Cunningham, & Sobell, 1996; Sobell, Ellingstad, & Sobell, 2000). Recent research indicated that even very-high-risk and high-risk drinkers are capable of reducing their drinking to less harmful levels (Hasin et al., 2017).

With regard to loss of control, empirical research beginning in the 1970s established that even in very severe cases, physical dependence is not initiated by a small amount of drinking (Marlatt, 1978; Pattison, Sobell, & Sobell, 1977); other factors, such as conditioned cues (Niaura et al., 1988) and positive consequences of drinking (Orford, 2001), are necessary to explain why some people continue drinking despite repeatedly suffering adverse consequences (Humphreys, 2009). Finally, considerable research shows that individuals with mildly to moderately severe alcohol use problems respond well to brief interventions, often by reducing their drinking to nonproblematic levels rather than ceasing their drinking altogether (Bien, Miller, & Tonigan, 1993; Cunningham, Wild, Cordingley, van Mierlo, & Humphreys, 2010; Hester, Delaney, Campbell, & Handmaker, 2009; Sobell & Sobell, 1993, 1995).

CLINICAL PICTURE

The focus point in the clinical picture of alcohol use disorders is ambivalence. Individuals with alcohol problems are very ambivalent about changing their alcohol use. Unless their reasons to stop drinking are extremely and consistently and personally compelling, they are unlikely to reduce or curtail their use of alcohol. Drinking is widespread in our society, and even those with severe alcohol problems enjoy the subjective experience of drinking. For individuals at the less severe end of the alcohol problem continuum, ambivalence can be very pronounced, as the decision to stop or reduce drinking is based on probable future risks, rather than on certain immediate (and extremely and consistently and personally compelling) consequences. A failure to recognize this logical and predictable ambivalence can seriously compromise the success of the assessment and treatment process.

Traditional conceptualizations of alcohol use problems assume and assert that individuals enter treating "in denial;" that is, they fail to recognize that their drinking is a problem (Nowinski, Baker, & Carroll, 1992). In response, traditional interventions attempt to break through the denial using confrontation; the rationale behind confrontation of denial, in part, derives from the first step of AA (i.e., recognizing that one is powerless over alcohol; Nowinski et al., 1992). For some individuals with alcohol problems, confrontation of denial produces favorable results. Moreover, AA has helped millions of women and men recover from alcoholism, is extremely cost-effective (Kelly, 2017), and can lead to short- and long-term changes in alcohol consumption (Humphreys, Blodgett, & Wagner, 2014). However, for some people with alcohol problems, AA can be off-putting given its "religio-guese" language and practices (Kelly, 2017; Verderhus, 2016). For many (perhaps most) people with alcohol use problems, confrontation of denial is especially off-putting, and elicits resentment, retaliation, and resistance to change. Somewhat paradoxically, a confrontational approach is likely to cause otherwise receptive patients to deny that they have an alcohol problem.

In contrast to the confrontation of denial approach, contemporary approaches to treating alcohol use problems are "motivational," concentrate on clients' ambivalence, and avoid the use of confrontation, labeling, or other tactics that provoke defensiveness and resistance. This alternative, nonthreatening, nonconfrontational, patient-centered style of interviewing is called motivational interviewing (MI; Miller & Rollnick, 1991, 2002, 2013). MI is often employed as a therapeutic intervention, and its clinical effectiveness for alcohol use problems, as well as other drug use problems, is well established across several hundred randomized controlled trials conducted around the globe.

Motivational interviewing is a collaborative, goal-oriented conversation style designed to strengthen intrinsic motivation for and commitment to change. The spirit of MI includes four elements: partnership, acceptance, compassion, and evocation. In contrast to traditional approaches, motivational interventions are intended, through support and persuasion, to increase the likelihood that people will reduce or end their drinking. MI focuses on helping patients (a) to recognize that problems exist in their lives and (b) to overcome ambivalence about changing drinking. Ambivalence is expressed through patient change talk (pro-change arguments) and sustain talk (pro-status quo, anti-change arguments), and is considered a normal part of the change process. Change talk, which MI is designed to promote, is captured by the acronym DARN-CAT; when preparing to make changes, change talk is evidenced by statements expressing: desire, ability, reasons, and need; when mobilizing for change, change talk is evidenced by statements expressing commitment, activation, and taking steps.

DIAGNOSTIC CONSIDERATIONS

Diagnostic formulations play an integral role in decisions about treatment goals and intensities, and are a requirement of insurance and clinical recording. An accurate diagnosis defines the problem in a way that can be communicated and understood by clinicians and researchers. A diagnostic formulation coupled with an assessment provides an initial understanding of the problem as well as a foundation for initial treatment planning. The two major diagnostic classifications of mental disorders are the *Diagnostic and Statistical Manual of Mental Disorders* (DSM) and the "Mental Disorder" section of the *International Classification of Diseases* (ICD). The first DSM (DSM-I) was published in 1952 by the American Psychiatric Association and was a variant of the ICD-6. Over the past few decades, changes in the DSM alcohol use disorder classification criteria have reflected both the state of knowledge and contemporary attitudes. For example, while the *DSM-III-R* viewed alcohol dependence as a graded phenomenon ranging from mild (enough consequences to meet criteria but no major withdrawal symptoms) to severe (several negative consequences and withdrawal symptoms), the *DSM-IV* separated psychological from physiological dependence by making physical dependence a specifier rather than a central symptom. Presently, the *DSM-5* eliminates the distinction between alcohol dependence and alcohol abuse, and instead views alcohol use disorders as varying only in terms of severity.

Several common clinical features of alcohol use disorders complicate their diagnosis and treatment. First, there is a high prevalence of co-occurring psychiatric disorders among individuals with alcohol problems (Batki et al., 2009; Bradizza, Stasiewicz, & Dermen, 2014; González-Pinto et al., 2010; McDonell et al., 2017; Nunes, Selzer, Levounis, & Davies, 2010). For example, Grant et al. (2015), using National Epidemiologic Survey on Alcohol and Related Conditions III (NESARC-III) data, found significant associations between 12-month and lifetime alcohol use disorder and co-occurring other substance use disorders, major depression, bipolar I disorder, antisocial personality disorder, and borderline personality disorder. This co-occurrence appeared across all levels of alcohol use disorder severity, with odds ratios as high as 6.4. Grant et al. (2015) found more modest, yet still significant, associations between alcohol use disorder and co-occurring panic disorder, specific phobia, and generalized anxiety disorder. Given the frequent co-occurrence with psychiatric disorders, the alcohol use disorder diagnostic formulation must assess three things: (1) the extent and nature of the alcohol problem; (2) the extent and nature of psychiatric disorders; and (3) the extent and nature of interaction between alcohol problems and psychiatric problems (Boden & Moos, 2009; Mack, Harrington, & Frances, 2010). Ideally, individuals should be alcohol free for several weeks in order to accurately assess for co-occurring psychiatric diagnoses, because active alcohol use can mask or exacerbate psychiatric symptoms (Schuckit, 2006).

Several studies have shown that co-occurring psychiatric problems are associated with poorer treatment outcomes among people with alcohol problems receiving treatment (Nunes et al., 2010; SAMHSA, 2015). An integrated treatment approach involving additional and specialized counseling is suggested for alcohol use disorder clients who have co-occurring disorders (SAMHSA, 2005, 2009). It should be noted, however, that additional research is needed on how, and to what degree, integrated services are effective for addressing alcohol use problems and co-occurring psychiatric problems.

Second, many individuals with alcohol use problems also have other drug use problems. Grant et al. (2015), for example, found that having a lifetime diagnosis of severe alcohol use disorder increases more than six-fold the risk for having a second substance use disorder. For people with alcohol problems who use other drugs (including nicotine in any form), it is important to gather a comprehensive profile of all types of psychoactive substance use and substance use problems. Over the course of an intervention, drug use patterns may change (e.g., decreased alcohol use, increased smoking or vaping; decreased alcohol use, increased cannabis use). Furthermore, alcohol abusers who use other drugs may experience pharmacological synergism (i.e., a multiplicative effect of similarly acting drugs taken concurrently) and/or cross-tolerance (i.e., lessened drug effect because of past heavy use of pharmacologically similar drugs). Both synergism and cross-tolerance must be considered when treating those with alcohol problems who use other drugs. The foregoing speaks to important differences between the treatment of individuals with alcohol use problems only and treatment of individuals who have other substance use problems in addition to their alcohol use problems (Pakula, MacDonald, & Stockwell, 2009).

Third, people who drink alcohol daily and in large quantities are likely to experience withdrawal symptoms when access to alcohol is restricted. These symptoms can range from minor withdrawal symptoms (e.g., psychomotor agitation) to, in the most severe cases, delirium tremens (DTs), a medical emergency with a high mortality rate. A history of past withdrawal symptoms, coupled with reports of recent heavy ethanol consumption, can alert clinicians that withdrawal symptoms are likely to occur upon cessation of drinking; such symptoms can be successfully managed with medical interventions. Given the foregoing, important diagnostic goals when assessing individuals with alcohol problems are to determine (a) the severity of the problem and (b) whether withdrawal symptoms are likely to occur when drinking is reduced.

EPIDEMIOLOGY

Problems with alcohol use have been described as the major behavioral disorders of our time (Tyburski, Sokolowski, Samochowiec, & Samochowiec, 2014). The 2014 Global Drug Survey (GDS, 2014), the biggest survey of current drug use ever conducted, found that 91% of its nearly 80,000 international respondents reported using alcohol in the past year. According to the World Health Organization (WHO, 2015), total alcohol per-capita consumption worldwide in 2010 averaged 21.2 liters of pure alcohol for males and 8.9 liters for females. While alcohol is used worldwide, often without notable negative consequence to the drinker, excessive alcohol use is a causal factor in more than 200 disease and injury conditions. WHO estimates that 3.3 million alcohol-related deaths (5.9% of deaths worldwide) occur annually. Drinking alcohol heightens the risk of developing mental and behavioral disorders, including alcohol dependence, major noncommunicable diseases such as liver cirrhosis, some cancers and cardiovascular diseases, and injuries resulting from violence and road clashes and collisions. Measured in disability-adjusted life-years (DALYs), 5.1% of the global burden of disease and injury is from alcohol. Alcohol-related death and disability occur relatively early in life; among 20- to 39-year-olds, one out of every four deaths is attributable to alcohol. Alcohol-attributable deaths among men amount to 7.6% of all global deaths compared with 4.0% of all deaths among women.

Among people aged 18 years of age or older in the US, epidemiological data indicate that 86.4% drank alcohol at some point in their lifetime, 70.1% drank in the past year, and 56.0% drank in the past month (National Institute on Alcohol Abuse and Alcoholism [NIAAA], 2017; SAMHSA, 2015; Office of the Surgeon General, 2016). Moreover, 26.9% engaged in binge drinking (over 66 million people) in the past month (five or more drinks on one occasion for males and four or more for females), and 7.0% (9.3% of men, 3.2% of women) engaged in heavy alcohol use in the past month (binge drinking on 5 or more days in the past month). It should be noted, however, that differences between men and women in alcohol consumption and alcohol problems, across nearly all indicators, have been narrowing in the US (White et al., 2015). Moreover, there appears to be an upward trend in drinking among women over 60 years old (Breslow, Castle, Chen, & Graubard, 2017). Heavy alcohol use also varies by race/ethnicity, with American Indians/Alaska Natives and non-Hispanic Whites reporting the highest rates. Across genders and races/ethnicities, the lifetime prevalence of alcohol use disorder is 29.1% and the 12-month prevalence is 13.9%, representing approximately 68.5 million and 32.6 million adults, respectively (Grant et al., 2015).

In 2015, the Office of the Surgeon General (2016) estimates that there were 15.7 million people in need of treatment for an alcohol use disorder (7.8% of men and 4.1% of women).

Regardless of age, less than 1 in 10 of those suffering with an alcohol use disorder received treatment for the disorder (NIAAA, 2017). Moreover, alcohol misuse contributes to 88,000 deaths in the US each year; 1 in 10 deaths among working adults is due to alcohol misuse (Office of the Surgeon General, 2016).The annual societal cost of alcohol use problems in the US is more than $249.0 billion (NIAAA, 2017).

From the standpoint of symptom-based prevalence, the ratio of alcohol misusers to severely dependent drinkers is a function of the definitions used and the populations sampled. Regardless of the definitions, on a problem severity continuum, it has been long known that the population of persons with identifiable problems but no severe signs of alcohol use problems is much larger than the population with severe alcohol use problems. Risky drinkers (misusers) constitute one out of three individuals with drinking problems, whereas severely dependent drinkers account for less than one out of 14 (CDC, 2015; Esser et al., 2014; Institute of Medicine, 1990). Individuals with low severity alcohol use problems are better captured with the *DSM-5* alcohol use disorder diagnostic criteria than with previous criteria, particularly when applied in college student (Hagman & Cohn, 2011) and older adult populations (Kuerbis, Hagman, & Sacco, 2013).

PSYCHOLOGICAL AND BIOLOGICAL ASSESSMENT

Thorough and careful assessments are critical to the development of meaningful treatment plans, and an accurate diagnosis of alcohol use disorder and co-occurring disorders is integral to the assessment process. Assessment serves several critical functions; it provides clinicians with: (a) an in-depth picture of a person's alcohol use, problem severity, and related consequences—this picture can be used to develop an individualized treatment plan tailored to the specific needs of each client; (b) an objective process by which to gauge treatment progress; and (c) empirical feedback about how a treatment plan already in place might be improved. The depth and intensity of an assessment will be related to problem severity, the complexity of the presenting case, and the specific interests of the clinician or researcher conducting the assessment. The instruments and methods described in this chapter can be used clinically to gather information that is relevant to the assessment and treatment planning process. The implications of assessment data for treatment issues, such as drinking goals and treatment intensity, show how the clinical interview can significantly affect treatment.

CRITICAL ISSUES IN ASSESSMENT

In the alcohol field, most research and clinical information is obtained through retrospective self-reports. Clients are asked to recount their use of alcohol and any alcohol-related negative consequences over a specified time period, such as the past month, the past 90 days, or the past year. Research has confirmed that self-reports by people with drinking problems are generally accurate if:

1. they are interviewed in clinical or research settings;
2. they are interviewed as per the precepts and principles of MI;
3. they are alcohol-free (i.e., there is no alcohol in their system);
4. they are given assurances of confidentiality.

Self-reports are inherently prone to some degree of inaccuracy, due to recall biases, social desirability biases, misinterpretation of questions, and the like. One way to confirm the accuracy of self-reports is to obtain overlapping information from different sources, such as chemical tests, collateral reports, and official records. Data from different sources are then compared and contrasted, and conclusions as to the presenting problems are based on a convergence of information. When the measures converge, one can have confidence in the accuracy of the reports.

Getting accurate information during the assessment of alcohol use problems is essential to the success of treatment. Information gathered through the assessment process can be used to provide feedback to clients to enhance their commitment to change. In order to make the assessment and feedback about the assessment most beneficial to clients, they should be delivered in a nonconfrontational manner using MI principles (for an introduction to MI, see http://www.integration.samhsa.gov/clinical-practice/motivational-interviewing). With respect to the length of an assessment, the breadth and depth of an assessment for alcohol use disorders will vary due to heterogeneity in alcohol problem severity across clients. Because persons with less severe alcohol problems often respond well to a brief intervention, an assessment that is longer than the intervention makes little sense. In contrast, individuals with severe alcohol use disorder may require a more intensive assessment covering such areas as organic brain dysfunction, psychiatric comorbidity, social needs, and medical status (e.g., liver function). Ultimately, an assessment should be based on clinical judgment and the client's individual needs. The next section describes different assessment areas and reviews relevant assessment instruments, scales, and questionnaires that can be used for assessing alcohol use and abuse. Only instruments that have sound psychometric properties and clinical utility are discussed. With respect to selecting an appropriate instrument for clinical or research purposes, it is helpful to ask, "What will I learn from using the instrument that I would not otherwise know from a routine clinical interview?"

ALCOHOL USE

Assessing alcohol consumption involves measuring the quantity and frequency of past and present use. When choosing an instrument to assess drinking, level of precision and time frame are key considerations. Two major dimensions along which measures differ are: (1) whether they gather summarized information (e.g., "How many days per week on average do you drink any alcohol?") versus specific information (e.g., "How many drinks did you have on each day of the past month?"); and (2) whether the information is recalled retrospectively or recorded in real time as it occurs. Specific measures are preferred over summary measures for pretreatment and within-treatment assessments because they provide information about patterns of drinking and opportunities to inquire about events associated with problem drinking that are not possible using summary data (e.g., "What was happening on Friday when you had 12 drinks?").

In terms of key instruments, there are four long-established approaches to assessing alcohol consumption: (1) lifetime drinking history (LDH; Skinner & Sheu, 1982; Sobell & Sobell, 1995); (2) quantity-frequency methods (QF; Room, 1990; Sobell & Sobell, 1995); (3) timeline follow-back (TLFB; Sobell & Sobell, 1993, 1995); and (4) self-monitoring (SM; Sobell, Bogardis, Schuller, Leo, & Sobell, 1989; Sobell & Sobell, 1995), including ecological momentary assessment (EMA; Morgenstern, Kuerbis, & Muench, 2015). The first three are retrospective estimation methods (i.e., they obtain information about alcohol use after it has occurred). The TLFB can also be used in treatment as an advice-feedback tool to help increase clients' motivation to change (Sobell & Sobell, 1995).

The fourth method, self-monitoring, asks clients to record their drinking at or about the same time that it occurred. The self-monitoring approach possesses several clinical advantages: (a) it provides feedback about treatment effectiveness; (b) it identifies situations that pose a high risk of relapse; and (c) it gives outpatient clients an opportunity to discuss drinking that has taken place since the previous session. EMA extends self-monitoring using smart phone technology, which can capture real-time data on human behavior inexpensively, efficiently, and accurately, using a device familiar to the respondent (Morgenstern, Kuerbis, & Muench, 2015). As a result, the past decade has seen a dramatic increase in the clinical and research uses of EMA for self-monitoring.

Alcohol Use Consequences

One of the key defining characteristics of a *DSM-5* diagnosis is alcohol-related consequences. Several short self-administered scales have been developed to assess alcohol-related biopsychosocial consequences and symptoms including: (1) the Alcohol Use Disorders Identification Test (AUDIT; Saunders, Aasland, Babor, De La Fuente, & Grant, 1993; http://auditscreen.org/); (2) the Severity of Alcohol Dependence Questionnaire (SADQ; Stockwell, Murphy, & Hodgson, 1983; Stockwell, Sitharthan, McGrath, & Lang, 1994); (3) the Alcohol Dependence Scale (ADS; Murphy & MacKillop, 2011; Skinner & Allen, 1982); and (4) the Short Alcohol Dependence Data Questionnaire (SADD; McMurran & Hollin, 1989; Raistrick, Dunbar, & Davidson, 1983). These scales take about 5 minutes to administer and range from 10 to 25 items in length. Given the elimination of the alcohol dependence diagnosis in the *DSM-5*, these "dependence" scales may well be in need of retitling. However, the types of symptoms these scales measure remain relevant for identifying people with alcohol use disorders of greater severity.

The AUDIT stands out for its psychometric characteristics, convenience, and cross-cultural validation. The AUDIT, developed as a multinational WHO project, is a brief screening test for the early detection of harmful and hazardous alcohol use in primary health care settings (Saunders et al., 1993). The 10 questions are scored based on the frequency of the experience (i.e., from 0 ["never"] to 4 ["daily"]). The AUDIT has been shown to be as good as or better than other screening tests (e.g., CAGE, MAST, ADS) in identifying individuals with probable alcohol problems (Barry & Fleming, 1993; Fleming, Barry, & MacDonald, 1991). According to the authors, the differences between the AUDIT and most other screening tests are that it: (a) detects drinkers along the entire severity continuum from mild to severe; (b) emphasizes hazardous consumption and frequency of intoxication compared with drinking behavior and adverse consequences; (c) uses a time frame that asks questions about current (i.e., past year) and lifetime use; and (d) avoids using a "yes/no" format and instead uses Likert rating scales.

The AUDIT is also noteworthy for being incorporated into NIAAA's (2005) *Helping Patients Who Drink Too Much: A Clinician's Guide* (see www.niaaa.nih.gov/Guide). The guide is written for primary care and mental health clinicians providing treatment to adults, and is premised on the notion that alcohol screening, combined with intervention and referral, has the potential to significantly reduce alcohol-related harm. The guide provides two methods for screening: a single question (about heavy drinking days) and a written self-report instrument—the AUDIT. The single interview question can be used at any time, either in conjunction with the AUDIT or alone. NIAAA also has published a parallel guide for youth entitled *Alcohol Screening and Brief Intervention for Youth: A Practitioner's Guide* (NIAAA, 2011; see https://niaaa.nih.gov/publications/clinical-guides-and-manuals/alcohol-screening-and-brief-intervention-youth), with developmentally appropriate screening items. Notably, both of the NIAAA guides also incorporate MI.

Co-occurring Disorders

As noted earlier, a substantial number of people with alcohol problems have co-occurring psychiatric problems. Although several diagnostic interviews and scales exist for assessing psychiatric comorbidity among individuals with alcohol disorder, the comprehensiveness of these assessments will vary depending on the resources available, specificity of the information required, treatment setting, and the assessor's skill level. Several brief and widely available questionnaires can assess for symptoms of co-occurring disorders. These instruments include the Beck Depression Inventory (Beck, Steer, & Garbin, 1988), the Beck Anxiety Inventory (Beck, Epstein, Brown, & Steer, 1988), the Hamilton Rating Scale for Depression (Hamilton, 1960), and the Symptom Checklist-90-R (Derogatis, 1983). Personality tests, especially objective tests rather than projective tests, also have clinical utility in assessing psychiatric disorder among individuals with alcohol use disorder. Prominent examples of objective personality tests include the Minnesota Multiphasic Personality Inventory–2 and Minnesota Multiphasic Personality Inventory–2-RF (Ben-Porath & Tellegen, 2008; Hathaway & McKinley, 1989) and the Millon Clinical Multiaxial Inventory–III (Millon, Millon, Davis, & Grossman, 2006).

High-Risk Situations and Self-Efficacy

Because relapse rates among individuals treated for alcohol problems are extremely high, the identification of high-risk situations for drinking has long been recognized as important at assessment and during treatment (Marlatt & Gordon, 1985; Sobell & Sobell, 1993). The Situational Confidence Questionnaire (SCQ-39) assesses self-efficacy to resist drinking by asking clients to rate their self-efficacy across a variety of situations on a scale ranging from 100% confident to 0% confident. The SCQ-39 can be completed in less than 20 minutes and contains eight subscales (e.g., unpleasant emotions, pleasant emotions, testing personal control) based on Marlatt and Gordon's (1985) classic relapse research. For clinical purposes, the Brief SCQ (BSCQ), a variant of the SCQ that is easy to score and interpret, was developed and consists of eight items that represent the eight subscales (Breslin, Sobell, Sobell, & Agrawal, 2000). Although the BSCQ can be used clinically to enhance treatment planning, it only identifies generic situations and problem areas. To examine clients' individual high-risk situations or areas where they lack self-confidence, clinicians should explore in depth specific high-risk situations with clients. For example, clients can be asked to describe their two or three highest-risk situations for alcohol use in the past year, with attention to the similarities and differences across the situations.

Neuropsychological Functioning

Numerous neurophysiological and neuropsychological studies have identified negative consequences from both acute and chronic alcohol consumption in areas of brain functioning, including attention, auditory working memory, verbal processing, abstraction/cognitive flexibility, psychomotor function, immediate memory, delayed memory, reaction time, and spatial processing. Moreover, it is well documented that individuals with alcohol use disorder are at elevated risk for neuropsychological problems, which can prove to be barriers to treatment success if they are not identified and addressed. Thus, a comprehensive alcohol use disorders assessment should include neuropsychological screening. Multiple screening tests are available for measuring neuropsychological functioning, but the most widely used include the Digit Span, Letter Number Sequencing, and Symbol Search subscales from the Wechsler Adult Intelligence

Scale (WAIS-IV; Wechsler, 2008), the Trail Making Test (Davies, 1968), the Wisconsin Card Sorting Test-64 (Kongs, Thompson, Iverson, & Heaton, 2000), and subscales from the Wechsler Memory Scale (WMS-IV; Wechsler, 2009). These screening tests are relatively easy and quick to administer (e.g., about 5 minutes) and are highly sensitive to alcohol-related brain dysfunction.

BARRIERS TO CHANGE

In developing a treatment plan, it is helpful to anticipate possible barriers that clients might encounter with respect to changing their behavior. Barriers can be both motivational and practical. If an individual is not motivated to change, there is little reason to expect that change will occur. Because many alcohol abusers are coerced into treatment (e.g., courts, significant others), such individuals might not have a serious interest in changing. Thus, it is important to evaluate a client's motivation for and commitment to change. According to Miller and Rollnick (1991), "motivation is a state of readiness or eagerness to change, which may fluctuate from one time or situation to another. This state is one that can be influenced" (p. 14). Thus, rather than a trait, motivation is a state that can be influenced by several variables, one of which is the therapist.

An easy way to assess readiness to change is to use a Readiness Ruler. The Readiness Ruler asks clients to indicate their readiness to change using a five-point scale ranging from "not ready to change" (1) to "unsure" (3) to "very ready to change" (5). The ruler has face validity, is user-friendly, and takes only a few seconds to complete. Environmental factors can also present formidable obstacles to change. For example, individuals in an environment where alcohol is readily available, and where there are many cues to drink, may find it difficult to abstain. For some individuals, social avoidance strategies (e.g., avoiding bars, no alcohol in the house) may be the only effective alternative. Finally, clinicians should attend to individual barriers that can also affect a person's ability to enter and complete treatment (e.g., child care, transportation, inability to take time off from work, unwillingness to adopt an abstinence goal) (CSAT, 2009).

BIOCHEMICAL MEASURES

Both unintentional and intentional recall biases can lead to inaccuracies in the self-report measurement of alcohol use. The use of alcohol, tobacco, and other drugs can be detected in different bodily fluids (e.g., breath, blood, urine, hair, saliva) and by several biochemical detection methods. In situations where there are concerns about the validity of self-reports (e.g., drug use among criminal offenders), a convergent validity approach relying on biochemical measures is often employed. Although there has been a tendency to consider biochemical measures as "gold standards" that are superior to self-reports, it is important to note that biochemical measures can suffer from validity and implementation problems. In fact, in some settings, self-reports may be superior to certain biochemical measures (Gmel, Wicki, Rehm, & Heeb, 2008). Moreover, issues of self-report accuracy take on different meanings for clinical versus research purposes, where different levels of reporting precision are required. For example, clinicians do not routinely have to obtain information to confirm their clients' alcohol use unless the situation warrants it. However, in clinical trials, researchers typically choose to verify their clients' self-reports using biochemical or other alternative measures (e.g., collateral reports).

Urinalysis can provide qualitative (i.e., which substances are currently in the body) and quantitative (i.e., how much of a substance is currently in the body) information. The detection of alcohol in the urine typically uses ethyl glucuronide (EtG), a direct metabolite of ethanol alcohol. EtG is present in the urine roughly 80 hours after alcohol has been metabolized. Given its relatively high reliability and sensitivity, and low expense, EtG testing is often used in situations where alcohol consumption is prohibited, such as by the military or in recovering alcoholic patients. However, all urine tests have limitations. Urinalyses cannot specify when a drug was taken. Rather, it only provides evidence of whether consumption occurred and the amount of drug or the drug's metabolite in the system at the time of testing. Moreover, urine tests are not able to distinguish between alcohol absorbed into the body from the actual consumption of alcohol and exposure to any of the many common commercial and household products containing alcohol. A final problem with urine testing is the urine specimen itself, which can be embarrassing to obtain, adulterated or substituted, and present a biological hazard during shipping and disposal.

Breath and hair analysis can also provide reliable information on alcohol use. A breath analyzer will yield reasonably accurate readings of a person's blood alcohol concentration (BAC), which is measured indirectly by analyzing the amount of alcohol in one's breath. Breath alcohol testers are noninvasive, inexpensive, easy to use, portable, and provide an immediate determination of BAC. Several portable testers differing in cost and precision are commercially available. Although they are relatively robust measures of BAC, breath analyzers can produce false readings due to tobacco smoke, recent drinking, a person's breathing rate, or equipment or operator error. Hair analysis tests whether two markers of alcohol use, EtG and fatty acid ethyl esters (FAEEs), are present. Only scalp hair can be used, and a sample approximately the diameter of a pencil and about 1.5 inches long is required. Hair analysis is relatively noninvasive and highly accurate, and it can provide a history of alcohol consumption for up to several years. Moreover, hair samples are nearly impossible to adulterate and are highly stable and transportable. Despite these advantages, hair analysis is several times more expensive than urine analysis, and it will not work if a person has very short hair or a shaved head.

Very recently, wearable real-time alcohol biosensors have started appearing as another noninvasive means to measure alcohol use. In 2015, NIAAA announced the Wearable Alcohol Biosensor Challenge (NIAAA, 2015). The challenge was to design a discreet device capable of measuring blood alcohol levels in near real-time. While still in prototype, NIAAA expects the wearable biosensor to improve on existing technology by providing real-time monitoring, in a manner that is inconspicuous and appealing to the general public. Ultimately, the device will be able to measure blood alcohol level, interpret and store the data, and transmit it to a smartphone or other device by wireless transmission.

Liver function problems are highly prevalent in alcoholics, so physicians routinely assess hepatic dysfunction when presented with a patient with chronic drinking problems. Elevated liver enzymes, which indicate liver dysfunction, are seen among alcohol-dependent drinkers. However, most problem drinkers (i.e., those who are not severely dependent on alcohol) do not show elevations on liver function tests (Sobell, Agrawal, & Sobell, 1999). In addition, alcohol-dependent women, more so than alcoholic men, are likely to demonstrate hepatic dysfunction (Schenker, 1997; Vatsalya et al. 2016; Wagnerberger, Schafer, Schwarz, Bode, & Parlesak, 2008). Cirrhosis, permanent and nonreversible cellular liver damage, typically occurs among only those with the heaviest drinking patterns. Unlike assessment of acute hepatic dysfunction, which can be done through a blood test, cirrhosis must be diagnosed through a liver biopsy.

ETIOLOGICAL CONSIDERATIONS

BEHAVIORAL GENETICS AND MOLECULAR GENETICS

Research has consistently shown that genes are responsible for about half of the risk for an alcohol use disorder; environmental factors (including social and cultural factors), as well interactions between genes and environmental factors, are responsible for the remaining half of the risk. Close relatives of persons with alcohol problems, adopted-away children of men and women with alcohol problems, and identical twins whose parents had alcohol problems have all been found to demonstrate a much higher likelihood of experiencing alcohol use problems than the general population (Foroud, Edenberg, & Crabbe, 2010). Two endophenotypes—or subconditions that increase the risk for a disorder—have produced replicable genetic associations in regard to alcohol problems—(1) level of response to alcohol and (2) neurophysiology markers (Salvatore, Gottesman & Dick, 2015). Additional candidate endophenotypes from the cognitive, sensory, and neuroimaging literatures show promise, but are in need of additional investigation. The absence or limited production of alcohol-metabolizing enzymes (most common among Asians), low response level to alcohol (i.e., needing a greater number of drinks to have an effect), low amplitude of the P300 wave component of event-related potentials, and low alpha activity and voltage on electroencephalograms all are associated with an increased risk of drinking problems, and all have strong genetic influences.

With regard to specific genes, the genes encoding two alcohol-metabolizing enzymes—alcohol dehydrogenase and aldehyde dehydrogenase—appear to have the strongest relation to alcohol use disorder; other gene variants associated with alcohol use disorder demonstrate much weaker relations (Foroud et al., 2010). In terms of mechanisms of action, the genetic variants associated with alcohol use disorder affect the metabolism and pharmacokinetics of alcohol, as well as the subjective response to alcohol (Ray, MacKillop, & Monti, 2010; Salvatore, Gottesman, & Dick, 2015). Although genetic studies have documented genetic influences on the risk of alcohol problems in men, this has occurred less so with women (Prescott, 2002). In a notable exception, Hardie, Moss, and Lynch (2008) found provisional support for gender differences in heritability with regard to specific symptoms of alcohol use problems.

NEUROANATOMY AND NEUROBIOLOGY

Multiple biological and physiological systems are impacted by and influence alcohol consumption. As noted earlier, biological factors found to be associated with the development of alcohol problems include the absence or limited production of alcohol-metabolizing enzymes, low level of response to alcohol (i.e., needing more drinks to have an effect), low amplitude of the P300 wave component of event-related potentials, and low alpha activity and voltage on electroencephalograms. These factors all substantially raise the likelihood that an individual will develop alcohol problems, but none, alone or in combination, is a sufficient or necessary determinant of alcohol abuse or dependence.

In addition, two other biological systems are currently receiving considerable research attention. The hypothalamic–pituitary–adrenal (HPA) axis is a hormone system that plays a central role in the body's response to stress. Alcohol consumption has been shown to stimulate the HPA axis system, and several studies suggest that individuals who demonstrate greater HPA activity in response to various stimuli may find alcohol consumption more reinforcing than individuals who demonstrate lower HPA activity (Becker, 2012). However, it is important to note that there are large individual differences in the response of the HPA axis to either stress or alcohol, and HPA dysfunction may play a role in only a subgroup of individuals with alcohol use problems. The endogenous opioid system plays a central role in various physiological processes, including pain relief, euphoria, and the rewarding and reinforcing effect of psychoactive substances (Volkow, 2010). Alcohol consumption also stimulates the endogenous opioid system, and it appears that endogenous opioids help to mediate the reinforcing effects of alcohol (Le Merrer, Becker, Befort, & Kieffer, 2009). Specifically, alcohol consumption increases dopamine in the nucleus accumbens, which may account for some of its reinforcing effects among some individuals. As with HPA, the endogenous opioid system may be most influential among a subgroup of individuals with alcohol use problems (Volkow, 2010).

LEARNING, MODELING, AND LIFE EVENTS

Learning theory, as applied to alcohol use, assumes that drinking is largely learned and that basic learning principles guide the acquisition, maintenance, and modification of drinking behavior. Classical conditioning models posit that the development of a drinking problem occurs largely through the pairing of conditioned stimuli, such as locations or people, with the unconditioned stimulus of alcohol. Through repeated pairings with alcohol, the conditioned stimuli come to elicit a conditioned response, which is manifested in craving for alcohol. Tolerance to alcohol has also been explained using a classical conditioning model, where the conditioned stimuli come to elicit a conditioned compensatory response (i.e., an opposite reaction to the initial drug effects) that resembles the unconditioned compensatory response elicited by alcohol consumption (Sherman, Jorenby, & Baker, 1988; Wikler, 1973). Operant conditioning models assume that alcohol consumption is governed by its reinforcing effects, including physiological and phenomenological changes in response to drinking, the social consequences of drinking, and/or the avoidance or cessation of withdrawal symptoms. In summary, learning models may explain how drinking problems may develop, and provide guidance in the design of interventions to modify drinking.

An especially influential variable in alcohol use and abuse which appears to be governed by basic learning principles is alcohol expectancy. Alcohol expectancies are the effects (positive and negative) attributed to alcohol that an individual anticipates experiencing when drinking (Goldman, Del Boca, & Darkes, 1999). Expectancies appear to develop early in life, are consistent across gender, and are learned according to social learning principles, including classical conditioning, operant conditioning, and modeling. In several different studies, alcohol expectancies have been shown to be highly related to adult and adolescent drinking practices, including drinking problems and relapse to drinking following a period of abstinence (Marlatt & Witkiewitz, 2005; Witkiewitz & Marlatt, 2007).

Research on the modeling of alcohol consumption emerged from Bandura's (1969) social learning theory, which posits that modeling influences the acquisition and performance of a variety of social behaviors. Caudill and Marlatt (1975) were among the first to experimentally study the influence of social modeling on drinking behavior, and they found that participants exposed to a heavy drinking model (a research confederate) consumed significantly more wine than those exposed to a light drinking or no model. Collins and Marlatt (1981) reviewed the research in 1981 and concluded that modeling was a powerful influence on drinking that occurred regardless of study setting or moderating variables (e.g., gender, age). Quigley and Collins (1999) performed a meta-analysis on published studies concerning the modeling of alcohol consumption and found "a definitive effect" of modeling on drinking behavior. Large effect sizes for both amount of alcohol consumed and BAC were documented. Modeling effects appear to be particularly influential among underage and young adult drinkers (Ennett et al., 2008).

For centuries, stress from life events has been thought to be related to alcohol consumption, and drinking has been seen as relieving stress (Sayette, 1999). The relationship between drinking and stress can be traced to the sociological literature of the 1940s and the emergence of the tension-reduction hypothesis in the 1950s (Pohorecky, 1991). This hypothesis proposes that (a) alcohol consumption will reduce stress under most circumstances, and (b) people will be motivated to drink in times of stress. This hypothesis forms the basis of current research about the relationship between drinking and stress (Sayette, 1999). Although studies indicate that drinking can reduce stress related to life events in certain people and under certain circumstances, the relationship between drinking and life events is far more complex than originally thought. Individual differences, including a family history of alcohol problems, certain personality traits (e.g., impulsivity), extent of self-consciousness, level of cognitive functioning, gender, and situational factors, including distraction and the timing of drinking and stress, have all been shown to be important moderators of the degree to which alcohol will reduce the subjective, behavioral, neurochemical, and immunological consequences of stress.

COGNITIVE INFLUENCES

An extensive literature exists regarding the role of cognitive influences on alcohol use. Among the earliest cognitive models of alcohol use is Hull's (1981) Self-Awareness Model. This model proposes that alcohol interferes with the process of encoding information, which subsequently decreases self-awareness by preventing the encoding of failures or poor evaluative feedback. Furthermore, the Self-Awareness Model postulates that people drink to reduce self-evaluative forms of stress. Although influential in stimulating research into cognitive influences on alcohol use problems, empirical evidence in support of the Self-Awareness Model has been inconsistent (Bacon & Ham, 2010), and other cognitive models have subsequently been proposed. The Attentional Allocation Model and Appraisal Disruption Model are especially notable.

Steele and Josephs' (1988, 1990) Attentional Allocation Model (see also Josephs & Steele, 1990) proposes that alcohol consumption reduces an individual's capacity for controlled and effortful information processing and for paying attention. Alcohol consumption results in "alcohol myopia," where attention is focused only on cues that are immediately salient and require little effortful processing. Depending on how attention is focused during intoxication (e.g., on a distraction or on current stressors), attention allocation can account for both increases and decreases in perceived stress and subjective wellbeing from drinking. Sayette's (1993) Appraisal-Disruption Model includes aspects of both the Self-Awareness Model and the Attention-Allocation Model, but it uniquely proposes that alcohol interferes with cognitive processing at the level of appraisal, which occurs early in information processing and involves the determination of the personal valence and relevance of stimuli and cues. The Appraisal-Disruption Model focuses on alcohol's effects on information organization, as opposed to self-awareness or attentional allocation, and includes a temporal dimension (i.e., before or during intoxication) in predicting how cue appraisal will influence drinking and its subjective consequences.

SEX AND RACIAL-ETHNIC CONSIDERATIONS

Whenever and wherever women's and men's alcohol use has been measured, results show that women drink less than men, and women's drinking leads to fewer social problems than does men's drinking (CSAT, 2009; NIAAA, 2017; SAMHSA, 2015; Office of the Surgeon General, 2016; Wilsnack, Vogeltanz, Wilsnack, & Harris, 2000). However, these gender differences are disappearing quickly, with drinking rates and alcohol use problems among women now approaching, and in some case equaling, those found among men (White et al., 2015). With more women experiencing drinking problems, it has become increasingly apparent that women present for treatment with gender-specific symptoms and needs. For example, Nichol, Krueger, and Iacono (2007) found that one-third of the symptoms typically used to diagnose alcohol problems concerned problems experienced almost exclusively by males (e.g., fighting while drinking). Moreover, depression appears to be particularly associated with women's drinking and drinking problems (Conner, Pinquart, & Gamble, 2009; Nichol et al., 2007). Gender differences in biological and social-structural factors associated with alcohol also contribute. For example, women are more susceptible to alcoholic liver injury than are men (Schenker, 1997; Vatsalya et al. 2016; Wagnerberger et al., 2008), likely due to less metabolism of alcohol in the stomach, and thus greater exposure to high alcohol concentrations. Gender differences in social roles vis-à-vis alcohol may remain an influence as well, though their influence appears to be waning (White et al., 2015).

While many studies have examined racial and/or ethnic differences in regard to alcohol use, the methods used for categorizing respondents' cultural/ethnic backgrounds have been rudimentary. Consequently, data on racial and/or ethnic differences must be considered preliminary. That said, across racial/ethnic groups, national epidemiological studies consistently document racial/ethnic variation in drinking, alcohol use disorders, alcohol use, and treatment engagement and retention (Chartier & Caetano, 2010; Jetelina et al., 2016). Compared with other ethnic groups, (a) Native Americans and Hispanics report higher rates of high-risk drinking; (b) Native Americans and Whites have a greater risk for alcohol use disorders; (c) Native Americans, Hispanics, and Blacks experience more severe drinking-related consequences; and (d) Hispanic problem drinkers are less likely to enter and stay in treatment. Moreover, among alcohol-dependent drinkers, Blacks and Hispanics are more likely to demonstrate recurrent or persistent alcohol dependence. Alcohol problem rates are generally lower among Asian Americans than among other ethnic and cultural groups (Cheng, Lee, & Iwamoto, 2012; Galvan & Caetano, 2003; Makimoto, 1998). However, there is some evidence to suggest that Asian Americans of mixed ethnic heritage may be at elevated risk for alcohol use problems (Price, Risk, Wong, & Klingle, 2002), and that Asian Americans may be uniquely vulnerable to both mental and physical problems when they misuse alcohol (Cheng et al., 2012). In sum, there appears to be variation in the US by race/ethnicity not only in alcohol consumption patterns, but also in the processes by which alcohol use can lead to alcohol problems.

Among individuals from Central and South America, knowing countries of origin is especially important as there are substantial between-country differences in migratory processes and experiences, as well as drinking prevalence and customs (Ramisetty-Mikler, Caetano, & Rodriguez, 2010). For example, Jetelina et al. (2016) examined putative between-country differences and found: (a) depression was significantly more prevalent among Puerto Ricans; (b) severe alcohol use disorder (i.e., with dependence) was significantly more prevalent among Mexicans; (c) volume of consumption was greater, and age of first use was younger, among Mexicans; and (d) alcohol dependence was nearly four times more likely among Hispanics with depression than among Hispanics without depression, regardless of national origin. While there were no significant differences in the proportion of current drinkers, former drinkers, lifetime abstainers, or binge drinkers across national groups, Jetelina et al. (2016) found that Mexicans were significantly more likely to meet diagnostic criteria for alcohol use problems than were other Hispanics. Mexicans also began drinking at an earlier age and consumed more alcohol. Why this might be so remains unknown, and deserves additional research attention. It is likely that social determinants play a role, including socioeconomic polarization, criminal justice problems, stresses related to immigration and/or acculturation, perceived discrimination and distrust of the dominant culture, and the lack of appropriate treatment options. Jetelina et al. also found Puerto Ricans were significantly more likely to meet diagnostic criteria for depression; this was not explained by alcohol dependence, nativity, or demographic differences. Again, why this might be so remains unknown, and merits additional research.

COURSE AND PROGNOSIS

Based largely on Jellinek's work on the progression of alcoholism (Jellinek, 1952), mid-20th-century thinking about the course of alcohol problems was that such problems develop in early adulthood (i.e., 20–30 years of age) and increase in severity over the course of several years. As noted earlier in this chapter, the notion of progressivity in alcohol problems has not been supported by research, although some alcohol problems do worsen over time. Moreover, research has shown that among those with alcohol use disorder, the severity of alcohol problems can be variable over time, sometimes improving, at other times worsening. If an individual is experiencing alcohol problems at one point, it is not possible to predict that, in the absence of treatment, the problems will worsen. However, it has long been known that men whose alcohol problems are severe are likely to continue to worsen over time if they continue to drink (Fillmore & Midanik, 1984). More recent research indicates that gender differences in the course of alcohol use and alcohol use problems are decreasing (White et al., 2015), whereas gender differences in time from first use to dependence are increasing, with an accelerated time to dependence among men (Keyes, Martins, Blanco, & Hasin, 2010).

Alcohol problems have been characterized as difficult to treat and seldom cured, with high rates of recurrence. Clinically, early recognition of the high likelihood of recurrence led to the development of relapse prevention procedures (Marlatt & Gordon, 1985). Such procedures include advising clients that setbacks may occur during recovery from the disorder and that they should use these setbacks as learning experiences to prevent future relapses, rather than as evidence that recovery is impossible. Recent research, however, has found that the probability of relapse in persons who have been in remission for several years is low (Finney & Moos, 2001; Schuckit & Smith, 2011). Moreover, a 16-year-long study of individuals treated for alcohol problems found predictors of long-term success to include first-year post-treatment engagement in AA, reduced depressive symptoms, improved stress coping, and enhanced social support for nondrinking (McKellar, Ilgen, Moos, & Moos, 2008).

CASE STUDY

The following case study provides an example of a typical client presenting for outpatient treatment of alcohol use problems.

CASE IDENTIFICATION

The patient is a single, 27-year-old, White male who voluntarily entered treatment at the Guided Self-Change (GSC) Clinic of the Addiction Research Foundation (Toronto, Canada). GSC treatment, a motivationally based cognitive-behavioral intervention, emphasizes helping clients to help themselves (Sobell & Sobell, 1993). Several published RCTs support GSC's efficacy for addressing alcohol and other drug problems. GSC employs a motivational client–therapist interactional style (see Miller & Rollnick, 2013); a cognitive-behavioral approach to planning, implementing, and maintaining changes; and a harm-reduction perspective for the treatment of alcohol use problems. GSC's major treatment components include: (a) weekly self-monitoring of behaviors targeted for change; (b) treatment goal advice, with clients selecting their own goal; (c) brief readings and homework assignments exploring high-risk situations, options, and action plans; (d) motivational strategies to increase clients' commitment to change; and (e) cognitive relapse prevention procedures.

PRESENTING COMPLAINTS

The patient was in his last year of graduate school and was planning to pursue a postdoctoral fellowship in the coming year. He reported seeking treatment because of "hitting a personal rock bottom" and an "ultimatum from my girlfriend." The client reported that 2 years prior to treatment, the frequency and quantity of his drinking had increased; personally concerned, he had tried to cut down and stop, but his own efforts had failed. He also reported that his graduate school friends and colleagues drank heavily after weekly seminars. He felt pressured to do the same, and feared negative stigmatization if he did not join in drinking with his colleagues. At treatment entry, on a readiness ruler, he reported he was "extremely ready" to take action to change his drinking. At the intake assessment he asserted, "I've started working on my problem, but I need some help." When asked why he decided to seek treatment, he replied as follows:

> A series of events which started with increased drinking, more and more drinking and not doing anything else, fights when I was intoxicated, or "drunk" for a better word, breakups with friends, stupid arguments with friends, arguments with girlfriends—just a lot of bad times and a lot of problems. I usually go for maybe 2 or 3 weeks and say, "I'm positively not going to have anything to drink again," but after a while I would say to myself, "Okay, well I can handle this now," but every time the drinking seemed to get worse, so I thought it's time to talk to somebody about it.

HISTORY

Although he reported drinking heavily for 8 years, he felt that his drinking had only been a problem for the last 4 years. At treatment entry, his scores on standardized alcohol and drug use screening questionnaires indicated a mild alcohol use problem and no current drug use problems. The patient also reported no current use of prescription medications or other psychoactive substances, including nicotine. He reported no current health problems or past treatment for mental health or substance use problems. He also reported never having attended self-help group meetings (e.g., AA) and had no prior alcohol-related hospitalizations or arrests. He reported no morning drinking in the past year, and, in terms of family history, reported that his father and grandfather had both been heavy drinkers. He reported experiencing several alcohol-related consequences in the 6 months prior to the assessment (e.g., fights in bars, personal problems, verbally abusive to others, spending too much money on alcohol). He reported that his highest-risk situations for problem drinking were when he was home alone, bored and stressed, and when out with friends after seminars. He also reported that on about half the days when he drank alcohol, he drank alone. Although this was his first treatment experience, he reported several prior unsuccessful attempts to reduce his alcohol use.

Assessment

At treatment entry, his subjective evaluation of the severity of his alcohol problem was "major" and he rated the overall quality of his life as "very unsatisfactory." Self-report of his drinking in the past year using the Timeline Follow-back assessment (Sobell & Sobell, 2000) was as follows: (1) abstinence—59% of the days; (2) drinks per drinking day—4.5 standard drinks (SDs; 1 SD = 13.6 g of absolute ethanol); (3) average weekly consumption—13 SDs; (4) highest single drinking day in the past year—14 SDs; (5) low consumption days (1–3 SDs) —42% of all days; and (6) heavy consumption—22% of all days (20% = 4–9 SDs, 2% were 10 SDs). As per GSC, he was provided with personalized feedback based on his self-reports of drinking, including descriptive drinking norms for his age and gender. In response, he said: "I'm a little alarmed. More than a little alarmed. I'm especially alarmed that I'm at the high end, but I know that's why I'm here. The other part that alarms me is that most of the people I know, I would put them in that—the high end." Based on the assessment interview, this patient met the criteria for a *DSM*-5 diagnosis of alcohol use disorder. On a continuum of alcohol use problems, the severity of his problem would be evaluated as mild.

SUMMARY

Conceptualizations of alcohol problems have improved markedly over the past several decades, affecting research and practice in regard to alcohol use disorders and their treatment. In particular, it is now recognized that severely dependent alcoholics represent only a small proportion of individuals suffering with alcohol problems. A one-size-fits-all approach is no longer appropriate for all individuals with alcohol problems. Residential treatment has lost favor, while brief screening and motivational interviewing have gained in favor. The concept that alcohol problems can be scaled along a continuum of severity is now widely accepted and has led to advances in assessment and treatment. For example, a continuum of disorder severity implies a continuum of treatment intensity, consistent with a stepped-care model where the first treatment is the least intensive, costly, and invasive, has demonstrated effectiveness at the assessed severity level, and is appealing and engaging to consumers. If treatment is not successful, then it can be stepped up to include longer, more intensive, or different components.

Assessment of alcohol problems is critical to good treatment planning and is a process that carries on throughout treatment. Besides using sound psychometric assessment instruments, the instruments should be clinically useful, feasible, and practical. Several important issues also need to be addressed at assessment. Chief among these is the assessment of co-occurring psychiatric disorders and other drug and nicotine use. Although many people with alcohol problems voluntarily seek treatment, many are coerced to seek treatment (e.g., by the courts, significant others, employers). In this regard, they often exhibit resistance and a lack of commitment to change. Motivational enhancement techniques and a motivational interviewing style are best practice for decreasing patients' resistance and increasing their commitment to change. Lastly, although alcohol use disorder can be treated successfully, there is still a high rate of relapse that must be addressed in treatment. However, a recurrence of problems does not mean the disorder is worsening; there is now abundant evidence that alcohol problems are not necessarily progressive, and across time may vary in severity, including periods of nondrinking or drinking limited quantities without problems.

REFERENCES

American Psychiatric Association. (2013). *Diagnostic and statistical manual of mental disorders* (5th ed.). Washington, DC: Author.

Bacon, A. K., & Ham, L. S. (2010). Attention to social threat as a vulnerability to the development of comorbid social anxiety disorder and alcohol use disorders: An avoidance-coping cognitive model. *Addictive Behaviors, 35*, 925–939.

Bandura, A. (1969). *Principles of behavior modification.* New York, NY: Holt, Rinehart & Winston.

Barry, K. L., & Fleming, M. F. (1993). The Alcohol Use Disorders Identification Test (AUDIT) and the SMAST-13: Predictive validity in a rural primary care sample. *Alcohol and Alcoholism, 28*, 33–42.

Batki, S. L., Meszaros, Z. S., Strutynski, K., Dimmock, J. A., Leontieva, L., Ploutz-Snyder, R., . . . Drayer, R. A. (2009). Medical comorbidity in patients with schizophrenia and alcohol dependence. *Schizophrenia Research, 107*(2), 139–146.

Beck, A. T., Epstein, N., Brown, G., & Steer, R. A. (1988). An inventory for measuring clinical anxiety: Psychometric properties. *Journal of Consulting and Clinical Psychology, 56*, 893–897.

Beck, A. T., Steer, R. A., & Garbin, M. G. (1988). Psychometric properties of the Beck Depression Inventory: Twenty-five years of evaluation. *Clinical Psychology Review, 8*, 77–100.

Becker, H. C. (2012). Effects of alcohol dependence and withdrawal on stress responsiveness and alcohol consumption. *Alcohol Research Current Reviews, 34*, 448–458.

Ben-Porath, Y., & Tellegen, A. (2008). *Minnesota Multiphasic Personality Inventory-2 Restructured Form (MMPI-2-RF).* Minneapolis, MN: University of Minnesota Press.

Bien, T. H., Miller, W. R., & Tonigan, J. S. (1993). Brief interventions for alcohol problems: A review. *Addiction, 88*, 315–336.

Bischof, G., Rumpf, H.-J., Hapke, U., Meyer, C., & John, U. (2003). Types of natural recovery from alcohol dependence: A cluster analytic approach. *Addiction, 98*(12), 1737–1746.

Boden, M. T., & Moos, R. (2009) Dually diagnosed patients' responses to substance use disorder treatment. *Journal of Substance Abuse Treatment, 37*(4), 335–345.

Bradizza C. M., Stasiewicz, P. R., & Dermen, K. H. (2014) Behavioral interventions for individuals dually-diagnosed with a severe mental illness and a substance use disorder. *Current Addiction Reports, 1*, 243–250.

Breslin, F. C., Sobell, L. C., Sobell, M. B., & Agrawal, S. (2000). A comparison of a brief and long version of the Situational Confidence Questionnaire. *Behaviour Research and Therapy, 38*, 1211–1220.

Breslow, R. A., Castle, I. P., Chen, C. M., & Graubard, B. I. (2017). Trends in alcohol consumption among older Americans: National health interview surveys, 1997 to 2014. *Alcoholism: Clinical and Environmental Research, 41*(5), 976–986.

Cahalan, D. (1970). *Problem drinkers: A national survey.* San Francisco, CA: Jossey-Bass.

Caudill, B. D., & Marlatt, G. A. (1975). Modeling influences in social drinking: An experimental analogue. *Journal of Clinical & Consulting Psychology, 43*, 405–415.

Centers for Disease Control and Prevention (CDC) (2015) *Fact sheets – alcohol use and your health.* Retrieved from https://www.cdc.gov/alcohol/fact-sheets/alcohol-use.htm.

Center for Substance Abuse Treatment (CSAT) (2009). *Substance abuse treatment: Addressing the specific needs of women.* Treatment Improvement Protocol (TIP) Series 51. HHS Publication No. (SMA) 09–4426. Rockville, MD: Substance Abuse and Mental Health Services Administration. Retrieved from http://kap.samhsa.gov/products/manuals/tips/pdf/TIP51.pdf.

Chartier, K., & Caetano, R. (2010). Ethnicity and health disparities in alcohol research. *Alcohol Research & Health, 33*(1), 152–160.

Cheng, A. W., Lee, C. S., & Iwamoto, D. K. (2012). Heavy drinking, poor mental health, and substance use among Asian Americans in the NLAAS: A gender-based comparison. *Asian American Journal of Psychology, 3,* 160–167.

Collins, R. L., & Marlatt, G. A. (1981). Social modeling as a determinant of drinking behavior: Implications for prevention and treatment. *Addictive Behaviors, 6,* 233–239.

Conner, K. R., Pinquart, M., & Gamble, S. A. (2009). Meta-analysis of depression and substance use among individuals with alcohol use disorders. *Journal of Substance Abuse Treatment, 37,* 127–137.

Cunningham, J. A., Wild, T. C., Cordingley, J., vanMierlo, T., & Humphreys, K. (2010). Twelve month follow-up results from a randomized controlled trial of a brief personalized feedback intervention for problem drinkers. *Alcohol and Alcoholism, 45,* 258–262.

Dahl, J. P., Doyle, G. A., Oslin, D. W., Buono, R. J., Ferraro, T. N., Lohoff, F. W., & Berrettini, W. H. (2005). Lack of association between single nucleotide polymorphisms in the corticotrophin releasing hormone receptor 1 (CRHR1) gene and alcohol dependence. *Journal of Psychiatric Research, 39,* 475–479.

Davies, A. D. M. (1968). The influence of age on trail making test performance. *Journal of Clinical Psychology, 24,* 96–98.

Dawson, D. A. (2000). Drinking patterns among individuals with and without *DSM-IV* alcohol use disorders. *Journal of Studies on Alcohol, 61,* 111–120.

Dawson, D. A., Goldstein, R. B., & Grant, B. F. (2013). Differences in the profiles of DSM-IV and DSM-5 Alcohol Use Disorders: Implications for clinicians. *Alcoholism: Clinical and Experimental Research, 37,* E305–E313.

Dawson, D. A., Grant, B. F., Stinson, F. S., Chou, P. S., Huang, B., & Ruan, W. J. (2005). Recovery from *DSM-IV* alcohol dependence: United States, 2001–2002. *Addiction, 100,* 281–292.

Derogatis, L. R. (1983). *SCL-90 Revised Version Manual-1.* Baltimore, MD: Johns Hopkins University, School of Medicine.

Di Giacomo, E., Zappa, L., Madeddu, F., Colmegna, F., & Clerici, M. (2017). Agreement between DSM-IV and DSM-5 criteria for alcohol use disorder among outpatients suffering from depressive and anxiety disorders. *The American Journal on Addictions, 26,* 53–56.

Edwards, A. C., Gillespie, N. A., Aggen, S. H., & Kendler, K. S. (2013). Assessment of a modified DSM-5 diagnosis of alcohol use disorder in a genetically informative population. *Alcoholism: Clinical and Experimental Research, 37,* 443–451.

Ennett, S. T., Foshee, V. A., Bauman, K. E., Hussong, A., Cai, L., Reyes, H. L. M., . . . DuRant, R. (2008). The social ecology of adolescent alcohol misuse. *Child Development, 79*(6), 1777–1791.

Esser M. B., Hedden, S. L., Kanny, D., Brewer, R. D., Gfroerer, J. C., & Naimi. T. S. (2014). Prevalence of alcohol dependence among US adult drinkers, 2009–2011. *Preventing Chronic Disease, 11,* 140329.

Fillmore, K. M., & Midanik, L. (1984). Chronicity of drinking problems among men: A longitudinal study. *Journal of Studies on Alcohol, 45,* 228–236.

Finney, J. W., & Moos, R. H. (1991). The long-term course of treated alcoholism, I: Mortality, relapse and remission rates and comparisons with community controls. *Journal of Studies on Alcohol, 52,* 44–54.

Fleming, M. F., Barry, K. L., & MacDonald, R. (1991). The Alcohol Use Disorders Identification Test (AUDIT) in a college sample. *International Journal of Addictions, 26,* 1173–1185.

Foroud, T., Edenberg, H. J., & Crabbe, J. C. (2010). Who is at risk for alcoholism? *Alcohol Research & Health, 33*(1), 64–75.

Galvan, F. H., & Caetano, R. (2003). Alcohol use and related problems among ethnic minorities in the United States. *Alcohol Research & Health, 27*(1), 87–94.

Global Drug Survey (2014). *Reflections on the results of the world's biggest ever drug survey by Dr Adam Winstock.* Retrieved from https://www.globaldrugsurvey.com/past-findings/the-global-drug-survey-2014-findings/.

Gmel, G., Wicki, M., Rehm, J., & Heeb, J. L. (2008). Estimating regression to the mean and true effects of an intervention in a four-wave panel study. *Addiction, 103*(1), 32–41.

Goldman, M. S., DelBoca, F. K., & Darkes, J. (1999). Alcohol expectancy theory: The application of cognitive neuroscience. In K. E. Leonard & H. T. Blane (Eds.), *Psychological theories of drinking and alcoholism* (2nd ed., pp. 203–246). New York, NY: Guilford Press.

González-Pinto, A., Alberich, S., Barbeito, S., Alonso, M., Vieta, E., Martínez-Arán, A., . . . López, P. (2010). Different profile of substance abuse in relation to predominant polarity in bipolar disorder: The Vitoria long-term follow-up study. *Journal of Affective Disorders, 124*, 250–255.

Grant, B. F., Goldstein, R. B., Saha, T. D., Chou, S. P., Jung, J., Zhang, H., . . . Hasin, D. S. (2015) Epidemiology of DSM-5 alcohol use disorder: Results from the National Epidemiologic Survey on Alcohol and Related Conditions III. *JAMA Psychiatry, 72*, 757–766.

Hagman, B. T. & Cohn, A. M. (2011). Toward DSM-V: Mapping the alcohol use disorder continuum in college students. *Drug and Alcohol Dependence, 118*, 202–208.

Hamilton, M. (1960). A rating scale for depression. *Journal of Neurology, Neurosurgery and Psychiatry, 23*, 56–62.

Hardie, T. L., Moss, H. B., & Lynch, K. G. (2008). Sex differences in the heritability of alcohol problems. *The American Journal on Addictions, 17*, 319–327.

Hasin, D. S., Wall, M., Witkiewitz, K., Kranzler, H. R., Falk, D., Litten, R., . . . Anton, R. (2017). Change in non-abstinent WHO drinking risk levels and alcohol dependence: A 3 year follow-up study in the US general population. *The Lancet Psychiatry, 4*, 469–476.

Hathaway, S. R., & McKinley, J. C. (1989). Restandardized by J. N. Butcher, W. G. Dahlstrom, J. R. Graham, A. Tellegen, & B. Kaemmer. (2001). *The Minnesota Multiphasic Personality Inventory.* Minneapolis: University of Minnesota Press.

Hester, R. K., Delaney, H. D., Campbell, W., & Handmaker, N. (2009). A web application for moderation training: Initial results of a randomized clinical trial. *Journal of Substance Abuse Treatment, 37*(3), 266–276.

Hull, J. G. (1981). A self-awareness model of the causes and effects of alcohol consumption. *Journal of Abnormal Psychology, 90*(6), 586–600.

Humphreys, K. (2009). Searching where the light is worse: Overemphasizing genes and under-playing environment in the quest to reduce substance misuse. *Clinical Pharmacology and Therapeutics, 85*, 357–358.

Humphreys, K., Blodgett, J. C., & Wagner, T. H. (2014). Estimating the efficacy of Alcoholics Anonymous without self-selection bias: An instrumental variables re-analysis of randomized clinical trials. *Alcoholism: Clinical and Experimental Research, 38*, 2688–2694.

Institute of Medicine. (1990). *Broadening the base of treatment for alcohol problems.* Washington, DC: National Academy Press.

Jellinek, E. M. (1942). *Alcohol addiction and chronic alcoholism.* New Haven, CT: Yale University Press.

Jellinek, E. M. (1952). Phases of alcohol addiction. *Quarterly Journal of Studies on Alcohol, 13*, 673–684.

Jellinek, E. M. (1960). *The disease concept of alcoholism.* New Brunswick, NJ: Hillhouse Press.

Jetelina, K. K., Reingle Gonzalez, J. M., Vaeth, P. A. C., Mills, B. A., & Caetano, R. (2016). An Investigation of the relationship between alcohol use and Major Depressive Disorder across Hispanic national groups. *Alcoholism: Clinical and Experimental Research, 40*, 536–542.

Josephs, R. A., & Steele, C. M. (1990). The two faces of alcohol myopia: Attentional mediation of psychological stress. *Journal of Abnormal Psychology, 99*, 115–126.

Kelly, J. F. (2017). Are societies paying unnecessarily for an otherwise free lunch? Final musings on the research on alcoholics anonymous and its mechanisms of behavior change. *Addiction, 112*, 943–945.

Keyes, K. M., Martins, S. S., Blanco, C., & Hasin, D. S. (2010). Telescoping and gender differences in alcohol dependence: New evidence from two national surveys. *American Journal of Psychiatry, 167*, 969–976.

King, M. P., & Tucker, J. A. (2000). Behavior change patterns and strategies distinguishing moderation drinking and abstinence during the natural resolution of alcohol problems without treatment. *Psychology of Addictive Behaviors, 14*, 48–55.

Klingemann, H. K., Sobell, L. C., Barker, J., Blomquist, J., Cloud, W., Ellinstad, D., . . . Tucker, J. (2001). *Promoting self-change from problem substance use: Practical implications for policy, prevention and treatment.* Boston, MA: Kluwer Academic.

Klingemann, H., Sobell, M. B., & Sobell, L. C. (2009). Continuities and changes in self-change research. *Addiction, 105*, 1510–1518.

Kongs, S. K., Thompson, L. L., Iverson, G. L., & Heaton, R. K. (2000). *Wisconsin Card Sorting Test - 64 card version: Professional manual.* Odessa, Ukraine: Psychological Assessment Resources.

Kuerbis, A. N., Hagman, B. T., & Sacco, P. (2013) Functioning of alcohol use disorders criteria among middle-aged and older adults: Implications for DSM-5. *Substance Use & Misuse, 48*, 309–322.

Le Merrer, J., Becker, J. A., Befort, K., & Kieffer, B. L. (2009). Reward processing by the opioid system in the brain. *Physiological Research, 89*, 1379–1412.

Mack, A. H., Harrington, A. L., & Frances, R. J. (2010). *Clinical manual for treatment of alcoholism and addictions.* Arlington, VA: American Psychiatric.

Makimoto, K. (1998). Drinking patterns and drinking problems among Asian-Americans and Pacific Islanders. *Alcohol Health & Research World, 22*(4), 270–275.

Marlatt, G. A. (1978). *Craving for alcohol, loss of control, and relapse.* New York, NY: Plenum Press.

Marlatt, G. A., & Gordon, J. R. (1985). *Relapse prevention.* New York, NY: Guilford Press.

Marlatt, G. A., & Witkiewitz, K. (2005). Relapse prevention for alcohol and drug problems. In G. A. Marlatt & D. M. Donovan (Eds.), *Relapse prevention: Maintenance strategies in the treatment of addictive behaviors* (2nd ed., pp. 1–44). New York, NY: Guilford Press.

McDonell, M. G., Leickly, E., McPherson, S., Skalisky, J., Srebnik, D., Angelo, F., . . . Ries, R. K. (2017). A randomized controlled trial of ethyl glucuronide-based contingency management for outpatients with co-occurring alcohol use disorders and serious mental illness. *American Journal of Psychiatry, 174*, 370–377.

McKellar, J., Ilgen, M., Moos, B. S., & Moos, R. (2008). Predictors of changes in alcohol-related self-efficacy over 16 years. *Journal of Substance Abuse Treatment, 35*, 148–155.

McMurran, M. & Hollin, C. R. (1989). The Short Alcohol Dependence Data (SADD) Questionnaire: norms and reliability data for male young offenders. *British Journal of Addiction, 84*: 315–318.

Mewton, L., Slade, T., McBride, O., Grove, R., & Teesso, M. (2011). An evaluation of the proposed DSM-5 alcohol use disorder criteria using Australian national data. *Addiction, 106*, 941–950.

Miller, W. R., & Rollnick, S. (1991). *Motivational interviewing: Preparing people to change addictive behavior.* New York, NY: Guilford Press.

Miller, W. R., & Rollnick, S. (2002). *Motivational interviewing: Preparing people for change* (2nd ed.). New York, NY: Guilford Press.

Miller, W. R., & Rollnick, S. (2013). *Motivational interviewing: Helping people change* (3rd ed.). New York, NY: Guilford Press.

Millon, T., Millon, C., Davis, R., & Grossman, S. (2006). *Millon Clinical Multiaxial Inventory-III (MCMI-III).* San Antonio, TX: Pearson.

Mohatt, G. V., Rasmus, S. M., Thomas, L., Allen, J., Hazel, K., & Marlatt, G. A. (2007). Risk, resilience, and natural recovery: A model of recovery from alcohol abuse for Alaska natives. *Addiction, 103,* 205–215.

Morgenstern, J., Kuerbis, A., & Muench, F. (2015). Ecological momentary assessment and alcohol use disorder treatment. *Alcohol Research: Current Reviews, 36*(1), 101–109.

Murphy, C. M., & MacKillop, J. (2011). Factor Structure Validation of the Alcohol Dependence Scale in a Heavy Drinking College Sample. *Journal of Psychopathology and Behavioral Assessment, 33,* 523–530.

National Institute on Alcohol Abuse and Alcoholism. (2011). *Alcohol Screening and Brief Intervention for Youth: A Practitioner's Guide.* Rockville, MD: US Department of Health & Human Services.

National Institute on Alcohol Abuse and Alcoholism. (2005). *Helping patients who drink too much: A clinician's guide.* Rockville, MD: US Department of Health & Human Services.

National Institute on Alcohol Abuse and Alcoholism. (2015). *Transcript: Wearable alcohol biosensor video description.* Retrieved from https://www.niaaa.nih.gov/transcript-wearable-alcohol-biosensor-video-description.

National Institute on Alcohol Abuse and Alcoholism. (2017). *Alcohol facts and statistics.* Retrieved from https://pubs.niaaa.nih.gov/publications/AlcoholFacts&Stats/AlcoholFacts&Stats.pdf.

Niaura, R. S., Rohsenow, D. J., Binkoff, J. A., Monti, P. M., Abrams, D. A., & Pedraza, M. (1988). Relevance of cue reactivity to understanding alcohol and smoking relapse. *Journal of Abnormal Psychology, 97,* 133–152.

Nichol, P. E., Krueger, R. F., & Iacono, W. G. (2007). Investigating gender differences in alcohol problems: A latent trait modeling approach. *Alcoholism: Clinical and Experimental Research, 31*(5), 783–794.

Nowinski, J., Baker, S. C., & Carroll, K. (1992). *Twelve step facilitation therapy manual* (Project MATCH Monograph Vol. 1). Rockville, MD: National Institute on Alcohol Abuse and Alcoholism.

Nunes, E. V., Selzer, J., Levounis, P., & Davies, C. (2010). *Substance dependence and co-occurring psychiatric disorders: Best practices for diagnosis and clinical treatment.* New York, NY: Civic Research Institute.

Office of the Surgeon General (2016). *Facing addiction in America: The Surgeon General's report on alcohol, drugs, and health.* Washington, DC: U.S. Department of Health and Human Services.

Orford, J. (2001). Addiction as excessive appetite. *Addiction, 96,* 15–31.

Pakula, B., Macdonald, S., & Stockwell, T. (2009). Settings and functions related to simultaneous use of alcohol with marijuana or cocaine among clients in treatment for substance abuse. *Substance Use & Misuse, 44*(2), 212–226.

Pattison, E. M., Sobell, M. B., & Sobell, L. C. (1977). *Emerging concepts of alcohol dependence.* New York, NY: Springer.

Pohorecky, L. A. (1991). Stress and alcohol interaction: An update of human research. *Alcoholism: Clinical and Experimental Research, 15,* 438–459.

Prescott, C. A. (2002). Sex differences in the genetic risk for alcoholism. *Alcohol Research & Health, 26*(4), 264–273.

Price, R. K., Risk, N. K., Wong, M. W., & Klingle, R. S. (2002). Substance use and abuse in Asian American and Pacific Islanders (AAPIs): Preliminary results from four national epidemiologic Studies. *Public Health Reports, 17,* S39–S50.

Quigley, B. M., & Collins, R. L. (1999). The modeling of alcohol consumption: A meta-analytic review. *Journal of Studies on Alcohol, 60,* 90–98.

Raistrick, D., Dunbar, G., & Davidson, R. (1983). Development of a questionnaire to measure alcohol dependence. *British Journal of Addiction, 78,* 89–95.

Ramisetty-Mikler, S., Caetano, R., & Rodriguez, L. A. (2010). The Hispanic Americans Baseline Alcohol Survey (HABLAS): Alcohol consumption and sociodemographic predictors across Hispanic national groups. *Journal of Substance Use, 15,* 402–416.

Ray, L. A., MacKillop, J., & Monti, P. M. (2010). Subjective responses to alcohol consumption as endophenotypes: Advancing behavioral genetics in etiological and treatment models of alcoholism. *Substance Use & Misuse, 45*, 1742–1765.

Room, R. (1990). *Measuring alcohol consumption in the United States: Methods and rationales.* New York, NY: Plenum Press.

Salvatore, J. E., Gottesman, I. I., & Dick, D. M. (2015). Endophenotypes for alcohol use disorder: An update on the field. *Current Addiction Reports, 2*(1), 76–90.

Saunders, J. B., Aasland, O. G., Babor, T. F., De LaFuente, J. R., & Grant, M. (1993). Development of the Alcohol Use Disorders Identification Test (AUDIT): WHO collaborative project on early detection of persons with harmful alcohol consumption. *Addiction, 88*, 791–804.

Sayette, M. A. (1993). An appraisal-disruption model of alcohol's effects on stress responses in social drinkers. *Psychological Bulletin, 114*(3), 459–476.

Sayette, M. A. (1999). Does drinking reduce stress? *Alcohol Health and Research World, 23*, 250–255.

Schenker, S. (1997). Medical consequences of alcohol abuse: Is gender a factor? *Alcoholism: Clinical and Experimental Research, 21*, 179–181.

Schuckit, M. A. (2006). *Drug and alcohol abuse: A clinical guide to diagnosis and treatment* (6th ed.). New York, NY: Springer.

Schuckit, M. A., & Smith, T. L. (2011). Onset and course of alcoholism over 25 years in middle class men. *Drug and Alcohol Dependence, 113*, 21–28.

Sherman, J. E., Jorenby, D. E., & Baker, T. B. (1988). Classical conditioning with alcohol: Acquired preferences and aversions, tolerance, and urges/cravings. In C. D. Chaudron & D. A. Wilkinson (Eds.), *Theories on alcoholism* (pp. 173–237). Toronto, Canada: Addiction Research Foundation.

Skinner, H. A. & Allen, B. A. (1982). Alcohol dependence syndrome: Measurement and validation. *Journal of Abnormal Psychology, 91*, 199–209.

Skinner, H. A., & Sheu, W. J. (1982). Reliability of alcohol use indices: The Lifetime Drinking History and the MAST. *Journal of Studies on Alcohol, 43*, 1157–1170.

Sobell, L. C., Agrawal, S., & Sobell, M. B. (1999). Utility of liver function tests for screening "alcohol abusers" who are not severely dependent on alcohol. *Substance Use & Misuse, 34*, 1723–1732.

Sobell, L. C., Cunningham, J. A., & Sobell, M. B. (1996). Recovery from alcohol problems with and without treatment: Prevalence in two population surveys. *American Journal of Public Health, 86*, 966–972.

Sobell, L. C., Ellingstad, T. P., & Sobell, M. B. (2000). Natural recovery from alcohol and drug problems: Methodological review of the research with suggestions for future directions. *Addiction, 95*, 749–764.

Sobell, L. C., & Sobell, M. B. (1995). Alcohol consumption measures. In J. P. Allen & M. Columbus (Eds.), *Assessing alcohol problems: A guide for clinicians and researchers* (pp. 55–73). Rockville, MD: National Institute on Alcohol Abuse and Alcoholism.

Sobell, L. C., & Sobell, M. B. (2000). Alcohol Timeline Followback (TLFB) In American Psychiatric Association (Ed.), *Handbook of psychiatric measures* (pp. 477–479). Washington, DC: Author.

Sobell, M. B., Bogardis, J., Schuller, R., Leo, G. I., & Sobell, L. C. (1989). Is self-monitoring of alcohol consumption reactive? *Behavioral Assessment, 11*, 447–458.

Sobell, M. B., & Sobell, L. C. (1993). *Problem drinkers: Guided self-change treatment.* New York, NY: Guilford Press.

Sobell, M. B., & Sobell, L. C. (1995). Controlled drinking after 25 years: How important was the great debate? *Addiction, 90*, 1149–1153.

Steele, C. M., & Josephs, R. A. (1988). Drinking your troubles away, II: An attention allocation model of alcohol's effect on psychological stress. *Journal of Abnormal Psychology, 97*(2), 196–205.

Steele, C. M., & Josephs, R. A. (1990). Alcohol myopia: Its prized and dangerous effects. *The American Psychologist, 45*(8), 921–933.

Stockwell, T., Murphy, D., & Hodgson, R. (1983). The Severity of Alcohol Dependence Questionnaire: Its use, reliability and validity. *British Journal of Addiction*, *78*, 145–155.

Stockwell, T., Sitharthan, T., McGrath, D., & Lang, E. (1994). The measurement of alcohol dependence and impaired control in community samples. *Addiction*, *89*, 167–174.

Substance Abuse and Mental Health Services Administration (SAMHSA). (2015). *2015 National Survey on Drug Use and Health (NSDUH)*. Retrieved from https://www.samhsa.gov/data/sites/default/files/NSDUH-FFR1-2015/NSDUH-FFR1-2015/NSDUH-FFR1-2015.pdf.

Substance Abuse and Mental Health Services Administration. (2009). *Integrated treatment for co-occurring disorders: The evidence*. DHHS Publication No. SMA-08-4366, Rockville, MD: Center for Mental Health Services, Substance Abuse and Mental Health Services Administration, U.S. Department of Health and Human Services.

Substance Abuse and Mental Health Services Administration. (2005). *Substance abuse treatment for persons with co-occurring disorders*. Treatment Improvement Protocol (TIP) Series, No. 42. HHS Publication No. (SMA) 133992. Rockville, MD: Substance Abuse and Mental Health Services Administration.

Tyburski, E. M., Sokolowski, A., Samochowiec, J., & Samochowiec, A. (2014). New diagnostic criteria for alcohol use disorders and novel treatment approaches – 2014 update. *Archives of Medical Science*, *10*(6), 1191–1197.

Vatsalya, V., Song, M., Schwandt, M. L., Cave, M. C., Barve, S. S., George, D. T., . . . McClain, C. J. (2016). Effects of sex, drinking history, and omega-3 and omega-6 fatty acids dysregulation on the onset of liver injury in very heavy drinking alcohol-dependent patients. *Alcoholism, Clinical and Experimental Research*, *40*, 2085–2093.

Verderhus, J. (2016). Mind the gap – a European viewpoint on alcoholics anonymous. *Addiction*, *112*, 937–938.

Volkow, N. L. (2010). Opioid-dopamine interactions: Implications for substance use disorders and their treatment. *Biological Psychiatry*, *68*, 685–686.

Wagnerberger, S., Schafer, C., Schwarz, E., Bode, C., & Parlesak, A. (2008). Is nutrient intake a gender-specific cause for enhanced susceptibility to alcohol-induced liver disease in women? *Alcohol & Alcoholism*, *43*(1), 9–14.

Wechsler, D. (2008). *Wechsler Adult Intelligence Scale-Fourth Edition (WAIS-IV)*. San Antonio, TX: Pearson.

Wechsler, D. (2009). *Wechsler Memory Scale – Fourth Edition (WMS-IV)*. San Antonio, TX: Pearson.

White, A., Castle, I. J., Chen, C. M., Shirley, M., Roach, D., Hingson, R. (2015) Converging patterns of alcohol use and related outcomes among females and males in the United States, 2002 to 2012. *Alcoholism, Clinical and Experimental Research*, *39*, 1712–1726.

Wikler, A. (1973). Dynamics of drug dependence. *Archives of General Psychiatry*, *28*, 611–616.

Wilsnack, R. W., Vogeltanz, N. D., Wilsnack, S. C., & Harris, T. R. (2000). Gender differences in alcohol consumption and adverse drinking consequences: Cross-cultural patterns. *Addiction*, *95*, 251–265.

Witkiewitz, K., & Marlatt, G. A. (2007). Overview of relapse prevention. In K. A. Witkiewitz & G. A. Marlatt (Eds.), *Therapist's guide to evidence-based relapse prevention* (pp. 3–17). San Diego, CA: Elsevier Academic Press.

World Health Organization. (2015). *Alcohol fact sheet*. Geneva, Switzerland: WHO, Media Centre. Retrieved from http://www.who.int/mediacentre/factsheets/fs349/en/

CHAPTER 19

Substance-Related and Addictive Disorders: Drugs

STACEY B. DAUGHTERS and JENNIFER Y. YI

INTRODUCTION

Substance use disorder is a prevalent and pervasive public health concern in the United States, incurring major costs to individuals, families, and society at large. In 2014, approximately 21.5 million Americans age 12 or older had a substance use disorder in the past year (SAMHSA, 2015). The financial burden on society from substance use is estimated to be greater than $600 billion annually in substance use-related treatment and prevention, health care expenditures, lost wages, reduced job production, accidents, and crime (SAMHSA, 2014a). In addition to the substantial economic cost, substance use disorder is associated with engagement in multiple health-compromising and risk-taking behaviors (e.g., condom nonuse, multiple partners, impulsive spending, driving while intoxicated) that contribute significantly to public health costs (Office of National Drug Control Policy [ONDCP], 2004).

DIAGNOSTIC CONSIDERATIONS

The *Diagnostic and Statistical Manual* (*DSM-5*; APA, 2013) provides a comprehensive classification system for the assessment and subsequent diagnosis of a *substance use disorder* across 10 drug classes, including alcohol, cannabis, phencyclidine, other hallucinogens, inhalants, opioids, sedatives, stimulants, tobacco, and other/unknown. Each substance is defined as a separate substance use disorder. The essential feature of a substance use disorder is continued substance use in spite of clinically and functionally significant impairment or distress, such as negative social and financial consequences, legal problems, and failure to meet responsibilities at work, school, or home. A key characteristic of a substance use disorder is an underlying change in the user's neurological circuitry, a side-effect that may persist even after substance use is discontinued, especially in individuals with a severe substance use disorder. This altered circuitry is believed to increase the vulnerability for repeated relapse, particularly when individuals encounter substances or substance-related stimuli.

Adult Psychopathology and Diagnosis, Eighth Edition. Edited by Deborah C. Beidel and B. Christopher Frueh.
© 2018 John Wiley & Sons, Inc. Published 2018 by John Wiley & Sons, Inc.
Companion website: www.wiley.com/go/beidel/psychopathology8e

The diagnostic criteria for a substance use disorder specify a maladaptive pattern of behaviors related to substance use. These behaviors fall into four categories: *impaired control, social impairment, risky use,* and *pharmacological criteria.*

Impaired control (criteria 1–4) is often characterized by using for longer periods of time or using larger amounts than intended, or engaging in unsuccessful efforts to follow through with intended plans to reduce use. Impaired control may also be evidenced by spending an excessive amount of time getting, using, or recovering from substance use. Additionally, impaired control can involve craving, a perceived need to engage in substance use operationalized as the extent to which the desire to use consumes an individual's thoughts. Craving often arises in the context of prior use (e.g., the presence of people with whom one had used; being in a location where one had previously used).

Social impairment (criteria 5–7) pertains to an inability to carry out the needs of daily life in all facets of one's environment, whether it involves failing to fulfill obligations or opting to use rather than engaging in social activities. It may also include giving up or reducing engagement in important and meaningful social activities. Further, social impairment is characterized by persistent substance use in spite of the negative social impact (e.g., having arguments and losing relationships with loved ones due to substance use).

Risky use (criteria 8, 9) involves the continued use of a substance that is known to present a danger to the user. This risk might entail using in a dangerous situation (e.g., driving, using machinery, unsafe sex) or using with a known vulnerability to a physical or psychological issue that would likely be made worse by further use.

Pharmacological criteria (criteria 10, 11) focus on tolerance and withdrawal. Tolerance is a state that develops wherein the user needs progressively larger doses of the drug in order to feel the desired effect. Withdrawal is a physical response to specific substances that can occur after extended, consistent use.

Substance use disorders can be further defined on a continuum as mild (two to three symptoms), moderate (four to five symptoms), or severe (six or more symptoms), indicating the level of severity that is determined by the number of 11 possible diagnostic criteria met. Substance use disorders can also be detailed by specifying "in early remission" (at least 3 months but less than 12 months without meeting criteria), "in sustained remission" (at least 12 months without meeting criteria), "on maintenance therapy," and/or "in a controlled environment."

CLINICAL PICTURE

In 2015, there were an estimated 2.3 million admissions to treatment for substance use at a specialty facility (Lipari, Park-Lee, & Van Horn, 2016). Between 2004 and 2014, five substance categories, alcohol, opiates, marijuana, cocaine, and methamphetamine/amphetamines accounted for between 96% and 97% of treatment admissions for substance use (SAMHSA, 2016). Among the different treatment settings available, most admissions (61%) received ambulatory care. In addition, 22% received detoxification and 17% received rehabilitation or residential treatment.

Specific populations are more vulnerable to initiation and continued substance use. In particular, youth and young adults are special populations of interest, because early use increases the likelihood of developing substance use problems. In 2014, approximately 1.3 million (5.0%) adolescents between the ages of 12 and 17 had a substance use disorder (SAMHSA, 2015).

PHYSIOLOGICAL AND PSYCHOLOGICAL EFFECTS

Substance use disorder can involve the recurrent use of a single or multiple substances. Commonly, substances are grouped based on categories that vary in their physiological and behavioral effects. In this section, we discuss the different substance categories, excluding nicotine and alcohol, which are discussed in other chapters. This discussion includes street and slang names, physiological and psychological effects of each category, and the withdrawal symptoms that occur with continued use and as tolerance develops. Interested readers are referred to Advokat, Comaty, & Julien (2014) for an extensive review.

Cannabinoids, such as marijuana, sinsemilla, and hashish (street names include dope, pot, weed, grass, hash), produce mild euphoria, sedation, enhanced sensory perception, increased appetite and pulse, psychomotor impairment, and confusion. Tolerance can occur with habitual use, and discontinuation of use can result in uncomfortable withdrawal effects, including anxiety, depression, irritability, and insomnia. Although cannabinoids are increasingly being used for medical purposes, they are still considered illegal under federal law.

Alternatively, hallucinogens, which include LSD (acid, blotter), mescaline (buttons, peyote, mesc), and psilocybin (magic mushrooms, shrooms), create an altered state of consciousness, detachment from self and environment, and dissociative symptoms. Hallucinogens are not physically addictive; however, LSD and mescaline produce negative physiological reactions such as increased body temperature, blood pressure, and heart rate. Psychologically, hallucinogen use can result in persistent mental disorders characterized by panic attacks and psychosis.

While both cannabinoids and hallucinogens are illegal street drugs, central nervous system (CNS) depressants, including benzodiazepines (e.g., alprazolam [Xanax], diazepam [Valium], lorazepam [Ativan], clonazepam [Klonopin]; benzos, xannies), and barbiturates (Seconal, Amytal, Phenobarbital; reds, yellows, yellow jackets, barbs) are legal substances which can be prescribed by a medical doctor. With low or moderate doses, they produce euphoria and disinhibition as well as decreased respiration, pulse, and blood pressure. At higher doses, confusion, impaired judgment, coordination, and memory loss occur. CNS depressants are particularly dangerous when combined because this increases the risk of respiratory depression and arrest. With long-term use, tolerance occurs and discontinuation of use can cause symptoms ranging from anxiety, insomnia, nausea, and muscle tension to more severe symptoms such as seizures, hallucinations, and psychosis.

Opioids (e.g., codeine, fentanyl, oxycodone) can be prescribed by a medical doctor for pain relief, yet are also commonly misused. Illicit opioids include opium (big O, tar) and heroin (dope, H, junk, smack). The effects of intoxication include euphoria, sedation, drowsiness, confusion, nausea, constipation, and respiratory depression. High doses of opioids can lead to coma and death. With prolonged use, tolerance occurs and, in the absence of the drug, users experience craving, sweating, fever, diarrhea, vomiting, and pain.

Unlike CNS depressants and opiates, stimulants increase respiration, heart rate, and blood pressure, and decrease appetite. Stimulants include cocaine (crack, coke, blow, yayo), methamphetamine (meth, speed, crystal, crank), MDMA (ecstasy, E, X, Adam), amphetamines (e.g., Adderall, Dexedrine; speed), and methylphenidate (e.g., Ritalin, Concerta, Daytrana; vitamin R, skippy, R-ball). Some stimulants can be obtained with a prescription from a medical doctor (e.g., amphetamines, methylphenidate), although they are categorized as controlled substances and their use is illegal without the appropriate prescription. Meanwhile, other stimulants (e.g., cocaine, methamphetamine) are illegal. Stimulant intoxication produces euphoria, mental alertness, and increased energy. Impulsive behavior, aggressiveness, anxiety, and irritability are also common features experienced by users. Additionally, prolonged use or high doses of stimulants can result in stimulant-induced psychosis. Due to the stress placed on the cardiovascular system, stimulant use can cause cardiac arrest, stroke, and death. Tolerance can occur quickly, and withdrawal symptoms include anxiety, anhedonia, irritability, insomnia, and depression.

Dissociative anesthetics include ketamine (special K, vitamin K) and PCP (angel dust, hog, ozone, rocket fuel, wack). They can be, but are rarely, prescribed by a medical doctor for mental health conditions. They create a dream-like state, euphoria, numbness, increased heart rate and blood pressure, and impaired memory and motor function. At high doses, ketamine can cause delirium, respiratory depression, and arrest. PCP use can result in panic, aggression, depression, and violence. Users of dissociative anesthetics quickly experience increasing tolerance, and a permanent tolerance may develop after several months of use. Although tolerance occurs, these drugs do not appear to have withdrawal symptoms.

Inhalants include a range of obtainable solvents (e.g., glues, paint thinners, gasoline, lighter fluid), gases (e.g., propane, butane, aerosol propellants, nitrous oxide; laughing gas, whippets, chloroform), nitrates (isobutyl, isoamyl; poppers, snappers), and aerosols (e.g., hair spray, spray paint). Inhalants are "huffed" through the nose and mouth and enter the lungs and subsequently the bloodstream rather quickly. The effects of intoxication include loss of motor skills and inhibition, slurred speech, headache, nausea, wheezing, and loss of consciousness. Extended use can lead to muscle weakness, memory impairment, depression, damage to the nervous and cardiovascular systems, and sudden death. There is little known about the tolerance and withdrawal of inhalants.

Synthetic cathinones (bath salts, vanilla sky, cloud nine, plant food) typically take the form of white or brown crystal-like powder that can be used in a variety of methods such as swallowing, snorting, smoking, or injection. They were originally manufactured and marketed as "legal highs," but have since been subject to federal bans. The physiological effect of synthetic cathinones is still largely unknown, but they are known to have similar chemical properties to amphetamines, cocaine, and MDMA. Users of synthetic cathinones report increased energy and agitation, accompanied by increased heart rate and blood pressure. Additional effects include paranoia, hallucinations, increased sociability and sex drive, panic attacks, and excited delirium (e.g., extreme agitation and violent behavior). Withdrawal symptoms include depression, anxiety, tremors, insomnia, and paranoia.

COMORBIDITY

Substance use disorders co-occur with many clinical disorders, ranging from depression and anxiety disorders to personality disorders. National epidemiological data suggest that among individuals with any substance use disorder, the prevalence rates for any mood and anxiety disorder are 40.9% and 29.9%, respectively (Conway, Compton, Stinson, & Grant, 2006). Mood and anxiety disorders are the most common comorbidities, followed by antisocial personality disorder (Jane-Llopis & Matysina, 2006) and schizophrenia-spectrum disorders (Kushner, Abrams, & Borchardt, 2000). Among personality disorders, borderline and antisocial personality disorders have the highest rates of co-occurrence with substance use disorders, with estimates ranging from 5% to 32% and 14% to 69%, respectively (e.g., Goldstein et al., 2007; Trull, Sher, Minks-Brown,

Durbin, & Burr, 2000). Additionally, prevalence of disorders differs by substance. For example, among individuals with *DSM-IV* lifetime opioid abuse or dependence, nearly 50% met the criteria for a personality disorder (Grella, Karno, Warda, Niv, & Moore, 2009b). These statistics are particularly alarming given that individuals with co-occurring disorders generally have worse treatment outcomes (e.g., noncompliance and relapse), higher rates of suicidal ideation, chronic physical health problems, distorted perception and cognition, social exclusion, aggression, legal problems, and homelessness (e.g., Horsfall, Cleary, Hunt, & Walter, 2009; McCauley, Killeen, Gros, Brady, & Back, 2012).

The causal direction of co-occurring conditions is mixed, with some evidence that mental disorders serve as risk factors predicting the onset of substance use disorders (Kessler, 2004; NIDA, 2009). Stronger predictors of the onset of substance use disorders include major depression, disruptive behavior disorders, bipolar disorder, as well as anxiety disorders, excluding generalized anxiety disorder, post-traumatic stress disorder (PTSD), and agoraphobia (Swendsen et al., 2010). Alternatively, other studies have found that substance use disorders predict later mental illness (Kessler, 2004; NIDA, 2009), as well as suicide (Yen et al., 2004) and mortality (Clark, Martin, & Cornelius, 2008). In addition, there is growing evidence for substance-induced disorders, such as stimulant- and cannabinoid-induced psychosis. Psychotic symptoms are estimated to occur in approximately 40% of amphetamine-dependent patients, although these symptoms are very likely to dissipate in 1–3 days. Cannabinoid use has been found to exacerbate the risk for psychosis in individuals who already carry a predisposition for psychosis. Additional studies have found differences in demographic (e.g., homelessness, older), familial (e.g., less family support), and clinical characteristics (e.g., greater awareness of psychotic symptoms) distinguishing substance-induced psychosis from a primary psychotic disorder (Caton et al., 2005). Temporary substance-induced depressive and anxiety symptoms have also been reported in the context of drug intoxication and withdrawal (Ahmadi & Ahmadi, 2005; Schuckit, 2006).

ASSESSMENT

Several variables need to be considered when determining the best method of assessment. It is important to determine if the goal of the assessment is to screen for potential substance use problems, to determine if an individual meets diagnostic criteria for a substance use disorder, to develop treatment goals and a treatment plan, or to assess treatment outcome. Commonly used psychological measures for screening, diagnosis, treatment planning, and post-treatment outcome measurement in line with *DSM-5* criteria and diagnoses are outlined in Table 19.1.

Screening and Treatment Planning

Given the high rate of comorbidity between substance use disorders and other psychological disorders, particularly mood, anxiety, or thought disorders, patients often present to treatment for problems other than substance use. As such, screening measures are useful for identifying substance use disorders in other settings. Several diagnostic instruments are available for use in both research and clinical settings, with advantages and disadvantages inherent in each instrument with regard to administration, cost, and interviewer qualification and training requirements.

Once a substance use problem or diagnosis is established, it is important to assess how the patient's frequency and severity of substance use has affected other life areas

Table 19.1

Instruments for the Screening and Diagnosis of *DSM-5* Substance Use Disorders

Instrument	Summary	Method of Administration	Population
Screening			
CAGE-AID (Brown & Rounds, 1995)	A four-item screener for substance use problems. Each "have you ever?" question can be answered either "yes" or "no," and each positive response gets one point. A score of 1 out of 4 indicates "possible" and a score of 2 detects most cases of substance misuse.	Interview or self-report	Adults; Adolescents
Drug Abuse Screening Test – 10 (DAST-10) (Skinner, 1982)	A 10-item measure adapted from the original DAST to be a brief screening tool for drug use in the past 12 months.	Interview or self-report	Adults
National Institute on Drug Abuse (NIDA) Quick Screen (NIDA, 2009)	An online, clinician screening tool used in general medical settings to identify risky substance use. It generates a substance involvement score (SI), determines risk and a recommended level of intervention, and provides additional resources.	Interview; clinician-administered	Adults
Diagnostic status			
Structured Clinical Interview for DSM-5 (SCID-5; First, Williams, Karg, & Spitzer, 2014)	A precise method for identifying substance use disorder across 10 drug classes according to *DSM-5* criteria. It is the most frequently used instrument in clinical trials.	Interview; clinician-administered	Adults: Adolescents
Mini International Neuropsychiatric Interview 7.0 (MINI 7.0; Sheehan, 2014)	A structured interview used for identifying substance use disorder and severity according to *DSM-5* criteria.	Interview; clinician-administered	Adults
Treatment planning and outcome			
Addiction Severity Index (ASI; McLellan et al., 1992)	The most comprehensive and widely used measure. Assesses substance use in the context of seven domains: medical status, employment status, family history, legal status, psychiatric status, and family and social relationships. It identifies problem areas in need of targeted intervention and is often used in clinical settings for treatment planning and outcome evaluation.	Interview or self-report	Adults
Drug Use Screening Inventory (revised) (DUSI-R; Kirisci, Hsu, & Tarter, 1994)	A 149-item measure assessing the severity of drug and alcohol problem in 10 psychosocial and psychiatric domains: behavior patterns, drug consequences, health status, psychiatric disorder, social competency, family system, school performance, work adjustments, recreation, and peer relationships. A "lie scale" is built in to ensure truthfulness and increase reliability by identifying inconsistencies.	Interview or self-report	Adults; Adolescents

Table 19.1
continued

Instrument	Summary	Method of Administration	Population
Inventory of Drug Use Consequences (InDUC-2R for recent or -2L for lifetime use; Tonigan & Miller, 2002)	A 50-item inventory of alcohol-related consequences. It is distinct from screening instruments in that it measures adverse consequences of substance use, including items referring to pathological use practices (e.g., rapid use), items reflecting dependence symptoms (e.g., craving), and items concerning help-seeking (e.g., Narcotics Anonymous). Includes five scales including impulse control, social responsibility, and physical, interpersonal, and intrapersonal domains.	Self-report	Adults
Timeline Followback (TLFB; Fals-Stewart, O'Farrell, & Freitas, 2000)	Assesses recent substance use by asking the client to retrospectively report use in a defined period prior to the interview date. In addition to capturing use, the TLFB can also identify frequency of use.	Interview or self-report	Adults; Adolescents
Motivation and treatment readiness			
University of Rhode Island Change Assessment (URICA; McConnaughy, Prochaska, & Velicer, 1983)	Measures the stages of change (pre-contemplation, contemplation, action, and maintenance) using a five-point Likert scale. Assesses readiness to change when clients enter treatment.	Self-report	Adults; Co-occurring disorders
Stages of Change Readiness and Treatment Eagerness Scale (SOCRATES; Miller & Tonigan, 1996)	Assesses motivation for change, in relation to alcohol and drug use, using three factorially derived scores: (1) recognition, (2) ambivalence, and (3) taking steps.	Self-report	Adults
Circumstances, Motivation, Readiness, and Suitability (CMRS) Scales (De Leon, Melnick, Kressel, & Jainchill, 1994)	Scales used to predict retention in therapeutic community treatment across four interrelated domains: (1) circumstances (external pressures), (2) motivation (intrinsic pressures), (3) readiness, and (4) suitability.	Self-report	Adults; Adolescents

(e.g., social and occupational functioning) in order to develop appropriate treatment goals and a treatment plan. For example, by assessing how much time the patient spends obtaining and using the substance, in addition to time spent recovering, the clinician will likely gain a better sense of the extent of impairment and, as such, which intervention might be most efficacious. Additional assessment techniques are utilized prior to and during treatment in order to target processes such as treatment planning, utilization of services, and goal attainment. Traditional models of substance use assessment and treatment planning have been based upon the transtheoretical model, which outlines stages of change in behavior in efforts to improve treatment outcomes (DiClemente & Prochaska, 1998). However, more recent evidence suggests that these models need to be reconsidered in order to integrate factors that will more clearly characterize the development and maintenance of substance use (Sutton, 2001), such as cognitive (e.g., executive control dysfunction; Blume & Marlatt, 2009), environmental, and social components (Selbekk, Sagvaag, & Fauske, 2015).

Functional analysis is often employed in substance use treatment to help patients effectively problem-solve ways to reduce the probability of future use. Within this model, an analysis of the antecedents and consequences of substance use is used to develop alternative cognitive and behavioral skills to reduce the risk of future substance use. Working together, the therapist and patient identify five high-risk situations and the (1) trigger for that situation, (2) thoughts during that situation, (3) feelings/emotions experienced in response to the trigger and thoughts, (4) substance use behavior, and (5) positive and negative consequences of substance use. In the context of consequences, emphasis is placed on acknowledging the short-term and immediate positives (e.g., relief) versus the larger-magnitude and longer-term negative (e.g., legal trouble, relationship problems, health) consequences. After constructing this personalized behavior chain, the therapist and patient engage in treatment planning to develop empirically supported strategies for altering behaviors and/or thoughts when faced with those same situations. Such strategies include behavioral activation (i.e., generating value-based alternative behaviors), mindfulness, assertiveness training, and fostering social support. Those interested in the use of functional analysis in treatment are directed to Marlatt and Donovan (2007).

Comprehensive outcome assessments include a wide range of dimensions beyond substance use behavior, such as changes in social, occupational, and psychological functioning. It is therefore ideal to readminister comprehensive measures such as the *Addiction Severity Index (ASI)*, *Drug Use Screening Inventory – Revised (DUSI-R)*, and *Inventory of Drug Use Consequences (InDUC-2R)* (see Table 19.1). In addition, self-report and biological indicators can be used to determine return to substance use, substance use behavior, and psychiatric symptoms.

Recent developments in Ecological Momentary Assessment (EMA) provide a suitable method to collect data on substance use behaviors, prompting individuals to answer brief information about their behaviors, thoughts, and feelings while continuing to interact in their natural environment (see Ferguson & Shiffman, 2011 for a detailed discussion). It provides the unique opportunity to track episodic behavior, emphasizing the role of immediate situations, while also recording information on an individual's internal experience (e.g., mood, craving). Notably, this assessment method avoids the pitfalls of retrospective recall and the difficulty of cultivating ecological validity in laboratory or medical settings. In addition, EMA boasts high compliance by utilizing signaled assessments, prompting individuals to report symptomology and measures of functioning in real time.

BIOLOGICAL DETECTION

The following is a brief overview of recent trends in the biological assessment of substance use (for a review, see Vearrier, Curtis, & Greenberg, 2010). Although recent work has identified cutting-edge technologies for biological testing of substance use, *urinalysis* remains the preferred method of detection for several reasons. First, because urinalysis has been used historically, it is well known and many of the problems associated with it have been addressed. Second, urine contains high concentrations of the target substance or its metabolites. Third, it is inexpensive and may be acquired in a minimally invasive manner compared with other biological approaches. Self-contained urine-based testing kits that can reliably detect the most commonly used psychoactive substances are becoming increasingly available, allowing practitioners and researchers to conduct on-site testing across a wide range of settings. Finally, recently developed quantitative and semi-quantitative tests are more sensitive to changes in the pattern, frequency, and amount of use (Preston, Silverman, Schuster, & Charles, 2002). Thus, in addition to indicating the presence or absence of a drug, quantitative urinalysis can be useful in detecting initial efforts to reduce substance use and monitor the effects of treatments.

While urinalysis has several advantages and obvious clinical utility, several limitations remain. Urine can only reliably indicate drug use in the previous 1–3 days (except for cannabis, methadone, and diazepam), thereby increasing the reliance on self-report for longer-term follow-up periods. In addition, urine is easily adulterated by using chemicals such as bleach, vinegar, or liquid soap, and can be easily diluted by using old urine or someone else's urine. Conversely, over-the-counter medications and certain foods can produce positive test results in the absence of illicit drug use. As such, careful attention to detail and procedures is needed to ensure accurate collection, and positive tests may need additional confirmation.

Blood collection can detect very recent drug use and is considered an ideal method for assessing quantitative levels when accuracy is the primary criterion for measure selection. However, blood is often not collected due to its invasive nature and reliance on trained personnel. Accordingly, blood is predominately used in forensic environments.

Saliva is the only body fluid that can be used as a substitute for blood, as drug concentration levels are comparable. Saliva collection has the advantage of being easy to obtain and is cost-effective because, similar to urinalysis, self-contained testing kits are widely available, eliminating the need for trained personnel and off-site testing. Saliva testing is typically used in outreach units and prisons. One collection procedure often utilized is the Salivette sampling device. It consists of a cotton wool swab, which is placed in the patients' buccal (cheek) cavity for saliva collection by absorption. Drawbacks to saliva collection include difficulty collecting an adequate amount for drug detection, and the possible contamination of the oral cavity as a result of oral, intranasal, and nicotine drug use. In addition, the validity of saliva collection is not yet well established.

Hair testing has been developed and theorized to have the potential benefits of drug detection over a longer period of time (up to 3 months), which is not possible with the aforementioned methods. However, quality control criteria and standard laboratory methods have yet to be established. In addition, evidence indicates that drug detection may differentially appear in darker hair (e.g., black), leading to a bias toward missing drug use in blond individuals or those with treated (e.g., bleached) hair. In addition, hair is sensitive to smoke in the air, resulting in a false-positive for individuals who abstain yet are surrounded by people who have smoked drugs.

Sweat testing may be used for detection of recent drug use (i.e., < 24 hours) using a cotton wipe or by utilizing "patch technology," during which individuals wear a patch for a period of several weeks, providing a longer time period than other testing methods previously discussed (for a review, see De Giovanni & Fucci, 2013). Patch technology is often utilized for surveillance (i.e., continuous monitoring) of drug use. While oxygen, carbon dioxide, and water vapor are able to escape through the patch, drugs are retained in the patch. Advantages of this method include minimal invasiveness and fewer ethical issues than those surrounding blood or urine testing. Challenges utilizing sweat testing include difficulties creating a sweat collection device that is universal despite intra- and interindividual variation in sweat drug concentrations, environmental contamination of patches before application and after removal, and the unknown effect of vigorous or prolonged exercise on the deposition of drugs onto the patch. Further research needs to be conducted in order to more precisely establish the permeability of the patch membranes, as well as to characterize reabsorption properties of the patches across different drug classes.

ETIOLOGICAL CONSIDERATIONS

GENETICS

Behavioral Genetics   Findings from twin, adoption, and family studies suggest that genetic factors account for a significant portion of the variance in liability for substance use disorders. Indeed, substance use disorders are some of the most highly heritable psychiatric disorders, with heritability estimates of 0.40 for stimulant use disorder, 0.43 for cannabis use disorder, 0.51 for sedative use disorder, 0.56 for alcohol use disorder, and 0.72 for cocaine use disorder (for a review, see Bienvenu, Davydow, & Kendler, 2011). The magnitude of genetic influence on substance use varies over the course of development, beginning with a negligible amount of genetic influence during early adolescence that increases over time until it stabilizes by age 35–40 years (Kendler, Schmitt, Aggen, & Prescott, 2008). Some research suggests that the majority of the genetic vulnerability for substance use disorders can be accounted for by shared genetic influences that are common across substance classes (Agrawal, Neale, Prescott, & Kendler, 2004; True et al., 1999; Tsuang et al., 1998), while other research demonstrates support for substance-specific genetic factors (Agrawal & Lynskey, 2008), such as genetic differences in metabolism and hedonic effects (Lyons et al., 1997). These findings point to significance of genetic factors in addiction liability, as well as the importance of studying genes that are involved in neurobiological substrates that are common and specific to substance use disorders.

Molecular Genetics   Evidence exists for a relationship between substance use disorder and specific genetic polymorphisms (variations in DNA structure), in particular the γ-aminobutyric acid (GABA) receptor genes on chromosome 4. Convergent evidence suggests that polymorphisms, specifically in GABA2, are associated with cannabis use and polysubstance abuse (Agrawal et al., 2008a,b; Drgon, D'Addario, & Uhl, 2006). In addition, dynorphin peptides, derived from the prodynorphin (PDYN) precursor polymorphisms are associated with opioid addiction (Clarke et al., 2012). Evidence from genome wide association studies (GWAS) has converged to implicate a cluster of nicotinic acetylcholine receptor (nAChR) subunit genes in drug use. More specific to heroin addiction, GWAS have provided evidence for the involvement of multiple genes, including μ-opioid receptor coding genes, metabotrpic receptors mGluR6 and mGluR8, nuclear receptor NR4A2, and cryptochrome 1 (Nielson et al., 2008). Meta-analytic approaches have also provided convergent evidence for the role of nAChR subunit genes, including CHRNA3 and CHRNA5, in cocaine dependence (Grucza et al., 2008).

Additional genes that increase the risk of substance use disorders include polymorphisms in dopamine receptor genes that play a role in reward and reinforcement behavior (Blum et al., 2000). A meta-analysis including 55 studies confirmed the A1[+] allele of DRD2 as a marker of substance use and severe substance misuse (Young, Lawford, Nutting, & Noble, 2004). Similarly, a polymorphism in the DAT1 gene has been associated with cocaine use (Guindalini et al., 2006). Furthermore, the CNR1 gene has been associated with several types of substance use, including cocaine, amphetamine, heroin, and cannabis (Comings et al., 1997; Proudnikov et al., 2010). Recent meta-analyses provide additional support for the involvement of genes that play a role in reward and reinforcement behavior in the development and maintenance of substance use across substance classes (reviewed by Li & Burmeister, 2009), suggesting that genes encoding for dopaminergic functioning may modulate substance use disorder liability across substance classes.

Gene–Environment Interactions   Beyond examining genetic factors in isolation, environmental risk factors have been shown to interact with genes to contribute to the development of substance use disorders. Although the majority of research examining gene–environment interactions in substance use has focused on alcohol use disorder, accumulating evidence suggests that early-life stress may result in widespread alterations in stress circuitry, increasing the likelihood of physical changes serving as risk factors for substance use. For example, the GABRA2 gene has been associated with substance use, namely heroin and cocaine, particularly for individuals who have experienced severe childhood maltreatment (Enoch et al., 2010; Soyka et al., 2008). In addition, there is a significant interaction between the 7R+ genotype (variation in the DRD4 dopamine receptor gene) and attachment history, more specifically for avoidant and anxious attachments in predicting cannabis use in young adulthood (Olsson et al., 2011). Taken together, genetic risk factors for substance use may be moderated by environmental variables, suggesting that as genetic researchers continue to incorporate environmental measures into their studies, additional gene–environment interactions may be revealed.

Learning and Habituation

Theories of learning and conditioning have been utilized to understand the development and maintenance of substance use disorders, and as a result, studies have been initially conducted in laboratory animals and humans that support the notion of drugs as reinforcers (for a review, see Higgins, Heil, & Lussier, 2004), with drug use theorized to be a form of operant behavior influenced by antecedents and consequences. Drug self-administration studies with humans have been used to examine the powerful influence of nondrug reinforcers on heroin and cocaine use (Comer, Collins, & Fischman, 1997; Greenwald & Steinmiller, 2009; Higgins et al., 1994). Thus, with continued substance use, substance use-seeking and -taking become habit-based processes formed from reinforcement learning (McKim, Bauer, & Boettiger, 2016).

Accordingly, the behavioral economics perspective posits that delayed reinforcers are discounted by individuals with substance use disorders (Bickel & Marsch, 2001). In other words, the value of delayed reinforcers is discounted compared with immediate reinforcers. Most notably, during the development of substance use disorders, the more immediate and hedonic expectancies surrounding the effects of drugs are valued over the more long-term and positive consequences of being abstinent. Accordingly, substance users demonstrate higher discount rates for delayed rewards across substance classes (e.g., heroin, such that there is greater reduction in the value of a future reward as the delay to obtain that reward increases; for a review, see MacKillop et al., 2011).

In line with the behavioral economics perspective, the reinforcing value of drug use is critically influenced by the environmental context of other available reinforcers. Accordingly, research has revealed a relationship between the degree of substance use and engagement in substance-free activities. High rates of drug use are most likely in contexts without substance-free sources of reinforcement, and drug use will generally decrease if access to alternative reinforcers is increased (Higgins et al., 2004). Individuals with fewer alternative behavioral choices will be more likely to develop a substance use disorder. Additionally, clinical research has reported positive outcomes for treatments based upon reinforcement theories such as contingency management (e.g., Prendergast, Podus, Finney, Greenwell, & Roll, 2006), behavioral activation (Daughters, Magidson, Lejuez, & Chen, 2016a), and a community reinforcement approach (e.g., Abbott, 2009).

EXECUTIVE FUNCTIONING

Executive functioning is implicated in behavior and emotion regulation and control, and includes the constructs of impulsivity, decision-making, and attentional bias. Neurobiological research has identified disruption of the prefrontal cortex (PFC), integrally involved in executive functioning processes, as a central feature of substance use disorders. Accordingly, disruption of the PFC is thought to lead to the impaired response inhibition and salience attribution syndrome (Goldstein & Volkow, 2011), which is characterized by behavioral manifestations of four core clinical symptoms: intoxication, bingeing, withdrawal, and craving. Through altered attentional processes, substance users attribute excessive salience to substances and substance-related cues, decreasing their ability to inhibit maladaptive behaviors. After habitual use, substance-seeking and -taking become the main motivational drive, culminating in persistent use despite experiencing negative consequences associated with substance use.

As a result of PFC disruption, processes critical to emotion, cognitive, and behavioral functioning are negatively affected, such as impulsivity, decision-making, and attention. Impulsivity has been associated with the initiation and continued use of substances (De Wit, 2009; Field, Schoenmakers, & Wiers, 2008; Johnson, Bickel, Moore, Badger, & Budney, 2010; Petry & Casarella, 1999), as well as the severity of substance use (Hester, Nestor, & Garavan, 2009). Such deficits in impulsivity have been evidenced by poorer behavioral performance on impulsivity tasks and aberrant activation in neural regions associated with impulsivity among substance users. In addition to impulsivity, reduced ability in decision-making has been found in substance users, such that chronic administration of substance use causes neuronal changes that alter a person's ability to choose nonrisky alternative behaviors, though others argue that the decision-making mechanism is already weak in individuals who are prone to addiction (Bechara, 2005). For instance, using the Game of Dice Task (Brand et al., 2004), Brand et al. (2008) found that opiate users exhibited a preference for decisions that led to more negative long-term consequences and made riskier choices compared with matched controls. In addition to impulsivity and decision-making, attentional processes have a central role in the development and maintenance of substance use disorders. The relationship between attentional bias and substance use disorders has demonstrated that substance users attend more to substances and substance-related stimuli, and this, in turn, is associated with greater subjective craving (Costantinou et al., 2010; Field, Munafo, & Franken, 2009;

Hester, Dixon, & Garavan, 2006; McCusker & Gettings, 1997) and substance use (Stacey & Wiers, 2010). Thus, individuals with deficits in executive function are more likely to develop a substance use disorder, and also more likely to relapse after attempted abstinence. Additionally, clinical research utilizing brain stimulation techniques, such as transcranial magnetic stimulation and transcranial direct current stimulation, targeting the PFC and reward-related regions, report positive outcomes, such as reduced substance use and related symptomology as treatments (for a review, see Feil & Zangen, 2010).

NEUROANATOMY AND NEUROBIOLOGY

Several neurobiological models have been proposed to explain how chronic substance use contributes to the development of substance use disorders and vulnerability to relapse, with a great deal of emphasis placed on the role of neuroadaptive changes that take place in brain reward and stress, incentive salience and habit formation, and executive function circuits over the course of chronic substance use (e.g., Koob & LeMoal, 2001, 2008; Koob & Volkow, 2016; Li & Sinha, 2008; Robinson & Berridge, 1993, 2001; Wise, 1980, 2002). The following sections will discuss neurobiological mechanisms that increase liability to substance use across substance classes, as well as the neurobiological changes that contribute to development and maintenance of substance use disorders.

Brain Reward Circuits   One pharmacological effect that is common to all drug addiction is increased activation in the mesocorticolimbic dopamine pathway of the brain (Koob & Volkow, 2010; Pierce & Kumaresan, 2006) underlying motivational and reward-related processes in substance use (Salamone & Correa, 2012). Dopamine neurons project from the ventral tegmental area to the ventral striatum and PFC, and dopaminergic functioning in these regions is believed to be a key component of the brain reward systems, which are critical for the reinforcing properties of drugs. Human neuroimaging studies show that acute administration of nearly all substances leads to increased activation in mesolimbic dopaminergic regions, and that this activation correlates with subjective ratings of high or euphoria and craving. However, chronic drug administration and acute withdrawal are associated with alterations in this pathway, characterized by decreases in extracellular dopamine, reduced D2 receptor availability, and reduced dopamine transmission in frontal and ventral striatal regions (for detailed reviews, see Koob & LeMoal, 2008; Sinha, 2008; Volkow, Wang, Fowler, Tomasi, & Telang, 2011). In sum, neuroadaptive changes take place in dopaminergic circuits over the course of chronic drug use. These changes contribute to the aversive affective symptoms that are common during withdrawal, which may drive individuals to relapse to drug use in order to escape this aversive state (Koob & LeMoal, 2008; Koob & Volkow, 2010). As such, alterations in dopaminergic functioning appear to be an important neurobiological mechanism underlying the development and maintenance of substance use disorders.

Brain Stress Circuits   The hypothalamic–pituitary–adrenal (HPA) axis and its primary hormone, cortisol, play a central role in mediating the body's response to stress, including behavioral, emotional, and additional physiological changes. The HPA axis is extremely sensitive to inputs from the limbic system and PFC, two brain areas that are important for modulating reinforcement and motivational processes (e.g., Li & Sinha, 2008; Schwabe, Dickinson, & Wolf, 2011). In animal models of substance use, evidence suggests that rats with elevated HPA axis reactivity to stress show greater self-administration of addictive substances (Piazza, Deminiere, Le Moal, & Simon, 1989, 1990; Piazza, Derouche, Rouge-Pont, & Le Moal, 1998; Piazza et al., 1991, 1996), and administration of exogenous corticosteroids to rats that were low-level responders led to an increased risk that these rats would begin to self-administer amphetamines (Piazza et al., 1991). Evidence also suggests that HPA axis activation, and subsequent release of adrenocorticotropic hormone and cortisol in response to stress, is associated with increased dopaminergic neurotransmission in mesolimbic reward circuits (Dunn, 1988; Kalivas & Duffy, 1989; Piazza & LeMoal, 1996; Prasad, Sorg, Ulibarri, & Kalivas, 1995; Thierry, Tassin, Blanc, & Glowinski, 1976), suggesting that reactivity in brain stress circuits plays an important role in both substance use liability and reinforcement.

Accordingly, population-based and epidemiological studies show evidence for the role of elevated stress, in the form of early life stress, trauma, and accumulated adversity in the development and maintenance of substance use, as well as substance use outcomes (Fox & Sinha, 2009; Sinha, 2008). Adolescent exposure to stressful life events, such as parental alcoholism or financial difficulty, has been shown to increase emotional and behavioral problems that intensify the risk for developing a substance use disorder (King & Chassin, 2007). Furthermore, populations dealing with chronic stress, including emotional stressors ranging from violence and loss to trauma, poor social support, and interpersonal conflict, have evidenced higher vulnerability to substance use disorders (Sinha, 2008).

Neuroadaptation in Reward and Stress Circuitry   Neurobiological models of drug addiction hypothesize that reward and stress circuits in the brain become dysregulated in response to chronic substance use, and this dysregulation contributes to the establishment of a "negative affect" or psychologically distressed state during withdrawal and continued abstinence, which increases the reinforcing effects of drugs and thus vulnerability to relapse following cessation (Koob, 2009; Koob & Le Moal, 2001, 2008; Koob & Volkow, 2010). Specifically, when reward pathways (i.e., the mesocorticolimbic dopamine system discussed previously) are activated by drug administration, opposing anti-reward systems (i.e., brain stress systems localized in the central nucleus of the amygdala and the bed nucleus of the stria terminalis) are recruited to limit reward function and maintain homeostasis. Over the course of chronic drug administration, neuroadaptive changes occur in response to the excessive utilization of brain reward systems, including subsequent decreases in activation of brain reward systems and increases in opposing brain stress circuits. Such a combination of depressed reward circuits and elevated anti-reward circuits is hypothesized to be the driving force motivating continued drug-seeking and -taking behaviors (Koob, 2008; Koob & Le Moal, 2008).

Furthermore, elevated brain stress activation is hypothesized to reduce an individual's ability to adapt to or cope with additional stressors during abstinence, thereby driving vulnerability to stress-induced relapse. This is in line with the negative reinforcement theory of addiction, which states that the motivation for substance use is the reduction or avoidance of negative emotional states (Baker, Piper, McCarthy, Majeskie, & Fiore, 2004). Similarly, evidence indicates that a behavioral proxy of negative reinforcement, namely low distress tolerance, is associated with poor substance use outcomes (Daughters et al., 2005a; Daughters, Lejuez, Kahler, Strong, & Brown, 2005b; Strong et al., 2012). In addition, reduced functional connectivity between neural regions is associated with goal-directed behavior during affective distress (Daughters et al., 2016b). Similarly, other studies have examined disruptions in medial prefrontal activity, implicated in self-control among substance users while under stress and during increased craving (Sinha, 2013). Taken together, neurobiological models suggest that chronic substance use is associated with neuroadaptive changes, including decreases in reward system activation and increases in anti-reward system functioning, particularly under the experience of stress and craving, which may serve to maintain compulsive drug-seeking and -taking behaviors, even after protracted periods of abstinence.

SPECIFIC POPULATIONS

Sex and Gender   Existing research has demonstrated that women differ from men in their pathways to drug addiction. Compared with men, women are less likely to have a substance use disorder, and onset of their substance use disorder tends to be later in life. Yet women become dependent at a quicker rate and experience more severe consequences of substance use over shorter periods of time (e.g., Hser, Huang, Teruya, & Anglin, 2004). This accelerated development to chronic use has been termed *telescoping*, and this trend has been consistently documented (Greenfield, Back, Lawson, & Brady, 2010). For women, the pathway to substance use is often relationship-based; for instance, women are more likely to initiate and continue substance use in the context of an intimate partner relationship (Frajzyngier, Neaigus, Gyarmathy, Miller, & Friedman, 2007; Tuchman, 2010), and following treatment, women's substance use is more likely to be influenced by their partners' continued substance use, as compared with men (Grella, Scott, Foss, & Dennis, 2008). Furthermore, women with substance use disorders are also more likely than men with substance use disorders to have a partner who uses illegal drugs (Westermeyer & Boedicker, 2000).

With regard to treatment, co-occurring psychiatric disorders are more common among women and also create a barrier to treatment. As indicated in a review by Greenfield et al. (2007), women have higher rates of comorbid eating disorders, mood and anxiety disorders, and PTSD, which subsequently make it difficult for them to find appropriate treatment to manage both disorders. Gender differences in stress reactivity may be one important mechanism underlying these differences. In a review, Fox and Sinha (2009) reported that, compared with substance-abusing men, women may experience increased emotional sensitivity to changes in the stress system, and the resulting neuroadaptations in autonomic function and affect may alter vulnerability to co-occurring disorders, possible relapse, and treatment outcome.

Women also face unique barriers to treatment engagement that may explain a reduced likelihood to enter treatment compared with men. For instance, barriers relating to child-rearing responsibilities, including limited access to child care services, as well as society's punitive attitude toward substance use by women as child bearers, present just some of the major treatment barriers for women suffering from substance use disorders (e.g., Greenfield et al., 2007). Moreover, women also differ from men in their response to treatment. Data on this topic have proven to be somewhat conflicting: whereas some researchers have reported that women are more likely than men to drop out of substance abuse treatment (King & Canada, 2004), others have proposed a complex interaction of gender and treatment modality (e.g., methadone vs. drug-free programs; Joe, Simpson, & Broome, 1999; McCaul, Svikis, & Moore, 2001; Simpson, Joe, Rowan-Szal, & Greener, 1997). There is also evidence that women are more likely than men to complete treatment (Hser, Huang, Teruya, & Anglin, 2004). The reasons underlying these discrepancies are unknown, but highlight the importance of investigating sex and gender differences in future research, which is particularly critical given the increasing prevalence of women with substance use disorders (Tuchman, 2010).

Race and Ethnicity   Studies suggest there are unique risk and protective factors arising from cultural differences such as acculturation-related stressors, cultural orientation, parenting styles, and discrimination that influence the developmental trajectories of substance use through adulthood (e.g., Gibbons et al., 2010; Kulis, Marsiglia, & Nieri, 2009; Thai, Connell, & Tebes, 2010), resulting in differential needs among minority substance users. For instance, racial-ethnic minorities who reside in inner city areas are particularly vulnerable to substance use and risky sexual behavior as a result of higher levels of poverty, violence, general risk practices, and availability of street drugs (e.g., Avants, Marcotte, Arnold, & Margolin, 2003). Importantly, there are large racial-ethnic disparities in access, referral, and utilization of treatment services, and evaluations of the substance abuse treatment system have shown that racial-ethnic minorities are under-served (Delphin-Rittmon et al., 2012; Marsh, Cao, Guerro, & Shin, 2009). Aside from Asian Americans, all racial groups have a larger treatment gap than Whites (Schmidt & Mulia, 2009), and among treatment-seeking individuals, African Americans and His-panics are more likely than Whites to report unmet needs (Wells, Klap, Koike, & Sherbourne, 2001). Moreover, these differences exist even after adjusting for other demographic factors such as criminal history and socioeconomic status (Le Cook & Alegria, 2011).

As with other health care access issues, racial-ethnic differences in accessing substance use treatment services may result from underlying differences in barriers to care. Factors such as perceived discrimination, prior negative experiences associated with services, and limited knowledge of available services may provide a better understanding of why there is an unmet need among those who perceive need for substance use treatment in minority groups (Grella, Karno, Warda, Moore, & Niv, 2009a), and data indicate that Whites experience half the rate of barriers than do African Americans and Hispanics (Perron et al., 2009). Looking beyond access and utilization of treatment, treatment outcome studies suggest mixed findings when exploring racial-ethnic minorities com-pared with Whites. Some data indicate that members of minority groups are less likely to complete and/or seek treatment, receive fewer treatment services, and are less likely to achieve recovery (Jerrell & Wilson, 1997; Rebach, 1992). However, research indicates that minority clients do not differ from nonminority clients in their response to treatment (e.g., Pickens & Fletcher, 1991) and in treatment outcomes (Niv, Pham, & Hser, 2009).

Sexual Orientation   Adults and adolescents with a minority sexual orientation (e.g., lesbian, gay, bisexual) are at greater risk for substance use and are more likely to use substances than are their heterosexual peers (for reviews, see Green & Feinstein, 2012; Marshal et al., 2008). Some data indicate that increased odds of substance use among lesbian, gay, and bisexual adults may be due to experiences such as discrimination (McCabe, Bostwick, Hughes, West, & Boyd, 2010) and other stigma-related social stressors (Meyer, 2003). Additional studies focus on the central role of social influences, consistent with social learning theories suggesting that increased risk for substance use may result from importance of use among peers, expectancies, and social triggers (Green & Feinstein, 2012). Although there has been substantially less research on treatment utilization among sexual minority subgroups, what research there is suggests higher rates of substance use treatment utilization (McCabe, West, Hughes, & Boyd, 2013). However, increased prevalence does not ensure receipt of comparable treatment quality, due to high levels of discrimination against individuals with minority sexual orientations and a lack of knowledge among providers about their unique mental health needs (Eliason & Hughes, 2004). More research is needed to elucidate the contributing factors to disproportionate risk for substance use and improving treatment outcomes among individuals with minority sexual orientations.

COURSE AND PROGNOSIS

By the 12th grade, about half of adolescents have used an illicit substance at least once (Johnston, O'Malley, Miech, Bachman, & Schulenberg, 2016). The most common substance used by adolescents is marijuana; however, additional drugs are easily found in the home, such as prescription medications and an assortment of inhalants. It should be noted that although many adolescents may experiment with drugs, most do not progress to abuse or dependence (Newcomb & Richardson, 1995). There is an ongoing debate about the development and progression of substance use among adolescents. Some researchers subscribe to the "gateway theory," which hypothesizes that for adolescents there is a distinct sequential pattern of substance use, beginning with licit substances (i.e., tobacco, alcohol) and progressing to illicit substance (e.g., marijuana), and finally advancing through a hierarchy of illicit substances (e.g., cocaine, heroin; Kandel, Yamaguchi, & Chen, 1992). However, more recent research finds that adolescent substance use does not always evidence a temporal sequence from licit to illicit substances, and the choice of substance used by adolescents is a function of contextual variables (e.g., availability, parental supervision) and association with other mental health symptoms (e.g., Lee, Humphreys, Flory, Liu, & Glass, 2011; Marmorstein, White, Loeber, & Stouthamer-Loeber, 2010) more than a normative sequential order (Tarter, Vanyukov, Kirisci, Reynolds, & Clark, 2006).

Although there are conflicting hypotheses as to adolescent use and progression, research has consistently evidenced similar risk factors for the development and maintenance of substance use disorders. Two primary risk factors include age of initiation and frequency of use during adolescence (Behrendt, Wittchen, Hofler, Lieb, & Beesdo, 2009; Degenhardt et al., 2009; King & Chassin, 2007). Age of initiation increases risk, in part, because earlier age of substance use allows for greater exposure to the substance. Considering that adolescence is a time of substantial neurological development, the adolescent brain may be particularly susceptible to substance use and addiction (Winters & Lee, 2008). In addition, substance-related problems (i.e., negative consequences of substance use) in adolescence significantly predict a future substance use disorder, elevated levels of depression, and antisocial and borderline personality disorder symptoms by age 24 (Rohde, Lewinsohn, Kahler, Seeley, & Brown, 2001).

Once a substance use disorder is present, recovery is notoriously difficult, even with exceptional treatment resources. For those who receive treatment, the next challenge is staying in treatment. Treatment dropout rates range from 21.5% to 43% for detoxification, 21.7% to 57% for inpatient treatment, and 23% to 50% for outpatient treatment (for a review, see Brorson, Arnevik, Rand-Hendriksen, & Duckert, 2013). Such high rates of premature treatment termination are of concern, because time in treatment is related to positive outcomes (e.g., Garner, Godley, Funk, Lee, & Garnick, 2010; Simpson, Joe, & Brown, 1997). As for relapse rates, estimates suggest that 90% of heroin- and cocaine-dependent users experience at least one relapse within 4 years after treatment, with many relapsing considerably sooner. Furthermore, of the patients admitted to the US public treatment system in 2007, approximately 57% were re-entering treatment (Office of Applied Studies, 2009). Retrospective and prospective treatment studies report that most participants initiate three to four episodes of treatment over multiple years before attaining abstinence (Hser, Maglione, Polinsky, & Anglin, 1998), and as many as 80% transition between treatment, recovery, using, and incarceration at least once over a 4-year follow-up period (Grella, Scott, Foss, & Dennis, 2008).

Treatment outcomes are dependent on a variety of factors, including individual characteristics and life problems, severity of addiction and substance use, aptness of treatment and linkage to services to treat other problems, and the quality of the transaction between the individual and the treatment program (NIDA, 2009). As previously stated, better treatment outcomes are related to length of stay, and for residential/ inpatient and outpatient programs, treatment participation of 90 days or longer is recommended for sustaining recovery and positive results (NIDA, 2009). However, treatment duration of 90 days is not always feasible (i.e., lack of insurance and prohibitive cost). From 2010 to 2013, the most commonly reported barrier to receiving treatment was inability to afford the cost of treatment and lack of insurance coverage (SAMHSA, 2014b). Historically, persons with substance use disorders receive a traditional acute treatment approach involving assessment, treatment, and discharge all within a short time frame (i.e., 28 days or 2 months), with the supposition that the patient is treated and will be able to maintain abstinence following the single treatment episode (Dennis & Scott, 2007).

However, recent literature addresses substance use disorders as a chronic condition, analogous to other chronic medical diseases. For example, McLellan et al. (2000) illustrate the similarities in genetic heritability, environmental factors, and personal choice within addiction and other medical conditions with chronic care treatment (e.g., type 2 diabetes mellitus, hypertension, and asthma). Of note, they found that treatment compliance for individuals with a substance use disorder is no better than adherence rates to prescribed treatments for these other medically accepted chronic diseases. Similar to chronic diseases such as diabetes and congestive heart failure, multiple relapses are common (Saitz, Larson, LaBelle, Richardson, & Samet, 2008); therefore, adjusting treatment to involve a continuum of care may improve long-term outcomes for people with substance use disorders.

CASE STUDY

CASE IDENTIFICATION

The patient (Alaina) is a 38-year-old African American female who entered treatment voluntarily at an intensive outpatient substance use treatment center.

PRESENTING COMPLAINTS

Alaina reported that she relapsed to substance use 8 months ago, and her preferred drug is crack/cocaine accompanied by frequent alcohol use. She reported that she had success in treatment for the first time 4 years ago and she would like to try to get back on track, as she has hit a low point in the past few months. At the time of treatment entry, Alaina reported no stable living arrangement and that she has recently been splitting her time between the homes of her friends, ex-boyfriend, and uncle. She has one child, age 6, who lives temporarily with her aunt, and with whom she has intermittent contact. In her current environment, she reported spending most of her time alone, as she has lost contact with her sober friends.

HISTORY

Alaina was raised by her mother and her grandmother and has never met her father. She reported an extensive family history of substance use, including heroin and crack/ cocaine use by her mother who still actively uses. Alaina first began using substances in high school. She graduated from high school, but at the age of 18 was arrested and spent a year in prison on a charge related to theft and possession of cocaine. Since that time, she reported regular crack/cocaine and alcohol use. She has worked intermittently as a hair stylist over the course of her life. Her most stable employment was during the past 4 years after she successfully completed a court-mandated treatment at a residential substance use treatment facility. She reported that she is committed to "learning from my mistakes" and "getting her daughter back" at this time, and that she had successfully remained abstinent up until her most recent relapse.

ASSESSMENT

The Addiction Severity Index and a clinical interview for *DSM-5* were administered to determine existing psychopathology, including substance use history, frequency, and severity, environmental strengths and stressors, legal issues, and psychiatric symptoms. During the interview, Alaina displayed psychomotor retardation, clear thought processes, and no obvious perceptual abnormalities. Her speech volume and tone were within normal limits, yet her speech rate was somewhat slower than normal. Based on this assessment, Alaina met criteria for current cocaine use disorder (severe), current alcohol use disorder (mild), and major depressive disorder (MDD). She reported past crack/cocaine and alcohol use beginning at age 15 when using with peers. Her MDD symptoms include depressed mood most of the day, nearly every day, markedly diminished interest in almost all activities, feelings of worthlessness and excessive guilt, and a diminished ability to think or concentrate. After a careful assessment of her symptom timeline, it was concluded that her MDD was not substance-induced, as her symptoms preceded the onset of her relapse to substance use.

The assessment of legal issues indicated that she is not on probation with the court system and entered treatment voluntarily. Alaina evidenced difficulty in identifying strengths, but with some additional probing she was able to acknowledge potential support from her aunt, as well as the importance of her spirituality. She reported that her Narcotics Anonymous (NA) sponsor was a source of support but moved away from the area about 6 months ago. She would like to begin attending NA meetings and looking for a new sponsor.

It was determined that a functional analysis to identify the antecedents and consequences of her substance use and depression would provide the most useful information for treatment planning. First, following the loss of her job at a local hair salon, she reported that she had a lot of free time and got bored easily. She felt hopeless that she couldn't find a new job and often ruminated over the guilt she felt about her choices in life and her inability to provide for her daughter. She contacted her old friends, which was soon followed by cocaine and alcohol use. She also reported feeling lonely, guilty, and worthless when she realized she could not adequately support her daughter financially, so drug use helped her "bury" these feelings, although they would always resurface when she was sober, leading to a cycle of negative reinforcement. Finally, she reported intensifying feelings of sadness and shame that she had used crack/cocaine and alcohol again given how much progress she had made in the past few years. She felt that she had let her daughter and aunt down. Taken together, it appeared that a lack of substance-free environmental reinforcements following the loss of her job was strongly associated with her relapse to substance use. This was soon thereafter compounded by the negative thoughts and feelings surrounding her parenting skills, resulting in repeated substance use and the cycle of negative reinforcement.

SUMMARY

Substance use problems are complex, and a comprehensive understanding requires knowledge of biological, genetic, neural, behavioral, and cognitive factors. This chapter provides an overview of current practices and cutting-edge advancements for understanding and assessing substance use disorders. Although much work is still needed, great progress has been made in understanding the etiology of substance use, with greatest promise evident in approaches that consider the interactive influence of multiple factors. Additionally, clear advances have been made in both initial and ongoing assessments using self-report, interview, behavioral, and biological methods. Also of great promise is the greater attention to neurobiological, genetic, sex and gender, and diversity issues when considering vulnerabilities to developing substance use disorders, as well as barriers to assessment and proper treatment. In summary, although the challenges of understanding and assessing substance use disorders remain, it is clear that the field has seen important advancements aimed at addressing these challenges.

REFERENCES

Abbott, P. J. (2009). A review of the community reinforcement approach in the treatment of opioid dependence. *Journal of Psychoactive Drugs, 41*(4), 379–385.

Advokat, C. D., Comaty, J. E., & Julien, R. M. (2014). *Julien's primer to drug action: A comprehensive guide to the actions, uses, and side effects of psychoactive drugs.* New York, NY: Worth.

Agrawal, A., & Lynskey, M. T. (2008). Are there genetic influences on addiction: Evidence from family, adoption and twin studies. *Addiction, 103*(7), 1069–1081.

Agrawal, A., Neale, M. C., Prescott, C. A., & Kendler, K. S. (2004). A twin study of early cannabis use and subsequent use and abuse/dependence of other illicit drugs. *Psychological Medicine, 34,* 1227–1237.

Agrawal, A., Pergadia, M. L., Saccone, S. F., Hinrichs, A. L., Lessov-Schlaggar, C. N., Saccone, N., . . . Madden, P. A. (2008a). Gamma-aminobutyric acid receptor genes and nicotine dependence: Evidence for association from a case-control study. *Addiction, 103*(6), 1027–1038.

Agrawal, A., Pergadia, M. L., Saccone, S. F., Lynskey, M. T., Wang, J. C., Martin, N. G., . . . Madden, P. A. (2008b). An autosomal linkage scan for cannabis use disorders in the nicotine addiction genetics project. *Archives of General Psychiatry, 65*(6), 713–721.

Ahmadi, M., & Ahmadi, J. (2005). Substance-induced anxiety disorder in opioid dependents. *Addictive Disorders & Their Treatment, 4*(4), 157–159.

American Psychiatric Association (APA) (2013). *Diagnostic and statistical manual of mental disorders* (5th ed.). Washington, DC: Author.

Avants, S. K., Marcotte, D., Arnold, R., & Margolin, A. (2003). Spiritual beliefs, world assumptions, and HIV risk behavior among heroin and cocaine users. *Psychology of Addictive Behaviors, 17*(2), 159–162.

Baker, T. B., Piper, M. E., McCarthy, D. E., Majeskie, M. R., & Fiore, M. C. (2004). Addiction motivation reformulated: An affective processing model of negative reinforcement. *Psychological Review, 111*(1), 33–51.

Bechara, A. (2005). Decision making, impulse control and loss of willpower to resist drugs: A neurocognitive perspective. *Nature Neuroscience, 8*(11), 1458–1463.

Behrendt, S., Wittchen, H.-U., Hofler, M., Lieb, R., & Beesdo, K. (2009). Transitions from first substance use to substance use disorders in adolescence: Is early onset associated with rapid escalation? *Drug and Alcohol Dependence, 99,* 68–78.

Bickel, W. K., & Marsch, L. A. (2001). Toward a behavioral economic understanding of drug dependence: Delay discounting processes. *Addiction, 96,* 73–86.

Bienvenu, O. J., Davydow, D. S., & Kendler, K. S. (2011). Psychiatric 'diseases' versus behavioral disorders and degree of genetic influence. *Psychological Medicine, 41*, 33–40.

Blum, K., Braverman, E. R., Holder, J. M., Lubar, J. F., Monastra, V. J., Miller, D., . . . Comings, D. (2000). Reward deficiency syndrome: A biogenetic model for the diagnosis and treatment of impulsive, addictive, and compulsive behaviors. *Journal of Psychoactive Drugs, 32*(Suppl.), 1–68.

Blume, A. W., & Marlatt, G. A. (2009). The role of executive cognitive functions in changing substance use: What we know and what we need to know. *Annals of Behavioral Medicine, 37*(2), 117–125.

Brand, M., Labudda, K., Kalbe, E., Hilker, R., Emmans, D., Fuchs, G., . . . Markowitsch, H. J. (2004). Decision-making impairments in patients with Parkinson's disease. *Behavioral Neurology, 15*, 77–85.

Brand, M., Roth-Bauer, M., Driessen, M., & Markowitsch, H. J. (2008). Executive functions and risky decision-making in patients with opiate dependence. *Drug and Alcohol Dependence, 97*, 64–72.

Brorson, H. H., Arnevik, E. A., Rand-Hendriksen, K., & Duckert, F. (2013). Drop-out from addiction treatment: A systematic review of risk factors. *Clinical Psychology Review, 33*, 1010–1024.

Brown, R. L., & Rounds, L. A. (1995). Conjoint screening questionnaires for alcohol and other drug abuse: Criterion validity in a primary care practice. *Wisconsin Medical Journal, 94*, 135–140.

Caton, C. L. M., Drake, R. E., Hasin, D. S., Dominguez, B., Shrout, P. E., Samet, S., & Schanzer, W. B. (2005). Differences between early-phase primary psychotic disorders with concurrent substance use and substance-induced psychoses. *Archives of General Psychology, 62*(2), 137–145.

Clark, D. B., Martin, C. S., & Cornelius, J. R. (2008). Adolescent-onset substance use disorders predict young adult mortality. *Journal of Adolescent Health, 42*(6), 637–639.

Clarke, T. K., Ambrose-Lanci, L., Ferraro, T. N., Berrettini, W. H., Kampman, K. M., Dackis, C. A., . . . Lohoff, F. W. (2012). Genetic association analyses of PDYN polymorphisms with heroin and cocaine addiction. *Genes, Brain and Behavior, 11*, 415–423.

Comer, S. D., Collins, E. D., & Fischman, M. W. (1997). Choice between money and intranasal heroin in morphine-maintained humans. *Behavioural Pharmacology, 8*(8), 677–690.

Comings, D. E., Muhleman, D., Gade, R., Johnson, P., Verde, R., Saucier, G., & MacMurray, J. (1997). Cannabinoid receptor gene (CNR1): Association with IV drug use. *Molecular Psychiatry, 2*, 161–168.

Conway, K. P., Compton, W., Stinson, F. S., & Grant, B. F. (2006). Lifetime comorbidity of DSM-IV mood and anxiety disorders and specific drug use disorders: Results from the National Epidemiologic Survey on Alcohol and Related Conditions. *Journal of Clinical Psychiatry, 67*(2), 247–257.

Costantinou, N., Morgan, C. J. A., Battistella, S., O'Ryan, D., Davis, P., & Curran, H. V. (2010). Attentional bias, inhibitory control and acute stress in current and former opiate addicts. *Drug and Alcohol Dependence, 109*, 220–225.

Daughters, S. B., Lejuez, C. W., Bornovalova, M. A., Kahler, C., Strong, D. R., & Brown, R. (2005a). Distress tolerance as a predictor of early treatment dropout in a residential substance abuse treatment facility. *Journal of Abnormal Psychology, 114*, 729–734.

Daughters, S. B., Lejuez, C. W., Kahler, C., Strong, D., & Brown, R. (2005b). Psychological distress tolerance and duration of most recent abstinence attempt among residential treatment seeking substance abusers. *Psychology of Addictive Behaviors, 19*, 208–211.

Daughters, S. B., Magidson, J. F., Lejuez, C. W., & Chen, Y. (2016a). LETS ACT: A behavioral activation treatment for substance use and depression. *Advances in Dual Diagnosis, 9*(2/3), 74–84.

Daughters, S. B., Ross, T. J., Bell, R. P., Yi, J. Y., Ryan, J., & Stein, E. A. (2016b). Distress tolerance among substance users is associated with functional connectivity between prefrontal regions during a distress tolerance task. *Addiction Biology.*

De Giovanni, N., & Fucci, N. (2013). The current status of sweat testing for drugs of abuse: A review. *Current Medicinal Chemistry*, 20(4), 545–561.

Degenhardt, L., Chiu, W. T., Conway, K., Dierker, L., Glantz, M., Kalaydjian, A., . . . Kessler, R. C. (2009). Does the "gateway" matter? Associations between the order of drug use initiation and the development of drug dependence in the National Comorbidity Study replication. *Psychological Medicine*, 39, 157–167.

De Leon, G., Melnick, G., Kressel, D., Jainchill, N. (1994). Circumstances, motivation, readiness, and suitability (the CMRS scales): Predicting retention in therapeutic community treatment. *American Journal of Drug and Alcohol Abuse*, 20(4), 495–515.

Delphin-Rittmon, M., Andres-Hyman, R., Flanagan, E. H., Ortiz, J., Amer, M. M., & Davidson, L. (2012). Racial-ethnic differences in referral source, diagnosis, and length of stay in inpatient substance abuse treatment. *Psychiatric Services*, 63(6), 612–615.

Dennis, M., & Scott, C. K. (2007). Managing addiction as a chronic condition. *Addiction Science and Clinical Practice*, 4(1), 56–57.

De Wit, H. (2009). Impulsivity as a determinant and consequence of drug use: A review of underlying processes. *Addiction Biology*, 14(1), 22–31.

DiClemente, C. C., & Prochaska, J. O. (1998). Toward a comprehensive, transtheoretical model of change: Stages of change and addictive behaviors. In W. R. Miller & N. Heather (Eds.), *Treating addictive behaviors* (2nd ed., pp. 3–24). New York, NY: Plenum Press.

Drgon, T., D'Addario, C., & Uhl, G. R. (2006). Linkage disequilibrium, haplotype and association studies of a chromosome 4 GABA receptor gene cluster: Candidate gene variants for addictions. *American Journal of Medical Genetics Part B: Neuropsychiatric Genetics*, 141B(8), 854–860.

Dunn, A. (1988). Stress related activation of cerebral dopaminergic systems. *Annals of the New York Academy of Sciences*, 537, 188–205.

Eliason, M., & Hughes, T. L. (2004). Treatment counselor's attitudes about lesbian, gay, bisexual and transgender clients: Urban vs. rural settings. *Substance Use and Misuse*, 39, 625–644.

Enoch, M. A., Hodgkinson, C. A., Qiaoping, Y., Shen, P-H., Goldman, D., & Roy, A. (2010). The influence of GABRA2, childhood trauma, and their interaction on alcohol, heroin, and cocaine dependence. *Biological Psychiatry*, 67(1), 20–27.

Fals-Stewart, W., O'Farrell, T. J., & Freitas, T. T. (2000). The timeline followback reports of psychoactive substance use by drug-abusing patients: Psychometric properties. *Journal of Consulting and Clinical Psychology*, 68(1), 134–144.

Feil, J., & Zangen, A. (2010). Brain stimulation in the study and treatment of addiction. *Neuroscience and Biobehavioral Reviews*, 34, 559–574.

Ferguson, S. G., & Shiffman, S. (2011). Using the methods of ecological momentary assessment in substance dependence research – Smoking cessation as a case study. *Substance Use & Misuse*, 46(1), 87–95.

Field, M., Munafo, M. R., & Franken, I. (2009). A meta-analytic investigation of the relationship between attentional bias and subjective craving in substance abuse. *Psychological Bulletin*, 135(4), 589–607.

Field, M., Schoenmakers, T., & Wiers, R. W. (2008). Cognitive processes in alcohol binges: A review and research agenda. *Current Drug Abuse Reviews*, 1, 263–279.

First, M. B., Williams, J. B., Karg, R. S., & Spitzer, R. L. (2014). *Structured Clinical Interview for DSM-5 Disorders*. Arlington, VA: American Psychiatric Association (APA).

Fox, H. C., & Sinha, R. (2009). Sex differences in drug-related stress-system changes: Implications for treatment in substance abusing women. *Harvard Review of Psychiatry*, 17, 103–119.

Frajzyngier, V., Neaigus, A., Gyarmathy, V. A., Miller, M., & Friedman, S. R. (2007). Gender differences in injections risk behaviors at the first injection episode. *Drug and Alcohol Dependence*, 89, 145–152.

Garner, B., Godley, M., Funk, R., Lee, M., & Garnick, D. (2010). The Washington Circle continuity of care performance measure: Predictive validity with adolescents discharged from residential treatment. *Journal of Substance Abuse Treatment, 38*(1), 3–11.

Gibbons, F. W., Etcheverry, P. E., Stock, M. L., Gerrard, M., Weng, C. Y., Kiviniemi, M., & O'Hara, R. E. (2010). Exploring the link between racial discrimination and substance use: What mediates? What buffers? *Journal of Personality and Social Psychology, 99*(5), 785–801.

Goldstein, R., Compton, W. M., Pulay, A. J., Ruana, W. J., Pickering, R. P., Stinson, F. S., & Grant, B. F. (2007). Antisocial behavioral syndromes and DSM-IV drug use disorders in the United States: Results from the National Epidemiologic Survey on Alcohol and Related Conditions. *Drug and Alcohol Dependence, 90*, 145–158.

Goldstein, R. Z., & Volkow, N. D. (2011). Dysfunction of the prefrontal cortex in addiction: Neuroimaging findings and clinical implications. *Nature Reviews Neuroscience, 12*(11), 652–669.

Green, K. E., & Feinstein, B. (2012). Substance use lesbian, gay, and bisexual populations: An update on empirical research and implications for treatment. *Psychology of Addictive Behaviors, 26*(2), 265–278.

Greenfield, S., Back, S., Lawson, K., & Brady, K. (2010). Substance abuse in women. *Psychiatric Clinics of North America, 33*(2), 339–355.

Greenfield, S., Brooks, A., Gordon, S., Green, C., Kropp, F., McHugh, R., . . . Miele, G. M. (2007). Substance abuse treatment entry, retention, and outcome in women: A review of the literature. *Drug and Alcohol Dependence, 86*(1), 1–21.

Greenwald, M. K., & Steinmiller, C. L. (2009). Behavioral economic analysis of opioid consumption in heroin-dependent individuals: Effects of alternative reinforcer magnitude and post-session drug supply. *Drug and Alcohol Dependence, 104*, 84–93.

Grella, C. E., Karno, M. P., Warda, U. S., Moore, M. D., & Niv, N. (2009a). Perceptions of need and help received for substance dependence in a national probability survey. *Psychiatric Services, 60*, 1068–1074.

Grella, C. E., Karno, M. P., Warda, U. S., Niv, N., & Moore, A. A. (2009b). Gender comorbidity among individuals with opioid use disorders in the NESARC Study. *Addictive Behaviors, 34*(6–7), 498–504.

Grella, C. E., Scott, C. K., Foss, M. A., & Dennis, M. L. (2008). Gender similarities and differences in the treatment, relapse and recovery cycle. *Evaluation Review, 32*, 113–137.

Grucza, R. A., Wang, J. C., Stitzel, J. A., Hinrichs, A. L., Saccone, S. F., Saccone, N. L., . . . Bierut, L. J. (2008). A risk allele for nicotine dependence in CHRNA5 is a protective allele for cocaine dependence. *Biological Psychiatry, 64*(11), 922–929.

Guindalini, C., Howard, M., Haddley, K., Laranjeira, R., Collier, D., Ammar, N., . . . Breen, G. (2006). A dopamine transporter gene functional variant associated with cocaine abuse in a Brazilian sample. *Proceedings of the National Academy of Sciences of the United States of America, 103*(12), 4552–4557.

Hester, R., Dixon, V., & Garavan, H. (2006). A consistent attentional bias for drug-related material in active cocaine users across word and picture versions of the emotional Stroop task. *Drug and Alcohol Dependence, 81*, 251–257.

Hester, R., Nestor, L., & Garavan, H. (2009). Impaired error awareness and anterior cingulate cortex hypoactivity in chronic cannabis users. *Neuropsychopharmacology, 34*(11), 2450–2458.

Higgins, S. T., Budney, A. J., Bickel, W. K., Foerg, F. E., Donham, R., & Badger, G. J. (1994). Incentives improve outcome in outpatient behavioral treatment of cocaine dependence. *Archives of General Psychiatry, 51*(7), 568–576.

Higgins, S. T., Heil, S. H., & Lussier, J. P. (2004). Clinical implications of reinforcement as a determinant of substance use disorders. *Annual Review of Psychology, 55*, 431–461.

Horsfall, J., Cleary, M., Hunt, G. E., & Walter, G. (2009). Psychosocial treatments for people with co-occurring severe mental illnesses and substance use disorders (dual diagnosis): A review of empirical evidence. *Harvard Review of Psychiatry, 17*(1), 24–34.

Hser, Y. I., Huang, Y. C., Teruya, C., & Anglin, M. D., (2004). Gender differences in treatment outcomes over a three-year period: A PATH model analysis. *Journal of Drug Issues, 34*(2), 419–439.

Hser, Y., Maglione, M., Polinsky, M., & Anglin, M. (1998). Predicting drug treatment entry among treatment-seeking individuals. *Journal of Substance Abuse Treatment, 15*(3), 213–220.

Jane-Llopis, E., & Matysina, I. (2006). Mental health and alcohol, drugs and tobacco: A review of the comorbidity between mental disorders and the use of alcohol, tobacco and illicit drugs. *Drug and Alcohol Review, 25*, 515–536.

Jerrell, J. M., & Wilson, J. L. (1997). Ethnic differences in the treatment of dual mental and substance disorders. *Journal of Substance Abuse Treatment, 14*(2), 133.

Joe, G. W., Simpson, D. D., & Broome, K. M. (1999). Retention and patient engagement models for different treatment modalities in DATOS. *Drug and Alcohol Dependence, 57*, 113–125.

Johnson, M. W., Bickel, W. K., Moore, B. A., Badger, G. J., & Budney, A. J. (2010). Delay discounting in current and former marijuana-dependent individuals. *Experimental and Clinical Psychopharmacology, 18*(1), 99–107.

Johnston, L. D., O'Malley, P. M., Miech, R. A., Bachman, J. G., & Schulenberg, J. E. (2016). *Monitoring the Future national survey results on drug use, 1975–2015: Overview of key findings on adolescent drug use.* Ann Arbor: Institute for Social Research, The University of Michigan. Retrieved January 23, 2016 from http://www.monitoringthefuture.org/pubs/monographs/mtf-overview2015.pdf.

Kalivas, P. W., & Duffy, P. (1989). Similar effects of daily cocaine and stress on mesocorticolimbic dopamine neurotransmission in the rat. *Biological Psychiatry, 25*(7), 913–928.

Kandel, D. B., Yamaguchi, K., & Chen, K. (1992). Stages of progression in drug involvement from adolescence to adulthood: Further evidence for the gateway theory. *Journal of Studies on Alcohol, 53*(5), 447–457.

Kendler, K. S., Schmitt, E., Aggen, S. H., & Prescott, C. A. (2008). Genetic and environmental influences on alcohol, caffeine, cannabis, and nicotine use from early adolescence to middle adulthood. *Archives of General Psychiatry, 65*(6), 674–682.

Kessler, R. C. (2004). The epidemiology of dual diagnosis. *Biological Psychology, 56*, 730–737.

King, A. C., & Canada, S. A., (2004). Client-related predictors of early treatment drop-out in a substance abuse clinic exclusively employing individual therapy. *Journal of Substance Abuse Treatment, 26*, 189–195.

King, K. M., & Chassin, L. (2007). A prospective study of the effects of age of initiation of alcohol and drug use on young adult substance dependence. *Journal of Studies on Alcohol and Drugs, 68*(20), 256–265.

Kirisci, L., Hsu, T., & Tarter, R. (1994). Fitting a two-parameter logistic item response model to clarify the psychometric properties of the Drug Use Screening Inventory for adolescent alcohol and drug abusers. *Alcoholism Clinical & Experimental Research, 18*, 1335–1341.

Koob, G. F. (2008). A role for brain stress systems in addition. *Neuron, 59*(1), 11–34.

Koob, G. F. (2009). Neurobiological substrates for the dark side of compulsivity in addiction. *Neuropharmacology, 56*(Suppl. 1), 18–31.

Koob, G. F., & LeMoal, M. (1997). Drug abuse: Hedonic homeostatic dysregulation. *Science, 278*, 52–58.

Koob, G. F., & LeMoal, M. (2001). Drug addiction, dysregulation of reward, and allostasis. *Neuropsychopharmacology, 24*, 97–129.

Koob, G. F., & LeMoal, M. (2008). Addiction and the brain antireward system. *Annual Review of Psychology, 59*, 29–53.

Koob, G. F., & Volkow, N. D. (2016). Neurobiology of addiction: A neurocircuitry analysis. *The Lancet Psychiatry, 3*(8), 760–773.

Koob, G. F., & Volkow, N. D. (2010). Neurocircuitry of addiction. *Neuropsychopharmacology, 35*, 217–238.

Kulis, S., Marsiglia, F. F., & Nieri, T. (2009). Perceived ethnic discrimination versus acculturation stress: Influences on substance use among Latino youth in the Southwest. *Journal of health and Social Behavior, 50*(4), 443–459.

Kushner, M. G., Abrams, K., & Borchardt, C. (2000). The relationship between anxiety disorders and alcohol use disorders: a review of major perspectives and findings. *Clinical psychology review, 20*(2), 149–171.

Le Cook, B. & Alegria, M. (2011). Racial-ethnic disparities in substance abuse treatment: The role of criminal history and socioeconomic status. *Psychiatric Services, 62*(11), 1273–1281.

Lee, S. S., Humphreys, K. L., Flory, K., Liu, R., & Glass, K. (2011). Prospective association of childhood attention-deficit/hyperactivity disorder (ADHD) and substance use and abuse/dependence: A meta-analytic review. *Clinical Psychology Review, 31*(3), 328–341.

Li, M. D., & Burmeister, M. (2009). New insights into the genetics of addiction. *Nature Reviews Genetics, 10*, 225–231.

Li, C. R., & Sinha, R. (2008). Inhibitory control and emotional stress regulation: Neuroimaging evidence for frontal-limbic dysfunction in psycho-stimulant addiction. *Neuroscience and Biobehavioral Reviews, 32*(3), 581–597.

Lipari, R. N., Park-Lee, E., & Van Horn, S. (2016). American's need for and receipt of substance use treatment in 2015. *The CBHSQ Report:* September 29, 2016. Center for Behavioral Health Statistics and Quality, Substance Abuse and Mental Health Services Administration, Rockville, MD.

Lyons, M. J., Toomey, R., Meyer, J. M., Green, A. I., Eisen, S. A., . . . Tsuang, M. T. (1997). How do genes influence marijuana use? The role of subjective effects. *Addiction, 92*(4), 409–417.

MacKillop, J., Amlung, M. T., Few, L. R., Ray, L. A., Sweet, L. H., & Munafo, M. R. (2011). Delayed reward discounting and addictive behavior: A meta-analysis. *Psychopharmacology, 216*(3), 305–321.

Marlatt, G. A., & Donovan, D. M. (2007). *Relapse prevention: Maintenance strategies in the treatment of addictive behaviors* (2nd ed.) New York, NY: Guildford Press.

Marmorstein, N. R., White, H. R., Loeber, R., & Stouthamer-Loeber, M. (2010). Anxiety as a predictor of age at first use of substances and progression to substance use problems among boys. *Journal of Abnormal Child Psychology, 38*(2), 211–223.

Marsh, J. C., Cao, D., Guerro, E., & Shin, H-C. (2009). Need-service matching in substance abuse treatment: Racial/ethnic differences. *Evaluation and Program Planning, 32*, 43–51.

Marshal, M. P., Friedman, M. S., Stall, R., King, K. M., Miles, J., Gold, M. A., . . . Morse, J. Q. (2008). Sexual orientation and adolescent substance use: A meta-analysis and methodological review. *Addiction, 103*(4), 546–556.

McCabe, S. E., Bostwick, W. B., Hughes, T. L., West, B. T., & Boyd, C. J. (2010). The relationship between discrimination and substance use disorders among lesbian, gay, and bisexual adults in the United States. *American Journal of Public Health, 100*(10), 1946–1952.

McCabe, S. E., West, B. T., Hughes, T. L., & Boyd, C. J. (2013). Sexual orientation and substance abuse treatment utilization in the United States: Results from a national survey. *Journal of Substance Abuse Treatment, 44*(1), 4–12.

McCaul, M. E., Svikis, D. S., & Moore, R. D. (2001). Predictors of outpatient treatment retention: Patient versus substance use characteristics. *Drug and Alcohol Dependence, 62*, 9–17.

McCauley, J. L., Killeen, T., Gros, D. F., Brady, K. T., & Back, S. E. (2012). Posttraumatic stress disorder and co-occurring substance use disorders: Advances in assessment and treatment. *Clinical Psychology, 19*(3), 10.1111/cpsp. 12006

McConnaughy, E. A., Prochaska, J. O., & Velicer, W. F. (1983). Stages of change in psychotherapy: Measurement and sample profiles. *Psychotherapy: Theory, Research & Practice, 20*(3), 368–375.

McCusker, C. G., & Gettings, B. (1997). Automaticity of cognitive biases in addictive behaviours: Further evidence with gamblers. *British Journal of Clinical Psychology, 36*(4), 543–554.

McKim, T. H., Bauer, D. J., & Boettiger, C. A. (2016). Addiction history associates with the propensity to form habits. *Journal of Cognitive Neuroscience, 28*(7), 1024–1038.

McLellan, A. T., Kushner, H., Metzger, D., Peters, R., Smith, I., & Grissom, G., (1992). The fifth edition of the Addiction Severity Index. *Journal of Substance Abuse Treatment, 9*(3), 199–213.

McLellan, A. T., Lewis, D. C., O'Brien, C. P., & Kleber, H. D. (2000). Drug dependence, a chronic medical illness: Implications for treatment, insurance and outcome evaluation. *Journal of the American Medical Association, 28*(13), 1689–1695.

Meyer, I. H. (2003). Prejudice, social stress, and mental health in lesbian, gay, and bisexual populations: Conceptual issues and research evidence. *Psychological Bulletin, 129*, 674–697.

Miller, W. R., & Tonigan, J. S. (1996). Assessing drinkers' motivations for change: The Stages of Change Readiness and Treatment Eagerness Scale (SOCRATES). *Psychology of Addictive Behaviors, 10*(2), 81–89.

National Institute on Drug Abuse (NIDA). (2009). *Comorbidity: Addiction and Other Mental Illnesses.* (NIH Publication Number 08–5771.) Bethesda, MD: National Institute on Drug Abuse (NIDA).

Newcomb, M. D., & Richardson, M. A. (1995). In M. Hersen & R. T. Ammerman (Eds.), *Advanced Abnormal Child Psychology* (pp. 411–431). Hillsdale, NJ: Erlbaum.

Nielson, D. A., Ji, F., Yuferov, A., Ho, A., Chen, O., Levran, O., . . . Kreek, M. J. (2008). Genotype patterns that contribute to increased risk for or protection from developing heroin addiction. *Molecular Psychiatry, 13*(4), 417–428.

Niv, N., Pham, R., & Hser, Y. (2009). Racial and ethnic differences in substance abuse service needs, utilization, and outcomes in California. *Psychiatric Services, 60*(10), 1350–1356.

Office of Applied Studies (2009). *Results from the 2008 survey on drug use and health: National findings.* Rockville, MD: Substance Abuse and Mental Health Services Administration, Department of Health and Human Services.

Office of National Drug Control Policy (ONDCP). (2004). *The economic costs of drug abuse in the United States, 1992–2002.* Washington, DC: Executive Office of the President (Publication No. 207303).

Olsson, C. A., Moyzis, R. K., Williamson, E., Ellis, J. E., Parkinson-Bates, M., Patton, G. C., Moore, E. E. (2011). Gene-environment interaction in problematic substance use: Interaction between DRD4 and insecure attachments. *Human Genetic Study, 18*(4), 717–726.

Perron, B. E., Mowbray, O. P., Glass, J. E., Delva, J., Vaughn, M. G., & Howad, M. O. (2009). Differences in service utilization and barriers among Blacks, Hispanics, and Whites with drug use disorders. *Substance Abuse Treatment, Prevention, and Policy, 4*(1), 3.

Petry, N. M., & Casarella, T. (1999). Excessive discounting of delayed rewards in substance abusers with gambling problems. *Drug and Alcohol Dependence, 56*, 25–32.

Piazza, P. V., Deminiere, J. M., LeMoal, M., & Simon, H. (1989). Factors that predict individual vulnerability to amphetamine self-administration. *Science, 245*, 1511–1513.

Piazza, P. V., Deminiere, J. M., LeMoal, M., & Simon, H. (1990). Stress- and pharmacologically-induced behavioral sensitization increases vulnerability to acquisition of amphetamine self-administration. *Brain Research, 514*(1), 22–26.

Piazza, P. V., Derouche, V., Rouge-Pont, F., & LeMoal, M. (1998). Behavioral and biological factors associated with individual vulnerability to psychostimulant abuse. *NIDA Research Monographs, 169*, 105–133.

Piazza, P. V., & LeMoal, M. L. (1996). Pathophysiological basis of vulnerability to drug abuse: Role of an interaction between stress, glucocorticoids, and dopaminergic neurons. *Annual Review of Pharmacology and Toxicology, 36*, 359–378.

Piazza, P. V., Maccari, S., Deminiere, J. M., LeMoal, M., Mormede, P., & Simon, H., (1991). Corticosterone levels determine individual vulnerability to amphetamine self-administration. *Proceedings of the National Academy of Sciences of the United States of America, 88*(6), 2088–2092.

Piazza, P. V., Marinelli, M., Rougé-Pont, F., Deroche, V., Maccari, S., Simon, H., & LeMoal, M. (1996). Stress, glucocorticoids, and mesencephalic dopaminergic neurons: A pathophysiological chain determining vulnerability to psychostimulant abuse. *NIDA Research Monograph, 163,* 277–299.

Pickens, R., & Fletcher, B. (1991). Overview of treatment issues. In R. Pickens, C. Leukefeld, & C. Schuster (Eds.), *Improving drug abuse treatment* (pp. 1–19). National Institute on Drug Abuse (NIDA) Research Monograph no. 106, Rockville, MD: NIDA.

Pierce, R. C., & Kumaresan, V. (2006). The mesolimbic dopamine system: The final common pathway for the reinforcing effect of drugs of abuse? *Neuroscience and Biobehavioral Reviews, 30,* 215–238.

Prasad, B., Sorg, B., Ulibarri, C., & Kalivas, P. (1995). Sensitization to stress and psychostimulants: Involvement of dopamine transmission versus the HPA axis. *Annals of the New York Academy of Science, 771,* 617–625.

Prendergast, M., Podus, D., Finney, J., Greenwell, L., & Roll, J. (2006). Contingency management for treatment of substance use disorders: a meta-analysis. *Addiction, 101*(11), 1546–1560.

Preston, K. L., Silverman, K., Schuster, C. R., & Charles, R. (2002). Assessment of cocaine use with quantitative urinalysis and estimation of new uses. *Addiction, 92*(6), 717–727.

Proudnikov, D., Kroslak, T., Sipe, J. C., Randesi, M., Li, D., Hamon, S., . . . Kreek, M. J. (2010). Association of polymorphisms of the cannabinoid receptor (CNR1) and fatty acid amide hydrolase (FAAH) genes with heroin addiction: Impact of long repeats of CNR1. *The Pharmacogenomics Journal, 10,* 232–242.

Rebach, H. (1992). Alcohol and drug use among ethnic minorities. In J. Trimble, C. Bolek, & S. Niemcryk (Eds.), *Ethnic and multicultural drug abuse: Perspective on current research* (pp. 23–57). New York, NY: Haworth Press.

Robinson, T. E., & Berridge, K. C. (1993). The neural basis of drug craving: An incentive-sensitization theory of addiction. *Brain Research Reviews, 18*(3), 247–291.

Robinson, T. E., & Berridge, K. C. (2001). Incentive-sensitization and addiction. *Addiction, 96,* 103–114.

Rohde, P., Lewinsohn, P. M., Kahler, C. W., Seeley, J. R., & Brown, R. A. (2001). Natural course of alcohol use disorders from adolescence to young adulthood. *Journal of the American Academy of Child & Adolescent Psychiatry, 40*(1), 83–90.

Saitz, R., Larson, M. J., LaBelle, C., Richardson, J., & Samet, J. H. (2008). The case for chronic disease management for addiction. *Journal of Addiction Medicine, 2*(2), 55–65.

Salamone, J. D., & Correa, M. (2012). The mysterious motivational functions of mesolimbic dopamine. *Neuron, 76*(3), 470–485.

Schmidt, L. A., & Mulia, N. (2009) Racial and ethnic disparities in AOD treatment. Robert Wood Johnson Foundation's Substance Abuse Policy Research Program. Retrieved July 15, 2010 from http://saprp.org/knowledgeassets/knowledge_detail.cfm?KAID=11.

Schuckit, M. A. (2006). Comorbidity between substance use disorders and psychiatric conditions. *Addiction, 101*(1), 76–88.

Schwabe, L., Dickinson, A., & Wolf, O. T. (2011). Stress, habits, and drug addiction: A psycho-neuroendocrinological perspective. *Experimental and clinical psychopharmacology, 19*(1), 53–63.

Selbekk, A. S., Sagvaag, H., & Fauske, H. (2015). Addiction, families and treatment: A critical realist search for theories that can improve practice. *Addiction Research & Theory, 23*(3), 196–204.

Sheehan, D. V. (2014). The Mini-International Neuropsychiatric Interview, Version 7. 0 for DSM-5 (M. I. N. I. 7. 0). Jacksonville, FL: Medical Outcomes Systems.

Simpson, D. D., Joe, G. W., & Brown, B. S. (1997). Treatment retention and follow-up outcomes in the drug abuse treatment outcome study (DATOS). *Psychology of Addictive Behaviors, 11*(4), 294–307.

Simpson, D. D., Joe, G. W., Rowan-Szal, G. R., & Greener, J. (1997). Drug abuse treatment process components that improve retention. *Journal of Substance Abuse Treatment, 14*(6), 565–572.

Sinha, R. (2008). Chronic stress, drug use, and vulnerability to addiction. *Annals of the New York Academy of Sciences, 1141*, 105–113.

Sinha, R. (2013). The clinical neurobiology of drug craving. *Current Opinion in Neurobiology, 23*(4), 649–654.

Skinner, H. A. (1982). The drug abuse screening test. *Addictive Behaviors, 7*(4), 363–371.

Soyka, M., Preuss, U. W., Hesselbrock, V., Zill, P., Koller, G., & Bondy, B. (2008). GABA-A2 receptor subunit gene (GABRA2) polymorphisms and risk for alcohol dependence. *Journal of Psychiatric Research, 42*(3), 184–191.

Stacey, A., & Wiers, R. (2010). Implicit cognition and addiction: A tool for explaining paradoxical behavior. *Annual Review of Clinical Psychology, 6*, 551–575.

Strong D. R., Brown R. A., Sims M., Herman D. S., Anderson B. J., & Stein, M. D. (2012) Persistence on a stress-challenge task before initiating buprenorphine treatment was associated with successful transition from opioid use to early abstinence. *Journal of Addiction Medicine, 6*(3), 219–25.

Substance Abuse and Mental Health Services Administration (SAMHSA), Center for Behavioral Statistics and Quality. (2015). *Behavioral health trends in the United States: Results from the 2014 National Survey on Drug Use and Health* (HHS Publication No. SMA 15–4927, NSDUH Series H-50). Rockville, MD: Substance Abuse and Mental Health Services Administration.

Substance Abuse and Mental Health Services Administration (SAMHSA). (2014a). *Prevention of substance abuse and mental illness.* Retrieved from http://www.samhsa.gov/prevention.

Substance Abuse and Mental Health Services Administration (SAMHSA), Center for Behavioral Statistics and Quality. (2014b). *Results from the 2013 National Survey on Drug Use and Health: Summary of national findings* (HHS Publication No. SMA 14–4863, NSDUH Series H-48). Rockville, MD: SAMHSA.

Substance Abuse and Mental Health Services Administration (SAMHSA), Center for Behavioral Statistics and Quality. (2016). *Treatment Episode Data Set (TEDS) National Admissions to Substance Abuse Treatment Services.* BHSIS Series S-84, HHS Publication No. (SMA) 16–4986. Rockville, MD: SAMHSA.

Sutton, S. (2001). Back to the drawing board? A review of applications of the transtheoretical model to substance use. *Addiction, 96*, 175–186.

Swendsen, J., Conway, K. P., Degenhardt, L., Glantz, M., Jin, R., Merikangas, K. . . . Kessler, R. C. (2010). Mental disorders as risk factors for substance use, abuse and dependence: Results from the 10-year follow-up of the national comorbidity survey. *Addiction, 105*(6), 1117–1128.

Tarter, R. E., Vanyukov, M., Kirisci, L., Reynolds, M., & Clark, D. B. (2006). Predictors of marijuana use in adolescents before and after licit drug use: Examination of the gateway hypothesis. *American Journal of Psychiatry, 163*, 2134–2140.

Thai, N. D., Connell, C. M., & Tebes, J. T. (2010). Substance use among Asian American adolescents: Influence of race, ethnicity, and acculturation in the context of key risk and protective factors. *Asian American Journal of Psychology, 1*(4), 261–274.

Thierry, A. M., Tassin, J. P., Blanc, G., & Glowinski, J. (1976). Selective activation of the mesocortical dopamine system by stress. *Nature, 263*, 242–244.

Tonigan, J. S., & Miller, W. R. (2002). The inventory of drug use consequences (InDUC): Test-retest stability and sensitivity to detect change. *Psychologically Addictive Behavior, 16*(2), 165–168.

True, W. R., Xian, H., Scherrer, J. F., Madden, P. A. F., Bucholz, K. K., Heath, A. C., . . . Tsuang, M. (1999). Common genetic vulnerability for nicotine and alcohol dependence in men. *Archives of General Psychiatry, 56*, 655–661.

Trull, T. J., Sher, K. J., Minks-Brown, C., Durbin, J., & Burr, R. (2000). Borderline personality disorder and substance use disorders: A review and integration. *Clinical Psychology Review, 20,* 235–253.

Tsuang, M. T., Lyons, M. J., Meyer, J. M., Doyle, T., Eisen, S. A., GoldbergJ., . . . Eaves, L. (1998). Co-occurrence of abuse of different drugs in men: The role of drug- specific and shared vulnerabilities. *Archives of General Psychiatry, 55,* 967–972.

Tuchman, E. (2010). Women and addiction: The importance of gender issues in substance abuse research. *Journal of Addictive Diseases, 29*(2), 127–138.

Vearrier, D., Curtis, J. A., Greenberg, M. I. (2010). Biological testing for drugs of abuse. In A. Luch (Ed.), *Molecular, Clinical and Environmental Toxicology* (pp. 489–517). Birkhauser Verlag: Birkhauser Basel.

Volkow, N. D., Wang, G. J., Fowler, J. S., Tomasi, D., & Telang, F. (2011). Addiction: Beyond dopamine reward circuitry. *Proceedings of the National Academy of Sciences, 108*(37), 15037–15042.

Wells, K., Klap, R., Koike, A., & Sherbourne, C. (2001). Ethnic disparities in unmet need for alcoholism, drug abuse, and mental health care. *American Journal of Psychiatry, 158,* 2027–2032.

Westermeyer, J., & Boedicker, A. E. (2000). Course, severity, and treatment of substance abuse among women verses men. *American Journal of Drug Alcohol Abuse, 26*(4), 523–535.

Winters, K. C., & Lee, C. S. (2008). Likelihood of developing an alcohol and cannibis use disorder during youth: Association with recent use and age. *Drug and Alcohol Dependence, 92,* 239–247.

Wise, R. A. (1980). The dopamine synapse and the notion of "pleasure centers" in the brain. *Trends in Neuroscience, 3*(4), 91–95.

Wise, R. A. (2002). Brain reward circuitry. *Neuron, 36*(2), 229–240.

Yen, S., Shea, M. T., Pagano, M., Sanislow, C. A., Grilo, C. M., McGlashan, T. H., . . . Morey, L. C. (2004). Axis I and axis II disorders as predictors of prospective suicide attempts: Findings from the collaborative longitudinal personality disorders study. *Journal of Abnormal Psychology, 113* (2), 301.

Young, R. M., Lawford, B. R., Nutting, A., & Noble, E. P. (2004). Advances in molecular genetics and the prevention and treatment of substance misuse: Implications of association studies of the A_1 allele of the D_2 dopamine receptor gene. *Addictive Behavior, 29*(7), 1275–1294.

CHAPTER 20

Neurocognitive Disorders

GERALD GOLDSTEIN[1]

INTRODUCTION AND RECENT DEVELOPMENTS

Most neurological disorders are ancient diseases, and developments in treatment and cure have been painfully slow. However, we continue to learn more about these disorders, and in previous versions of this chapter (Goldstein, 1997, 2007, 2014) we highlighted substantive developments. A new disorder, acquired immunodeficiency syndrome (AIDS) dementia, had appeared, and the marker for the Huntington's disease gene had been discovered. At the time of the 1997 writing, it was mentioned that a still mysterious and controversial disorder appeared, sustained by military personnel during the war with Iraq in the Persian Gulf area, popularly known as the Gulf War syndrome. An aspect of this syndrome has been said to involve impaired brain function (Goldstein, 2011; Goldstein, Beers, Morrow, Shemansky, & Steinhauer, 1996). A more readily understood condition emerging from the recent Iraq and Afghanistan wars involves the blast injuries caused largely by roadside bombs. These injuries appeared to have different characteristics from those associated with the open or closed head injuries associated with previous wars and accidents in civilian life (Belanger, Kretzmer, Vanderploeg, & French, 2010).

Another consequence of the Iraq and Afghanistan wars has been a reconsideration of the problem of mild traumatic brain injury (TBI), often called concussion. Concussion is a common sports injury, but it also appears to be a common consequence of sustaining a blast injury. It is sometimes complicated by its association with post-traumatic stress disorder (PTSD) acquired in reaction to the injury, and diagnostic difficulties have been created regarding whether the victim sustained brain injury, developed PTSD, or both. It was commonly accepted that concussion was a self-limiting disorder, and that essentially full recovery could be expected within no more than 90 days. Recently, however, it has been observed that some individuals with histories of concussion do not fully recover and continue to have complaints of cognitive problems, notably in attention, memory,

---

[1] Editor's note: Sadly, Dr. Goldstein passed away in 2017 after completing a draft of this chapter, but before the editing process began.

Adult Psychopathology and Diagnosis, Eighth Edition. Edited by Deborah C. Beidel and B. Christopher Frueh.
© 2018 John Wiley & Sons, Inc. Published 2018 by John Wiley & Sons, Inc.
Companion website: www.wiley.com/go/beidel/psychopathology8e

and organizational abilities. Individuals with multiple concussions appear to experience a cumulative and long-lasting effect.

Initially, these symptoms were attributed to stress, but neuroimaging studies using advanced technologies have found that identifiable brain damage may result from concussion, involving the upper brain stem, base of the frontal lobe, hypothalamic–pituitary axis, medial temporal lobe, fornix, and corpus callosum. Bigler (2008) has written a review of this area, using the phrase "persistent postconcussive syndrome" to describe this condition. Substantial support for the neurological basis for this disorder comes from use of a technology that was just beginning its development and widespread use at the last writing, called diffusion tensor imaging (DTI). DTI is an magnetic resonance imaging (MRI)-related procedure that tracks axonal white matter, identifying misalignments.

In the Gulf War, concussion and more serious trauma were associated with blast injuries sustained mainly as a result of roadside bombing. Blast injuries remain a controversial area, with some authorities claiming they are no different from the commonly accepted types of brain injury (Hoge et al., 2008; Wilk et al., 2010), whereas others claim they are a unique form of trauma not identified previously. The matter is further complicated by the fact that the bombs used were sometimes loaded with depleted uranium or possibly infectious agents. Thus, the understanding of head injury has changed in recent years, with the development of methods that can detect persistent neurological consequences of concussion, producing a new diagnosis called persistent postconcussive syndrome, and the problem of blast injury among military personnel, which is still under intensive investigation.

DIAGNOSTIC CONSIDERATIONS

With the publication of *DSM-5*, there are substantial changes from *DSM-IV* in terminology and content. The name of the category "Delirium, Dementia, Amnestic, and Other Cognitive Disorders" has been replaced by the phrase "Neurocognitive Disorders." The term *delirium* remains as part of a set of three major subcategories: major neurocognitive disorder, minor neurocognitive disorder, and delirium. The term *dementia* has been eliminated.

It may be useful to review the rationale for the changes made in *DSM-5*. The *DSM-5* Neurocognitive Disorders Work Group prepared a document that contains their proposals for changes and their rationales for proposing them (American Psychiatric Association, 2010). We summarize some of their major points here:

1. Efforts were made to eliminate demeaning or stigmatizing terminology. Just as the term *mental retardation* has been replaced by *intellectual disability* in the neuro-developmental disorders section, the term *dementia* has been replaced by *major and mild neurocognitive disorders*. These new terms are felt to reflect more accurately the nature of the disorder and a general attempt made by the writers of *DSM-5* to correct for the demeaning, stigmatizing connotations of the names of some psychiatric disorders. The change from *mental retardation* to *intellectual disability* has already been widely accepted.

2. Diagnostic criteria wording was changed to increase precision. Thus, for example, the term *consciousness* has been changed to *level of awareness*. The changes in cognition specified in *DSM-IV* mention only memory, orientation, and language. In *DSM-5* the domains of executive ability and visuospatial impairment are also specified.

3. Mention of severity is added to characterize development of a disturbance.
4. Specific symptoms of delirium are provided, such as hallucinations, delusions, and sleep–wake cycle disturbances.
5. Delirium is subcategorized into hyperactive, hypoactive, and mixed groups, again providing greater specificity.
6. There is a major reconceptualization regarding characterization of cognitive changes. The term *cognitive decline* replaces *cognitive deficits* to emphasize that major cognitive disorder is acquired and reflects a decline from previous level of performance. The previous model, based on Alzheimer's disease, requires that memory impairment must be present. However, data now indicate that in other neurocognitive disorders, other domains such as language or executive functions may be impaired first, and most prominently. The changed wording calls for decline from previous performance in one or more specified domains including memory, but also language (aphasia), disturbances of skilled movement (apraxia) or of recognition (agnosia) and executive function.
7. Emphasis is placed on objective assessment of performance that may include neuropsychological testing.
8. Emphasis is placed on independent performance of instrumental activities of daily living.

There have been changes in the number and description of the neurocognitive disorders. Dementia of the Alzheimer type has been renamed major or mild neurocognitive disorder due to Alzheimer's disease. The term *vascular dementia* has been replaced with *major* or *mild vascular neurocognitive disorder*. Other neurocognitive disorders/diagnoses now include frontotemporal, Lewy bodies disease, Huntington's disease, Parkinson's disease, TBI, substance/medication use, HIV infection, and prion disease neurocognitive disorders, each of which can be modified by a major or mild descriptor (see clinical presentation section).

The diagnosis of mild neurocognitive disorder is new to the *DSM* system. The distinction is a matter of severity. Cognitive decline is characterized as modest or mild, it should not interfere with capacity for independence in everyday living, and delirium or another mental disorder can make a better explanation of the condition. This change allows for the diagnosis of less disabling syndromes that may still benefit from treatment.

In general, the changes in *DSM-5* have gone in the direction of increased specificity, including more detailed documentation of symptoms, description of cognitive domains involved, providing an etiological diagnosis, consideration of subtypes and use of more precise terminology. The distinction between major and mild disorders allows for diagnosis of individuals with mild impairment who would not meet criteria for a diagnosable neurological disorder, but who have experienced cognitive decline associated with brain dysfunction that would benefit from programs of treatment and management, such as cognitive rehabilitation.

CLINICAL PRESENTATION

The theoretical approach taken here will be neuropsychological in orientation, and based on the assumption that clinical problems associated with brain damage can be understood best in the context of the relationship between brain function and behavior. Thus, we expand our presentation beyond the descriptive psychopathology of *DSM-5*

(APA, 2013) in order to provide some material related to basic brain–behavior mechanisms. There are many sources of brain dysfunction, and the nature of the source has a great deal to do with determining behavioral consequences: morbidity and mortality. Thus, understanding key neuropathological processes is crucial to understanding the differential consequences of brain damage, and, in turn, that requires an understanding of how the brain functions, and in some cases the genetics and neurochemistry of how memories and other cognitive abilities are preserved in brain tissue.

In recent years, knowledge of the neurological systems important for such areas as memory and language has been substantially expanded. It seems clear now that there are several separate memory systems located in different areas of the brain, notably the hippocampus, the amygdala, the neocortex, and the cerebellum. Each system interacts with the others but supports a different form of memory, such as immediate recall, remote recall, and the brief storage of information during ongoing cognitive activity known as working memory (Baddeley, 1986).

Initially, two major methodologies were used to assess brain dysfunction: direct investigations of brain function through lesion generation or brain stimulation in animal subjects; and studies of patients who had sustained brain damage, particularly localized brain damage. The latter method can be dated back to 1861 when Paul Broca produced his case report (Broca, 1861) on a patient who had suddenly developed speech loss. An autopsy revealed that he had sustained an extensive infarct in the area of the third frontal convolution of the left cerebral hemisphere. Thus, an important center in the brain for speech had been discovered, but perhaps more significantly, this case produced what many would view as the first reported example of a neuropsychological or brain–behavior relationship in a human. Indeed, to this day, the third frontal convolution of the left hemisphere is known as Broca's area, and the type of speech impairment demonstrated by the patient is known as Broca's aphasia.

Following Broca's discovery, much effort was devoted to relating specific behaviors to discrete areas of the brain. These early neuropsychological investigations not only provided data concerning specific brain–behavior relationships, but also explicitly or implicitly evolved a theory of brain function, now commonly known as classical localization theory. In essence, the brain was viewed as consisting of centers for various functions connected by neural pathways. In human subjects, the presence of these centers and pathways was documented through studies of individuals who had sustained damage to either a center or the connecting links between one center and another such that they became disconnected. To this day, the behavioral consequences of this latter kind of tissue destruction are referred to as a disconnection syndrome (Geschwind, 1965). For example, there are patients who can speak and understand, but who cannot repeat what was just said to them. In such cases, it is postulated that there is a disconnection between the speech and auditory comprehension centers.

Not all investigators advocated localization theory. The alternative view is that the brain functions as a whole in an integrated manner, currently known as mass action, holistic, or organismic theories of brain function. In contemporary neuropsychology the strongest advocates of holistic theory were Kurt Goldstein, Martin Scheerer, and Heinz Werner. Goldstein and Scheerer (1941) are best known for their distinction between abstract and concrete behavior, their description of the "abstract attitude," and the tests they devised to study abstract and concrete functioning in brain-damaged patients. Their major proposition was that many of the symptoms of brain damage could be viewed not as specific manifestations of damage to centers or connecting pathways but as some form of impairment of the abstract attitude. The abstract attitude is not localized in any region of the brain but depends upon the functional integrity of the brain as a whole. Goldstein

(1959) describes the abstract attitude as the capacity to transcend immediate sensory impressions and consider situations from a conceptual standpoint. Generally, it is viewed as underlying such functions as planning, forming intentions, developing concepts, and separating ourselves from immediate sensory experience.

The notion of a nonlocalized generalized deficit underlying many of the specific behavioral phenomena associated with brain damage has survived to some extent in contemporary neuropsychology, but in a greatly modified form. Similarly, some aspects of classical localization theory are still with us, but also with major changes (Mesulam, 1985). None of the current theories accepts the view that there is no localization of function in the brain, and correspondingly, none of them would deny that some behaviors cannot be localized to some structure or group of structures. This synthesis is reflected in several modern concepts of brain function, the most explicit of these probably being that of Luria (1973). Luria has developed the concept of functional systems as an alternative to both strict localization and mass action theories. Basically, a functional system consists of several elements involved in the mediation of some complex behavior. For example, there may be a functional system for auditory comprehension of language. Thus, no structure in the brain is only involved in a single function. Depending upon varying conditions, the same structure may play a role in several functional systems. With regard to clinical neuropsychology, the main point is that there are both specific and nonspecific effects of brain damage. Evidence for this point of view has been presented most clearly by Teuber and his associates (Teuber, 1959) and by Satz (1966). The Teuber group was able to show that patients with penetrating brain wounds that produced very focal damage had symptoms that could be directly attributed to the lesion site, but they also had other symptoms that were shared by all patients studied, regardless of their specific lesion sites.

An old principle of brain function in higher organisms that has held up well and that is commonly employed in clinical neuropsychology involves contralateral control: the right half of the brain controls the left side of the body and vice versa. The contralateral control principle is important for clinical neuropsychology because it explains why patients with damage to one side of the brain may become paralyzed only on the opposite side of their body or may develop sensory disturbances on that side. We see this condition most commonly in individuals who have had strokes, but it is also seen in some patients who have open head injuries or who have brain tumors.

Although aphasia, or impaired communicative abilities as a result of brain damage, was recognized before Broca (Benton & Joynt, 1960), it was not recognized that it was associated with destruction of a particular area of one side of the brain. Thus, the basic significance of Broca's discovery was the discovery not of aphasia, but of cerebral dominance. Cerebral dominance is the term that has been commonly employed to denote the fact that the human brain has a hemisphere that is dominant for language and a nondominant hemisphere. In most people, the left hemisphere is dominant, and left hemisphere brain damage may lead to aphasia. However, some individuals have dominant right hemispheres, while others do not appear to have a dominant hemisphere. Although it remains unknown why most people are left-hemisphere dominant, what is clear is that for individuals who sustain left hemisphere brain damage, aphasia is a common symptom, while aphasia is a rare consequence of damage to the right hemisphere.

Following Broca's discovery, other neuroscientists discovered that just as the left hemisphere has specialized function in the area of language, the right hemisphere also has its own specialized functions. These functions seem to relate to nonverbal abilities such as visual-spatial skills, perception of complex visual configurations, and, to some extent, appreciation of nonverbal auditory stimuli such as music. Some investigators have conceptualized the problem in terms of sequential as opposed to simultaneous abilities. The left hemisphere is said to deal with material in a sequential, analytic manner, while the right hemisphere functions more as a detector of patterns or configurations (Dean, 1986). Thus, while patients with left hemisphere brain damage tend to have difficulty with language and other activities that involve sequencing, patients with right hemisphere brain damage have difficulties with such tasks as copying figures and producing constructions, because such tasks involve either perception or synthesis of patterns. In view of these findings regarding specialized functions of the right hemisphere, many neuropsychologists now prefer to use the expression functional asymmetries of the cerebral hemispheres rather than cerebral dominance.

With this basic brain–behavior background in mind, we now turn to a clinical description of the individual disorders that are included in the broad diagnostic category of neurocognitive disorders. This includes delirium and a number of individual disorders included under the major categories of major or mild neurocognitive disorders.

DELIRIUM

The first disorder listed in the *DSM-5* is delirium. This temporary condition is basically a loss of capacity to maintain attention with corresponding reduced awareness of the environment. Tremors and lethargy may be accompanying symptoms. Delirium is reversible in most cases but may evolve into a permanent neurocognitive or other neurological disorder. *DSM-5* allows for the specification of the cause of delirium, whether it is due to substance intoxication, substance withdrawal, medication-induced delirium due to another medical condition, or delirium due to multiple etiologies. Typically, delirium is an acute phenomenon and does not persist beyond a matter of days. However, delirium, notably when it is associated with alcohol abuse, may eventually evolve into permanent disorders in the form of a persistent neurocognitive disorder (formerly dementia). The behavioral correlates of delirium generally involve personality changes such as euphoria, agitation, anxiety, hallucinations, and depersonalization.

MAJOR AND MILD NEUROCOGNITIVE DISORDERS

There are several types of neurocognitive disorders, but they all involve the usually slowly progressive deterioration of intellectual function. The deterioration is frequently patterned, with loss of memory generally being the first function to decline, and other abilities deteriorating at later stages of the illness. As noted in *DSM-5*, the term *major or mild neurocognitive disorder* replaces the term *dementia* in an effort to eliminate stigmatization. The *DSM-5* approach to the diagnosis of the major and mild neurocognitive disorders is that there is first a determination of whether the individual is suffering from a major or mild type of cognitive impairment, and then the reason for the impairment is added (e.g., due to Alzheimer's disease) to indicate the distinct behavioral features and likely etiology. Furthermore, for either the major or mild types, there are "probable" or "possible" specifiers depending upon the strength of the evidence for the etiological factor (genetics, neuroimaging).

Major or Mild Neurocognitive Disorders of the Alzheimer's Type   One class of neurocognitive disorders, major or mild neurocognitive disorder of the Alzheimer's type, arises most commonly in late life, either during late middle age or old age, although it may occur at any age. In children it is differentiated from intellectual disability on the basis of the presence of deterioration from a formerly higher level. These disorders are defined as those conditions in which, for no exogenous reason, the brain begins to deteriorate and continues to do so until death. As indicated in the psychological and biological assessment section, a diagnostic method has recently become available to specifically diagnose Alzheimer's disease in the living patient. Its presence also becomes apparent on examination of the brain at autopsy.

Clinically, the course of the Alzheimer's type generally begins with signs of impairment of memory for recent events, followed by deficits in judgment, visual-spatial skills, and language. The language deficit has become a matter of particular interest, perhaps because the communicative difficulties of patients with major or mild neurocognitive disorders of the Alzheimer's type are becoming increasingly recognized. Generally, the language difficulty does not resemble aphasia, but can perhaps be best characterized as an impoverishment of speech, with word-finding difficulties and progressive inability to produce extended and comprehensible narrative speech as illustrated in the descriptive writing of Alzheimer's disease patients (Neils, Boller, Gerdeman, & Cole, 1989). The patients wrote shorter descriptive paragraphs than did age-matched controls, and they also made more handwriting errors of various types. The end state is generalized, severe intellectual impairment involving all areas, with the patient sometimes surviving for various lengths of time in a persistent vegetative state.

Criteria for the Alzheimer's disease subtype include meeting criteria for major or minor neurocognitive disorder, early and prominent impairment in memory, deficits in at least one other domain in the case of the major form of the disorder, a course of gradual onset and continuing cognitive decline, and a ruling out of the condition being attributable to other disorders (APA, 2013). The diagnosis may indicate whether it occurs with or without behavioral disturbance. Separate criteria for psychosis and depression have been written.

Major or Mild Frontotemporal Neurocognitive Disorder   In this disorder, there is specific impairment of social judgment, decision-making, and particular language and memory skills. The decline in language can take the form of speech production, word finding, object naming, grammar, or word comprehension (APA, 2013). Frontotemporal neurocognitive disorder is only diagnosed when Alzheimer's disease has been ruled out, and the patient must have symptoms that can be characterized as forming a "frontal lobe syndrome" (Rosenstein, 1998). The generic term commonly used to characterize the behaviors associated with this syndrome is executive dysfunction, a concept originally introduced by Luria (1966). Executive function is progressively impaired, and personality changes involving either apathy and indifference or childishness and euphoria occur. Compared with patients with Alzheimer's disease, frontal dementia patients have greater impairment of executive function but relatively better memory and visuoconstructional abilities. The outstanding features may all be viewed as relating to impaired ability to control, regulate, and program behavior. This impairment is manifested in numerous ways, including poor abstraction ability, impaired judgment, apathy, and loss of impulse control. Language is sometimes impaired, but in a rather unique way. Rather than having a formal language disorder, the patient loses the ability to control behavior through language. There is also often a difficulty with narrative speech, which has been interpreted as a problem in forming the intention to speak or in formulating a plan for a narrative. Such terms as lack of insight or of the ability to produce goal-oriented behavior are used to describe the frontal lobe patient. In many cases, these activating, regulatory, and programming functions are so impaired that the outcome looks like a generalized dementia with implications for many forms of cognitive, perceptual, and motor activities. Frontal dementia may occur as a result of several processes, such as head trauma, tumor, or stroke, but the syndrome produced is more or less the same.

Major or Mild Neurocognitive Disorder With Lewy Bodies   This disorder has a different pathology from Alzheimer's disease, being associated more with Parkinson's disease (Becker, Farbman, Hamilton, & Lopez, 2011; McKeith et al., 2004). The major symptoms are variations in alertness, recurrent hallucinations, and Parkinsonian symptoms (e.g., tremor, rigidity). Lewy bodies are intraneuron inclusion bodies first identified in the substantia nigra of patients with Parkinson's disease.

Major or Mild Vascular Neurocognitive Disorder   This is a progressive condition based on a history of small strokes associated with hypertension. Patients with vascular neurocognitive disorder experience a stepwise deterioration of function, with each small stroke making the dementia worse in some way. There are parallels between this disorder and the older concept of cerebral arteriosclerosis in that they both relate to the role of generalized cerebral vascular disease in producing progressive brain dysfunction. However, vascular neurocognitive disorder is actually a much more precisely defined syndrome that, although not rare, is not extremely common either. Furthermore, although it continues to be a separate diagnosis, there is substantial evidence that vascular neurocognitive disorder overlaps a great deal with Alzheimer's disease. Autopsy studies often show that there is evidence of vascular pathology in individuals diagnosed with Alzheimer's disease, and the reverse is also true. It has been suggested that cardiovascular illness may be a risk factor for Alzheimer's disease. Moreover, there appears to have been an increased focus of interest in the specific vascular disorders, including heart failure, stroke, and arteriovenous malformations, each of which has different cognitive consequences (Festa, 2010; Lantz, Lazar, Levine, & Levine, 2010; Pavol, 2010).

Because this disorder is known to be associated with hypertension and a series of strokes, the end result is substantial deterioration in cognitive functioning. However, the course of the deterioration is not thought to be as uniform as is the case in Alzheimer's disease, but rather is generally described as stepwise and patchy. The patient may remain relatively stable between strokes, and the symptomatology produced may be associated with the site of the strokes. It should be noted that whereas these distinctions between vascular and Alzheimer's type dementia are clearly described, in individual patients it is not always possible to make a definitive differential diagnosis. Even such sophisticated radiological methods as the computed tomography (CT) scan and MRI do not always contribute to the diagnosis. *DSM-5* recognizes the significance of comorbidity with the statement "Most individuals with Alzheimer's disease are elderly and have multiple medical conditions that can complicate diagnosis and influence the clinical course. Major or mild NCD [neurocognitive disorder] due to Alzheimer's disease commonly co-occurs with cerebrovascular disease which contributes to the clinical picture" (p. 614).

Major or Mild Neurocognitive Disorder due to Huntington's Disease   The progressive cognitive deterioration seen in Huntington's disease also involves significant impairment of memory, with other abilities becoming gradually affected through the course of the illness. However, it differs from Alzheimer's disease in that it is accompanied by choreic movements and by the fact that the age of onset is substantially earlier than is the case for Alzheimer's disease. Because of the chorea, a difficulty in speech articulation is also frequently seen, which is not the case for Alzheimer's patients.

There are other major or minor neurocognitive disorders listed in the *DSM-5*, including major or mild neurocognitive disorder due to TBI, substance/medication-induced major or mild neurocognitive disorder, major or mild neurocognitive disorder due to HIV infection, major or mild neurocognitive disorder due to prion disease, and major or mild neurocognitive disorder due to Parkinson's disease. Patients diagnosed with these syndromes do not have the specific syndromes of the type described earlier. The deficit pattern tends to be global in nature, with all functions more or less involved, even though some investigators have attempted to identify syndromal subtypes, with some having more deficit in the area of abstraction and judgment, some in the area of memory, and some in regard to affect and personality changes. This typology has recently received support from studies delineating frontotemporal dementia, semantic dementia, and Lewy body dementia as separate entities, but most patients have difficulties with all three areas.

OTHER CONDITIONS IMPORTANT FOR UNDERSTANDING BRAIN FUNCTIONING

In this section we will provide descriptions of the more commonly occurring disorders associated with structural brain damage. It is clear that what is common in one setting may be rare in another. Thus, we will focus on what is common in an adult neuropsychiatric setting. The neuropsychological syndromes found in childhood are often quite different from what is seen in adults and deserve separate treatment. Furthermore, the emphasis will be placed on chronic rather than acute syndromes because, with relatively rare exceptions, the psychologist and psychiatrist encounter the former type far more frequently than the latter.

THE COMMUNICATIVE DISORDERS

In general, aphasia and related language disorders are associated with unilateral brain damage to the dominant hemisphere, which in most individuals is the left hemisphere. Most aphasias result from stroke, but they can be acquired on the basis of left hemisphere head trauma or from brain tumor. Whereas the definition has changed over the years, the most current one requires the presence of impairment of communicative ability associated with focal, structural brain damage. Thus, the term is not coextensive with all disorders of communicative ability and does not include, for example, the language disorders commonly seen in demented individuals with diffuse brain damage. The study of aphasia has in essence become a separate area of scientific inquiry, having its own literature and several theoretical frameworks. The term *aphasia* does not convey a great deal of clinically significant information, because the various subtypes are quite different from each other.

Numerous attempts have been made to classify the aphasias, and there is no universally accepted system. Contemporary theory indicates that perhaps the most useful major distinction is between fluent and nonfluent aphasias. To many authorities, this distinction is more accurate than that previously more commonly drawn between expressive and receptive aphasias. The problem is that people with aphasia with primarily expressive problems do not generally have normal language comprehension, and it is almost always true that people with aphasia with major speech comprehension disturbances do not express themselves normally. However, there are individuals with aphasia who talk fluently and others whose speech is labored, very limited, and halting, if present at all in a meaningful sense. In the case of the former group, while speech is fluent, it is generally more or less incomprehensible because of a tendency to substitute incorrect words for correct ones—a condition known as verbal paraphasia. However, the primary disturbance in these patients involves profoundly impaired auditory comprehension. This combination of impaired comprehension and paraphasia is generally known as Wernicke's aphasia. The responsible lesion is generally in the superior gyrus of the left temporal lobe. In nonfluent aphasia, comprehension is generally somewhat better, but speech is accomplished with great difficulty and is quite limited. This condition is generally known as Broca's aphasia, the responsible lesion being in the lower, posterior portion of the left frontal lobe (i.e., Broca's area). Several other types of aphasia are relatively rare and will not be described here. However, it is important to point out that most aphasias are mixed, having components of the various pure types. Furthermore, the type of aphasia may change in the same patient, particularly during the course of recovery.

The disorders of reading, writing, and calculation may also be divided into subtypes. In the case of reading, our interest here is in the so-called acquired alexias, whereby an individual who was formerly able to read has lost that ability because of focal, structural brain damage. The ability to read letters, words, or sentences may be lost. Handwriting disturbances, or agraphia, might involve a disability in writing words from dictation or a basic disability in forming letters. Thus, some agraphic patients can write, but with omissions and distortions relative to what was dictated.

However, some can no longer engage in the purposive movements needed to form letters. Calculation disturbances, or acalculias, are also of several types. The patient may lose the ability to read numbers, to calculate even if the numbers can be read, or to arrange numbers in a proper spatial sequence for calculation. The various syndromes associated with communicative disorders, while sometimes existing in pure forms, often merge together. For example, alexia is frequently associated with Broca's aphasia, and difficulty with handwriting is commonly seen in patients with Wernicke's aphasia. However, there is generally a pattern in which there is a clear primary disorder, such as impaired auditory comprehension, with other disorders, such as difficulty with reading or writing, occurring as associated defects. Sometimes rather unusual combinations occur, as in the case of the syndrome of alexia without agraphia. In this case, the patient can write but cannot read, often to the extent that the patient cannot read what she or he just wrote. Based upon recent research, we would add that academic deficits that are not the product of brain damage acquired during adulthood, or of inadequate educational opportunity, are frequently seen in adults. Rather, people with these deficits have developmentally based learning disabilities that they never outgrew. The view that learning disability is commonly outgrown has been rejected by most students of this area (Katz, Goldstein, & Beers, 2001).

DISORDERS OF PERCEPTION AND MOTILITY

The disorders of perception can involve perception of one's body as well as perception of the external world. In the case of the external world, the disorder can involve some class of objects or some geographic location. The disorders of motility to be discussed here will not be primary losses of motor function as in the cases of paralysis or paresis, but losses in the area of the capacity to perform skilled, purposive acts. The set of impairments found in this area is called apraxia. There is also the borderline area in which the neuro-psychological defect has to do with the coordination of a sense modality, usually vision, and purposive movement. These disorders are sometimes described as impairment of constructional or visual-spatial relations ability. In some patients, the primary difficulty is perceptual, whereas in others it is mainly motoric. The body schema disturbances most commonly seen are of three types. The first has to do with the patient's inability to point to his or her own body parts on command. The syndrome is called autotopognosia, meaning lack of awareness of the surface of one's body. A more localized disorder of this type is finger agnosia, in which, while identification of body parts is otherwise intact, the patient cannot identify the fingers of his or her own hands, or the hands of another person. Finger agnosia has been conceptualized as a partial dissolution of the body schema. The third type of body schema disturbance is right–left disorientation, in which the patient cannot identify body parts in regard to whether they are on the right or left side. For example, when the patient is asked to show the right hand, he or she may become confused or show the left hand. More commonly, however, a more complex command is required to elicit this deficit, such as asking the patient to place the left hand on the right shoulder. The traditional thinking about this disorder is that both finger agnosia and right–left disorientation are part of a syndrome, the responsible brain damage being in the region of the left angular gyrus. However, Benton (1985) has pointed out that the matter is more complicated than that, and the issue of localization involves the specific nature of these defects in terms of the underlying cognitive and perceptual processes affected.

The perceptual disorders in which the difficulty is in recognizing some class of external objects are called gnostic disorders or agnosias. These disorders may be classified with regard to modality and verbal or nonverbal content. Thus, one form of the disorder might involve visual perception of nonverbal stimuli, and would be called visual agnosia. By definition, an agnosia is present when primary function of the affected modality is intact, but the patient cannot recognize or identify the stimulus. For example, in visual agnosia, the patient can see but cannot recognize what he or she has seen. In order to assure oneself that visual agnosia is present, it should be determined that the patient can recognize and name the object in question when it is placed in his or her hand, so that it can be recognized by touch, or when it produces some characteristic sound, so that it can be recognized by audition. The brain lesions involved in the agnosias are generally in the association areas for the various perceptual modalities. Thus, visual agnosia is generally produced by damage to association areas in the occipital lobes. When language is involved, there is obviously a great deal of overlap between the agnosias and the aphasias. For example, visual-verbal agnosia can really be viewed as a form of alexia. In these cases, it is often important to determine through detailed testing whether the deficit is primarily a disturbance of perceptual recognition or a higher-level conceptual disturbance involving language comprehension. There is a wide variety of gnostic disorders reported in the literature involving such phenomena as the inability to recognize faces, colors, or spoken words. However, these are relatively rare conditions and, when present, they may only persist during the acute phase of the illness. In general, agnosia has been described as "perception without meaning," and it is important to remember that it is quite a different phenomenon from what we usually think of as blindness or deafness.

Sometimes a perceptual disorder does not involve a class of objects but a portion of geographic space. The phenomenon itself is described by many terms, the most frequently used ones being neglect and inattention. It is seen most dramatically in vision, where the patient may neglect the entire right or left side of the visual world. It also occurs in the somatosensory modality, in which case the patient may neglect one side or the other of his or her body. Neglect can occur on either side, but it is more common on the left side, because it is generally associated with right hemisphere brain damage. In testing for neglect, it is often useful to employ the method of double stimulation, for example, in the form of simultaneous finger wiggles in the areas of the right and left visual fields. Typically, the patient may report seeing the wiggle in the right field but not in the left. Similarly, when the patient with neglect is touched lightly on the right and left hands at the same time, he or she may report feeling the touch in only one hand or the other. As in the case of the gnostic disorders, neglect is defined in terms of the assumption of intactness of the primary sensory modalities. Thus, the patient with visual neglect should have otherwise normal vision in the neglected half field, while the patient with tactile neglect should have normal somatosensory function. Clinically, neglect may be a symptom of some acute process and should diminish in severity or disappear as the neuropathological condition stabilizes. For example, visual neglect of the left field is often seen in individuals who have recently sustained right hemisphere strokes, but it can be expected to disappear as the patient recovers.

The apraxias constitute a group of syndromes in which the basic deficit involves impairment of purposive movement occurring in the absence of paralysis, weakness, or unsteadiness. For some time, the distinction has been made among three major types of apraxia: ideomotor, limb-kinetic, and ideational. In ideomotor apraxia, the patient has difficulty in performing a movement to verbal command. In the case of limb-kinetic apraxia, movement is clumsy when performed on command or when the patient is asked to imitate a movement. In ideational apraxia, the difficulty is with organizing the correct motor sequences in response to language. In other words, it may be viewed as a disability in regard to carrying out a series of acts. In addition, there are facial apraxias, in which the patient cannot carry out facial movements to command. These four types are thought to involve different brain regions and different pathways. However, they are all generally conceptualized as a destruction or disconnection of motor engrams or traces that control skilled, purposive movement. Certain of the visual-spatial disorders are referred to as apraxias, such as constructional or dressing apraxia, but they are different in nature from the purer motor apraxias described earlier.

The basic difficulty the patient with a visual-spatial disorder has relates to comprehension of spatial relationships, and, in most cases, coordination between visual perception and movement. In extreme cases, the patient may readily become disoriented and lose his or her way when going from one location to another. However, in most cases, the difficulty appears to be at the cognitive level and may be examined by asking the patient to copy figures or solve jigsaw or block design type puzzles. Patients with primarily perceptual difficulties have problems in localizing points in space, judging direction, and maintaining geographic orientation, as tested by asking the patient to describe a route or use a map. Patients with constructional difficulties have problems with copying and block building. So-called dressing apraxia may be seen as a form of constructional disability in which the patient cannot deal effectively with the visual-spatial demands involved in such tasks as buttoning clothing. Whereas visual-spatial disorders can arise from lesions found in most parts of the brain, they are most frequently seen, and seen with the greatest severity, in patients with right hemisphere brain damage. Generally, the area that will most consistently produce the severest deficit is the posterior portion of the right hemisphere. In general, although some patients show a dissociation between visual-spatial and visual-motor or constructional aspects of the syndrome of constructional apraxia, most patients have difficulties on both purely perceptual and constructional tasks.

AMNESIA

Whereas some degree of impairment of memory is a part of many brain disorders, there are some conditions in which loss of memory is clearly the most outstanding deficit.

When the loss of memory is particularly severe and persistent, and other cognitive and perceptual functions are relatively intact, the patient can be described as having an amnesic syndrome. Dementia patients are often amnesic, but their memory disturbance is embedded in significant generalized impairment of intellectual and communicative abilities. The amnesic patient generally has normal language and may be of average intelligence. As in the case of aphasia and several of the other disorders, there is more than one amnesic syndrome. The differences among them revolve around what the patient can and cannot remember. The structures in the brain that are particularly important for memory are the limbic system, especially the hippocampus, and certain brain stem structures, including the mammillary bodies and the dorsomedial nucleus of the thalamus.

There are many systems described in the literature for distinguishing among types of amnesia and types of memory. With regard to the amnesias, perhaps the most basic distinction is between anterograde and retrograde amnesia. Anterograde amnesia involves the inability to form new memories from the time of the onset of the illness producing the amnesia, whereas retrograde amnesia refers to the inability to recall events that took place before the onset of the illness. This distinction dovetails with the distinction between recent and remote memory. It is also in some correspondence with the distinction made between short-term and long-term memory in the experimental literature. However, various theories define these terms somewhat differently, and it is perhaps best to use the more purely descriptive terms *recent* and *remote memory* in describing the amnesic disorders. It can then be stated that the most commonly appearing amnesic disorders involve dramatic impairment of recent memory with relative sparing of remote memory. This sparing becomes greater as the events to be remembered become more remote. Thus, most amnesic patients can recall their early lives, but they may totally forget what occurred during the last several hours. This distinction between recent and remote memory possibly helps to explain why most amnesic patients maintain normal language function and average intelligence. In this respect, an amnesic disorder is not so much an obliteration of the past as it is an inability to learn new material.

Probably the most common type of relatively pure amnesic disorder is alcoholic Korsakoff's syndrome. These patients, while often maintaining average levels in several areas of cognitive function, demonstrate a dense amnesia for recent events with relatively well-preserved remote memory. Alcoholic Korsakoff's syndrome has been conceptualized by Butters and Cermak (1980) as an information-processing defect in which new material is encoded in a highly degraded manner leading to high susceptibility of interference. Butters and Cermak (1980), as well as numerous other investigators, have accomplished detailed experimental studies of alcoholic Korsakoff's patients in which the nature of their perceptual, memory, and learning difficulties has been described in detail. The results of this research help to explain numerous clinical phenomena noted in Korsakoff's patients, such as their capacity to perform learned behaviors without recall of when or if those behaviors were previously executed, or their tendency to confabulate or "fill in" for the events of the past day that they do not recall. It may be noted that although confabulation was once thought to be a cardinal symptom of Korsakoff's syndrome, it is only seen in some patients. Another type of amnesic disorder is seen when there is direct, focal damage to the temporal lobes, and most important, to the hippocampus. These temporal lobe or limbic system amnesias are less common than Korsakoff's syndrome, but they have been well studied because of the light they shed on the neuropathology of memory. These patients share many of the characteristics of Korsakoff's patients but have a much more profound deficit in regard to basic consolidation and storage of new material. When Korsakoff's patients are sufficiently cued and given enough time, they can learn. Indeed, sometimes they can demonstrate normal recognition memory. However, patients with temporal lobe amnesias may find it almost impossible to learn new material under any circumstances.

In some cases, amnesic disorders are modality specific. If one distinguishes between verbal and nonverbal memory, the translation can be made from the distinction between language and nonverbal abilities associated with the specialized functions of each cerebral hemisphere. In fact, it has been reported that patients with unilateral lesions involving the left temporal lobe may have memory deficits for verbal material only, whereas right temporal patients have corresponding deficits for nonverbal material. Thus, the left temporal patient may have difficulty with learning word lists, while the right temporal patient may have difficulty with geometric forms. In summary, whereas there are several amnesic syndromes, they all have in common the symptom of lack of ability to learn new material following the onset of the illness. Sometimes the symptom is modality-specific, involving only verbal or nonverbal material, but more often than not it involves both modalities. There are several relatively pure types of amnesia, notably Korsakoff's syndrome, but memory difficulties are cardinal symptoms of many other brain disorders, notably the progressive dementias and certain disorders associated with infection. For example, people with herpes encephalitis frequently have severely impaired memories, but they have other cognitive deficits as well.

PSEUDODEMENTIA

Although alterations in brain function can give rise to symptoms that look like functional personality changes, the reverse can also occur. That is, a nonorganic personality change, notably the acquisition of a depression, can produce symptoms that look like they have been produced by alterations in brain function. The term generally applied to this situation is pseudodementia, and it is most frequently seen in elderly people who become depressed. The concept of pseudodementia or depressive pseudodementia is not universally accepted, but it is not uncommon to find elderly patients diagnosed as demented when in fact the symptoms of dementia are actually produced by depression. The point is proven when the symptoms disappear or diminish substantially after the depression has run its course or the patient is treated with antidepressant medication. Wells (1979, 1980) has pointed out that this differential diagnosis is a difficult one to make, and it cannot be accomplished satisfactorily with the usual examinational, laboratory, and psychometric methods. He suggests that perhaps the most useful diagnostic criteria are clinical features. For example, patients with pseudodementia tend to complain about their cognitive losses, whereas patients with dementia tend not to complain. In a more recent formulation, Caine (1986) pointed to the many complexities of differential diagnosis in the elderly, referring in particular to the abundant evidence for neuropsychological deficits in younger depressed patients, and to the not uncommon coexistence of neurological and psychiatric impairments in the elderly.

In recent years there has been substantial rethinking about the concept of pseudodementia in the direction of characterizing it as a neurobiological disorder associated with demonstrable changes in brain structure. Clinicians have observed that depression may sometimes be the first indicator of Alzheimer's disease, and Nussbaum (1994), based on an extensive review of the literature, concluded that pseudodementia or late-life depression has a neurological substrate involving subcortical structures and the frontal lobes. He indicated that the probable pathology is leukoaraiosis, diminution in the density of white matter, which particularly involves the subcortex in this disorder. Leukoaraiosis is frequently seen in the MRIs of elderly depressed individuals.

EPIDEMIOLOGY

Returning to the *DSM-5* disorders, the epidemiology of the neurocognitive disorders varies with the underlying disorder, and so is unlike what is found for most of the other diagnostic categories in the *DSM* system. Here, we will only sample from those disorders in which epidemiological considerations are of particular interest. There are some exceptionally interesting and well-documented findings for multiple sclerosis, in which prevalence is directly related to the latitude at which one resides; the further from the equator, the higher the prevalence (Koch-Henriksen & Sørensen, 2010). Further study of this phenomenon has tended to implicate an environmental rather than an ethnic factor.

The epidemiology of head trauma has been extensively studied, with gender, age, and social class turning out to be important considerations. Head trauma has a higher incidence in males than in females (274 per 100,000 in males and 116 per 100,000 in females in one study; Levin, Benton, & Grossman, 1982). It is related to age, with risk peaking between the ages of 15 and 24, and occurs more frequently in individuals from lower social classes. Alcohol is a major risk factor, but marital status, pre-existing psychiatric disorder, and previous history of head injury have also been implicated. The major causes of head injury are motor vehicle accidents, falls, assaults, and recreational or work activities, with motor vehicle accidents clearly being the major cause (50–60%; Smith, Barth, Diamond, & Giuliano, 1998). The epidemiology of Huntington's disease has also been extensively studied. The disease is transmitted as an autosomal dominant trait, and the marker for the gene has been located on the short arm of chromosome 4 (Gusella et al., 1983). Prevalence estimates vary between 5 and 7 per 100,000. There are no known risk factors for acquiring the disorder, the only consideration being having a parent with the disease. If that is the case, the risk of acquiring the disorder is 50%. A test is now available to detect carriers of the defective gene, and its availability and usage may eventually reduce the prevalence of Huntington's disease.

There is great interest in the epidemiology of Alzheimer's disease, because the specific cause of the disease is not fully understood, and prevention of exposure to risk factors for Alzheimer's disease and related disorders remains a possibility. General health status considerations do not appear to constitute risk factors, but some time ago there were beliefs that there was transmissible infective agent, and that exposure to aluminum might be a risk factor. The aluminum hypothesis has largely been discarded. Recently, episodes of head trauma have been implicated as a possible risk factor for Alzheimer's disease (Lye & Shores, 2000). A reasonably solid genetic association involving chromosome 21 trisomy has been formed between what appears to be an inherited form of Alzheimer's disease and Down syndrome.

Much of the epidemiology of the organic mental disorders merges with general considerations regarding health status. Cardiovascular risk factors such as obesity and hypertension put one at greater than usual risk for stroke. Smoking is apparently a direct or indirect risk factor for several disorders that eventuate in brain dysfunction. The association of alcoholism and diagnosis of substance/medication-induced major or mild neurocognitive disorder is now relatively widely accepted, although it was controversial at one time. Alcohol most clearly—and, perhaps, several other abused substances—make for significant risk factors.

Until recently, the risk of acquiring brain disease by infection had diminished substantially, but that situation has changed markedly with the appearance of human immunodeficiency virus, or HIV-1 infection, or AIDS dementia (Bornstein, Nasrallah, Para, & Whitacre, 1993; Grant et al., 1987; Van Gorp, Miller, Satz, & Visscher, 1989; Woods et al., 2009). It has become increasingly clear that AIDS is frequently transmitted to children during pregnancy or in association with breastfeeding. New anti-infection medication is in use or in the process of going through extensive clinical trials, and there is great promise of effectiveness.

In summary, the prevalence and incidence of the neurocognitive disorders vary substantially, ranging from very rare to common diseases. The number of risk factors also varies, ranging from complete absence to a substantial number. The genetic and degenerative diseases, notably Huntington's and Alzheimer's disease, possess little in the way of risk factors, and there is not much that can be done to prevent their occurrence. The development of a test for risk of transmitting Huntington's disease has opened up the admittedly controversial and complex matter of genetic counseling.

PSYCHOLOGICAL AND BIOLOGICAL ASSESSMENT

In recognition of the complexities involved in relating structural brain damage to behavioral consequences, the field of clinical neuropsychology has emerged as a specialty area within psychology. Clinical neuropsychological research has provided specialized instruments for assessment of brain-damaged patients and a variety of rehabilitation methods aimed at remediation of neuropsychological deficits. This research has also pointed out that brain damage, far from being a single clinical entity, actually represents a wide variety of disorders.

Initially, neuropsychologists were strongly interested in the relationship between localization of the brain damage and behavioral outcome. In recent years, however, it has become evident that localization is only one determinant of outcome, albeit often a very important one. Other considerations include the individual's current age, age when the brain damage was acquired, the premorbid personality and level of achievement, and the pathological process producing the dysfunction. Furthermore, neuropsychologists are now cognizant of the possible influence of various nonorganic factors on their assessment methods, such as educational level, socioeconomic status, and mood states. There has been increasing interest in sociocultural aspects of neuropsychological assessment, particularly with reference to research and testing in cultures throughout the world that are experiencing significant effects of some brain disease, such as AIDS dementia (Heaton, 2006).

More recently, a third major methodology, neuroradiology is available for the study of neurocognitive disorders. Beyond the earlier development of the CT scan, positron emission tomography (PET) and functional MRI (fMRI) now allow direct observation of brain function in living individuals while they are engaged in some targeted activity. Using different technologies, these procedures can detect changes when the brain is behaviorally activated. It is now also possible to track conduction from one structure to another while some complex behavior is being performed, such as listening to a word and saying what it is. These methods are known as online procedures because the individual is having recordings made at the same time as the behavior is performed.

A second new development is magnetic resonance spectroscopy (MRS). MRS uses MRI technology, but instead of producing a visualization of brain structure or activity, it generates a chemical profile of the brain. While the individual lies under the magnet, a surface coil placed around the head generates various chemical spectra that provide data about underlying tissue at a microbiological level. In the brain, the phosphorous spectrum produces information about brain metabolism based on the activity of phospholipids that exist in cell membranes. The hydrogen spectrum is most often used to determine the level of a substance called N-acetylaspartate (NAA). NAA level has been found to be associated with integrity of neurons and thus provides an index of neuronal loss, deterioration, or maldevelopment. Therefore, we have a way of examining brain tissue at a molecular biological level in a living individual. PET, fMRI, and MRS have substantially advanced our capability of assessing brain function. DTI is an MRI-related technique that can evaluate misalignment of axonal white matter, as may be found with head injury or some developmental disorders. It evaluates anisotropy associated with diffusion of water mainly in white matter.

In this author's judgment, the major developments over recent years continue to be technological in nature. Increasingly sophisticated techniques have been developed to image the brain, not only structurally as in an X-ray but also functionally. We now have very advanced capacities to image brain activity while the individual is engaging in some form of behavior. At present, fMRI is the most widely used of these procedures. It involves performing MRI while the individual is given tasks to perform and recording changes in brain activity. Thus, for example, it is possible to observe increased activity in the language area of the brain while the person is performing a language task.

There have also been new developments in the techniques used to make a pathological diagnosis of Alzheimer's disease in a living person. Previously, the diagnosis could only be made at autopsy. Now there is a neuroimaging procedure that can visualize neurochemical changes in the brain which can make a specific diagnosis. It involves an amyloid-imaging PET tracer called Pittsburgh Compound B that detects amyloid in the brain. Amyloid is known to be central to the pathogenesis of Alzheimer's disease (Fagan et al., 2005; Klunk et al., 2004). There have been advances in the genetics of Alzheimer's disease, with great interest in the apolipoprotein E epsilon 4 allele (APOE4) which appears to be associated with age of onset of the disorder. There has also been substantial interest in mild cognitive impairment (MCI), the mild cognitive deficits that frequently appear in elderly people. The question raised has involved whether occurrence of MCI results in conversion to Alzheimer's disease. The degree of deficits noted on neuropsychological testing has been found to be significantly associated with conversion to Alzheimer's disease, thereby constituting a significant risk factor.

ETIOLOGICAL CONSIDERATIONS

The brain may incur many of the illnesses that afflict other organs and organ systems. It may be damaged by trauma or it may become infected. The brain can become cancerous or it can lose adequate oxygen through occlusion of the blood vessels that supply it. The brain can be affected by acute or chronic exposure to toxins, such as carbon monoxide or other poisonous substances. Nutritional deficiencies can alter brain function just as they alter the function of other organs and organ systems. The brain may mature abnormally during pregnancy for various reasons, producing different developmental disorders. Aside from these general systemic and exogenous factors, there are diseases that more or less specifically have the central nervous system as their target. These conditions, generally known as degenerative and demyelinating diseases, include Huntington's disease, multiple sclerosis, Parkinson's disease, and disorders associated with aging.

From the point of view of neuropsychological considerations, it is useful to categorize the various disorders according to temporal and topographical parameters. Thus, certain neuropathological conditions are static and do not change substantially; others are slowly progressive; and some are rapidly progressive. With regard to topography, certain conditions tend to involve focal, localized disease, others involve multifocal lesions, and still others involve diffuse brain damage without specific localization. Another very important consideration has to do with morbidity and mortality. Some brain disorders are more or less reversible, some are static and do not produce marked change in the patient over lengthy periods, and some are rapidly or slowly progressive, producing increasing morbidity and eventually leading to death. Thus, some types of brain damage produce a stable condition with minimal changes, some types permit substantial recovery, and other types are in actuality terminal illnesses. It is, therefore, apparent that the kind of brain disorder the patient suffers from is a crucial clinical consideration in that it has major implications for treatment, management, and planning.

HEAD TRAUMA

Although the skull affords the brain a great deal of protection, severe blows to the head can produce temporary brain dysfunction or permanent brain injury. The temporary conditions, popularly known as concussions, are generally self-limiting and involve a period of confusion, dizziness, and perhaps double vision. However, there seems to be complete recovery in most cases. In concussion, the brain is not thought to be permanently damaged, but there are exceptions. More serious trauma is generally classified as closed or open head injury. In closed head injury, which is more common, the vault of the skull is not penetrated, but the impact of the blow crashes the brain against the skull and thus may create permanent structural damage. In the case of open head injury, the skull is penetrated by a missile of some kind. Open head injuries occur most commonly during wartime as a result of bullet wounds. They sometimes occur as a result of vehicular or industrial accidents, if some rapidly moving object penetrates the skull. Open head injuries are characterized by the destruction of brain tissue in a localized area. It is generally thought that there are more remote effects as well, but the most severe symptoms are usually associated with the track of the missile through the brain. Thus, an open head injury involving the left temporal lobe could produce aphasia, whereas similar injury to the back of the head could produce a visual disturbance.

A major neuropsychological difference between open and closed head injury is that although the open injury typically produces specific, localized symptoms, the closed head injury, with the possible exception of subdural hematoma, produces diffuse dysfunction without specific focal symptoms. In both cases, some of these symptoms may disappear with time, whereas others may persist. There is generally a sequence of phases that applies to the course of both closed and open head injuries. Often, the patient is initially unconscious and may remain that way for an widely varying amount of time, ranging from minutes to weeks or even months. After consciousness is regained, the patient generally goes through a so-called acute phase, during which there may be confusion and disorientation.

The cognitive residual symptoms of head trauma are extremely varied, because they are associated with whether the injury was open head or closed head and whether there was clear tissue destruction. Most often, patients with closed head injury have generalized intellectual deficits involving abstract reasoning ability, memory, and judgment. Sometimes, marked personality changes are noted, often having the characteristic of increased impulsiveness and exaggerated affective responsivity. Patients suffering from the residual of open head injury may have classic neuropsychological syndromes such as aphasia, visual-spatial disorders, and specific types of memory or perceptual disorders. In these cases, the symptoms tend to be strongly associated with the lesion site. For example, a patient with left hemisphere brain damage may have an impaired memory for verbal material such as names of objects, whereas the right hemisphere patient may have an impaired memory for nonverbal material such as pictures or musical compositions. In these cases there is said to be both modality (e.g., memory) and material (e.g., verbal stimuli) specificity. Head trauma is generally considered to be the most frequent type of brain damage in adolescents and young adults. Therefore, it generally occurs in a reasonably healthy brain. When the combination of a young person and a healthy brain exists, the prognosis for recovery is generally good if the wound itself is not devastating in terms of its extent or the area of the brain involved. For practical purposes, residual brain damage is a static condition that does not generate progressive changes for the worse, although there is some research evidence (Walker, Caveness, & Critchley, 1969) that, following a long quiescent phase, head-injured individuals may begin to deteriorate more rapidly than normal when they become elderly, and also that brain injury may be a risk factor for Alzheimer's disease (Lye & Shores, 2000). However, head-injured individuals may nevertheless have many years of productive functioning. There has been a strong interest in outcome following mild head injury (Levin, Eisenberg, & Benton, 1989), as well as in the specific problems associated with head injury in children (Noggle & Pierson, 2010). It has been frequently pointed out in recent years that trauma is the major cause of death in children, and head trauma among children is not uncommon. Most recently, a marked interest has developed in sports injuries (e.g., Schatz, Pardini, Lovell, Collins, & Podell, 2006), with most studies assessing athletes shortly after sustaining a concussion and evaluating future outcome.

Since the Persian Gulf War era, there has been a substantial increase in the study of head injury, particularly head injuries sustained by veterans and, more specifically, those who had blast injuries or concussions. Thus far, the results are mixed and the characteristics of persistent postconcussion syndrome and its association with PTSD are far from fully understood. Although standard neuroimaging procedures are typically normal following concussion, studies with DTI show some abnormal findings, as reviewed in Bigler (2008). However, in an individual study by Levin et al. (2010), there were no consequential findings with DTI, with head-injured subjects showing normal functional anisotropy, suggesting the absence of axonal misalignment. Wilk et al. (2010) found no or inconsistent association between self-reported concussion and the presence of persistent postconcussive symptoms. However, Mayer et al. (2010) did report finding white-matter abnormalities based upon DTI studies in patients with mild TBI. The roles of PTSD and depression as mediators of these associations have been stressed (Belanger et al., 2010).

DISEASES OF THE CIRCULATORY SYSTEM

Current thinking about the significance of vascular disease has changed from the time when it was felt that cerebral arteriosclerosis, or "hardening of the arteries," was the major cause of generalized brain dysfunction in the middle-aged and elderly. Although this condition is less common, the status of the heart and the blood vessels is significantly related to the intactness of brain function. Basically, the brain requires oxygen to function, and oxygen is distributed to the brain through the cerebral blood vessels. When these vessels become occluded, circulation is compromised and brain function is correspondingly impaired. This impairment occurs in several ways, perhaps the most serious and abrupt being stroke. A stroke is a sudden total blockage of a cerebral artery caused by blood clot or hemorrhage. The clot may be a thrombosis formed out of atherosclerotic plaques at branches and curves in the cerebral arteries, or an embolism, which is a fragment that has broken away from a thrombus in the heart and migrated to the brain.

Cerebral hemorrhages are generally fatal, but survival from thrombosis or embolism is not at all uncommon. Following a period of stupor or unconsciousness, the most common and apparent postacute symptom is hemiplegia—paralysis of one side of the body. There is also a milder form of stroke known as a transient ischemic attack (TIA), which is basically a temporary, self-reversing stroke that does not produce severe syndromes or may be essentially asymptomatic. The phrase "silent stroke" or "silent cerebral infarction" is used when stroke-type neuropathology is detected by MRI or related procedures, but there are no apparent symptoms (Das et al., 2008).

Other relatively common cerebrovascular disorders are associated with aneurysms and other vascular malformations in the brain. An aneurysm is an area of weak structure in a blood vessel that may not produce symptoms until it balloons out to the extent that it creates pressure effects or it ruptures. A ruptured aneurysm is an extremely serious medical condition which may lead to sudden death. However, surgical intervention in which the aneurysm is ligated is often effective. Arteriovenous malformations are congenitally acquired tangles of blood vessels. They may be asymptomatic for many years, but they can eventually rupture and hemorrhage. They may appear anywhere in the brain, but they commonly occur in the posterior half. The symptoms produced, when they occur, may include headache and neurological signs associated with the particular site.

There are major neuropsychological differences between the individual with a focal vascular lesion, most commonly associated with stroke, and the patient with generalized vascular disease such as vascular dementia. The stroke patient is characterized not only by the hemiplegia or hemiparesis, but also sometimes by an area of blindness in the right or left visual fields and commonly by a pattern of behavioral deficits associated with the hemisphere of the brain affected and the locus within that hemisphere. If the stroke involves a blood vessel in the left hemisphere, the patient will be paralyzed or weak on the right side of the body, the area of blindness, if present, will involve the right field of vision, and there will frequently be aphasia. Right hemisphere strokes may produce left-sided weakness or paralysis and left visual field defects but no aphasia. Instead, a variety of phenomena may occur. The patient may acquire a severe difficulty with spatial relations—a condition known as *constructional apraxia*. The ability to recognize faces or to appreciate music may be affected. A phenomenon known as *unilateral neglect* may develop, in which the patient does not attend to stimuli in the left visual field, although it may be demonstrated that basic vision is intact. Sometimes affective changes occur in which the patient denies that he or she is ill and may even develop euphoria.

In contrast with this specific, localized symptom picture seen in the stroke patient, the individual with vascular dementia or other generalized cerebral vascular disease has a quite different set of symptoms. Generally, there is no unilateral paralysis, no visual field deficit, no gross aphasia, and none of the symptoms characteristic of patients with right hemisphere strokes. Rather, there is a picture of generalized intellectual, and to some extent physical, deterioration. If weakness is present, it is likely to affect both sides of the body, and typically there is general diminution of intellectual functions, including memory, abstraction ability, problem-solving ability, and speed of thought and action. In the case of the patient with vascular dementia, there may be localizing signs, but there would tend to be several of them, and they would not point to a single lesion in one specific site. The more common forms of cerebral vascular disease are generally not seen until at least middle age, and for the most part they are diseases of the elderly. Clinically significant cerebral vascular disease is often associated with a history of generalized cardiovascular or other systemic diseases, notably hypertension and diabetes. Some genetic or metabolic conditions promote greater production of atheromatous material than is normal, and some people are born with arteriovenous malformations or aneurysms, placing them at higher than usual risk for serious cerebral vascular disease. When a stroke is seen in a young adult, it is usually because of an aneurysm or other vascular malformation. Most authorities agree that stroke is basically caused by atherosclerosis, and so genetic and acquired conditions that promote atherosclerotic changes in blood vessels generate risk of stroke. With modern medical treatment there is a good deal of recovery from stroke with substantial restoration of function. However, in the case of the diffuse disorders, there is really no concept of recovery because they tend to be slowly progressive. The major hope is to minimize the risk of future strokes, through such means as controlling blood pressure and weight. An area of particular interest is the long-term effects of hypertension on cerebral function, as well as the long-term effects of antihypertensive medication. Reviews written some time ago (Elias & Streeten, 1980; King & Miller, 1990) have demonstrated that hypertension in itself, as well as antihypertensive medication, can impair cognitive function, but there are no definite conclusions in this area as yet, with studies reporting mixed as well as benign outcomes associated with prudent use of the newer antihypertensive medications (Goldstein, 1986).

Degenerative and Demyelinating Diseases

The degenerative and demyelinating diseases constitute a variety of disorders that have several characteristics in common but that are also widely different from each other in many ways. What they have in common is that they specifically attack the central nervous system, they are slowly progressive and incurable, and although they are not all hereditary diseases, they appear to stem from some often unknown but endogenous defect in physiology. Certain diseases, once thought to be degenerative, have been found not to be so, or are thought not to be so at present. For example, certain dementias have been shown to be caused by so-called slow viruses, whereas multiple sclerosis, the major demyelinating disease, is strongly suspected to have a viral etiology. Thus, in these two examples, the classification would change from degenerative to infectious disease.

The term *degenerative disease* means that, for some unknown reason, the brain or the entire central nervous system gradually wastes away. In some cases, this wasting, or atrophy, resembles what happens to the nervous system in very old people, but substantially earlier than the senile period, perhaps as early as the late 40s. The previous distinction between presenile and senile dementia is not currently used much, apparently based upon the understanding that it is the same disease, most often neurocognitive disorder of the Alzheimer's type, but the research literature continues to be controversial, showing some important neurobiological differences between those who demonstrate presence of the disease before and during late life.

Senile dementia is generally diagnosed in elderly individuals when the degree of cognitive deficit is substantially greater than one would expect with normal aging. In other words, not all old people become significantly demented before death. Most of those who do, but who do not have another identifiable disease of the central nervous system, are generally thought to have neurocognitive disorder of the Alzheimer's type, which is thought to account for more cases of cognitive dysfunction than does vascular disease. There is another disorder related to Alzheimer's disease called Pick's disease, but it is difficult to distinguish from Alzheimer's disease in living individuals. The distinction only becomes apparent on autopsy, as the neuropathological changes in the brain are different. Within psychiatry, there is no longer an attempt to differentiate clinically among Alzheimer's, Pick's, and some rarer degenerative diseases. *DSM-5* considers all of these diseases as underlying the disorder known as major or mild neurocognitive disorder due to Alzheimer's disease.

Although much is still not known about the degenerative disorders, a lot has been discovered in recent years. The major discovery was that Alzheimer's and Huntington's disease (a frequently occurring degenerative disease found in younger adults) are apparently based on neurochemical deficiencies. In the case of Alzheimer's disease, the deficiency is thought to be primarily the group of substances related to choline, one of the neurotransmitters. The disease process itself is characterized by progressive death of the choline neurons—the cells that serve as receptor sites for cholinergic agents, and the presence of a gene that produces amyloid plaques in the brain. Huntington's disease is more neurochemically complex because three neurotransmitters are involved: choline, GABA, and substance P. The reasons for these neurochemical deficiency states remain unknown, but the states themselves have been described, and treatment efforts have been initiated based on this information. For example, some Alzheimer's patients have been given choline or lecithin, a substance related to choline, and other newer drugs such as Aricept, in the hope of slowing down the progression of the illness.

Most recently, an extensive literature has developed around progressive dementias that resemble but are pathologically or behaviorally different from Alzheimer's disease. One group is now known as prion diseases. Prions are proteins that are infectious and can transmit biological information. They also are apparently associated with Creutzfeldt–Jakob disease, a progressive dementia.

ALCOHOLISM

The term *alcoholism* in the context of central nervous system function involves not only the matter of excessive consumption of alcoholic beverages, but also a complex set of considerations involving nutritional status, related disorders such as head trauma, physiological alterations associated with the combination of excessive alcohol consumption and malnutrition, and possible genetic factors. What is frequently observed in long-term chronic alcoholism is a pattern of deterioration of intellectual function not unlike that seen in patients with major or minor neurocognitive disorders of the Alzheimer's type. However, it is not clear that the deteriorative process is associated with alcohol consumption *per se*. Thus, although some clinicians use the term *alcoholic dementia*, this characterization lacks sufficient specificity, because it is rarely at all clear that the observed dementia is in fact solely a product of excessive use of alcohol. Looking at the matter in temporal perspective, there may, first of all, be a genetic propensity for the acquisition of alcoholism that might ultimately have implications for central nervous system function (Goodwin, 1979). Second, Tarter (1976) has suggested that there may be an association between having minimal brain damage or a hyperactivity syndrome as a child and the acquisition of alcoholism as an adult. These two considerations suggest the possibility that at least some individuals who eventually become alcoholics may not have completely normal brain function preceding the development of alcoholism. Third, during the course of becoming chronically alcoholic, dietary habits tend to become poor, and multiple head injuries may be sustained as a result of fights or accidents. As the combination of excessive alcohol abuse and poor nutrition progresses, major physiological changes may occur, particularly in the liver, and to some extent in the pancreas and gastrointestinal system. Thus, the dementia seen in long-term patients with alcoholism may well involve a combination of all of these factors in addition to the always-present possibility of other neurological complications.

The majority of alcoholics who develop central nervous system complications manifest it in the form of general deterioration of intellectual abilities, but some develop specific syndromes. The most common of these is the Wernicke–Korsakoff syndrome, which begins with the patient going into a confusional state, accompanied by difficulty in walking and controlling eye movements, and by polyneuritis, a condition marked by pain or loss of sensation in the arms and legs. The latter symptoms may gradually disappear, but the confusional state may evolve into a permanent, severe amnesia. When this transition has taken place, the patient is generally described as having Korsakoff's syndrome or alcohol amnestic disorder, and is treated with large dosages of thiamine, because the etiology of the disorder appears to be a thiamine deficiency rather than a direct consequence of alcohol ingestion. Data reported previously (Blass & Gibson, 1977) indicate that the thiamine deficiency must be accompanied by an inborn metabolic defect related to an enzyme that metabolizes thiamine and is associated with thiamine transport genes (Guerrini, Thomson, & Gurling, 2009). It should be noted that the amnesic and intellectual disorders found in chronic alcoholics are permanent and present even when the patient is not intoxicated. The acute effects of intoxication or withdrawal (e.g., delirium tremens [DTs]) are superimposed on these permanent conditions. These disorders are also progressive as long as the abuse of alcohol and malnutrition persist. Other than abstinence and improved nutrition, there is no specific treatment. Even thiamine treatment for the Korsakoff patient does not restore memory; it is used primarily to prevent additional brain damage.

It is probably fair to say that a major interest in recent years has been the genetics of alcoholism. There is a growing, probably well-justified, belief that a positive family history of alcoholism puts an individual at increased risk for becoming alcoholic, if exposed to alcoholic beverages. The body of supporting research done is broad-ranging, including extensive family adoption studies (Goodwin, Schulsinger, Hermansen, Guze, & Winokur, 1973); neuropsychological studies of relatives (Schaeffer, Parsons, & Yohman, 1984) and children of alcoholics (Tarter, Hegedus, Goldstein, Shelly, & Alterman, 1984); psychophysiological studies, emphasizing brain event-related potentials in siblings (Steinhauer, Hill, & Zubin, 1987) and children of alcoholics (Begleiter, Porjesz, Bihari, & Kissin, 1984); and laboratory genetic studies. In summary, an extensive effort is being made to find biological markers of alcoholism (Hill, Steinhauer, & Zubin, 1987) and to determine the transmission of alcoholism in families. At this time, several susceptibility genes have been identified (Hill et al., 2004). One reasonable assumption is that alcoholism is a heterogeneous disorder, and there may be both hereditary and non-hereditary forms of it (Cloninger, Bohman, & Sigvardsson, 1981).

Toxic, Infectious, and Metabolic Illnesses

Exogenous or endogenous agents may poison the brain or it may become infected. Sometimes these events occur with such severity that the person dies, but more often, the individual survives with a greater or lesser degree of neurological dysfunction. Beginning with the exogenous toxins, we have already discussed the major one: alcohol. However, excessive use of drugs such as bromides and barbiturates may produce at least temporary brain dysfunction, such as delirium.

In psychiatric settings, a fairly frequently seen type of toxic disorder is carbon monoxide poisoning. This disorder and its treatment are quite complex, because it usually occurs in an individual with a major mood or psychotic disorder who attempted to commit suicide by inhaling car fumes in a closed garage. The brain damage sustained during the episode may often be permanent, resulting in significant intellectual and physical dysfunction in addition to the previously existing psychiatric disorder. Other toxic substances that may affect central nervous system function include certain sedative and hypnotic drugs, plant poisons, heavy metals, and toxins produced by certain bacteria, leading to such conditions as tetanus and botulism. The specific effects of these substances themselves, as well as whether exposure is acute (as in the case of tetanus or arsenic poisoning) or chronic (as in the case of addiction to opiates and related drugs), are often crucial.

Many brain disorders are associated with inborn errors of metabolism. In some way, a fault in metabolism produces a detrimental effect on the nervous system, generally beginning in early life. There are so many of these disorders that we will only mention two of the more well-known ones as illustrations. The first is phenylketonuria (PKU). PKU is an amino acid uria, a disorder that involves excessive excretion of an amino acid into the urine. It is genetic and, if untreated, can produce intellectual disability accompanied by poor psychomotor development and hyperactivity. The treatment involves a diet low in a substance called phenylalanine. The second disorder is Tay–Sachs disease. The enzyme abnormality here is a deficiency in a substance called hexasaminidase A, which is important for the metabolism of protein and polysaccharides. It is hereditary, occurs mainly in Jewish children, and is present from birth. The symptoms are initially poor motor development and progressive loss of vision, followed by dementia, with death usually occurring before the age of 5 years. These two examples illustrate similarity in process, which is basically an inherited enzyme deficiency, but variability in outcome. PKU is treatable, with a relatively favorable prognosis, whereas Tay–Sachs is a rapidly progressive, incurable terminal illness.

Bacterial infections of the brain are generally associated with epidemics but are sometimes seen when there are no epidemics at large. They are generally referred to as encephalitis, when the brain is infected, or meningitis, when the infection is in the membranous tissue that lines the brain, known as the meninges. Infections, of course, are produced by microorganisms that invade tissue and cause inflammation. During the acute phase of the bacterial infections, the patient may be quite ill, and survival is an important issue. Headaches, fever, and a stiff neck are major symptoms. There may be delirium, confusion, and alterations in state of consciousness ranging from drowsiness, through excessive sleeping, to coma. Some forms of encephalitis were popularly known as "sleeping sickness." Following the acute phase of bacterial infection, the patient may be left with residual neurological and neuropsychological disabilities and personality changes. Sometimes infections are local, and the patient is left with neurological deficits that correspond with the lesion site. The irritability, restlessness, and aggressiveness of postencephalitic children are mentioned in the literature. Jervis (1959) described them as overactive, restless, impulsive, assaultive, and wantonly destructive.

Neurosyphylis is another type of infection that has a relatively unique course. Most interesting, aside from the progressive dementia that characterizes this disorder, there are major personality changes involving the acquisition of delusions and a tendency toward uncritical self-aggrandizement. Although neurosyphilis or general paresis played a major role in the development of psychiatry, it is now a relatively rare disease and is seldom seen in clinical practice. Similarly, the related neurosyphilitic symptoms, such as tabes dorsalis and syphilitic deafness, are also rarely seen.

The incidence of and perhaps the interest in the bacterial infections and neurosyphilis have diminished, but interest in viral infections has increased substantially during recent years. There are perhaps four reasons for this phenomenon: (1) Jonas Salk's discovery that poliomyelitis was caused by a virus and could be prevented by vaccination; (2) the recent increase in the incidence of herpes simplex, which is a viral disorder; (3) the appearance of AIDS; and (4) the discovery of the "slow viruses." The latter two reasons are probably of greatest interest in the present context. With regard to the slow viruses, it has been discovered that certain viruses have a long incubation period and may cause chronic degenerative disease, resembling Alzheimer's disease in many ways. Thus, some neurocognitive disorders may be produced by a transmittable agent. One of these disorders appears to be a disease known as kuru, and another is known as Creutz-feldt–Jakob disease. Recently, there has been an outbreak of a related disorder called mad cow disease, or bovine spongiform encephalopathy (Balter, 2001). The discovery of infection as the cause of disease is important because it opens up the possibility of the development of a preventive treatment in the form of a vaccine.

Major and mild neurocognitive disorder due to AIDS is another form of viral encephalopathy. It is a consequence of HIV infection and apparently represents an illness that has not appeared on the planet previously. It has been characterized as a progressive subcortical dementia of the type seen in patients with Huntington's disease and other neurological disorders in which the major neuropathology is in the subcortex. The syndrome has not been completely described, but there is substantial evidence of neuropsychological abnormalities. The first papers in this area appeared around 1987, with the best-known study being that of Grant et al. (1987). A review is contained in Bornstein et al. (1993), and recent updates have been provided by Heaton (2006) and Woods et al. (2009).

GENETIC FACTORS

The neurocognitive disorders are based on some diseases of known genetic origin, some diseases in which a genetic or familial component is suspected, and some that are clearly acquired disorders. It is well established that Huntington's disease and certain forms of intellectual disability, notably Down syndrome, are genetic disorders. There appears to be evidence that there is a hereditary form of Alzheimer's disease, although the genetic contribution to Alzheimer's disease in general is not fully understood. A relatively rare genetic subtype has been identified consisting of patients who develop psychosis (DeMichele-Sweet & Sweet, 2010). The great majority of individuals with this subtype and other individuals with Alzheimer's disease have a gene on chromosome 14 called apolipoprotein E that promotes development of the amyloid plaques that constitute the major brain pathology associated with the disease. Whether multiple sclerosis has a genetic component remains under investigation, although it is clearly not a hereditary disorder like Huntington's disease.

Of great recent interest is the role of genetics in the acquisition of alcoholism, and subsequently dementia associated with alcoholism or alcohol amnestic disorder. Evidence suggests that having an alcoholic parent places one at higher than average risk for developing alcoholism. The specific genetic factors are far from understood, but there does appear to be an association in families. Whether having a family history of alcoholism increases the risk of acquiring dementia associated with alcoholism is not clear, but it has been shown that nonalcoholic sons of alcoholic fathers do more poorly on some cognitive tests than do matched controls. The matter is substantially clearer in the case of alcohol amnestic disorder or Korsakoff's syndrome. A widely cited study by Blass and Gibson (1977) showed that acquisition of Korsakoff's syndrome is dependent upon the existence of a genetic defect in a liver enzyme called transketolase in combination with a thiamine deficiency.

Other genetic and familial factors associated with the organic mental disorders relate largely to the genetics of underlying systemic disorders. Thus, the genetics of cancer might have some bearing on the likelihood of acquiring a brain tumor, while the genetics of the cardiovascular system might have some bearing on the risk for stroke. Disorders such as hypertension and diabetes appear to run in families and have varying incidences in different ethnic groups. Ethnic specificity is sometimes quite precise (but this is rare), as in the case of Tay–Sachs disease, a degenerative disorder of early childhood that is found almost exclusively in eastern European Jews.

COURSE AND PROGNOSIS

Course and prognosis for the neurocognitive disorders also vary with the underlying disorder. We will review the basic considerations here by first introducing some stages of acceleration and development. Then we will provide examples of disorders that have courses and prognoses consistent with various acceleration and developmental combinations. The acceleration stages are steady state, slow, moderate, and rapid. The developmental stages are the perinatal period, early childhood, late childhood and adolescence, early adulthood, middle age, and old age. The acceleration stages have to do with the rate of progression of the disorder, whereas the developmental stages characterize the age of onset of symptoms.

Intellectual disability would be a disorder with a course involving onset during the perinatal period and steady-state acceleration. Intellectual disability is one of those disorders in which there is little if any progression of neuropathology, but there may be a slowly progressive disability because of increasing environmental demands for cognitive abilities that the individual does not possess. Other developmental disorders, such as specific learning disability, do not have their onsets during the perinatal period but rather during early childhood when academic skills are first expected to be acquired.

In contrast to these disorders, stroke is typically characterized by onset during middle age. The acceleration of the disorder is extremely rapid at first and then slows down, gradually reaching steady state. Thus, the stroke patient, at the time of the stroke, becomes seriously ill very rapidly, and this is followed by additional destructive processes in the brain. Assuming a good outcome, a gradual recovery period follows, and there is restoration of the brain to a relatively normal steady state. On the other hand, malignant brain tumors, which also tend to appear during middle age, progress rapidly and do not decelerate unless they are successfully surgically removed.

The progressive dementias generally appear during middle or old age and accelerate slowly or moderately. Huntington's disease generally progresses less rapidly than Alzheimer's disease, and so the Huntington's patient may live a long life with his or her symptoms. Head trauma is a disorder that may occur at any age, but once the acute phase of the disorder is over, the brain typically returns to a steady state. Thus, the head trauma patient, if recovery from the acute condition is satisfactory, may have a normal life expectancy with an often dramatic picture of deterioration immediately following the trauma until completion of resolution of the acute phase, followed by substantial recovery. However, the degree of residual disabilities may vary widely.

Briefly summarizing these considerations from a developmental standpoint, the most common organic mental disorder associated with the perinatal period is intellectual disability and its variants. During early childhood, the specific and pervasive developmental disorders begin to appear. Head trauma typically begins to appear during late childhood and adolescence, and incidence peaks during young adulthood. Systemic illnesses, notably cardiovascular, cardiopulmonary, and neoplastic disease, most commonly impact negatively on brain functions during middle age. Dementia associated with alcoholism also begins to appear during early middle age. The progressive degenerative dementias are largely associated with old age.

With regard to acceleration, following the time period surrounding the acquisition of the disorder, developmental, vascular, and traumatic disorders tend to be relatively stable. Malignant tumors and certain infectious disorders may be rapidly progressive, and the degenerative disorders progress at a slow to moderate pace. Although the connotation of the term *progressive* is progressively worse, not all the neurocognitive disorders remain stable or get worse. There is recovery of certain disorders as a natural process or with the aid of treatment. In the case of head trauma, there is a rather typical history of initial unconsciousness, lapsing into coma for varying lengths of time, awakening, a period of memory loss and incomplete orientation called post-traumatic amnesia, and resolution of the amnesia. Rehabilitation is often initiated at some point in this progression, sometimes beginning while the patient is still in a coma. The outcome of this combination of spontaneous recovery and rehabilitation is rarely, if ever, complete return to pre-injury status, but often allows for a return to productive living in the community. Recovery from stroke is also common, and many post-stroke patients can return to community living. Among the most important prognostic indicators for head trauma are length of time in coma and length of post-traumatic amnesia. General health status is a good predictor for stroke outcome and potential for recurrence. Patients who maintain poor cardiac status, hypertension, inappropriate dietary habits, or substance abuse are poorer candidates for recovery than are post-stroke patients who do not have these difficulties. Some patients, particularly those with chronic, severe hypertension, may have multiple strokes, resolving into a vascular dementia.

There is increasing evidence that rehabilitation of head trauma may often have beneficial effects over and above spontaneous recovery. With regard to the developmental disorders, enormous efforts have been made in institutional and school settings to provide appropriate educational remediation for developmentally disabled children, often with some success. Effective treatment at the time of onset of acute disorder also has obvious implications for prognosis. Use of appropriate medications and management following trauma or stroke, and the feasibility and availability of neurosurgery, are major considerations. Tumors can be removed, aneurysms can be repaired, and increased pressure can be relieved by neurosurgeons. These interventions during the acute phase of a disorder are often mainly directed toward preservation of life, but they also have important implications for the outcomes of surviving patients.

SUMMARY

The diagnostic category of neurocognitive disorders, formerly known as delirium, dementia, and amnestic and other cognitive disorders—and as organic mental disorders before that—consists of many conditions in which behavioral changes may be directly associated with some basis in altered brain function. Although the general diagnostic term *organic brain syndrome* has commonly been used to describe these conditions, the wide variability in the manifestations of brain dysfunction makes this term insufficiently precise in reference to clinical relevance, and it has been abandoned. It was pointed out that the variability is attributable to several factors, including the following considerations: (a) the location of the damage in the brain, (b) the neuropathological process producing the damage; (c) the length of time the brain damage has been present; (d) the age and health status of the individual at the time the damage is sustained; and (e) the individual's premorbid personality and level of function.

The neuropsychological approach to the conceptualization of these disorders has identified behavioral parameters along which the manifestations of brain dysfunction can be described and classified. The most frequently considered dimensions are intellectual function, language, attention, memory, visual-spatial skills, perceptual skills, and motor function. Some important concepts related to brain function and brain disorders include the principle of contralateral control of perceptual and motor functions and functional hemisphere asymmetries. In addition, studies of brain-damaged patients have shown that particular structures in the brain mediate relatively discrete behaviors. Neurologists and neuropsychologists have identified several syndromes in such areas as language dysfunction, memory disorder, and general intellectual impairment. It was pointed out that there are also major variations in the courses of neurocognitive disorders. Some are transient, leaving little or no residua; some are permanent but not progressive; while others are either slowly or rapidly progressive. Whereas these disorders most profoundly and commonly involve impairment of cognitive, perceptual, and motor skills, sometimes personality changes of various types are the most prominent symptoms. More often than not, personality and affective changes appear in brain-damaged patients along with their cognitive, perceptual, and motor disorders. Thus, a mood disorder or such symptoms as delusions and hallucinations may be sequelae of brain damage for various reasons.

During the years spanning the writing of the various editions of this chapter, there have been several major developments in the area of what was originally called the organic mental disorders. There has been the appearance of at least one new disorder, AIDS dementia, major discoveries in the genetics of Huntington's disease and alcoholism, enormous developments in the technology of neuroimaging, growth of a field of neurotoxicology producing knowledge about the epidemiology of neurodevelopmental disorders in particular, and a reconceptualization by psychiatry of the previously held distinction between functional and organic disorders. The work in neuroimaging is particularly exciting, because it goes beyond obtaining more refined pictures of the brain and now allows us to observe the working of the brain during ongoing behavior through fMRI, and to examine the molecular biology of brain function through MRS.

REFERENCES

American Psychiatric Association. (2010). *Proposed revision/APA DSM-V*. Washington, DC: Author.

American Psychiatric Association. (2013). *Diagnostic and statistical manual of mental disorders* (5th ed.). Arlington, VA: American Psychiatric Publishing.

Baddeley, A. (1986). *Working memory*. New York, NY: Oxford University Press.

Balter, M. (2001). Genes and disease: Immune gene linked to vCJD susceptibility. *Science, 294,* 1438–1439.

Becker, J. T., Farbman, E. S., Hamilton, R. L., & Lopez, O. L. (2011). Dementia with Lewy bodies. In G. Goldstein, T. M. Incagnoli, & A. E. Puente (Eds.), *Contemporary neurobehavioral syndromes* (pp. 111–129). New York, NY: Psychology Press.

Begleiter, H., Porjesz, B., Bihari, B., & Kissin, B. (1984). Event-related potentials in boys at high risk for alcoholism. *Science, 225,* 1493–1496.

Belanger, H. G., Kretzmer, T., Vanderploeg, R. D., & French, L. M. (2010). Symptom complaints following combat-related traumatic brain injury: Relationship to traumatic brain injury severity and posttraumatic stress disorder. *Journal of the International Neuropsychological Society, 16,* 194–199.

Benton, A. L. (1985). Perceptual and spatial disorders. In K. Heilman & E. Valenstein (Eds.), *Clinical neuropsychology* (2nd ed., pp. 151–185). New York, NY: Oxford University Press.

Benton, A. L., & Joynt, R. J. (1960). Early descriptions of aphasia. *Archives of Neurology, 3,* 205–222.

Bigler, E. D. (2008). Neuropsychology and clinical neuroscience of persistent post-concussive syndrome. *Journal of the International Neuropsychological Society, 14,* 1–22.

Blass, J. P., & Gibson, G. E. (1977). Abnormality of a thiamine-requiring enzyme in patients with Wernicke-Korsakoff syndrome. *New England Journal of Medicine, 297,* 1367–1370.

Bornstein, R. A., Nasrallah, H. A., Para, M. F., & Whitacre, C. C. (1993). Neuropsychological performance in symptomatic and asymptomatic HIV infection. *AIDS, 7,* 519–524.

Broca, P. (1861). Perte de la parole. Ramollissement chronique et destruction partielle du lobe antérieur gauche du cerveau. [Loss of speech. Chronic softening and partial destruction of the left frontal lobe of the brain.] *Bulletin de la Société Anthropologique, 2,* 235–238.

Butters, N., & Cermak, L. S. (1980). *Alcoholic Korsakoff's syndrome.* New York, NY: Academic Press.

Caine, E. D. (1986). The neuropsychology of depression: The pseudodementia syndrome. In Grant & K. M. Adams (Eds.), *Neuropsychological assessment of neuropsychiatric disorders* (pp. 221–243). New York, NY: Oxford University Press.

Cloninger, C. R., Bohman, M., & Sigvardsson, S. (1981). Inheritance of alcohol abuse: Cross-fostering analysis of adopted men. *Archives of General Psychiatry, 38,* 861–868.

Das, R. R., Seshadri, S., Beiser, A. S., Kelly-Hayes, M., Au, R., Himali, J. J., . . . Wolf, P. A. (2008). Prevalence and correlates of silent cerebral infarcts in the Framingham offspring study. *Stroke, 39,* 2929–2935.

Dean, R. S. (1986). Lateralization of cerebral functions. In D. Wedding, A. M. Horton Jr., & J. Webster (Eds.), *The neuropsychology handbook: Behavioral and clinical perspectives* (pp. 80–102). New York, NY: Springer.

DeMichelle-Sweet, M. A., & Sweet, R. A. (2010). Genetics of psychosis in Alzheimer's disease: A review. *Journal of Alzheimer's Disease, 19,* 761–780.

Elias, M. F., & Streeten, D. H. P. (1980). *Hypertension and cognitive processes.* Mount Desert, ME: Beech Hill.

Fagan, A. M., Mintun, M. A., Mach, R. H., Lee, S. Y., Dence, C. S., Shah, A. R., . . . Holtzman, D. M. (2005). Inverse relation between in vivo amyloid imaging load and cerebrospinal fluid A beta42 in humans. *Annals of Neurology, 59,* 512–519.

Festa, J. R. (2010). Cognitive dysfunction in heart failure. *Division of Clinical Neuropsychology Newsletter, 28,* 3–9.

Geschwind, N. (1965). Disconnection syndromes in animals and man. *Brain, 88,* 237–294.

Goldstein, G. (1986). *Neuropsychological effects of five antihypertensive agents.* Poster session presented at the *annual meeting of the International Neuropsychological Society, Denver, CO.*

Goldstein, G. (1997). Delirium, dementia, and amnestic and other cognitive disorders. In S. M. Turner & M. Hersen (Eds.), *Adult psychopathology and diagnosis* (3rd ed., pp. 89–127). New York, NY: Wiley.

Goldstein, G. (2011). Persian Gulf and other "deployment" syndromes. In G. Goldstein, T. M. Incagnoli, & A. E. Puente (Eds.), *Contemporary neurobehavioral syndromes* (pp. 131–150). New York, NY: Psychology Press.

Goldstein, G., Beers, S. R., Morrow, L. A., Shemansky, W. J., & Steinhauer, S. R. (1996). A preliminary neuropsychological study of Persian Gulf veterans. *Journal of the International Neuropsychological Society, 2,* 368–371.

Goldstein, K. (1959). Functional disturbances in brain damage. In S. Arieti (Ed.), *American handbook of psychiatry.* New York, NY: Basic Books.

Goldstein, K., & Scheerer, M. (1941). Abstract and concrete behavior: An experimental study with special tests. *Psychological Monographs, 53*(2, Whole No. 239).

Goodwin, D. W. (1979). Alcoholism and heredity: A review and hypothesis. *Archives of General Psychiatry, 36*, 57–61.

Goodwin, D. W., Schulsinger, F., Hermansen, L., Guze, S. B., & Winokur, G. (1973). Alcohol problems in adoptees raised apart from alcoholic biological parents. *Archives of General Psychiatry, 28*, 238–243.

Grant, I., Atkinson, J. H., Hesselink, J. R., Kennedy, C. J., Richman, D. D., Spector, S. A., & McCutchan, J. A. (1987). Evidence for early central nervous system involvement in the acquired immunodeficiency syndrome (AIDS) and other human immunodeficiency virus (HIV) infections. *Annals of Internal Medicine, 107*, 828–836.

Guerrini, I., Thomson, A. D., & Gurling, H. M. (2009). Molecular genetics of alcohol-related brain damage. *Alcohol and Alcoholism, 44*, 166–170.

Gusella, J. F., Wexler, N. S., Conneally, P. M., Naylor, S. L., Anderson, M. A., Tanzi, R. E., . . . Martin, J. B. (1983). A polymorphic DNA marker genetically linked to Huntington's disease. *Nature, 306*, 234–238.

Heaton, R. K. (2006, February 1–4). *Presidential address given at the annual meeting of the International Neuropsychological Society, Boston, MA.*

Hill, S. Y., Shen, S., Zezza, N., Hoffman, E. K., Perlin, M., & Alan, W. (2004). A genome wide search for alcoholism susceptibility genes. *American Journal of Medical Genetics B: Neuropsychiatric Genetics, 128*, 102–113.

Hill, S. Y., Steinhauer, S. R., & Zubin, J. (1987). Biological markers for alcoholism: A vulnerability model conceptualization. In C. Rivers (Ed.), *Nebraska symposium on motivation: Vol. 34. Alcohol and addictive behavior* (pp. 207–256). Lincoln: University of Nebraska Press.

Hoge, C. W., McGurk, D., Thomas, J. J., Cox, A. L., Engel, C. C., & Castro, C. A. (2008). Mild traumatic brain injury in U.S. soldiers returning from Iraq. *New England Journal of Medicine, 358*, 453–463.

Jervis, G. A. (1959). The mental deficiencies. In S. Arieti (Ed.), *American handbook of psychiatry.* (Vol. 2) New York, NY: Basic Books.

Katz, L., Goldstein, G., & Beers, S. (2001). *Learning disabilities in older adolescents and adults: Clinical utility of the neuropsychological perspective.* New York, NY: Plenum Press.

King, H. E., & Miller, R. E. (1990). Hypertension: Cognitive and behavioral considerations. *Neuropsychology Review, 1*, 31–73.

Klunk, W. E., Engler, H., Nordberg, A., Wang, Y., Blomqvist, G., Holt, D. P., . . . Långström, B. (2004). Imaging brain amyloid in Alzheimer's disease with Pittsburgh Compound-B. *Annals of Neurology, 5*, 306–319.

Koch-Henriksen, N., & Sørensen, P. S. (2010). The changing demographic pattern of multiple sclerosis epidemiology. *Lancet Neurology, 9*, 520–532.

Lantz, E. R., Lazar, R. M., Levine, R., & Levine, J. (2010). Cerebrovascular anomalies: Brain AVMSs and cerebral aneurysms and brain arteriovenous malformations. *Division of Clinical Neuropsychology Newsletter, 28*, 17–23.

Levin, H. S., Benton, A. L., & Grossman, R. G. (1982). *Neurobehavioral consequences of closed head injury.* New York, NY: Oxford University Press.

Levin, H. S., Eisenberg, H. M., & Benton, A. L. (1989). *Mild head injury.* New York, NY: Oxford University Press.

Levin, H. S., Wilde, E., Troyanskaya, M., Petersen, N. J., Scheibel, R., Newsome, M., . . . Li, X. (2010). Diffusion tensor imaging of mild to moderate blast-related traumatic brain injury and its sequelae. *Journal of Neurotrauma, 27*, 683–694.

Luria, A. R. (1966). *Higher cortical functions in man* (B. Haigh, Trans.) New York, NY: Basic Books.

Luria, A. R. (1973). *The working brain.* New York, NY: Basic Books.

Lye, T. C., & Shores, E. A. (2000). Traumatic brain injury as a risk factor for Alzheimer's disease: A review. *Neuropsychology Review, 10*, 115–129.

Mayer, A. R., Ling, J., Mannell, M. V., Gasparovic, C., Phillips, J. P., Doezema, D., . . . Yeo, R. A. (2010). A prospective diffusion tensor imaging study in mild traumatic brain injury. *Neurology, 74*, 643–650.

McKeith, I., Mintzer, J., Aarsland, D., Burn, D., Chiu, H., Cohen-Mansfield, J., Reid, W., . . . International Psychogeriatric Association Expert Meeting on DLB. (2004). Dementia with Lewy bodies. *Lancet Neurology, 3*, 19–28.

Mesulam, M. M. (1985). *Principles of behavioral neurology.* Philadelphia, PA: F. A. Davis.

Neils, J., Boller, F., Gerdeman, B., & Cole, M. (1989). Descriptive writing abilities in Alzheimer's disease. *Journal of Clinical and Experimental Neuropsychology, 11*, 692–698.

Noggle, C. A., & Pierson, E. E. (2010). Pediatric TBI: Prevalence and functional ramifications. *Applied Neuropsychology, 17*, 81–82.

Nussbaum, P. D. (1994). Pseudodementia: A slow death. *Neuropsychology Review, 4*, 71–90.

Pavol M. (2010). Neuropsychology of ischemic stroke. *Division of Clinical Neuropsychology Newsletter, 28*, 12–16.

Rosenstein, L. D. (1998). Differential diagnosis of the major progressive dementias and depression in middle and late adulthood: A summary of the literature of the early 1990s. *Neuropsychology Review, 8*, 109–167.

Satz, P. (1966). Specific and nonspecific effects of brain lesions in man. *Journal of Abnormal Psychology, 71*, 65–70.

Schaeffer, K. W., Parsons, O. A., & Yohman, J. R. (1984). Neuropsychological differences between male familial and nonfamilial alcoholics and nonalcoholics. *Alcoholism: Clinical and Experimental Research, 8*, 347–351.

Schatz, P., Pardini, J. F., Lovell, M. R., Collins, M. W., & Podell, K. (2006). Sensitivity and specificity of the ImPACT Test Battery for concussion in athletes. *Archives of Clinical Neuropsychology, 21*, 91–99.

Smith, R. J., Barth, J. T., Diamond, R., & Giuliano, A. J. (1998). Evaluation of head trauma. In G. Goldstein, P. D. Nussbaum, & S. R. Beers (Eds.), *Neuropsychology* (pp. 135–170). New York, NY: Plenum Press.

Steinhauer, S. R., Hill, S. Y., & Zubin, J. (1987). Event related potentials in alcoholics and their first-degree relatives. *Alcoholism, 4*, 307–314.

Tarter, R. E. (1976). Neuropsychological investigations of alcoholism. In G. Goldstein & C. Neuringer (Eds.), *Empirical studies of alcoholism* (pp. 231–256). Cambridge, MA: Ballinger.

Tarter, R. E., Hegedus, A., Goldstein, G., Shelly, C., & Alterman, A. I. (1984). Adolescent sons of alcoholics: Neuropsychological and personality characteristics. *Alcoholism: Clinical and Experimental Research, 8*, 216–222.

Teuber, H.-L. (1959). Some alterations in behavior after cerebral lesions in man. In A. D. Bass (Ed.), *Evolution of nervous control from primitive organisms to man.* Washington, DC: American Association for the Advancement of Science.

Van Gorp, W. G., Miller, E. N., Satz, P., & Visscher, B. (1989). Neuropsychological performance in HIV-1 immunocompromised patients: A preliminary report. *Journal of Clinical and Experimental Neuropsychology, 11*, 763–773.

Walker, A. E., Caveness, W. F., & Critchley, M. (Eds.). (1969). *Late effects of head injury.* Springfield, IL: Charles C. Thomas.

Wells, C. E. (1979). Pseudodementia. *American Journal of Psychiatry, 136*, 895–900.

Wells, C. E. (1980). The differential diagnosis of psychiatric disorders in the elderly. In J. O. Cole & J. E. Barrett (Eds.), *Psychopathology in the aged* (pp. 19–31). New York, NY: Raven Press.

Wilk, J. E., Thomas, J. L., McGurk, D. M., Riviere, L. A., Castro, C. A., & Hoge, C. W. (2010). Mild traumatic brain injury (concussion) during combat: Lack of association of blast mechanism with persistent postconcussive symptoms. *Journal of Head Trauma Rehabilitation, 25*, 9–14.

Woods, S. P., Carey, C. L., Iudicello, J. E., Letendre, S. L., Fennema-Notestine, C., & Grant, I. (2009). Neuropsychological aspects of HIV infection. In I. Grant & K. M. Adams (Eds.), *Neuropsychological assessment of neuropsychiatric and neuromedical disorders* (3rd ed., pp. 366–397). New York, NY: Oxford University Press.

CHAPTER 21

Personality Disorders

J. CHRISTOPHER FOWLER, JOHN M. OLDHAM,
CHRISTOPHER J. HOPWOOD, and KATHERINE M. THOMAS

PERSONALITY DISORDERS (PDs) represent a major public health concern, as more than 1 in 10 adults in the community meet the diagnostic criteria for at least one PD (Torgersen, 2005; Torgersen, Kringlen, & Cramer, 2001) and PD diagnoses are associated with increased risk for hospitalization (Bender et al., 2001), criminal behavior (Johnson et al., 2000), suicidal behavior (Soloff, Lis, Kelly, & Cornelius, 1994), and dysfunction at work and in relationships (Grant et al., 2004; Skodol et al., 2002; Torgersen, 2005). Relatively few evidence-based treatments are available for the broad spectrum of PDs (McMain & Pos, 2007; Matusiewicz, Hopwood, Banducci, & Lejuez, 2010), which are notoriously difficult to treat and interfere with treatment of other kinds of disorders (Cyranowski et al., 2004; Feske et al., 2004; Reich, 2003). The single exception is borderline personality disorder (BPD), which has a strong evidence base for efficacious psychological treatments (Leichensring et al., 2011). The clinical importance of normative personality traits thought potentially to predispose to PDs and other forms of psychopathology is also well documented (e.g., Lahey, 2009; Ozer & Benet-Martinez, 2006; Roberts, Kuncel, Shiner, Caspi, & Goldberg, 2007). For instance, Cuijpers et al. (2010) estimated that the direct and indirect medical costs for individuals in the top 5% of neuroticism scores are $12,362 per person per year, compared with $7,851 for individuals with mood disorders and $3,641 for the average person.

Despite the clinical and economic impact of personality pathology, there is no shortage of controversy regarding how best to characterize and model dimensions of pathology and diagnosis—the *Diagnostic and Statistical Manual of Mental Disorders*, 5th edition (*DSM-5*), with its traditional categorical and alternative hybrid/dimensional models, the dimensional model of the *International Classification of Diseases*, 11th edition (*ICD-11*), the National Institute of Mental Health Research Domain Criteria initiative (RDoC; NIMH, 2008; Insel et al., 2010), and the new Hierarchical Taxonomy of Psychopathology (HiTOP; Kotov et al., 2016) all approach the characterization of personality pathology from different angles. With distinct major systems and numerous subsystems, representing PDs in a manner that is scientifically valid and clinically useful continues to suffer from conceptual and structural inconsistencies. In the historical run-up to the publication of *DSM-5*, the view that the *DSM-III* and *DSM-IV* polythetic

Adult Psychopathology and Diagnosis, Eighth Edition. Edited by Deborah C. Beidel and B. Christopher Frueh.
© 2018 John Wiley & Sons, Inc. Published 2018 by John Wiley & Sons, Inc.
Companion website: www.wiley.com/go/beidel/psychopathology8e

categorical model was irreparably flawed led to the proposal of alternative models (Borsnstein, 1997; Clark, 2007; Hopwood et al., 2011; Krueger et al., 2011b; Westen, Shedler, & Bradley, 2006; Widiger & Mullins-Sweat, 2009). Although most experts anticipated dramatic changes to diagnosing PDs in *DSM-5* (Bender et al., 2011; Krueger et al., 2011a; Skodol et al., 2011), in the end the Board of Trustees of the American Psychiatric Association voted to retain the *DSM-IV* system in *DSM-5*. However, they also included an alternative model in *DSM-5*, Section III. The new framework has the potential to increase clinical utility (Morey et al., 2014), more closely link the PDs with evidence-based models of personality and personality pathology, and ultimately lead to an increased focus on personality and PD among clinicians and scholars, with a corresponding improvement in practice and research. However, the proposed *DSM-5* model is not without critics, who have expressed concerns about both its clinical utility (Bornstein, 2011b; Clarkin & Huprich, 2011; Shedler et al., 2010) and its evidentiary basis (Samuel, 2011; Widiger, 2011; Zimmerman, 2011). With the publication of *DSM-5*, a host of questions emerge in relation to the diagnosis of PDs with the alternative model, and the scientific community is compelled to examine the reliability, validity, and clinical utility of the alternative model under varying conditions.

We begin this chapter by discussing several concepts relevant to the definition of personality pathology and PD. We next describe the *DSM-IV* PDs in an historical context, review research on the prevalence, etiology, and course of personality pathology, and describe several approaches to its assessment. Next, we review the *DSM-5* alternative model, highlighting differences between the *DSM-IV* and *DSM-5* approaches to PD diagnosis in the context of a clinical case. We then close with a discussion of the potential synergies between the alternative model and the NIMH RDoC initiative.

DEFINING PERSONALITY: TRAITS, DYNAMICS, PATHOLOGY, AND DISORDERS

Personality is a broad concept with considerable theoretical variation in terms of emphasis on different, even nonoverlapping, components. One way to organize divergent theoretical perspectives is to differentiate those aspects of personality on which they focus. For instance, a protracted rivalry exists in academic personality psychology between those who focus on its more stable or dynamic aspects that extend to the problem of how to classify personality pathology (Wright, 2011). There are also vigorous debates between those who would prefer a more conservative approach to diagnosis involving the retention of categorical PD constructs (e.g., Bornstein, 2011a; Gunderson, 2010; Shedler et al., 2010) and those who would overhaul the model by utilizing a completely dimensional approach (e.g., Widiger & Mullins-Sweat, 2009; Krueger et al., 2011).

The *DSM-III* and *DSM-IV* were based on atheoretical descriptions of personality pathology. The *DSM-IV* defines PD as "an enduring pattern of inner experience and behavior that deviates markedly from the expectations of the individual's culture, is pervasive and inflexible, has an onset in adolescence or early adulthood, is stable over time, and leads to distress or impairment" (APA, 2000, p. 685). The *DSM-IV* describes 10 instantiations of PD, organized into three clusters: cluster A (schizotypal, schizoid, and paranoid), cluster B (antisocial, borderline, histrionic, and narcissistic), and cluster C (avoidant, dependent, and obsessive-compulsive).

These specific PDs, their clustering, and their criteria were selected as much based on clinical legacy in the medical and psychoanalytic perspectives on personality and the collective wisdom of a specific group of committee members with diverse theoretical perspectives, as for their empirical support or conceptual coherence (Widiger, 1993). While this strategy had advantages (notably increasing PD research), it has become clear that important conceptual issues must be addressed more directly for PD classification to move forward. To clarify some of these conceptual issues, we begin by distinguishing four broad domains of personality that are relevant to debates on the nature of personality and related pathology: traits, dynamics, pathology, and disorders. These definitions provide a framework for discussing various perspectives on PD classification in the remainder of this chapter.

PERSONALITY TRAITS

Personality traits are enduring features of personality that are: (a) culturally universal (McCrae & Terracciano, 2005); (b) heritable (Jang, Livesley, & Vernon, 1996); (c) linked to specific neurobiological structures (DeYoung, 2010) and pathways (Depue & Lenzenweger, 2005); (d) well-characterized in terms of content and course (Soldz & Valliant, 2002); (e) valid for predicting a host of important life outcomes (Roberts et al., 2007); and (f) amenable to reliable assessment, particularly via self-report questionnaires (Samuel & Widiger, 2006). The Five-Factor Model (FFM) currently represents the most viable model of normative personality traits, having the advantage of decades of empirical justification (Digman, 1990) and extensive theoretical articulation (Costa & McCrae, 2006). In the FFM, five normally distributed traits represent the broadest level of variation in personality: neuroticism, extraversion, openness to experience, agreeableness, and conscientiousness. These traits provide a context for much of human behavior, and certain constellations of these traits make personality pathology in general and certain forms of PD more or less likely (Morey et al., 2002; Samuel & Widiger, 2008; Saulsman & Page, 2004).

From the perspective of the *DSM-IV*, personality traits such as those of the FFM are enduring features with broad implications for behavior across many situations. These features become clinically relevant when they are "inflexible and maladaptive and cause significant functional impairment or subjective distress" (APA, 2000, p. 686). This qualification implies a distinction between normal traits and severe inflexible maladaptive traits that are associated with impairment in functioning. However, an explicit linkage between traits and associated dysfunction invites a dimensional view of personality pathology, in which differences between trait and PD are quantitative rather than qualitative. Indeed, evidence suggests that the cluster model of the *DSM-IV* is not valid (Lenzenweger & Clarkin, 2005) and that the disorders are overlapping blends of polythetic and potentially common traits (Widiger et al., 1991), suggesting scientific advantages to viewing personality pathology dimensionally. These potential advantages have led some theorists to suggest defining PDs as reflecting extreme or maladaptive variants of normative traits (Widiger, 1993).

However, several research findings prescribe a pause in equating personality pathology with extreme scores on normative traits (Hopwood, 2011). First, relations between normative traits and PDs are not unique or special; normative traits relate systematically to most forms of psychopathology (Cuijpers et al., 2010; Kotov, Gomez, Schmidt, & Watson, 2010), just as they relate to a wide variety of individual differences in human behavior (Ozer & Benet-Martinez, 2006). Second, there are potential structural differences between normal and pathological personality traits (Krueger et al., 2011b). Third, personality traits and disorders can be distinguished empirically in terms of stability and incremental validity (Hopwood & Zanarini, 2010; Morey et al., 2012; Morey & Hopwood, 2013; Morey & Zanarini, 2000). Stable trait concepts are also limited for conceptualizing dynamic and contingent aspects of social behavior and emotional experiences related to personality and related pathology.

While the clinical utility and predictive validity for the categorical diagnosis of PDs has substantial empirical support (Blashfield & Intoccia, 2000), there are glaring short-comings of the polythetic categorical approach, including high rates of comorbidity among PDs, the loss of clinically relevant information inherent in all-or-nothing diagnosis (Krueger et al., 2007), excessive heterogeneity within PDs (Skodol, 2012) and the fact that all of the PD categories have diagnostic thresholds based upon committee opinion rather than empirically derived cut-points.

The strongest evidence in favor of abandoning the categorical approaches is the superiority of dimensional models in terms of predictive and incremental validity of associated personality constructs (Hopwood & Zanarini. 2010; Spitzer et al., 2008; Morey et al., 2007; Morey et al., 2012; Samuel & Widiger, 2006, 2008; Skodol et al., 2005; Widiger & Samuel, 2005; Fowler et al., 2015); clinical syndromes of depression, anxiety and substance abuse (Kotov et al., 2010); well-being, interpersonal and occupational functioning in prospective longitudinal studies (Morey et al., 2007; Skodol et al., 2005; Ozer & Benet-Martinez, 2006); and a variety of health, morbidity, and physical diseases (Deary et al., 2010).

PERSONALITY DYNAMICS

Mischel's (1968) text *Personality and Assessment* initiated a major conflict in personality psychology between those who view personality as made up of stable traits and those who see it primarily as a function of situational contingencies (see *Journal of Research in Personality, 43*[2]). Although it has been difficult and contentious, this debate has had several positive consequences. With regard to personality stability, trait psychologists were prompted to develop methods that could more convincingly show that traits can be reliably assessed, are stable, and are valid predictors of important behaviors. Equally relevant to contemporary models of PD, this debate led to the development of new models for understanding how traits and situations interact in *if . . . then* behavioral signatures (Mischel & Shoda, 1995). For instance, *if* a conscientious person is on the clock, *then* she will typically attend to her work. This logic extends to PD (Wright, 2011): *if* a person with BPD is exposed to rejection, *then* he will tend to react in a self-damaging manner. Notably, this formulation, while inconsistent with a simple trait-behavior formulation of personality (Clarkin & Huprich, 2011), is consonant with several previous models, including Lewin's (1936) classic equation that personality is a function of the person and the environment, or object-relations models asserting that behavior is influenced by the elicitation of self–other dyad units by the parameters of current, actual social situations (Kernberg & Caligor, 2005). As such, the concept of the behavioral signature both re-emphasizes and builds upon a long tradition in personality and clinical psychology that emphasizes the moderation of trait-relevant behavior by situational contingencies.

Understanding dynamic elements of personality may be particularly important given recent research suggesting that PD symptoms vary in their stabilities (McGlashan et al., 2005). However, research aimed at conceptualizing the behavioral signatures associated with PDs is just beginning. Most of the work in this area has involved borderline PD, likely because temporal variability in emotion and behavior is thematic of the disorder (Schmideberg, 1959). Research using ecological momentary assessment—in which assessments occur several times per day over several days—has generally shown excessive variability in mood, interpersonal behavior, and self-esteem among borderline individuals (Sadikaj, Russell, Moskowitz, & Paris, 2010; Trull et al., 2008; Zeigler-Hill & Abraham, 2006).

Organizing PD variation around an evidence-based model of individual differences may enable models of personality dynamics that can better connect personality research and clinical practice (e.g., Hopwood, Zimmermann, Pincus, & Krueger, 2015). Ongoing and future work exploring the individual dynamics associated with particular kinds of personality problems will be important for assimilating dynamic behavioral signatures into conceptualizations of personality pathology and PD.

SEVERITY OF PERSONALITY PATHOLOGY

Several PD theorists have emphasized the clinical utility of assessing the prototypic features that define personality pathology (whether a PD is present or not) and identifying features that distinguish PDs from one another (Bornstein, 2011a; Kernberg, 1984; Livesley, 1998; Pincus, 2005; Pincus & Hopwood, 2012). From this perspective, individuals can manifest clinically significant personality disturbance without triggering a diagnosable PD, whereas PDs (described later) reflect clinically significant distress or impairment in social, occupational, or other important areas of functioning with specific symptom constellations that vary across individuals. For example, the *DSM-IV* distinguishes the defining characteristics of PD in general from symptom criteria for 10 specific PD types. However, in the *DSM-IV* model, the level of personality pathology is not directly quantified but is left to the subjective judgement of the assessor to determine what constitutes clinically significant distress and impairment. A likely outcome is the conflation of PD criteria with aspects of pathological severity and its stylistic manifestations. This conflation likely contributes to unnecessarily high comorbidity among the PDs (Parker et al., 1998). The alternative model (discussed below) quantitatively addresses the severity of personality pathology.

Research supports the distinction between personality pathology and stylistic aspects of PDs. Parker et al. (2004) derived two higher-order factors from an assessment of the basic elements of personality pathology, which they labeled cooperativeness (ability to love) and coping (ability to work). These factors correlated nonspecifically with PDs and differentiated clinical and nonclinical samples. Hopwood et al. (2011) factor-analyzed PD symptoms after variance in each symptom associated with a general pathology factor was removed. The severity composite explained most of the variance in functional outcomes, but the five stylistic dimensions, which were labeled peculiarity, deliberateness, instability, withdrawal, and fearfulness, incremented this composite for predicting several specific outcomes. Importantly, these stylistic dimensions were completely independent of the overall level of personality pathology severity and were mostly independent of normative traits. Morey et al. (2011) assessed personality pathology with items from questionnaires designed to assess global personality dysfunction. By refining these item sets using a host of psychometric procedures, they showed, in two large and diverse samples, that greater severity was associated with greater likelihood of PD diagnosis and higher rates of comorbidity.

Finally, a growing body of longitudinal evidence indicates that severity of personality pathology may be far more important in determining treatment outcome than specific disorders. In a 2-year follow-up of subjects with BPD, the Collaborative Longitudinal PDs Study (CLPS) found that severity of BPD (as manifested by higher number of BPD criteria, greater functional impairment, and greater interpersonal relationship instability) predicted poorer outcome (Gunderson et al., 2006). A second line of evidence supporting the presence of a global psychopathology factors within psychiatric disorders carries the implication that categorical diagnoses may function as stylistic markers of more global latent factors. A recent cross-sectional factor-analytic study of PD criteria (Sharp et al. 2015) identified a general personality pathology factor that cuts across specific PDs and captures the vast majority of the variance of personality pathology. This general factor captured common variance in diverse expressions of personality pathology, with five second-order factors that capture unique variance. Similarly, a factor-analytic study of psychiatric diagnostic comorbidity utilizing longitudinal data from the Dunedin Multi-disciplinary Health and Development Study found that a general pathology factor accounted for the vast majority of variance, with second-order factors (externalizing and internalizing disorders) accounting for the remaining variance (Caspi et al., 2014).

PERSONALITY DISORDER STYLE

Delineating stylistic aspects of PD would represent a significant challenge even if global personality pathology were effectively separated from PD features. The *DSM-IV* pro-poses 10 PDs, but given the conflation of severity and style in the *DSM-IV* (Parker et al., 1998), it is possible that fewer than 10 stylistic dimensions would be sufficient for depicting the stylistic variability in PD expression. The Hopwood et al. (2011) study discussed identified five reliable PD dimensions, although that study was constrained by the *DSM-IV* content that was factor-analyzed. To the degree that the *DSM-IV* symptom criteria are not comprehensive (e.g., they do not include symptoms from appendicized diagnoses and may not fully capture the content of some disorders [e.g., Pincus, Wright, Hopwood, & Krueger, 2011]), it is possible that other important dimensions exist. Thus, an important question for ongoing research is: how many PD dimensions are there? In the current iteration of the *DSM-5* alternative model, based on a thorough review of the above models and feedback from practitioners, a hybrid dimensional-categorical model for personality and PD assessment and diagnosis was implemented in the *DSM-5* field testing. Based on a review of field test data and feedback from practitioners in a three-wave community survey (Krueger et al. 2011a, 2012) *DSM-5* introduced an alternative hybrid model for diagnosing PDs, located in Section 3 of the manual (the section containing "Emerging Measures and Models"). The *alternative model* consists of assessing: (1) level of personality functioning; (2) polythetic diagnostic criteria for seven PDs (antisocial, avoidant, borderline, narcissistic, obsessive-compulsive, schizotypal, and per-sonality disorder-trait specified); and (3) five personality trait domains and 25 facets for pathological personality trait assessment. Diagnostic criteria and thresholds for the six specific PDs are compatible with the defining criteria of the same disorders in *DSM-IV*.

Given that evidence is currently insufficient for such decisions, contemporary deci-sions about how to slice up the stylistic variance in PD will be necessarily questionable and temporary. For this reason, it is wise that the *DSM-5* is conceived as a living document subject to ongoing empirical and conceptual refinement (Krueger et al., 2011b). From our perspective, the process for making decisions about which PD constructs are sufficiently valid for routine clinical consideration should be regarded as a psychometric matter (Loevinger, 1957).

The PDs listed in the *DSM-IV* and its appendix offer a reasonable starting point as a list of hypothetical constructs in the PD domain (MacCorquodale & Meehl, 1948). The first step in establishing their construct validity would involve describing their theoretical contents thoroughly. Next, these contents would be measured using multiple assessment methods in diverse samples. The constructs would then be refined based on the psychometric considerations, including (a) replicability of factor structure; (b) discrimi-nant validity relative to one another, personality pathology, and normative traits;

(c) freedom from bias; (d) reliability; and (e) criterion validity. Clinically efficient methods for their assessment would then be developed and field-tested, permitting subjugation to further refinement through psychometric procedures. Ideally, the resulting constructs would provide a means for developing a coherent theory of PD style that could facilitate clinical formulations, future research, and testable inferences about dynamic processes.

Several investigators have undertaken projects along these lines, leading to the development of Clark's (1993) *Schedule for Nonadaptive and Adaptive Personality*, Livesley and Jackson's (2006) *Dimensional Assessment of Personality Problems*, the *Personality Inventory for DSM-5* (PID-5; Krueger et al., 2012). This line of work provides an important foundation for the process of depicting PD and delineates areas needing further study. For example, because all of these research programs have relied nearly exclusively on self-report questionnaires, which may be limited in some respects for assessing PD (Huprich & Bornstein, 2007), future investigations should employ multiple assessment methods. Second, variance in the structure of each of these models needs to be resolved to build consensual models of PD. Third, each of these models has been guided by an underlying trait perspective on PD classification, and the integration of these approaches with other theoretical approaches, including those that emphasize dynamic or potentially discontinuous aspects of PD or that separate personality pathology from PD, remains unclear.

The Separation of Personality Pathology and Disorder

Separating severity and style, as is done in *DSM-5* Section III "Alternative Model and Emerging Measures", has the potential to improve diagnostic efficiency and predictive validity. This two-part model of personality pathology and PD is analogous to common conceptions of intelligence involving a general component (i.e., g or IQ) and specific components (e.g., verbal vs. nonverbal abilities). Clinical diagnosis is determined by the presence of quantifiable severity threshold on the general component—just as mental retardation is defined by a particularly low IQ score. Thus, the diagnosis of personality pathology could be defined by a particularly low score on a measure of general personality functioning such as the Levels of Personality Functioning scale (Bender, Morey & Skodol, 2011). More specific predictions about impairment can be made when severity and stylistic elements are distinguished. For example, clinicians would predict that any individual with intellectual disabilities would do poorly in schoolwork relative to most other students, but they would further predict that individuals with personal strengths in verbal versus nonverbal abilities would perform relatively better in reading than in mathematics classes. Analogously, severity of personality pathology may permit predictions about the overall level of treatment needed (e.g., inpatient vs. outpatient), whereas PD style permits predictions about how pathology will manifest (e.g., as impulsive social behavior or social withdrawal) and what treatment techniques might be most effective (e.g., group vs. individual therapy, pharmacotherapy).

One general issue that requires reconciliation in distinguishing personality pathology severity from style involves their differential association with some PD constructs. Specifically, the terms *borderline* and *narcissism* are treated as distinct disorders in the *DSM-IV*, but they have historically been employed as a general term for personality pathology in several major theories (e.g., Kernberg, 1984; Kohut, 1971). Indeed, empirical models of personality organization appear to relate, conceptually and empirically, to these two PDs (Morey, 2005; Morey et al., 2011). So are narcissistic and borderline PDs discrete, stylistic elements of PD, or are they proxies for personality pathology? These are the kinds of theoretical questions that require resolution through empirical procedures if the field is to make progress toward a more scientifically valid and clinically useful model of personality pathology and disorder. We will return to contemporary issues in PD classification at the end of the chapter. First, we review the historical context of current operationalization and empirical evidence relating to the prevalence, etiology, and course of PDs as defined by the *DSM-IV*.

DIAGNOSTIC CONSIDERATIONS: AN HISTORICAL BACKDROP TO THE *DSM-IV*

Clinicians have been interested in pathological manifestations of personality for as long as they have been deriving psychopathology taxonomies. Among the first material approaches on record (from the fourth century BC) is Hippocrates' translation of the philosophies of ancient Mesopotamia (Sudhoff, 1926) into a taxonomy consisting of four temperaments that he believed corresponded to imbalance in bodily humors: choleric (irritable), melancholic (sad), sanguine (optimistic), and phlegmatic (apathetic). It is notable how similar these temperaments are to contemporary models of human personality (i.e., irritable ~ disagreeable, sad ~ neurotic, sanguine ~ extraverted, and phlegmatic ~ [un]conscientious). Hippocrates developed a taxonomy for psychiatric conditions based on these temperamental factors and other conditions, which included six classes of disease: phrenitis, mania, melancholia, epilepsy, hysteria, and Scythian disease (Menninger, 1963). Clinical theorists such as Galen added complexity to early Greek models throughout the Middle Ages and Renaissance, but the quasi-medical approach to classification and basic categories remained fairly similar and continued to be influenced somewhat by supernatural assumptions.

In the 17th century, scientific approaches began to supplant concepts that were rooted in clinical descriptions colored by metaphysical theories. The enhanced focus on falsifiable methods from the 17th century onward paved the way for contemporary models in descriptive psychiatry. Emil Kraepelin, who produced nine volumes of clinical psychiatry textbooks from 1883 to 1927 that represented a standard text on psychiatric classification during his lifetime and for many years to follow, is widely regarded as the pioneer of this movement. The aspect of his approach that set him apart from previous theorists was his focus on the course of disorders, in addition to their signs and symptoms. The concept of course is particularly important for PDs, which have been distinguished from other disorders based on the presumption that they are relatively more enduring. Given his focus on course and the historical importance of personality pathology, it is not surprising that many of the concepts in Kraepelin's textbook are easily identified in the *DSM* PDs. This link is also due to Kraepelin's influence on early 20th-century efforts to categorize mental disorders in the United States (Menninger, 1963). In the middle of that century, Kraepelinian concepts were blended with psychoanalytic ideas by major figures such as Adolf Meyer and William Alanson White, who contributed significantly to the conceptual models of psychopathology underlying the first *DSM*. (Kraepelin's conceptualizations also profoundly influenced theories of psychiatric classification in other countries, and the World Health Organization's *ICD* PD model significantly parallels that of the *DSM-IV*.)

DSM-I AND *DSM-II*

Personality disorders have appeared in every edition of the *DSM* (American Psychiatric Association [APA], 1952, 1968, 1980, 1987, 1994, 2000). In the *DSM-I*, they were characterized by developmental defects or pathological trends in personality structure, with minimal subjective anxiety and little or no sense of distress. In most instances, the disorder is manifested by a lifelong pattern of action or behavior, rather than by mental or emotional symptoms (APA, 1952, p. 34). These three pillars of PD definition have persisted in subsequent editions: PDs are thought to be developmental, stable, and ego-syntonic.

The *DSM-I* employed a narrative rating system for diagnosing PDs, meaning that clinicians were expected to determine a diagnosis based on the perceived match between a patient's behavior and a description of pathological prototypes in the manual. PDs in *DSM-I* were separated into distinct groups. Personality pattern disturbances were regarded as "deep-seated," "with little room for regression." These included the inadequate, schizoid, cyclothymic, and paranoid types. Personality trait disturbances referred to conditions brought about by stress, which were thought to indicate latent weaknesses in the underlying personality structure. These included emotional instability, passive aggression, compulsivity, and an "other" category. Sociopathic personality disturbances were similar to personality trait disturbances, but their manifestation was thought to be driven primarily by a mismatch between an individual's behavior and cultural norms. Such disturbances included antisocial and dyssocial reactions, sexual deviance, and substance abuse.

Although the second edition of the *DSM* (APA, 1968) brought with it some theoretical and classificatory changes to the PDs, it remained very similar to the first edition in its underlying approach and content. The primary change was the removal of the three diagnostic subcategories in favor of the more straightforward depiction of 10 distinct types, largely carried over from *DSM-I*. Specifically, dependent and aggressive subtypes of passive aggressive personality were collapsed, compulsive personality was reconceptualized and renamed obsessive-compulsive personality, dyssocial personality was renamed explosive personality, and asthenic personality, conceptualized as involving dependency and compromised character strength, was added. Finally, although PDs continued to be differentiated from other disorders in terms of their supposed ego-syntonicity, the assertion that patients with PDs routinely did not experience distress as a result of their personality pathology was tempered (Oldham, 2005).

DSM-III AND DSM-IV

In order to improve diagnostic reliability, *DSM-III* categories were rated based on atheoretical, behavioral symptom criteria rather than on prototype descriptions that were rooted in the formulations of specific theories and required relatively more clinical inference. The *DSM-III* also introduced the multiaxial system, in which a distinction was made between Axis I conditions (thought to be acute, ego-dystonic, and relatively amenable to treatment) and Axis II conditions (thought to be enduring, ego-syntonic, and relatively resistant to treatment), with PDs belonging to Axis II. Four *DSM-II* PDs were either eliminated (inadequate and asthenic) or moved to Axis I (cyclothymic and explosive). Schizoid PD was separated into schizoid (defined by interpersonal aloofness), schizotypal (defined by odd behavior), and avoidant PDs (defined by fear of interpersonal criticism/embarrassment). Two new PD diagnoses, borderline and narcissistic, were introduced in *DSM-III*. Finally, the PDs were grouped into three clusters based on their degree of shared phenomenology: cluster A consisted of schizoid, schizotypal, and paranoid; cluster B consisted of borderline, histrionic, narcissistic, and antisocial; and cluster C consisted of obsessive-compulsive, avoidant, dependent, and passive-aggressive.

The *DSM-IV* largely retained this system, with three major exceptions: (1) the antisocial criteria were simplified somewhat; (2) a paranoid/dissociation criterion was added to borderline; and (3) passive-aggressive PD was appendicized. The rationale for removing passive-aggressive PD was that it referred to a narrow behavioral tendency, rather than to a broad personality syndrome (Millon & Radovanov, 1995), although this view has been challenged on rational (Wetzler & Morey, 1999) and empirical (Hopwood et al., 2009) grounds. Finally, personality pathology was formally operationalized, separately from the criteria of each specific PD. It was defined as: (a) an enduring pattern of inner experience and behavior that deviates markedly from the expectations of the individual's culture and is manifested in at least two of the following areas: cognition, affectivity, interpersonal functioning, or impulsive control; (b) pervasive across a broad range of personal and social situations; (c) leading to clinically significant impairment in social, occupational, or other important areas of functioning; (d) stable with an onset that can be traced back to at least adolescence or early adulthood; (e) not better accounted for by another mental disorder; and (f) not due to the direct physiological effects of a substance or medical condition. Criteria sets were polythetic for all PDs, whereas in the *DSM-III*, criteria for some PDs had been more typological and impressionistic due to limited theoretical and empirical understanding. For example, a patient would have to meet all three of the *DSM-III-R* dependent PD criteria for the diagnosis, including passively allowing others to assume responsibility, subordinating needs to others, and lacking self-confidence. In the *DSM-IV*, a patient would need to meet five of eight symptoms, including difficulties initiating projects on one's own and urgently seeking new relationships for support when old relationships end. While this change enhanced the reliability of the PDs (Pfohl, Coryell, Zimmerman, & Stangl, 1986), the increased use of polythetic criteria may also have worsened the problems of construct heterogeneity, prevalence rates and diagnostic overlap (Gunderson, 2010).

CLINICAL PICTURE: THE *DSM-5* SECTION II PERSONALITY DISORDERS

Having described the clinical importance of personality pathology, defined the central concepts of personality and related pathology, and reviewed the history of PD taxonomy, we will now focus on clinical manifestations of the PDs listed in Section III of the *DSM-5* (APA, 2013). Cluster A consists of paranoid, schizoid, and schizotypal PDs, which are thought to share odd and eccentric features. These disorders are associated with psychotic disorders phenomenologically and etiologically (Maier, Lichtermann, Minges, & Heun, 1994) but are distinguished by their lack of persistent psychotic symptoms (i.e., hallucinations and delusions). *Paranoid* PD is defined by a pervasive pattern of distrust and beliefs that others' motives are malevolent. Symptoms involve suspiciousness and consequent social dysfunction, loose and hypervigilant thinking, and resentment. *Schizoid* PD is characterized by a pervasive pattern of social detachment and restricted emotional expression. Symptoms include disinterest in relationships and preference for solitude, limited pleasure in sex or other activities commonly regarded as pleasurable, and emotional flatness. The defining feature of *schizotypal* PD is a pervasive pattern of interpersonal deficits, cognitive or perceptual distortions, and eccentric behavior. It is diagnosed by symptoms related to eccentric perceptions and cognitions, flat affect, mistrustfulness, and profound social dysfunction.

Antisocial, borderline, histrionic, and narcissistic PDs comprise cluster B, which is regarded as the "dramatic, erratic, and emotional" group (APA, 2000). Individuals with these disorders tend to experience emotional dysregulation and behave impulsively. *Antisocial* PD is marked by a pervasive pattern of disregard for the rights and wishes of others (APA, 2000). The *DSM-IV* requires evidence of childhood conduct disorder for a diagnosis of antisocial PD, and additionally includes symptoms of socially nonnormative behavior, dishonesty, impulsivity, aggression, lack of empathy, and irresponsibility.

Borderline PD is characterized by "stable instability" (Schmideberg, 1959) in emotions, interpersonal behavior, and identity. Emotion dysregulation, including anger and emptiness, is thought to be triggered by concerns about abandonment, which is followed by maladaptive coping, including impulsive and suicidal/self-injurious behavior (Zanarini & Frankenburg, 2007). *Histrionic* PD is characterized by excessive emotionality and attempts to obtain attention from others. This desire to be the center of attention often comes at the cost of deep and meaningful interpersonal relationships, as histrionic individuals tend to have relatively superficial interpersonal interactions and shallow emotions. The core of *narcissistic* PD involves grandiose thoughts and behaviors, a need for excessive admiration from others, and a lack of empathy. It is commonly believed that arrogant and haughty behavior is undergirded by feelings of vulnerability and inadequacy.

Cluster C includes avoidant, dependent, and obsessive-compulsive PDs, which are grouped together based on their common thread of anxiety and fearfulness. *Avoidant* PD is characterized by social inhibition rooted in feelings of inadequacy and fears of negative evaluations from others (APA, 2000). Symptoms include avoidance of social and occupational opportunities, fears of shame and ridicule, and negative self-concept. *Dependent* PD is defined by an excessive need to be cared for by others that leads to submissive, clingy behavior. Symptoms include difficulties making autonomous decisions or expressing disagreement with others, nonassertiveness, preoccupation with abandonment, and maladaptive or self-defeating efforts to seek and maintain relationships. *Obsessive-compulsive* PD is defined by a preoccupation with order, perfection, and control in which flexibility, efficiency, and even task completion are often sacrificed. Symptoms include preoccupation with rules and order, perfectionism, workaholism, interpersonal inflexibility, frugality, and stubbornness.

RESEARCH ON THE *DSM-5* SECTION II PERSONALITY DISORDERS

EPIDEMIOLOGY

One of the principal advantages of the *DSM-III* and *DSM-IV* model of PDs that is being carried over to *DSM-5* Section II, has been its contribution to the increase in PD research. However, to the extent that a majority of this research has been based on a flawed conception of PDs, its utility is constrained by the validity of the model. Epidemiological studies instantiate this paradox. Although the development of reliable PD criteria has made it more possible to evaluate the prevalence of PDs, calculating the prevalence of PDs assumes that they are categorical taxa, even though the weight of evidence suggests they are not (Trull & Durrett, 2005), and diagnostic cutoffs in the *DSM-IV* are thus essentially arbitrary (Cooper, Balsis, & Zimmerman, 2010). As such, it is not clear what to make of PD prevalence rates. With this caveat in mind, we review the results of several epidemiological studies on PD based on *DSM* diagnostic cutoffs.

Overall prevalence rates estimate that more than 10% of individuals suffer from a PD during their lifetime (Grant et al., 2004; Lenzenweger, Loranger, Korfine, & Neff, 1997; Samuels et al., 2002; Torgersen, 2005; Torgerson et al., 2001). Although rates for individual PDs are more variable across studies, research suggests that most PDs have prevalence rates of between 0.5% and 5%, with paranoid, avoidant, and obsessive-compulsive PDs being relatively common and dependent, and narcissistic PDs being relatively uncommon. PD prevalence is considerably higher in psychiatric settings: research indicates that nearly half of clinical outpatients and more than half of clinical inpatients meet the diagnostic criteria for a PD (Molinari, Ames, & Essa, 1994;

Zimmerman, Rothschild, & Chelminski, 2005), making PDs among the most commonly encountered disorders in psychiatric settings. The two most commonly occurring PDs among psychiatric patients are borderline (10–20%; APA, 2000; Zimmerman et al., 2005), and dependent PD. Rates of dependent PD are particularly high among inpatients (15–25%; Jackson et al., 1991; Oldham, 2005) relative to outpatients (0–7%; Mezzich, Fabrega, & Coffman, 1987; Poldrugo & Forti, 1988; Zimmerman et al., 2005).

In contrast, somewhat lower occurrence rates have been observed for paranoid (2–4%; Zimmerman et al., 2005), schizoid, and schizotypal (1–2%; Stuart et al., 1998; Zimmerman et al., 2005) patients in clinical settings. These relatively low rates may relate to the impact of the paranoia and social avoidance that characterizes these disorders on treatment-seeking. Indeed, prevalence estimates for schizoid PD among a homeless population are as high as 14% (Rouff, 2000). Likewise, antisocial PD is seen in 1–4% of individuals in a clinical population (Zimmerman et al., 2005), but estimates are considerably higher in prison and substance abuse populations, indicating that individuals with this type of pathology are unlikely to initiate psychological treatment. Somewhat low rates have also been observed for narcissistic (2%; Torgersen et al., 2001) and obsessive-compulsive (3–9%; Zimmerman et al., 2005) PDs in clinical settings, perhaps owing to the limited functional impact of these PDs relative to others. Rates of histrionic and avoidant PD in clinical patients have been estimated at 10–15% (APA, 2000; Zimmerman et al., 2005).

ETIOLOGY

Despite extensive theorizing, empirical evidence regarding the etiology of PDs is quite limited (Paris, 2011; Skodol et al., 2011). Factors contributing to this gap between theory and evidence include a history of underfunding for PD research relative to research on other psychiatric conditions and various conceptual problems discussed throughout this chapter. Nevertheless, we briefly review etiological contributions related to genes, neurobiology, learning, and cognition presently.

Genetics   While the broad heritability of personality traits is well established (Lo et al., 2016; McGue, Bacon, & Lykken, 1993; Plomin, DeFries, Craig, & McGuggin, 2003), the heritability of personality pathology and disorders remains more ambiguous (Lenzenweger & Clarkin, 2005). A twin study by Torgersen et al. (2000) indicated that the overall 58% of the variance in PDs was due to genes, with specific heritability estimates for each PD as follows: paranoid (0.30), schizoid (0.31), schizotypal (0.62), borderline (0.69), histrionic (0.67), narcissistic (0.77), avoidant (0.31), dependent (0.55), and obsessive-compulsive (0.78). Notably, shared family environment influences were also particularly important in predicting borderline PD. These results led the researchers to conclude that PDs may have even stronger genetic influences than most other disorders, similar to broad dimensions of normative personality. Rates of antisocial PD were too low to be included in the Torgersen et al. (2000) study; however, work by other researchers has broadly evidenced that the heritability of aggression is between 44% and 72% (Siever, 2008). A meta-analysis suggests the importance of both genetic and environmental influences on antisocial behavior in men and women, although this influence was measured on antisocial behaviors as opposed to antisocial PD (Rhee & Waldman, 2002). Evidence also suggests higher rates of schizotypal (Kendler et al., 2006) and borderline PDs (Links, Steiner, & Huxley, 1988) among family members of individuals with those disorders, and increased rates of cluster C PDs among individuals who have relatives with Axis I anxiety disorders (Reich, 1991).

Evidence also suggests there are interactive effects between genes and the environment, such as the finding that associations between a polymorphism on the MAOA gene are associated with antisocial traits only in individuals who have been exposed to trauma (Caspi et al., 2002). Evidence suggesting an interaction between genes and the early attachment environment may also be crucial in subsequent development of PDs (Siever & Weinstein, 2009). The interplay of genes and environment in the genesis of psychopathology is quite complicated (e.g., Burt, 2009), and much more research is needed with respect to the etiology of PDs. Beyond a basic decomposition of the etiological components of personality pathology and specific PDs, research should begin focusing more on molecular models and the interplay between behavior genetic and environmental risk factors.

Neurobiology   As with etiology and despite a recent rise in interest in understanding neurological risk factors for the development of PDs (for a review, see Siever & Weinstein, 2009), potential neurobiological endophenotypes for PDs are largely unknown (Paris, 2011; Skodol et al., 2011). It is widely presumed that endophenotypes are more likely to reflect neurobiological dimensions that underlie personality pathology rather than point to pathways to specific PDs. Potential dimensions include those related to cognitive dysregulation, impulsivity, and emotion dysregulation (Depue & Lenzenweger, 2005; Siever & Weinstein, 2009). We will briefly review these three classes of potential endophenotypes and their implications for PDs.

Cluster A PDs, and particularly schizotypal PDs, share features of *cognitive dysregulation* with schizophrenia, including distorted perception and disrupted attention. Cognitive dysregulation is thought to relate to reduced dopamine reactivity in the frontal cortex (Abi-Dargham et al., 1998; Seiver & Weinstein, 2009), as well as structural anomalies found in psychotic disorders, such as increased ventricular volume (Hazlett et al., 2008). The influence of common endophenotypes represents a promising explanation for descriptive and phenomenological similarities between cluster A PDs and psychotic disorders (Depue & Lenzenweger, 2005).

Impulsivity is a reaction to emotional provocation, implicating a failure in higher-order mental processes that may predispose to several PDs, and particularly those in cluster B (Siever & Weinstein, 2009). Indeed, there is evidence of reduced cortical activation during impulsive behavior (New et al., 2004), and evidence that serotonin plays an important mediating role in the top-down regulation of impulsive, and particularly aggressive, impulses (Brown et al., 1982; Coccaro, Gabriel, & Siever, 1989; Winstanley, Theobald, Dalley, Glennon, & Robbins, 2004) generated from limbic structures (Herpetz et al., 2001).

Emotion dysregulation is also related to cluster B PDs, and it often takes the form of aggressive behavior, making it difficult to distinguish descriptively from impulsivity. Emotional dysregulation is associated with amygdala hyperreactivity (Donegan et al., 2003; Herpertz et al. 2001), suggesting that it may be dynamically related to impulsive behavior: hypersensitivity to threat leads to emotion dysregulation, and failure to modulate the urge to act based on dysregulated emotion by cortical structures leads to impulsive, often aggressive, behavior. Anxiety is thought to underlie cluster C PDs, which are responsive to chemical manipulations of serotonin and dopamine (Schneier, Blanco, Anita, & Liebowitz, 2002), suggesting common endophenotypes with mood and anxiety disorders (DeYoung, 2010).

Learning and Cognition   A large body of theory and empirical evidence supports links among attachment patterns, developmental trauma, and PDs. In particular, attachment patterns are related to the stylistic expression of PD (Meyer & Pilkonis, 2005), and childhood maltreatment is associated with the development of personality pathology in general (Johnson, Cohen, Brown, Smailes, & Bernstein, 1999) and some PDs specifically (e.g., borderline; Zanarini, Gunderson, Marino, & Schwartz, 1989). Several theories have been organized specifically around the interpersonal antecedents of personality pathology. For instance, Benjamin (1996) has formulated each of the *DSM-IV* PDs in terms of specific and testable developmental patterns. She has also outlined a broad framework for conceptualizing developmental "copy processes" that could usefully inform research in this area (Critchfield & Benjamin, 2010). Unfortunately, research is currently too limited to speak with confidence regarding the interpersonal mechanisms that generate or maintain PD; more research is needed on this important but neglected issue.

Cognitive theorists implicate three fundamental aspects of cognition in the development of PDs: automatic thoughts, cognitive distortions, and interpersonal strategies (Pretzer & Beck, 2005). From this perspective, individuals apply automatic (i.e., implicit or unconscious) thoughts to events they encounter that are rooted in deep-seated ways of interpreting the world, learned in early childhood. For some individuals, these automatic thoughts may lead to cognitive distortions, which, in turn, result in maladaptive interpersonal strategies that reinforce and maintain an individual's personality pathology. Several automatic thoughts and cognitive distortions have been hypothesized for specific PDs (Beck & Freeman, 1990). For example, individuals with avoidant PD may be prone to automatic thoughts such as "I am incompetent," whereas individuals with obsessive-compulsive PD are more likely to employ dichotomous thinking (Beck & Freeman, 1990). As with interpersonal models, further research is needed on cognitive models of the genesis and maintenance of personality pathology.

Course and Prognosis

According to the *DSM-5* Section II, for a PD to be diagnosed in an individual younger than 18 years, the maladaptive personality features must have been present for at least 1 year. The single exception to this rule is antisocial PD, which cannot be diagnosed before age 18. There is no upper restriction on PD diagnosis in the *DSM-5*, but most PDs tend to decline in middle age (although see Tackett, Balsis, Oltmanns, & Krueger, 2009). As such, PDs as conceptualized in the *DSM-5* Section II can generally be regarded as disorders of young to middle adulthood. Within this period, PDs have long been presumed to be stable and pervasive. This assumption has caused significant skepticism regarding prognosis. However, recent research suggests some optimism for therapeutic improvement in that the stability of PDs seems to be lower than was once thought, and treatments have shown benefit for at least some PD symptoms. This research and its implications for conceptualizing personality pathology are discussed presently.

Course   Several longitudinal studies of PD in adult clinical samples in the past few decades have shed significant light on the course of PDs (Morey & Hopwood, 2013). The Collaborative Longitudinal Personality Disorders (CLPS) study followed individuals with PDs or major depression for 10 years. Early research from this study found that PDs declined rapidly over the first 2 years of follow-up (Grilo et al., 2004). Later research showed that PD features were less stable than personality traits (Morey et al., 2007), and that some PD features declined more rapidly than others (McGlashan et al., 2005), leading to the proposal that personality pathology reflects a hybrid combination of stable, enduring personality traits and dynamic, environmentally contingent symptoms. Zanarini's McLean Study of Adult Development (MSAD) is an ongoing study that has followed individuals with borderline PD and a comparison clinical sample without borderline PD for more than 16 years. As in CLPS, remission from borderline PD was more rapid than anticipated in the MSAD (Zanarini, Frankenburg, Hennen, Reich, & Silk, 2007), and again temperamental and acute symptoms were identified (Hopwood, Donnellan, & Zanarini, 2010; Zanarini et al., 2007). Lenzenweger's Longitudinal Study of Personality Disorder similarly showed, in a college student sample followed for 4 years, that there is "compelling evidence of change in PD features over time and does not support the assumption that PD features are trait-like, enduring, and stable over time" (Lenzenweger, 2006, p. 662).

Overall, these findings suggest that some aspects of personality pathology are stable, as has been historically assumed, whereas other aspects appear to operate more like the symptoms of Axis I disorders: they are malleable and perhaps reactive to the influence of environmental dynamics. Thus it may be possible, diagnostically, to distinguish aspects of PD that are due to temperamental diatheses from those that are due to dynamic environmental processes, or the interaction between traits and contexts. These promising findings also suggest that some aspects of PD may be subject to change through psychological treatment, a topic to which we now turn.

Treatment Effects   There is limited evidence that psychopharmacology is effective for treating PD, with results mostly suggesting that targeted use of medication may benefit certain symptom constellations (e.g., the emotional lability of BPD or the cognitive slippage of schizotypal PD; Siever & Weinstein, 2009) but not treat the totality of PD symptoms. Nevertheless, polypharmacy for PDs is common (Zanarini, Frankenburg, Hennen, & Silk, 2004). Perhaps in part because of the longstanding belief that PDs are intractable, relatively few psychosocial treatments have been developed for personality pathology, and most of them have been developed for a single disorder, BPD (Cristea et al., 2017; Leichsenring et al., 2011; Matusiewicz et al., 2010). Several issues complicate the effectiveness of psychosocial treatments, including relatively high rates of early dropout (particularly in BPD, cf. Skodol, Buckley, & Charles, 1983), substantial diagnostic complexity (McGlashan et al., 2000), and the tendency for PD treatment to be challenging for clinicians, who may consequently exhibit maladaptive behavior that could have negative, iatrogenic consequences

That said, some headway is being made with regard to borderline PD (for a thorough review of the evidence, see Leichensring et al., 2011), with several treatments showing benefit in controlled research, including dialectical behavior therapy (Linehan, 1993), transference-focused therapy (Clarkin, Levy, Lenzenweger, & Kernberg, 2007), schema-focused therapy (Giesen-Bloo et al., 2006), good psychiatric management (Gunderson, 2014), and mentalization-based therapy (Bateman & Fonagy, 2004). It is notable that these therapeutic models come from very different theoretical backgrounds, yet they share several features, including a highly structured therapeutic frame, a focus on the relationship between therapist and client, and a focus on managing self-damaging behavior through contracting and explicit crisis plans. The treatments also tend to show similar effects in controlled research (Clarkin et al., 2007). One potential conclusion to draw from the similarity of these treatments is that, in dealing with complex phenomena such as PDs, it is more helpful to integrate the wisdom of multiple perspectives than to cling to theoretical dogma. This lesson may fruitfully translate to the issue of PD classification, to which we now turn.

ASSESSMENT

The manner in which personality pathology and PD are assessed varies across theoretical and measurement approaches, with preferences for particular methods often being related to underlying theoretical assumptions. Common assessment methods are thus organized as follows according to their underlying theoretical foundation. Specifically, we distinguish *DSM*-based, trait, and psychoanalytic approaches to the assessment of personality pathology and PD.

DSM

The most common and widely accepted method for assessing personality pathology and PD involves translating the *DSM* PD symptoms into questions that individuals can endorse, and then determining whether they meet criteria based on the number of symptoms endorsed. Assessing PDs based on *DSM* symptoms can occur via either interview or questionnaire; clinicians tend to prefer unstructured interviews, whereas researchers tend to prefer semistructured interviews or self-report inventories (Widiger & Samuel, 2005). Structured and semistructured interviews are more reliable than unstructured interviews (Rogers, 2001), but unstructured interviews may have the advantages of allowing dynamics between patients and clinicians to occur more naturally and of not requiring patients to have insight into their own personality pathology (Westen, 1997). Conventionally, clinician or research interviews have been regarded as the criterion method for determining whether an individual has a PD. This is partially based on the belief that clinicians are better able to infer meanings and motivations behind client behaviors than are individuals with PDs, who are commonly thought to lack insight regarding their pathology.

Numerous measures exist for assessing PDs using the *DSM* model (Widiger & Samuel, 2005). Among the more commonly employed instruments are the clinician-administered *Structured Clinical Interview for DSM-IV TR Axis II Personality Disorders* (SCID-II; First, Gibbon, Spitzer, Williams, & Benjamin, 1997) and the self-report *Personality Disorder Questionnaire* (Hyler, 1994). A new diagnostic interview for the alternative model has been developed (SCID-AMPD; First et al., 2014) and is currently undergoing field testing. Given that rates of PD are lower by interview than self-report (Clark & Harrison, 2001; Hopwood et al., 2008), a method advocated by First et al. (1997) and others is to screen for PDs using a self-report questionnaire and then to use a clinician-administered semi-structured interview as a follow-up procedure to determine whether an individual meets diagnostic criteria for disorders endorsed by self-report.

A primary advantage of the *DSM* symptom-based method is that it provides a consensual way to evaluate PDs and thus increases confidence among clinicians and researchers that they are assessing the same constructs. However, agreement among *DSM*-based measures is poor (Skodol, Rosnick, Kellman, Oldham, & Hyler, 1991), and assessing PDs from the *DSM* perspective is limited to the degree that the *DSM* model is of questionable validity, as many have suggested. Several authors have argued that a more theoretically coherent model is needed to improve methods for assessing personality pathology and disorders. Trait and psychoanalytic models, which are described as follows, may offer desirable theoretical coherence.

Trait Models

Building upon consistent evidence that personality traits such as those of the FFM systematically relate to *DSM* PDs (Samuel & Widiger, 2008; Saulsman & Page, 2004), trait researchers have developed methods for deriving PD scores from FFM-based assessments (Miller, Bagby, Pilkonis, Reynolds, & Lynam, 2005). A potential advantage to FFM assessment methods is that normal and pathological personality can be evaluated within the same model. This would permit, for example, an assessment of personality strengths that may not be afforded by an exclusive focus on PD constructs (Samuel, 2011). However, one potential limitation to this approach is the possibility that normative measures such as those based on the FFM do not effectively assess some important aspects of personality pathology and disorder (Hopwood, 2011; Krueger et al., 2011b; although see also Haigler & Widiger, 2001). It is also possible that the self-report method, on which most trait research heavily relies, may be limited for some aspects of personality pathology assessment (Huprich & Bornstein, 2007).

A related approach to PD assessment involves focusing on maladaptive traits rather than general personality, as in the FFM. The two predominant measures that are used in this regard are the *Dimensional Assessment of Personality Pathology* (Livesley & Jackson, 2006), which was initially developed to test the structure of the *DSM* model but later reformulated as a trait model, and the *Schedule for Nonadaptive and Adaptive Personality* (Clark, 1993), which was developed to provide a means for dimensionally assessing clinically relevant personality and personality pathology traits. Both measures consist of higher-order factors that resemble subsets of FFM traits (Widiger, Livesley, & Clark, 2009) and lower-order factors that assess pathological personality traits. Recently, Krueger and colleagues have developed a questionnaire that is similar to these measures to serve as the basis for pathological trait assessment in the *DSM-5* (Krueger et al., 2011a,b, 2012).

PSYCHOANALYTIC ASSESSMENT

Unlike trait psychologists, psychoanalytically oriented clinicians and researchers tend to prefer clinician ratings or performance-based assessment over self-report methods. There has also been increased interest among psychoanalytic researchers and clinicians in using prototypes to assess PDs. The *Shedler and Westen Assessment Procedure* (SWAP; Westen & Shedler, 1999) is a prototype-based clinician rating method informed by psychoanalytic theory. On the SWAP, clinicians describe their patients' personalities by sorting 200 cards that are applicable to varying degrees to the patient being rated. These sorts can then be compared with prototypes to determine the most likely diagnosis. Evidence suggesting that clinicians tend to think of patients in prototypical terms rather than trait profiles (Rottman, Woo-kyoung, Sanislow, & Kim, 2009; Westen et al., 2006) makes the SWAP and similar procedures appealing. However, prototypes are not without limitations, mainly owing to their potential unreliability (Zimmerman, 2011) and the loss of information that occurs when ratings are made globally (Samuel, Hopwood, Krueger, Thomas, & Ruggero, 2013). For instance, if a patient is a good match to a given prototype, that could mean the patient either moderately matches nearly all features of the description or matches some features of the description extremely well and others not so well.

Another approach involves using measures that assess features of psychoanalytic theories that deviate from the *DSM* model. For instance, psychoanalysts have developed the *Psychodynamic Diagnostic Manual* (PDM Task Force, 2006; see also *Journal of Personality Assessment*, special issue 2, 2011) for this purpose. Other examples include the *Structured Interview of Personality Organization* (Stern et al., 2010) and the *Inventory of Personality Organization* (Kernberg & Clarkin, 1995), which are based on Kernberg's (1984) model of personality pathology. An appealing feature of this model is that it explicitly separates personality pathology (i.e., personality organization) from PDs. However, thus far these measures have been subjected to limited psychometric research.

A third historically psychoanalytic approach to assessing personality pathology involves performance-based assessment methods in which individuals provide open-ended responses to novel stimuli. For example, the *Rorschach Inkblot Method* (Huprich, 2005), in which individuals describe what images they see in a series of inkblots, the *Thematic Apperception Test*, in which individuals produce stories to go along with pictures, and sentence completion tests (e.g., Hy & Loevinger, 1996) are commonly employed performance-based assessments. Scoring methods have also been developed to score patient narratives as a way of evaluating concepts that are important in psychoanalytic theory, such as defense mechanisms (Cramer, 1991) and the quality of object relations (Westen, 1995).

The primary strengths of psychoanalytic approaches to PD assessment include the fact that they are embedded in a coherent theory of personality pathology and also that they may be better suited than interviews and self-reports to identifying pathological personality processes that are outside of individuals' awareness (Huprich & Bornstein, 2007). However, there is limited empirical support for psychoanalytic approaches to PD assessment over *DSM*-based and trait assessment instruments, and using methods that are informed heavily by nonconsensual theories risks returning to a time when clinicians used the same terms to mean different things. Furthermore, clinician ratings and performance-based methods are time-consuming relative to questionnaires. Thus, the utility of psychoanalytic approaches could be better judged if they were made as efficient as possible and linked better empirically to other approaches to PD assessment.

SUMMARY

Overall, any assessment method designed to evaluate complicated constructs such as personality pathology and PDs is likely to have strengths and weaknesses. The optimal strategy is therefore to use multiple assessment methods from varying theoretical perspectives. One example of a more comprehensive approach is the LEAD standard (Pilkonis, Heape, Ruddy, & Serrao, 1991), in which all available current and historical data from any methods are evaluated by a team of expert clinicians to derive the most reliable possible diagnosis.

THE *DSM-5*

Personality pathology is significantly reconceptualized in the *DSM-5* Section III (Skodol et al., 2011). It is likely that something like this reconceptualization will ultimately replace the problematic *DSM-5* Section II model in future editions of the *DSM*. In this section, we describe widely recognized problems with the *DSM-IV* model that led to this reconceptualization, the *DSM-5* Section III alternative, and the impact of the *DSM-5* on scientific validity and clinical utility. We conclude by highlighting differences between the *DSM-5* Section II and III approaches to PD diagnosis with a case study.

CRITICISMS OF THE *DSM-5* SECTION II PDs

Although the Section II model, derived from *DSM-III* and *DSM-IV*, has catalyzed PD research, the research it has stimulated has contributed to the identification of several limitations of the system (Clark, 2007). Many limitations relate to the categorical conceptualization of PD, which appears to fit nature poorly (Trull & Durrett, 2005), worsens reliability (Heumman & Morey, 1990), and necessitates arbitrary diagnostic cutoffs (Skodol et al., 2011). Others, such as profound diagnostic overlap (Clark, 2007; Oldham, Skodol, Kellman, Hyler, & Rosnick, 1992) and the common use of a not-otherwise-specified category (Verheul & Widiger, 2004), appear to relate to the questionable empirical structure of the PDs (Hopwood et al., 2011). The polythetic format of PD criteria (Krueger et al., 2011b), conflation of personality severity and style in PD symptoms (Parker et al., 1998), and the arbitrary diagnostic cutoffs contribute to problematic diagnostic heterogeneity. *DSM-IV* constructs also conflate relatively stable traits with more dynamic symptoms (McGlashan et al., 2005; Zanarini et al., 2007). Finally, as discussed previously, although the *DSM-III* and *DSM-IV* have promoted PD research in general, some PDs are woefully neglected in the research literature, and the *DSM-IV* has not led to the development of effective treatments for most PDs (Widiger & Mullins-Sweatt, 2009).

DSM-5 Section III PDs

The *DSM-5* Section III model was designed to address some of these problems with a view to improving the scientific validity and clinical utility of PD diagnosis. We will first describe the basic elements of this model, and we will then describe the degree to which it improves the scientific validity and clinical utility of PD assessment.

The *DSM-5* Section III model (Krueger et al., 2011a; Morey et al., 2011; Skodol et al., 2011) includes a general definition of personality pathology which is quantified, six PDs defined by a mix of symptom deficits and pathological traits, and a hierarchical system of pathological traits. The general definition of personality pathology is quantified in terms of levels of functioning on two dimensions rated on a five-point scale: self (i.e., identity and self-direction) and interpersonal (i.e., empathy and intimacy). Any patient in the diagnostic range would be assessed for the presence of six potential PDs: antisocial, avoidant, borderline, narcissistic, obsessive-compulsive, and schizotypal. Reviews of the literature by the *DSM-5* Workgroup revealed a lack of persuasive data to establish the construct validity of the other four *DSM-IV* PDs (schizoid, paranoid, histrionic, and dependent). These PD types were not included as distinct PDs; however, traits reflecting these conditions can be specified using the PD-trait specified diagnosis. There are five criteria for each PD. Criterion A involves the core deficits in self and interpersonal functioning that are specific to that disorder. Criterion B lists the traits that are also thought to undergird each disorder. Criteria C–E specify that these features must be stable, deviant, and not better accounted for by other conditions, respectively. Any patient with personality pathology who does meet the criteria for a specific disorder would be classified as PD-trait specified. This specification would be based on a hierarchical model with five higher-order traits (negative affectivity, detachment, antagonism, disinhibition, and psychoticism) and 25 lower order traits (Krueger et al., 2011a,b, in review). These traits could also be used to supplement PD diagnoses, for instance when a patient meets criteria for a certain PD and has several other significant traits, or to describe a patient without any PD diagnosis but with some pathological traits.

The Scientific Validity of *DSM-5* Section III PDs

The *DSM-5* Section III model appears to improve the scientific validity of PD diagnosis in several respects relative to its predecessor. Research discussed earlier supports the quantification of a general personality pathology factor in terms of levels of functioning, and the contents of this rating scale are based on empirical evidence (Morey et al., 2011) rooted in a large body of theoretical considerations and clinical observations (Bender et al., 2011). The PDs that are included retain several concepts such as borderline personality, psychopathy, and schizotypy, with considerable construct validity, and the transition to a more personality-based model of psychopathy (Hare, 1991) improves the definition of that construct considerably. The traits incorporate a dimensional perspective and appear to capture the major traits of other dimensional models (Krueger et al., 2012; Wright et al., 2012), addressing the most common evidence-based critique of the *DSM-IV* PDs.

Because the model is so new and uses a somewhat novel approach to PD assessment, critics have argued that not enough is known about its validity (Shedler et al., 2010; Zimmerman, 2011). Early evidence suggests that the *DSM-5* alternative model covers the content described in the *DSM-IV* relatively well (Hopwood et al., 2011), and mental health clinicians generally judged the *DSM-5* alternative PD model as more useful than the *DSM-IV-TR* Axis II (Morey et al., 2014).

The *DSM-5* alternative model for PD operationalizes core impairments in identity/ self-direction and empathy/intimacy in the form of a five-point rating scale, the Level of Personality Functioning Scale (LFSP; Bender et al 2011). The LFSP has been shown to be easily scored, even with minimal training by novices (Zimmerman et al., 2013). The LFSP demonstrated adequate to good sensitivity and specificity in predicting the presence of a PD, and was correlated with markers of personality pathology (Morey et al., 2013). The LFSP also demonstrated a medium to large effect size correlation with the sum of all *DSM-IV* PD symptoms (Few et al., 2013).

Dimensional personality trait domains embedded in the alternative model are assessed via the PID-5 (Krueger et al., 2012). Emerging evidence indicates that PID-5 trait domains are linked to internalizing symptoms, externalizing behaviors, and severity of personality pathology (Few et al., 2013), and that domains predict *DSM-IV* PDs (Bastiaens et al., 2015; Hopwood, Thomas, Markon, Wright, & Krueger, 2012), as well as functional impairment (Fowler et al., 2016; Keeley, Flanagan, & McCluskey, 2014). At the present time only one longitudinal study has been published. This study indicated that PID-5 traits were highly stable and predicted future psychosocial functioning (Wright et al., 2015).

Despite the growing evidence in support of the alternative model, questions remain regarding how the restructured criteria A and B will affect prevalence of the PDs, and how the trait structure will hold up in future research. This approach also likely contributes to some odd facet–domain relationships, such as the loading of submissiveness onto negative affectivity (Widiger, 2011, although see also Krueger et al., 2011a).

There is also significant controversy regarding decisions about which PD constructs to retain. The response from the clinical and research community to an initial proposal to delete narcissistic PD (e.g., Pincus, 2011) contributed to the *DSM-5* workgroup's decision to include that disorder in its second proposal. However, paranoid, schizoid, histrionic, and dependent PDs were reconceptualized as pathological personality traits rather than distinct PDs. Decisions regarding which PDs to retain were based primarily on evidence concerning the prevalence of these conditions and the overall body of research for each PD (Skodol et al., 2011). However, it is predictable that clinicians and researchers would hesitate to delete PDs to which they have grown accustomed. Furthermore, de-emphasizing constructs such as dependent and histrionic PDs may inadvertently limit assessment of related pathology of excessive need for affiliation and reassurance (Wright et al., 2012), a central feature of this disorder (Widiger, 2010), which is not well represented in the pathological trait model (Pincus et al., 2011).

THE CLINICAL UTILITY OF *DSM-5* SECTION III PDs

According to First et al. (2004), clinical utility involves the clinician's ability to communicate; select effective interventions; predict course, prognosis, and future management needs; and differentiate disorder from nondisorder to determine who might benefit from treatment. The degree to which the *DSM-5* model improves upon the *DSM-IV* can be evaluated in each of these areas.

In terms of communication, the levels of functioning index and any reduction in diagnostic overlap and construct heterogeneity that results from the move from polythetic to type diagnosis would tend to facilitate communication. However, trait ratings solve the problem posed by the regular diagnosis of PD-not otherwise specified (Krueger et al., 2011b), and over time clinicians will likely become more familiar with the *DSM-5* traits. It is also useful to note that the 25 facets of the *DSM-5* represent a dramatic reduction from the 79 to 99 symptom criteria of *DSM-III* and *DSM-IV* (Krueger et al., 2011a). Finally, although it is clinically important to depict personality-related strengths (e.g., Bornstein, 2011a; Hopwood, 2011), the *DSM-5* provides no mechanism for doing so, as all of the elements of PD diagnosis are pathological.

Overall, the *DSM-5* Section II model has not been particularly useful to clinicians wishing to select effective interventions, as there are no evidence-based interventions for most PDs, and treatments that do exist are only modestly helpful (Matusiewicz et al., 2010). There are reasons to think that the *DSM-5* Section III model could lead to more effective interventions. For instance, the development of treatment methods to differentially target personality pathology or particular types/traits of PD style could enhance the specificity of therapeutic techniques. However, the issue of treatment selection has rarely been discussed in debates about how to classify PDs, suggesting that improvements in this regard attributable to the *DSM-5* Section III are likely to be modest (Clarkin & Huprich, 2011).

The *DSM-5* has perhaps made the most significant progress in terms of helping clinicians differentiate disorder from nondisorder. The quantification of levels provides clinicians with a clear basis for determining a patient's diagnostic standing. Several aspects of the *DSM-5* Section III model may also improve clinical predictions about course and prognosis. Dimensional models of PD are more stable and more valid for predicting prospective outcomes (Morey et al., 2007), suggesting that their incorporation into the *DSM-5* should improve clinical predictions. The separation of levels of functioning from PD styles may improve prognostic predictions if, for instance, it is shown that personality pathology is more stable than PD instantiations.

Thus far, the concerns expressed by critics regarding the burdensome complexity of the alternative model have failed to emerge, according to surveys of psychiatrists, psychologists and other mental health care providers. As noted earlier, clinicians found the alternative model preferable to the well-known *DSM-IV-TR* in every category except communication (Morey et al., 2014). As discussed earlier, it is wise that the *DSM-5* be regarded as a living document that can be modified in order to incorporate new information, such as the stability and long-term predictive validity of different elements of PD diagnosis (Krueger et al., 2011b).

CASE STUDY

We will demonstrate differences between the *DSM-5* Section II and III models using the case of Elaine, a 28-year-old single, unemployed woman. Elaine presented for an evaluation at a low-fee outpatient clinic, unkempt and in clear distress, although her behavior was appropriate and she established rapport readily. The clinician experienced her as thoughtful, warm, and insightful and reported that she had provoked in him a strong desire to be helpful to her. Elaine sought psychotherapy shortly after her life circumstances had worsened considerably. She had been evicted from her apartment 1 month prior and had been living in a homeless shelter. During that time, she had stolen money to buy alcohol and food. She had begun cutting herself on her arms and legs with thumb tacks and broken glass in moments of acute despair, something she had done on a few occasions during dramatic romantic break-ups in adolescence, but which she had discontinued since that time. She denied suicidal intent but acknowledged multiple potentially self-harming behaviors, such as promiscuous sex and careless substance use, in the past and present.

Elaine described being the lone child in an intact, middle-class family as "mostly okay," although she also reported being estranged from her physically abusive father for the 10 years since she had moved out of her parents' house. She maintained a close relationship with her mother, but their contact was somewhat limited due to the ongoing rupture between Elaine and her father. She also had several close friends whom she felt she could trust, although she reported feeling too ashamed to turn to them for help when she really needed it. During adolescence and early adulthood, Elaine had been convicted several times for petty theft. She reported that she had generally stolen or shoplifted with or for her boyfriends in the distant past, but that in the previous few years she had primarily shoplifted alcohol or food for her own consumption. Elaine did well academically and reported many positive social experiences and stable friendships during adolescence, although this time was also colored by several emotionally charged and disruptive romantic breakups. She described several instances in which she behaved in a manner she later regarded as embarrassing in order to attract the attention of a potential suitor. For instance, when Elaine was 16, she shared seductive pictures of herself with a boy that she liked, who then showed the pictures to his friends. When she learned he had done this, she drank heavily, had a sexual liaison with the boy's friend, and threw a rock through his bedroom window. She was charged, convicted, and put on probation, which she later violated; her social reputation also predictably suffered.

Elaine's personality problems were exacerbated 3 years prior to her visit when she witnessed the death of her daughter in an automobile accident. Elaine had been driving, but the accident was not her fault. After being left by her daughter's father shortly after conception, she had cared for her daughter alone and reported that doing so was her main motivation to limit her drinking and work reliably. Following the accident, Elaine had persistent post-traumatic symptoms, including re-experiencing, avoidance of social events, exaggerated startle, nightmares, and generalized anxiety. She had a history of alcohol abuse that had reached dependence in the last 2 years and had become sufficiently severe to cost her a job 6 months prior to her presentation. She also reported that following the accident, she became disinterested in a committed relationship with a man, although she continued to have multiple sexual relationships.

In terms of personality diagnosis, Elaine has several borderline characteristics with some historical precedent but which had become more severe following her daughter's death. She claimed that every man with whom she had ever had a close romantic relationship had been verbally or physically abusive. She described a host of brief and volatile relationships characterized by a pattern of events involving intense anger over seemingly minor issues, followed by impulsive behavior such as substance abuse or infidelity, and a deep sense of emptiness and regret. She reported feeling so ashamed of herself and angry at her partner following these episodes that she would end relationships rather than acknowledge her behavior or attempt to repair the relationship.

Notably, Elaine also reported impulsive, and often attention-seeking, behavior associated with a particularly positive mood. She said that when she felt good, she "just doesn't want it to end," so she "lets it all hang out," which typically involves behaviors such as substance abuse and promiscuous sex that ultimately lead to her feeling lonely and empty.

DSM-IV DIAGNOSIS

From the perspective of the *DSM-5* Section II, Elaine would meet seven of nine criteria for BPD: unstable relationships, identity disturbance, impulsivity, suicidal gestures, affective instability, emptiness, and anger. She would not meet the criteria for dissociative symptoms/paranoid ideation. Although her thinking became somewhat loose during moments of extreme distress, this symptom was not severe enough to be rated as fully present. She also denied abandonment concerns. Elaine would also meet criteria for antisocial PD, having met criteria for adolescent conduct disorder and six of seven antisocial criteria (failure to conform, deceitfulness, impulsivity, irritability, recklessness, irresponsibility), and for histrionic PD, having five of eight symptoms (inappropriate sexuality, rapidly shifting emotions, use of appearance for attention, impressionistic speech, and theatricality). She would, therefore, be well categorized as having prominent cluster B personality pathology and, in particular, borderline, antisocial, and histrionic features.

DSM-5 DIAGNOSIS

DSM-5 Section III PD diagnosis occurs in several steps. The first involves rating overall personality pathology. A rating of 3, indicating serious impairment, seemed most appropriate for Elaine in terms of both self- and interpersonal functioning. Her self-system was poorly regulated and unstable, with some boundary definition problems and a fragile self-concept. Her sense of agency was weak, and she commonly felt empty. She often experienced life as meaningless or dangerous. There was sufficient self-functioning that a rating of 4, indicating extreme impairment, did not seem warranted. She was able to regulate her self-states more often than not, and she was able to articulate a unique identity. There was some evidence of agency and transient fulfillment. Interpersonally, she was able to have stable attachments to individuals outside of romantic relationships, and in these contexts she was generally able to understand others' behaviors and motivations empathically. However, she was not able to use these relationships when she needed social support the most, and the negative impacts of her interpersonal dysfunction in romantic relationships were profound.

Elaine met criteria A for moderate or greater impairment in personality (self/interpersonal) functioning; however, she did not meet the criteria for a specific PD. For example, she did not have the required criterion B traits of risk-taking or hostility (scores on these traits range from 0 [not present] to 3 [present]). Most of the criterion A and B features for antisocial behavior were absent. Thus, she would be classified as PD-trait specified, with prominent negative affectivity (emotional lability) and disinhibition (recklessness, impulsivity, and irresponsibility).

Is this an improvement? Section III appears to offer a richer description than does Section II, in that it quantifies personality pathology, separates personality pathology from PD features, and lists PD features in more detail. Furthermore, the Section II antisocial diagnosis was accurate given her symptoms but did not seem to capture her very well. That said, from a clinical perspective the term borderline does seem to describe Elaine overall, and perhaps more efficiently than the trait-specified diagnosis. The question of optimal models of PD diagnosis cannot be answered using a single study or single case example, and it is likely that there will be strengths and weaknesses of any model of PD. Thus this question will need to be answered by the future researchers and clinicians who use the *DSM-5*.

NIMH RESEARCH DOMAIN CRITERIA INITIATIVE

The RDoC initiative takes a basic science approach to psychiatric disturbance by utilizing results from genetics, neuroimaging, and behavioral studies to identify "tipping points" (disruptions of the normal-range operation) in the full range of cognitive and emotional functioning to identify pathological processes of five broad systems. The RDoC incorporates a dimensional approach to study the full range of variation from normal to psychopathological expression (Cuthbert & Insel, 2013). It is assumed that extremes of function (genetic, neurological, and behavioral) may be implicated in psychopathology. For example, a complete lack of response to social rejection may be associated with psychopathy while extreme hypersensitivity to rejection may be a marker for internalizing disorders, including some variants of psychiatric conditions such as personality, anxiety and depressive disorders.

The RDoC currently consists of five major domains with constructs embedded within those domains. The negative valance domain includes acute threat or fear response, potential threat, anxiety and anticipatory anxiety reactions, sustained threat, and frustrated nonreward. Positive valence system includes approach motivation, initial response to reward, sustained response to reward, reward learning, and habit. Cognitive systems include attention, perception, working memory, declarative memory, language behavior, and cognitive controls. The systems for social processes include constructs such as affiliation, attachment, social communication, perceptions and understanding of self and others. Arousal and modulatory systems include constructs of arousal, biological rhythms, and sleep–wake cycles and architecture.

A potential limitation of the RDoC as it pertains to clinical practice with PDs is that, because it is focused on underlying mechanisms, the constructs and methods promoted by the initiative tend to be somewhat far from the lived experience of patients. Evidence-based models of the structure of psychopathology that are based to a greater degree than RDoC on patient-reported presenting are needed to fill the gap between diagnostic schemes, such as the *DSM*, built primarily on clinical observation and expertise, and bottom-up models such as the RDoC, built primarily on neuroscience research. The HiTOP (Kotov et al., 2017) is a model of individual differences in mental disorder with significant content resemblance to both the RDoC and the alternative model of the *DSM-5*, Section III. This model is organized hierarchically, with broad concepts such as internalizing and externalizing at the top, and narrow concepts such as specific symptoms at the bottom. It is similar to the RDoC and unlike the *DSM* Section II model in identifying empirically based and transdiagnostic markers for a range of mental disorders. It is similar to both *DSM-5* PD frameworks and unlike the RDoC in focusing on constructs and methods that are easily implemented in clinical settings. Overall, HiTOP offers significant potential for reorganizing the diagnosis of both PDs and other mental health conditions in a way that improves science and practice.

DSM-5 and *RDoC*

Prior to the publication of *DSM-5*, Kupfer & Rieger (2011) anticipated that the RDoC initiative to reclassify mental disorders on the basis of neuroscience evidence could contribute significantly to the future iterations of the *DSM*. In turn, dimensions identified in the *DSM-5* personality trait model could potentially contribute to the scientific evidence for the RDoC, because aspects of the PD trait dimensions share conceptual features with the consensus domains proposed by NIMH to frame their Research Domain Criteria or RDoC initiative (Trull & Widiger, 2013). For example, the processes underlying the *DSM-5* trait domain of negative affectivity may be associated with features of the RDoC negative valence systems, and the *DSM-5* trait domain of impulsivity may map onto features of the RDoC effortful control systems. The Levels of Personality Functioning constructs align well with the NIMH Research Domain Criterion of Systems for Social Processes (Sanislow et al. 2010). The interpersonal dimension of personality pathology (particularly the regulatory processes associated with affiliative behavior in BPD) has been hypothesized to be regulated by opioid and oxytocin neuropeptides (Stanley & Siever 2010). Variation in the encoding of receptors for these neuropeptides may contribute to variation in complex human social behavior and social cognition, such as trust, altruism, social bonding, and the ability to infer the emotional state of others (Donaldson & Young 2008). Furthermore, facets of the RDoC social processes domain may be examined utilizing constructs such as hypersensitivity to rejection (an element of negative affectivity) and the facet of separation insecurity. In the next section, two study designs will be briefly outlined, each targeting an RDoC domain utilizing *DSM-5* alternative model measures and trait domain scores to further neuro-science research into personality pathology.

Interpersonal Hypersensitivity and the RDoC Negative Valence System Impairment in interpersonal relationships is a hallmark of PDs and is one of two prepotent criteria for diagnosing a PD in the alternative model. One facet of interpersonal impairment is hypersensitivity to rejection. Hypersensitivity to interpersonal stressors in the form of rejection sensitivity, abandonment fears, and separation insecurity is especially prominent among patients with BPD and has been proposed as a phenotype for the disorder (Gunderson, Lyons-Ruth, 2004). This phenomenon has been widely studied among individuals with BPD and there is ample evidence linking interpersonal hypersensitivity in response to angry faces (Levine et al., 1997; Wagner & Linehan 1999), abandonment scripts (Herpertz, Sass, & Favazza, 1997), and negative interpersonal events (Jovev & Jackson, 2006). Longitudinal outcome studies indicate that symptom remission among borderline patients appears to be responsive to positive interpersonal events (Links & Heslegrave, 2000), whereas negative relationship events predict worsening psychosocial functioning (Pagano et al., 2004).

While BPD has been the primary target population for studying rejection sensitivity among psychiatric samples, social psychologists probe the neurological and health impact of social ostracism across healthy individuals. Relatively healthy individuals experience pain response when socially excluded. In fact, several studies demonstrated that social exclusion activates brain regions that process and regulate the unpleasantness of physical pain, including the dorsal anterior cingulate cortex and the right ventral lateral prefrontal cortex (Eisenberger, Lieberman, & Williams, 2003; Riva et al., 2012). It stands to reason that hypersensitivity to negative interpersonal events may constitute an underlying latent dimension that predicts emergence of a broad spectrum of psychopathology.

Table 21.1

Elaine's *DSM-5* Personality Disorder Trait Profile

Negative affectivity	3
Emotional liability	3
Anxiousness	2
Submissiveness	1
Separation insecurity	2
Perseveration	0
Hostility	1
Restricted affectivity	0
Detachment	1
Social withdrawal	1
Suspiciousness	2
Depressivity	2
Anhedonia	1
Intimacy avoidance	0
Antagonism	1
Callousness	0
Manipulativeness	1
Grandiosity	0
Attention-seeking	2
Deceitfulness	1
Disinhibition	3
Impulsivity	3
Distractibility	2
Recklessness	3
Irresponsibility	3
Rigid perfectionism	0
Risk-taking	0
Psychoticism	1
Unusual perceptions/experiences	0
Eccentricity	0
Perceptual dysregulation	2

Conceptualizing interpersonal hypersensitivity as one element of the negative valence system could be tested in the following manner. All adult patients admitted to a single psychiatric hospital are invited to participate in a study assessing psychiatric treatment response, neuroimaging and genomics. A cohort of 200 matched controls screened for major psychopathology is included to broaden the range of normal response set. Consented participants undergo a battery of self-report and interview measures assessing a broad spectrum of psychiatric disorders and symptoms. Key measures include the PID-5 (Krueger et al., 2012) and the Level of Personality Functioning scale (Morey et al., 2012) as well as a specific self-report measure of rejection sensitivity (Downey &

Feldman, 1996). Patients then undergo an functional magnetic resonance imaging (fMRI) procedure including a well-validated task (in the imaging environment) that evokes social ostracism or rejection—the Cyberball task (Williams, Cheung, & Choi, 2000). *Cyberball* is a computerized game designed to experimentally induce social rejection or ostracism. It has been used in fMRI environments with considerable success. Subjects are informed they will be playing a ball toss game with two other participants in adjoining rooms. The game begins with three players (in actuality two are computer-generated and controlled confederates). The start position has one of the computer confederates throwing the ball to the participant. The participant is then required to indicate to whom he or she would like to throw the ball by clicking on the appropriate player icon. In the social rejection condition, the participant receives the ball twice and is then completely excluded from the game (i.e., not receiving the ball ever again). In the inclusion condition, the participant randomly received the ball approximately 33% of the time. The social rejection condition has been shown to activate dorsal anterior cingulate cortex and right ventral lateral prefrontal cortex, areas of the brain that process unpleasant experience and physical pain (Eisenberger et al., 2003; Riva et al., 2012). Finally, genetic testing is conducted on all consented participants and exon-wide association for targeted genes (serotonin transporter [5-HT] and dopamine receptor D4 [DRD4 exon III]). 5-HT has been implicated in reactivity to stressful life events (Caspi et al., 2003), and DRD4 exon III is related to resilience against traumatic interpersonal events (Das et al., 2011). In this study, the behavioral marker of rejection sensitivity as measured by the Rejection Sensitivity Questionnaire (Downey & Feldman, 1996) will serve as the dependent variable and all other variables will serve as independent variables that potentially predict rejection sensitivity.

Statistical analysis of all independent variables utilizing structural equation modeling allows for the clustering of data from distinct measures to form latent factors that contribute to the prediction of the dependent variable (in this case the dimensional measure of rejection sensitivity). Thus, inputs from subjective, conscious-level experience of interpersonal hypersensitivity, dimensional representations of personality trait domains, global ratings of severity of personality pathology, neuroimaging data from event-related potentials, and exon-wide genetic factors can coalesce in unanticipated patterns to predict the outcome. Importantly, this modeling procedure allow for the cross-cutting assessment of this domain of functioning, breaking out of conventional categorical definitions and allowing for an assessment of cross-diagnostic indicators of this specific psychological process.

Recruiting all patients in a hospital setting ($N = 3,000$) as well as screened healthy control participants ($N = 200$) maximizes the likelihood of assessing a broad range of experience of rejection sensitivity. Rejection sensitivity may be expressed as a curvilinear function with pathology expressed at both extremes—pathological lack of reactivity (possibly individuals high in callous indifference) through a more normative range, including the healthy controls, to the extreme of rejection sensitivity often found among individuals with internalizing disorders. Exon-level sequencing, multiple regions of interest from fMRI, and measures of personality trait domains will provide a robust test of the specific genetic and neurobiological circuitry for rejection sensitivity.

The value of assessing personality traits within this paradigm is clear. The personality trait domains may aggregate, providing a latent construct for rejection sensitivity linking a latent factor (perhaps internalizing personality pathology) to genetic and neurocircuit-level data to identify the underlying factors associated with extremes of rejection sensitivity.

Detachment and the RDoC System for Social Processes   Research indicates that positive social support reduces stress. Positive social support promotes self-regulation strategies in response to stressful events (Aspinwall & Taylor, 1997; Uchino, Carlisle & Birmingham, 2011) and appears to buffer acute and chronic stress effects on health and physiological markers (Uchino, 2009). Even recollection of past positive social support of a loved one helps to downregulate negative emotions among individuals with relatively secure attachment styles (Mikulincer & Shaver, 2008; Selcuk et al., 2012). By contrast, psychological detachment is linked to a variety of negative outcomes. For example, detachment (indicated by a dismissive/detached attachment style) among diabetic patients is linked to greater interpersonal distance, dissatisfaction and difficulty forming collaborative relationships with health care providers, poorer adherence to exercise protocols, and poorer medication compliance (Ciechanowski et al., 2004) as well as a 33% increased risk of death compared with diabetic individuals with more interactive attachment styles (Ciechanowski et al., 2010).

Among individuals with psychiatric disturbance, dismissive/detached individuals are less likely to seek psychotherapy treatment for distress (Riggs & Jacobvitz, 2002) and when they do seek treatment are more prone to become distressed when faced with difficult issues in treatment, which may lead to higher rates of dropout (Dozier et al., 2001). While less is known about the genetic and neurobiological factors associated with *detachment* as a cross-cutting personality trait, at least one study indicates that people with a dismissive/detached attachment style show decreased activity of the striatum and ventral tegmental area, suggesting decreased responsivity to social rewards (Vrtička et al., 2008).

Detachment as a personality trait domain may be particularly well suited as a behavioral variable for examining the neurobiological correlates involved in the RDoC system for social processing. The proposed study will utilize the social avoidance subscale of the Liebowitz Social Anxiety Scale Self-Report (dos Santos et al., 2013) as the dependent variable. All domains and trait facets of the PID-5 (with particular emphasis on detachment domain scores), and the Level of Personality Functioning Scale will be used to assess level of impairment associated with detachment. Additionally, a measure of attachment style (Relationship Questionnaire; Bartholemew & Horowitz, 1991) and a measure of the FFM of personality (Big Five Inventory; John et al., 2008) will provide a broad spectrum of personality functioning as potential independent variables associated with fMRI and genetic data.

Specific regions of interest for fMRI resting state network analysis include the anterior cingulate, nucleus accumbens, orbitofrontal cortex, and amygdala which are implicated in processing of social emotions (Britton et al., 2006). Abnormal resting state connectivity between the amygdala and the inferior temporal gyrus is related to social anxiety disorder (Liao et al., 2010) and therefore may be related to detachment as a broader, cross-cutting domain of personality functioning. Biological markers will include oxytocin and vasopressin due to the hypothesized balance between these neuropeptides in regulating social behavior in humans (Neumann & Landgraf, 2012).

Structural equation modeling will be utilized to estimate the multiple inputs from subjective, conscious-level experience of detachment, dimensional representations of this personality trait domain, global ratings of severity of personality pathology, neuroimaging data, and genetic influences in identifying detachment. Again utilizing a sample of consented adults($N = 3,000$) in a psychiatric hospital and healthy controls ($N = 200$) will provide a full spectrum of levels of detachment from high engagement to extreme detachment.

Given the profound negative health impact that detachment imparts to those at the extreme range (Ciechanowski et al., 2010), efforts to uncover genetic and neurocircuitry structures associated with detachment, establishing cut-points of severity based on these biomarkers, and linking these to a variety of health outcomes could lead to novel treatment interventions targeting the function of those structures. Some early translational and intervention research on the effects of oxytocin have yielded promising results. Intranasal administration of oxytocin has demonstrated increased specific prosocial behavior such as social decision-making, processing of social stimuli, eye gazing, and social memory.

Use of oxytocin in the treatment of post-traumatic stress disorder has been reported in clinical populations (Pitman et al., 1993); however, results are equivocal for BPD. Oxytocin reduced stress reaction (cortisol level) for BPD subjects engaged in a stress paradigm (Simeon et al., 2011); however, oxytocin hindered trust and social cooperation in a subset of BPD subjects with an anxious attachment style and heightened rejection sensitivity (Bartz et al., 2011), implying that cognitive bias and expectation may have colored the reaction to oxytocin.

SUMMARY

In this chapter, we have described personality pathology and PDs, reviewed their history, clinical presentation, and construct validity, and compared the *DSM-5* Section II and III models of PD with a clinical case. In general, it can be concluded that personality pathology is common and associated with profound functional impairments and personal and societal costs. Although recent research provides new, promising methods for assessing and treating PDs, much remains unknown about how to assess and treat personality problems. The alternative model for *DSM-5* PDs could contribute to further understanding and clinical utility. However, there is a long history of research and clinical neglect in relation to PDs, so understanding of many aspects of personality pathology is severely limited. Future directions for research include obtaining a better understanding of associations between normative traits and personality-related impairments, developing stronger links between research and practice, and incorporating dynamic elements of personality into existing models. Advances in these areas should contribute to an improved understanding of etiology and ultimately to more effective assessment and treatment methods. Two examples of potential research designs are included in the chapter.

REFERENCES

Abi-Dargham, A., Gil, R., Krystal, J., Baldwin, R. M., Seibyl, J. P., Bowers, M., . . . Laruelle, M. (1998). Increased striatal dopamine transmission in schizophrenia: Confirmed in a second cohort. *American Journal of Psychiatry, 155,* 761–767.

American Psychiatric Association. (1952). *Diagnostic and statistical manual of mental disorders.* Washington, DC: Author.

American Psychiatric Association. (1968). *Diagnostic and statistical manual of mental disorders* (2nd ed.). Washington, DC: Author.

American Psychiatric Association. (1980). *Diagnostic and statistical manual of mental disorders* (3rd ed.). Washington, DC: Author.

American Psychiatric Association. (1987). *Diagnostic and statistical manual of mental disorders* (3rd ed., text rev.). Washington, DC: Author.

American Psychiatric Association. (1994). *Diagnostic and statistical manual of mental disorders* (4th ed.). Washington, DC: Author.

American Psychiatric Association. (2000). *Diagnostic and statistical manual of mental disorders* (4th ed., text rev.). Washington, DC: Author.

American Psychiatric Association. (2013). *Diagnostic and statistical manual of mental disorders* (5th ed.). Arlington, VA: American Psychiatric Press.

Aspinwall, L. G., & Taylor, S. E. (1997). A stitch in time: self-regulation and proactive coping. *Psychological bulletin, 121*(3), 417.

Bartholomew, K., & Horowitz, L. M. (1991). Attachment styles among young adults: a test of a four-category model. *Journal of Personality and Social Psychology, 61*(2), 226.

Bartz, J., Simeon, D., Hamilton, H., Kim, S., Crystal, S., Braun, A., . . . Hollander, E. (2010). Oxytocin can hinder trust and cooperation in borderline personality disorder. *Social cognitive and Affective Neuroscience*, nsq085.

Bastiaens, T., Claes, L., Smits, D., De Clercq, B., De Fruyt, F., Rossi, G., Vanwalleghem, D., Vermote, R., Lowyck, B., Claes, S., & De Hert, M. (2015). The construct validity of the Dutch Personality Inventory for DSM-5 Personality Disorders (PID-5) in a clinical sample. *Assessment, 23*, 42–51.

Bateman, A. W., & Fonagy, P. (2004). Mentalization-based treatment of BPD. *Journal of Personality Disorders, 18*, 36–51.

Beck, A. T., & Freeman, A. F. (1990). *Cognitive therapy of personality disorders*. New York, NY: Guilford Press.

Bender, D. S., Dolan, R. T., Skodol, A. E., Sanislow, C. A., Dyck, I. R., McGlasgan, T. H., . . . Gunderson, J. G. (2001). Treatment utilization by patients with personality disorders. *The American Journal of Psychiatry, 158*, 295–302.

Bender, D. S., Morey, L. C., & Skodol, A. E. (2011). Toward a model for assessing level of personality functioning in *DSM-5*: An empirical review. *Journal of Personality Assessment, 93*, 332–346.

Benjamin, L. S. (1996). *Interpersonal diagnosis and treatment of personality disorders* (2nd ed.). New York, NY: Guilford Press.

Blashfield, R. K., & Intoccia, V. (2000). Growth of the literature on the topic of personality disorders. *American Journal of Psychiatry, 157*(3), 472–473.

Bornstein, R. F. (1997). Dependent personality disorder in the *DSM-IV* and beyond. *Clinical Psychology: Science and Practice, 4*, 175–187.

Bornstein, R. F. (2011a). Toward a multidimensional model of personality disorder diagnosis: Implications for *DSM-5*. *Journal of Personality Assessment, 93*, 362–369.

Bornstein, R. F. (2011b). Reconceptualizing personality pathology in *DSM-5*: Limitations in evidence for eliminating dependent personality disorder and other *DSM-IV* syndromes. *Journal or Personality Disorders, 25*, 235–247.

Britton, J. C., Phan, K. L., Taylor, S. F., Welsh, R. C., Berridge, K. C., & Liberzon, I. (2006). Neural correlates of social and nonsocial emotions: An fMRI study. *Neuroimage, 31*(1), 397–409.

Brown, G. L., Eberth, M. H., Goyer, P. F., Jimerson, D. C., Klein, W. J., Bunney, W. E., & Goodwin, F. K. (1982). Aggression, suicide, and serotonin: Relationships to CSF amine metabolites. *American Journal of Psychiatry, 139*, 741–746.

Burt, S. A. (2009). Rethinking environmental contributions to child and adolescent psychopathology: A meta-analysis of shared environmental influences. *Psychological Bulletin, 135*, 608–637.

Caspi, A., Houts, R. M., Belsky, D. W., Goldman-Mellor, S. J., Harrington, H., Israel, S., . . . Moffitt, T. E. (2014). The p factor: one general psychopathology factor in the structure of psychiatric disorders? *Clinical Psychological Science, 2*(2), 119–137.

Caspi, A., McClay, J., Moffitt, T. E., Mill, J., Martin, J., Craig, I. W., . . . Poulton, R. (2002). Role of genotype in the cycle of maltreated children. *Science, 297*, 851–854.

Caspi, A., Sugden, K., Moffitt, T. E., Taylor, A., Craig, I. W., Harrington, H., . . . Poulton, R. (2003). Influence of life stress on depression: moderation by a polymorphism in the 5-HTT gene. *Science, 301*(5631), 386–389.

Ciechanowski, P., Russo, J., Katon, W. J., Lin, E. H., Ludman, E., Heckbert, S., . . . Young, B. A. (2010). Relationship styles and mortality in patients with diabetes. *Diabetes Care, 33*(3), 539–544.

Ciechanowski, P., Russo, J., Katon, W., Von Korff, M., Ludman, E., Lin, E., . . . Bush, T. (2004). Influence of patient attachment style on self-care and outcomes in diabetes. *Psychosomatic Medicine, 66*(5), 720–728.

Clark, L. A. (1993). *Manual for the schedule for nonadaptive and adaptive personality.* Minneapolis: University of Minnesota Press.

Clark, L. A. (2007). Assessment and diagnosis of personality disorder: Perennial issues and emerging conceptualization. *Annual Review of Psychology, 58*, 227–258.

Clark, L. A., & Harrison, J. A. (2001). Assessment instruments. In W. J. Livesley (Ed.), *Handbook of personality disorders: Theory, research, and treatment* (pp. 277–306). New York, NY: Guilford Press.

Clarkin, J. F., & Huprich, S. K. (2011). Do DSM-V personality disorder proposals meet criteria for clinical utility? *Journal of Personality Disorders, 25*(2), 192–205.

Clarkin, J. F., Levy, K. N., Lenzenweger, M. F., & Kernberg, O. (2007). Evaluating three treatments for borderline personality disorder: A multiwave study. *The American Journal of Psychiatry, 164*, 6922–6928.

Coccaro, E. F., Gabriel, S., & Siever, L. J. (1990). Buspirone challenge: Preliminary evident for a role for 5-HT-1A receptors in impulsive aggressive behavior in humans. *Psychopharmacology Bulletin, 26*, 393–405.

Cooper, L. D., Balsis, S., & Zimmerman, M. (2010). Challenges associated with a polythetic diagnostic system: Criteria combinations in the personality disorders. *Journal of Abnormal Psychology, 119*(4), 886–895.

Costa, P. T., Jr. & McCrae, R. R. (2006). Trait and factor theories. In M. Hersen & J. C. Thomas (Eds.), *Comprehensive handbook of personality and psychopathology, Vol. 1: Personality and everyday functioning* (pp. 96–114). Hoboken, NJ: John Wiley & Sons.

Cramer, P. (1991). Anger and the use of defense mechanisms in college students. *Journal of Personality, 59*, 39–55.

Cristea, I. A., Gentili, C., Cotet, C. D., Palomba, D., Barbui, C., & Cuijpers, P. (2017). Efficacy of Psychotherapies for Borderline Personality Disorder: A Systematic Review and Meta-analysis. *JAMA Psychiatry, 74*(4), 319–328.

Critchfield, K. L., & Benjamin, L. S. (2010). Assessment of repeated relational patterns for individual cases using the SASB-Based Intrex Questionnaire. *Journal of Personality Assessment, 92*, 480–489.

Cuijpers, P., Smit, F., Penninx, B. W. J. H., DeGraaf, R., tenHave, M., & Beekman, A. T. F. (2010). Economic costs of neuroticism: A population-based study. *Archives of General Psychiatry, 67*, 1086–1093.

Cuthbert, B. N., & Insel, T. R. (2013). Toward the future of psychiatric diagnosis: the seven pillars of RDoC. *BMC Medicine, 11*(1), 126.

Cyranowski, J. M., Frank, E., Winter, E., Rucci, P., Novick, D., Pilkonis, P., . . . Kupfer, D. J. (2004). Personality pathology and outcome in recurrently depressed women over 2 years of maintenance interpersonal psychotherapy. *Psychological Medicine, 34*, 659–669.

Das, D., Cherbuin, N., Tan, X., Anstey, K. J., & Easteal, S. (2011). DRD4-exonIII-VNTR moderates the effect of childhood adversities on emotional resilience in young-adults. *PLoS One, 6*(5), e20177.

Deary, I. J., Weiss, A., & Batty, G. D. (2010). Intelligence and personality as predictors of illness and death how researchers in differential psychology and chronic disease epidemiology are collaborating to understand and address health inequalities. *Psychological Science in the Public Interest, 11*(2), 53–79.

Depue, R. A., & Lenzenweger, M. F. (2005). A neurobehavioral dimensional model of personality disturbance. In M. F. Lenzenweger & J. F. Clarkin (Eds.), *Major theories of personality disorder* (2nd ed., pp. 391–453). New York, NY: Guilford Press.

DeYoung, C. G. (2010). Mapping personality traits onto brain systems: BIS, BAS, FFFS, and beyond. *European Journal of Personality, 24,* 404–422.

Digman, J. M. (1990). Personality structure: Emergence of the five-factor model. *Annual Review of Psychology, 41,* 417–440.

Donaldson, Z. R., & Young, L. J. (2008). Oxytocin, vasopressin, and the neurogenetics of sociality. *Science, 322*(5903), 900–904.

Donegan, N. H., Sanislow, C. A., Blumberg, H. P., Fulbright, R. K., Lacadie, C., Skudlarski, P., . . . Wexler, B. E. (2003). Amygdala hyperreactivity in borderline personality disorder: implications for emotional dysregulation. *Biological Psychiatry, 54,* 1284–1293.

dos Santos, L. F., Loureiro, S. R., Crippa, J. A. S., & de Lima Osório, F. (2013). Adaptation and initial psychometric study of the self-report version of Liebowitz Social Anxiety Scale (LSAS-SR). *International Journal of Psychiatry in Clinical Practice, 17*(2), 139–143.

Downey, G., & Feldman, S. I. (1996). Implications of rejection sensitivity for intimate relationships. *Journal of Personality and Social Psychology, 70*(6), 1327.

Dozier, M., Lomax, L., Tyrrell, C. L., & Lee, S. W. (2001). The challenge of treatment for clients with dismissing states of mind. *Attachment & Human Development, 3*(1), 62–76.

Eisenberger, N. I., Lieberman, M. D., & Williams, K. D. (2003). Does rejection hurt? *An fMRI study of social exclusion. Science, 302*(5643), 290–292.

Feske, U., Mulsant, B. H., Pilkonis, P. A., Soloff, P., Dolata, D., Sackeim, H. A., & Haskett, R. F. (2004). Clinical outcome of ECT in patients with major depression and comorbid borderline personality disorder. *The American Journal of Psychiatry, 161,* 2073–2080.

Few, L. R., Miller, J. D., Rothbaum, A. O., Meller, S., Maples, J., Terry, D. P., Collins, B., & MacKillop, J. (2013). Examination of the Section III DSM-5 diagnostic system for personality disorders in an outpatient clinical sample. *Journal of Abnormal Psychology, 122,* 1057–1069.

First, M. B., Gibbon, R. L., Spitzer, R. L., Williams, J. B. W., & Benjamin, L. S. (1997). *Structured Clinical Interview for DSM-IV Axis II personality disorders (SCID-II).* Washington, DC: American Psychiatric Press.

First, M. B., Pincus, H. A., Levine, J. B., Williams, J. B. W., Ustun, B., & Peele, R. (2004). Clinical utility as a criterion for revising psychiatric diagnoses. *American Journal of Psychiatry, 161,* 946–954.

First, M. B., Skodol, A. E., Bender, D. S., & Oldham, J. M. (2014). *Structured clinical interview for the DSM-5 alternative model for personality disorders (SCID–AMPD).* New York: New York State Psychiatric Institute.

Fowler, J. C., Patriquin, M. A., Madan, A., Allen, J. G., Frueh, B. C., & Oldham, J. M. (2016). Incremental validity of the PID-5 in relation to the five factor model and traditional polythetic personality criteria of the DSM-5. *International Journal of Methods in Psychiatric Research.*

Fowler, J. C., Sharp, C., Kalpakci, A., Madan, A., Clapp, J., Allen, J. G., . . . Oldham, J. M. (2015). A dimensional approach to assessing personality functioning: examining personality trait domains utilizing DSM-IV personality disorder criteria. *Comprehensive Psychiatry, 56,* 75–84.

Giesen-Bloo, J., vanDyck, R., Spinhoven, P., vanTilburg, W., Dirksen, C., vanAsselt, T., . . . Arntz, A. (2006). Outpatient psychotherapy for borderline personality disorder: Randomized trial of schema-focused therapy vs transference-focused psychotherapy. *Archives of General Psychiatry, 63,* 649–658.

Grant, B. F., Hasin, D. S., Stinson, F. S., Dawson, D. A., Chou, S. P., Ruan, W. J., & Pickering, R. P. (2004). Prevalence, correlates, and disability of personality disorders in the United States: Results from the National Epidemiologic Survey on alcohol and related conditions. *Journal of Clinical Psychiatry, 65,* 948–958.

Grilo, C. M., Shea, M. T., Sanislow, C. A., Skodol, A. E., Gunderson, J. G., Stout, R. L., . . . McGlashan, T. H. (2004). Two-year stability and change of schizotypal, borderline, avoidant, and obsessive-compulsive personality disorders. *Journal of Consulting and Clinical Psychology, 72,* 767–775.

Gunderson, J. G. (2010). Commentary on "Personality traits and the classification of mental disorders: Toward a more complete integration in *DSM-5* and an empirical model of psychopathology." *Personality Disorders: Theory, Research, and Treatment, 1,* 119–122.

Gunderson, J. G. (2014). *Handbook of good psychiatric management for borderline personality disorder.* American Psychiatric Pub.

Gunderson, J. G., Daversa, M. T., Grilo, C. M., McGlashan, T. H., Zanarini, M. C., Shea, M. T., . . . Dyck, I. R. (2006). Predictors of 2-year outcome for patients with borderline personality disorder. *American Journal of Psychiatry, 163*(5), 822–826.

Gunderson, J. G., & Lyons-Ruth, K. (2008). BPD's interpersonal hypersensitivity phenotype: A gene-environment-developmental model. *Journal of Personality Disorders, 22*(1), 22–41.

Haigler, E. D., & Widiger, T. A. (2001). Experimental manipulations of NEO PI-R items. *Journal of Personality Assessment, 77,* 339–358.

Hare, R. D. (1991). *The Hare psychopathy checklist—Revised manual.* Toronto, Canada: Multi-Health Systems.

Hazlett, E. A., Buchsbaum, M. S., Mehmet, H. M., Newmark, R., Goldstein, K. E., Zelmanova, Y., . . . Siever, L. J. (2008). Cortical gray and white matter volume in unmedicated schizotypal and schizophrenia patients. *Schizophrenia Research, 1,* 111–123.

Herpertz, S. C., Dietrich, T. M., Wenning, B., Krings, T., Erberich, S. G., Willmes, K., . . . Sass, H. (2001). Evidence of abnormal amygdala functioning in borderline personality disorder: A functional MRI study. *Biological Psychiatry, 50,* 292–298.

Herpertz, S., Sass, H., & Favazza, A. (1997). Impulsivity in self-mutilative behavior: psychometric and biological findings. *Journal of psychiatric research, 31*(4), 451–465.

Heumman, K. A., & Morey, L. C. (1990). Reliability of categorical and dimensional judgments of personality disorder. *American Journal of Psychiatry, 147,* 498–500.

Hopwood, C. J. (2011). Personality traits in the DSM-5. *Journal of Personality Assessment, 93,* 398–405.

Hopwood, C. J., Donnellan, M. B., & Zanarini, M. C. (2010). Temperamental and acute symptoms of borderline personality disorder: associations with normal personality traits and dynamic relations over time. *Psychological Medicine, 40,* 1871–1878.

Hopwood, C. J., Malone, J. C., Ansell, E. B., Sanislow, C. A., Grilo, C. M., McGlashan, T. H., . . . Morey, L. C. (2011). Personality assessment in DSM-V: Empirical support for rating severity, style, and traits. *Journal of Personality Disorders, 25,* 305–320.

Hopwood, C. J., Morey, L. C., Edelen, M. O., Shea, M. T., Grilo, C. M., Sanislow, C. A., . . . Skodol, A. E. (2008). A comparison of interview and self-report methods for the assessment of borderline personality disorder criteria. *Psychological Assessment, 20,* 81–85.

Hopwood, C. J., Morey, L. C., Markowitz, J. C., Pinto, A., Skodol, A. E., Gunderson, J. G., . . . Sanislow, C. A. (2009). The construct validity of passive-aggressive personality disorder. *Psychiatry: Interpersonal and Biological Processes, 72,* 256–267.

Hopwood, C. J., Thomas, K. M., Markon, K. E., Wright, A. G., & Krueger, R. F. (2012). DSM-5 personality traits and DSM–IV personality disorders. *Journal of Abnormal Psychology, 121,* 424–432.

Hopwood, C. J., & Zanarini, M. C. (2010). Five-factor trait instability in borderline relative to other personality disorders. *Personality Disorders: Theory, Research, and Treatment, 1,* 158–166.

Hopwood, C. J., Zimmermann, J., Pincus, A. L., & Krueger, R. F. (2015). Connecting personality structure and dynamics: Towards a more evidence-based and clinically useful diagnostic scheme. *Journal of Personality Disorders, 29*(4), 431–448.

Huprich, S. K. (2005). *Rorschach assessment of personality disorders.* Mahwah, NJ: Erlbaum.

Huprich, S. K. & Bornstein, R. F. (2007). An overview of issues related to categorical and dimensional models of personality disorders assessment. *Journal of Personality Assessment, 89,* 3–15.

Hy, L. X., & Loevinger, J. (1996). *Measuring ego development* (2nd ed.). Mahwah, NJ: Erlbaum.

Hyler, S. E. (1994). *Personality Diagnostic Questionnaire-4 (PDQ-4)* New York: New York State Psychiatric Institute.

Insel, T.R., Cuthbert, B.N., Garvey, M.A., Heinssen, R.K., Pine, D.S., Quinn, K.J., Sanislow, C.A., & Wang, P.S. (2010). Research domain criteria (RDoC): toward a new classification framework for research on mental disorders. *American Journal of Psychiatry, 167*(7): 748–751.

Jackson, H. J., Whiteside, H. L., Bates, G. W., Bell, R., Rudd, R. P., & Edwards, J. (1991). Diagnosing personality disorders in psychiatric inpatients. *Acta Psychiatrica Scandinavica, 83,* 206–213.

Jang, K. L., Livesley, W. J., & Vernon, P. A. (1996). Heritability of the big five personality dimensions and their facets: A twin study. *Journal of Personality, 64,* 577–591.

John, O. P., Naumann, L. P., & Soto, C. J. (2008). Paradigm shift to the integrative big five trait taxonomy. *Handbook of Personality: Theory and Research, 3,* 114–158.

Johnson, J. G., Cohen, P., Brown, J., Smailes, E., & Bernstein, D. P. (1999). Childhood maltreatment increases risk for personality disorders during early adulthood. *Archives of General Psychiatry, 56,* 600–606.

Johnson, J. G., Cohen, P., Kasen, S., Skodol, A. E., Hamagami, F., & Brook, J. S. (2000). Age-related change in personality disorder trait levels between early adolescence and adulthood: A community-based longitudinal investigation. *Acta Psychiatrica Scandinavica, 102,* 265–275.

Jovev, M., & Jackson, H. J. (2006). The relationship of borderline personality disorder, life events and functioning in an Australian psychiatric sample. *Journal of Personality Disorders, 20*(3), 205–217.

Keeley, J. W., Flanagan, E. H., & McCluskey, D. L. (2014). Functional impairment and the DSM-5 dimensional system for personality disorder. *Journal of Personality Disorders, 28,* 657–674.

Kendler, K. S., Czajkowski, N., Tambs, K., Torgersen, S., Aggen, S. H., Neale, M. C., & Reichborn-Kjennerud, T. (2006). Dimensional representations of *DSM-IV* Cluster A personality disorders in a population-based sample of Norwegian twins: A multivariate study. *Psychological Medicine, 36,* 1583–1591.

Kernberg, O. F. (1984). *Severe personality disorders.* New Haven, CT: Yale University Press.

Kernberg, O. F., & Caligor, E. (2005). A psychoanalytic theory of personality disorders. In M. F. Lenzenweger & J. F. Clarkin (Eds.), *Major theories of personality disorder* (2nd ed., pp. 391–453). New York, NY: Guilford Press.

Kernberg, O. F., & Clarkin, J. F. (1995). *The inventory of personality organization.* White Plains, NY: Hospital-Cornell Medical Center.

Kohut, H. (1971). *The analysis of the self.* New York, NY: International Universities Press.

Kotov, R., Gomez, W., Schmidt, F., & Watson, D. (2010). Linking "big" personality traits to anxiety, depressive, and substance use disorders: A meta-analysis. *Psychological Bulletin, 136*(5), 768–821.

Kotov, R., Krueger, R. F., Watson, D., Achenbach, T. M., Althoff, R. R., Bagby, M., . . . Zimmerman, M. (2016). The Hierarchical Taxonomy of Psychopathology (HiTOP): A dimensional alternative to traditional nosologies. *Journal of Abnormal Psychology, 126*(4), 454–477.

Krueger, R. F., Eaton, N. R., Clark, L. A., Watson, D. W., Derringer, J., Skodol, A., & Livesley, W. J. (2011a). Deriving an empirical structure of personality pathology for *DSM-5. Journal of Personality Disorders, 25*(2), 170–191.

Krueger, R. F., Eaton, N. R., Derringer, J., Markon, K. E., Clark, L. A., Watson, D., & Livesley, W. J. (2011b). Personality in *DSM-5:* Helping delineate personality disorder content and framing the meta-structure. *Journal of Personality Assessment, 93,* 325–331.

Krueger, R. F., Derringer, J., Markon, K. E., Watson, D., & Skodol, A. E. (2012). Constructing a personality inventory for DSM-5. *Psychological Medicine, 42*(9), 1879–1890.

Krueger, R. F., Skodol, A. E., Livesley, W. J., Shrout, P. E., & Huang, Y. (2007). Synthesizing dimensional and categorical approaches to personality disorders: refining the research agenda for DSM-V Axis II. *International Journal of Methods in Psychiatric Research, 16,* (S1).

Kupfer, D. J., & Regier, D. A. (2011). Neuroscience, clinical evidence, and the future of psychiatric classification in DSM-5. *American Journal of Psychiatry, 168*(7), 672–674.

Lahey, B. B. (2009). The public health significance of neuroticism. *American Psychologist, 4,* 241–256.

Leichsenring, F., Leibing, E., Kruse, J., New, A. S., & Leweke, F. (2011). Borderline personality disorder. *The Lancet, 377*(9759), 74–84.

Lenzenweger, M. F. (2006). The longitudinal study of personality disorders: History, design considerations, and initial findings. *Journal of Personality Disorders, 20,* 645–670.

Lenzenweger, M. F., & Clarkin, J. F. (2005). The personality disorders: History, classification, and research issues. In M. F. Lenzenweger & J. F. Clarkin (Eds.), *Major theories of personality disorder* (2nd ed., pp. 391–453). New York, NY: Guilford Press.

Lenzenweger, M. F., Loranger, A. W., Korfine, L., & Neff, C. (1997). Detecting personality disorders in a nonclinical population: Application of a 2-stage for case identification. *Archives of General Psychiatry, 54,* 4345–4351.

Levine, D., Marziali, E., & Hood, J. (1997). Emotion processing in borderline personality disorders. *The Journal of Nervous and Mental Disease, 185*(4), 240–246.

Lewin, K. (1936). *Principles of topological psychology.* New York, NY: McGraw-Hill.

Liao, W., Qiu, C., Gentili, C., Walter, M., Pan, Z., Ding, J., . . . Chen, H. (2010). Altered effective connectivity network of the amygdala in social anxiety disorder: a resting-state FMRI study. *PloS one, 5*(12), e15238.

Linehan, M. (1993). *Cognitive-behavioral treatment of borderline personality disorder.* New York, NY: Guilford Press.

Links, P. S., & Heslegrave, R. J. (2000). Prospective studies of outcome: Understanding mechanisms of change in patients with borderline personality disorder. *Psychiatric Clinics of North America, 23* (1), 137–150.

Links, P. S., Steiner, M., & Huxley, G. (1988). The occurrence of borderline personality disorder in the families of borderline patients. *Journal of Personality Disorders, 2,* 14–20.

Livesley, W. J. (1998). Suggestions for a framework for an empirically based classification of personality disorder. *The Canadian Journal of Psychiatry, 43,* 137–147.

Livesley, W. J., & Jackson, D. N. (2006). *Dimensional assessment of personality problems.* Port Huron, MI: Sigma Assessment Systems.

Lo, M. T., Hinds, D. A., Tung, J. Y., Franz, C., Fan, C. C., Wang, Y., . . . Sanyal, N. (2016). Genomewide analyses for personality traits identify six genomic loci and show correlations with psychiatric disorders. *Nature Genetics, 49*(1), 152–156.

Loevinger, J. (1957). Objective tests as instruments of psychological theory. *Psychological Reports, 3,* 635–694.

MacCorquodale, K., & Meehl, P. E. (1948). On a distinction between hypothetical constructs and intervening variables. *Psychological Review, 55,* 95–107.

Maier, W., Lichtermann, D., Minges, J., & Heun, R. (1994). Personality disorders among the relatives of schizophrenia patients. *Schizophrenia Bulletin, 20,* 481–493.

Matusiewicz, A. K., Hopwood, C. J., Banducci, A. N., & Lejuez, C. W. (2010). The effectiveness of cognitive behavioral therapy for personality disorders. *Psychiatric Clinics of North America, 33,* 657–685.

McCrae, R. R., & Terracciano, A. (2005). Universal features of personality traits from the observer's perspective: Data from 50 cultures. *Journal of Personality and Social Psychology, 88,* 547–561.

McGlashan, T. H., Grilo, C. M., Sanislow, C. A., Ralevski, E., Morey, L. C., Gunderson, J. G., . . . Pagano, M. (2005). Two-year prevalence and stability of individual *DSM-IV* criteria for schizotypal, borderline, avoidant, and obsessive-compulsive personality disorders: Toward a hybrid model of axis II disorders. *American Journal of Psychiatry, 162,* 883–889.

McGlashan, T. H., Grilo, C. M., Skodol, A. E., Gunderson, J. G., Shea, M. T., Morey, L. C., . . . Stout, R. L. (2000). The Collaborative Longitudinal Personality Disorders Study: Baseline Axis I/II and II/II diagnostic co-occurrence. *Acta Psychiatrica Scandinavica, 102,* 256–264.

McGue, M., Bacon, S., & Lykken, D. T. (1993). Personality stability and change in early adulthood: A behavioral genetic analysis. *Developmental Psychology, 29,* 196–109.

McMain, S., & Pos, A. E. (2007). Advances in psychotherapy of personality disorders: a research update. *Current Psychiatry Reports, 9*(1), 46–52.

Menninger, K. A. (1963). *The vital balance: The life process in mental health and illness.* New York, NY: Viking Press.

Meyer, B., & Pilkonis, P. A. (2005). An attachment model of personality. In M. F. Lenzenweger & J. F. Clarkin (Eds.), *Major theories of personality disorder* (2nd ed., pp. 231–281). New York, NY: Guilford Press.

Mezzich, J. E., Fabrega, H., Jr. & Coffman, G. A. (1987). Multiaxial characterization of depressive patients. *Journal of Nervous and Mental Disease, 175,* 339–346.

Mikulincer, M., & Shaver, P. R., (2008). Adult attachment and affect regulation. In J. Cassidy & P. R. Shaver (Eds.), *Handbook of attachment: Theory, research, and clinical applications* (2nd ed.). (pp. 503–531). New York, NY: Guilford Press.

Miller, J. D., Bagby, R. M., Pilkonis, P. A., Reynolds, S. K., & Lynam, D. R. (2005). A simplified technique for scoring *DSM-IV* personality disorders with the five-factor model. *Assessment, 12,* 404–415.

Millon, T., & Radovanov, J. (1995). Passive-aggressive (negativistic) personality disorder. In W. Livesley (Ed.), *The DSM-IV personality disorders: Diagnosis and of self-defeating personality disorder* (pp. 312–325). New York, NY: Guilford Press.

Mischel, W. (1968). *Personality and assessment.* New York, NY: John Wiley & Sons.

Mischel, W., & Shoda, Y. (1995). A cognitive-affective system theory of personality: Reconceptualizing situations, dispositions, dynamics, and invariance in personality structure. *Psychological Review, 102,* 246–268.

Molinari, V., Ames, A., & Essa, M. (1994). Prevalence of personality disorders in two geropsychiatric inpatient units. *Journal of Geriatric Psychiatry and Neurology, 7,* 209–215.

Morey, L. C. (2005). Personality pathology as pathological narcissism. In M. Maj, H. S. Akiskal, J. E. Mezzich, & A. Okasha (Eds.), *Evidence and experience in psychiatry, Vol. 8: Personality disorders* (pp. 328–331). Hoboken, NJ: John Wiley & Sons.

Morey, L. C., Bender, D. S., & Skodol, A. E. (2013). Validating the proposed diagnostic and statistical manual of mental disorders, severity indicator for personality disorder. *The Journal of nervous and mental disease, 201*(9), 729–735.

Morey, L. C., Berghuis, H., Bender, D. S., Verheul, R., Krueger, R. F., & Skodol, A. E. (2011). Empirical articulation of a core dimension of personality pathology. *Journal of Personality Assessment, 93,* 347–353.

Morey, L. C., Gunderson, J. G., Quigley, B. D., Shea, M. T., Skodol, A. E., McGlashan, T. H., . . . Zanarini, M. C. (2002). The representation of borderline, avoidant, obsessive-compulsive, and schizotypal personality disorders by the five-factor model. *Journal of Personality Disorders, 16,* 215–234.

Morey, L. C., & Hopwood, C. J. (2013). Stability and change in personality disorders. *Annual Review of Clinical Psychology, 9,* 499–528.

Morey, L. C., Hopwood, C. J., Gunderson, J. G., Skodol, A. E., Shea, M. T., Yen, S., McGlashan, T. H. (2007). Comparison of alternate models for personality disorders. *Psychological Medicine, 37,* 7983–7994.

Morey, L. C., Hopwood, C. J., Markowitz, J. C., Gunderson, J. G., Grilo, C. M., McGlashan, T. H., . . . Skodol, A. E. (2012). Comparison of alternative models for personality disorders, II: 6-, 8-, and 10-year follow-up. *Psychological Medicine, 42*(8), 1705–1713.

Morey, L. C., Skodol, A. E., & Oldham, J. M. (2014). Clinician judgments of clinical utility: A comparison of DSM-IV-TR personality disorders and the alternative model for DSM-5 personality disorders. *Journal of Abnormal Psychology, 123*(2), 398.

Morey, L. C., & Zanarini, M. C. (2000). Borderline personality: Traits and disorder. *Journal of Abnormal Psychology, 109,* 733–737.

Neumann, I. D., & Landgraf, R. (2012). Balance of brain oxytocin and vasopressin: implications for anxiety, depression, and social behaviors. *Trends in Neurosciences, 35*(11), 649–659.

New, A. S., Buchsbaum, M. S., Hazlett, E. A., Goodman, M., Koenigsberg, H., Lo, J., . . . Siever, L. J. (2004). Fluoxetine increases relative metabolic rate in prefrontal cortex in impulsive aggression. *Psychopharmacology, 176,* 451–458.

National Institute of Mental Health. (2008). *The National Institute of Mental Health strategic plan.* Bethesda, MD: National Institute of Mental Health. Retrieved from http://www.nimh.nih.gov/about/strategic-planning-reports/index.shtml.

Oldham, J. M. (2005). Guideline watch: Practice guideline for the treatment of patients with borderline personality disorder. *Focus, 3,* 396–400.

Oldham, J. M., Skodol, A. E., Kellman, H. D., Hyler, S. E., & Rosnick, L. (1992). Diagnosis of DSM-III-R personality disorders by two structured interviews: Patterns of comorbidity. *American Journal of Psychiatry, 149,* 213–220.

Ozer, D. J., & Benet-Martinez, V. (2006). Personality and the prediction of consequential outcomes. *Annual Review of Psychology, 57,* 401–421.

Pagano, M. E., Skodol, A. E., Stout, R. L., Shea, M. T., Yen, S., Grilo, C. M., . . . Gunderson, J. G. (2004). Stressful life events as predictors of functioning: findings from the Collaborative Longitudinal Personality Disorders Study. *Acta Psychiatrica Scandinavica, 110*(6), 421–429.

Paris, J. (2011). Endophenotypes and the diagnosis of personality disorders. *Journal of Personality Disorders, 25*(2), 260–268.

Parker, G., Hadzi-Pavlovic, D., Both, L., Kumar, S., Wilhelm, K., & Olley, A. (2004). Measuring disordered personality functioning: To love and to work reprised. *Acta Psychiatrica Scandinavica, 110,* 230–239.

Parker, G., Roussos, J., Wilhelm, K., Mitchell, P., Austin, M. P., & Hadzi-Pavlovic, D. (1998). On modelling personality disorders: Are personality style and disordered functioning independent or interdependent constructs? *Journal of Nervous and Mental Disease, 186,* 709–715.

PDM Task Force. (2006). *Psychodynamic diagnostic manual.* Silver Springs, MD: Alliance of Psychoanalytic Organizations.

Pfohl, B., Coryell, W., Zimmerman, M., & Stangl, D. (1986). *DSM-III* personality disorders: Diagnostic overlap and internal consistency of individual *DSM-III* criteria. *Comprehensive Psychiatry, 27,* 21–34.

Pilkonis, P. A., Heape, C. L., Ruddy, J., & Serrao, P. (1991). Validity in the diagnosis of personality disorders: The use of the LEAD standard. *Psychological Assessment: A Journal of Consulting and Clinical Psychology, 3,* 46–54.

Pincus, A. L. (2005). A contemporary integrative interpersonal theory of personality disorders. In M. F. Lenzenweger & J. F. Clarkin (Eds.), *Major theories of personality disorder* (2nd ed., pp. 391–453). New York, NY: Guilford Press.

Pincus, A. L. & Hopwood, C. J. (2012). A contemporary interpersonal model of personality pathology and personality disorder. In T. A. Widiger (Ed.), *Oxford handbook of personality disorders* (pp. 372–398). Oxford, England: Oxford University Press.

Pincus, A. L., Wright, A. G. C., Hopwood, C. J., & Krueger, R. F. (2011). *An interpersonal analysis of pathological personality traits in DSM-5.* Zurich, Switzerland: Society for Interpersonal Theory and Research.

Pitman, R. K., Orr, S. P., & Lasko, N. B. (1993). Effects of intranasal vasopressin and oxytocin on physiologic responding during personal combat imagery in Vietnam veterans with post-traumatic stress disorder. *Psychiatry Research, 48*(2), 107–117.

Plomin, R., DeFries, J. C., Craig, I. W., & McGuggin, P. (2003). Behavioral genetics. In R. Plomin, J. C. DeFries, I. W. Craig, & P. McGuggin (Eds.), *Behavioral genetics in the postgenomic era* (pp. 531–540). Washington, DC: American Psychological Association.

Poldrugo, F., & Forti, B. (1988). Personality disorders and alcoholism treatment outcome. *Drug and Alcohol Dependence, 21*, 171–176.

Pretzer, J. L., & Beck, A. T. (2005). A cognitive theory of personality disorders. In M. F. Lenzenweger & J. F. Clarkin (Eds.), *Major theories of personality disorder* (2nd ed., pp. 391–453). New York, NY: Guilford Press.

Reich, J. (1991). Using the family history method to distinguish relatives of patients with dependent personality disorder from relatives of controls. *Psychiatry Research, 39*, 227–237.

Reich, J. (2003). The effects of Axis II disorders on the outcome of treatment of anxiety and unipolar depressive disorders: A review. *Journal of Personality Disorders, 17*, 387–405.

Rhee, S. H., & Waldman, I. D. (2002). Genetic and environmental influences on antisocial behavior: A meta-analysis of twin and adoption studies. *Psychological Bulletin, 128*, 490–529.

Riggs, S. A., & Jacobvitz, D. (2002). Expectant parents' representations of early attachment relationships: associations with mental health and family history. *Journal of Consulting and Clinical Psychology, 70*(1), 195.

Riva, P., Romero Lauro, L. J., DeWall, C. N., & Bushman, B. J. (2012). Buffer the pain away: stimulating the right ventrolateral prefrontal cortex reduces pain following social exclusion. *Psychological science, 23*(12), 1473–1475.

Roberts, B. W., Kuncel, N. R., Shiner, R., Caspi, A., & Goldberg, L. R. (2007). The power of personality: The comparative validity of personality traits, socioeconomic status, and cognitive ability for predicting important life outcomes. *Perspectives on Psychological Science, 2*, 313–345.

Rogers, R. (2001). *Diagnostic and structured interviewing: A handbook for psychologists.* New York, NY: Guilford Press.

Rottman, B. M., Woo-kyoung, A., Sanislow, C. A., & Kim, N. S. (2009). Can clinicians recognize *DSM-IV* personality disorders from five-factor model descriptions of patient cases. *American Journal of Psychiatry, 166*, 427–433.

Rouff, L. (2000). Schizoid personality traits among the homeless mentally ill: A quantitative and qualitative report. *Journal of Social Distress & the Homeless, 9*, 127–141.

Sadikaj, G., Russell, J. J., Moskowitz, D. S., & Paris, J. (2010). Affect dysregulation in individuals with borderline personality disorder: Persistence and interpersonal triggers. *Journal of Personality Assessment, 92*, 490–500.

Samuel, D. B. (2011). Assessing personality in the *DSM-5*: The utility of bipolar constructs. *Journal of Personality Assessment, 93*, 390–397.

Samuel, D. B., Hopwood, C. J., Krueger, R. F., Thomas, K. M., & Ruggero, C. J. (2013). Comparing methods for scoring personality disorder types using maladaptive traits in DSM-5. *Assessment, 20*, 353–361.

Samuel, D. B., & Widiger, T. A. (2006). Clinician's judgments of clinical utility: A comparison of the *DSM-IV* and five-factor models of personality. *Journal of Abnormal Psychology, 115*, 298–308.

Samuel, D. B., & Widiger, T. A. (2008). A meta-analytic review of the relationships between the five-factor model and DSM-IV-TR personality disorders: A facet level analysis. *Clinical Psychology Review, 28*, 1326–1342.

Samuels, J., Eaton, W. W., Bienvenu, O. J., III Brown, C. H., Costa, P. T., Jr. & Nestadt, G. (2002). Prevalence and correlates of personality disorders in a community sample. *British Journal of Psychiatry, 180*, 536–542.

Sanislow, C. A., Pine, D. S., Quinn, K. J., Kozak, M. J., Garvey, M. A., Heinssen, R. K., . . . Cuthbert, B. N. (2010). Developing constructs for psychopathology research: research domain criteria. *Journal of abnormal psychology, 119*(4), 631.

Saulsman, L. M., & Page, A. C. (2004). The five-factor model and personality disorder empirical literature: A meta-analytic review. *Clinical Psychology Review, 23*, 1055–1085.

Schmideberg, M. (1959). The borderline patient. In S. Arieti (Ed.), *American handbook of psychiatry* (Vol. *I* pp. 398–416). New York, NY: Basic Books.

Schneier, F. R., Blanco, C., Anita, S. X., & Liebowitz, M. R. (2002). The social anxiety spectrum. *Psychiatric Clinics of North America, 25*, 757–774.

Selcuk, E., Zayas, V., Günaydin, G., Hazan, C., & Kross, E. (2012). Mental representations of attachment figures facilitate recovery following upsetting autobiographical memory recall. *Journal of Personality and Social Psychology, 103*(2), 362–378.

Sharp, C., Wright, A. G., Fowler, J. C., Frueh, B. C., Allen, J. G., Oldham, J., & Clark, L. A. (2015). The structure of personality pathology: Both general ('g') and specific ('s') factors?. *Journal of Abnormal Psychology, 124*, 387.

Shedler, J., Beck, A., Fonagy, P., Gabbard, G. O., Gunderson, J., Kernberg, O. F., . . . Westen, D. (2010). Personality disorders in *DSM-5. The American Journal of Psychiatry, 167*, 1026–1028.

Siever, L. J. (2008). Neurobiology of aggression and violence. *The American Journal of Psychiatry, 165*, 429–442.

Siever, L. J., & Weinstein, L. N. (2009). The neurobiology of personality disorders: Implications for psychoanalysis. *Journal of the American Psychoanalytic Association, 57*, 361–398.

Simeon, D., Bartz, J., Hamilton, H., Crystal, S., Braun, A., Ketay, S., & Hollander, E. (2011). Oxytocin administration attenuates stress reactivity in borderline personality disorder: a pilot study. *Psychoneuroendocrinology, 36*(9), 1418–1421.

Skodol, A. E. (2012). Personality disorders in DSM-5. *Annual Review of Clinical Psychology, 8*, 317–344.

Skodol, A. E., Bender, D. S., Morey, L. C., Clark, L. A., Oldham, J. M., Alarcon, R. D., . . . Siever, L. J. (2011). Personality disorder types proposed for *DSM-5. Journal of Personality Disorders, 25*(2), 136–169.

Skodol, A. E., Buckley, P., & Charles, E. (1983). Is there a characteristic pattern to the treatment of history of clinic outpatients with borderline personality? *Journal of Nervous and Mental Disease, 171*, 405–410.

Skodol, A. E., Gunderson, J. G., Shea, M. T., McGlashan, T. H., Morey, L. C., Sanislow, C. A., . . . Pagano, M. E. (2005). The collaborative longitudinal personality disorders study (CLPS): Overview and implications. *Journal of Personality Disorders, 19*(5), 487–504.

Skodol, A. E., Rosnick, L., Kellman, D., Oldham, J. M., & Hyler, S. (1991). Development of a procedure for validating structured assessments of Axis II. In A. E. Skodol, L. Rosnick, D. Kellman, J. M. Oldham, & S. Hyler (Eds.), *Personality disorders: New perspectives on diagnostic validity*. Washington, DC: American Psychiatric Association.

Skodol, A. E., Siever, L. J., Livesley, W. J., Gunderson, J. G., Pfohl, B., & Widiger, T. A. (2002). The borderline diagnosis II: Biology, genetics, and clinical course. *Biological Psychiatry, 51*, 951–963.

Soldz, S., & Valliant, G. E. (2002). The big five personality traits and the life course: A 45-year longitudinal study. *Journal of Research in Personality, 33*, 208–232.

Soloff, P. H., Lis, J. A., Kelly, T., & Cornelius, J. R. (1994). Risk factors for suicidal behavior borderline personality disorder. *The American Journal of Psychiatry, 151*, 1316–1323.

Spitzer, R. L., First, M. B., Shedler, J., Westen, D., & Skodol, A. E. (2008). Clinical utility of five dimensional systems for personality diagnosis: a "consumer preference" study. *The Journal of Nervous and Mental Disease, 196*(5), 356–374.

Stanley, B., & Siever, L. J. (2009). The interpersonal dimension of borderline personality disorder: toward a neuropeptide model. *American Journal of Psychiatry, 167*(1), 24–39.

Stern, B. L., Caligor, E., Clarkin, J. F., Critchfield, K. L., Horz, S., MacCornack, V., . . . Kernberg, O. F. (2010). Structured Interview of Personality Organization (STIPO): Preliminary psychometrics in a clinical sample. *Journal of Personality Assessment, 92*, 35–44.

Stuart, S., Pfohl, B., Battaglia, M., Bellodi, L., Grove, W., & Cadoret, R. (1998). The cooccurrence of DSM-III-R personality disorders. *Journal of Personality Disorders, 12*, 302–315.

Sudhoff, K. (1926). *Essays in the history of medicine* (pp. 67–87). New York, NY: Medical Life Press.

Tackett, J. L., Balsis, S., Oltmanns, T. F., & Krueger, R. F. (2009). A unifying perspective on personality pathology across the life span: Developmental considerations for the fifth edition of the *Diagnostic and Statistical Manual for Mental Disorders. Developmental Psychopathology, 21*, 687–713.

Torgersen, S. (2005). Epidemiology. In J. M. Oldham, A. E. Skodol, & D. Bender (Eds.), *Textbook of personality disorders* (pp. 129–141). Washington, DC: American Psychiatric Press.

Torgersen, S., Kringlen, E., & Cramer, V. (2001). The prevalence of personality disorders in a community sample. *Archives of General Psychiatry, 58*, 590–596.

Torgersen, S., Lygren, S., Oien, P. A., Skre, I., Onstad, S., Edvardsen, J., . . . Kringlen, E. (2000). A twin study of personality disorders. *Comprehensive Psychiatry, 41*, 416–425.

Trull, T. J., & Durrett, C. A. (2005). Categorical and dimensional models of personality disorder. *Annual Review of Clinical Psychology, 1*, 355–380.

Trull, T. J., Solhan, M. B., Tragesser, S. L., Jahng, S., Wood, P. K., Piasecki, T. M., & Watson, D. (2008). Affective instability: Measuring a core feature of borderline personality disorder with ecological momentary assessment. *Journal of Abnormal Psychology, 117*, 647–661.

Trull, T. J., & Widiger, T. A. (2013). Dimensional models of personality: the five-factor model and the DSM-5. *Dialogues in Clinical Neuroscience, 15*(2), 135–146.

Uchino, B. N. (2009). Understanding the links between social support and physical health: A lifespan perspective with emphasis on the separability of perceived and received support. *Perspectives on Psychological Science, 4*(3), 236–255.

Uchino, B. N., Carlisle, M., Birmingham, W., & Vaughn, A. A. (2011). Social support and the reactivity hypothesis: Conceptual issues in examining the efficacy of received support during acute psychological stress. *Biological Psychology, 86*(2), 137–142.

Verheul, R., & Widiger, T. A. (2004). A meta-analysis of the prevalence and usage of the Personality Disorder Not Otherwise Specified (PDNOS) diagnosis. *Journal of Personality Disorders, 18*, 309–319.

Vrtička, P., Andersson, F., Grandjean, D., Sander, D., & Vuilleumier, P. (2008). Individual attachment style modulates human amygdala and striatum activation during social appraisal. *PLoS One, 3*(8), e2868.

Wagner, A. W., & Linehan, M. M. (1999). Facial expression recognition ability among women with borderline personality disorder: implications for emotion regulation?. *Journal of personality disorders, 13*(4), 329–344.

Westen, D. (1995). A clinical-empirical model of personality: Life after the Mischelian ice and the NEO-lithic era. *Journal of Personality, 63*, 495–591.

Westen, D. (1997). Divergences between clinical and research methods for assessing personality disorders: Implications for research and the evolution of Axis II. *American Journal of Psychiatry, 154*, 895–903.

Westen, D., & Shedler, J. (1999). Revising and assessing Axis II, part II: Toward an empirically-based and clinically useful classification of personality disorders. *American Journal of Psychiatry, 156*, 273–285.

Westen, D., Shedler, J., Bradley, R. (2006). A prototype approach to personality disorder diagnosis. *The American Journal of Psychiatry, 163*, 846–856.

Wetzler, S., & Morey, L. C. (1999). Passive-aggressive personality disorder: The demise of a syndrome. *Psychiatry: Interpersonal and Biological Processes, 62*, 49–59.

Widiger, T. A. (1993). The DSM-III-R categorical personality disorder diagnoses: A critique and an alternative. *Psychological Inquiry, 4*, 75–90.

Widiger, T. A. (2010). Personality, interpersonal circumplex, and *DSM-5*: A commentary on five studies. *Journal of Personality Assessment, 92*, 528–532.

Widiger, T. A. (2011). The *DSM-5* dimensional model of personality disorder: Rationale and empirical support. *Journal of Personality Disorders, 25*(2), 222–234.

Widiger, T. A., Frances, A. J., Harris, M., Jacobsberg, L., Fyer, M., & Manning, D. (1991). Comorbidity among Axis II disorders. In J. Oldham (Ed.), *Personality disorders: New perspectives on diagnostic validity* (pp. 163–194). Washington, DC: American Psychiatric Press.

Widiger, T. A., Livesley, W. J., & Clark, L. E. A. (2009). An integrative dimensional classification of personality disorder. *Psychological Assessment, 21*, 243–255.

Widiger, T. A., & Mullins-Sweatt, S. N. (2009). Five-factor model of personality disorders: A proposal for DSM-V. *Annual Review of Clinical Psychology, 5*, 197–220.

Widiger, T. A., & Samuel, D. B. (2005). Evidence-based assessment of personality disorders. *Psychological Assessment, 17*, 278–287.

Williams, K. D., Cheung, C. K., & Choi, W. (2000). Cyberostracism: effects of being ignored over the Internet. *Journal of Personality and Social Psychology, 79*(5), 748.

Winstanley, C. A., Theobald, D. E., Dalley, J. W., Glennon, J. C., & Robbins, T. W. (2004). 5-HT$_{2A}$ and 5-HT$_{2C}$ receptor antagonists have opposing effects on a measure of impulsivity: Interactions with global 5-HT depletion. *Psychopharmacology, 176*, 379–385.

Wright, A. G. C. (2011). Qualitative and quantitative distinctions in personality disorder. *Journal of Personality Assessment, 93*, 370–379.

Wright, A. C., Calabrese, W. R., Rudick, M. M., Yam, W. H., Zelazny, K., Williams, T. F., . . . Simms, L. J. (2015). Stability of the DSM-5 Section III pathological personality traits and their longitudinal associations with psychosocial functioning in personality disordered individuals. *Journal of Abnormal Psychology, 124*, 199–207.

Wright, A. G. C., Thomas, K. M., Hopwood, C. J., Markon, K. E., Pincus, A. L., & Krueger, R. F. (2012). Empirical examination of the DSM-5 personality trait structure. *Journal of Abnormal Psychology, 121*(4), 951–957.

Zanarini, M. C., & Frankenburg, F. R. (2007). The essential nature of borderline psychopathology. *Journal of Personality Disorders, 21*, 518–535.

Zanarini, M. C., & Frankenburg, F. R., Hennen, J., Reich, D. B., & Silk, K. R. (2007). Prediction of the 10-year course of borderline personality disorder. *The American Journal of Psychiatry, 163*, 827–832.

Zanarini, M. C., Frankenburg, F. R., Hennen, J., & Silk, K. R. (2004). Mental health service utilization by borderline personality disorder patients and Axis II comparison subjects followed prospectively for 6 years. *Journal of Clinical Psychiatry, 65*, 28–36.

Zanarini, M. C., Gunderson, J. G., Marino, M. F., & Schwartz, E. O. (1989). Childhood experiences of borderline patients. *Comprehensive Psychiatry, 30*, 18–25.

Zeigler-Hill, V., & Abraham, J. (2006). Borderline personality features: Instability of self-esteem and affect. *Journal of Social and Clinical Psychology, 25*, 668–687.

Zimmerman, M. (2011). A critique of the proposed prototype rating system for personality disorders in *DSM-5*. *Journal of Personality Disorders, 25*(2), 206–221.

Zimmerman, M., Rothschild, L., & Chelminski, I. (2005). The prevalence of *DSM-IV* personality disorders in psychiatric outpatients. *American Journal of Psychiatry, 162*, 1911–1918.

Author Index

Aalbers, A., 468
Aalto-Setälä, T., 299
Aasland, O. G., 677
Abbott, D. W., 524
Abbott, P. J., 706
Abel, G. G., 600, 602, 604, 605, 606, 607, 609, 611
Abelson, J. M., 139
Abi-Dargham, A., 769
Aboud, A., 65
Aboujaoude, E., 366
Abraham, J. 2006, 761
Abramovitch, A., 368, 377
Abramowitz, J. S., 316, 322, 375, 376
Abramowitz, S. I., 644
Abrams, K., 82, 305, 698
Abramson, L. Y., 274
Abugel, J., 457
Abujaoude, E., 365
Abukmeil, S. S., 173
Abuzzahab, F., Sr., 594
Accurso, E. C., 499
Acebo, C., 557
Acierno, R., 413, 419
Acocella, J., 459, 473
Acosta, F. X., 180
Adams, C., 161
Adams, G. L., 180, 181
Adams, N. E., 325
Addington, D., 63
Addington, J., 62, 63, 182
Adelmann, M., 511
Aderibigbe, Y. A., 457
Adler, L. E., 79, 80
Advokat, C. D., 697
Aerts, L., 585
Aeschbach, D., 557
Aggarwal, A., 379
Aggen, S. H., 670, 704

Agnello, C., 589
Agras, S., 436
Agras, W., 499, 505
Agras, W. S., 501, 502
Agrawal, A., 704
Agrawal, S., 678, 680
Agresta, J., 177
Aguilar-Bolaños, M., 469
Aguilar-Gaxiola, S., 262
Aguilera, A., 179
Aharonovich, E., 62
Aharonovsky, O., 374
Ahern, D. K., 440
Ahlers, C. J., 604, 643
Ahmadi, J., 699
Ahmadi, M., 699
Ahn, C. W., 55
Ahrens, C., 70
Ai, A. L., 133
Aidroos, N., 60
Aizenstein, H. J., 272
Akagi, H., 436
Akio, I., 511
Akiskal, H. S., 10, 220, 221
Akkermann, K., 513, 517
Aksan, N., 322
Akyüz, G., 452, 459
Alarcón, R.D., 146
Alatiq, Y., 217
Albert, P. S., 217
Albertini, R. S., 371, 382
Alcaine, O., 301
Aldao, A., 254
Alden, L. E., 326, 328
Alderete, E., 262
Aldhoon, B., 513
Aldridge-Morris, R., 472
Alegria, M., 132, 148, 263, 501, 521, 522, 710
Alevizios, B., 227

Alexandra Burt, S., 517
Alexopoulos, G. S., 271, 272, 278
Alfano, C. A., 554
Alfano, L., 512
Ali, M., 555
Ali, S., 264
Allan, T., 317
Allen, B. A., 677
Allen, J. G., 453
Allen, J. J. B., 470, 474, 475
Allen, J. L., 329
Allen, L. A., 436, 440
Allgulander, C., 312
Allness, D. J., 165
Alloy, L. B., 215, 216, 254, 274
Allsworth, J., 317
Almay, S., 313
Almeida, J. R., 227
Almeida, O., 183
Aloi, M., 518, 520
Alonso, J., 641
Alphs, L. D., 60
Altenburger, L. E., 601
Altenor, A., 275
Alterman, A. I., 60, 65, 747
Althof, S., 577
Althof, S. E., 587, 588
Altice, F.L., 54, 55
Altinay, M., 271
Altman, E., 166
Altshuler, L., 218
Altshuler, L. L., 213, 227
Altus, L., 468
Alvidrez, J., 140, 147
Alvir, J. M. J., 173
Alyanak, B., 452
Amador, X. F., 162, 170
Ambrose, M. L., 62
Ambrosini, P. J., 10

Adult Psychopathology and Diagnosis, Eighth Edition. Edited by Deborah C. Beidel and B. Christopher Frueh.
© 2018 John Wiley & Sons, Inc. Published 2018 by John Wiley & Sons, Inc.
Companion website: www.wiley.com/go/beidel/psychopathology8e

Subject Index

Adult Psychopathology and Diagnosis, Eighth Edition. Edited by Deborah C. Beidel and B. Christopher Frueh.
© 2018 John Wiley & Sons, Inc. Published 2018 by John Wiley & Sons, Inc.
Companion website: www.wiley.com/go/beidel/psychopathology8e